*This book is dedicated to my wife Lindy
and to the memory of my mother Rene*

Foreword

The field of systems programming primarily grew out of the efforts of many programmers and managers whose creative energy went into producing practical, utilitarian systems programs needed by the rapidly growing computer industry. Programming was practiced as an art where each programmer invented his own solutions to problems, with little guidance beyond that provided by his immediate associates. In 1968, the late Ascher Opler, then at IBM, recognized that it was necessary to bring programming knowledge together in a form that would be accessible to all systems programmers. Surveying the state of the art, he decided that enough useful material existed to justify a significant codification effort. On his recommendation, IBM decided to sponsor The Systems Programming Series as a long term project to collect, organize, and publish those principles and techniques that would have lasting value throughout the industry. Since 1968 nineteen titles have been published in the Series including *An Introduction to Database Systems, Sixth Edition,* the most thoroughly revised of all previous editions. Like its predecessors, the book provides the basis for a solid education in the fundamentals of database technology and reflects the latest developments in the field.

The Series consists of an open-ended collection of text-reference books. The contents of each book represent the individual author's view of the subject area and do not necessarily reflect the views of the IBM Corporation. Each is organized for course use but is detailed enough for reference.

Representative topic areas already published, or that are contemplated to be covered by the Series, include: database systems, communication systems, graphics systems, expert systems, and programming process management. Other topic areas will be included as the systems programming discipline evolves and develops.

The Editorial Board

About the Author

C. J. Date is an independent author, lecturer, and consultant, specializing in relational database systems. He is based in Healdsburg, California.

In 1967, following several years spent working as a mathematical programmer and programming instructor for Leo Computers Ltd. (London, England), Mr. Date moved to the IBM (UK) Development Laboratories, where he worked on the integration of database functions into PL/I. In 1974 he moved to the IBM Systems Development Center in California, where he was responsible for the design of a database language known as the Unified Database Language, UDL. He was subsequently involved in technical planning and externals design for the IBM relational database products SQL/DS (announced in 1981 for VSE and in 1983 for VM) and DB2 (announced in 1983 for MVS). He left IBM in May 1983.

Mr. Date has been active in the database field for some 25 years. He was one of the first people anywhere to recognize the significance of Codd's pioneering work on the relational model. He has lectured widely on technical subjects—principally on database topics, and especially on relational database—throughout North America and also in Europe, Australia, Latin America, and the Far East. In addition to the present book, he is author or coauthor of several other database books, including *An Introduction to Database Systems: Volume II* (1983), which covers advanced aspects of the subject; *Database: A Primer* (1983), which treats database systems from the nonspecialist's point of view; *Relational Database: Selected Writings* (1986), *Relational Database Writings 1985–1989* (1990), and *Relational Database Writings 1989–1991* (1992), which treat various aspects of relational technology in depth; and a series of books on specific systems and languages—*A Guide to DB2* (4th edition, 1993), *A Guide to SYBASE and SQL Server* (1992), *A Guide to SQL/DS* (1988), *A Guide to INGRES* (1987), and *A Guide to the SQL Standard* (3rd edition, 1993). His books have been translated into many languages, including Chinese, Dutch, French, Italian, Japanese, Polish, Portuguese, Russian, Spanish, and Braille.

Mr. Date has also published well over 100 technical papers and articles and has made a variety of contributions to database theory. He is a regular columnist for *Database Programming & Design* magazine. His professional seminars on database technology (offered both in North America and overseas) are widely considered to b second to none for the quality of their material content and the clarity of the expositio

Preface to the Sixth Edition

The field of database technology is suffering from an information explosion—ironically enough, since information processing is what database technology is supposed to be all about. Here, for example, is a partial list of professional publications in the field that appear in the United States on a regular basis:

- *ACM Transactions on Database Systems* (TODS), published quarterly—around 700 pages per year
- *ACM SIGMOD Record,* published quarterly—around 250 pages per year
- Proceedings of the *Annual ACM SIGMOD International Conference on Management of Data*—around 450 pages per year
- Proceedings of the *Annual ACM SIGACT-SIGMOD Symposium on Principles of Database Systems*—around 350 pages per year
- Proceedings of the *Annual International Conference on Very Large Data Bases* (VLDB)—around 650 pages per year
- *The VLDB Journal,* published quarterly—around 450 pages per year

Add to the foregoing the various more specialized conferences on distributed database systems, or CAD/CAM databases, or expert database systems, or client/server systems, or object-oriented systems (etc.)—say eight or ten conferences a year, with proceedings typically running at around 300–350 pages . . . add too the huge number of technical reports from universities and industrial research laboratories . . . add the occasional papers that appear in the publications of related disciplines, such as office automation, artificial intelligence, and programming languages . . . add the trade journals such as *Data Base Newsletter, Database Review, InfoDB, Database Programming & Design,* etc., etc., which together represent many thousands of pages per year . . . add the trade shows such as *Database World* and *DB/Expo,* each with its own voluminous set of proceedings . . . add the vendor reference manuals and other documents describing various commercial products, each with a new release every 18 months or so . . . add the numerous textbooks now available that have the word "database" somewhere in their title . . . and it becomes apparent that there are (conservatively) somewhere in excess of 100,000 pages of new material published *every year.* It is thus clearly impossible to keep abreast of everything that is happening in the database field.

From all of the above, it follows that the present book—despite its inordinate length, for which I apologize—can only be, as its title indicates, an introduction to the subject, not an exhaustive treatment. Because of the explosive growth of the field, moreover, even what it is that constitutes "a good introduction" to the subject changes fairly rapidly; as a result, this new (sixth) edition of the book is once again so different from its predecessor that it is to all intents and purposes a brand new book. The overall objective remains the same, however—namely, to provide the basis for a solid education in the fundamentals of database technology, and in particular to pave the way for an understanding of the directions in which the field is currently developing and is likely to develop in the future. The book is intended primarily as a textbook, not a work of reference, though to some extent I am hopeful that it can serve the latter purpose also. The emphasis is on insight, not algorithms.

Prerequisites: Readers are assumed to be professionally interested in some aspect of data processing; they may, for example, be systems analysts or designers, application programmers, systems programmers, students following a college or similar course in computer science, or teachers of such a course. They are expected:

■ To have a reasonable appreciation of the capabilities of a modern computer system, especially the file-management features of such a system (though the book does include an appendix that provides a tutorial overview of this latter topic);

■ To have some familiarity with at least one high-level programming language.

Since these prerequisites are not particularly demanding, however, I am hopeful that the book will prove suitable as an introductory text for anyone concerned with using or implementing a database system, or for anyone who simply wishes to broaden a general knowledge of the computer science field.

The book is divided into six major parts, as follows:

   I. Basic Concepts
  II. The Relational Model
 III. Database Design
 IV. Data Protection
  V. Further Topics
 VI. Object-Oriented Systems

Each part in turn is divided into several chapters:

■ Part I (three chapters) provides a broad introduction to the concepts of database systems in general and relational database systems in particular.

■ Part II (five chapters), which is the longest part of the book—indeed, it is almost a book within a book—consists of a detailed and very careful examination of **the relational model,** which is not only the theoretical foundation underlying today's relational products, but is in fact the theoretical foundation for the entire database field.* A lengthy chapter on the major concepts of the standard relational language SQL is also included.

- Part III (four chapters) discusses the general question of **database design;** three chapters are devoted to design theory and one to the **entity/relationship model.**

- Part IV (four chapters) is concerned with various aspects of the **data protection** problem. Specifically, it discusses the concepts of recovery, concurrency, security, and integrity in a database environment.

- Part V (five chapters) shows how the ideas of the relational model are relevant to a variety of further aspects of database technology—optimization, distributed database processing, view support, and so on.

- Finally, Part VI (four chapters) describes the important new **object-oriented** approach to database systems. Chapter 25 in particular (the last in the book) considers the possibility of a rapprochement between object-oriented and relational technology.

In addition, there are four appendixes—one on file management and physical storage structures (as already mentioned), one on a commercial relational system (IBM's DB2 product), one on the comparatively new field of logic-based systems, and one that lists some important abbreviations and acronyms.

The book overall is meant to be read in sequence more or less as written. Each chapter opens with an introduction and closes with a summary; in addition, most chapters include a set of exercises, usually with answers (often the answers give additional information about the subject of the exercise). Most chapters also include an extensive list of references, many of them annotated. This structure allows the subject matter to be treated in a multilevel fashion, with the most important concepts and results being presented "in line" in the main body of the text and various subsidiary issues and more complex aspects being deferred to the Exercises, Answers, or References sections, as appropriate.

Note: References are identified in the text by two-part numbers in square brackets. For example, the reference "[4.1]" refers to the first item in the list of references at the end of Chapter 4, namely, a paper by E. F. Codd published in *Communications of the ACM* (CACM), Vol. 13, No. 6 (June 1970).

For readers who might be familiar with the previous edition of the book, the major differences from that edition are summarized below.

- *Part I:* Chapters 1–2 cover roughly the same ground as Chapters 1–2 in the previous edition, but they have been rewritten, and the treatment of certain topics (e.g.,

---

* By happy coincidence, this book's planned publication date coincides almost exactly with the relational model's silver anniversary (Codd's first publication on the subject [4.2] was dated August 19th, 1969).

client/server processing) has been improved and amplified. Chapter 3 is new; it provides a gentle introduction to some of the material to be covered in more detail in later parts of the book (especially Part II).

■ *Part II:* Chapter 4–7 (on the relational model) represent a completely rewritten, considerably expanded, and very much improved version of Chapters 11–15 from the previous edition. Chapter 8 (on the SQL language) is a condensed and considerably revised version of material from Chapters 5–6 and 9 (and elsewhere) from that edition.

Note: Some words of explanation are in order here. Previous editions of this book discussed commercial relational systems, and in particular the commercial SQL language, before getting into details of the theoretical relational model; this was done in the belief that it is usually easier on the student to show the concrete before the abstract. Unfortunately, however, the gulf between SQL and the relational model has grown so wide that I now feel it would be actively misleading to treat SQL first. In fact, SQL in its present form is so far from being a true embodiment of relational principles—it suffers from so many sins of both omission and commission—that I would have preferred to relegate it to an appendix in this edition; but the language is so important from a commercial point of view (and every database professional needs to have some familiarity with it) that it would simply not be appropriate to treat it in so dismissive a manner. I have therefore settled on a compromise—a long chapter on SQL basics in this part of the book, and individual sections in subsequent chapters describing those aspects of SQL that are specific to the subject of the chapter in question (where applicable).

Incidentally, all SQL discussions in this edition are at the level of the current SQL standard known informally as "SQL/92."

■ *Part III:* Chapter 9 (on functional dependencies) is almost entirely new. Chapters 10 and 11 represent a major revision and expansion of the old Chapter 21. Chapter 12 is a rewrite of the old Chapter 22 (the material on the entity/relationship model has been amplified and the material on RM/T has been dropped).

Again, some explanation is in order. Many reviewers complained that the previous edition treated database design issues far too late. It is my own feeling that students are simply not ready to design databases properly or to appreciate design issues until they have some understanding of what databases are and how they are used; in other words, I believe it is important to spend some time on the relational model and related matters before exposing the student to database design questions. However, I do agree that it is possible to treat design matters earlier than the previous edition did, and I have accordingly done so in this edition.

■ *Part IV:* The four chapters of this part represent a major revision and expansion of Chapters 16 and 17 from the previous edition.

■ *Part V:* Chapters 18 (on optimization) and 21 (on distributed database) are expanded and significantly revised versions of the old Chapters 18 and 23, respectively. Chapter 17 (on views) is almost completely new (it replaces the old Chapter

8); in particular, it includes some important new results regarding view updatability. Chapters 19 (on domains) and 20 (on missing information) are both new.

■ *Part VI:* This part is almost completely new, though certain portions of the material did appear in Chapter 25 in the previous edition.

Finally, Appendixes A, B, and C replace the old Chapters 3, 4, and 24, respectively, and Appendix D is an updated version of the old Appendix D.

In addition to the changes sketched above, the following topics have been (mostly) dropped from this edition:

■ INGRES (old Chapter 10)
■ Frontend subsystems (old Chapter 19)
■ Administration facilities (old Chapter 20)
■ RM/T (part of the old Chapter 22)
■ Further research topics (old Chapter 26)
■ Prerelational systems (old Appendixes A, B, and C)

Several readers of the previous edition felt that these topics were somewhat peripheral to the book's main theme; in an attempt to keep the book down to a comparatively manageable size, therefore (and also to keep it more focused), it seemed reasonable to drop them from this new edition.

One further introductory remark: The previous edition included the qualifier *Volume I* in its title. That was because at that time there was a sequel, *An Introduction to Database Systems: Volume II* (first edition, Addison-Wesley, 1983). Volume II is still in print and is still reasonably current; over the years, however, much of the material of Volume II has found its way into Volume I as well, with the result that the "Volume I *vs.* Volume II" split no longer makes much sense. I have therefore decided to drop the "Volume I" qualifier from the title of this edition.

I would like to close these prefatory notes with the following edited extract from another preface—Bertrand Russell's own preface to *The Bertrand Russell Dictionary of Mind, Matter and Morals* (ed., Lester E. Denonn), Citadel Press, 1993, reprinted here by permission:

> *I have been accused of a habit of changing my opinions. . . . I am not myself in any degree ashamed of [that habit]. What physicist who was already active in 1900 would dream of boasting that his opinions had not changed during the last half century? . . . The kind of philosophy that I value and have endeavoured to pursue is scientific, in the sense that there is some definite knowledge to be obtained and that new discoveries can make the admission of former error inevitable to any candid mind. For what I have said, whether early or late, I do not claim the kind of truth which theologians claim for their creeds. I claim only, at best, that the opinion expressed was a sensible one to hold at the time. . . . I should be much surprised if subsequent research did not show that it needed to be modified. [Such opinions*

were not] intended as pontifical pronouncements, but only as the best I could do at
the time towards the promotion of clear and accurate thinking. Clarity, above all,
has been my aim.

Readers of earlier editions of this book, if they study the present edition, will find that
I too have changed my opinions on many matters (and will no doubt continue to do so).
I hope they will accept the remarks quoted above as adequate justification for this state
of affairs. I share Bertrand Russell's perception of what the field of scientific inquiry is
all about, but he expresses that perception far more eloquently than I could hope to do.

The on-line Instructor's Manual, which complements this book, is available by
anonymous ftp from the Internet site `ftp aw.com` in the directory `cseng/au-`
`thors/date/intro6e/im.txt`. To obtain a copy of the Solutions Manual, con-
tact your Addison-Wesley sales representative.

Acknowledgments

Once again it is a pleasure to acknowledge my debt to the many people involved, directly or indirectly, in the production of this book. First, the text has certainly benefited
from the comments of students on the seminars I have been teaching over the past
several years. It has also benefited enormously from the comments of, and discussions
with, numerous friends and reviewers, including Nagraj Alur, Marilyn Bohl, Charley
Bontempo, Daniel Cooke, Hugh Darwen (alias Andrew Warden), David Embley,
Henry Etlinger, Bill Grosky, Tim Hartley, Sebastian Holst, Tom Johnston, Won Kim,
Roger King, Adrian Larner, Tim Martyn, Nelson Mattos, David McGoveran, Jim
Panttaja, Fabian Pascal, Arnie Rosenthal, Sharon Salveter, Martin Solomon, Alan
Tharp, Colin White, Paul Winsberg, and Salih Yurttas. Each of these people reviewed
at least some portion of the manuscript of this edition or made technical material available or otherwise helped me find answers to my many technical questions, and I am
very grateful to all of them. I would particularly like to thank my friends Hugh Darwen
and David McGoveran for numerous illuminating conversations and much stimulating
correspondence. I would also like to thank my wife Lindy for contributing the cover art
once again. Finally, I am grateful (as always) to everyone at Addison-Wesley—especially Lynne Doran Cote and Katherine Harutunian—for all of their encouragement
and support throughout this project, and to my editor Elydia Davis for her usual sterling
job.

Healdsburg, California   C. J. Date

Contents

PART **I**

BASIC CONCEPTS

Part I consists of three introductory chapters.

- Chapter 1 sets the scene by explaining what a database is and why database systems are generally desirable. It also very briefly discusses the difference between *relational* database systems and others.
- Next, Chapter 2 presents a general architecture for database systems, the so-called *ANSI/SPARC architecture*. That architecture serves as a framework on which all later chapters in the book will build.
- Chapter 3 then presents a broad overview of relational systems, in order to serve as a gentle introduction to the much more comprehensive discussions of the same subject to follow in later parts of the book. It also provides a brief introduction to the standard relational language SQL, and introduces and explains the running example (the suppliers-and-parts database).

1 | An Overview of Database Management

1.1 An Introductory Example

A **database system** is essentially nothing more than a *computerized record-keeping system*. The **database** itself can be regarded as a kind of electronic filing cabinet; in other words, it is a repository for a collection of computerized data files. The user of the system will be given facilities to perform a variety of operations on such files, including the following among others:

- Adding new, empty files to the database
- Inserting new data into existing files
- Retrieving data from existing files
- Updating data in existing files
- Deleting data from existing files
- Removing existing files, empty or otherwise, from the database

By way of illustration, Fig. 1.1 shows a very small database containing just a single file, called CELLAR, which in turn contains data concerning the contents of a wine cellar. Fig. 1.2 shows an example of a **retrieval** operation against that database, together with the data (more accurately, the *result*—but it is usual in database contexts to refer to results as data also) returned from that retrieval. *Note:* Throughout this book we show all database operations and suchlike material in upper case for clarity. In practice, it is often more convenient to enter such material in lower case. Most systems will accept both.

Fig. 1.3 gives examples, all more or less self-explanatory, of **insert, update,** and **delete** operations on the wine cellar database. Examples of adding and removing entire files will be given later, in Chapters 3 and 4.

To conclude this introductory section, a few final remarks:

- First, for obvious reasons, computerized files such as CELLAR in the example are frequently referred to as **tables** rather than files (in fact, they are **relational** tables—see Section 1.6).

BIN	WINE	PRODUCER	YEAR	BOTTLES	READY
2	Chardonnay	Buena Vista	92	1	94
3	Chardonnay	Geyser Peak	92	5	94
6	Chardonnay	Stonestreet	91	4	93
12	Jo. Riesling	Jekel	93	1	94
21	Fumé Blanc	Ch. St. Jean	92	4	94
22	Fumé Blanc	Robt. Mondavi	91	2	93
30	Gewurztraminer	Ch. St. Jean	93	3	94
43	Cab. Sauvignon	Windsor	86	12	95
45	Cab. Sauvignon	Geyser Peak	89	12	97
48	Cab. Sauvignon	Robt. Mondavi	88	12	99
50	Pinot Noir	Gary Farrell	91	3	94
51	Pinot Noir	Stemmler	88	3	95
52	Pinot Noir	Dehlinger	90	2	93
58	Merlot	Clos du Bois	89	9	95
64	Zinfandel	Lytton Spring	89	9	98
72	Zinfandel	Rafanelli	90	2	98

FIG. 1.1 The wine cellar database (CELLAR file)

■   Second, the rows of such a table can be thought of as representing the **records** of the file (sometimes referred to explicitly as *logical* records, to distinguish them from other kinds of records to be discussed later). Likewise, the columns can be regarded as representing the **fields** of those logical records. In this book, we will tend to use the "record" and "field" terminology when we are talking about database systems in general, the "row" and "column" terminology when we are talking about relational systems specifically. (Actually, when we get to our more formal relational discussions in later parts of the book, we will switch to more formal terms anyway.)

```
Retrieval:

SELECT WINE, BIN, PRODUCER
FROM    CELLAR
WHERE   READY = 95 ;
```

Result (as shown on, e.g., a display screen):

WINE	BIN	PRODUCER
Cab. Sauvignon	43	Windsor
Pinot Noir	51	Stemmler
Merlot	58	Clos du Bois

FIG. 1.2 Sample retrieval against the wine cellar database

```
Inserting new data:

INSERT
INTO    CELLAR ( BIN, WINE, PRODUCER, YEAR, BOTTLES, READY )
        VALUES ( 53, 'Pinot Noir', 'Saintsbury', 92, 1, 96 ) ;
```

```
Updating existing data:

UPDATE CELLAR
SET    BOTTLES = 4
WHERE  BIN = 3 ;
```

```
Deleting existing data:

DELETE
FROM    CELLAR
WHERE   BIN = 2 ;
```

FIG. 1.3 INSERT, UPDATE, and DELETE examples

■   Third, the SELECT, INSERT, UPDATE, and DELETE operations shown in Figs.
    1.2 and 1.3 above are actually all examples of statements from a database language
    called **SQL**. SQL is the language currently supported by most commercial
    database products; in fact, it is the official standard language for dealing with rela-
    tional systems (see further discussion in Section 1.6 below). The name "SQL" was
    originally an abbreviation for "Structured Query Language," and was pronounced
    "sequel." Now that the language has become a standard, however, the name is just
    a name—it is not officially an abbreviation for anything at all—and the pendulum
    has swung in favor of the pronunciation "ess-cue-ell." We will assume this latter
    pronunciation in this book.

1.2   What Is a Database System?

To repeat from Section 1.1, a database system is basically a computerized record-
keeping system; that is, it is a computerized system whose overall purpose is to maintain information and to make that information available on demand. The information
concerned can be anything that is deemed to be of significance to the individual or
organization the system is intended to serve—anything, in other words, that is needed to
assist in the general process of running the business of that individual or organization.

   Note: The terms "data" and "information" are treated as synonymous in this book.
Some writers prefer to distinguish between the two, using "data" to refer to the values
actually stored in the database and "information" to refer to the *meaning* of those values
as understood by some user. The distinction is clearly important—so important that it
seems preferable to make it explicit, where relevant, instead of relying on a somewhat
arbitrary differentiation between two essentially similar terms.

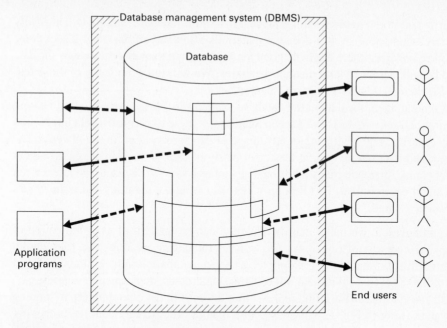

FIG. 1.4 Simplified picture of a database system

    Fig. 1.4 shows a greatly simplified view of a database system. The figure is intended to illustrate the point that a database system involves four major components, namely, **data, hardware, software,** and **users**. We consider these four components briefly below. Later, of course, we will discuss each in much more detail (except for the hardware component, most details of which are beyond the scope of this book).

Data

Database systems are available on machines that range all the way from quite small micros (even portable PCs) to the largest mainframes. Needless to say, the facilities provided by any given system are to some extent determined by the size and power of the underlying machine. In particular, systems on large machines ("large systems") tend to be *multi-user,* whereas those on smaller machines ("small systems") tend to be *single-user.* A **single-user system** is a system in which at most one user can access the database at any given time; a **multi-user system** is a system in which many users can access the database concurrently. As Fig. 1.4 suggests, we will normally assume the latter case in this book, for generality, but in fact the distinction is largely irrelevant so far as most users are concerned: A major objective of most multi-user systems is precisely to allow each individual user to behave as if he or she were working with a *single*-user system. The special problems of multi-user systems are primarily problems that are internal to the system, not ones that are visible to the user (see Part IV of this book, especially Chapter 14).

    Incidentally, it is usually convenient to assume for the sake of simplicity that the totality of data stored in the system is all held in a single database, and we will normally make this assumption, since it does not materially affect any of our other discussions. In practice, however, there might be good reasons, even in a small system, why the data should be split across several distinct databases. We will touch on some of those reasons elsewhere in this book (e.g., in Chapter 2).

In general, then, the data in the database—at least in a large system—will be both *integrated* and *shared*. As we will see in Section 1.4, these two aspects, data integration and data sharing, represent a major advantage of database systems in the "large" environment; and data integration, at least, can be significant in the "small" environment also. Of course, there are many additional advantages also (to be discussed later), even in the small environment. But first let us explain what we mean by the terms "integrated" and "shared."

■ By **integrated,** we mean that the database can be thought of as a unification of several otherwise distinct data files, with any redundancy among those files wholly or partly eliminated. For example, a given database might contain both an EMPLOYEE file, giving employee names, addresses, departments, salaries, etc., and an ENROLLMENT file, representing the enrollment of employees in training courses (refer to Fig. 1.5). Now suppose that, in order to carry out the process of training course administration, it is necessary to know the department for each enrolled student. Then there is clearly no need to include that information, redundantly, in the ENROLLMENT file, because it can always be discovered by referring to the EMPLOYEE file instead.

■ By **shared,** we mean that individual pieces of data in the database can be shared among several different users, in the sense that each of those users can have access to the same piece of data (and different users can use it for different purposes). As indicated earlier, different users can even be accessing the same piece of data *at the same time* ("concurrent access"). Such sharing (concurrent or otherwise) is partly a consequence of the fact that the database is integrated. In the EMPLOYEE-ENROLLMENT example cited above, the department information in the EMPLOYEE file would typically be shared by users in the Personnel Department and users in the Education Department—and, as suggested above, those two classes of users would typically use that information for different purposes.

Another consequence of the fact that the database is integrated is that any given user will typically be concerned only with some small portion of the total database

EMPLOYEE	NAME	ADDRESS	DEPARTMENT	SALARY	. . .
ENROLLMENT	NAME	COURSE	. . .		

FIG. 1.5 The EMPLOYEE and ENROLLMENT files

(moreover, different users' portions will overlap in many different ways). In other words, a given database will be perceived by different users in a variety of different ways. In fact, even when two users share the same portion of the database, their views of that portion might differ considerably at a detailed level. This latter point is discussed more fully in Section 1.5 and in the next chapter.

Hardware

The hardware portions of the system consist of:

- The secondary storage volumes—typically moving-head magnetic disks—that are used to hold the stored data, together with the associated I/O devices (disk drives, etc.), device controllers, I/O channels, and so forth; and
- The processor(s) and associated main memory that are used to support the execution of the database system software (see the next subsection below).

This book does not concern itself very greatly with the hardware portions of the system, for the following reasons among others: First, these aspects form a major topic in their own right; second, the problems encountered in this area are not peculiar to database systems; and third, those problems have been very thoroughly investigated and documented in numerous other places.

Software

Between the physical database itself (i.e., the data as actually stored) and the users of the system is a layer of software, the **database manager** (DB manager) or, more usually, **database management system** (DBMS). All requests from users for access to the database are handled by the DBMS; the facilities sketched in Section 1.1 for adding and removing files (or tables), retrieving data from and updating data in such files or tables, and so forth, are all facilities provided by the DBMS. One general function provided by the DBMS is thus *the shielding of database users from hardware-level details* (much as programming-language systems shield application programmers from hardware-level details). In other words, the DBMS provides users with a view of the database that is elevated somewhat above the hardware level, and supports user operations (such as the SQL operations discussed briefly in Section 1.1) that are expressed in terms of that higher-level view. We shall discuss this function, and other functions of the DBMS, in considerably more detail throughout the body of this book.

Note: The DBMS is easily the most important software component in the overall system, but it is not the only one. Others include utilities, application development tools, design aids, report writers, and so on. See Chapter 2 for further discussion.

Users

We consider three broad classes of users:

- First, there are the **application programmers,** who are responsible for writing application programs that use the database, typically in a language such as COBOL or PL/I or some more modern language such as C or Pascal. Those programs operate on the data in all the usual ways—retrieving existing information, inserting new information, deleting or changing existing information. All of these functions are of course performed by issuing the appropriate request to the DBMS. The programs themselves may be conventional batch applications, or they may be **online** applications, whose function is to support an end user (see the next paragraph) who is accessing the database from an online workstation or terminal. Most modern applications are of the online variety.

■ The second class of user, then, is **end users,** who interact with the system from online workstations or terminals. A given end user can access the database via one of the online applications mentioned in the previous paragraph, or he or she can use an interface provided as an integral part of the database system software. Such interfaces are also supported by means of online applications, of course, but those applications are **builtin,** not user-written. Most systems provide at least one such builtin application, namely an interactive **query language processor,** by which the user is able to issue high-level commands or statements (such as SELECT, INSERT, etc.) to the DBMS. The language SQL mentioned in Section 1.1 can be regarded as a typical example of a database query language.

   Note: The term "query language," common though it is, is really a misnomer, inasmuch as the English verb "query" suggests *retrieval* (only), whereas query languages typically provide UPDATE, INSERT, and DELETE operations (and probably other operations) as well.

   Most systems also provide additional builtin interfaces in which users do not issue explicit commands such as SELECT at all, but instead operate by (e.g.) choosing items from a menu or filling in boxes on a form. Such **menu-** or **forms-driven** interfaces tend to be easier to use for people who do not have a formal training in IT (IT = Information Technology; the abbreviation IS = Information Systems is often used with much the same meaning). By contrast, **command-driven interfaces**—i.e., query languages—do tend to require a certain amount of professional IT expertise, though perhaps not a very great deal (obviously not as much as is needed to write an application program in a language like COBOL). Then again, a command-driven interface is likely to be more flexible than a menu- or forms-driven one, in that query languages typically provide certain functions that are not supported by those other interfaces.

■ The third class of user (not shown in Fig. 1.4) is the **database administrator** or DBA. Discussion of the DBA function—and the associated (very important) **data** administrator function—is deferred to Sections 1.4 and 2.7.

This completes our preliminary description of the major aspects of a database system. We now go on to discuss the ideas in somewhat more detail.

1.3 What Is a Database?

Persistent Data

It is customary to refer to the data in a database as "persistent" (even though it might not actually persist for very long!). By "persistent," we mean to suggest that database data differs in kind from other, more ephemeral, data, such as input data, output data, control statements, work queues, software control blocks, intermediate results, and more generally any data that is transient in nature. Let us elaborate briefly on the terms "input data" and "output data":

- "Input data" refers to information entering the system for the very first time (typically from a terminal or workstation). Such information might cause a change to be made to the persistent data (it might *become* part of the persistent data), but it is not initially part of the database as such.

- Similarly, "output data" refers to messages and results emanating from the system (typically printed or displayed on a screen). Again, such information might be *derived from* the persistent data, but it is not itself considered to be part of the database.

Of course, the distinction between persistent and transient data is not a hard and fast one—it depends to some extent on context (i.e., how the data is being used). However, assuming that the distinction does at least make some intuitive sense, we can now give a slightly more precise definition of the term "database":

- A **database** consists of some collection of persistent data that is used by the application systems of some given enterprise.

The term "enterprise" here is simply a convenient generic term for any reasonably self-contained commercial, scientific, technical, or other organization. An enterprise might be a single individual (with a small private database), or a complete corporation or similar large body (with a very large shared database), or anything in between. Here are some examples:

1. A manufacturing company
2. A bank
3. A hospital
4. A university
5. A government department

Any enterprise must necessarily maintain a lot of data about its operation. This is the "persistent data" referred to above. The enterprises just mentioned would typically include the following among their persistent data:

1. Product data
2. Account data
3. Patient data

4. Student data

5. Planning data

Note: The first few editions of this book used the term "operational data" in place of "persistent data." That earlier term reflected the original emphasis in database systems on **operational** or **production** applications—i.e., routine, highly repetitive applications that were executed over and over again to support the day-to-day operation of the enterprise (for example, an application to support the deposit or withdrawal of cash in a banking system). Now that databases are increasingly being used for other kinds of application as well—i.e., **decision support** applications—the term "operational data" is no longer entirely appropriate. Indeed, enterprises nowadays often maintain two distinct databases, one containing operational data and one containing decision support data. The decision support database frequently consists of *summary information* (e.g., totals, averages), where that summary information in turn is extracted from the operational database on a periodic basis—say once a day or once a week.

Entities and Relationships

Let us consider the example of a manufacturing company in a little more detail. Such an enterprise will typically wish to record information about the *projects* it has on hand; the *parts* used in those projects; the *suppliers* who supply those parts; the *warehouses* in which the parts are stored; the *employees* who work on the projects; and so on. Projects, parts, suppliers, etc., thus constitute the basic **entities** about which the company needs to record information (the term "entity" is widely used in database circles to mean any distinguishable object that is to be represented in the database). Refer to Fig. 1.6.

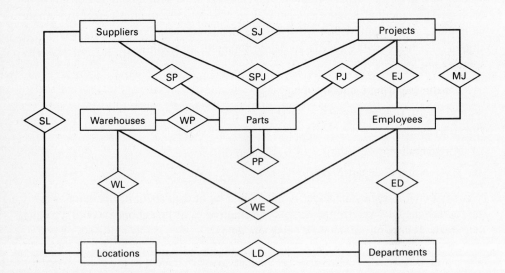

FIG. 1.6 A simple entity/relationship (E/R) diagram

It is important to understand that, in addition to the basic entities themselves, there will also be **relationships** linking those basic entities together. Such relationships are represented by diamonds and connecting lines in Fig. 1.6. For example, there is a relationship ("SP") between suppliers and parts: Each supplier supplies certain parts, and conversely each part is supplied by certain suppliers (more accurately, each supplier supplies certain *kinds* of parts, each *kind* of part is supplied by certain suppliers). Similarly, parts are used in projects, and conversely projects use parts (relationship PJ); parts are stored in warehouses, and warehouses store parts (relationship WP); and so on. Note that these relationships are all *bidirectional*—that is, they can be traversed in either direction. For example, relationship SP between suppliers and parts can be used to answer either of the following questions:

■ Given a supplier, find the parts supplied by that supplier

■ Given a part, find the suppliers who supply that part

The significant point about this relationship, and all of the others illustrated in the figure, is that *they are just as much a part of the data as are the basic entities*. They must therefore be represented in the database, just like the basic entities. Later in this book we will consider ways in which this can be done.

Incidentally, Fig. 1.6 is a simple example of what is called (for obvious reasons) an **entity/relationship diagram** (E/R diagram for short). In Chapter 12 we will consider such diagrams in some detail.

Fig. 1.6 also illustrates a number of other points:

1. Although most of the relationships in the diagram involve *two* types of entity—i.e., they are *binary* relationships—it is by no means the case that all relationships must necessarily be binary in this sense. In the example there is one relationship ("SPJ") involving three types of entity (suppliers, parts, and projects)—a *ternary* relationship. The intended interpretation is that certain suppliers supply certain parts to certain projects. Note carefully that this ternary relationship ("suppliers supply parts to projects") is *not* equivalent, in general, to the combination of the three binary relationships "suppliers supply parts," "parts are used in projects," and "projects are supplied by suppliers." For example, the statement that

   (a) Smith supplies monkey wrenches to the Manhattan project

   tells us *more* than the following three statements do:

   (b) Smith supplies monkey wrenches,

   (c) Monkey wrenches are used in the Manhattan project, and

   (d) The Manhattan project is supplied by Smith

   —we cannot (validly!) infer (a) knowing only (b), (c), and (d). More precisely, if we know (b), (c), and (d), then we might be able to infer that Smith supplies monkey wrenches to *some* project (say project Jz), that *some* supplier (say supplier Sx) supplies monkey wrenches to the Manhattan project, and that Smith supplies *some* part (say part Py) to the Manhattan project—but we cannot validly infer that Sx is Smith or that Py is monkey wrenches or that Jz is the Manhattan project. False inferences such as these are examples of what is sometimes called **the connection trap**.

2. The diagram also includes one relationship (PP) involving just *one* type of entity (parts). The relationship here is that certain parts include other parts as immediate components (the so-called **bill-of-materials** relationship)—for example, a screw is a component of a hinge assembly, which is also considered as a part and might in turn be a component of some higher-level part such as a lid. Note that this relationship is still binary; it is just that the two types of entity that are linked together, namely parts and parts, happen to be one and the same.

3. In general, a given set of entity types might be linked together in any number of distinct relationships. In the diagram, there are two relationships between projects and employees: One (EJ) represents the fact that employees are assigned to projects, the other (MJ) represents the fact that employees manage projects.

Note carefully that a relationship can be regarded as an entity in its own right. If we take as our definition of entity "any object about which we wish to record information," then a relationship certainly fits the definition. For instance, "part P4 is stored in warehouse W8" is an entity about which we might well wish to record information—e.g., the corresponding quantity. Moreover, there are definite advantages (beyond the scope of the present chapter) to be obtained by not making any unnecessary distinctions between entities and relationships. In this book, therefore, we will generally treat relationships as just a special kind of entity.

Properties

As just indicated, we regard an entity as any object about which we wish to record information. In other words, entities (and hence relationships also) have **properties**. For example, suppliers have *locations;* parts have *weights;* projects have *priorities;* assignments have *start dates;* and so on. Such properties must therefore be represented in the database also. For example, the database might include a record type S representing the "suppliers" entity type, and that record type in turn might include a field type CITY representing the "location" property.

Properties in turn might be very simple in nature, or they might have an internal structure of arbitrary complexity. For example, the "supplier location" property is presumably quite simple, consisting as it does of just a city name, and can be represented in the database by a simple character string. By contrast, a warehouse might have a "floor plan" property, and that property might be quite complex, consisting perhaps of an entire architectural drawing plus associated descriptive text. Current database products are mostly not very good at dealing with complex properties such as drawings or text. We will return to this topic later in this book (especially in Chapter 19 and Chapters 22-25); until then, we will generally assume (where it makes any difference) that all properties are "simple" and can be represented by "simple" data types in the database. Examples of such "simple" data types include numbers, strings, dates, times, etc.

1.4 Why Database?

Why use a database system? What are the advantages? To some extent the answer to these questions depends on whether the system in question is single- or multi-user (or rather, to be more accurate, there are numerous *additional* advantages in the multi-user case). Let us consider the single-user case first.

Refer back to the wine cellar example once again (Fig. 1.1), which we can regard as typical of a single-user database. Now, that particular database is so small and so simple that the advantages might not be very immediately obvious. But imagine a similar database for a large restaurant, with a stock of perhaps thousands of bottles and with very frequent changes to that stock; or think of a liquor store, with again a very large stock and with high turnover on that stock. (These would typically still be single-user systems, incidentally, even though the database is larger.) The advantages of a database system over traditional, paper-based methods of record-keeping will perhaps be more readily apparent in these examples. Here are some of them:

- *Compactness:* No need for possibly voluminous paper files.
- *Speed:* The machine can retrieve and change data far faster than a human can. In particular, *ad hoc,* spur-of-the-moment queries (e.g., "Do we have more Zinfandel than Pinot Noir?") can be answered quickly without any need for time-consuming manual or visual searches.
- *Less drudgery:* Much of the sheer tedium of maintaining files by hand is eliminated. Mechanical tasks are always better done by machines.
- *Currency:* Accurate, up-to-date information is available on demand at any time.

The foregoing benefits apply with even more force in a multi-user environment, of course, where the database is likely to be much larger and much more complex than in the single-user case. However, there is one overriding additional advantage in such an environment, namely as follows: *The database system provides the enterprise with centralized control of its data* (which, as the reader should realize from Section 1.3, is one of its most valuable assets). Such a situation contrasts sharply with that found in an enterprise without a database system, where typically each application has its own private files—quite often its own private tapes and disks, too—so that the data is widely dispersed and might thus be difficult to control in any systematic way.

Data Administration and Database Administration

Let us elaborate a little on this concept of centralized control. The concept implies that (in an enterprise with a database system) there will be some identifiable person who has this central responsibility for the data. That person is the **data administrator** (sometimes abbreviated DA) mentioned briefly at the end of Section 1.2. Given that (as indicated above) the data is one of the enterprise's most valuable assets, it is imperative that there should be some person who understands the data, and the needs of the enterprise with respect to the data, *at a senior management level*. The data administrator is that person. Thus, it is the data administrator's job to decide what data should be stored in the database in the first place, and to establish policies for maintaining and dealing with that data once it has been stored. An example of such a policy would be one that dictates who can perform what operations on what data in what circumstances—in other words, a *data security* policy (see further discussion below).

Note carefully that the data administrator is a manager, not a technician (although he or she certainly does need to have some appreciation of the capabilities of database systems at a technical level). The *technical* person responsible for implementing the data administrator's decisions is the **data***base* **administrator** (usually abbreviated DBA). Thus, the DBA, unlike the data administrator, is an *IT professional*. The job of the DBA is to create the actual database and to implement the technical controls needed to enforce the various policy decisions made by the data administrator. The DBA is also responsible for ensuring that the system operates with adequate performance and for providing a variety of other related technical services. The DBA will typically have a staff of systems programmers and other technical assistants (i.e., the DBA function will typically be performed in practice by a team of several people, not just by one person); for simplicity, however, it is convenient to assume that the DBA is indeed a single individual. We will discuss the DBA function in more detail in Chapter 2.

Benefits of the Database Approach

We close this section by identifying some of the specific advantages that accrue from the notion of centralized control of the data.

- Redundancy can be reduced.

   In nondatabase systems each application has its own private files. This fact can often lead to considerable redundancy in stored data, with resultant waste in storage space. For example, a personnel application and an education-records application might both own a file that includes department information for employees. As suggested in Section 1.2, those two files can be integrated, and the redundancy eliminated, *if* the data administrator is aware of the data requirements for both applications—i.e., *if* the enterprise has the necessary overall control.

   Incidentally, we do not mean to suggest that *all* redundancy can or necessarily should be eliminated. Sometimes there are sound business or technical reasons for maintaining several distinct copies of the same stored data. However, we do mean to suggest that any such redundancy should be carefully *controlled*—that is, the DBMS should be aware of it, if it exists, and should assume responsibility for "propagating updates" (see the next point below).

- Inconsistency can be avoided (to some extent).

   This is really a corollary of the previous point. Suppose that a given fact about the real world—say the fact that employee E3 works in department D8—is represented by two distinct entries in the stored database. Suppose also that the DBMS is not aware of this duplication (i.e., the redundancy is not controlled). Then there will necessarily be occasions on which the two entries will not agree—namely, when one of the two has been updated and the other has not. At such times the database is said to be *inconsistent.* Clearly, a database that is in an inconsistent state is capable of supplying incorrect or contradictory information to its users.

It should also be clear that if the given fact is represented by a single entry (i.e., if the redundancy is removed), then such an inconsistency cannot occur. Alternatively, if the redundancy is not removed but is controlled (by making it known to the DBMS), then the DBMS could guarantee that the database is never inconsistent *as seen by the user,* by ensuring that any change made to either of the two entries is automatically applied to the other one also. This process is known as **propagating updates**—where (as is usually the case) the term "update" is taken to include all of the operations of insertion, deletion, and modification. Note, however, that few commercially available systems today are capable of automatically propagating updates in this manner; that is, most current products do not support controlled redundancy at all, except in certain special situations.

■   The data can be shared.

We discussed this point in Section 1.2, but for completeness we mention it again here. Sharing means not only that existing applications can share the data in the database, but also that new applications can be developed to operate against that same stored data. In other words, it might be possible to satisfy the data requirements of new applications without having to create any additional stored data.

■   Standards can be enforced.

With central control of the database, the DBA (under the direction of the data administrator) can ensure that all applicable standards are observed in the representation of the data. Applicable standards might include any or all of the following: corporate, installation, departmental, industry, national, and international standards. Standardizing data representation is particularly desirable as an aid to *data interchange,* or migration of data between systems (this consideration is becoming particularly important with the advent of distributed processing technology—see Section 2.12). Likewise, data naming and documentation standards are also very desirable as an aid to data sharing and understandability.

■   Security restrictions can be applied.

Having complete jurisdiction over the database, the DBA (a) can ensure that the only means of access to the database is through the proper channels, and hence (b) can define security rules to be checked whenever access is attempted to sensitive data (again, under appropriate direction from the data administrator). Different rules can be established for each type of access (retrieve, insert, delete, etc.) to each piece of information in the database. Note, however, that without such rules the security of the data might actually be *more* at risk than in a traditional (dispersed) filing system; that is, the centralized nature of a database system in a sense *requires* that a good security system be in place also.

■   Integrity can be maintained.

The problem of integrity is the problem of ensuring that the data in the database is accurate. Inconsistency between two entries that purport to represent the same "fact" is an example of lack of integrity (see the discussion of this point above); of course, that particular problem can arise only if redundancy exists in the stored data. Even if there is no redundancy, however, the database might still contain incorrect information. For example, an employee might be shown as having worked 400 hours in the week instead of 40, or as belonging to a department D9 when no such department exists. Centralized control of the database can help in avoiding such problems—insofar as they can be avoided—by permitting the data administrator to define (and the DBA to implement) integrity rules to be checked whenever any data update operation is attempted. (Again we are using the term "update" generically to cover all of the operations of insertion, deletion, and modification.)

It is worth pointing out that data integrity is even more important in a multiuser database system than it is in a "private files" environment, precisely because the database is shared. For without appropriate controls it would be possible for one user to update the database incorrectly, thereby generating bad data and so "infecting" other innocent users of that data. It should also be mentioned that most database products tend to be somewhat weak in their support for integrity controls, although there have been some recent improvements in this area.

■ Conflicting requirements can be balanced.

Knowing the overall requirements of the enterprise—as opposed to the requirements of individual users—the DBA (under the data administrator's direction, as always) can so structure the system as to provide an overall service that is "best for the enterprise." For example, a representation can be chosen for the data in storage that gives fast access for the most important applications (possibly at the cost of poorer performance for certain other applications).

Most of the advantages listed above are probably fairly obvious. However, one further point, which might not be so obvious (although it is in fact implied by several of the others) needs to be added to the list—namely, *the provision of data independence*. (Strictly speaking, this is an *objective* for database systems, rather than an advantage necessarily.) The concept of data independence is so important that we devote a separate section to it.

1.5 Data Independence

Data independence can most easily be explained by first explaining its opposite. Applications implemented on older systems tend to be data-dependent. What this means is that the way in which the data is organized in secondary storage, and the technique for accessing it, are both dictated by the requirements of the application under consideration, and moreover that *knowledge of that data organization and that access technique is built into the application logic and code*.

■ *Example:* Suppose we have an application that processes the EMPLOYEE file, and suppose it is decided, for performance reasons, that the file is to be stored indexed on the "employee name" field. In an older system, the application in question will typically be aware of the fact that the index exists, and aware also of the file sequence as defined by that index, and the internal structure of the application will be built around that knowledge. In particular, the precise form of the various data access and exception-checking procedures within the application will depend very heavily on details of the interface presented to the application by the data management software.

We say that an application such as the one in this example is **data-dependent,** because it is impossible to change the storage structure (how the data is physically stored) or access technique (how it is accessed) without affecting the application, probably drastically. For instance, it would not be possible to replace the indexed file in the example by a hash-addressed file without making major modifications to the application. What is more, the portions of the application requiring alteration in such a case are precisely those portions that communicate with the data management software; the difficulties involved are quite irrelevant to the problem the application was originally written to solve—i.e., they are difficulties *introduced* by the nature of the data management interface.

In a database system, however, it would be extremely undesirable to allow applications to be data-dependent, for at least the following two reasons:

1. Different applications will need different views of the same data. For example, suppose that before the enterprise introduces its integrated database, there are two applications, A and B, each owning a private file that includes the field "customer balance." Suppose, however, that application A records this field in decimal, whereas application B records it in binary. It will still be possible to integrate the two files, and to eliminate the redundancy, provided the DBMS is ready and able to perform all necessary conversions between the stored representation chosen (which might be decimal or binary or something else again) and the form in which each application wishes to see it. For example, if it is decided to store the field in decimal, then every access by B will require a conversion to or from binary.

    This is a fairly trivial example of the kind of difference that might exist in a database system between the data as seen by a given application and the data as physically stored. Many other possible differences will be considered later.

2. The DBA must have the freedom to change the storage structure or access technique in response to changing requirements, without having to modify existing applications. For example, new kinds of data might be added to the database; new standards might be adopted; application priorities (and therefore relative performance requirements) might change; new types of storage device might become available; and so on. If applications are data-dependent, such changes will typically require corresponding changes to be made to programs, thus tying up programmer effort that would otherwise be available for the creation of new applications. It is still not uncommon, even today, to find that 25 percent or even more of the programming effort available in the installation is devoted to this kind of maintenance activity—clearly a waste of a scarce and valuable resource.

It follows that the provision of data independence is a major objective of database systems. Data independence can be defined as **the immunity of applications to change in storage structure and access technique**—which implies, of course, that the applications concerned do not depend on any one particular storage structure or access technique. In Chapter 2, we describe an architecture for database systems that provides a basis for achieving the data independence objective. Before then, however, let us consider in more detail some examples of the types of change that the DBA might wish to make, and that we might therefore wish applications to be immune to.

We start by defining three terms: *stored field, stored record,* and *stored file* (refer to Fig. 1.7).

■ A **stored field** is the smallest unit of stored data. The database will, in general, contain many **occurrences** (or **instances**) of each of several **types** of stored field. For example, a database containing information about parts would probably include a stored field type called "part number," and there would be one occurrence of this stored field for each kind of part (screw, hinge, lid, etc.).

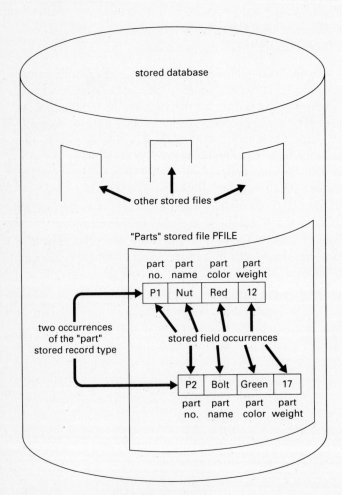

FIG. 1.7 Stored fields, records, and files

■   A **stored record** is a collection of related stored fields. Again we distinguish between type and occurrence. A stored record **occurrence** (or **instance**) consists of a
group of related stored field occurrences. For example, a stored record occurrence
in the "parts" database might consist of an occurrence of each of the following
stored fields: part number, part name, part color, and part weight. We say that the
database contains many occurrences of the "part" stored record **type** (again, one
occurrence for each distinct kind of part).

   As an aside, we note that it is common to drop the qualifiers "type" and "occurrence" and to rely on context to indicate which is meant. Although there is a
slight risk of confusion, the practice is convenient, and we will adopt it ourselves
from time to time in this book.

■   Finally, a **stored file** is the collection of all occurrences of one type of stored record. *Note:* We deliberately ignore the possibility of a stored file containing more
than one type of stored record. This is another simplifying assumption that does not
materially affect any of our subsequent discussions.

Now, in nondatabase systems it is usually the case that an application's *logical*
record is identical to some corresponding *stored* record. As we have already seen, however, this is not necessarily the case in a database system, because the DBA might need
to be able to make changes to the storage structure—that is, to the stored fields, records,
and files—while the corresponding logical structure does *not* change. For example, the
"part weight" field mentioned above might be stored in binary to economize on storage
space, whereas a given COBOL application might see it as a PICTURE item (i.e., as a
character string). And later the DBA might decide for some reason to change the stored
representation of that field from binary to decimal, and yet still allow the application to
see it in character form.

   As stated earlier, a difference such as this one, involving data type conversion on a
particular field on each access, is comparatively minor; in principle, however, the difference between what the application sees and what is actually stored might be quite
considerable. To amplify this remark, we present below a list of aspects of the database
storage structure that might be subject to variation. The reader should consider in each
case what the DBMS would have to do to protect an application from such variation
(and indeed whether such protection can always be achieved).

■   Representation of numeric data

   A numeric field might be stored in internal arithmetic form (e.g., in packed
decimal) or as a character string. Either way, the DBA must choose an appropriate
base (e.g., binary or decimal), scale (fixed or floating point), mode (real or complex), and precision (number of digits). Any of these aspects might be changed to
improve performance or to conform to a new standard or for many other reasons.

■   Representation of character data

   A character string field might be stored using any of several distinct coded
character sets or "forms-of-use" (e.g., ASCII, EBCDIC).

- Units for numeric data

  The units in a numeric field might change—from inches to centimeters, for example, during a process of metrication.

- Data encoding

  In some situations it might be desirable to represent data in storage by coded values. For example, the "part color" field, which an application sees as a character string ("Red" or "Blue" or "Green" ...), might be stored as a single decimal digit, interpreted according to the coding scheme 1 = "Red," 2 = "Blue," and so on.

- Data materialization

  In practice the logical field seen by an application will usually correspond to some specific stored field (although, as we have already seen, there might be differences in data type, units, and so on). In such a case, the process of materialization—that is, constructing an occurrence of the logical field from the corresponding stored field occurrence and presenting it to the application—can be said to be *direct*. Sometimes, however, a logical field will have no single stored counterpart; instead, its values will be materialized by means of some computation performed on a set of several stored field occurrences. For example, values of the logical field "total quantity" might be materialized by summing a number of individual stored quantity values. "Total quantity" here is an example of a **virtual** field, and the materialization process is said to be *indirect*. Note, however, that the user might see a difference between real and virtual fields, inasmuch as it might not be (directly) possible to insert or modify an occurrence of a virtual field.

- Structure of stored records

  Two existing stored records might be combined into one. For example, the stored records

| Part Number | Color |

and

| Part Number | Weight |

could be combined to form

| Part Number | Color | Weight |

Such a change might occur as predatabase applications are brought into the database system. It implies that an application's logical record might consist of a subset of the corresponding stored record—that is, certain fields in that stored record would be invisible to the application in question.

Alternatively, a single stored record type might be split into two. Reversing the previous example, the stored record type

| Part Number | Color | Weight |

could be broken down into

Part Number	Color	and	Part Number	Weight

Such a split would allow less frequently used portions of the original record to be stored on a slower device, for example. The implication is that an application's logical record might contain fields from several distinct stored records—that is, it would be a superset of any given one of those stored records.

■ Structure of stored files

A given stored file can be physically implemented in storage in a wide variety of ways. For example, it might be entirely contained within a single storage volume (e.g., a single disk), or it might be spread across several volumes on several different device types; it might or might not be physically sequenced according to the values of some stored field; it might or might not be sequenced in one or more additional ways by some other means, e.g., by one or more indexes or one or more embedded pointer chains (or both); it might or might not be accessible via hash-addressing; the stored records might or might not be physically blocked (several per physical record); and so on. But none of these considerations should affect applications in any way (other than in performance, of course).

This concludes our list of aspects of the storage structure that are subject to possible change. The list implies (among other things) that the database should be able to **grow** without affecting existing applications; indeed, enabling the database to grow without logically impairing existing applications is probably the single most important reason for requiring data independence in the first place. For example, it should be possible to extend an existing stored record by the addition of new stored fields, representing, typically, further information concerning some existing type of entity (e.g., a "unit cost" field might be added to the "part" stored record). Such new fields should simply be invisible to existing applications. Likewise, it should be possible to add entirely new types of stored record (and hence new stored files), again without requiring any change to existing applications; such records would typically represent new types of entity (e.g., a "supplier" record type could be added to the "parts" database). Again, such additions should be invisible to existing applications.

We close this section by noting that data independence is not an absolute—different systems provide it in different degrees. To put this another way, few systems, if any, provide no data independence at all; it is just that some systems are less data-independent than others. Modern systems tend to be more data-independent than older systems, but they are still not perfect, as we will see in some of the chapters to come.

1.6   Relational Systems and Others

Almost all of the database products developed since the late 1970s have been based on what is called **the relational approach;** what is more, the vast majority of database research over the last 25 years has also been based—albeit a little indirectly, in some cases—on that approach. In fact, it is undeniable that the relational approach represents the dominant trend in the marketplace today, and that the "relational model" (see Part II of this book) is the single most important development in the entire history of the database field. For these reasons, plus the additional reason that the relational model is solidly based on certain aspects of mathematics and therefore provides an ideal vehicle for teaching the concepts and principles of database systems, the emphasis in this book is very heavily on relational systems and the relational approach.

What then does it mean to say that a system is relational? It is unfortunately not possible to answer this question fully at this early point in our discussions; however, it is possible, and desirable, to give a rough-and-ready answer, which we can make more precise later. Briefly, a relational system is a system in which:

1. The data is perceived by the user as tables (and nothing but tables); and

2. The operators at the user's disposal (e.g., for data retrieval) are operators that generate new tables from old. For example, there will be one operator to extract a subset of the rows of a given table, and another to extract a subset of the columns— and of course a row subset and a column subset of a table can both in turn be regarded as tables themselves.

The reason such systems are called "relational" is that the term "relation" is essentially just a mathematical term for a table. For most practical purposes, indeed, the terms "relation" and "table" can be taken as synonymous. See Part II of this book for further discussion.

As indicated, we will make the foregoing definition considerably more precise later, but it will serve for the time being. Fig. 1.8 provides an illustration. The data—see part (a) of the figure—consists of a single table, named CELLAR (in fact, it is a scaled-down version of the CELLAR table from Fig. 1.1, reduced in size to make it a little more manageable). Two sample retrievals—one involving a row-subsetting operation and the other a column-subsetting operation—are shown in part (b) of the figure. *Note:* Once again, the two retrievals are in fact examples of the SELECT statement of the language SQL first mentioned in Section 1.1.

We can now distinguish between relational and nonrelational systems, as follows. As already stated, the user of a relational system sees the data as tables, and nothing but tables. The user of a nonrelational system, by contrast, sees other data structures, either instead of or in addition to the tables of a relational system. Those other structures, in turn, require other operators to manipulate them. For example, in a **hierarchic** system, the data is represented to the user in the form of a set of tree structures (hierarchies), and the operators provided for manipulating such structures include operators for traversing hierarchic paths up and down the trees.

To pursue the point a little further: Database systems can in fact be conveniently categorized according to the data structures and operators they present to the user. First of all, older (prerelational) systems fall into three broad categories, namely **inverted**

a) *Given table:*

CELLAR

WINE	YEAR	BOTTLES
Chardonnay	91	4
Fumé Blanc	91	2
Pinet Noir	88	3
Zinfandel	89	9

b) *Operators (examples):*

1. *Row subset:*

```
SELECT  WINE, YEAR, BOTTLES
FROM    CELLAR
WHERE   YEAR > 90 ;
```

Result:

WINE	YEAR	BOTTLES
Chardonnay	91	4
Fumé Blanc	91	2

2. *Column subset:*

```
SELECT  WINE, BOTTLES
FROM    CELLAR ;
```

Result:

WINE	BOTTLES
Chardonnay	4
Fumé Blanc	2
Pinot Noir	3
Zinfandel	9

FIG. 1.8 Data structure and operators in a relational system (examples)

list, hierarchic, and **network** systems. Examples of commercially available products in these three categories include:

Inverted list:	CA-DATACOM/DB, from Computer Associates International Inc. (previously known as DATACOM/DB, from Applied Data Research)
Hierarchic:	IMS, from IBM Corporation
Network:	CA-IDMS/DB, from Computer Associates International Inc. (previously known as IDMS, from Cullinet Software Inc.)

The first **relational** products began to appear in the late 1970s and early 1980s. At the time of writing (1993), there are well over 100—perhaps as many as 200—such products commercially available, and those products run on just about every kind of hardware and software platform imaginable. Examples of such products include DB2 from IBM Corporation; Rdb/VMS from Digital Equipment Corporation; ORACLE from Oracle Corporation; INGRES from the Ingres Division of The ASK Group Inc.; SYBASE from Sybase Inc.; and many, many more.

More recently, research has proceeded on a variety of what might be called "postrelational" systems, some of them based on upward-compatible extensions to the original relational approach, others consisting of attempts at doing something entirely different. We content ourselves for now with merely mentioning some of these more recent approaches by name, without making any attempt at this point to explain what the names mean or what the researchers are trying to achieve:

- Deductive DBMSs
- Expert DBMSs
- Extendable DBMSs
- Object-oriented DBMSs
- Semantic DBMSs
- Universal relation DBMSs

In the case of **object-oriented** systems, in fact, some products have begun to appear, including GemStone from Servio Corporation, ObjectStore from Object Design Corporation, and OpenODB from Hewlett-Packard Corporation. We will examine some of these newer directions—object-oriented systems in particular—in later parts of the book.

1.7   Summary

We close this introductory chapter by summarizing the main points discussed. First, a **database system** can be thought of as a computerized record-keeping system. Such a system involves the **data** itself (stored in the **database**), **hardware, software** (in particular the **database management system** or DBMS), and—most important!—**users**. Users in turn can be divided into **application programmers, end users,** and the **database administrator** or DBA. The DBA is responsible for administering the database and database system in accordance with policies established by the **data administrator**.

Databases are **integrated** and (usually) **shared;** they are used to store **persistent** data. Such data can be usefully (albeit informally) considered as representing **entities**, together with **relationships** among those entities—although in fact a relationship is really just a special kind of entity. We very briefly examined the idea of **entity/relationship diagrams**.

Database systems provide a number of benefits, of which one of the most important is **data independence** (the immunity of applications to changes in the way the data is stored and accessed).

Finally, database systems can be based on a number of different approaches, including in particular the **relational** approach. From both an economic and a theoretical perspective, the relational approach is easily the most important (and this state of affairs is not likely to change in the foreseeable future). In a relational system, the data is seen by the user as **tables,** and the operators available to the user for dealing with the data are operators that manipulate tables. We have seen a few simple examples of **SQL,** the standard language for dealing with relational systems. This book will be heavily based on the relational approach, although *not*—for reasons explained in the Preface—on SQL *per se*.

Exercises

1.1 Define the following terms:

binary relationship	menu-driven interface
command-driven interface	multi-user system
concurrent access	online application
data administration	persistent data
database	property
database system	query language
data independence	redundancy
DBA	relationship
DBMS	security
entity	sharing
entity/relationship diagram	stored field
forms-driven interface	stored file
integration	stored record
integrity	

1.2 What are the advantages of using a database system?

1.3 What are the disadvantages of using a database system?

1.4 What do you understand by the term "relational system"? Distinguish between relational and nonrelational systems.

1.5 Show the effects of the following SQL retrieval operations on the wine cellar database of Fig. 1.1.

(a)
```
SELECT  WINE, PRODUCER
FROM    CELLAR
WHERE   BIN = 72 ;
```

(b)
```
SELECT  WINE, PRODUCER
FROM    CELLAR
WHERE   YEAR > 91 ;
```

(c)
```
SELECT  BIN, WINE, YEAR
FROM    CELLAR
WHERE   READY < 94 ;
```

(d)
```
SELECT  WINE, BIN, YEAR
FROM    CELLAR
WHERE   PRODUCER = 'Robt. Mondavi'
AND     BOTTLES > 6 ;
```

1.6 Show the effects of the following SQL update operations on the wine cellar database of Fig. 1.1.

(a)
```
INSERT
INTO    CELLAR ( BIN, WINE, PRODUCER, YEAR, BOTTLES, READY )
        VALUES ( 80, 'Syrah', 'Meridian', 89, 12, 94 ) ;
```

(b)
```
DELETE
FROM    CELLAR
WHERE   READY > 95 ;
```

(c)
```
UPDATE  CELLAR
SET     BOTTLES = 5
WHERE   BIN = 50 ;
```

(d) UPDATE CELLAR
　　　SET　　BOTTLES = BOTTLES + 2
　　　WHERE　BIN = 50 ;

1.7　Write SQL statements to perform the following operations on the wine cellar database:

(a) Retrieve bin number, name of wine, and number of bottles for all Geyser Peak wines.

(b) Retrieve bin number and name of wine for all wines for which there are more than five bottles in stock.

(c) Retrieve bin number for all red wines.

(d) Add three bottles to bin number 30.

(e) Remove all Chardonnay from stock.

(f) Add an entry for a new case (12 bottles) of Gary Farrell Merlot: bin number 55, year 91, ready in 96.

1.8　Suppose you have a classical music collection consisting of CDs and/or LPs and/or audio tapes, and you want to build a database that will let you find which recordings you have for a specific composer (e.g., Sibelius) or conductor (e.g., Simon Rattle) or soloist (e.g., Arthur Grumiaux) or work (e.g., Beethoven's Fifth) or orchestra (e.g., the NYPO) or kind of work (e.g., violin concerto) or chamber group (e.g., the Kronos Quartet). Draw an entity/relationship diagram like that of Fig. 1.6 for this database.

Answers to Selected Exercises

1.1　We make one remark here: The trade press, sales brochures, etc., very frequently use the term *database* when they really mean *DBMS* (e.g., "vendor *X*'s database outperformed vendor *Y*'s database by a factor of two to one"). This usage is sloppy, and deprecated, but very, very common. *Caveat lector.*

1.3　Some disadvantages are as follows:

- Security might be compromised (without good controls)
- Integrity might be compromised (without good controls)
- Additional hardware might be required
- Performance overhead might be significant
- Successful operation is crucial (the enterprise might be highly vulnerable to failure)
- The system is likely to be complex (though such complexity should be concealed from the user)

1.5　(a)

WINE	PRODUCER
Zinfandel	Rafanelli

(b)

WINE	PRODUCER
Chardonnay	Buena Vista
Chardonnay	Geyser Peak
Jo. Riesling	Jekel
Fumé Blanc	Ch. St. Jean
Gewurztraminer	Ch. St. Jean

(c)

BIN	WINE	YEAR
6	Chardonnay	91
22	Fumé Blanc	91
52	Pinot Noir	90

(d)

WINE	BIN	YEAR
Cab. Sauvignon	48	88

1.6 (a) Row for bin 80 added to the CELLAR table.

(b) Rows for bins 45, 48, 64, and 72 deleted from the CELLAR table.

(c) Row for bin 50 has number of bottles set to 5.

(d) Same as (c).

1.7 (a)
```
SELECT  BIN, WINE, BOTTLES
FROM    CELLAR
WHERE   PRODUCER = 'Geyser Peak' ;
```

(b)
```
SELECT  BIN, WINE
FROM    CELLAR
WHERE   BOTTLES > 5 ;
```

(c)
```
SELECT  BIN
FROM    CELLAR
WHERE   WINE = 'Cab. Sauvignon'
OR      WINE = 'Pinot Noir'
OR      WINE = 'Zinfandel'
OR      WINE = 'Syrah'
OR      ....... ;
```

There is no shortcut answer to this question, because "color of wine" is not explicitly recorded in the database.

(d)
```
UPDATE  CELLAR
SET     BOTTLES = BOTTLES + 3
WHERE   BIN = 30 ;
```

(e)
```
DELETE
FROM    CELLAR
WHERE   WINE = 'Chardonnay' ;
```

(f)
```
INSERT
INTO    CELLAR ( BIN, WINE, PRODUCER, YEAR, BOTTLES, READY ) ·
        VALUES ( 55, 'Merlot', 'Gary Farrell', 91, 12, 96 ) ;
```

2 An Architecture for a Database System

2.1 Purpose

We are now in a position to introduce an architecture for a database system. Our aim in presenting this architecture is to provide a framework on which we can build in subsequent chapters. Such a framework is useful for describing general database concepts and for explaining the structure of specific database systems—but we do not claim that every system can neatly be matched to this particular framework, nor do we mean to suggest that this particular architecture provides the only possible framework. "Small" systems, in particular, will probably not support all aspects of the architecture. However, the architecture in question does seem to fit most systems (relational or otherwise) reasonably well; moreover, it is in broad agreement with that proposed by the ANSI/SPARC Study Group on Data Base Management Systems (the so-called ANSI/SPARC architecture—see references [2.1–2.2]). We choose not to follow the ANSI/SPARC terminology in every detail, however.

One additional preliminary remark: The material of this chapter (and the preceding chapter) is of course fundamental to a full appreciation of the structure and capabilities of modern database systems. However, it is also somewhat abstract, and hence rather dry, and it does tend to involve a large number of concepts and terms that are probably new to the novice reader. In later parts of the book, you will find material that is much less abstract, and thus perhaps more immediately understandable. You might therefore prefer just to give the present chapter a "once over lightly" reading for now, and to reread individual sections more carefully later as they become more directly relevant to the topics at hand.

2.2 The Three Levels of the Architecture

The ANSI/SPARC architecture is divided into three levels, known as the internal, conceptual, and external levels (see Fig. 2.1). Broadly speaking:

- The **internal level** is the one closest to physical storage—i.e., it is the one concerned with the way the data is physically stored;

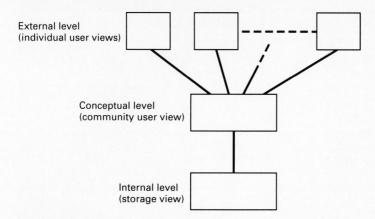

External level
(individual user views)

Conceptual level
(community user view)

Internal level
(storage view)

FIG. 2.1   The three levels of the architecture

■   The **external level** is the one closest to the users—i.e., it is the one concerned with the way the data is viewed by individual users; and

■   The **conceptual level** is a "level of indirection" between the other two.

If the external level is concerned with *individual* user views, then the conceptual level is concerned with a *community* user view. In other words, there will be many distinct external views, each consisting of a more or less abstract representation of some portion of the total database, and there will be precisely one conceptual view, consisting of a similarly abstract representation of the database in its entirety. (Remember that most users will not be interested in the total database, but only in some restricted portion of it.) Likewise, there will be precisely one internal view, representing the total database as physically stored. *Note:* When we describe some representation as abstract here, we merely mean that it involves user-oriented constructs such as logical records and fields instead of machine-oriented constructs such as bits and bytes.

An example will help to make these ideas clearer. Fig. 2.2 shows the conceptual view, the corresponding internal view, and two corresponding external views (one for a PL/I user and one for a COBOL user), all for a simple personnel database. Of course, the example is completely hypothetical—it is not intended to resemble any actual system—and many irrelevant details have deliberately been omitted.

We explain the example as follows.

■   At the conceptual level, the database contains information concerning an entity type called EMPLOYEE. Each individual EMPLOYEE occurrence has an EMPLOYEE_NUMBER (six characters), a DEPARTMENT_NUMBER (four characters), and a SALARY (five decimal digits).

■   At the internal level, employees are represented by a stored record type called STORED_EMP, twenty bytes long. STORED_EMP contains four stored fields: a six-byte prefix (presumably containing control information such as flags or pointers), and three data fields corresponding to the three properties of employees. In

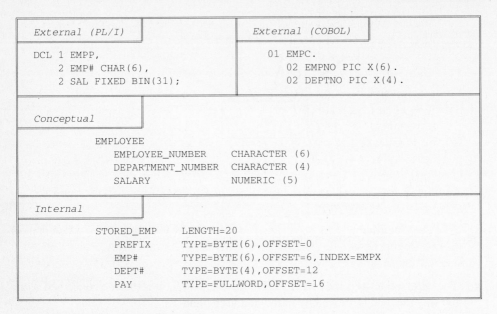

```
External (PL/I)                      External (COBOL)

DCL 1 EMPP,                            01 EMPC.
   2 EMP# CHAR(6),                        02 EMPNO PIC X(6).
   2 SAL FIXED BIN(31);                   02 DEPTNO PIC X(4).


Conceptual

           EMPLOYEE
               EMPLOYEE_NUMBER     CHARACTER (6)
               DEPARTMENT_NUMBER   CHARACTER (4)
               SALARY              NUMERIC (5)

Internal

           STORED_EMP     LENGTH=20
               PREFIX     TYPE=BYTE(6),OFFSET=0
               EMP#       TYPE=BYTE(6),OFFSET=6,INDEX=EMPX
               DEPT#      TYPE=BYTE(4),OFFSET=12
               PAY        TYPE=FULLWORD,OFFSET=16
```

FIG. 2.2   An example of the three levels

addition, STORED_EMP records are indexed on the EMP# field by an index called EMPX, whose definition is not shown.

■ The PL/I user has an external view of the database in which each employee is represented by a PL/I record containing two fields (department numbers are of no interest to this user and have therefore been omitted from the view). The record type is defined by an ordinary PL/I structure declaration in accordance with the normal PL/I rules.

■ Similarly, the COBOL user has an external view in which each employee is represented by a COBOL record containing, again, two fields (this time, salaries have been omitted). The record type is defined by an ordinary COBOL record description in accordance with the normal COBOL rules.

Notice that corresponding objects can have different names at each point. For example, the employee number is referred to as EMP# in the PL/I view, as EMPNO in the COBOL view, as EMPLOYEE_NUMBER in the conceptual view, and as EMP# (again) in the internal view. Of course, the system must be aware of the correspondences. For example, it must be told that the COBOL field EMPNO is derived from the conceptual field EMPLOYEE_NUMBER, which in turn is represented at the internal level by the stored field EMP#. Such correspondences, or **mappings,** are not shown in Fig. 2.2. See Section 2.6.

Now, it makes little difference for the purposes of the present chapter whether the system under consideration is relational or otherwise. But it might be helpful to indicate briefly how the three levels of the architecture will typically be realized in a relational system:

- First, the conceptual level in such a system *will* definitely be relational, in the sense that the objects visible at that level will be relational tables (also, the operators will be relational operators, i.e., operators that work on such tables, such as the row- and column-subsetting operators discussed briefly in Section 1.6).

- Second, a given external view will typically either be relational also, or else something very close to it; for example, the PL/I and COBOL record declarations of Fig. 2.2 can be regarded as, respectively, the PL/I and COBOL equivalents of the declaration of a relational table in a relational system. *Note:* In passing we should mention the point that the term "external view" (usually abbreviated to just "view") unfortunately has a rather specific meaning in relational contexts that is *not* identical to the meaning ascribed to it in this chapter. See Chapter 3 for an explanation of the relational meaning.

- Third, the internal level will *not* be "relational," because the objects at that level will not be just (stored) relational tables—instead, they will be the same kinds of object found at the internal level of any other kind of system (stored records, pointers, indexes, hashes, etc.). In fact, relational theory as such has *nothing whatsoever* to say about the internal level; it is, to repeat from Chapter 1, concerned with how the database looks to the *user*.

We now proceed to examine the three levels of the architecture in considerably more detail, starting with the external level. Fig. 2.3 (overleaf) shows the major components of the architecture and their interrelationships. That figure will be referenced repeatedly throughout the remainder of this chapter.

2.3   The External Level

The external level is the individual user level. As explained in Chapter 1, a given user can be either an application programmer or an end user of any degree of sophistication. The DBA is an important special case. (Unlike other users, however, the DBA will need to be interested in the conceptual and internal levels also. See the next two sections.)

Each user has a **language** at his or her disposal:

- For the application programmer, that language will be either one of the conventional programming languages such as C, COBOL, or PL/I, or else a proprietary language that is specific to the system in question. Such proprietary languages are often called "fourth generation" languages (4GLs), on the (very informal!) grounds that (a) machine code, assembler language, and languages such as COBOL can be regarded as three earlier language "generations," and (b) the proprietary languages represent the same kind of improvement over "third generation" languages as those languages did over assembler language.

- For the end user, the language will be either a query language or some special-purpose language, perhaps forms- or menu-driven, tailored to that user's requirements and supported by some online application program (see Section 1.2).

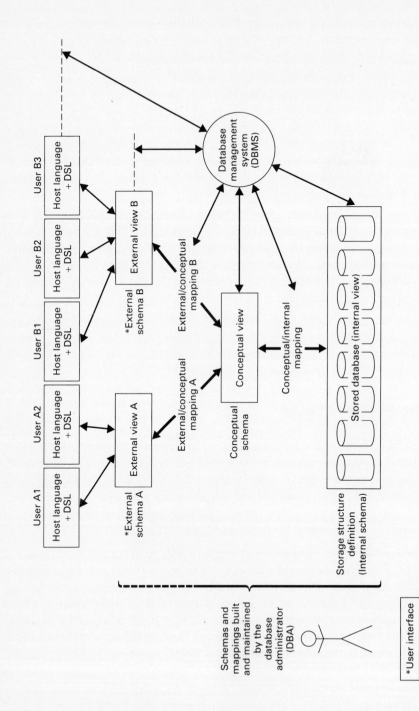

FIG. 2.3 Detailed system architecture

* User interface

For our purposes, the important thing about all such languages is that they will include a **data sublanguage**—i.e., a subset of the total language that is concerned specifically with database objects and operations. The data sublanguage (abbreviated DSL in Fig. 2.3) is said to be **embedded** within the corresponding **host language**. The host language is responsible for providing various nondatabase facilities, such as local (temporary) variables, computational operations, if-then-else logic, and so on. A given system might support any number of host languages and any number of data sublanguages; however, one particular data sublanguage that is supported by almost all current systems is the language SQL discussed very briefly in Chapter 1. Most such systems allow SQL to be used both interactively (as a standalone query language) and also embedded in other languages such as C and COBOL. See Chapter 8 for further discussion.

Now, although it is convenient for architectural purposes to distinguish between the data sublanguage and its containing host language, the two might in fact be *in*distinguishable so far as the user is concerned; indeed, it is preferable from the user's point of view if they *are* indistinguishable. If they are, or if they can be separated only with difficulty, we say the two are **tightly coupled**. If they are clearly and easily separable, then we say they are **loosely** coupled. Most systems today support loose coupling only. A tightly coupled system would provide a more uniform set of facilities for the user, but obviously involves more effort on the part of the system designers and developers (which presumably accounts for the status quo); however, there is evidence to suggest that there will or may be a gradual movement toward more tightly coupled systems over the next few years.

In principle, any given data sublanguage is really a combination of at least two subordinate languages—a **data definition language** (DDL), which supports the definition or declaration of database objects, and a **data manipulation language** (DML), which supports the manipulation or processing of such objects. For example, consider the PL/I user of Fig. 2.2 in Section 2.2. The data sublanguage for that user consists of those PL/I features that are used to communicate with the DBMS:

- The DDL portion consists of those declarative constructs of PL/I that are needed to declare database objects—the DECLARE (DCL) statement itself, certain PL/I data types, possibly special extensions to PL/I to support new objects that are not handled by existing PL/I.

- The DML portion consists of those executable statements of PL/I that transfer information to and from the database—again, possibly including special new statements.

Note: Current PL/I does not in fact include any specific database features at all. The "DML" statements in particular are typically just calls to the DBMS (though those calls might be syntactically disguised in some manner to make them a little more user-friendly; see, e.g., the discussion of embedded SQL in Chapter 8). This is because PL/I systems, like most other systems today, currently provide only very loose coupling between the data sublanguage and its host.

To return to the architecture: We have already indicated that an individual user will generally be interested only in some portion of the total database; moreover, that user's view of that portion will generally be somewhat abstract when compared with the way the data is physically stored. The ANSI/SPARC term for an individual user's view is an **external view**. An external view is thus the content of the database as seen by some particular user (that is, to that user the external view *is* the database). For example, a user from the Personnel Department might regard the database as a collection of department record occurrences plus a collection of employee record occurrences, and might be quite unaware of the supplier and part record occurrences seen by users in the Purchasing Department.

In general, then, an external view consists of many occurrences of each of many types of **external record** (*not* necessarily the same thing as a stored record). The user's data sublanguage is defined in terms of external records; for example, a DML *retrieve* operation will retrieve external record occurrences, not stored record occurrences. *Note:* For the time being we assume that all information is represented at the external level in the form of records. Some systems allow information to be represented in other ways as well, e.g., in the form of "links" or pointers. For a system using such alternative methods, the definitions and explanations given in this section will require suitable modification. Analogous remarks apply to the conceptual and internal levels also (see Sections 2.4 and 2.5).

Incidentally, we can now see that the term "logical record" used at several points in Chapter 1 actually referred to an external record. From this point forward, in fact, we will generally avoid the term "logical record."

Each external view is defined by means of an **external schema,** which consists basically of definitions of each of the various external record types in that external view (refer back to Fig. 2.2 for a couple of simple examples). The external schema is written using the DDL portion of the user's data sublanguage. (That DDL is therefore sometimes referred to as an *external DDL.*) For example, the employee external record type might be defined as a six-character employee number field plus a five-digit (decimal) salary field, and so on. In addition, there must be a definition of the *mapping* between the external schema and the underlying *conceptual* schema (see the next section). We will consider that mapping later, in Section 2.6.

2.4   The Conceptual Level

The **conceptual view** is a representation of the entire information content of the database, again (as with an external view) in a form that is somewhat abstract in comparison with the way in which the data is physically stored. It will also be quite different, in general, from the way in which the data is viewed by any particular user. Broadly speaking, the conceptual view is intended to be a view of the data "as it really is," rather than as users are forced to see it by the constraints of (for example) the particular language or hardware they might be using.

The conceptual view consists of many occurrences of each of many types of **conceptual record**. For example, it might consist of a collection of department record occurrences plus a collection of employee record occurrences plus a collection of supplier record occurrences plus a collection of part record occurrences (etc., etc.). A conceptual record is not necessarily the same as either an external record, on the one hand, or a stored record, on the other.

Note: It should be pointed out that there might well be other ways of representing data at the conceptual level—ways, that is, that do not involve records as such at all, and hence might be preferable in some respects for that very reason [2.7]. For example, instead of dealing in terms of "conceptual records," it might be preferable to consider entities, and perhaps relationships too, in some more direct fashion. However, such considerations are beyond the scope of this early part of the book. See Chapters 12 and 22–25 for further discussion.

The conceptual view is defined by means of the **conceptual schema,** which includes definitions of each of the various conceptual record types (again, refer to Fig. 2.2 for a simple example). The conceptual schema is written using another data definition language, the *conceptual DDL.* If data independence is to be achieved, then those conceptual DDL definitions must not involve any considerations of storage structure or access technique—they must be definitions of information content *only.* Thus there must be no reference in the conceptual schema to stored field representations, stored record sequence, indexing, hash-addressing, pointers, or any other storage and access details. If the conceptual schema is made truly data-independent in this way, then the external schemas, which are defined in terms of the conceptual schema (see Section 2.6), will *a fortiori* be data-independent too.

The conceptual view, then, is a view of the total database content, and the conceptual schema is a definition of that view. However, it would be misleading to suggest that the conceptual schema is nothing more than a set of definitions much like the simple record definitions found in (e.g.) a COBOL program today. The definitions in the conceptual schema are intended to include a great many additional features, such as the security and integrity rules mentioned in Chapter 1. Some authorities would go so far as to suggest that the ultimate objective of the conceptual schema is to describe the complete enterprise—not just its data *per se,* but also how that data is used: how it flows from point to point within the enterprise, what it is used for at each point, what audit or other controls are to be applied at each point, and so on [2.3]. It must be emphasized, however, that no system today actually supports a conceptual level of anything approaching this degree of comprehensiveness; in most existing systems, the "conceptual schema" is really little more than a simple union of all individual external schemas, with the addition of certain security and integrity rules. But it seems clear that systems of the future will eventually be far more sophisticated in their support of the conceptual level.

2.5   The Internal Level

The third level of the architecture is the internal level. The **internal view** is a low-level representation of the entire database; it consists of many occurrences of each of many types of **internal record**. "Internal record" is the ANSI/SPARC term for the construct that we have been calling a *stored* record (and we will continue to use this latter term).

The internal view is thus still at one remove from the physical level, since it does not deal in terms of *physical* records—also called **blocks** or **pages***—nor with any device-specific considerations such as cylinder or track sizes. In other words, the internal view effectively assumes an infinite linear address space; details of how that address space is mapped to physical storage are highly system-specific and are deliberately omitted from the general architecture.

The internal view is described by means of the **internal schema,** which not only defines the various stored record types but also specifies what indexes exist, how stored fields are represented, what physical sequence the stored records are in, and so on (once again, see Fig. 2.2 for a simple example). The internal schema is written using yet another data definition language—the *internal DDL. Note:* In this book we will normally use the more intuitive terms "stored database" in place of "internal view" and "storage structure definition" in place of "internal schema."

In closing, we remark that, in certain exceptional situations, application programs—in particular, applications of a "utility" nature (see Section 2.11)—might be permitted to operate directly at the internal level rather than at the external level. Needless to say, the practice is not recommended; it represents a security risk (since the security rules are bypassed) and an integrity risk (since the integrity rules are bypassed likewise), and the program will be data-dependent to boot; but sometimes it might be the only way to obtain the required function or performance—just as the user in a high-level programming language system might occasionally need to descend to assembler language in order to satisfy certain function or performance objectives today.

2.6 Mappings

Referring again to Fig. 2.3, the reader will observe two levels of **mapping** in the architecture, one from the conceptual level to the internal level and one from the external level to the conceptual level. The *conceptual/internal* mapping defines the correspondence between the conceptual view and the stored database; it specifies how conceptual records and fields are represented at the internal level. If the structure of the stored database is changed—i.e., if a change is made to the storage structure definition—then the conceptual/internal mapping must be changed accordingly, so that the conceptual schema can remain invariant. (It is the responsibility of the DBA to manage such changes, of course.) In other words, the effects of such changes must be isolated below the conceptual level, in order that data independence might be preserved.

An *external/conceptual* mapping defines the correspondence between a particular external view and the conceptual view. In general, the differences that can exist between these two levels are similar to those that can exist between the conceptual view and the stored database. For example, fields can have different data types, field and record names can be changed, several conceptual fields can be combined into a single (virtual) external field, and so on. Any number of external views can exist at the same

---

* The block or page is *the unit of I/O*—i.e., it is the amount of data transferred between secondary storage and main memory in a single secondary storage access. Typical page sizes are 1K, 2K, or 4K bytes (K = 1024).

time; any number of users can share a given external view; different external views can overlap.

Incidentally, most systems permit the definition of one external view to be expressed in terms of others (in effect, via an *external/external* mapping), rather than always requiring an explicit definition of the mapping to the conceptual level—a useful feature if several external views are rather similar to one another. Relational systems in particular typically do provide such a capability.

2.7 The Database Administrator

As explained in Chapter 1, the *data* administrator is the person who makes the strategic and policy decisions regarding the data of the enterprise, and the data*base* administrator (DBA) is the person who provides the necessary technical support for implementing those decisions. Thus, the DBA is responsible for the overall control of the system at a technical level. We can now describe some of the functions of the DBA in a little more detail. In general, those functions will include the following.

■ Defining the conceptual schema

It is the *data* administrator's job to decide exactly what information is to be held in the database—in other words, to identify the entities of interest to the enterprise and to identify the information to be recorded about those entities. This process is usually referred to as **logical**—sometimes *conceptual*—**database design**. Once the data administrator has thus decided the content of the database at an abstract level, the DBA will then create the corresponding conceptual schema, using the conceptual DDL. The object (compiled) form of that schema will be used by the DBMS in responding to access requests. The source (uncompiled) form will act as a reference document for the users of the system.

(In practice, matters will rarely be as clearcut as the foregoing remarks suggest. In some cases, the data administrator will create the conceptual schema directly. In others, the DBA will do the logical design.)

■ Defining the internal schema

The DBA must also decide how the data is to be represented in the stored database. This process is usually referred to as **physical** database design. Having done the physical design, the DBA must then create the corresponding storage structure definition (i.e., the internal schema), using the internal DDL. In addition, he or she must also define the associated mapping between the internal and conceptual schemas. In practice, either the conceptual DDL or the internal DDL—most likely the former—will probably include the means for defining that mapping, but the two functions (creating the schema, defining the mapping) should be clearly separable. Like the conceptual schema, the internal schema and corresponding mapping will exist in both source and object form.

■ Liaising with users

It is the business of the DBA to liaise with users, to ensure that the data they require is available, and to write (or help the users write) the necessary external schemas, using the applicable external DDL. (As already mentioned, a given system might support several distinct external DDLs.) In addition, the mapping between any given external schema and the conceptual schema must also be defined. In practice, the external DDL will probably include the means for specifying that mapping, but once again the schema and the mapping should be clearly separable. Each external schema and corresponding mapping will exist in both source and object form.

Other aspects of the user liaison function include consulting on application design, providing technical education, assisting with problem determination and resolution, and similar system-related professional services.

- Defining security and integrity rules

    As already discussed, security and integrity rules can be regarded as part of the conceptual schema. The conceptual DDL should include facilities for specifying such rules.

- Defining backup and recovery procedures

    Once an enterprise is committed to a database system, it becomes critically dependent on the successful operation of that system. In the event of damage to any portion of the database—caused by human error, say, or a failure in the hardware or supporting operating system—it is essential to be able to repair the data concerned with the minimum of delay and with as little effect as possible on the rest of the system. For example, the availability of data that has *not* been damaged should ideally not be affected. The DBA must define and implement an appropriate recovery scheme, involving, e.g., periodic unloading or "dumping" of the database to backup storage, and procedures for reloading the database when necessary from the most recent dump.

    Incidentally, the foregoing discussion provides one reason why it might be a good idea to spread the total data collection across several databases, instead of keeping it all in one place; the individual database might very well form the unit for dump and reload purposes. Nevertheless, we will continue to talk as if there were in fact just a single database, for simplicity.

- Monitoring performance and responding to changing requirements

    As indicated in Section 1.4, the DBA is responsible for so organizing the system as to get the performance that is "best for the enterprise," and for making the appropriate adjustments as requirements change. For example, it might be necessary to **reorganize** the stored database on a periodic basis to ensure that performance levels remain acceptable. As already mentioned, any change to the physical storage (internal) level of the system must be accompanied by a corresponding change to the definition of the mapping from the conceptual level, so that the conceptual schema can remain constant.

Of course, the foregoing is not an exhaustive list—it is merely intended to give some idea of the extent and nature of the DBA's responsibilities.

2.8   The Database Management System

The **database management system** (DBMS) is the software that handles all access to the database. Conceptually, what happens is the following.

1. A user issues an access request, using some particular data sublanguage (typically SQL).
2. The DBMS intercepts that request and analyzes it.
3. The DBMS inspects, in turn, the external schema for that user, the corresponding external/conceptual mapping, the conceptual schema, the conceptual/internal mapping, and the storage structure definition.
4. The DBMS executes the necessary operations on the stored database.

By way of an example, consider what is involved in the retrieval of a particular external record occurrence. In general, fields will be required from several conceptual record occurrences, and each conceptual record occurrence in turn will require fields from several stored record occurrences. Conceptually, then, the DBMS must first retrieve all required stored record occurrences, then construct the required conceptual record occurrences, and then construct the required external record occurrence. At each stage, data type or other conversions might be necessary.

Of course, the foregoing description is very much simplified; in particular, it implies that the entire process is interpretive, inasmuch as it suggests that the processes of analyzing the request, inspecting the various schemas, etc., are all done at execution time. Interpretation, in turn, usually implies poor performance, because of the execution-time overhead. In practice, however, it might be possible for access requests to be *compiled* in advance of execution time. A concrete example of a system that employs this latter approach, IBM's DB2, is briefly described in Appendix B.

Let us now examine the functions of the DBMS in a little more detail. Those functions will include support for at least all of the following.

■ Data definition

The DBMS must be able to accept data definitions (external schemas, the conceptual schema, the internal schema, and all associated mappings) in source form and convert them to the appropriate object form. In other words, the DBMS must include *language processor* components for each of the various data definition languages (DDLs). The DBMS must also "understand" the DDL definitions, in the sense that, for example, it "understands" that EMPLOYEE external records include a SALARY field; it must then be able to use this knowledge in interpreting and responding to user requests (e.g., a request for all employees with salary less than $50,000).

■ Data manipulation

The DBMS must be able to handle requests from the user to retrieve, update, or delete existing data in the database, or to add new data to the database. In other words, the DBMS must include a data manipulation language (DML) processor component.

In general, DML requests may be "planned" or "unplanned":

1. A **planned** request is one for which the need was foreseen well in advance of the time at which the request is actually to be executed. The DBA will probably have tuned the physical database design in such a way as to guarantee good performance for such requests.

2. An **unplanned** request, by contrast, is an *ad hoc* query, i.e., a request for which the need was not seen in advance, but instead arose in a spur-of-the-moment fashion. The physical database design might or might not be ideally suited for the specific request under consideration. In general, obtaining the best possible performance for unplanned requests represents a significant challenge for the DBMS. See Chapter 18 for an extensive discussion of this problem.

To use the terminology introduced in Section 1.3, planned requests are characteristic of "operational" or "production" applications, while unplanned requests are characteristic of "decision support" applications. Furthermore, planned requests will typically be issued from prewritten application programs, whereas unplanned requests, by definition, will be issued interactively.

■ Data security and integrity

The DBMS must monitor user requests and reject any attempts to violate the security and integrity rules defined by the DBA (see Section 2.7).

■ Data recovery and concurrency

The DBMS—or else some other related software component, usually called the **transaction manager**—must enforce certain recovery and concurrency controls. Details of these aspects of the system are beyond the scope of this chapter; see Part IV of this book for further information (Chapters 13 and 14).

■ Data dictionary

The DBMS must provide a **data dictionary** function. The data dictionary can be regarded as a database in its own right (but a system database, rather than a user database). The dictionary contains "data about the data" (sometimes called *metadata*)—that is, *definitions* of other objects in the system—rather than just "raw data." In particular, all the various schemas and mappings (external, conceptual, etc.) will physically be stored, in both source and object form, in the dictionary. A comprehensive dictionary will also include cross-reference information, showing, for instance, which programs use which pieces of the database, which users require which reports, what terminals are connected to the system, and so on. The dictionary might even—in fact, probably should—be integrated into the database it defines, and thus include its own definition. It should certainly be possible to query the dictionary just like any other database, so that, for example, it is possible to tell which programs and/or users are likely to be affected by some proposed change to the system. See Chapter 3 for further discussion.

Note: We are touching here on an area in which there is much terminological confusion. Some people would refer to what we are calling the dictionary as a *directory* or a *catalog*—with the implication that directories and catalogs are somehow inferior to a true dictionary—and would reserve the term "dictionary" to refer to a specific (important) kind of application development tool [2.6]. Other terms that are also sometimes used to refer to this latter kind of object are "data repository" and "data encyclopedia." See references [2.4–2.6].

■ Performance

It goes without saying that the DBMS should perform all of the functions identified above as efficiently as possible.

We can summarize all of the foregoing by saying that the overall function of the DBMS is to provide the **user interface** to the database system. The user interface can be defined as a boundary in the system below which everything is invisible to the user. By definition, therefore, the user interface is at the *external* level. However, as we shall see in Chapter 17, there are some situations in which the external view is unlikely to differ very significantly from the relevant portion of the underlying conceptual view, at least in today's commercial products.

We conclude this section by briefly contrasting database management systems as discussed above with **file** management systems (file managers for short). Basically, the file manager is that component of the overall system that manages stored files; loosely speaking, therefore, it is "closer to the disk" than the DBMS is. (In fact, Appendix A explains how the DBMS is typically built *on top of* some kind of file manager.) Thus, the user of a file management system will be able to create and destroy stored files and perform simple retrieval and update operations on stored records in such files. In contrast to the DBMS, however:

■ File managers are not aware of the internal structure of stored records, and hence cannot handle requests that rely on a knowledge of that structure (such as "Find all employees with salary less than $50,000").

■ They typically provide little or no support for security and integrity rules.

■ They typically provide little or no support for recovery and concurrency controls.

■ There is no true data dictionary concept at the file manager level.

■ They provide much less data independence than the DBMS does.

2.9 The Data Communications Manager

In this section, we briefly consider the topic of **data communications**. Database requests from an end user are actually transmitted (from that user's workstation—which might be physically remote from the system itself—to some online application, builtin or otherwise, and thence to the DBMS) in the form of *communication messages*. Likewise, responses back to the user (from the DBMS and online application back to the user's workstation) are also transmitted in the form of such messages. All such message transmissions take place under the direction of another software component, the **data communications manager** (DC manager).

The DC manager is not part of the DBMS but is an autonomous system in its own right. However, since the DC manager and the DBMS are clearly required to work harmoniously together, they are sometimes regarded as equal partners in a higher-level cooperative venture called the **database/data-communications system** (DB/DC system), in which the DBMS looks after the database and the DC manager handles all messages to and from the DBMS, or more accurately to and from applications that use the DBMS. In this book, however, we shall have comparatively little to say about message-handling as such (it is a large subject in its own right). Section 2.12 does briefly discuss the question of communication *between distinct systems* (i.e., between distinct machines in a communications network), but that is really a separate topic.

2.10 Client/Server Architecture

Preceding sections of this chapter have discussed the so-called ANSI/SPARC architecture for database systems in some detail. In particular, Fig. 2.3 gave a simplified picture of that architecture. In this section we take a look at database systems from a slightly different perspective. The overall purpose of such systems, of course, is to support the development and execution of database applications. From a high-level point of view, therefore, a database system can be regarded as having a very simple two-part structure, consisting of a **server** (also called the **backend**) and a set of **clients** (also called **frontends**). Refer to Fig. 2.4.

We explain the figure as follows.

■ The server is the DBMS itself. It supports all of the basic DBMS functions discussed in Section 2.8—data definition, data manipulation, data security and integrity, and so on. In particular, it provides all of the external, conceptual, and internal

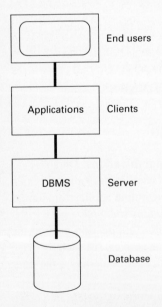

End users

Applications Clients

DBMS Server

Database

FIG. 2.4 Client/server architecture

level support discussed in Sections 2.3–2.6. Thus, "server" in this context is just another name for the DBMS.

■ The clients are the various applications that run on top of the DBMS—both user-written applications and builtin applications, i.e., applications provided either by the vendor of the DBMS or by some "third-party" software vendor. As far as the server is concerned, of course, there is no difference between user-written and builtin applications—they all use the same interface to the server, namely the external-level interface discussed in Section 2.3.

   Note: Certain special "utility" applications might constitute an exception to the foregoing. As mentioned in Section 2.5, such applications sometimes need to operate directly at the internal level of the system. Such utilities are best regarded as integral components of the DBMS, rather than as applications in the usual sense. Utilities are discussed in more detail in the next section.

Applications in turn can be divided into several reasonably well-defined categories, as follows.

1. First, *user-written applications*. These are basically regular application programs, written (typically) either in a conventional programming language such as C or COBOL or in some proprietary language such as FOCUS—though in both cases the language needs to be coupled somehow with an appropriate data sublanguage, as explained in Section 2.3.

2. Second, *vendor-provided applications* (often called **tools**). The overall purpose of such tools is to assist in the process of creating and executing other applications!—i.e., applications that are tailored to some specific task (though the created application might not look much like an application in the conventional sense; indeed, the whole point of the tools is to allow users, especially end users, to create applications *without* having to write conventional programs). For example, one of the vendor-provided tools will be a query language processor, whose purpose of course is to allow end users to issue *ad hoc* queries to the system. Each such query is basically nothing more than a small (or maybe not so small) tailored application that is intended to perform some specific application function.

   Vendor-provided tools in turn divide into a number of distinct classes:

   ▪ query language processors
   ▪ report writers
   ▪ business graphics subsystems
   ▪ spreadsheets
   ▪ natural language processors
   ▪ statistical packages
   ▪ copy management tools
   ▪ application generators (including "4GL" processors)
   ▪ other application development tools, including computer-aided software engineering (CASE) products

and so on. Details of such tools are beyond the scope of this book; however, we remark that since (as stated above) the whole point of a database system is to support the creation and execution of applications, the quality of the available frontend tools is, or should be, a major factor in "the database decision" (i.e., the process of choosing the right system for a given customer). In other words, the DBMS *per se* is not the only factor that needs to be taken into account, nor even necessarily the most significant factor.

We close this section with a forward pointer. Since the overall system can be so neatly divided into two parts (server and clients), the possibility arises of running the two on *different machines*. In other words, the potential exists for **distributed processing**. Distributed processing means that distinct machines can be connected together into some kind of communications network, in such a way that a single data processing task can be spread across several machines in the network. (In fact, so attractive is this possibility—for a variety of reasons, mainly economic—that the term "client/server" has come to apply almost exclusively to the case where the server and clients are indeed on different machines. This usage is sloppy but very, very common.) We will discuss distributed processing in more detail in Section 2.12.

2.11 Utilities

Utilities are programs designed to help the DBA with various administration tasks. As mentioned in Section 2.10, some utility programs operate at the external level of the system, and thus are effectively nothing more than special-purpose applications; some might not even be provided by the DBMS vendor, but rather by some third-party software supplier. Other utilities, however, operate directly at the internal level (in other words, they are really part of the server), and hence must be provided by the DBMS vendor.

Here are some typical examples of the kind of utilities that are frequently needed in practice:

- **Load** routines, to create the initial version of the database from one or more non-database files

- **Unload/reload** routines, to unload the database, or portions thereof, to backup storage for recovery purposes and to reload data from such backup copies (of course, the "reload utility" is basically identical to the load utility just discussed)

- **Reorganization** routines, to rearrange the data in the database for various reasons (usually having to do with performance)—e.g., to cluster data together in some particular way on the disk, or to reclaim space occupied by data that has become obsolete

- **Statistical** routines, to compute various performance statistics such as file sizes or data value distributions or I/O counts, etc.

- **Analysis** routines, to analyze the statistics just mentioned

The foregoing list represents just a small sample of the range of functions that utilities typically provide. A wealth of other possibilities exist.

2.12   Distributed Processing

To repeat from Section 2.10, the term "distributed processing" means that distinct machines can be connected together into a communications network such that a single data processing task can span several machines in the network. (The term "parallel processing" is also sometimes used with essentially the same meaning, except that the distinct machines tend to be physically close together in a "parallel" system and need not be so in a "distributed" system—e.g., they might be geographically dispersed in the latter case.) Communication between the various machines is handled by some kind of network management software—possibly an extension of the DC manager discussed in Section 2.9, possibly a separate software component.

Many levels or varieties of distributed processing are possible. As mentioned in Section 2.10, one simple case involves running the DBMS backend (the server) on one machine and the application frontends (the clients) on another. Refer to Fig. 2.5.

As mentioned at the end of Section 2.10, "client/server"—although strictly speak-

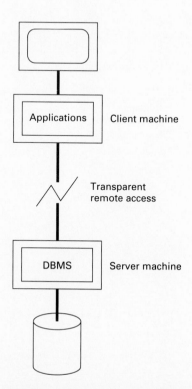

FIG. 2.5 Client and server running on different machines

ing a purely architectural term—has come to be virtually synonymous with the arrangement illustrated in Fig. 2.5, in which client and server run on different machines. Indeed, there are many arguments in favor of such a scheme:

- The first is basically just the usual parallel processing argument—namely that many processors are now being applied to the overall task, and server (database) and client (application) processing are being done in parallel. Response time and throughput should thus be improved.

- Furthermore, the server machine might be a custom-built machine that is tailored to the DBMS function (a "database machine"), and might thus provide better DBMS performance.

- Likewise, the client machine might be a personal workstation, tailored to the needs of the end user and thus able to provide better interfaces, high availability, faster responses, and overall improved ease of use to the user.

- Several different client machines might be able (in fact, probably will be able) to access the same server machine. Thus, a single database might be shared across several distinct client systems (see Fig. 2.6).

In addition to the foregoing arguments, there is also the point that running the client(s) and the server on separate machines matches the way many enterprises actually

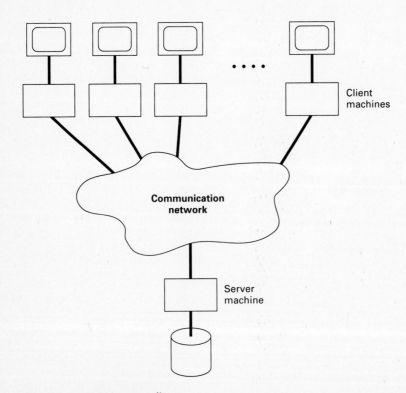

FIG. 2.6 One server, many clients

operate. It is quite common for a single enterprise—a bank, for example—to operate many computers, such that the data for one portion of the enterprise is stored on one computer and that for another portion is stored on another. It is also quite common for users on one computer to need at least occasional access to data stored on another. To pursue the banking example for a moment, it is very likely that users at one branch office will occasionally need access to data stored at another. Note, therefore, that the client machines might have stored data of their own, and the server machine might have applications of its own. In general, therefore, each machine will act as a server for some users and a client for others (see Fig. 2.7); in other words, each machine will support *an entire database system* (in the sense of earlier sections of this chapter).

The final point is that a single client machine might be able to access several dif-

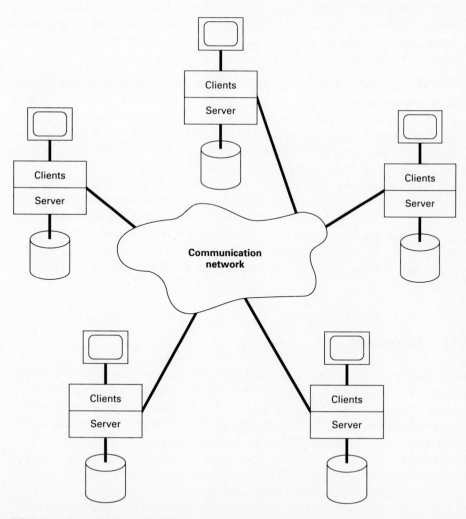

FIG. 2.7 Each machine is both client and server

ferent server machines (the converse of the case illustrated in Fig. 2.6). This capability is desirable because, as mentioned above, enterprises do typically operate in such a manner that their total data collection is not stored on one single machine but rather is spread across many distinct machines, and applications will sometimes need the ability to access data from more than one machine. Such access can basically be provided in two ways:

1. A given client might be able to access any number of servers, but only one at a time (i.e., each individual database request must be directed to just one server). In such a system it is not possible, within a single request, to combine data from two or more different servers. Furthermore, the user in such a system has to know which particular machine holds which pieces of data.

2. The client might be able to access many servers simultaneously (i.e., a single database request might be able to combine data from several servers). In this case, the servers look to the client as if they were really a single server (from a logical point of view), and the user does not have to know which machines hold which pieces of data.

The second case here is an example of what is usually referred to as a **distributed database system**. Distributed database is a big topic in its own right; carried to its logical conclusion, full support for distributed database implies that a single application should be able to operate "transparently" on data that is spread across a variety of different databases, managed by a variety of different DBMSs, running on a variety of different machines, supported by a variety of different operating systems, and connected together by a variety of different communication networks—where "transparently" means that the application operates from a logical point of view as if the data were all managed by a single DBMS running on a single machine. Such a capability might sound like a pretty tall order!—but it is highly desirable from a practical perspective, and vendors are working hard to make such systems a reality. We will discuss distributed database in detail in Chapter 21.

2.13 Summary

In this chapter we have taken a look at database systems from an overall architectural point of view. First, we described the **ANSI/SPARC architecture,** which divides a database system into three **levels,** as follows: The **internal** level is the one closest to physical storage (i.e., it is the one concerned with the way the data is physically stored); the **external** level is the one closest to the users (i.e., it is the one concerned with the way the data is viewed by individual users); and the **conceptual** level is a level of indirection between the other two (it provides a *community view* of the data). The data as perceived at each level is described by a **schema** (or several schemas, in the case of the external level). **Mappings** describe the correspondence between (a) a given external schema and the conceptual schema, and (b) the conceptual schema and the internal schema.

Users—i.e., end users and application programmers, both of whom operate at the external level—interact with the data by means of a **data sublanguage,** which breaks down into at least two components, a **data definition language** (DDL) and a **data manipulation language** (DML). The data sublanguage is embedded in a **host language.** *Note:* The dividing lines between the host language and the data sublanguage, and between the DDL and the DML, are primarily conceptual in nature; ideally they should be "transparent to the user."

We also took a closer look at the functions of the **DBA** and the **DBMS.** Among other things, the DBA is responsible for creating the internal schema (**physical database design**); creating the conceptual schema (**logical** or **conceptual** database design), by contrast, is the responsibility of the *data* administrator. And the DBMS is responsible (among other things) for implementing DDL and DML requests from the user. The DBMS is also responsible for providing some kind of **data dictionary** function.

Database systems can also be conveniently thought of as consisting of a **server** (the DBMS itself) and a set of **clients** (the applications). Client and server can and often will run on separate machines, thus providing one simple kind of **distributed processing.** In general, each server can serve many clients, and each client can access many servers. If the system provides total "transparency"—meaning that each client can behave as if it were dealing with a single server on a single machine, regardless of the actual physical state of affairs—then we have a true **distributed database system.**

Exercises

2.1 Draw a diagram of the database system architecture presented in this chapter (the ANSI/SPARC architecture).

2.2 Define the following terms:

backend	frontend
client	host language
conceptual DDL, schema, view	load
conceptual/internal mapping	logical database design
data definition language	internal DDL, schema, view
data dictionary	physical database design
data manipulation language	planned request
data sublanguage	reorganization
DB/DC system	server
DC manager	storage structure definition
distributed database	unload/reload
distributed processing	unplanned request
external DDL, schema, view	user interface
external/conceptual mapping	utility

2.3 Explain the sequence of steps involved in retrieving a particular external record occurrence.

2.4 List the major functions performed by the DBMS.

2.5 List the major functions performed by the DBA.

2.6 Distinguish between the DBMS and a file management system.

2.7 Give some examples of vendor-provided frontends or tools.

2.8 Give some examples of database utilities.

2.9 Examine any database system that might be available to you. Try to map that system to the ANSI/SPARC architecture as described in this chapter. Does it cleanly support the three levels of the architecture? How are the mappings between levels defined? What do the various DDLs (external, conceptual, internal) look like? What data sublanguage(s) does the system support? What host languages? Who performs the DBA function? Are there any security or integrity facilities? Is there a dictionary? What vendor-provided applications does the system support? What utilities? Is there a separate DC manager? Are there any distributed processing capabilities?

References and Bibliography

Some of the following references are beginning to show their age, but they are all still relevant to the concepts introduced in the present chapter.

2.1 ANSI/X3/SPARC Study Group on Data Base Management Systems. *Interim Report. FDT* (ACM SIGMOD bulletin) *7,* No. 2 (1975).

2.2 Dionysios C. Tsichritzis and Anthony Klug (eds.). "The ANSI/X3/SPARC DBMS Framework: Report of the Study Group on Data Base Management Systems." *Information Systems 3* (1978).

These two documents [2.1–2.2] are the Interim and Final Reports, respectively, of the so-called ANSI/SPARC Study Group. The ANSI/X3/SPARC Study Group on Data Base Management Systems (to give it its full title) was established in late 1972 by the Standards Planning and Requirements Committee (SPARC) of ANSI/X3, the American National Standards Committee on Computers and Information Processing. The objectives of the Study Group were to determine which areas, if any, of database technology were appropriate for standardization, and to produce a set of recommendations for action in each such area. In working to meet these objectives, the Study Group took the position that *interfaces* were the only aspect of a database system that could possibly be suitable for standardization, and accordingly defined a generalized database system architecture, or framework, that emphasized the role of such interfaces. The Final Report provides a detailed description of that architecture and of some of the 42 identified interfaces. The Interim Report is an earlier working document that is still of some interest; in some areas it provides additional detail.

2.3 J. J. van Griethuysen (ed.). *Concepts and Terminology for the Conceptual Schema and the Information Base.* International Organization for Standardization Document No. ISO/TC97/SC5-N695 (March 1982).

ISO/TC97/SC5/WG3 is an ISO Working Group whose objectives include "the definition of concepts for conceptual schema languages." This Working Group report includes an introduction to three competing candidates (more accurately, three *sets* of candidates) for an appropriate conceptual schema formalism, and applies each of the three to a common example involving the activities of a hypothetical Car Registration Authority. The three sets of contenders are (1) "entity-attribute-relationship" approaches, (2) "binary relationship" approaches, and (3) "interpreted predicate logic" approaches. The report also includes a discussion of the fundamental concepts underlying the notion of the conceptual schema, and offers some principles for implementation of a system that properly supports that notion. Heavy going in places, but an important document for anyone seriously interested in the conceptual level of the system.

2.4 Data Dictionary Systems Working Party of the British Computer Society. *Report.* Joint Issue: *Data Base* (ACM SIGBDP newsletter) *9,* No. 2; *SIGMOD Record* (ACM SIGMOD bulletin) *9,* No. 4 (December 1977).

An excellent description of the role of the data dictionary; includes a brief but good discussion of the conceptual schema.

2.5 P. P. Uhrowczik. "Data Dictionary/Directories." *IBM Sys. J. 12,* No. 4 (1973).

A good introduction to the basic concepts of a data dictionary system. An implementation is outlined based on IMS (IBM's original Data Dictionary product in fact conformed to that broad outline).

2.6 Paul Winsberg. *Dictionary Standards: ANSI, ISO, and IBM;* and *Industry Views of the Dictionary Standards Muddle.* Both in *InfoDB 3,* No. 4 (Winter 1988/89).

An excellent introduction to, and analysis of, the world of dictionary standards—including, in particular, the ANSI Information Resource Dictionary Systems (IRDS) standard.

2.7 William Kent. *Data and Reality.* Amsterdam, Netherlands: North-Holland/New York, NY: Elsevier Science (1978).

A stimulating and thought-provoking discussion of the nature of information, and in particular of the conceptual schema. The book can be regarded in large part as a compendium of real-world problems that (it is suggested) existing database formalisms—in particular, formalisms that are based on conventional record-like structures, which includes the relational approach—have difficulty in dealing with. Recommended.

3 | An Introduction to Relational Databases

3.1 Introduction

As explained in Chapter 1, the emphasis in this book is very much on the relational approach. In particular, the next part of the book, Part II, covers the theoretical foundations of that approach—namely, the relational model—in depth. The purpose of the present chapter is just to give a preliminary and very informal introduction to the material to be addressed in Part II (and to some extent in subsequent parts also), in order to pave the way for a better understanding of those later parts of the book. Most of the topics mentioned will be discussed again more formally, and in much more detail, in those later chapters.

3.2 Relational Systems

We begin by defining a **relational database management system** ("relational system" for short) as a system in which, at a minimum:

1. The data is perceived by the user as tables (and nothing but tables); and
2. The operators at the user's disposal—e.g., for data retrieval—are operators that generate new tables from old, and those operators include at least SELECT (also known as RESTRICT), PROJECT, and JOIN.

This definition, though still very brief, is slightly more specific than the one given in Chapter 1.

A sample relational database, the departments-and-employees database, is shown in Fig. 3.1. As you can see, that database is indeed "perceived as tables" (and the meaning of those tables is intended to be self-explanatory). Fig. 3.2 shows some sample SELECT, PROJECT, and JOIN operations against that database. Here are (very loose!) definitions of those operations:

■ The **SELECT** operation (also known as **RESTRICT**) extracts specified rows from a table.

DEPT	DEPT#	DNAME	BUDGET
	D1	Marketing	10M
	D2	Development	12M
	D3	Research	5M

EMP	EMP#	ENAME	DEPT#	SALARY
	E1	Lopez	D1	40K
	E2	Cheng	D1	42K
	E3	Finzi	D2	30K
	E4	Saito	D2	35K

FIG. 3.1 The departments-and-employees database (sample values)

- The **PROJECT** operation extracts specified columns from a table.
- The **JOIN** operation joins together two tables on the basis of common values in a common column.

Of the three examples, the only one that seems to need any further explanation is the JOIN example. First of all, observe that the two tables DEPT and EMP do indeed have a common column, namely DEPT#, so they can be joined together on the basis of

SELECT (RESTRICT):   Result:

DEPTs where BUDGET > 8M

DEPT#	DNAME	BUDGET
D1	Marketing	10M
D2	Development	12M

PROJECT: Result:

DEPTs over DEPT#, BUDGET

DEPT#	BUDGET
D1	10M
D2	12M
D3	5M

JOIN:

DEPTs and EMPs over DEPT#

Result:

DEPT#	DNAME	BUDGET	EMP#	ENAME	SALARY
D1	Marketing	10M	E1	Lopez	40K
D1	Marketing	10M	E2	Cheng	42K
D2	Development	12M	E3	Finzi	30K
D2	Development	12M	E4	Saito	35K

FIG. 3.2 SELECT, PROJECT, and JOIN (examples)

common values in that column. That is, a given row from table DEPT will join to a given row in table EMP—to produce a new, wider row—if and only if the two rows in question have a common DEPT# value. For example, the DEPT and EMP rows

DEPT#	DNAME	BUDGET
D1	Marketing	10M

EMP#	ENAME	DEPT#	SALARY
E1	Lopez	D1	40K

(column names shown for explicitness) can be joined together to produce the result row

DEPT#	DNAME	BUDGET	EMP#	ENAME	SALARY
D1	Marketing	10M	E1	Lopez	40K

because they have the same value, D1, in the common column. The set of all possible such joined rows constitutes the overall result. Observe that the common (DEPT#) value appears just once, not twice, in each result row. Observe too that since no EMP row has a DEPT# value of D3 (i.e., no employee is currently assigned to that department), no row for D3 appears in the result, even though there *is* a row for D3 in table DEPT.

One point that Fig. 3.2 clearly illustrates is that *the result of each of the three operations is another table.* This is the relational property of **closure,** and it is very important. Basically, because the output of any operation is the same kind of object as the input—they are all tables—so *the output from one operation can become input to another.* Thus it is possible (for example) to take a projection of a join, or a join of two restrictions, etc., etc. In other words, it is possible to write *nested expressions*—i.e., expressions in which the operands themselves are represented by expressions, instead of just simple table names. This fact in turn has numerous important consequences, as we will see later (both in this chapter and in many subsequent ones).

Note: When we say that the output from each operation is another table, it is very important to understand that we are talking *from a conceptual point of view.* We do not necessarily mean to imply that the system actually has to materialize the result of every individual operation in its entirety. For example, suppose we are trying to compute a restriction of a join. Then, as soon as a given row of the join is constructed, the system can immediately apply the restriction to that row to see whether it belongs in the final result, and immediately discard it if not. In other words, the intermediate result that is the output from the join might never exist as a fully materialized table in its own right at all. As a general rule, in fact, the system tries very hard *not* to materialize intermediate results in their entirety, for obvious performance reasons.

Another point that Fig. 3.2 also clearly illustrates is that the operations are all **set-at-a-time,** not row-at-a-time; that is, the operands and results are all entire tables, not just single rows, and tables contain *sets* of rows. For example, the JOIN in Fig. 3.2 operates on two tables of three and four rows respectively, and returns a result table of four rows. This **set processing capability** is a major distinguishing characteristic of relational systems (see further discussion in Section 3.6 below). By contrast, the operations in nonrelational systems are typically at the row- or record-at-a-time level.

Let us return to Fig. 3.1 for a moment. There are a few additional points to be made in connection with the sample database of that figure:

- First, note that the "relational system" definition requires only that the database be *perceived by the user* as tables. Tables are the **logical** structure in a relational system, not the physical structure. At the physical level, in fact, the system is free to use any or all of the usual storage structures—sequential files, indexing, hashing, pointer chains, compression, etc.—provided only that it can map those structures into tables at the logical level. Another way of saying the same thing is that tables represent an *abstraction* of the way the data is physically stored—an abstraction in which numerous storage-level details, such as stored record placement, stored record sequence, stored data encodings, stored record prefixes, stored access structures such as indexes, and so forth, are all *hidden from the user*.

  Incidentally, the term "logical structure" in the foregoing paragraph is intended to encompass both the conceptual and external levels, in ANSI/SPARC terms. The point is that—as explained in Chapter 2—the conceptual and external levels in a relational system will be relational, but the internal or physical level will not. In fact, relational theory as such has nothing to say about the internal level at all; it is, to repeat, concerned with how the database looks to the *user*.

- Second, relational databases like that of Fig. 3.1 satisfy a very nice property: *The entire information content of the database is represented in one and only one way, namely as explicit data values.* This method of representation (as explicit values in column positions in rows in tables) is the *only* method available in a relational database. In particular, there are no *pointers* connecting one table to another. For example, there is a connection between the D1 row of table DEPT and the E1 row of table EMP, because employee E1 works in department D1; but that connection is represented, not by a pointer, but by the appearance of the *value* D1 in the DEPT# position of the EMP row for E1. In nonrelational systems, by contrast, such information is typically represented by some kind of pointer that is explicitly visible to the user.

  Note: When we say there are no pointers in a relational database, we do not mean that there cannot be pointers *at the physical level*—on the contrary, there certainly can be pointers at that level, and indeed there certainly will be. But as already explained, all such physical storage details are concealed from the user in a relational system.

- Finally, note that *all data values are atomic* (or **scalar**). That is, at every row-and-column position in every table there is always exactly one data value, never a group of several values. Thus, for example, in table EMP (considering the DEPT# and EMP# columns only, and for clarity showing them in that left-to-right order), we have

DEPT#	EMP#
D1	E1
D1	E2
. .	. .

instead of

DEPT#	EMP#
D1	E1,E2
..	..

Column EMP# in the second version of this table is an example of what is usually called a **repeating group**. A repeating group is a column, or combination of columns, that contains several data values in each row (different numbers of values in different rows, in general). *Relational databases do not allow repeating groups;* the second version of the table above would not be permitted in a relational system. (The reason for this apparent limitation is basically *simplicity*. See Chapters 4 and 19 for further discussion.)

We close this section by remarking that the definition given for "relational system" at the beginning of the section is only a *minimal* definition (it is taken from reference [3.1], and is essentially the definition that was current in the early 1980s). There is, of course, far more to a relational system than we can or need to describe in the present section. In particular, please note that the relational model consists of much more than just "tables plus SELECT, PROJECT, and JOIN." See Section 3.4.

3.3   A Note on Terminology

If it is true that a relational database is basically just a database in which the data is perceived as tables—and of course it *is* true—then a good question to ask is: Why exactly do we call such a database relational anyway? The answer is simple: "Relation" is just a mathematical term for a table (to be precise, a table of a certain specific kind—details to be discussed in Chapter 4). Thus, for example, we can say that the departments-and-employees database of Fig. 3.1 contains two *relations.*

Now, in informal contexts it is usual to treat the terms "relation" and "table" as if they were synonymous; indeed, the term "table" is used much more frequently than the term "relation" in such contexts. But it is worth taking a moment to understand why the latter term was introduced in the first place. Briefly, the explanation is as follows.

- As already indicated, relational systems are based on what is called *the relational model of data.* The relational model, in turn, is an abstract theory of data that is based on certain aspects of mathematics (principally set theory and predicate logic).

- The principles of the relational model were originally laid down in 1969–70 by Dr. E. F. Codd, at that time a researcher in IBM. It was late in 1968 that Codd, a mathematician by training, first realized that the discipline of mathematics could be used to inject some solid principles and rigor into a field—database management—that, prior to that time, was all too deficient in any such qualities. Codd's ideas were first widely disseminated in a now classic paper, "A Relational Model of Data for Large Shared Data Banks" (see reference [4.1] in Chapter 4).

- Since that time, those ideas—by now almost universally accepted—have had a wide-ranging influence on just about every aspect of database technology, and indeed on other fields as well, such as the fields of artificial intelligence, natural language processing, and hardware system design.

Now, the relational model as originally formulated by Codd very deliberately made use of certain terms, such as the term "relation" itself, that were not familiar in IT circles at that time, even though the concepts in some cases were. The trouble was, many of the more familiar terms were very *fuzzy*—they lacked the precision necessary to a formal theory of the kind that Codd was proposing.

- *Example:* Consider the term "record." At different times that single term can mean either a record *occurrence* or a record *type;* a *COBOL-style* record (which allows repeating groups) or a *flat* record (which does not); a *logical* record or a *physical* record; a *stored* record or a *virtual* record; and perhaps other things as well.

The formal relational model therefore does not use the term "record" at all; instead, it uses the term "tuple" (short for "*n*-tuple"), which was given a precise definition by Codd when he first introduced it. We do not give that definition here; for present purposes, it is sufficient to say that the term "tuple" corresponds approximately to the notion of a *flat record instance* (just as the term "relation" corresponds approximately to the notion of a table). When we move on (in Part II) to study the more formal aspects of relational systems, we will make use of the formal terminology, but in this chapter we are not trying to be very formal, and we will mostly stick to terms such as "table," "row," and "column" that are reasonably familiar.

3.4 The Relational Model

So what exactly is the relational model? A good way to characterize it is as follows: The relational model is *a way of looking at data*—that is, it is a prescription for a way of representing data (namely, by means of tables), and a prescription for a way of manipulating such a representation (namely, by means of operators such as JOIN). More precisely, the relational model is concerned with three aspects of data: data **structure,** data **integrity,** and data **manipulation**. The structural and manipulative aspects have already been illustrated; to illustrate the integrity aspect (*very* superficially, please note!), we consider the departments-and-employees database of Fig. 3.1 once again. In all likelihood, that database would be subject to numerous integrity rules; for example, employee salaries might have to be in the range 25K to 95K, department budgets might have to be in the range 1M to 15M, and so on. However, there are certain rules that the database *must* obey if it is to conform to the prescriptions of the relational model. To be specific:

1. Each row in table DEPT must include a unique DEPT# value; likewise, each row in table EMP must include a unique EMP# value.
2. Each DEPT# value in table EMP must exist as a DEPT# value in table DEPT (to reflect the fact that every employee must be assigned to an existing department).

Columns DEPT# in table DEPT and EMP# in table EMP are the **primary keys** for their respective tables. Column DEPT# in table EMP is a **foreign** key, referencing the primary key of table DEPT. *Note:* The reader might already have noticed that we indicate primary keys by double underlining in our figures (see, e.g., Fig. 3.1). We will follow this convention throughout this book.

A word of warning is appropriate at this point. The relational model is, as already indicated, a *theory.* Note carefully, however, that (as suggested at the end of Section 3.2) it is not necessary for a system to support that theory in its entirety in order to qualify as relational according to the definition. Indeed, so far as this writer is aware, *there is no product on the market today that supports every last detail of the theory.* This is not to say that some parts of the theory are unimportant; on the contrary, *every detail* of the theory is important, and important, moreover, for genuinely practical reasons. Indeed, the point cannot be stressed too strongly that the purpose of the theory is not just "theory for its own sake"; rather, the purpose is to provide a base on which to build systems that are *100 percent practical.* But the sad fact is that the vendors have not yet really stepped up to the challenge of implementing the theory in its entirety. As a consequence, the relational products of today all fail, in one way or another, to deliver on the full promise of relational technology.

Note: When we say that every detail of the theory is important, we do not mean to imply that every portion of the theory is as important as every other. The fact is, some portions are not as widely accepted as others; indeed, there are some, such as the treatment of missing information, that are still subject to a considerable degree of controversy. Details of such matters are beyond the scope of the present chapter; see Parts II and V of this book (especially Chapters 5 and 20) for further discussion.

3.5 Optimization

As explained in Section 3.2, relational operations such as SELECT, PROJECT, and JOIN are all *set-level* operations. As a consequence, relational languages such as SQL are often said to be *nonprocedural,* on the grounds that users specify *what,* not *how*—i.e., they say what they want, without specifying a procedure for getting it. The process of "navigating" around the stored database in order to satisfy the user's request is performed automatically by the system, not manually by the user. For this reason, relational systems are sometimes referred to as **automatic navigation** systems. In nonrelational systems, by contrast, such navigation is generally the responsibility of the user. A striking illustration of the benefits of automatic navigation is shown in Fig. 3.3, which contrasts a certain SQL INSERT statement with the "manual navigation" code the user might have to write to achieve an equivalent effect in a nonrelational system.

Despite the remarks of the previous paragraph, it has to be said that "nonprocedural" is not a very satisfactory term—common though it is—because procedurality and nonprocedurality are not absolutes. The best that can be said is that some language *A* is either more or less procedural than some other language *B*. Perhaps a better way of putting matters would be to say that relational languages such as SQL are at *a higher*

```
INSERT INTO SP ( S#, P#, QTY )
        VALUES ( 'S4', 'P3', 1000 ) ;
```

```
MOVE 'S4' TO S# IN S
FIND CALC S
ACCEPT S-SP-ADDR FROM S-SP CURRENCY
FIND LAST SP WITHIN S-SP
while SP found PERFORM
   ACCEPT S-SP-ADDR FROM S-SP CURRENCY
   FIND OWNER WITHIN P-SP
   GET P
   IF P# IN P < 'P3'
      leave loop
   END-IF
   FIND PRIOR SP WITHIN S-SP
END-PERFORM
MOVE 'P3' TO P# IN P
FIND CALC P
ACCEPT P-SP-ADDR FROM P-SP CURRENCY
FIND LAST SP WITHIN P-SP
while SP found PERFORM
   ACCEPT P-SP-ADDR FROM P-SP CURRENCY
   FIND OWNER WITHIN S-SP
   GET S
   IF S# IN S < 'S4'
      leave loop
   END-IF
   FIND PRIOR SP WITHIN P-SP
END-PERFORM
MOVE 1000 TO QTY IN SP
FIND DB-KEY IS S-SP-ADDR
FIND DB-KEY IS P-SP-ADDR
STORE SP
CONNECT SP TO S-SP
CONNECT SP TO P-SP
```

FIG. 3.3 Automatic *vs.* manual navigation

level of abstraction than programming languages such as C and COBOL (or data sub-languages such as are typically found in nonrelational DBMSs, come to that—see Fig. 3.3). Fundamentally, it is this raising of the level of abstraction that is responsible for the increased productivity that relational systems can provide.

Deciding just how to perform the automatic navigation referred to above is the responsibility of a very important DBMS component called the **optimizer**. In other words, for each relational request from the user, it is the job of the optimizer to choose an efficient way to implement that request. By way of an example, let us suppose the user issues the following request:

```
RESULT := ( EMP WHERE EMP# = 'E4' ) [ SALARY ] ;
```

Explanation: The expression in parentheses ("EMP WHERE ...") requests a *re-striction* of the EMP table to just the row where EMP# is E4. The column name in square brackets ("SALARY") then requests a *projection* of the result of that restriction over the SALARY column. Finally, the *assignment* operation (":=") requests the result of that projection to be assigned to table RESULT. In other words, RESULT is a single-column, single-row table that— after the request has been executed—will contain employee E4's salary. (We are making use here of the syntax for relational operations to be described in detail in Chapter 6. Note too, incidentally, that we are implicitly making use of the relational *closure* property—we have written a nested expression, in which the input to the projection operation is the output from the restriction operation.)

Now, even in this very simple example, there are probably at least two ways of performing the necessary data access:

1. By doing a physical sequential scan of (the stored version of) table EMP until the required record is found;

2. If there is an index on (the stored version of) the EMP# column of that table— which in practice there probably will be, because it is the primary key, and most systems in fact *require* an index on the primary key—then by using that index and thus going directly to the E4 data.

The optimizer will choose which of these two strategies to adopt. More generally, given any particular relational request, the optimizer will make its choice of strategy for implementing that request on the basis of such considerations as the following:

■   Which tables are referenced in the request (there may be more than one if, e.g., there are any joins involved)

■   How big those tables are

■   What indexes exist

■   How selective those indexes are

■   How the data is physically clustered on the disk

■   What relational operations are involved

and so on. To repeat, therefore: User requests specify only what data the user wants, not how to get to that data; the access strategy for getting to the data is chosen by the optimizer ("automatic navigation"). Users and user programs are thus independent of such access strategies, which is of course essential if data independence is to be achieved.

We will have a lot more to say about the optimizer in Chapter 18.

3.6   The Catalog

As explained in Chapter 2 (Section 2.8), every DBMS must provide a **catalog** or **dictionary** function. The catalog is the place where—among other things—all of the various schemas (external, conceptual, internal) and all of the corresponding mappings (external/conceptual, conceptual/internal) are kept. In other words, the catalog contains detailed information (sometimes called **descriptors**) regarding the various objects that are of interest to the system itself. Examples of such objects are tables, indexes, users, integrity rules, security rules, and so on. Descriptor information is essential if the system is to be able to do its job properly. For example, the optimizer uses catalog information about indexes (see Chapter 18), as well as much other information, to help it decide how to implement user requests. Likewise, the security subsystem uses catalog information about users and security rules (see Chapter 15) to grant or deny such requests in the first place.

Now, one of the nice features of relational systems is that, in such a system, *the catalog itself consists of tables* (more precisely, *system* tables, so called to distinguish them from ordinary user tables). As a result, users can interrogate the catalog in exactly the same way as they interrogate their own data. For example, the catalog will typically include two system tables called TABLES and COLUMNS, the purpose of which is to describe the tables known to the system and the columns of those tables. (We say "typically" because the catalog is not the same in every system; this is because the catalog for a particular system necessarily contains a good deal of information that is specific to that system.) For the departments-and-employees database, the TABLES and COLUMNS tables might look in outline as shown in Fig. 3.4.

Note: It would be more accurate to say that the TABLES and COLUMNS tables describe the *named* tables known to the system, as opposed to the *un*named tables that result from the evaluation of some relational expression. Note too that the category "named tables" includes the catalog tables themselves—i.e., the catalog is *self-describing*. The entries for the catalog tables themselves are not shown in Fig. 3.4, however.

Now suppose some user of the departments-and-employees database wants to know exactly what columns the DEPT table contains (obviously we are assuming that for some reason the user does not already have this information). Then the expression

TABLES	TABNAME	COLCOUNT	ROWCOUNT	. . . . .
	DEPT	3	3	. . . . .
	EMP	4	4	. . . . .
	. . . .	. . . .	. . . .	. . . . .

COLUMNS	TABNAME	COLNAME	. . . . .
	DEPT	DEPT#	. . . . .
	DEPT	DNAME	. . . . .
	DEPT	BUDGET	. . . . .
	EMP	EMP#	. . . . .
	EMP	ENAME	. . . . .
	EMP	DEPT#	. . . . .
	EMP	SALARY	. . . . .
	. . . .	. . . .	. . . . .

FIG. 3.4 Catalog for the departments-and-employees database (in outline)

```
( COLUMNS WHERE TABNAME = 'DEPT' ) [ COLNAME ]
```

provides exactly what is required. *Note:* If we had wanted to *keep* the result of this query in some more permanent fashion, we could have assigned the value of the expression to some other table, say RESULT, as in the example in Section 3.5. However, we will omit this final assignment step from most of our examples (both here and in later chapters).

Here is another example: "Which tables include a column called EMP#?"

```
( COLUMNS WHERE COLNAME = 'EMP#' ) [ TABNAME ]
```

Exercise for the reader: What does the following do?

```
( ( TABLES JOIN COLUMNS )
        WHERE COLCOUNT < 5 ) [ TABNAME, COLNAME ]
```

3.7 Base Tables and Views

We have seen that, starting with a given set of tables such as DEPT and EMP, relational expressions allow us to obtain further tables from that given set—e.g., by joining two of the given tables together. It is time to introduce a little more terminology. The original (given) tables are called **base** tables; a table that is obtained from those base tables by means of some relational expression is called a **derived** table. Thus, base tables have *independent existence,* while derived tables do not—they depend on the base tables. Observe, therefore, that a derived table is, precisely, a table that is defined in terms of other tables—ultimately, in terms of base tables—and a base table is, precisely, a table that is not a derived table.

Now, relational systems obviously have to provide a means for creating the base tables in the first place. In SQL, for example, this function is performed by the CREATE TABLE statement (TABLE here meaning, very specifically, a *base* table). And base tables obviously have to be *named* (indeed, their name is specified in the statement that creates them). Most derived tables, by contrast, are not named. However, relational systems usually support one particular kind of derived table, called a *view,* that does have a name. A **view** is thus a named table that—unlike a base table—does not have an independent existence of its own, but is instead defined in terms of one or more underlying named tables (base tables or other views).

An example is in order. The statement

```
CREATE VIEW TOPEMPS AS
    ( EMP WHERE SALARY > 33K ) [ EMP#, ENAME, SALARY ] ;
```

might be used to define a view called TOPEMPS. When this statement is executed, the expression following the AS—which is in fact the view definition—is not evaluated but is merely "remembered" by the system in some way (actually by saving it in the catalog, under the specified name TOPEMPS). To the user, however, it is now as if there really were a table in the database called TOPEMPS, with rows and columns as shown in the unshaded portions (only) of Fig. 3.5 below. In other words, the name TOPEMPS

TOPEMPS	EMP#	ENAME	DEPT#	SALARY
	E1	Lopez	D1	40K
	E2	Cheng	D1	42K
	E3	Finzi	D2	30K
	E4	Saito	D2	35K

FIG. 3.5 TOPEMPS as a view of base table EMP (unshaded portions)

denotes a *virtual* table, *viz.* the table that would result if the view-defining expression were actually evaluated.

Note carefully, however, that although we say that the name TOPEMPS denotes "the table that would result if the view-defining expression were actually evaluated," we definitely do not mean to suggest that it refers to *a separate copy* of the data—i.e., we do not mean to suggest that the view-defining expression actually *is* evaluated. On the contrary, the view is effectively just a *window* into the underlying table EMP. Furthermore, of course, any changes to that underlying table will be automatically and instantaneously visible through that window (provided, of course, that those changes lie within the unshaded portion of EMP); likewise, changes to TOPEMPS will automatically and instantaneously be applied to the real table EMP, and hence of course be visible through the window.

Here then is an example of a query involving view TOPEMPS:

```
( TOPEMPS WHERE SALARY < 42K ) [ EMP#, SALARY ]
```

The result will look like this:

EMP#	SALARY
E1	40K
E4	35K

Operations against a view like that just shown are effectively handled by replacing *references* to the view by the expression that *defines* the view (i.e., the expression that was saved in the catalog). In the example, therefore, the expression

```
( TOPEMPS WHERE SALARY < 42K ) [ EMP#, SALARY ]
```

is modified by the system to become

```
( ( EMP WHERE SALARY > 33K ) [ EMP#, ENAME, SALARY ] )
                    WHERE SALARY < 42K ) [ EMP#, SALARY ]
```

which, after a certain amount of rearrangement (see Chapter 18), can be simplified to just

```
( EMP WHERE SALARY > 33K AND SALARY < 42K ) [ EMP#, SALARY ]
```

And this expression evaluates to the result shown earlier. In other words, the original operation against the view is effectively converted into an equivalent operation against the underlying base table. That equivalent operation is then executed in the normal way (more accurately, *optimized and* executed in the normal way).

Now, the view TOPEMPS is very simple, consisting as it does just of a row-and-column-subset of a single underlying base table. In principle, however, a view definition—since it is essentially just a named relational expression—can be *of arbitrary complexity*. For example, here is a view whose definition includes a join of two underlying base tables:

```
CREATE VIEW JOINEX1 AS
    ( ( EMP JOIN DEPT ) WHERE BUDGET > 7M ) [ EMP#, DEPT# ] ;
```

We will return to the general question of view definition and view processing in Chapter 17.

Incidentally, we can now explain the remark in Chapter 2 (Section 2.2) to the effect that the term "view" has a rather specific meaning in relational contexts that is not identical to the meaning ascribed to it in the ANSI/SPARC architecture. At the external level of that architecture, the database is perceived as an "external view," defined by an external schema (and different users can have different external views). In relational systems, by contrast, a view (as explained above) is, specifically, a *named, derived, virtual table*. Thus, the relational analog of an ANSI/SPARC "external view" is (typically) a collection of several tables, each of which is a view in the relational sense. The "external schema" consists of definitions of those views.

Now, the ANSI/SPARC architecture is quite general and allows for arbitrary variability between the external and conceptual levels. In principle, even the *types* of data structure supported at the two levels could be different—for example, the conceptual level could be based on relations, while a given user could have an external view of the database as a hierarchy. In practice, however, most systems use the same type of structure as the basis for both levels, and relational products are no exception to this general rule—a view is still a table, like a base table. And since the same type of object is supported at both levels, the same data sublanguage (usually SQL) applies at both levels. Indeed, the fact that a view is a table is precisely one of the strengths of relational systems; it is important in just the same way that the fact that a subset is a set is important in mathematics. *Note:* SQL products, and the SQL standard (see Chapter 8) often seem to miss this point, however, inasmuch as they refer repeatedly to "tables and views" (with the implication that a view is not a table). The reader is advised *not* to fall into this common trap of taking "tables" to mean, specifically, *base tables only*.

There is one final point that needs to be made on the subject of base tables and views, as follows. The base table *vs.* view distinction is frequently characterized thus:

■ Base tables "really exist," in the sense that they represent data that is actually stored in the database;

■ Views, by contrast, do not "really exist" but merely provide different ways of looking at the "real" data.

However, this characterization, though arguably useful in an informal sense, does not accurately reflect the true state of affairs. It is true that users can *think* of base tables as if they physically existed; in a way, in fact, the whole point of the relational approach is to allow users to think of base tables as physically existing, while not having to concern themselves with how those tables are physically represented in storage. But— and it is a big but!—this way of thinking should *not* be construed as meaning that a base table is a physically stored table (i.e., a collection of physically adjacent, physically stored records, each one consisting of a direct copy of a row of the base table). As explained in Section 3.2, base tables are best thought of as an *abstraction* of some collection of stored data—an abstraction in which all storage-level details are concealed. In principle, there can be an arbitrary degree of differentiation between a base table and its stored counterpart.

A simple example might help to clarify this point. Consider the departments-and-employees database once again. Most of today's relational systems would probably implement that database with two stored files, one for each of the two base tables. But there is absolutely no reason why there should not be just one stored file of *hierarchic* stored records, each one consisting of department number, name, and budget for some given department, followed by employee number, name, and salary for each employee who happens to be in that department.

3.8   The SQL Language

Most current relational products support some dialect of the standard relational language SQL. SQL was originally developed in IBM Research in the early 1970s; it was first implemented on a large scale in the IBM relational prototype System R, and subsequently reimplemented in numerous commercial products, from both IBM and other vendors. Dialects of SQL have since become an American national (ANSI) standard, an international (ISO) standard, a UNIX (X/Open) standard, an IBM standard (it forms the "common database interface" portion of IBM's System Applications Architecture, SAA), and a federal information processing standard (FIPS)—see the References and Bibliography section in Chapter 8. In this section we take a very brief look at the SQL language.

SQL is used to formulate relational operations (i.e., operations that define and manipulate data in relational form). We consider the definitional operations first. Fig. 3.6 shows how the departments-and-employees database of Fig. 3.1 might be defined, using SQL *data definition* operations.

As you can see, the definition includes one CREATE TABLE statement for each of the two tables. The CREATE TABLE statement is, as already indicated, an example of an SQL data definition operation. Each CREATE TABLE statement specifies the name of the (base) table to be created, the names and data types of the columns of that table, and the primary key and any foreign keys in that table (possibly some additional information also, not illustrated in Fig. 3.6). Refer back to Section 3.4 if you need to refresh your memory regarding primary and foreign keys.

```
CREATE TABLE DEPT
     ( DEPT#    CHAR(2),
       DNAME    CHAR(20),
       BUDGET   DECIMAL(7),
     PRIMARY KEY ( DEPT# ) ) ;

CREATE TABLE EMP
     ( EMP#     CHAR(2),
       ENAME    CHAR(20),
       DEPT#    CHAR(2),
       SALARY   DECIMAL(5),
     PRIMARY KEY ( EMP# ),
     FOREIGN KEY ( DEPT# ) REFERENCES DEPT ) ;
```

FIG. 3.6 The departments-and-employees database (SQL data definition)

Having created the tables, we can now start operating on them by means of the SQL *data manipulation* operations SELECT, INSERT, UPDATE, and DELETE. In particular, we can perform relational SELECT, PROJECT, and JOIN operations on the data, in each case by using the SQL data manipulation statement SELECT. Fig. 3.7 shows how the SELECT, PROJECT, and JOIN examples of Fig. 3.2 could be formu-

```
SELECT (RESTRICT):       Result:
SELECT DEPT#, DNAME, BUDGET
FROM    DEPT
WHERE   BUDGET > 8M ;
```

DEPT#	DNAME	BUDGET
D1	Marketing	10M
D2	Development	12M

```
PROJECT:                 Result:
SELECT DEPT#, BUDGET
FROM    DEPT ;
```

DEPT#	BUDGET
D1	10M
D2	12M
D3	5M

```
JOIN:
SELECT DEPT.DEPT#, DNAME, BUDGET, EMP#, ENAME, SALARY
FROM    DEPT, EMP
WHERE   DEPT.DEPT# = EMP.DEPT# ;
```

Result:

DEPT#	DNAME	BUDGET	EMP#	ENAME	SALARY
D1	Marketing	10M	E1	Lopez	40K
D1	Marketing	10M	E2	Cheng	42K
D2	Development	12M	E3	Finzi	30K
D2	Development	12M	E4	Saito	35K

FIG. 3.7 SELECT, PROJECT, and JOIN examples in SQL

lated using SQL. *Note:* The join example in that figure illustrates the point that **quali-fied names** (e.g. DEPT.DEPT#, EMP.DEPT#) are sometimes necessary in SQL to "disambiguate" column references. If unqualified names were used—i.e., if the WHERE clause were of the form "WHERE DEPT# = DEPT#"—then the two "DEPT#" references would be ambiguous (it would not be clear in either case whether the reference stood for DEPT.DEPT# or EMP.DEPT#).

The reader will observe that the SELECT statement of SQL and the SELECT operation of the relational model are not the same thing! Indeed, SQL supports all three of the relational operations SELECT, PROJECT, and JOIN (and more besides), all within its own SELECT statement. For this reason among others, RESTRICT is to be preferred over SELECT as the name of the relational operation; referring to the two distinct operations by two distinct names should reduce the chance of confusion between them. (In fact, RESTRICT was the original name for the relational operation; furthermore, it is an intuitively good name, inasmuch as the operation has the effect of—for example—*restricting* the set of departments to just those with a budget in excess of 8M.)

We close this brief discussion of SQL with a few miscellaneous observations:

1. *Update operations:* Examples of the SQL update operations INSERT, UPDATE, and DELETE have already been given in Chapter 1. However, the examples in the body of that chapter happened all to be single-row operations. Like SELECT, however, INSERT, UPDATE, and DELETE are *set-level* operations, in general (and some of the exercises and answers in Chapter 1 did in fact illustrate this point). Here are some set-level update examples for the departments-and-employees database:

   ```
   INSERT
   INTO    TEMP ( EMP# )
           SELECT EMP#
           FROM   EMP
           WHERE  DEPT# = 'D1' ;
   ```

   This example assumes that we have previously created another table TEMP with just one column, called EMP#. The INSERT statement inserts into that table employee numbers for all employees in department D1.

   ```
   UPDATE EMP
   SET    SALARY = SALARY * 1.1
   WHERE  DEPT# = 'D1' ;
   ```

   This UPDATE statement updates the database to reflect the fact that all employees in department D1 have been given a ten percent salary increase.

   ```
   DELETE
   FROM    EMP
   WHERE   DEPT# = 'D2' ;
   ```

   This DELETE statement deletes all EMP rows for employees in department D2.

2. *Catalog:* The SQL standard does include specifications for a standard catalog

called the *Information Schema* (see Chapter 8). At the time of writing, however, few products if any have actually implemented the standard Information Schema.

3. *Views:* Here are SQL analogs of the CREATE VIEW statement for TOPEMPS and the sample query against that view from Section 3.7:

```
CREATE VIEW TOPEMPS AS
       SELECT EMP#, ENAME, SALARY
       FROM   EMP
       WHERE  SALARY > 33K ;

SELECT EMP#, SALARY
FROM   TOPEMPS
WHERE  SALARY < 42K ;
```

4. *Means of invocation:* Most SQL products allow SQL statements to be executed both (a) "directly," i.e., interactively from an online terminal, and (b) as part of an application program (i.e., the SQL statements can be "embedded," meaning they can be intermixed with the programming language statements of such a program). In case (b), moreover, the program can typically be written in a variety of host languages (C, COBOL, Pascal, PL/I, etc.).

5. *SQL is not perfect:* We include numerous SQL examples in this book because SQL is the standard relational language and because its use and implementation are both very widespread. But it must be emphasized that SQL is very far from being the "perfect" relational language: It suffers from numerous sins of both omission and commission. See Chapter 8 for further discussion.

3.9   The Suppliers-and-Parts Database

Our running example throughout most of this book is the well-known **suppliers-and-parts** database. The purpose of this section is to introduce that database, in order to serve as a point of reference for later chapters. Fig. 3.8 shows a set of sample data values; subsequent examples will actually assume these specific values, where it makes any difference. Fig. 3.9 shows the database definition, expressed in a syntax to be explained in Chapter 4. Note the primary and foreign key specifications in particular.

The intended semantics of the database are as follows.

■ Table S represents *suppliers.* Each supplier has a supplier number (S#), unique to that supplier; a supplier name (SNAME), not necessarily unique (though SNAME values do happen to be unique in Fig. 3.8); a rating or status value (STATUS); and a location (CITY). We assume that each supplier is located in exactly one city.

■ Table P represents *parts* (more accurately, kinds of part). Each kind of part has a part number (P#), which is unique; a part name (PNAME); a color (COLOR); a weight (WEIGHT); and a location where parts of that type are stored (CITY). We assume—where it makes any difference—that part weights are given in pounds.

S	S#	SNAME	STATUS	CITY
	S1	Smith	20	London
	S2	Jones	10	Paris
	S3	Blake	30	Paris
	S4	Clark	20	London
	S5	Adams	30	Athens

P	P#	PNAME	COLOR	WEIGHT	CITY
	P1	Nut	Red	12	London
	P2	Bolt	Green	17	Paris
	P3	Screw	Blue	17	Rome
	P4	Screw	Red	14	London
	P5	Cam	Blue	12	Paris
	P6	Cog	Red	19	London

SP	S#	P#	QTY
	S1	P1	300
	S1	P2	200
	S1	P3	400
	S1	P4	200
	S1	P5	100
	S1	P6	100
	S2	P1	300
	S2	P2	400
	S3	P2	200
	S4	P2	200
	S4	P4	300
	S4	P5	400

FIG. 3.8 The suppliers-and-parts database (sample values)

```
CREATE DOMAIN S#      CHAR(5) ;
CREATE DOMAIN NAME    CHAR(20) ;
CREATE DOMAIN STATUS NUMERIC(5) ;
CREATE DOMAIN CITY    CHAR(15) ;
CREATE DOMAIN P#      CHAR(6) ;
CREATE DOMAIN COLOR  CHAR(6) ;
CREATE DOMAIN WEIGHT NUMERIC(5) ;
CREATE DOMAIN QTY     NUMERIC(9) ;

CREATE BASE RELATION S
    ( S#      DOMAIN ( S# ),
      SNAME   DOMAIN ( NAME ),
      STATUS  DOMAIN ( STATUS ),
      CITY    DOMAIN ( CITY ) )
    PRIMARY KEY ( S# ) ;

CREATE BASE RELATION P
    ( P#      DOMAIN ( P# ),
      PNAME   DOMAIN ( NAME ),
      COLOR   DOMAIN ( COLOR ),
      WEIGHT  DOMAIN ( WEIGHT ),
      CITY    DOMAIN ( CITY ) )
    PRIMARY KEY ( P# ) ;

CREATE BASE RELATION SP
    ( S#      DOMAIN ( S# ),
      P#      DOMAIN ( P# ),
      QTY     DOMAIN ( QTY ) )
    PRIMARY KEY ( S#, P# )
    FOREIGN KEY ( S# ) REFERENCES S
    FOREIGN KEY ( P# ) REFERENCES P ;
```

FIG. 3.9 The suppliers-and-parts database (data definition)

We also assume that each kind of part comes in exactly one color and is stored in a warehouse in exactly one city.

■ Table SP represents *shipments*. It serves in a sense to connect the other two tables together. For example, the first row of table SP in Fig. 3.8 connects a specific supplier from table S (namely, supplier S1) with a specific part from table P (namely, part P1)—in other words, it represents a shipment of parts of kind P1 by the supplier called S1 (and the shipment quantity is 300). Thus, each shipment has a supplier number (S#), a part number (P#), and a quantity (QTY). We assume that there can be at most one shipment at any given time for a given supplier and a given part; for a given shipment, therefore, the combination of S# value and P# value is unique with respect to the set of shipments currently appearing in the SP table.

We remark that (as already pointed out in Section 1.3) suppliers and parts can be regarded as **entities,** and a shipment can be regarded as a **relationship** between a particular supplier and a particular part. As also pointed out in Section 1.3, however, relationships are best regarded as just a special case of entities. One advantage of relational databases is precisely that all entities, regardless of whether they are in fact relationships, are represented in the same uniform way—namely, by means of tables, as the example shows.

One final remark: The suppliers-and-parts database is of course extremely simple, much simpler than any real database is likely to be in practice; most real databases will involve many more entities and relationships than this one does. Nevertheless, it is at least adequate to illustrate most of the points that we need to make in the next few parts of the book, and (as already stated) we will use it as the basis for most—not all—of our examples in the next few chapters. And another editorial comment: There is of course nothing wrong with using more descriptive names such as SUPPLIERS, PARTS, and SHIPMENTS in place of the rather terse names S, P, and SP used above; indeed, descriptive names are generally to be recommended in practice. But in the case of suppliers-and-parts specifically, the three tables are referenced so frequently in the chapters that follow that very short names seemed desirable. Long names tend to become irksome with much repetition.

3.10   Summary

This brings us to the end of our short overview of relational technology. Obviously we have barely scratched the surface of what by now has become a very extensive subject, but the whole point of the chapter has been to serve as a gentle introduction to the much more comprehensive discussions that follow in the remainder of the book. Even so, we have managed to cover quite a lot of ground. Here is a summary of the major topics we have discussed.

A **relational database** is a database that is perceived by its users as a collection of **relations** or tables. All values in a relation are atomic or **scalar** (there are no repeating groups). A **relational system** is a system that supports relational databases and operations on such databases, including in particular the operations **RESTRICT** (often called SELECT), **PROJECT,** and **JOIN**. These operations, and others like them, are all **set-level**. The **closure** property of relational systems means that the output from every operation is the same kind of object as the input (they are all relations), which implies that we can write **nested relational expressions**.

The formal theory underlying relational systems is called **the relational model**. The relational model is concerned with logical matters only, not physical matters. It addresses three aspects of data—data **structure** (or **objects**), data **integrity,** and data **manipulation** (or **operators**). The *objects* are basically the tables; the *integrity* portion has to do with **primary and foreign keys;** and the *operators* are RESTRICT, PROJECT, JOIN, etc.

The **optimizer** is the system component that determines how to implement user requests (which are concerned with "what," not "how"). Since relational systems therefore assume responsibility for "navigating" around the stored database to locate the desired data, such systems are sometimes described as **automatic navigation** systems. Optimization and automatic navigation are prerequisites for **data independence** in a relational system.

The **catalog** is a set of system tables that contain **descriptors** for the various items that are of interest to the system (base tables, views, indexes, users, etc.). Users can interrogate the catalog in exactly the same way they interrogate their own data.

A **derived** table is a table that is derived from other tables by means of some relational expression. A **base** table is a table that is not a derived table. A **view** is a **named** derived table, whose definition in terms of other tables is kept in the catalog. Users can operate on views in much the same way as they operate on base tables. The system implements operations on views by replacing references to the name of the view by the expression that defines the view, thereby converting the operation into an equivalent operation on the underlying base tables. We will refer to this method of implementation as the **substitution** method.

The standard language for interacting with relational databases is **SQL**. The SQL operation for creating a new base table is **CREATE TABLE**. The SQL retrieval operation is **SELECT** (often referred to as SELECT - FROM - WHERE); this operation provides the functionality of the relational RESTRICT, PROJECT, and JOIN operations, and more besides. The SQL update operations are **INSERT, UPDATE,** and **DELETE**. SQL is extremely important from a commercial point of view but is very far from being the "perfect" relational language.

Finally, the base example for much of the remainder of this book is **the suppliers-and-parts database**. It is worth taking the time to familiarize yourself with this example now, if you have not already done so. That is, you should at least know which columns exist in which tables and what the primary and foreign keys are (it is not so important to know exactly which scalar values occur where!).

By way of conclusion, let us try to relate the material discussed in this chapter to the components of the ANSI/SPARC architecture discussed in Chapter 2. The correspondence is not entirely clearcut, as will be seen, but it can nevertheless be useful as an aid to understanding.

1. Base tables correspond to the ANSI/SPARC conceptual level.

2. Views correspond to the ANSI/SPARC external level, as already explained in Section 3.7. *Note:* Actually, most relational products on the market today muddy the external/conceptual distinction somewhat, because they allow users to operate directly on base tables as well as on views.

3. The relational model has nothing to say regarding the ANSI/SPARC internal level. In principle—as explained in Section 3.2—the system is free to employ any storage structures it likes at the internal level, provided only that it can abstract from those storage structures and present the data at the conceptual level in pure tabular form. Unfortunately, this is another area where today's products have muddied the waters somewhat: Most of those products tend to map *one* base table to *one* stored file, and are far too inflexible with respect to the degree of difference they can tolerate between the two. In other words, those products do not provide as much data independence as we would really like, or as relational systems are theoretically capable of providing.

   Note: It is at least true, however, that user requests—i.e., SQL statements—in those products make no direct reference to access structures such as indexes. As a result, the DBA or DBMS can create and destroy such structures freely, for performance and tuning reasons, without invalidating existing applications. (At least, this is true in the SQL standard, though here again some products unfortunately violate the principle and do not conform to the standard in this regard.)

4. SQL is a typical (in fact, the standard) data sublanguage. As such, it includes both a **data definition** language (DDL) component and a **data manipulation** language (DML) component. As already indicated, the SQL DML can operate at both the external and the conceptual level. The SQL DDL, similarly, can be used to define objects at the external level (views), the conceptual level (base tables), and even—in most systems, though not in the standard—the internal level (e.g., indexes). Moreover, SQL also provides certain "data control" facilities—that is, facilities that cannot really be classified as belonging to either the DDL or the DML. An example of such a facility is the GRANT statement, which allows one user to grant certain *access privileges* to another (see Chapter 15).

5. Application programs in an SQL system can access the database from a host language such as COBOL by means of *embedded SQL statements* (see Chapter 8). Embedded SQL represents a "loose coupling" between SQL and the host language. Basically, any statement that can be used in interactive SQL can be used in embedded SQL also. In addition, certain special statements, also discussed in Chapter 8, are provided for use in the embedded environment only.

Exercises

3.1 Define the following terms:

automatic navigation	primary key
base table	projection
catalog	relational database
closure	relational DBMS
derived table	relational model
foreign key	restriction
join	set-level operation
optimization	view

3.2 Sketch the contents of the catalog tables TABLES and COLUMNS for the suppliers-and-parts database.

3.3 As explained in Section 3.6, the catalog is self-describing—i.e., it includes entries for the catalog tables themselves. Extend Fig. 3.4 to include the necessary entries for the TABLES and COLUMNS tables themselves.

3.4 Here is a query on the suppliers-and-parts database. What does it do?

```
RESULT  :=  ( ( S JOIN SP ) WHERE P# = 'P2' ) [ S#, CITY ] ;
```

3.5 Suppose the expression on the right-hand side of the assignment in Exercise 3.4 is used in a view definition:

```
CREATE VIEW V AS
   ( ( S JOIN SP ) WHERE P# = 'P2' ) [ S#, CITY ] ;
```

Now consider the query

```
ANSWER  :=  ( V WHERE CITY = 'London' ) [ S# ] ;
```

What does this query do? Show what is involved on the part of the DBMS in processing this query.

References and Bibliography

3.1 E. F. Codd. "Relational Database: A Practical Foundation for Productivity." *CACM 25*, No. 2 (February 1982). Republished in Robert L. Ashenhurst (ed.), *ACM Turing Award Lectures: The First Twenty Years 1966–1985*. Reading, Mass.: Addison-Wesley ACM Press Anthology Series (1987).

This is the paper that Codd presented on the occasion of his receiving the 1981 ACM Turing Award. It discusses the well-known *application backlog* problem. To paraphrase: "The demand for computer applications is growing fast—so fast that information systems departments (whose responsibility it is to provide those applications) are lagging further and further behind in their ability to meet that demand." There are two complementary ways of attacking this problem:

1. Provide IT professionals with new tools to increase their productivity;

2. Allow end users to interact directly with the database, thus bypassing the IT professional entirely.

Both approaches are needed, and in this paper Codd gives evidence to suggest that the necessary foundation for both is provided by relational technology.

3.2 C. J. Date. "Why Relational?" In C. J. Date, *Relational Database Writings 1985–1989*. Reading, Mass.: Addison-Wesley (1990).

An attempt to provide a succinct yet reasonably comprehensive summary of the major advantages of the relational approach. The following observation from the paper is worth repeating here: Among all the numerous advantages of "going relational," there is one in particular that cannot be overemphasized, and that is *the existence of a sound theoretical base*. To quote:

"... relational really is different. It is different because it is not *ad hoc*. Older systems, by contrast, were *ad hoc;* they may have provided solutions to certain important problems of their day, but they did not rest on any solid theoretical base. Relational systems, by contrast, do rest on such a base . . . which means that [they] are *rock solid*.

"Thanks to this solid foundation, relational systems behave in well-defined ways; and (possibly without realizing the fact) users have a simple model of that behavior in their mind, one that enables them to predict with confidence what the system will do in any given situation. There are (or should be) no surprises. This predictability means that user interfaces are easy to understand, document, teach, learn, use, and remember."

3.3 C. J. Date. "Relational Technology: A Brief Introduction." In C. J. Date and Hugh Darwen, *Relational Database Writings 1989–1991*. Reading, Mass.: Addison-Wesley (1992).

Portions of the present chapter were originally published in somewhat different form in this paper.

Answers to Selected Exercises

3.3 Fig. 3.10 shows the entries for the TABLES and COLUMNS tables (only; i.e., the entries for the user's own tables are omitted). It is obviously not possible to give precise COL-COUNT and ROWCOUNT values.

TABLES	TABNAME	COLCOUNT	ROWCOUNT	. . . . .
	TABLES	(>3)	(>2)	. . . . .
	COLUMNS	(>2)	(>5)	. . . . .
	. . . . . .	. . . .	. . . .	. . . . .

COLUMNS	TABNAME	COLNAME	. . . . .
	TABLES	TABNAME	. . . . .
	TABLES	COLCOUNT	. . . . .
	TABLES	ROWCOUNT	. . . . .
	COLUMNS	TABNAME	. . . . .
	COLUMNS	COLNAME	. . . . ·
	. . . .	. . . .	. . . . .

FIG. 3.10 Catalog entries for TABLES and COLUMNS themselves (in outline)

3.4 The query retrieves supplier number and city for suppliers who supply part P2.

3.5 The meaning of the query is: "Retrieve supplier number for London suppliers who supply part P2." The first step in processing the query is to replace the name V by the expression that defines V, giving:

```
( ( ( ( S JOIN SP ) WHERE P# = 'P2' ) [ S#, CITY ] )
                              WHERE  CITY = 'London' ) [ S# ]
```

This simplifies to:

```
( ( S WHERE CITY = 'London' ) JOIN ( SP WHERE P# = 'P2' ) ) [ S# ]
```

For further discussion and explanation, see Chapters 17 and 18.

PART **II**

THE RELATIONAL MODEL

The foundation of modern database technology is without question the relational model; it is that foundation that makes the field a science. Thus, any treatment of the field that does not include thorough coverage of the model is by definition shallow. Likewise, any claim to skill or expertise in the field is less than fully justified if the claimant does not understand the model in depth. Not that the material is difficult to understand, we hasten to add—it certainly is not—but, to repeat, it *is* fundamental.

As explained in Chapter 3, the relational model is concerned with three aspects of data—data *structure* (or *objects*), data *integrity,* and data *manipulation* (or *operators*). In this part of the book, we consider each of these aspects in turn: Chapter 4 discusses objects, Chapter 5 discusses integrity, and Chapters 6 and 7 discuss operators. (We devote two chapters to the last of these topics because the operators part of the model can be realized in two distinct but equivalent fashions, known respectively as the *relational algebra* and the *relational calculus.*) Chapter 8 is explained below.

Note: It is important to understand that the model is not a static thing—it has changed somewhat over the years, and indeed continues to do so. The definitions, descriptions, and explanations given in this book reflect the most recent thinking of the present writer and other workers in this field. However, it is only fair to mention that, while most of the material to be discussed is indeed rock solid (the changes referred to above have indeed been evolutionary, not revolutionary, in nature), there are still a few issues where some controversy exists. Such issues are appropriately flagged in the text.

As stated above, the relational model is not inherently difficult to understand. But it is a theory, and most theories tend to come equipped with their own special terminology—and (for reasons already explained in Section 3.3) the relational model is no exception to this general rule. And, of course, we will be using that special terminology very heavily in this part of the book. Now, it cannot be denied that the terminology can be a little bewildering at first, and indeed can serve as a barrier to understanding (this latter fact is particularly unfortunate, given that the underlying ideas in most cases are not difficult at all). So if you are having trouble in understanding some of the discussions that follow, please have patience: You will probably find that the concepts do become very straightforward, once you have become familiar with the terminology.

As the reader will soon see, the chapters here are very long (this is almost a book within a book). But the length reflects the importance of the subject matter, plus a desire on the part of the writer to provide a treatment that is comprehensive (even definitive). The reader might like to take the material one section at a time rather than one chapter at a time. Of course, it is quite possible to provide an overview of the model in just one or two pages; indeed, it is a major strength of the relational approach that its basic ideas can be explained and understood very easily. However, a one- or two-page treatment cannot really do justice to the subject, nor truly illustrate its wide range of applicability. The considerable length of this part of the book should thus be seen, not as a comment on the model's complexity, but rather as a tribute to its importance and to its success as a foundation for numerous far-reaching developments.

Finally, regarding Chapter 8: We have already explained in Part I of this book that, despite its numerous deficiencies (in particular, despite the fact that it is very far from being a true implementation of the relational model), just about every database product on the market today supports some version of the standard language SQL. As a consequence, no modern database textbook would be complete without some reasonably detailed introduction to that language, and such indeed is the aim of Chapter 8.

4 | Relational Data Objects: Domains and Relations

4.1 An Introductory Example

As explained in Chapter 3, the relational model is divided into three parts, having to do with *objects, integrity,* and *operators,* respectively. All three parts have their own special terms. The most important of the terms used in connection with the "objects" part (the subject of the present chapter) are shown in Fig. 4.1, using relation S from the suppliers-and-parts database by way of illustration. The terms in question are *relation* itself (of course), *tuple, cardinality, attribute, degree, domain,* and *primary key.* (Of these terms, *relation* and *primary key,* at least, should already be reasonably familiar to you.) We explain each term very informally here, then go on to give more formal definitions in subsequent sections. In brief:

■ A **relation** corresponds to what so far in this book we have mostly been calling a table.

■ A **tuple** (usually pronounced to rhyme with "couple") corresponds to a row of such a table and an **attribute** to a column. The number of tuples is called the **cardinality** and the number of attributes is called the **degree**.

■ The **primary key** is a unique identifier for the table—that is, a column or column combination with the property that, at any given time, no two rows of the table contain the same value in that column or column combination.

■ Finally, a **domain** is a pool of values, from which specific attributes of specific relations draw their actual values. For example, the domain labeled S# in Fig. 4.1 is the set of all legal supplier numbers, and the set of S# values appearing in relation S at any given time is constrained to be some subset of that set. Likewise, the set of S# values appearing in relation SP at any given time is also constrained to be some subset of that set.

These terms are summarized in Fig. 4.2. A couple of points arising from that figure:

1. Please understand that the "equivalences" shown are all only approximate, because the formal relational terms on the left have precise definitions, whereas the infor-

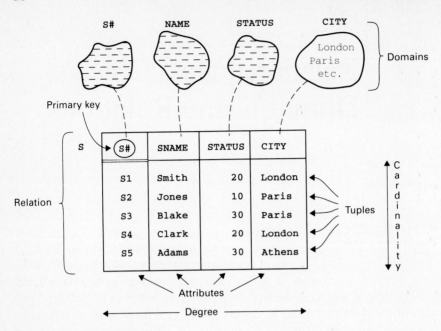

FIG. 4.1 The suppliers relation S

mal "equivalents" on the right have only rough-and-ready definitions. Thus, e.g., a relation and a table are not really the same thing, although in practice it is frequently convenient to pretend that they are. (We will explain the precise difference between a relation and a table in Section 4.3.)

2. The notion of "domain," in particular, serves right away to illustrate the important point that—as mentioned in Chapter 3—*not all relational systems support all aspects of the relational model.* Indeed, we managed to give a general overview of relational systems in Chapter 3 without ever mentioning domains at all (except in the CREATE DOMAIN statements in Fig. 4.8, and even there we did not explain the concept). The fact is, most of today's relational systems do not really support

Formal relational term	Informal equivalents
relation	table
tuple	row or record
cardinality	number of rows
attribute	column or field
degree	number of columns
primary key	unique identifier
domain	pool of legal values

FIG. 4.2 Relational data objects: terminology

domains, even though they are actually one of the most fundamental ingredients of the entire relational model. Please understand, therefore, that in the next few chapters we are describing the relational model *per se;* we are *not* necessarily describing the way any given relational system actually behaves.

Now we proceed with our formal development.

4.2   Domains

We take as our starting point *the smallest semantic unit of data,* which we assume to be the individual data value (such as the individual supplier number or the individual part weight or the individual city name or the individual shipment quantity). We will refer to such values as **scalars** (although this term is not much used in the relational literature). Scalar values represent "the smallest semantic unit of data" in the sense that they are *atomic:* They have no internal structure (i.e., they are nondecomposable) so far as the relational model—and hence the relational DBMS—is concerned. Note very carefully, however, that having no internal structure so far as the model or DBMS is concerned is not the same as having no internal structure at all. For example, a city name certainly does have an internal structure (it consists of a sequence of letters); however, if we decompose such a city name into its constituent letters, then *we lose meaning.* It is only if the letters all appear together, in the right sequence, that the meaning becomes apparent.

Note: We remark in passing that the concept "atomicity of scalar values" is actually a rather slippery one [4.8,4.15]. However, we choose to defer further discussion of this point to Chapter 19; for present purposes, we simply assume that the concept is at least intuitively understandable.

Next, we define a **domain** to be a named set of scalar values, all of the same type. For example, the domain of supplier numbers is the set of all possible supplier numbers, the domain of shipment quantities is the set of all integers greater than zero and less than 10,000 (say). Thus domains are *pools of values,* from which actual attribute values are drawn. More precisely, each attribute must be "defined on" exactly one underlying domain, meaning that values of that attribute must be taken from that domain. For example, the part number attribute in relation P and the part number attribute in relation SP will both be defined on the domain of part numbers (because, of course, both of those attributes represent part numbers). In other words, at any given time, every P# value in relation P must be a value from the part number domain, and similarly for the P# values in relation SP. Another way of saying the same thing—as already suggested in Section 4.1—is that, at any given time, the set of P# values in relation P must be some subset of the set of values appearing in the part number domain, and similarly for the P# values in relation SP.

Note, incidentally, that at any given time there will typically be values in a given domain that do not currently appear as a value for any of the attributes that correspond to that domain. For example, if the value P8 is a legal part number, then it will appear in the part number domain, even though no part P8 actually appears in relation P in our sample suppliers-and-parts database (Fig. 4.1)—i.e., no part P8 actually exists at this time.

Domain-Constrained Comparisons

So what is the significance of domains? One important answer to this question is that **domains constrain comparisons,** as we now explain. Consider the following two SQL queries against the suppliers-and-parts database (note that both queries involve a join):

```
SELECT  . . . . .              SELECT  . . . . .
FROM    P, SP                   FROM    P, SP
WHERE   P.P# = SP.P# ;          WHERE   P.WEIGHT = SP.QTY  ;
```

Of these two queries, the one on the left probably makes sense, whereas the one on the right probably does not. How do we know this? From a formal point of view, the answer is that the query on the left involves a comparison between two attributes, P.P# and SP.P#, that are (as explained above) *defined on the same domain,* whereas the one on the right involves a comparison between two attributes, P.WEIGHT and SP.QTY, that are presumably defined on different domains. (We say "presumably" here because, although it is true that weights and quantities are both numbers, they are different *kinds* of numbers. It does not make much sense to compare a weight and a quantity. The weight and quantity domains would therefore presumably be distinct.)

As the foregoing discussion suggests, therefore, if two attributes draw their values from the same domain, then comparisons—and hence joins, unions, and many other operations (see Chapter 6)—involving those two attributes probably make sense, because they are comparing like with like. Conversely, if two attributes draw their values from different domains, then comparisons (etc.) involving those two attributes probably do not make sense. Thus, one advantage of having the system support domains is that it would enable the system to prevent users from making silly mistakes. Note that it is very easy to make silly mistakes!—e.g., by typing "S#" when "P#" is intended. If the user tried to execute an operation involving a cross-domain comparison, the system could interrupt and inform the user of the probable error. (We say "probable" error, because there might in fact be circumstances in which it is not an error at all. See Chapter 19.)

Incidentally, we should make it clear that although our examples were expressed in terms of SQL, SQL in fact does *not* provide the kind of domain support we are describing here. Both of the queries above would be legal in SQL. The one on the right would deliver a meaningless answer, of course.

Data Definition

One point that might not yet be clear to the reader is that domains are primarily conceptual in nature. They might or might not be explicitly stored in the database as actual sets of values; in most cases, in fact, they probably will not be. But they should at least be specified as part of the database definition (in a system that supports the concept at all—but, as already explained, most systems currently do not); and then each attribute definition should include a reference to the corresponding domain, so that the system is aware of which attributes are comparable with one another and which not.

Now, in order to make the ideas of the relational model a little more concrete (both in the present section and throughout this part of the book), we will make use of a hypothetical relational language to illustrate those ideas. We will introduce the language in piecemeal fashion as we go along. Clearly, the first thing we need is a way of creating a new domain:

```
CREATE DOMAIN domain data-type ;
```

Here *domain* is the name of the new domain and *data-type* is the corresponding data type—e.g., CHAR(*n*) or NUMERIC(*n*). *Note:* In Chapters 16 and 19 we will discuss some additional components of the CREATE DOMAIN statement, not shown above.

Fig. 4.3 (a repeat of Fig. 3.9) shows how the suppliers-and-parts database might be defined using this language. Note that the example makes use of CREATE BASE RELATION statements (of course) as well as CREATE DOMAIN statements. A fuller explanation of CREATE BASE RELATION is given in Section 4.3; here we just point out that each attribute definition within those CREATE BASE RELATION statements includes a reference to the corresponding domain.

Creating a new domain via CREATE DOMAIN will cause the DBMS to make an entry in the catalog to describe that new domain. (Refer back to Section 3.6 if you need to refresh your memory regarding the catalog.) Likewise, creating a new base relation via CREATE BASE RELATION will cause the DBMS to make a set of entries describing that new relation. See Exercise 4.2 at the end of this chapter.

A note on naming: For definiteness, we will make the following assumptions regarding scope of names:

- Domains have names that are unique within the database.
- Named relations have names that are unique within the database.
- Attributes have names that are unique within the containing relation (even if that containing relation itself is *un*named!—see Chapter 6, Section 6.2).

In general, a given attribute can have the same name as the corresponding domain or a different name. Obviously it must have a different name if any ambiguity would otherwise result—in particular, if two attributes in the same relation are both based on the same domain (see the definition of *relation* in the next section, and note the phrase "not necessarily all distinct"). Generally speaking, however, it is a good idea if attributes do have the same name as the underlying domain wherever possible, or at least include the name of that domain as (say) the trailing portion of their own name. We have followed this convention in the example of Fig. 4.3 (an example illustrating the "trailing portion" idea is given later, in Fig. 4.4).

We might additionally have followed another common convention and omitted the reference to the underlying domain altogether from the definition of any attribute that

```
CREATE DOMAIN S#      CHAR(5) ;
CREATE DOMAIN NAME    CHAR(20) ;
CREATE DOMAIN STATUS NUMERIC(5) ;
CREATE DOMAIN CITY    CHAR(15) ;
CREATE DOMAIN P#      CHAR(6) ;
CREATE DOMAIN COLOR   CHAR(6) ;
CREATE DOMAIN WEIGHT NUMERIC(5) ;
CREATE DOMAIN QTY     NUMERIC(9) ;

CREATE BASE RELATION S
     ( S#       DOMAIN ( S# ),
       SNAME    DOMAIN ( NAME ),
       STATUS   DOMAIN ( STATUS ),
       CITY     DOMAIN ( CITY ) )
     PRIMARY KEY ( S# ) ;

CREATE BASE RELATION P
     ( P#       DOMAIN ( P# ),
       PNAME    DOMAIN ( NAME ),
       COLOR    DOMAIN ( COLOR ),
       WEIGHT   DOMAIN ( WEIGHT ),
       CITY     DOMAIN ( CITY ) )
     PRIMARY KEY ( P# ) ;

CREATE BASE RELATION SP
     ( S#       DOMAIN ( S# ),
       P#       DOMAIN ( P# ),
       QTY      DOMAIN ( QTY ) )
     PRIMARY KEY ( S#, P# )
     FOREIGN KEY ( S# ) REFERENCES S
     FOREIGN KEY ( P# ) REFERENCES P ;
```

FIG. 4.3 The suppliers-and-parts database (data definition)

bears the same name as that domain. For example, the CREATE BASE RELATION
for base relation S might have been simplified to just:

```
CREATE BASE RELATION S
     ( S#, SNAME DOMAIN (NAME), STATUS, CITY )
     PRIMARY KEY ( S# ) ;
```

Destroying domains: We have seen how to create a new domain. It must also be
possible to destroy an existing domain if we have no further use for it:

```
DESTROY DOMAIN domain ;
```

This operation will delete the catalog entry describing the domain, so that the domain in question is no longer known to the system. (We assume until further notice that
DESTROY DOMAIN will simply fail if any base relation currently includes an attribute that is defined on the specified domain. See Chapter 19 for further discussion.)

Domain-based queries: Here is another example of the practical significance of
domains. Consider the query:

"Which relations in the database contain any information pertaining to suppliers?"

This query can be stated more precisely:

"Which relations in the database include an attribute that is defined on the supplier numbers domain?"

In a system that supports the domain concept, the query thus translates into a simple interrogation against the catalog. In a system that does not support domains, it is obviously not possible to interrogate the catalog regarding domains as such—it is only possible to interrogate it regarding *attributes*. Only if the database designer has followed the naming convention recommended above—in other words, if he or she has in effect imposed the domain discipline on the database, without any support for that discipline from the system—will that attribute interrogation serve the intended purpose.

Domains and Data Types

We conclude this section by calling out explicitly a fact that many readers will already have realized for themselves—namely, a domain is really nothing more nor less than a **data type** (as that term is understood in modern programming languages). For example, the following is legal in the programming language Pascal:

```
type Day = ( Sun, Mon, Tue, Wed, Thu, Fri, Sat ) ;
var Today : Day ;
```

Here we have a *user-defined data type* called "Day" (with exactly seven legal values) and a variable called "Today" that is defined to be of that data type (and hence is constrained to those seven legal values). The situation is obviously analogous to a relational database in which we have a *domain* called "Day" and an *attribute* called "Today" that is defined on that domain. Furthermore, there are in fact some programming languages—e.g., SIMULA 67, MODULA-2, and Ada, though not however Pascal—that support some or all of the various other functions usually ascribed to domains in the relational model [4.8].

Given that a domain is basically just a data type, therefore, it is after all not quite fair to say that current DBMSs provide no domain support at all. The fact is, such systems do support domains in a very primitive sense, inasmuch as they do at least provide certain builtin (i.e., system-defined) primitive data types such as INTEGER and FLOAT. But when we talk about domain support in the context of relational systems, we really mean more than this primitive level of support—we mean that the system should provide a facility by which users can define their own more sophisticated data types, such as "supplier numbers," "part numbers," "city names," "colors," etc., etc., with all that such a facility implies.

So what *does* such a facility imply? There is certainly much more to it than just domain-constrained comparisons as discussed earlier in this section. Indeed, the domain concept is in fact considerably more complex than it might appear at first sight (which is perhaps why most systems currently do not support it). Precisely because there is so much more to the subject, however, we choose to ignore such further implications for the time being. Until further notice, therefore, we will assume only that domain support means that if two scalar values are to be compared, then they must come from the same domain. But please understand that this is a fairly major simplification, and we make it only to simplify the overall exposition. See Chapter 19 for further elaboration.

4.3 Relations

We are now in a position to examine exactly what is meant by the term "relation." It is as well to admit right at the outset, however, that historically there has been a certain amount of confusion surrounding this apparently simple concept (not least in previous editions of this book). The root of the confusion lies in a failure to distinguish clearly between relation *variables* and relation *values*. A **relation variable** is a variable in the usual programming language sense—i.e., it is a named object whose value changes over time. And the value of such a variable at any given time is, precisely, a **relation value**. For example, the statement

```
CREATE BASE RELATION S ... ;
```

creates a relation variable called S, whose value at any given time is some specific relation value.*

Note, therefore, that *base relation* (or "base table") is not really a very accurate term; base relation *variable,* though cumbersome, would be more specific. After all, if we say in some programming language

```
DECLARE QTY INTEGER ... ;
```

we do not call QTY an *integer,* we call it an *integer variable.* It is the *values* of that variable that are the actual integers; in other words, the unqualified term *integer* is used to mean, specifically, an integer *value.* Throughout the rest of this book, therefore, we will use the term *relation variable* when we wish to stress the point that we are referring to a variable *per se;* we will use the unqualified term *relation* to mean a relation value specifically (unless there is no risk of confusion in using it to mean a variable—in particular, we will continue to talk in terms of "base relations" rather than "base relation variables," for brevity and familiarity.)

Relation Values

Here then is the definition of the term *relation* (meaning, specifically, a relation *value*):

■ A **relation,** *R* say, on a collection of domains *D1, D2, . . . Dn*—not necessarily all distinct—consists of two parts, a *heading* and a *body.* (In terms of the tabular representation of a relation, the heading is the row of column headings and the body is the set of data rows.) To elaborate:

---

* If we think of relations as tables, then we could say that (e.g.) the relation variable S will have different tables as its value at different times. Note, however, that those different tables will all have the same columns; it is in their rows that they will differ.

1. The **heading** consists of a fixed set of **attributes,** or more precisely <attribute-name:domain-name> pairs,

   ```
   { <A1:D1>, <A2:D2>, ..., <An:Dn> }
   ```

   such that each attribute Aj corresponds to exactly one of the underlying domains Dj ($j = 1, 2, \ldots n$). The attribute names $A1, A2, \ldots An$ are all distinct.

2. The **body** consists of a set of **tuples** (sometimes *n-tuples,* but it is usual to drop the "*n-*" prefix). Each tuple in turn consists of a set of <attribute-name:attribute-value> pairs

   ```
   { <A1:vi1>, <A2:vi2>, ..., <An:vin> }
   ```

   ($i = 1, 2, \ldots m$, where m is the number of tuples in the set). In each such tuple, there is one such <attribute-name:attribute-value> pair $<Aj:vij>$ for each attribute Aj in the heading. For any given pair $<Aj:vij>$, vij is a value from the unique domain Dj that is associated with the attribute Aj.

The values m and n are called the **cardinality** and the **degree,** respectively, of relation R.

By way of example, let us examine table S from Fig. 4.1 (we deliberately do not refer to it as a relation for the moment) to see how it measures up to this definition.

■ First, that table does have four underlying domains, namely the domain of supplier numbers (S#), the domain of names (NAME), the domain of status values (STATUS), and the domain of city names (CITY). (When we draw a relation as a table on paper, we normally do not bother to show the underlying domains, but we must understand that, at least conceptually, they are always there.)

■ Next, the table certainly does have two parts—it has a row of column headings, and it has a set of data rows. We consider the row of column headings first:

   ```
   ( S#, SNAME, STATUS, CITY )
   ```

What this row really represents is the following set of ordered pairs:

   ```
   { < S#     : S#     >,
     < SNAME  : NAME   >,
     < STATUS : STATUS >,
     < CITY   : CITY   > }
   ```

The first component in each pair is the attribute name, the second is the corresponding domain name. Thus, we can agree that the row of column headings does indeed represent a *heading,* in the sense of the definition. *Note:* As the foregoing might suggest, it is common in practice to think of the heading of a relation as consisting just of a set of attribute names (i.e., the domain names are often omitted), except when precision is particularly important. This practice is sloppy but convenient, and we will frequently adopt it ourselves in what follows.

■ As for the rest of the table, it certainly does consist of a set, namely a set of rows. Let us now concentrate on just one of the rows in that set, say the row

```
( S1, Smith, 20, London )
```

What this row really represents is the following set of ordered pairs:

```
{ < S#      : 'S1'     >,
  < SNAME   : 'Smith'  >,
  < STATUS  : 20       >,
  < CITY    : 'London' > }
```

The first component in each pair is the attribute name, the second is the corresponding attribute value. It is normal to omit the attribute names in informal contexts, of course, because we have a convention that says that each individual value in the table is actually a value of the attribute whose name appears at the top of the relevant column; furthermore, that value is indeed a value from the relevant underlying domain. For example, the value "S1" is a value of the S# attribute, and it is drawn from the appropriate underlying domain, namely the domain of supplier numbers (which is also called S#). So we can agree that each row does indeed represent a *tuple,* in the sense of the definition.

It follows from all of the above that we can agree that table S of Fig. 4.1 can indeed be regarded as a picture of a relation in the sense of the definition—*provided* we can agree on how to "read" such a picture (i.e., *provided* we can agree on certain **rules of interpretation** for such pictures). In other words, we have to agree that yes, there are some underlying domains; yes, each column corresponds to exactly one of those domains; yes, each row represents a tuple; yes, each attribute value is drawn from the appropriate domain; and so on. If we can agree on all of these "rules of interpretation," then—*and only then*—we can agree that a "table" is a reasonable picture of a relation.

So we can now see that a table and a relation are not really quite the same thing (even though we pretended in earlier chapters that they were). Rather, a **relation** is what the definition given earlier says it is, namely a rather abstract kind of object; and a **table** is a concrete picture (typically on paper) of such an abstract object. They are not (to repeat) quite the same. Of course, they are very similar . . . and in informal contexts, at least, it is usual, and perfectly acceptable, to say they are the same. But when we are trying to be more formal and more precise (and right now, of course, we are trying to be more precise), then we do have to recognize that the two concepts are not exactly identical.

Note: If you are having difficulty with this idea that there are some differences between a relation and a table, the following might help. First, it is undeniably a major advantage of the relational model that its basic abstract object (i.e., the relation) does have such a simple representation (as a table) on paper; it is that simple representation that makes relational systems easy to use and easy to understand, and makes it easy to reason about the way relational systems behave. However, it is unfortunately also the case that the tabular representation *suggests some things that are not true*. For example, it clearly suggests that the rows of the table (i.e., the tuples of the relation) are in a certain top-to-bottom order, but they are not. See the further discussion of this point later in this section.

Relation Variables

In his original paper [4.1], Codd talked about something he called "time-varying" relations. What he really meant by this term was what at the beginning of this section we called relation *variables*—i.e., variables whose *value* was a relation (different relations at different times, in general). For example, as explained earlier, the statement

```
CREATE BASE RELATION S ... ;
```

defines a variable called S whose value at any given time is a relation as defined above. However, that value is "time-varying," because as time goes by new supplier tuples will be inserted and/or existing supplier tuples will be modified or deleted (as a consequence, incidentally, the cardinality is "time-varying" too).

"Time-varying" is really not a very good term, however. After all, given the programming language declaration shown previously, *viz.*:

```
DECLARE QTY INTEGER ... ;
```

we do not call QTY a "time-varying integer," we call it an *integer variable*. In this book, therefore, we will (as already stated) use the "relation variable" terminology, not the "time-varying" terminology; but the reader should at least be aware of the existence of this latter terminology.

Now let R be a relation variable; R will have different values at different times. However, all possible values of R will have **the same heading**. For example, all possible values of base relation S will have the heading {S#,SNAME,STATUS,CITY}.*

More Terminology

As already explained, the number of attributes in a given relation, or equivalently the number of underlying domains, is called the **degree** (sometimes the **arity**) of the relation. A relation of degree one is said to be *unary,* a relation of degree two *binary,* a relation of degree three *ternary,* . . . and a relation of degree n *n-ary.* (The relational model is thus concerned with *n*-ary relations, in general, for arbitrary nonnegative integer n.) In the suppliers-and-parts database, relations S, P, and SP have degrees 4, 5, and 3, respectively.

Now, confusion sometimes arises between the two notions of *domain* and *unary relation* (after all, a domain does look superficially something like a table with one column). Note, however, that there is a definite and important distinction to be drawn between the two concepts, namely as follows: *Domains are static, relations are dynamic* (speaking rather loosely!—"relation" here really means a relation *variable*). In other words, the content of a relation (variable) changes over time, whereas the content

---

* For the benefit of readers who might be familiar with SQL, we should mention the fact that it is possible in SQL to add a new column to, or remove an existing column from, an existing base table by means of an operation called ALTER TABLE. However, that operation is best regarded, not as changing the heading of the existing table, but rather as destroying the existing table and then creating a new one with the same name and a new heading.

of a domain does not (remember that a domain contains *all possible* values of the relevant type). See reference [4.8] for further discussion of this point.

"Nondistinct Domains"

To return to the definition of *relation* yet again: Note that the underlying domains of a relation are not necessarily all distinct. In other words, several attributes in the same relation might all be drawn from the same domain. An example of such a relation is shown in Fig. 4.4. (That relation, PART_STRUCTURE, in fact shows how *bill-of-materials* data—see Section 1.3, subsection "Entities and Relationships"—is typically represented in a relational system.)

If the same domain is used more than once within some given relation, then (as pointed out earlier) it is not possible to give all attributes of that relation the same name as the underlying domain. Fig. 4.4 illustrates the recommended approach in such a situation: Generate distinct attribute names by prefixing a common domain name with distinct *role names* to indicate the distinct roles being played by that domain in each of its appearances. In fact, if we agreed always to follow this convention, and furthermore always to use some reserved distinguishing character (such as the underscore character) to separate the role name, if present, from the trailing domain name, then the specification "DOMAIN (*domain*)" would never be explicitly needed in the definition of an attribute.

Data Definition

Here then is the syntax of CREATE BASE RELATION:

```
CREATE BASE RELATION base-relation
    ( attribute-definition-commalist )
      candidate-key-definition-list
      foreign-key-definition-list ;
```

A new base relation is created, named *base-relation,* with the specified attributes, candidate keys, and foreign keys. The relation is initially empty (i.e., contains no tuples). For some examples, refer back to Fig. 4.3. Points arising:

PART_STRUCTURE	MAJOR_P#	MINOR_P#	QTY
	P1	P2	2
	P1	P3	4
	P2	P3	1
	P2	P4	3
	P3	P5	9
	P4	P5	8
	P5	P6	3

FIG. 4.4 The PART_STRUCTURE relation

1. The terms *list* and *commalist* are useful syntactic shorthands (they will be used not only here but throughout this book). In general:

   ▪ If *xyz* is a syntactic unit, then *xyz-list* is a syntactic unit consisting of a sequence of zero or more *xyz's* in which each pair of adjacent *xyz's* is separated by at least one blank.

   ▪ If *xyz* is a syntactic unit, then *xyz-commalist* is a syntactic unit consisting of a sequence of zero or more *xyz's* in which each pair of adjacent *xyz's* is separated by a comma (and optionally one or more blanks).

   So, for example, an *attribute-definition-commalist* consists of a sequence of *attribute-definitions,* each except the last being separated from the next by a comma, and a *candidate-key-definition-list* consists of a sequence of *candidate-key-definitions,* each except the last being separated from the next by at least one blank. *Note:* Henceforth we will usually omit the hyphens from expressions such as "candidate key definition" (except in formal syntax), provided no ambiguity results from such omission.

2. An *attribute definition* takes the form:

   ```
   attribute DOMAIN ( domain )
   ```

   If the "DOMAIN (*domain*)" specification is omitted, the attribute is assumed to be defined on a domain with the same name.

3. Candidate key definitions will be explained in detail in the next chapter. Prior to that point, we will simply assume that each CREATE BASE RELATION contains exactly one such definition, of the following particular form:

   ```
   PRIMARY KEY ( attribute-commalist )
   ```

4. Foreign key definitions will also be explained in the next chapter.

Destroying base relations: Here is the syntax for destroying an existing base relation:

```
DESTROY BASE RELATION base-relation ;
```

This operation will delete all tuples in the specified base relation, and then delete all relevant catalog entries for that relation. The relation will now no longer be known to the system. (We assume until further notice that DESTROY BASE RELATION will simply fail if any view definition—or snapshot definition [see Section 4.4]—currently refers to the base relation in question. See Chapter 17 for further discussion.)

Properties of Relations

Relations possess certain properties, all of them immediate consequences of the definition of *relation* given earlier, and all of them very important. We first briefly state those properties, then discuss them in detail. The properties, four in number, are as follows. Within any given relation:

■   There are no duplicate tuples

- Tuples are unordered, top to bottom
- Attributes are unordered, left to right
- All attribute values are atomic

1. *There are no duplicate tuples*

This property follows from the fact that the body of the relation is a mathematical set (of tuples), and sets in mathematics by definition do not include duplicate elements.

Incidentally, this first property serves right away to illustrate the point that a relation and a table are not the same thing, because a table (in general) might contain duplicate rows—in the absence of any discipline to prevent such a thing—whereas a relation *cannot* contain any duplicate tuples. (For if a "relation" does contain duplicate tuples, then *it is not a relation!*—by definition.) It is very unfortunately the case that SQL does permit tables to contain duplicate rows. This is not the place to go into all of the reasons why duplicate rows are a mistake (see references [4.5] and [4.11] for a comprehensive discussion); for present purposes, we content ourselves with observing that the relational model does not recognize duplicate rows, and hence that in this book we will take care to ensure that duplicate rows never occur. (This remark applies primarily to our discussions of SQL in Chapter 8. So far as the relational model is concerned, of course, no special care is necessary.)

An important corollary of the fact that there are no duplicate tuples is that *there is always a primary key.** Since tuples are unique, it follows that at least the combination of *all* attributes of the relation has the uniqueness property, so that at least the combination of all attributes can (if necessary) serve as the primary key. In practice, of course, it is usually not necessary to involve all the attributes—some lesser combination is usually sufficient. Indeed, the primary key will be defined in Chapter 5 not to include any attributes that are superfluous for the purposes of unique identification; thus, for example, the combination {S#,CITY}, though "unique," is not the primary key for relation S, because the CITY attribute can be discarded without destroying the uniqueness property. (Note, however, that primary keys can certainly be composite, i.e., involve more than one attribute. Relation SP is a case in point.)

2. *Tuples are unordered (top to bottom)*

This property also follows from the fact that the body of the relation is a mathematical set; sets in mathematics are not ordered. In Fig. 4.1, for example, the tuples of relation S could just as well have been shown in reverse sequence—it would still have been the same relation. Thus, there is no such thing as "the fifth tuple" or "the 97th tuple" or "the first tuple" of a relation, and there is no such thing as "the next tuple"; in other words, there is no concept of positional addressing, and there is no concept of

---

* More accurately, there is always at least one *candidate* key. We are assuming here that one of those candidate keys is chosen as the primary key. See Chapter 5 for further discussion.

"nextness".* Reference [4.11], already mentioned above in connection with the "no duplicate tuples" property, shows why the "no tuple ordering" property is important too (indeed, the two properties are interrelated).

As mentioned earlier in this section, this second property also serves to illustrate the point that a relation and a table are not the same thing, because the rows of a table obviously do have a top-to-bottom ordering, whereas the tuples of a relation do not.

3. *Attributes are unordered (left to right)*

This property follows from the fact that the heading of a relation is also defined as a set (of attributes). In Fig. 4.1, for example, the attributes of relation S could just as well have been shown in the order (say) SNAME, CITY, STATUS, S#—it would still have been the same relation, at least so far as the relational model is concerned (see the annotation to reference [4.1]). Thus, there is no such thing as "the first attribute" or "the second attribute" (etc.), and there is no "next attribute" (again, there is no concept of "nextness"); in other words, attributes are always referenced by name, never by position. As a result, the scope for errors and obscure programming is reduced. For example, there is—or should be—no way to subvert the system by somehow "flopping over" from one attribute into another. This situation contrasts with that found in many programming systems, where it often is possible to exploit the physical adjacency of logically discrete items (deliberately or otherwise) in a variety of subversive ways.

Observe that this question of attribute ordering is yet another area where the concrete representation of a relation as a table suggests something that is not really true: The columns of a table obviously do have a left-to-right ordering, but the attributes of a relation do not.

4. *All attribute values are atomic*

This last property is, of course, a consequence of the fact that all underlying domains contain atomic values only. We can state the property differently (and very informally) as follows: At every row-and-column position within the table, there is always exactly one value, never a collection of several values. Or equivalently again: *Relations do not contain repeating groups*. A relation satisfying this condition is said to be **normalized,** or equivalently to be in **first normal form** (further normal forms—second, third, etc.—are discussed in Part III of this book).

The foregoing implies that *all* relations are normalized so far as the relational model is concerned, and indeed so they are. In fact, the unqualified term "relation" is *always* taken to mean a "normalized relation" in the context of the relational model. The point is, however, that a *mathematical* relation need not be normalized. Consider relation BEFORE of Fig. 4.5. Mathematically speaking, BEFORE *is* a relation, of de-

---

* It is true that some concept of "nextness" is required in the interface between the relational database and host languages such as C and COBOL (see, e.g., the discussion of SQL cursors in Chapter 8). But it is the host languages, not the relational model, that impose this requirement. In effect, those languages require *un*ordered sets to be converted into *ordered* lists, so that operations such as "FETCH next tuple" can have a meaning. Note too that such facilities form part of the application programming interface only—they are not exposed to end users.

BEFORE	S#	PQ			AFTER	S#	P#	QTY

BEFORE	S#	PQ
	S1	P# / QTY
		P1 300
		P2 200
		P3 400
		P4 200
		P5 100
		P6 100
	S2	P# / QTY
		P1 300
		P2 400
	S3	P# / QTY
		P2 200
	S4	P# / QTY
		P2 200
		P4 300
		P5 400

AFTER	S#	P#	QTY
	S1	P1	300
	S1	P2	200
	S1	P3	400
	S1	P4	200
	S1	P5	100
	S1	P6	100
	S2	P1	300
	S2	P2	400
	S3	P2	200
	S4	P2	200
	S4	P4	300
	S4	P5	400

FIG. 4.5 An example of normalization

gree two, but it is a relation for which one of the underlying domains is *relation-valued.* A relation-valued domain is a domain whose elements are themselves relations, instead of simple scalars. In the example, attribute PQ is defined on a relation-valued domain, whose elements are binary relations; those binary relations in turn are defined on two scalar-valued domains, namely P# and QTY. The relational model does not permit relation-valued domains (but see Chapter 19).

A relation like BEFORE is thus not permitted in a relational database. Instead, it must be replaced by some normalized relation that carries the same information. Relation AFTER in the figure is such a relation (in fact, of course, it is the familiar shipments relation SP). The degree of relation AFTER is three, and the three underlying domains are all scalar-valued, as required. As already explained, a relation such as AFTER is said to be normalized; by contrast, a relation such as BEFORE is said to be *un*normalized, and the process of converting BEFORE into AFTER is called **normalization**. As the example shows, it is a trivial matter to cast an unnormalized relation into an equivalent normalized form; however, we will have a lot more to say about the overall normalization process in Part III of this book.

The reason for insisting that all relations be normalized is as follows. Basically, a normalized relation has a *simpler structure,* mathematically speaking, than an unnormalized one. As a result, the corresponding operators are simpler too, and there are fewer of them. For example, consider the following two tasks:

1. Create a new shipment for supplier S5, part P5, quantity 500.
2. Create a new shipment for supplier S4, part P5, quantity 500.

With relation AFTER, there is no qualitative difference between these two tasks—each involves the insertion of a single tuple into the relation. With relation BEFORE, by contrast, task 1 involves the same kind of single-tuple insertion, but task 2 involves *a totally different operation*—namely, an operation to insert a new entry into a set of entries (i.e., a repeating group) within an existing tuple. Thus, two qualitatively different "INSERT" operations are needed to support unnormalized relations. For exactly analogous reasons, two different UPDATE operations, two different DELETE operations, etc., etc., are also needed. And note clearly that these remarks apply, not only to the data manipulation operations, but to *all* operations in the system; for example, additional data security operations are needed, additional data integrity operations are needed, etc., etc. (In fact, it is an axiom that if there are *n* ways of representing data, then *n* sets of operators are needed.) Hence, the one-word answer to the question "Why do we insist on normalization?" is *simplicity*—simplicity, that is, in the basic data objects we have to deal with, which leads in turn to corresponding simplifications everywhere else in the system.

4.4 Kinds of Relations

In this section we identify some of the various kinds of relations that might exist in a relational system (note that not all systems support all kinds, however).

1. First, a *named* relation is a relation variable that has been defined to the DBMS—in our syntax, by means of CREATE BASE RELATION or CREATE VIEW or CREATE SNAPSHOT (see paragraph 6 below for CREATE SNAPSHOT, and Chapter 3 for CREATE VIEW).

2. A *base* relation is a named relation that is not a derived relation (in other words, base relations are *autonomous*). In practice, the base relations are those relations that have been judged to be sufficiently important (for the database at hand) that the database designer has decided it is worth giving them a name and making them a direct part of the database—as opposed to other relations that are more ephemeral in nature, such as the result of a query.

3. A *derived* relation is a relation that is defined (by means of some relational expression) in terms of other, named relations—ultimately, in terms of base relations. *Caveat:* Be warned, however, that some writers use "derived" to mean what we call "expressible" (see next paragraph).

4. An *expressible* relation is a relation that can be obtained from the set of named relations by means of some relational expression. Of course, every named relation is an expressible relation, but the converse is not true. Base relations, views, snap-

shots (see paragraph 6 below), and intermediate and final query results are all expressible relations. In other words, the set of all expressible relations is, precisely, the set of all base relations and all derived relations.

5. A *view* is a named derived relation. (Views, of course, like base relations, are really relation *variables*.) Views are also *virtual*—they are represented within the system solely by their definition in terms of other named relations.

6. A *snapshot* is also a named derived relation, like a view (it is also really a relation *variable*). Unlike a view, however, a snapshot is real, not virtual—i.e., it is represented not only by its definition in terms of other named relations, but also (at least conceptually) by its own separate data. Here is an example:

```
CREATE SNAPSHOT SC AS
        ( ( S JOIN SP ) WHERE P# = 'P2' ) [ S#, CITY ]
        REFRESH EVERY DAY ;
```

Creating a snapshot is much like executing a query, except that (a) the result of that query is kept in the database under the specified name (SC in the example) as a *read-only* relation, and (b) periodically (EVERY DAY in the example) the snapshot is "refreshed"—i.e., its current value is discarded, the query is executed again, and the result of that new execution becomes the new value of the snapshot. Refer to Chapter 17 for a discussion of when snapshots might be useful.

7. A *query result* is the unnamed derived relation that results from executing some specified query. Query results do not have persistent existence within the database (though they can, of course, be assigned to some named relation that does).

8. An *intermediate result* is an unnamed derived relation that results from the evaluation of some relational expression that is nested within some larger such expression. For example, consider the expression

```
( ( S JOIN SP ) WHERE P# = 'P2' ) [ S#, CITY ]
```

The relation resulting from the expression S JOIN P is an intermediate result; let us refer to it as TEMP1. Then the relation resulting from the expression TEMP1 WHERE P# = 'P2' is also an intermediate result; let us refer to it as TEMP2. Then the relation resulting from the expression TEMP2 [S#, CITY] is the final result. Intermediate results, like final results, have no persistent existence within the database (in fact, as mentioned in Chapter 3, Section 3.2, they might never be materialized in their entirety at all).

9. Finally, a *stored* relation is an expressible relation that is supported in physical storage in some "direct, efficient" manner (with appropriate definitions of "direct" and "efficient," of course—details beyond the scope of this chapter).

We close this section by pointing out that there is *not* necessarily a one-to-one correspondence between stored and base relations. The set of stored relations must naturally be such that all base relations, and hence all expressible relations, can be derived from them—but there is no requirement that all stored relations be base relations, nor that all base relations be stored relations. Refer back to Chapter 3 (end of Section 3.7) for an extended discussion of this point in different terms, with an example.

4.5 Relations and Predicates

We have not stressed the point thus far, but it should be intuitively obvious to the reader that every relation, base or derived, has an intended *interpretation* or *meaning*. Moreover, users must be aware of those meanings if they are to use the database effectively. The meaning of base relation S, for example, is something like the following:

> *The supplier with the specified supplier number (S#) has the specified name (SNAME) and the specified status value (STATUS), and is located in the specified city (CITY); moreover, no two suppliers have the same supplier number.*

This statement is not very precise, but it will serve for present purposes.

Formally, the foregoing statement is an example of what is called a **predicate,** or truth-valued function—a function of four arguments, in this particular case. Substituting values for the arguments is equivalent to *invoking* the function (or "instantiating" the predicate), thereby yielding an expression, called a **proposition,** that is either *true* or *false*. For example, the substitution

```
S# = 'S1' SNAME = 'Smith' STATUS = 20 CITY = 'London'
```

yields a proposition that is *true*. By contrast, the substitution

```
S# = 'S1' SNAME = 'Abbey' STATUS = 45 CITY = 'Tucson'
```

yields a proposition that is *false* (it is not the case that supplier S1 has name Abbey, status 45, and location Tucson). And at any given time, of course, the relation contains exactly those tuples that make the predicate evaluate to *true* at that time.

It follows from the foregoing that if (for example) a tuple is presented as a candidate for insertion into some relation, the DBMS should accept that tuple only if it does not cause the corresponding predicate to be violated (i.e., only if the corresponding proposition is not *false*). More generally, the predicate for a given relation constitutes the **criterion for update acceptability** for that relation—that is, the criterion for deciding whether or not some proposed update is in fact valid (or at least plausible) for the given relation.

In order for it to be able to decide whether or not a given update is acceptable on a given relation, therefore, the DBMS needs to be aware of the predicate for that relation. Now, it is of course not possible for the DBMS to know *exactly* what the predicate is for a given relation. In the case of relation S, for example, the DBMS has no way of knowing *a priori* that the predicate is such that the tuple (S1,Smith,20,London) makes it *true* and the tuple (S1,Abbey,45,Tucson) does not.* However, the DBMS certainly *does* know a reasonably close approximation to that predicate. To be specific, it knows that, if a given tuple is to be deemed acceptable, all of the following must be true:

---

* We make use of an obvious shorthand here, by which, e.g., the expression (S1,Smith,20,London) stands for the tuple {<S#:'S1'>, <SNAME:'Smith'>, <STATUS:20>, <CITY:'London'>}.

■   The S# value must be a value from the domain of supplier numbers

■   The SNAME value must be a value from the domain of names

■   The STATUS value must be a value from the domain of status values

■   The CITY value must be a value from the domain of city names

■   The S# value is unique with respect to all such values in the relation

In other words, for a base relation such as S, the DBMS does at least know certain *integrity rules* that have been declared for that relation, such as the rule that S# values come from the domain of supplier numbers and must be unique. Formally, therefore, we can *define* the (DBMS-understood) "meaning" of a given base relation to be the logical AND of all DBMS-known rules that apply to that base relation. And it is this meaning that the DBMS will check whenever an update is attempted on the relation in question.

We will have more to say regarding the meaning of relations at various points in the chapters that follow. See in particular Chapter 6, Section 6.9 (on the meaning of derived relations), also Chapters 9-11 (on various kinds of "dependencies"), Chapter 16 (on integrity rules in general) and Chapter 17 (on views).

4.6   Relational Databases

In the light of the discussions and explanations of the previous two sections, it is now possible to give a slightly more formal definition—more formal, that is, than the one given in Section 4.2— of the term "relational database." The following definition is paraphrased from one originally given by Codd in reference [4.1]:

■   A **relational database** is a database that is perceived by the user as a collection of normalized relations (i.e., relation *variables*) of assorted degrees.

As pointed out earlier in this book, the phrase "perceived by the user" is crucial: The ideas of the relational model apply at the external and conceptual levels of the system, not the internal level. To put this another way, the relational model represents a database system at a level of abstraction that is somewhat removed from the details of the underlying machine—just as, for example, a language such as Pascal represents a programming system at a level of abstraction that is somewhat removed from the details of the underlying machine. Indeed, the relational model can be regarded as a rather abstract programming language that is oriented specifically toward database applications.

The distinction between domains and (named) relations can also do with a little elaboration. We refer to named relations as variables because their value changes with time. As pointed out in Section 4.3, the underlying domains are *not* variables in the same sense. For example, the set of *all possible* supplier numbers obviously does not change with time—or rather, if it does, then the change is a *definitional* change, i.e., a change at the type level rather than the occurrence level. It is a bit like changing the basic data type for a supplier number from CHAR(5) to CHAR(7). Note, incidentally, that such a change is likely to imply a database reorganization.

To sum up, then, we can say that, in traditional terms, a relation resembles a *file* (logical, not physical), a tuple a *record* (occurrence, not type), and an attribute a *field* (type, not occurrence). These correspondences are at best approximate, however. A relation should not be regarded as "just a file," but rather as a *disciplined* file—the discipline in question being one that results in a considerable simplification in the structure of the data objects with which the user must interact, and hence in a corresponding simplification in the operators needed to deal with those objects. To be specific, all data in a relational database is represented in *one and only one way,* namely by explicit value (this feature is sometimes referred to as "the basic principle of the relational model," also as "the information principle"). In particular, logical connections within and across relations are represented by such explicit values; there are no user-visible pointers between files or records, no user-visible record orderings, no user-visible repeating groups, etc., etc.

4.7 Summary

In this chapter we have taken a comprehensive look at the basic data **objects** of the relational model, *viz.* domains and relations. A **domain** is essentially a **data type** (possibly system-defined, more generally user-defined); it provides a set of **scalar values,** from which various attributes in various relations draw their actual values. Domains **constrain comparisons,** inasmuch as the comparands in such a comparison are generally required to come from the same domain. As a consequence, domains constrain various relational operations, such as join, union, and so forth (see Chapter 6).

A **relation** has two parts, a heading and a body. The **heading** is a set of **attributes** (more accurately, attribute-name/domain-name pairs), the **body** is a set of **tuples.** The number of attributes is called the **degree** and the number of tuples is called the **cardinality**. A relation can be thought of as a **table,** with the columns representing the attributes and the rows representing the tuples, but that representation is only approximate. Also, all relations satisfy four very important properties:

- They do not contain any duplicate tuples
- There is no ordering to the tuples, top to bottom
- There is no ordering to the attributes, left to right
- All attribute values are atomic (the relation is **normalized**)

Every relation has an associated *meaning* or **predicate,** which constitutes the **criterion for update acceptability** for that relation. At any given time, a given relation contains exactly those tuples that cause the corresponding predicate to evaluate to *true* at that time.

A **named** relation is really a **variable** (its heading is fixed but its body changes value over time). Examples of named relations are **base relations, views,** and **snapshots.** An **unnamed** relation is the result of evaluating some relational expression; it typically has a much more ephemeral existence than a named relation, and its body does not change so long as it exists. Examples of unnamed relations are intermediate and final query results.

We have also introduced the data definition statements of a hypothetical relational language that we will be using throughout this part of the book—**CREATE** and **DESTROY DOMAIN** and **CREATE** and **DESTROY BASE RELATION**. (We have also mentioned the CREATE and DESTROY operations for views and snapshots, but we will return to these later, in Chapter 17.)

Exercises

4.1 Refer to Fig. 3.3 in Chapter 3 (outline catalog structure for the departments-and-employees database). (a) Rename the various components of that catalog in accordance with the formal relational terms introduced in this chapter. (b) How should the structure of that catalog be extended to take account of domains? (c) Write a query against that extended catalog to find all named relations that make use of the EMP# domain.

4.2 (a) Write a CREATE BASE RELATION and appropriate set of CREATE DOMAINs for the relation PART_STRUCTURE illustrated in Fig. 4.4. (b) Assuming this relation is included in the departments-and-employees database of Exercise 4.1, show the updates the system must make to the catalog to reflect your answer to part (a). (c) Write an appropriate set of DESTROY statements to cause the catalog updates of part (b) to be undone.

4.3 As we have seen, data definition operations such as CREATE and DESTROY DOMAIN and CREATE and DESTROY BASE RELATION cause updates to be made to the catalog. But the catalog is only a collection of relations, just like ordinary user data; so could we not use the regular relational update operations (e.g., INSERT, UPDATE, and DELETE in SQL) to update the catalog appropriately? Discuss.

4.4 What domains are the catalog relations themselves defined on?

4.5 A relation is defined to have a *set* of attributes and a *set* of tuples. Now, in mathematics the empty set is a perfectly respectable set; indeed, it is usually desirable that results, theorems, etc., that hold true for a set of n elements should continue to hold true if $n = 0$. Can a relation have an empty set of tuples? Or an empty set of attributes?

4.6 Fig. 4.6 (opposite) shows some sample data values for an extended form of the suppliers-and-parts database called the *suppliers-parts-projects* database. Suppliers (S), parts (P), and projects (J) are uniquely identified by supplier number (S#), part number (P#), and project number (J#), respectively. The significance of an SPJ (shipment) tuple is that the specified supplier supplies the specified part to the specified project in the specified quantity (and the combination S#-P#-J# uniquely identifies such a tuple). Write a suitable data definition for this database. *Note:* This database will be used in numerous exercises in subsequent chapters.

4.7 State as precisely as you can the predicate for relation SPJ from the previous exercise.

References and Bibliography

Most of the following references are applicable to all three aspects of the relational model, not just to the "data objects" aspect.

4.1 E. F. Codd. "A Relational Model of Data for Large Shared Data Banks." *CACM 13,* No. 6 (June 1970). Republished in *Milestones of Research—Selected Papers 1958–1982 (CACM 25th Anniversary Issue), CACM 26,* No. 1 (January 1983).

S	S#	SNAME	STATUS	CITY
	S1	Smith	20	London
	S2	Jones	10	Paris
	S3	Blake	30	Paris
	S4	Clark	20	London
	S5	Adams	30	Athens

P	P#	PNAME	COLOR	WEIGHT	CITY
	P1	Nut	Red	12	London
	P2	Bolt	Green	17	Paris
	P3	Screw	Blue	17	Rome
	P4	Screw	Red	14	London
	P5	Cam	Blue	12	Paris
	P6	Cog	Red	19	London

J	J#	JNAME	CITY
	J1	Sorter	Paris
	J2	Display	Rome
	J3	OCR	Athens
	J4	Console	Athens
	J5	RAID	London
	J6	EDS	Oslo
	J7	Tape	London

SPJ	S#	P#	J#	QTY
	S1	P1	J1	200
	S1	P1	J4	700
	S2	P3	J1	400
	S2	P3	J2	200
	S2	P3	J3	200
	S2	P3	J4	500
	S2	P3	J5	600
	S2	P3	J6	400
	S2	P3	J7	800
	S2	P5	J2	100
	S3	P3	J1	200
	S3	P4	J2	500
	S4	P6	J3	300
	S4	P6	J7	300
	S5	P2	J2	200
	S5	P2	J4	100
	S5	P5	J5	500
	S5	P5	J7	100
	S5	P6	J2	200
	S5	P1	J4	100
	S5	P3	J4	200
	S5	P4	J4	800
	S5	P5	J4	400
	S5	P6	J4	500

FIG. 4.6 The suppliers-parts-projects database (sample values)

The paper that started it all. Although now some 25 years old, it stands up remarkably well to repeated rereading. Of course, many of the ideas have been refined somewhat since the paper was first published, but by and large the changes have been evolutionary, not revolutionary, in nature. Indeed, there are some ideas in the paper whose implications have still not been fully explored.

The paper is divided into two principal parts: "Relational Model and Normal Form" and "Redundancy and Consistency."

1. The first part includes a discussion of data independence (especially the lack of such independence in systems available at the time the paper was written), relational data objects (i.e., relations and domains), normalization (i.e., first normal form), linguistic aspects, and base relations *vs.* views *vs.* other derivable relations.

2. The second part introduces a number of relational operations—projection, join, etc. (see the annotation to reference [6.1] for additional commentary on these operations)—and uses them as a basis for discussing various kinds of redundancy and consistency in a relational database. A set of relations is said to be *strongly redundant* if it includes at least one relation that has a projection (possibly the identity projection, i.e., the projection over all attributes) that is derivable from other relations in the set. Note, incidentally, that the set of named relations available to the user of a given database might indeed be strongly redundant in this sense, inasmuch as it might include both base relations and views that are derivable from those base relations.

The definition of *relation* given in the paper is worth a brief discussion here. That definition runs somewhat as follows (paraphrasing slightly): Given sets *D1, D2, . . . Dn* (not necessarily distinct), *R* is a *relation* on those *n* sets if it is a set of *n*-tuples each of which has its first element from *D1,* its second element from *D2,* and so on. (The set *Dj* is said to be the *j*th *domain* of *R*.) More concisely, *R* is a subset of the Cartesian product of its domains.

Although mathematically respectable, this definition can be criticized from a database standpoint (with, of course, 20:20 hindsight) on a number of counts:

1. First, it does not clearly distinguish between domains and attributes. (Later in the paper Codd does use the term "active domain" for the set of values from a given domain actually appearing in the database at the current time, but "active domain" is still not quite equivalent to "attribute" as that term is now used.) As a result, there has been widespread confusion over domains and attributes, and such confusion still persists, even today.

2. Next, a relation according to the definition in fact does have a left-to-right ordering among its domains. Again, Codd states later in the paper that users should not have to deal with relations as such but rather with "their domain-unordered counterparts" (which he refers to as "relationships"), but that refinement seems to have escaped the attention of some database system designers. (SQL in particular does very unfortunately include a notion of left-to-right column ordering within a table. See Chapter 8.)

3. Finally, the definition does not adequately distinguish between the static and dynamic (or time-independent and time-dependent) aspects of relation variables (what we have called the "heading" and the "body"), although the distinction is clearly implied by later sections of the paper. This omission has also been a rich source of subsequent confusion.

It is probably worth mentioning a few additional points that the reader might otherwise find a little puzzling on reading the paper for the first time. *Note:* In making the following comments, we are of course liberally applying the "20:20 hindsight" principle once again!

1. Despite its title, the paper nowhere gives a succinct definition of the term "relational model" (nor indeed of the term "data model," although this paper was unquestionably the one that introduced the concept). On the contrary, it at least implies that the term includes the "objects" aspect only (i.e., the operators and integrity features are excluded). Also, it talks about "*a* relational model . . . *for [a database]*" (italics added), thus suggesting that the term "relational model" refers to an abstract view of the data *in a specific database* instead of to an abstract view of data in general. Both of these misinterpretations are still regrettably common in the database literature; the first in particular (i.e., the idea that "the relational model is just structure," sometimes expressed in the form "the relational model is just flat files") represents a *major* misconception. Reference [4.12] attempts to set the record straight regarding this particular error, in its discussion of "Myth No. 3."

2. The paper allows a relation to have *any number* of primary keys; in other words, it uses the term "primary key" for what we would now call a *candidate* key (see Chapter 5). It also does not require such a "primary" (i.e., candidate) key to be irreducible (again, see Chapter 5). However, it does also say that "[if] a relation has two or more [irreducible] primary keys, one of them is arbitrarily selected and called *the* primary key of that relation."

3. The definition given for foreign key is unnecessarily restrictive, in that it does not permit the primary key (or any candidate key?—see the previous paragraph) of a relation to be a foreign key, and it does not consider the case of a foreign key value that happens to be null. Again, see Chapter 5 for a detailed discussion of foreign keys in general, and null foreign key values in particular.

4.2 E. F. Codd. "Derivability, Redundancy, and Consistency of Relations Stored in Large Data Banks." IBM Research Report RJ599 (August 19th, 1969).

A preliminary version of reference [4.1]. There are a few differences of detail (particularly in terminology) between the two papers, but easily the most significant change is that reference [4.1] introduces, and justifies, the idea that all relations should be *normalized*. One major advantage claimed for normalization is that *first-order predicate calculus* is suitable and sufficient as a basis for a data sublanguage if all relations are normalized (see Chapter 7 for discussion of such a language).

4.3 E. F. Codd. "Data Models in Database Management." Proc. Workshop on Data Abstraction, Databases, and Conceptual Modelling (Michael L. Brodie and Stephen N. Zilles, eds.), Pingree Park, Colo. (June 1980): *ACM SIGART* Newsletter No. 74 (January 1981); *ACM SIGMOD Record 11,* No. 2 (February 1981); *ACM SIGPLAN Notices 16,* No. 1 (January 1981).

This paper appears to be the first in which a comprehensive definition of the term **data model** appeared. To paraphrase somewhat, a data model is defined to consist of a combination of three components:

1. A collection of data object types, which form the basic building blocks for any database that conforms to the model

2. A collection of general integrity rules, which constrain the set of occurrences of those object types that can legally appear in any such database

3. A collection of operators, which can be applied to such object occurrences for retrieval and other purposes

The paper then discusses what purpose data models in general (and the relational model in particular) are intended to serve, and offers evidence in support of the claim that—contrary to popular belief—the relational model was actually the *first* abstract data model to be defined; the so-called hierarchic and network (i.e., prerelational) "models" were defined *after the fact* by a process of abstraction from already existing implementations.

4.4 E. F. Codd. *The Relational Model for Database Management Version 2.* Reading, Mass.: Addison-Wesley (1990).

Codd spent much of the late 1980s revising and extending his original model (which he now refers to as "the Relational Model Version 1" or RM/V1), and this book is the result. It describes "the Relational Model Version 2" (RM/V2). The essential difference between RM/V1 and RM/V2 is as follows: Whereas RM/V1 was intended as an abstract blueprint for one particular aspect of the total database problem (essentially the foundational aspect), RM/V2 is intended as an abstract blueprint for *the entire system.* Thus, where RM/V1 contained just three parts—objects, or structure; operators, or manipulation; and integrity—RM/V2 contains 18; and those 18 parts include not only the original three (of course), but also parts having to do with views, the catalog, authorization, naming, distributed database, and various other aspects of database management. For purposes of reference, here is a complete list of the 18 parts:

A	Authorization	M	Manipulation
B	Basic operators	N	Naming
C	Catalog	P	Protection
D	Principles of DBMS design	Q	Qualifiers
E	Commands for the DBA	S	Structure
F	Functions	T	Data types
I	Integrity	V	Views
J	Indicators	X	Distributed database
L	Principles of language design	Z	Advanced operators

The ideas promulgated in this book are by no means universally accepted, however. See in particular references [4.15] and [4.16] by the present author.

4.5 Hugh Darwen. "The Duplicity of Duplicate Rows." In C. J. Date and Hugh Darwen, *Relational Database Writings 1989-1991.* Reading, Mass.: Addison-Wesley (1992).

This paper was written as further support for the arguments already presented in reference [4.11] in support of the relational model requirement that tables not contain any duplicate rows. The paper not only offers novel versions of some of those same arguments, it also manages to come up with some additional ones. In particular, it stresses the fundamental point that, in order to discuss (in any intelligent manner) the question of whether two objects are duplicates of each other, it is essential to have a clear *criterion of identity* for the class of objects under consideration. In other words, what does it mean for two objects, be they rows in a table or anything else, to be "the same"?

4.6 Hugh Darwen. "The Nullologist in Relationland." In C. J. Date and Hugh Darwen, *Relational Database Writings 1989–1991*. Reading, Mass.: Addison-Wesley (1992).

Nullology is (as Darwen puts it) "the study of nothing at all"—or, in other words, the study of the empty set. Sets are ubiquitous in relational theory, and hence the question as to what happens if one or more of those sets happens to be empty is far from being a frivolous one. In fact, several of the empty-set cases turn out to be absolutely fundamental.

So far as the present chapter ("Relational Data Objects") is concerned, the most immediately applicable portions of this paper are Section 2 ("Tables with No Rows") and Section 3 ("Tables with No Columns"). See also Exercise 4.5 and reference [4.7] below (item 6).

4.7 Hugh Darwen (writing as Andrew Warden). "Adventures in Relationland." In C. J. Date, *Relational Database Writings 1985–1989*. Reading, Mass.: Addison-Wesley (1990).

A series of short papers that examine various aspects of the relational model and relational DBMSs in an original, entertaining, and informative style. The papers have the following titles:

1. The Naming of Columns

2. In Praise of Marriage

3. The Keys of the Kingdom

4. Chivalry

5. A Constant Friend

6. Table_Dee and Table_Dum

7. Into the Unknown

Several of these papers are referenced elsewhere in the present book.

4.8 C. J. Date. "What Is a Domain?" In C. J. Date, *Relational Database Writings 1985–1989*. Reading, Mass.: Addison-Wesley (1990).

A systematic and comprehensive tutorial on the relational domain concept. The paper argues strongly that a domain is basically nothing more nor less than a data type, either builtin or (more generally, though few systems provide any such support today) user-defined. See Chapter 19 for further discussion.

4.9 C. J. Date. "Defining Data Types in a Database Language." In C. J. Date, *Relational Database Writings 1985–1989*. Reading, Mass.: Addison-Wesley (1990).

A complementary paper to reference [4.8], describing what is involved in adding new data types to a database language. By way of example, the specific case of adding support for dates and times to SQL is considered in detail (SQL did not include any date and time support when this paper was first written).

4.10 C. J. Date. "What Is a Relation?" In C. J. Date and Hugh Darwen, *Relational Database Writings 1989–1991*. Reading, Mass.: Addison-Wesley (1992).

This paper does for relations what reference [4.8] does for domains. To quote the abstract: "Despite the fact that the relational model has its foundations in mathematics, relations in the relational model and relations in mathematics are not the same thing. This paper discusses some of the differences between the two."

In particular, the paper stresses the point that stored and base relations are not necessarily in one-to-one correspondence (see Section 4.4 of the present chapter). And it goes on to say: "In most cases, of course, there does tend to be a one-to-one correspondence between stored and base relations, at least in those products on the market today, and no doubt this state of affairs accounts for the fact that many people do tend to confuse the two notions. Also, honesty compels me to confess that I might be partly responsible for the confusion: In several books . . . I have said that 'a base [relation] . . . physically exists, in the sense that there exist physically stored records . . . that directly represent that [relation] in storage.' My apologies to any reader who may have been led astray by such remarks in the past. *Mea culpa*."

4.11 C. J. Date. "Why Duplicate Rows Are Prohibited." In C. J. Date, *Relational Database Writings 1985–1989*. Reading, Mass.: Addison-Wesley (1990).

Presents an extensive series of arguments, with examples, in support of the requirement in the relational model that tables not contain any duplicate rows. In particular, the paper shows that duplicate rows constitute a major *optimization inhibitor* (see Chapter 18). See also reference [4.5].

4.12 C. J. Date. "Some Relational Myths Exploded." In C. J. Date, *Relational Database: Selected Writings*. Reading, Mass.: Addison-Wesley (1986).

An examination of some 26 popular misconceptions concerning relational database management systems.

4.13 C. J. Date. "Further Relational Myths." In C. J. Date, *Relational Database Writings 1985–1989*. Reading, Mass.: Addison-Wesley (1990).

A sequel to [4.12], examining eight additional "relational myths."

4.14 C. J. Date. "Relational Database: Further Misconceptions Number Three." In C. J. Date and Hugh Darwen, *Relational Database Writings 1989–1991*. Reading, Mass.: Addison-Wesley (1992).

Discusses yet more "relational myths."

4.15 C. J. Date. "Notes Toward a Reconstituted Definition of the Relational Model Version 1 (RM/V1)." In C. J. Date and Hugh Darwen, *Relational Database Writings 1989–1991*. Reading, Mass.: Addison-Wesley (1992).

Summarizes and criticizes Codd's "RM/V1" (see the annotation to reference [4.4]) and offers an alternative definition. The assumption is that it is crucially important to get "Version 1" right before we can even consider moving on to some "Version 2." *Note:* The version of the relational model described in the present book is essentially the "reconstituted" version as sketched in this paper.

4.16 C. J. Date. "A Critical Review of the Relational Model Version 2 (RM/V2)." In C. J. Date and Hugh Darwen, *Relational Database Writings 1989–1991*. Reading, Mass.: Addison-Wesley (1992).

Summarizes and criticizes Codd's "RM/V2" [4.4].

4.17 C. J. Date. Series of articles in *Database Programming & Design* (under the generic title *According to Date*), beginning with *5,* No. 9 (September 1992).

An informal series of articles on a variety of relational database issues. In fact, many of the topics discussed in the present book are covered, but in a much less rigorous manner. The common theme is that "theory is practical!"—i.e., IT professionals ignore the theoretical aspects of their field at their own peril.

4.18 D. J. McLeod. "High Level Definition of Abstract Domains in a Relational Data Base System." In *Computer Languages 2:* Pergamon Press (1977). An earlier version of this paper can be found in Proc. ACM SIGPLAN/SIGMOD Conference on Data: Abstraction,

Definition, and Structure, Salt Lake City, Ut. (March 1976): Joint Issue—*ACM SIGPLAN Notices 11* (Special Issue) / *FDT* (ACM SIGMOD bulletin) *8*, No. 2 (1976).

One of the first papers to examine the domain concept in detail.

Answers to Selected Exercises

4.1 (a) The obvious changes are summarized below:

```
Replace TABLES       by    RELATIONS
        COLUMNS            ATTRIBUTES
        TABNAME           RELNAME
        COLCOUNT          DEGREE
        ROWCOUNT          CARDINALITY (often abbreviated CARD)
        COLNAME           ATTRNAME
```

Note that RELATIONS here really means *named* relations. In fact, the RELATIONS relation should really have another attribute (RELTYPE) whose values indicate the type (base relation, view, or snapshot) of the corresponding named relation. The catalog structure thus now looks like this:

RELATIONS | RELNAME | DEGREE | CARDINALITY | RELTYPE | ... |

ATTRIBUTES | RELNAME | ATTRNAME | ..... |

(b) We need a new catalog relation (DOMAINS) containing an entry for each domain, and a new attribute (DOMNAME) in the ATTRIBUTES catalog relation giving the underlying domain for each attribute of each named relation. The catalog structure thus now looks like this:

DOMAINS | DOMNAME | DATATYPE | ..... |

RELATIONS | RELNAME | DEGREE | CARDINALITY | RELTYPE | ... |

ATTRIBUTES | RELNAME | ATTRNAME | DOMNAME | ..... |

As a subsidiary exercise, the reader might like to consider what further extensions to the catalog would be needed to represent information regarding primary and foreign keys.

(c) (ATTRIBUTES WHERE DOMNAME = 'EMP#') [RELNAME]

4.2 (a) Data definition:

```
CREATE DOMAIN P# CHAR(6) ;
CREATE DOMAIN QTY NUMERIC(9) ;

CREATE BASE RELATION PART_STRUCTURE
    ( MAJOR_P# DOMAIN ( P# ),
      MINOR_P# DOMAIN ( P# ),
      QTY      DOMAIN ( QTY ) )
    PRIMARY KEY ( MAJOR_P#, MINOR_P# ) ;
```

Note: If the PART_STRUCTURE relation were part of the suppliers-and-parts database, we would probably need the additional specifications

```
FOREIGN KEY ( RENAME MAJOR_P# AS P# ) REFERENCES P
FOREIGN KEY ( RENAME MINOR_P# AS P# ) REFERENCES P
```

in the relation definition (see Chapter 5 for an explanation of these specifications).

(b) We show the new catalog entries only (see Fig. 4.7). Note that the CARDINALITY entry in the RELATIONS relation for the RELATIONS relation itself will also need to be incremented by one. Also, we have shown the cardinality of PART_STRUCTURE as 0, not 7 (despite the fact that Fig. 4.4 shows it as containing seven tuples), because, of course, the relation will be empty when it is first created.

(c) `DESTROY BASE RELATION PART_STRUCTURE ;`
   `DESTROY DOMAIN QTY ;`
   `DESTROY DOMAIN P# ;`

```
DOMAINS

     DOMNAME   DATATYPE     . . . . .

     P#        CHAR(6)      . . . . .
     QTY       NUMERIC(9)   . . . . .


RELATIONS

     RELNAME          DEGREE   CARDINALITY   RELTYPE   . . .

     PART_STRUCTURE     3            0       Base      . . .


ATTRIBUTES

     RELNAME          ATTRNAME   DOMNAME   . . . . .

     PART_STRUCTURE   MAJOR_P#   P#        . . . . .
     PART_STRUCTURE   MINOR_P#   P#        . . . . .
     PART_STRUCTURE   QTY        QTY       . . . . .
```

FIG. 4.7 Catalog entries for PART_STRUCTURE

4.3 In principle, the answer is yes, it *might* be possible to update the catalog by means of regular INSERT, UPDATE, and DELETE operations. However, allowing such operations would potentially be very dangerous, because it would be all too easy to destroy information (inadvertently or otherwise) in the catalog so that the system would no longer be able to function correctly. Suppose, for example, that the SQL DELETE operation

```
DELETE
FROM    RELATIONS
WHERE   RELNAME = 'EMP' ;
```

were allowed on the departments-and-employees catalog. Its effect would be to remove the tuple describing the EMP relation from the RELATIONS relation. *As far as the system is concerned, the EMP relation would now no longer exist*—i.e., the system would no longer have any knowledge of that relation. Thus, all subsequent attempts to access that relation would fail.

In most real products, therefore, UPDATE, DELETE, and INSERT operations on the catalog *either* are not permitted at all—this is the normal case—*or* are permitted only to very highly authorized users (perhaps only to the DBA). Instead, catalog updates are performed by means of the *data definition* statements (CREATE DOMAIN, CREATE BASE RELATION, etc.). For example, the CREATE BASE RELATION statement for relation EMP causes (a) an entry to be made for EMP in the RELATIONS relation and (b) a set of four entries, one for each of the four attributes of EMP, to be made in the ATTRIBUTES relation. (It also causes a number of other things to happen, which are however of no concern to us here.) Thus CREATE is in some ways the analog of INSERT for the catalog. Likewise, DESTROY is the analog of DELETE; and in SQL, which provides a variety of ALTER statements—e.g., ALTER (base) TABLE—for changing catalog entries in various ways, ALTER is the analog of UPDATE.

> *Note:* The catalog also includes entries for the catalog relations themselves, as we have seen. However, those entries are not created by explicit CREATE operations. Instead, they are created automatically by the system itself as part of the system installation procedure. In effect, they are "hard-wired" into the system.

4.4 It is obviously not possible to give a definitive answer to this question. Here are some reasonable suggestions:

```
Domain DOMNAME is defined on NAME
       RELNAME              NAME
       ATTRNAME             NAME
       DATATYPE             DATATYPE
       DEGREE               CARDINALS
       CARDINALITY          CARDINALS
       RELTYPE              RELTYPE
```

These domains in turn are assumed to be defined as follows:

- NAME is the set of all legal names.
- DATATYPE is the set of all builtin scalar data types (CHAR(n), NUMERIC(n), etc.). Some additional design work is needed here to deal with the parameter n.
- CARDINALS is the set of all nonnegative integers less than some implementation-defined upper limit.
- RELTYPE is the set { "Base", "View", "Snapshot" }.

Note that we have (partly) violated our own principle in the foregoing!—the principle, that is, that each attribute should have the same name as the underlying domain. The exercise illustrates the point that such violations will tend to happen if relations are designed before the underlying domains have been pinned down (an observation that applies to all databases, of course, not just to the catalog).

4.5 A relation with an empty set of tuples is perfectly reasonable, and indeed common (it is analogous to a file with no records). In particular, of course, every base relation has an empty set of tuples when it is first created. It is usual, though a trifle imprecise, to refer to a relation with no tuples as *an empty relation.*

> What is perhaps less immediately obvious is that a relation with an empty set of attributes is perfectly reasonable too! In fact, such relations turn out to be of *crucial importance*—much as empty sets are crucially important in general set theory, or zero is important in ordinary arithmetic.

> In order to examine this notion in slightly more detail, we first have to consider the question of whether a relation with no attributes can have any tuples. In fact, such a relation can have *at most one* tuple, namely the 0-tuple (i.e., the tuple with no attribute values at all); it cannot contain more than one such tuple, because all 0-tuples are duplicates of one another. There are thus precisely two relations (i.e., relation *values*) of degree zero, one that contains just one tuple and one that contains no tuples at all. So important are these two relations that, following Darwen [4.6–4.7], we have pet names for them: We call the first

TABLE_DEE and the other TABLE_DUM, or DEE and DUM for short (DEE is the one with one tuple, DUM is the empty one).

It is not possible to go into much detail on this subject at this juncture; suffice it to say that one reason these relations are so important is that DEE corresponds to *true* (or *yes*) and DUM corresponds to *false* (or *no*). The Exercises and Answers sections in the next two chapters offer a little more insight. For further discussion, see references [4.6–4.7].

4.6
```
CREATE DOMAIN S#      CHAR(5) ;
CREATE DOMAIN NAME    CHAR(20) ;
CREATE DOMAIN STATUS  NUMERIC(5) ;
CREATE DOMAIN CITY    CHAR(15) ;
CREATE DOMAIN P#      CHAR(6) ;
CREATE DOMAIN COLOR   CHAR(6) ;
CREATE DOMAIN WEIGHT  NUMERIC(5) ;
CREATE DOMAIN J#      CHAR(4) ;
CREATE DOMAIN QTY     NUMERIC(9) ;

CREATE BASE RELATION S
    ( S#       DOMAIN ( S# ),
      SNAME    DOMAIN ( NAME ),
      STATUS   DOMAIN ( STATUS ),
      CITY     DOMAIN ( CITY ) )
    PRIMARY KEY ( S# ) ;

CREATE BASE RELATION P
    ( P#       DOMAIN ( P# ),
      PNAME    DOMAIN ( NAME ),
      COLOR    DOMAIN ( COLOR ),
      WEIGHT   DOMAIN ( WEIGHT ),
      CITY     DOMAIN ( CITY ) )
    PRIMARY KEY ( P# ) ;

CREATE BASE RELATION J
    ( J#       DOMAIN ( J# ),
      JNAME    DOMAIN ( NAME ),
      CITY     DOMAIN ( CITY ) )
    PRIMARY KEY ( J# ) ;

CREATE BASE RELATION SPJ
    ( S#       DOMAIN ( S# ),
      P#       DOMAIN ( P# ),
      J#       DOMAIN ( J# ),
      QTY      DOMAIN ( QTY ) )
    PRIMARY KEY ( S#, P#, J# )
    FOREIGN KEY ( S# ) REFERENCES S
    FOREIGN KEY ( P# ) REFERENCES P
    FOREIGN KEY ( J# ) REFERENCES J ;
```

4.7 A tuple {<S#:*s*,P#:*p*,J#:*j*,QTY:*q*>} appears in relation SPJ if and only if all of the following conditions are satisfied:

- The values *s, p, j, q* are all values from the appropriate domains
- The value *s* appears as a value of attribute S# in relation S, and similarly for the values *p* and *j*
- No tuple {<S#:*s*,P#:*p*,J#:*j*,QTY:*q'*>} with $q' \neq q$ appears in relation SPJ
- The given tuple does not violate any other applicable integrity rules (see Chapter 16)

Finally (and informally), supplier *s* supplies part *p* to project *j* in quantity *q*. This informal statement is not, of course, part of the *DBMS-understood* meaning of the relation.

5 | Relational Data Integrity: Candidate Keys and Related Matters

5.1 Introduction

The integrity part of the relational model is probably the part that has changed the most over the years. And this state of affairs is undoubtedly due to the fact that—to be blunt—the integrity part has less of a solid scientific basis than the other two parts. In particular, certain basic definitions have changed several times in this area, and certain aspects of certain versions of those definitions have tended to smack more of dogma than logic. In this chapter we will give our own currently preferred definitions and explanations, and will generally try to present the material in a way that seems the most satisfactory and coherent at the time of writing. Where the departures from earlier definitions and descriptions are particularly egregious, however, we will also offer some remarks regarding the changes and the reasons for them.

With that preamble out of the way, let us get on with the matter at hand. We begin with a little philosophy.

1. At any given time, any given database contains some particular configuration of data values, and of course that configuration is supposed to "reflect reality"—i.e., it is supposed to be a model or representation of some particular portion of the real world.

2. Now, certain configurations of values simply do not make sense, in that they do not represent any possible state of the real world. For example, a configuration for the suppliers-and-parts database in which there was a tuple in relation P saying "part P7 weighs minus 25 pounds" would presumably not make sense—weights cannot be negative in the real world.

3. The database definition therefore needs to be extended to include certain **integrity rules,** the purpose of which is to inform the DBMS of certain constraints in the real world (such as the constraint that part weights cannot be negative), so that it can prevent such impossible configurations of values from occurring. In the part weights example, of course, all the DBMS would have to do is monitor INSERTs and UPDATEs on relation P, and reject any operation that attempts to introduce a negative value for the WEIGHT attribute.

It is important to understand that most databases are subject to a very large number of integrity rules. For example, the list of rules for suppliers-and-parts might easily include all of the following (this list is taken from reference [5.5]):

- Supplier numbers must be of the form S*nnnn* (where *nnnn* stands for up to four decimal digits)

- Part numbers must be of the form P*nnnnn* (where *nnnnn* stands for up to five decimal digits)

- Supplier status values must be in the range 1–100

- Supplier and part cities must be drawn from a certain list

- Part colors must be drawn from a certain list

- Part weights must be greater than zero

- Shipment quantities must be a multiple of 100

- All red parts must be stored in London

- If the supplier city is London, then the supplier status must be 20

and so on.

Now, any given integrity rule is necessarily **database-specific,** in the sense that it applies to just one specific database; all of the examples above are obviously database-specific in this sense. However, in addition to its support for database-specific rules (which will be discussed briefly in the next chapter and described in depth in Chapter 16), the relational model does include two *general* integrity features—features, that is, that are relevant to the integrity of *every* database, not just to some specific database such as suppliers-and-parts. The two features in question are (a) *candidate* (and *primary*) *keys* and (b) *foreign keys*. We discuss candidate keys in Sections 5.2–5.3 and foreign keys in Sections 5.4–5.5.

Although the basic ideas of candidate and foreign keys are quite simple, there is unfortunately one significant complicating factor: *nulls.* The possibility that (e.g.) a given foreign key might permit nulls muddies the picture considerably. For pedagogic reasons, therefore, we ignore nulls entirely in Sections 5.2–5.5, introducing them (briefly) only in Section 5.6. Sections 5.7 and 5.8 then discuss the impact of nulls on candidate and foreign keys, respectively. Section 5.9 then presents a summary and some concluding remarks.

There is one more observation we need to make before we start getting into details, as follows. We tend to think primarily of integrity rules as they apply to base relations specifically. This is because, of course, it is the base relations that are supposed to reflect reality, and hence it is the base relations that must be constrained to contain correct, or at least plausible, configurations of values. In fact, however, derived relations are subject to integrity rules as well. For example, the rule that applies to base relation S that says that supplier numbers are unique also applies to every restriction of that relation, obviously.

As the example suggests, derived relations will automatically **inherit** certain integrity rules from the relations from which they are derived. But it is possible that certain derived relations will be subject to certain additional integrity rules, over and above the rules they automatically inherit. Thus, it might well be desirable to be able to state integrity rules explicitly for certain derived relations. An example might be a candidate key definition for a view.

We will have more to say regarding such matters in Chapters 6 and 17. In the present chapter, by contrast, we will limit our attention to base relations only, on the principle that if we get the base relations right, then we stand a chance of getting other things right too, but if we get the base relations wrong, it is a virtual certainty that everything else will be wrong as well.

5.2 Candidate Keys

We have referred informally to *primary* keys several times in this book already; informally, the primary key of a relation is just a unique identifier for that relation. However, primary keys are really only a special case of the more fundamental concept *candidate* key. Here then is a definition of this latter concept. Let R be a relation. Then a **candidate key** for R is a subset of the set of attributes of R, say K, such that:

1. *Uniqueness property:*
   No two distinct tuples of R have the same value for K.

2. *Irreducibility property:*
   No proper subset of K has the uniqueness property.

Note that (as pointed out in Chapter 4) *every* relation does have at least one candidate key, because relations do not contain duplicate tuples. That is, since tuples are unique, it follows that at least the combination of all attributes of the relation has the uniqueness property; hence, either

■   That combination also has the irreducibility property and so is a candidate key (in fact, the *only* candidate key), or

■   There exists at least one proper subset of that combination that *a fortiori* has the uniqueness property and also has the irreducibility property

(see below for further discussion of the irreducibility property). In practice, of course, it is usually not necessary to involve all the attributes—some lesser combination is usually sufficient. However, it is certainly possible to have a relation where the only candidate key is the combination of all the attributes—i.e., the relation is "all key." An example would be the relation that results from eliminating attribute QTY from relation SP in the suppliers-and-parts database.

Now, note very carefully that the definition of candidate key given above applies to relations *per se* (i.e., relation *values*), not to relation *variables*. When we consider relation variables—specifically, when we consider *base relations*—we are interested from an integrity point of view not so much in the particular relation that happens to be the value of that relation variable at some particular time, but rather in the set of *all possible relations* that can ever be values of that variable.

■ For example, if we say that the attribute combination {S#,P#} is a candidate key for base relation SP, we do not mean merely that no two tuples in the relation that happens to be the current value of SP have the same value for that combination; rather, we mean that all possible relations *R* that can be values of SP are such that no two distinct tuples of *R* have the same value for that combination.

To cater specifically for relation variables, therefore, we need to extend the candidate key definition as follows (the extensions are shown in **boldface**): Let *R* be a relation **variable** (in particular, a base relation). Then a candidate key for *R* is a subset of the set of attributes of *R,* say *K,* such that **for all time** it is the case that:

1. *Uniqueness property:*
   No two distinct tuples **in the current value** of *R* have the same value for *K.*

2. *Irreducibility property:*
   No proper subset of *K* has the uniqueness property.

Henceforth, we will take the term "candidate key" to have this latter, more demanding, meaning (barring explicit statements to the contrary).

Here then is the syntax for specifying a candidate key for a base relation (note that every CREATE BASE RELATION statement must include at least one candidate key definition):

```
candidate-key-definition
    ::=    CANDIDATE KEY ( attribute-commalist )
         | PRIMARY KEY ( attribute-commalist )
```

For some examples, refer back to Fig. 3.9 or Fig. 4.3. (Note, however, that those figures illustrate the PRIMARY KEY case only, not the CANDIDATE KEY case. The PRIMARY KEY case is discussed further in the next section.)

There are a few outstanding issues to clear up before we can move on to discuss why candidate keys are so important:

■ First, although it is true in practice that most relations tend to have *exactly* one candidate key, it is certainly possible to have more than one. We might, for example, have a relation ELEMENTS that represents the table of chemical elements. Now, every element has a unique name, a unique symbol (e.g., the symbol for lead is "Pb"), and a unique atomic number. The relation thus clearly has three distinct candidate keys:

```
CREATE BASE RELATION ELEMENTS
      ( NAME    ... ,
        SYMBOL ... ,
        NUMBER ... ,
        ...    ... )
      CANDIDATE KEY ( NAME )
      CANDIDATE KEY ( SYMBOL )
      CANDIDATE KEY ( NUMBER )
```

- Second, note that candidate keys are defined to be *sets* of attributes. It is thus appropriate to use "set brackets" or braces when referring to them. For example, in the suppliers-and-parts database, {S#} is a candidate key for relation S, {P#} is a candidate key for relation P, and {S#,P#} is a candidate key for relation SP. In informal contexts, however, it is usual to drop the braces in the common case where the set contains exactly one attribute. Thus, we might say (e.g.) that S#— instead of {S#}—is a candidate key for relation S. *Terminology:* A candidate key that involves more than one attribute is said to be **composite**. A candidate key that involves exactly one attribute is said to be **simple**.

- The **irreducibility** requirement needs a little elaboration. Basically, the point is that if we were to specify a "candidate key" that was *not* irreducible, the system would not be aware of the true state of affairs, and thus would not be able to enforce the associated integrity constraint properly. For example, suppose we were to define the combination {S#,CITY}—instead of S# alone—as a candidate key for base relation S. Then the system will not enforce the constraint that supplier numbers are "globally" unique; instead, it will enforce only the weaker constraint that supplier numbers are "locally" unique within city. Thus, true candidate keys do not include any attributes that are irrelevant for unique identification purposes.

    Note: In fact, there is another good reason why candidate keys are required to be irreducible, having to do with *foreign* keys (see Section 5.4). Basically, the point is that any foreign key that referenced a "reducible" candidate key (if such a thing were possible) would be "reducible" too, and the relation containing it would thus almost certainly be in violation of the principles of further normalization (see Chapter 10).

    Incidentally, irreducibility in the foregoing sense is referred to as *minimality* in most of the literature (including previous editions of this book). However, "minimality" is not really the *mot juste*, because to say that candidate key *K1* is "minimal" does not mean that another candidate key *K2* cannot be found that has fewer components; it is entirely possible that (e.g.) *K1* has four components and *K2* only two. We will stay with the term "irreducible."

- Finally, please note that the logical notion of a candidate key should not be confused with the physical notion of a "unique index," even though the latter is very often used to implement the former. In other words, there is no implication that there has to be an index (or any other special access path, come to that) on a candidate key. In practice, of course, there probably *will* be some such special access path, but whether there is or not is beyond the scope of the model as such.

What Are Candidate Keys For?

The reason candidate keys are so important is that they provide the basic **tuple-level addressing mechanism** in a relational system. That is, the only system-guaranteed way of pinpointing some specific tuple is *by some candidate key value*. For example, the expression

```
S WHERE S# = 'S3'
```

is guaranteed to yield at most one tuple.* Likewise, if SNAME is also a candidate key for relation S (note that the sample data of Fig. 4.7 is consistent with this hypothesis), the expression

```
S WHERE SNAME = 'Blake'
```

is also guaranteed to yield at most one tuple. By contrast, the expression

```
S WHERE CITY = 'Paris'
```

will yield an unpredictable number of tuples, in general. It follows that *candidate keys are just as fundamental to the successful operation of a relational system as main memory addresses are to the successful operation of the underlying machine.* As a consequence:

1. "Relations" that do not have a candidate key—i.e., "relations" that permit duplicate tuples—are bound to display strange and anomalous behavior in certain circumstances.

2. A system that has no knowledge of candidate keys is bound to display behavior on occasion that is not "truly relational," even if the relations it deals with are indeed true relations and do not permit duplicate tuples.

The behavior referred to above as "strange and anomalous" and "not truly relational" has to do with such matters as *view updating* and *optimization.* See Chapters 17 and 18, respectively.

5.3 Primary Keys and Alternate Keys

As we have seen, it is possible (though perhaps a little unusual) for a given base relation to have more than one candidate key. In such a case, the relational model has historically required that exactly one of those candidate keys be chosen as the **primary key** for that base relation; the remainder, if any, are then called **alternate keys**. In the ELEMENTS example, for instance, we might choose "element symbol" as the primary key; "element name" and "atomic number" would then be alternate keys. And in the case where there is only one candidate key anyway, the relational model has (again) historically required that that candidate key be designated the **primary** key for the base relation in question. Hence every base relation has always had a primary key.

Note: If the set of candidate keys actually does include more than one member, then the choice of which is to be primary is essentially arbitrary. To quote reference [5.2]: "The normal basis [for making the choice] is simplicity, but this aspect is outside the scope of the relational model."

---

* More precisely, it yields a *relation* that contains at most one tuple.

Our current position on such matters is as follows: Choosing one candidate key (in those cases where there is a choice) as the primary key might be a good idea in many cases—even in most cases—but it cannot be justified in *all* cases, unequivocally. Arguments in support of this position are given in reference [5.8].

Of course, if the relation has only one candidate key, there is little harm in calling that candidate key the primary key. And when there are several candidate keys, there might still be many situations where choosing one of those candidate keys as the primary key is a good idea (albeit for reasons—perhaps just pyschological reasons—that are beyond the scope of the model as such). In other words, primary keys might still be argued to have a considerable amount of *pragmatic* (or at least historical) importance. We therefore provide some syntax for declaring them (see below). But we no longer insist that every base relation have a primary key; rather, we insist only that every base relation have at least one candidate key.

As for our own examples, we will usually, but *not* invariably, follow the primary key discipline—that is, most of our base relations will indeed have a primary key (and we will continue to mark that primary key by double underlining in our figures).

Here then is the relevant syntax (repeated from Section 5.2):

```
candidate-key-definition
   ::=    CANDIDATE KEY ( attribute-commalist )
        | PRIMARY KEY ( attribute-commalist )
```

Within a given CREATE BASE RELATION statement there must be at least one candidate key definition. At most one of those definitions is permitted to be of the PRIMARY KEY form.

One final point regarding terminology: The terms "candidate key" and "primary key" should preferably *not* be abbreviated to just "key." The term *key* has far too many meanings already in the database world. In the relational model alone, we have candidate keys, alternate keys, primary keys, and foreign keys; in other contexts we have index keys, hash keys, sort keys, secondary keys, search keys, parent keys, child keys, encryption keys, decryption keys, privacy keys, . . . and so on, *ad nauseam*. Thus, it is preferable—in this writer's opinion—*always* to qualify the term appropriately, to avoid any possible confusion.

(In previous editions of this book, we have gone on to suggest that if any one key out of all that multiplicity of keys deserved to be called *the* key, it was clearly the primary key! We now feel that if the unqualified term "key" is used at all, it would be more appropriate to use it to mean a *candidate* key. The very fact that we have changed our opinion in this regard can be seen as lending further weight to the original argument that the term should always be qualified.)

5.4 Foreign Keys

Refer once again to the suppliers-and-parts database, and consider attribute S# of relation SP. It is clear that a given value for that attribute should be permitted to appear in the database only if that same value also appears as a value of the primary key S# of relation S (for otherwise the database cannot be considered to be in a state of integrity). For example, it would make no sense for relation SP to include a shipment for supplier S8, say, if there were no supplier S8 in relation S. Likewise, a given value for attribute P# of relation SP should be permitted to appear only if the same value also appears as a value of the primary key P# of relation P; for again it would make no sense for relation SP to include a shipment for part P8, say, if there were no part P8 in relation P. Attributes S# and P# of relation SP are thus examples of what are called *foreign keys*.

Before going any further, we must point out that once again we find ourselves in an area where there is a certain amount of controversy. The relational model has historically required that foreign keys match, very specifically, *primary* keys, not just candidate keys (see, e.g., reference [5.2]). And previous editions of this book, as well as other publications by this writer (see, e.g., references [5.3–5.4]), have supported this position. Our current position, by contrast, resembles our current position on primary keys in general: Requiring foreign keys to match primary keys specifically is probably a good idea in many cases—even in most cases—but it cannot be justified in *all* cases, unequivocally. Once again, arguments in support of this position can be found in reference [5.8]. As for our own examples in this book, we will in fact follow the discipline that foreign keys do indeed reference primary keys specifically; in large part, however, this is done purely to simplify the exposition.

Let us now make the basic ideas a little more precise. Here first is a definition of the term *foreign key*. Let *R2* be a base relation. Then a **foreign key** in *R2* is a subset of the set of attributes of *R2*, say *FK*, such that:

- There exists a base relation *R1* (*R1* and *R2* not necessarily distinct) with a candidate key *CK*, and

- For all time, each value of *FK* in the current value of *R2* is identical to the value of *CK* in some tuple in the current value of *R1*.

Points arising:

1. Note that foreign keys, like candidate keys, are defined to be *sets* of attributes. It is thus appropriate to use set brackets or braces when referring to them. Strictly speaking, for example, the foreign keys in relation SP in the suppliers-and-parts database are {S#} and {P#}, not S# and P#. In informal contexts, however, it is usual to drop the braces in the common case where the set contains exactly one attribute.

2. By definition, every value of a given foreign key is required to appear as a value of the matching candidate key. Note, however, that the converse is *not* a requirement; that is, the candidate key corresponding to some given foreign key might contain a value that does not currently appear as a value of that foreign key. In the case of suppliers-and-parts, for example (sample values as shown in Fig. 3.8), the supplier number S5 appears in relation S but not in relation SP, because supplier S5 does not currently supply any parts.

3. A given foreign key will be **composite**—i.e., will consist of more than one attribute—if and only if the candidate key it matches is composite too. It will be **simple** if and only if the candidate key it matches is simple too.

4. Each component attribute of a given foreign key must be defined on the same domain as the corresponding component of the matching candidate key (except as explained in Chapter 19).

5. There is no requirement that a foreign key be a component of the primary key—or of some candidate key—of its containing relation, although in the case of suppliers-and-parts it does so happen that both foreign keys in fact are (indeed, the two foreign keys in relation SP together *are* the primary key for that relation). Here is a counterexample (the departments-and-employees database definition from Chapter 3, Fig. 3.5, shown in a simplified form):

```
DEPT ( DEPT#, DNAME, BUDGET )
     PRIMARY KEY ( DEPT# )
EMP  ( EMP#, ENAME, DEPT#, SALARY )
     PRIMARY KEY ( EMP# )
     FOREIGN KEY ( DEPT# ) REFERENCES DEPT
```

In this database, attribute DEPT# of relation EMP is a foreign key, matching the primary key DEPT# of relation DEPT; however, it is certainly not a component of the primary key EMP# (nor of any other candidate key) of relation EMP. In fact, *any attribute or attribute combination whatsoever* (in a base relation) can be a foreign key, in general.

6. *Terminology:* A foreign key value represents a **reference** to the tuple containing the matching candidate key value (the **referenced tuple** or **target tuple**). The problem of ensuring that the database does not include any invalid foreign key values is therefore known as the **referential integrity** problem. The constraint that values of a given foreign key must match values of the corresponding candidate key is known as a **referential constraint**. We refer to the relation that contains the foreign key as the **referencing** relation and the relation that contains the corresponding candidate key as the **referenced relation** or **target relation**.

7. *Referential diagrams:* Consider suppliers-and-parts once again. We can represent the referential constraints that exist in that database by means of the following **referential diagram:**

```
S ← SP → P
```

Each arrow means there is a foreign key in the relation from which the arrow emerges that refers to—specifically—the primary key of the relation to which the arrow points. *Note:* For simplicity, we ignore here the slight refinement that is needed to deal with the case of a foreign key that references a candidate key that is not the primary key. But we do remark that it is sometimes a good idea to label each arrow in a referential diagram with the name(s) of the attribute(s) that constitute the relevant foreign key. For instance:

```
  S#    P#
S ← SP → P
```

In this book, however, we will show such labels only when omitting them might lead to confusion or ambiguity.

8. A given relation can of course be both a referenced relation and a referencing relation, as is the case with relation *R2* in the following diagram:

```
R3  →  R2  →  R1
```

It is convenient to introduce the term "referential path." Let relations *Rn, R(n − 1), ... R2, R1* be such that there is a referential constraint from *Rn* to *R(n − 1),* a referential constraint from *R(n −* 1) to *R(n − 2), . . .* and a referential constraint from *R2* to *R1:*

```
Rn  →  R(n - 1)  →  R(n - 2)  →   ...  →  R2  →  R1
```

Then the chain of arrows from *Rn* to *R1* represents a **referential path** from *Rn* to *R1.*

9. Note that relations *R1* and *R2* in the foreign key definition are *not necessarily distinct.* That is, a relation might include a foreign key whose values are required to match the values of some candidate key in that same relation. By way of example, consider the relation

```
EMP ( EMP#, ..., SALARY, ..., MGR_EMP#, ... )
    PRIMARY KEY ( EMP# )
    FOREIGN KEY ( RENAME MGR_EMP# AS EMP# ) REFERENCES EMP
```

in which attribute MGR_EMP# represents the employee number of the manager of the employee identified by EMP#. In this relation, EMP# is the primary key, and MGR_EMP# is a foreign key that refers to it. (For example, the tuple for employee E4 might include a MGR_EMP# value of E3, which represents a reference to the EMP tuple for employee E3. See the end of this section for an explanation of the RENAME construct.) Such a relation is sometimes said to be **self-referencing.** *Exercise:* Invent some sample data for this relation.

10. Self-referencing relations such as relation EMP in the foregoing example actually represent a special case of a more general situation—namely, there can exist referential *cycles.* Relations *Rn, R(n − 1), R(n − 2), . . . , R2, R1* form a **referential cycle** if *Rn* includes a foreign key referring to *R(n − 1), R(n − 1)* includes a foreign key referring to *R(n − 2), . . .* and so on, and finally *R1* includes a foreign key referring back to *Rn* again. More succinctly, a referential cycle exists if there is a referential path from some relation *Rn* to itself:

```
Rn  →  R(n - 1)  →  R(n - 2)  →   ...  →  R2  →  R1  →  Rn
```

11. Foreign-to-candidate-key matches are sometimes said to be the "glue" that holds the database together. Another way of saying the same thing is that such matches represent certain *relationships* between tuples. Note carefully, however, that not all such relationships are represented by such matches. For example, there is a relationship ("colocation") between suppliers and parts, represented by the CITY attributes of relations S and P; a given supplier and a given part are "colocated" if they are located in the same city. However, those CITY attributes are not foreign keys. Of course, they could *become* foreign keys if a relation with CITY as a candidate key were added to the database.

Here then is the syntax for specifying a foreign key (note that a given CREATE BASE RELATION statement can include zero or more foreign key definitions):

```
FOREIGN KEY ( element-commalist ) REFERENCES base-relation
```

The syntactic category *element* here is either the name of an attribute of the containing base relation (the normal case), or an expression of the form

```
RENAME attribute AS attribute
```

where the first *attribute* is the name of an attribute of the containing relation, and the second is a new name for that attribute that effectively replaces the first name so far as the foreign key in question is concerned. The complete set of attribute names for the foreign key must be identical to the set of attribute names for some candidate key of the base relation mentioned in the REFERENCES clause. For some examples, see Fig. 3.9 or Fig. 4.3 (for the normal case), and the MGR_EMP# example above (for the RENAME case). For further discussion of RENAME, see Chapter 6 (Section 6.2).

Referential Integrity

Along with the foreign key concept, the relational model includes the following rule (the **referential integrity** rule):

■ *Referential integrity:*
The database must not contain any unmatched foreign key values.

The term "unmatched foreign key value" here means a foreign key value for which there does not exist a matching value of the relevant candidate key in the relevant target relation. In other words, the rule simply says: If *B* references *A,* then *A* must exist.

Finally, we remark that the two concepts "foreign key" and "referential integrity" are *defined in terms of each other.* That is, it is not possible to explain what a foreign key is without mentioning the concept of referential integrity (at least tacitly), and likewise it is not possible to explain what referential integrity is without mentioning the concept of a foreign key (again, at least tacitly). Thus, the terms "support for referential integrity" and "support for foreign keys" mean *exactly the same thing.*

5.5 Foreign Key Rules

Now, the referential integrity rule as stated in the previous section is framed purely in terms of database *states.* Any state of the database that does not satisfy the rule is by definition incorrect; but how exactly are such incorrect states to be avoided? The rule itself does not say.

One possibility, of course, is that the system could simply reject any operation that, if executed, would result in an illegal state. In some cases, however, a preferable alternative would be for the system to accept the operation but to perform certain additional compensating operations, if necessary, in order to guarantee that the overall result is still a legal state. For example, if the user asks to delete supplier S1 from relation S, it should be possible to get the system to delete the shipments for supplier S1 from relation SP as well, without any further action on the part of the user (assuming that such a "cascade delete" effect is what is wanted).

It follows that, for any given database, it should be possible for the user—in this context, probably the *database designer*—to specify which operations should be rejected and which accepted, and, for those that are accepted, what compensating operations (if any) should be performed by the system. We therefore present a brief discussion of this possibility in the present section. Note clearly, however, that we are quite definitely stepping outside the bounds of the original relational model in this discussion.

The basic idea is as follows. For each foreign key, there are two broad questions that need to be answered:

1. What should happen on an attempt to delete the target of a foreign key reference?—for example, an attempt to delete a supplier for which there exists at least one matching shipment? For definiteness let us consider this case explicitly. In general there are at least two possibilities:

   - RESTRICTED—The delete operation is "restricted" to the case where there are no such matching shipments (it is rejected otherwise)

   - CASCADES—The delete operation "cascades" to delete those matching shipments also

2. What should happen on an attempt to update a candidate key that is the target of a foreign key reference?—for example, an attempt to update the supplier number for a supplier for which there exists at least one matching shipment? For definiteness, again, let us consider this case explicitly. In general there are the same possibilities as there are for DELETE:

   - RESTRICTED—The update operation is "restricted" to the case where there are no such matching shipments (it is rejected otherwise)

   - CASCADES—The update operation "cascades" to update the foreign key in those matching shipments also

For each foreign key in the design, therefore, the database designer should specify, not only the attribute or attribute combination constituting that foreign key and the corresponding target relation, but also the answers to the foregoing questions (i.e., the particular **foreign key rules** that apply to that foreign key). Hence we need to extend the syntax of a foreign key definition, as follows:

```
FOREIGN KEY ( ... ) REFERENCES base-relation
                    DELETE option
                    UPDATE option
```

where *option* is RESTRICTED or CASCADES. Points arising:

1. Of course, the RESTRICTED and CASCADES options for the foreign key delete and update rules do not exhaust the possibilities— they merely represent cases that are very commonly required in practice. In principle, however, there could be an arbitrary number of possible responses to, e.g., an attempt to delete a particular supplier. For example:

    - A conversation could be initiated with the end user
    - Information could be written to some archive database
    - The shipments for the supplier in question could be transferred to some other supplier

    It will never be feasible to provide declarative syntax for all conceivable responses. In general, therefore, *option* in the syntax above should include the possibility of invoking an installation-defined **database procedure** (sometimes called a "stored procedure" or "triggered procedure").

2. Let *R2* and *R1* be, respectively, a referencing relation and the corresponding refer-enced relation:

    ```
    R2 → R1
    ```

    Let the delete rule for this referential constraint be CASCADES. Thus, a DELETE on a given tuple of relation *R1* will imply a DELETE on certain tuples of relation *R2* (in general). Now suppose that relation *R2* in turn is referenced by some other relation *R3*:

    ```
    R3 → R2 → R1
    ```

    Then the effect of the implied DELETE on tuples of *R2* is defined to be exactly as if an attempt had been made to delete those tuples directly; i.e., it depends on the delete rule specified for the referential constraint from *R3* to *R2*. If that implied DELETE fails (because of the delete rule from *R3* to *R2* or for any other reason), then the entire operation fails and the database remains unchanged. And so on, recursively, to any number of levels.

    Analogous remarks apply to the CASCADES update rule also, *mutatis mu-tandis,* if the foreign key in relation *R2* has any attributes in common with the candidate key of that relation that is referenced by the foreign key in *R3*.

    It follows from the foregoing that, from a logical point of view, database up-date operations are always atomic (all or nothing), even if under the covers they involve several updates on several relations because of, e.g., a CASCADES delete rule.

3. The fact that referential cycles are possible probably means that some constraint checking cannot be done at the time of the individual update but must instead be deferred to some later time, e.g., to COMMIT time (see Chapter 16). For other-wise there will be no way to insert the first tuple into the database. See reference [5.4] for further discussion of such cases, also Exercise 5.4 at the end of the chapter.

5.6 Nulls (A Digression)

We have now explained the basic ideas underlying the candidate and foreign concepts in the relational model. Unfortunately, there is one major complicating factor that we have deliberately ignored up to this point—namely, **nulls**.

Now, the topic of nulls is a large subject in its own right; we will discuss it in detail in Chapter 20. But in order to explain the implications of nulls on the integrity part of the relational model, we obviously have to say something about nulls in general first. This section is thus intended as a brief introduction to the concept.

Basically, nulls are intended as a basis for dealing with the problem of **missing information**. This problem is one that is frequently encountered in the real world. For example, historical records sometimes include such entries as "Date of birth unknown"; meeting agendas often show a speaker as "To be announced"; and police records might include the entry "Present whereabouts unknown." Hence it is necessary to have some way of dealing with such situations in our formal database systems.

In reference [5.1], Codd proposes an approach to this issue that makes use of special markers called *nulls* to represent such missing information. The idea is that if a given tuple has a null in a given attribute position, it means that the value of that attribute is missing for some reason for the tuple in question. For example, a shipment tuple might have a null QTY (we know that the shipment exists but we do not know the quantity shipped); or a part tuple might have a null COLOR (perhaps COLOR does not apply to some kinds of part). Note carefully that nulls are not the same as (e.g.) blank or zero; in fact, they are not really values at all in the usual sense of that term, which is why we called them "markers" above (and why, incidentally, the commonly encountered term "null value" is deprecated).

In general, a given attribute might or might not be allowed to contain nulls—it will depend on the definition of the attribute in question, at least for base relations. (In other words, the syntax of an "attribute definition" in CREATE BASE RELATION will have to be extended to include a specification of the form NULLS ALLOWED or NULLS NOT ALLOWED.) If a given attribute is allowed to contain nulls, and a tuple is inserted into the relation and no value is provided for that attribute, the system will automatically place a null in that position. If a given attribute is *not* allowed to contain nulls, the system will reject any attempt to introduce a null into that position.

As already indicated, we do not wish to discuss the implications of the null concept in full detail here. But we do wish to make it very clear that in our opinion, nulls—and the entire theory of **three-valued logic** on which they are based—are *fundamentally misguided* and have no place in a clean formal system such as the relational model is intended to be. In fact, it is our opinion that (a) the missing information problem is still not fully understood; (b) *no* fully satisfactory solution to the problem is known at this time; and therefore (c) incorporation of nulls or any similar feature into the model is premature at this time. But it must also be emphasized that other writers—Codd in particular—believe exactly the opposite; in fact, Codd now regards nulls as an integral part of the relational model [4.4].

Be that as it may, let us now return to the main thread of our discussion and examine the effect of nulls on the candidate and foreign key concepts as previously described.

5.7 Candidate Keys and Nulls

As explained in Section 5.3, the relational model has historically required that (in the case of base relations, at least) exactly one candidate key be chosen as the *primary* key for the relation in question; the remaining candidate keys, if any, are then *alternate* keys. And then, along with the primary key concept, the model has included the following rule (the **entity integrity** rule):

■   *Entity integrity:*
   No component of the primary key of a base relation is allowed to accept nulls.

In other words, the definition of every attribute involved in the primary key of any base relation must explicitly or implicitly include the specification NULLS NOT ALLOWED.

The rationale for this rule runs somewhat as follows:

■   Base relations—more precisely, tuples within base relations—correspond to *entities* in the real world. For example, base relation S corresponds to suppliers in the real world.

■   By definition, entities in the real world are *distinguishable* —that is, they are *identifiable* in some way.

■   Therefore, entity representatives within the database must be distinguishable (identifiable) also.

■   Primary keys perform this unique identification function in the relational model (i.e., they serve to represent the necessary entity identifiers).

■   Suppose, therefore, by way of example, that base relation S included a tuple for which the S# value was null. Then that would be like saying that there was a supplier in the real world that had no *id*entity (or at least no known identity).

■   Furthermore, what does that null mean? If it means "property does not apply," then clearly the tuple makes no sense; as explained above, entities must have *id*entity,' and hence the property *must* apply. If it means "value unknown," then all kinds of problems arise. For example, we now do not even know (in general) whether the tuple represents one of the suppliers we *do* know about (because we don't know!— that's what "don't know" means). Thus, for example, the query "How many suppliers are there?" also has to respond "don't know."

■   Similar arguments apply to all the other possible interpretations of null. In fact, an entity with missing *id*entity is a contradiction in terms: An entity without identity *does not exist* (this is why the rule is called "entity integrity").

■   Arguments analogous to the foregoing can be used to show that in a base relation with a composite primary key, primary key values that are *partially* null must be prohibited also.

■   To sum up: If an entity is important enough in the real world to require explicit representation in the database, then that entity must be definitely and unambiguously identifiable—for otherwise it would be impossible even to talk about it in any sensible manner. For this reason, the entity integrity rule is sometimes stated in the form:

In a relational database, we never record information about something we cannot identify.

In passing, we remark that it is commonly but erroneously thought that the entity integrity rule says something along the lines of "Primary key values must be unique." It does not. That uniqueness requirement is part of the basic definition of the primary key concept *per se*. The entity integrity rule says (to repeat) that primary keys in base relations must not contain any nulls.

Now let us examine the rule more closely. Since it involves not one but two concepts, primary keys and nulls, both of which we find somewhat suspect, the reader will not be surprised that we do not wholeheartedly subscribe to the rule. We offer the following observations:

■   The rule applies only to *base relations*. Other relations might indeed have a primary key for which nulls are allowed. As a trivial example, suppose that part colors have "nulls allowed," and suppose moreover that relation P has an additional tuple, for part P7 say, in which COLOR is in fact given as null. Now consider the relation that results from the query "List all part colors." That relation has just one attribute, which is the only candidate key and is therefore the primary key—and one of the tuples in the relation has a null in that primary key position. So the entity integrity rule implies an unpleasant (and not well justified) distinction between base relations and others. What would happen, for example, if we tried to save the result of the query "List all part colors" as a new base relation?

■   The rule applies only to *primary* keys. *Alternate* keys might or might not have nulls allowed. But if *AK* is an alternate key that has nulls allowed, then *AK* could not have been chosen as the primary key, because of the entity integrity rule; so in what sense exactly was *AK* a "candidate" key in the first place? Alternatively, if we have to say that alternate keys cannot have nulls allowed either, then the entity integrity rule applies to *all candidate keys,* not just to the primary key.

■   In fact, as this writer has pointed out elsewhere [20.8], the rationale given above for the entity integrity rule can be applied with equal justification to *every attribute of every base relation*—implying that nulls should be disallowed everywhere! So what purpose exactly do they serve?

■   Regarding primary keys specifically, it has been suggested [5.2] that primary keys that have nulls allowed should be referred to not as primary keys at all but as "weak identifiers." In other words, some relations do not have a proper unique identifier after all? In our opinion, this is nothing but a very suspect attempt to shore up an already suspect position. Furthermore, reference [4.4] goes on to require that a tuple that contains nothing but nulls in every attribute position "softly and suddenly vanish away," which to this writer seems more suspect still.

■ Suppose we agreed to drop the whole idea of nulls, and used *default values* instead
to represent missing information (just as we do in the real world, in fact). For example, if employee Joe's salary is unknown for some reason, we might represent it
in the database by the value "minus 1" (see Chapter 20 for further discussion).
Then the entity integrity rule would no longer have any meaning and could safely
be dropped.

Note: We might want to retain a modified version of the rule—"No base relation primary key is allowed to accept default values"—as a *guideline,* but *not* as an
inviolable rule (much as the ideas of further normalization [see Chapters 10–11]
serve as a guideline, but not as an inviolable rule). Fig. 5.1 gives an example (taken
from reference [4.15]) of a relation called SURVEY for which we might well want
to violate such a guideline; it represents the results of a salary survey, showing the
average, maximum, and minimum salary by birth year for a certain sample popu-
lation (BIRTHYEAR is the primary key). And the tuple with a default
BIRTHYEAR value ("????") represents people who declined to answer the question "When were you born?"

SURVEY	BIRTHYEAR	AVGSAL	MAXSAL	MINSAL
	1940	85K	130K	33K
	1941	82K	125K	32K
	1942	77K	99K	32K
	1943	78K	97K	35K
	....	...	...	...
	1970	29K	35K	12K
	????	56K	117K	20K

FIG. 5.1 The SURVEY relation

5.8 Foreign Keys and Nulls

Consider the departments-and-employees database from Chapter 3 once again. Suppose it is possible, in the company represented by that database, for certain employees
not to be assigned to any department. In the EMP tuple corresponding to such an employee, therefore, there is no genuine department number that can serve as the appropriate value for the DEPT# foreign key.

By way of another example, consider the *self-referencing* EMP relation discussed
in Section 5.4 above. What is the value of MGR_EMP# for the president of the company?

In order to deal with examples such as the foregoing, therefore, the relational
model has historically permitted nulls to appear in foreign key positions. (It is worth
pointing out, incidentally, that those nulls are likely to be of the "value does not exist"
variety, not the "value unknown" variety; see Chapter 20 for further discussion.) The
foreign key definition we gave earlier thus requires some slight refinement, as follows

(the extensions are shown in **boldface**). Let *R2* be a base relation. Then a *foreign key* in *R2* is a subset of the set of attributes of *R2*, say *FK*, such that:

- There exists a base relation *R1* (*R1* and *R2* not necessarily distinct) with a candidate key *CK*, and

- For all time, each value of *FK* in the current value of *R2* **either is null or** is identical to the value of *CK* in some tuple in the current value of *R1*.

The referential integrity rule—"The database must not contain any unmatched foreign key values"—remains unchanged, but the meaning of the term "unmatched foreign key value" is extended to refer to a **nonnull** foreign key value for which there does not exist a matching value of the relevant candidate key in the relevant target relation. Points arising:

1. There is now another foreign key rule (in addition to the delete and update rules discussed in Section 5.5) to be considered, namely the *nulls rule*. That is, for each foreign key, the database designer needs to decide whether or not that foreign key can accept nulls. And we need to extend the foreign key definition syntax once again, as follows—

```
FOREIGN KEY ( ... ) REFERENCES base-relation
                    DELETE option
                    UPDATE option
                    NULLS  null-option
```

(where *null-option* is either ALLOWED or NOT ALLOWED)— in order to allow the designer to record his or her decision accordingly.

2. If a given foreign key *FK* is composite and does in fact permit nulls, there is some controversy over whether it should be legal for a given *FK* value to have some components null and others nonnull, or whether we should insist that each *FK* value must be either wholly null or wholly nonnull. For the purposes of the present discussion, we adopt the latter (simpler) position. See references [5.4] and [5.7] for detailed discussion of this issue.

3. Consider once again the question of what should happen on an attempt to delete the target of a foreign key reference—for example, an attempt to delete a supplier for which there exists at least one matching shipment. For definiteness let us consider this case explicitly once again. If the foreign key in question—SP.S# in the example—permits nulls, there is now another possibility for the delete rule (i.e., another possible value for *option* in the syntax), namely NULLIFIES:

   - NULLIFIES—The foreign key is set to null in all such matching shipments and the supplier is then deleted

4. Consider once again also the question of what should happen on an attempt to update a candidate key that is the target of a foreign key reference—for example, an attempt to update the supplier number for a supplier for which there exists at least one matching shipment. For definiteness let us consider this case explicitly once again. If the foreign key in question—SP.S# in the example—permits nulls,

there is now another possibility for the update rule (i.e., another possible value for *option* in the syntax), namely NULLIFIES:

- NULLIFIES—The foreign key is set to null in all such matching shipments and the supplier is then updated

An Opinion

It is our general opinion that nulls are such a bad idea that it is not worth wrecking the whole relational model over them, just because a suitable target tuple sometimes does not exist for some particular foreign key (thereby making it appear that some foreign keys must have NULLS ALLOWED). *Note:* We will explain in Chapter 20 just why we think nulls "wreck the model."

Suppose, therefore, that (as suggested earlier) we agree to drop the whole idea of nulls, and use *default values* instead to represent missing information. Then it is obviously possible to construct a "default target tuple" with a default value for the relevant candidate key, and use that same default value (instead of null) for the matching foreign key when necessary. This approach is not very elegant, but it does have the overwhelming advantage of *not undermining the logical foundations of the relational model.* Until further notice, therefore, we will simply ignore all aspects of null support; in particular, we will not entertain the possibility that a given foreign key might permit nulls.

5.9 Summary

If this chapter has seemed a little confusing, it is because of the necessity of presenting a historical as well as a current perspective on the subject. The material has indeed changed quite considerably over time. Anyway, to summarize:

- We began by discussing **integrity rules** in general, and pointing out that any given rule is necessarily **database-specific**. We then focused on the "general" integrity features of the relational model. We defined **candidate keys,** both for relations in general and relation variables (especially base relations) in particular. Candidate keys are required to be **unique** and **irreducible,** and every relation has at least one. No exceptions!

- Candidate keys are important because they provide the **tuple-level addressing mechanism** in the relational model.

- Historically, the model has required that one candidate key be designated as the **primary** key (at least for base relations); any other candidate keys were then said to be **alternate** keys. However, recent investigations [5.8] indicate that primary keys in particular are not nearly so important as candidate keys in general (especially since there is no formal basis for choosing which candidate key is to be primary). But since there might be pragmatic arguments (and there are certainly historical arguments) in favor of retaining the primary key concept, we will at least continue to use primary keys in examples in this book.

- Next, we defined **foreign keys** and several related concepts—**referential con-**

straint, **referential path, referential cycle,** and others. Historically, the model has required that foreign keys refer specifically to primary keys, not just to candidate keys; however, recent investigations [5.9] indicate that this requirement is too strong, and that there are sometimes good reasons to have a foreign key that refers to a candidate key that is not the primary key. In this book, however, we will continue to show foreign keys as referring to primary keys specifically, since it tends to simplify the exposition.

■ We then described two **foreign key rules**—the delete and update rules—which, though not part of the relational model as such, are desirable in practice as a basis for a declarative mechanism for maintaining referential integrity as required by the model. Each of these rules can specify either the **RESTRICTED** option or the **CASCADES** option.

■ Next, we digressed briefly to introduce the concept of **nulls,** which are intended as a basis for dealing with **missing information**. We claimed (without providing much in the way of supporting evidence, however) that the whole nulls idea should be dropped, and that a scheme based on **default values** is to be preferred.

■ Last, we discussed the effect of nulls on candidate and foreign keys. In particular, we explained the **entity integrity** rule, and concluded that a version of that rule might serve as a useful database design guideline but could not be regarded as a hard-and-fast requirement. We also explained the **NULLIFIES** option on the foreign key delete and update rules.

The whole question of missing information will be discussed again in much more detail in Chapter 20; from this point forward, we will completely ignore the concept of nulls (until we reach that chapter). In particular, we will not consider the effect of nulls on the relational operators in Chapters 6 and 7.

There are a couple of final remarks to be made by way of closing. First, the relational model is frequently described as including "two general integrity rules," namely the entity and referential integrity rules. However, it would really be more appropriate to refer to those two rules as *meta*rules, not as rules *per se,* as we now explain.

■ Consider the referential integrity rule, for example. That rule says that foreign key values are supposed to match candidate key values (speaking very loosely, of course).

■ Now consider the suppliers-and-parts database. Because of the referential integrity rule, that database must have a *database-specific* rule saying that values of attribute S# in relation SP must match values of attribute S# in relation S; it must also have another similar rule for attribute P# in relation SP and attribute P# in relation P. Thus, the referential integrity rule is a different *kind* of rule from the database-specific rules; in effect, it is *a rule that says there must be certain other rules*—which is what we mean by a **metarule**.

■ Analogous remarks apply to the entity integrity rule also.

The other closing remark is as follows. We said at the start of this chapter that the relational model has two general integrity features, candidate keys and foreign keys. However, it would be more accurate to say that it has *three*. The third is **domains,** and this feature too has an associated metarule—one that is in fact more fundamental than the other two:

■ *Attribute integrity:*
Every attribute is required to satisfy the constraint that its values are drawn from the relevant domain.

In the case of suppliers-and-parts, for example, this metarule requires that there be database-specific rules saying that values of attribute S# in relation S are drawn from the domain of supplier numbers, values of attribute SNAME in relation S are drawn from the domain of names, etc., etc.

Exercises

5.1 Modify your answer to Exercise 4.6 in Chapter 4 to include a suitable set of foreign key rules for the suppliers-parts-projects database.

5.2 Using the sample suppliers-parts-projects data values from Fig. 4.6, say what the effect of each of the following operations is:

(a) UPDATE project J7, setting CITY to New York

(b) UPDATE part P5, setting P# to P4

(c) UPDATE supplier S5, setting S# to S8, if the relevant update rule is RESTRICTED

(d) DELETE supplier S3, if the relevant delete rule is CASCADES

(e) DELETE part P2, if the relevant delete rule is RESTRICTED

(f) DELETE project J4, if the relevant delete rule is CASCADES

(g) UPDATE shipment S1-P1-J1, setting S# to S2

(h) UPDATE shipment S5-P5-J5, setting J# to J7

(i) UPDATE shipment S5-P5-J5, setting J# to J8

(j) INSERT shipment S5-P6-J7

(k) INSERT shipment S4-P7-J6

(l) INSERT shipment S1-P2-*jjj* (where *jjj* stands for a default project number)

5.3 An education database contains information about an inhouse company education training scheme. For each training course, the database contains details of all prerequisite courses for that course and all offerings for that course; and for each offering it contains details of all teachers and all student enrollments for that offering. The database also contains information about employees. The relevant relations are as follows, in outline:

```
COURSE      ( COURSE#, TITLE )
PREREQ      ( SUP_COURSE#, SUB_COURSE# )
OFFERING    ( COURSE#, OFF#, OFFDATE, LOCATION )
TEACHER     ( COURSE#, OFF#, EMP# )
ENROLLMENT  ( COURSE#, OFF#, EMP#, GRADE )
EMPLOYEE    ( EMP#, ENAME, JOB )
```

The meaning of the PREREQ relation is that the superior course (SUP_COURSE#) has the subordinate course (SUB_COURSE#) as an immediate prerequisite; the other relations are intended to be self-explanatory. Draw a suitable referential diagram for this database. Give the corresponding database definition (i.e., write the corresponding CREATE DOMAIN and CREATE BASE RELATION statements).

5.4 The following two relations represent a database containing information about departments and employees:

```
DEPT ( DEPT#, ..., MGR_EMP#, ... )
EMP  ( EMP#, ..., DEPT#, ... )
```

Every department has a manager (MGR_EMP#); every employee has a department (DEPT#). Again, draw a referential diagram and write a suitable database definition for this database.

5.5 The following two relations represent a database containing information about employees and programmers:

```
EMP  ( EMP#, ..., JOB, ... )
PGMR ( EMP#, ..., LANG, ... )
```

Every programmer is an employee, but the converse is not the case. Once again, draw a referential diagram and write a suitable database definition.

5.6 The body of the chapter discussed foreign key delete and update rules, but it did not mention any foreign key "insert rule." Why not?

5.7 In the answer to Exercise 4.5 in Chapter 4 we introduced the special (very important) degree-0 relations DEE and DUM. What candidate keys do these relations possess?

5.8 Let R be a relation of degree n. What is the maximum number of candidate keys relation R might possess?

References and Bibliography

5.1 E. F. Codd. "Extending the Relational Database Model to Capture More Meaning." *ACM TODS 4,* No. 4 (December 1979).

The overall purpose of this paper is (as the title indicates) to present some preliminary "semantic" extensions to the basic relational model. Before getting into details of the proposed extensions, however, the paper first establishes its starting point by summarizing the features of the basic model (as of 1979), and in so doing provides the first published statement of the entity integrity and referential integrity rules (not however in quite the form given in the present chapter). The rules were implicit, more or less, in the model as originally formulated in reference [4.1] but had not previously been spelled out explicitly. The paper also contains the first version of Codd's proposals regarding the use of *nulls* and *three-valued logic* as an attack on the missing information problem.

Another term occasionally encountered in the literature, *primary domain,* was also first defined in this paper. A **primary domain** is a domain on which at least one single-attribute (i.e., noncomposite) primary key is defined. In the case of suppliers-and-parts, for example, the primary domains are S# and P#.

See the References and Bibliography sections of Chapters 12, 19, and 20 for additional commentary on this paper.

5.2 E. F. Codd. "Domains, Keys, and Referential Integrity in Relational Databases." *InfoDB 3,* No. 1 (Spring 1988).

An attempt to clarify the domain, primary key, and foreign key concepts. The paper is obviously authoritative, since Codd was the inventor of all three concepts; in the present writer's opinion, however, it unfortunately still leaves too many issues unresolved or unexplained. Incidentally, it gives the following argument in favor of the discipline of requiring one candidate key to be selected as the primary key: "Failure to support this discipline is something like trying to use a computer with an addressing scheme for its memory and for its auxiliary storage that changes radix whenever a particular kind of event occurs (for example, encountering an address that happens to be a prime number)." But if we accept this argument, why not take it to its logical conclusion and use an identical addressing scheme for *all* objects? Is it not very awkward to have to address suppliers by 5-character supplier numbers and parts by 6-character part numbers?—not to mention shipments, which involve "addresses" that are *composite*. (In fact, there is much to be said for this idea of a globally uniform addressing scheme. See the discussion of *object IDs* in Part VI of this book.)

5.3 C. J. Date. "Referential Integrity." Proc. 7th International Conference on Very Large Data Bases, Cannes, France (September 1981). Republished in revised form in C. J. Date, *Relational Database: Selected Writings*. Reading, Mass: Addison-Wesley (1986).

The paper that introduced the foreign key rules (RESTRICTED, CASCADES, NULLIFIES) discussed in Sections 5.5 and 5.8 of the present chapter. The main difference between the original (VLDB 1981) version of the paper and the revised version is that the original version, following reference [5.1], permitted multiple target relations per foreign key, whereas—for reasons explained in detail in reference [5.4]—the revised version backed off from that excessively general position.

5.4 C. J. Date. "Referential Integrity and Foreign Keys. Part I: Basic Concepts; Part II: Further Considerations." In C. J. Date, *Relational Database Writings 1985–1989*. Reading, Mass: Addison-Wesley (1990).

Part I of this lengthy paper (over 80 pages in total) discusses the history of the referential integrity concept and offers a preferred set of basic definitions (with rationale). Part II provides further arguments in favor of those preferred definitions and gives some specific practical recommendations; in particular, it discusses problems caused by (a) overlapping foreign keys, (b) composite foreign key values that are partly null, and (c) *conterminous* referential paths (i.e., distinct referential paths that have the same start point and the same end point). *Note:* Certain of the positions of this paper are slightly (but not very seriously) undermined by the arguments of reference [5.8].

5.5 C. J. Date. "Integrity." Chapter 11 of C. J. Date and Colin J. White: *A Guide to DB2* (4th edition). Reading, Mass: Addison-Wesley (1993).

At the time of writing, IBM's DB2 product provides more than most other commercial systems in the way of *declarative* primary and foreign key support. This reference includes a comprehensive description of that support.

It is worth pointing out that the DB2 support does suffer from a number of implementation restrictions, the general purpose of which is *to guarantee predictable behavior*. As a simple example, suppose relation R contains just two tuples, with primary key values 1 and 2 respectively, and consider the update request "Double every primary key value in R." The correct result is that the tuples should now have primary key values 2 and 4, respectively. If DB2 were to update the "2" first (replacing it by "4") and then update the "1" second (replacing it by "2"), the request would succeed. If, on the other hand, it were to update— or, rather, attempt to update—the "1" first (replacing it by "2"), it would run into a uniqueness violation, and the request would fail (the database would remain unchanged). In other words, *the result of the request would be unpredictable*. In order to avoid such unpredictability, DB2 simply outlaws any situations in which it might otherwise occur. Unfortunately, however, some of the resulting restrictions are quite severe [5.11].

Note that, as the foregoing example suggests, DB2 typically does "inflight checking"—i.e., it applies integrity checks to each individual tuple *as it updates that tuple*. Such inflight checking is logically incorrect (see the discussion of update operations in Chapter 6, Section 6.9) but is done for performance reasons.

5.6 C. J. Date. "Composite Keys." In C. J. Date and Hugh Darwen, *Relational Database Writings 1989–1991*. Reading, Mass.: Addison-Wesley (1992).

To quote from the abstract: "Arguments for and against the inclusion of composite [primary and foreign keys] in the design of a relational database are summarized and some . . . recommendations offered."

5.7 C. J. Date. "Composite Foreign Keys and Nulls." In C. J. Date and Hugh Darwen, *Relational Database Writings 1989–1991*. Reading, Mass.: Addison-Wesley (1992).

5.8 C. J. Date. "The Primacy of Primary Keys: An Investigation." *InfoDB 7,* No. 3 (Summer 1993).

5.9 Bruce M. Horowitz. "A Run-Time Execution Model for Referential Integrity Maintenance." Proc. 8th International Data Engineering Conference, Phoenix, Ariz. (February 1992).

It is well known that certain combinations of

1. referential structures (i.e., collections of relations that are interrelated via referential constraints),

2. foreign key delete and update rules, and

3. actual data values in the database

can together lead to certain conflict situations and can potentially cause unpredictable behavior on the part of the implementation; see, e.g., reference [5.4] for further explanation. There are three broad approaches to dealing with this problem: (a) leave it to the user, (b) have the system detect and reject attempts to define structures that might potentially lead to conflicts at run time, or (c) have the system detect and reject *actual* conflicts at run time. Option (a) is a nonstarter and option (b) tends to be excessively cautious [5.5,5.11]; Horowitz therefore proposes option (c). The paper gives a set of rules for such run-time actions and proves their correctness. Note, however, that the question of performance overhead of such run-time checking is not considered.

Horowitz was an active member of the committee that defined the current version of the SQL standard [8.1], and the proposals of this paper are effectively assumed by the referential integrity portions of that standard.

5.10 Victor M. Markowitz. "Referential Integrity Revisited: An Object-Oriented Perspective." Proc. 16th International Conference on Very Large Data Bases, Brisbane, Australia (August 1990).

The "object-oriented perspective" of this paper's title reflects the author's opening position statement that "referential integrity underlies the relational representation of object-oriented structures." The paper is not, however, really about object-orientation at all. Rather, it presents an algorithm that, starting from an entity/relationship diagram (see Chapters 1 and 12), will generate a relational database definition in which certain of the problem cases identified in reference [5.4] (overlapping keys, partly null foreign key values) do not arise.

The paper also discusses three commercial products (DB2, SYBASE, and INGRES) from a referential integrity viewpoint. DB2, which provides *declarative* support, is shown to be unduly restrictive; SYBASE and INGRES, which provide *procedural* support (via "triggers" and "rules," respectively), are shown to be less restrictive than DB2 but cumbersome and difficult to use (though the INGRES support is said to be "technically superior" to that of SYBASE).

5.11 Victor M. Markowitz. "Safe Referential Integrity Structures in Relational Databases." Proc. 17th International Conference on Very Large Data Bases, Barcelona, Spain (September 1991).

Proposes two formal "safeness conditions" that will guarantee that certain of the problem situations discussed in (e.g.) references [5.4] and [5.9] cannot occur. The paper also considers what is involved in satisfying those conditions in DB2, SYBASE, and INGRES. Regarding DB2, it is shown that some of the implementation restrictions imposed in the interests of safety [5.5] are logically unnecessary, while at the same time others are inadequate (i.e., DB2 still permits certain unsafe situations). Regarding SYBASE and INGRES, it is claimed that the procedural support found in those products does not provide for the detection of unsafe—or even incorrect!—referential specifications.

Answers to Selected Exercises

5.1 We show a possible CREATE BASE RELATION statement for relation SPJ (only).

```
CREATE BASE RELATION SPJ
     ( S#        DOMAIN ( S# ),
       P#        DOMAIN ( P# ),
       J#        DOMAIN ( J# ),
       QTY       DOMAIN ( QTY ) )
     PRIMARY KEY ( S#, P#, J# )
     FOREIGN KEY ( S# ) REFERENCES S
                  DELETE CASCADES
                  UPDATE RESTRICTED
     FOREIGN KEY ( P# ) REFERENCES P
                  DELETE CASCADES
                  UPDATE RESTRICTED
     FOREIGN KEY ( J# ) REFERENCES J
                  DELETE CASCADES
                  UPDATE RESTRICTED ;
```

5.2 (a) Accepted.

    (b) Rejected (candidate key uniqueness violation).

    (c) Rejected (violates RESTRICTED update rule).

    (d) Accepted (supplier S3 and all shipments for supplier S3 are deleted).

    (e) Rejected (violates RESTRICTED delete rule).

    (f) Accepted (project J4 and all shipments for project J4 are deleted).

    (g) Accepted.

    (h) Rejected (candidate key uniqueness violation).

    (i) Rejected (referential integrity violation).

    (j) Accepted.

    (k) Rejected (referential integrity violation).

    (l) Rejected (referential integrity violation—the default project number *jjj* does not exist in relation J).

5.3 The referential diagram is shown in Fig. 5.2. A possible database definition follows. *Note:* For emphasis, the sole candidate key for each relation is defined explicitly by a CANDIDATE KEY clause. There would be no harm done (indeed, it would make no difference at all) if we replaced all or any of those clauses by a PRIMARY KEY clause instead.

```
CREATE DOMAIN COURSE# CHAR(5) ;
CREATE DOMAIN TITLE   CHAR(256) ;
CREATE DOMAIN OFF#    CHAR(5) ;
CREATE DOMAIN OFFDATE DATE ;
CREATE DOMAIN CITY    CHAR(15) ;
CREATE DOMAIN EMP#    CHAR(6) ;
CREATE DOMAIN NAME    CHAR(20) ;
CREATE DOMAIN JOB     CHAR(48) ;
CREATE DOMAIN GRADE   CHAR(1) ;
```

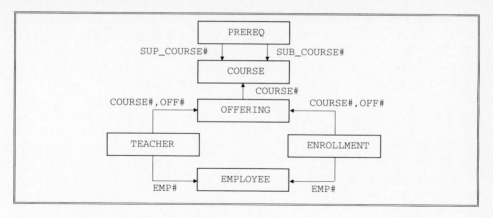

FIG. 5.2 Referential diagram for the education database

```
CREATE BASE RELATION COURSE
    ( COURSE# DOMAIN ( COURSE# ),
      TITLE   DOMAIN ( TITLE ) )
    CANDIDATE KEY ( COURSE# ) ;


CREATE BASE RELATION PREREQ
    ( SUP_COURSE# DOMAIN ( COURSE# ),
      SUB_COURSE# DOMAIN ( COURSE# ) )
    CANDIDATE KEY ( SUP_COURSE#, SUB_COURSE# )
    FOREIGN KEY ( RENAME SUP_COURSE# AS COURSE# )
                                REFERENCES COURSE
                                DELETE CASCADES
                                UPDATE CASCADES
    FOREIGN KEY ( RENAME SUB_COURSE# AS COURSE# )
                                REFERENCES COURSE
                                DELETE CASCADES
                                UPDATE CASCADES ;


CREATE BASE RELATION OFFERING
    ( COURSE#  DOMAIN ( COURSE# ),
      OFF#     DOMAIN ( OFF# ),
      OFFDATE  DOMAIN ( OFFDATE ),
      LOCATION DOMAIN ( CITY ) )
    CANDIDATE KEY ( COURSE#, OFF# )
    FOREIGN KEY ( COURSE# ) REFERENCES COURSE
                      DELETE CASCADES
                      UPDATE CASCADES ;


CREATE BASE RELATION EMPLOYEE
    ( EMP#  DOMAIN ( EMP# ),
      ENAME DOMAIN ( NAME ),
      JOB   DOMAIN ( JOB ) )
    CANDIDATE KEY ( EMP# ) ;
```

```
CREATE BASE RELATION TEACHER
      ( COURSE# DOMAIN ( COURSE# ),
        OFF#    DOMAIN ( OFF# ),
        EMP#    DOMAIN ( EMP# ) )
      CANDIDATE KEY ( COURSE#, OFF#, EMP# )
      FOREIGN KEY ( COURSE#, OFF# ) REFERENCES OFFERING
                                        DELETE CASCADES
                                        UPDATE CASCADES
         FOREIGN KEY ( EMP# ) REFERENCES EMP
                                 DELETE CASCADES
                                 UPDATE CASCADES ;

CREATE BASE RELATION ENROLLMENT
      ( COURSE# DOMAIN ( COURSE# ),
        OFF#    DOMAIN ( OFF# ),
        EMP#    DOMAIN ( EMP# ),
        GRADE   DOMAIN ( GRADE )
      CANDIDATE KEY ( COURSE#, OFF#, EMP# )
      FOREIGN KEY ( COURSE#, OFF# ) REFERENCES OFFERING
                                        DELETE CASCADES
                                        UPDATE CASCADES
         FOREIGN KEY ( EMP# ) REFERENCES EMP
                                 DELETE CASCADES
                                 UPDATE CASCADES ;
```

Points arising:

1. The attributes COURSE# in relation TEACHER and COURSE# in relation ENROLLMENT could also be regarded as foreign keys, both of them referring to COURSE. However, if the referential constraints from TEACHER to OFFERING, ENROLLMENT to OFFERING, and OFFERING to COURSE are all properly maintained, the referential constraints from TEACHER to COURSE and ENROLLMENT to COURSE will be maintained automatically. See reference [5.4] for further discussion.

2. Relation OFFERING is an example of a relation that is simultaneously both a *referenced* and a *referencing* relation: There is a referential constraint *to* OFFERING from ENROLLMENT (also from TEACHER, as a matter of fact), and a referential constraint *from* OFFERING to COURSE:

   ```
   ENROLLMENT  →  OFFERING  →  COURSE
   ```

3. Note that there are two distinct referential paths from ENROLLMENT to COURSE— one direct (foreign key COURSE# in ENROLLMENT), and the other indirect via OFFERING (foreign keys {COURSE#,OFF#} in ENROLLMENT and COURSE# in OFFERING):

   ```
              ┌────────────────────────┐
              │                        ▼
   ENROLLMENT  →  OFFERING  →  COURSE
   ```

   However, the two paths are not truly independent of one another (the upper path is implied by the combination of the lower two). For further discussion of this point, see reference [5.4] once again.

4. There are also two distinct referential paths from PREREQ to COURSE, but this time the two paths are totally independent (they have totally separate meanings). See reference [5.4] yet again.

5.4 The referential diagram is shown in Fig. 5.3. Since the database involves a referential cycle (there is a referential path from each of the two relations to itself), *either* one of the two foreign keys must be permitted to accept nulls (deprecated solution) *or* the integrity check-

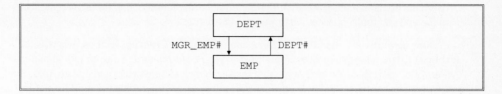

FIG. 5.3 Referential diagram involving a cycle

ing must be deferred (see Chapter 16). Apart from this consideration, the database definition is essentially straightforward. We omit the details.

5.5 We show just the CREATE BASE RELATION statements (and those only in outline):

```
CREATE BASE RELATION EMP
     ( EMP# ... ,
          ...... ,
       JOB   ... )
     PRIMARY KEY ( EMP# ) ) ;

CREATE BASE RELATION PGMR
     ( EMP# ... ,
          ...... ,
       LANG ... )
     PRIMARY KEY ( EMP# )
     FOREIGN KEY ( EMP# ) REFERENCES EMP
                  DELETE CASCADES
                  UPDATE CASCADES ;
```

Points arising:

1. This example illustrates the point that a foreign key can in fact also be a candidate key
   of its containing relation. Relation EMP lists all employees, and relation PGMR lists
   just those employees that are programmers; thus, every employee number appearing in
   PGMR must also appear in EMP (but the converse is not true). The primary key of
   PGMR is also a foreign key, referring to the primary key of EMP. Note that the two
   relations can be regarded as representing, respectively, an entity supertype (employees) and an entity subtype (programmers). In fact, the example is typical of the way
   entity supertypes and subtypes would be represented in a relational database. See
   Chapter 19 for further discussion of supertypes and subtypes.

2. Note that there is another integrity constraint that also needs to be maintained in this
   example—namely, the constraint that a given employee must be represented in relation
   PGMR if and only if the value of EMP.JOB for that employee is "Programmer." This
   constraint is not a *referential* constraint, however. See Chapter 16 for a discussion of integrity constraints in general.

5.6 There is no explicit foreign key "insert rule," because INSERTs on the referencing relation
(also UPDATEs on the foreign key in the referencing relation) are governed by the basic
referential integrity rule itself, i.e., the requirement that there be no unmatched foreign key
values. In other words, taking suppliers-and-parts as a concrete example:

- An attempt to INSERT a shipment (SP) tuple will succeed only if (a) the supplier number
  in that tuple exists as a supplier number in relation S, *and* (b) the part number in that tuple
  exists as a part number in relation P.

- An attempt to UPDATE a shipment (SP) tuple will succeed only if (a) the supplier number in the updated tuple exists as a supplier number in relation S, *and* (b) the part number in the updated tuple exists as a part number in relation P.

Note carefully also that the foregoing applies to the *referencing* relation, whereas the (explicit) delete and update rules apply to the *referenced* relation. Thus, to talk about an "insert rule," as if that rule were somehow similar to the existing delete and update rules, is really a rather confusing thing to do. This fact provides additional justification for not including any explicit "insert rule" in the concrete syntax.

5.7 Both relations have exactly one candidate key, namely the empty set of attributes { } (usually written ø).

The concept of an empty (or *nullary*) candidate key is worth some slight elaboration. DEE and DUM are not the only relations that can have such a candidate key. However, if ø is a candidate key for relation *R*, then:

■ It must be the *only* candidate key for *R*, because any other set of attributes of *R* would be a proper superset of ø, thus violating the irreducibility requirement for candidate keys. (It is therefore in fact the *primary* key, if a primary key must be chosen.)

■ *R* is constrained to contain at most one tuple, because every tuple has the same value for the empty set of attributes.

Note that our syntax certainly does permit the declaration of such a relation—for example:

```
CREATE BASE RELATION R ( X ..., Y ..., Z ... )
      PRIMARY KEY ( ) ;
```

It also permits the declaration of a relation with no attributes at all—i.e., a relation whose only possible values are DEE and DUM:

```
CREATE BASE RELATION R ( )
      PRIMARY KEY ( ) ;
```

To revert to the question of empty candidate keys: Of course, if a candidate key can be empty, then so can a matching foreign key. Reference [4.6] discusses this possibility in some detail. We remark that (according to our definitions of the terms) an empty candidate or foreign key is neither simple nor composite.

5.8 Let m be the largest integer greater than or equal to $n/2$. Relation R will have the maximum possible number of candidate keys if either (a) every distinct set of m attributes is a candidate key or (b) n is odd and every distinct set of $m-1$ attributes is a candidate key. Either way, it follows that the maximum number of candidate keys in R is $n! / (m! * (n-m)!)$.

Here are two examples of relations with the maximum possible number of candidate keys. The first is a simplified form of the ELEMENTS example from the body of the chapter:

```
CREATE BASE RELATION ELEMENTS
      ( NAME    ... , SYMBOL ... , NUMBER ... )
      CANDIDATE KEY ( NAME )
      CANDIDATE KEY ( SYMBOL )
      CANDIDATE KEY ( NUMBER )
```

The second is a relation concerning marriages:

```
CREATE BASE RELATION MARRIAGES
      ( WIFE    ... , HUSBAND ... , WEDDING_DATE ... )
      CANDIDATE KEY ( WIFE, HUSBAND )
      CANDIDATE KEY ( HUSBAND, WEDDING_DATE )
      CANDIDATE KEY ( WEDDING_DATE, WIFE )
```

We are assuming that no two distinct marriages involve the same husband and wife.

6 | Relational Operators I: Relational Algebra

6.1 Introduction

The third and last part of the relational model, the operators part, has evolved considerably since the publication of Codd's original paper [6.1]. However, it is still the case, as it always has been, that the principal component of this piece of the model is what is called the **relational algebra,** which essentially consists of a collection of operators, such as *join,* that take relations as their operands and return relations as their result. In Chapter 3 we discussed three such operators—*restrict, project,* and *join*—rather briefly; in the present chapter we will examine those operators and certain others in considerable depth.

In reference [6.2], Codd defined what is usually regarded as the "original" algebra, *viz.* the set of eight operators shown symbolically in Fig. 6.1. Now, Codd had a specific purpose in mind, which we will examine in the next chapter, for defining precisely those eight. But the reader should understand that those eight are by no means the end of the story; in fact, any number of operators could be defined that satisfy the simple requirement of "relations in, relations out" (and many such operators have indeed been proposed, by many different writers—see, e.g., references [6.9–6.11]). In this chapter we will first discuss Codd's original operators (or at least our version of them), and use them as the basis for discussing a variety of algebraic ideas; we will then go on to consider ways in which that original set of eight might usefully be extended.

An Overview of the Original Algebra

As stated above, the relational algebra as defined by Codd in reference [6.2] consisted of eight operators, two groups of four each:

1. The traditional set operations *union, intersection, difference,* and *Cartesian product* (all of them modified somewhat to take account of the fact that their operands are, specifically, relations, not arbitrary sets);

2. The special relational operations *restrict, project, join,* and *divide.*

Here are simplified definitions of these eight operators (refer to Fig. 6.1):

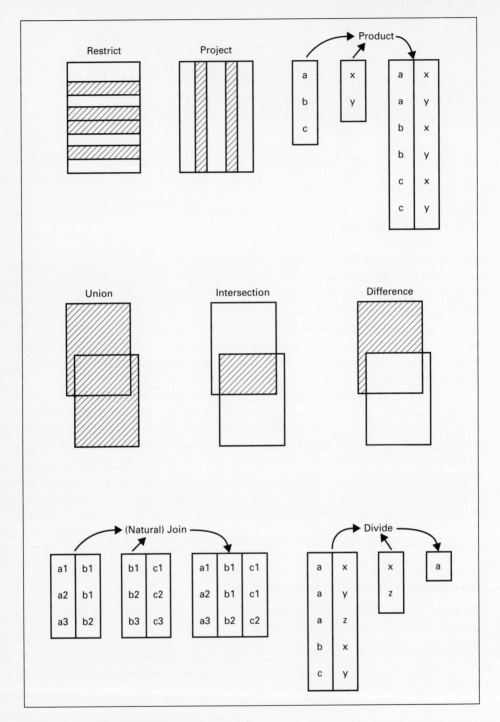

FIG. 6.1 The original eight operators (overview)

Restrict: Returns a relation consisting of all tuples from a specified relation that satisfy a specified condition.*

Project: Returns a relation consisting of all tuples that remain as (sub)tuples in a specified relation after specified attributes have been eliminated.

Product: Returns a relation consisting of all possible tuples that are a combination of two tuples, one from each of two specified relations.

Union: Returns a relation consisting of all tuples appearing in either or both of two specified relations.

Intersect: Returns a relation consisting of all tuples appearing in both of two specified relations.

Difference: Returns a relation consisting of all tuples appearing in the first and not the second of two specified relations.

Join: Returns a relation consisting of all possible tuples that are a combination of two tuples, one from each of two specified relations, such that the two tuples contributing to any given combination have a common value for the common attribute(s) of the two relations (and that common value appears just once, not twice, in the result tuple). *Note:* Strictly speaking, this is the *natural* join. See Section 6.5 for further explanation.

Divide: Takes two relations, one binary and one unary, and returns a relation consisting of all values of one attribute of the binary relation that match (in the other attribute) all values in the unary relation.

So much for our quick overview of the original operators. The plan of the remainder of the chapter is as follows. Following this introductory section, Section 6.2 discusses the question of *closure* once again and elaborates on it considerably. Sections 6.3–6.5 then discuss Codd's original eight operators in detail, and Section 6.6 gives some examples of how those operators can be used to formulate queries. Next, Section 6.7 considers the question "What is the algebra for?" Then Section 6.8 describes two more important operators called EXTEND and SUMMARIZE. Section 6.9 then discusses relational assignment and update operations, and Section 6.10 considers relational comparisons. Finally, Section 6.11 offers a brief summary.

6.2 Closure

We have explained several times already that the output from each relational operation is another relation. This is the relational **closure** property, first mentioned in Chapter 3. To recap from that chapter: Because the output of any operation is the same kind of

---

* As explained in Chapter 3, *restrict* was the original name for this operation, but nowadays it is more usually referred to as *select*. This latter name is a little unfortunate, however, in that it is too easily confused with the SELECT of SQL, which is not the same thing at all. In fact, the SELECT of SQL is *strictly more powerful* than the algebraic *restrict*—basically, it includes the functionality of all of the original eight algebraic operations, and more besides. In this book we will favor *restrict* over *select* when we mean the algebraic operation.

object as the input (they are all relations), so *the output from one operation can become input to another*. Thus it is possible, e.g., to take a projection of a union, or a join of two restrictions, or the union of a join and an intersection, etc., etc. In other words, it is possible to write **nested expressions**—that is, expressions in which the operands are themselves represented by expressions, instead of just by relation names. We will see many examples of such nested expressions in this chapter (indeed, throughout this book).

Note: There is an obvious analogy between the ability to nest relational expressions in the relational algebra and the ability to nest arithmetic expressions in ordinary arithmetic. Indeed, the fact that relations are closed under the algebra is important for exactly the same kinds of reasons that the fact that numbers are closed under ordinary arithmetic is important.

Now, when we discussed closure in Chapter 3, there was one very significant point that we deliberately glossed over. As explained in Chapter 4, a relation has two parts, a heading and a body; loosely speaking, the heading is the set of attributes and the body is the data. Now, the heading for a *base* relation is obviously well-defined and known to the system, because it is specified as part of the relevant CREATE BASE RELATION operation (see Chapter 4). But what about *derived* relations? For example, consider the expression

```
S JOIN P
```

which represents the join of suppliers and parts over matching cities (CITY being the only attribute common to the two relations). What is the heading for the result of this join? Closure dictates that it must *have* a heading, and the system needs to know what it is (so does the user, come to that, as we will see in a moment).

If we are to take closure seriously, therefore, every relational operation must be defined in such a way as to produce a result with a proper relational heading (i.e., a proper set of proper attribute names). And the reason every result relation is required to have such a set of proper attribute names is, of course, to allow us to *refer* to those attribute names in subsequent operations—e.g., in further relational operations nested deeper within the overall expression. For example, we could not sensibly even *write* an expression such as

```
( S JOIN P ) WHERE WEIGHT > 18
```

if we did not know that the result of evaluating the expression S JOIN P had an attribute called WEIGHT. In other words, what we need is a set of **attribute name inheritance rules** built into the algebra, such that if we know the attribute names of the input to any relational operation, we can predict the attribute names of the output from that operation. Given such rules for an arbitrary operation, it will then follow that an arbitrary *expression,* no matter how complex, will produce a result that also has a well-defined set of attribute names.

Before going any further, we remark that this is an aspect of the algebra that has been overlooked in most treatments in the literature—with the notable exception of the treatment found in Hall *et al.* [6.9] and Darwen [4.7]. The version of the algebra we present in this chapter is very much influenced by Darwen's work. (Earlier editions of this book did address the attribute name inheritance problem, but the approach they proposed was very much inferior to Darwen's scheme.)

Our version of the relational algebra, then, is defined in such a way as to guarantee that all relations do have proper headings—i.e., headings in which each attribute does have a proper attribute name that is unique within its containing relation. As a preparatory step to achieving this goal, we introduce a new operator, RENAME, whose purpose is basically to rename attributes within a specified relation. More precisely, the RENAME operator takes a specified relation and—conceptually, at least—returns a new copy of that relation in which some attribute has been given a different name. (The "specified relation" might be the result of an expression, of course, involving other algebraic operations.) For example, we might write:

```
S RENAME CITY AS SCITY
```

This expression (please note that it *is* an expression, not a "command" or statement, and hence that it can be nested within other expressions) evaluates to a relation having the same body as relation S but with its city attribute named SCITY instead of CITY:

S#	SNAME	STATUS	SCITY
S1	Smith	20	London
S2	Jones	10	Paris
S3	Blake	30	Paris
S4	Clark	20	London
S5	Adams	30	Athens

The other attributes of this relation have names that are inherited without change from their counterparts in relation S. The relation itself is unnamed. (We remind the reader that we made use of a variant of RENAME in our syntax for foreign key definitions. Refer back to Section 5.6 if you need to refresh your memory.)

In closing this section, it is worth pointing out that it is possible to carry the closure notion still further. As we saw in Chapter 5, every relation not only has a heading and a body, it also has *a set of candidate keys*. A strong case can therefore be made that the system should know the candidate keys, as well as the attribute names, for every result relation. In other words, it would be very desirable to have a set of **candidate key inheritance rules,** by which the system could deduce the candidate keys for the result of an arbitrary expression. See Exercise 6.11 at the end of this chapter, also reference [9.6] in Chapter 9.

6.3 A Syntax for the Relational Algebra

We are now in a position to introduce a concrete syntax for the operations of the relational algebra (see the BNF grammar in Fig. 6.2). Please note that the syntax is not intended as a serious candidate for an end user language—it is not particularly user-

```
expression
    ::=   monadic-expression | dyadic-expression

monadic-expression
    ::=   renaming  |  restriction  |  projection

renaming
    ::=   term RENAME attribute AS attribute

term
    ::=   relation | ( expression )

restriction
    ::=   term WHERE condition

projection
    ::=   term | term [ attribute-commalist ]

dyadic-expression
    ::=   projection dyadic-operation expression

dyadic-operation
    ::=   UNION | INTERSECT | MINUS | TIMES | JOIN | DIVIDEBY
```

FIG. 6.2 A BNF grammar for the relational algebra

friendly—but it *is* intended as a sound basis for the discussions that follow in the rest of the chapter, and of course it could be made more user-friendly by means of appropriate "syntactic sugar." Indeed, we will make a few simple syntactic improvements of our own later in the chapter.

Some Notes on the Grammar

1. Refer back to Chapter 4 (Section 4.3) for an explanation of the "commalist" convention.

2. The categories *relation* and *attribute* are both defined to be *identifiers* (a terminal category with respect to this grammar). They represent a relation name and an attribute name, respectively.

3. See the subsection "Restriction" in Section 6.5 for an explanation of the category *condition*.

Now, the grammar as defined above requires heavy use of parentheses in complex expressions in order to enforce a desired order of evaluation. Later in this chapter we will introduce a few simplifications that will have the effect of reducing the total number of parentheses in many cases. One such simplification we introduce right away—**multiple renaming**. Consider the following example:

```
( S RENAME CITY AS SCITY ) RENAME S# AS SNUM
```

As explained earlier, the inner expression here evaluates to a relation having the same body as relation S but with its city attribute named SCITY instead of CITY. The overall expression then evaluates to a relation that again has the same body but now additionally has its supplier number attribute named SNUM instead of S#. In order to allow several attributes to be renamed at the same time without having to nest expressions several levels deep, we introduce an extended version of the RENAME operator, which in the example looks like this:

```
( S RENAME CITY AS SCITY, S# AS SNUM )
```

In other words, another legal syntax for the syntactic category *renaming* is:

```
( term RENAME rename-commalist )
```

where *rename* is:

```
attribute AS attribute
```

6.4   Traditional Set Operations

We now consider the individual operations of the original algebra in some detail, using the concrete syntax introduced in Section 6.3. The present section is concerned with the traditional set operations and the next section with the special relational operations.

The traditional set operations are union, intersection, difference, and product (more precisely, *extended Cartesian* product). Let us concentrate first on *union*.

In mathematics, the union of two sets is the set of all elements belonging to either or both of the original sets. Since a relation is a set, loosely speaking (a set of tuples), it is obviously possible to construct the union of two relations; the result will be a set consisting of all tuples appearing in either or both of the original relations. For example, the union of the set of supplier tuples in relation S and the set of part tuples in relation P is certainly a set.

However, although that result is a set, *it is not a relation;* relations cannot contain a mixture of different kinds of tuples, they must be *tuple-homogeneous.* And, of course, we do want the result to be a relation, because we want to preserve the closure property. Therefore, the union in the relational algebra is not the completely general mathematical union; rather, it is a special form of union, in which we require the two input relations to be what we might loosely call "the same shape"—meaning, for example, that they both contain supplier tuples, or both contain part tuples, but not a mixture of the two. If the two relations are the same shape in this sense, then we can take their union, and the result will also be a relation of the same shape; in other words, the closure property will be preserved.

A more precise term for the "same shape" concept is **type-compatibility.*** We will

---

* Previous editions of this book, following reference [6.2], used the term **union-compatibility** for this concept, and indeed this latter term is found throughout the literature. Our reasons for now preferring the term "type-compatibility" are explained in Chapter 19, where we also explore the possibility of extending the definition of the term (and thereby relaxing somewhat the rather stringent requirements on union, intersection, and difference).

say that two relations are type-compatible if they have *identical headings*—meaning, precisely, that:

1. They each have the same set of attribute names (note, therefore, that they must *a fortiori* have the same degree);

and

2. Corresponding attributes (i.e., attributes with the same name in the two relations) are defined on the same domain.

Union, intersection, and difference all require their operands to be type-compatible; arguments analogous to those presented above for union apply to intersection and difference also. (Cartesian product by contrast has no such requirement, though it does have a different requirement of its own, as we will see.) If we need to take a union or intersection or difference of two relations that would be type-compatible except for some differences in attribute names, we can use the RENAME operator introduced in Section 6.2 to make them type-compatible first, before performing the desired operation.

Now we can proceed with our definitions of the traditional set operations, or rather the variants thereof that are supported in the relational algebra.

Union

The **union** of two type-compatible relations *A* and *B* (*A* UNION *B*) is a relation with the same heading as each of *A* and *B* and with a body consisting of the set of all tuples *t* belonging to *A* or *B* or both.

Example: Let relations *A* and *B* be as shown in Fig. 6.3 (*A* is the suppliers in London, and *B* is the suppliers who supply part P1, intuitively speaking). Then *A* UNION *B*—see part (a) of the figure—is the suppliers who *either* are located in London *or* supply part P1 (or both). Notice that the result has three tuples, not four—duplicate tuples are eliminated, by definition.

Note: The question of duplicate elimination does not arise with the other traditional set operations (intersection, difference, product). In fact, the only other operation where it does arise is projection.

Intersection

The **intersection** of two type-compatible relations *A* and *B* (*A* INTERSECT *B*) is a relation with the same heading as each of *A* and *B* and with a body consisting of the set of all tuples *t* belonging to both *A* and *B*.

Example: Again, let *A* and *B* be as shown in Fig. 6.3. Then *A* INTERSECT *B*—see part (b) of the figure—is the suppliers who are located in London *and* supply part P1.

Difference

The **difference** between two type-compatible relations *A* and *B*, in that order (*A* MINUS *B*), is a relation with the same heading as each of *A* and *B* and with a body consisting of the set of all tuples *t* belonging to *A* and not to *B*.

A

S#	SNAME	STATUS	CITY
S1	Smith	20	London
S4	Clark	20	London

B

S#	SNAME	STATUS	CITY
S1	Smith	20	London
S2	Jones	10	Paris

(a) *Union*
    (A UNION B)

S#	SNAME	STATUS	CITY
S1	Smith	20	London
S4	Clark	20	London
S2	Jones	10	Paris

(b) *Intersection*
    (A INTERSECT B)

S#	SNAME	STATUS	CITY
S1	Smith	20	London

(c) *Difference*
    (A MINUS B)

S#	SNAME	STATUS	CITY
S4	Clark	20	London

(d) *Difference*
    (B MINUS A)

S#	SNAME	STATUS	CITY
S2	Jones	10	Paris

FIG. 6.3 Union, intersection, and difference examples

Example: Let *A* and *B* again be as shown in Fig. 6.3. Then *A* MINUS *B*—see part (c) of the figure—is the suppliers who are located in London and do *not* supply part P1, and *B* MINUS *A*—see part (d) of the figure—is the suppliers who supply part P1 and are *not* located in London. Observe that MINUS has a directionality to it, just like subtraction does in ordinary arithmetic (e.g., "5 − 2" and "2 − 5" are not the same thing).

Product

In mathematics, the Cartesian product (product for short) of two sets is the set of all ordered pairs of elements such that the first element in each pair comes from the first set and the second element in each pair comes from the second set. Thus, the Cartesian product of two relations would be a set of ordered pairs of tuples. But again we want to preserve the closure property; in other words, we want the result to consist of *tuples,* not ordered pairs of tuples. Therefore, the relational algebra version of Cartesian product is an *extended form* of the operation, in which each ordered pair of tuples is replaced by the single tuple that is the *coalescing* of the two tuples in question. "Coalescing" here basically means *union* (in the set theory sense, not the relational algebra sense); that is, given the two tuples

    { <A1:a1>, <A2:a2>, ..., <Am:am> }

and

```
{ <B1:b1>, <B2:b2>, ..., <Bn:bn> }
```

(attribute names shown for explicitness), the coalescing of the two is the single tuple

```
{ <A1:a1>, <A2:a2>, ..., <Am:am>, <B1:b1>, <B2:b2>, ..., <Bn:bn> }
```

Another problem that arises in connection with Cartesian product is that (of course) we require the result relation to have a well-formed heading. Now, clearly the heading of the result is basically just the coalescing of the headings of the two input relations. A problem will therefore arise if those two headings have any attribute names in common—if the operation were permitted, the result heading would have two identical attribute names and would thus not be "well-formed." If we need to construct the Cartesian product of two relations that do have any such common attribute names, therefore, we must use the RENAME operator to rename attributes appropriately first.

We therefore define the **Cartesian product** of two relations *A* and *B* (*A* TIMES *B*), where *A* and *B* have no common attribute names, to be a relation with a heading that is the coalescing of the headings of *A* and *B* and with a body consisting of the set of all tuples *t* such that *t* is the coalescing of a tuple *a* belonging to *A* and a tuple *b* belonging to *B*. Note that the cardinality of the result is the product of the cardinalities of *A* and *B*, and the degree of the result is the sum of their degrees.

Example: Let relations *A* and *B* be as shown in Fig. 6.4 (*A* is all current supplier numbers and *B* is all current part numbers, intuitively speaking). Then *A* TIMES *B*—see the lower part of the figure—is all current supplier-number/part-number pairs.

A	S#		B	P#
	S1			P1
	S2			P2
	S3			P3
	S4			P4
	S5			P5
				P6

Cartesian product (A TIMES B)

S#	P#		..	..		..	..		..	..		..	..
S1	P1		S2	P1		S3	P1		S4	P1		S5	P1
S1	P2		S2	P2		S3	P2		S4	P2		S5	P2
S1	P3		S2	P3		S3	P3		S4	P3		S5	P3
S1	P4		S2	P4		S3	P4		S4	P4		S5	P4
S1	P5		S2	P5		S3	P5		S4	P5		S5	P5
S1	P6		S2	P6		S3	P6		S4	P6		S5	P6
..	..		..	..		..	..		..	..			

FIG. 6.4 Cartesian product example

We should not leave this discussion without mentioning that, in practice, only fairly complex queries need to make explicit use of the Cartesian product operation (see the Exercises and Answers at the end of this chapter for some examples). In other words, it is comparatively unusual—though *not* totally unknown, please note—for a real query to require the use of Cartesian product. The operation is included in the relational algebra mainly for conceptual reasons. In particular, it will turn out in Section 6.5 that Cartesian product is required as an intermediate step on the way to defining the θ-*join* operation (and θ-join, by contrast, *is* needed fairly frequently).

We remark that one reason why Cartesian product is not very important in practice is that *there is no more information in the output than there was in the input.* In the case of the example of Fig. 6.4, for instance, the result does not tell us anything we did not already know—it simply tells us what supplier numbers exist and what part numbers exist.

Some Syntactic Shorthands

It is easy to verify that UNION is **associative**—that is, if *A, B,* and *C* are arbitrary expressions (yielding type-compatible relations), then the expressions

```
( A UNION B ) UNION C
```

and

```
A UNION ( B UNION C )
```

are equivalent. For convenience, therefore, we allow a sequence of UNIONs to be written without any embedded parentheses; thus each of the foregoing expressions can unambiguously be simplified to just

```
A UNION B UNION C
```

Analogous remarks apply to INTERSECT and TIMES (but not to MINUS). We remark too that UNION, INTERSECT, and TIMES (but not MINUS) are also **commutative**—that is, the expressions

```
A UNION B
```

and

```
B UNION A
```

are also equivalent, and similarly for INTERSECT and TIMES. *Note:* We will revisit the whole question of associativity and commutativity in Chapter 18. Regarding TIMES, incidentally, we remark that the Cartesian product operation of set theory is neither associative nor commutative, but the extended version as we have defined it is both.

6.5   Special Relational Operations

Now we turn our attention to the special relational operations restrict, project, join (various kinds), and divide.

Restriction

"Restriction" is really an abbreviation for θ-*restriction*, where "θ" stands for any simple scalar comparison operator (=, ≠, >, ≥, etc.). The **θ-restriction** of relation A on attributes X and Y (in that order)—

```
A WHERE X θ Y
```

—is a relation with the same heading as A and with a body consisting of the set of all tuples t of A such that the condition "$X \theta Y$" evaluates to *true* for that tuple t. Attributes X and Y must be defined on the same domain, and the operator must make sense for that domain. (Note that not all "θ"s do make sense for all domains. For example, consider the domain SEX, with values "Male" and "Female." We take it as self-evident that the only "θ"s that make sense for this domain are *equals* and *not equals; less than* does *not* make sense. Refer to Chapter 19 for further discussion.)

A scalar literal value can be specified in place of either attribute X or attribute Y (or both, of course); indeed, this is the normal case in practice.* For example:

```
A WHERE X θ literal
```

The restriction operator effectively yields a "horizontal" subset of a given relation—that is, that subset of the tuples of the given relation for which a specified condition is satisfied.

Now, restriction as just defined permits only a simple comparison in the WHERE clause. However, it is possible—by virtue of the closure property—to extend the definition unambiguously to a form in which the condition in the WHERE clause consists of an arbitrary Boolean combination of such simple comparisons, thanks to the following equivalences:

1. `A WHERE c1 AND c2` ≡ `( A WHERE c1 ) INTERSECT ( A WHERE c2 )`
2. `A WHERE c1 OR c2` ≡ `( A WHERE c1 ) UNION ( A WHERE c2 )`
3. `A WHERE NOT c` ≡ `A MINUS ( A WHERE c )`

Henceforth we will therefore assume that the condition in the WHERE clause of a restriction consists of such an arbitrary Boolean combination of simple comparisons (with parentheses if necessary in order to indicate a desired order of evaluation). Such a condition—i.e., one that can be established as *true* or *false* for a given tuple by examining just that tuple in isolation—is said to be a **restriction condition**. And so we have now (as promised in "Some notes on the grammar" following Fig. 6.2) defined the syntactic category *condition*.[†]

Some examples of restriction are given in Fig. 6.5.

---

* We should point out that replacing X or Y by a literal is really just another syntactic shorthand. For example, the restriction S WHERE CITY = 'London' can be regarded as shorthand for an expression of the form (EXTEND S ADD 'London' AS LONDON) WHERE CITY = LONDON. See the discussion of the EXTEND operator in Section 6.8.

[†] Well, not quite. In a system that supports a truth-valued data type, a "simple comparison" might also consist of just the name of an attribute, or a literal, of that data type.

S WHERE CITY = 'London'	S#	SNAME	STATUS	CITY
	S1	Smith	20	London
	S4	Clark	20	London

P WHERE WEIGHT < 14	P#	PNAME	COLOR	WEIGHT	CITY
	P1	Nut	Red	12	London
	P5	Cam	Blue	12	Paris

SP WHERE S# = 'S1' AND P# = 'P1'	S#	P#	QTY
	S1	P1	300

FIG. 6.5 Restriction examples

Projection

The **projection** of relation A on $X, Y, \ldots, Z$ (where each of $X, Y, \ldots, Z$ is an attribute of A)—

```
A [ X, Y, ..., Z ]
```

—is a relation with heading $\{X, Y, \ldots, Z\}$ and body consisting of the set of all tuples $\{X{:}x, Y{:}y, \ldots, Z{:}z\}$ such that a tuple appears in A with X-value x, Y-value y, $\ldots$, and Z-value z. Thus, the projection operator effectively yields a "vertical" subset of a given relation—that is, that subset obtained by eliminating all attributes not specified in the attribute commalist and then eliminating duplicate (sub)tuples from what is left.

No attribute can be specified more than once in the attribute commalist (why not?). However, note the following:

1. Our syntax does allow the attribute commalist (and enclosing square brackets) to be omitted entirely; the effect is equivalent to specifying a commalist of *all* the attributes of the original relation, i.e., it represents the *identity projection*. In other words, a relation *name* is (of course) a valid relational *expression*.

2. A projection of the form $R[]$—i.e., one in which the attribute commalist is not omitted but is empty—is also legal. It represents a *nullary* projection. See Exercise 6.7 at the end of the chapter.

Some examples of projection are given in Fig. 6.6. Notice in the first example (the projection of suppliers over the CITY attribute) that, although relation S has five tuples and hence five cities, there are only three cities in the result—duplicate tuples are eliminated. Analogous remarks apply to the other examples also, of course.

We remark that it is often convenient in practice to be able to specify, not the attributes over which the projection is to be taken, but rather the attributes that are to be "projected away." Thus we might say, for example, "Project the WEIGHT attribute

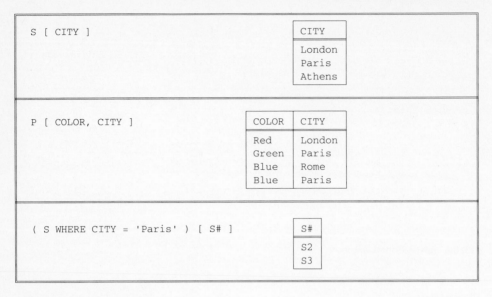

FIG. 6.6 Projection examples

away from relation P" instead of "Project relation P over the P#, PNAME, COLOR, and CITY attributes." However, we do not propose any concrete syntax here for this alternative—but of course equivalent—version of projection.

Natural Join

The join operation comes in several different varieties. Easily the most important, however, is the *natural* join—so much so, that the unqualified term "join" is taken almost invariably to mean the natural join specifically, and we follow this common usage in taking the unqualified keyword JOIN to represent natural join in our syntax. Here then is the definition (it is a little abstract, but we assume that readers are already familiar with natural join at an intuitive level from our discussions in Chapter 3). Let relations *A* and *B* have headings

```
{ X1, X2, ..., Xm, Y1, Y2, ..., Yn }
```

and

```
{ Y1, Y2, ..., Yn, Z1, Z2, ..., Zp }
```

respectively; i.e., attributes $Y1, Y2, \ldots, Yn$ (only) are common to the two relations, attributes $X1, X2, \ldots, Xm$ are the other attributes of *A*, and attributes $Z1, Z2, \ldots, Zp$ are the other attributes of *B*. Suppose also that corresponding attributes (i.e., attributes with the same name) are defined on the same domain. Let us now regard $\{X1, X2, \ldots, Xm\}$, $\{Y1, Y2, \ldots, Yn\}$, and $\{Z1, Z2, \ldots, Zp\}$ as three *composite* attributes X, Y, and Z, respectively. Then the **natural join** of *A* and *B*—

```
A JOIN B
```

—is a relation with heading $\{X,Y,Z\}$ and body consisting of the set of all tuples $\{X:x,Y:y,Z:z\}$ such that a tuple appears in A with X-value x and Y-value y and a tuple appears in B with Y-value y and Z-value z.

An example of a natural join (the natural join S JOIN P, over the common attribute CITY) is given in Fig. 6.7.

Note: We have illustrated the point several times—indeed, it is illustrated by Fig. 6.7—but it is still worth explicitly stating that joins are *not* always between a foreign key and a matching candidate key (possibly a matching primary key), even though such joins are a very common and important special case.

Join as we have defined it is both associative and commutative. As a result, the expressions

```
( A JOIN B ) JOIN C
```

and

```
A JOIN ( B JOIN C )
```

can both be unambiguously simplified to

```
A JOIN B JOIN C
```

Also, the expressions

```
A JOIN B
```

and

```
B JOIN A
```

are equivalent. We remark that, if A and B have no attribute names in common, then A JOIN B is equivalent to A TIMES B (i.e., natural join degenerates to Cartesian product in this case).

S#	SNAME	STATUS	CITY	P#	PNAME	COLOR	WEIGHT
S1	Smith	20	London	P1	Nut	Red	12
S1	Smith	20	London	P4	Screw	Red	14
S1	Smith	20	London	P6	Cog	Red	19
S2	Jones	10	Paris	P2	Bolt	Green	17
S2	Jones	10	Paris	P5	Cam	Blue	12
S3	Blake	30	Paris	P2	Bolt	Green	17
S3	Blake	30	Paris	P5	Cam	Blue	12
S4	Clark	20	London	P1	Nut	Red	12
S4	Clark	20	London	P4	Screw	Red	14
S4	Clark	20	London	P6	Cog	Red	19

FIG. 6.7 The natural join S JOIN P

θ-Join

Now we turn to the θ-*join* operation. θ-join is intended for those occasions (comparatively rare, but by no means unknown) where we need to join two relations together on the basis of some condition other than equality. Let relations A and B have no attribute names in common (as in the discussion of Cartesian product in Section 6.4), and let θ be as defined under the discussion of restriction above. Then the **θ-join** of relation A on attribute X with relation B on attribute Y is defined to be the result of evaluating the expression

```
( A TIMES B ) WHERE X θ Y
```

In other words, it is a relation with the same heading as the Cartesian product of A and B, and with a body consisting of the set of all tuples t such that t belongs to that Cartesian product and the condition "X θ Y" evaluates to *true* for that tuple t. Attributes X and Y must be defined on the same domain, and the operation must make sense for that domain.

By way of example, suppose we wish to compute the *greater-than join* of relation S on CITY with relation P on CITY (we assume that ">" makes sense for cities, and interpret it to mean simply "greater in alphabetic ordering"). An appropriate relational algebra expression is

```
( ( S RENAME CITY AS SCITY )
    TIMES
    ( P RENAME CITY AS PCITY ) )
  WHERE SCITY > PCITY
```

The result is shown in Fig. 6.8. Of course, it would be sufficient to rename just one of the two CITY attributes; the only reason for renaming both is symmetry.

Observe that θ-join is not a primitive operation; instead, it is always equivalent to taking the extended Cartesian product of the two relations (with appropriate attribute renaming if necessary), and then performing an appropriate restriction on the result.

If θ is "equals," the θ-join is called an **equijoin**. It follows from the definition that the result of an equijoin must include two attributes with the property that the values in those two attributes are equal in every tuple in the relation. If one of those two attributes is eliminated (which can be done via projection), the result is the natural join! Thus the natural join is also not a primitive operation; instead, it is a projection of a restriction of

S#	SNAME	STATUS	SCITY	P#	PNAME	COLOR	WEIGHT	PCITY
S2	Jones	10	Paris	P1	Nut	Red	12	London
S2	Jones	10	Paris	P4	Screw	Red	14	London
S2	Jones	10	Paris	P6	Cog	Red	19	London
S3	Blake	30	Paris	P1	Nut	Red	12	London
S3	Blake	30	Paris	P4	Screw	Red	14	London
S3	Blake	30	Paris	P6	Cog	Red	19	London

FIG. 6.8 Greater-than join of suppliers and parts on cities

a product (with, again, some appropriate attribute renaming operations). For example, the expression representing the natural join of suppliers and parts (over cities)—

```
S JOIN P
```

—is equivalent to the following more complex expression:

```
( ( S TIMES ( P RENAME CITY AS PCITY ) ) WHERE CITY = PCITY  )
        [ S#, SNAME, STATUS, CITY, P#, PNAME, COLOR, WEIGHT  ]
```

Division

Let relations *A* and *B* have headings

```
{ X1, X2, ..., Xm, Y1, Y2, ..., Yn }
```

and

```
{ Y1, Y2, ..., Yn }
```

respectively; i.e., attributes *Y1, Y2, . . . , Yn* are common to the two relations, *A* additionally has attributes *X1, X2, . . . , Xm,* and *B* has no other attributes. (Relations *A* and *B* represent the dividend and the divisor, respectively.) Suppose also that corresponding attributes (i.e., attributes with the same name) are defined on the same domain. Let us now regard {*X1,X2, . . . , Xm*} and {*Y1,Y2, . . . , Yn*} as two *composite* attributes *X* and *Y,* respectively. Then the division of *A* by *B*—

```
A DIVIDEBY B
```

—is a relation with heading {*X*} and body consisting of the set of all tuples {*X:x*} such that a tuple {*X:x,Y:y*} appears in *A* for *all* tuples {*Y:y*} appearing in *B*. In other words, the result consists of those *X*-values from *A* whose corresponding *Y*-values (in *A*) include *all* *Y*-values from *B,* loosely speaking.

Fig. 6.9 shows some simple examples of division. The dividend (DEND) in each case is the projection of SP over S# and P#; the divisors (DOR) are as indicated in the figure. Notice the last example in particular, in which the divisor is a relation containing part numbers for all currently known parts; the result (obviously) shows supplier numbers for suppliers who supply all those parts. As this example suggests, the DIVIDEBY operator is useful for queries of this kind; indeed, whenever the natural language version of the query includes a condition that involves the word "all" ("Get suppliers who supply *all* parts"), then that is a very strong hint that division is the operation that is required.

Before closing this section, we must mention that the division operator does hold some traps for the unwary; specifically, difficulties arise in connection with *empty relations.* A revised form of the operator, DIVIDEBY PER, which avoids those difficulties but is unfortunately somewhat more complex than the original operator, is described in the annotation to reference [6.4]. It is perhaps worth pointing out that division-type queries are often more readily expressed in terms of relational comparisons anyway (see Section 6.10).

DEND	S#	P#
	S1	P1
	S1	P2
	S1	P3
	S1	P4
	S1	P5
	S1	P6
	..	..

	..	..
	S2	P1
	S2	P2
	S3	P2
	S4	P2
	S4	P4
	S4	P5

DOR	P#
	P1

DOR	P#
	P2
	P4

DOR	P#
	P1
	P2
	P3
	P4
	P5
	P6

DEND DIVIDEBY DOR

S#
S1
S2

S#
S1
S4

S#
S1

FIG. 6.9 Division examples

6.6 Examples

In this section we present a few examples of the use of the relational algebra in formulating queries. The reader is recommended to check these examples against the sample data values of Fig. 3.8. *Note:* Any of the examples could be extended to include a final *assignment* operation, assigning the value of the expression to some named relation (see Section 6.9). For brevity, we usually omit this step.

6.6.1 Get supplier names for suppliers who supply part P2.

```
( ( SP JOIN S ) WHERE P# = 'P2' ) [ SNAME ]
```

Explanation: First the natural join of relations SP and S over supplier numbers is constructed, which has the effect (conceptually) of extending each SP tuple with the corresponding supplier information (i.e., the appropriate SNAME, STATUS, and CITY values). That join is then restricted to just those tuples in which the P# value is P2. Finally, that restriction is projected over the SNAME attribute. The final result has a sole attribute, called SNAME.

6.6.2 Get supplier names for suppliers who supply at least one red part.

```
( ( ( ( P WHERE COLOR = 'Red' ) JOIN SP ) [ S# ] JOIN S ) [ SNAME ]
```

The sole attribute of the result is SNAME again.

Here, by the way, is a different formulation of the same query:

```
( ( ( ( P WHERE COLOR = 'Red' ) [ P# ] JOIN SP ) JOIN S ) [ SNAME ]
```

The example thus illustrates the important point that there will often be several different ways of formulating any given query. See Chapter 18 for a discussion of some of the implications of this point.

6.6.3 Get supplier names for suppliers who supply all parts.

```
( ( SP [ S#, P# ] DIVIDEBY P [ P# ] ) JOIN S ) [ SNAME ]
```

Once again the result has a sole attribute called SNAME. *Note:* The characterization of the meaning of this expression as "supplier names for suppliers who supply all parts" is slightly inaccurate. See the annotation to reference [6.4] for further explanation.

6.6.4 Get supplier numbers for suppliers who supply at least all those parts supplied by supplier S2.

```
SP [ S#, P# ] DIVIDEBY ( SP WHERE S# = 'S2' ) [ P# ]
```

The result has a sole attribute called S#. (Once again the stated characterization of the meaning of the expression is slightly inaccurate. Again, see the annotation to reference [6.4].)

6.6.5 Get all pairs of supplier numbers such that the two suppliers concerned are colocated (i.e., located in the same city).

```
( ( ( S RENAME S# AS FIRSTS# ) [ FIRSTS#, CITY ] JOIN
    ( S RENAME S# AS SECONDS# ) [ SECONDS#, CITY ] )
            WHERE FIRSTS# < SECONDS# ) [ FIRSTS#, SECONDS# ]
```

The result relation has two attributes, called FIRSTS# and SECONDS#. It would be sufficient, of course, to rename the S# attribute in just one of the two operands of the join.

6.6.6 Get supplier names for suppliers who do not supply part P2.

```
( ( S [ S# ] MINUS ( SP WHERE P# = 'P2' ) [ S# ] )
                                    JOIN S ) [ SNAME ]
```

The result has a sole attribute called SNAME.

We elaborate a little on this last example in order to illustrate another point. It is not always easy to see immediately how to formulate a given query as a single nested expression (especially when the query is somewhat complex). Nor should it be necessary to do so, either. Here is a step-at-a-time solution to the same problem:

```
T1  :=  S [ S# ] ;
T2  :=  SP WHERE P# = 'P2' ;
T3  :=  T2 [ S# ] ;
T4  :=  T1 MINUS T3 ;
```

```
T5  :=  T4 JOIN S ;
T6  :=  T5 [ SNAME ] ;
```

T6 contains the desired result.

Explanation: Here ":=" represents the relational assignment operator (discussed in more detail in Section 6.9). We assume for the sake of the example that relation names of the form *Ti* are taken by the system to apply to *temporary* relations, which are created automatically by the system when they are first assigned a value and are destroyed automatically at some suitable time (e.g., end-of-session). Now, if the system includes a delayed evaluation feature (as, for example, the PRTV system did [6.8]), then breaking the query down into a sequence of small steps in this fashion need have absolutely no undesirable performance implications. Instead, the overall query can be processed as follows.

1. Let us assume that the sequence of steps shown is followed by a request to DISPLAY T6. This DISPLAY request implies that the system cannot delay evaluation any further but instead must somehow compute the value of T6.

2. In order to evaluate T6, which is the projection of T5 over SNAME, the system must first evaluate T5; in order to evaluate T5, which is the join of T4 and S, the system must first evaluate T4; . . .; and so on. In other words, the system effectively has to evaluate the original nested expression, exactly as if the user had written that nested expression in the first place.

See the next section for a brief discussion of the general question of evaluating such nested expressions, also Chapter 18 for an extended treatment of the same topic.

6.7   What Is the Algebra For?

To summarize this chapter so far: We have defined a *relational algebra,* i.e., a collection of operations on relations. The operations in question are restriction (also known as selection), projection, product, union, intersection, difference, join (natural join and θ-join), and divide, plus an attribute renaming operator, RENAME. (This is essentially the set that Codd originally defined in reference [6.2], except for RENAME.) We have also presented a possible syntax for those operations, and used that syntax as a basis for a number of examples and illustrations.

As pointed out in Section 6.5, however, Codd's eight operations do not constitute a *minimal* set (nor were they ever intended to), because some of them are not primitive—they can be defined in terms of the others. For example, natural join is a projection of a restriction of a product. In fact, of the set of eight, three, *viz.* join, intersection, and divide, can be defined in terms of the other five (see Exercise 6.2 at the end of the chapter). Those other five operations (restriction, projection, product, union, and difference), by contrast, can be regarded as **primitive,** in the sense that none of them can be defined in terms of the other four. Thus, a minimal set of operations would be the set consisting of the five primitives. In practice, however, the other three operations (especially join) are so useful that a good case can be made for supporting them directly, despite the fact that they are not primitive.

We are now in a position to clarify one very important point. Although we have never said as much explicitly, the body of the chapter up to now has certainly suggested that the primary purpose of the algebra is merely *data retrieval*. Such is not the case, however. The fundamental intent of the algebra is to allow **the writing of expressions**. Those expressions in turn are intended to serve a variety of purposes, including retrieval of course, but certainly not limited to that function alone. The following list indicates some possible applications for such expressions. (Basically, of course, such expressions represent *relations*, and those relations in turn define the scope for the retrieval, update, etc., operations shown in the list.)

- Defining a scope for **retrieval**—i.e., defining the data to be fetched as the result of a retrieval operation

- Defining a scope for **update**—i.e., defining the data to be inserted, modified, or deleted as the result of an update operation (see Section 6.9)

- Defining **(named) virtual relations**—i.e., defining the data to be made visible through a view (see Chapter 17)

- Defining **snapshots**—i.e., defining the data to be kept in the form of a "snapshot" relation (again, see Chapter 17)

- Defining **security rules**—i.e., defining the data over which authorization of some kind is to be granted (see Chapter 15)

- Defining **stability requirements**—i.e., defining the data that is to be the scope of some concurrency control operation (see Chapter 14)

- Defining **integrity rules**—i.e., defining some specific rule that the database must satisfy, over and above the general rules (or "metarules") that are part of the relational model and apply to every database (see Chapter 16)

In general, in fact, the expressions serve as *a high-level and symbolic representation of the user's intent* (with regard to some particular query, for example). And precisely because they are high-level and symbolic, they can be manipulated in accordance with a variety of high-level, symbolic **transformation rules**. For example, the expression

```
( ( SP JOIN S ) WHERE P# = 'P2' ) [ SNAME ]
```

("names of suppliers who supply part P2"—Example 6.6.1) can be transformed into the logically equivalent, but probably more efficient, expression

```
( ( SP WHERE P# = 'P2' ) JOIN S ) [ SNAME ]
```

(*Exercise:* In what sense is the second of these two expressions probably more efficient? Why only "probably"?)

The algebra thus serves as a convenient basis for **optimization** (refer back to Chapter 3, Section 3.5, if you need to refresh your memory regarding the concept of optimization). That is, even if the user expresses the query by means of the first of the two expressions shown above, the optimizer should convert it into the second before executing it (the performance of a given query should ideally not depend on the particular form in which the user happens to express that query). See Chapter 18 for further discussion.

We conclude this section by noting that, precisely because of its fundamental nature, the algebra is often used as a kind of *yardstick* against which the expressive power of some given relational language (e.g., SQL) can be measured. Basically, a language is said to be **relationally complete** [6.2] if it is at least as powerful as the algebra—i.e., if its expressions permit the definition of every relation that can be defined by means of expressions of the algebra. We will discuss this notion of relational completeness in more detail in the next chapter.

6.8   Extend and Summarize

Numerous writers have proposed new algebraic operators since Codd defined his original eight. In this section we examine two such operators in detail, *viz.* EXTEND and SUMMARIZE, that are generally agreed to represent desirable additions to the original set. Our descriptions follow the general outline of the descriptions given by Darwen in reference [4.7]; Darwen in turn was heavily influenced by the work of Todd and others on the PRTV system [6.7–6.9].

Extend

The reader will probably have noticed that the algebra as we have described it so far includes no scalar computational capabilities. In practice, however, such capabilities are obviously desirable. For example, we would like to be able to retrieve the value of an arithmetic expression such as WEIGHT * 454 from the database, or to refer to such a value in a WHERE clause in a restriction (recall that part weights are given in pounds; the expression WEIGHT * 454 will convert such a weight to grams). The purpose of the **extend** operation is to support such capabilities. More precisely, EXTEND takes a specified relation and—conceptually, at least—makes a new relation that is similar to the original relation but includes an additional attribute, values of which are obtained by evaluating some scalar computational expression. For example, we might write:

```
EXTEND P ADD ( WEIGHT * 454 ) AS GMWT
```

This expression evaluates to a relation with the same heading as P, except that it additionally includes an attribute called GMWT. Each tuple of that relation is the same as the corresponding tuple of P, except that it additionally includes a GMWT value, computed in accordance with the specified scalar expression. See Fig. 6.10.

Now we can use attribute GMWT in projections, restrictions, etc. For example:

```
( EXTEND P ADD ( WEIGHT * 454 ) AS GMWT ) WHERE GMWT > 10000
```

Note: Of course, a more user-friendly language would allow the scalar expression to appear directly in the WHERE clause:

```
P WHERE ( WEIGHT * 454 ) > 10000
```

However, such a capability is really just syntactic sugar.

P#	PNAME	COLOR	WEIGHT	CITY	GMWT
P1	Nut	Red	12	London	5448
P2	Bolt	Green	17	Paris	7718
P3	Screw	Blue	17	Rome	7718
P4	Screw	Red	14	London	6356
P5	Cam	Blue	12	Paris	5448
P6	Cog	Red	19	London	8626

FIG. 6.10 An example of EXTEND

We can incorporate EXTEND into the syntax of Fig. 6.2 by adding a new kind of *monadic expression,* with syntax as follows:

```
EXTEND term ADD scalar-expression AS attribute
```

For example:

```
EXTEND A ADD exp AS Z
```

The result of this expression (note that it *is* an expression, not a "command" or statement) is a relation with heading equal to the heading of *A* extended with the new attribute *Z*,* and with body consisting of all tuples *t* such that *t* is a tuple of *A* extended with a value for the new attribute *Z* that is computed by evaluating the scalar expression *exp* on that tuple of *A*. Relation *A* must not have an attribute called *Z,* and *exp* must not refer to *Z*. Observe that the cardinality of the result is equal to the cardinality of *A* and the degree of the result is equal to the degree of *A* plus one.

Here are some more examples:

1. `EXTEND S ADD 'Supplier' AS TAG`

   This expression effectively "tags" each tuple of relation S with the literal value "Supplier" (a scalar literal is a simple case of a scalar expression, of course).

2. `EXTEND ( P JOIN SP ) ADD ( WEIGHT * QTY ) AS SHIPWT`

   The *term* operand of EXTEND can be an arbitrary relational expression enclosed in parentheses.

3. `( EXTEND S ADD CITY AS SCITY ) [ S#, SNAME, STATUS, SCITY ]`

   An attribute name such as CITY is also a legal scalar expression. Observe that this example is equivalent to

   `S RENAME CITY AS SCITY`

   In other words, RENAME is not primitive!—it can be defined in terms of EXTEND.

---

* The system needs to know the domain for attribute Z. We defer detailed discussion of this issue (and many related issues) to Chapter 19.

4. `EXTEND S ADD COUNT ( ( SP RENAME S# AS X ) WHERE X = S# ) AS NP`

The result of this expression is shown in Fig. 6.11. *Explanation:*

- For a given supplier in relation S, the expression

  `( ( SP RENAME S# AS X ) WHERE X = S# )`

  yields the set of shipments corresponding to that supplier.

- The "aggregate function" COUNT is then applied to that set of shipments and returns the corresponding cardinality (which is a scalar value, of course).

Attribute NP in the result thus represents the number of parts supplied by the supplier identified by the corresponding S# value. Notice the NP value for supplier S5 in particular; the set of SP tuples for supplier S5 is empty, of course, and so the COUNT function returns zero.

Note: As indicated above, COUNT is an example of an *aggregate function.* Other well-known examples of such functions include SUM, AVG, MAX, and MIN. If the argument to such a function happens to be an empty set, COUNT (as we have seen) returns zero, and so does SUM; MAX and MIN return, respectively, the lowest and the highest value in the relevant domain, and AVG raises an exception.

To return to EXTEND *per se:* Subexpressions such as the one shown in the example—

`( ( SP RENAME S# AS X ) WHERE X = S# )`

(i.e., expressions that involve an attribute renaming, followed by an equality comparison that compares that renamed attribute with an attribute of the relation to be "extended" that has the same name as the renamed attribute before the renaming)—are needed sufficiently often in practice that it seems worthwhile to introduce an appropriate shorthand. Let us therefore agree to define

`( MATCHING expression )`

(where *expression* is an arbitrary relational expression) to be an expression that is permitted as an argument to an aggregate function reference within an EXTEND, with interpretation as follows. First, let the EXTEND be

`EXTEND R1 ADD agg-fun ( MATCHING R2 ) AS ...`

S#	SNAME	STATUS	CITY	NP
S1	Smith	20	London	6
S2	Jones	10	Paris	2
S3	Blake	30	Paris	1
S4	Clark	20	London	3
S5	Adams	30	Athens	0

FIG. 6.11 Another EXTEND example

Let the set of attributes common to *R1* and *R2* be *Y*. Then the appearance of the subexpression "(MATCHING *R2*)" is defined to be shorthand for the expression

```
( ( R2 RENAME Y AS X ) WHERE X = Y )
```

for some appropriate (but essentially arbitrary) name *X*. With this simplification, the overall expression for the original query becomes just

```
EXTEND S ADD COUNT ( MATCHING SP ) AS NP
```

5. Finally, we can also provide a shorthand for a **multiple EXTEND** operation as suggested by the following example (compare the discussion of multiple renaming in Section 6.2):

```
( EXTEND P ADD CITY AS PCITY, ( WEIGHT * 454 ) AS GMWT )
```

Summarize

As we have seen, the extend operation provides a way of incorporating "horizontal" or "row-wise" computations into the algebra. The **summarize** operation performs the analogous function for "vertical" or "column-wise" computations. For example, the expression

```
SUMMARIZE SP BY ( P# ) ADD SUM ( QTY ) AS TOTQTY
```

evaluates to a relation with heading {P#,TOTQTY}, in which there is one tuple for each distinct P# value in SP, containing that P# value and the corresponding total quantity (see Fig. 6.12). In other words, relation P is conceptually "grouped" into sets of tuples (one set for each distinct value of P#), and then each group is used to generate one tuple in the overall result.*

In terms of the syntax of Fig. 6.2, we are introducing another new kind of *monadic expression,* as follows:

```
SUMMARIZE term BY ( attribute-commalist )
             ADD aggregate-expression AS attribute
```

For example:

```
SUMMARIZE A BY ( A1, A2, ..., An ) ADD exp AS Z
```

Here *A1, A2, . . ., An* are distinct attributes of *A*. The result of the expression (note that it *is* an expression, not a "command" or statement) is a relation with heading {*A1,A2, . . ., An,Z*},[†] and with body consisting of all tuples *t* such that *t* is a tuple of the projection of *A* over *A1, A2, . . . An,* extended with a value for the new attribute *Z;* that new *Z*-value is computed by evaluating the aggregate expression *exp* on all tuples of *A* that have the same values for *A1, A2, . . . An* as tuple *t*. The *attribute-commalist* must not include an attribute called *Z*, and *exp* must not refer to *Z*. Observe that the

---

* In fact, the previous edition of this book (following SQL—see Chapter 8) used the keyword GROUPBY instead of BY, but "GROUPBY" has slightly procedural connotations, and in any case BY is shorter.

† As with EXTEND, the system needs to know the domain for the new attribute *Z*. Again, we defer detailed discussion of such matters to Chapter 19.

P#	TOTQTY
P1	600
P2	1000
P3	400
P4	500
P5	500
P6	100

FIG. 6.12 An example of SUMMARIZE

cardinality of the result is equal to the cardinality of the projection of A over $A1$, $A2, \ldots An$ and the degree of the result is equal to the degree of that projection plus one.

Here is another example, to illustrate the point that the *term* operand of SUMMARIZE can be an arbitrary relational expression enclosed in parentheses:

```
SUMMARIZE ( P JOIN SP ) BY ( CITY ) ADD COUNT AS NSP
```

The result looks like this:

CITY	NSP
London	5
Paris	6
Rome	1

In other words, the result contains one tuple for each of the three part cities (London, Paris, and Rome), showing in each case the number of shipments of parts stored in that city.

The point should be stressed that SUMMARIZE is a far less straightforward operator than EXTEND. Here are some examples that illustrate some of the possible pitfalls.

1. `SUMMARIZE SP BY ( ) ADD SUM ( QTY ) AS GRANDTOTAL`

   In this first example, the summarization is by *no attributes at all*. Assuming for the moment that relation SP does contain at least one tuple, all of those SP tuples "have the same value" for no attributes at all; hence there is just one group, and so just one tuple in the result—in other words, the aggregate computation is performed precisely once for the entire relation. The overall expression thus evaluates to a relation with one attribute and one tuple; the attribute is called GRANDTOTAL, and the single scalar value in the single result tuple is the total of all QTY values in the original SP relation.

   If on the other hand the original SP relation has no tuples at all, then there are no groups, and hence no result tuples—i.e., the result relation is empty too. Thus, a slight weakness of SUMMARIZE is that it cannot be used to obtain an aggregation (e.g., a COUNT) of an empty set.

2. `SUMMARIZE SP BY ( S# ) ADD COUNT AS NP`

The result of this second example looks like this:

S#	NP
S1	6
S2	2
S3	1
S4	3

The reader will observe that the result does *not* include a tuple for supplier S5 (with a count of zero), despite the fact that supplier S5 does indeed supply zero parts. The reason is, of course, that supplier S5 does not appear in relation SP. The overall result is thus at least arguably a little counterintuitive. (Of course, we have already seen a way of producing an analogous result that does include supplier S5. Refer back to the fourth EXTEND example if you need to refresh your memory.)

Incidentally, note that COUNT (unlike the other aggregate functions) requires no argument. In fact, COUNT is strictly unnecessary anyway, since it is equivalent to SUM(1).

3. Consider the query "Get part cities that store more than five red parts":

```
( ( SUMMARIZE ( P WHERE COLOR = 'Red' )
          BY ( CITY ) ADD COUNT AS N ) WHERE N > 5 ) [ CITY  ]
```

Now suppose we change the query to "Get part cities that store five red parts or less." Simply replacing ">" by "≤" in the foregoing expression—

```
( ( SUMMARIZE ( P WHERE COLOR = 'Red' )
          BY ( CITY ) ADD COUNT AS N ) WHERE N ≤ 5 ) [ CITY ]
```

—does *not* produce the correct answer, because it fails to include part cities that store no red parts at all. A correct formulation of this second query would be:

```
P [ CITY ] MINUS xyz
```

where *xyz* is the expression given above for the first query.

Note: The problem illustrated by this example is not actually a problem of SUMMARIZE itself—it is caused by the fact that the SUMMARIZE argument (the restriction of relation P to red parts) already excludes parts that are not red. This fact does not make the result any less counterintuitive, however.

4. Finally, we can also provide a shorthand for a **multiple SUMMARIZE** operation as suggested by the following example (compare the earlier discussions of the multiple renaming and multiple EXTEND operations):

```
( SUMMARIZE SP BY ( P# ) ADD SUM ( QTY ) AS TOTQTY,
                            AVG ( QTY ) AS AVGQTY )
```

We conclude this section with the following two observations.

1. First, we have seen that SUMMARIZE (like DIVIDEBY) gets into difficulties over empty relations. A revised form of the operator, which avoids those difficulties but is unfortunately somewhat more complex than the original operator, is described in the annotation to reference [6.3].

2. As the reader might have realized, SUMMARIZE is not a primitive operator—it can be simulated by means of EXTEND (provided care is taken over the definitions of the aggregate functions; refer to Chapter 7 for further discussion). But SUMMARIZE is a very convenient shorthand.

6.9 Update Operations

It is usual to consider the "relational operators" portion of the relational model as including a **relational assignment** operation in addition to the operations of the relational algebra. In fact, we have already given several examples of such an operation in Section 6.6 above, when we discussed step-at-a-time query formulations (we also gave some examples in Chapter 3). Here is the syntax:

```
target   :=   source ;
```

Here *source* and *target* are relational expressions that evaluate to type-compatible relations (in practice, the *target* will usually be just a named relation, typically a base relation). The *source* is evaluated and the result is assigned to the *target,* replacing the previous value.

The assignment operation makes it possible to "remember" the value of some algebraic expression in the database, and thereby to change the database state—in other words, to *update* the database.* But assignment is somewhat of a sledgehammer operation, inasmuch as it supports only the wholesale replacement of an entire relation value. In practice, of course, some finer-precision update operations are clearly desirable.

Now, the assignment operation theoretically *could* be used as the basis for such finer-precision operations. For example, it would theoretically be possible to perform insertions and deletions as suggested by the following examples:

```
S   :=   S UNION { { < S#      : 'S6'     >,
                     < SNAME  : 'Baker' >,
                     < STATUS :   50      >,
                     < CITY   : 'Madrid' > } } ;

SP  :=   SP MINUS { { < S#  : 'S1' >,
                      < P#  : 'P1' >,
                      < QTY :   300 > } } ;
```

The first of these two assignments inserts a tuple for supplier S6 into relation S, the second deletes the shipment for supplier S1 and part P1 from relation SP. And if we can

---

* The operation also serves as a basis for *retrieval* operations, of course (i.e., queries), as we have seen many times already in this chapter.

simulate INSERT and DELETE operations in this manner, we can obviously simulate UPDATE operations too, by first deleting and then inserting. (Incidentally, notice the use of tuple and relation literals in the examples. Such literals must clearly be supported in any real relational implementation.)

However, using UNION and MINUS in this manner as a substitute for explicit INSERT and DELETE operations is not really satisfactory, because UNION and MINUS do not handle error situations appropriately—that is, UNION and MINUS fail to balk at situations that are customarily treated as errors by INSERT and DELETE. Specifically, UNION will not reject an attempt to insert a tuple that is a duplicate of one that already exists, and MINUS will not reject an attempt to delete a nonexistent tuple. In practice, therefore, a relational system should obviously provide explicit INSERT and DELETE and UPDATE operations as well. So let us propose some appropriate syntax.

- **INSERT:** The **insert** statement takes the form

```
INSERT source INTO target ;
```

  where *source* and *target* are relational expressions that evaluate to type-compatible relations (in practice, the *target* will usually be just a named relation). The *source* is evaluated and all tuples of the result are inserted into the *target*. Here is an example:

```
INSERT ( S WHERE CITY = 'London') INTO TEMP ;
```

  TEMP here is assumed to be type-compatible with relation S.

- **UPDATE:** The **update** statement takes the form

```
UPDATE target assignment-commalist ;
```

  where each *assignment* is of the form

```
attribute := scalar-expression
```

  The *target* is a relational expression, and each *attribute* is an attribute of the relation that results from evaluating that expression. All tuples in the target relation are updated in accordance with the specified *assignments*. Here is an example:

```
UPDATE P WHERE COLOR = 'Red'
       CITY  :=  'Paris' ;
```

  In practice the *target* will often be just a restriction of some named relation, as the example suggests.

- **DELETE:** The **delete** statement takes the form

```
DELETE target ;
```

  The *target* is a relational expression; all tuples in the target relation are deleted. Here is an example:

```
DELETE S WHERE STATUS < 20 ;
```

  As with UPDATE, the *target* will often be just a restriction of some named relation, as the example suggests.

We defer to Chapter 17 discussion of what happens if the *targets* are more complex than those shown in the examples (for all three of INSERT, UPDATE, and DELETE, and indeed for relational assignments in general). However, we stress the point that all of these operations are **set-level**. DELETE, for example, deletes a *set* of tuples from the target relation. Informally, we often talk of (e.g.) updating an individual tuple within a relation, but it must be clearly understood that:

1. We are really talking about updating a *set* of tuples within the relation, a set that just happens to have cardinality one; and

2. Sometimes updating a set of tuples of cardinality one is impossible!

Suppose, for example, that the suppliers relation is subject to the integrity constraint that suppliers S1 and S4 must have the same status. Then any "tuple-level" UPDATE that tries to change the status of just one of those two suppliers must necessarily fail. Instead, both must be updated simultaneously, as in the following example:

```
UPDATE S WHERE S# = 'S1' OR S# = 'S4'
        STATUS  :=  STATUS + 5 ;
```

A Note on the Meaning of Relations

We pointed out in Chapter 4 that every relation has an associated meaning or predicate, and users must pay attention to those predicates in order to use the database sensibly. Note carefully that this remark applies just as much to retrieval as it does to update. However, the question does come to the fore in connection with update, because as explained in Chapter 4 the predicate is the *criterion for update acceptability* for the relation in question—it dictates, for example, whether a particular UPDATE operation will succeed (as indeed we saw in the discussion of UPDATE operations in the example just above).

Now, the predicates for *base* relations are presumed to be known—they consist essentially of whatever integrity constraints (e.g., candidate key constraints, foreign key constraints, probably others as well) are declared for the base relation in question. But what about *derived* relations? Here we clearly need a set of rules, such that if we know the predicate(s) for the input(s) to any relational operation, we can state the predicate for the output from that operation.

It is in fact very easy to find such a set of rules—they follow immediately from the definitions of the operations. For example, if *A* and *B* are any two type-compatible relations and their respective predicates are *PA* and *PB,* then the predicate *PC* for the expression (call it *C*) *A* INTERSECT *B* is obviously (*PA*) AND (*PB*); that is, a tuple *t* will appear in *C* if and only if *PA*(*t*) is *true* and *PB*(*t*) is *true*. So if, for example, we define *C* as a **view** and try to insert tuple *t* into that view, *t* must satisfy the predicate for *A* and the predicate for *B,* or the INSERT will fail. See Chapter 17 for further discussion of updates on views.

Here is another example: The predicate for the relation that results from the *restriction* expression

```
R WHERE condition
```

is (*PR*) AND (*condition*), where *PR* is the predicate for *R*.

Stating the predicates corresponding to the other relational algebra operators is left as an exercise for the reader.

6.10   Relational Comparisons

The relational algebra as originally defined did not include any direct way of comparing two relations (e.g., testing them for equality, or testing to see whether one was a subset of the other). One consequence of this omission is that certain queries were extremely awkward to express (see Exercise 6.48 at the end of this chapter for an illustration and further discussion). However, the omission is easily repaired. First we define a new kind of *condition,* a **relational comparison,** with syntax as follows:

```
expression θ expression
```

Here the two *expressions* are expressions of the relational algebra that evaluate to type-compatible relations, and θ is any of the following comparison operators:

```
= (equals)
≠ (not equals)
≤ (subset of)
< (proper subset of)
≥ (superset of)
> (proper superset of)
```

Note: The choice of operator symbols is perhaps a little unwise, since, e.g., the negation of "*A* is a proper subset of *B*" is certainly not "*A* is a superset of *B*" (i.e., "<" and "≥" are not inverses of each other). However, we will stay with those symbols for the purposes of this book.

Here are some examples:

1. `S [ CITY ] = P [ CITY ]`

   Meaning: Is the projection of suppliers over CITY the same as the projection of parts over CITY?

2. `S [ S# ] > SP [ S# ]`

   Meaning (considerably paraphrased): Are there any suppliers who don't supply any parts?

Next we permit this new kind of condition to be used in **restriction** operations.*
For example:

```
S WHERE ( ( SP RENAME S# AS X ) WHERE X = S# ) [ P# ] = P [  P# ]
```

---

  * Observe, however, that those new conditions are not *restriction conditions* as that term was defined in Section 6.5. In fact, our explanations here are deliberately simplified. What we really need to do is the following. First, we need to permit *relation-valued attributes*—i.e., attributes that contain values that are relations (and we need to do this without violating the requirements of normalization!). Next we need to extend the EXTEND operator so that it can generate such attributes. Then we can use such attributes as comparands in restrictions in the usual way, *without* having to invent something that is not a genuine restriction condition. This whole topic is discussed further in Chapter 19.

This expression evaluates to a relation containing supplier tuples for suppliers who supply all parts. *Explanation:*

■ For a given supplier, the expression

```
( ( SP RENAME S# AS X ) WHERE X = S# ) [ P# ]
```

yields the set of part numbers for parts supplied by that supplier.

■ That set of part numbers is then compared with the set of *all* part numbers. If the two sets are equal, the corresponding supplier tuple appears in the result.

Of course, we can make use of the same MATCHING shorthand introduced in the section on EXTEND, thereby simplifying the overall expression to just

```
S WHERE ( MATCHING SP ) [ P# ] = P [ P# ]
```

Some More Shorthands

One particular relational comparison that is needed very often in practice is a test to see whether a given relation is empty (i.e., contains no tuples). Once again, therefore, it seems worthwhile to introduce a shorthand. Let us therefore define a truth-valued function

```
IS_EMPTY ( expression )
```

which returns *true* if the result of evaluating the relational *expression* argument is empty, and *false* otherwise.

Another common requirement is to be able to test whether a given tuple *t* appears within a given relation *R*. Assuming that we can construct a relation containing just a specified tuple by enclosing the specified tuple in set brackets, the following relational comparison will suffice:

```
{ t } ≤ R
```

However, the following shorthand—which will be very familiar if the reader knows SQL—is a little more user-friendly:

```
t IN R
```

IN here is really the **set membership** operator, usually represented as ∈.

6.11 Summary

We have discussed the **relational algebra**. We began by reemphasizing the importance of **closure** and **nested expressions,** and explained that if we are going to take closure seriously, then we need a set of **attribute name inheritance rules**. In passing, we also mentioned the possibility of **candidate key** inheritance rules.

The original algebra consisted of eight operations—the traditional set operations **union, intersection, difference,** and **product** and the special relational operations **restrict, project, join,** and **divide**. To this original set we added **RENAME, EXTEND,** and **SUMMARIZE**. For certain of these operations the two operands are required to be **type-compatible** (previously called *union*-compatible). We also pointed out that these operations are not all **primitive** (some of them can be defined in terms of others). We then showed how the operations can be combined together into expressions that serve a variety of purposes—**retrieval, update,** and several others. We also very briefly discussed the idea of **transforming** these expressions for **optimization** purposes (but we will discuss this idea in much more detail in Chapter 18). And we considered the possibility of using a **step-at-a-time** approach to deal with complex queries.

The relational model also includes a **relational assignment** operation, which might possibly be used as the basis for update operations. However, explicit **INSERT, UPDATE,** and **DELETE** operations are clearly to be preferred in practice. We stressed the point that these operations are all **set-level,** and we noted also that they must be controlled by the **predicate** for the relation in question. Finally, we discussed the idea of **relational comparisons,** which frequently make queries somewhat easier to express.

Exercises

Exercises 6.13–6.48 ask the reader to formulate some sample queries as relational algebra expressions. (By way of an interesting variation on these "query" exercises, the reader might like to try looking at some of the answers first and stating what the given expression means in English.) Exercises 6.1–6.12, by contrast, are concerned with some slightly more theoretical aspects of the algebra.

6.1 In the body of the chapter we stated that union, intersection, product, and (natural) join are all both commutative and associative. Verify these assertions to your own satisfaction.

6.2 Of Codd's original set of eight algebraic operations, the five operations union, difference, product, restriction, and projection can be considered as primitives. Give definitions of natural join, intersection, and (harder!) division in terms of those primitives.

6.3 Consider the expression A JOIN B. If A and B have disjoint headings (i.e., have no attributes in common), this expression is equivalent to the expression A TIMES B. What is it equivalent to if instead A and B have *identical* headings?

6.4 Show that the five primitive operators mentioned in Exercise 6.2 truly are primitive, in the sense that none of them can be expressed in terms of the other four.

6.5 In ordinary arithmetic, multiplication and division are inverse operations. Are TIMES and DIVIDEBY inverse operations in the relational algebra?

6.6 Given the usual suppliers-and-parts database, what is the value of the expression S JOIN SP JOIN P? *Warning:* There is a trap here.

6.7 Let A be a relation of degree n. How many different projections of A are there?

6.8 In ordinary arithmetic there is a special number, 1, with the property that

```
n * 1 = 1 * n = n
```

for all numbers n. We say that 1 is the **identity** with respect to multiplication. Is there any relation that plays an analogous role in the relational algebra? If so, what is it?

6.9 In ordinary arithmetic there is another special number, 0, with the property that

```
n * 0 = 0 * n = 0
```

for all numbers *n*. Is there any relation that plays an analogous role in the relational algebra? If so, what is it?

6.10 Investigate the effect of the algebraic operations discussed in this chapter on the relations that are the answers to the two previous exercises.

6.11 Let *A* and *B* be two arbitrary relations. State the candidate key(s) for each of the following:

    (a) An arbitrary restriction of *A*

    (b) An arbitrary projection of *A*

    (c) *A* TIMES *B*

    (d) *A* UNION *B*

    (e) *A* INTERSECT *B*

    (f) *A* MINUS *B*

    (g) *A* JOIN *B*

    (h) *A* DIVIDEBY *B*

    (i) An arbitrary extension of *A*

    (j) An arbitrary summarization of *A*

    Assume in each case that *A* and *B* meet the requirements for the operation in question (e.g., they are type-compatible, in the case of UNION).

6.12 In Section 6.2, we said that the relational closure property was important for the same kind of reason that the arithmetic closure property was important. In arithmetic, however, there is one unpleasant situation where the closure property breaks down—namely, division by zero. Is there any analogous situation in the relational algebra?

Query Exercises

The remaining exercises are all based on the suppliers-parts-projects database. In each case you are asked to write either a relational algebra expression or a sequence of relational assignments (whichever you prefer) for the indicated operation. You can make use of relational comparison operations also if you wish. For convenience we repeat the structure of the database (in outline) below:

```
S    ( S#, SNAME, STATUS, CITY )
     PRIMARY KEY ( S# )
P    ( P#, PNAME, COLOR, WEIGHT, CITY )
     PRIMARY KEY ( P# )
J    ( J#, JNAME, CITY )
     PRIMARY KEY ( J# )
SPJ ( S#, P#, J#, QTY )
     PRIMARY KEY ( S#, P#, J# )
     FOREIGN KEY ( S# ) REFERENCES S
     FOREIGN KEY ( P# ) REFERENCES P
     FOREIGN KEY ( J# ) REFERENCES J
```

6.13 Get full details of all projects.

6.14 Get full details of all projects in London.

6.15 Get supplier numbers for suppliers who supply project J1.

6.16 Get all shipments where the quantity is in the range 300 to 750 inclusive.

6.17 Get all part-color/part-city combinations. *Note:* Here and in subsequent exercises, the term "all" is to be taken to mean "all currently represented in the database," not "all possible."

6.18 Get all supplier-number/part-number/project-number triples such that the indicated supplier, part, and project are all colocated.

6.19 Get all supplier-number/part-number/project-number triples such that the indicated supplier, part, and project are not all colocated.

6.20 Get all supplier-number/part-number/project-number triples such that no two of the indicated supplier, part, and project are colocated.

6.21 Get part numbers for parts supplied by a supplier in London.

6.22 Get part numbers for parts supplied by a supplier in London to a project in London.

6.23 Get all pairs of city names such that a supplier in the first city supplies a project in the second city.

6.24 Get part numbers for parts supplied to any project by a supplier in the same city as that project.

6.25 Get project numbers for projects supplied by at least one supplier not in the same city.

6.26 Get all pairs of part numbers such that some supplier supplies both the indicated parts.

6.27 Get the total number of projects supplied by supplier S1.

6.28 Get the total quantity of part P1 supplied by supplier S1.

6.29 For each part being supplied to a project, get the part number, the project number, and the corresponding total quantity.

6.30 Get part numbers of parts supplied to some project in an average quantity of more than 320.

6.31 Get project names for projects supplied by supplier S1.

6.32 Get colors of parts supplied by supplier S1.

6.33 Get part numbers for parts supplied to any project in London.

6.34 Get project numbers for projects using at least one part available from supplier S1.

6.35 Get supplier numbers for suppliers supplying at least one part supplied by at least one supplier who supplies at least one red part.

6.36 Get supplier numbers for suppliers with a status lower than that of supplier S1.

6.37 Get project numbers for projects whose city is first in the alphabetic list of such cities.

6.38 Get project numbers for projects supplied with part P1 in an average quantity greater than the greatest quantity in which any part is supplied to project J1.

6.39 Get supplier numbers for suppliers supplying some project with part P1 in a quantity greater than the average shipment quantity of part P1 for that project.

6.40 Get project numbers for projects not supplied with any red part by any London supplier.

6.41 Get project numbers for projects supplied entirely by supplier S1.

6.42 Get part numbers for parts supplied to all projects in London.

6.43 Get supplier numbers for suppliers who supply the same part to all projects.

6.44 Get project numbers for projects supplied with at least all parts available from supplier S1.

6.45 Get all cities in which at least one supplier, part, or project is located.

6.46 Get part numbers for parts that are supplied either by a London supplier or to a London project.

6.47 Get supplier-number/part-number pairs such that the indicated supplier does not supply the indicated part.

6.48 Get all pairs of supplier numbers, Sx and Sy say, such that Sx and Sy supply exactly the same set of parts each. (Thanks to a correspondent, Fatma Mili of Oakland University, Rochester, Michigan, for this problem.)

References and Bibliography

6.1 E. F. Codd. "A Relational Model of Data for Large Shared Data Banks." *CACM 13,* No. 6 (June 1970). Republished in *Milestones of Research—Selected Papers 1958–1982* (CACM 25th Anniversary Issue), *CACM 26,* No. 1 (January 1983).

Codd's original paper on the relational model included definitions of the following algebraic operations. It is interesting to note that the definitions proposed for *restriction* and *join* were rather different from the definitions usually given today, also that the list of operations included a couple, *tie* and *composition,* that are now rarely considered. We assume throughout what follows that *X, Y, . . .* etc., represent attributes or attribute combinations, as necessary.

■ *Permutation* (i.e., reordering the attributes of a relation, left to right; this operation was intended for use purely at the internal level of the system, since of course the left-to-right ordering of attributes is irrelevant so far as the user is concerned)

■ *Restriction* (given relations $A\{X,Y\}$ and $B\{Y\}$, the paper defines the restriction of A by B to be the maximal subset of A such that $A[Y]$ is a subset—not necessarily a proper subset—of B)

■ *Projection* (more or less as understood today)

■ Several types of *join* (see below)

■ *Tie* (given a relation $A\{X1,X2, . . ., Xn\}$, the *tie* of A is the restriction of A to that subset in which $A[Xn] = A[X1]$—using "restriction" in the sense in which we used that term in the body of this chapter, not in the special sense defined above)

■ *Composition* (given relations $A\{X,Y\}$ and $B\{Y,Z\}$, the composition of A with B is the projection on $\{X,Z\}$ of a join of A on Y with B on $Y;$ our reason for saying "a" join is explained below)

We elaborate slightly on the question of join, as follows. Given relations $A\{X,Y\}$ and $B\{Y, Z\}$, the paper defines a *join* of A with B to be any relation $C\{X,Y,Z\}$ such that $C[X,Y] = A$ and $C[Y, Z] = B$. The natural join (called the *linear* natural join in the paper, in order to distinguish it from another kind of join that the paper refers to as a *cyclic* join) is an important special case, but it is not the only possibility, in general. Note that θ-joins (as opposed to "linear" joins)—i.e., joins involving scalar comparison operators other than "equals"—are not discussed.

6.2 E. F. Codd. "Relational Completeness of Data Base Sublanguages." In *Data Base Systems, Courant Computer Science Symposia Series 6.* Englewood Cliffs, N.J.: Prentice-Hall (1972).

Includes a formal definition of the original version of the relational algebra, which is close to the version discussed in Sections 6.4 and 6.5 of the present chapter. The operators defined are union, intersection, difference, extended (here called *expanded*) Cartesian product, projection, θ-join (and natural join), division, and θ-restriction. The principal differences between the algebra as defined in this paper and the version discussed in the body of the chapter are as follows:

■ *Projection:* The paper permits a given attribute of the original relation to appear any number of times in the result, instead of at most once.

■ *Restriction:* The paper permits an arbitrary scalar comparison between two attribute values (more generally, between two subtuples) of a given tuple but not between an attribute value of such a tuple and a literal.

■ *Attribute naming:* The paper does not consider the question of result attribute names at all. Instead, the attributes of a relation are assumed to be ordered left to right, and hence to be identifiable by their ordinal position.

■ *Other extensions:* The paper does not discuss EXTEND, SUMMARIZE, relational comparisons, or explicit update operations.

Additional commentary on this paper appears in Chapter 7—see reference [7.2] and (especially) Section 7.4.

6.3 Hugh Darwen. Private communication (December 7th, 1992).

Proposes a generalized version of SUMMARIZE that overcomes certain of the problems discussed in Section 6.8. The basic idea is to replace the parenthesized commalist of attributes in the BY clause by a *relational expression:*

```
SUMMARIZE term BY relational-expression
          ADD aggregate-expression AS attribute
```

For example:

```
SUMMARIZE SP BY S [ S# ] ADD COUNT AS NP
```

The result here includes a tuple for supplier S5, with a count of zero. In general, the expression

```
SUMMARIZE A BY B ADD exp AS Z
```

is defined as follows:

- *B* must be type-compatible with some projection of *A* (i.e., every attribute of *B* must be an attribute of *A*). Let the attributes of that projection of *A* be *A1, A2, . . . , An*.
- The heading of the result consists of all attributes of *B* plus the new attribute *Z*.
- The body of the result consists of all tuples *t* such that *t* is a tuple of *B* extended with a value for the new attribute *Z;* that new *Z*-value is computed by evaluating the aggregate expression *exp* on all tuples of *A* that have the same values for *A1, A2, . . . , An* as does tuple *t*.

The crucial difference between this revised SUMMARIZE and the version described in Section 6.8 is that the result has the same cardinality as *B*. Points arising:

- If the set "all tuples of *A* that have the same values for *A1, A2, . . . , An* as does tuple *t*" is empty, the aggregate expression *exp* will be applied to an empty set of values. As explained in the body of the chapter, for COUNT and SUM, the result will be zero; for MAX, it will be "minus infinity" (where "minus infinity" is the smallest value in the applicable domain); for MIN it will be "plus infinity" (analogously defined); and for AVG, an exception will be raised.
- If *B* is not just type-compatible with some projection of *A* but actually *is* such a projection, as in, e.g.,

  ```
  SUMMARIZE SP BY SP [ S# ] ADD COUNT AS NP
  ```

  then we effectively return to the original SUMMARIZE.

Observe in particular that with this revised form of SUMMARIZE, the operation

```
SUMMARIZE SP BY TABLE_DEE ADD SUM ( QTY ) AS GRANDTOTAL
```

will work—i.e., will return the correct answer, *viz.* zero—even if relation SP is empty (contrast the situation with SUMMARIZE as described in the body of the chapter). See Chapter 4 for a discussion of TABLE_DEE.

6.4 Hugh Darwen and C. J. Date. "Into the Great Divide." In C. J. Date and Hugh Darwen, *Relational Database Writings 1989–1991*. Reading, Mass.: Addison-Wesley (1992).

The division operator as defined in Section 6.5 applies only to dividend and divisor relations that satisfy the property that the heading of the divisor is a proper subset of the heading of the dividend. This paper discusses a generalized division operator (due to Stephen Todd) that applies to *any pair of relations whatsoever*. That operator is defined as follows. Given relations $A\{X,Y\}$ and $B\{Y,Z\}$, the expression

```
A DIVIDEBY B
```

yields a relation with the heading $\{X,Z\}$ and a body consisting of all tuples $\{X:x,Z:z\}$ such that a tuple $\{X:x,Y:y\}$ appears in *A* for all tuples $\{Y:y,Z:z\}$ appearing in *B*. For example, suppose we have two relations SP{S#,P#} and PJ{P#,J#}, where SP shows which suppliers supply which parts and PJ shows which parts are used in which projects. Then the expression

```
SP DIVIDEBY PJ
```

yields a relation with heading {S#,J#} showing pairs of supplier numbers and project numbers such that the indicated supplier supplies all parts that are used by the indicated project. Likewise, the expression

```
PJ DIVIDEBY SP
```

yields a relation with heading {J#,S#} showing pairs of project numbers and supplier numbers such that the indicated project uses all parts that are supplied by the indicated supplier.

At least, such was the intent. This paper [6.4] shows that neither Codd's original version of division, nor Todd's generalized version, quite solves the problem it was intended to solve (the characterizations of the two DIVIDEBY expressions above are neither of them totally accurate). It also shows that Todd's divide is not quite an upward-compatible extension of Codd's, and further that if the operator definitions are revised so that they *can* be used to solve the problem they were intended to (see below), then they no longer merit the name "division"!

To explain why DIVIDEBY does not quite solve the problem it was intended to, let us revert to Codd's original version of the operator. Consider the query "Get supplier numbers for suppliers who supply all purple parts." Suppose relation PP, the restriction of the parts relation to just the tuples for purple parts, has already been constructed. Then the query would typically be expressed as follows:

```
SP [ S#, P# ] DIVIDEBY PP [ P# ]
```

Now assume—as is in fact the case with our usual sample data—that there *are* no purple parts, so that relation PP, and hence the projection of that relation PP over P#, are both empty. If there are no purple parts, then *every supplier supplies all of them*—even suppliers, such as S5 in our sample data, who supply no parts at all! But suppliers who supply no parts at all are not represented in relation SP, and hence there is no way the DIVIDEBY expression above can possibly produce a result that includes such suppliers.

We can fix this problem by defining a new "divide per" operator, as follows. Let relations *A, AB,* and *B* have headings {X}, {X,Y}, and {Y}, respectively. Then the division of *A* by *B* per *AB, A* DIVIDEBY *B* PER *AB,* is a relation with heading {X} and body consisting of all tuples {X:x} such that a tuple {X:x,Y:y} appears in *AB* for *all* tuples {Y:y} appearing in *B*—loosely:

```
A.X WHERE FORALL B EXISTS AB ( A.X = AB.X AND AB.Y = B.Y )
```

(see Chapter 7 for an explanation of FORALL and EXISTS). The query "supplier numbers for suppliers who supply all purple parts" can now be simply (and correctly) expressed as

```
S [ S# ] DIVIDEBY PP [ P# ] PER SP [ S#, P# ]
```

This fix solves the problem with Codd's divide; the fix for Todd's divide is analogous. *Note:* It would obviously be possible to extend the definition of "divide per" to allow the headings of *A, B,* and *AB* to be *supersets* of {X}, {Y}, and {X,Y}, respectively. We omit the details here

The reason "divide per" no longer merits the name of division is explained at the end of the answer to Exercise 6.5.

6.5 R. C. Goldstein and A. J. Strnad. "The MacAIMS Data Management System." Proc. 1970 ACM SICFIDET Workshop on Data Description and Access (November 1970).

6.6 A. J. Strnad. "The Relational Approach to the Management of Data Bases." Proc. IFIP Congress, Ljubljana, Yugoslavia (August 1971).

MacAIMS [6.5–6.6] appears to have been the earliest example of a system supporting both *n*-ary relations and a set-level language. The language was algebraic. Two particularly interesting features of the system were the following:

- The storage structure could vary from stored relation to stored relation. Each type of structure was managed by a component called a "relational strategy module," specific to that structure, which hid the storage details of that structure from the rest of the system (and of course from the user).

- Attributes were stored as "data element sets." Each data element (i.e., attribute value) was assigned a unique fixed-length *reference number,* and all references to the data element within any relation were via that reference number. The algorithm for assigning reference numbers was such that, if *a* and *b* belonged to the same data element set, then the reference number for *a* would be greater than that for *b* if and only if *a* was greater than *b*. As a result, any comparison operation between two data elements (from the same data element set) could be made directly on the corresponding reference numbers; moreover, the actual comparison itself was likely to be more efficient, because reference numbers were fixed-length whereas data elements could be variable-length. This point is particularly significant in view of the fact that such comparisons were easily the operations most frequently performed in the internals of the system (as indeed they probably are in any database system).

6.7 M. G. Notley. "The Peterlee IS/1 System." IBM (UK) Scientific Centre Report UKSC-0018 (March 1972).

See the annotation to reference [6.8].

6.8 S. J. P. Todd. "The Peterlee Relational Test Vehicle—A System Overview." *IBM Sys. J. 15,* No. 4 (1976).

The Peterlee Relational Test Vehicle (PRTV) was an experimental system developed at the IBM UK Scientific Centre in Peterlee, England. It was based on an earlier prototype called IS/1 [6.7]. It supported *n*-ary relations and a version of the algebra called ISBL (Information System Base Language), which was based on proposals documented in reference [6.9]. The ideas discussed in the present chapter regarding result attribute names and operators based on matching attribute names can be traced back to ISBL and the proposals of reference [6.9].

Three significant aspects of PRTV were the following:

- It incorporated some sophisticated expression transformation techniques (see Chapter 18).
- It included a delayed evaluation feature, which was important both for optimization and for the support of named virtual relations (i.e., views).
- It provided "function extensibility"—i.e., the ability to extend the system to include an arbitrary set of user-defined computational functions.

6.9 P. A. V. Hall, P. Hitchcock, and S. J. P. Todd. "An Algebra of Relations for Machine Computation." Conference Record of the 2nd ACM Symposium on Principles of Programming Languages, Palo Alto, Calif. (January 1975).

6.10 Antonio L. Furtado and Larry Kerschberg. "An Algebra of Quotient Relations." Proc. 1977 ACM SIGMOD International Conference on Management of Data, Toronto, Canada (August 1977).

Presents a revised relational algebra for operating directly on "quotient relations." Given a relation *R,* a quotient relation can be derived from *R* by grouping tuples on the basis of the values of some attribute of *R* (along the lines of the BY clause in SUMMARIZE, as discussed in Section 6.8 of the present chapter). For example, the quotient relation derived from the supplier relation S on the basis of CITY values is a set of three groups of tuples—one containing two London tuples, one containing two Paris tuples, and one containing a single Athens tuple. The authors claim that operating directly on such quotient relations leads both to more natural query formulation and to a potential for more efficient implementation.

6.11 T. H. Merrett. "The Extended Relational Algebra, A Basis for Query Languages." In *Databases: Improving Usability and Responsiveness* (ed., B. Shneiderman). New York, N.Y.: Academic Press (1978).

Proposes the introduction of *quantifiers* into the algebra—not just the existential and universal quantifiers of the calculus (see Chapter 7), but the more general quantifiers "the number of" and "the proportion of." Such quantifiers would allow the expression of such conditions as "at least three of," "not more than half of," "an odd number of," etc.

6.12 Patrick A. V. Hall. "Relational Algebras, Logic, and Functional Programming." Proc. 1984 ACM SIGMOD International Conference on Management of Data, Boston, Mass. (June 1984).

Presents a functional interpretation of the relational algebra, with the aims (paraphrasing from the paper) of (a) providing a theoretical basis for the so-called "fourth generation languages" (4GLs—see Chapter 2), and (b) integrating functional, logic, and relational languages so that they can share implementation technology. The author claims that, whereas logic programming and databases have been moving toward each other for some time, at the time of writing the functional or applicative languages have paid little heed to database requirements or technology. The paper is therefore presented principally as a contribution toward a rapprochement between the latter two.

6.13 Anthony Klug. "Equivalence of Relational Algebra and Relational Calculus Query Languages Having Aggregate Functions." *JACM 29,* No. 3 (July 1982).

Defines a set of extensions to both the relational algebra and the relational calculus (see Chapter 7) to incorporate aggregate function support—somewhat along the lines of the SUMMARIZE operator of Section 6.8, in the case of the algebra—and demonstrates the equivalence of the two extended languages.

Answers to Selected Exercises

6.2 JOIN is discussed in Section 6.5. INTERSECT can be defined as follows:

```
A INTERSECT B  ≡  A MINUS ( A MINUS B )
```

or

```
A INTERSECT B  ≡  B MINUS ( B MINUS A )
```

These equivalences, though valid, are slightly unsatisfactory, since *A* INTERSECT *B* is symmetric in *A* and *B* and the other two expressions are not. Here by contrast is a symmetric equivalent:

```
( A MINUS ( A MINUS B ) ) UNION ( B MINUS ( B MINUS A ) )
```

Note: Given that *A* and *B* must be type-compatible, we also have:

```
A INTERSECT B  ≡  A JOIN B
```

As for division, assume that *A, B, X,* and *Y* are as in the discussion of DIVIDEBY in Section 6.5. Then:

```
A DIVIDEBY B  ≡  A [ X ] MINUS
                 ( ( A [ X ] TIMES B ) MINUS A ) [ X ]
```

We remark that since JOIN can be defined in terms of TIMES and TIMES is a special case of JOIN, we could regard JOIN as a primitive in place of TIMES.

We remark also that if we were allowed to refer to relation **complements,** we could alternatively regard UNION and INTERSECT as primitives and define MINUS in terms of them. Let us use NOT(*R*) to mean the complement of *R*, i.e., the set of all possible tuples that are type-compatible with *R* but are not in fact tuples of *R*. Then:

```
A MINUS B  ≡  NOT ( ( NOT ( A ) ) UNION ( A INTERSECT B ) )
```

6.3 *A* INTERSECT *B* (see the answer to Exercise 6.2 above).

6.4 We give an intuitive "proof" only.

- Product is the only operator that increases the number of attributes, so it cannot be simulated by any combination of the other operators. Therefore product is primitive.

- Projection is the only operator that reduces the number of attributes, so it cannot be simulated by any combination of the other operators. Therefore projection is primitive.

- Union is the only operator that increases the number of tuples, apart from product, and product increases the number of attributes as well. Let the two relations to be "unioned" be *A* and *B*. Note that *A* and *B* must be type-compatible, and their union has exactly the same attributes as each of them. If we form the *product* of *A* and *B,* and then use projection to reduce the set of attributes in the product to just the set of attributes in *A* (or in *B*), we simply get back to the original relation *A* (or *B*) again. Therefore product cannot be used to simulate union, and union is primitive.

- Difference cannot be simulated via product (because product increases the number of tuples) or union (likewise) or projection (because projection reduces the number of attributes). Nor can it be simulated by restriction, because difference is sensitive to the values appearing in the second relation, whereas restriction cannot be (by virtue of the nature of a restriction condition). Therefore difference is primitive.

- Restriction is the only operator that allows attribute values to be compared with externally specified literals (i.e., values that are not already part of some relation). Therefore restriction is primitive.

6.5 Not quite. DIVIDEBY is perhaps more analogous to *integer* division in ordinary arithmetic (i.e., it ignores the remainder). It is true that if A and B are two relations, then forming the Cartesian product of A and B and then dividing the result by B will take us back to A again:

```
( A TIMES B ) DIVIDEBY B = A
```

However, dividing A by B and then forming the Cartesian product of the result with B will yield a relation that *might* be identical to A, but is more likely to be some proper subset of A:

```
( A DIVIDEBY B ) TIMES B ≤ A
```

Let us agree to refer to this latter fact for the moment as "the pseudoinverse property." Then we can say that the result of dividing A by B is the maximal subset of the projection $A[X]$ (where X is the set of common attributes in A and B) such that the pseudoinverse property holds.

  We remark that an analogous property does *not* hold for the "divide per" operation defined in reference [6.4].

6.6 The trap is that the join involves the CITY attributes as well as the S# and P# attributes (because of the way we defined the JOIN operator). The result looks like this:

S#	SNAME	STATUS	CITY	P#	QTY	PNAME	COLOR	WEIGHT
S1	Smith	20	London	P1	300	Nut	Red	12
S1	Smith	20	London	P4	200	Screw	Red	14
S1	Smith	20	London	P6	100	Cog	Red	19
S2	Jones	10	Paris	P2	400	Bolt	Green	17
S3	Blake	30	Paris	P2	200	Bolt	Green	17
S4	Clark	20	London	P4	200	Screw	Red	14

6.7 2^n. This count includes the *identity* projection (i.e., the projection on all n attributes, which yields a result that is identical to the original relation A) and the *nullary* projection (i.e., the projection on no attributes at all, which yields TABLE_DUM if the original relation A is empty, and TABLE_DEE otherwise).

6.8 Yes, there is such a relation, namely TABLE_DEE. TABLE_DEE (DEE for short) is the analog of 1 with respect to multiplication in ordinary arithmetic because

```
R TIMES DEE = DEE TIMES R = R
```

for all relations R. In other words, DEE is the **identity** with respect to TIMES (and indeed with respect to JOIN also).

6.9 There is no relation that behaves with respect to TIMES in a way that is *exactly* analogous to the way that 0 behaves with respect to multiplication. However, the behavior of TABLE_DUM (DUM for short) is somewhat reminiscent of the behavior of 0, inasmuch as

```
R TIMES DUM = DUM TIMES R = an empty relation with
                            the same heading as R
```

for all relations R.

6.10 First, the only relations that are compatible with DEE and DUM for the purposes of union, intersection, and difference are DEE and DUM themselves. We have:

UNION	DEE DUM
DEE	DEE DEE
DUM	DEE DUM

INTERSECT	DEE DUM
DEE	DEE DUM
DUM	DUM DUM

MINUS	DEE DUM
DEE	DUM DEE
DUM	DUM DUM

In the case of difference, the first operand is shown at the left of the table and the second at the top (for the other operators, of course, the operands are interchangeable). Notice how reminiscent these tables are of the truth tables for OR, AND, and AND NOT, respectively; of course, the resemblance is not a coincidence.

Turning now to restrict and project, we have:

- Any restriction of DEE yields DEE if the restriction condition is *true*, DUM if it is *false*.
- Any restriction of DUM yields DUM.
- Projection of any relation over no attributes yields DUM if the original relation is empty, DEE otherwise. In particular, projection of DEE or DUM, necessarily over no attributes at all, returns its input.

The following remarks on division assume Todd's generalized form of the division operator as discussed in reference [6.4]:

- Any relation *R* divided by DEE yields *R*.
- Any relation *R* divided by DUM yields an empty relation with the same heading as *R*.
- DEE divided by any relation *R* yields *R*.
- DUM divided by any relation *R* yields an empty relation with the same heading as *R*.
- Any nonempty relation divided by itself yields DEE. An empty relation divided by itself yields DUM.

Extend and summarize:

- Extending DEE or DUM to add a new attribute yields a relation of one attribute and the same number of tuples as its input.
- Summarizing DEE or DUM (necessarily by no attributes at all) yields a relation of one attribute and the same number of tuples as its input.

6.11 We are concerned here (of course) with "time-independent" candidate keys. With that caveat in mind, we offer the following as a "first cut' set of answers (but see the note at the end).

(a) Any restriction of *A* inherits all of the candidate keys of *A*.

(b) If the projection includes any candidate key *K* of *A*, then *K* is a candidate key for the projection. Otherwise the only candidate key is the combination of all attributes of the projection.

(c) Every combination *K* of a candidate key *KA* of *A* and a candidate key *KB* of *B* is a candidate key for the product *A* TIMES *B*.

(d) The only candidate key for the union *A* UNION *B* is the combination of all attributes.

(e) Left as an exercise for the reader (intersection is not a primitive).

(f) Every candidate key of *A* is a candidate key for the difference *A* MINUS *B*.

(g) We leave the general case as an exercise for the reader (natural join is not a primitive). However, we remark that in the particular case where the joining attribute in *A* is a candidate key of *A*, every candidate key of *B* is a candidate key for the join.

(h) Left as an exercise for the reader (division is not a primitive).

(i) The candidate keys for an arbitrary extension of *A* are the same as the candidate keys of *A*.

(j) The only candidate key for an arbitrary summarization of *A* is the set of attributes specified in the BY clause.

However, many of the foregoing statements can be refined somewhat in certain situations. For example:

- The combination {S#,P#,J#} is *not* a candidate key for the restriction SPJ WHERE S# = 'S1'—rather, the combination {P#,J#} is

- If relation *A* has heading {*X,Y,Z*} and sole candidate key *X* and satisfies the "functional dependency" $Y \rightarrow Z$ (see Chapter 9), then *Y* is a candidate key for the projection of *A* over *Y* and *Z*

- If *A* and *B* are both restrictions of some relation *C*, then every candidate key of *C* is a candidate key of *A* UNION *B*

And so on. The whole question of candidate key inheritance is discussed in some detail in reference [9.6] in Chapter 9.

6.12 No!

6.13 J

6.14 J WHERE CITY = 'London'

6.15 (SPJ WHERE J# = 'J1') [S#]

6.16 SPJ WHERE QTY ≥ 300 AND QTY ≤ 750

6.17 P [COLOR, CITY]

6.18 (S JOIN P JOIN J) [S#, P#, J#]

6.19 (((S RENAME CITY AS SCITY) TIMES
        (P RENAME CITY AS PCITY) TIMES
        (J RENAME CITY AS JCITY))
    WHERE SCITY ≠ PCITY
    OR   PCITY ≠ JCITY
    OR   JCITY ≠ SCITY) [S#, P#, J#]

6.20 (((S RENAME CITY AS SCITY) TIMES
        (P RENAME CITY AS PCITY) TIMES
        (J RENAME CITY AS JCITY))
    WHERE SCITY ≠ PCITY
    AND   PCITY ≠ JCITY
    AND   JCITY ≠ SCITY) [S#, P#, J#]

6.21 (SPJ JOIN (S WHERE CITY = 'London')) [P#]

6.22 ((SPJ JOIN (S WHERE CITY = 'London')) [P#, J#]
                JOIN (J WHERE CITY = 'London')) [P#]

6.23 ((S RENAME CITY AS SCITY) JOIN SPJ JOIN
        (J RENAME CITY AS JCITY)) [SCITY, JCITY]

6.24 (J JOIN SPJ JOIN S) [P#]

6.25 (((J RENAME CITY AS JCITY) JOIN SPJ JOIN
        (S RENAME CITY AS SCITY))
                        WHERE JCITY ≠ SCITY) [J#]

6.26 (((SPJ [S#, P#] RENAME S# AS XS#, P# AS XP#))
    TIMES
    ((SPJ [S#, P#] RENAME S# AS YS#, P# AS YP#)))
                    WHERE XS# = YS#
                    AND   XP# < YP#) [XP#, YP#]

6.27 (SUMMARIZE ((SPJ WHERE S# = 'S1') [J#]) BY ( )
                            ADD COUNT AS N) [N]

As pointed out in Section 6.8, this expression will unfortunately *not* return zero (more precisely, a relation of one attribute and one tuple, containing the single value zero) if supplier S1 supplies no projects at all; rather, it will return an empty relation. The following solution is therefore preferable:

```
( EXTEND ( S WHERE S# = 'S1' )
  ADD COUNT ( ( MATCHING SPJ ) [ P# ] ) AS N ) [ N ]
```

6.28
```
( SUMMARIZE ( SPJ WHERE S# = 'S1' AND P# = 'P1' ) BY ( )
                        ADD SUM ( QTY ) AS Q ) [ Q ]
```

The following solution is preferable (why, exactly?). Note the syntax of the SUM argument; see Chapter 7 for an explanation.

```
( EXTEND ( S WHERE S# = 'S1')
  ADD SUM ( ( MATCHING SPJ ) WHERE P# = 'P1', QTY )
                                        AS Q ) [ Q ]
```

6.29
```
SUMMARIZE SPJ BY ( P#, J# ) ADD SUM ( QTY ) AS Q
```

6.30
```
( ( SUMMARIZE SPJ BY ( P#, J# )
                  ADD AVG ( QTY ) AS Q )
                           WHERE Q > 320 ) [ P# ]
```

6.31
```
( J JOIN ( SPJ WHERE S# = 'S1' ) ) [ JNAME ]
```

6.32
```
( P JOIN ( SPJ WHERE S# = 'S1' ) ) [ COLOR ]
```

6.33
```
( SPJ JOIN ( J WHERE CITY = 'London' ) ) [ P# ]
```

6.34
```
( SPJ JOIN ( SPJ WHERE S# = 'S1' ) [ P# ] ) [ J# ]
```

6.35
```
( ( ( SPJ JOIN ( P WHERE COLOR = 'Red' ) [ P# ] )
              [ S# ] JOIN SPJ ) [ P# ] JOIN SPJ ) [ S# ]
```

6.36
```
( ( S [ S#, STATUS ] RENAME S# AS XS#, STATUS AS XSTATUS )
  TIMES
  ( S [ S#, STATUS ] RENAME S# AS YS#, STATUS AS YSTATUS ) )
  WHERE XS# = 'S1' AND XSTATUS > YSTATUS ) [ YS# ]
```

6.37
```
J [ J# ] MINUS
  ( ( J [ J#, CITY ] RENAME CITY AS XCITY )
          TIMES J [ CITY ] ) WHERE XCITY > CITY ) [ J# ]
```

6.38
```
( ( ( SUMMARIZE ( SPJ WHERE P# = 'P1' ) BY ( J# )
                        ADD AVG ( QTY ) AS QX )
      TIMES
      ( SUMMARIZE ( SPJ WHERE J# = 'J1' ) BY ( )
                        ADD MAX ( QTY ) AS QY ) [ QY ] )
      WHERE QX > QY ) [ J# ]
```

Note: The foregoing expression does not adequately handle the case in which there are no shipments for project J1. The following solution might therefore be preferable:

```
( EXTEND ( SPJ WHERE P# = 'P1' )
  ADD AVG ( ( SPJ RENAME J# AS ZJ# )
          WHERE ZJ# = J# AND P# = 'P1', QTY ) AS QX )
                                        [ J#, QX ]
  TIMES
( EXTEND ( SPJ WHERE J# = 'J1' )
  ADD MAX ( ( SPJ WHERE J# = 'J1', QTY ) AS QY ) [ QY ] )
  WHERE QX > QY ) [ J# ]
```

6.39 (((((SPJ WHERE P# = 'P1') [S#, J#, QTY])

RENAME J# AS XJ#, QTY AS XQ)

TIMES

(SUMMARIZE (SPJ WHERE P# = 'P1') BY (J#)

ADD AVG (QTY) AS Q))

WHERE XJ# = J# AND XQ > Q) [S#]

6.40 J [J#] MINUS

((S WHERE CITY = 'London') [S#]

JOIN SPJ JOIN (P WHERE COLOR = 'Red')) [J#]

6.41 J [J#] MINUS (SPJ WHERE S# ≠ 'S1') [J#]

6.42 (P WHERE (MATCHING SPJ) [J#] ≥

(J WHERE CITY = 'London') [J#]) [P#]

6.43 (SPJ [S#, P#, J#] DIVIDEBY J [J#]) [S#]

Note: The foregoing solution assumes that relation SPJ is nonempty.

6.44 (J WHERE (MATCHING SPJ) [P#] ≥

(SPJ WHERE S# = 'S1') [P#]) [J#]

6.45 S [CITY] UNION P [CITY] UNION J [CITY]

6.46 (SPJ JOIN (S WHERE CITY = 'London')) [P#]

UNION

(SPJ JOIN (J WHERE CITY = 'London')) [P#]

6.47 (S TIMES P) [S#, P#] MINUS SP [S#, P#]

6.48 We show two solutions to this problem. The first, which is due to Hugh Darwen, uses only the operators of Sections 6.3–6.5; for clarity, we give it in step-at-a-time form, with comments.

```
T1   :=  ( SP RENAME S# AS SA ) [ SA, P# ] ;
         /* T1 {SA,P#} : SA supplies part P# */

T2   :=  ( SP RENAME S# AS SB ) [ SB, P# ] ;
         /* T2 {SB,P#} : SB supplies part P# */

T3   :=  T1 [ SA ] ;
         /* T3 {SA} : SA supplies some part */

T4   :=  T2 [ SB ] ;
         /* T4 {SB} : SB supplies some part */

T5   :=  T1 TIMES T4 ;
         /* T5 {SA,SB,P#} : SA supplies some part and
                           SB supplies part P# */

T6   :=  T2 TIMES T3 ;
         /* T6 {SA,SB,P#} : SB supplies some part and
                           SA supplies part P# */

T7   :=  T1 JOIN T2 ;
         /* T7 {SA,SB,P#} : SA and SB both supply part P# */

T8   :=  T3 TIMES T4 ;
         /* T8 {SA,SB} : SA supplies some part and
                         SB supplies some part */

T9   :=  SP [ P# ] ;
         /* T9 {P#} : part P# is supplied by some supplier */
```

```
T10  :=  T8 TIMES T9 ;
         /* T10 {SA,SB,P#} :
            SA supplies some part,
            SB supplies some part, and
            part P# is supplied by some supplier */

T11  :=  T10 MINUS T7 ;
         /* T11 {SA,SB,P#} : part P# is supplied,
                             but not by both SA and SB */

T12  :=  T6 INTERSECT T11 ;
         /* T12 {SA,SB,P#} : part P# is supplied by SA
                             but not by SB */

T13  :=  T5 INTERSECT T11 ;
         /* T13 {SA,SB,P#} : part P# is supplied by SB
                             but not by SA */

T14  :=  T12 [ SA, SB ] ;
         /* T14 {SA,SB} :
            SA supplies some part not supplied by SB */

T15  :=  T13 [ SA, SB ] ;
         /* T15 {SA,SB} :
            SB supplies some part not supplied by SA */

T16  :=  T14 UNION T15 ;
         /* T16 {SA,SB} : some part is supplied by SA or SB
                          but not both */

T17  :=  T7 [ SA, SB ] ;
         /* T17 {SA,SB} :
            some part is supplied by both SA and SB */

T18  :=  T17 MINUS T16 ;
         /* T18 {SA,SB} :
            some part is supplied by both SA and SB,
            and no part supplied by SA is not supplied by SB,
            and no part supplied by SB is not supplied by SA
            — so SA and SB each supply exactly the same parts */

T19  :=  T18 WHERE SA < SB ;
         /* tidy-up step */
```

The second solution—which is much more straightforward!—makes use of the relational comparisons introduced in Section 6.10. Let RA denote relation S with attribute S# renamed as SA, projected over that renamed attribute, and let RB be defined analogously. Then the required result is given by

```
( RA TIMES RB )
  WHERE ( SP WHERE S# = SA ) [ P# ] =
        ( SP WHERE S# = SB ) [ P# ]
  AND   SA < SB
```

The purpose of the final restriction—"SA < SB"—in both solutions is simply to produce a slightly tidier result. Specifically, (a) it eliminates pairs of the form (S*a*,S*a*), and (b) it ensures that the pairs (S*a*,S*b*) and (S*b*,S*a*) do not both appear.

7 | Relational Operators II: Relational Calculus

7.1 Introduction

In Chapter 6 we said that the operators part of the relational model was based on the relational algebra, but we might equally well have said it was based on the relational *calculus*. In other words, the algebra and the calculus are alternatives to one another. The principal distinction between them is as follows: Whereas the algebra provides a collection of explicit operations—join, union, projection, etc.—that can be used to tell the system how actually to *build* some desired relation from the given relations in the database, the calculus merely provides a notation for formulating the *definition* of that desired relation in terms of those given relations. For example, consider the query "Get supplier numbers and cities for suppliers who supply part P2." An algebraic version of this query might look somewhat as follows (we deliberately do not use the formal syntax of Chapter 6):

- First, form the natural join of relations S and SP on S#.
- Next, restrict the result of that join to tuples for part P2.
- Finally, project the result of that restriction over S# and CITY.

A calculus formulation, by contrast, might look something like this:

- Get S# and CITY for suppliers such that there exists a shipment SP with the same S# value and with P# value P2.

Here the user has merely stated the defining characteristics of the desired result, and has left it to the system to decide exactly what joins, projections, etc., must be executed in order to construct that result. Thus, we might say that—at least superficially—the calculus formulation is *descriptive* where the algebraic one is *prescriptive:* The calculus simply describes what the problem *is,* the algebra prescribes a procedure for *solving* that problem. Or, *very* informally: The algebra is procedural (admittedly high-level, but still procedural); the calculus is nonprocedural.

However, we stress the point that the foregoing distinctions *are* only superficial. The fact is, *the algebra and the calculus are precisely equivalent to one another.* For every expression of the algebra, there is an equivalent expression in the calculus; likewise, for every expression of the calculus, there is an equivalent expression in the algebra. There is a one-to-one correspondence between the two. The different formalisms simply represent different styles of expression—the calculus is arguably closer to natural language, the algebra is perhaps more like a programming language. But, to repeat, all such distinctions are more apparent than real; in particular, neither approach is genuinely more nonprocedural than the other. We will examine this question of the equivalence between the two approaches in more depth in Section 7.4.

Now, relational calculus is founded on a branch of mathematical logic called the *predicate* calculus. The idea of using predicate calculus as the basis for a database language appears to have originated in a paper by Kuhns [7.8]. The concept of a *relational* calculus—i.e., an applied predicate calculus specifically tailored to relational databases—was first proposed by Codd in reference [7.2]; a language explicitly based on that calculus called "Data Sublanguage ALPHA" was also presented by Codd in another paper [7.3]. ALPHA itself was never implemented, but a language called QUEL [7.7,7.12-7.14], which certainly was implemented and for some time was a serious competitor to SQL, was very similar to it—indeed, the design of QUEL was much influenced by ALPHA.

A fundamental feature of the calculus as defined in reference [7.2] is the notion of the **tuple variable** (also known as a **range variable**). Briefly, a tuple variable is a variable that "ranges over" some relation—i.e., a variable whose only permitted values are tuples of that relation. In other words, if tuple variable *T* ranges over relation *R,* then, at any given time, *T* represents some tuple *t* of *R*. For example, the query "Get supplier numbers for suppliers in London" can be expressed in QUEL as follows:

```
RANGE OF SX IS S
RETRIEVE ( SX.S# ) WHERE SX.CITY = "London"
```

The tuple variable here is SX, and it ranges over relation S (the RANGE statement is a *definition* of that variable). The RETRIEVE statement can be paraphrased: "For each possible value of the variable SX, retrieve the S# component of that value, if and only if the CITY component has the value London."

Because of its reliance on tuple variables (and to distinguish it from the domain calculus—see below), the original relational calculus has come to be known as the **tuple calculus**. The tuple calculus is described in detail in Section 7.2.

In reference [7.9], Lacroix and Pirotte proposed an alternative version of the calculus called the **domain calculus**, in which tuple variables are replaced by **domain variables**—i.e., variables that range over a domain instead of a relation. A language called ILL based on the domain calculus is presented by the same authors in reference [7.10]. Other examples of domain calculus languages are FQL [7.11], DEDUCE [7.1], and (arguably) Query-By-Example, QBE [7.15]. Of these languages, QBE is probably the best known, and several commercial QBE implementations exist. We sketch the domain calculus in Section 7.6; QBE is discussed briefly in the annotation to reference [7.15].

Note: In an attempt to keep this chapter a little shorter than Chapter 6, we deliberately omit detailed discussion of relational assignment, relational comparisons, and update operations. All of these items could be grafted on to the relational calculus (tuple or domain version) in a fairly obvious manner.

7.2 Tuple-Oriented Relational Calculus

As with the algebra in Chapter 6, we introduce a concrete syntax for the relational calculus in order to provide a basis for the discussions that follow in the rest of the chapter. The syntax is defined by the BNF grammar of Fig. 7.1. *Note:* Square brackets "[" and "]" are used in that grammar not as symbols of the language being defined, but rather to indicate that the material they enclose can optionally be omitted.

```
range-variable-definition
    ::=    RANGE OF variable IS range-item-commalist ;

range-item
    ::=    relation | expression

expression
    ::=    ( target-item-commalist ) [ WHERE wff ]

target-item
    ::=    variable | variable . attribute [ AS attribute ]

wff
    ::=    condition
        | NOT wff
        | condition AND wff
        | condition OR wff
        | IF condition THEN wff
        | EXISTS variable ( wff )
        | FORALL variable ( wff )
        | ( wff )
```

FIG. 7.1   A BNF grammar for the tuple calculus

Some Notes on the Grammar

1. Refer back to Chapter 4 (Section 4.3) for an explanation of the "commalist" convention.

2. The categories *relation, variable,* and *attribute* are each defined to be *identifiers* (a terminal category with respect to this grammar). They represent a relation name, a tuple variable name, and an attribute name, respectively.

3. The category *condition* represents either a WFF enclosed in parentheses (see below for an explanation of WFFs) or a simple scalar comparison of the form

comparand θ *comparand*

Here "θ" is any of the usual scalar comparison operators (=, ≠, >, ≥, etc.), and each *comparand* is either (a) a scalar literal or (b) an attribute value, represented by an attribute reference of the form *variable.attribute* (sometimes called a "qualified attribute name").

   Note: In a system that supports a truth-valued data type, a *condition* might also consist of just a reference to an attribute, or a literal, of that data type.

4. The category *wff* represents a "well-formed formula" (WFF, pronounced "weff"). WFFs are discussed in detail in the following subsections. *Note:* We adopt the usual conventions for dropping unnecessary parentheses from WFFs. We omit the details here.

Tuple Variables

A **tuple** (or **range**) **variable** is defined by means of a statement of the form

```
RANGE OF T IS X1, X2, ..., Xn ;
```

where *T* is the tuple variable being defined, and each *Xi* ($i = 1, 2, \ldots, n$) is either a relation name or a tuple calculus expression. Let *Xi* evaluate to relation *Ri* ($i = 1, 2, \ldots, n$). Relations *R1, R2, . . . , Rn* must be type-compatible in the sense of Chapter 6; that is, they must have *identical headings*. Then tuple variable *T* ranges over the union of those relations—i.e., its value at any given time is some tuple currently appearing within at least one of those relations. Of course, if the commalist of expressions identifies just one named relation *R* (this is the normal case), then the tuple variable *T* ranges over just the tuples currently appearing in that single relation *R*.

   Here are examples of both the normal case and the "union" case:

```
RANGE OF SX  IS S ;
RANGE OF SPX IS SP ;
RANGE OF SY  IS ( SX ) WHERE SX.CITY = 'London',
                ( SX ) WHERE EXISTS SPX ( SPX.S# = SX.S# AND
                                          SPX.P# = 'P1' ) ;
```

The tuple variable SY ranges over the set of S tuples for suppliers who either are located in London or supply part P1 (or both). See later for further explanation.

   Note: In the interests of historical accuracy, we observe that the calculus as originally defined in reference [7.2] did not include tuple variables that ranged over anything other than a single named relation. As a consequence, the original calculus did not support UNION, nor—much more important!—did it support the (effective) ability to create nested expressions.

   Throughout the rest of this chapter, we assume that the following range variable definitions are in effect:

```
RANGE OF SX IS S ;
RANGE OF SY IS S ;
RANGE OF SZ IS S ;
```

```
RANGE OF PX IS P ;
RANGE OF PY IS P ;
RANGE OF PZ IS P ;

RANGE OF SPX IS SP ;
RANGE OF SPY IS SP ;
RANGE OF SPZ IS SP ;
```

We remark that in a real calculus-based language there would have to be some rules regarding the *scope* of such range variable names. We ignore such matters in the present chapter.

Free and Bound Variables

Each occurrence of a tuple variable within a WFF is either **free** or **bound**. We explain this notion in purely syntactic terms first, with examples, then go on to discuss its significance afterwards.

By *occurrence of a tuple variable within a WFF*, we mean an appearance of the variable *name* within the WFF under consideration. A tuple variable T occurs within a given WFF either (a) in the context of an attribute reference of the form $T.A$ (where A is an attribute of the relation over which T ranges) or (b) as the variable immediately following one of the **quantifiers** EXISTS and FORALL (quantifiers are explained in the next subsection below). Here then are the rules governing whether a given tuple variable occurrence ("occurrence" for short) is free or bound:

1. Within a simple comparison such as "$T.A < U.A$," all occurrences are free.
2. Occurrences in the WFFs "(f)" and "NOT f" are free or bound according as they are free or bound in f. Occurrences in the WFFs "f AND g," "f OR g," and "IF f THEN g" are free or bound according as they are free or bound in f or g, as applicable.
3. Occurrences of T that are free in f are bound in the WFFs "EXISTS $T(f)$" and "FORALL $T(f)$." Other occurrences in f are free or bound in these WFFs according as they are free or bound in f.

Examples:

■ Simple comparisons:

```
SX.S# = 'S1'
SX.S# = SPX.S#
SPX.P# ≠ PX.P#
```

All occurrences of SX, PX, and SPX are free in these examples.

■ Boolean WFFs:

```
PX.WEIGHT < 15 OR PX.WEIGHT > 25
NOT ( SX.CITY = 'London' )
SX.S# = SPX.S# AND SPX.P# ≠ PX.P#
IF PX.COLOR = 'Red' THEN PX.CITY = 'London'
```

Again, all occurrences of SX, PX, and SPX here are free.

■   Quantified WFFs:

```
EXISTS SPX ( SPX.S# = SX.S# AND SPX.P# = 'P2' )
FORALL PX ( PX.COLOR = 'Red' )
```

See the next subsection below for an explanation of these two examples.

Quantifiers

There are two quantifiers, EXISTS and FORALL. Basically, if f is a WFF in which variable x is free, then

```
EXISTS x ( f )
```

and

```
FORALL x ( f )
```

are both legal WFFs, and x is bound in both of them. The first means: **There exists at least one value** of the variable x such that the WFF f evaluates to *true*. The second means: **For all values** of the variable x, the WFF f evaluates to *true*. For example, suppose the variable x ranges over the set "Members of the US Senate in 1993," and suppose f is the WFF "x is female".* Then "EXISTS x (f)" is a legal WFF, and it evaluates to *true;* and "FORALL x (f)" is also a legal WFF, and it evaluates to *false*.

We now examine the quantifiers a little more carefully. First we consider the **existential** quantifier EXISTS. Here again is the EXISTS example from the end of the previous subsection:

```
EXISTS SPX ( SPX.S# = SX.S# AND SPX.P# = 'P2' )
```

This WFF can be read as follows:

There exists an SP tuple, SPX say, such that the S# value in that tuple is equal to the value of SX.S#—whatever that is—and the P# value in that tuple is equal to P2.

Each occurrence of SPX in this example is bound. The single occurrence of SX is free.

We define EXISTS formally as *an iterated OR*. In other words, if (a) R is a relation with tuples $T1, T2, \ldots, Tm$, (b) T is a tuple variable that ranges over that relation, and (c) $f(T)$ is a WFF in which T occurs as a free variable, then the WFF

```
EXISTS T ( f ( T ) )
```

is defined to be equivalent to the WFF

```
false OR ( f ( T1 ) ) OR ... OR ( f ( Tm ) )
```

Observe in particular that this expression evaluates to *false* if R is empty.

Example: Let relation R contain the following tuples:

---

* The observant reader will notice that, strictly, this is not a legal WFF according to the syntax of Fig. 7.1. However, it is a trivial matter to convert it into a legal WFF.

```
( 1, 2, 3 )
( 1, 2, 4 )
( 1, 3, 4 )
```

For simplicity, let us assume that tuple components can be identified by their ordinal position, so that we can refer to them by subscripted references of the form $T[i]$. Then the following expressions have the indicated values:

```
EXISTS T ( T[3] > 1 )                 : true
EXISTS T ( T[2] > 3 )                 : false
EXISTS T ( T[1] > 1 OR T[3] = 4 ) : true
```

Turning now to the **universal** quantifier FORALL, here to repeat is the FORALL example from the end of the previous subsection:

```
FORALL PX ( PX.COLOR = 'Red' )
```

This WFF can be read as follows:

For all P tuples, PX say, the COLOR value in that tuple is Red.

The two occurrences of PX in this example are both bound.

Just as we define EXISTS as an iterated OR, so we define FORALL as *an iterated AND*. In other words, if R, T, and $f(T)$ are as in our discussion of EXISTS above, then the WFF

```
FORALL T ( f ( T ) )
```

is defined to be equivalent to the WFF

```
true AND ( f ( T1 ) ) AND ... AND ( f ( Tm ) )
```

Observe that this expression evaluates to *true* if R is empty.

Example: If relation R contains the same tuples as before, then the following expressions have the indicated values:

```
FORALL T ( T[1] > 1 )                 : false
FORALL T ( T[2] > 1 )                 : true
FORALL T ( T[1] = 1 AND T[3] > 2 ) : true
```

Note: FORALL is included in the calculus purely for convenience; it is not essential—the identity

```
FORALL x ( f ) ≡ NOT EXISTS x ( NOT f )
```

(loosely, "all x's satisfy f" is the same as "no x's do not satisfy f") shows that any WFF involving FORALL can always be replaced by an equivalent WFF involving EXISTS instead. For example, the (true) statement

"For all integers x, there exists an integer y such that $y > x$"

is equivalent to the statement

"There does not exist an integer x such that there does not exist an integer y such that $y > x$"

But it is usually easier to think in terms of FORALL than in terms of EXISTS and a double negative; in other words, it is desirable in practice to support both quantifiers.

More on Free and Bound Variables

Suppose variable x ranges over the set of all integers, and consider the WFF

```
EXISTS x ( x > 3 )
```

The bound variable x in this WFF is a kind of *dummy*—it serves only to link the expression inside the parentheses to the quantifier outside. The WFF simply states that there exists some integer, say x, that is greater than three. *Observe, therefore, that the meaning of this WFF would remain totally unchanged if all occurrences of x were replaced by occurrences of some other variable y.* In other words, the WFF

```
EXISTS y ( y > 3 )
```

is semantically identical to the one above.

Now consider the WFF

```
EXISTS x ( x > 3 ) AND x < 0
```

Here there are three occurrences of x, *referring to two different variables*. The first two occurrences are bound, and could be replaced by some other variable y without changing the overall meaning of the WFF. The third occurrence is free, and *cannot* be replaced with impunity. Thus, of the two WFFs below, the first is equivalent to the one just shown and the second is not:

```
EXISTS y ( y > 3 ) AND x < 0
EXISTS y ( y > 3 ) AND y < 0
```

Note, moreover, that the truth value of the original WFF cannot be determined without knowing the value of the free variable x. By contrast, a WFF in which all variables are bound is *true* or *false,* unequivocally. *More terminology:* A WFF in which all variables are bound is called a **closed WFF.** An **open WFF** is a WFF that is not closed, i.e., one that contains at least one free variable.

Target Item Commalists

Each **target item** in a target item commalist is either a simple variable name such as T (see below) or an expression of the form

```
T.A [ AS X ]
```

Here T is a tuple variable, A is an attribute of the associated relation (remember that, in general, the "associated relation" is the union of a set of type-compatible relations represented by tuple calculus expressions—see below), and X is an attribute name for the corresponding attribute in the result of evaluating the target item commalist (again, see below). Note that the "AS X" portion can be omitted; if it is, the corresponding attribute of the result inherits its name in the obvious way (the inherited name would be A in the case above). A new name *must* be specified if the target item commalist would otherwise include any duplicate attribute names.

A target item that is just a variable name *T* is defined to be shorthand for the commalist of target items

```
T.A1, T.A2, ..., T.An
```

where *A1, A2, . . . , An* are all of the attributes of the relation associated with *T*.
Examples:

```
SX.S#
SX.S# AS SNO
SX
SX.S#, SX.CITY AS SCITY, PX.P#, PX.CITY AS PCITY
```

Strictly speaking, a target item commalist has meaning only in the context of a containing tuple calculus expression. In outline, however, what happens in evaluating such an expression is the following: Let the tuple variables specified within the specified target item commalist be *T, U, . . . , V*. Let the corresponding relations (i.e., the relations over which the tuple variables range) be *TR, UR, . . . , VR*, respectively. Let the result attributes have names (explicitly specified or inherited) *X1, X2, . . . , Xr*. Then:

1. First, the extended Cartesian product *TR* TIMES *UR* TIMES . . . TIMES *VR* is constructed.

2. Second, tuples that do not satisfy the WFF in the WHERE clause (if any) are eliminated from the result of Step 1.

3. Finally, the result from Step 2 is projected over the attributes *X1, X2, . . . , Xr*.

Expressions

A tuple calculus expression is an expression of the form

```
( target-item-commalist ) [ WHERE f ]
```

in which every free variable in *f* (if any) must be mentioned in the target item commalist. As explained above, the value of this expression is defined to be a projection of that subset of the extended Cartesian product *TR* TIMES *UR* TIMES . . . TIMES *VR* for which *f* evaluates to *true*—or, if "WHERE *f* " is omitted, a projection of that entire Cartesian product. The projection in question is taken over the attributes *X1, X2, . . . , Xr*, where the *Xi*'s are as defined above. *Note:* We will frequently make use of a convenient shorthand by which the parentheses enclosing the target item commalist can optionally be dropped if that commalist contains exactly one target item.
Examples:

```
( SX.S# )
( SX.S# ) WHERE SX.CITY = 'London'
( SX.S# AS SNO ) WHERE SX.CITY = 'London'
( SX.S#, SX.CITY ) WHERE EXISTS SPX ( SPX.S# = SX.S# AND
                                       SPX.P# = 'P2' )
( SX.S#, PX.P# ) WHERE SX.CITY ≠ PX.CITY
( SX )
```

Loosely speaking, the first of these denotes the set of all supplier numbers in relation S; the second denotes that subset of those supplier numbers for which the city is London. The third is the same as the second, except that the sole attribute of the result has been renamed SNO. The fourth is a tuple calculus representation of the query "Get supplier numbers and cities for suppliers who supply part P2" (which is of course the sample query we started with, at the beginning of Section 7.1; note that this example is the first in which the parentheses surrounding the target item commalist are actually required). The fifth is a tuple calculus representation of the query "Get supplier-number/ part-number pairs such that the supplier and part are not colocated." The last denotes the entire suppliers relation.

7.3 Examples

We present a few examples of the use of the tuple relational calculus in formulating queries. To facilitate comparisons with the relational algebra, we also give references to the corresponding examples in Chapter 6, where applicable. As in that chapter, any of the examples could be extended to include a final *assignment* step, assigning the value of the expression to some named relation; we omit this step for brevity.

7.3.1 Get supplier numbers for suppliers in Paris with status > 20.

```
SX.S# WHERE SX.CITY = 'Paris' AND SX.STATUS > 20
```

7.3.2 Get all pairs of supplier numbers such that the two suppliers are located in the same city. (Example 6.6.5)

```
( SX.S# AS FIRSTS#, SY.S# AS SECONDS# )
   WHERE SX.CITY = SY.CITY AND SX.S# < SY.S#
```

Note: The specifications "AS FIRSTS#" and "AS SECONDS#" give names to attributes of the *result;* those names are thus not available for use in the WHERE clause, which is why the second comparison in that WHERE clause is "SX.S# < SY.S#," not "FIRSTS# < SECONDS#."

7.3.3 Get supplier names for suppliers who supply part P2. (Example 6.6.1)

```
SX.SNAME WHERE EXISTS SPX ( SPX.S# = SX.S# AND SPX.P# = 'P2' )
```

The WFF in the WHERE clause here is identical to the first example in the subsection "Quantifiers" in Section 7.2; refer to that example if you require further explanation.

7.3.4 Get supplier names for suppliers who supply at least one red part. (Example 6.6.2)

```
SX.SNAME WHERE EXISTS SPX ( SX.S# = SPX.S# AND
                           EXISTS PX ( PX.P# = SPX.P# AND
                                       PX.COLOR = 'Red' ) )
```

Or equivalently (but in **prenex normal form,** in which all quantifiers appear at the front of the WFF):

```
SX.SNAME WHERE EXISTS SPX ( EXISTS PX ( SX.S# = SPX.S# AND
                                        SPX.P# = PX.P# AND
                                        PX.COLOR = 'Red' ) )
```

Prenex normal form is not inherently more or less correct than any other form, but with a little practice it does tend to become the most natural formulation in many cases. Furthermore, it introduces the possibility of reducing the number of parentheses, as follows. The WFF

```
quant-1 vble-1 ( quant-2 vble-2 ( wff ) )
```

(where each of *quant-1* and *quant-2* is either EXISTS or FORALL) can optionally, and unambiguously, be abbreviated to just

```
quant-1 vble-1 quant-2 vble-2 ( wff )
```

Thus we can rewrite the calculus expression above (if desired) as

```
SX.SNAME WHERE EXISTS SPX EXISTS PX ( SX.S# = SPX.S# AND
                                      SPX.P# = PX.P# AND
                                      PX.COLOR = 'Red' )
```

For clarity, however, we will continue to show all parentheses in all remaining examples in this section.

7.3.5 Get supplier names for suppliers who supply at least one part supplied by supplier S2.

```
SX.SNAME WHERE EXISTS SPX ( EXISTS SPY ( SX.S# = SPX.S# AND
                                         SPX.P# = SPY.P# AND
                                         SPY.S# = 'S2' ) )
```

7.3.6 Get supplier names for suppliers who supply all parts. (Example 6.6.3)

```
SX.SNAME WHERE FORALL PX ( EXISTS SPX ( SPX.S# = SX.S# AND
                                        SPX.P# = PX.P# ) )
```

Or equivalently, but without using FORALL:

```
SX.SNAME WHERE NOT EXISTS PX ( NOT EXISTS SPX
                                   ( SPX.S# = SX.S# AND
                                     SPX.P# = PX.P# ) )
```

We remark that the characterization of this expression as representing "supplier names for suppliers who supply all parts" is *100 percent accurate* (contrast the situation with the algebraic counterpart, using DIVIDEBY).

7.3.7 Get supplier names for suppliers who do not supply part P2. (Example 6.6.6)

```
SX.SNAME WHERE NOT EXISTS SPX
                 ( SPX.S# = SX.S# AND SPX.P# = 'P2' )
```

Notice how easily this solution is derived from the solution given in Example 7.3.3 above.

7.3.8 Get supplier numbers for suppliers who supply at least all those parts supplied by supplier S2. (Example 6.6.4)

```
SX.S# WHERE FORALL SPY ( SPY.S# ≠ 'S2' OR
                         EXISTS SPZ ( SPZ.S# = SX.S# AND
                                      SPZ.P# = SPY.P# ) )
```

Paraphrasing: "Get supplier numbers for suppliers, say SX, such that, for all shipments SPY, either that shipment is not from supplier S2, or if it is, then there exists a shipment SPZ of the SPY part from supplier SX."

We introduce another syntactic convention to help with complex queries such as this one, namely an explicit syntactic form for the **logical implication** operator. If f and g are WFFs, then the logical implication expression

```
IF f THEN g
```

is also a WFF, with semantics identical to those of the WFF

```
( NOT f ) OR g
```

The expression above can thus be rewritten (if desired):

```
SX.S# WHERE FORALL SPY ( IF SPY.S# = 'S2' THEN
                         EXISTS SPZ ( SPZ.S# = SX.S# AND
                                      SPZ.P# = SPY.P# ) )
```

Paraphrasing: "Get supplier numbers for suppliers, say SX, such that, for all shipments SPY, if that shipment SPY is from supplier S2, then there exists a shipment SPZ of the SPY part from supplier SX."

7.3.9 Get part numbers for parts that either weigh more than 16 pounds or are supplied by supplier S2, or both.

```
RANGE OF PU IS PX.P# WHERE PX.WEIGHT > 16,
             SPX.P# WHERE SPX.S# = 'S2' ;
PU.P#
```

The relational algebra equivalent here would involve an explicit union.

For interest, we show an alternative formulation of this query. However, this second formulation relies on the fact that every part number in relation SP also appears in relation P, which the "union-style" formulation does not.

```
PX.P# WHERE PX.WEIGHT > 16
      OR   EXISTS SPX ( SPX.P# = PX.P# AND SPX.S# = 'S2' )
```

7.4 Relational Calculus *vs.* Relational Algebra

We claimed in the introduction to this chapter that the relational algebra and the relational calculus are fundamentally equivalent to each other. We now examine that claim in more detail. First, Codd showed in reference [7.2] that the algebra is at least as powerful as the calculus. (For brevity, we will use the unqualified term "calculus" to refer to the tuple calculus specifically throughout this section.) He did this by giving an algorithm—"Codd's reduction algorithm"—by which an arbitrary expression of the calculus could be reduced to a semantically equivalent expression of the algebra. We do not present Codd's algorithm in detail here, but content ourselves with a reasonably complex example that illustrates in broad terms how that algorithm works.*

As a basis for our example we use, not the familiar suppliers-and-parts database, but the extended suppliers-parts-projects version from the exercises in Chapter 4 and elsewhere. For convenience we show in Fig. 7.2 a set of sample values for that database (repeated from Fig. 4.6).

S	S#	SNAME	STATUS	CITY
	S1	Smith	20	London
	S2	Jones	10	Paris
	S3	Blake	30	Paris
	S4	Clark	20	London
	S5	Adams	30	Athens

P	P#	PNAME	COLOR	WEIGHT	CITY
	P1	Nut	Red	12	London
	P2	Bolt	Green	17	Paris
	P3	Screw	Blue	17	Rome
	P4	Screw	Red	14	London
	P5	Cam	Blue	12	Paris
	P6	Cog	Red	19	London

J	J#	JNAME	CITY
	J1	Sorter	Paris
	J2	Display	Rome
	J3	OCR	Athens
	J4	Console	Athens
	J5	RAID	London
	J6	EDS	Oslo
	J7	Tape	London

SPJ	S#	P#	J#	QTY
	S1	P1	J1	200
	S1	P1	J4	700
	S2	P3	J1	400
	S2	P3	J2	200
	S2	P3	J3	200
	S2	P3	J4	500
	S2	P3	J5	600
	S2	P3	J6	400
	S2	P3	J7	800
	S2	P5	J2	100
	S3	P3	J1	200
	S3	P4	J2	500
	S4	P6	J3	300
	S4	P6	J7	300
	S5	P2	J2	200
	S5	P2	J4	100
	S5	P5	J5	500
	S5	P5	J7	100
	S5	P6	J2	200
	S5	P1	J4	100
	S5	P3	J4	200
	S5	P4	J4	800
	S5	P5	J4	400
	S5	P6	J4	500

FIG. 7.2   The suppliers-parts-projects database (sample values)

---

* Actually, the algorithm presented in reference [7.2] had a slight error in it [7.4]. Furthermore, the version of the calculus defined in that paper did not include an analog of the union operation, so that in fact Codd's calculus was strictly less powerful than Codd's algebra. The claim that the algebra and the calculus, enhanced to include an analog of union, are equivalent is nevertheless true, as several writers have demonstrated; see, e.g., Klug [6.13].

Now consider the query: "Get names and cities for suppliers who supply at least one Athens project with at least 50 of every part." A calculus expression for this query is:

```
( SX.SNAME, SX.CITY ) WHERE EXISTS JX FORALL PX EXISTS SPJX
                          ( JX.CITY = 'Athens' AND
                            JX.J# = SPJX.J# AND
                            PX.P# = SPJX.P# AND
                            SX.S# = SPJX.S# AND
                            SPJX.QTY ≥ 50 )
```

where SX, PX, JX, and SPJX are tuple variables ranging over S, P, J, and SPJ, respectively. We now show how this expression can be evaluated to yield the desired result.

Step 1: For each tuple variable, retrieve the range (i.e., the set of possible values for that variable), restricted if possible. By "restricted if possible," we mean that there might be a restriction condition embedded within the WHERE clause that can be used right away to eliminate certain tuples from all further consideration. In the case at hand, the sets of tuples retrieved are as follows:

```
SX   : All tuples of S                           5 tuples
PX   : All tuples of P                           6 tuples
JX   : Tuples of J where CITY = 'Athens'         2 tuples
SPJX : Tuples of SPJ where QTY ≥ 50             24 tuples
```

Step 2: Construct the Cartesian product of the ranges retrieved in Step 1, to yield:

S#	SN	STATUS	CITY	P#	PN	COLOR	WEIGHT	CITY	J#	JN	CITY	S#	P#	J#	QTY
S1	Sm	20	Lon	P1	Nt	Red	12	Lon	J3	OR	Ath	S1	P1	J1	200
S1	Sm	20	Lon	P1	Nt	Red	12	Lon	J3	OR	Ath	S1	P1	J4	700
..	..	..	..	..	..	...	..	...	..	..	...	..	..	..	...
..	..	..	...	..	..	...	..	...	..	..	...	..	..	..	...
..	..	..	...	..	..	...	..	...	..	..	...	..	..	..	...
..	..	..	...	..	..	...	..	...	..	..	...	..	..	..	...

(etc., etc.). The complete product contains 5 * 6 * 2 * 24 = 1440 tuples. *Note:* We have made a number of obvious abbreviations here in the interests of space. Also, we have not bothered to rename attributes (as we really ought to have done, to avoid ambiguity), but instead are relying on ordinal position to show (e.g.) which "S#" comes from relation S and which from relation SPJ. This unorthodox trick is adopted purely to shorten the exposition.

Step 3: Restrict the Cartesian product constructed in Step 2 in accordance with the "join condition" portion of the WHERE clause. In the example, that portion is

```
JX.J# = SPJX.J# AND PX.P# = SPJX.P# AND SX.S# = SPJX.S#
```

We therefore eliminate tuples from the product for which the supplier S# value is not equal to the shipment S# value or the part P# value is not equal to the shipment P# value or the project J# value is not equal to the shipment J# value, to yield a subset of the Cartesian product consisting (as it happens) of just ten tuples:

S#	SN	STATUS	CITY	P#	PN	COLOR	WEIGHT	CITY	J#	JN	CITY	S#	P#	J#	QTY
S1	Sm	20	Lon	P1	Nt	Red	12	Lon	J4	Cn	Ath	S1	P1	J4	700
S2	Jo	10	Par	P3	Sc	Blue	17	Rom	J3	OR	Ath	S2	P3	J3	200
S2	Jo	10	Par	P3	Sc	Blue	17	Rom	J4	Cn	Ath	S2	P3	J4	200
S4	Cl	20	Lon	P6	Cg	Red	19	Lon	J3	OR	Ath	S4	P6	J3	300
S5	Ad	30	Ath	P2	Bt	Green	17	Par	J4	Cn	Ath	S5	P2	J4	100
S5	Ad	30	Ath	P1	Nt	Red	12	Lon	J4	Cn	Ath	S5	P1	J4	100
S5	Ad	30	Ath	P3	Sc	Blue	17	Rom	J4	Cn	Ath	S5	P3	J4	200
S5	Ad	30	Ath	P4	Sc	Red	14	Lon	J4	Cn	Ath	S5	P4	J4	800
S5	Ad	30	Ath	P5	Cm	Blue	12	Par	J4	Cn	Ath	S5	P5	J4	400
S5	Ad	30	Ath	P6	Cg	Red	19	Lon	J4	Cn	Ath	S5	P6	J4	500

(This relation of course represents an equijoin.)

Step 4: Apply the quantifiers from right to left, as follows.

- For the quantifier "EXISTS *RX*" (where *RX* is a tuple variable that ranges over some relation *R*), *project* the current intermediate result to eliminate all attributes of relation *R*.

- For the quantifier "FORALL *RX*," *divide* the current intermediate result by the "restricted range" relation associated with *RX* as retrieved in Step 1. This operation will also have the effect of eliminating all attributes of relation *R*.

In the example, the quantifiers are:

```
EXISTS JX FORALL PX EXISTS SPJX
```

Hence:

1. *(EXISTS SPJX)* Project away the attributes of SPJ (SPJ.S#, SPJ.P#, SPJ.J#, and SPJ.QTY). Result:

S#	SN	STATUS	CITY	P#	PN	COLOR	WEIGHT	CITY	J#	JN	CITY
S1	Sm	20	Lon	P1	Nt	Red	12	Lon	J4	Cn	Ath
S2	Jo	10	Par	P3	Sc	Blue	17	Rom	J3	OR	Ath
S2	Jo	10	Par	P3	Sc	Blue	17	Rom	J4	Cn	Ath
S4	Cl	20	Lon	P6	Cg	Red	19	Lon	J3	OR	Ath
S5	Ad	30	Ath	P2	Bt	Green	17	Par	J4	Cn	Ath
S5	Ad	30	Ath	P1	Nt	Red	12	Lon	J4	Cn	Ath
S5	Ad	30	Ath	P3	Sc	Blue	17	Rom	J4	Cn	Ath
S5	Ad	30	Ath	P4	Sc	Red	14	Lon	J4	Cn	Ath
S5	Ad	30	Ath	P5	Cm	Blue	12	Par	J4	Cn	Ath
S5	Ad	30	Ath	P6	Cg	Red	19	Lon	J4	Cn	Ath

2. *(FORALL PX)* Divide by relation P. Result:

S#	SNAME	STATUS	CITY	J#	JNAME	CITY
S5	Adams	30	Athens	J4	Console	Athens

(We now have room to show this relation without any abbreviations.)

3. *(EXISTS JX)* Project away the attributes of J (J.J#, J.JNAME, and J.CITY). Result:

S#	SNAME	STATUS	CITY
S5	Adams	30	Athens

Step 5: Project the result of Step 4 in accordance with the specifications in the target item commalist. In our example, the target item commalist is:

```
SX.SNAME, SX.CITY
```

Hence the final result is:

SNAME	CITY
Adams	Athens

It follows from all of the foregoing that the original calculus expression is semantically equivalent to a certain nested algebraic expression—to be precise, a projection of a projection of a division of a projection of a restriction of a product of four restrictions (!).

This concludes the example. Of course, many improvements to the algorithm are possible (see Chapter 18—in particular, reference [18.15]—for some ideas for such improvements), and many details have been glossed over in our explanation; nevertheless, the example should be adequate to give the general idea of how the reduction works.

Incidentally, we are now able to explain one of the reasons (not the only one) why Codd defined precisely the eight algebraic operators he did: Those eight operators provided a convenient **target language** as a vehicle for a possible implementation of the calculus. In other words, given a language such as QUEL [7.7] that is founded on the calculus, one possible approach to implementing that language would be to take the query as submitted by the user—which is basically just a calculus expression—and apply the reduction algorithm to it, thereby obtaining an equivalent algebraic expression. That algebraic expression of course consists of a set of algebraic operations, which are by definition inherently implementable. (The next step is to go on to *optimize* that algebraic expression. See Chapter 18.)

Another point to note is that Codd's eight algebraic operators also provide a *yardstick* for measuring the expressive power of any given database language (existing or proposed). We mentioned this issue briefly at the end of Section 6.7; let us now examine it in a little more depth.

First, a language is said to be **relationally complete** if it is at least as powerful as the relational calculus—that is, if any relation definable by some expression of the relational calculus is also definable by some expression of the language in question [7.2]. (In Section 6.7 we said that "relationally complete" meant as powerful as the *algebra*, not the calculus, but it comes to the same thing, as the reader will soon see. In fact, it follows immediately from the existence of Codd's reduction algorithm that the relational algebra is relationally complete.)

Relational completeness can be regarded as a basic measure of selective or expressive power for database languages in general. In particular, since the calculus and the algebra are both relationally complete, they both provide a basis for designing languages that provide this power of expressiveness *without having to resort to the use of loops*—a particularly important consideration in the case of a language that is intended for end users, though it is not irrelevant for application programmers as well.

Next, since the algebra is relationally complete, it follows that, to show that any given language *L* is also complete, it is sufficient to show (a) that *L* includes analogs of each of the eight algebraic operations (indeed, it is sufficient to show that it includes analogs of the five *primitive* algebraic operations), and (b) that the operands of any operation in *L* can be arbitrary *L* expressions. SQL is an example of a language that can be shown to be relationally complete in this manner—see Exercise 8.6 in Chapter 8— and QUEL is another. Indeed, it is often easier in practice to show that a given language has equivalents of the algebraic operations than to show that it has equivalents of the expressions of the calculus. This is why we typically define relational completeness in algebraic rather than calculus terms.

Incidentally, please understand that relational completeness does not necessarily imply any other kind of completeness. For example, it is desirable that a language provide "computational completeness" also—i.e., it should be capable of computing all computable functions. Observe that the calculus as we have defined it is *not* complete in this sense, though in practice real database languages ought preferably to be so; indeed, computational completeness was one of the motivations for the EXTEND and SUMMARIZE operations that we added to the algebra in Section 6.8. In the next section, we will consider what is involved in extending the calculus to provide analogs of those operations.

To return to the question of the equivalence of the algebra and the calculus: We have shown by example that any calculus expression can be reduced to an algebraic equivalent, and hence that the algebra is at least as powerful as the calculus. Conversely, it is possible to show that any algebraic expression can be reduced to a calculus equivalent, and hence that the calculus is at least as powerful as the algebra; for proof, see, e.g., Ullman [7.16]. It follows that the two formalisms are logically equivalent.

7.5   Computational Capabilities

Adding computational capabilities to the calculus is basically straightforward: We simply extend the definition of *comparands* and *target-items* to include a new category, *scalar-expression,* where the operands of such an expression in turn can include literals, attribute references, and/or aggregate function references. In the case of target-items, we also require that a specification of the form "AS attribute" be used to provide a proper attribute name for the result attribute if there is no obvious name to inherit.

We assume that scalar expressions in general are well understood, and omit the specifics here. However, we do show the syntax for *aggregate function reference:*

```
aggregate-function ( expression [, attribute ] )
```

Here *aggregate-function* is COUNT, SUM, AVG, MAX, or MIN (possibly others besides, of course), *expression* is an expression of the tuple calculus (thus evaluating to a relation), and *attribute* is that attribute of that result relation over which the aggregation is to be done. For COUNT, the *attribute* argument is irrelevant and must be omitted; for the other aggregate functions, it can optionally be omitted if and only if the *expression* argument evaluates to a relation of degree one, in which case the sole attribute of the result of *expression* is assumed by default. Observe, incidentally, that an aggregate function reference returns a *scalar* value, which is why such a reference is permitted as an operand in a scalar expression.

Two points arise from the foregoing:

1. The aggregate functions act in certain respects as a new kind of quantifier. In particular, if the *expression* argument in a given aggregate function reference is of the form "*(tic)* WHERE *f* " (where *tic* is a target item commalist and *f* is a WFF), and if an occurrence of the tuple variable *T* is free in *f*, then that occurrence of *T* is bound in the aggregate function reference

   ```
   aggregate-function ( ( tic ) WHERE f [, attribute ] )
   ```

2. For the benefit of readers who might be familiar with SQL, we remark that by allowing two arguments in an aggregate function reference, *expression* and *attribute,* we avoid the need for SQL's *ad hoc* trick of using a DISTINCT operator to eliminate duplicates, if required, before the aggregation is done. The *expression* argument evaluates to a relation, from which duplicate tuples are always eliminated by definition. The *attribute* argument then specifies the attribute of that relation over which the aggregation is to be performed, and duplicate values are *not* eliminated from that attribute before the aggregation is done. Of course, the attribute might not contain any duplicates anyway; in particular, this will be the case if the attribute in question is a candidate key.

Now let us take a look at some examples. To facilitate comparisons with the relational algebra, we also give references to the corresponding examples in Chapter 6.

7.5.1 Get the part number and the weight in grams for each part with gram weight > 10000. (Variation on the second example in the introductory text to EXTEND subsection, Section 6.8)

```
( PX.P#, PX.WEIGHT * 454 AS GMWT )
   WHERE PX.WEIGHT * 454 > 10000
```

Observe that the specification "AS GMWT" gives a name to the applicable attribute of the *result*. That name is thus not available for use in the WHERE clause, which is why the expression "PX.WEIGHT * 454" appears in two places.

7.5.2 Get every supplier, each one tagged with the literal value "Supplier." (Example 1 from EXTEND subsection, Section 6.8)

```
( SX, 'Supplier' AS TAG )
```

7.5.3 Get each shipment, plus corresponding part details and total shipment weight. (Example 2 from EXTEND subsection, Section 6.8)

```
( SPX.S#, SPX.QTY, PX, PX.WEIGHT * SPX.QTY AS SHIPWT )
  WHERE PX.P# = SPX.P#
```

7.5.4 For each part, get the part number and the total shipment quantity. (First example in the introductory text to SUMMARIZE subsection, Section 6.8)

```
( PX.P#, SUM ( SPX WHERE SPX.P# = PX.P#, QTY ) AS TOTQTY )
```

Notice that instead of a clause of the form "BY (P#)", the aggregate function reference includes as its first argument a calculus expression that evaluates (for a given part) to exactly the set of tuples over which the aggregation is to be done. Notice too that the result will include one tuple for each part, even parts that are currently supplied by no supplier (the sum for such a part will be zero).

7.5.5 Get the total shipment quantity. (Example 1 from SUMMARIZE subsection, Section 6.8)

```
SUM ( SPX, QTY ) AS GRANDTOTAL
```

Unlike its SUMMARIZE counterpart, this expression will return the correct result (*viz.*, zero) if relation SP is empty.

7.5.6 For each supplier, get the supplier number and the total number of parts supplied. (Variation on Example 2 from SUMMARIZE subsection, Section 6.8)

```
( SX.S#, COUNT ( SPX WHERE SPX.S# = SX.S# ) AS #_OF_PARTS )
```

Unlike its SUMMARIZE counterpart, this expression will produce a result that does include a tuple for supplier S5 (with a count of zero).

7.5.7 Get part cities that store (a) more than five red parts, (b) five red parts or less. (Example 3 from SUMMARIZE subsection, Section 6.8)

```
PX.CITY WHERE COUNT ( PY WHERE PY.CITY = PX.CITY
                         AND PY.COLOR = 'Red' ) > 5
```

This expression represents a solution to part (a) of the problem. Unlike its SUMMARIZE counterpart, this solution can be converted into a solution for part (b) by simply replacing ">" by "≤".

7.6   Domain-Oriented Relational Calculus

As indicated in Section 7.1, the domain-oriented relational calculus (domain calculus for short) differs from the tuple calculus in that it has *domain* variables instead of tuple variables—i.e., variables that range over domains instead of over relations. (*Note:* "Scalar variable" would be a better name than "domain variable," since the values are domain *elements*—i.e., scalars—not domains *per se.*) We discuss the domain calculus only rather briefly here.

From a practical standpoint, the most immediately obvious distinction between the domain and tuple versions of the calculus is that the domain version supports an additional form of *condition*, which we will refer to as a **membership condition**. A membership condition takes the form

```
R ( pair, pair, ... )
```

where *R* is a relation name, and each *pair* is of the form *A:v*, where *A* in turn is an attribute of *R* and *v* is either a domain variable or a literal. The condition evaluates to *true* if and only if there exists a tuple in relation *R* having the specified values for the specified attributes. For example, the expression

```
SP ( S#:'S1', P#:'P1' )
```

is a membership condition that evaluates to *true* if and only if there exists a tuple in relation SP with S# value S1 and P# value P1. Likewise, the membership condition

```
SP ( S#:SX, P#:PX )
```

evaluates to *true* if and only if there exists an SP tuple with S# value equal to the current value of domain variable SX (whatever that might be) and P# value equal to the current value of domain variable PX (again, whatever that might be).

For the remainder of this section we assume the existence of domain variables with names formed by appending X, Y, Z, . . . to the corresponding domain names—except that, for domains whose names end in "#", we drop that "#". We remind the reader that in the suppliers-and-parts database each attribute has the same name as its underlying domain, except for attributes SNAME and PNAME, for which the underlying domain is called simply NAME.

Examples of domain calculus expressions:

```
( SX )
( SX ) WHERE S ( S#:SX )
( SX ) WHERE S ( S#:SX, CITY:'London' )
( SX, CITYX ) WHERE S ( S#:SX, CITY:CITYX )
              AND  SP ( S#:SX, P#:'P2' )
( SX, PX ) WHERE S ( S#:SX, CITY.CITYX )
           AND   P ( P#:PX, CITY:CITYY )
           AND   CITYX ≠ CITYY
```

Loosely speaking, the first of these denotes the set of all supplier numbers;* the second denotes the set of all supplier numbers in relation S; the third denotes that subset of those supplier numbers for which the city is London. The next is a domain calculus representation of the query "Get supplier numbers and cities for suppliers who supply part P2" (note that the tuple calculus version of this query required an existential quantifier; note too that this example is the first one in which the parentheses surrounding the target item commalist are actually required). The last is a domain calculus representation of the query "Get supplier-number/part-number pairs such that the supplier and part are not colocated."

---

* And might not be a supported query in an implemented system, given that domains themselves are typically not stored in the database.

We give domain calculus versions of some of the examples from Section 7.3.

7.6.1 Get supplier numbers for suppliers in Paris with status > 20. (Example 7.3.1)

```
SX WHERE EXISTS STATUSX
  ( STATUSX > 20 AND S ( S#:SX, STATUS:STATUSX, CITY:'Paris' ) )
```

Observe that quantifiers are still needed. This particular example is somewhat clumsier than its tuple calculus counterpart. On the other hand, there are also cases where the reverse is true; see especially some of the more complex examples later.

7.6.2 Get all pairs of supplier numbers such that the two suppliers are located in the same city. (Example 7.3.2)

```
( SX AS FIRSTS#, SY AS SECONDS# )
                WHERE EXISTS CITYZ
                  ( S ( S#:SX, CITY:CITYZ ) AND
                    S ( S#:SY, CITY:CITYZ ) AND
                    SX < SY )
```

7.6.3 Get supplier names for suppliers who supply at least one red part. (Example 7.3.4)

```
NAMEX WHERE EXISTS SX EXISTS PX
          ( S ( S#:SX, SNAME:NAMEX )
            AND SP ( S#:SX, P#:PX )
            AND P ( P#:PX, COLOR:'Red' ) )
```

7.6.4 Get supplier names for suppliers who supply at least one part supplied by supplier S2. (Example 7.3.5)

```
NAMEX WHERE EXISTS SX EXISTS PX
          ( S ( S#:SX, SNAME:NAMEX )
            AND SP ( S#:SX, P#:PX )
            AND SP ( S#:'S2', P#:PX ) )
```

7.6.5 Get supplier names for suppliers who supply all parts. (Example 7.3.6)

```
NAMEX WHERE EXISTS SX ( S ( S#:SX, SNAME:NAMEX )
            AND FORALL PX ( IF P ( P#:PX )
                            THEN SP ( S#:SX, P#:PX ) ) )
```

7.6.6 Get supplier names for suppliers who do not supply part P2. (Example 7.3.7)

```
NAMEX WHERE EXISTS SX ( S ( S#:SX, SNAME:NAMEX )
                  AND NOT SP ( S#:SX, P:'P2' ) )
```

7.6.7 Get supplier numbers for suppliers who supply at least all those parts supplied by supplier S2. (Example 7.3.8)

```
SX WHERE FORALL PX ( IF SP ( S#:'S2', P#:PX )
                THEN SP ( S#:SX, P#:PX ) )
```

7.6.8 Get part numbers for parts that either weigh more than 16 pounds or are supplied by supplier S2, or both. (Example 7.3.9)

```
PX WHERE EXISTS WEIGHTX
         ( P ( P#:PX, WEIGHT:WEIGHTX )
              AND WEIGHTX > 16 )
         OR SP ( S#:'S2', P#:PX )
```

The domain calculus, like the tuple calculus, is formally equivalent to the relational algebra (i.e., it is relationally complete). For proof see, e.g., Ullman [7.16].

7.7 Summary

We have briefly considered the **relational calculus,** an alternative to the relational algebra. Superficially, the two look very different—the calculus is **descriptive** where the algebra is **prescriptive**—but at a deep level they are the same thing, because any expression of the calculus can be converted into a semantically equivalent expression in the algebra, and *vice versa.*

The calculus exists in two forms, **tuple** calculus and **domain** calculus. The key difference between them is that the variables of the tuple calculus are **tuple** variables (they range over relations, and their values are tuples), while the variables of the domain calculus are **domain** variables (they range over domains, and their values are scalars; for this reason, in fact, "domain variable" is not really a very accurate term).

An expression of the tuple calculus consists of a parenthesized **target item commalist** and an optional WHERE clause containing a **WFF** ("well-formed formula"). That WFF is constructed from **quantifiers** (EXISTS and FORALL), **free** and **bound variables,** literals, comparison operators, logical (Boolean) operators, and parentheses. Every free variable mentioned in the WFF must also be mentioned in the target item commalist. *Note:* We did not explicitly discuss the point in the body of the chapter, but expressions of the algebra are intended to serve essentially the same purposes as expressions of the algebra (see Section 6.7).

We showed by example how Codd's **reduction algorithm** can be used to convert an arbitrary expression of the calculus to an equivalent expression of the algebra, thus paving the way for a possible implementation strategy for the calculus. And we mentioned once again the issue of **relational completeness,** and discussed briefly what is involved in proving that some given language L is complete in this sense.

We also considered how the calculus might be extended to provide **computational** capabilities (analogous to the capabilities provided by EXTEND and SUMMARIZE in the algebra). And we saw how many of the counterintuitive aspects of SUMMARIZE in the algebra had no counterpart in the calculus, thus lending weight to the contention that the calculus tends to be a little more user-friendly [7.2].

Finally, we presented a brief introduction to the **domain** calculus, and claimed (without attempting to prove as much) that it too was relationally complete. Thus, the tuple calculus, the domain calculus, and the algebra are all equivalent to one another.

Exercises

Exercises 7.9 and 7.11 ask the reader to formulate some sample queries as relational calculus expressions. (By way of an interesting variation on those exercises, the reader might like to try looking at some of the answers first and stating what the given expression means in English.) Exercises 7.1–7.8 and 7.10, by contrast, are concerned with some slightly more theoretical aspects of the calculus.

7.1 Let $f(x)$ and g be arbitrary WFFs in which x does and does not occur, respectively, as a free variable. Which of the following statements are valid? (The symbol $\Rightarrow$ means "implies"; the symbol $\equiv$ means "is equivalent to.")

(a) `EXISTS x ( g ) ≡ g`

(b) `FORALL x ( g ) ≡ g`

(c) `EXISTS x ( f(x) AND g ) ≡ EXISTS x ( f(x) ) AND g`

(d) `FORALL x ( f(x) AND g ) ≡ FORALL x ( f(x) ) AND g`

(e) `FORALL x ( f(x) ) ⇒ EXISTS x ( f(x) )`

7.2 Let $f(x,y)$ be an arbitrary WFF with free variables x and y. Which of the following statements are valid?

(a) `EXISTS x EXISTS y ( f(x,y) ) ≡ EXISTS y EXISTS x ( f(x,y) )`

(b) `FORALL x FORALL y ( f(x,y) ) ≡ FORALL y FORALL x ( f(x,y) )`

(c) `FORALL x ( f(x,y) ) ≡ NOT EXISTS x ( NOT f(x,y) )`

(d) `EXISTS x ( f(x,y) ) ≡ NOT FORALL x ( NOT f(x,y) )`

(e) `EXISTS x FORALL y ( f(x,y) ) ≡ FORALL y EXISTS x ( f(x,y) )`

(f) `EXISTS y FORALL x ( f(x,y) ) ⇒ FORALL x EXISTS y ( f(x,y) )`

7.3 Let $f(x)$ and $g(y)$ be arbitrary WFFs with free variables x and y, respectively. Which of the following statements are valid?

(a) `EXISTS x ( f(x) ) AND EXISTS y ( g(y) ) ≡`
    `EXISTS x EXISTS y ( f(x) AND g(y) )`

(b) `EXISTS x ( IF f(x) THEN g(x) ) ≡`
    `IF FORALL x ( f(x) ) THEN EXISTS x ( g(x) )`

7.4 Consider once again the query in Example 7.3.8—"Get supplier numbers for suppliers who supply at least all those parts supplied by supplier S2"—for which a possible tuple calculus formulation is

```
SX.S# WHERE FORALL SPY ( IF SPY.S# = 'S2' THEN
                         EXISTS SPZ ( SPZ.S# = SX.S# AND
                                      SPZ.P# = SPY.P# ) )
```

What will this query return if supplier S2 currently supplies no parts at all? What difference would it make if we replaced SX by SPX throughout?

7.5 Here is a sample query against the suppliers-parts-projects database (the usual conventions apply regarding range variable names):

```
( PX.PNAME, PX.CITY ) WHERE FORALL SX FORALL JX EXISTS SPJX
                          ( SX.CITY = 'London' AND
                            JX.CITY = 'Paris' AND
                            SPJX.S# = SX.S# AND
                            SPJX.P# = PX.P# AND
                            SPJX.J# = JX.J# AND
                            SPJX.QTY < 500 )
```

    (a) Translate this query into English.

    (b) Play DBMS and "execute" the reduction algorithm on this query. Can you see any improvements that might be made to that algorithm?

7.6 Give a tuple calculus formulation of the query "Get the three heaviest parts."

7.7 Consider the *bill-of-materials* relation PART_STRUCTURE of Chapter 4 (the data definition is given in the answer to Exercise 4.2 and some sample values are given in Fig. 4.4). The well-known **part explosion** query "Get part numbers for all parts that are components, *at any level,* of some given part, say part P1"—the result of which, PART_LIST say, is certainly a relation that can be derived from PART_STRUCTURE—cannot be formulated as a single expression of the original relational calculus (or algebra). In other words, PART_LIST is a derivable relation that nevertheless *cannot* be derived by means of a single expression of the original calculus (or algebra). Why is this?

7.8 Suppose the suppliers relation S were to be replaced by a set of relations LS, PS, AS, . . . (one for each distinct supplier city; the LS relation, for example, contains just the supplier tuples for the suppliers in London). Suppose too that we are unaware of exactly what supplier cities exist, and are therefore unaware of exactly how many such relations there are. Consider the query "Does supplier S1 exist in the database?" Can this query be expressed in the calculus (or algebra)? Justify your answer.

7.9 Give tuple calculus solutions to Exercises 6.13–6.48.

7.10 Design a suitable set of computational capabilities for the domain calculus along the lines of those discussed for the tuple calculus in Section 7.5.

7.11 Give domain calculus solutions to Exercises 6.13–6.48.

References and Bibliography

7.1 C. L. Chang. "DEDUCE—A Deductive Query Language for Relational Data Bases." In *Pattern Recognition and Artificial Intelligence* (ed., C. H. Chen). New York: Academic Press (1976).

7.2 E. F. Codd. "Relational Completeness of Data Base Sublanguages." In *Data Base Systems, Courant Computer Science Symposia Series 6.* Englewood Cliffs, N.J.: Prentice-Hall (1972).

The paper that introduced the notion of relational completeness. It includes the original definitions of both the tuple relational calculus and the relational algebra (i.e., the eight operations described in Sections 6.3 and 6.4). It also presents the details of the reduction algorithm sketched in Section 7.4, thereby proving that the algebra is at least as expressive as the calculus. (For the version of the calculus defined in the paper, incidentally, the converse is not true, because that version did not include any equivalent of the algebraic UNION operator.) The paper concludes with some brief arguments in favor of using the calculus over the algebra as a basis for a practical database language. The arguments are (paraphrasing):

    1. *Extendability:* A calculus-based language is more suitable than an algebraic one for

extension via the incorporation of scalar computational operators, aggregate functions, etc.

2. *Ease of capturing the user's intent* (important for optimization, authorization, etc.): The calculus, because it permits the user to request data by its properties instead of by a sequence of manipulative operations, is a better basis than the algebra for this purpose.

3. *Closeness to natural language:* Codd recognizes that most users should not have to deal directly with either the algebra or the calculus as such. But the idea of requesting data by its properties is more natural than that of having to devise an appropriate sequence of manipulative operations. Thus the calculus should prove more suitable as a target for some more user-friendly higher-level language.

However, it is not clear that any of these arguments really stands up, given the formal equivalence of the two approaches. Regarding the third argument, however, it is perhaps worth observing that the calculus and the algebra—because they are more systematically defined—are *both* much more suitable than SQL as such a target language! It is noteworthy that many SQL systems effectively convert SQL internally into something rather close to the algebra for implementation purposes.

7.3 E. F. Codd. "A Data Base Sublanguage Founded on the Relational Calculus." Proc. 1971 ACM SIGFIDET Workshop on Data Description, Access and Control, San Diego, Calif. (November 1971).

The paper that defined "Data Sublanguage ALPHA." One small point regarding ALPHA is worth elaborating on briefly here—the use of *implicit range variables.* The basic idea is to allow a relation name to be used to stand for an implicit range variable that ranges over the relation in question, provided no ambiguity results. Both QUEL and SQL adopted this fairly obvious shorthand. In QUEL, for example, we might write simply

```
RETRIEVE ( S.S# ) WHERE S.CITY = "London"
```

instead of

```
RANGE OF SX IS S
RETRIEVE ( SX.S# ) WHERE SX.CITY = "London"
```

But it has to be clearly understood in the first of these formulations that the "S" in (e.g.) "S.S#" does *not* represent relation S—it represents a *range variable* called S that ranges over the relation with the same name.

7.4 C. J. Date. "A Note on the Relational Calculus." *ACM SIGMOD Record 18,* No. 4 (December 1989). Republished as "An Anomaly in Codd's Reduction Algorithm" in C. J. Date and Hugh Darwen, *Relational Database Writings 1989–1991.* Reading, Mass.: Addison-Wesley (1992).

Identifies and explains a minor anomaly in Codd's reduction algorithm [7.2].

7.5 C. J. Date. "Why Quantifier Order Is Important." In C. J. Date and Hugh Darwen, *Relational Database Writings 1989–1991.* Reading, Mass.: Addison-Wesley (1992).

7.6 C. J. Date. "Relational Calculus as an Aid to Effective Query Formulation." In C. J. Date and Hugh Darwen, *Relational Database Writings 1989–1991.* Reading, Mass.: Addison-Wesley (1992).

Just about every relational product on the market currently supports SQL, not the relational calculus (or the relational algebra). This paper nevertheless advocates (and illustrates) the use of relational calculus as an intermediate step in the construction of "complex" SQL queries.

7.7   G. D. Held, M. R. Stonebraker, and E. Wong. "INGRES—A Relational Data Base System." Proc. NCC *44,* Anaheim, Calif. Montvale, N.J.: AFIPS Press (May 1975).

There were two major relational prototypes under development in the mid to late 1970s: System R at IBM, and INGRES at the University of California at Berkeley. Both of those projects became extremely influential in the research world, and both subsequently led to commercial systems, including DB2 in the case of System R and the commercial INGRES product in the case of INGRES. *Note:* The INGRES prototype is sometimes referred to as "University INGRES," in order to distinguish it from the commercial version of the system.

   INGRES was not originally an SQL system; instead, it supported a language called QUEL ("Query Language"), which in many respects was technically superior to SQL. Indeed, QUEL still forms the basis of a certain amount of current database research, and examples expressed in QUEL still appear in the research literature. This paper [7.7], which was the first to describe the INGRES prototype, includes a preliminary definition of QUEL. See also references [7.12–7.14].

7.8   J. L. Kuhns. "Answering Questions by Computer: A Logical Study." Report RM-5428-PR, Rand Corp., Santa Monica, Calif. (1967).

7.9   M. Lacroix and A. Pirotte. "Domain-Oriented Relational Languages." Proc. 3rd International Conference on Very Large Data Bases (October 1977).

7.10 M. Lacroix and A. Pirotte. "ILL: An English Structured Query Language for Relational Data Bases." In *Architecture and Models in Data Base Management Systems* (ed., G. M. Nijssen). Amsterdam, Netherlands: North-Holland / New York, NY: Elsevier Science (1977).

7.11 A. Pirotte and P. Wodon. "A Comprehensive Formal Query Language for a Relational Data Base." *R.A.I.R.O. Informatique/Computer Science 11,* No. 2 (1977).

The "formal query language" FQL is based (like ILL) on the domain calculus but is much more formal (less "English-like") than ILL.

7.12 Michael Stonebraker (ed.). *The INGRES Papers: The Anatomy of a Relational Database Management System.* Reading, Mass.: Addison-Wesley (1986).

A collection of some of the major papers from the University INGRES project, edited and annotated by one of the original INGRES designers. (References [7.13–7.14] below are included in the collection.) To this writer's knowledge, this is the only book available that describes the design and implementation of a full-scale relational DBMS in detail. Essential reading for the serious student.

7.13 Michael Stonebraker, Eugene Wong, Peter Kreps, and Gerald Held. "The Design and Implementation of INGRES." *ACM TODS 1,* No. 3 (September 1976). Republished in reference [7.12].

A detailed description of the INGRES prototype.

7.14 Michael Stonebraker. "Retrospection on a Data Base System." *ACM TODS 5,* No. 2 (June 1980). Republished in reference [7.12].

An account of the history of the INGRES prototype project (to January 1979). The emphasis is on mistakes and lessons learned, rather than on successes.

7.15 Moshé M. Zloof. "Query By Example." Proc. NCC 44, Anaheim, Calif. (May 1975). Montvale, N.J.: AFIPS Press (1977).

The relational language **Query-By-Example** (QBE) incorporates elements of both the tuple and the domain calculus (with the emphasis on the latter). Its syntax, which is attractive and intuitively very simple, is based on the idea of making entries in "skeleton tables" on the screen instead of writing linear statements. For example, a QBE formulation of the query "Get supplier names for suppliers who supply at least one part supplied by supplier S2" (a fairly complex query) might look like this:

S	S#	SNAME
	_SX	P._NX

SP	S#	P#
	_SX	_PX

SP	S#	P#
	S2	_PX

Explanation: The user asks the system to display three skeleton tables on the screen, one for relation S and two for relation SP, and makes entries in them as shown. Entries beginning with a leading underscore represent "examples" (i.e., domain variables); other entries represent literals. The user is asking the system to "present" ("P.") supplier name values (_NX) such that, if the supplier is _SX, then _SX supplies some part _PX, and part _PX in turn is also supplied by supplier S2. Notice that the existential quantifiers are all implicit (as they are also in QUEL, incidentally)—another reason why the syntax is intuitively easy to understand.

Here is another example: "Get pairs of supplier numbers such that the suppliers concerned are colocated."

S	S#	CITY
	_SX	_CZ
	_SY	_CZ

P.	_SX	_SY

Unfortunately QBE is not relationally complete. To be specific, it does not (properly) support the negated existential quantifier (NOT EXISTS). As a result, certain queries (e.g., "Get names of suppliers who supply all parts") cannot be expressed in QBE.

(Actually QBE did originally "support" NOT EXISTS, at least implicitly, but the construct was always somewhat troublesome. The basic problem was that there was no way to specify the order in which the various implicit quantifiers were to be applied, and unfortunately the order is significant—see reference [7.5] or Exercise 7.2(e). As a result, certain queries were ambiguous [7.5].)

Zloof was the original inventor and designer of QBE. This paper was the first of many by Zloof on the subject.

7.16 Jeffrey D. Ullman. *Principles of Database and Knowledge-Base Systems: Volume I.* Rockville, Md.: Computer Science Press (1988).

Ullman's book includes a more formal treatment of relational calculus and related matters than the present book does. In particular, it discusses the concept of **safety** of calculus expressions. This topic is of concern if we adopt a slightly different version of the calculus, one in which range variables are not defined by separate RANGE statements but instead are bound to their range by means of explicit conditions within the WHERE clause. In such a version of the calculus, the query "Get suppliers in London" (for example) might look something like this—

```
SX WHERE SX ∈ S AND SX.CITY = 'London'
```

—instead of the following:

```
RANGE OF SX IS S ;
SX WHERE SX.CITY = 'London'
```

One problem with this version of the calculus (not the only one) is that it would apparently permit a query such as

```
SX WHERE NOT ( SX ∈ S )
```

Such an expression is said to be "unsafe," because it does not return a finite answer (the set of all things that are not tuples of S is infinite). As a consequence, certain rules have to be imposed to guarantee that all legal expressions are safe. Such rules are described in Ullman's book (for both tuple and domain calculus).

Answers to Selected Exercises

7.1　(a) Valid. (b) Valid. (c) Valid. (d) Valid. (e) Not valid. *Note:* The reason that (e) is not valid is that FORALL applied to an empty set always yields *true*. By contrast, EXISTS applied to an empty set yields *false*. Thus, e.g, the fact that the statement "All purple parts weigh over 100 pounds" is *true* does not necessarily mean that there actually exist any purple parts.

We remark that the (valid!) equivalences can be used as a basis for a set of calculus expression transformation rules, much like the algebraic expression transformation rules mentioned in Chapter 6 (and discussed in detail in Chapter 18). An analogous remark applies to the answers to Exercises 7.2 and 7.3 as well.

7.2　(a) Valid. (b) Valid. (c) Valid (this one was discussed in the body of the chapter). (d) Valid (hence each of the quantifiers can be defined in terms of the other). (e) Not valid. (f) Valid. Observe that (as (a) and (b) show) a sequence of *like* quantifiers can be written in any order without changing the meaning, whereas (as (e) shows) for *unlike* quantifiers the order is significant. By way of illustration of this latter point, suppose that x and y range over the set of integers and f is the WFF "$y > x$". It should be clear that the WFF

```
FORALL x EXISTS y ( y > x )
```

("for all integers x, there exists a larger integer y") evaluates to *true,* whereas the WFF

```
EXISTS y FORALL x ( y > x )
```

("there exists an integer x that is larger than every integer y") evaluates to *false*. Hence interchanging unlike quantifiers changes the meaning. In a calculus-based query language, therefore, interchanging unlike quantifiers in a WHERE clause will change the meaning of the query [7.5].

7.3　(a) Valid. (b) Valid.

7.4　If supplier S2 currently supplies no parts, the original query will return all supplier numbers in relation S (including in particular S2, who presumably appears in S but not in SP). If we replace SX by SPX throughout, it will return all supplier numbers in relation SP. The difference between the two formulations is thus as follows: The first means "Get supplier numbers for suppliers who supply at least all those parts supplied by supplier S2" (as required). The second means "Get supplier numbers for suppliers who *supply at least one part and* supply at least all those parts supplied by supplier S2."

7.5　(a) Get part name and city for parts supplied to every project in Paris by every supplier in London in a quantity < 500. (b) The result of this query is empty.

7.6　This exercise is very difficult!—especially when we take into account the fact that part weights are not unique. (If they were unique, we could paraphrase the query as "Get all parts such that the count of heavier parts is less than three.") The exercise is so difficult, in fact, that we do not attempt to give a pure calculus solution here. It illustrates very well the point that relational completeness is only a *basic* measure of expressive power, not necessarily a sufficient one. (The next two exercises also illustrate this point.)

　　The fact is that comparatively few systems are capable of dealing well with the kind of problem of which this particular exercise is an illustration, even though such problems are very common in practice. We refer to such problems as **quota queries**. Interestingly enough, Codd's ALPHA language [7.3] did include facilities for quota queries, but (as already stated) ALPHA was never implemented. The example might look something like this in ALPHA:

```
(3) ( PX.P#, PX.PNAME, PX.COLOR, PX.WEIGHT, PX.CITY )
       DOWN PX.WEIGHT
```

The initial "(3)" is the quota (it means the *first* three); "DOWN PX.WEIGHT" means "for the purposes of filling the quota, conceptually sequence tuples of the parts relation by descending WEIGHT value."

DEC's Rdb/VMS product is one example of a commercial system that does support quota queries.

7.7 Let PSA, PSB, PSC, . . . , PSn be tuple variables for relation PART_STRUCTURE, and suppose the given part is part P1. Then:

(a) A calculus expression for the query "Get part numbers for all parts that are components, at the *first* level, of part P1" is:

```
PSA.MINOR_P# WHERE PSA.MAJOR_P# = 'P1'
```

(b) A calculus expression for the query "Get part numbers for all parts that are components, at the *second* level, of part P1" is:

```
PSB.MINOR_P# WHERE EXISTS PSA
                 ( PSA.MAJOR_P# = 'P1' AND
                   PSB.MAJOR_P# = PSA.MINOR_P# )
```

(c) A calculus expression for the query "Get part numbers for all parts that are components, at the *third* level, of part P1" is:

```
PSC.MINOR_P# WHERE EXISTS PSA EXISTS PSB
                 ( PSA.MAJOR_P# = 'P1' AND
                   PSB.MAJOR_P# = PSA.MINOR_P# AND
                   PSC.MAJOR_P# = PSB.MINOR_P# )
```

And so on. A calculus expression for the query "Get part numbers for all parts that are components, at the *n*th level, of part P1" is:

```
PSn.MINOR_P# WHERE EXISTS PSA EXISTS PSB ... EXISTS PS(n-1)
                 ( PSA.MAJOR_P# = 'P1' AND
                   PSB.MAJOR_P# = PSA.MINOR_P# AND
                   PSC.MAJOR_P# = PSB.MINOR_P# AND
                   .....................  AND
                   PSn.MAJOR_P# = PS(n-1).MINOR_P# )
```

All of these result relations (a), (b), (c), . . . then need to be UNIONed together to construct the relation PART_LIST.

The problem is, of course, that there is no way to write n such expressions if the value of n is unknown. Thus, the part explosion query is a classic illustration of a problem that cannot be formulated by means of a single expression in a language that is only relationally complete—i.e., a language that is no more powerful than the original calculus (or algebra). In other words, we need another extension—details beyond the scope of this chapter—to the original calculus (and algebra).

Note: Although this problem is usually referred to as "bill of materials" or "parts explosion," it is actually of much wider applicability than those names might suggest. In fact, the kind of relationship typified by the "parts contain parts" structure occurs in a very wide range of applications. Other examples include management hierarchies, family trees, security graphs, communication networks, software module calling structures, transportation networks, etc., etc.

7.8   This query cannot be expressed in either the calculus or the algebra. For example, to express it in the calculus, we would basically need to be able to say something like the following:

Does there exist a relation *R* such that there exists a tuple *T* in *R* such that *T*.S# = 'S1'?

In other words, we would need to be able to quantify over *relations* instead of over tuples, and we would therefore need a new kind of range variable, one whose value is some (named) relation. The query therefore cannot be expressed in the relational calculus, since the relational calculus supports only range variables whose values are tuples (and therefore allows us to quantify over *tuples* but not relations).

Note, incidentally, that the query under discussion is a "yes/no" query (the desired answer is basically a truth value). The reader might be tempted to think, therefore, that the reason the query cannot be handled in the calculus or the algebra is that calculus and algebra expressions are relation-valued, not truth-valued. However, yes/no queries *can* be handled in the calculus and algebra if properly implemented! The crux of the matter is to recognize that yes and no (equivalently, *true* and *false*) are *representable as relations*. The relations in question are TABLE_DEE and TABLE_DUM, respectively. For further discussion, see Chapter 4.

7.9   We have numbered the following solutions as 7.9.*n,* where 6.*n* is the number of the original exercise in Chapter 6. We assume that SX, SY, PX, PY, JX, JY, SPJX, SPJY (etc.) are tuple variables ranging over relations S, P, J, SPJ, respectively; definitions of those range variables are not shown.

7.9.13 JX

7.9.14 JX WHERE JX.CITY = 'London'

7.9.15 SPJX.S# WHERE SPJX.J# = 'J1'

7.9.16 SPJX WHERE SPJX.QTY ≥ 300 AND SPJX.QTY ≤ 750

7.9.17 (PX.COLOR, PX.CITY)

7.9.18 (SX.S#, PX.P#, JX.J#) WHERE SX.CITY = PX.CITY
                                 AND   PX.CITY = JX.CITY
                                 AND   JX.CITY = SX.CITY

7.9.19 (SX.S#, PX.P#, JX.J#) WHERE SX.CITY ≠ PX.CITY
                                 OR   PX.CITY ≠ JX.CITY
                                 OR   JX.CITY ≠ SX.CITY

7.9.20 (SX.S#, PX.P#, JX.J#) WHERE SX.CITY ≠ PX.CITY
                                 AND   PX.CITY ≠ JX.CITY
                                 AND   JX.CITY ≠ SX.CITY

7.9.21 SPJX.P# WHERE EXISTS SX (SX.S# = SPJX.S# AND
                                    SX.CITY = 'London')

7.9.22 SPJX.P# WHERE EXISTS SX EXISTS JX
            (SX.S# = SPJX.S# AND SX.CITY = 'London' AND
              JX.J# = SPJX.J# AND JX.CITY = 'London')

7.9.23 (SX.CITY AS SCITY, JX.CITY AS JCITY)
          WHERE EXISTS SPJX (SPJX.S# = SX.S# AND SPJX.J# = JX.J#)

7.9.24 SPJX.P# WHERE EXISTS SX EXISTS JX
                    (SX.CITY = JX.CITY AND
                      SPJX.S# = SX.S# AND
                      SPJX.J# = JX.J#)

7.9.25 SPJX.J# WHERE EXISTS SX EXISTS JX
                    (SX.CITY ≠ JX.CITY AND
                      SPJX.S# = SX.S# AND
                      SPJX.J# = JX.J#)

7.9.26 (SPJX.P# AS XP#, SPJY.P# AS YP#)
          WHERE SPJX.S# = SPJY.S# AND SPJX.P# < SPJY.P#

7.9.27 COUNT (SPJX.J# WHERE SPJX.S# = 'S1') AS N

7.9.28 SUM (SPJX WHERE

        SPJX.S# = 'S1' AND SPJX.P# = 'P1', QTY) AS Q

The following "solution" is *not* correct (why not?):

    SUM (SPJX.QTY WHERE

        SPJX.S# = 'S1' AND SPJX.P# = 'P1', QTY) AS Q

(*Answer:* Because duplicate QTY values will now be eliminated before the sum is computed.)

7.9.29 (SPJX.P#, SPJX.J#,

      SUM (SPJY WHERE SPJY.P# = SPJX.P#

              AND   SPJY.J# = SPJX.J#, QTY) AS Q)

7.9.30 SPJX.P#

    WHERE AVG (SPJY WHERE SPJY.P# = SPJX.P#

              AND   SPJY.J# = SPJX.J#, QTY) > 320

7.9.31 JX.JNAME WHERE EXISTS SPJX (SPJX.J# = JX.J# AND

                            SPJX.S# = 'S1')

7.9.32 PX.COLOR WHERE EXISTS SPJX (SPJX.P# = PX.P# AND

                            SPJX.S# = 'S1')

7.9.33 SPJX.P# WHERE EXISTS JX (JX.CITY = 'London' AND

                        JX.J# = SPJX.J#)

7.9.34 SPJX.J# WHERE EXISTS SPJY (SPJX.P# = SPJY.P# AND

                          SPJY.S# = 'S1')

7.9.35 SPJX.S# WHERE EXISTS SPJY EXISTS SPJZ EXISTS PX

              (SPJX.P# = SPJY.P# AND

                SPJY.S# = SPJZ.S# AND

                SPJZ.P# = PX.P# AND

                PX.COLOR = 'Red')

7.9.36 SX.S# WHERE EXISTS SY (SY.S# = 'S1' AND

                          SX.STATUS < SY.STATUS)

7.9.37 JX.J# WHERE FORALL JY (JY.CITY ≥ **JX.CITY)**

Or: JX.J# WHERE JX.CITY = MIN (JY.CITY)

7.9.38 SPJX.J# WHERE SPJX.P# = 'P1' AND

        AVG (SPJY WHERE SPJY.P# = 'P1'

              AND   SPJY.J# = SPJX.J#, QTY) >

        MAX (SPJZ.QTY WHERE SPJZ.J# = 'J1')

7.9.39 SPJX.S# WHERE SPJX.P# = 'P1'

    AND   SPJX.QTY >

            AVG (SPJY

                WHERE SPJY.P# = 'P1'

                AND   SPJY.J# = SPJX.J#, QTY)

7.9.40 JX.J# WHERE NOT EXISTS SPJX EXISTS SX EXISTS PX

              (SX.CITY = 'London' AND

                PX.COLOR = 'Red' AND

                SPJX.S# = SX.S# AND

                SPJX.P# = PX.P# AND

                SPJX.J# = JX.J#)

7.9.41 JX.J# WHERE FORALL SPJY (IF SPJY.J# = JX.J#

                            THEN SPJY.S# = 'S1')

7.9.42 PX.P# WHERE FORALL JX

          (IF JX.CITY = 'London' THEN

            EXISTS SPJY (SPJY.P# = PX.P# AND

                        SPJY.J# = JX.J#))

7.9.43 SX.S# WHERE EXISTS PX FORALL JX EXISTS SPJY
        (SPJY.S# = SX.S# AND
        SPJY.P# = PX.P# AND
        SPJY.J# = JX.J#)

7.9.44 JX.J# WHERE FORALL SPJY (IF SPJY.S# = 'S1' THEN
                               EXISTS SPJZ
                          (SPJZ.J# = JX.J# AND
                          SPJZ.P# = SPJY.P#))

7.9.45 RANGE OF VX IS (SX.CITY), (PX.CITY), (JX.CITY) ;
VX.CITY

7.9.46 SPJX.P# WHERE EXISTS SX (SX.S# = SPJX.S# AND
                       SX.CITY = 'London')
        OR   EXISTS JX (JX.J# = SPJX.J# AND
                       JX.CITY = 'London')

7.9.47 (SX.S#, PX.P#) WHERE NOT EXISTS SPJX
                (SPJX.S# = SX.S# AND SPJX.P# = PX.P#)

7.9.48 (SX.S# AS XS#, SY.S# AS YS#) WHERE FORALL PZ
((IF   EXISTS SPJX (SPJX.S# = SX.S# AND SPJX.P# = PZ.P#)
   THEN EXISTS SPJY (SPJY.S# = SY.S# AND SPJY.P# = PZ.P#))
  AND
  (IF   EXISTS SPJY (SPJY.S# = SY.S# AND SPJY.P# = PZ.P#)
   THEN EXISTS SPJX (SPJX.S# = SX.S# AND SPJX.P# = PZ.P#)))

7.10 Left to the reader.

7.11 We have numbered the following solutions as 7.11.*n*, where 6.*n* is the number of the original exercise in Chapter 6. We follow the same conventions as in Section 7.6 regarding the definition and naming of domain variables.

7.11.13 (JX, NAMEX, CITYX)
    WHERE J (J#:JX, JNAME:NAMEX, CITY:CITYX)

7.11.14 (JX, NAMEX, 'London' AS CITY)
    WHERE J (J#:JX, JNAME:NAMEX, CITY:'London')

7.11.15 SX WHERE SPJ (S#:SX, J#:'J1')

7.11.16 (SX, PX, JX, QTYX)
    WHERE SPJ (S#:SX, P#:PX, J#:JX, QTY:QTYX)
    AND   QTYX ≥ 300 AND QTYX ≤ 750

7.11.17 (COLORX, CITYX) WHERE P (COLOR:COLORX, CITY:CITYX)

7.11.18 (SX, PX, JX) WHERE EXISTS CITYX
                     (S (S#:SX, CITY:CITYX) AND
                      P (P#:PX, CITY:CITYX) AND
                      J (J#:JX, CITY:CITYX))

7.11.19 (SX, PX, JX) WHERE EXISTS CITYX EXISTS CITYY EXISTS CITYZ
                     (S (S#:SX, CITY:CITYX) AND
                     P (P#:PX, CITY:CITYY) AND
                     J (J#:JX, CITY:CITYZ)
                  AND (CITYX ≠ CITYY OR
                         CITYY ≠ CITYZ OR
                         CITYZ ≠ CITYX))

7.11.20 (SX, PX, JX) WHERE EXISTS CITYX EXISTS CITYY EXISTS CITYZ
                     (S (S#:SX, CITY:CITYX) AND
                       P (P#:PX, CITY:CITYY) AND
                       J (J#:JX, CITY:CITYZ)
                       AND (CITYX ≠ CITYY AND
                             CITYY ≠ CITYZ AND
                             CITYZ ≠ CITYX))

7.11.21 PX WHERE EXISTS SX (SPJ (P#:PX, S#:SX) AND
                         S (S#:SX, CITY:'London'))

7.11.22 PX WHERE EXISTS SX EXISTS JX
             (SPJ (S#:SX, P#:PX, J#:JX)
               AND S (S#:SX, CITY:'London')
               AND J (J#:JX, CITY:'London'))

7.11.23 (CITYX AS SCITY, CITYY AS JCITY)
             WHERE EXISTS SX EXISTS JY
                (S (S#:SX, CITY:CITYX)
                  AND J (J#:JY, CITY:CITYY)
                  AND SPJ (S#:SX, J#:JY))

7.11.24 PX WHERE EXISTS SX EXISTS JX EXISTS CITYX
             (S (S#:SX, CITY:CITYX)
               AND J (J#:JX, CITY:CITYX)
               AND SPJ (S#:SX, P#:PX, J#:JX))

7.11.25 JY WHERE EXISTS SX EXISTS CITYX EXISTS CITYY
             (SPJ (S#:SX, J#:JY)
               AND S (S#:SX, CITY:CITYX)
               AND J (J#:JY, CITY:CITYY)
               AND CITYX ≠ CITYY)

7.11.26 (PX AS XP#, PY AS YP#) WHERE EXISTS SX
                            (SPJ (S#:SX, P#:PX)
                              AND SPJ (S#:SX, P#:PY)
                              AND PX < PY)

7.11.27–30 Solutions omitted.

7.11.31 NAMEX WHERE EXISTS JX
                (J (J#:JX, JNAME:NAMEX)
                  AND SPJ (S#:'S1', J#:JX))

7.11.32 COLORX WHERE EXISTS PX
                  (P (P#:PX, COLOR:COLORX) AND
                    SPJ (S#:'S1', P#:PX))

7.11.33 PX WHERE EXISTS JX
             (SPJ (P#:PX, J#:JX) AND
               J (J#:JX, CITY:'London'))

7.11.34 JX WHERE EXISTS PX
             (SPJ (P#:PX, J#:JX) AND
               SPJ (P#:PX, S#:'S1'))

7.11.35 SX WHERE EXISTS PX EXISTS SY EXISTS PY
             (SPJ (S#:SX, P#:PX) AND
               SPJ (P#:PX, S#:SY) AND
               SPJ (S#:SY, P#:PY) AND
               P (P#:PY, COLOR:'Red'))

7.11.36 SX WHERE EXISTS STATUSX EXISTS STATUSY
              (S (S#:SX, STATUS:STATUSX) AND
              S (S#:'S1', STATUS:STATUSY) AND
              STATUSX < STATUSY)

7.11.37 JX WHERE EXISTS CITYX
              (J (J#:JX, CITY:CITYX) AND
              FORALL CITYY (IF J (CITY:CITYY)
                                  THEN CITYY ≥ CITYX))

7.11.38–39 Solutions omitted.

7.11.40 JX WHERE J (J#:JX) AND
              NOT EXISTS SX EXISTS PX
                 (SPJ (S#:SX, P#:PX, J#:JX) AND
                 S (S#:SX, CITY:'London') AND
                 P (P#:PX, COLOR:'Red'))

7.11.41 JX WHERE J (J#:JX)
         AND   FORALL SX (IF SPJ (S#:SX, J#:JX)
                          THEN SX = 'S1')

7.11.42 PX WHERE P (P#:PX)
         AND   FORALL JX (IF J (J#:JX, CITY:'London')
                          THEN SPJ (P#:PX, J#:JX))

7.11.43 SX WHERE S (S#:SX)
         AND   EXISTS PX FORALL JX
            (SPJ (S#:SX, P#:PX, J#:JX))

7.11.44 JX WHERE J (J#:JX)
         AND   FORALL PX (IF SPJ (S#:'S1', P#:PX)
                          THEN SPJ (P#:PX, J#:JX))

7.11.45 CITYX WHERE S (CITY:CITYX)
           OR   P (CITY:CITYX)
           OR   J (CITY:CITYX)

7.11.46 PX WHERE EXISTS SX (SPJ (S#:SX, P#:PX) AND
                            S (S#:SX, CITY:'London'))
           OR   EXISTS JX (SPJ (J#:JX, P#:PX) AND
                            J (J#:JX, CITY:'London'))

7.11.47 (SX, PX) WHERE S (S#:SX) AND P (P#:PX)
               AND   NOT SPJ (S#:SX, P#:PX)

7.11.48 (SX AS XS#, SY AS YS#) WHERE S (S#:SX) AND S (S#:SY)
         AND FORALL PZ
           ((IF SPJ (S#:SX, P#:PZ) THEN SPJ (S#:SY, P#:PZ))
             AND
             (IF SPJ (S#:SY, P#:PZ) THEN SPJ (S#:SX, P#:PZ)))

8 | The SQL Language

8.1 Introduction

As mentioned in the introduction to this part of the book, SQL is very far from being a faithful implementation of the relational model. Nevertheless, it *is* the standard relational language, it is supported by just about every product on the market today, and so every database professional needs to know something about it. Hence this chapter.

The first thing that must be said is that SQL is an enormous language. The standard document itself [8.1] is well over 600 pages long. As a consequence, it is not possible in a book of this nature to treat the subject exhaustively; all we can hope to do is describe major aspects in a reasonably comprehensive manner, but the reader is warned that our discussions are necessarily sketchy and superficial in many places. In particular, we have not hesitated to omit material that is irrelevant to the purpose at hand, nor to make significant simplifications in the interests of brevity. More complete (but still tutorial) descriptions can be found in references [8.5–8.7].

The plan of the chapter is as follows. Following this introductory section, Section 8.2 treats SQL's data definition facilities and Sections 8.3–8.4 treat SQL's data manipulation facilities (Section 8.3 covers retrieval operations and Section 8.4 update operations). Sections 8.5–8.7 then focus on three key SQL constructs, namely table expressions (including in particular *select* expressions), conditional expressions, and scalar expressions, respectively. Next, Section 8.8 describes the special considerations that apply to "embedded" SQL (i.e., the facilities for embedding SQL statements in a host language program). Section 8.9 presents a brief summary. *Note:* Additional aspects of SQL, having to do with matters such as recovery, concurrency, etc., will be described briefly in subsequent chapters devoted to those topics.

A few further preliminary remarks are in order. First, our discussions are all at the level of the current standard [8.1] known informally as "SQL/92," also as "SQL-92" or just "SQL2"; the official name is **International Standard Database Language SQL (1992)**. The presentation is loosely based on material from reference [8.5], though it has been considerably revised to suit the needs of the present book. Please note also that:

- The "#" character, much used in our example domain and column names, is in fact not legal in SQL/92.

- We use the semicolon ";" as a statement terminator, but SQL/92 actually prescribes such a terminator only in the case of embedded SQL, and then only for certain host languages.

- We often use names for syntactic categories that are different from those of the standard, because the standard terminology is often not very apt.

Although our discussions are all at the SQL/92 level, we should make it clear that no product actually supports the whole of SQL/92 at the time of writing. Instead, products typically support what might be called "a superset of a subset" of SQL/92. In other words, any given product, while it fails to support certain aspects of the standard, will at the same time probably go beyond the standard in certain other respects. IBM's DB2 product, for example, certainly does not support all of the SQL/92 integrity features, but it does go beyond the standard in its rules regarding view updatability.

One final introductory remark: SQL uses the terms *table, row,* and *column* in place of the relational terms *relation, tuple,* and *attribute.* For consistency with the SQL standard and SQL products, therefore, we will do likewise in this chapter (and elsewhere in this book whenever we are concerned with SQL specifically).

8.2 Data Definition

In this section we examine the **basic data objects** and corresponding **data definition language (DDL) statements** of SQL. The principal DDL statements are as follows:

```
CREATE DOMAIN    CREATE TABLE
ALTER DOMAIN     ALTER TABLE
DROP DOMAIN      DROP TABLE
```

There are also statements for creating and destroying ("dropping") views, but we defer discussion of views to Chapter 17.

Domains

SQL's "domains" are unfortunately a long way from being true relational domains as described in Chapters 4 and 19; in fact, the two concepts are so far apart that it would have been preferable to use some other name for the SQL construct. Almost the sole purpose of domains in SQL is to allow a simple data type specification (such as "S# CHAR(5)") to be defined once and then shared by several columns in several base tables. For purposes of reference, we list below some of the principal differences between true domains and the SQL construct (many of these points will not make much sense until the reader has studied Chapter 19):

- As already suggested, SQL domains are really just a syntactic shorthand. They are certainly not true user-defined data types.

- There is no requirement that SQL domains even be used—columns in base tables can be defined directly in terms of the builtin, system-defined data types such as FLOAT or INTEGER.

- There is no SQL support for "domains on domains": An SQL domain must be defined in terms of one of the builtin, system-defined data types, not another user-defined domain.

- SQL does not provide anything like *strong typing*. There is no true type checking. In particular, domains do not "constrain comparisons"—the only requirement on comparisons is that the comparands must be of the same *basic* type, i.e., both numeric or both character strings or (etc.). An analogous remark applies to numeric expressions, character string expressions, bit string expressions, . . . (etc., etc.): In all cases, domains as such are essentially irrelevant.

- SQL does not support the ability for users to define the operations that apply to a given domain.

- SQL does not make a clear distinction between a domain as such (i.e., a user-defined data type) and the *representation* of that domain in terms of one of the system-defined data types.

- SQL does not have any concept of subtypes and supertypes, nor of inheritance.

- Finally, SQL does not even support what is arguably the most fundamental domain of all, *viz.* the domain of truth values!

Here is the syntax for creating an SQL domain. *Note:* As in Chapter 7 we use square brackets "[" and "]" to indicate optional material, and we will continue to do so throughout this chapter.

```
CREATE DOMAIN domain data-type
            [ default-definition ]
            [ domain-constraint-definition-list ] ;
```

Explanation:

1. SQL supports the following **scalar data types,** most of them self-explanatory. (A number of defaults, abbreviations, and alternative spellings—e.g., CHAR for CHARACTER—are also supported. We omit the details here.)

```
CHARACTER [ VARYING ] (n)     INTEGER      DATE
BIT [ VARYING ] (n)           SMALLINT     TIME
NUMERIC (p,q)                 FLOAT (p)    TIMESTAMP
DECIMAL (p,q)                              INTERVAL
```

2. The optional *default-definition* specifies a default value that applies to every column that is defined on the domain and does not have an explicit default value of its own. It takes the form "DEFAULT *default*"—where *default* in turn is a literal, a reference to a niladic builtin function (e.g., CURRENT_DATE), or NULL.* *Note:* A niladic function is a function that takes no arguments.

---

* We defer detailed discussion of SQL's support for nulls to Chapter 20. Passing references to nulls in the present chapter are unavoidable, however.

3. The optional list of *domain constraint definitions* specifies a set of integrity constraints that apply to every column defined on the domain. Now, we will explain in Chapter 16 that a domain integrity constraint is—or, rather, should be—conceptually nothing more than an enumeration of the values that go to make up that domain. SQL, however, allows a domain constraint to involve a truth-valued expression *of arbitrary complexity*. We leave it as an exercise for the reader to meditate on some of the unfortunate implications of this unwarranted permissiveness.

Here is an example:

```
CREATE DOMAIN COLOR CHAR(6) DEFAULT '???'
       CONSTRAINT VALID_COLORS
       CHECK ( VALUE IN
               ( 'Red', 'Yellow', 'Blue', 'Green', '???' ) ) ;
```

Now the CREATE TABLE for base table P, the parts table, might look like this:

```
CREATE TABLE P ( ... , COLOR COLOR, ... ) ;
```

If the user inserts a row into table P and does not provide a value for the COLOR column within that row, then the value "???" will be placed in that position by default. Alternatively, if the user *does* provide a COLOR value but it is not one of the legal set, the operation will fail, of course, and the system will produce a diagnostic that mentions the VALID_COLORS constraint.

Next, an existing domain can be **altered** at any time in a variety of ways by means of the statement ALTER DOMAIN. Specifically, ALTER DOMAIN allows a new default definition to be specified for an existing domain (replacing the previous one, if any) or an existing one to be deleted. It also allows a new integrity constraint to be specified for an existing domain or an existing one to be deleted. The details of these various options are surprisingly complex, however, and beyond the scope of this book; the interested reader is referred to reference [8.1] or reference [8.5] for further discussion.

Finally, an existing domain can be **destroyed** by means of the statement DROP DOMAIN—syntax:

```
DROP DOMAIN domain option ;
```

where *option* is either RESTRICT or CASCADE. The general idea here is as follows: (a) If RESTRICT is specified, the DROP will fail if the domain is referenced anywhere; (b) if CASCADE is specified, the DROP will succeed and will "cascade" in various ways (for example, columns that were previously defined on the domain will now be considered to be directly defined on the domain's underlying data type instead). Once again the details are quite complex, and we omit them here. See reference [8.1] or reference [8.5] for further information.

Base Tables

Before we get into the details of base tables specifically, there are a couple of points to be made on the topic of SQL tables in general. First, SQL tables—unlike true relations—are allowed to include **duplicate rows;** they therefore do not necessarily have any candidate keys. Second, SQL tables—unlike true relations—are considered to have a **left-to-right column ordering;** in the suppliers table S, for example, column S# might be the first column, column SNAME might be the second column, and so on.

Turning to base tables specifically: Base tables are defined by means of the CREATE TABLE statement (note, therefore, that the keyword TABLE here refers to a base table specifically; the same is true of ALTER TABLE and DROP TABLE, *q.v.*). The syntax is as follows:

```
CREATE TABLE base-table ( base-table-element-commalist ) ;
```

where each *base-table-element* is either a *column-definition* or a *base-table-constraint-definition.* Each *column-definition* in turn (there must be at least one such) looks like this:

```
column representation [ default-definition ]
```

Here *representation* specifies the relevant data type or domain, and the optional *default-definition* specifies a default for the column, overriding any default specified at the domain level, if applicable. If a given column does not have an explicit default of its own and does not inherit one from an underlying domain, it is implicitly assumed to have a default of NULL—i.e., NULL is the "default default."

Each *base-table-constraint-definition* is one of the following:

- a candidate key definition
- a foreign key definition
- a "check constraint" definition

We proceed to discuss each of these in more detail. *Note:* Each can optionally be preceded by the phrase "CONSTRAINT *constraint,*" thereby providing a name for the new constraint (the same is true for domain constraints, as we saw in the VALID_COLORS example earlier). For brevity, we ignore this option in our further discussions below.

Candidate keys: A candidate key definition takes the form

```
UNIQUE ( column-commalist )
```

or the form

```
PRIMARY KEY ( column-commalist )
```

The *column-commalist* must not be empty in either case. A given base table can have at most one PRIMARY KEY specification but any number of UNIQUE specifications. In the case of PRIMARY KEY, each specified column is additionally assumed to be NOT NULL, even if NOT NULL is not specified explicitly (see "Check constraints" below).

Foreign keys: A foreign key definition takes the form

```
FOREIGN KEY ( column-commalist )
        REFERENCES base-table [ ( column-commalist ) ]
        [ ON DELETE option ]
        [ ON UPDATE option ]
```

where *option* is NO ACTION or CASCADE or SET DEFAULT or SET NULL. CAS-
CADE and SET NULL correspond directly to our CASCADES and NULLIFIES (refer
back to Chapter 5 if you need to refresh your memory); NO ACTION, which is the
default, is similar but not identical to our RESTRICTED (see reference [8.5] for an
explanation of the differences), and SET DEFAULT is self-explanatory. *Note:* The second *column-commalist* is required if the foreign key references a candidate key that is
not a primary key.

Check constraints: A "check constraint definition" takes the form

```
CHECK ( conditional-expression )
```

An attempt to create a row within base table *B* is considered to violate a check constraint for *B* if it causes the conditional expression specified within that constraint to
evaluate to *false*. Note that the conditional expression can be arbitrarily complex; it is
specifically *not* limited to a restriction condition referring just to table *B*, but can instead
refer to anything in the database. Reference [8.19] offers some critical comments regarding this unnecessary generality.

Here is an example of CREATE TABLE:

```
CREATE TABLE SP
     ( S# S# NOT NULL, P# P# NOT NULL, QTY QTY NOT NULL,
       PRIMARY KEY ( S#, P# ),
       FOREIGN KEY ( S# ) REFERENCES S
                          ON DELETE CASCADE
                          ON UPDATE CASCADE,
       FOREIGN KEY ( P# ) REFERENCES P
                          ON DELETE CASCADE
                          ON UPDATE CASCADE,
       CHECK ( QTY > 0 AND QTY < 5001 ) ) ;
```

We are assuming here that (a) domains S#, P#, and QTY have already been defined,
and (b) S# and P# have been explicitly defined to be the primary keys for tables S and
P, respectively. Also, we have deliberately made use of the convenient shorthand by
which a check constraint of the form

```
CHECK ( column IS NOT NULL )
```

can be replaced by a simple NOT NULL specification in the definition of the column
in question. In the example, we have thus replaced three slightly cumbersome check
constraints by three simple NOT NULLs.

Next, an existing base table can be **altered** at any time by means of the ALTER
TABLE statement. The following alterations are supported:

- A new column can be added
- A new default can be defined for an existing column (replacing the previous one,
  if any)
- An existing column default can be deleted
- An existing column can be deleted

■   A new base table integrity constraint can be specified

■   An existing base table integrity constraint can be deleted

We give an example of the first case only:

```
ALTER TABLE S ADD COLUMN DISCOUNT INTEGER DEFAULT -1 ;
```

This statement adds a DISCOUNT column (of type INTEGER) to the suppliers base table. All existing rows in that table are extended from four columns to five; the value of the new fifth column is minus 1 in every case.

Finally, an existing base table can be **destroyed** by means of DROP TABLE— syntax:

```
DROP TABLE base-table option ;
```

where (as with DROP DOMAIN) *option* is either RESTRICT or CASCADE. If RESTRICT is specified and the base table is referenced in any view definition or integrity constraint, the DROP will fail; if CASCADE is specified, the DROP will succeed (destroying the table along with all of its rows), and any referencing view definitions and integrity constraints will be dropped also.

The Information Schema

The SQL analog of what is more conventionally known as the *catalog* is called the **Information Schema**. In fact, the familiar terms "catalog" and "schema" are both used in SQL, but with highly SQL-specific meanings. Loosely speaking, a **catalog** in SQL consists of the descriptors for an individual database,* and a **schema** consists of the descriptors for that portion of that database that belongs to some individual user. In other words, there can be any number of catalogs, each divided up into any number of schemas. However, each catalog is required to include exactly one schema called INFORMATION_SCHEMA, and from the user's perspective it is that schema (as already indicated) that performs the normal "catalog" function.

The Information Schema thus consists of a set of SQL tables whose contents effectively echo, in a precisely defined way, all of the definitions from all of the other schemas in the catalog in question. More precisely, the Information Schema is defined to contain a set of **views** of a hypothetical "Definition Schema." The implementation is not required to support the Definition Schema as such, but it is required (a) to support *some* kind of "Definition Schema," and (b) to support views of that "Definition Schema" that do look like those of the Information Schema. Points arising:

1. The rationale for stating the requirement in terms of two separate pieces (a) and (b) as just described is as follows. First, existing products certainly do support something akin to the "Definition Schema." However, those "Definition Schemas" vary widely from one product to another (even when the products in question come

---

* In the interests of accuracy, we should point out that there is actually no such thing as a "database" in the SQL standard! Exactly what the collection of data is that is described by a given catalog is implementation-defined. However, it is not unreasonable to think of it as a database.

from the same vendor). Hence the idea of requiring only that the implementation support certain predefined views of its "Definition Schema" makes sense.

2. We should really say "an" (not "the") Information Schema, since as we have seen there is one such schema in every catalog. In general, therefore, the totality of data available to a given user will *not* be described by a single Information Schema. To simplify our discussion, however, we will continue to talk as if there really were just one such schema.

It is not worth going into great detail on the content of the Information Schema here. Instead, we simply list some of the more important Information Schema views, in the hope that their names alone will be sufficient to give some idea of what that schema covers (we remark, however, that the TABLES view includes information regarding *all* named tables, views as well as base tables; the VIEWS view contains information for views only, of course). We deliberately ignore some of the more esoteric features.

```
SCHEMATA                       REFERENTIAL_CONSTRAINTS
DOMAINS                        CHECK_CONSTRAINTS
TABLES                         KEY_COLUMN_USAGE
VIEWS                          ASSERTIONS
COLUMNS                        VIEW_TABLE_USAGE
TABLE_PRIVILEGES               VIEW_COLUMN_USAGE
COLUMN_PRIVILEGES              CONSTRAINT_TABLE_USAGE
USAGE_PRIVILEGES               CONSTRAINT_COLUMN_USAGE
DOMAIN_CONSTRAINTS             CONSTRAINT_DOMAIN_USAGE
TABLE_CONSTRAINTS
```

8.3   Data Manipulation: Retrieval Operations

Now we turn to the **data manipulation language (DML)** statements of SQL. The principal DML statements are SELECT, INSERT, UPDATE, and DELETE. The present section considers retrieval operations (SELECT) and the next section considers update operations (INSERT, UPDATE, DELETE). For simplicity, we assume throughout that all statements are entered interactively; the special considerations that apply to SQL statements embedded in application programs are discussed in Section 8.8.

A retrieval operation in SQL is essentially just a **table expression,** of potentially arbitrary complexity. We do not get into all of that complexity here; rather, we simply present a set of examples, in the hope that those examples will serve to highlight some of the most important points. (To facilitate comparisons with the relational algebra and relational calculus, we also give references to the corresponding examples in Chapters 6 and 7, where applicable.) A more complete, and more formal, treatment of table expressions in general is given in Section 8.5.

8.3.1 Get color and city for "nonParis" parts with weight greater than ten.

```
SELECT  P.COLOR, P.CITY
FROM    P
WHERE   P.CITY <> 'Paris'
AND     P.WEIGHT > 10 ;
```

First of all, note the use of the symbol <> (not equals) in this example. The usual scalar comparison operators are written as follows in SQL: =, <>, <, >, <=, and >=.

Next (and much more important), note that—given our usual sample data—this query will return *four* rows, not two, even though three of those four rows are identical, all being of the form (Red,London). SQL does not eliminate redundant duplicate rows from the result of a SELECT unless the user explicitly requests it to do so via the keyword **DISTINCT**, as in:

```
SELECT DISTINCT P.COLOR, P.CITY
FROM     P
WHERE    P.CITY <> 'Paris'
AND      P.WEIGHT > 10 ;
```

This query will return two rows only.

Incidentally, we could perfectly well have omitted the "P." qualifiers throughout this example. The general rule regarding **name qualification** in SQL is that unqualified names are acceptable if they cause no ambiguity. In our examples, however, we will generally include all qualifiers, even when they are technically redundant. (Unfortunately, however, there are certain contexts in which column names are explicitly required to be *un*qualified! An example is the ORDER BY clause—see below.)

Finally, note that the sequence of rows in a given result table is unpredictable, in general, *unless* the user explicitly requests some particular sequence, as here:

```
SELECT DISTINCT P.COLOR, P.CITY
FROM     P
WHERE    P.CITY <> 'Paris'
AND      P.WEIGHT > 10
ORDER    BY CITY DESC ;
```

In general, the **ORDER BY** clause takes the form

```
ORDER BY order-item-commalist
```

where (a) the commalist must not be empty, and (b) each *order-item* consists of an *un*qualified column name, optionally followed by ASC or DESC (where ASC and DESC mean ascending and descending, respectively, and ASC is the default).

8.3.2 For all parts, get the part number and the weight of that part in grams.

```
SELECT P.P#, P.WEIGHT * 454 AS GMWT
FROM     P ;
```

The specification AS GMWT introduces an appropriate result column name for the "computed column." The two columns of the result table are thus called P# and GMWT, respectively. If the AS GMWT specification had been omitted, the corresponding result column would effectively have been unnamed. Observe, therefore, that SQL does not actually require the user to provide a result column name in such circumstances, but we will always do so in our examples.

8.3.3 Get full details of all suppliers.

```
SELECT *    — or "SELECT S.*" (i.e., the "*" can be qualified)
FROM     S ;
```

The result is a copy of the entire S table; the star or asterisk is shorthand for a list of all column names in the table(s) referenced in the FROM clause, in the left-to-right order in which those column(s) are defined within those table(s). Notice the **comment** in this example, incidentally (SQL comments are introduced with a double hyphen and terminate with a newline character).

We remark that the star notation is convenient for interactive queries, since it saves keystrokes. However, it is potentially dangerous in embedded SQL—i.e., SQL within an application program—because the meaning of the "*" might change (e.g., if a column is added to or dropped from some table, via ALTER TABLE).

Note: In SQL/92 the expression SELECT * FROM *T* (where *T* is a table name) can be further abbreviated to just TABLE *T*.

8.3.4 Get all combinations of supplier and part information such that the supplier and part in question are colocated. SQL provides several different ways of formulating this query. We give three of the simplest here.

```
1. SELECT  S.S#, S.SNAME, S.STATUS, S.CITY,
           P.P#, P.PNAME, P.COLOR, P.WEIGHT
   FROM    S, P
   WHERE   S.CITY = P.CITY ;
2. S JOIN P USING CITY ;
3. S NATURAL JOIN P ;
```

The result in each case is the **natural join** of tables S and P (on cities).

The first of the foregoing formulations—which is the only one of the three that would have been valid in SQL as originally defined (the explicit JOIN support was added in SQL/92)—merits further discussion. Conceptually, we can think of that version of the query as being implemented as follows:

- First, the FROM clause is executed, to yield the **Cartesian product** S TIMES SP.

- Next, the WHERE clause is executed, to yield a **restriction** of that product in which the two CITY values in each row are equal (in other words, we have now constructed the *equijoin* of suppliers and parts over cities).

- Finally, the SELECT clause is executed, to yield a **projection** of that restriction over the columns mentioned in the SELECT clause. The final result is the natural join.

Loosely speaking, therefore, FROM in SQL corresponds to Cartesian product, WHERE to restrict, and SELECT to project, and the SQL SELECT–FROM–WHERE represents a projection of a restriction of a product.

8.3.5 Get all pairs of city names such that a supplier located in the first city supplies a part stored in the second city.

```
SELECT DISTINCT S.CITY AS SCITY, P.CITY AS PCITY
FROM   S JOIN SP USING S# JOIN P USING P# ;
```

Notice that the following is *not* correct, because it includes CITY as a joining column in the second join:

```
SELECT DISTINCT S.CITY AS SCITY, P.CITY AS PCITY
FROM    S NATURAL JOIN SP NATURAL JOIN P ;
```

8.3.6 Get all pairs of supplier numbers such that the two suppliers concerned are colocated. (Examples 6.6.5, 7.3.2)

```
SELECT FIRST.S# AS SA, SECOND.S# AS SB
FROM   S AS FIRST, S AS SECOND
WHERE  FIRST.CITY = SECOND.CITY
AND    FIRST.S# < SECOND.S# ;
```

Note the explicit **range variables** FIRST and SECOND in this example. The range variables have all been implicit in our previous examples (see the annotation to reference [7.3] if you need to refresh your memory regarding implicit range variables). Note too that the introduced column names SA and SB refer to columns of the *result table*, and so cannot be used in the WHERE clause.

8.3.7 Get the total number of suppliers.

```
SELECT COUNT(*) AS N
FROM   S ;
```

The result here is a table with one column, called N, and one row, containing the value 5. SQL supports the usual set of **aggregate functions** (COUNT, SUM, AVG, MAX, and MIN), but there are a few SQL-specific points the user needs to be aware of, *viz.*:

■ In general, the argument of the function can optionally be preceded by the keyword DISTINCT, to indicate that duplicates are to be eliminated before the function is applied. For MAX and MIN, however, DISTINCT is irrelevant and has no effect.

■ The special function COUNT(*)—DISTINCT not allowed— is provided to count all rows in a table without any duplicate elimination.

■ Any nulls in the argument column are always eliminated before the function is applied, regardless of whether DISTINCT is specified, except for the case of COUNT(*), where nulls are handled just like nonnull values.

■ If the argument happens to be an empty set, COUNT returns a value of zero; the other functions all return null. (We have argued elsewhere that this behavior is logically incorrect—see reference [8.19]—but it is the way SQL is defined.)

8.3.8 Get the maximum and minimum quantity for part P2.

```
SELECT MAX ( SP.QTY ) AS MAXQ, MIN ( SP.QTY ) AS MINQ
FROM   SP
WHERE  SP.P# = 'P2' ;
```

Observe that the FROM and WHERE clauses here both effectively provide part of the argument to the two aggregate functions. They should therefore logically appear within the argument-enclosing parentheses. Nevertheless, the query is indeed written as shown. This unorthodox approach to syntax has significant negative repercussions on the structure, usability, and orthogonality* of the SQL language. For instance, one immediate consequence is that aggregate functions cannot be nested, with the result that a query such as "Get the average total-part-quantity" cannot be formulated without cumbersome circumlocutions (because the expression AVG(SUM(QTY)) is not legal). Further details of such matters are beyond the scope of this book.

8.3.9 For each part supplied, get the part number and the total shipment quantity. (Example 7.5.4)

```
SELECT  SP.P#, SUM ( SP.QTY ) AS TOTQTY
FROM    SP
GROUP   BY SP.P# ;
```

The foregoing is the SQL analog of the relational algebra expression

```
SUMMARIZE SP BY ( P# ) ADD SUM ( QTY ) AS TOTQTY
```

Observe in particular that if the GROUP BY clause is specified, expressions in the SELECT clause must be **single-valued per group**.

Here is an alternative formulation of the same query:

```
SELECT  P.P#, ( SELECT SUM ( SP.QTY )
                FROM    SP
                WHERE   SP.P# = P.P# ) AS TOTQTY
FROM    P ;
```

The ability to use nested select expressions to represent scalar items (e.g., within the SELECT clause, as here) was added in SQL/92 and represents a major improvement over SQL as originally defined. In the example, it allows us to generate a result that includes rows for parts that are not supplied at all, which the previous formulation (using GROUP BY) does not. (The TOTQTY value for such parts will unfortunately be given as null, however, not zero.)

8.3.10 Get part numbers for all parts supplied by more than one supplier.

```
SELECT  SP.P#
FROM    SP
GROUP   BY SP.P#
HAVING COUNT ( SP.S# ) > 1 ;
```

The HAVING clause is to groups what the WHERE clause is to rows; in other words, HAVING is used to eliminate groups, just as WHERE is used to eliminate rows. Expressions in a HAVING clause must be single-valued per group.

8.3.11 Get supplier names for suppliers who supply part P2. (Examples 6.6.1, 7.3.3)

---

* **Orthogonality** means *independence*. A language is orthogonal if independent concepts are kept independent, not mixed together in confusing ways. Orthogonality is desirable because the less orthogonal a language is, the more complicated it is and— paradoxically but simultaneously—the less powerful it is.

```
SELECT DISTINCT S.SNAME
FROM    S
WHERE   S.S# IN
      ( SELECT SP.S#
        FROM    SP
        WHERE   SP.P# = 'P2' ) ;
```

Explanation: This example makes use of what is called a **subquery**. Loosely speaking, a subquery is a SELECT–FROM–WHERE–GROUP BY–HAVING expression that is nested inside another such expression. Subqueries are typically used to represent the set of values to be searched via an **IN condition,** as the example illustrates. The system evaluates the overall query by evaluating the subquery first (at least conceptually). That subquery returns the set of supplier *numbers* for suppliers who supply part P2, namely the set {S1,S2,S3,S4}. The original expression is thus equivalent to the following simpler one:

```
SELECT DISTINCT S.SNAME
FROM    S
WHERE   S.S# IN ( 'S1', 'S2', 'S3', 'S4' ) ;
```

It is worth pointing out that the original problem—"Get supplier names for suppliers who supply part P2"—can equally well be formulated by means of a *join,* e.g., as follows:

```
SELECT DISTINCT S.SNAME
FROM    S, SP
WHERE   S.S# = SP.S#
AND     SP.P# = 'P2' ;
```

8.3.12 Get supplier names for suppliers who supply at least one red part. (Examples 6.6.2, 7.3.4)

```
SELECT DISTINCT S.SNAME
FROM    S
WHERE   S.S# IN
      ( SELECT SP.S#
        FROM    SP
        WHERE   SP.P# IN
              ( SELECT P.P#
                FROM    P
                WHERE   P.COLOR = 'Red' ) ) ;
```

Subqueries can be nested to any depth. *Exercise:* Give some equivalent join formulations of this query.

8.3.13 Get supplier numbers for suppliers with status less than the current maximum status in the S table.

```
SELECT S.S#
FROM    S
WHERE   S.STATUS <
      ( SELECT MAX ( S.STATUS )
        FROM    S ) ;
```

This example involves *two distinct implicit range variables,* both denoted by the same symbol "S" and both ranging over the S table.

8.3.14 Get supplier names for suppliers who supply part P2. (Same as Example 8.3.11)

```
SELECT DISTINCT S.SNAME
FROM    S
WHERE   EXISTS
      ( SELECT *
        FROM    SP
        WHERE   SP.S# = S.S#
        AND     SP.P# = 'P2' ) ;
```

Explanation: The SQL expression "EXISTS (SELECT . . . FROM . . .)" evaluates to *true* if and only if the result of evaluating the "SELECT . . . FROM . . ." is not empty. In other words, the SQL **EXISTS** *function* corresponds to the *existential quantifier* of relational calculus (but see Chapter 20).

8.3.15 Get supplier names for suppliers who do not supply part P2. (Examples 6.6.6, 7.3.7)

```
SELECT DISTINCT S.SNAME
FROM    S
WHERE   NOT EXISTS
      ( SELECT *
        FROM    SP
        WHERE   SP.S# = S.S#
        AND     SP.P# = 'P2' ) ;
```

Alternatively:

```
SELECT DISTINCT S.SNAME
FROM    S
WHERE   S.S# NOT IN
      ( SELECT SP.S#
        FROM   SP
        WHERE  SP.P# = 'P2' ) ;
```

8.3.16 Get supplier names for suppliers who supply all parts. (Examples 6.6.3, 7.3.6)

```
SELECT DISTINCT S.SNAME
FROM    S
WHERE   NOT EXISTS
      ( SELECT *
        FROM   P
        WHERE  NOT EXISTS
             ( SELECT *
               FROM   SP
               WHERE  SP.S# = S.S#
               AND    SP.P# = P.P# ) ) ;
```

SQL does not include any direct support for the universal quantifier FORALL; hence,

"FORALL-type" queries typically have to be expressed in terms of a negated existential quantifier, as in this example.

It is worth pointing out that expressions such as the one just shown, daunting though they might appear at first glance, are easily constructed by a user who is familiar with relational calculus, as explained in reference [7.6]. Alternatively—if they are still thought too daunting—then there are several "workaround" approaches that can be used that avoid the need for negated quantifiers. In the example, for instance, we might write:

```
SELECT  DISTINCT S.SNAME
FROM    S
WHERE   ( SELECT COUNT ( SP.P# )
          FROM    SP
          WHERE   SP.S# = S.S# ) = ( SELECT COUNT ( P.P# )
                                     FROM    P ) ;
```

("names of suppliers where the count of the parts they supply is equal to the count of all parts"). Note, however, that:

- First, this latter formulation relies—as the NOT EXISTS formulation did not—on the fact that no part number appears in relation SP that does not also appear in relation P. In other words, the two formulations are equivalent (and the second is correct) only because a certain integrity constraint is in effect.

- Second, the technique used in the second formulation to compare two counts was not supported in SQL as originally defined but was added in SQL/92. It is still not supported in all products.

- We remark too that what we would *really* like to do is to compare two *tables* (see the discussion of relational comparisons in Chapter 6), thereby expressing the query as follows:

```
SELECT  DISTINCT S.SNAME
FROM    S
WHERE   ( SELECT SP.P#
          FROM    SP
          WHERE   SP.S# = S.S# ) = ( SELECT P.P#
                                     FROM    P ) ;
```

SQL does not directly support comparisons between tables, however, and so we have to resort to the trick of comparing table cardinalities instead (relying on our own external knowledge to ensure that if the cardinalities are the same then the tables are the same too, at least in the situation under consideration). See Exercise 8.8 at the end of the chapter.

8.3.17 Get part numbers for parts that either weigh more than 16 pounds or are supplied by supplier S2, or both. (Example 7.3.9)

```
SELECT  P.P#
FROM    P
WHERE   P.WEIGHT > 16
UNION
```

```
SELECT  SP.P#
FROM    SP
WHERE   SP.S# = 'S2' ;
```

Redundant duplicate rows are always eliminated from the result of an unqualified **UNION, INTERSECT,** or **EXCEPT** (EXCEPT is the SQL analog of our MINUS). However, SQL also provides the qualified variants **UNION ALL, INTERSECT ALL,** and **EXCEPT ALL,** where duplicates (if any) are retained. We deliberately omit examples of these variants.

This brings us to the end of our list of retrieval examples. The list is rather long; nevertheless, there are numerous SQL features that we have not even mentioned. The fact is, SQL is an extremely *redundant* language, in the sense that it almost always provides numerous different ways of formulating the same query, and space simply does not permit us to describe all possible formulations and all possible options, even for the comparatively small number of examples we have discussed in this section.

8.4   Data Manipulation: Update Operations

As already mentioned, the SQL DML includes three update operations: INSERT, UPDATE (i.e., modify), and DELETE. We content ourselves here with a few simple examples, all of them (we trust) self-explanatory.

8.4.1 Single-row INSERT.

```
INSERT
INTO    P ( P#, PNAME, COLOR, WEIGHT, CITY )
VALUES ('P8', 'Sprocket', 'Pink', 14, 'Nice' ) ;
```

8.4.2 Multi-row INSERT.

```
INSERT
INTO    TEMP ( S#, CITY )
        SELECT S.S#, S.CITY
        FROM   S
        WHERE  S.STATUS > 15 ;
```

8.4.3 Multi-row UPDATE.

```
UPDATE P
SET    COLOR = 'Yellow',
       WEIGHT = P.WEIGHT + 5
WHERE  P.CITY = 'Paris' ;
```

8.4.4 Multi-row UPDATE.

```
UPDATE P
SET    CITY = ( SELECT S.CITY
               FROM    S
               WHERE   S.S# = 'S5' )
WHERE  P.COLOR = 'Red' ;
```

8.4.5 Multi-row DELETE.

```
DELETE
FROM    SP
WHERE   'London' =
      ( SELECT  S.CITY
        FROM    S
        WHERE   S.S# = SP.S# ) ;
```

8.5   Table Expressions

An exhaustive treatment of table expressions would be out of place in this book. For purposes of reference, however, we do at least give in Fig. 8.1 (overleaf) a fairly complete BNF grammar for such expressions (the grammar is complete except for a few options having to do with nulls). And we elaborate on one special case—arguably the most important case in practice—namely, *select expressions.*

A select expression can be thought of, loosely, as a table expression that does not involve any UNIONs, EXCEPTs, or INTERSECTs ("loosely," because, of course, such operators might be involved in expressions that are *nested inside* the select expression). As Fig. 8.1 indicates, a select expression consists of several components: a SELECT clause, a FROM clause, a WHERE clause, a GROUP BY clause, and a HAVING clause (the last three of these clauses are optional). We now proceed to explain each of these components one by one.

The SELECT Clause

The SELECT clause takes the form

```
SELECT [ ALL | DISTINCT ] select-item-commalist
```

Explanation:

1. The *select-item-commalist* must not be empty. See below for a detailed discussion of select-items.

2. If neither ALL nor DISTINCT is specified, ALL is assumed.

3. We assume for the moment that the FROM, WHERE, GROUP BY, and HAVING clauses have already been evaluated. No matter which of those clauses are specified and which omitted, the conceptual result of evaluating them is always a table (possibly a "grouped" table—see later), which we will refer to as table *T1* (though the conceptual result is in fact unnamed).

4. Let *T2* be the table that is derived from *T1* by evaluating the specified select-items against *T1* (see below).

5. Let *T3* be the table that is derived from *T2* by eliminating redundant duplicate rows from *T2* if DISTINCT is specified, or a table that is identical to *T2* otherwise.

6. Table *T3* is the final result.

We turn now to an explanation of select-items. There are two cases to consider, of

```
table-expression
    ::=   join-table-expression
        | nonjoin-table-expression

join-table-expression
    ::=   table-reference [ NATURAL ] JOIN
                table-reference [ ON conditional-expression
                                | USING ( column-commalist ) ]
        | table-reference CROSS JOIN table-reference
        | ( join-table-expression )

table-reference
    ::=   table [ [ AS ] range-variable
                    [ ( column-commalist ) ] ]
        | ( table-expression ) [ AS ] range-variable
                                    [ ( column-commalist ) ]
        | join-table-expression

nonjoin-table-expression
    ::=   nonjoin-table-term
        | table-expression UNION [ ALL ]
                [ CORRESPONDING [ BY ( column-commalist ) ] ]
                    table-term
        | table-expression EXCEPT [ ALL ]
                [ CORRESPONDING [ BY ( column-commalist ) ] ]
                    table-term

nonjoin-table-term
    ::=   nonjoin-table-primary
        | table-term INTERSECT [ ALL ]
                [ CORRESPONDING [ BY ( column-commalist ) ] ]
                    table-primary

table-term
    ::=   nonjoin-table-term
        | join-table-expression

table-primary
    ::=   nonjoin-table-primary
        | join-table-expression

nonjoin-table-primary
    ::=   TABLE table
        | table-constructor
        | select-expression
        | ( nonjoin-table-expression )

table-constructor
    ::=   VALUES row-constructor-commalist

row-constructor
    ::=   scalar-expression
        | ( scalar-expression-commalist )
        | ( table-expression )

select-expression
    ::=   SELECT [ ALL | DISTINCT ] select-item-commalist
            FROM table-reference-commalist
                [ WHERE conditional-expression ]
                    [ GROUP BY column-commalist ]
                        [ HAVING conditional-expression ]

select-item
    ::=   scalar-expression [ [ AS ] column ]
        | [ range-variable . ] *
```

FIG. 8.1 A BNF grammar for SQL table expressions

which the second is just shorthand for a commalist of select-items of the first form; thus, the first case is really the more fundamental.

Case 1: The select-item takes the form

```
scalar-expression [ [ AS ] column ]
```

- The scalar expression will typically (but not necessarily) involve one or more columns of table *T1* (see paragraph 2 above). For each row of *T1*, the scalar expression is evaluated, to yield a scalar result. The commalist of such results (corresponding to evaluation of all select-items in the SELECT clause against a single row of *T1*) constitutes a single row of table *T2* (see paragraph 3 above). If the select-item includes an AS clause, the *un*qualified name *column* from that clause is assigned as the name of the corresponding column of table *T2** (the optional keyword AS is just noise and can be omitted without affecting the meaning). If the select-item does not include an AS clause, then (a) if it consists simply of a (possibly qualified) column name, that column name is assigned as the name of the corresponding column of table *T2;* (b) otherwise the corresponding column of table *T2* effectively has no name.

- If a select-item includes an aggregate function reference *and* the select expression does not include a GROUP BY clause (see below), then no select-item in the SELECT clause can include any reference to a column of table *T1* unless that column reference is the argument (or part of the argument) to an aggregate function reference.

Case 2: The select-item takes the form

```
[ range-variable . ] *
```

- If the qualifier is omitted (i.e., the select-item is just an unqualified asterisk), then this select-item must be the only select-item in the SELECT clause. This form is shorthand for a commalist of all of the columns of table *T1*, in left-to-right order.

- If the qualifier is included (i.e., the select-item consists of an asterisk qualified by a range variable name *R,* thus: "*R.**"), then the select-item represents a commalist of all of the columns of the table associated with range variable *R,* in left-to-right order. (Recall that a table name can and often will be used as an implicit range variable. Thus, the select-item will frequently be of the form "*T.**" rather than "*R.**".)

The FROM Clause

The FROM clause takes the form

```
FROM table-reference-commalist
```

---

* Because it is, specifically, the name of a column of table *T2*, not table *T1*, any name introduced by such an AS clause cannot be used in the WHERE, GROUP BY, and HAVING clauses (if any) directly involved in the construction of that table *T1*. It can, however, be referenced in an associated ORDER BY clause, and also in an "outer" table expression that contains the select expression under discussion nested within it.

The *table-reference-commalist* must not be empty. Let the specified table references evaluate to tables *A, B, . . . C*, respectively. Then the result of evaluating the FROM clause is a table that is equal to the Cartesian product of *A, B, . . . C. Note:* The Cartesian product of a single table *T* is defined to be equal to *T;* in other words, it is (of course) legal for the FROM clause to contain just a single table reference.

The WHERE Clause

The WHERE clause takes the form

```
WHERE conditional-expression
```

Let *T* be the result of evaluating the immediately preceding FROM clause. Then the result of the WHERE clause is a table that is derived from *T* by eliminating all rows for which the conditional expression does not evaluate to *true*. If the WHERE clause is omitted, the result is simply *T*.

The GROUP BY Clause

The GROUP BY clause takes the form

```
GROUP BY column-commalist
```

The *column-commalist* must not be empty. Let *T* be the result of evaluating the immediately preceding FROM clause and WHERE clause (if any). Each *column* mentioned in the GROUP BY clause must be the optionally qualified name of a column of *T*. The result of the GROUP BY clause is a **grouped table**—i.e., a set of groups of rows, derived from *T* by conceptually rearranging it into the minimum number of groups such that within any one group all rows have the same value for the combination of columns identified by the GROUP BY clause. Note carefully, therefore, that the result is thus *not* a proper table. However, a GROUP BY clause never appears without a corresponding SELECT clause whose effect is to derive a proper table from that improper intermediate result, so little harm is done by this temporary deviation from the pure tabular framework.

If a select expression includes a GROUP BY clause, then there are restrictions on the form that the SELECT clause can take. To be specific, each select-item in the SELECT clause (including any that are implied by an asterisk shorthand) must be **single-valued per group**. Thus, such select-items must not include any reference to any column of table *T* that is not mentioned in the GROUP BY clause itself—*unless* that reference is the argument, or part of the argument, to one of the aggregate functions COUNT, SUM, AVG, MAX, or MIN, whose effect is to reduce some collection of scalar values from a group to a single such value.

The HAVING Clause

The HAVING clause takes the form

```
HAVING conditional-expression
```

Let *G* be the grouped table resulting from the evaluation of the immediately preceding FROM clause, WHERE clause (if any), and GROUP BY clause (if any). If there is no GROUP BY clause, then *G* is taken to be the result of evaluating the FROM and WHERE clauses alone, considered as a grouped table that contains exactly one group;* in other words, there is an implicit, conceptual GROUP BY clause in this case that specifies *no grouping columns at all.* The result of the HAVING clause is a grouped table that is derived from *G* by eliminating all groups for which the conditional expression does not evaluate to *true.*

Note 1: If the HAVING clause is omitted but the GROUP BY clause is included, the result is simply *G.* If the HAVING and GROUP BY clauses are both omitted, the result is simply the "proper"—i.e., nongrouped—table *T* resulting from the FROM and WHERE clauses.

Note 2: Scalar expressions in a HAVING clause must be single-valued per group (like scalar expressions in the SELECT clause if there is a GROUP BY clause, as discussed above).

Note 3: It is worth mentioning that the HAVING clause is totally redundant—i.e., for every select expression that involves such a clause, there is a semantically identical select expression that does not (exercise for the reader!).

A Comprehensive Example

We conclude our discussion of select expressions with a reasonably complex example that illustrates some (by no means all) of the points explained above. The query is as follows:

For all red and blue parts such that the total quantity supplied is greater than 350 (excluding from the total all shipments for which the quantity is less than or equal to 200), get the part number, the weight in grams, the color, and the maximum quantity supplied of that part.

```
SELECT  P.P#,
        'Weight in grams =' AS TEXT1,
        P.WEIGHT * 454 AS GMWT,
        P.COLOR,
        'Max quantity =' AS TEXT2,
        MAX ( SP.QTY ) AS MQY
FROM  .P, SP
WHERE   P.P# = SP.P#
AND   ( P.COLOR = 'Red' OR P.COLOR = 'Blue')
AND     SP.QTY > 200
GROUP  BY P.P#, P.WEIGHT, P.COLOR
HAVING SUM ( SP.QTY ) > 350 ;
```

Explanation: First, note that (as explained above) the clauses of a select expression are conceptually executed in the order in which they are written—with the sole exception

---

* This is what SQL says, though logically it should say *at most* one group (there should be no group at all if the FROM and WHERE clauses yield an empty table).

of the SELECT clause itself, which is executed last. In the example, therefore, we can imagine the result being constructed as follows:

1. **FROM:** The FROM clause is evaluated to yield a new table that is the Cartesian product of tables P and SP.

2. **WHERE:** The result of Step 1 is reduced by the elimination of all rows that do not satisfy the WHERE clause. In the example, therefore, rows not satisfying the conditional expression

   ```
   P.P# = SP.P# AND
   ( P.COLOR = 'Red' OR P.COLOR = 'Blue') AND
   SP.QTY > 200
   ```

   are eliminated.

3. **GROUP BY:** The result of Step 2 is grouped by values of the column(s) named in the GROUP BY clause. In the example, those columns are P.P#, P.WEIGHT, and P.COLOR. *Note:* In theory P.P# alone would be sufficient as the grouping column here, since P.WEIGHT and P.COLOR are themselves single-valued per part number. However, SQL is not aware of this latter fact, and will raise an error condition if P.WEIGHT and P.COLOR are omitted from the GROUP BY clause, because they *are* mentioned in the SELECT clause. See reference [9.6] in Chapter 9.

4. **HAVING:** Groups not satisfying the condition

   ```
   SUM ( SP.QTY ) > 350
   ```

   are eliminated from the result of Step 3.

5. **SELECT:** Each group in the result of Step 4 generates a single result row, as follows. First, the part number, weight, color, and maximum quantity are extracted from the group. Second, the weight is converted to grams. Third, the two literal strings "Weight in grams =" and "Max quantity =" are inserted at the appropriate points in the row. Note, incidentally, that—as the phrase "appropriate points in the row" suggests—we are relying here on the fact that columns of tables have a left-to-right ordering in SQL. The literal strings would not make much sense if they did not appear at those "appropriate points."

The final result looks like this:

P#	TEXT1	GMWT	COLOR	TEXT2	MQY
P1	Weight in grams =	5448	Red	Max quantity =	300
P5	Weight in grams =	5448	Blue	Max quantity =	400
P3	Weight in grams =	7718	Blue	Max quantity =	400

In conclusion, please understand that the algorithm just described is intended purely as a **conceptual** explanation of how the SELECT statement is evaluated. The algorithm is certainly correct, in the sense that it is guaranteed to produce the correct result. However, it would probably be rather inefficient if actually executed. For example, it would be very unfortunate if the system were actually to construct the Cartesian product in Step 1. Considerations such as these are exactly the reason why relational systems require an optimizer (see Chapter 18). Indeed, the task of the optimizer in an SQL system can be characterized as that of finding an implementation procedure that will produce the same result as the conceptual algorithm sketched above but is more efficient than that algorithm.

8.6 Conditional Expressions

Like table expressions, conditional expressions appear in numerous contexts through-out the SQL language; in particular, of course, they are used in WHERE clauses to qualify or disqualify rows for subsequent processing. Here we discuss some of the most important features of such expressions. Please note, however, that our treatment is definitely *not* meant to be exhaustive; in particular, we ignore everything to do with nulls. (Conditional expressions, perhaps more than most other parts of the language, require significantly extended treatment when the implications and complications of nulls are taken into account, and certain conditional expression formats, not discussed in this chapter, are provided purely to deal with certain aspects of null support.)

As in the previous section, we begin with a BNF grammar (Fig. 8.2, overleaf). The reader will see that most conditional expression formats either have already been illustrated in earlier sections or else are self-explanatory; here we just offer a few words of explanation regarding a couple of specific cases, namely MATCH conditions and all-or-any conditions.

MATCH Conditions

A MATCH condition takes the form

```
row-constructor MATCH UNIQUE ( table-expression )
```

Let *r1* be the row that results from evaluating *row-constructor* and let *T* be the table that results from evaluating *table-expression*. Then the MATCH condition evaluates to *true* if and only if *T* contains exactly one row, *r2* say, such that the comparison

```
r1 = r2
```

evaluates to *true*. Here is an example:

```
SELECT SP.*
FROM   SP
WHERE  NOT ( SP.S# MATCH UNIQUE ( SELECT S.S# FROM S ) ) ;
```

("Get shipments that do not have exactly one matching supplier in the suppliers table"). Such a query might be useful in checking the integrity of the database, because, of course, there should not *be* any such shipments if the database is correct. Note, however, that an IN condition could be used to perform the same check.

Incidentally, the UNIQUE can be omitted from MATCH UNIQUE, but then MATCH becomes synonymous with IN (at least in the absence of nulls).

```
conditional-expression
    ::=    conditional-term
        |  conditional-expression OR conditional-term

conditional-term
    ::=    conditional-factor
        |  conditional-term AND conditional-factor

conditional-factor
    ::=    [ NOT ] conditional-primary

conditional-primary
    ::=    simple-condition | ( conditional-expression )

simple-condition
    ::=    comparison-condition
        |  in-condition
        |  match-condition
        |  all-or-any-condition
        |  exists-condition

comparison-condition
    ::=    row-constructor comparison-operator row-constructor

comparison-operator
    ::=    = | < | <= | > | >= | <>

in-condition
    ::=    row-constructor [ NOT ] IN ( table-expression )
        |  scalar-expression [ NOT ] IN
                            ( scalar-expression-commalist )

match-condition
    ::=    row-constructor MATCH UNIQUE ( table-expression )

all-or-any-condition
    ::=    row-constructor
                comparison-operator ALL ( table-expression )
        |  row-constructor
                comparison-operator ANY ( table-expression )

exists-condition
    ::=    EXISTS ( table-expression )
```

FIG. 8.2 A BNF grammar for SQL conditional expressions

All-or-Any Conditions

An all-or-any condition has the general form

```
row-constructor
    comparison-operator qualifier ( table-expression )
```

where *comparison-operator* is any of the usual set (=, <>, etc.), and *qualifier* is ALL or ANY. In general, an all-or-any condition evaluates to *true* if and only if the corresponding comparison without the ALL (respectively ANY) evaluates to *true* for all (respectively any) of the rows in the table represented by *table-expression*. (If that table is empty, the ALL conditions evaluate to *true,* the ANY conditions evaluate to *false.*) Here is an example ("Get part names for parts whose weight is greater than that of every blue part"):

```
SELECT DISTINCT PX.PNAME
FROM    P AS PX
WHERE   PX.WEIGHT >ALL ( SELECT PY.WEIGHT
                         FROM    P AS PY
                         WHERE   PY.COLOR = 'Blue' ) ;
```

The result looks like this:

PNAME
Cog

Explanation: The nested table expression returns the set of weights for blue parts, namely the set {17,12}. The outer SELECT then returns the name of the only part whose weight is greater than every value in this set, namely part P6. In general, of course, the final result might contain any number of part names (including zero).

A word of caution is appropriate here, at least for native English speakers. The fact is, all-or-any conditions are seriously error-prone. A very natural English formulation of the foregoing query would use the word "any" in place of "every," which could easily lead to the (incorrect) use of >ANY instead of >ALL. Analogous criticisms apply to every one of the ANY and ALL operators.

8.7 Scalar Expressions

Scalar expressions in SQL are essentially straightforward. We content ourselves in this section with a list of some of the most important operators that can be used in the construction of such expressions, and offering a few additional comments on a couple of those operators—CASE and CAST—whose meaning is perhaps not immediately apparent. Note that the aggregate functions also can appear within such expressions, since they return a scalar result. Furthermore, a table expression enclosed in parentheses can also be treated as a scalar value, so long as it evaluates to a table of exactly one row and one column. As mentioned earlier (in the discussion of Example 8.3.9), this last possibility, which was introduced with SQL/92, represents a *major* improvement over SQL as originally defined.

Here then is the list of operators, in alphabetic order.

```
arithmetic operators (+, -, *, /)    OCTET_LENGTH
BIT_LENGTH                           POSITION
CASE                                 SESSION_USER
```

```
CAST                               SUBSTRING
CHARACTER_LENGTH                   SYSTEM_USER
concatenation (||)                 TRIM
CURRENT_USER                       UPPER
LOWER                              USER
```

We now elaborate slightly on the operators CASE and CAST.

CASE Operations

A CASE operation returns one of a specified set of values, depending on a specified condition. For example:

```
CASE
    WHEN S.STATUS <   5 THEN 'Last resort'
    WHEN S.STATUS < 10 THEN 'Dubious'
    WHEN S.STATUS < 15 THEN 'Not too good'
    WHEN S.STATUS < 20 THEN 'Mediocre'
    WHEN S.STATUS < 25 THEN 'Acceptable'
    ELSE                    'Fine'
END
```

CAST Operations

CAST converts a specified scalar value to a specified scalar data type (possibly a user-defined domain). For example:

```
CAST ( 'S8' AS S# )
```

Not all pairs of data types are mutually convertible; for example, conversions between numbers and bit strings are not supported. The reader is referred to reference [8.1] for details of precisely which data types can be converted to which.

8.8 Embedded SQL

As explained in Chapter 3, SQL statements can be executed interactively, or they can be executed as part of an application program (in which case the SQL statements are physically embedded within the program source code, intermixed with the statements of the host language). Up to this point, however, we have ignored the latter case and have tacitly assumed—where it made any difference—that the language was being used interactively. Now we turn our attention to embedded SQL specifically.

The fundamental principle underlying embedded SQL, which we refer to as **the dual-mode principle,** is that *any SQL statement that can be used interactively can also be used in an application program.* Of course, there are various differences of detail between a given interactive SQL statement and its embedded counterpart, and retrieval operations in particular require significantly extended treatment in a host program environment (see later); but the principle is nevertheless broadly true. (Its converse is not, by the way; that is, there are a number of embedded SQL statements that cannot be used interactively, as we will see.)

Note clearly also that the dual-mode principle applies to the entire SQL language, not just to the data manipulation operations. It is true that the DML operations are far and away the ones most frequently used in a programming context, but there is nothing wrong in embedding (for example) a CREATE TABLE statement in a program, if it makes sense to do so for the application at hand.

Before we can discuss the actual statements of embedded SQL, it is necessary to cover a number of preliminary details. Most of those details are illustrated by the program fragment shown in Fig. 8.3. (To fix our ideas we assume that the host language is PL/I. Most of the ideas translate into other host languages with only minor changes.) Points arising:

1. Embedded SQL statements are prefixed by **EXEC SQL,** so that they can easily be distinguished from statements of the host language, and are terminated by a special **terminator** symbol (a semicolon for PL/I).

2. An *executable* SQL statement (from now on we will usually drop the "embedded") can appear wherever an executable host statement can appear. Note the qualifier "executable" here: Unlike interactive SQL, embedded SQL includes some statements that are purely declarative, not executable. For example, DECLARE CURSOR is not an executable statement (see later), nor are BEGIN and END DECLARE SECTION (see paragraph 5 below), and nor is WHENEVER (see paragraph 9 below).

3. SQL statements can include references to **host variables;** such references must include a colon prefix to distinguish them from SQL column names. Host variables

```
EXEC SQL BEGIN DECLARE SECTION ;

   DCL SQLSTATE CHAR(5) ;
   DCL P#       CHAR(6) ;
   DCL WEIGHT   FIXED DECIMAL(3) ;

EXEC SQL END DECLARE SECTION ;

P# = 'P2' ;                      /* for example             */
EXEC SQL SELECT P.WEIGHT
         INTO   :WEIGHT
         FROM   P
         WHERE  P.P# = :P# ;
IF SQLSTATE = '00000'
THEN ... ;                       /* WEIGHT = retrieved value */
ELSE ... ;                       /* some exception occurred  */
```

FIG. 8.3   Fragment of a PL/I program with embedded SQL

can appear in embedded SQL (DML statements only) wherever a literal can appear in interactive SQL. They can also appear in an INTO clause on SELECT (see paragraph 4 below) or FETCH (see later) to designate targets for retrieval, and in certain "dynamic SQL" statements (again, see later).

4. Notice the **INTO clause** on the SELECT statement in Fig. 8.3. The purpose of that clause is (as just indicated) to specify the target variables into which values are to be retrieved; the ith target variable mentioned in the INTO clause corresponds to the ith value to be retrieved as specified by the SELECT clause.

5. All host variables that will be referenced in SQL statements must be defined within an **embedded SQL declare section,** which is delimited by the **BEGIN** and **END DECLARE SECTION** statements.

6. Every embedded SQL program must include a host variable called **SQLSTATE.*** After any SQL statement has been executed, a status code is returned to the program in that variable; in particular, a status code of 00000 means that the statement executed successfully, and a value of 02000 means that the statement did execute but no data was found to satisfy the request. In principle, therefore, every SQL statement in the program should be followed by a test on SQLSTATE, and appropriate action taken if the value is not what was expected. In practice, however, such testing is usually implicit. See paragraph 9 below.

7. Host variables must have a **data type** appropriate to the uses to which they are put. In particular, a host variable that is to be used as a target (e.g., on FETCH) must have a data type that is compatible with that of the expression that provides the value to be assigned to that target; likewise, a host variable that is to be used as a source (e.g., on UPDATE) must have a data type that is compatible with that of the SQL column to which values of that source are to be assigned. Similar remarks apply to a host variable that is to be used in a comparison, or indeed in any kind of scalar expression. For details of what it means for data types to be compatible in the foregoing sense, the reader is referred to the official standard document [8.1].

8. Host variables and SQL columns can have the same name.

9. As already mentioned, every SQL statement should in principle be followed by a test of the returned SQLSTATE value. The **WHENEVER** statement is provided to simplify this process. The WHENEVER statement has the syntax:

```
EXEC SQL WHENEVER condition action terminator
```

where *terminator* is as explained in paragraph 1 above, *condition* is either SQLERROR or NOT FOUND, and "action" is either CONTINUE or a GO TO statement. WHENEVER is not an executable statement; rather, it is a directive to

---

* Earlier versions of SQL used a variable called SQLCODE in place of SQLSTATE; SQLSTATE was added in SQL/92, and SQLCODE is now officially "deprecated," because most of its values (unlike those of SQLSTATE) are implementation-defined instead of being prescribed by the standard.

the SQL language processor. "WHENEVER *condition* GO TO *label*" causes that processor to insert an "IF *condition* GO TO *label*" statement after each executable SQL statement it encounters; "WHENEVER *condition* CONTINUE" causes it not to insert any such statements, the implication being that the programmer will insert such statements by hand. The two *conditions* are defined as follows:

```
NOT FOUND    means    no data was found
                      (SQLSTATE = 02000)
SQLERROR     means    an error occurred
                      (see reference [8.1] for SQLSTATE)
```

Each WHENEVER statement the SQL processor encounters on its sequential scan through the program text (for a particular condition) overrides the previous one it found (for that condition).

So much for the preliminaries. In the rest of this section we concentrate on DML operations specifically. As already indicated, most of those operations can be handled in a fairly straightforward fashion (i.e., with only minor changes to their syntax). Retrieval operations require special treatment, however. The problem is that such operations retrieve many rows (in general), not just one, and host languages are typically not equipped to handle the retrieval of more than one row at a time. It is therefore necessary to provide some kind of bridge between the set-at-a-time retrieval level of SQL and the row-at-a-time retrieval level of the host; and **cursors** provide such a bridge. A cursor is a new kind of SQL object, one that applies to embedded SQL only (because of course interactive SQL has no need of it). It consists essentially of a kind of *pointer* that can be used to run through a collection of rows, pointing to each of the rows in turn and thus providing addressability to those rows one at a time. However, we defer detailed discussion of cursors to a later subsection, and consider first those statements that have no need of them.

Operations Not Involving Cursors

The data manipulation statements that do not need cursors are as follows:

- "Singleton SELECT"
- INSERT
- UPDATE (except the CURRENT form—see later)
- DELETE (again, except the CURRENT form—see later)

We give examples of each of these statements in turn.

8.8.1 (Singleton SELECT) Get status and city for the supplier whose supplier number is given by the host variable GIVENS#.

```
EXEC SQL SELECT  STATUS, CITY
         INTO    :RANK, :CITY
         FROM    S
         WHERE   S# = :GIVENS# ;
```

We use the term **singleton SELECT** to mean a select expression* that evaluates to a table containing at most one row. In the example, if there exists exactly one row in table S satisfying the WHERE condition, then the STATUS and CITY values from that row will be assigned to the host variables RANK and CITY as requested, and SQLSTATE will be set to 00000. If no S row satisfies the WHERE condition, SQLSTATE will be set to 02000; and if more than one does, the program is in error, and SQLSTATE will be set to an error code.

8.8.2 (INSERT) Insert a new part (part number, name, and weight given by host variables P#, PNAME, PWT, respectively; color and city unknown) into table P.

```
EXEC SQL INSERT
        INTO   P ( P#, PNAME, COLOR, WEIGHT, CITY )
        VALUES ( :P#, :PNAME, DEFAULT, :PWT, DEFAULT ) ;
```

8.8.3 (UPDATE) Increase the status of all London suppliers by the amount given by the host variable RAISE.

```
EXEC SQL UPDATE S
        SET    STATUS = STATUS + :RAISE
        WHERE  CITY = 'London' ;
```

If no supplier rows satisfy the WHERE condition, SQLSTATE will be set to 02000.

8.8.4 (DELETE) Delete all shipments for suppliers whose city is given by the host variable CITY.

```
EXEC SQL DELETE
        FROM   SP
        WHERE  :CITY =
             ( SELECT CITY
               FROM   S
               WHERE  S.S# = SP.S# ) ;
```

Again SQLSTATE will be set to 02000 if no rows satisfy the WHERE condition.

Operations Involving Cursors

Now we turn to the question of set-level retrieval—i.e., retrieval of an entire set of many rows, instead of just one row. As explained earlier, what is needed here is a mechanism for accessing the rows in the set one by one, and **cursors** provide such a mechanism. The process is illustrated in outline by the example of Fig. 8.4, which is intended to retrieve supplier details (S#, SNAME, and STATUS) for all suppliers in the city given by the host variable Y.

Explanation: The DECLARE X CURSOR . . . statement defines a cursor called X, with an associated table expression as specified by the SELECT that forms part of that DECLARE. That table expression is not evaluated at this point; DECLARE CURSOR is a purely declarative statement. The expression *is* evaluated when the cursor is opened. The FETCH statement is then used to retrieve rows one at a time from the

---

* It is not quite a select expression as defined in Section 8.5, owing to the presence of the INTO clause.

```
   EXEC SQL DECLARE X CURSOR FOR      — define the cursor    */
            SELECT S.S#, S.SNAME, S.STATUS
            FROM    S
            WHERE   S.CITY = :Y ;

   EXEC SQL OPEN X ;                        /* execute the query    */
            DO for all S rows accessible via X ;
                EXEC SQL FETCH X INTO :S#, :SNAME, :STATUS ;
                                         /* fetch next supplier */
                .........
            END ;
   EXEC SQL CLOSE X ;                       /* deactivate cursor X */
```

FIG. 8.4 Multi-row retrieval

resulting set, assigning retrieved values to host variables in accordance with the specifications of the INTO clause in that statement. (For simplicity we have given the host
variables the same names as the corresponding database columns. Notice that the
SELECT in the cursor declaration does not have an INTO clause of its own.) Since
there will be many rows in the result set, the FETCH will normally appear within a loop
(DO . . . END in PL/I); the loop will be repeated so long as there are more rows still to
come in that result set. On exit from the loop, cursor X is closed.

   Now let us consider cursors and cursor operations in more detail. First, a cursor is
declared by means of a **DECLARE CURSOR** statement, which takes the general form

```
EXEC SQL DECLARE cursor CURSOR
         FOR table-expression
       [ ORDER BY order-item-commalist ] ;
```

where *table-expression* and *order-item-commalist* are as described earlier in this chapter. For an example, see Fig. 8.4. *Note:* We are ignoring a few optional specifications
in the interests of brevity. See reference [8.1] or reference [8.5] for further details.

   As previously stated, the DECLARE CURSOR statement is declarative, not executable; it declares a cursor with the specified name and having the specified table
expression permanently associated with it. The table expression can include host variable references. A program can include any number of DECLARE CURSOR statements, each of which must (of course) be for a different cursor.

   Three executable statements are provided to operate on cursors: **OPEN, FETCH,**
and **CLOSE**.

1. The statement

```
EXEC SQL OPEN cursor ;
```

   opens or *activates* the specified cursor (which must not currently be open). In effect, the table expression associated with the cursor is evaluated (using the current
   values for any host variables referenced within that expression); a set of rows is
   thus identified and becomes the current **active set** for the cursor. The cursor also

identifies a *position* within that active set, namely the position just before the first row in the set. (Active sets are always considered to have an ordering, so that the concept of position has meaning. The ordering is either that defined by the ORDER BY clause, or a system-determined ordering in the absence of such a clause.)

2. The statement

```
EXEC SQL FETCH cursor INTO host-variable-commalist ;
```

advances the specified cursor (which must be open) to the next row in the active set and then assigns values from that row to host variables as specified in the INTO clause. If there is no next row when FETCH is executed, then SQLSTATE is set to 02000 and no data is retrieved.

3. The statement

```
EXEC SQL CLOSE cursor ;
```

closes or *deactivates* the specified cursor (which must currently be open). The cursor now has no current active set. However, it can subsequently be opened again, in which case it will acquire another active set—probably not exactly the same set as before, especially if the values of any host variables referenced in the cursor declaration have changed in the meantime. Note that changing the values of those host variables while the cursor is open has no effect on the current active set.

Two further statements can include references to cursors. These are the **CURRENT** forms of **UPDATE** and **DELETE**. If a cursor, X say, is currently positioned on a particular row, then it is possible to UPDATE or DELETE the "current of X," i.e., the row on which X is positioned. For example:

```
EXEC SQL UPDATE S
         SET    STATUS = STATUS + :RAISE
         WHERE  CURRENT OF X ;
```

UPDATE . . . WHERE CURRENT and DELETE . . . WHERE CURRENT are not permitted if the table expression in the cursor declaration would define a nonupdatable view if it were part of a CREATE VIEW statement (see Chapter 17).

Dynamic SQL

Dynamic SQL consists of a set of embedded SQL facilities that are provided specifically to allow the construction of generalized, online, and possibly interactive applications. (Recall from Chapter 1 that an online application is an application that supports access to the database from an online terminal.) Consider what a typical online application has to do. In outline, the steps it must go through are as follows.

1. Accept a command from the terminal.
2. Analyze that command.
3. Issue appropriate SQL statements to the database.
4. Return a message and/or results to the terminal.

If the set of commands the program can accept is fairly small, as in the case of (perhaps) a program handling airline reservations, then the set of possible SQL statements to be issued will probably also be small and can be "hardwired" into the program. In this case, Steps 2 and 3 above will consist simply of logic to examine the input command and then branch to the part of the program that issues the predefined SQL statement(s). If, on the other hand, there can be great variability in the input, then it might not be practicable to predefine and "hardwire" SQL statements for every possible command. Instead, it is probably much more convenient to *construct* the necessary SQL statements dynamically, and then to compile and execute those constructed statements dynamically. The facilities of dynamic SQL are provided to assist in this process.

The two principal dynamic statements are PREPARE and EXECUTE. Their use is illustrated in the following (unrealistically simple but accurate) example.

```
DCL SQLSOURCE CHAR VARYING (65000) ;

SQLSOURCE = 'DELETE FROM SP WHERE SP.QTY < 300' ;
EXEC SQL PREPARE SQLPREPPED FROM :SQLSOURCE ;
EXEC SQL EXECUTE SQLPREPPED ;
```

Explanation:

1. The name SQLSOURCE identifies a PL/I varying length character string variable in which the program will somehow construct the source form (i.e., character string representation) of some SQL statement—a DELETE statement, in our particular example.

2. The name SQLPREPPED, by contrast, identifies an *SQL* variable, not a PL/I variable, that will be used (conceptually) to hold the compiled form of the SQL statement whose source form is given in SQLSOURCE. The names SQLSOURCE and SQLPREPPED are arbitrary, of course.

3. The assignment statement "SQLSOURCE = . . . ;" assigns to SQLSOURCE the source form of an SQL DELETE statement. In practice, of course, the process of constructing such a source statement is likely to be much more complex—perhaps involving the input and analysis of some request from the end-user, expressed in natural language or some other form more "user-friendly" than plain SQL.

4. The PREPARE statement then takes that source statement and "prepares" (i.e., compiles) it to produce an executable version, which it stores in SQLPREPPED.

5. Finally, the EXECUTE statement executes that SQLPREPPED version and thus causes the actual DELETE to occur. SQLSTATE information from the DELETE is returned exactly as if the DELETE had been executed directly in the normal way.

Note that since it denotes an SQL variable, not a PL/I variable, the name SQLPREPPED does not have a colon prefix when it is referenced in the PREPARE and EXECUTE statements. Note too that such SQL variables are not explicitly declared.

Incidentally, the process just described is exactly what happens when SQL statements themselves are entered interactively. Most systems provide some kind of interactive SQL query processor. That processor is in fact just a particular kind of generalized online application; it is ready to accept an extremely wide variety of input, *viz.* any valid (or invalid!) SQL statement. It uses the facilities of dynamic SQL to construct suitable SQL statements corresponding to its input, to compile and execute those constructed statements, and to return messages and results back to the terminal.

For more information regarding dynamic SQL, see reference [8.1] or reference [8.5].

8.9 Summary

This concludes our survey of the major features of the SQL standard ("SQL/92"). We began by discussing the basic data objects. To review, the **principal DDL statements** are as follows:

```
CREATE DOMAIN    CREATE TABLE
ALTER DOMAIN     ALTER TABLE
DROP DOMAIN      DROP TABLE
```

Two further DDL statements, CREATE and DROP VIEW, are discussed in Chapter 17.

1. Regarding **domains,** we stressed the point that domains in SQL are very far from being true relational domains; in fact, SQL domains are basically little more than a shorthand. More precisely, they provide (a) domain-level **data type** specifications, (b) domain-level **default** definitions, and (c) domain-level **integrity constraints**. We summarized SQL's scalar data types, but omitted much of the complexity (unwarranted complexity, in this writer's opinion) that attaches to other aspects of SQL-style domains.

2. Regarding **base tables,** we first pointed out that SQL tables in general differ from true relations in at least two respects: They permit duplicate rows, and they have a left-to-right ordering to their columns. Base tables in particular have one or more columns, zero or more declared **candidate keys** (of which at most one can be declared to be the **primary** key), zero or more declared **foreign keys,** and zero or more declared **check constraints**. The following foreign key delete and update rules are supported: NO ACTION, CASCADE, SET DEFAULT, and SET NULL.

We also briefly described the **Information Schema,** which consists of a set of prescribed views of a hypothetical "Definition Schema."

Next we moved on to discuss **data manipulation** operations. To be specific:

1. We described **retrieval operations** (which basically means **table expressions**). Usually such an operation consists of a single **select expression,** but various kinds of explicit **JOIN** expressions are also supported, and join expressions and select expressions can be combined together in arbitrary ways using the **UNION, INTERSECT,** and **EXCEPT** operators. We also mentioned the use of **ORDER BY** to order the table resulting from a table expression (of any kind).

2. Regarding **select expressions** in particular, we described:

- The basic **SELECT clause** itself, including the use of **DISTINCT,** scalar expressions, the introduction of result column names, and "SELECT *"

- The **FROM clause,** including the use of range variables and the use of table references within the FROM clause that are more complex than just a simple table name

- The **WHERE clause,** including the use of **subqueries** and the **EXISTS** function

- The **GROUP BY** and **HAVING clauses,** including the use of the **aggregate functions** COUNT, SUM, AVG, MAX, and MIN

We also gave a **conceptual evaluation algorithm** (i.e., an outline of a formal definition) for select expressions.

3. We briefly described the update operations **INSERT, UPDATE,** and **DELETE.**

Next, we gave more details of (a) **table expressions** (including a BNF grammar); (b) **conditional expressions** (again including a BNF grammar, and elaborating on **MATCH conditions** and **all-or-any conditions** in particular); and (c) **scalar expressions** (elaborating on the operators **CASE** and **CAST**). We also stressed the point that a select expression that evaluates to a single-column, single-row table can be used as a scalar value (e.g., within a SELECT or WHERE clause).

Finally, we described the principal features of **embedded SQL.** The basic idea behind embedded SQL is **the dual-mode principle,** i.e., the principle that (insofar as possible) *any SQL statement that can be used interactively can also be used in an application program.* The major exception to this principle arises in connection with **multi-row retrieval operations,** which require the use of a **cursor** to bridge the gap between the set-at-a-time retrieval level of SQL and the row-at-a-time retrieval level of host languages such as PL/I. (Perhaps this is the place to mention that the SQL standard [8.1] also supports Ada, C, COBOL, Fortran, MUMPS, and Pascal in addition to PL/I.)

Following a number of necessary (though mostly syntactic) preliminaries—including in particular a brief explanation of **SQLSTATE**—we considered those operations, namely **singleton SELECT, INSERT, UPDATE,** and **DELETE,** that have no need for cursors. Then we turned to the operations that *do* need cursors, and discussed **DECLARE CURSOR, OPEN, FETCH, CLOSE,** and the **CURRENT** forms of **UPDATE** and **DELETE.** (The standard refers to the CURRENT forms of these operators as *positioned* UPDATE and DELETE, and uses the term *searched* UPDATE and DELETE for the nonCURRENT or "out of the blue" forms.) Finally, we gave a very brief introduction to the concept of **dynamic SQL,** mentioning the **PREPARE** and **EXECUTE** statements in particular.

Exercises

8.1 Give an SQL data definition for the suppliers-parts-projects database.

8.2 Write a sequence of DROP statements that will have the effect of destroying all of the contents of the suppliers-parts-projects database.

8.3　In Section 8.2 we described the CREATE TABLE statement as defined by the SQL standard [8.1]. Many commercial SQL products support additional options on that statement,
however, typically having to do with indexes, disk space allocation, and other implementation
matters, and thereby undermining the objectives of physical data independence and inter-
system compatibility. Investigate any SQL product that might be available to you. Do the
foregoing criticisms apply to that product? Specifically, what additional CREATE TABLE
options does that product support?

8.4　Once again, investigate any SQL product that might be available to you. Does that product
support the Information Schema? If not, what *does* its catalog support look like?

8.5　Show that SQL is *relationally complete* (see Chapter 6), in the sense that, for any arbitrary
expression of the relational algebra, there exists a semantically equivalent SQL expression.

8.6　Does SQL have equivalents of the relational EXTEND and SUMMARIZE operations?

8.7　Is there an SQL equivalent of the relational assignment operation?

8.8　Are there SQL equivalents of the relational comparison operations?

8.9　Give as many different SQL formulations as you can think of for the query "Get supplier
names for suppliers who supply part P2" (see Examples 8.3.11 and 8.3.14).

8.10　There are two formally equivalent approaches to the manipulative part of the relational
model, the calculus and the algebra. One implication is that there are therefore two styles
on which the design of a query language can be based. For example, QUEL is (at least
arguably) calculus-based, and so is QBE; by contrast, the language ISBL of the system
PRTV [6.8] is algebra-based. Is SQL algebra-based or calculus-based?

8.11　Give SQL solutions to Exercises 6.13-6.48.

8.12　Give SQL formulations for the following update problems.

(a) Insert a new supplier S10 into table S. The name and city are Smith and New York,
respectively; the status is not yet known.

(b) Change the color of all red parts to orange.

(c) Delete all projects for which there are no shipments.

8.13　Using the suppliers-parts-projects database, write a program with embedded SQL statements
to list all supplier rows, in supplier number order. Each supplier row should be immediately followed in the listing by all project rows for projects supplied by that supplier, in
project number order.

8.14　Given the tables

```
CREATE TABLE PARTS
    ( P# ... , DESCRIPTION ... ,
      PRIMARY KEY ( P# ) ) ;

CREATE TABLE PART_STRUCTURE
    ( MAJOR_P# ... , MINOR_P# ... , QTY ... ,
      PRIMARY KEY ( MAJOR_P#, MINOR_P# ),
      FOREIGN KEY ( MAJOR_P# ) REFERENCES PARTS,
      FOREIGN KEY ( MINOR_P# ) REFERENCES PARTS ) ;
```

where PART_STRUCTURE shows which parts (MAJOR_P#) contain which other parts
(MINOR_P#) as first-level components, write an SQL program to list all component parts
of a given part, to all levels (the **parts explosion** problem). The following sample values
(repeated from Fig. 4.4) might help you visualize this problem:

PART_STRUCTURE	MAJOR_P#	MINOR_P#	QTY
	P1	P2	2
	P1	P3	4
	P2	P3	1
	P2	P4	3
	P3	P5	9
	P4	P5˙	8
	P5	P6	3

References and Bibliography

8.1 International Organization for Standardization (ISO). *Database Language SQL*. Document ISO/IEC 9075:1992. Also available as American National Standards Institute (ANSI) Document ANSI X3.135-1992.

The current version of the official ISO/ANSI SQL standard, known informally as *SQL2, SQL-92,* or *SQL/92.* The point is worth mentioning that, although SQL is widely recognized as the international "relational" standard, the standard document does not describe itself as such; in fact, it never actually mentions the term "relation" at all!

8.2 X/Open. *Structured Query Language (SQL): CAE Specification C201* (September 1992).

Defines the X/Open SQL standard.

8.3 U.S. Department of Commerce, National Institute of Standards and Technology. *Database Language SQL*. FIPS PUB 127-2 (1992).

Defines the Federal Information Processing (FIPS) SQL standard.

8.4 IBM Corp.. *Systems Application Architecture Common Programming Interface: Database Reference*. IBM Document No. SC26-4348.

Defines the IBM SAA SQL standard.

8.5 C. J. Date and Hugh Darwen. *A Guide to the SQL Standard* (3rd edition). Reading, Mass.: Addison-Wesley (1993).

Portions of this chapter are based on material from this reference, which is intended as a comprehensive tutorial on SQL/92. References [8.6] and [8.7] below are also SQL/92 tutorials.

8.6 Stephen Cannan and Gerard Otten. *SQL—The Standard Handbook*. Maidenhead, UK: McGraw-Hill International (1993).

8.7 Jim Melton and Alan R. Simon. *Understanding The New SQL: A Complete Guide*. San Mateo, Calif.: Morgan Kaufmann (1993).

8.8 Donald D. Chamberlin and Raymond F. Boyce. "SEQUEL: A Structured English Query Language." Proc. ACM SIGMOD Workshop on Data Description, Access, and Control, Ann Arbor, Mich. (May 1974).

The paper that first introduced the SQL language (or SEQUEL, as it was originally called; the name was subsequently changed for legal reasons).

8.9 M. M. Astrahan and R. A. Lorie. "SEQUEL-XRM: A Relational System." Proc. ACM Pacific Regional Conference, San Francisco, Calif. (April 1975).

Describes the first prototype implementation of SEQUEL, the original version of SQL [8.8]. See also references [8.12–8.13], which perform an analogous function for System R.

8.10 Phyllis Reisner, Raymond F. Boyce, and Donald D. Chamberlin. "Human Factors Evaluation of Two Data Base Query Languages: SQUARE and SEQUEL." Proc. NCC 44, Anaheim, Calif. Montvale, N.J.: AFIPS Press (May 1975).

SQL's predecessor SEQUEL [8.8] was based on an earlier language called SQUARE. The two languages were fundamentally the same, in fact, but SQUARE used a rather mathematical syntax whereas SEQUEL was based on English keywords such as SELECT, FROM, WHERE, etc. The present paper reports on a set of experiments that were carried out on the usability of the two languages, using college students as subjects. A number of revisions were made to SEQUEL as a result of that work [8.11].

8.11 Donald D. Chamberlin *et al.* "SEQUEL/2: A Unified Approach to Data Definition, Manipulation, and Control." *IBM J. R&D. 20,* No. 6 (November 1976). See also errata: *IBM J. R&D. 21,* No. 1 (January 1977).

Experience from the early prototype implementation of SEQUEL discussed in reference [8.9] and results from the usability tests reported in reference [8.10] led to the design of a revised version of the language called SEQUEL/2. The language supported by System R [8.12–8.13] was basically SEQUEL/2 (with the conspicuous absence of the so-called "assertion" and "trigger" facilities), plus certain extensions suggested by early user experience [8.14].

8.12 M. M. Astrahan *et al.* "System R: Relational Approach to Database Management." *ACM TODS 1,* No. 2 (June 1976).

System R was *the* major prototype implementation of (an early version of) the SQL language. This paper describes the architecture of System R as originally planned.

8.13 M. W. Blasgen *et al.* "System R: An Architectural Overview." *IBM Sys. J. 20,* No. 1 (February 1981).

Describes the architecture of System R as it became by the time the system was fully implemented.

8.14 Donald D. Chamberlin. "A Summary of User Experience with the SQL Data Sublanguage." Proc. International Conference on Databases, Aberdeen, Scotland (July 1980). Also available as IBM Research Report RJ2767 (April 1980).

Discusses early user experience with System R and proposes some extensions to the SQL language in the light of that experience. A few of those extensions—EXISTS, LIKE (not discussed in the present chapter), PREPARE, and EXECUTE—were in fact implemented in the final version of System R.

8.15 Donald D. Chamberlin, Arthur M. Gilbert, and Robert A. Yost. "A History of System R and SQL / Data System." Proc. 7th International Conference on Very Large Data Bases, Cannes, France (September 1981).

Discusses the lessons learned from the System R prototype and describes the evolution of that prototype into the first of IBM's relational product family, namely SQL/DS (recently renamed "DB2 for VM and VSE").

8.16 Donald D. Chamberlin *et al.* "A History and Evaluation of System R." *CACM 24,* No. 10 (October 1981).

Describes the three principal phases of the System R project (preliminary prototype, multi-user prototype, evaluation), with emphasis on the technologies of compilation and optimization pioneered in System R. There is some overlap between this paper and reference

[8.15]. *Note:* It is interesting to compare and contrast this paper with reference [7.14], which performs an analogous function for the University INGRES project.

8.17 C. J. Date. "A Critique of the SQL Database Language." *ACM SIGMOD Record 14,* No. 3 (November 1984). Republished in C. J. Date, *Relational Database: Selected Writings,* Reading, Mass.: Addison-Wesley (1986).

SQL is very far from perfect. This paper presents a critical analysis of a number of the language's principal shortcomings (mainly from the standpoint of formal computer languages in general, rather than database languages specifically). *Note:* Certain of this paper's criticisms do not apply to SQL/92.

8.18 C. J. Date. "What's Wrong with SQL?" In C. J. Date, *Relational Database Writings 1985– 1989.* Reading, Mass.: Addison-Wesley (1990).

Discusses some additional shortcomings of SQL, over and above those identified in reference [8.17], under the headings "What's wrong with SQL *per se,*" "What's wrong with the SQL standard," and "Application portability." *Note:* Again, certain of this paper's criticisms do not apply to SQL/92.

8.19 C. J. Date. "How SQL Missed the Boat." *Database Programming & Design 6,* No. 9 (September 1993).

A succinct summary of SQL's shortcomings with respect to its support (or lack thereof) for the structural, manipulative, and integrity aspects of the relational model.

8.20 C. J. Date. "SQL Dos and Don'ts." In C. J. Date, *Relational Database Writings 1985– 1989.* Reading, Mass.: Addison-Wesley (1990).

This paper offers some practical advice on how to use SQL in such a way as (a) to avoid some of the potential pitfalls arising from the problems discussed in references [8.17– 8.19] and (b) to realize the maximum possible benefits in terms of productivity, portability, connectivity, and so forth.

8.21 M. Negri, S. Pelagatti, and L. Sbattella. "Formal Semantics of SQL Queries." *ACM TODS 16,* No. 3 (September 1991).

To quote from the abstract: "The semantics of SQL queries are formally defined by stating a set of rules that determine a syntax-driven translation of an SQL query to a formal model called Extended Three Valued Predicate Calculus (E3VPC), which is largely based on well-known mathematical concepts. Rules for transforming a general E3VPC expression to a canonical form are also given; . . . problems like equivalence analysis of SQL queries are completely solved." Note, however, that the SQL dialect considered is only the first version of the standard ("SQL/86"), not SQL/92.

Answers to Selected Exercises

8.1
```
CREATE DOMAIN S#     CHAR(5)  ;
CREATE DOMAIN NAME   CHAR(20) ;
CREATE DOMAIN STATUS NUMERIC(5)  ;
CREATE DOMAIN CITY   CHAR(15) ;
CREATE DOMAIN P#     CHAR(6)  ;
CREATE DOMAIN COLOR  CHAR(6)  ;
CREATE DOMAIN WEIGHT NUMERIC(5)  ;
CREATE DOMAIN J#     CHAR(4)  ;
CREATE DOMAIN QTY    NUMERIC(9)  ;
```

```
CREATE TABLE S
     ( S#      S#,
       SNAME   NAME,
       STATUS  STATUS,
       CITY    CITY,
     PRIMARY KEY ( S# ) ) ;

CREATE TABLE P
     ( P#      P#,
       PNAME   NAME,
       COLOR   COLOR,
       WEIGHT  WEIGHT,
       CITY    CITY,
     PRIMARY KEY ( P# ) ) ;

CREATE TABLE J
     ( J#      J#,
       JNAME   NAME,
       CITY    CITY,
     PRIMARY KEY ( J# ) ) ;

CREATE TABLE SPJ
     ( S#      S#,
       P#      P#,
       J#      J#,
       QTY     QTY,
     PRIMARY KEY ( S#, P#, J# ),
     FOREIGN KEY ( S# ) REFERENCES S,
     FOREIGN KEY ( P# ) REFERENCES P,
     FOREIGN KEY ( J# ) REFERENCES J ) ;
```

8.2
```
DROP TABLE SPJ RESTRICT ;
DROP TABLE S   RESTRICT ;
DROP TABLE P   RESTRICT ;
DROP TABLE J   RESTRICT ;

DROP DOMAIN S#     RESTRICT ;
DROP DOMAIN NAME   RESTRICT ;
DROP DOMAIN STATUS RESTRICT ;
DROP DOMAIN CITY   RESTRICT ;
DROP DOMAIN P#     RESTRICT ;
DROP DOMAIN COLOR  RESTRICT ;
DROP DOMAIN WEIGHT RESTRICT ;
DROP DOMAIN J#     RESTRICT ;
DROP DOMAIN QTY    RESTRICT ;
```

8.5 In order to show that SQL is relationally complete, we have to show first that there exist SQL expressions for each of the five primitive operations restrict, project, product, union, and difference, and then that the operands to those SQL expressions can be arbitrary SQL expressions in turn.

   We begin by observing that SQL effectively does support the relational algebra RENAME operator, thanks to the introduction in SQL/92 of the optional "AS *column*" specification on a select-item. We can therefore ensure that all tables do have proper column names, and in particular that the operands to product, union, and difference satisfy the requirements of (our version of) the algebra with respect to column naming. Furthermore—provided those operand column naming requirements are indeed satisfied—the SQL column name inheritance rules in fact coincide with those of (our version of) the algebra.

Here then are SQL expressions corresponding to the five primitive operations:

```
Algebra              SQL

A WHERE p            SELECT * FROM A WHERE p

A [x,y,...,z]        SELECT DISTINCT x,y,...,z  FROM A

A TIMES B            A CROSS JOIN B

A UNION B            SELECT * FROM A UNION SELECT * FROM B

A MINUS B            SELECT * FROM A EXCEPT SELECT * FROM B
```

Referring to the grammar of Fig. 8.1, we see that each of *A* and *B* in the SQL expressions above is a *table-reference*. We also see that if we enclose each of the five SQL expressions shown in parentheses, each in turn becomes a valid form of *table-reference*. It follows that SQL is indeed relationally complete.

8.6 The answer is yes in both cases. First, the expression

```
EXTEND A ADD exp AS Z
```

can be represented in SQL as

```
SELECT A.*, exp AS Z
FROM   ( A ) AS A
```

The parenthesized *A* in the FROM clause here is a table-reference of arbitrary complexity (corresponding to the *A* operand of the EXTEND); the second *A* in the FROM clause is a range variable.

Second, the expression

```
SUMMARIZE A BY ( A1, A2, ..., An ) ADD exp AS Z
```

can be represented in SQL as

```
SELECT A.A1, A.A2, ..., A.An, exp AS Z
FROM   ( A ) AS A
GROUP  BY A.A1, A.A2, ..., A.An
```

8.7 SQL does not support the relational assignment operation directly. Provided we assume the target is a named relation, however, it is possible to simulate such an operation in a fairly straightforward manner. For example, the assignment

```
R  :=  X ;
```

(where *R* is a named relation and *X* is an arbitrary relational expression) can be effectively simulated by the sequence of SQL operations

```
DELETE FROM R ;
INSERT INTO R QX ;
```

where *QX* is the SQL equivalent of *X*.

8.8 SQL does not support the relational comparison operations directly. However, such operations can be simulated, albeit only in a very cumbersome manner. For example, the comparison

```
A = B
```

(where *A* and *B* are relations) can be simulated by the SQL expression

```
NOT EXISTS ( SELECT * FROM A
             WHERE NOT EXISTS ( SELECT * FROM B
                                WHERE A-row = B-row ) )
```

(where *A-row* and *B-row* are row constructors representing an entire row of *A* and an entire row of *B*, respectively).

8.9   Here are a few such formulations. Note that the following list is not even close to being exhaustive. Note too that this is a very simple query!

```
SELECT DISTINCT S.SNAME
FROM    S
WHERE   S.S# IN
        ( SELECT SP.S#
          FROM    SP
          WHERE   SP.P# = 'P2' ) ;

SELECT DISTINCT T.SNAME
FROM ( S NATURAL JOIN SP ) AS T
WHERE   T.P# = 'P2' ;

SELECT DISTINCT T.SNAME
FROM ( S JOIN SP ON S.S# = SP.P# AND SP.P# = 'P2' ) AS T ;

SELECT DISTINCT T.SNAME
FROM ( S JOIN SP USING S# ) AS T
WHERE   T.P# = 'P2' ;

SELECT DISTINCT S.SNAME
FROM    S
WHERE   S.S# =ANY
        ( SELECT SP.S#
          FROM    SP
          WHERE   SP.P# = 'P2' ) ;

SELECT DISTINCT S.SNAME
FROM    S
WHERE   EXISTS
        ( SELECT *
          FROM    SP
          WHERE   SP.S# = S.S#
          AND     SP.P# = 'P2' ) ;

SELECT DISTINCT S.SNAME
FROM    S, SP
WHERE   S.S# = SP.S#
AND     SP.P# = 'P2' ;

SELECT DISTINCT S.SNAME
FROM    S
WHERE   0 <
        ( SELECT COUNT(*)
          FROM    SP
          WHERE   SP.S# = S.S#
          AND     SP.P# = 'P2' ) ;

SELECT DISTINCT S.SNAME
FROM    S
WHERE   'P2' IN
        ( SELECT SP.P#
          FROM    SP
          WHERE   SP.S# = S.S# ) ;
```

```
SELECT DISTINCT S.SNAME
FROM    S
WHERE   'P2' =ANY
      ( SELECT SP.P#
        FROM    SP
        WHERE   SP.S# = S.S# ) ;

SELECT S.SNAME
FROM    S, SP
WHERE   S.S# = SP.S#
AND     SP.P# = 'P2'
GROUP   BY S.SNAME ;
```

Subsidiary question: What are the implications of the foregoing?

8.10 SQL is really a hybrid of both the algebra and the calculus. For example, it provides both the existential quantifier EXISTS (calculus) and the UNION operator (algebra). Interestingly, SQL was originally intended to be distinct from both the algebra and the calculus (see reference [8.8]); it was felt that the "IN subquery" construct was more user-friendly than both the explicit joins (etc.) of the algebra and the quantifiers of the calculus. As it turned out, however, the "IN subquery" construct was (obviously) inadequate by itself, and so it became necessary to extend the original language in a variety of ways. The situation now, ironically enough, is that the "IN subquery" facility could be eliminated entirely from the SQL language with effectively no loss of function (though it might be argued that the "IN subquery" construct is sometimes intuitively easier to understand than the alternatives). See references [8.17–8.19] for further discussion of this point.

8.11 We have numbered the following solutions as 8.11.*n*, where 6.n is the number of the original exercise in Chapter 6.

8.11.13
```
SELECT *
FROM    J ;
```

Or simply:

```
TABLE J ;
```

8.11.14
```
SELECT J.*
FROM    J
WHERE   J.CITY = 'London' ;
```

8.11.15
```
SELECT DISTINCT SPJ.S#
FROM    SPJ
WHERE   SPJ.J# = 'J1' ;
```

8.11.16
```
SELECT SPJ.*
FROM    SPJ
WHERE   SPJ.QTY >= 300
AND     SPJ.QTY <= 750 ;
```

8.11.17
```
SELECT DISTINCT P.COLOR, P.CITY
FROM    P ;
```

8.11.18
```
SELECT S.S#, P.P#, J.J#
FROM    S, P, J
WHERE   S.CITY = P.CITY
AND     P.CITY = J.CITY ;
```

8.11.19 SELECT S.S#, P.P#, J.J#
         FROM   S, P, J
         WHERE   ·NOT (S.CITY = P.CITY AND
                        P.CITY = J.CITY) ;

8.11.20 SELECT S.S#, P.P#, J.J#
         FROM   S, P, J
         WHERE   S.CITY <> P.CITY
         AND   P.CITY <> J.CITY
         AND   J.CITY <> P.CITY ;

8.11.21 SELECT DISTINCT SPJ.P#
         FROM   SPJ
         WHERE   (SELECT S.CITY
                   FROM   S
                   WHERE S.S# = SPJ.S#) = 'London' ;

8.11.22 SELECT DISTINCT SPJ.P#
         FROM   SPJ
         WHERE   (SELECT S.CITY
                   FROM   S
                   WHERE S.S# = SPJ.S#) = 'London'
         AND   (SELECT J.CITY
                   FROM   J
                   WHERE J.J# = SPJ.J#) = 'London' ;

8.11.23 SELECT DISTINCT S.CITY AS SCITY, J.CITY AS JCITY
         FROM   S, J
         WHERE   EXISTS
               (SELECT *
                 FROM   SPJ
                 WHERE SPJ.S# = S.S#
                 AND   SPJ.J# = J.J#) ;

8.11.24 SELECT DISTINCT SPJ.P#
         FROM   SPJ
         WHERE   (SELECT S.CITY
                   FROM   S
                   WHERE S.S# = SPJ.S#) =
                 (SELECT J.CITY
                   FROM   J
                   WHERE J.J# = SPJ.J#) ;

8.11.25 SELECT DISTINCT SPJ.J#
         FROM   SPJ
         WHERE   (SELECT S.CITY
                   FROM   S
                   WHERE S.S# = SPJ.S#) <>
                 (SELECT J.CITY
                   FROM   J
                   WHERE J.J# = SPJ.J#) ;

8.11.26 SELECT DISTINCT SPJX.P# AS PA, SPJY.P# AS PB
         FROM   SPJ AS SPJX, SPJ AS SPJY
         WHERE   SPJX.S# = SPJY.S#
         AND   SPJX.P# < SPJY.P# ;

8.11.27 SELECT COUNT (DISTINCT SPJ.J#) AS N
         FROM   SPJ
         WHERE   SPJ.S# = 'S1' ;

8.11.28 SELECT SUM (SPJ.QTY) AS X
         FROM   SPJ
         WHERE   SPJ.S# = 'S1'
         AND   SPJ.P# = 'P1' ;

8.11.29 SELECT SPJ.P#, SPJ.J#, SUM (SPJ.QTY) AS Y
         FROM   SPJ
         GROUP   BY SPJ.P#, SPJ.J# ;

8.11.30 SELECT DISTINCT SPJ.P#
         FROM   SPJ
         GROUP   BY SPJ.P#, SPJ.J#
         HAVING   AVG (SPJ.QTY) > 320 ;

8.11.31 SELECT DISTINCT J.JNAME
         FROM   J, SPJ
         WHERE   J.J# = SPJ.J#
         AND   SPJ.S# = 'S1' ;

8.11.32 SELECT DISTINCT P.COLOR
         FROM   P, SPJ
         WHERE   P.P# = SPJ.P#
         AND   SPJ.S# = 'S1' ;

8.11.33 SELECT DISTINCT SPJ.P#
         FROM   SPJ, J
         WHERE   SPJ.J# = J.J#
         AND   J.CITY = 'London' ;

8.11.34 SELECT DISTINCT SPJX.J#
         FROM   SPJ AS SPJX, SPJ AS SPJY
         WHERE   SPJX.P# = SPJY.P#
         AND   SPJY.S# = 'S1' ;

8.11.35 SELECT DISTINCT SPJX.S#
         FROM   SPJ AS SPJX, SPJ AS SPJY, SPJ AS SPJZ
         WHERE   SPJX.P# = SPJY.P#
         AND   SPJY.S# = SPJZ.S#
         AND   (SELECT P.COLOR
                  FROM   P
                  WHERE   P.P# = SPJZ.P#) = 'Red' ;

8.11.36 SELECT S.S#
         FROM   S
         WHERE   S.STATUS < (SELECT S.STATUS
                               FROM   S
                               WHERE   S.S# = 'S1') ;

8.11.37 SELECT J.J#
         FROM   J
         WHERE   J.CITY = (SELECT MIN (J.CITY)
                             FROM   J) ;

8.11.38 SELECT DISTINCT SPJX.J#
         FROM   SPJ AS SPJX
         WHERE   SPJX.P# = 'P1'
         AND   (SELECT AVG (SPJY.QTY)
                  FROM   SPJ AS SPJY
                  WHERE   SPJY.J# = SPJX.J#
                  AND   SPJY.P# = 'P1') >
                (SELECT MAX (SPJZ.QTY)
                  FROM   SPJ AS SPJZ
                  WHERE   SPJZ.J# = 'J1') ;

```
8.11.39  SELECT  DISTINCT SPJX.S#
         FROM    SPJ AS SPJX
         WHERE   SPJX.P# = 'P1'
         AND     SPJX.QTY > ( SELECT AVG ( SPJY.QTY )
                              FROM    SPJ AS SPJY
                              WHERE   SPJY.P# = 'P1'
                              AND     SPJY.J# = SPJX.J# ) ;
8.11.40  SELECT  J.J#
         FROM    J
         WHERE   NOT EXISTS
             ( SELECT *
               FROM    SPJ, P, S
               WHERE   SPJ.J# = J.J#
               AND     SPJ.P# = P.P#
               AND     SPJ.S# = S.S#
               AND     P.COLOR = 'Red'
               AND     S.CITY = 'London' ) ;
8.11.41  SELECT  J.J#
         FROM    J
         WHERE   NOT EXISTS
             ( SELECT *
               FROM    SPJ
               WHERE   SPJ.J# = J.J#
               AND     NOT ( SPJ.S# = 'S1' ) ) ;
8.11.42  SELECT  P.P#
         FROM    P
         WHERE   NOT EXISTS
             ( SELECT *
               FROM    J
               WHERE   J.CITY = 'London'
               AND     NOT EXISTS
                   ( SELECT *
                     FROM    SPJ
                     WHERE   SPJ.P# = P.P#
                     AND     SPJ.J# = J.J# ) ) ;
8.11.43  SELECT  S.S#
         FROM    S
         WHERE   EXISTS
             ( SELECT *
               FROM    P
               WHERE   NOT EXISTS
                   ( SELECT *
                     FROM    J
                     WHERE   NOT EXISTS
                         ( SELECT *
                           FROM    SPJ
                           WHERE   SPJ.S# = S.S#
                           AND     SPJ.P# = P.P#
                           AND     SPJ.J# = J.J# ) ) ) ;
8.11.44  SELECT  J.J#
         FROM    J
         WHERE   NOT EXISTS
             ( SELECT *
```

```
                    FROM    SPJ AS SPJX
                    WHERE   SPJX.S# = 'S1'
                    AND     NOT EXISTS
                          ( SELECT *
                            FROM    SPJ AS SPJY
                            WHERE   SPJY.P# = SPJX.P#
                            AND     SPJY.J# = J.J# ) ) ;
```

8.11.45 `SELECT S.CITY FROM S`
```
         UNION
         SELECT P.CITY FROM P
         UNION
         SELECT J.CITY FROM J ;
```

8.11.46 `SELECT DISTINCT SPJ.P#`
```
         FROM    SPJ
         WHERE   ( SELECT S.CITY
                   FROM    S
                   WHERE   S.S# = SPJ.S# ) = 'London'
         OR      ( SELECT J.CITY
                   FROM    J
                   WHERE   J.J# = SPJ.J# ) = 'London' ;
```

8.11.47 `SELECT S.S#, P.P#`
```
         FROM    S CROSS JOIN P
         EXCEPT
         SELECT SPJ.S#, SPJ.P#
         FROM    SPJ ;
```

8.11.48 Left to the reader.

8.12 (a) `INSERT INTO S ( S#, SNAME, STATUS, CITY )`
```
                VALUES ( 'S10', 'Smith', DEFAULT, 'New York' ) ;
```

   (b) `UPDATE P`
```
        SET    COLOR = 'Orange'
        WHERE  P.COLOR = 'Red' ;
```

   (c) `DELETE`
```
        FROM    J
        WHERE   NOT EXISTS
              ( SELECT * FROM SPJ
                WHERE   SPJ.J# = J.J# ) ;
```

8.13 Note that there might be some suppliers who supply no projects at all; the following solution does deal with such suppliers satisfactorily (how, exactly?).

First we define two cursors, CS and CJ, as follows:

```
EXEC SQL DECLARE CS CURSOR FOR
        SELECT S.S#, S.SNAME, S.STATUS, S.CITY
        FROM    S
        ORDER   BY S# ;

EXEC SQL DECLARE CJ CURSOR FOR
        SELECT J.J#, J.JNAME, J.CITY
        FROM    J
        WHERE   J.J# IN
              ( SELECT SPJ.J#
                FROM    SPJ
                WHERE   SPJ.S# = :CS_S# )
        ORDER BY J# ;
```

When cursor CJ is opened, host variable CS_S# will contain a supplier number value, fetched via cursor CS. The procedural logic is essentially as follows:

```
EXEC SQL OPEN CS ;
DO for all S rows accessible via CS ;
   EXEC SQL FETCH CS INTO :CS_S#, :CS_SN, :CS_ST, :CS_SC ;
   print CS_S#, CS_SN, CS_ST, CS_SC ;
   EXEC SQL OPEN CJ ;
   DO for all J rows accessible via CJ ;
      EXEC SQL FETCH CJ INTO :CJ_J#, :CJ_JN, :CJ_JC ;
      print CJ_J#, CJ_JN, CJ_JC ;
   END ;
   EXEC SQL CLOSE CJ ;
END ;
EXEC SQL CLOSE CS ;
```

8.14 This is a good example of a problem that SQL in its current form does not handle well. The basic difficulty is as follows: We need to "explode" the given part to n levels, where the value of n is unknown at the time of writing the program. A comparatively straightforward way of performing such an n-level "explosion"—if it were possible—would be by means of a recursive program, in which each recursive invocation creates a new cursor, as follows:

```
GET LIST ( GIVENP# ) ;
CALL RECURSION ( GIVENP# ) ;
RETURN ;

RECURSION: PROC ( UPPER_P# ) RECURSIVE ;
   DCL UPPER_P# ... ;
   DCL LOWER_P# ... ;
   EXEC SQL DECLARE C "reopenable" CURSOR FOR
            SELECT MINOR_P#
            FROM   PART_STRUCTURE
            WHERE  MAJOR_P# = :UPPER_P# ;

   print UPPER_P# ;
   EXEC SQL OPEN C ;
   DO for all PART_STRUCTURE rows accessible via C ;
      EXEC SQL FETCH C INTO :LOWER_P# ;
      CALL RECURSION ( LOWER_P# ) ;
   END ;
   EXEC SQL CLOSE C ;
END ; /* of RECURSION */
```

We have assumed here that the (fictitious) specification "reopenable" on DECLARE CURSOR means that it is legal to OPEN that cursor even if it is already open, and that the effect of such an OPEN is to create a new *instance* of the cursor for the specified table expression (using the current values of any host variables referenced in that expression). We have assumed further that references to such a cursor in FETCH (etc.) are references to the "current" instance, and that CLOSE destroys that instance and reinstates the previous instance as "current." In other words, we have assumed that a reopenable cursor forms a *stack*, with OPEN and CLOSE serving as the "push" and "pop" operators for that stack.

Unfortunately, these assumptions are purely hypothetical today. There is no such thing as a reopenable cursor in SQL today (indeed, an attempt to OPEN a cursor that is already open will fail). The foregoing code is illegal. But the example makes it clear that "reopenable cursors" would be a very desirable extension to current SQL.

Since the foregoing procedure does not work, we give a sketch of one possible (but very inefficient) procedure that does.

```
GET LIST ( GIVENP# ) ;
CALL RECURSION ( GIVENP# ) ;
RETURN ;

RECURSION: PROC ( UPPER_P# ) RECURSIVE ;
   DCL UPPER_P# ... ;
   DCL LOWER_P# ... INITIAL ( '       ' ) ;
   EXEC SQL DECLARE C CURSOR FOR
                     SELECT MINOR_P#
                     FROM   PART_STRUCTURE
                     WHERE  MAJOR_P# = :UPPER_P#
                     AND    MINOR_P# > :LOWER_P#
                     ORDER  BY MINOR_P# ;

   print UPPER_P# ;
   DO "forever" ;
      EXEC SQL OPEN C ;
      EXEC SQL FETCH C INTO :LOWER_P# ;
      EXEC SQL CLOSE C ;
      IF no "lower P#" retrieved THEN RETURN ;
      IF "lower P#" retrieved THEN CALL RECURSION ( LOWER_P# ) ;
   END ;
END ; /* of RECURSION */
```

Observe in this solution that the same cursor is used on every invocation of RECURSION. (By contrast, new instances of UPPER_P# and LOWER_P# are created dynamically each time RECURSION is invoked; those instances are destroyed at completion of that invocation.) Because of this fact, we have to use a trick—

```
... AND MINOR_P# > :LOWER_P# ORDER BY MINOR_P#
```

—so that, on each invocation of RECURSION, we simply ignore all immediate components (LOWER_P#s) of the current UPPER_P# that have already been processed.

See reference [8.14] for a discussion of some alternative approaches to this problem.

PART III

DATABASE DESIGN

This part of the book is concerned with the general subject of database design (more specifically, *relational* database design). The database design problem can be stated very simply, as follows: Given some body of data to be represented in a database, how do we decide on a suitable logical structure for that data?—in other words, how do we decide what base relations should exist and what attributes those relations should have? The practical significance of this problem is obvious.

Before we start getting into details, a number of preliminary remarks are in order.

- First, note that we are concerned with **logical** design only, not physical design. Now, we obviously do not mean to suggest by this remark that physical design is not important—on the contrary, physical design is *very* important. However:

  - Physical design can be treated as a separate, follow-on activity. In other words, the "right" way to do database design is to do a clean logical (i.e., relational) design first, and then, as a separate and subsequent step, to map that logical design into whatever physical structures the target DBMS happens to support.

  - Physical design, by definition, tends to be somewhat DBMS-specific, and as a topic is thus not appropriate for a general textbook such as this one. Logical design, by contrast, is (or should be) quite DBMS-independent, and there are some solid theoretical principles that can be applied to the problem. And, of course, such principles definitely do have a place in a book of this kind.

  Unfortunately we live in an imperfect world, and in practice it will often be the case that design decisions made at the physical level will have an impact back on the logical level. In other words, several iterations will have to be made over the "logical-then-physical" design cycle, and compromises will probably have to be made. Nevertheless, we stand by our original contention that the right way to do database design is to get the logical design right first, without paying any attention whatsoever at the logical design stage to physical—i.e., performance—considerations. Thus, this part of the book is primarily concerned with what is involved in "getting the logical design right first."

- Although as already stated we are concerned primarily with *relational* design, it is our belief that the ideas to be discussed are relevant to the design of nonrelational databases also. In other words, the right way to do database design in a nonrelational system is to do a clean relational design first, and then, as a separate and subsequent step, to map that relational design into whatever nonrelational structures (e.g., hierarchies) the target DBMS happens to support.

- Having said all of the above, we must now also say that database design is still very much of an art, not a science. There *are* some scientific principles that can be brought to bear on the problem, and those principles are the subject of the next three chapters; however, there are many, many design issues that those principles simply do not address at all. As a consequence, numerous database theoreticians and practitioners have proposed design methodologies—some of them fairly rigorous, others less so, but all of them *ad hoc* to a degree—that can be used as an attack on what at the time of writing is still a rather intractable problem, *viz.*, the problem of finding "the" logical design that is incontestably the right one. Since those methodologies *are* all *ad hoc* to a greater or lesser extent, there can be few objective criteria for preferring any given approach over all the rest; nevertheless, we present (in Chapter 12) a well-known approach that is arguably a little less *ad hoc* than some.

■ We should also state explicitly a couple of assumptions that underlie most of the discussions in this part of the book:

▪ Database design is not just a question of getting the data structures right—data integrity is a key ingredient also. This remark will be amplified at several points in the chapters that follow.

▪ We will be concerned for the most part with what might be termed *application-independent* design. In other words, we are primarily concerned with what the data *is,* rather than how it will be used. Application independence in this sense is desirable for the very good reason that it is normally—perhaps always—the case that not all uses to which the data will be put are known at design time; thus, we want a design that will be *robust,* in the sense that it will not be invalidated by the advent of new application requirements that were not foreseen at the time of the original design. To put this another way (and to use the terminology of Chapter 2), what we are trying to do is to design the *conceptual schema;* that is, we are interested in producing a hardware-independent, operating-system-independent, DBMS-independent, language-independent, user-independent (etc., etc.) abstract logical design. In particular, we are *not* interested in making compromises for performance reasons, as already explained above.

■ We stated above that the problem of database design is the problem of deciding what base relations should exist and what attributes they should have. In fact, of course, it involves the problem of deciding what *domains* should exist as well. We will have little to say on this topic, however, since little relevant work seems to have been done on it at the time of writing (reference [12.26] is an exception).

The structure of this part is as follows. Chapter 9 lays some theoretical groundwork. Chapters 10 and 11 are concerned with the ideas of *further normalization,* which build directly on that groundwork to give formal meaning to informal claims to the effect that certain designs are "better" than certain others. Chapter 12 then describes the concepts of *entity/relationship modeling,* and shows how those concepts can be used to tackle the design problem "top down" (starting with real-world entities and ending up with a formal database design).

9 | Functional Dependencies

9.1 Introduction

In this chapter we will examine a concept that is "not quite fundamental, but very nearly so" [9.7]—the concept of **functional dependence**. This concept will turn out to be crucially important to a number of issues to be discussed in later chapters, including in particular the database design theory described in Chapter 10.

Basically, a functional dependence (usually abbreviated FD) is *a many-to-one relationship* from one set of attributes to another within a given relation. In the shipments relation SP, for example, there is a functional dependence from the set of attributes {S#,P#} to the set of attributes {QTY}. What this means is that for *many* values of the attribute pair S#-P# there is *one* corresponding value of the attribute QTY (refer to Fig. 3.8 if you want to check this point).

In Section 9.2, we define the concept of functional dependence more precisely, distinguishing carefully between those FDs that happen to be satisfied at some particular time and those that must be satisfied for *all* time. As already mentioned, it turns out that FDs provide a basis for a scientific attack on a number of practical problems. This is because FDs possess a rich set of interesting formal properties, which make it possible to treat the problems in question in a formal and rigorous manner. Sections 9.3–9.6 explore some of those formal properties in detail and explain some of their practical consequences. Finally, Section 9.7 presents a brief summary.

Note: Some readers might like to skip portions of this chapter on a first reading. Indeed, most of what you need from this chapter in order to understand the material of Chapters 10–12 is covered in Sections 9.2 and 9.3. You might therefore prefer to give the remaining sections a "once over lightly" reading for now, and come back to them later when you have assimilated the material of the next three chapters.

A small point regarding terminology: The terms functional **dependence** and functional **dependency** are used interchangeably in the technical literature. Customary English usage would suggest that the term "dependence" be used for the FD concept *per se* and would reserve the term "dependency" for "the object that depends." But we very frequently need to refer to FDs in the plural, and "dependencies" seems to trip off the tongue more readily than "dependences"; hence our use of both terms.

9.2   Basic Definitions

In order to illustrate the ideas of the present section, we make use of a slightly revised version of the shipments relation, one that includes, in addition to the usual attributes S#, P#, and QTY, an attribute CITY, representing the city for the relevant supplier. We will refer to this revised relation as SCP to avoid confusion. A possible tabulation of relation SCP is given in Fig. 9.1.

Now, it is very important in this area—as in so many others—to distinguish clearly between (a) the *value* of a given relation (i.e., relation variable) at a given point in time and (b) the *set of all possible values* that the given relation (variable) might assume at different times (see Chapter 4, Section 4.3). In what follows, we will first define the concept of functional dependency as it applies to Case (a), and then extend it to apply to Case (b). Here then is the definition for Case (a).

■   Let R be a relation, and let X and Y be arbitrary subsets of the set of attributes of R. Then we say that Y is **functionally dependent** on X—in symbols,

$$X \rightarrow Y$$

(read "X **functionally determines** Y," or simply "X arrow Y")—if and only if each X-value in R has associated with it precisely one Y-value in R.

In other words, whenever two tuples of R agree on their X-value, they also agree on their Y-value. For example, the tabulation of relation SCP shown in Fig. 9.1 satisfies the FD

    { S# } → { CITY }

because every SCP tuple with a given S# value also has the same CITY value. Indeed, it also satisfies several more FDs, the following among them:

SCP	S#	CITY	P#	QTY
	S1	London	P1	100
	S1	London	P2	100
	S2	Paris	P1	200
	S2	Paris	P2	200
	S3	Paris	P2	300
	S4	London	P2	400
	S4	London	P4	400
	S4	London	P5	400

FIG. 9.1   The relation SCP (sample tabulation)

```
{ S#, P# } → { QTY }
{ S#, P# } → { CITY }
{ S#, P# } → { CITY, QTY }
{ S#, P# } → { S# }
{ S#, P# } → { S#, P#, CITY, QTY }
{ S# }     → { QTY }
{ QTY }    → { S# }
```

(*Exercise:* Check these.)

The left-hand side and right-hand side of an FD are sometimes called the **determinant** and the **dependent,** respectively. As the definition states, the determinant and dependent are both *sets* of attributes. When the set contains just one attribute, however—i.e., when it is a **singleton set**—we will often drop the set brackets and write just, e.g.,

```
S# → CITY
```

As already explained, the foregoing definitions apply to "Case (a)"—i.e., to individual relation *values.* However, when we consider relation *variables*—in particular, when we consider *base relations*—we are usually interested not so much in the FDs that happen to hold in the particular value that the variable happens to have at some particular time, but rather in those FDs that hold for *all possible values* of that variable. In the case of SCP, for example, the FD

```
S# → CITY
```

holds for all possible values of SCP, because, at any given time, a given supplier has precisely one corresponding city, and so any two tuples appearing in SCP at the same time with the same supplier number must necessarily have the same city as well. In fact, the statement that this FD holds "for all time" (i.e., for all possible values of SCP) is an *integrity constraint* for SCP—it places limits on the values that SCP can legitimately assume.

Here then is the "Case (b)" definition of functional dependency (the extensions over the Case (a) definition are shown in **boldface**):

- Let R be a relation **variable,** and let X and Y be arbitrary subsets of the set of attributes of R. Then we say that Y is functionally dependent on X—in symbols,

```
X → Y
```

(read "X functionally determines Y," or simply "X arrow Y")—if and only if, **in every possible legal value of R,** each X-value has associated with it precisely one Y-value.

In other words, **in every possible legal value of R,** whenever two tuples agree on their X-value, they also agree on their Y-value.

Henceforth, we will usually take the term "functional dependency" to have this latter, more demanding, *time-independent* meaning (barring explicit statements to the contrary). Here are some time-independent FDs that apply to the relation variable SCP:

```
{ S#, P# } → QTY
{ S#, P# } → CITY
{ S#, P# } → { CITY, QTY }
{ S#, P# } → S#
{ S#, P# } → { S#, P#, CITY, QTY }
{ S# }     → CITY
```

Notice in particular that the following FDs, which do hold in the sample tabulation of Fig. 9.1, do *not* hold "for all time":

```
S#  → QTY
QTY → S#
```

In other words, the statement that (e.g.) "every shipment for a given supplier has the same shipment quantity" happens to be true for the sample values in Fig. 9.1, but it is not true for all possible legal values of SCP.

It is worth pointing out that if X is a candidate key of relation R—in particular, if it is the *primary* key—then all attributes Y of relation R must necessarily be functionally dependent on X (this fact follows from the definition of candidate key). In the usual parts relation P, for example, we must necessarily have:

```
P# → { P#, PNAME, COLOR, WEIGHT, CITY }
```

In fact, if relation R satisfies the FD $A \rightarrow B$ and A is *not* a candidate key,* then R will involve some **redundancy**. In the case of relation SCP, for example, the fact that a given supplier is located in a given city appears many times, in general (see Fig. 9.1). We will take up this point and discuss it in detail in Chapter 10.

Now, even if we restrict our attention to FDs that hold "for all time," the set of FDs satisfied by all legal values of a given relation can still be very large, as the SCP example suggests. (*Exercise:* Try writing down the complete set of FDs satisfied by SCP. See also Exercises 9.1 and 9.7 at the end of the chapter.) What we would like is to find some way of reducing that set to a manageable size—and, indeed, most of the remainder of this chapter is concerned with exactly this issue.

Why is this objective desirable? One reason is that (as already stated) FDs represent integrity constraints, and hence the DBMS needs to check them when updates are performed. Given a particular set S of FDs, therefore, it is desirable to find some other set T that is (ideally) much smaller than S and has the property that every FD in S is implied by the FDs in T. If such a set T can be found, it is sufficient that the DBMS enforce the FDs in T, and the FDs in S will then be enforced automatically. The problem of finding such a set T is thus of considerable practical interest.

9.3   Trivial and Nontrivial Dependencies

Note: In the remainder of this chapter, we will occasionally abbreviate "functional dependency" to just "dependency." Similarly for "functionally dependent on," "functionally determines," etc.

One obvious way to reduce the size of the set of FDs we have to deal with is to eliminate the *trivial* dependencies. A dependency is trivial if it cannot possibly not be

---

* And the FD is not *trivial* (see Section 9.3) and A is not a *superkey* (see Section 9.5) and R contains at least two tuples.

satisfied. Just one of the FDs shown for SCP in the previous section was trivial in this sense, *viz.* the FD

```
{ S#, P# } → S#
```

In fact, an FD is **trivial** if and only if the right-hand side is a subset (not necessarily a proper subset) of the left-hand side.

As the name implies, trivial dependencies are not very interesting in practice; we are usually more interested in practice in **nontrivial** dependencies (which are, of course, precisely the ones that are not trivial), because these are the ones that correspond to "genuine" integrity constraints. When we are dealing with formal dependency theory, however, we cannot necessarily assume that all dependencies are nontrivial.

9.4 Closure of a Set of Dependencies

We have already suggested (near the end of Section 9.2) that certain FDs imply others. As a simple example, the FD

```
{ S#, P# } → { CITY, QTY }
```

implies both the following FDs:

```
{ S#, P# } → CITY
{ S#, P# } → QTY
```

As a more complex example, suppose we have a relation R with three attributes A, B, and C, such that the FDs $A \rightarrow B$ and $B \rightarrow C$ both hold in R. Then it is easy to see that the FD $A \rightarrow C$ also holds in R. The FD $A \rightarrow C$ here is an example of a **transitive** FD—C is said to depend on A *transitively*, via B.

The set of all FDs that are implied by a given set S of FDs is called the **closure** of S, and is denoted S^+. Clearly we need a way of computing S^+ from S. The first attack on this problem appeared in a paper by Armstrong [9.1], which gave a set of *rules of inference* (more usually called *Armstrong's axioms*) by which new FDs can be inferred from given ones. Those rules can be stated in a variety of equivalent ways, one of the simplest of which is as follows:

- **Armstrong's inference rules:** Let A, B, and C be arbitrary subsets of the set of attributes of the given relation R, and let us agree to write (e.g.) AB to mean the union of A and B. Then:

  1. **Reflexivity:** If B is a subset of A, then $A \rightarrow B$.
  2. **Augmentation:** If $A \rightarrow B$, then $AC \rightarrow BC$.
  3. **Transitivity:** If $A \rightarrow B$ and $B \rightarrow C$, then $A \rightarrow C$.

Each of these three rules can be directly proved from the definition of functional dependence (the first is just the definition of a **trivial** dependence, of course). Moreover, the rules are **complete,** in the sense that, given a set S of FDs, all FDs implied by S can be derived from S using the rules. They are also **sound,** in the sense that no additional FDs (i.e., FDs not implied by S) can be so derived. In other words, the rules can be used to derive precisely the closure S^+.

Several further rules can be derived from the three given above, the following among them. These additional rules can be used to simplify the practical task of computing S^+ from S. (D is another arbitrary subset of the set of attributes of R.)

4. **Self-determination:** $A \to A$.
5. **Decomposition:** If $A \to BC$, then $A \to B$ and $A \to C$.
6. **Union:** If $A \to B$ and $A \to C$, then $A \to BC$.
7. **Composition:** If $A \to B$ and $C \to D$, then $AC \to BD$.

And in reference [9.6], Darwen proves the following rule, which he calls the *General Unification Theorem:*

8. If $A \to B$ and $C \to D$, then $A \cup (C - B) \to BD$ (where "$\cup$" is union and "$-$" is set difference).

The name "General Unification Theorem" refers to the fact that several of the earlier rules can be seen as special cases [9.6].

Example: Suppose we are given relation R with attributes A, B, C, D, E, F, and the FDs

```
A   → BC
B   → E
CD  → EF
```

Observe that we are extending our notation slightly (though not incompatibly) by writing, e.g., BC for the set consisting of attributes B and C—previously BC would have meant the *union* of B and C, where B and C were *sets* of attributes. *Note:* If you would prefer a more concrete example, take A as employee number, B as department number, C as manager's employee number, D as project number for a project directed by that manager (unique within manager), E as department name, and F as percentage of time allocated by the specified manager to the specified project.

We now show that the FD $AD \to F$ holds in R, and so is a member of the closure of the given set:

```
1. A   → BC   (given)
2. A   → C    (1, decomposition)
3. AD  → CD   (2, augmentation)
4. CD  → EF   (given)
5. AD  → EF   (3 and 4, transitivity)
6. AD  → F    (5, decomposition)   ∎
```

9.5 Closure of a Set of Attributes

We have not yet given an effective algorithm for computing the closure S^+ of a given set S of FDs. However, in this section we give an effective way of determining whether a given (specified) FD is *in* that closure. We begin our discussion with the notion of a *superkey*.

A **superkey** for a relation R is a set of attributes of R that includes at least one *candidate* key of R as a subset—not necessarily a proper subset, of course. (The definition of "superkey" can thus be derived from that of "candidate key" by simply deleting the irreducibility requirement.) It follows immediately that the superkeys for a given relation R are precisely those subsets K of the set of attributes of R such that the functional dependency

$$K \rightarrow A$$

holds true for every attribute A of R.

Now suppose we know the FDs that hold for some given relation, and we need to determine the candidate keys for that relation. The candidate keys are, by definition, those superkeys that are irreducible. So determining whether or not a given set of attributes K is a superkey is a big step toward determining whether K is in fact a candidate key.

To determine whether K is a superkey, we need to determine whether the set of all attributes functionally dependent on K is in fact the set of all attributes of R. And so, given a set S of FDs that hold in R, we need a way of determining the set of all attributes of R that are functionally dependent on K—the so-called **closure** K^+ of K under S. A simple algorithm for computing this closure is given in Fig. 9.2. *Exercise:* Prove that algorithm is correct.

Example: Suppose we are given relation R with attributes A, B, C, D, E, F, and FDs

$$
\begin{aligned}
A &\rightarrow BC \\
E &\rightarrow CF \\
B &\rightarrow E \\
CD &\rightarrow EF
\end{aligned}
$$

We now compute the closure $\{A,B\}^+$ of the set of attributes $\{A,B\}$ under this set of FDs.

1. We initialize the result CLOSURE[K,S] to $\{A,B\}$.

2. We now go round the inner loop four times, once for each of the given FDs. On the first iteration (for the FD $A \rightarrow BC$), we find that the left-hand side is indeed a subset

```
CLOSURE[K,S] := K ;
do "forever" ;
   for each FD X → Y in S
      do ;
         if X is a subset of CLOSURE[K,S]
         then CLOSURE[K,S] := CLOSURE[K,S] UNION Y ;
      end ;
   if CLOSURE[K,S] did not change on this iteration
   then /* computation complete */ leave loop ;
end ;
```

FIG. 9.2 Computing the closure K^+ of K under S

of CLOSURE[K,S] as computed so far, so we add attributes (B and) C to the result. CLOSURE[K,S] is now the set {A,B,C}.

3. On the second iteration (for the FD $E \rightarrow CF$), we find that the left-hand side is *not* a subset of the result as computed so far, which thus remains unchanged.

4. On the third iteration (for the FD $B \rightarrow E$), we add E to CLOSURE[K,S], which now has the value {A,B,C,E}.

5. On the fourth iteration (for the FD $CD \rightarrow EF$), CLOSURE[K,S] remains unchanged.

6. Now we go round the inner loop four times again. On the first iteration, the result does not change; on the second, it expands to {A,B,C,E,F}; on the third and fourth, it does not change.

7. Now we go round the inner loop four times again. CLOSURE[K,S] does not change, and so the whole process terminates, with {A,B}$^+$ = {A,B,C,E,F}. Note, therefore, that {A,B} is not a superkey (and hence not a candidate key *a fortiori*). ▮

An important corollary of the foregoing is as follows: Given a set S of FDs, we can easily tell whether a specific FD $X \rightarrow Y$ follows from S, because that FD will follow if and only if Y is a subset of the closure X^+ of X under S. In other words, we now have a simple way of determining whether a given FD $X \rightarrow Y$ is in the closure S^+ of S.

9.6 Irreducible Sets of Dependencies

Let $S1$ and $S2$ be two sets of FDs. If every FD implied by $S1$ is implied by the FDs in $S2$—i.e., if $S1^+$ is a subset of $S2^+$—we say that $S2$ is a **cover** for $S1$.* What this means is that if the DBMS enforces the constraints represented by the FDs in $S2$, then it will automatically be enforcing the FDs in $S1$.

Next, if $S2$ is a cover for $S1$ and $S1$ is a cover for $S2$—i.e., if $S1^+ = S2^+$—we say that $S1$ and $S2$ are **equivalent**. Clearly, if $S1$ and $S2$ are equivalent, then if the DBMS enforces the constraints represented by the FDs in $S2$ it will automatically be enforcing the FDs in $S1$, and *vice versa*.

Now we define a set S of FDs to be **irreducible**[†] if and only if it satisfies the following three properties:

1. The right-hand side (the dependent) of every FD in S involves just one attribute (i.e., is a singleton set).

2. The left-hand side (the determinant) of every FD in S is irreducible in turn—meaning that no attribute can be discarded from the determinant without changing the closure S^+ (i.e., without converting S into some set not equivalent to S). We will say that such an FD is **left-irreducible**.

3. No FD in S can be discarded from S without changing the closure S^+ (i.e., without converting S into some set not equivalent to S).

---

* Some writers use the term "cover" to mean what we will be calling an *equivalent* set.
[†] Usually called *minimal* in the literature.

For example, consider the familiar parts relation P. The following FDs (among others) hold in that relation:

```
P# → PNAME
P# → COLOR
P# → WEIGHT
P# → CITY
```

This set of FDs is easily seen to be irreducible: The right-hand side is a single attribute in each case, the left-hand side is obviously irreducible in turn, and none of the FDs can be discarded without changing the closure (i.e., without *losing some information*). By contrast, the following sets of FDs are not irreducible:

1. ```
   P# → { PNAME, COLOR }   : The right-hand side of this FD is not
   P# → WEIGHT                a singleton set
   P# → CITY
   ```

2. ```
   { P#, PNAME } → COLOR   : This FD can be simplified by
   P# → PNAME                dropping PNAME from the left-hand
   P# → WEIGHT               side without changing the closure
   P# → CITY                 (i.e., it is not left-irreducible)
   ```

3. ```
   P# → P#                 : This FD can be discarded without
   P# → PNAME                changing the closure
   P# → COLOR
   P# → WEIGHT
   P# → CITY
   ```

We now claim that for every set of FDs, there exists at least one equivalent set that is irreducible. In fact, this is easy to see. Let the original set of FDs be S. Thanks to the decomposition rule, we can assume without loss of generality that every FD in S has a singleton right-hand side. Next, for each FD f in S, we examine each attribute A in the left-hand side of f; if S and the set of FDs obtained by eliminating A from the left-hand side of f are equivalent, we delete A from the left-hand side of f. Then, for each FD f remaining in S, if S and $S - f$ are equivalent, we delete f from S. The final set S is irreducible and is equivalent to the original set S.

Example: Suppose we are given relation R with attributes $A, B, C, D,$ and FDs

```
A  → BC
B  → C
A  → B
AB → C
AC → D
```

We now compute an irreducible set of FDs that is equivalent to this given set.

1. The first step is to rewrite the FDs such that each one has a singleton right-hand side:

   ```
   A  → B
   A  → C
   B  → C
   A  → B
   AB → C
   AC → D
   ```
   ```

We observe immediately that the FD $A \rightarrow B$ occurs twice, so one occurrence can be eliminated.

2. Next, attribute C can be eliminated from the left-hand side of the FD $AC \rightarrow D$, because we have $A \rightarrow C$, so $A \rightarrow AC$ by augmentation, and we are given $AC \rightarrow D$, so $A \rightarrow D$ by transitivity; thus the C on the left-hand side of $AC \rightarrow D$ is redundant.

3. Next, we observe that the FD $AB \rightarrow C$ can be eliminated, because again we have $A \rightarrow C$, so $AB \rightarrow CB$ by augmentation, so $AB \rightarrow C$ by decomposition.

4. Finally, the FD $A \rightarrow C$ is implied by the FDs $A \rightarrow B$ and $B \rightarrow C$, so it can also be eliminated. We are left with:

```
A → B
B → C
A → D
```

This set is irreducible. ∎

A set I of FDs that is irreducible and is equivalent to some other set S of FDs is said to be an **irreducible cover** for S. Thus, given some particular set S of FDs that need to be enforced, it is sufficient for the system to find and enforce an irreducible cover I instead. We should make it clear, however, that a given set of FDs does not necessarily have a *unique* irreducible cover (see Exercise 9.12).

9.7 Summary

A **functional dependency** (FD) is a many-to-one relationship between two sets of attributes of a given relation. Given a relation R, the FD $A \rightarrow B$ (where A and B are subsets of the set of attributes of R) is said to hold in R if and only if, whenever two tuples of R have the same value for A, they also have the same value for B. We are normally interested only in those FDs that hold "for all time," i.e., for all possible values of the given relation (taking "relation" here to mean a relation *variable* specifically). Every relation necessarily satisfies certain **trivial** FDs; an FD is trivial if and only if the right-hand side (the **dependent**) is a subset of the left-hand side (the **determinant**).

Certain FDs imply others. Given a set S of FDs, the **closure** S^+ of that set is the set of all FDs implied by the FDs in S. S is necessarily a subset of S^+. **Armstrong's rules** provide a **sound** and **complete** basis for computing S^+ from S, though several additional rules of inference (easily derived from Armstrong's rules) make that computation a little more straightforward in practice.

Given a subset A of the set of attributes of relation R and a set S of FDs that hold in R, the **closure** A^+ of A under S is the set of all attributes B of R such that the FD $A \rightarrow B$ is a member of S^+. If A^+ consists of all attributes of R, A is said to be a **superkey** for R (and a **candidate key** is an irreducible superkey). We gave a simple algorithm for computing A^+ from A and S, and hence a simple way of determining whether a given

FD $X \rightarrow Y$ is a member of S^+ ($X \rightarrow Y$ is a member of S^+ if and only if Y is a subset of X^+).

Two sets of FDs $S1$ and $S2$ are **equivalent** if and only if they are **covers** for each other, i.e., if and only if $S1^+ = S2^+$. Every set of FDs is equivalent to at least one **irreducible** set. A set of FDs is irreducible if (a) every FD in the set has a singleton right-hand side, (b) no FD in the set can be discarded without changing the closure of the set, and (c) no attribute can be discarded from the right-hand side of any FD in the set without changing the closure of the set. If I is an irreducible set equivalent to S, then enforcing the FDs in I will automatically enforce the FDs in S.

In conclusion, we note that many of the foregoing ideas can be extended to apply to integrity constraints in general, not just to FDs. For example, it is true in general that (a) certain integrity constraints are trivial, (b) certain integrity constraints imply others, (c) the set of all constraints implied by a given set can be regarded as the closure of the given set, (d) the question of whether a specific constraint is in a certain closure—i.e., whether the specific constraint is implied by certain given constraints—is an interesting practical problem, (e) the question of finding an irreducible cover for certain given constraints is an interesting practical problem. What makes FDs in particular much more tractable than integrity constraints in general is the existence of a sound and complete set of inference rules for FDs. The References and Bibliography sections in this chapter and in Chapter 11 give references to papers describing several other specific kinds of constraints (MVDs, JDs, and INDs) for which such sets of inference rules also exist. In this book, however, we choose not to give those other kinds of constraints so extensive and so formal a treatment as we have given FDs.

Exercises

9.1 Let R be a relation of degree n. What is the maximum number of functional dependencies R can possibly satisfy (trivial as well as nontrivial)?

9.2 What does it mean to say that Armstrong's rules of inference are sound? Complete?

9.3 Prove the *reflexivity, augmentation,* and *transitivity* rules, assuming only the basic definition of functional dependence.

9.4 Prove that the three rules of the previous exercise imply the *self-determination, decomposition, union,* and *composition* rules.

9.5 Prove Darwen's "General Unification Theorem." Which of the rules of the previous two exercises did you use? Which rules can be derived as special cases of the theorem?

9.6 Define (a) the closure of a set of FDs; (b) the closure of a set of attributes under a set of FDs.

9.7 List the set of all FDs satisfied (for all time) by the shipments relation SP.

9.8 Here is a set of FDs for a relation $R\{A,B,C,D,E,F,G\}$.

```
A    → B
BC   → DE
AEF  → G
```

Compute the closure $\{A,C\}^+$ under this set. Is the FD $ACF \rightarrow DG$ implied by this set?

9.9 What does it mean to say that two sets *S1* and *S2* of FDs are equivalent?

9.10 What does it mean to say that a set of FDs is irreducible?

9.11 Here are two sets of FDs for a relation *R{A,B,C,D,E}*. Are they equivalent?

　1. $A \rightarrow B$　　$AB \rightarrow C$　　$D \rightarrow AC$　　$D \rightarrow E$

　2. $A \rightarrow BC$　　$D \rightarrow AE$

9.12 Here is a set of FDs for relation *R{A,B,C,D,E,F}*:

$$AB \rightarrow C$$
$$C \rightarrow A$$
$$BC \rightarrow D$$
$$ACD \rightarrow B$$
$$BE \rightarrow C$$
$$CE \rightarrow FA$$
$$CF \rightarrow BD$$
$$D \rightarrow EF$$

Find an irreducible cover for this set of FDs.

9.13 A relation TIMETABLE is defined with the following attributes:

D Day of the week (1–5)

P Period within day (1–8)

C Classroom number

T Teacher name

L Lesson name

The tuple *{D:d,P:p,C:c,T:t,L:l}* is an element of this relation if and only if at time *{D:d,P:p}* lesson *l* is taught by teacher *t* in classroom *c*. You can assume that lessons are one period in duration and that every lesson has a lesson name that is unique with respect to all lessons taught in the week. What functional dependencies hold in this relation? What are the candidate keys?

9.14 A relation NADDR is defined with attributes NAME (unique), STREET, CITY, STATE, and ZIP. For any given zipcode, there is just one city and state. Also, for any given street, city, and state, there is just one zipcode. Give an irreducible set of FDs for this relation. What are the candidate keys?

9.15 Relation *R* has attributes *A, B, C, D, E, F, G, H, I, J*, and satisfies the FDs

$$ABD \rightarrow E$$
$$AB \rightarrow G$$
$$B \rightarrow F$$
$$C \rightarrow J$$
$$CJ \rightarrow I$$
$$G \rightarrow H$$

Is this an irreducible set? What are the candidate keys?

References and Bibliography

9.1 W. W. Armstrong. "Dependency Structures of Data Base Relationships." Proc. IFIP Congress, Stockholm, Sweden (1974).

　The paper that first formalized the theory of FDs (it is the source of "Armstrong's axioms"). The paper also gives a precise characterization of candidate keys.

9.2 Marco A. Casanova, Ronald Fagin, and Christos H. Papadimitriou. "Inclusion Dependencies and Their Interaction with Functional Dependencies." Proc. 1st ACM SIGACT-SIGMOD Symposium on Principles of Database Systems, Los Angeles, Calif. (March 1982).

Inclusion dependencies (INDs) can be regarded as a generalization of the concept of referential constraints. For example, the IND

```
SP.S#  ⟶  S.S#
```

(not the notation used in the paper) states that the set of values appearing in attribute SP.S# must be a subset (not necessarily a proper subset) of the set of values appearing in attribute S.S#. This particular example is in fact a referential constraint, of course; in general, however, there is no requirement for an IND that the left-hand side be a foreign key or the right-hand side a candidate key. *Note:* INDs do have some points in common with FDs, since both represent many-to-one relationships.

The paper provides a sound and complete set of inference rules for INDs, which we may state (a little loosely) as follows:

1. $A \longrightarrow A$.
2. If $AB \longrightarrow CD$, then $A \longrightarrow C$ and $B \longrightarrow D$.
3. If $A \longrightarrow B$ and $B \longrightarrow C$, then $A \longrightarrow C$.

9.3 R. G. Casey and C. Delobel. "Decomposition of a Data Base and the Theory of Boolean Switching Functions." *IBM J. R&D 17,* No. 5 (September 1973).

Shows that for any given relation, the set of FDs (called *functional relations* in this paper) can be represented by a "Boolean switching function," and moreover that that function is unique in the following sense: The original FDs can be specified in many superficially different (but actually equivalent) ways, each one in general giving rise to a superficially different Boolean function—but all such functions can be reduced by the laws of Boolean algebra to the same canonical form. The problem of "decomposing" the original relation (i.e., in a nonloss way—see Chapter 10) is then shown to be logically equivalent to the well-understood Boolean algebra problem of finding "a covering set of prime implicants" for the Boolean function corresponding to that relation together with its FDs. Hence the original problem can be transformed into an equivalent problem in Boolean algebra, and well-known techniques can be brought to bear on it.

This paper was the first of several to draw parallels between dependency theory and a variety of other disciplines. See, for example, reference [9.8] below, also several of the references in Chapter 11.

9.4 E. F. Codd. "Further Normalization of the Data Base Relational Model." In *Data Base Systems, Courant Computer Science Symposia Series 6.* Englewood Cliffs, N.J.: Prentice-Hall (1972).

The paper that first introduced the concept of functional dependence. The "further normalization" of the title refers to the specific database design discipline discussed in Chapter 10; the purpose of the paper was, very specifically, to show the applicability of the ideas of functional dependence to the database design problem. (Indeed, FDs represented the first scientific attack on that problem.) However, the functional dependency idea has since shown itself to be of much wider applicability.

9.5 E. F. Codd. "Normalized Data Base Structure: A Brief Tutorial." Proc. 1971 ACM SIGFIDET Workshop on Data Description, Access, and Control, San Diego, Calif. (November 1971).

A tutorial introduction to the ideas of reference [9.4].

9.6   Hugh Darwen. "The Role of Functional Dependence in Query Decomposition." In C. J. Date and Hugh Darwen, *Relational Database Writings 1989–1991*. Reading, Mass.: Addison-Wesley (1992).

Gives a set of **FD inheritance rules,** by which FDs holding in an arbitrary derived relation can be deduced from those holding in the relation(s) from which the relation is derived. The set of FDs thus deduced can then be inspected to determine candidate keys for the derived relation, thus providing the **candidate key inheritance rules** mentioned in passing as "very desirable" in Chapter 6. The paper shows how these FD and candidate key inheritance rules can be used to provide significant improvements in DBMS performance, functionality, and usability.

9.7   Hugh Darwen. "OObservations of a Relational Bigot." Presentation to BCS Special Interest Group on Formal Aspects of Computing Science, London, UK (December 21st, 1990).

9.8   R. Fagin. "Functional Dependencies in a Relational Database and Propositional Logic." *IBM J. R&D 21,* No. 6 (November 1977).

Shows that "Armstrong's axioms" [9.1] are strictly equivalent to the system of implicational statements in propositional logic. In other words, the paper defines a mapping between FDs and propositional statements, and then shows that a given FD f is a consequence of a given set S of FDs if and only if the proposition corresponding to f is a logical consequence of the set of propositions corresponding to S.

9.9   Claudio L. Lucchesi and Sylvia L. Osborn. "Candidate Keys for Relations." *J. Comp. and Sys. Sciences 17,* No. 2 (1978).

Presents an algorithm for finding all candidate keys for a given relation, given the set of FDs that hold in that relation.

Answers to Selected Exercises

9.1   An FD is basically a statement of the form $A \to B$ where A and B are each subsets of the set of attributes of R. Since a set of n elements has 2^n possible subsets, each of A and B has 2^n possible values, and hence an upper limit on the number of possible FDs is 2^{2n}.

9.5

1. $A \to B$	(given)
2. $C \to D$	(given)
3. $A \to B \cap C$	(joint dependence, 1)
4. $C - B \to C - B$	(self-determination)
5. $A \cup (C - B) \to (B \cap C) \cup (C - B)$	(composition, 3, 4)
6. $A \cup (C - B) \to C$	(simplifying 5)
7. $A \cup (C - B) \to D$	(transitivity, 6, 2)
8. $A \cup (C - B) \to B \cup D$	(composition, 1, 7)

This completes the proof.   ■

The rules used in the proof are as indicated in the comments above. The following are all special cases of Darwen's theorem: union, transitivity, composition, and augmentation. So too is the following useful rule:

■ If $A \to B$ and $AB \to C$, then $A \to C$.

9.7   The complete set of FDs—i.e., the closure—for relation SP is as follows:

```
{ S#, P#, QTY } → { S#, P#, QTY }
{ S#, P#, QTY } → { S#, P# }
{ S#, P#, QTY } → { P#, QTY }
{ S#, P#, QTY } → { S#, QTY }
{ S#, P#, QTY } → { S# }
```

```
{ S#, P#, QTY } → { S# }
{ S#, P#, QTY } → { P# }
{ S#, P#, QTY } → { QTY }
{ S#, P#, QTY } → { }

{ S#, P# }      → { S#, P#, QTY }
{ S#, P# }      → { S#, P# }
{ S#, P# }      → { P#, QTY }
{ S#, P# }      → { S#, QTY }
{ S#, P# }      → { S# }
{ S#, P# }      → { P# }
{ S#, P# }      → { QTY }
{ S#, P# }      → { }

{ P#, QTY }     → { P#, QTY }
{ P#, QTY }     → { P# }
{ P#, QTY }     → { QTY }
{ P#, QTY }     → { }

{ S#, QTY }     → { S#, QTY }
{ S#, QTY }     → { S# }
{ S#, QTY }     → { QTY }
{ S#, QTY }     → { }

{ S# }          → { S# }
{ S# }          → { }

{ P# }          → { P# }
{ P# }          → { }

{ QTY }         → { QTY }
{ QTY }         → { }

{ }             → { }
```

9.8 $\{A,C\}^+ = \{A,B,C,D,E\}$. The answer to the second part of the question is yes.

9.11 They are equivalent. Let us number the FDs of the first set as follows:

1. $A \rightarrow B$
2. $AB \rightarrow C$
3. $D \rightarrow AC$
4. $D \rightarrow E$

First, 3. can be replaced by:

3. $D \rightarrow A$ and $D \rightarrow C$

Next, 1. and 2. together imply that 2. can be replaced by:

2. $A \rightarrow C$

But now we have $D \rightarrow A$ and $A \rightarrow C$, so $D \rightarrow C$ is implied (by transitivity) and so can be dropped, leaving:

3. $D \rightarrow A$

The first set of FDs is thus equivalent to the following irreducible set:

$A \rightarrow B$
$A \rightarrow C$
$D \rightarrow A$
$D \rightarrow E$

The second given set of FDs

$$A \rightarrow BC$$
$$D \rightarrow AE$$

is clearly also equivalent to this irreducible set. Thus, the two given sets are equivalent. ∎

9.12 The first step is to rewrite the given set such that every FD has a singleton right-hand side:

1. $AB \rightarrow C$
2. $C \rightarrow A$
3. $BC \rightarrow D$
4. $ACD \rightarrow B$
5. $BE \rightarrow C$
6. $CE \rightarrow A$
7. $CE \rightarrow F$
8. $CF \rightarrow B$
9. $CF \rightarrow D$
10. $D \rightarrow E$
11. $D \rightarrow F$

Now:

- 2. implies 6., so we can drop 6.
- 8. implies $CF \rightarrow BC$ (by augmentation), which with 3. implies $CF \rightarrow D$ (by transitivity), so we can drop 9.
- 8. implies $ACF \rightarrow AB$ (by augmentation), and 11. implies $ACD \rightarrow ACF$ (by augmentation), and so $ACD \rightarrow AB$ (by transitivity), and so $ACD \rightarrow B$ (by decomposition), so we can drop 4.

No further reductions are possible, and so we are left with the following irreducible set:

$$AB \rightarrow C$$
$$C \rightarrow A$$
$$BC \rightarrow D$$
$$BE \rightarrow C$$
$$CE \rightarrow F$$
$$CF \rightarrow B$$
$$D \rightarrow E$$
$$D \rightarrow F$$

Alternatively:

- 2. implies $CD \rightarrow ACD$ (by composition), which with 4. implies $CD \rightarrow B$ (by transitivity), so we can replace 4. by $CD \rightarrow B$.
- 2. implies 6., so we can drop 6. (as before).
- 2. and 9. imply $CF \rightarrow AD$ (by composition), which implies $CF \rightarrow ADC$ (by augmentation), which with (the original) 4. implies $CF \rightarrow B$ (by transitivity), so we can drop 8.

No further reductions are possible, and so we are left with the following irreducible set:

$$AB \rightarrow C$$
$$C \rightarrow A$$
$$BC \rightarrow D$$
$$CD \rightarrow B$$
$$BE \rightarrow C$$
$$CE \rightarrow F$$
$$CF \rightarrow D$$

$$D \rightarrow E$$
$$D \rightarrow F$$

Observe, therefore, that there are two distinct irreducible covers for the original set of FDs.

9.13 The candidate keys are *L, DPC,* and *DPT.*

9.14 Abbreviating NAME, STREET, CITY, STATE, and ZIP as *N, R, C, T,* and *Z,* respectively, we have:

$$N \rightarrow RCT \qquad RCT \rightarrow Z \qquad Z \rightarrow CT$$

An obviously equivalent irreducible set is:

$$N \rightarrow R \qquad N \rightarrow C \qquad N \rightarrow T \qquad RCT \rightarrow Z \qquad Z \rightarrow C \qquad Z \rightarrow T$$

The only candidate key is *N.*

9.15 We do not give a full answer to this exercise, but content ourselves with the following observations. First, the set is clearly not irreducible, since $C \rightarrow J$ and $CJ \rightarrow I$ together imply $C \rightarrow I$. Second, an obvious *superkey* is $\{A,B,C,D,G,J\}$ (i.e., the set of all attributes mentioned on the left-hand sides of the given FDs). We can eliminate J from this set because $C \rightarrow J$, and we can eliminate G because $AB \rightarrow G$. Since none of A, B, C, D appears on the right-hand side of any of the given FDs, it follows that $\{A,B,C,D\}$ is a candidate key.

10 | Further Normalization I: 1NF, 2NF, 3NF, BCNF

10.1 Introduction

Throughout this book so far we have made use of the suppliers-and-parts database as a running example, with logical design as follows:

```
S  ( S#, SNAME, STATUS, CITY )
   PRIMARY KEY ( S# )

P  ( P#, PNAME, COLOR, WEIGHT, CITY )
   PRIMARY KEY ( P# )

SP ( S#, P#, QTY )
   PRIMARY KEY ( S#, P# )
   FOREIGN KEY ( S# ) REFERENCES S
   FOREIGN KEY ( P# ) REFERENCES P
```

Now, this design does have a feeling of rightness about it: It is "obvious" that three relations, *viz.* S, P, and SP, are necessary; it is also "obvious" that the part COLOR attribute belongs in relation P, the supplier CITY attribute in relation S, the shipment QTY attribute in relation SP, and so on. But what is it that tells us these things are so? Some insight into this question can be gained by seeing what happens if the design is changed in some way. Suppose, for example, that the CITY attribute is moved out of the suppliers relation and into the shipments relation (intuitively the wrong place for it, since "supplier city" obviously concerns suppliers, not shipments). Fig. 10.1 shows a sample tabulation for this revised shipments relation. (In order to avoid confusion with our usual SP relation, we will refer to this revised relation as SCP, as we did in Chapter 9.)

A glance at the figure is sufficient to show immediately what is wrong with this design: **redundancy**. To be specific, every SCP tuple for supplier S1 tells us S1 is located in London, every SCP tuple for supplier S2 tells us S2 is located in Paris, and so on. More generally, the fact that a given supplier is located in a given city is stated as many times as there are shipments for that supplier. This redundancy in turn leads to several further problems. For example, after an update, supplier S1 might be shown as being located in London by one tuple and in Amsterdam by another. So perhaps a good

SCP	S#	CITY	P#	QTY
	S1	London	P1	300
	S1	London	P2	200
	S1	London	P3	400
	S1	London	P4	200
	S1	London	P5	100
	S1	London	P6	100
	S2	Paris	P1	300
	S2	Paris	P2	400
	S3	Paris	P2	200
	S4	London	P2	200
	S4	London	P4	300
	S4	London	P5	400

FIG. 10.1 Sample tabulation of relation SCP

design principle is "one fact in one place" (i.e., avoid redundancy). *The subject of further normalization is essentially just a formalization of simple ideas like this one*—a formalization, however, that does have very practical application in the area of database design.

Of course, relations in a relational database are *always* normalized, in the sense that they contain "scalar" values only.* Fig. 4.5 in Chapter 4 showed by example how an unnormalized relation—i.e., a relation that contains repeating groups, loosely speaking—can be reduced to an equivalent normalized form. However, a given relation might be normalized in this sense and yet still possess certain undesirable properties; relation SCP of Fig. 10.1 is a case in point. The principles of further normalization allow us to recognize such cases and show how to reduce such relations to a more desirable form. In the case of relation SCP, for example, those principles would tell us precisely what is wrong with that relation, and they would tell us how to break it down into two "more desirable" relations, one with heading {S#,CITY} and one with heading {S#,P#,QTY}.

Normal Forms

The process of further normalization—hereinafter abbreviated to just *normalization*—is built around the concept of **normal forms**. A relation is said to be in a particular normal form if it satisfies a certain prescribed set of conditions. For example, a relation is said to be in **first normal form** (abbreviated 1NF) if and only if it satisfies the condition that it contains scalar values only.

Note: It follows that *every* normalized relation is in first normal form, as already stated in Chapter 4; it is this fact that accounts for the term "first." In other words,

---

* Refer to Chapter 19 for an elaboration on the meaning of "scalar" in this context.

"normalized" and "1NF" mean *exactly the same thing*. However, the reader should be aware that the term "normalized" is very often used to mean one of the higher levels (especially *third* normal form, 3NF). This latter usage is sloppy, but very common.

Numerous normal forms have been defined (see Fig. 10.2). The first three (1NF, 2NF, 3NF) were defined by Codd in reference [9.4]. As Fig. 10.2 indicates, all normalized relations are in 1NF; some 1NF relations are also in 2NF; and some 2NF relations are also in 3NF. The motivation behind Codd's definitions was that 2NF was "more desirable" (in a sense to be explained) than 1NF, and 3NF in turn was more desirable than 2NF. That is, the database designer should generally aim for a design involving relations in 3NF, not relations that are merely in 2NF or 1NF.

Reference [9.4] also introduced the idea of a procedure, the so-called **normalization procedure,** by which a relation that happens to be in some given normal form, say 2NF, can be converted into a set of relations in a more desirable form, say 3NF. (The procedure as originally defined only went as far as 3NF, of course, but it was subsequently extended all the way to 5NF, as we will see in the next chapter.) We can characterize that procedure as *the successive reduction of a given collection of relations to some more desirable form*. Note that the procedure is **reversible;** that is, it is always possible to take the output from the procedure (say the set of 3NF relations) and convert them back into the input (say the original 2NF relation). Reversibility is important, of course, because it means that *no information is lost* in the normalization process.

To return to the topic of normal forms *per se:* Codd's original definition of 3NF [9.4] turned out to suffer from certain inadequacies, as we shall see in Section 10.5. A revised and stronger definition, due to Boyce and Codd, was given in reference [10.2]—stronger, in the sense that any relation that was 3NF by the new definition was certainly 3NF by the old, but a relation could be 3NF by the old definition and not by the new. The new 3NF is now usually referred to as **Boyce/Codd normal form** (BCNF) in order to distinguish it from the old form.

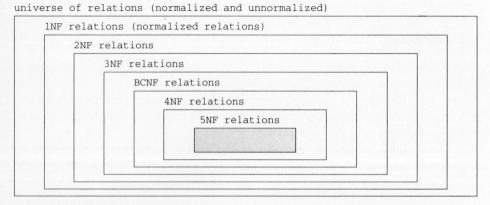

FIG. 10.2 Normal forms

Subsequently, Fagin [11.8] defined a new **"fourth" normal form** (4NF—"fourth" because at that time BCNF was still usually called "third"). More recently, Fagin again [11.9] defined yet another normal form which he called **projection-join normal form** (PJ/NF, also known as **"fifth"** normal form or 5NF). As Fig. 10.2 shows, some BCNF relations are also in 4NF, and some 4NF relations are also in 5NF.

By now the reader might well be wondering whether there is any end to this progression, and whether there might be a 6NF, a 7NF, and so on *ad infinitum*. Although this is a good question to ask, we are obviously not in a position to give it any detailed consideration as yet. We content ourselves with the rather equivocal statement that there are indeed additional normal forms not shown in Fig. 10.2, but that 5NF is actually the "final" normal form in a special (but important) sense. We will return to this question in Chapter 11.

Structure of the Chapter

The aim of this chapter is to examine the concepts of further normalization, up to and including Boyce/Codd normal form (we leave the other two to Chapter 11). The plan of the chapter is as follows. Following this somewhat lengthy introduction, Section 10.2 discusses the basic concept of **nonloss decomposition,** and demonstrates the crucial importance of **functional dependence** to this concept (indeed, functional dependence forms the basis for Codd's original three normal forms and for BCNF). Section 10.3 then describes the original three normal forms, showing by example how a given relation can be carried through the normalization procedure to achieve 3NF. Section 10.4 digresses slightly to consider the question of **alternative decompositions**—that is, the question of choosing the "best" decomposition of a given relation, when there is a choice. Next, Section 10.5 discusses BCNF. Finally, Section 10.6 provides a summary and offers a few concluding remarks.

The reader is warned that we make little attempt at rigor in what follows; rather, we rely to a considerable extent on plain intuition. Indeed, part of the point is that concepts such as nonloss decomposition, BCNF, etc., despite the somewhat esoteric terminology, are essentially very simple and commonsense ideas. Most of the references treat the material in a much more formal and rigorous manner. A good tutorial can be found in reference [10.5].

Two final introductory remarks:

1. As already suggested, the general idea of normalization is that the database designer should aim for relations in the "ultimate" normal form (5NF). However, this recommendation should not be construed as law. Occasionally there might be good reasons for flouting the principles of normalization (see Exercise 10.7 at the end of the chapter). The only hard requirement is that relations be in at least first normal form. Indeed, this is as good a place as any to make the point that database design can be an extremely complex task (at least in a "large database" environment; the design of "small" databases is usually fairly straightforward). Normalization is a useful aid in the process, but it is not a panacea; anyone designing a database is certainly advised to be familiar with the basic principles of normalization, but we

do not mean to suggest that the design should necessarily be based on those principles alone. Chapter 12 discusses a number of other aspects of design that have little
or nothing to do with normalization as such.

2. As indicated above, we will be using the normalization procedure as a basis for
   introducing and discussing the various normal forms. However, we do not mean to
   suggest that database design will actually be done in practice by applying that procedure; in fact, it probably will not—it is much more likely that some "top-down"
   scheme such as the one described in Chapter 12 will be used instead. The ideas of
   normalization can then be used to *verify* that the resulting design does not uninten-
   tionally violate any of the normalization principles. Nevertheless, the normalization procedure does provide a convenient framework in which to describe those
   principles; for the purposes of this chapter, therefore, we adopt the useful fiction
   that we are indeed carrying out the design process by applying that procedure.

10.2 Nonloss Decomposition and Functional Dependencies

Before we can get into the specifics of the normalization procedure, we need to examine one crucial aspect of that procedure more closely, namely the concept of **nonloss**
(also called **lossless**) **decomposition**. We have seen that the procedure involves breaking down or *decomposing* a given relation into other relations, and moreover that the
decomposition is required to be *reversible,* so that no information is lost in the process;
in other words, the only decompositions we are interested in are indeed those that are
nonloss. As we will see, the question of whether a given decomposition is nonloss is
intimately bound up with the concept of **functional dependence**.

By way of example, consider the familiar suppliers relation S, with heading
{S#,STATUS,CITY} (we ignore attribute SNAME for simplicity). Fig. 10.3 shows a
sample tabulation of this relation (a subset of our usual sample values) and—in the
parts of the figure labeled (a) and (b)—two possible decompositions corresponding to
that tabulation.

Examining those two decompositions, we observe that:

1. In Case (a), no information is lost; the two relations SST and SC still tell us that
   supplier S3 has status 30 and city Paris, and supplier S5 has status 30 and city
   Athens. In other words, this first decomposition is indeed nonloss.

2. In Case (b), by contrast, information definitely is lost; we can still tell that both
   suppliers have status 30, but we cannot tell which supplier has which city. In other
   words, the second decomposition is not nonloss but **lossy**.

What exactly is it here that makes the first decomposition nonloss and the other
lossy? Well, observe first that the process we have been referring to as "decomposition"
is really a process of **projection;** each of the relations SST, SC, and STC in the figure

S	S#	STATUS	CITY
	S3	30	Paris
	S5	30	Athens

(a) SST	S#	STATUS		SC	S#	CITY
	S3	30			S3	Paris
	S5	30			S5	Athens

(b) SST	S#	STATUS		STC	STATUS	CITY
	S3	30			30	Paris
	S5	30			30	Athens

FIG. 10.3 Relation S and two possible decompositions

is in fact a projection of the original relation S. So the decomposition operator in the normalization procedure is in fact *projection.*

Observe next that when we say in Case (a) that no information is lost, what we really mean is that *if we join relations SST and SC back together again, we get back the original relation S.* In Case (b), by contrast, if we join SST and SC together again, we do *not* get back the original relation S, and so we have lost information.* In other words, "reversibility" means, precisely, that *the original relation is equal to the join of its projections.* Thus, just as the decomposition operator in the normalization procedure is projection, so the *re*composition operator is **join** (meaning, of course, *natural* join over attributes with the same name).

So the interesting question is as follows: If *R1* and *R2* are projections of some relation *R,* and *R1* and *R2* between them include all of the attributes of *R,* what conditions have to be satisfied in order to guarantee that joining *R1* and *R2* back together takes us back to the original *R?* And this is where functional dependencies come in. Returning to our example, observe that relation S satisfies the irreducible set of FDs.[†]

```
S#  →  STATUS
S#  →  CITY
```

---

* More precisely, we get back all of the tuples in the original relation S, together with some additional "spurious" tuples. We can never get back anything *less* than the original relation. (*Exercise:* Prove this statement.) Since we have no way in general of knowing which tuples are spurious and which genuine, we have indeed lost information.

[†] Here and throughout this chapter we take "FDs" to mean, specifically, FDs that are *time-independent*—i.e., FDs that must be satisfied by *all legal values* of the relevant relation. Refer back to Chapter 9 if you need to refresh your memory regarding irreducible sets of FDs.

Given the fact that it satisfies these FDs, it surely cannot be coincidence that relation S is equal to the join of its projections on {S#,STATUS} and {S#,CITY}. And of course it is not. In fact, we have the following *theorem* (due to Heath [10.4]):

■   **Heath's theorem:** Let $R\{A,B,C\}$ be a relation, where A, B, and C are sets of attributes. If R satisfies the FD $A \to B$, then R is equal to the join of its projections on $\{A,B\}$ and $\{A,C\}$.

Taking A as S#, B as STATUS, and C as CITY, the theorem confirms what we have already observed, namely that relation S can be nonloss-decomposed into its projections on {S#,STATUS} and {S#,CITY}.

At the same time, we also know that relation S *cannot* be nonloss-decomposed into its projections on {S#,STATUS} and {STATUS,CITY}. Heath's theorem does not explain why this is so;* intuitively, however, we can see that the problem is that *one of the FDs is lost in this decomposition*. Specifically, the FD S# $\to$ STATUS is still represented (by the projection on {S#,STATUS}), but the FD S# $\to$ CITY has been lost.

More on Functional Dependencies

We conclude this section with a few additional remarks concerning FDs.

1. **Left-irreducible FDs:** Recall from Chapter 9 that an FD is said to be *left-irreducible* if its left-hand side is "not too big." For example, consider relation SCP once again from Section 10.1. That relation satisfies the FD

    ```
    { S#, P# } → CITY
    ```

    However, attribute P# on the left-hand side here is redundant for functional dependency purposes; that is, we also have the FD

    ```
    S# → CITY
    ```

    (CITY is also functionally dependent on S# alone). This latter FD is left-irreducible, but the previous one is not; equivalently, CITY is *irreducibly dependent* on S#, but not irreducibly dependent on {S#,P#}.[†]

    Left-irreducible FDs and irreducible dependencies will turn out to be important in the definition of second and third normal form (see Section 10.3).

2. **FD diagrams:** Let R be a relation and let I be some irreducible set of FDs that apply to R. It is convenient to represent the set I by means of a *functional dependency diagram* (FD diagram). FD diagrams for relations S, SP, and P—which should be self-explanatory—are given in Fig. 10.4. We shall make frequent use of such diagrams throughout the rest of this chapter.

---

* It does not do so because it is of the form "if . . . then . . . ," not "if *and only if* . . . then . . ." (see Exercise 10.1 at the end of the chapter). We will be discussing a stronger form of Heath's theorem in the next chapter (Section 11.2).

    [†] "Left-irreducible FD" and "irreducibly dependent" are our preferred terms for what are more usually called "**full** FD" and "**fully** dependent" in the literature (and were so called in previous editions of this book). These latter terms have the merit of brevity but are less descriptive and less apt.

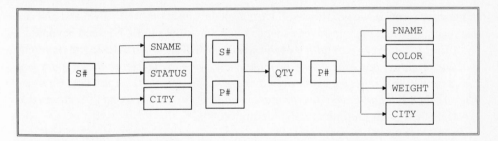

FIG. 10.4 FD diagrams for relations S, SP, P

As you can see, every arrow in the diagrams of Fig. 10.4 is *an arrow out of a candidate key* (actually the primary key) of the relevant relation. By definition, there will always be arrows out of each candidate key, because, for one value of each candidate key, there is always one value of everything else; those arrows can never be eliminated. *It is if there are any other arrows that difficulties arise.* Thus, the normalization procedure can be characterized, very informally, as a procedure for eliminating arrows that are not arrows out of candidate keys.

3. **FDs are a semantic notion:** FDs are, of course, a special kind of integrity constraint. As such, they are definitely a *semantic* notion. Recognizing the FDs is part of the process of understanding what the data *means;* the fact that relation S satisfies the FD S# $\rightarrow$ CITY, for example, means that each supplier is located in precisely one city. To look at this another way:

- There is a constraint in the real world that the database represents, namely that each supplier is located in precisely one city;
- Since it is part of the semantics of the situation, that constraint must somehow be observed in the database;
- The way to ensure that it is so observed is to specify it in the database definition, so that the DBMS can enforce it;
- The way to specify it in the database definition is to declare the FD.

And we will see later that the concepts of normalization lead to a very simple means of declaring FDs.

10.3 First, Second, and Third Normal Forms

We are now in a position to describe Codd's original three normal forms. We present a preliminary, very informal, definition of 3NF first in order to give some idea of the point we are aiming for. We then consider the process of reducing an arbitrary relation to an equivalent collection of 3NF relations, giving somewhat more precise definitions of the three forms as we go. However, we note at the outset that 1NF, 2NF, and 3NF are not very significant in themselves except as stepping-stones to BCNF (and beyond).

Caveat: Note very carefully that throughout this section we assume for simplicity that each relation has exactly one candidate key, which is therefore the primary key. This assumption is reflected in our definitions, which (we repeat) are not very rigorous. The case of a relation having two or more candidate keys is discussed in Section 10.5.

Here then is our preliminary 3NF definition:

■ **Third normal form** (very informal definition): A relation is in 3NF if and only if the nonkey attributes (if any) are

(a) mutually independent, and

(b) irreducibly dependent on the primary key.

We explain the terms "nonkey attribute" and "mutually independent" as follows.

■ A *nonkey attribute* is any attribute that does not participate in the primary key of the relation concerned.

■ Two or more attributes are *mutually independent* if none of them is functionally dependent on any combination of the others. Such independence implies that each such attribute can be updated independently of all the rest.

For example, relation P (the parts relation) is in 3NF according to the foregoing definition: Attributes PNAME, COLOR, WEIGHT, and CITY are certainly all independent of one another (it is possible to change, e.g., the color of a part without simultaneously having to change its weight), and of course they are all irreducibly dependent on the primary key P#.

The foregoing informal definition of 3NF can be interpreted, even more intuitively, as follows:

■ **Third normal form** (even more informal definition): A relation is in third normal form (3NF) if and only if, for all time, each tuple consists of a primary key value that identifies some entity, together with a set of zero or more mutually independent attribute values that describe that entity in some way.

Again, relation P fits the definition: Each tuple of P consists of a primary key value (a part number) that identifies some part in the real world, together with four additional values (part name, part color, part weight, and part city), each of which serves to describe that part, and each of which is independent of all the rest.

Now we turn to the normalization procedure. First we give a definition of first normal form.

■ **First normal form:** A relation is in 1NF if and only if all underlying domains contain scalar values only.

This definition merely states that *any* normalized relation is in 1NF, which is of course correct. However, a relation that is *only* in first normal form (that is, a 1NF relation that is not also in 2NF, and therefore not in 3NF either) has a structure that is undesirable for a number of reasons. To illustrate the point, let us suppose that information concerning suppliers and shipments, rather than being split into the two relations S and SP, is lumped together into a single relation as follows:

```
FIRST ( S#, STATUS, CITY, P#, QTY )
       PRIMARY KEY ( S#, P# )
```

This is an extended version of relation SCP from Section 10.1. The attributes have their usual meanings, except that for the sake of the example we introduce an additional constraint:

```
CITY → STATUS
```

(STATUS is functionally dependent on CITY; the meaning of this constraint is that a supplier's status is determined by the location of that supplier—e.g., all London suppliers *must* have a status of 20). Also, we ignore attribute SNAME for simplicity. The primary key of FIRST is the combination {S#,P#}; the FD diagram is shown in Fig. 10.5.

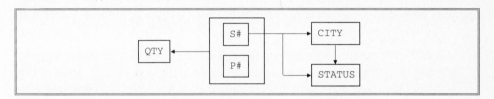

FIG. 10.5 Functional dependencies in relation FIRST

Notice that this FD diagram is "more complex" than the FD diagram for a 3NF relation. As suggested in the previous section, a 3NF diagram has arrows out of the primary key *only* (look at Fig. 10.4), whereas a non3NF diagram (such as the diagram for FIRST) has arrows out of the primary key *together with certain additional arrows*—and it is those additional arrows that cause all the trouble. In fact, relation FIRST violates both conditions (a) and (b) in the 3NF definition above—the nonkey attributes are not all mutually independent, because STATUS depends on CITY (one additional arrow), and they are not all irreducibly dependent on the primary key, because STATUS and CITY are each dependent on S# alone (two more additional arrows).

As a basis for illustrating some of the difficulties that arise from those additional arrows, Fig. 10.6 shows a sample tabulation for relation FIRST. The values shown are basically as usual, except that the status of supplier S3 has been changed from 30 to 10 to be consistent with the new constraint that CITY determines STATUS. The redundancies are obvious. For example, every tuple for supplier S1 shows CITY as London; likewise, every tuple for city London shows STATUS as 20.

The redundancies in relation FIRST lead to a variety of what for historical reasons are usually called **update anomalies**—that is, difficulties with the update operations

FIRST	S#	STATUS	CITY	P#	QTY
	S1	20	London	P1	300
	S1	20	London	P2	200
	S1	20	London	P3	400
	S1	20	London	P4	200
	S1	20	London	P5	100
	S1	20	London	P6	100
	S2	10	Paris	P1	300
	S2	10	Paris	P2	400
	S3	10	Paris	P2	200
	S4	20	London	P2	200
	S4	20	London	P4	300
	S4	20	London	P5	400

FIG. 10.6 Sample tabulation of FIRST

INSERT, DELETE, and UPDATE. To fix our ideas we concentrate first on the sup-plier-city redundancy (corresponding to the FD S# → CITY). Problems occur with each of the three operations.

- **INSERT:** We cannot insert the fact that a particular supplier is located in a partic-ular city until that supplier supplies at least one part. Indeed, the tabulation of Fig. 10.6 does not show that supplier S5 is located in Athens. The reason is that, until S5 supplies some part, we have no appropriate primary key value. (We are assum-ing here that we have decided that it is appropriate to enforce the *entity integrity* rule for relation FIRST. Refer to Chapter 5 if you need to refresh your memory regarding that rule.)

- **DELETE:** If we delete the only FIRST tuple for a particular supplier, we destroy not only the shipment connecting that supplier to some part but also the informa-tion that the supplier is located in a particular city. For example, if we delete the FIRST tuple with S# value S3 and P# value P2, we lose the information that S3 is located in Paris. (The insertion and deletion problems are really two sides of the same coin.)

    Note: The real problem here is that relation FIRST contains too much informa-tion all bundled together; hence, when we delete a tuple, *we delete too much*. To be more precise, relation FIRST contains information regarding shipments *and* infor-mation regarding suppliers, and so deleting a shipment causes supplier information to be deleted as well. The solution to this problem, of course, is to "unbundle"— that is, to place the shipment information in one relation and the supplier informa-tion in another (and this is exactly what we will do in just a moment). Thus, another informal way of characterizing the normalization procedure is to describe it as an *unbundling* procedure: Place logically separate information into separate relations.

- **UPDATE:** The city value for a given supplier appears in FIRST many times, in general. This redundancy causes update problems. For example, if supplier S1 moves from London to Amsterdam, we are faced with *either* the problem of searching FIRST to find every tuple connecting S1 and London (and changing it) *or* the possibility of producing an inconsistent result (the city for S1 might be given as Amsterdam in one tuple and London in another).

The solution to these problems, as already suggested, is to replace the relation FIRST by the two relations

```
SECOND { S#, STATUS, CITY }
```

and

```
SP { S#, P#, QTY }
```

The FD diagrams for these two relations are given in Fig. 10.7; sample tabulations are given in Fig. 10.8. Observe that information for supplier S5 has now been included (in relation SECOND but not in relation SP). Relation SP is now in fact exactly our usual shipments relation.

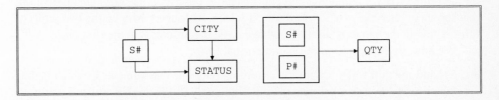

FIG. 10.7 Functional dependencies in the relations SECOND and SP

SECOND	S#	STATUS	CITY		SP	S#	P#	QTY
	S1	20	London			S1	P1	300
	S2	10	Paris			S1	P2	200
	S3	10	Paris			S1	P3	400
	S4	20	London			S1	P4	200
	S5	30	Athens			S1	P5	100
						S1	P6	100
						S2	P1	300
						S2	P2	400
						S3	P2	200
						S4	P2	200
						S4	P4	300
						S4	P5	400

FIG. 10.8 Sample tabulations of SECOND and SP

It should be clear that this revised structure overcomes all the problems with update operations sketched earlier:

■   **INSERT:** We can insert the information that S5 is located in Athens, even though S5 does not currently supply any parts, by simply inserting the appropriate tuple into SECOND.

■   **DELETE:** We can delete the shipment connecting S3 and P2 by deleting the appropriate tuple from SP; we do not lose the information that S3 is located in Paris.

■   **UPDATE:** In the revised structure, the city for a given supplier appears once, not many times, because there is precisely one tuple for a given supplier in relation SECOND (attribute S# is the primary key for that relation). In other words, the S#-CITY redundancy has been eliminated. Thus we can change the city for S1 from London to Amsterdam by changing it once and for all in the relevant SECOND tuple.

Comparing Figs. 10.7 and 10.5, we see that the effect of the decomposition of FIRST into SECOND and SP has been to eliminate the dependencies that were not irreducible, and it is that elimination that has resolved the difficulties. Intuitively, we can say that in relation FIRST the attribute CITY did not describe the entity identified by the primary key, namely a shipment; instead it described the *supplier* involved in that shipment (and likewise for attribute STATUS, of course). Mixing the two kinds of information in the same relation was what caused the problems in the first place.

We now give a definition of second normal form.

■   **Second normal form** (definition assuming only one candidate key, which is thus the primary key): A relation is in 2NF if and only if it is in 1NF and every nonkey attribute is irreducibly dependent on the primary key.

Relations SECOND and SP are both in 2NF (the primary keys are S# and the combination {S#,P#}, respectively). Relation FIRST is not in 2NF. A relation that is in first normal form and not in second can always be reduced to an equivalent collection of 2NF relations. The reduction process consists of replacing the 1NF relation by suitable projections; the collection of projections so obtained is equivalent to the original relation, in the sense that the original relation can always be recovered by joining those projections back together again. In our example, SECOND and SP are projections of FIRST,* and FIRST is the join of SECOND and SP over S#.

To summarize, the first step in the normalization procedure is to take projections to eliminate "nonirreducible" functional dependencies. Thus, given a relation R as follows—

```
R   ( A, B, C, D )
    PRIMARY KEY ( A, B )
    A → D
```

—the normalization discipline recommends replacing R by its two projections $R1$ and $R2$, as follows:

---

* Except for the fact that SECOND can include tuples—such as the tuple for supplier S5 in Fig. 10.8—that have no counterpart in FIRST. In other words, the new structure can represent information that could not be represented in the original. In this sense, the new structure can be regarded as a slightly more faithful representation of the real world.

```
R1 ( A, D )
   PRIMARY KEY ( A )

R2 ( A, B, C )
   PRIMARY KEY ( A, B )
   FOREIGN KEY ( A ) REFERENCES R1
```

Relation *R* can be recovered by taking the foreign-to-matching-primary-key join of *R2* and *R1*.

To return to the example: The SECOND-SP structure still causes problems, however. Relation SP is satisfactory; as a matter of fact, relation SP is now in third normal form, and we will ignore it for the remainder of this section. Relation SECOND, on the other hand, still suffers from a lack of mutual independence among its nonkey attributes. The FD diagram for SECOND is still "more complex" than a 3NF diagram. To be specific, the dependency of STATUS on S#, though it *is* functional, and indeed irreducible, is **transitive** (via CITY): Each S# value determines a CITY value, and that CITY value in turn determines the STATUS value. More generally, whenever the FDs $A \rightarrow B$ and $B \rightarrow C$ both hold, then it is a logical consequence that the transitive FD $A \rightarrow C$ holds also, as explained in Chapter 9. And transitive dependencies lead, once again, to update anomalies. (We now concentrate on the city-status redundancy, corresponding to the FD CITY $\rightarrow$ STATUS.)

- **INSERT:** We cannot insert the fact that a particular city has a particular status—e.g., we cannot state that any supplier in Rome must have a status of 50—until we have some supplier actually located in that city (assuming again that we wish to enforce the entity integrity rule).

- **DELETE:** If we delete the only SECOND tuple for a particular city, we destroy not only the information for the supplier concerned but also the information that that city has that particular status. For example, if we delete the SECOND tuple for S5, we lose the information that the status for Athens is 30. (Once again, the insertion and deletion problems are two sides of the same coin.)

  Note: Actually, the problem is bundling again: Relation SECOND contains information regarding suppliers *and* information regarding cities. And once again, of course, the solution is to "unbundle"—i.e., to place the supplier information in one relation and the city information in another.

- **UPDATE:** The status for a given city appears in SECOND many times, in general (the relation still contains some redundancy). Thus, if we need to change the status for London from 20 to 30, we are faced with *either* the problem of searching SECOND to find every tuple for London (and changing it) or the possibility of producing an inconsistent result (the status for London might be given as 20 in one tuple and 30 in another).

Again the solution to the problems is to replace the original relation (SECOND, in this case) by two projections, namely the projections

```
SC { S#, CITY }
```

and

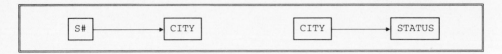

FIG. 10.9 Functional dependencies in the relations SC and CS

```
CS { CITY, STATUS }
```

The FD diagrams for these two relations are given in Fig. 10.9; sample tabulations are given in Fig. 10.10. Observe that status information for Rome has been included in relation CS. The reduction is reversible, once again, since SECOND is the join of SC and CS over CITY.

It should be clear, again, that this revised structure overcomes all the problems with update operations sketched earlier. Detailed consideration of those problems is left to the reader. Comparing Figs. 10.9 and 10.7, we see that the effect of the further decomposition is to eliminate the transitive dependence of STATUS on S#, and again it is that elimination that has resolved the difficulties. Intuitively, we can say that in relation SECOND the attribute STATUS did not describe the entity identified by the primary key, namely a supplier; instead it described the city in which that supplier happened to be located. Once again, mixing the two kinds of information in the same relation was what caused the problems.

We now give a definition of third normal form.

■ **Third normal form** (definition assuming only one candidate key, which is thus the primary key): A relation is in 3NF if and only if it is in 2NF and every nonkey attribute is nontransitively dependent on the primary key. ("No transitive dependencies" implies no *mutual* dependencies, in the sense of that term explained at the beginning of this section.)

Relations SC and CS are both in 3NF (the primary keys are S# and CITY, respectively). Relation SECOND is not in 3NF. A relation that is in second normal form and not in third can always be reduced to an equivalent collection of 3NF relations. We have already indicated that the process is reversible, and hence that no information is lost in

SC	S#	CITY		CS	CITY	STATUS
	S1	London			Athens	30
	S2	Paris			London	20
	S3	Paris			Paris	10
	S4	London			Rome	50
	S5	Athens				

FIG. 10.10 Sample tabulations of SC and CS

the reduction; however, the 3NF collection can contain information, such as the fact that the status for Rome is 50, that could not be represented in the original 2NF relation.*

To summarize, the second step in the normalization procedure is to take projections to eliminate transitive dependencies. In other words, given a relation R as follows—

```
R ( A, B, C )
   PRIMARY KEY ( A )
   B → C
```

—the normalization discipline recommends replacing R by its two projections $R1$ and $R2$, as follows:

```
R1 ( B, C )
   PRIMARY KEY ( B )

R2 ( A, B )
   PRIMARY KEY ( A )
   FOREIGN KEY ( B ) REFERENCES R1
```

Relation R can be recovered by taking the foreign-to-matching-primary-key join of $R2$ and $R1$.

We conclude this section by stressing the point that the level of normalization of a given relation is a matter of semantics, not merely a matter of the data values that happen to appear in that relation at some particular time. It is not possible just to look at the tabulation of a given relation at a given time and to say whether or not that relation is in (say) 3NF—it is also necessary to know the meaning of the data, i.e., the dependencies, before such a judgment can be made. Note too that even knowing the dependencies, it is never possible to *prove* from a given tabulation that a relation is in 3NF. The best that can be done is to show that the given tabulation does not violate any of the dependencies; assuming it does not, then the tabulation is *consistent with the hypothesis* that the relation is in 3NF, but that fact of course does not guarantee that the hypothesis is valid.

10.4   Dependency Preservation

During the reduction process it is frequently the case that a given relation can be non-loss-decomposed in a variety of different ways. Consider the relation SECOND from Section 10.3 once again, with FDs S# → CITY and CITY → STATUS and therefore also (by transitivity) S# → STATUS (see Fig. 10.11, in which the transitive FD is shown as a broken arrow). We showed in Section 10.3 that the update anomalies encountered with SECOND could be overcome by replacing it by its decomposition into the two 3NF projections

---

* It follows that, just as the SECOND-SP combination was a slightly better representation of the real world than the 1NF relation FIRST, so the SC-CS combination is a slightly better representation than the 2NF relation SECOND.

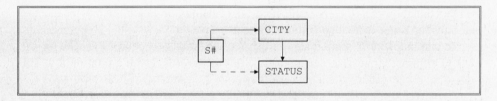

FIG. 10.11 Functional dependencies in the relation SECOND

```
SC { S#, CITY }    and    CS { CITY, STATUS }
```

Let us refer to this decomposition as "decomposition *A*." Here then is an alternative decomposition ("decomposition *B*"):

```
SC { S#, CITY }    and    SS { S#, STATUS }
```

(projection SC is the same for both *A* and *B*). Decomposition *B* is also nonloss, and the two projections are again both in 3NF. But decomposition *B* is less satisfactory than decomposition *A* for a number of reasons. For example, it is still not possible (in *B*) to insert the information that a particular city has a particular status unless some supplier is located in that city.

Let us examine this example a little more closely. First, note that the projections in decomposition *A* correspond to the *solid* arrows in Fig. 10.11, whereas one of the projections in decomposition *B* corresponds to the *broken* arrow. In decomposition *A,* the two projections are **independent** of one another, in the following sense: Updates can be made to either one without regard for the other.* Provided only that such an update is legal within the context of the projection concerned—which means only that it must not violate the primary key uniqueness constraint for that projection—then *the join of the two projections after the update will always be a valid SECOND* (i.e., the join cannot possibly violate the FD constraints on SECOND). In decomposition *B,* by contrast, updates to either of the two projections must be monitored to ensure that the FD CITY → STATUS is not violated (if two suppliers have the same city, then they must have the same status; consider, for example, what is involved in decomposition *B* in moving supplier S1·from London to Paris). In other words, the two projections are not independent of one another in decomposition *B.*

The basic problem is that, in decomposition *B,* the FD CITY → STATUS has become an *inter-relation constraint* (implying, incidentally, that in many products today it will have to be maintained by procedural application code). In decomposition *A,* by contrast, it is the *transitive* FD S# → STATUS that is the inter-relation constraint, and that constraint will be enforced automatically if the two *intra*-relation constraints S# → CITY and CITY → STATUS are enforced. And enforcing these two latter constraints is very simple, of course, involving as it does nothing more than the enforcement of the corresponding primary key uniqueness constraints.

---

* Except for the referential constraint from SC to CS, of course.

The concept of independent projections thus provides a guideline for choosing a particular decomposition when there is more than one possibility. Specifically, a decomposition in which the projections are independent in the sense described is generally preferable to one in which they are not. Rissanen [10.6] shows that projections *R1* and *R2* of a relation *R* are independent in the foregoing sense if and only if

- Every FD in *R* is a logical consequence of those in *R1* and *R2,* and
- The common attributes of *R1* and *R2* form a candidate key for at least one of the pair.

Consider decompositions *A* and *B* as defined earlier. In *A* the two projections are independent, because their common attribute CITY is the primary key for CS, and every FD in SECOND either appears in one of the two projections or is a logical consequence of those that do. In *B,* by contrast, the two projections are not independent, because the FD CITY $\rightarrow$ STATUS cannot be deduced from the FDs in those projections—though it is true that their common attribute, S#, is a candidate key for both.

(We remark that the third possibility, replacing SECOND by its two projections on {S#,STATUS} and {CITY,STATUS}, is not a valid decomposition, because it is not nonloss. *Exercise:* Prove this statement.)

Terminology: A relation that cannot be decomposed into independent projections is said to be **atomic** [10.6]. Note carefully, however, that the fact that some given relation is not atomic in this sense should not necessarily be taken to mean that it should be decomposed into atomic components. For example, relations S and P of the suppliers-and-parts database are not atomic, but there seems little point in decomposing them further. Relation SP, by contrast, *is* atomic.

The idea that the normalization procedure should decompose relations into projections that are independent in Rissanen's sense has come to be known as **dependency preservation**. We close this section by explaining this concept somewhat more precisely.

1. Suppose we are given some relation *R*, which—after we have applied all steps of the normalization procedure—we replace by a set of relations *R1, R2, . . . , Rn* (all projections of *R*, of course).

2. Let the set of given FDs for the original relation *R* be *S*, and let the sets of FDs that apply to relations *R1, R2, . . . , Rn* be *S1, S2, . . . , Sn*, respectively.

3. Each FD in the set *Si* will refer to attributes of *Ri* only (*i* = 1, 2, . . . , *n*). Enforcing the constraints (FDs) in any given set *Si* is thus a simple matter. But what we need to do is to enforce the constraints in the original set *S*. We would therefore like the decomposition into *R1, R2, . . . , Rn* to be such that enforcing the constraints in *S1, S2, . . . , Sn* individually is together equivalent to enforcing the constraints in the original set *S*—in other words, we would like the decomposition to be *dependency-preserving*.

4. Let *S'* be the union of *S1, S2, . . . , Sn*. Note that it is *not* the case that *S'* = *S*, in general; in order for the decomposition to be dependency-preserving, however, it

is sufficient that the *closures* of *S* and *S'* be equal (refer back to Section 9.4 if you need to refresh your memory regarding the notion of the closure of a set of FDs).

5. There is no efficient way of computing the closure S^+ of a set of FDs, in general, so actually computing the two closures and testing them for equality is infeasible. Nevertheless, there *is* an efficient way of testing whether a given decomposition is FD-preserving. Details of the algorithm are beyond the scope of this chapter; see, e.g., Ullman's book [7.16] for the specifics.

Note: The answer to Exercise 10.3 at the end of the chapter gives an algorithm by which an arbitrary relation can be nonloss-decomposed into a set of dependency-preserving 3NF projections.

10.5 Boyce/Codd Normal Form

In this section we drop our simplifying assumption that every relation has just one candidate key (namely, the primary key) and consider what happens in the general case. The fact is, Codd's original definition of 3NF [9.4] did not treat the general case satisfactorily. To be precise, it did not adequately deal with the case of a relation that

1. had two (or more) candidate keys, such that
2. the two candidate keys were composite, and
3. they overlapped (i.e., had at least one attribute in common).

The original definition of 3NF was therefore subsequently replaced by a stronger definition, due to Boyce and Codd, that catered for this case also [10.2]. However, since that new definition actually defines a normal form that is strictly stronger than the old 3NF, it is better to introduce a new name for it, instead of just continuing to call it 3NF; hence the term *Boyce/Codd normal form* (BCNF).* *Note:* The combination of conditions 1., 2., and 3. might not occur very often in practice. For a relation where it does not, 3NF and BCNF are equivalent.

In order to explain BCNF, we first remind the reader of the term **determinant,** which was introduced in Chapter 9 to refer to the left-hand side of an FD. We also remind the reader of the term **trivial FD,** which is an FD in which the left-hand side is a superset of the right-hand side. Now we can define BCNF:

■ **Boyce/Codd normal form:** A relation is in BCNF if and only if every nontrivial, left-irreducible FD has a candidate key as its determinant.

Or, less formally:

■ **Boyce/Codd normal form** (informal definition): A relation is in BCNF if and only if the only determinants are candidate keys.

---

* A definition of "third" normal form that was in fact equivalent to the BCNF definition was actually first given by Heath in 1971 [10.4]; "Heath normal form" might thus have been a more appropriate name.

In other words, the only arrows in the dependency diagram are arrows out of candidate keys. We have already explained that there will always be arrows out of candidate keys; the BCNF definition says there are *no other arrows,* and hence no arrows that can be eliminated by the normalization procedure. *Note:* The difference between the two BCNF definitions is that we tacitly assume in the informal case (a) that determinants are "not too big" and (b) that all FDs are nontrivial. In the interests of simplicity, we will continue to make these same assumptions throughout the rest of this chapter, except where otherwise indicated.

It is worth pointing out that the BCNF definition is conceptually simpler than the old 3NF definition, in that it makes no explicit reference to first and second normal forms as such, nor to the concept of transitive dependence. Furthermore, although (as already stated) BCNF is strictly stronger than 3NF, it is still the case that any given relation can be nonloss-decomposed into an equivalent collection of BCNF relations.

Before considering some examples involving more than one candidate key, let us convince ourselves that relations FIRST and SECOND, which were not in 3NF, are not in BCNF either; also that relations SP, SC, and CS, which were in 3NF, are also in BCNF. Relation FIRST contains three determinants, namely S#, CITY, and {S#,P#}; of these, only {S#,P#} is a candidate key, so FIRST is not in BCNF. Similarly, SECOND is not in BCNF either, because the determinant CITY is not a candidate key. Relations SP, SC, and CS, on the other hand, are each in BCNF, because in each case the (single) candidate key is the only determinant in the relation.

We now consider an example involving two disjoint—i.e., nonoverlapping—candidate keys. Suppose that in the suppliers relation

```
S { S#, SNAME, STATUS, CITY }
```

attributes S# and SNAME are both candidate keys (i.e., for all time, it is the case that every supplier has a unique supplier number and also a unique supplier name). Assume, however (as elsewhere in the book), that attributes STATUS and CITY are mutually independent—i.e., the FD CITY $\rightarrow$ STATUS, which we introduced purely for the purposes of Section 10.3, no longer holds. Then the FD diagram is as shown in Fig. 10.12.

Relation S is in BCNF. Although it is true that the FD diagram is superficially "more complex" than a 3NF diagram, it is nevertheless still the case that the only determinants are candidate keys; i.e., the only arrows are arrows out of those candidate keys. So the message of this first example is just that having more than one candidate key is not necessarily bad. But it is definitely desirable to specify the fact that SNAME *is* a candidate key in the database definition, so that the DBMS can enforce the required uniqueness. For example:

```
S ( S#, SNAME, STATUS, CITY )
  CANDIDATE KEY ( S# )
  CANDIDATE KEY ( SNAME )
```

Now we present some examples in which the candidate keys overlap. Two candidate keys overlap if they involve two or more attributes each and have at least one

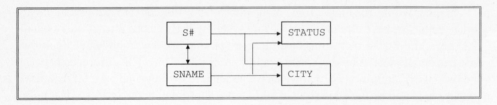

FIG. 10.12 Functional dependencies in relation S, if SNAME is a candidate key (and CITY $\to$ STATUS does not hold)

attribute in common.* For our first example, we suppose again that supplier names are unique, and we consider the relation

```
SSP { S#, SNAME, P#, QTY }
```

The candidate keys are {S#,P#} and {SNAME,P#}. Is this relation in BCNF? The answer is no, because it contains two determinants, S# and SNAME, that are not candidate keys for the relation (S# and SNAME are both determinants, because each of them determines the other). A partial tabulation of relation SSP is given in Fig. 10.13 (opposite). As that figure shows, relation SSP involves the same kind of redundancies as did relations FIRST and SECOND of Section 10.3 (and relation SCP of Section 10.1), and hence is subject to the same kind of update anomalies. For example, changing the name of supplier S1 from Smith to Robinson leads, once again, either to search problems or to possibly inconsistent results. Yet SSP *is* in 3NF by the old definition, because that definition did not require an attribute to be irreducibly dependent on each candidate key if it was itself a component of some candidate key of the relation, and so the fact that SNAME is not irreducibly dependent on {S#,P#} was ignored. (By "3NF" here we mean 3NF as originally defined by Codd in reference [9.4], not the simplified form of 3NF that we defined in Section 10.3.)

The solution to the SSP problems is, of course, to break the relation down into two projections, in this case the projections

```
SS { S#, SNAME }        and      SP { S#, P#, QTY }
```

—or alternatively the projections

```
SS { S#, SNAME }        and      SP { SNAME, P#, QTY }
```

(note that there are two equally valid decompositions in this example). All of these projections are in BCNF.

At this point, we should probably stop for a moment and consider what is "really" going on here. The original design, consisting of the single relation SSP, is *clearly* bad; the problems with it are intuitively obvious, and it is unlikely that any competent

---

* In accordance with our discussions on this subject in Chapter 5, we will not attempt to choose one of the candidate keys as the primary key in any of the examples that follow. We will therefore also not mark any columns with double underlining in our sample tabulations.

SSP	S#	SNAME	P#	QTY
	S1	Smith	P1	300
	S1	Smith	P2	200
	S1	Smith	P3	400
	S1	Smith	P4	200
	..	.....	..	...

FIG. 10.13 Partial tabulation of the relation SSP

database designer would ever seriously propose it, even if he or she had no exposure to the ideas of BCNF (etc.) at all. Common sense would tell the designer that the SS-SP design is better. But what do we mean by "common sense"? What are the *principles* (inside the designer's brain) that the designer is applying when he or she chooses the SS-SP design over the SSP design?

The answer is, of course, that they are exactly the principles of functional dependency and Boyce/Codd normal form. In other words, those concepts (FD, BCNF, and all the other formal ideas discussed in this chapter and the next) are nothing more nor less than *formalized common sense*. The whole point of the theory underlying this area is to try to identify such common sense principles and formalize them—which, of course, is not an easy thing to do! But if it can be done, then we can *mechanize* those principles; in other words, we can write a program and get the machine to do the work. Critics of normalization usually miss this point; they claim (quite rightly) that the ideas are all basically common sense, but they typically do not realize that it is a significant achievement to state what "common sense" means in a precise and formal way.

Let us now return to the main thread of our discussion. As a second example of overlapping candidate keys, we consider a relation SJT with attributes S, J, and T, standing for student, subject, and teacher, respectively (we warn the reader that some might regard this as a pathological example). The meaning of an SJT tuple {S:*s*,J:*j*,T:*t*} is that student *s* is taught subject *j* by teacher *t*. Suppose in addition that the following constraints apply:

- For each subject, each student of that subject is taught by only one teacher.

- Each teacher teaches only one subject (but each subject is taught by several teachers).

A sample tabulation of this relation is given in Fig. 10.14.

What are the FDs in relation SJT? From the first constraint, we have a dependency of T on the combination {S,J}. From the second constraint, we have a dependency of J on T. Finally, the fact that each subject is taught by several teachers tells us that there is *not* a dependency of T on J. So the FD diagram is as shown in Fig. 10.15.

Again we have two overlapping candidate keys, namely the combination {S,J} and the combination {S,T}. Once again the relation is in 3NF and not in BCNF; and once again the relation suffers from certain update anomalies. For example, if we wish to

SJT	S	J	T
	Smith	Math	Prof. White
	Smith	Physics	Prof. Green
	Jones	Math	Prof. White
	Jones	Physics	Prof. Brown

FIG. 10.14 Sample tabulation of the relation SJT

delete the information that Jones is studying physics, we cannot do so without at the same time losing the information that Professor Brown teaches physics. The difficulties are caused by the fact that attribute T is a determinant but not a candidate key. Again we can get over the problems by replacing the original relation by two BCNF projections, in this case the projections

ST { S, T }   and   TJ { T, J }

It is left as an exercise for the reader to give tabulations of these two relations corresponding to the data of Fig. 10.14, to draw a corresponding FD diagram, to show that the two projections are indeed in BCNF (what are the candidate keys?), and to check that this decomposition does in fact avoid the problems.

We cannot leave this example, however, without pointing out that, although the decomposition just discussed does solve certain problems, it unfortunately introduces different ones. The trouble is, the two projections ST and TJ are not *independent,* in Rissanen's sense (see Section 10.4). To be specific, the FD

{ S, J } → T

cannot be deduced from the FD

T → J

(which is the only FD represented in the two projections). As a result, the two projections cannot be independently updated. For example, an attempt to insert a tuple for Smith and Prof. Brown into relation ST must be rejected, because Prof. Brown teaches physics and Smith is already being taught physics by Prof. Green; yet the system cannot

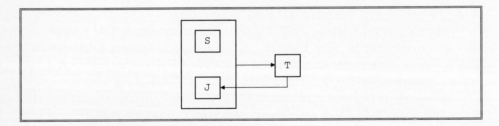

FIG. 10.15 Functional dependencies in the relation SJT

detect this fact without examining relation TJ. We are forced to the unpleasant conclusion that the two objectives of (a) decomposing a relation into BCNF components, and (b) decomposing it into independent components, can occasionally be in conflict; that is, it is not always possible to satisfy both objectives simultaneously.

Note: In fact, relation SJT is atomic (see Section 10.4), even though it is not in BCNF. Observe, therefore, that the fact that an atomic relation cannot be decomposed into independent components does not mean that it cannot be decomposed at all (where by "decomposed," of course, we mean decomposed in a nonloss way). "Atomic relation" is thus really not a very good term for the concept, at least from an intuitive point of view, since such atomicity is neither a necessary nor a sufficient criterion for a good database design.

Our third and final example of overlapping candidate keys concerns a relation EXAM with attributes S (student), J (subject), and P (position). The meaning of an EXAM tuple {S:*s*,J:*j*,P:*p*} is that student *s* was examined in subject *j* and achieved position *p* in the class list. For the purposes of the example, we assume that the following constraint holds.

■   There are no ties; that is, no two students obtained the same position in the same subject.

Then the FDs are as shown in Fig. 10.16.

Again we have two overlapping candidate keys, namely {S,J} and {J,P}, because (a) if we are given a student and a subject, then there is exactly one corresponding position, and equally (b) if we are given a subject and a position, there is exactly one corresponding student. However, the relation is in BCNF, because those candidate keys are the only determinants. The reader should check that update anomalies such as those discussed earlier in this chapter do not occur with this relation. Thus overlapping candidate keys do not *necessarily* lead to problems of the kind we have been discussing in this chapter so far.

In conclusion, we see that the concept of BCNF eliminates certain problem cases that could occur—at least theoretically—under the old definition of 3NF. Moreover, BCNF is conceptually simpler than 3NF, in that it makes no overt reference to the concepts of 1NF, 2NF, primary key, or transitive dependence. Furthermore, the reference it does make to candidate keys can be replaced by a reference to the more funda-

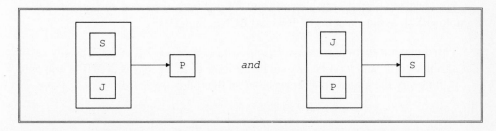

FIG. 10.16   Functional dependencies in the relation EXAM

mental notion of functional dependence (the definition given in [10.2] in fact makes this replacement). On the other hand, the concepts of primary key, transitive dependence, etc., are useful in practice, since they give some idea of the actual step-by-step process the designer must go through in order to reduce an arbitrary relation to an equivalent collection of BCNF relations.

We remark finally that the answer to Exercise 10.3 at the end of the chapter includes an algorithm by which an arbitrary relation can be nonloss-decomposed into a set of BCNF projections.

10.6   Summary

This brings us to the end of the first of our two chapters on further normalization. We have discussed the concepts of **first, second, third,** and **Boyce/Codd normal form**. The various levels of normalization form a total ordering, in the sense that every relation in $(n+1)$st normal form is automatically in nth normal form as well, whereas the converse is not true—there exist relations in nth normal form that are not in $(n+1)$st normal form.* Furthermore, reduction to BCNF is always possible; that is, any given relation can always be replaced by an equivalent set of relations in BCNF. And the purpose of such reduction is to **avoid redundancy,** and hence to avoid certain **update anomalies**.

The reduction process consists of replacing the given relation by certain **projections** in such a way that **joining** those projections back together again gives us back the original relation; in other words, the process is **reversible** (equivalently, the decomposition is **nonloss**). We also saw the crucial role that **functional dependencies** play in the procedure; in fact, **Heath's theorem** tells us that if a certain FD is satisfied, then a certain decomposition is nonloss. This state of affairs can be seen as further confirmation of the claim made in Chapter 9 to the effect that FDs are "not quite fundamental, but very nearly so."

We also discussed Rissanen's concept of **independent projections,** and suggested that it is better to decompose into such projections rather than into projections that are not independent, when there is a choice. A decomposition into such independent projections is said to be **dependency-preserving**. Unfortunately, we also saw that the two objectives of (a) nonloss decomposition to BCNF, and (b) dependency preservation, can occasionally conflict with one another.

We conclude with a very elegant (and fully accurate) pair of definitions, due to Zaniolo [10.7], of the concepts of 3NF and BCNF. First, 3NF:

■   **Third normal form** (Zaniolo's definition): Let R be a relation, let X be any set of attributes of $R,$ and let A be any single attribute of R. Then R is in 3NF if and only if, for every FD $X \rightarrow A$ in $R,$ at least one of the following is true:

---

* Interpreting "$(n+1)$st normal form" to mean BCNF, not true 4NF, if $n = 3$! See Chapter 11.

1. X contains A (so the FD is trivial)

2. X contains a candidate key of R (so X is a superkey)

3. A is contained in a candidate key of R

(Recall that a *superkey* is a set of attributes that includes the set of attributes constituting some candidate key as a subset—not necessarily a proper subset, of course.) The definition of **Boyce/Codd normal form** is obtained from the 3NF definition by simply dropping possibility number 3 above. Incidentally, possibility number 3 is precisely the cause of the "inadequacy" in Codd's original 3NF definition [9.4] that we referred to in the introduction to this chapter.

Exercises

10.1 Prove Heath's theorem. Is the converse of that theorem valid?

10.2 It is sometimes claimed that every binary relation is necessarily in BCNF. Is this claim valid?

10.3 Fig. 10.17 is a hierarchic (i.e., unnormalized) representation of a collection of information to be recorded in a company personnel database. The figure is intended to be read as follows.

- The company has a set of departments.

- Each department has a set of employees, a set of projects, and a set of offices.

- Each employee has a job history (set of jobs the employee has held). For each such job, the employee also has a salary history (set of salaries received while employed on that job).

- Each office has a set of phones.

The database is to contain the following information.

- For each department: department number (unique), budget, and the department manager's employee number (unique).

- For each employee: employee number (unique), current project number, office number,

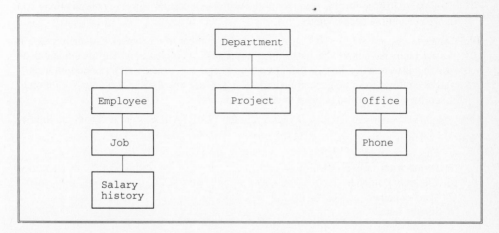

FIG. 10.17 A company database (unnormalized structure)

and phone number; also, title of each job the employee has held, plus date and salary for each distinct salary received in that job.

■ For each project: project number (unique) and budget.

■ For each office: office number (unique), area in square feet, and numbers (unique) of all phones in that office.

Design an appropriate set of normalized relations to represent this information. State any assumptions you make concerning the dependencies involved.

10.4 A database used in an order-entry system is to contain information about customers, items, and orders. The following information is to be included.

■ For each customer:
　Customer number (unique)
　"Ship-to" addresses (several per customer)
　Balance
　Credit limit
　Discount

■ For each order:
　Heading information: customer number
　　　　　　　　　　　ship-to address
　　　　　　　　　　　date of order
　Detail lines (several per order): item number
　　　　　　　　　　　　　　　　quantity ordered

■ For each item:
　Item number (unique)
　Manufacturing plants
　Quantity on hand at each plant
　Stock danger level for each plant
　Item description

For internal processing reasons a "quantity outstanding" value is associated with each detail line of each order. This value is initially set equal to the quantity of the item ordered and is (progressively) reduced to zero as (partial) shipments are made.

Design a database for this data. As in the previous question, state any assumptions you make concerning dependencies.

10.5 Suppose that in Exercise 10.4 only a very small number of customers, say one percent or less, actually have more than one ship-to address. (This is typical of real-life situations, in which it is frequently the case that just a few exceptions—usually rather important ones— fail to conform to some general pattern.) Can you see any drawbacks to your solution to Exercise 10.4? Can you think of any improvements?

10.6 (Modified version of Exercise 9.13.) A relation TIMETABLE is defined with the following attributes:

D Day of the week (1–5)
P Period within day (1–8)
C Classroom number
T Teacher name
S Student name
L Lesson name

The tuple $\{D{:}d, P{:}p, C{:}c, T{:}t, L{:}l\}$ is an element of this relation if and only if at time $\{D{:}d, P{:}p\}$ student s is attending lesson l which is being taught by teacher t in classroom c.

You can assume that lessons are one period in duration and that every lesson has a lesson name that is unique with respect to all lessons taught in the week. Reduce TIMETABLE to a more desirable structure.

10.7 (Modified version of Exercise 9.14.) A relation NADDR is defined with attributes NAME (unique), STREET, CITY, STATE, and ZIP. For any given zipcode, there is just one city and state. Also, for any given street, city, and state, there is just one zipcode. Is NADDR in BCNF? 3NF? 2NF? Can you think of a better design?

References and Bibliography

See also the references in Chapter 9, especially references [9.4–9.5] (Codd's original papers on 1NF, 2NF, and 3NF).

10.1 Philip A. Bernstein. "Synthesizing Third Normal Form Relations from Functional Dependencies." *ACM TODS 1,* No. 4 (December 1976).

In this chapter we have discussed techniques for decomposing large relations into smaller ones. In this paper, Bernstein considers the inverse problem of using small relations to construct larger ones. The problem is not actually characterized in this way in the paper; rather, it is described as the problem of synthesizing relations given a set of attributes and a set of corresponding FDs, with the constraint that the synthesized relations must be in 3NF. However, since attributes and FDs have no meaning outside the context of some containing relation, it would be more accurate to regard the primitive construct as a binary relation involving an FD, rather than as a pair of attributes plus an FD.

Note: It would equally well be possible to regard the given set of attributes and FDs as a **universal relation**—see the References and Bibliography section in Chapter 11—that satisfies a given set of dependencies, in which case the "synthesis" process can alternatively be perceived as a process of *decomposing* that universal relation into 3NF projections. But we stay with the original "synthesis" interpretation for the purposes of the present discussion.

The synthesis process, then, is one of constructing *n*-ary relations from binary relations, given a set of FDs that apply to those binary relations, and given the objective that all constructed relations be in third normal form. (BCNF had not been defined when this work was done.) Algorithms are presented for performing this task.

One objection to the approach (recognized by Bernstein) is that the manipulations performed by the synthesis algorithm are necessarily purely syntactic in nature and take no account of semantics. For instance, given the FDs

$A \rightarrow B$ in relation $R\{A, B\}$
$B \rightarrow C$ in relation $S\{B, C\}$
$A \rightarrow C$ in relation $T\{A, C\}$

the third might or might not be redundant—i.e., implied by the first and second—depending on the meaning of *R, S,* and *T*. As an example of where it is not so implied, take *A* as employee number, *B* as office number, *C* as department number; take *R* as "office of employee," *S* as "department owning office," *T* as "department of employee"; and consider the case of an employee working in an office belonging to a department not the employee's own. The synthesis algorithm simply assumes that (e.g.) *S.C* and *T.C* are one and the same (in fact, it does not recognize relation names at all); it thus relies on the existence of some external mechanism— i.e., human intervention—for avoiding semantically invalid manipulations. In the case at hand, it would be the responsibility of the person defining the original FDs to use distinct attribute names *C1* and *C2* (say) in place of *S.C* and *T.C*.

10.2 E. F. Codd. "Recent Investigations into Relational Data Base Systems." Proc. IFIP Congress, Stockholm, Sweden (1974), and elsewhere.

This paper consists of a survey of a somewhat miscellaneous collection of topics. In particular it gives "an improved definition of third normal form," where "third normal form" in fact refers to what is now known as Boyce/Codd normal form. Other topics discussed include views and view updating, data sublanguages, data exchange, and needed investigations (all as of 1974).

10.3 C. J. Date. "A Normalization Problem." *The Relational Journal 4,* No. 2, April/May 1992.

To quote the abstract, this paper "examines a simple problem of normalization and uses it to make some observations on the subject of database design and explicit integrity constraint declaration." The problem involves a simple airline application and the following FDs:

```
 1. { FLIGHT }  →  DESTINATION
 2. { FLIGHT }  →  HOUR
 3. { DAY, FLIGHT }  →  GATE
 4. { DAY, FLIGHT }  →  PILOT
 5. { DAY, HOUR, GATE }  →  DESTINATION
 6. { DAY, HOUR, GATE }  →  FLIGHT
 7. { DAY, HOUR, GATE }  →  PILOT
 8. { DAY, HOUR, PILOT }  →  DESTINATION
 9. { DAY, HOUR, PILOT }  →  FLIGHT
10. { DAY, HOUR, PILOT }  →  GATE
```

Among other things, this example serves as a good illustration of the point that the "right" database design can rarely be decided on the basis of normalization principles alone.

10.4 I. J. Heath. "Unacceptable File Operations in a Relational Database." Proc. 1971 ACM SIGFIDET Workshop on Data Description, Access, and Control, San Diego, Calif. (November 1971).

This paper gives a definition of "3NF" that was in fact the first published definition of *BCNF*. It also includes a proof of what we referred to in the body of the chapter as *Heath's theorem*. It is worth noting that the three steps in the normalization procedure as discussed in this chapter all represent applications of that theorem.

10.5 William Kent. "A Simple Guide to Five Normal Forms in Relational Database Theory." *CACM 26,* No. 2 (February 1983).

The source of the following intuitively attractive characterization of "3NF" (more accurately BCNF): **Each attribute must represent a fact about the key, the whole key, and nothing but the key** (slightly paraphrased).

10.6 Jorma Rissanen. "Independent Components of Relations." *ACM TODS 2,* No. 4 (December 1977).

10.7 Carlo Zaniolo. "A New Normal Form for the Design of Relational Database Schemata." *ACM TODS 7,* No. 3 (September 1982).

The source of the elegant definitions of 3NF and BCNF mentioned in Section 10.6. The principal purpose of the paper is to define a new normal form, *elementary key normal form* (EKNF), which lies between 3NF and BCNF and "captures the salient qualities of both" while avoiding the problems of both (namely that 3NF is "too forgiving" and BCNF is "prone to computational complexity"). The paper also shows that Bernstein's algorithm [10.1] in fact generates relations that are already in EKNF.

Answers to Selected Exercises

10.1 Heath's theorem states that if $R\{A,B,C\}$ satisfies the FD $A \rightarrow B$ (where A, B, and C are sets of attributes), then R is equal to the join of its projections $R1$ on $\{A,B\}$ and $R2$ on $\{A,C\}$.

In the following proof of this theorem, we adopt our usual informal shorthand for tuples, writing, e.g., (a,b,c) for $\{A:a,B:b,C:c\}$.

First we show that no tuple of R is lost by taking the projections and then joining those projections back together again. Let $(a,b,c) \in R$. Then $(a,b) \in R1$ and $(a,c) \in R2$, and so $(a,b,c) \in R1$ JOIN $R2$. ∎

Next we show that every tuple of the join is indeed a tuple of R (i.e., the join does not generate any "spurious" tuples). Let $(a,b,c) \in R1$ JOIN $R2$. In order to generate such a tuple in the join, we must have $(a,b) \in R1$ and $(a,c) \in R2$. Hence there must exist a tuple $(a,b^*,c) \in R$ for some b^*, in order to generate the tuple $(a,c) \in R2$. We therefore must have $(a,b^*) \in R1$. Now we have $(a,b) \in R1$ and $(a,b^*) \in R1$; hence we must have $b = b^*$, because $A \rightarrow B$. Hence $(a,b,c) \in R$. ∎

The converse of Heath's theorem would state that if $R\{A,B,C\}$ is equal to the join of its projections on $\{A,B\}$ and on $\{A,C\}$, then R satisfies the FD $A \rightarrow B$. This statement is false. For an example of a relation that *is* equal to the join of two of its projections and yet does not satisfy any (nontrivial) FDs at all, see relation CTX in Chapter 11 (Section 11.2).

10.2 The claim is almost but not quite valid. The following pathological counterexample is taken from reference [4.6]. Consider the relation USA {COUNTRY,STATE}, interpreted as "STATE is a member of COUNTRY," where COUNTRY is the United States of America in every tuple. Then the FD

```
{ }  →  COUNTRY
```

holds in this relation, and yet the empty set { } is not a candidate key. So USA is not BCNF.

Note, incidentally, that it is quite possible in general to have a candidate key that *is* the empty set! See the answer to Exercise 5.7 in Chapter 5 for further discussion.

10.3 Fig. 10.18 shows all of the most important functional dependencies, both those implied by the wording of the exercise and those corresponding to reasonable semantic assumptions (stated explicitly below). The attribute names are intended to be self-explanatory.

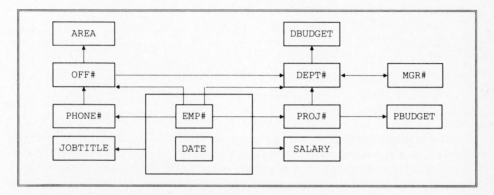

FIG. 10.18 Dependency diagram for Exercise 10.3

Semantic assumptions

- No employee is the manager of more than one department at a time.
- No employee works in more than one department at a time.
- No employee works on more than one project at a time.
- No employee has more than one office at a time.
- No employee has more than one phone at a time.
- No employee has more than one job at a time.
- No project is assigned to more than one department at a time.
- No office is assigned to more than one department at a time.

Step 0

First observe that the original hierarchic structure can be regarded as an *un*normalized relation
DEPT0:

```
DEPT0 ( DEPT#, DBUDGET, MGR#, XEMP0, XPROJ0, XOFFICE0 )
      CANDIDATE KEY ( DEPT# )
      CANDIDATE KEY ( MGR# )
```

Here DEPT#, DBUDGET and MGR# are self-explanatory, and the domains corresponding to
attributes XEMP0, XPROJ0, and XOFFICE0 are **relation-valued** and require further explanation.

Let us concentrate for the moment on the relation-valued domain corresponding to
XPROJ0. Define *PB* to be the set of all possible PROJ#-PBUDGET pairs (i.e., the Cartesian
product of the domains underlying PROJ# and PBUDGET). Then the XPROJ0 value corresponding to any given DEPT# value is some subset of the set of pairs in the set *PB*. The relation-
valued domain corresponding to XPROJ0 is thus *the set of all possible subsets* of the set *PB*—
the so-called **power set** of the set *PB*. (For simplicity, we ignore the fact that there is an FD from
PROJ# to PBUDGET, which means that in practice some subsets of the set *PB* are not legal
values for attribute XPROJ0.)

Analogous remarks apply to XEMP0, XOFFICE0, and indeed to all attributes in the example whose underlying domains are relation-valued; in each case, the domain is the power set of
the set of all possible tuples of some particular type (and those tuples are not necessarily normalized—i.e., they might contain repeating groups). We will indicate each such relation-valued
attribute by the prefix "X". Thus the given hierarchy can be represented as the following "nest"
of normalized and unnormalized relations. *Note:* We use *italics* to indicate attributes that are
"unique within parent," or globally unique if no such parent exists.

```
DEPT0 ( DEPT#, DBUDGET, MGR#,
        XEMP0 ( EMP#, PROJ#, OFF#, PHONE#,
                XJOB0 ( JOBTITLE,
                        XSALHIST0 ( DATE, SALARY ) ) ),
        XPROJ0 ( PROJ#, PBUDGET ),
        XOFFICE0 ( OFF#, AREA, XPHONE0 ( PHONE# ) ) )
```

Step 1

First, let us assume for simplicity that we wish every relation to have a *primary* key specifically—i.e., we will always designate one candidate key as the primary key. In the case of DEPT0,
in particular, let us choose DEPT# as the primary key (so that MGR# becomes an alternate key).
Now we can reduce that relation to a collection of 1NF relations. This preliminary reduction
process is explained by Codd [4.1] as follows.

- Starting with the relation at the top of the hierarchy, we take its primary key and expand each
  of the immediately subordinate relations by inserting that primary key. The primary key of

each such expanded relation is the combination of the attribute that gave "uniqueness within parent" before expansion, together with the primary key copied down from the parent relation. Note, however, that many of those "primary keys" will include attributes that are redundant for unique identification purposes and will be eliminated later in the overall procedure.

■ Now we strike out from the parent relation all relation-valued attributes (i.e., those attributes defined on relation-valued domains), remove the top node of the hierarchy, and repeat the same sequence of operations on each remaining subhierarchy.

We obtain the following collection of 1NF relations. Observe that we have lost all relation-valued attributes. (Incidentally, by considering each subhierarchy separately, we have also immediately eliminated any multivalued dependencies—MVDs—that are not also FDs. See Chapter 11.)

```
DEPT1 ( DEPT#, DBUDGET, MGR# )
      PRIMARY KEY ( DEPT# )
      ALTERNATE KEY ( MGR# )

EMP1 ( DEPT#, EMP#, PROJ#, OFF#, PHONE# )
     PRIMARY KEY ( DEPT#, EMP# )

JOB1 ( DEPT#, EMP#, JOBTITLE )
     PRIMARY KEY ( DEPT#, EMP#, JOBTITLE )

SALHIST1 ( DEPT#, EMP#, JOBTITLE, DATE, SALARY )
         PRIMARY KEY ( DEPT#, EMP#, JOBTITLE, DATE )

PROJ1 ( DEPT#, PROJ#, PBUDGET )
      PRIMARY KEY ( DEPT#, PROJ# )

OFFICE1 ( DEPT#, OFF#, AREA )
        PRIMARY KEY ( DEPT#, OFF# )

PHONE1 ( DEPT#, OFF#, PHONE# )
       PRIMARY KEY ( DEPT#, OFF#, PHONE# )
```

Step 2

We now reduce the 1NF relations to an equivalent 2NF collection by eliminating any dependencies that are not irreducible. We consider the 1NF relations one by one.

DEPT1:   This relation is already in 2NF.

EMP1:   First observe that DEPT# is actually redundant as a component of the primary key for this relation. We can take EMP# alone as the primary key, in which case the relation is in 2NF as it stands.

JOB1:   Again, DEPT# is not required as a component of the primary key. Since DEPT# is functionally dependent on EMP#, we have a nonkey attribute (DEPT#) that is not irreducibly dependent on the primary key (the combination {EMP#,JOBTITLE}), and hence JOB1 is not in 2NF. We can replace it by

```
JOB2A ( EMP#, JOBTITLE )
       PRIMARY KEY ( EMP#, JOBTITLE )
```

and

```
JOB2B ( EMP#, DEPT# )
       PRIMARY KEY ( EMP# )
```

However, JOB2A is a projection of SALHIST2 (see below), and JOB2B is a projection of EMP1 (renamed as EMP2 below), so both of these relations can be discarded.

SALHIST1:   As with JOB1, we can project out DEPT# entirely. Moreover, JOBTITLE is not required as a component of the primary key; we can take the combination {EMP#,DATE} as the primary key, to obtain the 2NF relation

```
SALHIST2 ( EMP#, DATE, JOBTITLE, SALARY )
         PRIMARY KEY ( EMP#, DATE )
```

PROJ1:   As with EMP1, we can consider DEPT# as a nonkey attribute; the relation is then in 2NF as it stands.

OFFICE1:   Similar remarks apply.

PHONE1:   We can project out DEPT# entirely, since the relation (DEPT#,OFF#) is a projection of OFFICE1 (renamed as OFFICE2 below). Also, OFF# is functionally dependent on PHONE#, so we can take PHONE# alone as the primary key, to obtain the 2NF relation

```
PHONE2 ( PHONE#, OFF# )
         PRIMARY KEY ( PHONE# )
```

Note that this relation is not necessarily a projection of EMP2 (phones or offices might exist without being assigned to employees), so that we cannot discard this relation.

Hence our collection of 2NF relations is

```
DEPT2 ( DEPT#, DBUDGET, MGR# )
      PRIMARY KEY ( DEPT# )
      ALTERNATE KEY ( MGR# )

EMP2 ( EMP#, DEPT#, PROJ#, OFF#, PHONE# )
     PRIMARY KEY ( EMP# )

SALHIST2 ( EMP#, DATE, JOBTITLE, SALARY )
         PRIMARY KEY ( EMP#, DATE )

PROJ2 ( PROJ#, DEPT#, PBUDGET )
      PRIMARY KEY ( PROJ# )

OFFICE2 ( OFF#, DEPT#, AREA )
        PRIMARY KEY ( OFF# )

PHONE2 ( PHONE#, OFF# )
        PRIMARY KEY ( PHONE# )
```

Step 3

Now we reduce the 2NF relations to an equivalent 3NF set by eliminating transitive dependencies. The only 2NF relation not already in 3NF is the relation EMP2, in which OFF# and DEPT# are both transitively dependent on the primary key EMP#—OFF# via PHONE#, and DEPT# via PROJ# and also via OFF# (and hence via PHONE#). The 3NF relations (projections) corresponding to EMP2 are

```
EMP3 ( EMP#, PROJ#, PHONE# )
     PRIMARY KEY ( EMP# )

X ( PHONE#, OFF# )
  PRIMARY KEY ( PHONE# )

Y ( PROJ#, DEPT# )
  PRIMARY KEY ( PROJ# )

Z ( OFF#, DEPT# )
  PRIMARY KEY ( OFF# )
```

However, X is PHONE2, Y is a projection of PROJ2, and Z is a projection of OFFICE2. Hence our collection of 3NF relations is simply

```
DEPT3 ( DEPT#, DBUDGET, MGR# )
     PRIMARY KEY ( DEPT# )
     ALTERNATE KEY ( MGR# )

EMP3 ( EMP#, PROJ#, PHONE# )
     PRIMARY KEY ( EMP# )

SALHIST3 ( EMP#, DATE, JOBTITLE, SALARY )
          PRIMARY KEY ( EMP#, DATE )

PROJ3 ( PROJ#, DEPT#, PBUDGET )
     PRIMARY KEY ( PROJ# )

OFFICE3 ( OFF#, DEPT#, AREA )
        PRIMARY KEY ( OFF# )

PHONE3 ( PHONE#, OFF# )
        PRIMARY KEY ( PHONE# )
```

Each of these 3NF relations is in fact in BCNF (and indeed in 4NF, because of the way we performed the reduction to 1NF in Step 1—see Chapter 11). ■

Note that, given certain (reasonable) additional semantic constraints, this collection of relations is **strongly redundant** [4.1], in that the projection of relation PROJ3 over {PROJ#,DEPT#} is at all times equal to a projection of the join of EMP3 and PHONE3 and OFFICE3.

Observe finally that it is possible to "spot" the BCNF relations from the FD diagram (how?). *Note:* We do not claim that it is *always* possible to "spot" a BCNF decomposition— only that it is often possible to do so in practical cases. A more precise statement is the following. Given a relation R satisfying a set of FDs S, the algorithm below (Steps 0–8) is guaranteed to produce a decomposition D of R into 3NF (not BCNF) relations that is both nonloss and dependency-preserving:

0. Initialize D to the empty set.

1. Let I be an irreducible cover for S.

2. Let X be a set of attributes appearing on the left-hand side of some FD $X \rightarrow Y$ in I.

3. Let the complete set of FDs in I with left-hand side X be $X \rightarrow Y1, X \rightarrow Y2, \ldots X \rightarrow Yn$.

4. Let the union of $Y1, Y2, \ldots Yn$ be Z.

5. Replace D by the union of D and the projection of R over X and Z.

6. Repeat Steps 3–5 for each distinct X.

7. Let $A1, A2, \ldots, An$ be those attributes of R (if any) still unaccounted for (i.e., still not included in any relation in D). Replace D by the union of D and the projection of R over $A1$, $A2, \ldots, An$.

8. If no relation in D includes a candidate key of R, replace D by the union of D and the projection of R over some candidate key of R.

And the following algorithm (Steps 0–3) is guaranteed to produce a decomposition D of R into BCNF relations that is nonloss but not necessarily dependency-preserving:

0. Initialize D to contain just R.

1. For each nonBCNF relation T in D, execute Steps 2–3.

2. Let $X \rightarrow Y$ be an FD in T that violates the requirements for BCNF.

3. Replace T in D by two of its projections, *viz.* that over X and Y and that over all attributes except those in Y.

To revert to the company personnel example: As a subsidiary exercise—not much to do with normalization as such, but very relevant to database design in general—the reader might like to try extending the foregoing design to incorporate the necessary *foreign key* specifications.

10.4 Fig. 10.19 shows the most important FDs for this exercise. The semantic assumptions are as follows:

- No two customers have the same ship-to address.

- Each order is identified by a unique order number.

- Each detail line within an order is identified by a line number, unique within the order.

An appropriate set of BCNF relations is as follows:

```
CUST ( CUST#, BAL, CREDLIM, DISCOUNT )
     PRIMARY KEY ( CUST# )

SHIPTO ( ADDRESS, CUST# )
     PRIMARY KEY ( ADDRESS )

ORDHEAD ( ORD#, ADDRESS, DATE )
        PRIMARY KEY ( ORD# )

ORDLINE ( ORD#, LINE#, ITEM#, QTYORD, QTYOUT )
        PRIMARY KEY ( ORD#, LINE# )

ITEM ( ITEM#, DESCN )
     PRIMARY KEY ( ITEM# )

IP ( ITEM#, PLANT#, QTYOH, DANGER )
   PRIMARY KEY ( ITEM#, PLANT# )
```

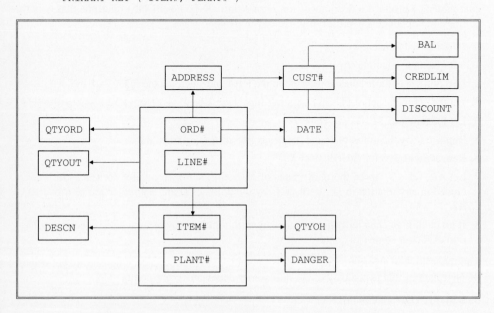

FIG. 10.19 Dependency diagram for Exercise 10.4

10.5 Consider the processing that must be performed by a program handling orders. We assume that the input order specifies customer number, ship-to address, and details of the items ordered (item numbers and quantities).

```
RETRIEVE CUST WHERE CUST# = input.CUST# ;
check balance, credit limit, etc. ;
RETRIEVE SHIPTO WHERE ADDRESS = input.ADDRESS
            AND    CUST#   = input.CUST#
/* this checks the ship-to address */ ;
if everything is OK then process the order ;
```

If 99 percent of customers actually have only one ship-to address, it would be rather inefficient to put that address in a relation other than CUST (if we consider only that 99 percent, ADDRESS is in fact functionally dependent on CUST#). We can improve matters as follows. For each customer we designate one valid ship-to address as that customer's *primary* address. For the 99 percent, of course, the primary address is the only address. Any other addresses we refer to as *secondary*. Relation CUST can then be redefined as

```
CUST ( CUST#, ADDRESS, BAL, CREDLIM, DISCOUNT )
     PRIMARY KEY ( CUST# )
```

and relation SHIPTO can be replaced by

```
SECOND ( ADDRESS, CUST# )
       PRIMARY KEY ( ADDRESS )
```

Here CUST.ADDRESS refers to the primary address, and SECOND contains all secondary addresses (and corresponding customer numbers). These relations are both in BCNF. The order-processing program now looks like this:

```
RETRIEVE CUST WHERE CUST# = input.CUST# ;
check balance, credit limit, etc. ;
if CUST.ADDRESS ≠ input.ADDRESS then
RETRIEVE SECOND WHERE ADDRESS = input.ADDRESS
            AND    CUST#   = input.CUST#
/* this checks the ship-to address */ ;
if everything is OK then process the order ;
```

The advantages of this approach include the following:

- Processing is simpler and marginally more efficient for 99 percent of customers.
- If the ship-to address is omitted from the input order, the primary address could be used by default.
- Suppose that the customer can have a different discount for each ship-to address. With the original approach (shown as the answer to the previous exercise), the DISCOUNT attribute would have to be moved to the SHIPTO relation, making processing still more complicated. With the revised approach, however, the primary discount (corresponding to the primary address) can be represented by an appearance of DISCOUNT in CUST, and secondary discounts by a corresponding appearance of DISCOUNT in SECOND. Both relations are still in BCNF, and processing is again simpler for 99 percent of customers.

To sum up: Isolating exceptional cases seems to be a valuable technique for obtaining the best of both worlds—i.e., combining the advantages of BCNF with the simplification in retrieval that can occur if the restrictions of BCNF are violated.

10.6 Fig. 10.20 shows the most important functional dependencies. A possible collection of relations is:

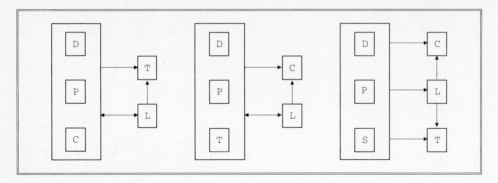

FIG. 10.20 Dependency diagram for Exercise 10.6

```
SCHED ( L, T, C, D, P )
      CANDIDATE KEY ( L )
      CANDIDATE KEY ( T, D, P )
      CANDIDATE KEY ( C, D, P )

STUDY ( S, L )
      CANDIDATE KEY ( S, L )
```

10.7 NADDR is 2NF but not 3NF or BCNF. A better design might be:

```
NSZ ( NAME, STREET, ZIP )
    PRIMARY KEY ( NAME )

ZCS ( ZIP, CITY, STATE )
    PRIMARY KEY ( ZIP )
```

These two relations are both BCNF. Note, however, that:

- Since STREET, CITY, and STATE are almost invariably required together (think of printing a mailing list), and since zipcodes do not change very often, it might be argued that such a decomposition is hardly worthwhile.

- In particular, retrieving the full address for a given NAME now requires a join (although that join could be concealed from the user by defining NADDR as a view of NSZ and ZCS). In other words, it might be argued that normalization to BCNF is *good for update but bad for retrieval*—i.e., the redundancy that occurs in the absence of full normalization certainly causes problems with update but might help with retrieval.* Redundancy causes difficulties if it is *uncontrolled;* but *controlled* redundancy (i.e., redundancy that is declared to the DBMS, and managed by the DBMS) might be acceptable in some situations.

- The FD {STREET,CITY,STATE} → ZIP is not directly represented by this design; instead, it will have to be maintained separately, either declaratively (if the DBMS supports a declarative integrity language along the lines of the one sketched in Chapter 16), or procedurally otherwise. In fact, of course, relations NSZ and ZCS are not *independent* in Rissanen's sense [10.6].

---

* On the other hand, such redundancy can actually hinder certain retrievals (i.e., make the corresponding queries more awkward to formulate).

11 | Further Normalization II: Higher Normal Forms

11.1 Introduction

In the previous chapter we discussed the ideas of further normalization up to and including Boyce/Codd normal form (which is as far as the functional dependency concept can carry us). Now we complete our discussions by examining **fourth** and **fifth** normal forms (4NF and 5NF). As we will see, the definition of fourth normal form makes use of a new kind of dependency, called a **multivalued** dependency (MVD); MVDs are a generalization of FDs. Likewise, the definition of fifth normal form makes use of another new kind of dependency, called a **join** dependency (JD); JDs are a generalization of MVDs, just as MVDs are a generalization of FDs. Section 11.2 discusses MVDs and 4NF, Section 11.3 discusses JDs and 5NF (and explains why 5NF is—in a certain special sense—the *final* normal form). Note that our discussions of MVDs and JDs are deliberately less formal and complete than our discussions of FDs in Chapter 9; we leave the formal treatment to the papers listed in the References and Bibliography section.

Section 11.4 then reviews the entire normalization procedure and makes some additional comments on it. Finally, Section 11.5 briefly examines some possible directions for future research in the normalization field, and Section 11.6 presents a summary.

11.2 Multivalued Dependencies and Fourth Normal Form

Suppose we are given an *unnormalized*—i.e., non1NF—relation UCTX containing information about courses, teachers, and texts (see Fig. 11.1). Each tuple in the relation consists of a course name, plus a repeating group of teacher names, plus a repeating group of text names (two such tuples are shown in the figure). The intended meaning of such a tuple is that the specified course can be taught by any of the specified teachers and uses all of the specified texts as references. We assume that, for a given course, there can exist any number of corresponding teachers and any number of corresponding texts. Moreover, we also assume—perhaps not very realistically!—that teachers and texts are quite independent of one another; that is, no matter who actually teaches any

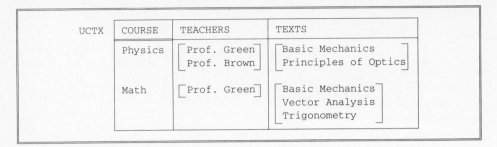

FIG. 11.1 Sample tabulation of the unnormalized relation UCTX

particular offering of the given course, the same texts are used. Finally, we also assume that a given teacher or a given text can be associated with any number of courses.

Now let us convert this structure into an equivalent normalized form. Observe first that there are no FDs in the data at all (apart from trivial ones such as COURSE $\rightarrow$ COURSE). The ideas discussed in the previous chapter therefore provide us with no formal basis by which to decompose the structure into projections; the only operation available to us of a normalizing nature is the elementary one of "flattening" the structure (as in Chapter 4), which for the data of Fig. 11.1 yields the relation CTX shown in Fig. 11.2.

The meaning of the normalized version CTX is loosely as follows: A tuple {COURSE:c,TEACHER:t,TEXT:x} appears in the relation if and only if course c can be taught by teacher t and uses text x as a reference. Observe that, for a given course, all possible combinations of teacher and text appear; that is, CTX satisfies the constraint

```
IF   tuples (c,t1,x1), (c,t2,x2) both appear
THEN tuples (c,t1,x2), (c,t2,x1) both appear also
```

(using our usual shorthand for representing tuples without showing attribute names).

It is apparent that relation CTX involves a good deal of **redundancy,** leading as

CTX	COURSE	TEACHER	TEXT
	Physics	Prof. Green	Basic Mechanics
	Physics	Prof. Green	Principles of Optics
	Physics	Prof. Brown	Basic Mechanics
	Physics	Prof. Brown	Principles of Optics
	Math	Prof. Green	Basic Mechanics
	Math	Prof. Green	Vector Analysis
	Math	Prof. Green	Trigonometry

FIG. 11.2 Sample tabulation of the normalized equivalent CTX

usual to certain **update anomalies**. For example, to add the information that the physics course can be taught by a new teacher, it is necessary to create *two* new tuples, one for each of the two texts. Nevertheless, CTX is in BCNF, since it is "all key."

Note: The reader might object here that it is not necessary to include all teacher-text combinations for a given course; for example, two tuples are sufficient to show that the physics course has two teachers and two texts. The problem is, *which* two tuples? Any particular choice leads to a relation having a very unobvious interpretation and very strange update behavior. To see that this is so, the reader should try the experiment of making such a choice and then stating the meaning of the relation that results—i.e., stating the criteria for deciding whether some given update is or is not an acceptable operation on that relation (see Section 4.5 in Chapter 4).

The existence of "problem" BCNF relations such as CTX was recognized very early on. Now, in the case of CTX in particular, it is intuitively clear that the difficulties are caused by the fact that teachers and texts are completely independent of one another; it is also easy to see that matters would be improved if CTX were replaced by its projections on {COURSE,TEACHER} and {COURSE,TEXT} (see Fig. 11.3). These two projections—let us call them CT and CX, respectively—are both "all key" and are both in BCNF; furthermore, relation CTX can be recovered by joining CT and CX back together again, so the decomposition is nonloss. However, it was not until 1977 that these intuitive ideas were put on a sound theoretical footing by Fagin's introduction of the notion of *multivalued dependencies*.

Note: We stress the point that the discussions that follow are intended to explain a *formal theory,* albeit in a fairly informal manner. Pragmatically speaking, however, all we need do is recognize that when we are trying to normalize some unnormalized relation, *the first thing to do is to separate independent repeating groups*—a rule that makes obvious intuitive sense. In the example, the original unnormalized relation UCTX should be converted into two unnormalized relations, UCT (containing courses and repeating groups of teachers) and UCX (containing courses and repeating groups of texts). Those two unnormalized relations can then be "flattened" and reduced to BCNF in the usual way, and the "problem" normalized relation CTX will simply not

CT

COURSE	TEACHER
Physics	Prof. Green
Physics	Prof. Brown
Math	Prof. Green

CX

COURSE	TEXT
Physics	Basic Mechanics
Physics	Principles of Optics
Math	Basic Mechanics
Math	Vector Analysis
Math	Trigonometry

FIG. 11.3 Sample tabulations of CT and CX

arise. But the theory gives us a formal basis for what would otherwise be a mere rule of thumb.

To revert to the example: The decomposition of Fig. 11.3 is indeed correct, and desirable. As we have already indicated, however, that decomposition cannot be made on the basis of functional dependencies, because there *are* no FDs in the relation (other than trivial ones). Instead, it is made on the basis of a new kind of dependency, the **multivalued** dependency (MVD) mentioned above. Multivalued dependencies are a generalization of functional dependencies, in the sense that every FD is an MVD (but the converse is not true; i.e., there exist MVDs that are not FDs). There are two MVDs in relation CTX:

```
COURSE  →→ TEACHER
COURSE  →→ TEXT
```

Notice the double-headed arrows; the MVD $A \twoheadrightarrow B$ is read as "*B* is **multidependent** on *A*," or, equivalently, "*A* **multidetermines** *B*."

For the moment we concentrate on the first of these two MVDs, which means intuitively that, although a course does not have a *single* corresponding teacher—i.e., the *functional* dependence COURSE → TEACHER does *not* hold—nevertheless, each course does have a well-defined *set* of corresponding teachers (several of them, in general). By "well-defined" here we mean, more precisely, that for a given course *c* and a given text *x*, the set of teachers *t* matching the pair (*c*,*x*) in CTX depends on the value *c* alone—it makes no difference what particular value of *x* we choose. The second MVD (of TEXT on COURSE) is interpreted analogously.

We now give a definition of MVD.

■   **Multivalued dependence:** Let *R* be a relation, and let *A*, *B*, and *C* be arbitrary subsets of the set of attributes of *R*. Then we say that *B* is **multidependent** on *A*—in symbols,

$$A \twoheadrightarrow B$$

(read "*A* multidetermines *B*," or simply "*A* double arrow *B*")—if and only if the set of *B*-values matching a given (*A*-value,*C*-value) pair in *R* depends only on the *A*-value and is independent of the *C*-value.

(As with functional dependencies, we are interested not so much in those multivalued dependencies that happen to be satisfied at some particular time but rather in those that must be satisfied for all time. Throughout this chapter we will consider MVDs only in this latter, more demanding, sense.)

It is easy to show (see Fagin [11.8]) that, given the relation $R\{A,B,C\}$, the MVD $A \twoheadrightarrow B$ holds if and only if the MVD $A \twoheadrightarrow C$ also holds. MVDs always go together in pairs in this way. For this reason it is common to represent both in a single joint statement, using the notation

$$A \twoheadrightarrow B \mid C$$

For example:

COURSE $\twoheadrightarrow$ TEACHER | TEXT

Now, we stated above that multivalued dependencies are a generalization of functional dependencies, in the sense that every FD is an MVD. More precisely, an FD is an MVD in which the set of dependent values matching a given determinant value is actually always a singleton set.

Returning to our original CTX problem, we can now see that the trouble with relations such as CTX is that they involve MVDs that are not also FDs. (In case it is not obvious, we point out that it is precisely the existence of those MVDs that leads to the necessity of—for example—inserting *two* tuples to add another physics teacher. Those two tuples are needed in order to maintain the integrity constraint that is represented by the MVD.) The two projections CT and CX do not involve any such MVDs, which is why they represent an improvement over the original design. We would therefore like to replace CTX by those two projections, and an important theorem proved by Fagin in reference [11.8] allows us to make exactly that replacement:

- **Theorem** (Fagin): Let $R\{A,B,C\}$ be a relation, where A, B, and C are sets of attributes. Then R is equal to the join of its projections on $\{A,B\}$ and $\{A,C\}$ if and only if R satisfies the MVD $A \twoheadrightarrow B \mid C$.

(Notice that this is a stronger version of Heath's theorem as defined in Chapter 10.) Following Fagin [11.8], we can now define *fourth normal form.**

- **Fourth normal form:** Relation R is in 4NF if and only if, whenever there exist subsets A and B of the attributes of R such that the (nontrivial) MVD $A \twoheadrightarrow B$ is satisfied, then all attributes of R are also *functionally* dependent on A.

In other words, the only nontrivial dependencies (FDs or MVDs) in R are of the form $K \rightarrow X$ (i.e., a *functional* dependency from a candidate key K to some other attribute X). Equivalently: R is in 4NF if it is in BCNF and all MVDs in R are in fact FDs "out of candidate keys." Note, therefore, that 4NF implies BCNF.

Relation CTX is not in 4NF, since it involves an MVD that is not an FD at all, let alone an FD "out of a candidate key." The two projections CT and CX are both in 4NF, however. Thus 4NF is an improvement over BCNF, in that it eliminates another form of undesirable structure. What is more, Fagin shows in reference [11.8] that 4NF is always achievable—that is, any relation can be nonloss-decomposed into an equivalent collection of 4NF relations—though our discussion of the SJT example in Section 10.5 shows that in some cases it might not be desirable to carry the decomposition that far (or even as far as BCNF).

We conclude this section by remarking that Rissanen's work on independent projections [10.6], though couched in terms of FDs, is applicable to MVDs also. Remember that a relation $R\{A,B,C\}$ satisfying the FDs $A \rightarrow B$ and $B \rightarrow C$ is better decomposed into its projections on $\{A,B\}$ and $\{B,C\}$ rather than into those on $\{A,B\}$ and $\{A,C\}$. The same holds true if the FDs are replaced by the MVDs $A \twoheadrightarrow B$ and $B \twoheadrightarrow C$.

---

* Fourth normal form was so called because at the time BCNF was still usually called *third* normal form.

11.3 Join Dependencies and Fifth Normal Form

So far in this chapter—and throughout the previous chapter—we have tacitly assumed that the sole operation necessary or available in the decomposition process is the replacement of a relation (in a nonloss way) by two of its projections. This assumption has successfully carried us as far as 4NF. It comes perhaps as a surprise, therefore, to discover that there exist relations that cannot be nonloss-decomposed into two projections but *can* be so decomposed into three or more. To coin an ugly but convenient term, we will describe such a relation as "*n*-decomposable" (for some $n > 2$)—meaning that the relation in question can be nonloss-decomposed into *n* projections but not into any number of projections less than *n*. A relation that can be nonloss-decomposed into two projections we will call "2-decomposable." *Note:* The phenomenon of *n*-decomposability for $n > 2$ was first noted by Aho, Beeri, and Ullman [11.1]. The particular case $n = 3$ was also studied by Nicolas [11.20].

Let us consider an example. Refer to relation SPJ of Fig. 11.4 (a simplified version of the shipments relation from the suppliers-parts-projects database). That relation is "all key" and involves no nontrivial FDs or MVDs, and is therefore in 4NF. The figure also shows (a) the three binary projections SP, PJ, and JS of SPJ, and (b) the effect of joining SP and PJ over P# and then (c) joining that result and JS over (J#,S#). Notice that the result of the first join is to produce a copy of the original SPJ relation plus one

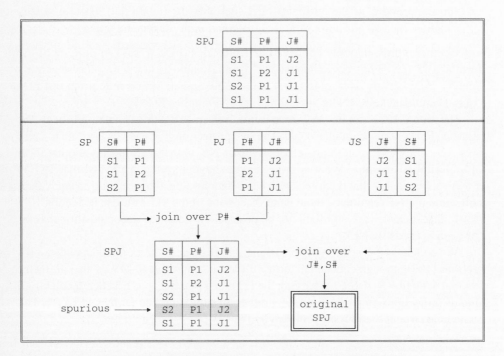

FIG. 11.4 SPJ is the join of all three of its binary projections but not of any two

additional (spurious) tuple, and the effect of the second join is then to eliminate that spurious tuple. *Note:* The net result is the same whatever pair of projections we choose for the first join, though the intermediate result is different in each case (the reader might care to check this statement).

The example of Fig. 11.4 is of course expressed in terms of a set of specific data values that happen to exist at some specific time. However, the 3-decomposability of relation SPJ could be a more fundamental, time-independent property—i.e., a property satisfied by all legal values of the relation—*if* that relation satisfies a certain time-independent constraint. To understand what that constraint must be, observe first that the statement "SPJ is equal to the join of its three projections SP, PJ, and JS" is precisely equivalent to the following statement:

```
IF   the pair  (s1,p1)    appears in SP
AND  the pair  (p1,j1)    appears in PJ
AND  the pair  (j1,s1)    appears in JS
THEN the triple (s1,p1,j1) appears in SPJ
```

because the triple $(s1,p1,j1)$ obviously appears in the join of SP, PJ, and JS. (The converse of this statement, that if $(s1,p1,j1)$ appears in SPJ then $(s1,p1)$ appears in projection SP (etc.) is obviously true for any degree-3 relation SPJ.) Since $(s1,p1)$ appears in SP if and only if $(s1,p1,j2)$ appears in SPJ for some $j2$, and similarly for $(p1,j1)$ and $(j1,s1)$, we can rewrite the statement above as a constraint on SPJ:

```
IF   (s1,p1,j2), (s2,p1,j1), (s1,p2,j1) appear in SPJ
THEN (s1,p1,j1) appears in SPJ also
```

And if *this* statement is true for all time—i.e., for all possible legal values of relation SPJ—then we do have a time-independent constraint on the relation (albeit a rather bizarre one). Notice the *cyclic nature* of that constraint ("if $s1$ is linked to $p1$ and $p1$ is linked to $j1$ and $j1$ is linked back to $s1$ again, then $s1$ and $p1$ and $j1$ must all coexist in the same tuple"). *A relation will be n-decomposable for some $n > 2$ if and only if it satisfies some such cyclic constraint.*

Suppose then that relation SPJ does in fact satisfy that time-independent constraint (the sample values in Fig. 11.4 are consistent with this hypothesis). For brevity, let us agree to refer to that constraint as *Constraint 3D* (for 3-decomposable). What does Constraint 3D mean in real-world terms? Let us try to make it a little more concrete by giving an example. The constraint says that, in the portion of the real world that relation SPJ is supposed to represent, it is a fact that, *if* (for example)

(a) Smith supplies monkey wrenches, and

(b) Monkey wrenches are used in the Manhattan project, and

(c) Smith supplies the Manhattan project,

then

(d) Smith supplies monkey wrenches to the Manhattan project.

Note that, as pointed out in Chapter 1 (Section 1.3), (a), (b), and (c) together normally do *not* imply (d); indeed, exactly this example was held up in that chapter as an illustration of "the connection trap." In the particular case at hand, however, we are saying *there is no such trap*—because there is an additional real-world constraint in effect, namely Constraint 3D, that makes the inference valid in this special case.

To return to the main topic of discussion: Because Constraint 3D is satisfied if and only if the relation concerned is equal to the join of certain of its projections, we refer to that constraint as a **join dependency** (JD). A JD is a constraint on the relation concerned, just as an MVD or an FD is a constraint on the relation concerned. Here is the definition:

■ **Join dependency:** Let R be a relation, and let A, B, . . . , Z be arbitrary subsets of the set of attributes of R. Then we say that R satisfies the JD

    `* ( A, B, ..., Z )`

if and only if R is equal to the join of its projections on A, B, . . . , Z.

For example, if we agree to use SP to mean the subset {S#,P#} of the set of attributes of SPJ, and similarly for PJ and JS, then relation SPJ satisfies the JD *(SP,PJ,JS).

We have seen, then, that relation SPJ, with its JD *(SP,PJ,JS), can be 3-decomposed. The question is, *should* it be? And the answer is "Probably yes." Relation SPJ suffers from a number of problems over update operations, problems that are removed when it is 3-decomposed. Some examples of such problems are shown in Fig. 11.5. Consideration of what happens after 3-decomposition is left as an exercise for the reader.

Fagin's theorem (discussed in Section 11.2), to the effect that $R\{A,B,C\}$ can be nonloss-decomposed into its projections on $\{A,B\}$ and $\{A,C\}$ if and only if the MVDs $A \twoheadrightarrow B$ and $A \twoheadrightarrow C$ hold in R, can now be restated as follows:

■ $R\{A,B,C\}$ satisfies the JD *(AB,AC) if and only if it satisfies the MVDs $A \twoheadrightarrow B \mid C$.

SPJ	S#	P#	J#
	S1	P1	J2
	S1	P2	J1

SPJ	S#	P#	J#
	S1	P1	J2
	S1	P2	J1
	S2	P1	J1
	S1	P1	J1

- If (S2,P1,J1) is inserted, (S1,P1,J1) must also be inserted

- Yet converse is not true

- Can delete (S2,P1,J1) without side effects

- If (S1,P1,J1) deleted, another tuple must also be deleted (which?)

FIG. 11.5 Examples of update problems in SPJ

Since this theorem can be taken as a *definition* of multivalued dependency, it follows that an MVD is just a special case of a JD, or that JDs are a generalization of MVDs (rather as MVDs are a generalization of FDs). What is more, it is immediate from the JD definition that JDs are **the most general form of dependency possible** (using, of course, the term "dependency" in a very specialized sense!). That is, there does not exist a still higher form of dependency such that JDs are merely a special case of that higher form—so long as we restrict our attention to dependencies that deal with a relation being decomposed via projection and recomposed via join. (However, if we permit other decomposition and recomposition operators, then other types of dependency might come into play. We discuss this possibility very briefly in Section 11.5.)

Returning now to our example, we can see that the problem with relation SPJ is that it involves a JD that is not an MVD, and hence not an FD either. (*Exercise for the reader: Why* is this a problem, exactly?) We have also seen that it is possible, and probably desirable, to decompose such a relation into smaller components—namely, into the projections specified by the join dependency. That decomposition process can be repeated until all resulting relations are in *fifth normal form:*

■ **Fifth normal form:** A relation *R* is in 5NF—also called **projection-join normal form** (PJ/NF)—if and only if every join dependency in *R* is implied by the candidate keys of *R*.

(The notion of a JD being implied by the candidate keys of a relation is explained below.)

Relation SPJ is not in 5NF; it satisfies a certain join dependency, namely Constraint 3D, that is certainly not implied by its sole candidate key (that key being the combination of all of its attributes). To state this differently, relation SPJ is not in 5NF, because (a) it *can* be 3-decomposed and (b) that 3-decomposability is not implied by the fact that the combination {S#,P#,J#} is a candidate key. By contrast, after 3-decomposition, the three projections SP, PJ, and JS are each in 5NF, since they do not involve any JDs at all.

Although it might not yet be obvious to the reader (because we have not yet explained what it means for a JD to be implied by candidate keys), it is a fact that any relation in 5NF is automatically in 4NF also, because an MVD is a special case of a JD. In fact, Fagin shows in reference [11.9] that any MVD that is implied by a candidate key must in fact be an FD in which that candidate key is the determinant. Fagin also shows in that same reference [11.9] that any given relation can be nonloss-decomposed into an equivalent collection of 5NF relations; that is, 5NF is always achievable.

We now explain what it means for a JD to be implied by candidate keys. First we consider a simple example. Suppose once again (as we did in Chapter 10, Section 10.5) that the familiar suppliers relation S has two candidate keys, S# and SNAME. Then that relation satisfies several join dependencies—for example, it satisfies the JD

```
* ( { S#, SNAME, STATUS }, { S#, CITY } )
```

That is, relation S is equal to the join of its projections on {S#,SNAME,STATUS} and {S#,CITY}, and hence can be nonloss-decomposed into those projections. (This fact does not mean that it *should* be so decomposed, only that it *could* be.) This JD is implied by the fact that S# is a candidate key (in fact it is implied by Heath's theorem [10.4]). Likewise, relation S also satisfies the JD

```
*  ( { S#, SNAME }, { S#, STATUS }, { SNAME, CITY } )
```

This JD is implied by the fact that S# and SNAME are *both* candidate keys.

For the general case, Fagin [11.9] gives an algorithm by which it is possible, given a JD and a set of candidate keys, to test whether that JD is implied by those candidate keys (it is not always immediately obvious—witness the second example above). Thus, given a relation *R*, we can tell if *R* is in 5NF, provided we know all candidate keys **and all JDs** in *R*. However, discovering all the JDs might itself be a nontrivial operation. That is, whereas it is relatively easy to identify FDs and MVDs (because they have a fairly straightforward real-world interpretation), the same cannot be said for JDs—JDs, that is, that are not MVDs and not FDs—because the intuitive meaning of JDs might not be obvious. Hence the process of determining when a given relation is in 4NF but not 5NF, and so could probably be decomposed to advantage, is *still unclear*. Experience suggests that such relations are pathological cases and likely to be rare in practice.

In conclusion, we note that it follows from the definition that 5NF is the **ultimate** normal form with respect to projection and join (which accounts for its alternative name, *projection-join* normal form). That is, a relation in 5NF is **guaranteed to be free of anomalies** that can be eliminated by taking projections.* For if a relation is in 5NF, the only join dependencies are those that are implied by candidate keys, and so the only valid decompositions are ones that are based on those candidate keys. (Each projection in such a decomposition will consist of one or more of those candidate keys, plus zero or more additional attributes.) For example, the suppliers relation S is in 5NF. It *can* be further decomposed in several nonloss ways, as we saw above, but every projection in any such decomposition will still include one of the original candidate keys, and hence there does not seem to be any particular advantage in that further reduction.

11.4   The Normalization Procedure Summarized

This chapter and its predecessor have been concerned with the technique of *nonloss decomposition* as an aid to database design. The basic idea is as follows: Given some first normal form relation $R^\dagger$ and some list of constraints (FDs, MVDs, and JDs) that apply to *R*, we systematically reduce *R* to a collection of smaller relations that are equivalent to *R* in a certain well-defined sense but are also in some way more desirable than *R*. Each step of the reduction process consists of taking projections of the relations resulting from the preceding step. The given constraints are used at each step to guide

---

* Of course, this remark does not mean that the relation is free of *all possible* anomalies. It just means (to repeat) that it is free of anomalies that can be removed by taking projections.

$\dagger$ The original 1NF relation might of course have been obtained by first "flattening" an unnormalized structure.

the choice of which projections to take next. The overall process can be stated informally as a set of rules, as follows.

1. Take projections of the original 1NF relation to eliminate any functional dependencies that are not irreducible. This step will produce a collection of 2NF relations.

2. Take projections of those 2NF relations to eliminate any transitive functional dependencies. This step will produce a collection of 3NF relations.

3. Take projections of those 3NF relations to eliminate any remaining functional dependencies in which the determinant is not a candidate key. This step will produce a collection of BCNF relations. *Note:* Rules 1–3 can be condensed into the single guideline "Take projections of the original relation to eliminate all FDs in which the determinant is not a candidate key."

4. Take projections of those BCNF relations to eliminate any multivalued dependencies that are not also functional dependencies. This step will produce a collection of 4NF relations. *Note:* In practice it is usual—by "separating independent repeating groups"—to eliminate such MVDs *before* applying Rules 1–3 above, as explained in our discussion of the CTX example in Section 11.2.

5. Take projections of those 4NF relations to eliminate any join dependencies that are not implied by the candidate keys—though perhaps we should add "if you can find them." This step will produce a collection of relations in 5NF.

Several points arise from the foregoing summary.

1. First of all, the process of taking projections at each step must of course be done in a nonloss way and (where possible) in a dependency-preserving way.

2. Notice that (as was first observed by Fagin in reference [11.9]) there is a very attractive parallelism among the definitions of BCNF, 4NF, and 5NF, *viz.:*

   - A relation R is in BCNF if and only if every FD in R is implied by the candidate keys of R

   - A relation R is in 4NF if and only if every MVD in R is implied by the candidate keys of R

   - A relation R is in 5NF if and only if every JD in R is implied by the candidate keys of R

   The update anomalies discussed in Chapter 10 and in earlier sections of the present chapter are precisely anomalies that are caused by FDs or MVDs or JDs that are not implied by candidate keys.

3. The overall objectives of the normalization process are as follows:

   - To eliminate certain kinds of redundancy

   - To avoid certain update anomalies

   - To produce a design that is a "good" representation of the real world—one that is intuitively easy to understand and a good base for future growth

   - To simplify the enforcement of certain integrity constraints

Let us elaborate a little on the last item in this list. The general point is that (as discussed elsewhere in this book) some integrity constraints imply others. As a trivial example, the constraint that salaries must be greater than $10,000 certainly implies the constraint that they must be greater than zero. Now, if constraint *A* implies constraint *B,* then *enforcing A will enforce B automatically* (it will not even be necessary to state *B* explicitly, except perhaps in the form of a comment). And normalization to 5NF gives us a simple way of enforcing certain important and commonly occurring constraints; basically, all we have to do is enforce uniqueness of candidate keys, and then all JDs (and all MVDs and all FDs) will be enforced automatically—because, of course, all of those JDs (and MVDs and FDs) will be implied by the candidate keys.

4. Once again, we stress the point that the normalization guidelines *are* only guidelines, and occasionally there might be good reasons for not normalizing "all the way." The classic example of a case where complete normalization *might* not be a good idea is provided by the name-and-address relation NADDR (see Exercise 10.7 in Chapter 10)—though, to be frank, the example is not very convincing. As a rule of thumb, *not* normalizing all the way is usually a bad idea.

5. We also repeat the point from Chapter 10 that the notions of dependency and further normalization are *semantic* in nature—in other words, they are concerned with what the data *means*. By contrast, the relational algebra and relational calculus, and languages such as SQL that are based on those formalisms, are concerned only with data *values;* any interpretation of those values is imposed from the outside (by the human user). Thus, those formalisms and languages do not and cannot require any particular level of normalization other than first. The normalization guidelines should be regarded primarily as a discipline to help the database designer (and hence the user)—a discipline by which the designer can capture a part, albeit a small part, of the semantics of the real world in a simple and straightforward manner.

6. Following on from the previous point: The ideas of normalization are useful in database design, but they are not a panacea. Here are some of the reasons why not:

   - It is true (as discussed above) that normalization can help to enforce certain integrity constraints very simply, but JDs and MVDs and FDs are not the only kind of constraint that can arise in practice.

   - The decomposition might not be unique (usually, in fact, there will be many ways of reducing a given collection of relations to 5NF), and there are few objective criteria by which to choose among alternative decompositions.

   - The BCNF and dependency-preservation objectives can occasionally be in conflict, as explained in Section 10.5 ("the SJT problem").

   - The normalization procedure eliminates redundancies by taking projections, but not all redundancies can be eliminated in this manner ("the CTXD problem"—see the annotation to reference [11.8]).

We should also mention the point that good top-down design methodologies tend to generate fully normalized designs anyway.

11.5 Other Normal Forms

Before closing this chapter, we remind the reader of our remark in the introduction to Chapter 10 to the effect that there do exist other normal forms, over and above those that we have been discussing. The fact is, the theory of normalization and related topics—now usually known as **dependency theory**—has grown into a very considerable field in its own right, with several distinct (though of course interrelated) aspects and with a very extensive literature. Research in the area is continuing, and indeed flourishing. It is beyond the scope of this chapter to discuss such research in any depth; a good survey of the field as of the mid 1980s can be found in reference [10.12]. Here we just mention a couple of specific examples.

1. **Domain-key normal form:** Domain-key normal form (DK/NF) was proposed by Fagin in reference [11.10]. DK/NF—unlike the normal forms we have been discussing—is not defined in terms of FDs, MVDs, or JDs at all. Instead, a relation R is said to be in DK/NF if and only if every constraint on R is a logical consequence of the *domain constraints* and *key constraints* that apply to R:

    - A *domain constraint*—as the term is used here—is a constraint to the effect that values of a given attribute are taken from some prescribed domain. (In Chapter 16, we will refer to such a constraint as an *attribute* constraint instead of a domain constraint.)

    - A *key constraint* is a constraint to the effect that a certain attribute or attribute combination constitutes a candidate key.

    Enforcing constraints on a DK/NF relation is thus conceptually simple, since it is sufficient to enforce just the domain and key constraints and all other constraints will then be enforced automatically. Note carefully too that "all other constraints" here means more than just FDs and MVDs and JDs—in fact, it means the *relation predicate* for the relation in question, as defined in Chapter 4 (and elaborated in Chapter 16).

    Fagin shows in reference [11.10] that any DK/NF relation is necessarily in 5NF (and therefore in 4NF, etc.), and indeed also in (3,3)NF (see below). However, DK/NF is not always achievable, nor has the question "Exactly when *can* it be achieved?" been answered.

2. **"Restriction-union" normal form:** Consider the suppliers relation S once again. Normalization theory as we have described it tells us that relation S is in a "good" normal form; indeed, it is in 5NF, and is therefore guaranteed to be free of anomalies that can be eliminated by taking projections. But why keep all suppliers in a single relation? What about a design in which London suppliers are kept in one relation (LS, say), Paris suppliers in another (PS, say), and so on? In other words, what about the possibility of decomposing the original suppliers relation via **restriction** instead of projection? Would the resulting structure be a good design or a bad one? (In fact it would almost certainly be bad, but the point is that classical normalization theory as such has absolutely nothing to say in answer to such questions.)

Another direction for normalization research therefore consists of examining the implications of decomposing relations by some operation other than projection. In the example, the decomposition operator is, as already mentioned, (disjoint) *restriction;* the corresponding recomposition operator is (disjoint) **union**. Thus, it might be possible to construct a "restriction-union" normalization theory, analogous *but orthogonal* to the projection-join normalization theory we have been discussing.* To this writer's knowledge no such theory has ever been worked out in detail, but some initial ideas can be found in a paper by Smith [11.26], where a new normal form called **"(3,3)NF"** is defined. (3,3)NF implies BCNF; however, a (3,3)NF relation need not be in 4NF, nor need a 4NF relation be in (3,3)NF, so that (as suggested above) reduction to (3,3)NF is orthogonal to reduction to 4NF (and 5NF). Further ideas on this topic appear in references [11.9] and [11.17].

11.6   Summary

In this chapter we have completed our discussion (begun in Chapter 10) of **further normalization**. We have discussed **multivalued dependencies** (MVDs), which are a generalization of functional dependencies, and **join dependencies** (JDs), which are a generalization of multivalued dependencies. Loosely speaking:

■   A relation $R\{A,B,C\}$ satisfies the MVDs $A \twoheadrightarrow B \mid C$ if and only if the set of B values matching a given (A,C) pair depends only on the A value, and similarly for the set of C values matching a given (A,B) pair. Such a relation can be nonloss-decomposed into its projections on $\{A,B\}$ and $\{A,C\}$; in fact, the MVDs are a necessary and sufficient condition for this decomposition to be valid (Fagin's theorem).

■   A relation $R\{A,B, \ldots ,Z\}$ satisfies the JD $*(A,B, \ldots ,Z)$ if and only if it is equal to the join of its projections on $A, B, \ldots Z$. Such a relation can (obviously) be nonloss-decomposed into those projections.

A relation is in 4NF if the only MVDs it satisfies are in fact FDs out of candidate keys. A relation is in 5NF (also called **projection-join** normal form, PJ/NF) if and only if the only JDs it satisfies are in fact FDs out of candidate keys. 5NF (which is always achievable) is the ultimate normal form with respect to projection and join.

We also summarized the **normalization procedure,** presenting it as an informal sequence of steps and offering a few relevant comments, and we briefly mentioned some *additional normal forms*.

In conclusion, we should perhaps point out that further research into such issues is very much a worthwhile activity. The reason is that the field of *further normalization,* or rather **dependency theory** as it is now more usually called, does represent the one

---

* Indeed, Fagin [11.9] originally called 5NF *projection-join* normal form precisely because it was **the** normal form with respect to the projection and join operators.

piece of science in a field—database design—that is regrettably still far too subjective and lacking in solid principles and guidelines. Thus, any further successes in dependency theory research are very much to be welcomed.

Exercises

11.1 Let C be a certain club, and let relation $R\{A,B\}$ be such that the tuple (a,b) is included in R if and only if a and b are both members of C. What FDs, MVDs, and JDs does R satisfy? What normal form is it in?

11.2 A database is to contain information concerning sales representatives, sales areas, and products. Each representative is responsible for sales in one or more areas; each area has one or more responsible representatives. Similarly, each representative is responsible for sales of one or more products, and each product has one or more responsible representatives. Every product is sold in every area; however, no two representatives sell the same product in the same area. Every representative sells the same set of products in every area for which that representative is responsible. Design a suitable relational structure for this data.

11.3 In the answer to Exercise 10.3 in Chapter 10, we gave an algorithm for nonloss decomposition of an arbitrary relation R into a set of BCNF relations. Revise that algorithm so that it yields 4NF relations instead.

11.4 (Modified version of Exercise 11.2.) A database is to contain information concerning sales representatives, sales areas, and products. Each representative is responsible for sales in one or more areas; each area has one or more responsible representatives. Similarly, each representative is responsible for sales of one or more products, and each product has one or more responsible representatives. Finally, each product is sold in one or more areas, and each area has one or more products sold in it. Moreover, if representative R is responsible for area A, and product P is sold in area A, and representative R is responsible for product P, then R sells P in A. Design a suitable relational structure for this data.

References and Bibliography

11.1 A. V. Aho, C. Beeri, and J. D. Ullman. "The Theory of Joins in Relational Databases." *ACM TODS 4*, No. 3 (September 1979). First published in Proc. 19th IEEE Symp. on Foundations of Computer Science (October 1977).

The paper that first pointed out that relations could exist that were not equal to the join of any two of their projections, but were equal to the join of three or more. The major objective of the paper was to present an algorithm, now generally called the **chase,** for determining whether or not a given JD is a logical consequence of a given set of FDs (an example of the **implication problem**—see reference [11.12]. This problem is equivalent to the problem of determining whether a given decomposition is nonloss, given a certain set of FDs. The paper also discusses the question of extending the algorithm to deal with the case where the given dependencies are not FDs but MVDs.

11.2 Catriel Beeri, Ronald Fagin, and John H. Howard. "A Complete Axiomatization for Functional and Multivalued Dependencies." Proc. 1977 ACM SIGMOD International Conference on Management of Data, Toronto, Canada (August 1977).

Extends the work of Armstrong [9.1] to include MVDs as well as FDs. In particular, it gives the following (sound and complete) set of inference rules for MVDs:

1. **Complementation:** If between them *A, B, C* include all attributes of the relation and *A* is a superset of $B \cap C$, then $A \twoheadrightarrow B$ if and only if $A \twoheadrightarrow C$.

2. **Reflexivity:** If *B* is a subset of *A* then $A \twoheadrightarrow B$.

3. **Augmentation:** If $A \twoheadrightarrow B$ and *C* is a subset of *D* then $AD \twoheadrightarrow BC$.

4. **Transitivity:** If $A \twoheadrightarrow B$ and $B \twoheadrightarrow C$ then $A \twoheadrightarrow C - B$.

The following additional (and useful) inference rules can be derived from those given above:

5. **Pseudotransitivity:** If $A \twoheadrightarrow B$ and $BC \twoheadrightarrow D$ then $AC \twoheadrightarrow D - BC$.

6. **Union:** If $A \twoheadrightarrow B$ and $A \twoheadrightarrow C$ then $A \twoheadrightarrow BC$.

7. **Decomposition:** If $A \twoheadrightarrow BC$ then $A \twoheadrightarrow B \cap C, A \twoheadrightarrow B - C$, and $A \twoheadrightarrow C - B$.

The paper then goes on to give two further rules by which certain FDs can be inferred from certain *combinations* of FDs and MVDs:

8. **Replication:** If $A \rightarrow B$ then $A \twoheadrightarrow B$.

9. **Coalescence:** If $A \twoheadrightarrow B$ and $C \rightarrow D$ and *D* is a subset of *B* and $B \cap C$ is empty, then $A \rightarrow D$.

Armstrong's rules (see Chapter 9) plus rules 1–4 and 8–9 above form a sound and complete set of rules for FDs and MVDs together.

The paper also derives one more useful rule relating FDs and MVDs:

10. If $A \twoheadrightarrow B$ and $AB \rightarrow C$ then $A \rightarrow C - B$.

11.3   Volkert Brosda and Gottfried Vossen. "Update and Retrieval Through a Universal Schema Interface." *ACM TODS 13,* No. 4 (December 1988).

Previous attempts at providing a universal relation interface (see reference [11.14]) deal with retrieval operations only. This paper develops an approach for dealing with update operations also—i.e., updates that are expressed (like retrievals) directly in terms of the universal relation.

11.4   C. Robert Carlson and Robert S. Kaplan. "A Generalized Access Path Model and Its Application to a Relational Data Base System." Proc. 1976 ACM SIGMOD International Conference on Management of Data, Washington, D.C. (June 1976).

See the annotation to reference [11.14].

11.5   C. J. Date. "Will the Real Fourth Normal Form Please Stand Up?" In C. J. Date and Hugh Darwen, *Relational Database Writings 1989–1991*. Reading, Mass.: Addison-Wesley (1992).

To paraphrase from the abstract: "There are several distinct notions in the database design world all laying claim to the title of *fourth normal form* (4NF). The purpose of this paper is to try to set the record straight."

11.6   C. J. Date and Ronald Fagin. "Simple Conditions for Guaranteeing Higher Normal Forms in Relational Databases." In C. J. Date and Hugh Darwen, *Relational Database Writings 1989–1991*. Reading, Mass.: Addison-Wesley (1992). Also in *ACM TODS 17,* No. 3 (September 1992).

Shows that if (a) relation *R* is in 3NF and (b) all candidate keys of *R* are simple (i.e., singleattribute), then *R* is automatically in 5NF. In other words, there is no need to worry in the case of such a relation about the comparatively complicated topics—MVDs, JDs, 4NF, 5NF—discussed in the present chapter. *Note:* The paper also proves another result, namely that if (a) *R* is in BCNF and (b) at least one of its candidate keys is simple, then *R* is automatically in 4NF, but not necessarily 5NF.

11.7   C. Delobel and D. S. Parker. "Functional and Multivalued Dependencies in a Relational Database and the Theory of Boolean Switching Functions." Tech. Report No. 142, Dept. Maths. Appl. et Informatique, Univ. de Grenoble, France (November 1978).

Extends the results of reference [9.3] to include MVDs as well as FDs.

11.8   Ronald Fagin. "Multivalued Dependencies and a New Normal Form for Relational Databases." *ACM TODS 2,* No. 3 (September 1977).

The new normal form was 4NF.

We add a note here on **embedded** multivalued dependencies. Suppose we extend relation CTX of Section 11.2 to include an additional attribute DAYS, representing the number of days spent with the indicated TEXT by the indicated TEACHER on the indicated COURSE. Let us refer to this relation as CTXD. Sample tabulation:

CTXD	COURSE	TEACHER	TEXT	DAYS
	Physics	Prof. Green	Basic Mechanics	5
	Physics	Prof. Green	Principles of Optics	5
	Physics	Prof. Brown	Basic Mechanics	6
	Physics	Prof. Brown	Principles of Optics	4
	Math	Prof. Green	Basic Mechanics	3
	Math	Prof. Green	Vector Analysis	3
	Math	Prof. Green	Trigonometry	4

The primary key here is the combination {COURSE,TEACHER,TEXT}, and we have the FD:

```
{ COURSE, TEACHER, TEXT } → DAYS
```

Observe that the relation *is* now in fourth normal form; it does not involve any MVDs that are not also FDs (refer back to the definitions of 4NF and MVD). However, it does include two *embedded* MVDs (of TEACHER on COURSE and TEXT on COURSE). The embedded MVD of *B* on *A* is said to hold in relation *R* if the "ordinary" MVD *A* → *B* holds in some projection of *R*. An ordinary MVD is a special case of an embedded MVD, but not all embedded MVDs are ordinary MVDs.

As the example illustrates, embedded MVDs imply redundancy, just like ordinary MVDs; however, that redundancy cannot be eliminated by taking projections. The relation shown above cannot be nonloss-decomposed into projections at all (in fact, it is in fifth normal form as well as fourth), because DAYS depends on all three of COURSE, TEACHER, and TEXT and so cannot appear in a relation with anything less than all three. Instead, therefore, the two embedded MVDs would have to be stated as additional, explicit constraints on the relation (see Chapter 16).

11.9   Ronald Fagin. "Normal Forms and Relational Database Operators." Proc. 1979 ACM SIGMOD International Conference on Management of Data, Boston, Mass. (May/June 1979).

This is the paper that introduced the concept of projection-join normal form (PJ/NF, or 5NF). However, it is also much more than that. It can be regarded as the definitive statement of what might be termed "classical" normalization theory—i.e., the theory of nonloss decomposition based on projection as the decomposition operator and natural join as the corresponding recomposition operator.

11.10   Ronald Fagin. "A Normal Form for Relational Databases That Is Based on Domains and Keys." *ACM TODS 6,* No. 3 (September 1981).

11.11   Ronald Fagin. "Acyclic Database Schemes (of Various Degrees): A Painless Introduction." IBM Research Report RJ3800 (April 1983). Republished in Proc. CAAP83 8th Colloquium on Trees in Algebra and Programming: Springer-Verlag Lecture Notes in Computer Science No. 159 (eds., G. Ausiello and M. Protasi). New York, N.Y.: Springer-Verlag (1983).

Section 11.3 of the present chapter showed how a certain ternary relation SPJ that satisfied a certain cyclic constraint could be nonloss-decomposed into its three binary projections. The resulting database structure (i.e., schema, called scheme in this paper) is said to be **cyclic,** because each of the three relations has an attribute in common with each of the other two. (If the structure is depicted as a *hypergraph,* in which edges represent individual relations and the node that is the intersection of two edges corresponds precisely to the attributes in common to those two edges, then it should be clear why the term "cyclic" is used.) By contrast, most of the structures that arise in practice tend to be acyclic. Acyclic structures enjoy a number of formal properties that do not apply to database structures in general. In this paper, Fagin presents and explains a list of such properties.

A helpful way to think about acyclicity is the following: Just as the theory of normalization can help in determining when *a single relation* should be restructured in some way, so the theory of acyclicity can help in determining when a *collection* of relations should be restructured in some way.

11.12   R. Fagin and M. Y. Vardi. "The Theory of Data Dependencies—A Survey." IBM Research Report RJ4321 (June 1984). Republished in *Mathematics of Information Processing: Proc. Symposia in Applied Mathematics 34,* American Mathematical Society (1986).

Provides a brief history of the subject of dependency theory as of the mid 1980s (note that "dependency" here does *not* refer to FDs only). In particular, the paper summarizes the major achievements in three specific areas within the overall field, and in so doing provides a good selected list of relevant references. The three areas are (1) the implication problem, (2) the universal relation model, and (3) acyclic schemas. The **implication problem** is the problem of determining, given a set of dependencies *D* and some specific dependency *d,* whether *d* is a logical consequence of *D* (see Section 9.7). The **universal relation model** and **acyclic schemas** (also known as acyclic *schemes*) are discussed, briefly, in the annotation to references [11.14] and [11.11], respectively.

11.13   Ronald Fagin, Alberto O. Mendelzon, and Jeffrey D. Ullman. "A Simplified Universal Relation Assumption and Its Properties." *ACM TODS 7,* No. 3 (September 1982).

Conjectures that the "real world" can always be represented by means of a universal relation [11.14] that satisfies precisely one join dependency plus a set of functional dependencies, and explores some of the consequences of that conjecture.

11.14   W. Kent. "Consequences of Assuming a Universal Relation." *ACM TODS 6,* No. 4 (December 1981).

The concept of the **universal relation** manifests itself in several different ways. First, the normalization discipline described in the last two chapters tacitly assumed that it is possible to define an initial universal relation that includes all of the attributes relevant to the database under consideration, and then showed how that relation can be replaced by successively smaller projections until some "good" structure is reached. But is that initial assumption realistic or justifiable? Reference [11.14] suggests not, on both practical and theoretical grounds. Reference [11.27] is a reply to reference [11.14], and reference [11.15] is a reply to that reply.

The second, and more pragmatically significant, manifestation of the universal relation concept is as a *user interface.* The basic idea here is quite straightforward, and indeed (from an intuitive standpoint) quite appealing: Users should frame their database requests, not in terms of relations and joins among those relations, but rather in terms of attributes alone. For example:

```
RETRIEVE STATUS WHERE COLOR = 'Red'
```

("Get status for suppliers who supply some red part"). At this point the idea forks into two more or less distinct interpretations:

1. One possibility is that the system should somehow determine for itself what logical access paths to follow (in particular, what joins to perform) in order to answer the query. This is the approach suggested in reference [11.4] (which seems to have been the first paper to discuss the possibility of a universal relation interface, although the term "universal relation" did not appear in the paper). This approach is critically dependent on proper naming of attributes. Thus, for example, the two supplier number attributes (in relations S and SP respectively) *must* be given the same name; conversely, the supplier city and part city attributes (in relations S and P respectively) must *not* be given the same name. If either of these two rules is violated, there will be certain queries that the system will be unable to handle properly.

2. The other, less ambitious, approach is simply to regard all queries as being formulated in terms of a *predefined* set of joins—in effect, a predefined view consisting of "the" join of all relations in the database.

While there is no question that either approach would greatly simplify the expression of many queries arising in practice—and indeed some such approach is essential to the support of any natural language interpreter—it is also clear that the system must support the ability to specify (logical) access paths explicitly as well, in general. To see that this must be so, consider the query

```
RETRIEVE STATUS WHERE COLOR ≠ 'Red'
```

Does this query mean "Get status of suppliers who supply a part that is not red" or "Get status of suppliers who do not supply a red part"? Whichever it is, there has to be some way of formulating the other. Come to that, the first example above is also susceptible to an alternative interpretation: "Get status for suppliers who supply *only* red parts." And here is a third example: "Get names of suppliers who are colocated." Here again it is clear that an explicit join will be necessary (because the problem involves a join of relation S with itself).

11.15 William Kent. "The Universal Relation Revisited." *ACM TODS 8,* No. 4 (December 1983).

11.16 Henry F. Korth *et al.* "System/U: A Database System Based on the Universal Relation Assumption." *ACM TODS 9,* No. 3 (September 1984).

Describes the theory, DDL, DML, and implementation of an experimental universal relation system built at Stanford University.

11.17 David Maier and Jeffrey D. Ullman. "Fragments of Relations." Proc. 1983 SIGMOD International Conference on Management of Data, San Jose, Calif. (May 1983).

11.18 David Maier, Jeffrey D. Ullman, and Moshe Y. Vardi. "On the Foundations of the Universal Relation Model." *ACM TODS 9,* No. 2 (June 1984). An earlier version of this paper, under the title "The Revenge of the JD," appeared in Proc. 2nd ACM SIGACT-SIGMOD Symposium on Principles of Database Systems, Atlanta, Ga. (March 1983).

11.19 David Maier and Jeffrey D. Ullman. "Maximal Objects and the Semantics of Universal Relation Databases." *ACM TODS 8,* No. 1 (March 1983).

Maximal objects represent an approach to the ambiguity problem that arises in universal relation systems when the underlying structure is not acyclic (see reference [11.11]). A maximal object corresponds to a predeclared subset of the attributes of the universal relation for which the underlying structure *is* acyclic. Such objects are then used to guide the interpretation of queries that would otherwise be ambiguous.

11.20 J. M. Nicolas. "Mutual Dependencies and Some Results on Undecomposable Relations." Proc. 4th International Conference on Very Large Data Bases, Berlin, FDR (September 1978).

Introduces the concept of "mutual dependency." A mutual dependency is actually a special case of the general join dependency—i.e., a JD that is not an MVD or FD—that happens to involve exactly three projections (like the JD example given in Section 11.3). It has nothing to do with the concept of mutual dependence discussed in Chapter 10.

11.21 Sylvia L. Osborn. "Towards a Universal Relation Interface." Proc. 5th International Conference on Very Large Data Bases, Rio de Janeiro, Brazil (October 1979).

The proposals of this paper assume that if there are two or more sequences of joins in a universal relation system that will generate a candidate answer to a given query, then the desired response is the union of all such candidates. Algorithms are given for generating all such sequences of joins.

11.22 D. Stott Parker and Claude Delobel. "Algorithmic Applications for a New Result on Multivalued Dependencies." Proc. 5th International Conference on Very Large Data Bases, Rio de Janeiro, Brazil (October 1979).

Applies the results of reference [11.7] to various problems, such as the problem of testing for a nonloss decomposition.

11.23 Y. Sagiv, C. Delobel, D. S. Parker, and R. Fagin. "An Equivalence between Relational Database Dependencies and a Subclass of Propositional Logic." *JACM 28*, No. 3 (June 1981).
Combines references [9.8] and [11.24].

11.24 Y. Sagiv and R. Fagin. "An Equivalence between Relational Database Dependencies and a Subclass of Propositional Logic." IBM Research Report RJ2500 (March 1979).

Extends the results of reference [9.8] to include MVDs as well as FDs.

11.25 E. Sciore. "A Complete Axiomatization of Full Join Dependencies." *JACM 29*, No. 2 (April 1982).

Extends the work of reference [11.2] to include JDs as well as FDs and MVDs.

11.26 J. M. Smith. "A Normal Form for Abstract Syntax." Proc. 4th International Conference on Very Large Data Bases, Berlin, FDR (September 1978).

The paper that introduced (3,3)NF.

11.27 Jeffrey D. Ullman. "On Kent's 'Consequences of Assuming a Universal Relation.'" *ACM TODS 8*, No. 4 (December 1983).

11.28 Jeffrey D. Ullman. "The U.R. Strikes Back." Proc. 1st ACM SIGACT-SIGMOD Symposium on Principles of Database Systems, Los Angeles, Calif. (March 1982).

Answers to Selected Exercises

11.1 Note first that R contains every possible A-value paired with every possible B-value, and further that the set of all A-values, S say, is the same as the set of all B-values. R is thus equal to the Cartesian product of set S with itself; equivalently, R is equal to the Cartesian product of the projection of R on A with the projection of R on B. R thus satisfies the following MVDs (which are *not* trivial, please observe, since they are certainly not satisfied by all relations):

$$\{ \ \} \ \twoheadrightarrow A \ | \ B$$

Equivalently, R satisfies the JD $*(A,B)$ (remember that join degenerates to Cartesian product when there are no common attributes).

It follows that R is not in 4NF. It is, however, in BCNF (it is all key), and it satisfies no nontrivial FDs.

Note: R also satisfies the MVDs

$A \twoheadrightarrow B \mid \{ \; \}$

and

$B \twoheadrightarrow A \mid \{ \; \}$

However, these MVDs *are* trivial, since they are satisfied by every binary relation with attributes A and B.

11.2 First we introduce three relations

```
REPS      ( REP#, ... )
          PRIMARY KEY ( REP# )

AREAS     ( AREA#, ... )
          PRIMARY KEY ( AREA# )

PRODUCTS ( PROD#, ... )
          PRIMARY KEY ( PROD# )
```

with the obvious interpretation. Second, we can represent the relationship between sales representatives and sales areas by a relation

```
RA ( REP#, AREA# )
   PRIMARY KEY ( REP#, AREA# )
```

and the relationship between sales representatives and products by a relation

```
RP ( REP#, PROD# )
   PRIMARY KEY ( REP#, PROD# )
```

(both of these are many-to-many relationships).

Next, we are told that every product is sold in every area. So if we introduce a relation

```
AP ( AREA#, PROD# )
   PRIMARY KEY ( AREA#, PROD# )
```

to represent the relationship between areas and products, then we have the constraint (let us call it C)

```
FORALL AX FORALL PX EXISTS APX ( APX.AREA# = AX.AREA# AND
                                 APX.PROD# = PX.PROD# )
```

(where AX, PX, APX are tuple variables for relations AREAS, PRODUCTS, AP, respectively). Notice that constraint C implies that relation AP is not in 4NF (see Exercise 11.1). In fact, relation AP does not give us any information that cannot be obtained from the other relations; to be precise, AP is equal at all times to the Cartesian product

```
AREAS [ AREA# ] TIMES PRODUCTS [ PROD# ]
```

Nevertheless, let us assume for the moment that relation AP *is* included in our design anyway.

No two representatives sell the same product in the same area. In other words, given an {AREA#,PROD#} combination, there is exactly one responsible sales representative (REP#), so we can introduce a relation

```
APR ( AREA#, PROD#, REP# )
   PRIMARY KEY ( AREA#, PROD# )
```

in which (to make the FD explicit)

```
{ AREA#, PROD# } → REP#
```

(of course, specification of the combination {AREA#,PROD#} as primary key is sufficient to express this FD). Now, however, relations RA, RP, and AP are all redundant, since they are all projections of APR; they can therefore all be dropped. In place of constraint C, we now need constraint C1:

```
FORALL AX FORALL PX EXISTS APRX ( APRX.AREA# = AX.AREA# AND
                                  APRX.PROD# = PX.PROD# )
```

(where APRX is a tuple variable for relation APR). Constraint C1 certainly needs to be stated explicitly if it is to be enforced by the DBMS—see Chapter 16—but should be stated explicitly in any case since it represents part of the semantics of the situation and needs to be understood by the user.

Also, since every representative sells all of that representative's products in all of that representative's areas, we have the additional constraint C2 on relation APR:

```
REP# →→ AREA# | PROD#
```

(an MVD; relation APR is not in 4NF). Again the constraint should be stated explicitly.

Thus the final design consists of relations REPS, AREAS, PRODUCTS, and APR, together with explicit constraints C1 and C2.

This exercise illustrates very clearly the point that, in general, the normalization discipline is adequate to represent *some* semantic aspects of a given problem (basically, dependencies that are implied by candidate keys, where by "dependencies" we mean FDs, MVDs, or JDs), but that explicit statement of additional dependencies might also be needed for other aspects, and some aspects cannot be represented in terms of such dependencies at all. It also illustrates the point (once again) that it is not always desirable to normalize "all the way" (relation APR is in BCNF but not in 4NF).

11.3 The revision is straightforward—all that is necessary is to replace the references to FDs and BCNF by analogous references to MVDs and 4NF, thus:

0. Initialize D to contain just R.

1. For each non4NF relation T in D, execute Steps 2–3.

2. Let $X →→ Y$ be an MVD in T that violates the requirements for 4NF.

3. Replace T in D by two of its projections, *viz.* that over X and Y and that over all attributes except those in Y.

11.4 This is a "cyclic constraint" example. The following design is therefore suitable:

```
REPS  ( REP#, ... )
      PRIMARY KEY ( REP# )

AREAS ( AREA#, ... )
      PRIMARY KEY ( AREA# )

PRODUCTS ( PROD#, ... )
         PRIMARY KEY ( PROD# )

RA ( REP#, AREA# )
   PRIMARY KEY ( REP#, AREA# )

RP ( REP#, PROD# )
   PRIMARY KEY ( REP#, PROD# )

AP ( AREA#, PROD# )
   PRIMARY KEY ( AREA#, PROD# )
```

Also, the user needs to be informed that the join of RA, RP, and AP does *not* involve any "connection trap."

12 | The Entity/Relationship Model

12.1 Introduction

The principal topic of this chapter, the entity/relationship model, is the best-known example of a class of data models usually known as "extended" or **semantic** models. Semantic modeling was the subject of much research in the late 1970s and early 1980s. The motivation for that research (i.e., the problem that the researchers were trying to solve) was as follows: Database systems generally—relational or otherwise—typically have only a very limited understanding of what the data in the database *means;* they typically "understand" certain simple atomic data values, and perhaps certain simple integrity constraints that apply to those values, but very little else (any more sophisticated interpretation is left to the human user). And it would be nice if systems could understand a little more, so that they could respond a little more intelligently to user interactions, and perhaps support more sophisticated (i.e., higher-level) user interfaces. For example, it would be nice if SQL could understand that part weights and shipment quantities, though of course both numeric values, are different in kind—i.e., *semantically* different—so that (e.g.) a request to join parts and shipments on the basis of matching weights and quantities could at least be questioned, if not rejected outright.

Of course, the notion of *domains* is very relevant to the foregoing example—which serves to illustrate the important point that existing data models are not totally devoid of all semantic aspects. For instance, domains, candidate keys, and foreign keys are all semantic aspects of the existing relational model. To put this another way, the various "extended" models that have been developed to address the semantics issue are only slightly more semantic than earlier models; to paraphrase Codd [12.5], capturing the meaning of the data is a never-ending task, and we can expect to see continuing developments in this area as our understanding continues to evolve. The term **semantic model,** often used (as already mentioned) to refer to one or other of the "extended" models, is thus not particularly apt, because it suggests that the model in question has somehow managed to capture *all* of the semantics of the situation under consideration. On the other hand, "semantic modeling" *is* an appropriate label for the overall activity of attempting to represent meaning. In this chapter we first present a short introduction to some of the ideas underlying that activity; we then examine one particular approach, the entity/relationship approach, in some depth.

Note: Semantic modeling is also known by a variety of other names (especially when the activity is being carried out in the context of database design for some specific enterprise or application—see later). Other terms that are frequently heard include *data* modeling, *entity/relationship* modeling, and *entity* modeling. We prefer the term *semantic* modeling for the following reasons:

■   We dislike "data modeling" because (a) it clashes with our previously established use of the term "data model" to mean a formal system consisting of objects, integrity rules, and operators, also because (b) it tends to reinforce the popular misconception—see, e.g., reference [4.12]—that a data model (in our sense) involves data structure *only*.

■   We also dislike "entity/relationship modeling" because it tends to suggest that there is just one specific approach to the problem, whereas, of course, many different approaches are possible in practice. However, the term "entity/relationship modeling" is well established, and indeed very popular and commonly encountered.

■   We have no deep-rooted objections to "entity modeling," except that it seems a little more specific as a label than "semantic modeling," and thus might suggest an emphasis that is not quite appropriate.

Anyway, let us return to the main thread of the discussion. Our reason for including this material in this part of the book is as follows: *Semantic modeling ideas can be useful as an aid to systematic database design, even in the absence of direct DBMS support for those ideas.* Thus, just as the ideas of the original relational model were used as a primitive database design aid well before there were any commercial implementations of that model, so the ideas of some given "extended" model can be useful as a design aid even if there are no commercial implementations of those ideas. At the time of writing, in fact, it is probably fair to say that the *major* impact of semantic modeling ideas has been in the area of database design—several design methodologies have been proposed that are based on one semantic modeling approach or another. For this reason, the major emphasis of this chapter is, specifically, on the application of semantic modeling ideas to the problem of database design.

Note: Design methodologies that are based on semantic modeling ideas are often referred to as **top-down** methodologies, because they start at a high level of abstraction with "real-world" constructs ("entities," etc.) and finish at the comparatively low level of abstraction represented by a specific concrete database design.

The plan of the chapter is as follows. Following this introductory section, Section 12.2 explains in general terms what is involved in semantic modeling. Section 12.3 then discusses the best known of the extended models, Chen's *entity/relationship* (E/R) model, and Sections 12.4 and 12.5 consider the application of that model to database design. Finally, Section 12.6 offers a brief analysis of certain aspects of the E/R model, and Section 12.7 gives a summary.

12.2 The Overall Approach

We can characterize the overall approach to the semantic modeling problem in terms of the following four steps.

1. First, we attempt to identify a set of *semantic* concepts that seem to be useful in talking informally about the real world.

   - For example, we might agree that the world is made up of **entities** (even though it is impossible to state with any precision exactly what an entity is and what it is not; despite this lack of precision, the entity concept does seem to be useful in talking about the world, at least intuitively).

   - We might go further and agree that entities can usefully be grouped into **entity types**. For example, we might agree that all individual employees are **instances** of the generic EMPLOYEE entity **type**. The advantage of such grouping is that all entities of a given type will have certain **properties** in common—e.g., all employees have a salary—and hence that the grouping can lead to some (fairly obvious) *economies of representation*. In relational terms, for example, the commonality is factored up into the relation heading.

   - We might go still further and agree that every entity has a special property that serves to *identify* that entity—i.e., every entity has an **identity**.

   - We might go further again and agree that any entity can be related to other entities by means of **relationships**.

   And so on. But note carefully that all of these terms (entity instance, entity type, property, relationship, etc.) are *not* precisely or formally defined—they are semantic terms merely, not formal terms. Step 1 is not a formal step. Steps 2–4 below, by contrast, are formal.

2. Next, we try to devise a set of corresponding *symbolic* (i.e., formal) **objects** that can be used to represent the foregoing semantic concepts. For example, the extended relational model RM/T [12.5] provides some special kinds of relations called *E-* and *P-relations*. Roughly speaking, E-relations represent entities and P-relations represent properties; however, E- and P-relations of course have formal definitions, whereas, as explained above, entities and properties do not.

3. We also devise a set of formal **integrity rules** to go along with those formal objects. For example, RM/T provides an integrity rule called *property integrity,* which says that every entry in a P-relation must have a corresponding entry in an E-relation (to reflect the fact that every property must be a property of some entity).

4. Finally, we also develop a set of formal **operators** for manipulating those formal objects. For example, RM/T provides a *PROPERTY* operator, which can be used to join together an E-relation and all of its corresponding P-relations, and thus to collect together all of the properties for a given entity.

The objects, rules, and operators of Steps 2–4 above together constitute an extended data model—"extended," that is, if those constructs are truly a superset of those of one of the basic models, such as the basic relational model; but there is not really a clear distinction in this context between what is extended and what is basic. *Note carefully, however, that the rules and operators are just as much part of the model as are the objects* (just as they are in the basic relational model). This fact notwithstanding, however, the operators are perhaps less important than the objects and integrity rules from the point of view of database design; the emphasis in the rest of this chapter is therefore on objects and rules rather than on operators, though we will offer a few comments regarding operators on occasion.

Step 1, to repeat, involves an attempt to identify a set of semantic concepts that seem to be useful in talking about the world. A few such concepts—entity, property, relationship, subtype—are shown in Fig. 12.1 by way of illustration. For each concept, the figure also gives an informal definition and a few typical examples. Note that the examples are deliberately chosen to illustrate the point that the very same object in the real world might legitimately be regarded as an entity by some people, as a property by others, and as a relationship by still others. (This point shows why it is impossible to

Concept	Informal definition	Examples
ENTITY	A distinguishable object	Supplier, Part, Shipment Employee, Department Person Composition, Concerto Orchestra, Conductor Purchase order, Order line
PROPERTY	A piece of information that describes an entity	Supplier number Shipment quantity Employee department Person height Concerto type Purchase order date

RELATIONSHIP	An entity that serves
	to interconnect two or
	more other entities
		Shipment (supplier-part)
		Assignment (employee-
		       department)
		Recording (composition-
		       orchestra-
		       conductor)

SUBTYPE	Entity type Y is a subtype
	of entity type X if and only
	if every Y is necessarily
	an X
		Employee is a subtype
		    of Person
		Concerto is a subtype
		    of Composition

FIG. 12.1 Some useful semantic concepts

give terms such as "entity" a precise definition, by the way.) It is a goal of semantic modeling—not yet fully achieved—to support such *flexibility of interpretation.*

One final remark: We pointed out in Chapter 1 that relationships are best regarded as entities in their own right, and said that we would generally treat them that way throughout this book. We also pointed out in Chapter 3 that one advantage of the relational model was precisely that it represented all entities, including relationships, in the same way—namely, by means of relations. Nevertheless, the relationship concept (like the entity concept) does seem to be *intuitively* useful in talking about the world; moreover, the approach to database design to be discussed in Sections 12.3–12.5 does rely heavily on the entity *vs.* relationship distinction. We therefore adopt the relationship terminology for the purposes of the next few sections. However, we will have more to say on this question in Section 12.6.

12.3   An Overview of the E/R Model

We turn now to the application of semantic modeling ideas to the problem of database design. As indicated in Section 12.1, one of the best known approaches—certainly one of the most widely used—is the so-called **entity/relationship** (E/R) approach, based on the "entity/relationship model" introduced by Chen in 1976 [12.3] and refined in various ways by Chen and numerous others since that time (see, e.g., references [12.4] and [12.28–12.29]). The remainder of this chapter is therefore devoted to a discussion of the E/R approach. (We should stress, however, that the E/R model is very far from being the only "extended" model—many, many others have been proposed. See, e.g., references [12.5], [12.13], [12.25], and particularly [12.19] for introductions to several others, also references [12.15] and [12.20] for tutorial surveys of the field.)

The E/R model includes analogs of all of the semantic objects listed in Fig. 12.1. Let us examine those objects one by one. (We should say immediately that most of the ideas to be discussed in what follows will already be broadly familiar to anyone who knows the relational model, although there are certain differences in terminology, as will be seen.) *Note:* Reference [12.3] not only introduced the E/R model *per se,* it also introduced a corresponding **diagramming technique** ("E/R diagrams"). We will discuss E/R diagrams in some detail in the next section; however, a simple example of such a diagram, based on a figure from reference [12.3], is shown in Fig. 12.2, and the reader might find it helpful to study that example in conjunction with the discussions below. The example represents the data for a simple manufacturing company (it is an extended version of the simple E/R diagram given in Chapter 1, Fig. 1.6).

Entities

Chen [12.3] begins by defining an entity as "a thing which can be distinctly identified." He then goes on to classify entities into **regular entities** and **weak entities**. A weak entity is an entity that is existence-dependent on some other entity, in the sense that it cannot exist if that other entity does not also exist. For example, referring to Fig. 12.2,

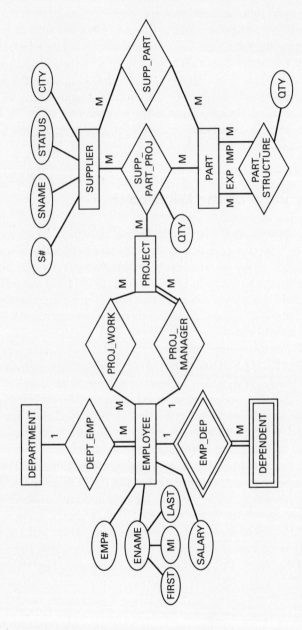

FIG. 12.2 Entity/relationship diagram (example)

an employee's dependents might be weak entities—they cannot exist (so far as the database is concerned) if the relevant employee does not exist. In particular, if a given employee is deleted, all dependents of that employee must be deleted also. A regular entity, by contrast, is an entity that is not weak; e.g., employees might be regular entities. Some writers use the term "strong entity" instead of "regular entity."

Properties

Entities (and relationships, *q.v.*) have properties (also known as *attributes;* we avoid this term since it already has a specific meaning in the relational model). All entities of a given type have certain kinds of properties in common—for example, all employees have an employee number, a name, a salary, and so on. (*Note:* We deliberately do not include "department number" as a property of employees in this example. See the discussion of relationships below.) Each kind of property draws its values from a corresponding **value set** (i.e., domain, in relational terms). Furthermore, properties can be:

- **Simple** or **composite** (e.g., the composite property "employee name" might be made up of the simple properties "first name," "middle initial," and "last name")
- **Key** (i.e., unique, possibly within some context; e.g., a dependent's name might be unique only within the context of a given employee)
- **Single-** or **multi-valued** (i.e., repeating groups are permitted; this concept is not illustrated in Fig. 12.2)
- **Missing** (e.g., "unknown" or "not applicable"; this concept is not illustrated in Fig. 12.2)
- **Base** or **derived** (e.g., "total quantity" for a given part might be derived as the sum of the individual shipment quantities for that part; this concept is not illustrated in Fig. 12.2)

Relationships

Reference [12.3] defines a relationship as "an association among entities." For example, there is a relationship (DEPT_EMP) between departments and employees, representing the fact that a given department employs a given set of employees. As with entities, it is necessary in principle to distinguish between relationship *types* and relationship *instances,* but it is common to ignore such refinements in informal discussion, and we will often do so ourselves.

The entities involved in a given relationship are said to be the **participants** in that relationship. The number of participants in a given relationship is called the **degree** of that relationship. Note that this term therefore does not mean quite the same thing as "degree" in the relational model.

Let R be a relationship type that involves entity type E as a participant. If every instance of E participates in at least one instance of R, then the participation of E in R is said to be **total,** otherwise it is said to be **partial**. For example, if every part must be supplied by at least one supplier, then the participation of parts in SUPP_PART is total;

but if it is possible for a given part to be supplied by no supplier at all, then the participation of parts in SUPP_PART is partial.

An E/R relationship can be **one-to-one, one-to-many** (also known as **many-to-one**), or **many-to-many** (we assume for simplicity that all relationships are binary, i.e.,
degree two; extending the concepts, and the terminology, to relationships of degree
greater than two is essentially straightforward, of course). Now, a reader familiar with
the relational model might be tempted to think of the many-to-many case as the only
one that is a genuine relationship, since that case is the only one that demands representation by means of a separate relation (one-to-one and one-to-many relationships can
always be represented by means of a foreign key in one of the participant relations).
However, there are good reasons to treat the one-to-one and one-to-many cases just like
the many-to-many case, at least if there is any possibility that they could ever evolve
and become many-to-many over time. Only if there is no such possibility is it safe to
treat them differently. (Of course, sometimes there *is* no such possibility. For example,
it will always be true that a circle has exactly one point that is its center.)

Subtypes

*Note: The ideas discussed in this subsection were not included in the original E/R
model of reference [12.3] but were added later. See, e.g., Teorey, Yang, and Fry
[12.28].*

Any given entity is of at least one entity type, but an entity can be of several types
simultaneously. For example, if some employees are programmers (and all programmers are employees), then we might say that PROGRAMMER is a **subtype** of the
EMPLOYEE **supertype**. All properties of employees apply automatically to programmers, but the converse is not true (e.g., programmers might have a property "primary
programming language skill," which does not apply to employees in general). Likewise, programmers automatically participate in all relationships in which employees
participate, but the converse is not true (e.g., programmers might belong to some professional computer society, while employees in general do not). We say that properties
and relationships that apply to the supertype are **inherited** by the subtype. *Note:* Inheritance will be discussed in more detail in Chapter 19.

Note further that some programmers might be application programmers and others
might be system programmers; thus we might say that APPLICATION_PROGRAMMER
and SYSTEM_PROGRAMMER are both subtypes of the PROGRAMMER supertype
(and so on). In other words, an entity subtype is still an entity *type,* and can thus have
subtypes of its own. A given entity type and its immediate subtypes, their immediate
subtypes, and so on, together constitute the **type hierarchy** for the entity type in question. See Fig. 12.3 for an example.

For the benefit of readers who might be familiar with IMS (or some other system
that supports a hierarchic data structure), we remark that type hierarchies should not be
confused with IMS-style hierarchies. In Fig. 12.3, for example, there is no suggestion
that for one EMPLOYEE there are many corresponding PROGRAMMERs (as there
would be if the figure was meant to represent an IMS-style hierarchy); on the contrary,

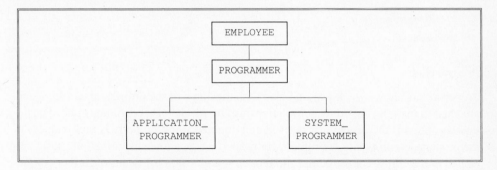

FIG. 12.3 Example of a type hierarchy

for one instance of EMPLOYEE there is *at most one* corresponding PROGRAMMER, representing that same EMPLOYEE in his or her PROGRAMMER role.

This brings us to the end of our brief discussion of the major structural features of the E/R model. Now let us turn our attention to E/R diagrams.

12.4   E/R Diagrams

As explained in the previous section, reference [12.3] not only introduced the E/R model *per se,* it also introduced the concept of **entity/relationship diagrams**. E/R diagrams constitute a technique for representing the logical structure of a database in a pictorial manner. As such, they provide a simple and readily understood means of communicating the salient features of the design of any given database ("a picture is worth a thousand words"). Indeed, the popularity of the E/R model as an approach to database design can probably be attributed more to the existence of the E/R diagramming technique than to any other cause. We describe the rules for constructing an E/R diagram in terms of the examples already given in Figs. 12.2 and 12.3.

Note: Like the E/R model itself, the E/R diagramming technique has evolved somewhat over time. The version we describe in this section differs in certain important respects from the one originally described by Chen in reference [12.3].

Entities

Each entity type is shown as a rectangle, labeled with the name of the entity type in question. For a weak entity type, the rectangle is doubled.

Examples (see Fig. 12.2):

■   Regular entities:

DEPARTMENT
EMPLOYEE
SUPPLIER
PART
PROJECT

■   Weak entity:

DEPENDENT

Properties

Properties are shown as ellipses, labeled with the name of the property in question and attached to the relevant entity (or relationship) by means of a continuous line. The ellipse is dotted if the property is derived and doubled if the property is multivalued. If the property is composite, its component properties are shown as further ellipses, connected to the ellipse for the composite property in question by means of further continuous lines. Key properties are underlined. Value sets are not shown.

Examples (see Fig. 12.2):

■   For EMPLOYEE:

EMP# (key)
ENAME (composite, consisting of FIRST, MI, and LAST)
SALARY

■   For SUPPLIER:

S# (key)
SNAME
STATUS
CITY

■   For SUPP_PART_PROJ:

QTY

■   For PART_STRUCTURE:

QTY

All other properties are omitted from Fig. 12.2 for reasons of space.

Relationships

Each relationship type is shown as a diamond, labeled with the name of the relationship type in question. The diamond is doubled if the relationship in question is that between a weak entity type and the entity type on which its existence depends. The participants in each relationship are connected to the relevant relationship by means of continuous lines; each such line is labeled "1" or "M" to indicate whether the relationship is one-to-one, many-to-one, etc. The line is doubled if the participation is total.

Examples (see Fig. 12.2):

■   DEPT_EMP (one-to-many relationship between DEPARTMENT and EMPLOYEE)

■   EMP_DEP (one-to-many relationship between EMPLOYEE and DEPENDENT, a weak entity type)

■   PROJ_WORK and PROJ_MANAGER (both relationships between EMPLOYEE and PROJECT, the former many-to-many, the latter one-to-many)

- SUPP_PART_PROJ (many-to-many-to-many relationship involving SUPPLIER, PART, and PROJECT)

- SUPP_PART (many-to-many relationship between SUPPLIER and PART)

- PART_STRUCTURE (many-to-many relationship between PART and PART)

  Observe in this last case that the two lines from PART to PART_STRUCTURE are distinguished by labeling them with two distinct "role names" (EXP and IMP, for "part explosion" and "part implosion" respectively). PART_STRUCTURE is an example of what is sometimes called a **recursive relationship**.

Subtypes and Supertypes

Let *Y* be a subtype of *X*. Then we draw a continuous line from *Y* to *X,* marked with a hook to represent the mathematical "subset of" operator (because the set of all *Y*'s is a subset of the set of all *X*'s).

Examples (see Fig. 12.3—but note that the hooks are omitted in that figure):

- PROGRAMMER is a subtype of EMPLOYEE

- APPLICATION_PROGRAMMER and SYSTEM_PROGRAMMER are subtypes of PROGRAMMER

12.5 Database Design with the E/R Model

In a sense, an entity/relationship diagram constructed in accordance with the rules described in the previous section *is* a (rather abstract) database design. If we attempt to map such a design into the formalisms of a specific DBMS, however, we will soon discover that the E/R diagram is still very imprecise in certain respects and leaves a number of details unspecified (especially integrity details). To illustrate the point, we consider what is involved in mapping a design such as that of Fig. 12.2 into a relational database definition.

Regular Entities

To repeat, the regular entities in Fig. 12.2 are as follows:

```
DEPARTMENT
EMPLOYEE
SUPPLIER
PART
PROJECT
```

Each regular entity type maps into a base relation. The database will thus contain five base relations, say DEPT, EMP, S, P, and J, corresponding to these five entity types. Furthermore, each of those base relations will have a primary key—DEPT#, EMP#, S#, P#, and J#, say—corresponding to the "keys" identified in the E/R diagram. We will document these facts by writing an appropriate set of data definition language

(DDL) statements, or at least the beginnings of such a set of statements.* Here, for example, is the statement for the DEPT relation (in outline):

```
CREATE BASE RELATION DEPT
     ( DEPT# DOMAIN ( DEPT# ) ... )
       PRIMARY KEY ( DEPT# ) ;
```

The others are left as an exercise for the reader to complete. *Note:* The domains or "value sets" need to be documented too. We omit detailed discussion of this aspect, since as already mentioned the value sets are not shown in the E/R diagram.

Many-to-Many Relationships

The many-to-many (or many-to-many-to-many, etc.) relationships in the example are as follows:

```
PROJ_WORK (involving employees and projects)
SUPP_PART (involving suppliers and parts)
SUPP_PART_PROJ (involving suppliers, parts, and projects)
PART_STRUCTURE (involving parts and parts)
```

Each such relationship also maps into a base relation. We therefore introduce four more base relations corresponding to these four relationships. Let the relation for the SUPP_PART association be SP (the usual suppliers-and-parts relation). Let us defer for a moment the question of the primary key for this relation, and concentrate instead on the matter of the *foreign* keys that are necessary in order to identify the participants in the relationship:

```
CREATE BASE RELATION SP
     ( S# ... , P# ... , ... )
       .....
       FOREIGN KEY ( S# ) REFERENCES S
       FOREIGN KEY ( P# ) REFERENCES P ;
```

Clearly, the relation must include two foreign keys (S# and P#) corresponding to the two participants (suppliers and parts), and those foreign keys must reference the corresponding participant relations S and P. Furthermore, an appropriate set of foreign key rules—i.e., a delete rule and an update rule[†]—must be specified for each of those foreign keys (refer to Chapter 5 if you need to refresh your memory regarding these rules). In the case of relation SP, we might specify the following rules. (The specific rules shown are only by way of illustration, of course; note in particular that they are *not* pinned down by the E/R diagram.)

---

* In other words, we are suggesting the use of DDL statements as a means for recording design decisions. DDL statements are not the only way of performing this function, of course, but whatever formalism is used must be functionally equivalent to such statements. Our use of DDL statements in the present section should be interpreted in this light.

[†] We remind the reader that we are ignoring null support until Chapter 20. In particular, we do not entertain the possibility that a foreign key might permit nulls, which implies that we ignore both the foreign key nulls rule and the NULLIFIES option on the foreign key delete and update rules.

```
CREATE BASE RELATION SP
     ( S# ... , P# ... , ... )
     .....
          FOREIGN KEY ( S# ) REFERENCES S
                    DELETE RESTRICTED
                    UPDATE CASCADES
          FOREIGN KEY ( P# ) REFERENCES P
                    DELETE RESTRICTED
                    UPDATE CASCADES ;
```

What about the primary key for this relation? One possibility would be to take the combination of the participant-identifying foreign keys (S# and P#, in the case of SP)— *if* that combination has a unique value for each instance of the relationship (which might or might not be the case, but usually is), and *if* it has NULLS NOT ALLOWED (which also might or might not be the case, but usually is),* and *if* the database designer has no objection to composite primary keys (which might or might not be the case). Alternatively, a new noncomposite attribute, "shipment number" say, might be introduced to serve as the primary key. For the sake of the example, we will go with the first of these two possibilities, and so add the clause

```
PRIMARY KEY ( S#, P# )
```

to the CREATE BASE RELATION statement for relation SP.

Consideration of the PROJ_WORK, PART_STRUCTURE, and SUPP_PART_PROJ relationships is left as an exercise for the reader.

Many-to-One Relationships

There are three many-to-one relationships in the example:

PROJ_MANAGER (from projects to managers)
DEPT_EMP (from employees to departments)
EMP_DEP (from dependents to employees)

Of these three, the last involves a weak entity type (DEPENDENT), the other two involve only regular entity types. We will discuss the weak entity case in a moment; for now, let us concentrate on the other two cases. Consider the DEPT_EMP example. This example does *not* cause the introduction of any new relations. Instead, we simply introduce a foreign key in the relation on the "many" side of the relationship (EMP) that references the relation on the "one" side (DEPT), as follows:

```
CREATE BASE RELATION EMP
     ( EMP# ... , DEPT# ... , ... )
        PRIMARY KEY ( EMP# )
        FOREIGN KEY ( DEPT# ) REFERENCES DEPT
                  DELETE ...
                  UPDATE ... ;
```

---

* This condition is required if we wish to satisfy the entity integrity rule for relation SP. In any case (as mentioned earlier), all foreign keys *will* have NULLS NOT ALLOWED so far as we are concerned, so the point is irrelevant anyway.

The foreign key rule possibilities here are exactly the same as those for a foreign key that represents a participant in a many-to-many relationship (in general). Observe once again that they are not pinned down by the E/R diagram.

Note: For the sake of the present exposition, we will assume that one-to-one relationships (which in any case are not all that common in practice) are treated in exactly the same way as many-to-one relationships. Reference [12.9] contains an extended discussion of the special problems of the one-to-one case.

Weak Entities

The relationship from a weak entity type to the entity type on which it depends is of course a many-to-one relationship, as indicated in the previous subsection. However, the foreign key rules for that relationship *must* be as follows:*

```
DELETE CASCADES
UPDATE CASCADES
```

These rules together capture and reflect the necessary existence dependence. Here is an example:

```
CREATE BASE RELATION DEPENDENT
     ( EMP# ... )
     .....
        FOREIGN KEY ( EMP# ) REFERENCES EMP
                   DELETE CASCADES
                   UPDATE CASCADES ;
```

What is the primary key for such a relation? As with the case of many-to-many relationships, it turns out we have a choice. One possibility is to take the combination of the foreign key and the weak entity "key" from the E/R diagram—*if* (once again) the database designer has no objection to composite primary keys. Alternatively, we might introduce a new, noncomposite attribute to serve as the primary key. For the sake of the example again, we will go with the first of the two possibilities, and so add the clause

```
PRIMARY KEY ( EMP#, DEP_NAME )
```

(where DEP_NAME is the name of the employee's dependent) to the CREATE BASE RELATION statement for relation DEPENDENT.

Properties

Each property shown in the E/R diagram maps into an attribute in the appropriate relation—except that, if the property is multivalued, we create a new relation for it in accordance with the principles of normalization. Domains are created for value sets in the obvious way (though deciding the value sets in the first place might not be quite so obvious, of course!). Details of these steps are straightforward and are omitted here.

---

* Also, the nulls rule, if specified, *must* be NULLS NOT ALLOWED.

Supertypes and Subtypes

Since Fig. 12.2 does not involve any supertypes and subtypes, let us switch to the example of Fig. 12.3. Each entity type in that figure will map into a base relation of its own; each such relation will contain attributes corresponding to the properties that apply at the relevant position within the type hierarchy (and hence to all subordinate positions, by inheritance, but not to any superior positions). Let us concentrate on the relations, EMP and PGMR say, corresponding to the entity types EMPLOYEE and PROGRAMMER:

```
CREATE BASE RELATION EMP
     ( EMP#    ... , DEPT# ... , SALARY ... , ... )
       PRIMARY KEY ( EMP# ) ;
CREATE BASE RELATION PGMR
     ( EMP#    ... , LANG ... , ... )
       PRIMARY KEY ( EMP# )
       FOREIGN KEY ( EMP# ) REFERENCES EMP ... ;
```

Here the attribute LANG represents the property "primary programming language skill," which applies only to those employees that happen to be programmers. Observe that relations EMP and PGMR both have the same primary key (EMP#), and furthermore that the primary key for the subtype (PGMR) also serves as a foreign key, referring back to the primary key of the supertype (EMP). Deciding an appropriate set of foreign key rules for that foreign key is left as an exercise for the reader (see Chapter 19, Exercise 19.4). Consideration of the other entity types in Fig. 12.3 (APPLICATION_PROGRAMMER and SYSTEM_PROGRAMMER) is left as an exercise also.

12.6   A Brief Analysis

In this section we briefly examine certain aspects of the E/R model in a little more depth. The discussions that follow are taken for the most part from an extended examination of the same topics by the present author in reference [12.7].

The E/R Model as a Foundation for the Relational Model?

We begin by considering the E/R approach from a slightly different perspective. It is probably obvious to the reader that the ideas of the E/R approach, or something very close to those ideas, must have been the *in*formal underpinnings in Codd's mind when he first developed the *formal* relational model. As explained in Section 12.2, the overall approach to semantic modeling involves four broad steps, which we can summarize as follows:

1. Identify useful semantic concepts
2. Devise formal objects
3. Devise formal integrity rules
4. Devise formal operators

Observe that these four steps are also applicable to the design of the *basic* relational model (and indeed to any formal data model), not just to "extended" models such as the E/R model. In other words, in order for Codd to have constructed the (formal) basic relational model in the first place, he must have had some (informal) "useful semantic concepts" in his mind, and those concepts must basically have been those of the E/R model, or something very like them. Indeed, Codd's own writings support this contention. In his very first paper on the relational model (reference [4.2]), we find the following:

> "The set of entities of a given entity type can be viewed as a relation, and we shall call such a relation an *entity type relation* . . . The remaining relations . . . are between entity types and are . . . called *inter-entity relations* . . . An essential property of every inter-entity relation is that [it includes at least two foreign keys that] either refer to distinct entity types or refer to a common entity type serving distinct roles."

Here Codd is clearly proposing that relations be used to model both "entities" and "relationships." But—and it is a very big but—the point is that *relations are formal objects, and the relational model is a formal system*. The essence of Codd's contribution was that he found a good *formal* model of certain aspects of the real world.

In contrast to the foregoing, the entity/relationship model is *not* (or, at least, not primarily) a formal model. Instead, it consists primarily of a set of *in*formal concepts, corresponding to Step 1 (only) of the four steps mentioned above. (Furthermore, what formal aspects it does possess do not seem to be significantly different from the corresponding aspects of the basic relational model— see the further discussion of this point in the next subsection below.) And while it is unquestionably useful to have an armory of "Step 1" concepts at one's disposal for database design purposes (among others), the fact remains that database designs cannot be completed without the formal objects and rules of Steps 2 and 3, and numerous other tasks cannot be performed at all without the formal operators of Step 4.

Please note that the foregoing remarks are not intended to suggest that the E/R model is not useful. It is. But it is not the whole story. Moreover, it is a little strange to realize that the first published description of the *in*formal E/R model appeared several years after the first published description of the *formal* relational model, given that (as we have seen) the latter was originally founded on some rather E/R-like ideas.

Is the E/R Model a Data Model?

In the light of the discussions above, it is not even clear that the E/R "model" is truly a data model at all, at least in the sense in which we have been using that term in this book so far (i.e., as a formal system involving structural, integrity, and manipulative aspects). Certainly the term "E/R modeling" is usually taken to mean the process of deciding the *structure* (only) of the database, although we did include some consideration of integrity aspects also in our discussions in Sections 12.3-12.5. However, a charitable reading of Chen's original paper would suggest that the E/R model is indeed a data model, but one that is essentially just *a thin layer on top of the basic relational model* (it is certainly not a candidate for replacing the relational model, as some people seem to think). We justify this claim as follows.

■ First, the fundamental E/R data object—that is, the fundamental *formal* object, as opposed to the informal objects "entity," "relationship," etc.—is the *n*-ary relation.

■ The E/R operators are basically the operators of the relational algebra. (Actually, reference [12.3] is not very clear on this point, but it seems to propose a set of operators that are strictly less powerful than those of the relational algebra; for example, there is apparently no union and no explicit join.)

■ It is in the area of integrity that the two approaches differ from each other somewhat: The E/R model includes a set of *builtin* integrity rules, corresponding to some but not all of the foreign key rules discussed in Chapter 5 of this book. Thus, where a "pure" relational system would require the user to formulate certain foreign key rules explicitly, an E/R system would require only that the user state that a given relation represents a certain kind of relationship, and certain foreign key rules would then be understood.

Entities *vs.* Relationships

We have indicated several times already in this book that "relationships" are best regarded merely as a special kind of entity. By contrast, it is a *sine qua non* of the E/R approach that the two concepts be distinguished somehow. In this writer's opinion, any approach that insists on making such a distinction is seriously flawed, because (as mentioned in Section 12.2) *the very same object* can quite legitimately be regarded as an entity by some users and a relationship by others. Consider the case of a marriage, for example:

■ From one perspective, a marriage is clearly a relationship between two people. Sample query: "Who was Elizabeth Taylor married to in 1975?"

■ From another perspective, a marriage is equally clearly an entity in its own right. Sample query: "How many marriages have been performed in this church since April?"

If the design methodology insists on the "entity *vs.* relationship" distinction, then (at best) the two interpretations will be treated asymmetrically (i.e., "entity" queries and "relationship" queries will take quite different forms); at worst, one interpretation will not be supported at all (i.e., one class of query will be impossible to formulate).

As a further illustration of the point, consider the following statement from a tutorial on the E/R approach in reference [12.10]:

"It is common *initially* to represent some relationships as attributes [meaning, specifically, foreign keys] during conceptual schema design and then to convert these attributes into relationships as the design progresses and is better understood."

But what happens if an attribute *becomes* a foreign key at some later time?—i.e., if the database evolves after it has already been in existence for some time? If we take this argument to its logical conclusion, database designs should involve only relationships, no attributes at all!

12.7   Summary

We opened this chapter by presenting a brief introduction to the general idea of **semantic modeling**. There are four broad steps involved, of which the first is informal and the rest are formal:

1. Identify useful semantic concepts
2. Devise corresponding symbolic objects
3. Devise corresponding integrity rules
4. Devise corresponding operators

Some useful semantic concepts are **entity, property, relationship,** and **subtype**.

The ultimate objective of semantic modeling research is to make database systems a little more intelligent. A more immediate objective is to provide a basis for a systematic attack on the problem of **database design**. We described the application of one particular "semantic" model, Chen's **entity/relationship (E/R) model,** to the design problem.

In connection with the foregoing, the point is worth repeating from Section 12.3 that Chen's original paper [12.3] actually contained two distinct, and more or less independent, proposals: It proposed the E/R model *per se,* and it also proposed **the E/R diagramming technique**. As we stated in Section 12.4, the popularity of the E/R model can probably be attributed more to the existence of that diagramming technique than to any other cause. But the point is, it is not necessary to adopt all of the ideas of the *model* in order to use the *diagrams;* it is quite possible to use E/R diagrams as a basis for *any* design methodology—an RM/T-based methodology, for example, as described in reference [12.6]. Arguments regarding the relative suitability of the E/R and other models as a basis for database design often seem to miss this point.

Let us also contrast the ideas of semantic modeling (and of the E/R model in particular) with the normalization discipline as described in Chapters 10–11. The normalization discipline involves reducing large relations to smaller ones; it assumes that we have some small number of large relations as input, and it manipulates that input to produce a large number of small relations as output—i.e., it maps large relations into small ones (speaking *very* loosely, of course!). But the normalization discipline has absolutely nothing to say about how we arrive at those large relations in the first place. Top-down methodologies such as the one described in the present chapter, by contrast, address exactly that problem; they map the real world into large relations. In other words, the two approaches (top-down design and normalization) *complement each other*. The overall suggested design procedure thus runs as follows:

1. Use the E/R approach or some other top-down methodology to generate "large" relations representing regular entities, weak entities, etc., and then
2. Use the ideas of further normalization to break those "large" relations down into "small" ones.

However, the reader will have realized from the quality of the discussions in the body of the chapter that semantic modeling as a discipline is not nearly so rigorous or clearcut as the further normalization discipline discussed in Chapters 10–11. The reason for this state of affairs is that (as indicated in the introduction to this part of the book) database design is still very much a subjective exercise, not an objective one; there is comparatively little by way of really solid principles that can be brought to bear on the problem (the few principles that do exist being, of course, basically the principles of normalization). The ideas of the present chapter can be regarded as more in the way of rules of thumb, albeit ones that do seem to work reasonably well in practical situations.

There is one final point that is worth calling out explicitly. Despite the unfortunate fact that the whole field is still somewhat subjective, there is one specific area in which semantic modeling ideas can be very relevant and useful today—namely, the **data dictionary** area. The data dictionary can be regarded in some respects as "the database designer's database"; it is after all a database in which the database designer records his or her design decisions [12.2]. The study of semantic modeling can thus be extremely useful in the design of the dictionary system, because it identifies the kinds of object the dictionary itself needs to support and "understand"—for example, entity categories (such as the E/R model's regular and weak entities), integrity rules (such as the E/R model's notion of total *vs.* partial participation in a relationship), entity supertypes and subtypes, and so forth.

Exercises

12.1 What do you understand by the term "semantic modeling"?

12.2 Identify the four broad steps involved in defining an "extended" model such as the E/R model.

12.3 Define the following E/R terms:

   entity

   regular entity

   weak entity

   relationship

   property

   key property

   supertype, subtype

   type hierarchy

   inheritance

12.4 Give examples of:

   (a) a many-to-many relationship in which one of the participants is a weak entity;

   (b) a many-to-many relationship in which one of the participants is another relationship;

   (c) a many-to-many relationship that has a subtype;

   (d) a subtype that has an associated weak entity that does not apply to the supertype.

12.5 Draw an E/R diagram for the education database from Exercise 5.3 in Chapter 5.

12.6 Draw an E/R diagram for the company personnel database from Exercise 10.3 in Chapter 10. Use that diagram to derive an appropriate set of base relations.

12.7 Draw an E/R diagram for the order-entry database from Exercise 10.4 in Chapter 10. Use that diagram to derive an appropriate set of base relations.

12.8 Draw an E/R diagram for the sales database from Exercise 11.2 in Chapter 11. Use that diagram to derive an appropriate set of base relations.

12.9 Draw an E/R diagram for the revised sales database from Exercise 11.4 in Chapter 11. Use that diagram to derive an appropriate set of base relations.

References and Bibliography

See also some of the references in Chapter 2, especially the ISO report on the conceptual schema [2.3], Winsberg's overview of data dictionary standardization activities [2.6], and Kent's book *Data and Reality* [2.7].

12.1 J. R. Abrial. "Data Semantics." In J. W. Klimbie and K. L. Koffeman (eds.): *Data Base Management.* Amsterdam, Netherlands: North-Holland / New York, NY: Elsevier Science (1974).

One of the very earliest proposals in the semantic modeling area. The following quote nicely captures the general flavor of the paper (some might say of the subject in general): "Hint for the reader: If you are looking for a definition of the term *semantics,* stop reading because there is no such definition in this paper."

12.2 Frank W. Allen, Mary E. S. Loomis, and Michael V. Mannino. "The Integrated Dictionary-Directory System." *ACM Comp. Surv. 14,* No. 2 (June 1982).

A tutorial on the data dictionary, with a brief survey of available products as of 1982.

12.3 Peter Pin-Shan Chen. "The Entity-Relationship Model—Toward a Unified View of Data." *ACM TODS 1,* No. 1 (March 1976). Republished in M. Stonebraker (ed.): *Readings in Database Systems.* San Mateo, Calif.: Morgan Kaufmann (1988).

The paper that introduced the E/R model and E/R diagrams. As mentioned in the body of the chapter, the model has been revised and refined considerably over time; certainly the explanations and definitions given in this first paper were quite imprecise, so that such revisions were definitely needed. (One of the criticisms of the E/R model has always been that the terms do not seem to have a single, well-defined meaning but are instead interpreted in many different ways [12.4,12.17]. Of course, it is true that the whole database field is bedeviled by inaccurate and conflicting terminology, but this particular area is worse than most.) Here are some examples:

■ As stated in Section 12.3, an entity is defined as "a thing which can be distinctly identified" and a relationship as "an association among entities." The first question that arises, then, is the following: Is a relationship an entity? A relationship is clearly "a thing which can be distinctly identified," but later sections of the paper seem to reserve the term "entity" to mean something that is definitely *not* a relationship. Presumably this latter is the intended interpretation, for otherwise why "entity/relationship model"? But the paper really is not clear.

■ Entities and relationships can have *attributes* (we used the term "property" in the body of the chapter). Again, the paper is ambivalent as to the meaning of the term—at first it defines an attribute to be a property that is not the primary key, nor any component thereof (contrast the relational definition), but later it uses the term in the standard relational sense.

- The primary key for a relationship is assumed to be the combination of the foreign keys identifying the entities involved in the relationship (the term "foreign key" is not used, however). This assumption is appropriate only for many-to-many relationships, and not always even then. For example, consider the relation SPD {S#,P#,DATE,QTY}, representing shipments of certain parts by certain suppliers on certain dates; assume that the same supplier can ship the same part more than once, but not more than once on the same date. Then the primary key is the combination {S#,P#,DATE}; yet we might choose to regard suppliers and parts as entities but dates not.

12.4 Peter Pin-Shan Chen. "A Preliminary Framework for Entity-Relationship Models." In P. P.-S. Chen (ed.), *Entity-Relationship Approach to Information Modeling and Analysis.* ER Institute, PO Box 617, Saugus, Calif. 91350 (1981).

12.5 E. F. Codd. "Extending the Database Relational Model to Capture More Meaning." *ACM TODS 4,* No. 4 (December 1979).

The paper that introduced the extended relational model RM/T. Some immediate differences between RM/T and the E/R model are as follows. First, RM/T makes no unnecessary distinctions between entities and relationships (a relationship is regarded merely as a special kind of entity). Second, the structural and integrity aspects of RM/T are more extensive, and more precisely defined, than those of the E/R model. Third, RM/T includes its own special operators, over and above the operators of the basic relational model (though much additional work remains to be done in this last area).

In outline, RM/T works as follows:

- First, entities (including "relationships") are represented by *E-relations* and *P-relations,* both of which are special forms of the general *n*-ary relation. E-relations are used to record the fact that certain entities exist, and P-relations are used to record certain properties of those entities.

- Second, a variety of relationships can exist among entities—for example, entity types *A* and *B* might be linked together in an **association** (RM/T's term for a many-to-many relationship), or entity type *Y* might be a **subtype** of entity type *X*. RM/T includes a formal **catalog** structure by which such relationships can be made known to the system; the system is thus capable of enforcing the various **integrity constraints** that are implied by the existence of such relationships.

- Third, a number of high-level **operators** are provided to facilitate the manipulation of the various RM/T objects (E-relations, P-relations, catalog relations, etc.).

Like the E/R model, RM/T includes analogs of all of the constructs (entity, property, relationship, subtype) listed in Fig. 12.1. Specifically, it provides an **entity classification scheme,** which in many respects constitutes the most significant aspect—or, at least, the most immediately visible aspect—of the entire model. Entities are divided into three categories, namely *kernels, characteristics,* and *associations:*

- **Kernels:** Kernel entities are entities that have *independent existence;* they are "what the database is really all about." In other words, kernels are entities that are neither characteristic nor associative (see below).

- **Characteristics:** A characteristic entity is an entity whose primary purpose is to describe or "characterize" some other entity. Characteristics are *existence-dependent* on the entity they describe. The entity described can be kernel, characteristic, or associative.

- **Associations:** An associative entity is an entity whose function is to represent a *many-to-many* (or many-to-many-to-many, etc.) *relationship* among two or more other entities. The entities associated can each be kernel, characteristic, or associative.

In addition:

- Entities (regardless of their classification) can also have **properties**.

- In particular, any entity (again, regardless of its classification) can have a property whose function is to **designate** some other related entity. A designation represents a many-to-one relationship between two entities.

- Entity **supertypes** and **subtypes** are supported. If *B* is a subtype of *A,* then *B* is a kernel, a characteristic, or an association depending on whether *A* is a kernel, a characteristic, or an association.

    We can relate the foregoing concepts to their E/R analogs (somewhat loosely) as follows: A kernel corresponds to an E/R "regular entity," a characteristic to an E/R "weak entity," and an association to an E/R "relationship" (many-to-many variety only).

    In addition to the aspects discussed briefly above, RM/T also includes support for (a) *surrogates* (see reference [12.12]), (b) the *time* dimension, and (c) various kinds of *data aggregation* (see references [12.22–12.23]).

12.6   C. J. Date. "A Practical Approach to Database Design." In C. J. Date, *Relational Database: Selected Writings*. Reading, Mass.: Addison-Wesley (1986).

Describes a database design methodology based on the concepts of RM/T [12.5].

12.7   C. J. Date. "Entity/Relationship Modeling and the Relational Model." In C. J. Date and Hugh Darwen, *Relational Database Writings 1989–1991*. Reading, Mass.: Addison-Wesley (1992).

12.8   C. J. Date. "Don't Encode Information into Primary Keys!" In C. J. Date and Hugh Darwen, *Relational Database Writings 1989–1991*. Reading, Mass.: Addison-Wesley (1992).

Presents arguments against what are sometimes called "intelligent keys." See also references [5.6–5.7] for some related recommendations regarding foreign keys.

12.9   C. J. Date. "A Note on One-to-One Relationships." In C. J. Date, *Relational Database Writings 1985–1989*. Reading, Mass.: Addison-Wesley (1990).

An extensive discussion of the problem of one-to-one relationships, which turn out to be rather more complicated than they might appear at first sight.

12.10   Ramez Elmasri and Shamkant B. Navathe. *Fundamentals of Database Systems* (2nd edition). Redwood City, Calif.: Benjamin/Cummings (1994).

This general textbook on database management includes two chapters (out of a total of 25) on the use of E/R techniques for database design.

12.11   Candace C. Fleming and Barbara von Hallé. *Handbook of Relational Database Design*. Reading, Mass.: Addison-Wesley (1989).

A comprehensive and good pragmatic guide to database design in a relational system, with specific examples based on IBM's DB2 product and the Teradata (now NCR) DBC/1012 database machine. Both logical and physical design issues are addressed—though the book uses the term "logical design" to mean what we would call "relational design," and the term "relational design" to include at least some aspects of what we would call "physical design"! The specific design methodology advocated has several points in common with that described in reference [12.6].

12.12   P. Hall, J. Owlett, and S. J. P. Todd. "Relations and Entities." In G. M. Nijssen (ed.), *Modelling in Data Base Management Systems*. Amsterdam, Netherlands: North-Holland / New York, NY: Elsevier Science (1975).

The first paper to treat the idea of **surrogates** in detail (surrogates were incorporated later into RM/T). A surrogate is a system-assigned, system-maintained entity identifier;

in RM/T terms, every E- and P-relation has a surrogate as primary key, which in the case of P-relations serves as a foreign key also (referencing the corresponding E-relation). The paper discusses the advantages of surrogates at some length.

It is perhaps worth emphasizing the point that surrogates are *not* (as some writers seem to think) the same thing as "tuple IDs." For one thing—to state the obvious—tuple IDs identify tuples and surrogates identify entities, and there is certainly nothing like a one-to-one correspondence between the two. In fact, there is a one-to-one correspondence between entities and tuples *only* in the case of E-relations (in RM/T terms). It follows that tuples in base relations other than E-relations, and tuples in derived relations, have *no* obvious correspondence to surrogates at all.

Furthermore, tuple IDs have performance connotations, while surrogates do not; access to a tuple via its tuple ID is assumed to be fast (we are assuming here that [base relation] tuples map fairly directly to physical storage, as is in fact the case in most of today's relational products). Also, tuple IDs are usually concealed from the user, while surrogates are usually not; in other words, it is not possible to store a tuple ID as an attribute value, while it certainly is possible to store a surrogate as an attribute value.

In a nutshell: Surrogates are a logical concept; tuple IDs are a physical concept.

12.13   M. M. Hammer and D. J. McLeod. "The Semantic Data Model: A Modelling Mechanism for Database Applications." Proc. 1978 ACM SIGMOD International Conference on Management of Data, Austin, Texas (May/June 1978).

The Semantic Data Model (SDM) represents another proposal for a database design formalism. Like the E/R model, it concentrates on structural and integrity aspects and has little or nothing to say regarding manipulative aspects (operators). See also references [12.14] and [12.16].

12.14   Michael Hammer and Dennis McLeod. "Database Description with SDM: A Semantic Database Model." *ACM TODS 6,* No. 3 (September 1981).

See reference [12.13].

12.15   Richard Hull and Roger King. "Semantic Database Modeling: Survey, Applications, and Research Issues." *ACM Comp. Surv. 19,* No. 3 (September 1987).

A comprehensive tutorial on the semantic modeling field and related matters. This paper is a good place to start a deeper investigation into the issues and research problems surrounding semantic modeling activities.

12.16   D. Jagannathan *et al.* "SIM: A Database System Based on the Semantic Data Model." Proc. 1988 ACM SIGMOD International Conference on Management of Data, Chicago, Ill. (June 1988).

Describes a commercial DBMS product based on "a semantic data model similar to" the Semantic Data Model proposed by Hammer and McLeod in reference [12.13].

12.17   William Kent. "A Taxonomy of Entity-Relationship Models." Private communication (1982).

12.18   Heikki Mannila and Kari-Jouko Räihä. *The Design of Relational Databases.* Wokingham, UK: Addison-Wesley (1992).

To quote the preface, this book is "a graduate-level textbook and reference on the design of relational databases." It covers both dependency theory and normalization on the one hand, and the E/R approach on the other, in each case from a fairly formal perspective. The following (incomplete) list of chapter titles gives some idea of the book's scope:

- Design Principles

- Integrity Constraints and Dependencies

- Properties of Relational Schemas

- Axiomatizations for Dependencies
- Algorithms for Design Problems
- Mappings between ER-diagrams and Relational Database Schemas
- Schema Transformations
- Use of Example Databases in Design

The techniques described in the book have been implemented by the authors in the form of a tool called Design By Example.

12.19 T. W. Olle, H. G. Sol, and A. A. Verrijn-Stuart (eds.). *Information Systems Design Methodologies: A Comparative Review*. Amsterdam, Netherlands: North-Holland / New York, NY: Elsevier Science (1982).

The proceedings of an IFIP Working Group 8.1 conference. Some 13 different methodologies are described and applied to a standard benchmark problem. The book also includes a set of reviews of some of the proposed approaches.

12.20 Joan Peckham and Fred Maryanski. "Semantic Data Models." *ACM Comp. Surv. 20,* No. 3 (September 1988).

Another tutorial survey.

12.21 H. A. Schmid and J. R. Swenson. "On the Semantics of the Relational Data Base Model." Proc. 1975 ACM SIGMOD International Conference on Management of Data, San Jose, Calif. (May 1975).

This paper proposed a "basic semantic model" that predated Chen's work on the E/R model but in fact was very similar to that model (except in terminology, of course; Schmid and Swenson use *independent object, dependent object,* and *association* in place of Chen's terms *regular entity, weak entity,* and *relationship* (?), respectively).

12.22 J. M. Smith and D. C. P. Smith. "Database Abstractions: Aggregation." *CACM 20,* No. 6 (June 1977).

See reference [12.22].

12.23 J. M. Smith and D. C. P. Smith. "Database Abstractions: Aggregation and Generalization." *ACM TODS 2,* No. 2 (June 1977).

The proposals of these two papers [12.22] and [12.23] had a significant influence on RM/T [12.5], especially in the area of subtypes and supertypes.

12.24 Veda C. Storey. "Understanding Semantic Relationships." *The VLDB Journal 2,* No. 4 (October 1993).

To quote from the abstract: "Semantic data models have been developed [in the database community] using abstractions such as [subtyping], aggregation, and association. Besides these well-known relationships, a number of additional semantic relationships have been identified by researchers in other disciplines such as linguistics, logic, and cognitive psychology. This article explores some of [these latter] relationships and discusses . . . their impact on database design."

12.25 B. Sundgren. "The Infological Approach to Data Bases." In J. W. Klimbie and K. L. Koffeman (eds.), *Data Base Management*. Amsterdam, Netherlands: North-Holland / New York, NY: Elsevier Science (1974).

The "infological approach" is an approach to semantic modeling that has been successfully used for database design for many years in Scandinavia.

12.26 Dan Tasker. *Fourth Generation Data: A Guide to Data Analysis for New and Old Systems*. Sydney, Australia: Prentice-Hall of Australia Pty., Ltd. (1989).

A good pragmatic guide to database design, with the primary emphasis on individual data items. Data items are divided into three basic kinds: label, quantity, and description. *Label* items stand for entities; in relational terms, they correspond to primary and foreign keys. *Quantity* items represent amounts or measures or positions on a scale (possibly a date/time scale), and are subject to the usual arithmetic manipulations. *Description* items are all the rest. (Of course, there is much more to the classification scheme than this brief sketch can suggest.) The book goes on to deal with each kind in considerable detail. The discussions are not always "relationally pure"—for example, Tasker's use of the term "domain" does not fully coincide with the relational use of that term—but the book does contain a great deal of sound practical advice.

12.27 Toby J. Teorey and James P. Fry. *Design of Database Structures*. Englewood Cliffs, NJ: Prentice-Hall (1982).

A textbook on all aspects of database design. The book is divided into five parts: Introduction, Conceptual Design, Implementation Design (i.e., mapping the conceptual design to constructs that a specific DBMS can understand), Physical Design, and Special Design Issues.

12.28 Toby J. Teorey, Dongqing Yang, and James P. Fry. "A Logical Design Methodology for Relational Databases Using the Extended Entity-Relationship Model." *ACM Comp. Surv. 18,* No. 2 (June 1986).

The "extended E/R model" adds support for generalization and subset hierarchies (two variants on type hierarchies), nulls, and relationships involving more than two participants.

12.29 Toby J. Teorey. *Database Modeling and Design: The Entity-Relationship Approach*. San Mateo, Calif.: Morgan Kaufmann (1990).

A more recent textbook on the application of E/R and "extended" E/R concepts [12.28] to database design.

PART **IV**

DATA
PROTECTION

In this part of the book, we turn our attention to the question of **data protection**—that is, protecting the database against a variety of possible threats (both deliberate and accidental). The fact is, there are indeed many risks that the data might be exposed to. For example:

- The system might crash in the middle of executing some program, thereby leaving the database in an unpredictable state.

- Two programs executing concurrently might interfere with one another's operation, thereby producing incorrect results.

- Sensitive data might be exposed to—or, worse, changed by—an unauthorized user.

- Updates might change the database in an invalid way.

And so on (the possibilities are endless). The system therefore has to provide an extensive set of controls to protect the database against such threats—specifically, **recovery, concurrency, security,** and **integrity** controls. This part of the book examines such matters in detail: Chapter 13 deals with recovery, Chapter 14 with concurrency, Chapter 15 with security, and Chapter 16 with integrity.

13 Recovery

13.1 Introduction

The topics of this chapter and the next, recovery and concurrency, are very much inter-related, both of them being aspects of the more general topic of *transaction processing*. For pedagogic reasons, however, it is desirable to try to keep them separate as much as possible, at least until we have finished describing some of the basic concepts. In the present chapter, therefore, we will concentrate on recovery specifically, but a few references to concurrency will inevitably creep in from time to time.

Recovery in a database system means, primarily, recovering the database itself—that is, restoring the database to a state that is known to be correct* after some failure has rendered the current state incorrect, or at least suspect. And the underlying principles on which such recovery is based are quite simple, and can be summed up in a single word: **redundancy**. (Redundancy, that is, at the physical level; any such redundancy should of course be hidden from the user and thus not be visible at the logical level.) In other words, the way to make sure that the database is indeed recoverable is to make sure that any piece of information it contains can be reconstructed from some other information stored, redundantly, somewhere else in the system.

Before we go any further, we should make it clear that the ideas of recovery—indeed, the ideas of transaction processing in general—are somewhat independent of whether the underlying system is relational or something else. (On the other hand, we should also mention that much of the theoretical work on transaction processing has historically been done, and continues to be done, in a specifically relational context.) We should also make it clear that this is an enormous subject!—all we can hope to do here is introduce the reader to some of the most important and basic ideas. See the References and Bibliography section (especially reference [13.11]) for suggestions for further reading.

The plan of the chapter is as follows. Following this brief introduction, Sections 13.2 and 13.3 explain the fundamental notion of a *transaction* and the associated idea of *transaction recovery* (i.e., recovering the database after some individual transaction

---

* Or at least *assumed* to be correct. See Chapter 16 (Section 16.2) for a discussion of what "correct" means in this context.

has failed for some reason). Section 13.4 then goes on to expand the foregoing ideas into the broader sphere of *system* recovery (i.e., recovering after some kind of system crash has caused all currently running transactions to fail simultaneously). Section 13.5 takes a slight detour into the question of *media* recovery (i.e., recovering after the database has been physically damaged in some way, e.g., by a head crash on the disk). Section 13.6 then introduces the crucially important concept of *two-phase commit*. Section 13.7 describes the relevant aspects of SQL. Finally, Section 13.8 presents a summary and a few concluding remarks.

One last preliminary note: We assume throughout this chapter that we are in a "large" (shared, multi-user) database environment. "Small" (nonshared, single-user) DBMSs typically provide little or no recovery support—instead, recovery is regarded as the user's responsibility (implying that the user has to make periodic backup copies of the database and redo work manually if a failure occurs).

13.2 Transactions

As indicated in Section 13.1, we begin our discussions by introducing the fundamental notion of a **transaction**. A transaction is a **logical unit of work**. Consider the following example. Suppose first that relation P, the parts relation, includes an additional attribute TOTQTY, representing the total shipment quantity for the part in question; in other words, the value of TOTQTY for any given part is supposed to be equal to the sum of all QTY values, taken over all shipments for that part. Now consider the pseudocode of Fig. 13.1, the intent of which is to add a new shipment for supplier S5 and part P1, with quantity 1000, to the database (the INSERT adds the new shipment to the SP relation, the UPDATE updates the TOTQTY value for part P1 accordingly).

```
    BEGIN TRANSACTION ;

    INSERT ( { S#:'S5', P#:'P1', QTY:1000 } ) INTO SP ;
    IF any error occurred THEN GO TO UNDO ;

    UPDATE P WHERE P# = 'P1' TOTQTY := TOTQTY + 1000 ;
    IF any error occurred THEN GO TO UNDO ;

    COMMIT TRANSACTION ;
    GO TO FINISH ;

UNDO :
    ROLLBACK TRANSACTION ;

FINISH :
    RETURN ;
```

FIG. 13.1 A sample transaction (pseudocode)

The point of the example is that what is presumably intended to be a single, atomic operation—"Add a new shipment"—in fact involves *two* updates to the database (as always, we take the term "update" to include INSERTs and DELETEs as well as UPDATEs specifically). What is more, the database is not even consistent between those two updates; it temporarily violates the requirement that the value of TOTQTY for part P1 is supposed to be equal to the sum of all QTY values for part P1. Thus, a logical unit of work (i.e., a transaction) is not necessarily just a single database operation; rather, it is a *sequence* of several such operations, in general, that transforms a consistent state of the database into another consistent state, without necessarily preserving consistency at all intermediate points.

Now, it is clear that what must *not* be allowed to happen in the example is for one of the updates to be executed and the other not, because that would leave the database in an inconsistent state. Ideally, of course, we would like a cast-iron guarantee that both updates will be executed. Unfortunately, it is impossible to provide such a guarantee—there is always a chance that things will go wrong, and go wrong moreover at the worst possible moment. For example, a system crash might occur between the two updates, or an arithmetic overflow might occur on the second of them, etc.* But a system that supports **transaction processing** does provide the next best thing to such a guarantee. Specifically, it guarantees that if the transaction executes some updates and then a failure occurs (for whatever reason) before the transaction reaches its planned termination, *then those updates will be undone.* Thus the transaction *either* executes in its entirety *or* is totally canceled (i.e., made as if it never executed at all). In this way a sequence of operations that is fundamentally not atomic can be made to look as if it really were atomic from an external point of view.

The system component that provides this atomicity (or semblance of atomicity) is known as the **transaction manager,** and the operations COMMIT TRANSACTION and ROLLBACK TRANSACTION are the key to the way it works:

- The **COMMIT TRANSACTION** operation (COMMIT for short) signals *successful* end-of-transaction: It tells the transaction manager that a logical unit of work has been successfully completed, the database is (or should be) in a consistent state again, and all of the updates made by that unit of work can now be "committed" or made permanent.

- By contrast, the **ROLLBACK TRANSACTION** operation (ROLLBACK for short) signals *unsuccessful* end-of-transaction: It tells the transaction manager that something has gone wrong, the database might be in an inconsistent state, and all of the updates made by the logical unit of work so far must be "rolled back" or undone.

In the example, therefore, we issue a COMMIT if we get through the two updates successfully, which will commit the changes in the database and make them permanent.

---

* System crash is referred to in Section 13.4 as a *global* or *system* failure. By contrast, an individual program failure such as overflow is referred to as a *local* failure.

If anything goes wrong, however—i.e., if either update statement raises an error condition—then we issue a ROLLBACK instead, to undo any changes made so far.

Incidentally, we should point out that a realistic application program will not only update the database (or attempt to), but will also send some kind of message back to the end user indicating what has happened. In the example, we might send the message "Shipment added" if the COMMIT is reached, or the message "Error—shipment not added" otherwise. Message-handling, in turn, has additional implications for recovery. See reference [13.11] for further discussion.

At this juncture, the reader might be wondering how it is possible to undo an update. The answer, of course, is that the system maintains a **log** or **journal** on tape or (more commonly) disk, on which details of all update operations—in particular, before and after values of the updated object—are recorded. Thus, if it becomes necessary to undo some particular update, the system can use the corresponding log entry to restore the updated object to its previous value.

(Actually the foregoing is somewhat oversimplified. In practice, the log will consist of two portions, an *active* or online portion and an *archive* or offline portion. The online portion is the portion used during normal system operation to record details of updates as they are performed, and is normally held on disk. When the online portion becomes full, its contents are transferred to the offline portion, which—because it is always processed sequentially—is usually held on tape.)

One further (important) point: The system must guarantee that individual statements are themselves atomic (all or nothing). This consideration becomes particularly significant in a relational system, where statements are set-level and typically operate on many tuples at a time; it must not be possible for such a statement to fail in the middle and leave the database in an inconsistent state (e.g., with some tuples in the target set updated and others not). In other words, if an error does occur in the middle of such a statement, then the database must remain totally unchanged. Moreover, as mentioned in Chapter 5, the same is true even if the statement causes additional operations to occur "under the covers" because of, e.g., a foreign key cascade delete rule.

13.3 Transaction Recovery

A transaction begins with the successful execution of a BEGIN TRANSACTION statement (BEGIN for short), and it ends with the successful execution of either a COMMIT or a ROLLBACK statement. COMMIT establishes what is called, among many other things, a **commit point** (also—especially in commercial products—**syncpoint**). A commit point thus corresponds to the end of a logical unit of work, and hence to a point at which the database is or should be in a state of consistency.* ROLLBACK, by con-

---

* Throughout this discussion, the term "database" really means that portion of the database that is accessible to the transaction under consideration. Other transactions might be executing in parallel with that transaction and making changes in their own portions, and so "the total database" might *not* be in a state of consistency at this point. As explained in Section 13.1, however, we are ignoring the possibility of concurrent transactions (so far as possible) in the present chapter. This simplification does not materially affect the issue under discussion, of course.

trast, rolls the database back to the state it was in at BEGIN TRANSACTION, which effectively means back to the previous commit point. (The phrase "the previous commit point" is still accurate, even in the case of the first transaction in the program, if we agree to think of the first BEGIN TRANSACTION in the program as tacitly establishing an initial "commit point.")

When a commit point is established:

1. All updates made by the program since the previous commit point are committed; that is, they are **made permanent**. Prior to the commit point, all such updates should be regarded as *tentative only*—tentative in the sense that they might be undone (i.e., rolled back). Once committed, an update is guaranteed never to be undone (this is the definition of "committed").

2. All database positioning is lost and all tuple locks are released. "Database positioning" here refers to the idea that at any given time a given program will typically have addressability to certain tuples (e.g., via certain *cursors* in the case of SQL, as explained in Chapter 8); this addressability is lost at a commit point. Tuple locks are explained in the next chapter. *Note:* Some systems do provide an option by which the program in fact might be able to retain addressability to certain tuples (and therefore retain certain tuple locks) from one transaction to the next. See Section 13.7 for further discussion.

Paragraph 2 here—excluding the remark about possibly retaining some addressability and hence retaining corresponding tuple locks—also applies if a transaction terminates with ROLLBACK instead of COMMIT. Paragraph 1, of course, does not.

Note carefully that COMMIT and ROLLBACK terminate the *transaction,* not the program. In general, a single program execution will consist of a *sequence* of several transactions running one after another, as illustrated in Fig. 13.2.

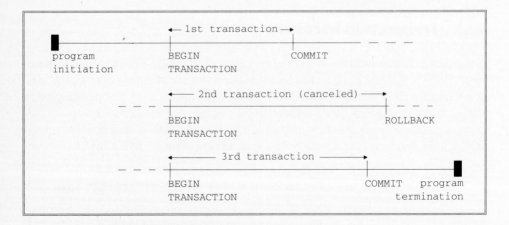

FIG. 13.2 Program execution is a sequence of transactions

Now let us return to the example of the previous section (Fig. 13.1). In that example, we included explicit tests for errors, and issued an explicit ROLLBACK if any error was detected. But, of course, the system cannot assume that application programs will always include explicit tests for all possible errors. Therefore, the system will issue an *implicit* ROLLBACK for any program that fails for any reason to reach its planned termination (in terms of Fig. 13.1, "planned termination" means the RETURN statement, which terminates the application and passes control back to the system).

We can now see, therefore, that transactions are not only the unit of work but also the unit of **recovery**. For if a transaction successfully commits, then the system will guarantee that its updates will be permanently installed in the database, even if the system crashes the very next moment. It is quite possible, for instance, that the system might crash after the COMMIT has been honored but before the updates have been physically written to the database—they could still be waiting in a main memory buffer and so be lost at the time of the crash. Even if that happens, the system's restart procedure will still install those updates in the database; it is able to discover the values to be written by examining the relevant entries in the log. (It follows that the log must be physically written before COMMIT processing can complete. This important rule is known as the **write-ahead log rule**.) Thus the restart procedure will recover any transactions that completed successfully but did not manage to get their updates physically written prior to the crash; hence, as stated earlier, transactions are indeed the unit of recovery. (In the next chapter we will see that they are the unit of *concurrency* also. Further, since they are supposed to transform a consistent state of the database into another consistent state, they can also be regarded as the unit of *integrity*—see Chapter 16.)

The ACID Properties

Following reference [13.13], we can summarize this section and the previous one by saying that transactions have four important properties—*atomicity, consistency, isolation,* and *durability* (referred to colloquially as "the ACID properties").

- **Atomicity:** Transactions are atomic (all-or-nothing).

- **Consistency:** Transformations preserve database consistency. That is, a transaction transforms a consistent state of the database into another consistent state, without necessarily preserving consistency at all intermediate points. Chapter 16 discusses database consistency in detail.

- **Isolation:** Transactions are isolated from one another. That is, even though in general there will be many transactions running concurrently, any given transaction's updates are concealed from all the rest, until that transaction commits. Another way of saying the same thing is that, for any two distinct transactions *T1* and *T2, T1* might be allowed to see *T2*'s updates (after *T2* has committed) or *T2* might be allowed to see *T1*'s updates (after *T1* has committed), but certainly not both. See Chapter 14 for further discussion.

- **Durability:** Once a transaction commits, its updates survive, even if there is a subsequent system crash.

13.4 System Recovery

The system must be prepared to recover, not only from purely local failures such as the occurrence of an overflow condition within an individual transaction, but also from "global" failures such as a power failure on the CPU (CPU = central processing unit). A local failure, by definition, affects only the transaction in which the failure has actually occurred; such failures have already been adequately discussed in Sections 13.2 and 13.3. A global failure, by contrast, affects all of the transactions in progress at the time of the failure, and hence has significant system-wide implications. In this section and the next, we briefly consider what is involved in recovering from a global failure.

Such failures fall into two broad categories:

- **System failures** (e.g., power failure), which affect all transactions currently in progress but do not physically damage the database. A system failure is sometimes called a *soft crash*.

- **Media failures** (e.g., head crash on the disk), which do cause damage to the database, or to some portion of it, and affect at least those transactions currently using that portion. A media failure is sometimes called a *hard crash*.

System failures are discussed below, media failures are discussed in Section 13.5.

The critical point regarding system failure is that *the contents of main memory are lost* (in particular, the database buffers are lost). The precise state of any transaction that was in progress at the time of the failure is therefore no longer known; such a transaction can therefore never be successfully completed, and so must be *undone* (rolled back) when the system restarts.

Furthermore, it might also be necessary (as mentioned in Section 13.3) to *redo* certain transactions at restart time that did successfully complete prior to the crash but did not manage to get their updates transferred from the database buffers to the physical database.

The question arises: How does the system know at restart time which transactions to undo and which to redo? The answer is as follows. At certain prescribed intervals—typically whenever some prescribed number of entries have been written to the log—the system automatically **takes a checkpoint**. Taking a checkpoint involves (a) physically writing ("force-writing") the contents of the database buffers out to the physical database, and (b) physically writing a special **checkpoint record** out to the physical log. The checkpoint record gives a list of all transactions that were in progress at the time the checkpoint was taken. To see how this information is used, consider Fig. 13.3, which is meant to be read as follows:

- A system failure has occurred at time *tf*.
- The most recent checkpoint prior to time *tf* was taken at time *tc*.
- Transactions of type *T1* completed (successfully) prior to time *tc*.
- Transactions of type *T2* started prior to time *tc* and completed (successfully) after time *tc* and before time *tf*.
- Transactions of type *T3* also started prior to time *tc* but did not complete by time *tf*.

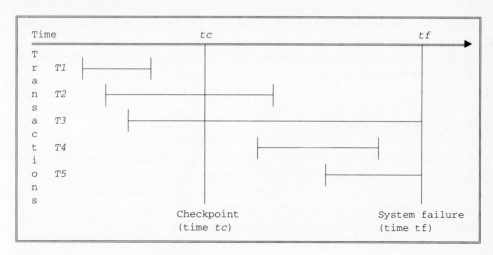

FIG. 13.3 Five transaction categories

- Transactions of type *T4* started after time *tc* and completed (successfully) before time *tf*.

- Finally, transactions of type *T5* also started after time *tc* but did not complete by time *tf*.

It should be clear that, when the system is restarted, transactions of types *T3* and *T5* must be undone, and transactions of types *T2* and *T4* must be redone. Note, however, that transactions of type *T1* do not enter into the restart process at all, because their updates were forced to the database at time *tc* as part of the checkpoint process. Note too that transactions that completed unsuccessfully (i.e., with a rollback) before time *tf* also do not enter into the restart process at all (why not?).

At restart time, therefore, the system first goes through the following procedure in order to identify all transactions of types *T2-T5:*

1. Start with two lists of transactions, the UNDO list and the REDO list. Set the UNDO list equal to the list of all transactions given in the most recent checkpoint record; set the REDO list to empty.

2. Search forward through the log, starting from the checkpoint record.

3. If a BEGIN TRANSACTION log entry is found for transaction *T,* add *T* to the UNDO list.

4. If a COMMIT log entry is found for transaction *T,* move *T* from the UNDO list to the REDO list.

5. When the end of the log is reached, the UNDO and REDO lists identify, respectively, transactions of types *T3* and *T5,* and transactions of types *T2* and *T4*.

The system now works backward through the log, undoing the transactions in the UNDO list; then it works forward again, redoing the transactions in the REDO list. *Note:* Restoring the database to a correct state by undoing work is sometimes called *backward recovery*. Similarly, restoring it to a correct state by redoing work is sometimes called *forward* recovery.

Finally, when all such recovery activity is complete, then (and only then) the system is ready to accept new work.

13.5 Media Recovery

Note: The topic of media recovery is somewhat different in kind from the topics of transaction and system recovery. We include it here for completeness.

To repeat from Section 13.4, a media failure is a failure such as a disk head crash, or a disk controller failure, in which some portion of the database has been physically destroyed. Recovery from such a failure basically involves reloading (or *restoring*) the database from a backup copy (or *dump*), and then using the log—both active and archive portions, in general—to redo all transactions that completed since that backup copy was taken. There is no need to undo transactions that were still in progress at the time of the failure, since by definition all updates of such transactions have been "undone" (actually lost) anyway.

The need to be able to perform media recovery implies the need for a *dump/restore* (or *unload/reload*) *utility*. The dump portion of that utility is used to make backup copies of the database on demand. (Such copies can be kept on tape or other archival storage; it is not necessary that they be on direct access media.) After a media failure, the restore portion of the utility is used to recreate the database from a specified backup copy.

13.6 Two-Phase Commit

In this section we briefly discuss a very important elaboration on the basic commit/rollback concept called **two-phase commit**. Two-phase commit is important whenever a given transaction can interact with several independent "resource managers," each managing its own set of recoverable resources and maintaining its own recovery log.* For example, consider a transaction running in IBM's MVS environment that updates both an IMS database and a DB2 database (such a transaction is perfectly legal, by the way). If the transaction completes successfully, then *all* of its updates, to both IMS data and DB2 data, must be committed; conversely, if it fails, then *all* of its updates must be rolled back. In other words, it must not be possible for the IMS updates to be committed and the DB2 updates rolled back, or *vice versa*—for then the transaction would no longer be atomic.

It follows that it does not make sense for the transaction to issue, say, a COMMIT to IMS and a ROLLBACK to DB2; and even if it issued the same instruction to both,

---

* In particular, it is important in the context of distributed database systems. See Chapter 21.

the system could still crash in between the two, with unfortunate results. Instead, there-fore, the transaction issues a single *system-wide* COMMIT (or ROLLBACK). That COMMIT or ROLLBACK is handled by a system component called the **Coordinator,** whose task it is to guarantee that both resource managers (i.e., IMS and DB2, in the example) commit or roll back the updates they are responsible for *in unison*—and furthermore to provide that guarantee *even if the system fails in the middle of the process*. And it is the two-phase commit protocol that enables it to provide such a guarantee.

Here is the way it works. Assume for simplicity that the transaction has completed its database processing successfully, so that the system-wide operation it issues is COMMIT, not ROLLBACK. On receiving that COMMIT request, the Coordinator goes through the following two-phase process:

1. First, it instructs all resource managers to get ready to "go either way" on the trans-action. In practice, this means that each **participant** in the process—i.e., each re-source manager involved—must force-write all log entries for local resources used by the transaction out to its own physical log (i.e., out to nonvolatile storage; what-ever happens thereafter, the resource manager will now have a *permanent record* of the work it did on behalf of the transaction, and so will be able to commit its updates or roll them back, as necessary). Assuming the force-write is successful, the resource manager now replies "OK" to the Coordinator, otherwise it replies "Not OK."

2. When the Coordinator has received replies from all participants, it force-writes an entry to its own physical log, recording its decision regarding the transaction. If all replies were "OK," that decision is "commit"; if any reply was "Not OK," the decision is "rollback." Either way, the Coordinator then informs each participant of its decision, and *each participant must then commit or rollback the transaction locally, as instructed*. Note that each participant *must* do what it is told by the Co-ordinator in Phase 2—that is the protocol. Note too that it is the appearance of the decision record in the Coordinator's physical log that marks the transition from Phase 1 to Phase 2.

Now, if the system fails at some point during the overall process, the restart proce-dure will look for the decision record in the Coordinator's log. If it finds it, then the two-phase commit process can pick up where it left off. If it does not find it, then it assumes that the decision was "rollback," and again the process can complete appropri-ately. *Note:* It is worth pointing out that if the Coordinator and the participants are executing on different machines, as they might be in a distributed system (see Chapter 21), then a failure on the part of the Coordinator might keep some participant waiting a long time for the Coordinator's decision—and, so long as it *is* waiting, any updates made by the transaction via that participant must be kept hidden from other transactions (i.e., those updates will probably have to be kept *locked,* as discussed in the next chap-ter).

We remark that the data communications manager (DC manager—see Chapter 2) can also be regarded as a resource manager in the sense described above. That is, messages too can be regarded as a recoverable resource, just as the database can, and the DC manager needs to be able to participate in the two-phase commit process. For further discussion of this point, and of the whole idea of two-phase commit, the reader is referred to reference [13.11].

13.7 SQL Support

SQL's support for transactions, and hence for transaction-based recovery, follows the general outline described in the foregoing sections. In particular, SQL does support the usual **COMMIT** and **ROLLBACK** statements; these statements force a CLOSE for every open cursor, thereby causing all database positioning to be lost. *Note:* Some SQL implementations provide an option to prevent this automatic CLOSE and loss of positioning on COMMIT (but not ROLLBACK). In IBM's DB2, for example, the WITH HOLD option on a cursor declaration has such an effect for the cursor in question. The intent is to avoid the need to provide repositioning code to be executed after each COMMIT. Such an option is likely to be added to the standard in some future release.

One difference between SQL's support for transactions and the general concepts outlined in this chapter is that SQL does not include any explicit BEGIN TRANSACTION statement. Instead, a transaction is begun implicitly whenever the program executes a **"transaction-initiating"** statement and does not already have a transaction in progress. (As with the "cursor hold" option discussed above, it is likely that support for an explicit BEGIN TRANSACTION statement will be added to the standard in some future release.) Details of exactly which SQL statements are "transaction-initiating" would be out of place here; suffice it to say that all of the data definition and data manipulation statements discussed in Sections 8.2–8.4 *are* transaction-initiating, and so too are the cursor operations (OPEN, FETCH, etc.) discussed in Section 8.8. A special statement called **SET TRANSACTION** is used to define certain characteristics of the next transaction to be initiated (SET TRANSACTION can be executed only when no transaction is in progress, and is not itself transaction-initiating). The only such characteristics we discuss here are the *access mode* and the *isolation level*. The syntax is:

```
SET TRANSACTION option-list ;
```

where *option-list* must include at least one option.

- The **access mode** option is either **READ ONLY** or **READ WRITE**. If neither is specified, READ WRITE is assumed, unless READ UNCOMMITTED isolation level is specified, in which case READ ONLY is assumed. If READ WRITE is specified, the isolation level must not be READ UNCOMMITTED.

- The **isolation level** option takes the form ISOLATION LEVEL *isolation,* where *isolation* is READ UNCOMMITTED, READ COMMITTED, REPEATABLE READ, or SERIALIZABLE. For further explanation, see Chapter 14.

13.8 Summary

In this chapter we have presented a necessarily brief introduction to the topic of **transaction management**. A transaction is a **logical unit of work,** also a **unit of recovery** (and a unit of concurrency and a unit of integrity—see Chapters 14 and 16, respectively). Transactions possess the **ACID properties** of **atomicity, consistency, isolation,** and **durability. Transaction management** is the task of supervising the execution of transactions in such a way that they can indeed be guaranteed to possess these important properties. In fact, the overall function of the system might well be defined as **the reliable execution of transactions**.

Transactions are initiated by **BEGIN TRANSACTION** and terminated either by **COMMIT TRANSACTION** (*successful* termination) or by **ROLLBACK TRANSACTION** (*unsuccessful* termination). COMMIT establishes a **commit point** (updates are made permanent), ROLLBACK rolls the database back to the previous commit point (updates are undone). If a transaction does not reach its planned termination, the system will *force* a ROLLBACK for it (**transaction recovery**). In order to be able to undo updates, the system maintains a recovery **log**. Moreover, the log records for a given transaction must be written to the physical log before COMMIT processing for that transaction can complete; this is the **write-ahead log rule**.

The system also guarantees the ACID properties of transactions in the face of a system crash. To provide such a guarantee, the system must (a) **redo** all work done by transactions that completed successfully prior to the crash, and (b) **undo** all work done by transactions that started but did not complete prior to the crash. This **system recovery** activity is carried out as part of the system's **restart** procedure (sometimes known as the *restart/recovery* procedure). The system discovers what work has to be redone and what undone by examining the most recent **checkpoint record**. Checkpoint records are written to the log at prescribed intervals.

The system also provides **media recovery** by restoring the database from a previous **dump** and then—using the log—redoing the work completed since that dump was taken. Dump/restore **utilities** are needed to support media recovery.

Systems that permit transactions to interact with multiple **resource managers**—for example, two different DBMSs, or a DBMS and a DC manager—must use a protocol called **two-phase commit** if they are to maintain the transaction atomicity property. The two phases are (a) the **prepare** phase, in which the **Coordinator** instructs all **participants** to "get ready to go either way," and (b) the **commit** phase, in which—assuming all participants responded satisfactorily during the prepare phase—the Coordinator then instructs all participants to perform the actual commit.

Regarding support for recovery in the SQL standard, SQL does provide explicit **COMMIT** and **ROLLBACK** statements (but no explicit BEGIN statement). It also supports a **SET TRANSACTION** statement, which allows the user to specify the **access mode** and **level of isolation** for the next transaction to begin.

One last point: We have tacitly been assuming an application programming environment throughout this chapter. However, all of the concepts discussed apply equally to the end user environment also (though they might be somewhat more concealed in that environment). For example, SQL products typically allow the user to enter SQL statements interactively from the terminal. Usually each such interactive SQL statement is treated as a transaction in its own right; the system will typically issue an automatic COMMIT on the user's behalf after the SQL statement has been executed (or an automatic ROLLBACK if it failed, of course). However, some systems do allow the user to inhibit those automatic COMMITs, and instead to execute a whole series of SQL statements (followed by an explicit COMMIT) as a single transaction. The practice is not generally recommended, however, since it might cause portions of the database to remain locked, and therefore inaccessible to other users, for excessively lengthy periods of time (see Chapter 14). In such an environment, moreover, it is possible for end users to *deadlock* with one another, which is another good argument for prohibiting the practice (again, see Chapter 14).

Exercises

13.1 Systems do not allow a given transaction to commit changes to databases (or relations or . . .) on an individual basis, i.e., without simultaneously committing changes to all other databases (or relations or . . .). Why not?

13.2 Transactions cannot be nested inside one another. Why not?

13.3 State the write-ahead log rule. Why is the rule necessary?

13.4 What are the recovery implications of (a) force-writing buffers to the database at COMMIT? (b) never physically writing buffers to the database prior to COMMIT?

13.5 State the two-phase commit protocol, and discuss the implications of a failure on the part of (a) the Coordinator, (b) a participant, during each of the two phases.

13.6 Using the suppliers-and-parts database, write an SQL program to read and print all parts in part number order, deleting every tenth one as you go, and beginning a new transaction after every tenth row. You can assume that the foreign key delete rule from parts to shipments is CASCADES (i.e., you can ignore shipments for the purposes of this exercise).

References and Bibliography

13.1 Philip A. Bernstein, Vassos Hadzilacos, and Nathan Goodman. *Concurrency Control and Recovery in Database Systems*. Reading, Mass.: Addison-Wesley (1987).

A textbook, covering (as the title indicates) not just recovery but the whole of transaction management, from a much more formal perspective than the present chapter.

13.2 L. A. Bjork. "Recovery Scenario for a DB/DC System." Proc. ACM National Conference, Atlanta, Ga. (August 1973).

This paper and its companion paper by Davies [13.6] represent probably the earliest theoretical work in the area of recovery.

13.3 R. A. Crus. "Data Recovery in IBM DATABASE 2." *IBM Sys. J. 23,* No. 2 (1984).

Describes the DB2 recovery mechanism in detail (and in so doing provides a good description of recovery techniques in general). In particular, the paper explains how DB2 recovers from a system crash during the recovery process itself, while some transaction is in the middle of a rollback. This problem requires special care to ensure that uncommitted updates from the transaction being rolled back are in fact undone (the opposite of the lost update problem, in a sense—see Chapter 14).

13.4 C. J. Date. "Recovery." Chapter 1 of C. J. Date, *An Introduction to Database Systems: Volume II*. Reading, Mass.: Addison-Wesley (1983).

Portions of the present chapter are based on this earlier tutorial treatment.

13.5 C. J. Date. "Distributed Database: A Closer Look." In C. J. Date and Hugh Darwen, *Relational Database Writings 1989–1991*. Reading, Mass.: Addison-Wesley (1992).

Section 13.6 of the present chapter describes what might be called the *basic* two-phase commit protocol. Several improvements on that basic protocol are possible. For example, if participant *P* responds to the Coordinator *C* in Phase 1 that it did no updates for the transaction under consideration (i.e., it was *read-only*), then *C* can simply ignore *P* in Phase 2. Further, if *all* participants respond *read-only* in Phase 1, then Phase 2 can be omitted entirely.

Other improvements and refinements are possible. This paper [13.5] includes a tutorial description of some of them. Specifically, it discusses the *presumed commit* and *presumed rollback* protocols (improved versions of the basic protocol), the *tree of processes* model (when a participant needs to serve as the Coordinator for certain portions of a transaction), and what happens if a *communication failure* occurs during the acknowledgment process from a participant to the Coordinator. *Note:* Although the discussions are presented in the context of a distributed database system (see Chapter 21), most of the concepts are actually of wider applicability.

13.6 C. T. Davies, Jr. "Recovery Semantics for a DB/DC System." Proc. ACM National Conference, Atlanta, Ga. (August 1973).

See the annotation to reference [13.2].

13.7 C. T. Davies, Jr. "Data Processing Spheres of Control." *IBM Sys. J. 17,* No. 2 (1978).

Spheres of control were the first attempt to investigate and formalize what later became transaction management. A sphere of control is an abstraction that represents a piece of work that (from the outside) can be viewed as atomic. Unlike transactions as usually implemented today, however, spheres of control can be nested inside others, to arbitrary depth (see Exercise 13.2).

13.8 Hector Garcia-Molina and Kenneth Salem. "Sagas." Proc. 1987 ACM SIGMOD International Conference on Management of Data, San Francisco, Calif. (May 1987).

A major problem with transactions as described in the body of this chapter is that they are tacitly assumed to be short in duration (milliseconds or even microseconds). For if a transaction lasts a long time (hours, days, weeks), then (a) if it has to be rolled back, a very great deal of work has to be undone, and (b) even if it succeeds, it still has to hold on to system resources (database data, etc.) for an inordinately long time, thereby locking out other users (see Chapter 14). Unfortunately, many "real-world" transactions tend to be longduration, especially in some of the newer application areas, such as hardware and software engineering.

Sagas are an attack on this problem. A saga is a sequence of short transactions (in the usual sense) with the property that the system guarantees that *either* (a) all the transactions in the sequence execute successfully, *or* (b) certain **compensating transactions** are executed in order to cancel the effects of sucessfully completed transactions in an overall incomplete execution of the saga (thereby making it as if the saga had not been executed in the first place). In a banking system, for example, we might have the transaction "Add $100 to account *A*"; the compensating transaction would obviously be "Subtract $100 from account *A*." An extension to the COMMIT statement allows the user to inform the system of the compensating transaction to be run should it be necessary later to cancel the effects of the now completed transaction. Note that a compensating transaction should ideally never terminate with rollback!

13.9 James Gray. "Notes on Data Base Operating Systems." In *Operating Systems: An Advanced Course* (eds., R. Bayer, R. M. Graham, and G. Seegmuller). New York, N.Y.: Springer-Verlag (1978). Also available as IBM Research Report RJ 2188 (February 1978).

One of the earliest—certainly one of the most approachable—sources for material on transaction management. It contains the first generally available description of the two-phase commit protocol. It is obviously not as comprehensive as the more recent reference [13.11], but is nevertheless still recommended.

13.10　Jim Gray. "The Transaction Concept: Virtues and Limitations." Proc. 7th International Conference on Very Large Data Bases, Cannes, France (September 1981).

A concise statement of various transaction-related concepts and problems, including a variety of implementation issues. One particular problem addressed is the following: Transactions as usually understood cannot be nested inside one another (see the answer to Exercise 13.2). Is there nevertheless some way of allowing transactions to be composed of smaller "subtransactions"? The answer is a limited "Yes"—it is possible for a transaction to establish intermediate **savepoints** while it is executing, and subsequently to rollback to a previously established savepoint if required, instead of having to rollback all the way to the beginning. In fact, a savepoint facility along such lines has been incorporated into several implemented systems, including (e.g.) INGRES—the commercial product, not the prototype—and System R (although not DB2). Such a concept seems a little closer to the notion of transactions as that term is usually understood in the real world. But note that establishing a savepoint is not the same as performing a COMMIT; updates made by the transaction are still not made visible to other transactions until (successful) end-of-transaction.

　　　Note: The "sagas" of reference [13.8]—which in some respects address the same problem as savepoints—were proposed after Gray first wrote this paper.

13.11　Jim Gray and Andreas Reuter. *Transaction Processing: Concepts and Techniques.* San Mateo, Calif.: Morgan Kaufmann (1993).

If any computer science text ever deserved the epithet "instant classic," it is surely this one. Its size is daunting at first (over 1000 pages), but the authors display an enviable lightness of touch that makes even the driest aspects of the subject enjoyable reading. In their preface, they state their intent as being "to help . . . solve real problems"; the book is "pragmatic, covering basic transaction issues in considerable detail"; and the presentation "is full of code fragments showing . . . basic algorithms and data structures" and is not "encyclopedic." Despite this last claim, the book is (not surprisingly) comprehensive, and is surely destined to become the standard work. Strongly recommended.

13.12　Jim Gray *et al.* "The Recovery Manager of the System R Data Manager." *ACM Comp. Surv. 13,* No. 2 (June 1981).

References [13.12] and [13.15] are both concerned with the recovery features of System R. Reference [13.12] provides an overview of the entire recovery subsystem; reference [13.15] describes a specific aspect, called the *shadow page* mechanism, in detail (see below).

13.13　Theo Härder and Andreas Reuter. "Principles of Transaction-Oriented Database Recovery." *ACM Comp. Surv. 15,* No. 4 (December 1983).

The source of the acronym ACID (atomicity, consistency, isolation, durability). The paper gives a very clear and careful tutorial presentation of the principles of recovery. It also provides a consistent terminological framework for describing a wide variety of recovery schemes and logging techniques in a uniform way, and classifies and describes a number of existing systems in accordance with that framework.

　　　The paper includes some interesting empirical figures regarding frequency of occurrence and typical (acceptable) recovery times for the three kinds of failure (local, system, media) in a typical large system:

Type of failure	Frequency of occurrence	Recovery time
Local	10–100 per minute	Same as transaction execution time
System	Several per week	Few minutes
Media	Once or twice per year	1–2 hours

13.14　Henry F. Korth, Eliezer Levy, and Abraham Silberschatz. "A Formal Approach to Recovery by Compensating Transactions." Proc. 16th International Conference on Very Large Data Bases, Brisbane, Australia (August 1990).

Formalizes the notion of **compensating transactions,** which are used in sagas [13.8] and elsewhere for "undoing" committed (as well as uncommitted) transactions.

13.15   Raymond A. Lorie. "Physical Integrity in a Large Segmented Database." *ACM TODS 2,* No. 1 (March 1977).

As explained in the annotation to reference [13.12], this paper is concerned with a specific aspect of the System R recovery subsystem, called the *shadow page* mechanism. (Note that the term "integrity" in the title is being used with a meaning different from that we ascribe to it in this book—see Chapters 5 and 16.)

The basic idea behind shadow pages is simple: When an (uncommitted) update is first written to the database, the system does not overwrite the existing page but stores a new page somewhere else on the disk. The old page is then the "shadow" for the new one. Committing the update involves updating various pointers to point to the new page and discarding the shadow; rolling back the update, on the other hand, involves reinstating the shadow page and discarding the new one.

Although conceptually simple, the shadow page scheme suffers from the serious drawback that it destroys any physical clustering that might previously have existed in the data. For this reason the scheme was not used in DB2 [13.3].

13.16   C. Mohan, Don Haderle, Bruce Lindsay, Hamid Pirahesh, and Peter Schwartz. "ARIES: A Transaction Recovery Method Supporting Fine-Granularity Locking and Partial Rollbacks Using Write-Ahead Logging." *ACM TODS 17,* No. 1 (March 1992).

ARIES stands for "Algorithm for Recovery and Isolation Exploiting Semantics." ARIES has been implemented ("to varying degrees") in several commercial and experimental systems, including in particular IBM's DB2. To quote from the paper: "Solutions to [the transaction management problem] may be judged using several metrics: degree of concurrency supported within a page and across pages, complexity of the resulting logic, space overhead on nonvolatile storage and in memory for data and the log, overhead in terms of the number of synchronous and asynchronous I/O's required during restart/recovery and normal processing, kinds of functionality supported (partial transaction rollbacks, etc.), amount of processing performed during restart/recovery, degree of concurrent processing supported during restart/recovery, extent of system-induced transaction rollbacks caused by deadlocks, restrictions placed on stored data (e.g., requiring unique keys for all records, restricting maximum size of objects to the page size, etc.), ability to support novel lock modes that allow the concurrent execution—based on commutativity and other properties—of operations like increment/decrement on the same data by different transactions, and so on. [ARIES] fares very well with respect to all these metrics." (Very slightly paraphrased.)

Answers to Selected Exercises

13.1   Such a feature would conflict with the objective of transaction atomicity. If a transaction could commit some but not all of its updates, then the uncommitted ones might subsequently be rolled back, whereas the committed ones of course could not be. Thus, the transaction would no longer be all-or-nothing.

13.2   Such a feature would conflict with the objective of atomicity for the *outer* transaction. For consider what would happen if transaction *B* were nested inside transaction *A* and the following sequence of events occurred:

```
BEGIN TRANSACTION (transaction A)
transaction A updates tuple a
   BEGIN TRANSACTION (transaction B)
   transaction B updates tuple b
   COMMIT (transaction B)
ROLLBACK (transaction A)
```

If tuple *b* is restored to its pre-*A* value at this point, then *B*'s COMMIT was not in fact a COMMIT at all. Conversely, if *B*'s COMMIT was genuine, then tuple *b* cannot be restored to its pre-*A* value, and hence *A*'s ROLLBACK cannot be honored.

Observe that to say that transactions cannot be nested is to say that a program can execute a BEGIN TRANSACTION operation only when it has no transaction currently running.

Actually, many writers (beginning with Davies in reference [13.6]) have proposed the ability to nest transactions by dropping the requirement for *durability* (the "D" property in ACID) on the part of an inner transaction. What this means is that COMMIT by an inner transaction will commit that transaction's updates, *but only to the next outer level*. If that outer level then terminates with rollback, the inner transaction will be rolled back too. In the example, *B*'s COMMIT would thus be a COMMIT to *A* only, not to the outside world, and it might indeed subsequently be revoked.

We remark that nested transactions will be awkward to implement—from a purely syntactic point of view!—in a language like SQL that lacks an explicit BEGIN TRANSACTION (there has to be *some* explicit way of indicating that an inner transaction is to be started, and marking the point to roll back to if that inner transaction fails).

13.4 (a) REDO is never necessary following system failure. (b) Physical UNDO is never necessary, and hence UNDO log records are also unnecessary.

13.6 This exercise is typical of a wide class of applications, and the following outline solution (written in PL/I with embedded SQL) is typical too.

```
EXEC SQL DECLARE CP CURSOR FOR
         SELECT P.P#, P.PNAME, P.COLOR, P.WEIGHT, P.CITY
         FROM    P
         WHERE   P.P# > previous_P#
         ORDER   BY P# ;

previous_P# = '        ' ;
eof = false ;
DO WHILE ( eof = false ) ;
EXEC SQL OPEN CP ;
   DO count = 1 TO 10 ;
      EXEC SQL FETCH CP INTO :P#, ... ;
      IF SQLSTATE = '02000' THEN
         DO ;
             EXEC SQL CLOSE CP ;
             EXEC SQL COMMIT ;
             eof = true ;
         END ;
      ELSE print P#, ... ;
   END ;
   EXEC SQL DELETE FROM P WHERE P.P# = :P# ;
   EXEC SQL CLOSE CP ;
   EXEC SQL COMMIT ;
   previous_P# = P# ;
END ;
```

Observe that we lose position within the parts table at the end of each transaction (even if we did not close cursor CP explicitly, the COMMIT would close it automatically anyway). The foregoing code will therefore not be particularly efficient, because each new transaction requires a search on the parts table in order to reestablish position. Matters might be improved somewhat if there happens to be an index on column P.P#—as in fact there probably will be, since that column is the primary key for table P—and the optimizer chooses that index as the access path for the table.

14 Concurrency

14.1 Introduction

As explained in the introduction to Chapter 13 on recovery, the topics of concurrency and recovery go hand in hand, both being part of the general topic of *transaction processing*. Now we turn our attention to concurrency specifically. The term **concurrency** refers to the fact that DBMSs typically allow many transactions to access the same data at the same time—and in such a system, as is well known, some kind of **concurrency control mechanism** is needed to ensure that concurrent transactions do not interfere with each other's operation. Examples of the kinds of interference that can occur (in the absence of suitable controls) are given later, in Section 14.2.

The structure of the chapter is as follows:

- In Section 14.2, as just indicated, we explain some of the problems that can arise if proper concurrency control is not provided.

- Section 14.3 then introduces the standard mechanism for dealing with such problems, *viz.* **locking**. *Note:* Locking is not the only possible approach to the concurrency control problem, but it is far and away the one most commonly encountered in practice. Some other approaches are described in the annotation to references [14.1–14.2], [14.6–14.7], and [14.11–14.12].

- Section 14.4 shows how locking can be used to solve the problems described in Section 14.2.

- Locking unfortunately introduces problems of its own, of which one of the best known is **deadlock**. Section 14.5 discusses this issue.

- Section 14.6 describes the concept of **serializability,** which is established as the formal criterion of correctness for the execution of a set of concurrent transactions.

- Sections 14.7 and 14.8 then go on to consider some important refinements on the basic idea of locking, *viz.* **levels of isolation** and **intent locking**.

- Section 14.9 describes the relevant features of SQL.

- Finally, Section 14.10 presents a summary and a few concluding observations.

Note: A couple of the general remarks from the introduction to Chapter 11 are applicable again here:

1. First, the ideas of concurrency, like those of recovery, are somewhat independent of whether the underlying system is relational or something else. However, it is significant that—as with recovery—much of the early theoretical work in the area was done in a specifically relational context ("for definiteness," as reference [14.5] puts it).

2. Second, concurrency, like recovery, is a very large subject, and all we can hope to do in this chapter is introduce some of its most important and basic ideas. The exercises, answers, and annotated references at the end of the chapter include some discussion of certain more advanced aspects of the subject.

14.2   Three Concurrency Problems

We begin by considering the problems that any concurrency control mechanism has to address. There are essentially three ways in which things can go wrong—three ways, that is, in which a transaction, though correct in itself, can nevertheless produce the wrong answer if interference occurs on the part of some other transaction.* The three problems are:

■   The *lost update* problem

■   The *uncommitted dependency* problem

■   The *inconsistent analysis* problem

We consider each in turn.

The Lost Update Problem

Consider the situation illustrated in Fig. 14.1. That figure is intended to be read as follows: Transaction *A* retrieves some tuple *p* at time *t1;* transaction *B* retrieves that same tuple *p* at time *t2;* transaction *A* updates the tuple (on the basis of the values seen at time *t1*) at time *t3;* and transaction *B* updates the same tuple (on the basis of the values seen at time *t2.* which are the same as those seen at time *t1*) at time *t4*. Transaction *A*'s update is lost at time *t4,* because transaction *B* overwrites it without even looking at it.

The Uncommitted Dependency Problem

The uncommitted dependency problem arises if one transaction is allowed to retrieve— or, worse, update—a tuple that has been updated by another transaction but has not yet been committed by that other transaction. For if it has not yet been committed, there is

---

* Note that the interfering transaction might also be correct in itself. It is the uncontrolled *interleaving* of operations from the two correct transactions that produces the overall incorrect result. See Chapter 16 for an explanation of what it means for a transaction to be "correct in itself."

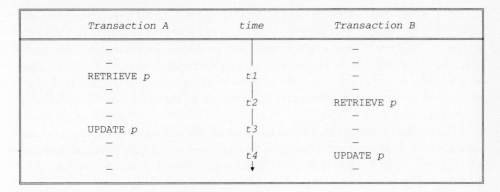

Transaction A	time	Transaction B
–		–
–		–
RETRIEVE p	t1	–
–		–
–	t2	RETRIEVE p
–		–
UPDATE p	t3	–
–		–
–	t4	UPDATE p
–		–

FIG. 14.1 Transaction *A* loses an update at time *t4*

always a possibility that it never will be committed but will be rolled back instead—in which case the first transaction will have seen some data that now no longer exists (and in a sense "never" existed). Consider Figs. 14.2 and 14.3.

In the first example (Fig. 14.2), transaction *A* sees an uncommitted update (also called an uncommitted change) at time *t2*. That update is then undone at time *t3*. Trans-

Transaction A	time	Transaction B
–		–
–		–
–	t1	UPDATE p
–		–
RETRIEVE p	t2	–
–		–
–	t3	ROLLBACK
–		

FIG. 14.2 Transaction *A* becomes dependent on an uncommitted change at time *t2*

Transaction A	time	Transaction B
–		–
–		–
–	t1	UPDATE p
–		–
UPDATE p	t2	–
–		–
–	t3	ROLLBACK
–		

FIG. 14.3 Transaction *A* updates an uncommitted change at time *t2*, and loses that update at time *t3*

action *A* is therefore operating on a false assumption—namely, the assumption that tuple *p* has the value seen at time *t2,* whereas in fact it has whatever value it had prior to time *t1.* As a result, transaction *A* might well produce incorrect output. Note, by the way, that the ROLLBACK of transaction *B* might be due to no fault of *B*'s—it might, for example, be the result of a system crash. (And transaction *A* might already have terminated by that time, in which case the crash would not cause a ROLLBACK to be issued for *A* also.)

The second example (Fig. 14.3) is even worse. Not only does transaction *A* become dependent on an uncommitted change at time *t2,* but it actually loses an update at time *t3*—because the ROLLBACK at time *t3* causes tuple *p* to be restored to its value prior to time *t1.* This is another version of the lost update problem.

The Inconsistent Analysis Problem

Consider Fig. 14.4, which shows two transactions *A* and *B* operating on account (ACC) tuples: Transaction *A* is summing account balances, transaction *B* is transferring an

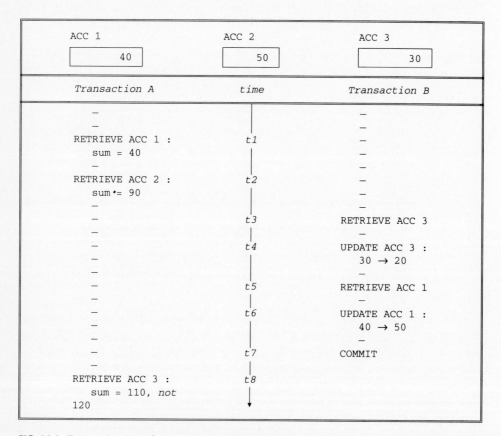

FIG. 14.4 Transaction *A* performs an inconsistent analysis

amount 10 from account 3 to account 1. The result produced by *A*, 110, is obviously incorrect; if *A* were to go on to write that result back into the database, it would actually leave the database in an inconsistent state. We say that *A* has seen an inconsistent state of the database and has therefore performed an inconsistent analysis. Note the difference between this example and the previous one: There is no question here of *A* being dependent on an uncommitted change, since *B* COMMITs all its updates before *A* sees ACC 3.

14.3 Locking

As indicated in Section 14.1, the problems of Section 14.2 can all be solved by means of a concurrency control technique called **locking**. The basic idea is simple: When a transaction needs an assurance that some object it is interested in—typically a database tuple—will not change in some unpredictable manner while its back is turned (as it were), it **acquires a lock** on that object. The effect of the lock is to "lock other transactions out of" the object, and thus in particular to prevent them from changing it. The first transaction is therefore able to carry out its processing in the certain knowledge that the object in question will remain in a stable state for as long as that transaction wishes it to.

We now give a more detailed explanation of the way locking works.

1. First, we assume the system supports two kinds of lock, **exclusive locks** (X locks) and **shared locks** (S locks), defined as indicated in the next two paragraphs. *Note:* X and S locks are sometimes called **write locks** and **read locks,** respectively. We assume until further notice that X and S locks are the only kinds available; see Section 14.8 for examples of other kinds. We also assume until further notice that tuples are the only kind of "lockable object"; again, see Section 14.8 for other possibilities.

2. If transaction *A* holds an exclusive (X) lock on tuple *p,* then a request from some distinct transaction *B* for a lock of either type on *p* will be denied.

3. If transaction *A* holds a shared (S) lock on tuple *p,* then:

   ▪ A request from some distinct transaction *B* for an X lock on *p* will be denied;

   ▪ A request from some distinct transaction *B* for an S lock on *p* will be granted (that is, *B* will now also hold an S lock on *p*).

These rules can conveniently be summarized by means of a *compatibility matrix* (Fig. 14.5). That matrix is interpreted as follows: Consider some tuple *p;* suppose transaction *A* currently holds a lock on *p* as indicated by the entries in the column headings (dash = no lock); and suppose some distinct transaction *B* issues a request for a lock on *p* as indicated by the entries down the left-hand side (for completeness we again include the "no lock" case). An "N" indicates a *conflict* (*B*'s request cannot be satisfied and *B* goes into a wait state), a "Y" indicates compatibility (*B*'s request is satisfied). The matrix is obviously symmetric.

	X	S	—
X	N	N	Y
S	N	Y	Y
—	Y	Y	Y

FIG. 14.5 Compatibility matrix for lock types X and S

Next, we introduce a **data access protocol** that makes use of X and S locks as just defined to guarantee that problems such as those described in Section 14.2 cannot occur:

1. A transaction that wishes to retrieve a tuple must first acquire an S lock on that tuple.

2. A transaction that wishes to update a tuple must first acquire an X lock on that tuple. Alternatively, if it already holds an S lock on the tuple, as it will in a RETRIEVE-UPDATE sequence, then it must *promote* that S lock to X level.

   Note: Transaction requests for tuple locks are normally implicit; a "tuple retrieve" request is an implicit request for an S lock, and a "tuple update" request is an implicit request for an X lock, on the relevant tuple. Also, of course (as always), we take the term "update" to include INSERTs and DELETEs as well as UPDATEs *per se,* but the protocol requires some slight refinement to take care of INSERTs and DELETEs. We omit the details here.

3. If a lock request from transaction *B* is denied because it conflicts with a lock already held by transaction *A,* transaction *B* goes into a wait state. *B* will wait until *A*'s lock is released. *Note:* The system must guarantee that *B* does not wait forever (a condition sometimes referred to as **livelock**). A simple way to provide such a guarantee is to service all lock requests in a first-come/first-served order.

4. X locks are held until end-of-transaction (COMMIT or ROLLBACK). S locks are normally held until that time also (but see Section 14.7).

14.4   The Three Concurrency Problems Revisited

Now we are in a position to see how the foregoing scheme solves the three problems described in Section 14.2. Again we consider them one at a time.

The Lost Update Problem

Fig. 14.6 is a modified version of Fig. 14.1, showing what would happen to the interleaved execution of that figure under the locking protocol described in Section 14.3. Transaction *A*'s UPDATE at time *t3* is not accepted, because it is an implicit request for an X lock on *R,* and such a request conflicts with the S lock already held by transaction *B;* so *A* goes into a wait state. For analogous reasons, *B* goes into a wait state at time *t4*. Now both transactions are unable to proceed, so there is no question of any update being lost. Locking thus solves the lost update problem by reducing it to another prob-

Transaction A	time	Transaction B
—		—
—		—
RETRIEVE p	t1	—
(acquire S lock on p)		—
—		—
—	t2	RETRIEVE p
—		(acquire S lock on p)
—		—
UPDATE p	t3	—
(request X lock on p)		—
wait		—
wait	t4	UPDATE p
wait		(request X lock on p)
wait		wait
wait		wait
wait		wait

FIG. 14.6   No update is lost, but deadlock occurs at time *t4*

lem!—but at least it does solve the original problem. The new problem is called **deadlock**. The problem of deadlock is discussed in Section 14.5.

The Uncommitted Dependency Problem

Figs. 14.7 and 14.8 are, respectively, modified versions of Figs. 14.2 and 14.3, showing what would happen to the interleaved executions of those figures under the locking protocol of Section 14.3. Transaction *A*'s operation at time *t2* (RETRIEVE in Fig. 14.7,

Transaction A	time	Transaction B
—		—
—		—
—	t1	UPDATE p
—		(acquire X lock on p)
—		—
RETRIEVE p	t2	—
(request S lock on p)		—
wait		—
wait	t3	COMMIT / ROLLBACK
wait		(release X lock on p)
resume : RETRIEVE p	t4	
(acquire S lock on p)		
—		

FIG. 14.7   Transaction *A* is prevented from seeing an uncommitted change at time *t2*

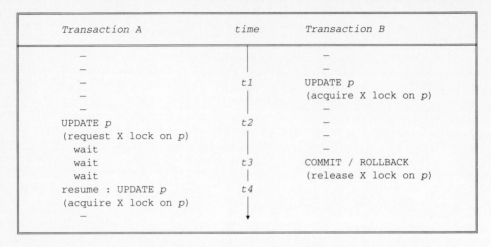

FIG. 14.8 Transaction *A* is prevented from updating an uncommitted change at time *t2*

UPDATE in Fig. 14.8) is not accepted in either case, because it is an implicit request for a lock on *R,* and such a request conflicts with the X lock already held by *B;* so *A* goes into a wait state. It remains in that wait state until *B* reaches its termination (either COMMIT or ROLLBACK), when *B*'s lock is released and *A* is able to proceed; and at that point *A* sees a *committed* value (either the pre-*B* value, if *B* terminates with a ROLLBACK, or the post-*B* value otherwise). Either way, *A* is no longer dependent on an uncommitted update.

The Inconsistent Analysis Problem

Fig. 14.9 (opposite) is a modified version of Fig. 14.4, showing what would happen to the interleaved execution of that figure under the locking protocol of Section 14.3. Transaction *B*'s UPDATE at time *t6* is not accepted, because it is an implicit request for an X lock on ACC 1, and such a request conflicts with the S lock already held by *A;* so *B* goes into a wait state. Likewise, transaction *A*'s RETRIEVE at time *t7* is also not accepted, because it is an implicit request for an S lock on ACC 3, and such a request conflicts with the X lock already held by *B;* so *A* goes into a wait state also. Again, therefore, locking solves the original problem (the inconsistent analysis problem, in this case) by forcing a deadlock. Again, see Section 14.5.

14.5   Deadlock

We have now seen how locking can be used to solve the three basic problems of concurrency. Unfortunately, however, we have also seen that locking can introduce problems of its own, principally the problem of deadlock. Two examples of deadlock were

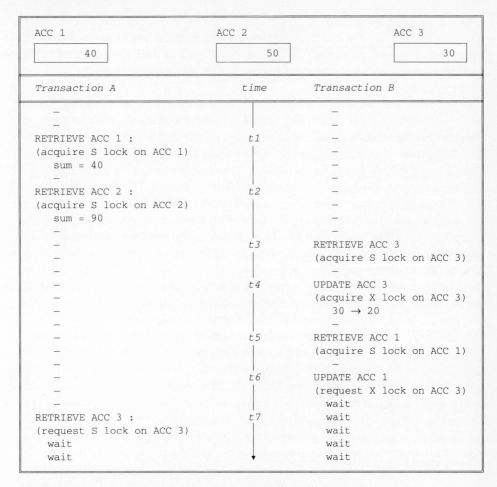

FIG. 14.9 Inconsistent analysis is prevented, but deadlock occurs at time *t7*

Transaction A	time	Transaction B
—		—
—		—
LOCK *p1* EXCLUSIVE	*t1*	—
—		—
—	*t2*	LOCK *p2* EXCLUSIVE
—		—
LOCK *p2* EXCLUSIVE	*t3*	—
wait		—
wait	*t4*	LOCK *p1* EXCLUSIVE
wait		wait
wait		wait

FIG. 14.10 An example of deadlock

given in the previous section. Fig. 14.10 shows a slightly more generalized version of the problem; *p1* and *p2* in that figure are intended to represent any lockable objects, not necessarily just database tuples (see Section 14.8), and the "LOCK . . . EXCLUSIVE" statements are intended to represent any operations that acquire (exclusive) locks, either explicitly or implicitly.

Deadlock is a situation in which two or more transactions are in a simultaneous wait state, each of them waiting for one of the others to release a lock before it can proceed. Fig. 14.10 shows a deadlock involving two transactions, but deadlocks involving three, four, . . . , transactions are also possible, at least in principle. As an aside, however, we remark that experiments with System R seemed to show that in practice deadlocks almost never do involve more than two transactions [14.4].

If a deadlock occurs, it is desirable that the system detect it and break it. Detecting the deadlock involves detecting a cycle in the **Wait-For Graph** (i.e., the graph of "who is waiting for whom"—see Exercise 14.4). Breaking the deadlock involves choosing one of the deadlocked transactions—i.e., one of the transactions in the cycle in the graph—as the **victim** and rolling it back, thereby releasing its locks and so allowing some other transaction to proceed. *Note:* In practice, not all systems do detect deadlocks—some just use a timeout mechanism and simply assume that a transaction that has done no work for some prescribed period of time is deadlocked.

Observe, incidentally, that the victim has "failed" and been rolled back *through no fault of its own.* Some systems will automatically restart such a transaction from the beginning, on the assumption that the conditions that caused the deadlock in the first place will probably not arise again. Other systems simply send a "deadlock victim" return code back to the application; it is then up to the program to deal with the situation in some graceful manner. The first of these two approaches is clearly preferable from the application programmer's point of view. But even if the programmer does sometimes have to get involved, it is *always* desirable to conceal the problem from the end user, for obvious reasons.

14.6   Serializability

We have now laid the groundwork for explaining the crucial notion of **serializability**. Serializability is the generally accepted **criterion for correctness** for concurrency control. More precisely, a given interleaved execution of a set of transactions is considered to be correct if it is serializable—i.e., if it produces the same result as some *serial* execution of the same transactions, running them one at a time. Here is the justification for this claim:

1. Individual transactions are assumed to be correct—i.e., they are assumed to convert a consistent state of the database into another consistent state, as explained in Chapter 13.

2. Running the transactions one at a time in any serial order is therefore also correct—

"any" serial order because individual transactions are assumed to be independent of one another.

3. An interleaved execution is therefore correct if it is equivalent to some serial execution—i.e., if it is serializable.

Referring back to the examples of Section 14.2 (Figs. 14.1–14.4), we can see that the problem in every case was that the interleaved execution was *not* serializable—that is, the interleaved execution was never equivalent to running either *A*-then-*B* or *B*-then-*A*. And the effect of the locking scheme discussed in Section 14.3 was precisely to *force* serializability in each case. In Figs. 14.7 and 14.8, the interleaved execution was equivalent to *B*-then-*A*. In Figs. 14.6 and 14.9, a deadlock occurred, implying that one of the two transactions would be rolled back and—presumably—run again later. If *A* is the one rolled back, then the interleaved execution again becomes equivalent to *B*-then-*A*.

Terminology: Given a set of transactions, any execution of those transactions (interleaved or otherwise) is called a **schedule**. Executing the transactions one at a time, with no interleaving, constitutes a **serial** schedule; a schedule that is not serial is an **interleaved** schedule (or simply a nonserial schedule). Two schedules are said to be **equivalent** if they are guaranteed to produce the same result, independent of the initial state of the database. Thus, a schedule is correct (i.e., serializable) if it is equivalent to some serial schedule.

The point is worth emphasizing that two different serial schedules involving the same set of transactions might very well produce different results, and hence that two different interleaved schedules involving those transactions might also produce different results and yet both be considered correct. For example, suppose transaction *A* is of the form "Add 1 to *x*" and transaction *B* is of the form "Double *x*" (where *x* is some item in the database). Suppose also that the initial value of *x* is 10. Then the serial schedule *A*-then-*B* gives *x* = 22, whereas the serial schedule *B*-then-*A* gives *x* = 21. These two results are equally correct, and any schedule that is guaranteed to be equivalent to either *A*-then-*B* or *B*-then-*A* is likewise correct. See Exercise 14.3.

The concept of serializability was first introduced (although not by that name) by Eswaran *et al.* in reference [14.5]. That same paper also proved an important theorem, called the **two-phase locking theorem,** which we state briefly as follows:*

> *If all transactions obey the "two-phase locking protocol," then all possible interleaved schedules are serializable.*

The **two-phase locking protocol,** in turn, is as follows:

1. Before operating on any object (e.g., a database tuple), a transaction must acquire a lock on that object.

2. After releasing a lock, a transaction must never go on to acquire any more locks.

---

* Two-phase locking is nothing to do with two-phase commit, by the way—they just have similar names.

A transaction that obeys this protocol thus has two phases, a lock acquisition phase and a lock releasing phase. *Note:* In practice the second phase is often compressed into the single operation of COMMIT (or ROLLBACK) at end-of-transaction. In fact, the locking protocol we discussed in Section 14.3 can be regarded as a strong form of the two-phase protocol.

The notion of serializability is a great aid to clear thinking in this potentially confusing area. We therefore offer a few additional comments on the subject here. Let E be an interleaved schedule involving some set of transactions $T1, T2, \ldots, Tn$. If E is serializable, then there exists some serial schedule S involving $T1, T2, \ldots, Tn$ such that E is equivalent to S. S is said to be a **serialization** of E. As we have already seen, S is not necessarily unique—i.e., a given E can have more than one serialization.

Now let Ti and Tj be any two transactions in the set $T1, T2, \ldots, Tn$. Assume without loss of generality that Ti precedes Tj in the serialization S. In the interleaved schedule E, therefore, the *effect* must be as if Ti really did execute before Tj. In other words, an informal—but very helpful—characterization of serializability is that, if A and B are any two transactions involved in some serializable schedule, then either A logically precedes B or B logically precedes A in that schedule; that is, **either B can see A's output or A can see B's**. (If A updates tuples $p, q, \ldots, r$, and if B sees any of these tuples as input, then B sees them *either* all as updated by A *or* all as they were before being updated by A—not a mixture of the two.) Conversely, if the effect is not as if either A ran before B or B ran before A, then the schedule is not serializable and not correct.

In conclusion, the point is worth stressing that if some transaction A is not two-phase (i.e., does not obey the two-phase locking protocol), then it is *always* possible to construct some other transaction B that can run interleaved with A in such a way as to produce an overall schedule that is not serializable and not correct. Now, in the interests of reducing resource contention and thereby improving performance and throughput, real systems typically do allow the construction of transactions that are not two-phase—i.e., transactions that "release locks early" (prior to COMMIT) and then go on to acquire more locks. However, it should be clearly understood that such transactions are a risky proposition. In effect, allowing a given transaction A to be non-two-phase amounts to a gamble that no interfering transaction B will ever coexist in the system with A (for if it does, then the system will potentially produce wrong answers).

14.7   Levels of Isolation

The term **isolation level** is used to refer to what might loosely be described as *the degree of interference* that a given transaction is prepared to tolerate on the part of concurrent transactions. Now, if serializability is to be guaranteed, the only amount of interference that can possibly be acceptable is none at all!—in other words, the isolation level should be the maximum possible. As indicated at the end of the previous section, however, real systems typically do permit transactions to operate at isolation levels that are less than this maximum, for a variety of pragmatic reasons.

Note: As the foregoing paragraph suggests, isolation level is generally regarded as a property of a *transaction.* Actually there is no reason why a given transaction should not operate at different levels at the same time on different parts of the database, at least in principle. For simplicity, however, we will continue to think of isolation level as a transaction-wide property.

Many different isolation levels can be defined; reference [14.4] discusses five, reference [14.9] and the SQL standard [8.1] both define four, IBM's DB2 product currently supports two. Generally speaking, the higher the isolation level, the less the interference (and the lower the concurrency); the lower the isolation level, the more the interference (and the higher the concurrency). By way of example, we consider the two levels supported by DB2, which are called **cursor stability** and **repeatable read,** respectively. *Repeatable read* (RR) is the maximum level; if all transactions operate at this level, all schedules are serializable (the explanations in Section 14.3 and 14.4 were tacitly assuming this isolation level). Under *cursor stability* (CS), by contrast, if a transaction *T1*

■ Obtains addressability to some tuple *p*,* and thus

■ Acquires a lock on *p,* and then

■ Relinquishes its addressability to *p* without updating it, and so

■ Does not promote its lock to X level, then

■ That lock can be released without having to wait for end-of-transaction.

But note that some other transaction *T2* can now update *p* and commit the change. If transaction *T1* now comes back and looks at *p* again, it will see that change, and so might see an inconsistent state of the database. Under repeatable read (RR), by contrast, *all* tuple locks (not just X locks) are held until end-of-transaction, and the problem just mentioned therefore cannot occur.

Note: The foregoing problem is *not* the only problem that can occur under CS—it just happens to be the easiest to explain. But it unfortunately suggests that RR is needed only in the comparatively unlikely case that a given transaction needs to look at the same tuple twice. On the contrary, there are arguments to suggest that RR is *always* a better choice than CS; a transaction running under CS is non-two-phase, and so (as explained in the previous section) serializability is no longer guaranteed. The counter-argument, of course, is that CS gives more concurrency than RR (probably but not necessarily).

In closing this section, we should note that the foregoing characterization of RR as the maximum isolation level refers to repeatable read as implemented in DB2. Unfortunately, the SQL standard [8.1] uses the same term "repeatable read" to mean an isolation level that is strictly lower than the maximum level. See Section 14.9.

---

* As explained in Chapter 8, it does this by setting a *cursor* to point to the tuple—hence the name "cursor stability." In the interests of accuracy, we should mention also that the lock *T1* acquires on *p* in DB2 is an "update" (U) lock, not an S lock. U locks are defined to be compatible with S locks but not with other U locks (and not with X locks, of course). We ignore the further implications of this refinement here.

14.8 Intent Locking

Up to this point we have been assuming that the unit for locking purposes is the individual tuple. In principle, however, there is no reason why locks should not be applied to larger or smaller units of data—an entire relation, or the whole database, or (going to the opposite extreme) a specific attribute value within a specific tuple. We speak of **locking granularity** [14.8]. As usual, there is a tradeoff: The finer the granularity, the greater the concurrency; the coarser, the fewer locks need to be set and tested and the lower the overhead. For example, if a transaction has an X lock on an entire relation, there is no need to set X locks on individual tuples inside that relation, which obviously reduces the overall number of locks; on the other hand, no concurrent transaction will be able to obtain any locks on that relation, or the tuples in that relation, at all.

Now suppose some transaction T requests an X lock on some relation R. On receipt of T's request, the system must be able to tell whether any other transaction already has a lock on any tuple of R—for if it does, then T's request cannot be granted at this time. How can the system detect such a conflict? It is obviously undesirable to have to examine every tuple of R to see whether any of them is locked by any other transaction, or to have to examine every existing lock to see whether any of them is for a tuple in R. Instead, we introduce another protocol, the **intent locking protocol,** according to which no transaction is allowed to acquire a lock on a tuple before first acquiring a lock—probably an *intent* lock (see below)—on the relation that contains it. Conflict detection in the example then becomes a comparatively simple matter of seeing whether any transaction has a conflicting lock *at the relation level*.

We have already implied that X and S locks make sense for whole relations as well as for individual tuples. Now—following references [14.8–14.9]—we introduce three new kinds of lock, called **intent locks,** that also make sense for relations, but not for individual tuples. The new kinds of lock are called **intent shared** (IS), **intent exclusive** (IX), and **shared intent exclusive** (SIX). They can be defined informally as follows (we suppose that transaction T has requested a lock of the indicated type on relation R; for completeness, we include definitions for types X and S as well).

■ IS
   T intends to set S locks on individual tuples of R, in order to guarantee the stability of those tuples while they are being processed.

■ IX
   Same as IS, *plus* T might update individual tuples of R and will therefore set X locks on those tuples.

■ S
   T can tolerate concurrent readers, but not concurrent updaters, in R. T itself will not update any tuples of R.

■ SIX
   Combines S and IX; i.e., T can tolerate concurrent readers, but not concurrent updaters, in R, *plus* T might update individual tuples of R and will therefore set X locks on those tuples.

- X

  T cannot tolerate any concurrent access to *R* at all; *T* itself might or might not update individual tuples of *R*.

The formal definitions of these five lock types are given by an extended form of the compatibility matrix first discussed in Section 14.3. Refer to Fig. 14.11.

	X	SIX	IX	S	IS	–
X	N	N	N	N	N	Y
SIX	N	N	N	N	Y	Y
IX	N	N	Y	N	Y	Y
S	N	N	N	Y	Y	Y
IS	N	Y	Y	Y	Y	Y
–	Y	Y	Y	Y	Y	Y

FIG. 14.11 Compatibility matrix extended to include intent locks

Here now is a more precise statement of the intent locking protocol:

1. Before a given transaction can acquire an S lock on a given tuple, it must first acquire an IS or stronger lock (see below) on the relation containing that tuple.

2. Before a given transaction can acquire an X lock on a given tuple, it must first acquire an IX or stronger lock (see below) on the relation containing that tuple.

(Note, however, that this is still not a complete definition. See the annotation to reference [14.8].)

We explain the notion of *relative lock strength* (as mentioned in the foregoing protocol) as follows. Refer to the **precedence graph** in Fig. 14.12. We say that lock type

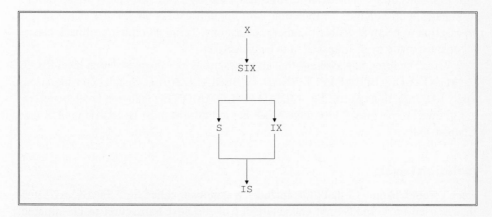

FIG. 14.12 Lock type precedence graph

L2 is stronger—i.e., higher in the graph—than lock type *L1* if and only if, whenever there is an "N" (conflict) in *L1*'s column in the compatibility matrix for a given row, there is also an "N" in *L2*'s column for that same row (see Fig. 14.11). Note that a lock request that fails for a given lock type will certainly fail for a stronger lock type (which implies that it is always safe to use a lock type that is stronger than strictly necessary). Note too that neither of S and IX is stronger than the other.

It is worth pointing out that, in practice, the relation-level locks required by the intent locking protocol will usually be acquired implicitly. For a read-only transaction, for example, the system will probably acquire an IS lock implicitly on every relation the transaction touches. For an update transaction, it will probably acquire IX locks instead. But the system will probably also have to provide an explicit LOCK statement of some kind in order to allow transactions to acquire S, X, or SIX locks at the relation level if they want them. Such an explicit LOCK statement is supported by DB2, for example (though not by the SQL standard).

We close this section with a remark on *lock escalation,* which is implemented in many systems and represents an attempt to balance the conflicting requirements of high concurrency and low lock management overhead. The basic idea is that when the system reaches some predefined threshold, it automatically replaces a set of fine-granularity locks by a single coarse-granularity lock—for example, by trading in a set of individual tuple-level S locks and converting the IS lock on the containing relation to an S lock. This technique seems to work well in practice.

14.9   SQL Support

The SQL standard does not provide any explicit locking capabilities (in fact, it does not mention locking as such at all). However, it does require the implementation to provide the usual guarantees regarding interference, or rather lack thereof, among concurrently executing transactions. Specifically, it requires that updates made by a given transaction *T1* not become visible to any distinct transaction *T2* until and unless transaction *T1* terminates with commit. Termination with commit causes all updates made by the transaction to become visible to other transactions. Termination with rollback causes all updates made by the transaction to be canceled.

Note: The foregoing assumes that all transactions execute at isolation level READ COMMITTED, REPEATABLE READ, or SERIALIZABLE. Special considerations apply to transactions executing at READ UNCOMMITTED isolation level, which (a) are allowed to perform "dirty reads" (see below) but (b) must be READ ONLY (see Chapter 13).

Isolation Levels

Recall from Chapter 13 that SQL includes a statement called SET TRANSACTION that is used to define certain characteristics of the next transaction to be initiated. One of those characteristics is *isolation level.* The possible levels are **READ**

UNCOMMITTED, READ COMMITTED, REPEATABLE READ, or SERIALIZABLE. The default is SERIALIZABLE; if any of the other three is specified, the implementation is free to assign some greater level, where "greater" is defined in terms of the ordering SERIALIZABLE > REPEATABLE READ > READ COMMITTED > READ UNCOMMITTED.

If all transactions execute at isolation level SERIALIZABLE (the default), then the interleaved execution of any set of concurrent transactions is guaranteed to be serializable. However, if any transaction executes at a lesser isolation level, then serializability can be violated in a variety of different ways. The standard defines three specific ways in which serializability might be violated, namely *dirty read, nonrepeatable read,* and *phantoms*:

- **Dirty read:** Suppose transaction *T1* performs an update on some row, transaction *T2* then retrieves that row, and transaction *T1* then terminates with rollback. Transaction *T2* has then seen a row that no longer exists, and in a sense never did exist (because transaction *T1* effectively never ran).

- **Nonrepeatable read:** Suppose transaction *T1* retrieves a row, transaction *T2* then updates that row, and transaction *T1* then retrieves the "same" row again. Transaction *T1* has now retrieved the "same" row twice but seen two different values for it.

- **Phantoms:** Suppose transaction *T1* retrieves the set of all rows that satisfy some condition (e.g., all supplier rows satisfying the condition that the supplier city is Paris). Suppose that transaction *T2* then inserts a new row satisfying that same condition. If transaction *T1* now repeats its retrieval request, it will see a row that did not previously exist—a "phantom."

The various isolation levels are defined in terms of which of the foregoing violations of serializability they permit. They are summarized in Fig. 14.13 ("Y" means the indicated violation can occur, "N" means it cannot).

An obvious question that arises is: How can the system prevent "phantoms" from occurring? The answer is that it must lock the *access path* used to get to the data under consideration. In the example mentioned above regarding Paris suppliers, for instance, if that access path happens to be an index on supplier cities, then the system must lock

isolation level	dirty read	nonrepeatable read	phantom
READ UNCOMMITTED	Y	Y	Y
READ COMMITTED	N	Y	Y
REPEATABLE READ	N	N	Y
SERIALIZABLE	N	N	N

FIG. 14.13 SQL isolation levels

the Paris entry in that index. Such a lock will prevent the creation of phantoms, because such creation would require the access path (the index entry, in our example) to be updated. See reference [13.11] or reference [14.4] for further discussion.

As mentioned in Section 14.8, a system that supports any isolation level other than SERIALIZABLE (which is, of course, the only totally *safe* level) would normally provide some explicit concurrency control facilities—typically explicit LOCK statements—in order to allow users to write their applications in such a way as to guarantee safety in the absence of such a guarantee from the system itself. However, the SQL standard does not include any such explicit mechanism.

We close this section by repeating the point that the REPEATABLE READ of SQL and the REPEATABLE READ of DB2 are not the same thing. In fact, DB2's REPEATABLE READ is the same as SQL's SERIALIZABLE.

14.10 Summary

We have examined the question of **concurrency control**. We began by looking at three problems that can arise in an interleaved execution of concurrent transactions if no such control is in place—the **lost update** problem, the **uncommitted dependency** problem, and the **inconsistent analysis** problem. All of these problems arise from schedules that are not **serializable**—i.e., not equivalent to some serial schedule involving the same transactions.

The most widespread technique for dealing with such problems is **locking**. There are two basic types of lock, **shared** (S) and **exclusive** (X). If a transaction has an S lock on an object, other transactions can also acquire an S lock on that object, but not an X lock; if a transaction has an X lock on an object, no other transaction can acquire a lock on the object of either type. Then we introduce a protocol for the use of these locks to ensure that the lost update problem and other problems cannot occur: Acquire an S lock on everything you retrieve, acquire an X lock on everything you update, and keep all locks until end-of-transaction. This protocol enforces serializability.

The protocol just described is a strong (and common) form of the **two-phase locking protocol**. It can be shown that if all transactions obey this protocol, then all schedules are serializable—the **two-phase locking theorem**. A serializable schedule implies that if A and B are any two transactions involved in that schedule, then either A can see B's output or B can see A's. Unfortunately, the two-phase locking protocol can lead to **deadlocks**. Deadlocks are resolved by choosing one of the deadlocked transactions as the **victim** and rolling it back.

Anything less than full serializability cannot be guaranteed to be safe (in general). However, systems typically allow transactions to operate at a **level of isolation** that is indeed unsafe, with the aim of reducing resource contention and increasing transaction throughput. We described one such "unsafe" level, *viz.* **cursor stability** (this is the DB2 term; the SQL standard analog is READ COMMITTED).

Next we briefly considered the question of **lock granularity** and the associated idea of **intent locking**. Basically, before a transaction can acquire a lock of any kind on some object, say a database tuple, it must first acquire an appropriate intent lock (at least) on the "parent" of that object (i.e., the containing relation, in the case of a tuple). In practice, such intent locks will usually be acquired implicitly, just as S and X locks on tuples are usually acquired implicitly. However, **explicit LOCK statements** of some kind should be provided in order to allow a transaction to acquire stronger locks (when needed) than the ones acquired implicitly.

Finally, we outlined SQL's concurrency control support. Basically, SQL does not provide any explicit locking capabilities at all. However, it does support various isolation levels—**READ UNCOMMITTED, READ COMMITTED, REPEATABLE READ,** and **SERIALIZABLE**—which the DBMS will probably implement by means of locking behind the scenes.

Exercises

14.1 Define the term *serializability*.

14.2 State (a) the two-phase locking protocol, (b) the two-phase locking theorem.

14.3 Let transactions *T1, T2,* and *T3* be defined to perform the following operations:

```
T1: Add one to A
T2: Double A
T3: Display A on the screen and then set A to one
```

(where *A* is some item in the database).

(a) Suppose transactions *T1, T2, T3* are allowed to execute concurrently. If *A* has initial value zero, how many possible correct results are there? Enumerate them.

(b) Suppose the internal structure of *T1, T2, T3* is as indicated below:

T1	T2	T3
R1: RETRIEVE A INTO *t1* *t1* := *t1* + 1 U1: UPDATE A FROM *t1*	R2: RETRIEVE A INTO *t2* *t2* := *t2* * 2 U2: UPDATE A FROM *t2*	R3: RETRIEVE A INTO *t3* display *t3* U3: UPDATE A FROM 1

If the transactions execute *without* any locking, how many possible schedules are there?

(c) With the given initial value for *A* (zero), are there any interleaved schedules that in fact produce a "correct" result and yet are not serializable?

(d) Are there any schedules that are in fact serializable but could not be produced if all three transactions obeyed the two-phase locking protocol?

14.4 The following represents the sequence of events in a schedule involving transactions *T1, T2, . . . , T12.* A, B, . . . , H are items in the database.

```
time t0     . . . . . . . . . .
time t1   (T1)   : RETRIEVE A
time t2   (T2)   : RETRIEVE B
    -     (T1)   : RETRIEVE C
    -     (T4)   : RETRIEVE D
    -     (T5)   : RETRIEVE A
    -     (T2)   : RETRIEVE E
```

```
-    (T2)    : UPDATE   E
-    (T3)    : RETRIEVE F
-    (T2)    : RETRIEVE F
-    (T5)    : UPDATE   A
-    (T1)    : COMMIT
-    (T6)    : RETRIEVE A
-    (T5)    : ROLLBACK
-    (T6)    : RETRIEVE C
-    (T6)    : UPDATE   C
-    (T7)    : RETRIEVE G
-    (T8)    : RETRIEVE H
-    (T9)    : RETRIEVE G
-    (T9)    : UPDATE   G
-    (T8)    : RETRIEVE E
-    (T7)    : COMMIT
-    (T9)    : RETRIEVE H
-    (T3)    : RETRIEVE G
-    (T10)   : RETRIEVE A
-    (T9)    : UPDATE   H
-    (T6)    : COMMIT
-    (T11)   : RETRIEVE C
-    (T12)   : RETRIEVE D
-    (T12)   : RETRIEVE C
-    (T2)    : UPDATE   F
-    (T11)   : UPDATE   C
-    (T12)   : RETRIEVE A
-    (T10)   : UPDATE   A
-    (T12)   : UPDATE   D
-    (T4)    : RETRIEVE G
time tn   .........
```

Assume that "RETRIEVE *R*" (if successful) acquires an S lock on *R,* and "UPDATE *R*" (if successful) promotes that lock to X level. Assume also that all locks are held until end-of-transaction. Are there any deadlocks at time *tn*?

14.5 Consider the concurrency problems illustrated in Figs. 14.1–14.4 once again. What would happen in each case if all transactions were executing under isolation level CS instead of RR?

14.6 Give both informal and formal definitions of the five lock types X, S, IX, IS, SIX. *Note:* The formal definitions are given by the compatibility matrix.

14.7 Define the notion of relative lock strength and give the corresponding precedence graph.

14.8 Define the intent locking protocol. What is the purpose of that protocol?

14.9 SQL defines three concurrency problems: *dirty read, nonrepeatable read,* and *phantoms.* How do these relate to the three concurrency problems identified in Section 14.2?

References and Bibliography

See also references [13.1], [13.9], and (especially) [13.11] in Chapter 13.

14.1 R. Bayer, M. Heller, and A. Reiser. "Parallelism and Recovery in Database Systems." *ACM TODS 5,* No. 2 (June 1980).

Proposes a concurrency control technique known as **multiversion locking** (also called **multiversion read,** and now implemented in several commercial products). The advantage of the technique is that read operations never have to wait—any number of readers *and one writer* can operate on the same logical object simultaneously. This advantage is particularly significant in distributed systems—see Chapter 21—where updates can take a long time and read-only queries might therefore otherwise be unduly delayed (and conversely). The basic idea is as follows:

1. If transaction *T2* asks to read an object that transaction *T1* currently has update access to, transaction *T2* is given access to a *previously committed* version of that object. Such a version must exist in the system somewhere—typically in the log—for recovery purposes.

2. If transaction *T2* asks to update an object that transaction *T1* currently has read access to, transaction *T2* is given access to that object, while transaction *T1* retains access to its own version of the object (which is now really the previous version).

Of course, the approach includes appropriate controls to ensure that each transaction always sees a consistent state of the database.

14.2 Philip A. Bernstein and Nathan Goodman. "Timestamp-Based Algorithms for Concurrency Control in Distributed Database Systems." Proc. 6th International Conference on Very Large Data Bases, Montreal, Canada (October 1980).

Discusses a collection of approaches to concurrency control based not on locking but on **timestamping**. The basic idea is that if transaction *A* starts execution before transaction *B,* then the system should behave as if *A* actually executed in its entirety before *B* started (as in a genuine serial schedule). Thus *A* should never be allowed to see any of *B*'s updates; likewise, *A* should never be allowed to update anything that *B* has already seen. Such controls can be enforced as follows. For any given database request, the system compares the timestamp of the requesting transaction with the timestamp of the transaction that last retrieved or updated the requested tuple. If there is a conflict, then the requesting transaction can simply be restarted with a new timestamp (as in the so-called *optimistic* methods [14.11]).

As the title of the paper suggests, timestamping was originally introduced in the context of a distributed system (where it was felt that locking imposed intolerable overheads, because of the messages needed to test and set locks, etc.). It is almost certainly not appropriate in a non-distributed system. Indeed, there is considerable skepticism as to its practicality in distributed systems also. One obvious problem is that each tuple has to carry the timestamp of the last transaction that last *retrieved* it (as well as the timestamp of the transaction that last updated it), which implies that every read becomes a write! In fact, Gray claims in reference [13.11] that timestamping schemes are really just a degenerate case of optimistic concurrency control schemes [14.11], which in turn suffer from problems of their own.

14.3 M. W. Blasgen, J. N. Gray, M. Mitoma, and T. G. Price. "The Convoy Phenomenon." *ACM Operating Systems Review 13,* No. 2 (April 1979).

The **convoy phenomenon** is a problem encountered with high-traffic locks, such as the lock needed to write a record to the log, in systems with *preemptive scheduling. Note:* "Scheduling" here refers to the problem of allocating machine cycles to transactions, not to the interleaving of database operations from different transactions as discussed in the body of the chapter.

The problem is as follows. If a transaction *T* is holding a high-traffic lock and is preempted by the system scheduler—i.e., forced into a wait state, perhaps because its time slice has expired—then a *convoy* of transactions will form, all waiting for their turn at the high-traffic lock. When *T* comes out of its wait state, it will soon release the lock, but (precisely because the lock is high-traffic) *T* itself will probably rejoin the convoy before the next transaction has finished with the resource, will therefore not be able to continue processing, and so will go into a wait state again.

The root of the problem is that in most cases (not all) the scheduler is part of the underlying operating system, not the DBMS, and is therefore designed to different performance parameters. As the authors observe, a convoy, once established, tends to be stable; the system is in a state of "lock thrashing," most of the machine cycles are devoted to process switching, and not much useful work is being done. A suggested solution—barring the possibility of replacing the scheduler—is to grant the lock not on a first-come/first-served basis but instead in random order.

14.4   C. J. Date. "Concurrency." Chapter 3 of C. J. Date, *An Introduction to Database Systems: Volume II*. Reading, Mass.: Addison-Wesley (1983).

Portions of the present chapter are based on this earlier tutorial treatment.

14.5   K. P. Eswaran, J. N. Gray, R. A. Lorie, and I. L. Traiger. "The Notions of Consistency and Predicate Locks in a Data Base System." *CACM 19*, No. 11 (November 1976).

The paper that first put the subject of concurrency control on a sound theoretical footing.

14.6   Peter Franaszek and John T. Robinson. "Limitations on Concurrency in Transaction Processing." *ACM TODS 10*, No. 1 (March 1985).

See the annotation to reference [14.11].

14.7   Peter A. Franaszek, John T. Robinson, and Alexander Thomasian. "Concurrency Control for High Contention Environments." *ACM TODS 17*, No. 2 (June 1992).

This paper claims that, for a variety of reasons, future transaction processing systems are likely to involve a significantly greater degree of concurrency than the systems of today, and that there is therefore likely to be substantially more data contention in such systems. The authors then present "a number of [nonlocking] concurrency control concepts and transaction scheduling techniques that are applicable to high contention environments" that—it is claimed, on the basis of experiments with simulation models—"can offer substantial benefits" in such environments.

14.8   J. N. Gray, R. A. Lorie, and G. R. Putzolu. "Granularity of Locks in a Large Shared Data Base." Proc. 1st International Conference on Very Large Data Bases, Framingham, Mass. (September 1975).

The paper that introduced the concept of **intent locking**. As explained in Section 14.8, the term "granularity" refers to the size of the objects that can be locked. Since different transactions obviously have different characteristics and different requirements, it is desirable that the system provide a range of different locking granularities (as indeed many systems do). This paper presents an implementation mechanism for such a multi-granularity system, based on intent locking.

We elaborate here on the **intent locking protocol,** since the explanations given in the body of the chapter were deliberately somewhat simplified. First of all, the lockable object types will not be limited to just relations and tuples, as we were assuming previously. Second, those lockable object types will (in general) not even form a strict hierarchy; the presence of indexes and other access structures will mean that they should rather be regarded as a *directed acyclic graph*. For example, the suppliers-and-parts database might contain both (a stored form of) the parts relation P and an index, XP say, on the P# attribute of that relation. To get to the tuples of relation P, we must start with the overall database, and then *either* go straight to the relation and do a sequential scan *or* go to index XP and thence to the required P tuples. So the tuples of P have two "parents" in the graph, P and XP, both of which have the database as a "parent" in turn.

We can now state the protocol in its most general form.

■ Acquiring an X lock on a given object implicitly acquires an X lock on all children of that object.

■ Acquiring an S or SIX lock on a given object implicitly acquires an S lock on all children of that lock.

■ Before a transaction can acquire an S or IS lock on a given object, it must first acquire an IS (or stronger) lock on at least one parent of that object.

■ Before a transaction can acquire an X, IX, or SIX lock on a given object, it must first acquire an IX (or stronger) lock on all parents of that object.

■ Before a transaction can release a lock on a given object, it must first release all locks it holds on all children of that object.

In practice, the protocol does not impose as much run-time overhead as might be thought, because at any given moment the transaction will probably already have most of the locks it needs. For example, an IX lock, say, will probably be acquired on the entire database just once, at program initiation time. That lock will then be held throughout all transactions executed during the lifetime of the program.

14.9 J. N. Gray, R. A. Lorie, G. R. Putzolu, and I. L. Traiger. "Granularity of Locks and Degrees of Consistency in a Shared Data Base." In *Proc. IFIP TC-2 Working Conference on Model-ling in Data Base Management Systems* (ed., G. M. Nijssen). Amsterdam, Netherlands: North-Holland/New York, N.Y.: Elsevier Science (1976).

The paper that introduced the concept of isolation level (under the name "degrees of consistency").

14.10 Theo Härder and Kurt Rothermel. "Concurrency Control Issues in Nested Transactions." *The VLDB Journal 2,* No. 1 (January 1993).

As explained in Chapter 13, several writers have suggested the idea of **nested transactions**. This paper proposes an appropriate set of locking protocols for such transactions.

14.11 H. T. Kung and John T. Robinson. "On Optimistic Methods for Concurrency Control." *ACM TODS 6,* No. 2 (June 1981).

Locking schemes can be described as *pessimistic,* inasmuch as they make the worst-case assumption that every piece of data touched by a given transaction might be needed by some concurrent transaction and had therefore better be locked. The **optimistic** schemes, by contrast, make the opposite assumption that conflicts are likely to be quite rare in practice. Thus, they operate by allowing transactions to run to completion completely unhindered, and then checking at commit time to see whether a conflict did in fact occur. If it did, the offending transaction is simply started again from the beginning. No updates are ever written to the database prior to successful completion of commit processing, so such restarts do not require any updates to be undone.

A subsequent paper [14.6] showed that under certain reasonable assumptions, optimistic methods enjoy certain inherent advantages over traditional locking methods in terms of the expected level of concurrency (i.e., number of simultaneous transactions) they can support, suggesting that optimistic methods might become the technique of choice in systems with large numbers of parallel processors. (Reference [13.11], by contrast, claims that optimistic methods in general are actually *worse* than locking in "hotspot" situations—where a hotspot is a data item that is updated very frequently, by many distinct transactions. See reference [14.12] for a discussion of a technique that works well on hotspots.)

14.12 Patrick E. O'Neil. "The Escrow Transactional Method." *ACM TODS 11,* No. 4 (December 1986).

Consider the following simple example. Suppose the database contains a data item *TC* representing "total cash on hand," and suppose almost every transaction in the system updates *TC,* decrementing it by some amount (corresponding to some payment to be made). *TC* is an example of a "hotspot," i.e., an item in the database that is touched by a significant percentage of the transactions running in the system. Under traditional locking, a hotspot can very quickly become a bottleneck (to mix metaphors horribly). But using traditional locking on a data item like *TC* is really overkill. If *TC* initially has a value of ten million dollars, and each individual transaction decrements it (on average) by only ten dollars, then we could run 1,000,000 such transactions, *and furthermore apply the 1,000,000 corresponding decrements in any order,* before running into trouble. There is thus no need to apply a traditional lock to *TC* at all; instead, all that is necessary is to make sure that the current value is large enough to permit the required decrement, and then do the update. (If the transaction subsequently fails, the amount of the decrement must be added back in again, of course.)

The **escrow** method applies to situations such as the one just described—i.e., situations in which the updates are of a certain special form, instead of being completely arbitrary. The system must provide a special new kind of update statement (e.g., "decrement by x, if and only if the current value is greater than y"). It can then perform the update by placing the decrement amount x "in escrow," taking it out of escrow at end-of-transaction (and committing the change if end-of-transaction is COMMIT, or adding the amount back into the original total if end-of-transaction is ROLLBACK).

The paper describes a number of cases in which the escrow method can be used. One example of a commercial product that supports the technique is IMS Fast Path from IBM. We remark that the technique might be regarded as a special case of optimistic concurrency control [14.11] (note, however, that the "special case" aspect—the provision of the special update statements—is critical).

14.13   Christos Papadimitriou. *The Theory of Database Concurrency Control*. Rockville, Md.: Computer Science Press (1986).

A textbook, with the emphasis on formal theory.

Answers to Selected Exercises

14.3   (a) There are six possible correct results, corresponding to the six possible serial schedules:

```
Initially  :  A = 0
T1-T2-T3   :  A = 1
T1-T3-T2   :  A = 2
T2-T1-T3   :  A = 1
T2-T3-T1   :  A = 2
T3-T1-T2   :  A = 4
T3-T2-T1   :  A = 3
```

Of course, the six possible correct results are not all distinct. As a matter of fact, it so happens in this particular example that the possible correct results are all independent of the initial state of the database, owing to the nature of transaction *T3*.

(b)   There are 90 possible distinct schedules. We can represent the possibilities as follows. (*Ri, Rj, Rk* stand for the three RETRIEVE operations *R1, R2, R3*, not necessarily in that order; similarly, *Up, Uq, Ur* stand for the three UPDATE operations *U1, U2, U3*, again not necessarily in that order.)

```
Ri-Rj-Rk-Up-Uq-Ur : 3 * 2 * 1 * 3 * 2 * 1 = 36 possibilities
Ri-Rj-Up-Rk-Uq-Ur : 3 * 2 * 2 * 1 * 2 * 1 = 24 possibilities
Ri-Rj-Up-Uq-Rk-Ur : 3 * 2 * 2 * 1 * 1 * 1 = 12 possibilities
Ri-Up-Rj-Rk-Uq-Ur : 3 * 1 * 2 * 1 * 2 * 1 = 12 possibilities
Ri-Up-Rj-Uq-Rk-Ur : 3 * 1 * 2 * 1 * 1 * 1 =  6 possibilities
                                    TOTAL = 90 combinations
```

(c)   Yes. For example, the schedule *R1-R2-R3-U3-U2-U1* produces the same result (one) as two of the six possible serial schedules (*Exercise:* Check this statement), and thus happens to be "correct" for the given initial value of zero. But it must be clearly understood that this "correctness" is a mere fluke, and results purely from the fact that the initial data value happened to be zero and not something else. As a counterexample, consider what would happen if the initial value of *A* were ten instead of zero. Would the schedule shown above still produce one of the genuinely correct results? (What *are* the genuinely correct results in this case?) If not, then the schedule *R1-R2-R3-U3-U2-U1* is not serializable.

(d)   Yes. For example, the schedule *R1-R3-U1-U3-R2-U2* is serializable (it is equivalent to the serial schedule *T1-T3-T2*), but it cannot be produced if *T1, T2,* and *T3* all obey the two-phase locking protocol. For, under that protocol, operation *R3* will acquire an S lock on *A* on behalf of transaction *T3;* operation *U1* in transaction *T1* will thus not be able to proceed until that lock has been released, and that will not happen until transaction *T3* terminates (in fact, transactions *T3* and *T1* will deadlock when operation *U3* is reached).

This exercise illustrates very clearly the following important point. Given a set of transactions and an initial state of the database: (1) Let ALL be the set of all possible schedules involving those transactions; (2) let "CORRECT" be the set of all schedules that are guaranteed to produce a correct final state or at least happen to do so from the given initial state; (3) let SERIALIZABLE be the set of all serializable schedules; and (4) let PRODUCIBLE be the set of all schedules producible under the two-phase locking protocol. Then, in general,

```
PRODUCIBLE ≤ SERIALIZABLE ≤ "CORRECT" ≤ ALL
```

(using "≤" to mean "is a subset of").

14.4 At time *tn* no transactions are doing any useful work at all! There is one deadlock, involving transactions *T2, T3, T9,* and *T8;* in addition, *T4* is waiting for *T9, T12* is waiting for *T4,* and *T10* and *T11* are both waiting for *T12.* We can represent the situation by means of a graph (the **Wait-For Graph**), in which the nodes represent transactions and a directed edge from node *Ti* to node *Tj* indicates that *Ti* is waiting for *Tj* (see Fig. 14.14). Edges are labeled with the name of the database item and level of lock they are waiting for.

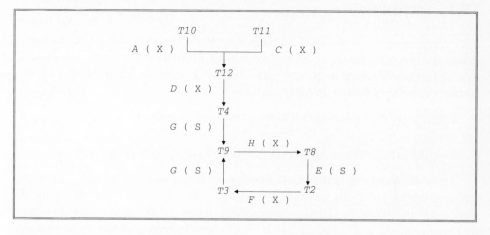

FIG. 14.14 The Wait-For Graph for Exercise 14.4

14.5 Isolation level CS has the same effect as isolation level RR on the problems of Figs. 14.1–14.3 (note, however, that this statement does *not* apply to CS as implemented in DB2, thanks to DB2's use of U locks in place of S locks). As for the inconsistent analysis problem (Fig. 14.4): Isolation level CS does not solve this problem; transaction *A* must execute under RR in order to retain its locks until end-of-transaction, for otherwise it will still produce the wrong answer. (Alternatively, of course, *A* could lock the entire accounts relation via some explicit lock request, if the system supports such an operation. This solution would work under both CS and RR isolation levels.)

14.9 The three concurrency problems identified in Section 14.2 were *lost update, uncommitted dependency,* and *inconsistent analysis.* Of these three:

■ *Lost updates:* The SQL implementation is required to guarantee (in all circumstances) that lost updates never occur.

■ *Uncommitted dependency:* This is just another name for dirty read.

■ *Inconsistent analysis:* This term covers both nonrepeatable read and phantoms.

15 | Security

15.1 Introduction

The terms *security* and *integrity* are frequently heard together in database contexts, though the two concepts are actually quite distinct. **Security** refers to the protection of data against unauthorized disclosure, alteration, or destruction; **integrity** refers to the accuracy or validity of data. In other words:

- Security involves ensuring that users are *allowed* to do the things they are trying to do;

- Integrity involves ensuring that the things they are trying to do are *correct*.

There are some similarities too, of course: In both cases, the system needs to be aware of certain *rules* that users must not violate; in both cases those rules must be specified (typically by the DBA) in some suitable language, and must be maintained in the system catalog; and in both cases the DBMS must monitor user operations in some way to ensure that the rules are enforced. In this chapter and the next we examine such ideas in some detail. The present chapter is concerned with security and the next with integrity.

15.2 General Considerations

There are numerous aspects to the security problem, among them the following:

- Legal, social, and ethical aspects (for example, does the person making the request, say for a customer's credit, have a legal right to the requested information?)

- Physical controls (for example, is the computer or terminal room locked or otherwise guarded?)

- Policy questions (for example, how does the enterprise owning the system decide who should be allowed access to what?)

- Operational problems (for example, if a password scheme is used, how are the passwords themselves kept secret? how often are they changed?)

- Hardware controls (for example, does the processing unit provide any security features, such as storage protection keys or a privileged operation mode?)

- Operating system security (for example, does the underlying operating system erase the contents of storage and data files when they are finished with?)

and finally

- Issues that are the specific concern of the database system itself (for example, does the database system have a concept of data ownership?)

For obvious reasons, we limit ourselves for the most part to issues in this last category only.

Now, modern DBMSs typically support either or both of two broad approaches to data security. The approaches are known as *discretionary* and *mandatory* control, respectively. In both cases, the unit of data or "data object" that might need to be protected can range all the way from an entire database or collection of relations on the one hand, to the specific data item at a specific attribute position within a specific tuple within a specific relation on the other. How the two approaches differ is indicated by the following brief outline:

- In the case of **discretionary** control, a given user will typically have different access rights (also known as **privileges** or **authorities**) on different objects; further, different users will typically have different rights on the same object. Discretionary schemes are thus very flexible.

- In the case of **mandatory** control, by contrast, each data object is tagged or labeled with a certain **classification** level, and each user is given a certain **clearance** level. A given data object can then be accessed only by users with the appropriate clearance. Mandatory schemes are thus comparatively rigid.

We will discuss discretionary schemes in Sections 15.3–15.4 and mandatory schemes in Section 15.5.

Regardless of whether we are dealing with a discretionary scheme or a mandatory scheme, all decisions as to which users are allowed to perform which operations on which objects are policy decisions, not technical ones. As such, they are clearly outside the jurisdiction of the DBMS per se; all the DBMS can do is enforce those decisions once they are made. It follows that:

1. The results of those policy decisions (a) must be made known to the system (this is done by means of statements in some appropriate definitional language), and (b) must be remembered by the system (this is done by saving them in the catalog in the form of **security rules,** also known as **authorization** rules).

2. There must be a means of checking a given access request against the applicable security rules. (By "access request" here we mean the combination of *requested operation* plus *requested object* plus *requesting user,* in general.) That checking is done by the DBMS's **security subsystem,** also known as the **authorization** subsystem.

3. In order that it may be able to decide which security rules are applicable to a given access request, the system must be able to recognize the *source* of that request—that is, it must be able to recognize the *requesting user*. For that reason, when users sign on to the system, they are typically required to supply, not only their user ID (to say who they are), but also a **password** (to prove they are who they say they are). The password is supposedly known only to the system and to legitimate users of the user ID concerned.

Regarding this last point, incidentally, note that any number of distinct users might be able to share the same group "user ID." In this way the system can support **user groups,** and can thus provide a way of allowing (say) everyone in the accounting department to share the same privileges. The operations of adding individual users to, or removing individual users from, a given group can then be performed independently of the operation of specifying the privileges that apply to that group. Note, however, that the obvious place to keep a record of which actual users are in which groups is again the catalog (or perhaps the database itself).

15.3 Discretionary Access Control

To repeat from the previous section, most DBMSs support either discretionary control or mandatory control or both. In fact it would be more accurate to say that most systems support discretionary control, and some systems support mandatory control as well; discretionary control is thus more likely to be encountered in practice, and so we deal with it first.

As already noted, there needs to be a language that supports the definition of (discretionary) security rules. We therefore begin by describing a hypothetical example of such a language. Here first is a simple example:

```
CREATE SECURITY RULE SR3
      GRANT RETRIEVE ( S#, SNAME, CITY ), DELETE
      ON    S WHERE S.CITY ≠ 'London'
      TO    Jim, Fred, Mary
      ON ATTEMPTED VIOLATION REJECT ;
```

This example is intended to illustrate the point that (in general) security rules have *five components*, as follows:

1. A **name** (SR3—"suppliers rule 3"—in the example). The rule will be registered in the system catalog under this name. The name will probably also appear in any message or diagnostics produced by the system in response to an attempted violation of the rule.

2. One or more **privileges** (RETRIEVE—on certain attributes only—and DELETE, in the example), specified by means of the GRANT clause.

3. The **scope** to which the rule applies, specified by means of the ON clause. In the example, the scope is supplier tuples where the city is not London.

4. One or more **"users"** (more accurately, user IDs) who are to be granted the specified privileges over the specified scope, specified by means of the TO clause.

5. A **violation response,** specified by the ON ATTEMPTED VIOLATION clause, telling the system what to do if a user attempts to violate the rule. In the example, the violation response is simply to reject the attempt (and to provide suitable diagnostic information, of course); such a response will surely be the one most commonly required in practice, so we might as well make it the default. But in general the response could be a procedure of arbitrary complexity.

Here then is the full syntax (using square brackets as in the BNF grammar in Chapter 7 to indicate that the material they enclose is optional):

```
CREATE SECURITY RULE rule
      GRANT privilege-commalist
      ON    expression
      TO    user-commalist
    [ ON ATTEMPTED VIOLATION action ] ;
```

Explanation:

1. The specified *rule* is the name of the new security rule.

2. Each *privilege* is one of the following:

```
RETRIEVE [ ( attribute-commalist ) ]
INSERT
UPDATE [ ( attribute-commalist ) ]
DELETE
ALL
```

RETRIEVE (unqualified), INSERT, UPDATE (unqualified), and DELETE are self-explanatory.* If a commalist of attributes is specified with RETRIEVE, then the privilege applies only to the attributes specified; UPDATE with a commalist of attributes is defined analogously. The specification ALL is shorthand for all privileges—RETRIEVE (all attributes), INSERT, UPDATE (all attributes), and DELETE.

Note that we are effectively limiting our discussion to *data manipulation* operations only. In practice, of course, there are many other operations that we would want to be subject to security rules as well, such as the operations of creating and destroying base relations—and the operations of creating and destroying security rules themselves, come to that. We omit detailed consideration of such operations for space reasons.

3. The *expression* is an expression of the relational calculus (or relational algebra—we use the calculus purely for reasons of definiteness) that defines the scope of the

---

* Well, perhaps not quite. The RETRIEVE privilege is needed just to *mention* the relevant object (e.g., in a view definition or an integrity constraint) as well as for retrieval *per se*. REFERENCE might have been a better keyword, had it not been for its referential integrity connotations.

rule. The target item commalist in that expression must identify exactly one range variable, referring to exactly one named relation; in other words, the scope of the rule is always some subset of the tuples of a single named relation. (It therefore makes sense to use the shorthand by which the name of a relation can be used as the name of an implicit range variable that ranges over the relation with the same name, as discussed in Chapter 7; we did this in our initial example, and we will continue to do the same in our other examples also.)

4. Each *user* is the ID of some user that is known to the system. The keyword ALL (meaning all known users) can also be specified.

5. The *action* is (in general) a procedure, of arbitrary complexity. As mentioned above, the default is just to reject the attempted operation, but in more sensitive situations some other action might be more appropriate—for example, it might be necessary to terminate the program or lock the user's keyboard. It might also be desirable to record attempted violations in a special log (*threat monitoring*), in order to permit subsequent analysis of such attempts and also to serve in itself as a deterrent against illegal infiltration; see the discussion of *audit trails* at the end of this section.

Of course, we also need a way of destroying existing rules:

```
DESTROY SECURITY RULE rule ;
```

For example:

```
DESTROY SECURITY RULE SR3 ;
```

For simplicity, we assume that destroying a given named relation will automatically destroy any security rules that apply to that relation.

Here are some further examples of security rules, most of them more or less self-explanatory.

1. ```
   CREATE SECURITY RULE EX1
          GRANT RETRIEVE ( S#, SNAME, CITY )
          ON     S
          TO     Jacques, Anne, Charley ;
   ```

   Users Jacques, Anne, and Charley can see a "vertical subset"—or (better) an attribute subset or value-independent subset—of base relation S. The example is thus an example of a **value-independent** security rule.

2. ```
   CREATE SECURITY RULE EX2
          GRANT RETRIEVE, INSERT, UPDATE ( SNAME, STATUS ), DELETE
          ON     S WHERE S.CITY = 'Paris'
          TO     Dan, Misha ;
   ```

   Users Dan and Misha can see a "horizontal subset"—or (better) a tuple subset or value-dependent subset—of base relation S. This is thus an example of a **value-dependent** security rule. Note that although users Dan and Misha can INSERT and DELETE supplier tuples, they cannot UPDATE attributes S# or CITY.

3. ```
CREATE SECURITY RULE EX3
      GRANT RETRIEVE
      ON   S WHERE EXISTS SP EXISTS P
            (S.S# = SP.S# AND SP.P# = P.P# AND P.CITY = 'Rome')
      TO   Giovanni ;
```

This is another value-dependent example: User Giovanni can retrieve supplier information, but only for suppliers who supply some part where the part city is Rome.

4. ```
CREATE SECURITY RULE EX4
      GRANT RETRIEVE ( S#, SNAME )
      ON    S WHERE S.STATUS > 50
      TO    Judy, Paul ;
```

Attribute STATUS here is used to define the scope but is nevertheless not visible to the users (Judy and Paul), who know at the most only that the suppliers whose name and number they can see have status greater than 50.

5. Suppose SSQ is a view, defined as follows:*

```
CREATE VIEW SSQ AS
    ( S.S#, SUM ( SP WHERE SP.S# = S.S#, QTY ) AS SQ ) ;
```

Then the following security rule—

```
CREATE SECURITY RULE EX5
      GRANT RETRIEVE
      ON    SSQ
      TO    Fidel ;
```

—will allow user Fidel to see total shipment quantities per supplier, but not individual shipment quantities. User Fidel thus sees a **statistical summary** of the underlying base relation SP. (Note that access to views is subject to the security mechanism, just as access to base relations is.)

6. Suppose SSS is a view, defined as follows:

```
CREATE VIEW SSS AS
    ( S.S#, S.SNAME ) WHERE S.STATUS > 50 ;
```

Then the following security rule—

```
CREATE SECURITY RULE EX6
      GRANT RETRIEVE
      ON    SSS
      TO    Judy, Paul ;
```

—has an effect similar to that of the security rule in Example 4 above. The effect is not identical, however: In Example 4, Judy and Paul can issue queries against base relation S directly; here they can issue queries only against view SSS. Note the use of a view to *hide information* in this example (and in the previous example too, of course).

---

* In Chapter 3 we used the algebra as a basis for defining views. Here we use the calculus instead, merely because we are using the calculus instead of the algebra as a basis for defining security rules.

7. ```
CREATE SECURITY RULE EX7
     GRANT RETRIEVE, UPDATE (STATUS)
     ON   S
     WHERE DAY () IN ('Mon', 'Tue', 'Wed', 'Thu', 'Fri')
           AND TIME () ≥ TIME '9:00 am'
           AND TIME () ≤ TIME '5:00 pm'
     TO   Purchasing ;
```

Here we are assuming that the system provides two niladic builtin functions (i.e., builtin functions that take no arguments) called DAY and TIME, with the obvious interpretations. This security rule guarantees that supplier status values can be changed by the user "Purchasing" (presumably meaning anyone in the purchasing department) only on a weekday, and only during working hours. This is an example of what is sometimes called a **context-dependent** rule, because a given access request will or will not violate the rule depending on the context—here the combination of day of the week and time of day—in which it is issued.

Other examples of builtin functions that the system probably ought to support anyway and could be useful for context-dependent rules include:

```
DATE()     —  value = the current date
USER()     —  value = the ID of the current user
TERMINAL() —  value = the ID of the originating terminal
                      for the current request
```

By now the reader has probably realized that, conceptually speaking, security rules are all "ORed" together. In other words, a given access request (meaning, again, the combination of requested operation plus requested object plus requesting user) is acceptable if and only if it does not violate the logical OR of all specified rules. For example, if (a) rule *R1* says user Nancy is allowed to retrieve P# and WEIGHT for parts in Paris, and (b) rule *R2* says she is allowed to retrieve P# and COLOR for parts in Paris or London, then (c) she will actually be allowed to retrieve P#, WEIGHT, and COLOR for parts in Paris, but only P# and COLOR for parts in London.

Finally, we have implied, but never quite stated as much, that users can do only the things they are explicitly allowed to do by the security rules. Anything not explicitly allowed is implicitly prohibited!

Audit Trails

It is important not to assume that the security system is perfect. A would-be infiltrator who is sufficiently determined will usually find a way of breaking through the controls, especially if the payoff for doing so is high. In situations where the data is sufficiently sensitive, therefore, or where the processing performed on the data is sufficiently critical, an **audit trail** becomes a necessity. If, for example, data discrepancies lead to a suspicion that the database has been tampered with, the audit trail can be used to examine what has been going on and to verify that matters are under control—or at least, if they are not, to help pinpoint the wrongdoer.

An audit trail is effectively a special file or database in which the system automat-
```

ically keeps track of all operations performed by users on the regular database.* A typical entry in the audit trail might contain the following information:

request (source text)

terminal from which the operation was invoked

user who invoked the operation

date and time of the operation

base relation(s), tuple(s), and attribute(s) affected

old values

new values

As mentioned earlier, the very fact that an audit trail is being maintained might be sufficient in itself to deter a would-be infiltrator in some situations.

15.4 Request Modification

In order to illustrate some of the ideas introduced in the previous section, we now briefly describe the security aspects of the INGRES language QUEL, since INGRES and QUEL adopt an interesting approach to the problem [15.16]. Basically, any given QUEL request is automatically *modified* before execution in such a way that it cannot possibly violate any security rule. For example, suppose user U is allowed to retrieve parts stored in London only:

```
DEFINE PERMIT RETRIEVE ON P TO U
       WHERE   P.CITY = "London"
```

(see below for a discussion of the DEFINE PERMIT operation). Now suppose user U issues the QUEL request:

```
RETRIEVE ( P.P#, P.WEIGHT )
WHERE       P.COLOR = "Red"
```

Using the "permit" for the combination of relation P and user U as stored in the catalog, INGRES automatically modifies this request to the form:

```
RETRIEVE ( P.P#, P.WEIGHT )
WHERE       P.COLOR = "Red"
AND         P.CITY  = "London"
```

And of course this modified request cannot possibly violate the security rule. Note, incidentally, that the modification process is "silent"—user U is not informed that the system has in fact executed a statement that is somewhat different from the original

---

* In some systems, the audit trail might be physically integrated with the recovery log (see Chapter 13); in others the two might be distinct. Either way, users should be able to interrogate the audit trail using their regular relational query language (provided they are suitably authorized, of course!).

request, because that fact in itself might be sensitive (user *U* might not even be allowed to know that there are any parts not stored in London).

The process of "request modification" just outlined is actually identical to the technique used for the implementation of *views* (see Chapters 3 and 17). So one advantage of the scheme is that it is very easy to implement—much of the necessary code exists in the system already. Another advantage is that it is comparatively efficient—the security enforcement overhead occurs at compilation time rather than execution time, at least in part (assuming a compiling system). Yet another advantage is that some of the awkwardnesses that can occur with the SQL approach when a given user needs different privileges over different portions of the same relation do not arise (see Section 15.7).

One *dis*advantage is that not all security rules can be handled in this simple fashion. As a trivial counterexample, suppose user *U* is not allowed to access relation P at all. Then no simple "modified" form of the RETRIEVE shown above can preserve the illusion that relation P does not exist. Instead, an explicit error message along the lines of "You are not allowed to access this relation" must necessarily be produced.

Security rules are expressed in QUEL by means of the DEFINE PERMIT statement—syntax as follows:

```
DEFINE PERMIT  operation-commalist
        ON       relation [ ( attribute-commalist ) ]
        TO       user
     [ AT       terminals ]
     [ FROM     time TO time ]
     [ ON       day TO day ]
     [ WHERE    condition ]
```

DEFINE PERMIT is thus very similar to our CREATE SECURITY RULE, except that special syntax is provided for contextual controls (such as time of day) instead of just using conditions in the WHERE clause to supply such information. Here is an example:

```
DEFINE PERMIT APPEND, RETRIEVE, REPLACE
        ON     S ( SNAME, CITY )
        TO     Joe
        AT     TTA4
        FROM   9:00 TO 17:30
        ON     Sat TO Sun
        WHERE  S.STATUS < 50
        AND    S.S# = SP.P#
        AND    SP.P# = P.P#
        AND    P.COLOR = "Red"
```

APPEND and REPLACE are the QUEL analogs of our INSERT and UPDATE, respectively.

Security rules are kept in the INGRES catalog under numeric identifiers (0, 1, 2, etc.). Those identifiers can be discovered by querying the catalog (a special HELP command is provided to assist in this process, though the conventional QUEL RETRIEVE statement could also be used). Thus, to destroy the rule just shown, it is first necessary to discover the applicable identifier. Suppose that identifier is 27. Then the statement

```
DESTROY PERMIT S 27
```

will remove the rule from the system.

15.5 Mandatory Access Control

Mandatory controls are applicable to databases in which the data has a rather static and rigid classification structure, as tends to be the case in (e.g.) military or government environments. As explained briefly in Section 15.2, the basic idea is that each data object has a **classification level** (e.g., top secret, secret, confidential, etc.), and each user has a **clearance level** (with the same possibilities as for the classification levels). The levels are assumed to form a strict ordering (e.g., top secret > secret > confidential, etc.). The simple rules are then imposed that:

1. User i can see object j only if the clearance level of i is greater than or equal to the classification level of j
2. User i can modify object j only if the clearance level of i is equal to the classification level of j

Number 1 here is obvious enough, but Number 2 requires a word of explanation. Observe first that another way of stating that second rule is to say that, by definition, anything written by user i automatically acquires a classification level equal to i's clearance level. Such a rule is necessary in order to prevent a user with, e.g., "secret" classification from copying secret data to a file of lower classification, thereby subverting the intent of the classification scheme.

Mandatory controls have received a lot of attention recently. This is because the U.S. Department of Defense (DoD) requires any system it uses to support certain mandatory controls, and hence DBMS vendors have been vying with one another to implement such controls. The controls in question are documented in two important DoD publications known informally as the **Orange Book** [15.1] and the **Lavender Book** [15.2], respectively; the Orange Book defines a set of security requirements for any "Trusted Computing Base" (TCB), and the Lavender Book defines an "interpretation" of the TCB requirements for database systems specifically.

The mandatory controls defined in references [15.1–15.2] in fact form part of a more general overall security classification scheme, which we summarize here for purposes of reference. First of all, the documents define four **security classes** (D, C, B, and A); broadly speaking, class D is the least secure, class C is more secure than class D, and so on. Class D is said to provide *minimal* protection, class C *discretionary* protection, class B *mandatory* protection, and class A *verified* protection.

- **Discretionary protection:** Class C is divided into two subclasses C1 and C2 (where C1 is *less* secure than C2). Each supports *discretionary* access control, meaning that access control is subject to the discretion of the data owner (effectively as described in Sections 15.3–15.4 above).

- Class C1 requires separation of data and users; i.e., it supports the concept of shared data, while allowing users to have private data of their own as well.

- Class C2 additionally requires accountability support through sign-on procedures, auditing, and resource isolation.

■ **Structured protection:** Class B is the class that deals with mandatory controls. It is further divided into subclasses B1, B2, and B3 (where B1 is the least secure of the three and B3 is the most).

- Class B1 requires "labeled security protection" (i.e., it requires each data object to be labeled with its classification level—secret, confidential, etc.). It also requires an informal statement of the security policy in effect.

- Class B2 additionally requires a *formal* statement of the same thing. It also requires that *covert channels* be identified and eliminated; an example of a covert channel might be the possibility of inferring the answer to an illegal query from the answer to a legal one (see the discusion of *inference controls* in the annotation to reference [15.6]).

- Class B3 specifically requires audit and recovery support, as well as a designated *security administrator.*

■ **Verified protection:** Class A, the most secure, requires a mathematical proof that (a) the security mechanism is consistent and that (b) it is adequate to support the specified security policy (!).

Several commercial DBMS products currently provide mandatory controls at the B1 level. They also typically provide discretionary controls at the C2 level. *Terminology:* DBMSs that support mandatory controls are often referred to as **multilevel secure** systems [15.12,15.15]. The term **trusted** system is also used with much the same meaning [15.17].

15.6 Data Encryption

Note: Much of the material of this section originally appeared in slightly different form in reference [15.4].

We have assumed so far in this chapter that any would-be infiltrator will be using the normal system facilities to access the database. We now turn our attention to the case of a "user" who attempts to bypass the system—e.g., by physically removing part of the database, or by tapping into a communication line. The most effective countermeasure against such threats is **data encryption**— that is, storing and transmitting sensitive data in an encrypted form.

In order to discuss some of the concepts of data encryption, we need to introduce some more terminology. The original (unencrypted) data is called the **plaintext**. The plaintext is **encrypted** by subjecting it to an **encryption algorithm,** whose inputs are the plaintext and an **encryption key;** the output from this algorithm—the encrypted form of the plaintext—is called the **ciphertext**. The details of the encryption algorithm are made public, or at least are not specially concealed, but the encryption key is kept secret. The ciphertext, which should be unintelligible to anyone not holding the encryption key, is what is stored in the database or transmitted down the communication line.

Example: Let the plaintext be the string

```
AS KINGFISHERS CATCH FIRE
```

(we assume for simplicity that the only data characters we have to deal with are upper-case letters and blanks). Let the encryption key be the string

```
ELIOT
```

and let the encryption algorithm be as follows.

1. Divide the plaintext into blocks of length equal to that of the encryption key:

   ```
   AS+KI   NGFIS   HERS+   CATCH   +FIRE
   ```

   (blanks now shown explicitly as "+").

2. Replace each character of the plaintext by an integer in the range 00–26, using blank = 00, A = 01, . . . , Z = 26:

   ```
   0119001109 1407060919 0805181900 0301200308 0006091805
   ```

3. Repeat Step 2 for the encryption key:

   ```
   0512091520
   ```

4. For each block of the plaintext, replace each character by the sum modulo 27 of its integer encoding and the integer encoding of the corresponding character of the encryption key:

   ```
   0119001109 1407060919 0805181900 0301200308 0006091805
   0512091520 0512091520 0512091520 0512091520 0512091520
   0604092602 1919152412 1317000720 0813021801 0518180625
   ```

5. Replace each integer encoding in the result of Step 4 by its character equivalent:

   ```
   FDIZB   SSOXL   MQ+GT   HMBRA   ERRFY
   ```

The decryption procedure for this example is straightforward, *given the key*. (*Exercise:* Decrypt the ciphertext shown above.) The question is, how difficult is it for a would-be infiltrator to determine the key without prior knowledge, given matching plaintexts and ciphertexts? In our simple example, the answer is, fairly obviously, "not very"; but, equally obviously, much more sophisticated schemes can easily be devised. Ideally the scheme employed should be such that the work involved in breaking it far outweighs any potential advantage to be gained in doing so. (In fact, a remark along the same general lines applies to all aspects of security: The intent should always be to make the cost of breaking the system significantly greater than the potential payoff.) The accepted ultimate objective for such schemes is that the *inventor* of the scheme, holding matching plaintext and ciphertext, should be unable to determine the key, and hence unable to decipher another piece of ciphertext.

The Data Encryption Standard

The example above made use of a **substitution** procedure: An encryption key was used to determine, for each character of the plaintext, a ciphertext character to be *substituted* for that character. Substitution is one of the two basic approaches to encryption as traditionally practiced; the other is **permutation,** in which plaintext characters are simply rearranged into some different sequence. Neither of these approaches is particularly secure in itself, but algorithms that combine the two can provide quite a high degree of security. One such algorithm is the **Data Encryption Standard** (DES), which was first adopted as a US federal standard in 1977 [15.3].

To use the DES, plaintext is divided into 64-bit blocks and each block is encrypted using a 64-bit key (actually the key consists of 56 data bits plus eight parity bits, so there are not 2^{64} but only 2^{56} possible keys). A block is encrypted by applying an initial permutation to it, then subjecting the permuted block to a sequence of 16 complex substitution steps, and finally applying another permutation, the inverse of the initial permutation, to the result of the last of those steps. The substitution at the ith step is not controlled directly by the original encryption key K but by a key Ki that is computed from the values K and i. For details, see reference [15.3].

The DES has the property that the decryption algorithm is identical to the encryption algorithm, except that the Ki's are applied in reverse order.

Public-Key Encryption

Over the years, many people have suggested that the DES might not be truly secure; indeed, the advent of very fast, highly parallel processors might very well mean that the DES could be broken by brute force, if by no more intelligent means. Many people also feel that the more recent "public-key" encryption schemes render the DES and similar traditional approaches technologically obsolete anyway. In a public-key scheme, both the encryption algorithm *and the encryption key* are made freely available; thus anyone can convert plaintext into ciphertext. But the corresponding **decryption key** is kept secret (public-key schemes involve *two* keys, one for encryption and one for decryption). Furthermore, the decryption key cannot feasibly be deduced from the encryption key; thus, even the person performing the original encryption cannot perform the corresponding decryption if not authorized to do so.

The original idea of public-key encryption is due to Diffie and Hellman [15.7]. We describe a specific approach, due to Rivest, Shamir, and Adleman [15.14], to show how such a scheme might work. Their approach (now usually referred to as *the RSA scheme,* from the initials of its originators) is based on the following two facts:

1. There is a known fast algorithm for determining whether a given number is prime;
2. There is no known fast algorithm for finding the prime factors of a given composite (i.e., nonprime) number.

Reference [15.10] gives an example in which determining (on a given machine) whether a given number of 130 digits is prime takes about seven minutes, whereas finding the two prime factors (on the same machine) of a number obtained by multiplying together two primes of 63 digits would take about 40 quadrillion years (one quadrillion = 1,000,000,000,000,000).

The RSA scheme works as follows.

1. Choose, randomly, two distinct large primes p and q, and compute the product $r = p * q$.

2. Choose, randomly, a large integer e that is relatively prime to the product $(p - 1)$ * $(q - 1)$. The integer e is the encryption key. *Note:* Choosing e is straightforward; e.g., any prime greater than both p and q will do.

3. Take the decryption key d to be the unique "multiplicative inverse" of e modulo $(p - 1) * (q - 1)$; i.e.,

   ```
   d * e = 1 modulo (p - 1) * (q - 1)
   ```

   The algorithm for computing d given e, p, and q is straightforward and is given in reference [15.14].

4. Publish the integers r and e but not d.

5. To encrypt a piece of plaintext P (which we assume for simplicity to be an integer less than r), replace it by the ciphertext C, computed as follows:

   ```
   C = P^e modulo r
   ```

6. To decrypt a piece of ciphertext C, replace it by the plaintext P, computed as follows:

   ```
   P = C^d modulo r
   ```

Reference [15.14] proves that this scheme works—i.e., that decryption of C using d does in fact recover the original P. However, computation of d knowing only r and e (and not p or q) is infeasible, as claimed earlier. Hence anyone can encrypt plaintext, but only authorized users (holding d) can decrypt ciphertext.

We give a trivial example to illustrate the foregoing procedure. For obvious reasons we restrict ourselves to very small numbers throughout.

Example: Let $p = 3$, $q = 5$; then $r = 15$, and the product $(p - 1) * (q - 1) = 8$. Let $e = 11$ (a prime greater than both p and q). To compute d, we have

```
d * 11 = 1 modulo 8
```

whence $d = 3$.

Now let the plaintext P consist of the integer 13. Then the ciphertext C is given by

```
C = P^e modulo r
  = 13^11 modulo 15
  = 1,792,160,394,037 modulo 15
  = 7
```

Now the original plaintext P is given by

```
P = C^d modulo r
  = 7^3 modulo 15
  = 343 modulo 15
  = 13   ∎
```

Because *e* and *d* are inverses of each other, public-key encryption schemes also permit encrypted messages to be **"signed"** in such a way that the recipient can be certain that the message originated with the person it purports to have done (i.e., "signatures" cannot be forged). Suppose that *A* and *B* are two users who wish to communicate with each other using a public-key encryption scheme. Then *A* and *B* will each publish an encryption algorithm (including in each case the corresponding encryption key), but of course will keep the decryption algorithm and key secret, even from each other. Let the encryption algorithms be ECA and ECB (for encrypting messages to be sent to *A* and *B,* respectively), and let the corresponding decryption algorithms be DCA and DCB, respectively. ECA and DCA are inverses of each other, as are ECB and DCB.

Now suppose that *A* wishes to send a piece of plaintext *P* to *B*. Instead of simply computing ECB(*P*) and transmitting the result, *A* first applies the *decryption* algorithm DCA to *P,* then encrypts the result and transmits that as the ciphertext *C:*

```
C = ECB ( DCA ( P ) )
```

On receipt of *C,* user *B* applies the decryption algorithm DCB and then the *encryption* algorithm ECA, producing the final result *P:*

```
ECA ( DCB ( C ) )
  = ECA ( DCB ( ECB ( DCA ( P ) ) ) )
  = ECA ( DCA ( P ) )               -- because DCB and ECB cancel
  = P                               -- because ECA and DCA cancel
```

Now *B* knows that the message did indeed come from *A,* because ECA will produce *P* only if the algorithm DCA was used in the encryption process, and that algorithm is known only to *A*. No one, *not even B,* can forge *A*'s signature.

15.7 SQL Support

The current SQL standard [8.1] supports discretionary access control only. Two more or less independent SQL features are involved—the **view mechanism,** which (as suggested in Section 15.3) can be used to hide sensitive data from unauthorized users, and the **authorization subsystem** itself, which allows users having specific privileges selectively and dynamically to grant those privileges to other users, and subsequently to revoke those privileges, if desired. Both features are discussed below.

Views and Security

To illustrate the use of views for security purposes, we give SQL analogs of Examples 1–5 (only) from Section 15.3.

```
1. CREATE VIEW EX1 AS
        SELECT S.S#, S.SNAME, S.CITY
        FROM   S ;
```

The view defines the data over which authorization is to be granted. The granting itself is done by means of the GRANT statement—e.g.:

```
GRANT SELECT ON EX1 TO Jacques, Anne, Charley ;
```

One difference between SQL and the hypothetical scheme described in Section 15.3 is worth pointing out explicitly: Because security rules are defined by means of the GRANT statement instead of by some kind of "CREATE RULE" statement, those rules are *unnamed* in SQL.*

2. CREATE VIEW EX2 AS
```
        SELECT S.S#, S.SNAME, S.STATUS, S.CITY
        FROM   S
        WHERE  S.CITY = 'Paris' ;
```

Corresponding GRANT:

```
GRANT SELECT, INSERT, UPDATE ( SNAME, STATUS ), DELETE
      ON EX2 TO Dan, Misha ;
```

3. CREATE VIEW EX3 AS
```
        SELECT S.S#, S.SNAME, S.STATUS, S.CITY
        FROM   S
        WHERE  EXISTS
             ( SELECT * FROM SP
               WHERE  EXISTS
                    ( SELECT * FROM P
                      WHERE  S.S# = SP.S#
                      AND    SP.P# = P.P#
                      AND    P.CITY = 'Rome' ) ) ;
```

Corresponding GRANT:

```
GRANT SELECT ON EX3 TO Giovanni ;
```

4. CREATE VIEW EX4 AS
```
        SELECT S.S#, S.SNAME
        FROM   S
        WHERE  S.STATUS > 50 ;
```

Corresponding GRANT:

```
GRANT SELECT ON EX4 TO Judy, Paul ;
```

5. CREATE VIEW SSQ AS
```
        SELECT S.S#, ( SELECT SUM ( SP.QTY )
                       FROM   SP
                       WHERE  SP.S# = S.S# ) AS SQ
        FROM   S ;
```

Corresponding GRANT:

```
GRANT SELECT ON SSQ TO Fidel ;
```

As the examples illustrate, the view mechanism of SQL provides an important measure of security "for free" ("for free" because the view mechanism is included in the system for other purposes anyway). What is more, many authorization checks—even value-dependent checks—can be applied at compilation time instead of execution time, a significant performance benefit. However, the view-based approach to security

---

* Integrity rules, by contrast, do have names in SQL. See Chapter 16.

does suffer from some slight awkwardness on occasion—in particular, if some particular user needs different privileges over different subsets of the same table at the same time. For example, consider the structure of an application that is allowed to scan and print all London parts and is also allowed to update some of them (just the red ones, say) during the scan.

GRANT and REVOKE

The SQL view mechanism allows the database to be conceptually divided up into pieces in various ways so that sensitive information can be hidden from unauthorized users. However, it does not allow for the specification of the operations that *authorized* users are allowed to execute against those pieces. That function (as we have already seen in the examples above) is performed by the **GRANT** statement, which we now discuss.

Note first that the creator of any object is automatically granted all privileges that make sense for that object. For example, the creator of a base table B is automatically granted the SELECT, INSERT, UPDATE, DELETE, and REFERENCES privileges on B (see below for an explanation of these privileges). Furthermore, these privileges are granted "with grant authority" in each case, which means that the privilege can be granted to some other user.

Here then is the syntax of the GRANT statement:

```
GRANT privilege-commalist ON object TO user-commalist
                             [ WITH GRANT OPTION ] ;
```

Explanation:

- The legal *privileges* include USAGE, SELECT, INSERT, UPDATE, DELETE, and REFERENCES. The USAGE privilege is needed to use a specific domain; the REFERENCES privilege is needed to refer to a specific named table in an integrity constraint; the other privileges should be self-explanatory. Note, however, that the INSERT and UPDATE privileges (but *not* the SELECT privilege, oddly enough) can be column-specific.

- *Object* can be either of the following:

```
DOMAIN domain
[ TABLE ] table
```

In this context—unlike most others in SQL—the (optional) keyword "TABLE" refers to views as well as base tables.

- The *user-commalist* can be replaced by the special keyword PUBLIC, meaning all users known to the system.

- WITH GRANT OPTION, if specified, means that the specified users are granted the specified privileges on the specified object **with grant authority**—meaning, as indicated above, that they can go on to grant those privileges on that object to some other user(s). Of course, WITH GRANT OPTION can be specified only if the user issuing the GRANT statement has the necessary grant authority.

Next, if user *A* grants some privilege to some other user *B,* user *A* can subsequently *revoke* that privilege from user *B.* Revoking privileges is done by means of the **REVOKE** statement—syntax:

```
REVOKE [ GRANT OPTION FOR ] privilege-commalist ON object
                           FROM user-commalist option ;
```

Here (a) GRANT OPTION FOR means that grant authority (only) is to be revoked; (b) *privilege-commalist, object,* and *user-commalist* are as for GRANT; and (c) *option* is either RESTRICT or CASCADE, and is discussed below. Examples:

1. `REVOKE SELECT ON EX1 FROM Jacques, Anne, Charley RESTRICT ;`
2. `REVOKE SELECT, INSERT, UPDATE ( SNAME, STATUS ), DELETE`
   `      ON EX2 FROM Dan, Misha CASCADE ;`
3. `REVOKE SELECT ON EX3 FROM Giovanni RESTRICT ;`
4. `REVOKE SELECT ON EX4 FROM Judy, Paul CASCADE ;`
5. `REVOKE SELECT ON SSQ FROM Fidel RESTRICT ;`

RESTRICT vs. CASCADE: Suppose *p* is some privilege on some object, and suppose user *A* grants *p* to user *B,* who in turn grants it to user *C.* What should happen if *A* now revokes *p* from *B?* Suppose for a moment that the REVOKE succeeds. Then the privilege *p* held by *C* would be "abandoned"—it would be derived from a user, namely *B,* who no longer holds it. The purpose of the RESTRICT *vs.* CASCADE option is to avoid the possibility of abandoned privileges, thus: RESTRICT causes the REVOKE to fail if it would lead to any abandoned privileges; CASCADE causes any such privileges to be revoked as well.

Finally, dropping a domain, base table, column, or view automatically revokes all privileges on the dropped object from all users.

15.8 Summary

We have discussed various aspects of the database **security** problem. We began by contrasting security and **integrity:** Security involves ensuring users are *allowed* to do the things they are trying to do, integrity involves ensuring the things they are trying to do are *correct.* Security, in other words, involves *the protection of data against unauthorized disclosure, alteration, or destruction.*

Security is enforced by the DBMS's **security subsystem,** which checks all access requests against the **security rules** stored in the system catalog. First we considered **discretionary** schemes, in which access to a given object is at the discretion of the object's owner. Each discretionary security rule has a **name,** a set of **privileges** (RETRIEVE, UPDATE, etc.), a **scope** (basically the data to which the rule applies, specified by a simple relational expression), a set of **users,** and a **violation response** (usually just REJECT). Such rules can be used to provide **value-dependent, value-independent, context-dependent,** and—through the use of views—**statistical**

summary controls. An **audit trail** can be used to record attempted security breaches. We took a brief look at an implementation technique for such rules known as **request modification**. This technique was pioneered by the INGRES prototype in connection with the QUEL language.

Next we took a brief look at **mandatory** controls, in which each object has a **classification** level and each user has a **clearance** level. We explained the rules for access under such a scheme. We also summarized the security classification scheme defined by the U.S. Department of Defense in references [15.1–15.2].

We then examined **data encryption,** touching on the basic ideas of **substitution** and **permutation**, explaining what the **Data Encryption Standard** is, and describing in outline how the **public-key** schemes work. In particular, we gave a simple example of the **RSA** (prime number) scheme. We also discussed the concept of **digital signatures**.

We also briefly described the security features of SQL—in particular, the use of **views** to hide information, and the use of **GRANT** and **REVOKE** to control which users have which privileges over which objects (domains, base tables, views).

In conclusion, it is perhaps worth pointing out that it is no good the DBMS providing an extensive set of security controls if it is possible to bypass those controls. In IBM's DB2 product, for example, the security mechanism would be almost useless if it were possible to access DB2 data from a conventional MVS program via conventional VSAM calls (the point being that DB2 data is physically stored in VSAM files, as we will see in Appendix B). For this reason, DB2 works in harmony with its various companion systems—MVS and VSAM, in particular—to guarantee that the total system is secure. The details are beyond the scope of this chapter, but the message should be clear.

Exercises

15.1 Base relation STATS looks like this:

```
STATS ( USERID, SEX, DEPENDENTS, JOB, SALARY, TAX, AUDITS )
     PRIMARY KEY ( USERID )
```

Using the hypothetical language introduced in Section 15.3, write security rules to give:

(a) User Ford RETRIEVE privileges over the entire relation.

(b) User Smith INSERT and DELETE privileges over the entire relation.

(c) Each user RETRIEVE privileges over that user's own tuple (only).

(d) User Nash RETRIEVE privileges over the entire relation and UPDATE privileges over the SALARY and TAX attributes (only).

(e) User Todd RETRIEVE privileges over the USERID, SALARY, and TAX attributes (only).

(f) User Ward RETRIEVE privileges as for Todd and UPDATE privileges over the SALARY and TAX attributes (only).

(g) User Pope full privileges (RETRIEVE, UPDATE, INSERT, DELETE) over tuples for preachers (only).

(h) User Jones DELETE privileges over tuples for people who perform a nonspecialist job, where a *nonspecialist job* is defined as one performed by more than ten people.

(i) User King RETRIEVE privileges for maximum and minimum salaries per job class.

15.2 Consider what is involved in extending the syntax of CREATE SECURITY RULE to include control over operations such as CREATE and DESTROY BASE RELATION, CREATE and DESTROY VIEW, CREATE and DESTROY SECURITY RULE (etc.).

15.3 Decrypt the following ciphertext, which was produced in a manner similar to that used in the "AS KINGFISHERS CATCH FIRE" example in Section 15.7, but using a different 5-character encryption key:

```
FNWAL  JPVJC  FPEXE  ABWNE  AYEIP  SUSVD
```

15.4 Work through the RSA public-key encryption scheme with $p = 7$, $q = 5$, and $e = 17$ for plaintext $P = 3$.

15.5 Can you think of any implementation problems or other disadvantages that might be caused by encryption?

15.6 Give SQL solutions to Exercise 15.1.

15.7 Write SQL statements to destroy the privileges granted in your solution to the previous exercise.

References and Bibliography

For a broad overview of security in general, see the book by Fernandez, Summers, and Wood [15.9]. For a much more detailed technical treatment, see the book by Denning [15.5]. The remaining references are either standards documents or technical papers (tutorials or research contributions) on various specific aspects of the security problem.

15.1 U.S. Department of Defense. *Trusted Computer System Evaluation Criteria* (the "Orange Book"). DoD National Computer Security Center (December 1985).

15.2 U.S. Department of Defense. *Trusted Database Management System Interpretation* (the "Lavender Book"). DoD National Computer Security Center (April 1991).

15.3 U.S. Department of Commerce/National Bureau of Standards. *Data Encryption Standard*. Federal Information Processing Standards Publication 46 (1977 January 15).

Defines the official Data Encryption Standard (DES), to be used by federal agencies and anyone else who wishes to do so. The encryption/decryption algorithm (see Section 15.6) is suitable for implementation on a hardware chip, which means that devices that incorporate it can operate at a high data rate. A number of such devices are commercially available.

15.4 C. J. Date. "Security." Chapter 4 of C. J. Date, *An Introduction to Database Systems: Volume II*. Reading, Mass.: Addison-Wesley (1983).

15.5 Dorothy E. Denning. *Cryptography and Data Security*. Reading, Mass.: Addison-Wesley (1983).

15.6 Dorothy E. Denning and Peter J. Denning. "Data Security." *ACM Comp. Surv. 11,* No. 3 (September 1979).

A good tutorial on security matters, covering discretionary access controls, mandatory access controls (here called *flow controls*), data encryption, and *inference controls* (the special problem of statistical databases). We offer a few words of explanation regarding the last of these, since they were not discussed in the body of the chapter. A statistical database (in the present context) is a database that permits queries that derive aggregated information (e.g., sums, averages) but not queries that derive individual information. For example, the query "What is the average salary of programmers?" might be permitted, while the query "What is the salary of programmer Mary?" would not be.

The problem with such databases is that it might be possible to make inferences from legal queries to deduce the answer to an illegal one. For example, the following two queries might both be legal:

1. How many female programmers are there aged between 25 and 30, living in Smallville, with a degree in modern languages from the University of Metropolis?

2. What is the average salary of female programmers aged between 25 and 30, living in Smallville, with a degree in modern languages from the University of Metropolis?

But if the answer to query Q1 is "one," then the security of the database will be compromised by query Q2. *Note:* An extended tutorial treatment of such problems, and approaches to their solution, is given by the present author in reference [15.4].

15.7 W. Diffie and M. E. Hellman. "New Directions in Cryptography." *IEEE Transactions on Information Theory* IT-22 (November 1976).

The paper that laid the theoretical groundwork for the so-called *public key* encryption schemes. As explained in the body of the chapter, ordinary encryption schemes such as the DES [15.3] require the encryption key to be kept secret. By contrast, the public key schemes use two different keys, one for encryption and one for decryption, and only the decryption key need be kept secret (and it is not possible to deduce the decryption key from the encryption key). In such schemes, therefore, anyone can generate encrypted messages, but no one—not even the message originator—is able to decrypt those messages except their intended recipient.

15.8 Ronald Fagin. "On an Authorization Mechanism." *ACM TODS 3,* No. 3 (September 1978).

An extended corrigendum to reference [15.11]. Under certain circumstances the mechanism of reference [15.11] would revoke a privilege that ought not to be revoked. This paper corrects that flaw.

15.9 Eduardo B. Fernandez, Rita C. Summers, and Christopher Wood. *Database Security and Integrity.* Reading, Mass.: Addison-Wesley (1981).

15.10 Martin Gardner. "A New Kind of Cipher That Would Take Millions of Years to Break." *Scientific American 237,* No. 2 (August 1977).

15.11 Patricia P. Griffiths and Bradford W. Wade. "An Authorization Mechanism for a Relational Data Base System." *ACM TODS 1,* No. 3 (September 1976).

Describes the GRANT and REVOKE mechanism originally proposed for System R. The scheme now included in the SQL standard is based on that mechanism, though significantly different in detail.

15.12 Sushil Jajodia and Ravi Sandhu. "Toward a Multilevel Secure Relational Data Model." Proc. 1991 ACM SIGMOD International Conference on Management of Data, Denver, Col. (June 1991).

As explained at the end of Section 15.5, "multilevel" in a security context refers to a system that supports mandatory access controls. This paper suggests that much of the current activity in the field is *ad hoc,* since there is very little consensus on basic concepts, and proposes a start at formalizing the principles of multilevel systems. The issues are more subtle than they might appear at first sight. For example, suppose some user is not allowed to know that certain suppliers exist (say suppliers with status greater than 20). Simply providing that user with a view of base relation S from which such suppliers are excluded is insufficient in itself to conceal the fact that such suppliers exist, because (for example) an attempt to insert a new supplier into that view will fail if the new supplier has the same supplier number as one of the hidden ones.

15.13 Abraham Lempel. "Cryptology in Transition." *ACM Comp. Surv. 11,* No. 4: Special Issue on Cryptology (December 1979).

A good tutorial on encryption and related matters.

15.14 R. L. Rivest, A. Shamir, and L. Adleman. "A Method for Obtaining Digital Signatures and Public-Key Cryptosystems." *CACM 21,* No. 2 (February 1978).

15.15 Ken Smith and Marianne Winslett. "Entity Modeling in the MLS Relational Model." Proc. 18th International Conference on Very Large Data Bases, Vancouver, Can. (August 1992).

"MLS" in the title of this paper stands for "multilevel secure" [15.12]. This paper focuses on the *meaning* of MLS databases, and proposes a new BELIEVED BY clause on retrieval and update operations to direct those operations to the particular state of the database understood or "believed [to be accurate] by" a specific user. This approach is claimed to solve a number of problems existing in prior approaches.

15.16 M. R. Stonebraker and E. Wong. "Access Control in a Relational Data Base Management System by Query Modification." Proc. ACM National Conference 1974.

The paper that introduced the INGRES request modification mechanism (here called *query* modification).

15.17 Bhavani Thuraisingham. "Current Status of R&D in Trusted Database Management Systems." *ACM SIGMOD Record 21,* No. 3 (September 1992).

A brief survey and extensive set of references on "trusted" or multilevel systems.

Answers to Selected Exercises

15.1 (a) CREATE SECURITY RULE AAA
```
         GRANT RETRIEVE ON STATS TO Ford ;
```

(b) CREATE SECURITY RULE BBB
```
         GRANT INSERT, DELETE ON STATS TO Smith ;
```

(c) CREATE SECURITY RULE CCC
```
         GRANT RETRIEVE
         ON    STATS WHERE STATS.USERID = USER ()
         TO    ALL ;
```

Note the use of the USER builtin function in this rule.

(d) CREATE SECURITY RULE DDD
```
         GRANT RETRIEVE, UPDATE ( SALARY, TAX )
         ON    STATS
         TO    Nash ;
```

(e) CREATE SECURITY RULE EEE
```
         GRANT RETRIEVE ( USERID, SALARY, TAX )
         ON    STATS
         TO    Todd ;
```

(f) CREATE SECURITY RULE FFF
      GRANT RETRIEVE (USERID, SALARY, TAX),
           UPDATE (SALARY, TAX)
      ON   STATS
      TO   Ward ;

(g) CREATE SECURITY RULE GGG
      GRANT ALL
      ON   STATS WHERE STATS.JOB = 'Preacher'
      TO   Pope ;

(h) RANGE OF TX IS STATS ;
  CREATE SECURITY RULE HHH
      GRANT DELETE
      ON   STATS WHERE
           COUNT (TX WHERE TX.JOB = STATS.JOB) > 10
      TO   Jones ;

(i) CREATE VIEW SALS AS
      (STATS.JOB,
        MAX (TX.SAL WHERE TX.JOB = STATS.JOB) AS MAXSAL,
        MIN (TX.SAL WHERE TX.JOB = STATS.JOB) AS MINSAL) ;

  CREATE SECURITY RULE III
      GRANT RETRIEVE ON SALS TO King ;

Note the need to use a view to express this rule.

15.2 We make just one point here: A user who has the authority to create a new base relation and in fact does create such a relation must be regarded as the **owner** of that new relation. The owner of a given base relation must automatically be granted all possible privileges on that relation, including not only the RETRIEVE, INSERT, UPDATE, and DELETE privileges (of course), but also the authority to create security rules granting privileges on that relation to other users.

15.3 The plaintext is

EYES I DARE NOT MEET IN DREAMS

What is the encryption key?

15.5 One problem is that, even in a system that supports encryption, data must still be processed in its plaintext form internally (e.g., for comparisons to operate correctly), and there is thus still a risk of sensitive data being accessible to concurrently executing applications or appearing in a memory dump. Also, there are severe technical problems in indexing encrypted data and in maintaining log records for such data.

15.6 (a) GRANT SELECT ON STATS TO Ford ;

(b) GRANT INSERT, DELETE ON STATS TO Smith ;

(c) CREATE VIEW MINE AS
      SELECT STATS.*
      FROM   STATS
      WHERE STATS.USERID = USER ;

  GRANT SELECT ON MINE TO PUBLIC ;

Note that SQL does support a USER builtin function.

(d) GRANT SELECT, UPDATE (SALARY, TAX) ON STATS TO Nash ;

(e) CREATE VIEW UST AS
            SELECT STATS.USERID, STATS.SALARY, STATS.TAX
            FROM   STATS ;

    GRANT SELECT ON UST TO Todd ;

(f) GRANT SELECT, UPDATE (SALARY, TAX) ON UST TO Ward ;

(g) CREATE VIEW PREACHERS AS
            SELECT STATS.*
            FROM   STATS
            WHERE   STATS.JOB = 'Preacher' ;

    GRANT ALL PRIVILEGES ON PREACHERS TO Pope ;

Observe the use of the shorthand "ALL PRIVILEGES" in this example. (ALL PRIVI-LEGES does not literally mean all privileges, however—it means all privileges on the relevant object for which the user issuing the GRANT has grant authority.)

(h) CREATE VIEW SPECIALISTS AS
            SELECT STX.*
            FROM   STATS AS STX
            WHERE   (SELECT COUNT(*)
                        FROM STATS AS STY
                        WHERE STY.JOB = STX.JOB) > 10 ;

    GRANT DELETE ON SPECIALISTS TO Jones ;

(i) CREATE VIEW SALS AS
            SELECT STATS.JOB,
                    MAX (STATS.SALARY) AS MAXSAL,
                    MIN (STATS.SALARY) AS MINSAL
            FROM   STATS
            GROUP   BY STATS.JOB ;

    GRANT SELECT ON SALS TO King ;

15.7 (a) REVOKE SELECT ON STATS FROM Ford RESTRICT ;

(b) REVOKE INSERT, DELETE ON STATS FROM Smith RESTRICT ;

(c) REVOKE SELECT ON MINE FROM PUBLIC RESTRICT ;

(d) REVOKE SELECT, UPDATE (SALARY, TAX)
                            ON STATS FROM Nash RESTRICT ;

(e) REVOKE SELECT ON UST FROM Todd RESTRICT ;

(f) REVOKE SELECT, UPDATE (SALARY, TAX)
                            ON UST FROM Ward RESTRICT ;

(g) REVOKE ALL PRIVILEGES ON PREACHERS FROM Pope RESTRICT ;

(h) REVOKE DELETE ON SPECIALISTS FROM Jones RESTRICT ;

(i) REVOKE SELECT ON SALS FROM King RESTRICT ;

16 | Integrity

16.1 Introduction

As explained in the introduction to the previous chapter, the term **integrity** is used to refer to the accuracy or correctness of the data in the database. It should not be confused with security, although there are certainly similarities between the two. To repeat from Chapter 15: In both cases (i.e., security and integrity), the system needs to be aware of certain rules that users must not violate; in both cases those rules must be specified (typically by the DBA) in some suitable language, and must be maintained in the system catalog; and in both cases the DBMS must monitor user operations in some way to ensure that the rules are enforced. One point of difference is that integrity rules, unlike security rules, are not user-specific—if they *were* user-specific, then by definition they would be security rules, not integrity rules!

In this chapter we turn our attention to integrity rules specifically. The structure of the chapter is as follows. Section 16.2 discusses the idea of integrity in general terms. Sections 16.3–16.7 then present a hypothetical language for the formulation of integrity rules, and use that language to introduce and illustrate an integrity rule *classification scheme*. Section 16.8 then distinguishes between *state* and *transition* rules. Section 16.9 revisits the candidate and foreign key concepts previously discussed in Chapter 5 and shows how they fit into the foregoing general framework. Finally, Section 16.10 describes the relevant aspects of SQL, and Section 16.11 presents a brief overview and summary of the entire chapter.

Note: Much of what follows is based on certain earlier publications by this author, reference [16.5] in particular. However, the integrity rule classification scheme presented herein represents a significant improvement over the scheme previously presented in reference [16.5]; at the time of writing, moreover, the new scheme (which is due to David McGoveran and the present writer) has not been described in detail elsewhere in the literature. One important difference between the new scheme and the earlier version is worth mentioning right away: The concept of a *checking time* specification (i.e., a clause such as ON UPDATE *R,* the purpose of which was to tell the DBMS when to check some associated constraint on some relation *R*), which was included in the earlier scheme, has been dropped in the new version. See the annotation to reference [16.4] for further explanation.

16.2   General Considerations

In this section we make a number of general preliminary remarks.

1. First of all, note that we are concerned in this chapter with **database-specific** integrity rules, of potentially arbitrary complexity—what are sometimes called *business rules.* We are not limiting ourselves to such matters as entity and referential integrity (see Chapter 5), which are merely special cases of the more general problem. As already indicated, however, we will have a few brief words to say regarding those special cases in Section 16.9.

2. We remind the reader of the following points, first made in Chapter 5.

   ▪ It is usual to think of integrity rules as applying to base relations specifically. This is because it is the base relations that are supposed to "reflect reality," and hence it is the base relations that must be constrained to contain correct, or at least plausible, values. In fact, however, derived relations are subject to integrity rules as well. For example, the rule that applies to base relation S that says that supplier numbers are unique also applies to every restriction of that relation, obviously.

   ▪ As the foregoing example suggests, derived relations will automatically **inherit** certain integrity rules from the relations from which they are derived. But it is possible that a derived relation will be subject to certain additional integrity rules, over and above the rules it automatically inherits. Thus, it might well be desirable to be able to state integrity rules explicitly for certain derived relations; an example might be a candidate key definition for a view.

   In this chapter, however, we will consider only integrity rules that do indeed apply to base relations *per se,* in order to simplify the exposition (and we will accordingly take the term "relation" to mean a base relation specifically, barring explicit statements to the contrary). The question of integrity rules for derived relations will come to the fore in the next chapter.

3. Please note that we are concerned very specifically with **declarative** integrity rule support. At the time of writing, unfortunately, few database products, relational or otherwise, provide much in the way of such declarative support. Several products, in fact, quite specifically emphasize the opposite approach—namely, procedural support, using **stored** or **triggered procedures**. (Stored and triggered procedures were mentioned briefly in Chapter 5 and are discussed further in Chapter 21 and Section 16.9, respectively.) But it has been suggested that if the DBMS did in fact provide declarative support, then as much as 90 percent of a typical database definition would consist of integrity rule declarations; thus, a system that supported

such declarations would relieve application programmers of a considerable burden. At the same time, it would also enable those programmers to become significantly more productive. Declarative integrity support is an important area for development.

4. We said in Section 16.1 that the term "integrity" refers to the accuracy or correctness of the data in the database. To say that the database is in a state of integrity means, therefore, that the database is **correct**—meaning, precisely, that it does not violate any known integrity rule. In other words, we regard the database as correct if and only if it satisfies the logical AND of all known rules. Clearly, however, a system that does not support much in the way of integrity support will have only a very weak sense of what it means for the database to be "correct." Since we said in Chapter 13 that *recovery* meant recovery to a previously known "correct state," and in Chapter 14 that *concurrency*—or, rather, concurrency *control*—meant that a serializable schedule transforms "a correct state" of the database into another "correct state," it can be seen that integrity is really a more fundamental issue than either recovery or concurrency. Indeed, integrity is an issue even in a single-user system.

5. We remind the reader that integrity is an important consideration at design time as well as at execution time. That is, database design is not just a matter of getting the data structures right—integrity rules need to be specified too. Note also that "integrity rules" here does *not* refer just to functional and other dependencies, which are just a special case of the more general problem; nor does it refer just to such matters as entity and referential integrity.

6. Finally, observe that (as already mentioned in Section 16.1) integrity rules, like security rules, are kept in the system catalog. They are enforced by the DBMS's **integrity subsystem,** which is responsible for monitoring user update operations (INSERTs, UPDATEs, and DELETEs) to ensure that such operations do not violate any known rules.

Note: We remind the reader that (as stated in Chapter 2) for performance reasons certain utilities, such as the load utility, might operate directly at the internal level of the system. Ensuring that such utilities do not violate integrity involves special considerations that are beyond the scope of this chapter. Appendix B includes a very brief discussion of this issue in the context of IBM's DB2 product specifically.

16.3   Integrity Rules

We begin with some observations that apply to integrity rules in general (later sections will be more specific). Here is a simple example of such a rule:

```
CREATE INTEGRITY RULE PR4
      FORALL PX ( PX.WEIGHT > 0 )
      ON ATTEMPTED VIOLATION REJECT ;
```

This statement, which is expressed in a hypothetical language originally proposed in reference [16.5] (somewhat modified here), is basically nothing more than a rather longwinded way of saying that part weights must be positive. We have deliberately spelled the rule out in detail, however, in order to illustrate the point that integrity rules in general have *three components,* as follows:

1. A **name** (PR4—"parts rule 4"—in the example). The rule will be registered in the system catalog under this name. The name will also appear in any diagnostics produced by the system in response to an attempted violation of the rule.

2. The **constraint** that must be satisfied, specified by means of a truth-valued expression. The integrity rule is said to be **satisfied** if and only if the constraint evaluates to *true,* and **violated** if and only if the constraint evaluates to *false. Note:* In the example, the constraint says that *all* parts must have a weight greater than zero, because of the universal quantifier FORALL PX.* Of course, it is sufficient in practice to check only the part that has just been inserted or has just had its weight updated, not all parts. But this can be regarded as an optimization!—conceptually, at least, it is nevertheless necessary to talk in terms of "all" parts. See "A note on syntax" later in this section for further discussion of this point.

   Observe that, strictly speaking, the constraint itself is just one component of the overall rule. Informally, however, the terms "integrity constraint" and "integrity rule" are often used as if they were synonymous.

3. A **violation response,** specified by the ON ATTEMPTED VIOLATION clause, telling the system what to do if a user attempts to violate the rule. In the example, the violation response is simply to reject the offending update (undoing any damage it might have done and providing suitable diagnostic information, of course); such a response will surely be the one most commonly required in practice, so we might as well make it the default. But in general the response could be a procedure of arbitrary complexity.

When a CREATE INTEGRITY RULE statement is executed, the system must first check to see whether the current state of the database satisfies the specified constraint. If it does not, the new rule must be rejected; otherwise it will be accepted (i.e., saved in the catalog) and enforced from that point forward. Enforcement in the example at hand will require the DBMS to monitor all operations that would insert a value into, or change a value in, attribute P.WEIGHT.

A note on syntax: In practice, the constraint portion of an integrity rule will almost always start with a universal quantifier—and in those cases where it does not, one can be assumed without changing the meaning. Consequently, that quantifier, and its asso-

---

* Here and throughout this chapter, we make use of our usual convention that SX, SY, . . . , represent range variables ranging over relation S; PX, PY, . . . , represent range variables ranging over relation P; and so on. We also frequently make use of the shorthand by which the name of a relation can be used as the name of an *implicit* range variable that ranges over the relation with the same name, as discussed in Chapter 7 and used extensively in Chapter 15.

ciated scoping parentheses, can optionally be omitted from the concrete syntax. In other words, we adopt the convention that any variable mentioned in the constraint that is not explicitly quantified is tacitly assumed to be *universally* quantified. Adopting this simplification, and making use of the shorthand that allows us to use a relation name to denote a range variable, and assuming we want the default violation response, our original example can be simplified to just:

```
CREATE INTEGRITY RULE PR4 P.WEIGHT > 0 ;
```

Of course, we also need a way of destroying existing rules:

```
DESTROY INTEGRITY RULE rule ;
```

For example:

```
DESTROY INTEGRITY RULE PR4 ;
```

We conclude this section with a quick overview of the integrity rule classification scheme mentioned in Section 16.1. The fact is, integrity rules can very conveniently be classified into four categories, *viz.* domain, attribute, relation, and database rules. Briefly:

1. A *domain* rule specifies the legal values for a given domain.

2. An *attribute* rule specifies the legal values for a given attribute.

3. A *relation* rule specifies the legal values for a given relation.

4. A *database* rule specifies the legal values for a given database.

The four cases are discussed in detail in the next four sections.

16.4 Domain Rules

The domain integrity rule for a given domain is, precisely, the definition of the set of values that go to make up that domain; in other words, it effectively just enumerates the values in the domain. There is thus no need for a separate "CREATE DOMAIN INTEGRITY RULE" statement—instead, the integrity rule can be specified as a direct part of the relevant CREATE DOMAIN statement. For example:

```
CREATE DOMAIN QTY NUMERIC (9)
           FORALL QTY ( QTY > 0 AND
                        QTY ≤ 5000 AND
                        MOD ( QTY, 50 ) = 0 ) ;
```

Points arising:

■   The name of the rule is just the name of the domain.

■   Since domains *per se* are never updated (attributes are updated instead), domain rules *per se* are never checked (*attribute* rules are checked instead—see the next section).

■   The concept of a violation response for a domain rule therefore does not arise.

- The constraint for a domain rule—sometimes referred to explicitly as a *domain constraint*—is specified by means of a formula of the relational calculus (actually the *domain* calculus) in which (a) there is exactly one variable, (b) that variable is universally quantified, and (c) it ranges over the domain in question. In the example, the constraint says that quantities must be positive multiples of 50 and must not exceed 5000. The quantifier could be omitted if desired.

- Destroying a domain integrity rule can be done only by destroying the domain itself. DESTROY DOMAIN is discussed in Chapters 4 and 19.

The expression "VALUES (*literal-commalist*)" is a useful shorthand for a particular common form of domain constraint. For example, the following CREATE DOMAIN statement—

```
CREATE DOMAIN COLOR CHAR(6)
            VALUES ( 'Red', 'Yellow', 'Blue',  'Green' ) ;
```

—is equivalent to:

```
CREATE DOMAIN COLOR CHAR(6)
            FORALL COLOR
                 ( COLOR = 'Red' OR
                   COLOR = 'Yellow' OR
                   COLOR = 'Blue' OR
                   COLOR = 'Green' ) ;
```

Other shorthands—range expressions (e.g., *a* TO *b*), pictures (e.g., PIC '999-99-9999'), etc.—could obviously be provided if desired.

Note: We should warn the reader that in our discussion of *domain/key normal form* in Chapter 11, we followed reference [11.10] in using the term "domain constraint" to mean not a domain constraint as defined above, but rather an *attribute* constraint as defined in the next section. We note too that domain constraints in SQL are also not identical to domain constraints as defined above. See Section 16.10.

16.5   Attribute Rules

The attribute integrity rule for a given attribute is, precisely, the specification of the domain from which that attribute draws its values. There is thus no need for a separate "CREATE ATTRIBUTE INTEGRITY RULE" statement; instead, the integrity rule is specified as a direct part of the applicable attribute definition. (Remember that we are taking "relation" to mean a base relation specifically, until further notice; by the same token, we will take "attribute" to mean an attribute of a base relation specifically, until further notice.) Here is an example:

```
SNAME DOMAIN ( NAME )
```

(part of the CREATE BASE RELATION for the suppliers relation S). If the "DOMAIN (*domain*)" specification is omitted from some attribute definition, the attribute is assumed to be defined on a domain with the same name.

Points arising:

■ The name of the rule is the same as the name of the corresponding domain rule, which is just the name of the domain.

■ Attribute rules are always checked **immediately;** that is, any attempt (via an INSERT or UPDATE operation) to introduce an attribute value into the database that is not a value from the relevant domain will simply be rejected (the operation will fail "immediately").

■ As just indicated, the violation response for an attribute rule is always simply REJECT.

■ The constraint for an attribute rule—sometimes referred to explicitly as an *attribute constraint*—is derived in an obvious way from the relevant domain constraint. (The derivation process basically involves modifying the domain constraint by replacing references to the domain by references to the attribute instead.)

■ An attribute integrity rule can be destroyed only by destroying the attribute itself (which in practice will usually be done by destroying the containing relation).

We remark that an attribute integrity rule is effectively nothing more nor less than an attribute *data type* specification (where the term *data type* refers to either a builtin data type such as NUMERIC(n) or a user-defined data type such as "supplier number"). See Chapter 19 for further discussion.

16.6 Relation Rules

A relation rule for a given relation is a rule that refers to the given relation *only*—not to any other relation, nor to any domain. Here is an example:

```
CREATE INTEGRITY RULE SR7
     FORALL S ( IF S.CITY = 'London' THEN S.STATUS = 20 )
     ON ATTEMPTED VIOLATION REJECT ;
```

("suppliers in London must have status 20"). Here is the general syntax (once again using square brackets to indicate optional material):

```
CREATE INTEGRITY RULE rule
     constraint
   [ ON ATTEMPTED VIOLATION action ] ;
```

Explanation:

■ The specified *rule* is the name of the new rule.

■ Relation rules are always checked **immediately;** that is, every update operation on a given relation conceptually includes as its final step the checking of all relation rules that apply to that relation.

■ The *constraint* (sometimes referred to explicitly as a *relation* constraint) is a **closed**

WFF of the tuple calculus.* In other words, it is a truth-valued expression that contains no free variables, and so evaluates to *true* or *false,* unequivocally. Furthermore, every bound—i.e., quantified—variable in that WFF must range over the same relation, namely the relation to which the integrity rule applies. In the example shown earlier (rule SR7), there is just one bound variable, namely S, which ranges over the relation with the same name.

Note: Recall from Section 16.3 that any apparently free variables in the WFF are implicitly universally quantified anyway, so that in fact the WFF *must* be closed.

■ The *action* is (in general) a procedure, of arbitrary complexity, that is to be invoked if the constraint evaluates to *false.* As mentioned in Section 16.3, the default is just to reject the attempted operation, but in more complex situations some other action might be more appropriate—for example, a procedure might be invoked to perform some **compensating** update somewhere else in the database. The foreign key CASCADES delete and update rules discussed in Chapter 5 provide simple examples of compensating procedures (declaratively specified, please note!).

Note: If some procedure other than REJECT is specified, the execution of that procedure must be considered part of the execution of the update operation that triggered the integrity check. Furthermore, that integrity check must be performed again after that procedure has executed (the procedure must obviously not leave the relation in a state that violates the constraint).

Here are some more examples of relation rules.

1. ```
CREATE INTEGRITY RULE RX1
        S.STATUS ≥ 0 AND S.STATUS ≤ 100 ;
```

("supplier status values must be in the range 1–100"). We are assuming here that the STATUS domain includes values not in the specified range, and are thus imposing an *additional* constraint on the STATUS attribute, over and above the applicable attribute constraint.

The point of this example is that a relation rule will very often refer not just to the single relation in question, but in fact just to one attribute of that relation. Integrity rule PR4 in Section 16.3 ("weights must be positive") is another case in point. In practice, relation rules are very often of this simple form; perhaps for this reason, some products do support this special case (e.g., in the form of "range checks" or "nulls not allowed" constraints), but do not support the more general case. Unfortunately, such products typically refer to that special case as an *attribute* (or *column*) rule. We feel that our use of this term as defined in Section 16.5 is more logical, but it is only fair to warn the reader of a potential source of confusion.

2. This next example makes use of the revised version of the shipments relation from

---

* Or a truth-valued expression of the relational algebra. We use the calculus merely for definiteness.
```

Chapter 9 called SCP (refer to Fig. 9.1 for a sample tabulation). Recall that relation SCP includes, in addition to the usual S#, P#, and QTY attributes, an attribute CITY, representing the city for the relevant supplier. So we have:

```
CREATE INTEGRITY RULE RX2
        FORALL SCPX ( FORALL SCPY
                    ( IF     SCPX.S# = SCPY.S#
                      THEN   SCPX.CITY = SCPY.CITY ) ) ;
```

Here we have two bound variables, SCPX and SCPY, that do indeed range over the same relation, *viz.* SCP. The constraint says that whenever two tuples of SCP agree on their S# value, they also agree on their CITY value; in other words, there is a **functional dependency** from S# to CITY in this relation. The more familiar notation "S# $\rightarrow$ CITY" can be regarded as shorthand for this longer formulation.

Here for interest is the same rule with the quantifiers implicit:

```
CREATE INTEGRITY RULE RX2
        IF SCPX.S# = SCPY.S# THEN SCPX.CITY = SCPY.CITY ;
```

3. ```
CREATE INTEGRITY RULE RX3
        IF SX.S# = SY.S# THEN SX.SNAME = SY.SNAME
                         AND SX.STATUS = SY.STATUS
                         AND SX.CITY   = SY.CITY ;
```

If two tuples of S agree on their S# value, they also agree on the value of everything else—in other words, they are the same tuple. The rule thus effectively states that S# is a **candidate key** for S. The more familiar notation "CANDIDATE KEY (S#)" can be regarded as shorthand for this longer formulation (see Section 16.9).

4. ```
CREATE INTEGRITY RULE RX4
        COUNT ( P WHERE P.COLOR = 'Red' ) > 1 ;
```

("there must exist at least two red parts"). Recall from Chapter 7 (Section 7.5) that the aggregate functions—COUNT, etc.—behave in certain respects like quantifiers; to be specific, the occurrence of the variable P in the subexpression P.COLOR = 'Red' (which is free in that subexpression) is indeed bound in the overall constraint. In fact, we could express this rule using EXISTS instead of COUNT:

```
CREATE INTEGRITY RULE RX4
        EXISTS PX ( EXISTS PY ( PX.P# ≠ PY.P# AND
                                PX.COLOR = 'Red' AND
                                PY.COLOR = 'Red' ) ) ;
```

Note, incidentally, that rule RX4 would have to be created *after* an appropriate set of tuples had been entered into relation P (why?). Note too that this example is different from all of the other examples we have seen so far, inasmuch as DELETE operations have the potential for violating the constraint (on the other hand, INSERT operations do not).

We close this section by reminding the reader that (as explained in Chapter 4, Section 4.5) every relation has an associated *predicate,* which constitutes the *criterion for update acceptability* for that relation. We can now make this concept more precise. In fact, the **relation predicate** for a given relation is defined to be, precisely, the logical

AND of all relation constraints and all attribute constraints that apply to the relation in question.

Incidentally, do not confuse relation *constraints* and relation *predicates*. Loosely speaking, a relation constraint is an individual integrity rule; a relation predicate is the logical AND of many rules, and is *what the relation (formally) means*.

16.7 Database Rules

A database rule is a rule that interrelates two or more distinct relations. Here is an example ("no supplier with status less than 20 can supply any part in a quantity greater than 500"):

```
CREATE INTEGRITY RULE C95
     FORALL SX ( FORALL SPX
               ( IF SX.STATUS < 20 AND SX.S# = SPX.S#
               THEN SPX.QTY ≤ 500 ) ) ;
```

Or omitting the quantifiers and corresponding parentheses:

```
CREATE INTEGRITY RULE C95
     IF SX.STATUS < 20 AND SX.S# = SPX.S#
     THEN SPX.QTY ≤ 500 ;
```

This example involves two bound variables, SX (ranging over relation S) and SPX (ranging over relation SP). *Exercise for the reader:* What operations does the DBMS have to monitor in order to enforce this constraint?

The general syntax for a database rule is superficially the same as that for a relation rule:

```
CREATE INTEGRITY RULE rule
     constraint
     [ ON ATTEMPTED VIOLATION action ] ;
```

However, there are some important differences, as follows:

■ The constraint must include at least one "join condition" involving two distinct bound variables, ranging over two distinct relations* (which are therefore *interrelated* under the constraint). Such a constraint is sometimes referred to explicitly as a *database constraint*.

■ **Database rules are not checked immediately**. Instead, the checking is **deferred** until end-of-transaction (COMMIT)—at least conceptually. Why is this? The answer is that database rules interrelate several distinct relations, and therefore several distinct update operations will be needed (in general) in order to update all of those relations in a consistent way. Now, it might well be the case with certain database rules—possibly even with most such rules—that the checking can in fact

---

* An example of such a join condition might be "SP.S# = S.S#."

be done "immediately" (as it is with all other kinds of rules), but we regard such early checking as an optimization, *not* as an intrinsic aspect of the rule in question.

■ The default *action* is not REJECT but ROLLBACK. Often, in fact, no other *action* will make much sense (we certainly must not leave the database in an incorrect state).

Note: If some procedure other than ROLLBACK is specified, the execution of that procedure must be considered part of the execution of the update operation that triggered the integrity check. Furthermore, that integrity check must be performed again after that procedure has executed (the procedure must obviously not leave the database in a state that violates the constraint).

Here are some more examples of database integrity rules:

1. CREATE INTEGRITY RULE DBX1
        FORALL SP (EXISTS S (S.S# = SP.S#) AND
                    EXISTS P (P.P# = SP.P#)) ;

("for every shipment, there exists a corresponding supplier and a corresponding part"). Given that S# is a candidate key for suppliers and P# is a candidate key for parts, this rule effectively defines the **referential constraints** from shipments to suppliers and parts. Note that the universal quantifier could be omitted in this example, but the existential quantifiers certainly cannot! For clarity, it seems better to include all quantifiers.

2. CREATE INTEGRITY RULE DBX2
        FORALL P EXISTS SP (SP.P# = P.P#) ;

("every part must have at least one shipment"). The checking *must* be deferred here in order to allow new parts to be inserted—because, of course, a new part will obviously violate the rule at the time it is first inserted, so such insertion must be followed by an operation to create at least one shipment for the new part before the integrity check is done.

3. CREATE INTEGRITY RULE DBX3
        FORALL P (SUM (SP WHERE SP.P# = P.P#, QTY) ≤ 2000)   ;

("no part can have a total shipment quantity exceeding 2000"). Note that the occurrence of range variable SP in the WHERE clause is bound by the "quantifier" SUM. Note also that (as in the previous examples) the initial universal quantifier FORALL P could safely be omitted, but to do so in examples like this one does seem to impair readability.

We close this section by pointing out that, just as every relation has an associated meaning (the *relation predicate* for that relation), so every database has an associated meaning too—the **database predicate** for that database, which we define to be, precisely, the logical AND of all database constraints and all relation predicates that apply to the database in question. (As with relations, do not confuse *constraints* and *predicates*. Loosely speaking, a database constraint is an individual integrity rule; a database predicate is the logical AND of many rules, and is *what the database formally means*.)

16.8 State *vs.* Transition Rules

All of the examples we have seen so far have been **state** rules—they have been concerned with correct *states* of the database. Sometimes, however, it is necessary to consider **transitions** from one state to another. In a database concerning people, for example, there might be a series of transition rules having to do with valid changes of marital status. For instance, the following transitions are all valid—

- Never-married to married
- Married to widowed
- Married to divorced
- Widowed to married

(etc., etc.), whereas the following are not—

- Never-married to widowed
- Never-married to divorced
- Widowed to divorced
- Divorced to widowed

(etc., etc.). Reverting to the suppliers-and-parts database, here is another example ("no supplier's status must ever decrease"):

```
CREATE INTEGRITY RULE SR9
     FORALL S' FORALL S
   ( IF S'.S# = S.S# THEN S'.STATUS ≤ S.STATUS ) ;
```

Explanation: We introduce the convention that a **primed** range variable (such as S′ in the example) is understood to range over the corresponding relation as it was *prior to the update operation under consideration*. (Note that up to this point we have tacitly been assuming that all range variables range over the corresponding relation as it is *after* the update in question.) Thus the constraint in the example means:

> *If S′ and S are supplier tuples before and after the update, respectively, and if they have the same supplier number (so they are in fact "the same" tuple), then the status of S′ must be less than or equal to that of S.*

Here is the same example with the quantifiers implicit:

```
CREATE INTEGRITY RULE SR9
     IF S'.S# = S.S# THEN S'.STATUS ≤ S.STATUS ;
```

Since this is a *relation* rule (it applies to just a single relation, namely the suppliers relation S), the checking is *immediate*. Here by contrast is an example of a *database* transition rule:

```
CREATE INTEGRITY RULE AR43
     FORALL S
           ( SUM ( SP  WHERE SP.S#  = S.S#, QTY ) ≥
             SUM ( SP' WHERE SP'.S# = S.S#, QTY ) ) ;
```

("the total quantity of any given part, taken over all suppliers, can only increase"). Since this is a database rule (it involves two distinct relations, S and SP), the checking is *deferred,* and the primed variable SP′ is taken to range over relation SP as it was at BEGIN TRANSACTION.

The concept of state *vs.* transition constraints has no meaning for domain and attribute rules.

16.9   Candidate and Foreign Keys

Since the most general (database) integrity rules do not logically belong to any single relation, symmetry suggests that they should be specified separately—i.e., by separate, standalone CREATE INTEGRITY RULE statements, as we have been doing. And then, since individual relation rules can obviously be specified in this same way, parsimony suggests that they *should* be—i.e., the language should not be cluttered up with numerous distinct ways of doing the same thing.*

However, this approach, although conceptually clean, unfortunately makes certain simple cases—arguably the commonest ones in practice, too—unduly cumbersome. By way of illustration, we repeat Example 3 from Section 16.6:

```
CREATE INTEGRITY RULE RX3
     IF SX.S# = SY.S# THEN SX.SNAME  = SY.SNAME
                       AND  SX.STATUS = SY.STATUS
                       AND  SX.CITY   = SY.CITY ;
```

As explained in Section 16.6, this is just a longwinded way of saying that S# is a candidate key for S, and the specification

```
CANDIDATE KEY ( S# )
```

(part of the definition of base relation S) seems preferable, at least from a human factors point of view. Logically speaking, however, this latter specification is nothing but shorthand for the more cumbersome formulation given above.

Analogous remarks apply to *foreign* keys also. For example, here is a general integrity language specification of the rule that says that attribute S# in relation SP is a foreign key referencing relation S:

```
CREATE INTEGRITY RULE SPSFK
     FORALL SP ( EXISTS S ( S.S# = SP.S# ) ) ;
```

Again, the specification

```
FOREIGN KEY ( S# ) REFERENCES S ...
```

(part of the definition of base relation SP) seems preferable.

---

* Some might argue the contrary position—namely, that domain rules are specified with the domain definition and attribute rules are specified with the attribute definition (and—arguably—database rules are specified with the database definition), and therefore relation rules should be specified with the relation definition. In any case, the point is not of fundamental importance; it is really a psychological issue, not a logical one.

To pursue this latter example a little further: The general integrity language version tacitly specifies RESTRICTED delete and update rules only. By contrast, consider the following extended specification:

```
CREATE INTEGRITY RULE SPSFK
      FORALL SP ( EXISTS S ( S.S# = SP.S# ) )
      ON ATTEMPTED VIOLATION
          DELETE SP WHERE NOT EXISTS S ( S.S# = SP.S# ) ;
```

The *conceptual*—i.e., unoptimized!—implications of this specification are as follows.

1. If we INSERT an SP tuple with no matching S tuple, that SP tuple will simply be deleted again. *Net effect:* No change to the database.

2. If we UPDATE the supplier number in an existing SP tuple to a value that does not match any S tuple, that SP tuple will be deleted. *Net effect:* The UPDATE has been converted into a DELETE.

3. If we UPDATE the supplier number in an existing S tuple, all SP tuples that previously matched that S tuple will be deleted. *Net effect:* The UPDATE has caused a cascaded *DELETE,* not a cascaded UPDATE.

4. If we DELETE an existing S tuple, all SP tuples that previously matched that S tuple will be deleted. *Net effect:* The DELETE has caused a cascaded DELETE.

Of the foregoing, Number 1 is clearly acceptable (it preserves the *status quo* and thereby certainly preserves referential integrity), and Number 4 is probably acceptable also (if cascade delete is what is wanted). But Numbers 2 and 3, while they do preserve referential integrity, are probably *not* acceptable; in particular, they do not correspond to any of the foreign key rules identified in Chapter 5 (not that those rules are necessarily complete in any sense, of course).

What this example shows is that, in order to specify "violation responses" (or compensating procedures) that are appropriate to the problem at hand, some finer-grained control is necessary. Specifically, we need to be able to control which updates invoke which compensating procedures, thus saying, for example, "ON UPDATE invoke procedure *A*" and "ON DELETE invoke procedure *B*." (Note that the UPDATE CASCADES, DELETE RESTRICTED, etc., specifications introduced in Chapter 5 provide precisely this kind of finer-grained control.) Further, we might very well want to specify whether a given procedure is to be invoked AFTER or BEFORE the corresponding update operation.

All of which leads us somewhat away from the realm of integrity rules as such and into the realm of **triggered procedures** [16.8]. A triggered procedure is a procedure that is to be invoked when a specified **trigger condition** occurs. In the case at hand, the trigger condition is an integrity constraint violation (or perhaps AFTER or BEFORE a specified update operation), and the purpose of the triggered procedure is to carry out a certain compensating action to bring the database back into a state of integrity again. In general, however, triggered procedures are applicable to a much wider variety of problems than just the integrity question that is the topic of the present chapter;* however, they represent a large subject in their own right, and one that is beyond the scope of this chapter. See reference [16.8] for further discussion.

16.10 SQL Support

SQL's integrity rule classification scheme is rather different from the scheme described in the foregoing sections. First, SQL divides such rules into three broad categories, as follows:

1. Domain rules

2. Base table rules

3. General rules ("assertions")

Domain and base table rules were discussed, albeit briefly, in Chapter 8; recall in particular that the category "base table rules" includes various candidate key, primary key, and foreign key specifications, also "CHECK constraints" (refer back to Section 8.2 for further discussion). Here we just offer a few additional comments on these first two cases:

■ An SQL domain rule is not (as it should be) limited to simply enumerating the values in the domain. Instead, it can involve a constraint of arbitrary complexity.

■ An SQL base table rule is not (as it should be) limited to referencing just the base table in question. Instead, it can involve a constraint of arbitrary complexity.

■ An SQL base table rule is *always* considered to be satisfied if the base table in question happens to be empty—even if the rule is of the form "this table must not be empty"!

See reference [16.6] for a discussion of some of the unfortunate implications of the foregoing points.

For the remainder of this section, we concentrate on the third case, general rules. General rules are created by means of **CREATE ASSERTION,** which corresponds, more or less, to our CREATE INTEGRITY RULE. The syntax is:

```
CREATE ASSERTION rule CHECK ( conditional-expression ) ;
```

Here *rule* is the name of the new rule, and *conditional-expression* defines the corresponding constraint (refer to Chapter 8 for an explanation of SQL conditional expressions). And here is the syntax of **DROP ASSERTION:**

```
DROP ASSERTION rule ;
```

---

* Triggered procedures are certainly useful for many purposes. However, it is the opinion of this writer that they are *not* usually a good approach to the problem of database integrity specifically, for reasons elaborated in reference [16.6]. Declarative specifications are always to be preferred if possible.

Note that, unlike all other forms of DROP discussed in this book, DROP ASSERTION does not offer a RESTRICT *vs.* CASCADE option.

Here are some examples of CREATE ASSERTION:

1. Every supplier has status at least five:

```
CREATE ASSERTION IC13 CHECK
      ( ( SELECT MIN ( S.STATUS ) FROM S ) > 4 ) ;
```

2. Every part has a positive weight:

```
CREATE ASSERTION IC18 CHECK
      ( NOT EXISTS ( SELECT * FROM P
                     WHERE  NOT ( P.WEIGHT > 0 ) ) ) ;
```

3. All red parts must be stored in London:

```
CREATE ASSERTION IC99 CHECK
      ( NOT EXISTS ( SELECT * FROM P
                     WHERE  P.COLOR = 'Red'
                     AND    P.CITY <> 'London' ) ) ;
```

4. No shipment has a total weight (part weight times shipment quantity) greater than 20,000:

```
CREATE ASSERTION IC46 CHECK
      ( NOT EXISTS ( SELECT * FROM P, SP
                     WHERE  P.P# = SP.P#
                     AND    ( P.WEIGHT * SP.QTY ) > 20000 ) ) ;
```

5. No supplier with status less than 20 can supply any part in a quantity greater than 500:

```
CREATE ASSERTION IC95 CHECK
      ( NOT EXISTS ( SELECT * FROM S, SP
                     WHERE  S.STATUS < 20
                     AND    S.S# = SP.S#
                     AND    SP.QTY > 500 ) ) ;
```

Deferred Checking

Any SQL integrity rule can be declared to be DEFERRABLE or NOT DEFERRABLE; if it is DEFERRABLE, it can further be declared to be INITIALLY DEFERRED or INITIALLY IMMEDIATE, which defines its state at beginning-of-transaction. DEFERRABLE rules can be dynamically switched on and off by means of the statement

```
SET CONSTRAINTS rules option ;
```

where *option* is IMMEDIATE or DEFERRED. For example:

```
SET CONSTRAINTS IC46, IC95 DEFERRED ;
```

COMMIT forces all rules into the IMMEDIATE state. And, of course, DEFERRABLE rules are checked only when they are in the IMMEDIATE state. NOT DEFERRABLE rules are always checked immediately.

16.11 Summary

In this chapter and its predecessor we have discussed the security and integrity aspects of database systems. We can distinguish between the two concepts, somewhat glibly, as follows:

- **Security** means protecting the database against unauthorized users;
- **Integrity** means protecting it against *authorized* users.

Both involve, among other things, (a) the definition of a set of appropriate rules, (b) a specification of what to do if those rules are violated, and (c) system monitoring of user operations to detect any such violations. In the specific case of integrity we have discussed:

- A hypothetical **language** for the expression of integrity rules
- The fact that, in general, each integrity rule has a **name,** a **constraint,** and a **violation response**
- **Domain** rules, which essentially just enumerate the values in the domain
- **Attribute** rules, which identify the domain from which the attribute draws its values
- **Relation** rules, which refer to the relation in question (only) and constrain the values that can appear in that relation
- **Database** rules, which refer to arbitrary combinations of relations and constrain the values that can appear in that combination of relations

We also explained that database rules are **deferred,** meaning that they are checked (at least conceptually) at end-of-transaction, whereas other rules are **immediate**. And we defined the important concepts **relation predicate** and **database predicate,** which correspond to the formal *meaning* of a given relation and a given database, respectively. In the case of relation and database rules, we also distinguished between **state** and **transition** constraints. In addition, we suggested that certain syntactic shorthands are desirable in practice, especially with respect to **candidate** and **foreign key** specifications. This discussion led us on a brief foray into the realm of **triggered procedures**.

As for SQL support: SQL provides **domain** rules, **base table** rules, and **general** rules (**assertions**). We concentrated on the general case (the other two cases were discussed previously, in Chapter 8); however, we should point out that general rules and base table rules are essentially interchangeable—i.e., they essentially represent two distinct ways of doing the same thing [16.6]. We also briefly discussed SQL's support for **deferred integrity checking** and the use of the **SET CONSTRAINTS** statement.

By way of conclusion, we stress the point once again that, whereas many systems are in fact quite strong on security, no system (at the time of writing) is really completely satisfactory in the area of integrity. It is to be hoped that this state of affairs will not persist for very much longer.

Exercises

For Exercises 16.1–16.16 you are asked to write integrity rules to enforce the indicated constraints on the suppliers-parts-projects database, using the hypothetical integrity language introduced in Sections 16.3–16.8.

16.1 The only legal cities are London, Paris, Rome, Athens, Oslo, Stockholm, Madrid, and Amsterdam.

16.2 All red parts weigh less than 50 pounds.

16.3 No two projects can be located in the same city.

16.4 At most one supplier can be located in Athens at any one time.

16.5 No shipment can have a quantity more than double the average of all such quantities.

16.6 The highest-status supplier must not be located in the same city as the lowest-status supplier.

16.7 Every project must be located in a city in which there is at least one supplier.

16.8 Every project must be located in a city in which there is at least one supplier of that project.

16.9 There must exist at least one red part.

16.10 The average supplier status must be greater than 15.

16.11 Every London supplier must supply part P2.

16.12 At least one red part weighs less than 50 pounds.

16.13 No shipment quantity can be reduced (in a single update) to less than half its current value.

16.14 Suppliers in London supply more different kinds of part than suppliers in Paris.

16.15 Suppliers in London supply more parts in total than suppliers in Paris.

16.16 Suppliers in Athens can move only to London or Paris, and suppliers in London can move only to Paris.

16.17 For each of your answers to Exercises 16.1–16.16, state whether the rule is a relation rule or a database rule.

16.18 For each of your answers to Exercises 16.1–16.16, state the operations that must be monitored by the DBMS to ensure that the applicable constraint is not violated. Assume in the case of the database rules that the checking is to be done "early," i.e., the operation to be monitored is not simply COMMIT!

16.19 One issue we did not discuss in the body of the chapter is the question of what should happen if the user attempts to destroy some relation or domain and some existing integrity rule refers to that relation or domain. What *should* happen in such a situation?

16.20 Give SQL solutions to Exercises 16.1–16.16.

References and Bibliography

16.1 D. Z. Badal and G. J. Popek. "Cost and Performance Analysis of Semantic Integrity Validation Methods." Proc. 1979 ACM International Conference on Management of Data, Boston, Mass. (May/June 1979).

Compares three different approaches to the implementation of integrity rules: checking at compilation time (that is, checking by examining database values and the effect of executing the transaction at the time it is compiled); run-time checking (that is, checking at COMMIT but before any writes have been made to the physical database); and post-execution checking (that is, checking after the physical writes have been done). Run-time validation is shown to give the best performance (based primarily on the number of I/O operations needed, but also taking into account such matters as lock duration).

16.2 Philip A. Bernstein, Barbara T. Blaustein, and Edmund M. Clarke. "Fast Maintenance of Semantic Integrity Assertions Using Redundant Aggregate Data." Proc. 6th International Conference on Very Large Data Bases, Montreal, Canada (October 1980).

Presents an efficient method of enforcement for integrity rules of a certain special kind. An example is "every value in set *A* must be less than every value in set *B*." The enforcement technique is based on the observation that (for example) the rule just given is logically equivalent to the rule "the *maximum* value in *A* must be less than the *minimum* value in *B*." By recognizing this class of rule and automatically deciding to keep the necessary maximum and minimum values as hidden variables, the system can reduce the number of comparisons involved in enforcing the constraint on a given update from something on the order of the cardinality of either *A* or *B* (depending which set the update applies to) to *one*—at the cost, of course, of having to maintain the stored maximum and minimum values.

16.3   O. Peter Buneman and Erik K. Clemons. "Efficiently Monitoring Relational Databases." *ACM TODS 4*, No. 3 (September 1979).

This paper is concerned with the efficient implementation of triggered procedures (here called *alerters*)—in particular, with the problem of deciding when the trigger condition is satisfied, without necessarily evaluating that condition. It gives a method (an *avoidance* algorithm) for detecting updates that cannot possibly satisfy a given trigger condition; it also discusses a technique for reducing the processing overhead in the event that the avoidance algorithm fails, by evaluating the trigger condition for some small subset (a *filter*) of the total set of relevant tuples.

16.4   Stefano Ceri and Jennifer Widom. "Deriving Production Rules for Constraint Maintenance." Proc. 16th International Conference on Very Large Data Bases, Brisbane, Australia (August 1990).

Describes an SQL-based integrity rules specification language and gives an algorithm for deriving all of the operations that might violate a given rule. (A preliminary outline of such an algorithm was given by the present writer in reference [16.5]. The existence of such an algorithm accounts for the removal—mentioned in Section 16.1—of the *checking time* component from the general integrity language of reference [16.5] in the version described in the present chapter.) The paper also addresses questions of optimization and correctness.

16.5   C. J. Date. "A Contribution to the Study of Database Integrity." In C. J. Date, *Relational Database Writings 1985–1989*. Reading, Mass.: Addison-Wesley (1990).

To quote from the abstract: "This paper attempts to impose some structure on the [database integrity] problem by (a) proposing a classification scheme for integrity rules, (b) using that scheme to clarify the principal underlying concepts of data integrity, (c) sketching an approach to a concrete language for formulating integrity rules, and (d) pinpointing some specific areas for further research." Portions of the present chapter are based on this earlier paper, but the classification scheme itself should be regarded as superseded by the revised version described in Sections 16.3–16.8 of the present chapter.

16.6   C. J. Date. "A Matter of Integrity, Part III." *Database Programming & Design 6*, No. 12 (December 1993).

16.7   K. P. Eswaran and D. D. Chamberlin. "Functional Specifications of a Subsystem for Data Base Integrity." Proc. 1st International Conference on Very Large Data Bases, Framingham, Mass. (September 1975).

An early proposal for a set of integrity facilities for SQL, including ASSERT and DROP ASSERTION statements (analogous to our CREATE and DROP INTEGRITY RULE statements, but without a violation response); a DEFINE TRIGGER statement (analogous to our CREATE INTEGRITY RULE *with* such a response), and a corresponding DROP TRIGGER statement; and an ENFORCE INTEGRITY statement to force the checking of deferred rules without actually causing a COMMIT. *Note:* The term TRIGGER as used in this paper would more accurately be called a triggered *procedure*.

16.8 K. P. Eswaran. "Specifications, Implementations, and Interactions of a Trigger Subsystem in an Integrated Data Base System." IBM Research Report RJ1820 (August 1976).

16.9 G. Gardarin and M. Melkanoff. "Proving Consistency of Database Transactions." Proc. 5th International Conference on Very Large Data Bases, Rio de Janeiro, Brazil (October 1979).

Presents a technique for verifying at compilation time that transactions cannot violate any integrity rules. The technique is based on Hoare's axiomatic approach to program correctness. It is suggested that such a technique could form the basis for a generalized compilation-time "transaction consistency verifier."

16.10 M. M. Hammer and S. K. Sarin. "Efficient Monitoring of Database Assertions." Proc. 1978 ACM SIGMOD International Conference on Management of Data, Austin, Texas (May/June 1978).

An algorithm is sketched for generating integrity-checking procedures (given appropriate integrity constraints) that are more efficient than the obvious "brute force" method of simply evaluating those constraints after an update has been performed. The checks are incorporated into transaction object code at compilation time. In some cases it is possible to detect that no run-time checks are needed at all. Even when they are needed, it is frequently possible to reduce the number of database accesses significantly in a variety of different ways.

16.11 M. R. Stonebraker and E. Wong. "Access Control in a Relational Data Base Management System by Query Modification." Proc. ACM National Conference 1974.

As mentioned in Chapter 15, this was the paper that introduced the INGRES request modification mechanism (it is the same as that chapter's reference [15.16]). That mechanism was used for integrity rules as well as security rules. Integrity rules were defined by means of the DEFINE INTEGRITY statement—syntax:

```
DEFINE INTEGRITY ON relation IS condition
```

For example:

```
DEFINE INTEGRITY ON S IS S.STATUS > 0
```

Suppose user U attempts the following REPLACE:

```
REPLACE S ( STATUS = S.STATUS - 10 )
WHERE    S.CITY = "London"
```

Then INGRES will automatically modify the REPLACE to the following:

```
REPLACE S ( STATUS = S.STATUS - 10 )
WHERE    S.CITY = "London"
AND      ( S.STATUS - 10 ) > 0
```

And of course this modified operation cannot possibly violate the integrity rule. (As in the security case, the modification process is "silent"—see Chapter 15.) The advantages and disadvantages of this scheme are very similar to those already mentioned in our discussion of the QUEL security mechanism in Chapter 15. Note in particular that not all integrity rules can be enforced in this simple way; as a matter of fact, QUEL supports only rules in which the constraint is a simple restriction condition. However, even that limited support represents more than is found in some systems.

16.12 A. Walker and S. C. Salveter. "Automatic Modification of Transactions to Preserve Data Base Integrity Without Undoing Updates." State University of New York, Stony Brook, N.Y.: Technical Report 81/026 (June 1981).

Describes a technique for automatically modifying any "transaction template" (i.e., transaction source code) into a corresponding *safe* template—safe, in the sense that no transaction instance conforming to that modified template can possibly violate any declared integrity rules. The method works by adding queries and tests to the original template to ensure *before* any updating is done that no rules will be violated. At run time, if any of those tests fails, the transaction is rejected and an error message is generated.

Answers to Selected Exercises

We adopt our usual conventions regarding range variable names.

16.1
```
CREATE DOMAIN CITY CHAR(15)
              VALUES ( 'London', 'Paris', 'Rome',
                       'Athens', 'Oslo', 'Stockholm',
                       'Madrid', 'Amsterdam' ) ;
```

16.2
```
CREATE INTEGRITY RULE IR2
      IF P.COLOR = 'Red' THEN P.WEIGHT < 50 ;
```

16.3
```
CREATE INTEGRITY RULE IR3
      FORALL JX FORALL JY
   ( IF JX.J# ≠ JY.J# THEN JX.CITY ≠ JY.CITY ) ;
```

16.4
```
CREATE INTEGRITY RULE IR4
      COUNT ( S WHERE S.CITY = 'Athens' ) < 2 ;
```

16.5
```
CREATE INTEGRITY RULE IR5
      SPJX.QTY ≤ 2 * AVG ( SPJY, QTY ) ;
```

16.6
```
CREATE INTEGRITY RULE IR6
      IF SX.STATUS = MAX ( S.STATUS ) AND
         SY.STATUS = MIN ( S.STATUS ) AND
         SX.STATUS ≠ SY.STATUS
      THEN SX.CITY ≠ SY.CITY ;
```

Actually, the terms "highest-status supplier" and "lowest-status supplier" are not well-defined, since status values are not unique. We have interpreted the requirement to be that if SX and SY are *any* suppliers with "highest status" and "lowest status," respectively, then SX and SY must not be colocated. We have also included a check to make sure that the "highest" status and "lowest status" are not equal!—for otherwise the requirement cannot possibly be satisfied.

16.7
```
CREATE INTEGRITY RULE IR7
      FORALL J EXISTS S ( S.CITY = J.CITY ) ;
```

16.8
```
CREATE INTEGRITY RULE IR8
      FORALL J EXISTS S EXISTS SPJ ( J.J# = SPJ.J# AND
                                     SPJ.S# = S.S# AND
                                     S.CITY = J.CITY ) ;
```

16.9
```
CREATE INTEGRITY RULE IR9
      IF EXISTS P ( true )
      THEN EXISTS P ( P.COLOR = 'Red' ) ;
```

The requirement as stated—"There must exist at least one red part"—is impossible to satisfy, if it is interpreted to mean *at all times.*

16.10
```
CREATE INTEGRITY RULE IR10
      ( IF EXISTS S ( true ) THEN AVG ( S, STATUS ) ELSE 20 ) > 15 ;
```

The parenthesized expression evaluates to the average supplier status so long as at least one supplier exists, or to the value 20 (an arbitrary value greater than 15) otherwise. *Note:* We must test for the existence of at least one supplier, because the AVG function will raise an exception if its argument is empty.

16.11 CREATE INTEGRITY RULE IR11
          IF S.CITY = 'London'
          THEN EXISTS SPJ (SPJ.S# = S.S# AND SPJ.P# = 'P2') ;

16.12 CREATE INTEGRITY RULE IR12
          IF EXISTS P (P.COLOR = 'Red')
          THEN EXISTS P (P.COLOR = 'Red' AND P.WEIGHT < 50) ;

16.13 CREATE INTEGRITY RULE IR13
          SP.QTY ≥ 0.5 * SP'.QTY

16.14 CREATE INTEGRITY RULE IR14
          COUNT (P WHERE EXISTS SPJ EXISTS S
                          (P.P# = SPJ.P# AND
                            SPJ.S# = S.S# AND
                            S.CITY = 'London')) >
          COUNT (P WHERE EXISTS SPJ EXISTS S
                          (P.P# = SPJ.P# AND
                            SPJ.S# = S.S# AND
                            S.CITY = 'Paris')) ;

16.15 CREATE INTEGRITY RULE IR15
          SUM (SPJ WHERE EXISTS S
                          (SPJ.S# = S.S# AND
                            S.CITY = 'London'), QTY) >
          SUM (SPJ WHERE EXISTS S
                          (SPJ.S# = S.S# AND
                            S.CITY = 'Paris'), QTY) ;

16.16 CREATE INTEGRITY RULE IR16
          IF S'.CITY = 'Athens'
          THEN S.CITY IN ('Athens', 'London', 'Paris')
          AND
          IF S'.CITY = 'London'
          THEN S.CITY IN ('London', 'Paris') ;

16.17 IR1 is neither a relation rule nor a database rule but a domain rule, of course. IR7, IR8, IR11, IR14, and IR15 are database rules. The rest are relation rules.

16.18 We have numbered the following solutions as 16.18.*n*, where 16.*n* is the number of the original exercise. As a subsidiary exercise, try stating the rules by which the DBMS can determine which operations need to be monitored for a given integrity constraint.

16.18.1 INSERTs on relations S, P, and J, and UPDATEs on attributes S.CITY, P.CITY, and J.CITY.

16.18.2 INSERTs on relation P, and UPDATEs on attributes P.COLOR and P.WEIGHT.

16.18.3 In principle, INSERTs on relation J, and UPDATEs on attributes J.J# and J.CITY. Provided the uniqueness of candidate key J.J# is enforced, however, it is sufficient (so far as rule IR3 is concerned) to check just UPDATEs on attribute J.CITY.

16.18.4 INSERTs on relation S, and UPDATEs on attribute S.CITY.

16.18.5 INSERTs and DELETEs on relation SPJ, and UPDATEs on attribute SPJ.QTY.

16.18.6 INSERTs and DELETEs on relation S, and UPDATEs on attributes S.STATUS and S.CITY.

16.18.7 INSERTs on relation J, DELETEs on relation S, and UPDATEs on attributes S.CITY and J.CITY.

16.18.8 INSERTs on relation J, DELETEs on relations S and SPJ, and UPDATEs on attributes S.S#, S.CITY, J.J#, J.CITY, SPJ.S#, and SPJ.J#.

16.18.9　INSERTs and DELETEs on relation P, and UPDATEs on attribute P.COLOR.

16.18.10　INSERTs and DELETEs on relation S, and UPDATEs on attribute S.STATUS.

16.18.11　INSERTs on relation S, DELETEs on relation SPJ, and UPDATEs on attributes S.S#, S.CITY, SPJ.S#, and SPJ.P#.

16.18.12　INSERTs and DELETEs on relation P, and UPDATEs on attributes P.COLOR and P.WEIGHT.

16.18.13　UPDATEs on attribute SP.QTY.

16.18.14　INSERTs and DELETEs on relations S, P, and SPJ, and UPDATEs on attributes S.S#, S.CITY, P.P#, SPJ.S#, and SPJ.P#.

16.18.15　INSERTs and DELETEs on relations S and SPJ, and UPDATEs on attributes S.S#, S.CITY, SPJ.S#, and SPJ.QTY.

16.18.16　UPDATEs on attribute S.CITY.

16.20　We have numbered the following solutions as 16.20.n, where 16.n is the number of the original exercise.

16.20.1
```
CREATE DOMAIN CITY CHAR(15)
        CONSTRAINT VALID_CITIES
        CHECK ( VALUE IN
            ( 'London', 'Paris', 'Rome',
              'Athens', 'Oslo', 'Stockholm',
              'Madrid', 'Amsterdam' ) ) ;
```

16.20.2
```
CREATE ASSERTION IR2 CHECK
    ( P.COLOR <> 'Red' OR P.WEIGHT < 50 ) ;
```

16.20.3
```
CREATE ASSERTION IR3 CHECK
    ( NOT EXISTS ( SELECT * FROM J JX WHERE
          EXISTS ( SELECT * FROM J JY WHERE
              ( JX.J# <> JY.J# AND
                JX.CITY <> JY.CITY ) ) ) ) ;
```

16.20.4
```
CREATE ASSERTION IR4 CHECK
    ( ( SELECT COUNT(*) FROM S
        WHERE S.CITY = 'Athens' ) < 2 ) ;
```

16.20.5
```
CREATE ASSERTION IR5 CHECK
    ( NOT EXISTS ( SELECT *
                   FROM   SPJ SPJX
                   WHERE  SPJX.QTY > 2 *
                       ( SELECT AVG ( SPJY.QTY )
                         FROM SPJ SPJY ) ) ) ;
```

16.20.6
```
CREATE ASSERTION IR6 CHECK
    ( NOT EXISTS ( SELECT * FROM S SX WHERE
          EXISTS ( SELECT * FROM S SY WHERE
                   SX.STATUS = ( SELECT MAX ( S.STATUS )
                                 FROM   S ) AND
                   SY.STATUS = ( SELECT MIN ( S.STATUS )
                                 FROM   S ) AND
                   SX.STATUS <> SY.STATUS AND
                   SX.CITY = SY.CITY ) ) ) ;
```

16.20.7
```
CREATE ASSERTION IR7 CHECK
    ( NOT EXISTS ( SELECT * FROM J WHERE
       NOT EXISTS ( SELECT * FROM S WHERE
                    S.CITY = J.CITY ) ) ) ;
```

16.20.8 CREATE ASSERTION IR8 CHECK
```
        ( NOT EXISTS ( SELECT * FROM J WHERE
          NOT EXISTS ( SELECT * FROM S WHERE
                       S.CITY = J.CITY AND
                       EXISTS ( SELECT * FROM SPJ
                                WHERE  SPJ.S# = S.S#
                                AND    SPJ.J# = J.J# ) ) ) ) ;
```

16.20.9 CREATE ASSERTION IR9 CHECK
```
        ( NOT EXISTS ( SELECT * FROM P )
          OR EXISTS ( SELECT * FROM P
                      WHERE  P.COLOR = 'Red' ) ) ;
```

16.20.10 CREATE ASSERTION IR10 CHECK
```
        ( ( SELECT AVG ( S.STATUS ) FROM S ) > 15 ) ;
```

If the suppliers table is empty, the SQL AVG function will return a null, the conditional expression will evaluate to *unknown* (see Chapter 20), and the constraint will *not* be regarded as violated.

16.20.11 CREATE ASSERTION IR11 CHECK
```
        ( NOT EXISTS ( SELECT * FROM S
                       WHERE  S.CITY = 'London'
                       AND    NOT EXISTS
                              ( SELECT * FROM SPJ
                                WHERE  SPJ.S# = S.S#
                                AND    SPJ.P# = 'P2' ) ) ) ;
```

16.20.12 CREATE ASSERTION IR12 CHECK
```
        ( NOT EXISTS ( SELECT * FROM P
                       WHERE  P.COLOR = 'Red' )
          OR EXISTS ( SELECT * FROM P
                      WHERE  P.COLOR = 'Red'
                      AND    P.WEIGHT < 50 ) ) ;
```

16.20.13 Cannot be done. SQL does not support transition rules.

16.20.14 CREATE ASSERTION IR14 CHECK
```
        ( ( SELECT COUNT(*) FROM P
            WHERE  EXISTS ( SELECT * FROM SPJ WHERE
                   EXISTS ( SELECT * FROM S WHERE
                            ( P.P# = SPJ.P# AND
                            SPJ.S# = S.S# AND
                            S.CITY = 'London' ) ) ) ) >
          ( SELECT COUNT(*) FROM P
            WHERE  EXISTS ( SELECT * FROM SPJ WHERE
                   EXISTS ( SELECT * FROM S WHERE
                            ( P.P# = SPJ.P# AND
                            SPJ.S# = S.S# AND
                            S.CITY = 'Paris' ) ) ) ) ) ;
```

16.20.15 CREATE ASSERTION IR15 CHECK
```
        ( ( SELECT SUM ( SPJ.QTY ) FROM SPJ
            WHERE  ( SELECT S.CITY FROM S
                     WHERE  S.S# = SPJ.S# ) = 'London' ) >
          ( SELECT SUM ( SPJ.QTY ) FROM SPJ
            WHERE  ( SELECT S.CITY FROM S
                     WHERE  S.S# = SPJ.S# ) = 'Paris' ) ) ;
```

16.20.16 Cannot be done. SQL does not support transition rules.

PART **V**

FURTHER TOPICS

We claimed in Part II of this book that the relational model is the foundation for modern database technology, and so it is. However, it is *only* the foundation: There is a lot more to relational technology than just the relational model as described in Part II, and database students and professionals need to be familiar with many additional concepts and facilities in order to be fully "relationally aware" (as indeed should be obvious from our discussions in Parts III and IV). We now turn our attention to a miscellaneous collection of further relational matters. The topics to be covered, in sequence, are as follows:

- Views (Chapter 17)
- Optimization (Chapter 18)
- Domains, relations, and data types (Chapter 19)
- Missing information (Chapter 20)
- Distributed databases (Chapter 21)

Actually the foregoing sequence is a little arbitrary, but the chapters have been written on the assumption that they will be read in order as written.

17 Views

17.1 Introduction

As explained in Chapter 3 (Section 3.7), a **view** is essentially just a named expression of the relational algebra or relational calculus. Here is a simple example, based for definiteness on the algebra:

```
CREATE VIEW GOOD_SUPPLIERS AS
    ( S WHERE STATUS > 15 ) [ S#, STATUS, CITY ] ;
```

When this statement is executed, the expression following the AS (which is the actual view definition) is not evaluated but is merely "remembered" by the system—actually by saving it in the catalog, under the specified name GOOD_SUPPLIERS. To the user, however, it is now as if there really were a relation in the database called GOOD_ SUPPLIERS, with tuples and attributes as shown in the unshaded portions (only) of Fig. 17.1 below. In other words, the name GOOD_SUPPLIERS denotes a **virtual** relation, *viz.* the relation that would result if the view-defining expression were indeed evaluated.

We also explained in Chapter 3 that a view such as GOOD_SUPPLIERS is effectively just a *window* into the underlying data. Any changes to that underlying data will be automatically and instantaneously visible through that window (provided, of course, that those changes lie within the scope of the view); likewise, changes to the view will automatically and instantaneously be applied to the underlying data, and hence of course be visible through the window.

GOOD_SUPPLIERS	S#	SNAME	STATUS	CITY
	S1	Smith	20	London
	S2	Jones	10	Paris
	S3	Blake	30	Paris
	S4	Clark	20	London
	S5	Adams	30	Athens

FIG. 17.1 GOOD_SUPPLIERS as a view of base relation S (unshaded portions)

Now, depending on the sophistication of the user (and perhaps also on the application at hand), the user might or might not realize that GOOD_SUPPLIERS really is a view; some users might be aware of that fact and might understand that there is a "real" relation S underneath, others might genuinely believe that GOOD_SUPPLIERS is a "real" relation in its own right. Either way, it makes little difference: The point is, users can operate on GOOD_SUPPLIERS just as if it *were* a real relation. For instance, here is an example of a query against GOOD_SUPPLIERS:

```
T1   :=   GOOD_SUPPLIERS WHERE CITY ≠ 'London' ;
```

Result:

```
T1   | S# | STATUS | CITY   |
     | S3 |     30 | Paris  |
     | S5 |     30 | Athens |
```

This query certainly looks just like a regular query on a regular "real" relation. And, as we saw in Chapter 3, the system handles such a query by converting it into an equivalent query on the underlying base relation (or base relations, plural). It does this by effectively replacing (within the query) each appearance of the **name** of the view by the expression that **defines** the view. In the example, this process gives

```
T1   :=   ( ( S WHERE STATUS > 15 ) [ S#, STATUS, CITY ] )
                                  WHERE CITY ≠ 'London' ;
```

which is readily seen to be equivalent to the simpler form

```
T1   :=   ( S WHERE STATUS > 15 AND CITY ≠ 'London' )
                              [ S#, STATUS, CITY ] ;
```

And this query produces the result shown earlier.

Incidentally, it is worth pointing out that this **substitution** process—i.e., the process of substituting the view-defining expression for the view name—works *precisely because of the relational closure property.* Closure implies (among many other things) that wherever a relation name *R* is permitted within an expression, a relational expression *X* is permitted instead (provided, of course, that expression *X* evaluates to a relation with the same heading as relation *R*). In other words, views work precisely because of the fact that relations are closed under the relational algebra—yet another illustration of the fundamental importance of the closure property.

Update operations are treated in a similar manner. For example, the operation

```
UPDATE GOOD_SUPPLIERS WHERE CITY = 'Paris'
       STATUS   :=   STATUS + 10 ;
```

will effectively be converted into

```
UPDATE S WHERE STATUS > 15 AND CITY = 'Paris'
       STATUS   :=   STATUS + 10 ;
```

INSERT and DELETE operations are handled analogously.

17.2   What Are Views For?

View support is desirable for a number of reasons, perhaps the most important of which is that views can provide what is called **logical data independence**—so called to distinguish it from *physical* data independence, as described in Section 1.5 (and discussed further in Appendix B). A system provides *physical* data independence if users and user programs are immune to changes in the physical structure of the stored database. A system provides **logical** data independence if users and user programs are also immune to changes in the *logical* structure of the database. There are two aspects to this latter kind of independence, namely **growth** and **restructuring**.

■ *Growth*

  Note: We discuss the question of growth in the database here only for completeness; it is important, but it has nothing to do with views as such.

  As the database grows to incorporate new kinds of information, so the definition of the database must also grow accordingly. There are two possible types of growth that can occur:

  1. The expansion of an existing base relation to include a new attribute, corresponding to the addition of new information concerning some existing type of object—e.g., the addition of a DISCOUNT attribute to the suppliers base relation.

      (The reader will realize that we are speaking rather loosely here. As explained in Chapter 4, relations cannot really "expand" to include new attributes. Rather, one relation can be replaced by another with the same name and with an "expanded" heading.)

  2. The inclusion of a new base relation, corresponding to the addition of a new type of object—e.g., the addition of project information to the suppliers-and-parts database.

  Neither of these two kinds of change should have any effect on existing users and user programs at all, at least in principle.*

■ *Restructuring*

  Occasionally it might become necessary to restructure the database in some way such that, although the overall information content remains the same, the *placement* of information within the database changes—i.e., the allocation of attributes to base relations is altered in some way. We consider just one simple example here. Suppose that for some reason (the precise reason is not important for present purposes) we wish to replace base relation S by the following two base relations:

```
SNC ( S#, SNAME, CITY )
    PRIMARY KEY ( S# )

ST  ( S#, STATUS )
    PRIMARY KEY ( S# )
```

---

* But see Example 8.3.3 in Chapter 8 for a warning regarding SQL specifically.

The crucial point to note is that *the old relation S is the join of the two new relations SNC and ST* (and SNC and ST are both *projections* of that old relation S). So we create a *view* that is exactly that join, and we name it S:

```
CREATE VIEW S AS SNC JOIN ST ;
```

Any program or interactive operation that previously referred to base relation S will now refer to view S instead. Hence—*provided the system supports data manipulation operations on views correctly*—users and user programs will indeed be logically immune to this particular restructuring of the database.*

As an aside, we must mention that the replacement of the original suppliers relation S by its two projections SNC and ST is not a totally trivial matter. In particular, observe that something must be done about the shipments relation SP, since that relation includes a foreign key that references the original suppliers relation. See Exercise 17.13 at the end of the chapter.

To revert to the main thread of the discussion: Note that it does not follow from the SNC-ST example that logical data independence can be achieved in the face of *all possible* restructurings. The critical issue is whether there exists an unambiguous mapping from the restructured version of the database back to the previous version (i.e., whether the restructuring is reversible), or in other words whether the two versions are **information-equivalent**. If not, logical data independence is clearly not achievable.

We conclude this section by briefly summarizing some other uses and advantages of views (logical data independence is the most important benefit, but it is not the only one).

■ They allow the same data to be seen by different users in different ways at the same time.

In other words, views allow users to focus on (and perhaps logically restructure) just that portion of the database that is of concern to them and to ignore the rest. This consideration is obviously important when there are many different users, in many different categories, all interacting simultaneously with a single integrated database.

■ They provide a shorthand or "macro" capability.

Consider the query "Get cities that store parts that are available from some supplier in London." In Section 17.3, Example 3, we will show how to define a view CITY_PAIRS with attributes SCITY and PCITY, such that a pair of city names {SCITY:*x*,PCITY:*y*} appears in the view if and only if a supplier located in

---

* In principle! Sadly, today's products—and the SQL standard—typically do *not* support data manipulation operations on views correctly, and hence often do not provide the desired degree of immunity to changes such as the one in the example. More specifically, most products (not all) do support view retrievals correctly, but not view updates; thus they might provide logical data independence for retrieval operations, but not for update operations.

city *x* supplies a part stored in city *y*. Given this view CITY_PAIRS, the following formulation of the query suffices:

```
( CITY_PAIRS WHERE SCITY = 'London' ) [ PCITY ]
```

Without the view, by contrast, the query is much more complex:

```
( ( ( S RENAME CITY AS SCITY )
     JOIN SP
     JOIN ( P RENAME CITY AS PCITY ) )
             WHERE SCITY = 'London' ) [ PCITY ]
```

While the user *could* use this second formulation directly—security rules permitting, of course—the first is obviously simpler. But the first is really just shorthand for the second; the system's view processing mechanism will effectively expand the first formulation into the second before it is executed.

There is a strong analogy here with **macros** in a programming language system. In principle, a user in a programming language system *could* write out the expanded form of a given macro directly in his or her source code—but it is much more convenient (for a variety of well understood reasons) not to do so, but rather to use the macro shorthand and let the system's macro processor do the expansion on the user's behalf. Analogous remarks apply to views. Thus, views in a database system play a role analogous to that of macros in a programming language system, and the well-known advantages and benefits of macros apply directly to views as well, *mutatis mutandis*. Note in particular that (as with macros) no run-time performance overhead attaches to the use of views—there is only a small overhead at view processing time (analogous to macro expansion time).

■ Automatic **security** is provided for hidden data.

"Hidden data" refers to data not visible through some given view. Such data is clearly secure from access through that particular view. Thus, forcing users to access the database via views is a simple but effective mechanism for authorization control. We have discussed this point already in Chapter 15.

17.3   Data Definition

The general syntax of CREATE VIEW is

```
CREATE VIEW view AS expression ;
```

where *view* is the name of the new view and *expression* (an expression of the relational algebra or relational calculus) is the definition of that view. Incidentally, notice how CREATE VIEW combines the *external schema* function and the *external/conceptual mapping* function (to use the ANSI/SPARC terminology of Chapter 2), since it defines both what the external object looks like and how that object maps to the conceptual level.

Here are some examples, expressed in the algebra for definiteness.

1. ```
   CREATE VIEW REDPARTS AS
        ( ( P WHERE COLOR = 'Red' ) [ P#, PNAME, WEIGHT, CITY ] )
                                    RENAME WEIGHT AS WT ;
   ```
   ```

The effect of this statement is to create a view called REDPARTS, containing tuples for red parts only, with four attributes called P#, PNAME, WT, and CITY, corresponding respectively to the four attributes P#, PNAME, WEIGHT, and CITY of the underlying base relation P. *Note:* The renaming of the WEIGHT attribute here is done purely for the sake of the example—it is obviously not required.

2.
```
CREATE VIEW PQ AS
        SUMMARIZE SP BY ( P# ) ADD SUM ( QTY ) AS TOTQTY ;
```

Unlike the previous example (REDPARTS), this view PQ is not just a simple subset—i.e., restriction and/or projection—of the underlying base relation. It can be regarded instead as a kind of *statistical summary* or *compression* of that underlying relation.

3.
```
CREATE VIEW CITY_PAIRS AS
   ( ( S RENAME CITY AS SCITY ) JOIN SP JOIN
     ( P RENAME CITY AS PCITY ) ) [ SCITY, PCITY ] ;
```

We mentioned this view earlier, in Section 17.2. As indicated previously, a pair of city names (x,y) will appear in the view if and only if a supplier located in city x supplies a part stored in city y. For example, supplier S1 supplies part P1; supplier S1 is located in London and part P1 is stored in London; and so the pair (London,London) appears in the view.

4.
```
CREATE VIEW LONDON_REDPARTS AS
        REDPARTS WHERE CITY = 'London' ;
```

The point of this example is that since the definition of a view can be any valid relational expression, and since such an expression can refer to views as well as base relations, it is perfectly possible to define a view in terms of other views.

The syntax of DESTROY VIEW is

```
DESTROY VIEW view ;
```

The specified view is destroyed (i.e., its definition is removed from the catalog). Here is an example:

```
DESTROY VIEW REDPARTS ;
```

In Chapter 4 we said that DESTROY BASE RELATION will fail if any view definition (or snapshot definition—see Section 17.8) currently refers to the base relation in question. By analogy, DESTROY VIEW will also fail if any view (or snapshot) definition currently refers to the view in question. Alternatively, we might consider extending CREATE VIEW (and CREATE SNAPSHOT) to include some kind of "RESTRICTED *vs.* CASCADES" option: RESTRICTED would mean that an attempt to destroy any underlying named relation will fail, CASCADES would mean that such an attempt will succeed and will "cascade" to destroy the view (or snapshot) as well.* RESTRICTED would then be the default.

---

* The SQL standard [8.1] does support such an option, but places it on DROP TABLE and DROP VIEW (= our DESTROY BASE RELATION and DESTROY VIEW), not on CREATE VIEW. There is no default—the required option must be stated explicitly. See Section 17.9.

17.4   Data Manipulation: Retrieval Operations

We have already explained in outline how a retrieval operation on a view is converted into an equivalent operations on the underlying base relation(s). We now make this explanation slightly more formal, as follows.

First, note that any given relational expression can be regarded as a relation-valued *function*—given values for the various relations mentioned in the expression (i.e., the arguments to the function), the expression evaluates to another relation. Now let D be a database (which for present purposes we regard as just a set of base relations) and let V be a view on D, i.e., a view whose definition X is a function on D:

```
V = X ( D )
```

Let R be a retrieval operation on V; R is of course another relation-valued function, and the result of the retrieval is

```
R ( V ) = R ( X ( D ) )
```

Thus the result of the retrieval is defined to be equal to the result of applying X to D—i.e., **materializing** the view V—and then applying R to that materialized relation. In practice, however, it is more efficient to apply the **substitution** procedure discussed earlier, which we can now see is equivalent to forming the function C that is the *composition* $R(X)$ of the functions X and R (in that order) and then applying C directly to D.

Now, the foregoing should effectively be familiar to the reader already from the discussions of the previous two sections. We nevertheless make it explicit here for the following reasons:

- First, it lays the groundwork for a similar discussion of update operations in Section 17.5 below.

- Second, it makes it clear that materialization (instead of substitution) is a perfectly legitimate view implementation technique, albeit one that is likely to be rather inefficient.

- Third, although in principle the substitution procedure is quite straightforward and works perfectly well in 100 percent of cases, the sad fact is that at the time of writing there are several SQL products for which this statement is not true!—that is, there are some products in which some retrievals on some views fail in surprising ways. The statement is also not true for versions of the SQL standard prior to SQL/92. And the reason for the failures is precisely that the products in question, and earlier versions of the SQL standard, do not fully support the relational closure property. See Exercise 17.14(a) at the end of the chapter.

17.5   Data Manipulation: Update Operations

The problem of view update can be loosely stated as follows: Given a particular update on a particular view, what updates need to be applied to what underlying base relations in order to implement the original view update? More precisely, let D be a database, and let V be a view on D, i.e., a view whose definition X is a function on D:

```
V = X ( D )
```

(as in Section 17.4). Now let U be an update operation on V; U is a relation-valued function, and the result of the update is

```
U ( V ) = U ( X ( D ) )
```

The problem of view update is then the problem of finding an update operation U' on D such that

```
U ( X ( D ) ) = X ( U' ( D ) )
```

because, of course, D is the only thing that "really exists" (views are virtual), and so updates cannot be directly implemented in terms of views *per se*. *Note:* In the interests of accuracy, we should point out that the database update operation U' might not be relation-valued—rather, it produces a result that is a *set* of several relations, in general (think of updating a join view, which might require updates to both component relations).

Before we go any further, we must emphasize the point that the view update problem has been the subject of considerable research over the years, and many different approaches have been proposed to its solution; see, e.g., references [17.3], [17.7], [17.8–17.9], [17.11], [17.13], and in particular Codd's proposals for RM/V2 [4.4]. In this chapter we describe a comparatively new approach [17.5–17.6], one that is less *ad hoc* than some previous proposals but does have the virtue of being upward-compatible with the best aspects of earlier approaches. It also has the virtue of treating as updatable a much wider class of views than earlier approaches do.

Some Important Principles

There are several important principles that must be satisfied by any systematic view updating mechanism. Of those principles, the first and overriding one is as follows:

> *A given tuple can appear in a given relation only if that tuple satisfies the relation predicate for that relation—and this observation is just as true for a view as it is for a base relation.*

(This principle is simply a restatement of the fact that, as explained in Chapter 4, the relation predicate for a given relation is the *criterion for update acceptability* for that relation.)

Observe, therefore, that in this chapter we will have to consider in some detail the question of what it is that constitutes the relation predicate for an arbitrary derived relation.

The remaining principles are as follows.

1. The updatability or otherwise of a given view is a semantic issue, not a syntactic one—i.e., it must not depend on the particular form in which the view definition happens to be stated. For example, the following two view definitions are semantically identical:

```
CREATE VIEW V AS
      S WHERE STATUS > 25 OR CITY = 'Paris' ;
```

```
CREATE VIEW V AS
    ( S WHERE STATUS > 25 ) UNION ( S WHERE CITY = 'Paris' ) ;
```

Obviously, both of these views should be updatable. (By contrast, the SQL standard, and most of today's SQL products, adopt the *ad hoc* position that the first is updatable and the second is not. See Section 17.9.)

2. It follows from the previous point that the view updatability rules must work correctly in the special case when the "view" is in fact a base relation. This is because any base relation *B* is semantically indistinguishable from a view *V* that is defined as *B* UNION *B*, or *B* INTERSECT *B*, or *B* MINUS *C* (if *C* is another base relation that has no tuples in common with *B*), or *B* WHERE *true*, or any of several other expressions that are identically equivalent to just *B*. Thus, for example, the rules for updating a union view, when applied to the view *V* = *B* UNION *B*, must yield exactly the same result as if the view updates had been applied directly to the base relation *B*.

3. The rules must preserve symmetry where applicable. For example, the DELETE rule for an intersection view *V* = *A* INTERSECT *B* must not arbitrarily cause a tuple to be deleted from *A* and not from *B*, even though such a one-sided delete would certainly have the effect of deleting the tuple from the view. Instead, the tuple must be deleted from both *A* and *B*. (In other words, there should be *no ambiguity*—there should always be exactly one way of implementing a given update, a way that works in all cases.)

4. The rules must take into account any applicable triggered actions, such as cascade DELETE. *Note:* For numerous well-documented reasons we would prefer such triggered actions to be specified *declaratively,* not procedurally. However, the view updating rules *per se* do not impose any such requirement.

5. For reasons of simplicity among others, it is desirable to regard UPDATE as shorthand for a DELETE-then-INSERT sequence (i.e., just as syntactic sugar), and we will so regard it. This shorthand is acceptable *provided* it is understood that:

   - No checking of relation predicates is done "in the middle of" any given update; that is, the expansion of UPDATE is DELETE-INSERT-check, not DELETE-check-INSERT-check. The reason is, of course, that the DELETE portion might temporarily violate the relation predicate while the UPDATE overall does not; e.g., suppose relation *R* contains exactly 10 tuples, and consider the effect of "UPDATE tuple *t*" on *R* if *R*'s relation predicate says that *R* must contain at least 10 tuples.

   - Triggered actions are likewise never performed "in the middle of" any given update (in fact they are done at the end, immediately prior to the relation predicate checking).

   - The shorthand requires some slight refinement in the case of projection views (see later).

We remark that treating UPDATEs as DELETEs-then-INSERTs implies that we conceive of UPDATEs as replacing entire tuples, not as replacing individual values within such a tuple.

6. All update operations on views are implemented by the same kind of update operations on the underlying relations. That is, INSERTs map to INSERTs and DELETEs to DELETEs (we can ignore UPDATEs, thanks to the previous point). For suppose, contrariwise, that there is some kind of view—say a union view—for which (say) INSERTs map to DELETEs. Then it must follow that INSERTs *on a base relation* must also sometimes map to DELETEs! This is because (as already observed under point 2 above) the base relation *B* is semantically identical to the union view *V = B* UNION *B*. An analogous argument applies to every other kind of view also (restriction, projection, intersection, etc.). The idea that an INSERT on a base relation might really be a DELETE we take to be self-evidently absurd; hence our position that (to repeat) INSERTs map to INSERTs and DELETEs to DELETEs.

7. In general, the rules when applied to a given view *V* will specify the operations to be applied to the relation(s) on which *V* is defined. And those rules must work correctly even when those underlying relations are themselves derived relations in turn. In other words, the rules must be capable of *recursive application*. Of course, if an attempt to update a given view leads to an attempt to update an underlying relation that is itself not updatable, the original update will fail.

8. The rules cannot assume that the database is well designed (e.g., fully normalized). However, they might on occasion produce a slightly surprising result if the database is *not* well designed—a fact that can be seen in itself as an additional argument in support of good design. We will give an example of such a "slightly surprising result" in the next section.

9. If a view is updatable, there should be no *prima facie* reason for permitting some updates but not others (e.g., DELETEs but not INSERTs).

10. INSERT and DELETE should be inverses of each other, insofar as possible.

We remind the reader of one other important principle, as follows. As explained in Chapter 6, relational operations are always set-at-a-time; a set containing a single tuple is merely a special case. What is more, a multi-tuple update is sometimes *required* (i.e., some updates cannot be simulated by a series of single-tuple operations). And this remark is true of both base relations and views, in general. For reasons of simplicity, we will for the most part present our view updating rules in terms of single-tuple operations, but the reader should not lose sight of the fact that considering single-tuple operations only is a slight oversimplification, and indeed a distortion of the truth.

We now consider the operations of the relational algebra one by one—union, intersection, and difference in Section 17.6, the rest in Section 17.7.

17.6 Updating Union, Intersection, and Difference Views

In this section, we assume we are updating a relation defined by means of an expression of the form *A* UNION *B* or *A* INTERSECT *B* or *A* MINUS *B* (as appropriate), where *A* and *B* are arbitrary relational expressions (i.e., they are not necessarily base relations).

A and *B* must represent type-compatible relations. The relation predicates corresponding to *A* and *B* are *PA* and *PB*, respectively.

Note: Several of the rules discussed in this section refer to the possibility of *side-effects*. Now, it is well known that side-effects are usually undesirable; the point is, however, that side-effects might be unavoidable if *A* and *B* happen to represent overlapping subsets of the same underlying relation, as will frequently be the case with union, intersection, and difference views. We will see some examples later.

Union

Here then is the INSERT rule for *A* UNION *B:*

■ **INSERT:** The new tuple must satisfy *PA* or *PB* or both. If it satisfies *PA*, it is inserted into *A* (note that this INSERT might have the side-effect of inserting the tuple into *B* also). If it satisfies *PB*, it is inserted into *B*, unless it was inserted into *B* already as a side-effect of inserting it into *A*.

   Note: The specific procedural manner in which this rule is stated ("insert into *A*, then insert into *B*") should be understood purely as a pedagogic device; it should not be taken to mean that the DBMS will execute exactly that procedure in practice. Indeed, the principle of symmetry—Principle No. 3 from the subsection "Some important principles" in the previous section—implies as much, because neither *A* nor *B* has priority over the other. Analogous remarks apply to all the rules discussed in the present section.

Explanation: The new tuple must satisfy at least one of *PA* and *PB* because otherwise it does not qualify for inclusion in *A* UNION *B*—i.e., it does not satisfy the relation predicate, *viz.* (*PA*) OR (*PB*), for *A* UNION *B*. (We note also that the new tuple must not already appear in either *A* or *B*, because otherwise we would be trying to insert a tuple that already exists.) Assuming the foregoing requirements are satisfied, the new tuple is inserted into whichever of *A* or *B* it logically belongs to (possibly both).

Examples: Let view UV be defined as

```
( S WHERE STATUS > 25 ) UNION ( S WHERE CITY = 'Paris' )
```

Fig. 17.2 shows a sample tabulation of this view, corresponding to the usual sample data values.

UV	S#	SNAME	STATUS	CITY
	S2	Jones	10	Paris
	S3	Blake	30	Paris
	S5	Adams	30	Athens

FIG. 17.2   View UV (sample values)

- Let the tuple to be inserted be (S6,Smith,50,Rome). This tuple satisfies the relation predicate for S WHERE STATUS > 25 (though not the relation predicate for S WHERE CITY = 'Paris'). It is therefore inserted into S WHERE STATUS > 25. Because of the rules regarding INSERT on a restriction (which are fairly obvious—see the next section), the effect is to insert the new tuple into the suppliers base relation.

- Now let the tuple to be inserted be (S7,Jones,50,Paris). This tuple satisfies the relation predicate for S WHERE STATUS > 25 *and* the relation predicate for S WHERE CITY = 'Paris'. It is therefore logically inserted into both. Note, however, that inserting it into either of the two restrictions has the side-effect of inserting it into the other anyway, so there is no need to perform the second INSERT explicitly.

Now suppose SA and SB are two distinct *base* relations, SA representing suppliers with status > 25 and SB representing suppliers in Paris (see Fig. 17.3); suppose view UV is defined as SA UNION SB, and consider again the two sample INSERTs previously discussed. Inserting the tuple (S6,Smith,50,Rome) into view UV will cause that tuple to be inserted into base relation SA, presumably as required. However, inserting the tuple (S7,Jones,50,Paris) into view UV will cause that tuple to be inserted into *both* base relations. This result is logically correct, although arguably counterintuitive (it is an example of what we called a "slightly surprising result" in Section 17.5). *It is our position that such surprises can occur only if the database is badly designed.* In particular, it is our position that a design that permits the very same tuple to appear in—i.e., to satisfy the relation predicate for—two distinct base relations is by definition a bad design. This (perhaps controversial!) position is elaborated in reference [17.12].

We turn now to the DELETE rule for A UNION B:

- **DELETE:** If the tuple to be deleted appears in A, it is deleted from A (note that this DELETE might have the side-effect of deleting the tuple from B also). If it (still) appears in B, it is deleted from B.

Examples to illustrate this rule are left as an exercise for the reader. Note that deleting a tuple from A or B might cause a cascade DELETE or some other triggered action to be performed.

Finally, the UPDATE rule:

SA					SB			
S#	SNAME	STATUS	CITY		S#	SNAME	STATUS	CITY
S3	Blake	30	Paris		S2	Jones	10	Paris
S5	Adams	30	Athens		S3	Blake	30	Paris

FIG. 17.3 Base relations SA and SB (sample values)

■ **UPDATE:** The tuple to be updated must be such that the updated version satisfies *PA* or *PB* or both. If the tuple to be updated appears in *A,* it is deleted from *A* **without** performing any triggered actions (cascade DELETE, etc.) that such a DELETE would normally cause, and likewise without checking the relation predicate for *A.* Note that this DELETE might have the side-effect of deleting the tuple from *B* also. If the tuple (still) appears in *B,* it is deleted from *B* (again without any triggered actions or relation predicate checks). Next, if the updated version of the tuple satisfies *PA,* it is inserted into *A* (note that this INSERT might have the side-effect of inserting the updated version into *B* also). Finally, if the updated version satisfies *PB,* it is inserted into *B,* unless it was inserted into *B* already as a side-effect of inserting it into *A.*

This UPDATE rule essentially consists of the DELETE rule followed by the INSERT rule, except that (as indicated) no triggered actions or relation predicate checks are performed after the DELETE (any triggered actions associated with the UPDATE are conceptually performed after all deletions and insertions have been done, just prior to the relation predicate checks).

It is worth pointing out that one important consequence of treating UPDATEs in this fashion is that a given UPDATE can cause a tuple to migrate from one relation to another. Given the database of Fig. 17.3, for example, updating the tuple (S5,Adams,30,Athens) within view UV to (S5,Adams,15,Paris) will delete the existing tuple for S5 from SA and insert the updated tuple for S5 into SB.

Intersect

Here now are the rules for updating *A* INTERSECT *B.* This time we simply state the rules without further discussion (they follow the same general pattern as the union rules), except to note that the relation predicate for *A* INTERSECT *B* is *(PA)* AND *(PB).* Examples to illustrate the various cases are left as an exercise for the reader.

■ **INSERT:** The new tuple must satisfy both *PA* and *PB.* If it does not currently appear in *A,* it is inserted into *A* (note that this INSERT might have the side-effect of inserting the tuple into *B* also). If it (still) does not appear in *B,* it is inserted into *B.*

■ **DELETE:** The tuple to be deleted is deleted from *A* (note that this DELETE might have the side-effect of deleting the tuple from *B* also). If it (still) appears in *B,* it is deleted from *B.*

■ **UPDATE:** The tuple to be updated must be such that the updated version satisfies both *PA* and *PB.* The tuple is deleted from *A* without performing any triggered actions or relation predicate checks (note that this DELETE might have the side-effect of deleting it from *B* also); if it (still) appears in *B,* it is deleted from *B,* again without any triggered actions or relation predicate checks. Next, if the updated version of the tuple does not currently appear in *A,* it is inserted into *A* (note that this INSERT might have the side-effect of inserting the tuple into *B* also). If it (still) does not appear in *B,* it is inserted into *B.*

Difference

Here are the rules for updating *A* MINUS *B* (the relation predicate is (*PA*) AND NOT (*PB*), of course):

- **INSERT:** The new tuple must satisfy *PA* and not *PB*. It is inserted into *A*.
- **DELETE:** The tuple to be deleted is deleted from *A*.
- **UPDATE:** The tuple to be updated must be such that the updated version satisfies *PA* and not *PB*. The tuple is deleted from *A* without performing any triggered actions or relation predicate checks; the updated version of the tuple is then inserted into *A*.

17.7 Updating Other Views

In this section we consider the remaining operations of the relational algebra—restriction, projection, join, etc.

Restriction

First of all, note that the relation predicate for the relation that results from the restriction operation

```
A WHERE condition
```

is (*PA*) AND (*condition*). For example, the relation predicate for the restriction S WHERE CITY = 'London' is (PS) AND (CITY = 'London'), where PS is the relation predicate for the suppliers relation S. It follows that (for example) any tuple *t* presented for insertion into a view defined by means of this restriction must be such that the conditions PS(*t*) and *t*.CITY = 'London' both evaluate to *true,* or the INSERT will fail.

Here then are the rules for updating *A* WHERE *condition:*

- **INSERT:** The new tuple must satisfy both *PA* and *condition*. It is inserted into *A*.
- **DELETE:** The tuple to be deleted is deleted from *A*.
- **UPDATE:** The tuple to be updated must be such that the updated version satisfies both *PA* and *condition*. The tuple is deleted from *A* without performing any triggered actions or relation predicate checks. The updated version of the tuple is then inserted into *A*.

Examples: Let view LS be defined as

```
S WHERE CITY = 'London'
```

Fig. 17.4 shows a sample tabulation of this view.

- An attempt to insert the tuple (S6,Green,20,London) into LS will succeed. The new tuple will be inserted into relation S, and will therefore be effectively inserted into the view as well.

LS	S#	SNAME	STATUS	CITY
	S1	Smith	20	London
	S4	Clark	20	London

FIG. 17.4 View LS (sample values)

- An attempt to insert the tuple (S1,Green,20,London) into LS will fail, because it violates the relation predicate for relation S (and hence for LS too)—specifically, it violates the candidate key uniqueness constraint on attribute S.S#.

- An attempt to insert the tuple (S6,Green,20,Athens) into LS will fail, because it violates the condition CITY = 'London'.

- An attempt to delete the LS tuple (S1,Smith,20,London) will succeed. The tuple will be deleted from relation S, and will therefore be effectively deleted from the view as well.

- An attempt to update the LS tuple (S1,Smith,20,London) to (S6,Green,20,London) will succeed. An attempt to update that same tuple (S1,Smith,20,London) to either (S2,Smith,20,London) or (S1,Smith,20,Athens) will fail (why, exactly, in each case?).

Projection

Again we start by considering the relevant relation predicate. Let the attributes of relation A be partitioned into two disjoint groups, X and Y say. Regard each of X and Y as a single **composite** attribute. It is clear, then, that a given tuple $\{X:x\}$ will appear in the projection $A[X]$ if and only if there exists some value y from the domain of Y-values such that the tuple $\{X:x,Y:y\}$ appears in A. For example, consider the projection of relation S over S#, SNAME, and CITY. Every tuple (s,n,c) appearing in that projection is such that there exists a status value t such that the tuple (s,n,t,c) appears in relation S.

Here then are the rules for updating $A[X]$:

- **INSERT:** Let the tuple to be inserted be (x). Let the default value of Y be y (it is an error if no such default value exists, i.e., if Y has "defaults not allowed"). The tuple (x,y) (which must satisfy PA) is inserted into A.

    Note: Since candidate keys will usually (but not invariably) have "defaults not allowed," a projection that does not include all candidate keys of the underlying relation will usually not permit INSERTs.

- **DELETE:** All tuples of A with the same X-value as the tuple to be deleted from $A[X]$ are deleted from A.

    Note: In practice, it will usually be desirable that X include at least one candidate key of A, so that the tuple to be deleted from $A[X]$ corresponds to exactly one tuple *a* of *A*. However, there is no logical reason to make this a hard requirement. Analogous remarks apply in the case of UPDATE also—see below.

■ **UPDATE:** Let the tuple to be updated be (x) and let the updated version be (*x′*). Let *a* be a tuple of *A* with the same *X*-value *x,* and let the value of *Y* in tuple *a* be *y.* All such tuples *a* are deleted from *A* without performing any triggered actions or relation predicate checks. Then, for each such value *y,* tuple (*x′*,y) (which must satisfy *PA*) is inserted into *A*.

Note: It is here that the "slight refinement" mentioned in Principle No. 5 in Section 17.5 shows itself. Specifically, observe that the final "INSERT" step in the UPDATE rule reinstates the previous *Y*-value in each inserted tuple—it does *not* replace it by the applicable default value, as a standalone INSERT would.

Examples: Let view SC be defined as

```
SC [ S#, CITY ]
```

Fig. 17.5 shows a sample tabulation of this view.

SC	S#	CITY
	S1	London
	S2	Paris
	S3	Paris
	S4	London
	S5	Athens

FIG. 17.5 View SC (sample values)

■ An attempt to insert the tuple (S6,London) into SC will succeed, and will have the effect of inserting the tuple (S6,*n,t,*London) into relation S, where *n* and *t* are the default values for attributes S.SNAME and S.STATUS, respectively.

■ An attempt to insert the tuple (S1,London) into SC will fail, because it violates the relation predicate for relation S (and hence for SC too)—specifically, it violates the candidate key uniqueness constraint on attribute S.S#.

■ An attempt to delete the tuple (S1,London) from SC will succeed. The tuple for S1 will be deleted from relation S.

■ An attempt to update the SC tuple (S1,London) to (S1,Athens) will succeed; the effect will be to replace the tuple (S1,Smith,20,London) in relation S by the tuple (S1,Smith,20,Athens)—*not* by the tuple (S1,*n,t,*Athens), please observe.

■ An attempt to update that same SC tuple (S1,London) to (S2,London) will fail (why, exactly?).

Consideration of the case in which the projection does not include a candidate key of the underlying relation—for example, the projection of relation S over STATUS and CITY—is left as an exercise for the reader.

Extension

The relation predicate *PE* for the relation *E* that results from the extension operation

```
EXTEND A ADD exp AS X
```

is as follows:

```
PA ( a ) AND e.X = exp ( a )
```

Here *e* is a tuple of relation *E* and *a* is the projection of that tuple *e* over all attributes of *A*. In stilted English:

"Every tuple *e* in the extension is such that (1) the tuple *a* that is derived from *e* by projecting away the value *e.X* satisfies *PA,* and (2) that value *e.X* is equal to the result of applying the expression *exp* to that tuple *a*."

Here then are the rules for *E* = EXTEND *A* ADD *exp* AS *X:*

- **INSERT:** Let the tuple to be inserted be *e; e* must satisfy *PE*. The tuple *a* that is derived from *e* by projecting away the value *e.X* is inserted into *A*.
- **DELETE:** Let the tuple to be deleted be *e*. The tuple *a* that is derived from *e* by projecting away the value *e.X* is deleted from *A*.
- **UPDATE:** Let the tuple to be updated be *e* and let the updated version be *e'*; *e'* must satisfy *PE*. The tuple *a* that is derived from *e* by projecting away the value *e.X* is deleted from *A* without performing any triggered actions or relation predicate checks. The tuple *a'* that is derived from *e'* by projecting away the value *e'.X* is inserted into *A*.

Examples: Let view PX be defined as

```
EXTEND P ADD ( WEIGHT * 454 ) AS GMWT
```

Fig. 17.6 shows a sample tabulation of this view.

- An attempt to insert the tuple (P7,Cog,Red,12,Paris,5448) will succeed, and will have the effect of inserting the tuple (P7,Cog,Red,12,Paris) into relation P.
- An attempt to insert the tuple (P7,Cog,Red,12,Paris,5449) will fail (why?).
- An attempt to insert the tuple (P1,Cog,Red,12,Paris,5448) will fail (why?).
- An attempt to delete the tuple for P1 will succeed, and will have the effect of deleting the tuple for P1 from relation P.
- An attempt to update the tuple for P1 to (P1,Nut,Red,10,Paris,4540) will succeed; the effect will be to replace the tuple (P1,Nut,Red,12,London) in relation P by the tuple (P1,Nut,Red,10,Paris).
- An attempt to update that same tuple to a tuple for P2 (with all other values unchanged) or a tuple in which the GMWT value is not equal to 454 times the WEIGHT value will fail (in each case, why?).

PX	P#	PNAME	COLOR	WEIGHT	CITY	GMWT
	P1	Nut	Red	12	London	5448
	P2	Bolt	Green	17	Paris	7718
	P3	Screw	Blue	17	Rome	7718
	P4	Screw	Red	14	London	6356
	P5	Cam	Blue	12	Paris	5448
	P6	Cog	Red	19	London	8626

FIG. 17.6   View PX (sample values)

Join

Most previous treatments of the view update problem—including those in previous editions of this book and in other books by the present author—have argued that the updatability or otherwise of a given join depends, at least in part, on whether the join is one-to-one, one-to-many, or many-to-many. In contrast to those previous treatments, we now contend that joins are *always* updatable. Moreover, the rules are identical in all three cases, and are essentially quite straightforward.

What makes this claim plausible—startling though it might seem at first sight—is the new perspective on the problem that is afforded by adoption of the fundamental principle stated in Section 17.5, to the effect that the relation predicate for a given relation is the criterion for update acceptability for that relation. Broadly speaking, the goal of view support has always been to make views look as much like base relations as possible, and this goal is indeed a laudable one. However:

- It is usually assumed (implicitly) that it is always possible to update an individual tuple of a base relation independently of all other tuples in that base relation.

- At the same time, it is realized (explicitly) that it is manifestly *not* always possible to update an individual tuple of a view independently of all other tuples in that view.

For example, Codd shows in reference [10.2] that it is not possible to delete just one tuple from a certain join, because the effect would be to leave a relation that "is not the join of any two relations whatsoever" (which means that the result could not possibly satisfy the relation predicate for the view). And the approach to such view updates historically has always been to reject them altogether, on the grounds that it is impossible to make them look completely like base relation updates.

Our approach is rather different. We recognize the fact that even with a base relation, it is not always possible to update individual tuples independently of all the rest. Typically, therefore, we accept those view updates that have historically been rejected, interpreting them in an obvious and logically correct way to apply to the underlying relation(s); we accept them, moreover, in full recognition of the fact that updating those underlying relations might well have side-effects on the view—*side-effects that are, however, required in order to avoid the possibility that the view might violate its own relation predicate.*

With that preamble out of the way, let us now get down to detail. In what follows, we first define our terms. Then we present the rules for updating join views. Then we consider the implications of those rules for each of the three cases (one-to-one, one-to-many, many-to-many) in turn.

Consider the join $J = A$ JOIN B, where (as in Chapter 6) relations A, B, and J have headings $\{X,Y\}$, $\{Y,Z\}$, and $\{X,Y,Z\}$, respectively. Let the relation predicates for A and B be PA and PB, respectively. Then the relation predicate PJ for J is

```
PA ( a ) AND PB ( b )
```

where for a given tuple j of the join, a is "the A-portion" of j (i.e., the tuple that is derived from j by projecting away the value $j.Z$) and b is "the B-portion" of j (i.e., the tuple that is derived from j by projecting away the value $j.X$). In other words:

"Every tuple in the join is such that the A-portion satisfies PA and the B-portion satisfies PB."

For example, the relation predicate for the join of relations S and SP over S# is as follows:

"Every tuple (s,n,t,c,p,q) in the join is such that the tuple (s,n,t,c) satisfies the relation predicate for S and the tuple (s,p,q) satisfies the relation predicate for SP."

Here then are the rules for updating $J = A$ JOIN B:

- **INSERT:** The new tuple j must satisfy PJ. If the A-portion of j does not appear in A, it is inserted into A.* If the B-portion of j does not appear in B, it is inserted into B.

- **DELETE:** The A-portion of the tuple to be deleted is deleted from A and the B-portion is deleted from B.

- **UPDATE:** The tuple to be updated must be such that the updated version satisfies PJ. The A-portion is deleted from A, without performing any triggered actions or relation predicate checks, and the B-portion is deleted from B, again without performing any triggered actions or relation predicate checks. Then, if the A-portion of the updated version of the tuple does not appear in A, it is inserted into A; if the B-portion does not appear in B, it is inserted into B.

Let us now examine the implications of these rules for the three different cases.

Case 1 (one-to-one): Note first that the term "one-to-one" here would more accurately be "(one-or-zero)-to-(one-or-zero)." In other words, there is a DBMS-known integrity constraint in effect that guarantees that for each tuple of A there is at most one

---

* Note that this INSERT might have the side-effect of inserting the B-portion into B also, as in the case of the views discussed in Section 17.6. Analogous remarks apply to the DELETE and UPDATE rules also; for brevity, we do not bother to spell out this possibility in detail in every case.

matching tuple in *B* and *vice versa*. More precisely, the set of attributes *Y* over which the join is performed must include a subset (not necessarily a proper subset) *K*, say, such that *K* is a candidate key for *A* and a candidate key for *B*.

Examples:

■   For a first example, the reader is invited to consider the effect of the foregoing rules on the join of the suppliers relation S to itself over supplier numbers (only).

■   By way of a second example, suppose the suppliers-and-parts database includes another base relation, SR { S#, REST }, where S# identifies a supplier and REST identifies that supplier's favorite restaurant. Assume that not all suppliers in relation S are represented in relation SR. The reader is invited to consider the effect of the foregoing rules on the join of relations S and SR (over S#). What difference would it make if a given supplier could be represented in relation SR and not in relation S?

Case 2 (one-to-many): The term "one-to-many" here would more accurately be "(zero-or-one)-to-(zero-or-more)." In other words, there is a DBMS-known integrity constraint in effect that guarantees that for each tuple of *B* there is at most one matching tuple in *A*. Typically, what this means is that the set of attributes *Y* over which the join is performed must include a subset (not necessarily a proper subset) *K*, say, such that *K* is a candidate key for *A* and a matching foreign key in *B*. *Note:* If the foregoing is in fact the case, and if that foreign key has NULLS NOT ALLOWED, we can replace the phrase "zero or one" by "exactly one."

Examples: Let view SSP be defined as

```
S JOIN SP
```

(this is a foreign-to-matching-candidate-key join, of course). Sample values are shown in Fig. 17.7.

■   An attempt to insert the tuple (S4,Clark,20,London,P6,100) into SSP will succeed, and will have the effect of inserting the tuple (S4,P6,100) into relation SP (thereby adding a tuple to the view).

■   An attempt to insert the tuple (S5,Adams,30,Athens,P6,100) into SSP will succeed, and will have the effect of inserting the tuple (S5,P6,100) into relation SP (thereby adding a tuple to the view).

■   An attempt to insert the tuple (S6,Green,20,London,P6,100) into SSP will succeed, and will have the effect of inserting the tuple (S6,Green,20,London) into relation S and the tuple (S6,P6,100) into relation SP (thereby adding a tuple to the view).

   Note: Suppose for the moment that it is possible for SP tuples to exist without a corresponding S tuple. Suppose moreover that relation SP already includes some tuples with supplier number S6 (but not one with supplier number S6 and part number P1). Then the INSERT in the example just discussed will have the effect of inserting some additional tuples into the view—namely, the join of the

SSP	S#	SNAME	STATUS	CITY	P#	QTY
	S1	Smith	20	London	P1	300
	S1	Smith	20	London	P2	200
	S1	Smith	20	London	P3	400
	S1	Smith	20	London	P4	200
	S1	Smith	20	London	P5	100
	S1	Smith	20	London	P6	100
	S2	Jones	10	Paris	P1	300
	S2	Jones	10	Paris	P2	400
	S3	Blake	30	Paris	P2	200
	S4	Clark	20	London	P2	200
	S4	Clark	20	London	P4	300
	S4	Clark	20	London	P5	400

FIG. 17.7   View SSP (sample values)

tuple (S6,Green,20,London) and those previously existing SP tuples for supplier S6.

■   An attempt to insert the tuple (S4,Clark,20,Athens,P6,100) into SSP will fail (why?).

■   An attempt to insert the tuple (S5,Adams,30,London,P6,100) into SSP will fail (why?).

■   An attempt to insert the tuple (S1,Smith,20,London,P1,400) into SSP will fail (why?).

■   An attempt to delete the tuple (S3,Blake,30,Paris,P2,200) from SSP will succeed, and will have the effect of deleting the tuple (S3,Blake,30,Paris) from relation S and the tuple (S3,P2,200) from relation SP.

■   An attempt to delete the tuple (S1,Smith,20,London,P1,300) from SSP will "succeed" (see the note below) and will have the effect of deleting the tuple (S1,Smith, 20,London) from relation S and the tuple (S1,P1,300) from relation SP.

   Note: Actually the overall effect of this attempted DELETE will depend on the foreign key delete rule from SP.S# to S.S#. If the rule is RESTRICT the overall operation will fail. If it is CASCADE it will have the side-effect of deleting all other SP tuples for supplier S1 as well.

■   An attempt to update the SSP tuple (S1,Smith,20,London,P1,300) to (S1,Smith,20, London,P1,400) will succeed, and will have the effect of updating the SP tuple (S1, P1,300) to (S1,P1,400).

■   An attempt to update the SSP tuple (S1,Smith,20,London,P1,300) to (S1,Smith,20, Athens,P1,400) will succeed, and will have the effect of updating the S tuple (S1,Smith,20,London) to (S1,Smith,20,Athens) and the SP tuple (S1,P1,300) to (S1,P1,400).

■   An attempt to update the SSP tuple (S1,Smith,20,London,P1,300) to (S6,Smith,20,

London,P1,300) will "succeed" (see the note below) and will have the effect of updating the S tuple (S1,Smith,20,London) to (S6,Smith,20,London) and the SP tuple (S1,P1,300) to (S6,P1,300).

Note: Actually, the overall effect of this attempted update will depend on the foreign key update rule for the referential constraint from SP.S# to S.S#. The details are left as an exercise for the reader.

Case 3 (many-to-many): The term "many-to-many" here would more accurately be "(zero-or-more)-to-(zero-or-more)." In other words, there is no DBMS-known integrity constraint in effect that guarantees that we are really dealing with a Case 1 or Case 2 situation.

Examples: Suppose we have a view defined as

```
S JOIN P
```

(join of S and P over CITY—a many-to-many join). Sample values are shown in Fig. 17.8.

■ Inserting the tuple (S7,Bruce,15,Oslo,P8,Wheel,White,25) will succeed, and will have the effect of inserting the tuple (S7,Bruce,15,Oslo) into relation S and the tuple (P8,Wheel,White,25,Oslo) into relation P (thereby adding the specified tuple to the view).

■ Inserting the tuple (S1,Smith,20,London,P7,Washer,Red,5) will succeed, and will have the effect of inserting the tuple (P7,Washer,Red,5,London) into relation P (thereby adding *two* tuples to the view—the tuple (S1,Smith,20,London,P7, Washer,Red,5), as specified, and the tuple (S4,Clark,20,London,P7,Washer, Red,5)).

■ Inserting the tuple (S6,Green,20,London,P7,Washer,Red,5) will succeed, and will have the effect of inserting the tuple (S6,Green,20,London) into relation S and the tuple (P7,Washer,Red,5,London) into relation P (thereby adding *six* tuples to the view).

S#	SNAME	STATUS	CITY	P#	PNAME	COLOR	WEIGHT
S1	Smith	20	London	P1	Nut	Red	12
S1	Smith	20	London	P4	Screw	Red	14
S1	Smith	20	London	P6	Cog	Red	19
S2	Jones	10	Paris	P2	Bolt	Green	17
S2	Jones	10	Paris	P5	Cam	Blue	12
S3	Blake	30	Paris	P2	Bolt	Green	17
S3	Blake	30	Paris	P5	Cam	Blue	12
S4	Clark	20	London	P1	Nut	Red	12
S4	Clark	20	London	P4	Screw	Red	14
S4	Clark	20	London	P6	Cog	Red	19

FIG. 17.8 The join of S and P over CITY

■ Deleting the tuple (S1,Smith,20,London,P1,Nut,Red,12) will succeed, and will have the effect of deleting the tuple (S1,Smith,20,London) from relation S and the tuple (P1,Nut,Red,12,London) from relation P (thereby deleting *four* tuples from the view).

Further examples are left as an exercise for the reader.

Other Operations

In this subsection, we briefly consider the remaining operations of the algebra (Cartesian product, θ-join, rename, divide, and summarize).

■ *Cartesian product:* Since Cartesian product is a special case of natural join (*A* JOIN *B* degenerates to *A* TIMES *B* if *A* and *B* have no attributes in common), the rules for *A* TIMES *B* are just a special case of the rules for *A* JOIN *B*. The details are left as another exercise for the reader.

■ θ-*join:* θ-join is a restriction of a Cartesian product. The rules for θ-join can therefore be derived from the rules for restriction and Cartesian product.

■ *Rename:* Trivial.

■ *Divide:* Divide (like θ-join) is not primitive, and hence the relevant rules can be derived from those already given (specifically those for difference, projection, and Cartesian product); the details are left as yet another exercise for the reader, but we observe that in practice it seems likely that most division views will not be updatable at all (why, exactly?).

■ *Summarize:* In general, the SUMMARIZE operation is not information-preserving—that is, there is no unambiguous reverse mapping from the result of a SUMMARIZE back to the original relation. As a consequence, views whose definition involves a SUMMARIZE are not updatable.

A Note on Target Relations

We conclude our discussions of view update with the following remark. Given that (e.g.) a join view is updatable, it follows that there is no reason why the target in an INSERT, UPDATE, or DELETE operation need be, specifically, a named relation. After all, if "INSERT INTO SSP" is legal (where SSP is as under the Case 2 join example above), then "INSERT INTO (S JOIN SP)" must surely be legal as well. The same is true for the target of a relational assignment operation, of course.

By way of illustration, suppose we have a view LSSP defined as

```
( S WHERE CITY = 'London' ) JOIN SP
```

With our usual sample values, an attempt to insert the tuple (S6,Green,20,London,P6,100) into this view will succeed; it will have the effect of inserting the tuple (S6,Green,20,London) into relation S and the tuple (S6,P6,100) into relation SP). More precisely, the first of these two tuples—(S6,Green,20,London)—will be inserted, not directly into base relation S, but rather into the restriction S WHERE CITY = 'London';

the rule for inserting a tuple into a restriction will then come into play, with the desired final effect. The point is, however, that the target of the intermediate INSERT is represented by a restriction expression, not by a named relation.

17.8   Snapshots (A Digression)

In this section we digress briefly to discuss **snapshots** [17.1], which do have some points in common with views (although the two concepts should certainly not be confused). As explained in Chapter 4, a snapshot is a named derived relation (i.e., a relation *variable*), like a view. Unlike a view, however, a snapshot is real, not virtual—i.e., it is represented not only by its definition in terms of other named relations, but also (at least conceptually) by its own separate data. Here is an example, repeated from Chapter 4:

```
CREATE SNAPSHOT SC AS
    ( ( S JOIN SP ) WHERE P# = 'P2' ) [ S#, CITY ]
        REFRESH EVERY DAY ;
```

Creating a snapshot is much like executing a query, except that (a) the result of the query is kept in the database under the specified name (SC in the example) as a *read-only relation,* and (b) periodically (EVERY DAY in the example) the snapshot is **refreshed**—i.e., its current value is discarded, the query is executed again, and the result of that new execution becomes the new value of the snapshot. Thus, the snapshot in the example represents the relevant data as it was at most 24 hours ago.

The point of the snapshot idea is that many applications—perhaps even most applications—can tolerate, or might even require, data as of some particular point in time. For example, reporting and accounting applications would typically fall into such a category; such applications typically require the data to be frozen at an appropriate moment (e.g., the end of an accounting period), and snapshots allow such freezing to occur without preventing other transactions from performing updates on the data in question. Similarly, it might be desirable, as mentioned in Chapter 1, to freeze large amounts of data for a complex query or decision support application, again without locking out updates. *Note:* This idea becomes particularly attractive in a distributed database context. See Chapter 21.

The syntax of CREATE SNAPSHOT is (as the example suggests)

```
CREATE SNAPSHOT snapshot AS expression
        REFRESH EVERY refresh-time ;
```

where *refresh-time* is, e.g., MONTH or WEEK or DAY or HOUR or *n* MINUTES or MONDAY or WEEKDAY . . . (etc.). And here is the syntax of the corresponding DESTROY operation:

```
DESTROY SNAPSHOT snapshot ;
```

The specified snapshot is destroyed (i.e., its definition is removed from the catalog). *Note:* DESTROY SNAPSHOT will fail if any view or snapshot definition currently refers to the snapshot in question. Alternatively (as mentioned in Section 17.3), we might consider extending CREATE SNAPSHOT to include some kind of "RESTRICTED *vs.* CASCADES" option. We do not consider this latter possibility further here.

17.9 SQL Support

In this section we summarize SQL's support for views (only—SQL does not currently support snapshots at all). First, the syntax of **CREATE VIEW** is:

```
CREATE VIEW view AS table-expression [ WITH CHECK OPTION ] ;
```

Explanation:

1. The *table-expression* is the view-defining expression. See Chapter 8 for a detailed explanation of SQL table expressions.

2. The WITH CHECK OPTION clause (if specified) means that INSERTs and UPDATEs on the view will be rejected if they violate the view-defining condition. Observe, therefore, that such operations will fail *only* if WITH CHECK OPTION is specified—i.e., by default, they will *not* fail. The reader will realize from previous sections of this chapter that we regard such behavior as logically incorrect. We would therefore strongly recommend that WITH CHECK OPTION *always* be specified if the view is updatable.*

   Note: WITH CHECK OPTION has numerous ramifications and subtleties that are beyond the scope of this book. See reference [8.5] for a comprehensive explanation (with examples), and reference [17.4] for some criticisms of the concept.

Examples:

1. ```
   CREATE VIEW REDPARTS
        AS SELECT P.P#, P.PNAME, P.WEIGHT, P.CITY
           FROM    P
           WHERE   P.COLOR = 'Red'
        WITH CHECK OPTION ;
   ```

2. ```
   CREATE VIEW LREDPARTS
        AS SELECT REDPARTS.P#, REDPARTS.WEIGHT
           FROM    REDPARTS
           WHERE   REDPARTS.CITY = 'London'
        WITH CHECK OPTION ;
   ```

3. ```
   CREATE VIEW CITYPAIRS
        AS SELECT DISTINCT S.CITY AS SCITY, P.CITY AS PCITY
           FROM    S, SP, P
           WHERE   S.S# = SP.S#
           AND     SP.P# = P.P# ;
   ```

---

* Of course, "updatable" here means "updatable according to SQL" (see later). Indeed, WITH CHECK OPTION is illegal if the view is not updatable according to SQL.
   ```

```
4. CREATE VIEW PQ
      AS SELECT SP.P#, SUM ( SP.QTY ) AS TOTQTY
         FROM   SP
         GROUP  BY SP.P# ;
```

An existing view can be destroyed by means of **DROP VIEW**—syntax:

```
DROP VIEW view option ;
```

where (as with DROP TABLE and DROP DOMAIN) *option* is either RESTRICT or CASCADE. If RESTRICT is specified and the view is referenced in any other view definition or in an integrity constraint, the DROP will fail; if CASCADE is specified, the DROP will succeed, and any referencing view definitions and integrity constraints will be dropped also.

View retrievals: As indicated in Section 17.4, all retrievals against all views are guaranteed to work correctly in the current version of the SQL standard (SQL/92). The same is unfortunately not true for certain current products, nor for earlier versions of the standard. See Exercise 17.14(a) at the end of the chapter.

View updates: SQL's support for view updating is quite limited. Basically, the only views that are considered to be updatable are views that are derived from a single base table via some combination of restrict and project operations. Furthermore, even this simple case is treated incorrectly, owing to SQL's lack of understanding of relation predicates—and in particular to the fact that SQL tables permit duplicate rows.

Here is a more precise statement of SQL's view updatability rules (this list is taken from reference [8.5]). In SQL, a view is updatable if and only if all of the following conditions 1-8 below apply:

1. The table expression that defines the scope of the view is a select expression; that is, it does not directly contain any of the keywords JOIN, UNION, INTERSECT, or EXCEPT.

2. The SELECT clause of that select expression does not directly contain the keyword DISTINCT.

3. Every select-item in that SELECT clause (after any necessary expansion of "asterisk-style" select-items) consists of a possibly qualified column name (option-ally accompanied by an AS clause), representing a simple reference to a column of the underlying table (see paragraph 5 below).

4. The FROM clause of that select expression contains exactly one table reference.

5. That table reference identifies either a base table or an updatable view. *Note:* The table identified by that table reference is *the* (single) underlying table for the updat-able view in question (see paragraph 3 above).

6. That select expression does not include a WHERE clause that includes a nested table expression that includes a FROM clause that includes a reference to the same table as is referenced in the FROM clause mentioned in paragraph 4 above.

7. That select expression does not include a GROUP BY clause.

8. That select expression does not include a HAVING clause.

Note 1: Updatability in SQL is "all or nothing," in the sense that *either* all three of INSERT, UPDATE, or DELETE can be applied to a given view *or* none of them can—it is not possible for (e.g.) DELETE to be applicable but INSERT not (although some commercial products do support such a capability).

Note 2: In SQL, the UPDATE operation either *can* or *cannot* be applied to a given view—it is not possible to have some columns updatable and others not within the same view (although, again, some commercial products do go beyond the standard in this respect).

Finally, it follows from all of the foregoing that the target of the SQL INSERT, DELETE, and UPDATE operations is always a named table (base table or view), not a more general expression.

17.10   Summary

A **view** is a named relational expression; it can be regarded as a **named virtual relation** (variable). Operations against a view are normally implemented by a process of **substitution;** that is, references to the *name* of the view are replaced by the expression that *defines* the view—and this substitution process works precisely because of **closure**. For **retrieval** operations, the substitution process works 100 percent of the time (at least in principle, though not necessarily in practice). For **update** operations, it works if the view is **information-preserving** (again in principle, though almost certainly not in practice at the time of writing).

We presented an extensive set of **principles** that should guide the design of any systematic view updating mechanism; the most important of those principles is the principle that the relation predicate for a given relation (in particular, for a given view) is the criterion for update acceptability for that relation. We then described a view updating mechanism that did indeed abide by those principles. Specifically, we presented rules for the updatability of views defined in terms of the **union, intersection, difference, restrict, project, join,** and **extend** operations and also (more briefly) the **product, θ-join, rename,** and **divide** operations.

We also examined the question of **logical data independence**. There are two aspects to such independence, **growth** and **restructuring,** both of which are important (but views are relevant only to the second of them). Other benefits of views include (a) their ability to hide data and thereby provide a certain measure of **security,** and (b) their ability to make life easier for the user, thanks to their "macro-like" properties.

We then digressed for a moment to give a brief discussion of **snapshots**. Finally, we described the relevant aspects of SQL (in outline).

There is one remaining point to be made, a point that is widely understood but only rarely appreciated. We state it explicitly here because it lends further support to the approach adopted in this chapter to the view update problem. The point is the following:

For any given database, the choice as to which relations are to be base relations and which are to be views is to some extent arbitrary.

In the case of suppliers, for example, we could make the familiar relation S a base relation and then define the two projections SNC (over S#, SNAME, and CITY) and ST (over S# and STATUS) as views; or we could define SNC and ST as base relations and then define S (the join of SNC and ST) as a view. And the point is, of course, that the updatability of a given database should not depend on the essentially arbitrary decision as to how we decide to represent that database—i.e., the decision as to which relations we decide to make base relations and which we decide to make views.* In the example, the updatability of relation S should in no way depend on whether S is a base relation or a view.

Exercises

17.1 Give calculus-based analogs of the algebraic view definitions shown in Section 17.3.

17.2 Create a view consisting of supplier numbers and part numbers for suppliers and parts that are not colocated.

17.3 Create a view consisting of supplier tuples for suppliers that are located in London.

17.4 Define relation SP of the suppliers-and-parts database as a view of relation SPJ of the suppliers-parts-projects database.

17.5 Create a view from the suppliers-parts-projects database consisting of all projects (project number and city attributes only) that are supplied by supplier S1 and use part P1.

17.6 Given the view definition—

```
CREATE VIEW HEAVYWEIGHTS AS
        ( ( ( P RENAME WEIGHT AS WT, COLOR AS COL ) )
                              WHERE WT > 14 ) [ P#, WT, COL ] ;
```

—show the operation actually executed (i.e., the converted form) for each of the following:

(a) `TA  :=  HEAVYWEIGHTS WHERE COL = 'Green' ;`

(b) `TB  :=  ( EXTEND HEAVYWEIGHTS ADD WT + 5 AS WTP ) [ P#, WTP ] ;`

(c) `UPDATE HEAVYWEIGHTS WHERE WT = 18 COL := 'White' ;`

(d) `DELETE HEAVYWEIGHTS WHERE WT < 10 ;`

(e) `INSERT ( { P#:'P99', WT:12, COL:'Purple' } )`
   `INTO  · HEAVYWEIGHTS ;`

17.7 Suppose the HEAVYWEIGHTS view definition is revised as follows:

```
CREATE VIEW HEAVYWEIGHTS AS
( ( ( EXTEND P ADD WEIGHT * 454 AS WT ) RENAME COLOR AS COL )
                      WHERE WT > 14 ) [ P#, WT, COL ] ;
```

Now repeat Exercise 17.6.

---

* We point out in passing that one objective of database design theory (meaning, specifically, the principles of further normalization and the principle described in reference [17.12]) is precisely to give some assistance with this decision-making process.

17.8 In Chapter 5 we suggested that it might sometimes be desirable to be able to declare candidate keys (or a primary key) for a view—i.e., to include CANDIDATE and/or PRIMARY KEY clauses within the CREATE VIEW statement. Why might such a facility be desirable?

17.9 What extensions to the system catalog as described in Chapters 3 and 4 are needed to support views? What about snapshots?

17.10 Suppose a given base relation R is replaced by two restrictions A and B such that A UNION B is always equal to R and A INTERSECT B is always empty. Is logical data independence achievable?

17.11 (a) The intersection A INTERSECT B is equivalent to the join A JOIN B (this join is one-to-one, but not *strictly* so, because there might exist tuples in A without counterparts in B and *vice versa*). Are the updatability rules given in Sections 17.6 and 17.7 for intersection and join views consistent with this equivalence?

(b) A INTERSECT B is also equivalent to A MINUS (A MINUS B) and to B MINUS (B MINUS A). Are the updatability rules given in Section 17.6 for intersection and difference views consistent with these equivalences?

17.12 One of the principles we laid down in Section 17.5 was that INSERT and DELETE should be inverses of each other, insofar as possible. Do the rules given in Section 17.6 for updating union, intersection, and difference views abide by this principle?

17.13 In Section 17.2 (in our discussion of logical data independence) we discussed the possibility of restructuring the suppliers-and-parts database by replacing base relation S by two of its projections SNC and ST. We also observed that such a restructuring was not a totally trivial matter. Discuss the implications.

17.14 Investigate any SQL product that might be available to you. (a) Can you find any examples of **view retrievals** that fail in that product? (b) What are the rules regarding **view updatability** in that product? (they are probably less stringent than those given in Section 17.9).

References and Bibliography

17.1 Michel E. Adiba and Bruce G. Lindsay. "Database Snapshots." IBM Research Report RJ2772 (March 7th, 1980).

The paper that proposed the snapshot concept. Semantics and implementation are both discussed. Regarding implementation, note in particular that various kinds of "differential refresh" are possible under the covers—it is not always necessary for the system to reexecute the original query in its entirety at refresh time.

17.2 H. W. Buff. "Why Codd's Rule No. 6 Must Be Reformulated." *ACM SIGMOD Record 17*, No. 4 (December 1988).

In 1985, Codd published a set of twelve rules to be used as "part of a test to determine whether a product that is claimed to be fully relational is actually so" [21.10]. His Rule No. 6 required that all views that are theoretically updatable also be updatable by the system. In this short note, Buff claims that the general view updatability problem is undecidable— i.e., no general algorithm exists to determine the updatability (in Codd's sense) or otherwise of an arbitrary view. Note, however, that the definition of view updatability adopted in the present chapter is somewhat different from Codd's, in that it explicitly pays attention to the applicable relation predicates.

17.3   D. D. Chamberlin, J. N. Gray, and I. L. Traiger. "Views, Authorization, and Locking in a Relational Data Base System." Proc. NCC *44,* Anaheim, Calif. Montvale, N.J.: AFIPS Press (May 1975).

Includes a brief rationale for the approach adopted to view updating in the System R prototype (and hence in SQL/DS, DB2, the SQL standard, etc.). See also reference [17.13], which performs the same function for the INGRES prototype.

17.4   Hugh Darwen. "Without Check Option." In C. J. Date and Hugh Darwen, *Relational Database Writings 1989–1991*. Reading, Mass.: Addison-Wesley (1992).

17.5   C. J. Date and David McGoveran. "Updating Union, Intersection, and Difference Views." *Database Programming & Design 7,* No. 6 (June 1994).

17.6   C. J. Date and David McGoveran. "Updating Joins and Other Views." *Database Programming & Design 7,* No. 8 (August 1994).

17.7   C. J. Date. "Updating Views." In C. J. Date, *Relational Database: Selected Writings*. Reading, Mass.: Addison-Wesley (1986).

An early treatment by the present author of the view updating rules (for restriction, projection, and join views only). We mention this paper here only so that we may make it clear that the ideas described therein should be considered superseded by the new approach described in the body of this chapter.

17.8   Umeshwar Dayal and Philip A. Bernstein. "On the Correct Translation of Update Operations on Relational Views." *ACM TODS 7,* No. 3 (September 1982).

The first really formal treatment of view updating rules (for restriction, projection, and join views only).

17.9   A. L. Furtado and M. A. Casanova. "Updating Relational Views." In *Query Processing in Database Systems* (eds., W. Kim, D. Reiner, and D. Batory). New York, N.Y.: Springer Verlag (1985).

There are two broad approaches to the view update problem. One (the only one discussed in any detail in the present book) attempts to provide a general mechanism that works regardless of the specific database involved; it is driven purely by the definitions of the views in question. The other, less ambitious, approach requires the DBA to specify, for each view, exactly what updates are allowed and what their semantics are, by (in effect) writing the procedural code to implement those updates in terms of the underlying base relations. This paper surveys work on each of the two approaches. An extensive set of references (to work prior to 1985) is included.

17.10   Nathan Goodman. "View Update Is Practical." *InfoDB 5,* No. 2 (Summer 1990).

A very informal, pragmatic overview of the problem of view updatability. To quote from the introduction: "Dayal and Bernstein [17.8] have proved that essentially no interesting views can be updated; Buff [17.2] has proved that no algorithm exists that can decide whether an arbitrary view is updatable. There seems little reason for hope. [But] nothing could be further from the truth. The fact is that view update is both possible and practical." (Somewhat paraphrased.)

17.11   Arthur M. Keller. "Algorithms for Translating View Updates to Database Updates for Views Involving Selections, Projections, and Joins." Proc. 4th ACM SIGACT-SIGMOD Symposium on Principles of Database Systems, Portland, Ore. (March 1985).

Proposes a set of five criteria that should be satisfied by view updating algorithms—no side-effects, one-step changes only, no unnecessary changes, no simpler replacements possible, and no DELETE-INSERT pairs instead of UPDATEs—and presents algorithms that satisfy those criteria. Among other things, the algorithms permit the implementation of one kind of update by another; for example, a DELETE on a view might translate into an UPDATE on the underlying base relation (e.g., a supplier could be deleted from the "London suppliers" view by changing the CITY value to Paris). As another example (beyond the scope of Keller's paper, however), a DELETE on *V* (where *V* is defined as the difference *A* MINUS *B*) might be implemented by means of an INSERT on *B* instead of a DELETE on *A*. Note that we rejected such possibilities in the body of this chapter, by virtue of our Principle No. 6.

17.12 David McGoveran and C. J. Date. "A New Database Design Principle." *Database Programming & Design 7,* No. 7 (July 1994).

Let *A* and *B* be any two relations, with associated relation predicates *PA* and *PB,* respectively. The meanings of *A* and *B* are said to **overlap** if and only if some tuple *t* can be constructed such that *PA(t)* and *PB(t)* are both true. The eponymous design principle then runs as follows:

> *Let* A' *and* B' *be any two base relations in the database, and let* A *and* B *be the projections of* A' *and* B' *(respectively) over all attributes that do not have a default value (i.e., all attributes that have "defaults not allowed"). Then there must not exist nonloss decompositions of* A *and* B *into* A1, A2, . . . , Am *and* B1, B2, . . . , Bn *(respectively) such that two distinct projections in the set* A1, A2, . . . , Am, B1, B2, . . . , Bn *have overlapping meanings.*

By "nonloss decomposition" here, we mean a decomposition of the given relation into a set of projections such that (a) the given relation can be reconstructed by joining those projections back together, and (b) none of those projections is redundant in that reconstruction process.

The paper presents a number of examples and arguments in support of this principle. It also points out that adherence to the principle has the consequence that if *A* and *B* are any two type-compatible base relations, then it will be true for all time that:

```
A UNION B      is a disjoint union
A INTERSECT B  is empty
A MINUS B      is equal to A
```

The paper also stresses the point that the principle is equally applicable to what might be called "individual user databases"—that is, an individual user's perception (as defined by views and/or base tables) of some underlying shared database. In other words, such an "individual user database" ought not to include any two views and/or base relations that violate the principle, for essentially all of the same reasons that the shared database ought not to include any two base relations that violate the principle.

17.13 M. R. Stonebraker. "Implementation of Views and Integrity Constraints by Query Modification." Proc. ACM SIGMOD International Conference on Management of Data, San Jose, Calif. (May 1975).

See the annotation to reference [17.3].

Answers to Selected Exercises

17.1 We have numbered the following solutions as 17.1.*n,* where *n* is the number of the original example in Section 17.3.

17.1.1
```
CREATE VIEW REDPARTS AS
      ( P.P#, P.PNAME, P.WEIGHT AS WT, P.CITY )
        WHERE P.COLOR = 'Red' ;
```

17.1.2 `CREATE VIEW PQ AS`
      `( SP.P#,`
            `SUM ( SPX WHERE SPX.P# = SP.P#, QTY ) AS TOTQTY ) ;`
It would be preferable to replace SP.P# by P.P# (twice) in the foregoing, but the resulting view would then not be a strict analog of the algebraic original.

17.1.3 `CREATE VIEW CITY_PAIRS AS`
      `( S.CITY AS SCITY, P.CITY AS PCITY )`
            `WHERE EXISTS ( SP WHERE SP.S# = S.S#`
                               `AND   SP.P# = P.P# ) ;`

17.1.4 `CREATE VIEW LONDON_REDPARTS AS`
      `( REDPARTS WHERE REDPARTS.CITY = «London« ) ;`

Note: Our answers to Exercises 17.2–17.5 below are also calculus-based.

17.2 `CREATE VIEW NON_COLOCATED AS`
      `( S.S#, P.P# ) WHERE S.CITY ≠ P.CITY ;`

17.3 `CREATE VIEW LONDON_SUPPLIERS AS`
      `( S.S#, S.SNAME, S.STATUS ) WHERE S.CITY = «London« ;`

We have omitted the CITY attribute from the view, since we know its value must be London for every tuple in the view. Note, however, that this omission means that any INSERT on the view will necessarily fail (unless the default value for attribute S.CITY happens to be London). In other words, a view like this one apparently cannot support INSERT operations at all. (Alternatively, there is the possibility of defining the default value for CITY *for tuples inserted via this view* to be London. This idea of **view-specific defaults** requires more study.)

17.4 The problem here is: How should attribute SP.QTY be defined? The sensible answer seems to be that, for a given S#-P# pair, SP.QTY should be the *sum* of all SPJ.QTY values, taken over all J#«s for that S#-P# pair:

```
CREATE VIEW SP AS
    ( SPJX.S#, SPJX.P#,
      SUM ( SPJY WHERE SPJY.S# = SPJX.S#
                 AND   SPJY.P# = SPJX.S#, QTY ) AS QTY ) ;
```

17.5 `CREATE VIEW JC AS`
      `( J.J#, J.CITY ) WHERE EXISTS SPJ ( SPJ.S# = «S1« AND`
                                          `SPJ.P# = «P1« AND`
                                          `SPJ.J# =  J.J# ) ;`

17.6 We leave it to the reader to show the converted forms. However, we remark that (e) will fail, because the tuple presented for insertion does not satisfy the relation predicate for the view.

17.7 Again (e) fails, though for a slightly different reason this time, namely as follows. First, the DBMS will provide a default WEIGHT value, w say, since the user has not provided a "real" value (and cannot, of course). Second, it will almost certainly not be the case that $w * 454$ is equal to the WT value the user *has* provided—even if that WT value were indeed greater than 14. Thus the tuple presented for insertion will again not satisfy the relation predicate for the view.

17.8 The following list of reasons is taken from reference [4.15]:

  ■ If users are to interact with views instead of base relations, then it is clear that those views should look to the user as much like base relations as possible. Ideally, in fact, the user should not even have to know that they *are* views, but should be able to treat them as if they actually were base relations. And just as the user of a base relation needs to know what candidate keys that base relation has (in general), so the user of a view needs to know what candidate keys that view has (again, in general). Explicitly declaring those keys is the obvious way to make that information available.

- The DBMS might not be able to deduce candidate keys for itself (this is certainly the case with every DBMS on the market today). Explicit declarations are thus likely to be the only means available (to the DBA, that is) of informing the DBMS—as well as the user—of the existence of such keys.

- Even if the DBMS were able to deduce candidate keys for itself, explicit declarations would at least enable the system to check that its deductions and the DBA's explicit specifications were not inconsistent.

- The DBA might have some knowledge that the DBMS does not, and might thus be able to improve on the DBMS's deductions. Reference [4.15] gives an example of this possibility.

And reference [10.3] offers another reason, which is essentially that such a facility would provide a simple and convenient way of stating certain important integrity constraints that otherwise could be stated only in a very circumlocutory fashion.

17.9   It is obviously impossible to provide a definitive answer to this question. We offer the following observations.

- Each view and each snapshot will have an entry in the RELATIONS relation, with a RELTYPE value of "View" or "Snapshot" as appropriate.

- Each view will also have an entry in a new catalog relation, which we might as well call VIEWS. That entry should include the relevant view-defining expression.

- Similarly, each snapshot will also have an entry in a new catalog relation (SNAP-SHOTS). That entry should include the relevant defining expression. It should also include information regarding the snapshot refresh interval.

- Yet another catalog relation will show which views and snapshots are defined in terms of which other relations. Note that the structure of this relation is somewhat similar to that of the PART_STRUCTURE relation (see Fig. 4.4 in Chapter 4): Just as parts can contain other parts, so views and snapshots can be defined in terms of other views and snapshots. Note, therefore, that the points discussed in the answer to Exercise 7.7 in Chapter 7 are relevant here.

17.10   Yes!—but note the following. Suppose we replace the suppliers relation S by two restrictions, SA and SB say, where SA is the suppliers in London and SB is the suppliers not in London. We can now define the union of SA and SB as a view called S. If we now try (through this view) to UPDATE a London supplier's city to something other than London, or a "nonLondon" supplier's city to London, the implementation must map that UPDATE to a DELETE on one of the two restrictions and an INSERT on the other. Now, the rules given in Section 17.6 do handle this case correctly—in fact, we (deliberately) *defined* UPDATE as a DELETE followed by an INSERT; however, there was a tacit assumption that the implementation would actually use an UPDATE, for efficiency reasons. This example shows that sometimes mapping an UPDATE to an UPDATE does not work; in fact, determining those cases in which it does work can be regarded as an optimization.

17.11   (a) Yes! (b) Yes!

17.12   For union and difference, INSERT and DELETE are always inverses of each other; however, for intersection they might not be (quite). For instance, if *A* and *B* are distinct base relations, inserting tuple *t* into *V = A* INTERSECT *B* might cause *t* to be inserted into *A* only (because it is already present in *B*); subsequently deleting *t* from *V* will now cause *t* to be deleted from both *A* and *B*. (On the other hand, deleting *t* and then reinserting it will always preserve the *status quo*.) Once again, it is our position that such an asymmetry can arise only if the database is badly designed [17.12].

17.13 We offer the following comments. First, the replacement process itself involves several steps, which might be summarized as follows. (This sequence of operations will be refined in a moment.)

```
CREATE BASE RELATION SNC
     ( S#     DOMAIN ( S# ),
       SNAME  DOMAIN ( NAME ),
       CITY   DOMAIN ( CITY ) )
     PRIMARY KEY ( S# ) ;

CREATE BASE RELATION ST
     ( S#     DOMAIN ( S# ),
       STATUS DOMAIN ( STATUS ) )
     PRIMARY KEY ( S# ) ;

INSERT S [ S#, SNAME, CITY ] INTO SNC ;

INSERT S [ S#, STATUS ] INTO ST ;

DESTROY BASE RELATION S ;
```

We can now create the desired view:

```
CREATE VIEW S AS SNC JOIN ST ;
```

We now observe that each of SNC.S# and ST.S# can be regarded as a foreign key referencing the other. Indeed, there is a strict one-to-one relationship between SNC and ST, and so we run into a variety of "one-to-one" difficulties that have been discussed in some detail by this writer elsewhere [12.9].

Note also that we must do something about the foreign key SP.S# in relation SP that references the old base relation S. It would be nice if that foreign key SP.S# could now be taken as referring to the view S instead; if this is not possible (as indeed it is typically not in today's products), then it would be better to add a third projection of base relation S to the database, as follows:

```
CREATE BASE RELATION SS
     ( S# DOMAIN ( S# ) )
     PRIMARY KEY ( S# ) ;

INSERT S [ S# ] INTO SS ;
```

(In fact, this design is recommended in reference [12.9] for several other reasons anyway.) We now change the definition of view S:

```
CREATE VIEW S AS SS JOIN SNC JOIN ST ;
```

We also add the following foreign key specification to the definitions of relations SNC and ST:

```
FOREIGN KEY ( S# ) REFERENCES SS
                   DELETE CASCADES
                   UPDATE CASCADES
```

Finally, we must change the specification for the foreign key SP.S# in relation SP to refer to relation SS instead of S.

Note: The idea of allowing a foreign key to reference a view instead of a base relation requires further study.

17.14 Here is one example of a view retrieval that certainly does fail in certain products at the time of writing. Consider the following view (Example 4 from Section 17.9):

```
CREATE VIEW PQ AS
       SELECT SP.P#, SUM ( SP.QTY ) AS TOTQTY
       FROM   SP
       GROUP  BY SP.P# ;
```

Consider also the following attempted query:

```
SELECT AVG ( PQ.TOTQTY ) AS PT
FROM   PQ ;
```

If we follow the simple substitution process explained in the body of the chapter (i.e., we try to replace references to the view name by the expression that defines the view), we obtain something like the following:

```
SELECT AVG ( SUM ( SP.QTY ) ) AS PT
FROM   SP
GROUP  BY SP.P# ;
```

And this is not a valid SELECT statement, because SQL does not allow aggregate functions to be nested in this fashion.

Here is another example of a query against the same view PQ that also fails in certain products (for much the same reason):

```
SELECT PQ.P#
FROM   PQ
WHERE  PQ.TOTQTY > 500 ;
```

Precisely because of the problem illustrated by these examples, incidentally, certain products—IBM's DB2 is a case in point—sometimes actually materialize the view (instead of applying the more usual substitution procedure) and then execute the query against that materialized version. This technique will always work, of course, but it is liable to incur a performance penalty. (Moreover, in the case of DB2 in particular, it is still true that some retrievals on some views do not work; i.e., DB2 does not *always* use materialization if substitution does not work, nor is it easy to characterize exactly which cases work and which do not. For instance, the second of the two examples given above still fails in DB2 at the time of writing. See reference [B.7] for further discussion.)

18 | Optimization

18.1 Introduction

Optimization represents both a challenge and an opportunity for relational systems—a challenge, because optimization is *required* in such a system if the system is ever to achieve acceptable performance; an opportunity, because it is precisely one of the strengths of the relational approach that relational expressions are at a sufficiently high semantic level that optimization is feasible in the first place. In a non-relational system, by contrast, where user requests are expressed at a lower semantic level, any "optimization" has to be done manually by the user ("optimization" in quotes, because the term is usually taken to mean *automatic* optimization). In such a system it is the user, not the system, who decides what low-level operations are needed and in what sequence those operations are to be executed—and if the user makes a bad decision, then there is nothing the system can do to improve matters. (Note too the implication that the user in such a system must have some programming expertise. This fact alone puts the system out of reach for many people who could otherwise benefit from it.)

The advantage of system-managed optimization is not just that users do not have to worry about how best to state their queries (i.e., how to phrase requests in order to get the best performance out of the system). The fact is, there is a real possibility that the optimizer might actually do *better* than a human programmer. There are several reasons for this state of affairs, the following among them:

1. A good optimizer—perhaps we should emphasize that "good"!—will have a wealth of information available to it that human programmers typically do not have. To be specific, it will have certain **statistical** information, such as the cardinality of each domain, the cardinality of each base relation, the number of distinct values in each attribute in each base relation, the number of times each distinct value occurs in each such attribute, and so on. (This information will be kept in the system catalog; see Section 18.5.) As a result, the optimizer should be able to make a more accurate assessment of the efficiency of any given strategy for implementing a particular request, and thus be more likely to choose the most efficient implementation.

2. Furthermore, if the database statistics change significantly over time (e.g., if the database is physically reorganized), then a different choice of strategy might become desirable; in other words, **reoptimization** might be required. In a relational system, reoptimization is trivial—it simply involves a reprocessing of the original relational request by the system optimizer. In a nonrelational system, by contrast, reoptimization involves rewriting the program, and will very likely not be done at all.

3. Third, the optimizer is a *program,* and is therefore by definition much more patient than a typical human programmer. The optimizer is quite capable of considering literally hundreds of different implementation strategies for a given request, whereas it is extremely unlikely that a human programmer would ever consider more than three or four (at least in any depth).

4. Fourth, the optimizer can be regarded in a sense as embodying the skills and services of "the best" human programmers. As a consequence, it has the effect of making those skills and services available to *everybody*—which means, of course, that it is making an otherwise scarce set of resources available to a wide range of users, in an efficient and cost-effective manner.

All of the above should serve as evidence in support of the claim at the beginning of this section to the effect that **optimizability**—i.e., the fact that relational requests are optimizable—is in fact a *strength* of relational systems.

The overall purpose of the optimizer, then, is to choose an efficient strategy for evaluating a given relational expression. In this chapter we describe some of the fundamental principles and techniques involved in the optimization process. Following an introductory motivating example in Section 18.2, Section 18.3 gives an overview of how optimizers work, and Section 18.4 then elaborates on one very important aspect of the process, *viz. expression transformation.* Section 18.5 briefly discusses the question (touched on above) of *database statistics.* Next, Section 18.6 describes one specific approach to optimization, called *query decomposition,* in some detail. Section 18.7 then addresses the question of how the relational operators (e.g., join) are actually implemented, and briefly considers the use of the statistics discussed in Section 18.5 to perform cost estimation. Finally, section 18.8 presents a summary of the entire chapter.

One final introductory remark: It is common to refer to this subject as *query* optimization specifically. This term is slightly misleading, however, inasmuch as the expression to be optimized—the "query"—might of course have arisen in some context other than interactive interrogation of the database; in particular, it might be part of an update operation rather than a query *per se.* What is more, the term *optimization* itself is somewhat of an overclaim, since there is usually no guarantee that the implementation strategy chosen is truly *optimal* in any measurable sense; it might in fact be so, but usually all that is known for sure is that the "optimized" strategy is an *improvement* on the original unoptimized version. (In certain rather limited contexts, however, it might be possible to claim legitimately that the chosen strategy is indeed optimal in a certain specific sense. See reference [18.27].)

18.2 An Introductory Example

We begin with a simple example in order to give some idea of the dramatic improvements that can be obtained. (The example is an elaboration of one already discussed briefly in Section 6.7.) The query is "Get names of suppliers who supply part P2." An algebraic expression for this query is:

```
( ( SP JOIN S ) WHERE P# = 'P2' ) [ SNAME ]
```

Suppose the database contains 100 suppliers and 10,000 shipments, of which only 50 are for part P2. Assume for simplicity that relations S and SP are both represented directly on the disk as "stored relations" (see Chapter 4). Then, if the system were simply to evaluate the expression "directly"—i.e., without any optimization at all—the sequence of events would be as follows:

1. **Join relations SP and S (over S#)**. This step involves reading the 10,000 shipments; reading each of the 100 suppliers 10,000 times (once for each of the 10,000 shipments); constructing an intermediate result consisting of 10,000 joined tuples; and writing those 10,000 joined tuples back out to the disk (for the sake of the example, we assume there is no room for this intermediate result relation in main memory).

2. **Restrict the result of Step 1 to just the tuples for part P2**. This step involves reading the 10,000 joined tuples back into memory again, but produces a relation consisting of only 50 tuples, which we assume is small enough to be kept in main memory.

3. **Project the result of Step 2 over SNAME**. This step produces the desired final result (50 tuples at most, which can stay in main memory).

The following procedure is equivalent to the one just described, in the sense that it necessarily produces the same final result, but is clearly much more efficient:

1. **Restrict relation SP to just the tuples for part P2**. This step involves reading 10,000 tuples but produces a relation consisting of only 50 tuples, which we assume will be kept in main memory.

2. **Join the result of Step 1 to relation S (over S#)**. This step involves the retrieval of the 100 suppliers (once only, not once per P2 shipment, because all the P2 shipments are in memory). The result contains 50 tuples (still in main memory).

3. **Project the result of Step 2 over SNAME** (same as Step 3 before). The desired final result (50 tuples at most) stays in main memory.

The first of these two procedures involves a total of 1,030,000 tuple I/O's, whereas the second involves only 10,100. It is clear, therefore, that if we take "number of tuple I/O's" as our performance measure, then the second procedure is a little over 100 times better than the first. (In practice, of course, it is *page* I/O's that matter, not tuple I/O's, but we can ignore this refinement for present purposes.) It is also clear that we would like the implementation to use the second procedure rather than the first!

So we see that a very simple change in the execution algorithm—doing a restriction and then a join, instead of a join and then a restriction—has produced a dramatic improvement in performance. And the improvement would be more dramatic still if relation SP were **indexed** or **hashed** on P#—the number of tuples read in Step 1 would be reduced from 10,000 to just 50, and the new procedure would then be nearly 7,000 times better than the original. Likewise, an index or hash on S.S# would help with Step 2 by reducing the 100 tuple I/O's to 50, so that the procedure would now be over 10,000 times better than the original. What this means is, if the original query took three hours to run, the final version will run in just over *one second*. And of course numerous further improvements are possible.

The foregoing example, simple though it is, should be sufficient to give some idea as to why optimization is necessary. It should also give some idea of the kinds of improvement that might be possible in practice. In the next section, we will present an overview of a systematic approach to the optimization problem; in particular, we will show how the overall problem can be divided into a number of more or less independent subproblems. That overview provides a convenient framework within which individual optimization strategies and techniques such as those discussed in later sections can be explained and understood.

18.3 The Optimization Process: An Overview

Following reference [18.3], we identify four broad stages in the overall optimization process, as follows:

1. Cast the query into some internal form
2. Convert to canonical form
3. Choose candidate low-level procedures
4. Generate query plans and choose the cheapest

We now proceed to amplify each of these four stages.

Stage 1: Cast the Query into Some Internal Form

The first stage involves the conversion of the original query into some internal representation that is more suitable for machine manipulation, thus eliminating purely external-level considerations (such as quirks of the concrete syntax of the query language under consideration) and paving the way for subsequent stages of the optimization process.

The obvious question is: What formalism should the internal representation be based on? Whatever formalism is chosen, it must of course be rich enough to represent all possible queries in the system's query language. It should also be as neutral as possible, in the sense that it should not prejudice any subsequent optimization choices. The internal form that is typically chosen is some kind of **abstract syntax tree** or **query tree**. For example, Fig. 18.1 (opposite) shows a possible query tree representation for the example from Section 18.2 ("Names of suppliers who supply part P2").

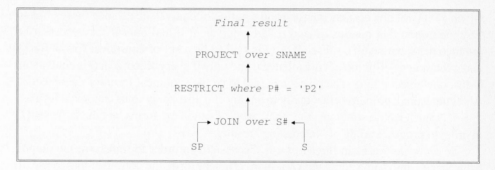

FIG. 18.1   Query tree for "Names of suppliers who supply part P2"

For our purposes, however, it is more convenient to assume that the internal representation employs one of the formalisms we are already familiar with—namely, the relational algebra or the relational calculus. A query tree such as that of Fig. 18.1 can be regarded as just an alternative, encoded representation of some expression in one of those two formalisms. To fix our ideas, we assume here that the formalism is the algebra specifically. Thus, we will assume henceforth that the internal representation of the query of Fig. 18.1 is precisely the algebraic expression shown earlier:

```
( ( SP JOIN S ) WHERE P# = 'P2' ) [ SNAME ]
```

Stage 2: Convert to Canonical Form

In this stage, the optimizer performs a number of optimizations that are "guaranteed to be good," regardless of the actual data values and access paths that exist in the stored database. The point is, relational languages typically allow all but the simplest of queries to be expressed in a variety of ways that are at least superficially distinct. In SQL, for example, even a query as simple as "Get names of suppliers who supply part P2" can be expressed in literally dozens of different ways*—not including trivial variations like replacing the condition $A = B$ by the condition $B = A$ or the condition p AND q by the condition q AND p (see Exercise 8.9 in Chapter 8). And the performance of a query really ought not to depend on the particular way the user chose to write it. The next step in processing the query is therefore to convert the internal representation into some equivalent **canonical form** (see below), with the objective of eliminating such superficial distinctions and—more important—finding a representation that is more efficient than the original in some respect.

A note regarding "canonical form": The notion of canonical form is central to many branches of mathematics and related disciplines. It can be defined as follows.

---

* We should point out, however, that the SQL language is exceptionally prone to this problem. Other languages (e.g., the algebra or the calculus) typically do not provide quite so many different ways of doing the same thing. This unnecessary "flexibility" on the part of SQL actually makes life harder for the *implementer*—not to mention the user—because it makes the optimizer's job more difficult.

Given a set Q of objects (say queries) and a notion of equivalence among those objects (say the notion that queries $q1$ and $q2$ are equivalent if and only if they necessarily produce the same result), subset C of Q is said to be a **set of canonical forms** for Q under the stated definition of equivalence if and only if every object q in Q is equivalent to just one object c in C. The object c is said to be the canonical form for the object q. All "interesting" properties that apply to an object q also apply to its canonical form c; thus it is sufficient to study just the small set C of canonical forms, not the large set Q, in order to prove a variety of "interesting" results.

To revert to the main thread of our discussion: In order to transform the output from Stage 1 into some equivalent but more efficient form, the optimizer makes use of certain well-defined **transformation rules** or **laws**. Here is an example of such a rule:

The expression

```
( A JOIN B ) WHERE restriction-on-A
```

can be transformed into the equivalent but more efficient expression

```
( A WHERE restriction-on-A ) JOIN B
```

We have already discussed this transformation briefly in Chapter 6 (Section 6.7); in fact, of course, it was the one we were using in our introductory example in Section 18.2, and that example showed clearly why such a transformation is desirable. Many more transformation rules are discussed in Section 18.4.

Stage 3: Choose Candidate Low-Level Procedures

Having converted the internal representation of the query into some more desirable (canonical) form, the optimizer must then decide how to execute the transformed query represented by that converted form. At this stage such considerations as the existence of indexes or other access paths, distribution of stored data values, physical clustering of stored data, etc., come into play. Note that we paid no heed to such matters in Stages 1 and 2 above.

The basic strategy is to consider the query expression as specifying a series of **"low-level" operations** (join, restriction, etc.), with certain interdependencies among them. An example of such an interdependency is the following: The code to perform a *projection* will typically require its input tuples to be in a certain sequence, to allow it to perform duplicate elimination, which means that the immediately preceding operation in the series must produce its output tuples in that same sequence.

Now, for each possible low-level operation, the optimizer will have available to it a set of predefined **implementation procedures**. For example, there will be a set of procedures for implementing the restriction operation—one for the case where the restriction is an equality condition on a candidate key, one where the restriction attribute is indexed, one where it is not indexed but the data is physically clustered on the restriction attribute, and so on. Examples of such procedures are given in Section 18.7 (see also references [18.4–18.14]).

Note: Each procedure will also have a (parameterized) **cost formula** associated with it, indicating the cost—typically in terms of disk I/O's, though some systems do take processor utilization and other factors into account also—of executing that procedure. These cost formulas are used in Stage 4 (see below). References [18.4–18.14] discuss and analyze the cost formulas for a number of different implementation procedures under a variety of different assumptions. See also Section 18.7.

Next, therefore, using information from the catalog regarding the current state of the database (existence of indexes, cardinalities of relations, etc.), and using also the interdependency information referred to above, the optimizer will choose one or more candidate procedures for implementing each of the low-level operations in the query expression. This process is sometimes referred to as **access path selection**. (See references [18.29–18.30]. Note, however, that in those papers the term is used to cover both Stage 3 and Stage 4, as we define those two stages here. Indeed, it might be difficult in practice to make a clean separation between the two; Stage 3 does flow more or less seamlessly into Stage 4.)

Stage 4: Generate Query Plans and Choose the Cheapest

The final stage in the optimization process involves the construction of a set of candidate **query plans,** followed by a choice of the best (i.e., cheapest) of those plans. Each query plan is built by combining together a set of candidate implementation procedures, one such procedure for each of the low-level operations in the query. Note that there will normally be many possible plans—probably embarrassingly many—for any given query. In fact, it might not be a good idea to generate all possible plans, since there will be combinatorially many of them, and the task of choosing the cheapest might well become prohibitively expensive in itself;* some heuristic technique for keeping the generated set within reasonable bounds is highly desirable, if not essential [18.3]. "Keeping the set within bounds" is usually referred to as *reducing the search space,* because it can be regarded as reducing the range ("space") of possibilities to be examined ("searched") by the optimizer to manageable proportions.

Choosing the cheapest plan naturally requires a method for assigning a cost to any given plan. Basically, of course, the cost for a given plan is just the sum of the costs of the individual procedures that go to make up that plan, so what the optimizer has to do is evaluate the cost formulas for those individual procedures. The problem is, those cost formulas will depend on the size of the relation(s) to be processed; since all but the simplest queries involve the generation of intermediate results during execution, the optimizer will have to estimate the size of those intermediate results in order to evaluate the formulas. Unfortunately, those sizes tend to be highly dependent on actual data values. As a consequence, accurate cost estimation can be a difficult problem. Reference [18.3] discusses some approaches to that problem and gives references to other research in the area.

---

* This is less of a consideration (though still not negligible) in a system like DB2 that does its optimization at compilation time rather than run time, as described in Appendix B.

18.4   Expression Transformation

In this section we present an introduction to some of the various transformation rules that might be useful in Stage 2 of the optimization process. Producing examples to illustrate the rules and deciding exactly why they might be useful are both left (in part) as exercises for the reader.

Of course, the reader should understand that, given a particular expression to transform, the application of one rule might generate an expression that is susceptible to transformation in accordance with some other rule. For example, it is unlikely that the original query will have been directly expressed in such a way as to require two successive projections—see item 2 under "Restrictions and Projections" below—but such an expression might arise internally as the result of applying certain other transformations. (An important case in point is provided by **view processing;** consider, for example, the query "Get all cities in view V," where view V is defined as the projection of relation S on S# and CITY.) In other words, starting from the original expression, the optimizer will apply its transformation rules repeatedly until it finally arrives at an expression that it judges—according to some builtin set of heuristics—to be "optimal" for the query under consideration.

Restrictions and Projections

We begin with some transformations involving restrictions and projections only.

1. A sequence of restrictions against a given relation can be transformed into a single ("ANDed") restriction against that relation; e.g., the expression

   ```
   ( A WHERE restriction-1 ) WHERE restriction-2
   ```

   is equivalent to the expression

   ```
   A WHERE restriction-1 AND restriction-2
   ```

2. In a sequence of projections against a given relation, all but the last can be ignored; e.g., the expression

   ```
   ( A [ projection-1 ] ) [ projection-2 ]
   ```

   is equivalent to the expression

   ```
   A [ projection-2 ]
   ```

   Of course, every attribute mentioned in *projection-2* must also be mentioned in *projection-1* for the first expression to make sense.

3. A restriction of a projection can be transformed into a projection of a restriction; e.g., the expression

   ```
   ( A [ projection ] ) WHERE restriction
   ```

   is equivalent to the expression

   ```
   ( A WHERE restriction ) [ projection ]
   ```

Note that it is generally a good idea to do restrictions before projections, because the effect of the restriction will be to reduce the size of the input to the projection, and hence to reduce the amount of data that might need to be sorted for duplicate elimination purposes in doing the projection.

Distributivity

The transformation rule used in the example in Section 18.2 (transforming a join followed by a restriction into a restriction followed by a join) is actually a special case of a more general law, called the *distributive* law. In general, the monadic operator *f* is said to **distribute** over the dyadic operator $\bigcirc$ if

```
f ( A O B )  ≡  f ( A ) O f ( B )
```

for all *A* and *B*. In ordinary arithmetic, for example, SQRT (square root) distributes over multiplication, because

```
SQRT ( A * B )  ≡  SQRT ( A ) * SQRT ( B )
```

for all *A* and *B*. Therefore an arithmetic expression optimizer can always replace either of these expressions by the other when doing arithmetic expression transformation. As a counterexample, SQRT does *not* distribute over addition, because the square root of $A + B$ is not equal to the sum of the square roots of *A* and *B,* in general.

In relational algebra, the **restriction** operator distributes over **union, intersection,** and **difference**. It also distributes over **join,** provided the restriction condition consists, at its most complex, of two separate restriction conditions ANDed together, one for each of the two join operands. In the case of the example in Section 18.2, this requirement was indeed satisfied—in fact, the condition was very simple and applied to just one of the operands—and so we could use the distributive law to replace the expression by a more efficient equivalent. The net effect was that we were able to "do the restriction early." Doing restrictions early is almost always a good idea, because it serves to reduce the number of tuples to be scanned in the next operation in sequence, and probably reduces the number of tuples in the output from that next operation too.

Here are a couple more specific cases of the distributive law, this time involving **projection**. First, the project operator distributes over **union** and **intersection** (but not **difference**). Second, it also distributes over **join,** so long as all of the join attributes are included in the projection; more precisely, the expression

```
( A JOIN B ) [ projection ]
```

is equivalent to the expression

```
( A [ A-projection ] ) JOIN ( B [ B-projection ] )
```

if and only if the set of attributes named in *projection* is (a) equal to the union of the sets of attributes named in *A-projection* and *B-projection,* and (b) includes all of the joining attributes. These laws can be used to "do projections early," which again is usually a good idea, for reasons similar to those given above for restrictions.

Commutativity and Associativity

Two more important general laws are the laws of *commutativity* and *associativity*. First, the dyadic operator $\bigcirc$ is said to be **commutative** if

```
A ◯ B  ≡  B ◯ A
```

for all *A* and *B*. In ordinary arithmetic, for example, multiplication and addition are commutative, but division and subtraction are not. In relational algebra, **union, inter-section,** and **join** are all commutative, but **difference** and **division** are not. So, for example, if a query involves a join of two relations *A* and *B*, the commutative law implies that it makes no difference which of *A* and *B* is taken as the "outer" relation and which the "inner." The system is therefore free to choose (say) the smaller relation as the "outer" one in computing the join (see Section 18.7).

Turning to associativity: The dyadic operator $\bigcirc$ is said to be **associative** if

```
A ◯ ( B ◯ C )  ≡  ( A ◯ B ) ◯ C
```

for all *A, B, C*. In arithmetic, multiplication and addition are associative, but division and subtraction are not. In relational algebra, **union, intersection,** and **join** are all as-sociative, but **difference** and **division** are not. So, for example, if a query involves a join of three relations *A, B,* and *C*, the associative and commutative laws together imply that it makes no difference in which order the relations are joined. The system is thus free to decide which of the various possible sequences is most efficient.

Idempotence

Another important general law is the law of *idempotence*. The dyadic operator $\bigcirc$ is said to be **idempotent** if

```
A ◯ A  ≡  A
```

for all *A*. As might be expected, the idempotence property can also be useful in expres-sion transformation. In relational algebra, **union, intersection,** and **join** are all idempo-tent, but **difference** and **division** are not.

Scalar Computational Expressions

It is not just relational expressions that are subject to transformation laws. For instance, we have already indicated that certain transformations are valid for *arithmetic* expres-sions. Here is a specific example: The expression

```
A * B + A * C
```

can be transformed into

```
A * ( B + C )
```

by virtue of the fact that "*" distributes over "+". A relational optimizer needs to know about such transformations because it will encounter computational expressions in the context of the **extend** and **summarize** operators.

Note, incidentally, that this example illustrates a slightly more general form of distributivity. Earlier, we defined distributivity in terms of a *monadic* operator distributing over a *dyadic* operator; in the case at hand, however, "*" and "+" are both *dyadic* operators. In general, the dyadic operator $\bigcirc$ is said to **distribute** over the dyadic operator $\circledast$ if

```
A ✳ ( B ○ C )  ≡  ( A ✳ B ) ○ ( A ✳ C )
```

for all *A*, *B*, *C* (in the arithmetic example above, take $\circledast$ as "*" and $\bigcirc$ as "+").

Conditional Expressions

We turn now to *conditional* or *truth-valued* expressions. Suppose *A* and *B* are attributes of two distinct relations. Then the truth-valued expression

```
A > B AND B > 3
```

(which might be part of a query) is clearly equivalent to—and can therefore be transformed into—the following:

```
A > B AND B > 3 AND A > 3
```

The equivalence is based on the fact that the comparison operator ">" is **transitive**. Note that this transformation is certainly worth making, because it enables the system to perform an additional restriction (using the condition "*A* > 3") before doing the greater-than join required by the condition "*A* > *B*". To repeat a point made previously, doing restrictions early is generally a good idea; having the system **infer** additional "early" restrictions, as here, is also a good idea. *Note:* This technique is implemented in several commercial products, including in particular DB2, where it is called *predicate transitive closure.*

Here is another example: The conditional expression

```
A > B OR ( C = D AND E < F )
```

can be transformed into

```
( A > B OR C = D ) AND ( A > B OR E < F )
```

by virtue of the fact that OR distributes over AND. This example illustrates another general law, *viz.*: Any conditional expression can be transformed into an equivalent expression in what is called **conjunctive normal form** (CNF). A CNF expression is an expression of the form

```
C1 AND C2 AND ... AND Cn
```

where each of *C1*, *C2*, . . . , *Cn* is, in turn, a conditional expression (called a **conjunct**) that involves no ANDs. The advantage of CNF is that a CNF expression is *true* only if every conjunct is *true;* equivalently, it is *false* if any conjunct is *false.* Since AND is commutative (*A* AND *B* is the same as *B* AND *A*), the optimizer can evaluate the individual conjuncts in any order it likes; in particular, it can do them in order of increasing difficulty (easiest first). As soon as it finds one that is *false,* the whole process can stop.

Furthermore, in a parallel processing environment, it might even be possible to evaluate all of the conjuncts in parallel. Again, as soon as one conjunct yields *false,* the whole process can stop.

It follows from this subsection and its predecessor that the optimizer needs to know how general properties such as distributivity apply not only to **relational** operators such as join, but also to **comparison** operators such as ">"; **logical** operators such as AND and OR; **arithmetic** operators such as "+"; and so on.

Semantic Transformations

Consider the following expression:

```
( SP JOIN S ) [ P# ]
```

The join here is a *foreign-to-matching-candidate-key join;* it matches a foreign key in relation SP with a corresponding candidate key in relation S. It follows that every tuple of relation SP does join to some tuple in relation S;* every tuple of relation SP therefore does contribute a P# value to the overall result. In other words, there is no need to do the join!—the expression can be simplified to just

```
SP [ P# ]
```

Note carefully, however, that this transformation is valid *only* because of the semantics of the situation. In general, each of the operands in a join will include some tuples that have no counterpart in the other operand, and hence some tuples that do not contribute to the overall result. In general, therefore, transformations such as the one just illustrated are not valid. In the case at hand, however, every tuple of relation SP *must* have a counterpart in relation S, because of the integrity constraint (actually a referential constraint) that says that every shipment must have a supplier, and so the transformation is valid after all.

A transformation that is valid only because a certain integrity constraint is in force is called a **semantic transformation** [18.23], and the resulting optimization is called a **semantic optimization**. Semantic optimization can be defined as the process of transforming a specified query into another, qualitatively different, query that is however guaranteed to produce the same result as the original one, thanks to the fact that the data is guaranteed to satisfy a certain integrity constraint.

It is important to understand that, in principle, *any integrity constraint whatsoever* can be used in semantic optimization (provided only that the constraint in question is immediate, not deferred—see Chapter 16). In other words, the technique is not limited just to referential constraints. Suppose, for example, that the suppliers-and-parts database is subject to the constraint "All red parts must be stored in London," and consider the query:

Find suppliers who supply only red parts and are located in the same city as at least one of the parts they supply.

---

* We ignore the possibility that the foreign key might have "nulls allowed."

This is a fairly complex query! By virtue of the integrity constraint, however, it can be transformed into the much simpler form:

Find London suppliers who supply only red parts.

Note: Many semantic transformations rely on a knowledge of functional dependencies and candidate keys. Once again, Darwen's work on such matters is relevant [14.7].

So far as this writer is aware, few commercial products currently do much in the way of semantic optimization. In principle, however, such optimization could provide very significant performance improvements—much greater improvements, very likely, than are obtained by any of today's more traditional optimization techniques. For further discussion of the semantic optimization idea, see references [18.24–18.28] and (especially) [18.23].

Concluding Remarks

In closing this section, we emphasize the fundamental importance of **closure** to everything we have been discussing. Closure means that we can write nested expressions, which means in turn that a single query can be represented by a single expression instead of a multi-statement procedure; thus, no flow analysis is necessary. Also, those nested expressions are recursively defined in terms of sub-expressions, which permits the optimizer to adopt a variety of "divide and conquer" evaluation tactics (see Section 18.6 below). And, of course, the various general laws (distributivity, etc.) would not even begin to make sense if we did not have the closure property.

18.5 Database Statistics

Stages 3 and 4 of the overall optimization process—the "access path selection" stages—make use of the so-called **database statistics** stored in the catalog (see Section 18.7 for a brief discussion of how those statistics are used). For purposes of illustration, we summarize below (with little further comment) some of the major statistics maintained by two commercial products, *viz.* DB2 and INGRES. Here first are some of the principal statistics kept by DB2:*

■ For each *base table:*
  ▪ cardinality
  ▪ number of pages occupied by this table
  ▪ fraction of table space occupied by this table

---

* Since they are SQL systems, both DB2 and INGRES use the terms table and column in place of relation and attribute. Also, note that they both effectively map one base table to one stored table.

- For each *column* of each base table:
  - number of distinct values in this column
  - second highest value in this column
  - second lowest value in this column
  - (for indexed columns only) the ten most frequently occurring values in this column and the number of times they occur
- For each *index:*
  - an indication of whether this is a "clustering index" (see Appendixes A and B)
  - if so, fraction of indexed table still in clustering sequence
  - number of leaf pages in this index
  - number of levels in this index

Note: The foregoing statistics are not updated every time the database is updated, because of the overhead such an approach would entail. Instead, they are updated, selectively, by means of a special system utility called RUNSTATS, which is executed on demand by the DBA—e.g., after a database reorganization (see Appendix B). An analogous remark applies to most other systems, including in particular INGRES (see below), where the utility is called OPTIMIZEDB.

Here then are some of the principal INGRES statistics. *Note:* In INGRES, an index is regarded as just a special kind of stored table. Thus, the statistics shown below for base tables and columns can be gathered for indexes too.

- For each *base table:*
  - cardinality
  - number of primary pages for this table
  - number of overflow pages for this table
- For each *column* of each base table:
  - number of distinct values in this column
  - maximum, minimum, and average value for this column
  - actual values in this column and their frequencies (a histogram)

18.6 A Divide and Conquer Strategy

As mentioned at the end of Section 18.4, relational expressions are recursively defined in terms of subexpressions, and this fact allows the optimizer to adopt a variety of "divide and conquer" strategies. Note that such strategies are likely to be especially attractive in a parallel processing environment—in particular, in a distributed database system—where different portions of the query can be executed in parallel on different processors. In this section we examine one such strategy, called **query decomposition,** which was pioneered by the INGRES prototype [18.31–18.32]. *Note:* Further information on optimization in INGRES (more specifically in the INGRES product, which is somewhat different from the INGRES prototype in this area) can be found in a paper by Kooi and Frankforth in reference [18.2]. See also reference [18.34].

The basic idea behind query decomposition is to break a query that involves many tuple variables down into a sequence of smaller queries involving (typically) one or two such variables each, using *detachment* and *tuple substitution* to achieve the desired decomposition:

- **Detachment** is the process of removing a component of the query that has just one variable in common with the rest of the query.

- **Tuple substitution** is the process of substituting for one of the variables in the query a tuple at a time.

Detachment is always applied in preference to tuple substitution so long as there is a choice (see example below). Eventually, however, the query will have been decomposed via detachment into a set of components that cannot be decomposed any further using that technique, and tuple substitution must be brought into play.

We give a single example of the decomposition process (based on an example from reference [18.31]). The query is "Get names of London suppliers who supply some red part weighing less than 25 pounds in a quantity greater than 200." Here is a QUEL formulation, which we refer to as query Q0:

```
Q0:   RETRIEVE (S.SNAME) WHERE S.CITY    = "London"
                         AND   S.S#      = SP.S#
                         AND   SP.QTY    > 200
                         AND   SP.P#     = P.P#
                         AND   P.COLOR   = "Red"
                         AND   P.WEIGHT < 25
```

The tuple variables here are S, P, and SP, each one ranging over the base relation with the same name.

Now, if we examine this query, we can see immediately from the last two comparison terms that the only parts we are interested in are parts that are red and weigh less than 25 pounds. So we can detach the "one-variable query" (actually a projection of a restriction) involving the variable P:

```
D1:   RETRIEVE INTO P' (P.P#) WHERE P.COLOR  = "Red"
                              AND    P.WEIGHT < 25
```

This one-variable query is detachable because it has just one variable, namely P itself, in common with the rest of the query. Since it links up to the rest of the original query via the attribute P# (in the comparison term SP.P# = P.P#), attribute P# is what must appear in the target commalist in the detached version; that is, the detached query must retrieve exactly the part numbers of red parts weighing less than 25 pounds. We save that detached query as a query D1 that retrieves its result into a temporary relation P' (the effect of the INTO clause is to cause a new relation P', with sole attribute P#, to be created automatically to hold the result of executing the RETRIEVE). Finally, we replace references to P in the reduced version of Q0 by references to P′. Let us refer to this new reduced query as query Q1:

```
Q1:   RETRIEVE (S.SNAME) WHERE  S.CITY = "London"
                         AND    S.S#   = SP.S#
                         AND    SP.QTY > 200
                         AND    SP.P#  = P'.P#
```

We now perform a similar process of detachment on query Q1, detaching the one-variable query involving variable SP as query D2 and leaving a modified version of Q1 (query Q2):

```
D2:   RETRIEVE INTO SP' (SP.S#, SP.P#) WHERE SP.QTY > 200

Q2:   RETRIEVE (S.SNAME) WHERE  S.CITY = "London"
                         AND    S.S#   = SP'.S#
                         AND    SP'.P# = P'.P#
```

Next we detach the one-variable query involving S:

```
D3:   RETRIEVE INTO S' (S.S#, S.SNAME) WHERE S.CITY = "London"

Q3:   RETRIEVE (S'.SNAME) WHERE  S'.S#  = SP'.S#
                          AND    SP'.P# = P'.P#
```

Finally we detach the two-variable query involving SP′ and P′:

```
D4:   RETRIEVE INTO SP'' (SP'.S#) WHERE SP'.P# = P'.P#

Q4:   RETRIEVE (S'.SNAME) WHERE S'.S# = SP''.S#
```

Thus, the original query Q0 has been decomposed into three one-variable queries D1, D2, and D3 (each of which is a projection of a restriction) and two two-variable queries D4 and Q4 (each of which is a projection of a join). We can represent the situation at this point by means of the tree structure shown in Fig. 18.2. That figure is meant to be read as follows:

- Queries D1, D2, and D3 take as input relations P, SP, and S respectively, and produce as output relations P′, SP′, and S′ respectively.

- Query D4 then takes as input relations P′ and SP′ and produces as output relation SP″.

- Finally, query Q4 takes as input relations S′ and SP″ and produces as output the overall required result.

Observe that queries D1, D2, and D3 are completely independent of one another and can be processed in any order (conceivably even in parallel). Likewise, queries D3 and D4 can be processed in any order once queries D1 and D2 have been processed. However, queries D4 and Q4 cannot be decomposed any further and must be processed by tuple substitution (which is really just the INGRES term for *brute force, index lookup,* or *hash lookup*—see Section 18.7). For example, consider query Q4. With our usual sample data, the set of supplier numbers in attribute SP″.S# will be the set

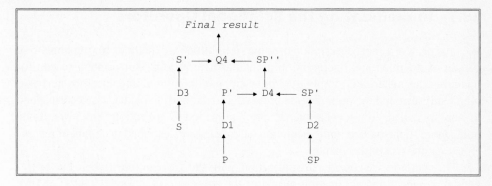

FIG. 18.2 Decomposition tree for query Q0

{S1,S2,S4}. Each of these three values will be substituted for SP″.S# in turn. Q4 will therefore be evaluated as if it had been written as follows:

```
RETRIEVE (S'.SNAME) WHERE S'.S# = "S1"
                    OR    S'.S# = "S2"
                    OR    S'.S# = "S4"
```

Reference [18.31] gives algorithms for breaking the original query down into irreducible components and for choosing the variable for tuple substitution. It is in that latter choice that much of the actual optimization resides; the paper [18.31] includes heuristics for making the cost estimates that drive the choice (INGRES will usually—but not always—try to choose the relation with the smallest cardinality as the one to do the substitution on). The principal objectives of the optimization process as a whole are to avoid having to build Cartesian products and to keep the number of tuples to be scanned to a minimum at each stage.

Reference [18.31] does not discuss the optimization of one-variable queries. However, information regarding that level of optimization is provided in the INGRES overview paper [8.13]. Basically it is similar to the analogous function in other systems, involving as it does the use of statistical information kept in the catalog and the choice of a particular access path (e.g., a hash or index) for scanning the relation.

Reference [18.32] presents some experimental evidence—namely, measurements from a benchmark set of queries—that suggests that the optimization techniques described above are basically sound and in practice quite effective. Some specific conclusions from that paper are the following:

1. Detachment is the best first move.

2. If tuple substitution *must* be done first, then the best choice of variable to be substituted for is a joining variable.

3. Once tuple substitution has been applied to one variable in a two-variable query, it is an excellent tactic to build an index or hash "on the fly" (if necessary) on the join attribute in the other relation. INGRES in fact often applies this tactic.

18.7   Implementing the Relational Operators

We now present a short description of some straightforward methods for implementing certain of the relational operators, in particular natural join. Our primary reason for including this material is simply to remove any possible remaining air of mystery that might still surround the optimization process. The methods to be discussed correspond to what we called "low-level implementation procedures" in Section 18.3. *Note:* Some much more sophisticated implementation techniques are described in certain of the references at the end of the chapter.

The operators we consider are projection, join, and aggregation—where by "aggregation" we mean the application of one of the aggregate functions (COUNT, SUM, MAX, etc.). There are two principal kinds of aggregation to consider:

1. Aggregation by no attributes

2. Aggregation by at least one attribute

Case 1 is straightforward: Basically, it involves scanning the entire relation over which the aggregation is to be done—except that, if the attribute to be aggregated happens to be indexed, it might be possible to compute the result directly from the index, without having to access the relation itself at all [18.30]. For example, the query

```
SUMMARIZE SP BY ( ) ADD AVG ( QTY ) AS AQ
```

can be answered by scanning the QTY index (assuming such an index exists) without touching relation SP at all. An analogous remark applies if AVG is replaced by COUNT or SUM (for COUNT, any index will do). As for MAX and MIN, the result can be found in *a single access* to the last index entry (for MAX) or the first (for MIN), assuming again that an index exists for the relevant attribute.

For the rest of this section we take "aggregation" to mean Case 2 specifically. Here is an example of Case 2:

```
SUMMARIZE SP BY ( P# ) ADD SUM ( QTY ) AS TOTQTY
```

From the user's point of view, projection, join, and Case 2 aggregation are of course very different from one another. From an implementation point of view, however, they do have certain similarities, because in every case the system needs to group tuples together on the basis of values of some attribute or attribute combination. In the case of projection, such grouping allows the system to eliminate duplicates; in the case of join, it allows it to find matching tuples; and in the case of aggregation, it allows it to compute the individual (i.e., per group) aggregate values. There are several techniques for performing such grouping:

1. Brute force

2. Index lookup

3. Hash lookup

4. Merge

5. Hash

6. Combinations of the above

   Figs. 18.3–18.7 give pseudocode procedures for the case of join specifically (projection and aggregation are left as exercises for the reader). The notation used in those figures is as follows. First, R and S are the relations—specifically, *stored* relations—to be joined, and C is their (possibly composite) common attribute. We assume that it is possible to access the tuples of each of R and S one at a time in some sequence, and we denote those tuples, in their access sequence, by $R[1]$, $R[2]$, ..., $R[m]$ and $S[1]$, $S[2]$, ..., $S[n]$, respectively. We use the expression $R[i] * S[j]$ to denote the joined tuple formed from the tuples $R[i]$ and $S[j]$. Finally, we refer to R as the **outer** relation and S as the **inner** relation (as Fig. 18.3 suggests).

Brute Force

Brute force is what might be called the "plain" case, in which all possible tuple combinations are inspected (i.e., every tuple of R is examined in conjunction with every tuple of S, as indicated in Fig. 18.3). *Note:* Brute force is often referred to as "nested loops," but this name is misleading, inasmuch as nested loops are in fact involved in all of the algorithms.

```
do i  := 1 to m ;                          /* outer loop */
   do j  := 1 to n ;                        /* inner loop */
      if R[i].C = S[j].C then
      add joined tuple R[i] * S[j] to result ;
   end ;
end ;
```

FIG. 18.3 Brute force

   Let us examine the costs associated with the brute force approach. First of all, the approach clearly requires a total of $m * n$ tuple read operations; but what about tuple writes?—i.e., what is the cardinality of the joined result? (The number of tuple writes will be equal to that cardinality if the result has to be written back out to the disk.)

- In the important special case of a many-to-one (i.e., foreign-to-matching-candidate-key) join, the cardinality of the result is clearly equal to (at most) the cardinality—*viz.*, m or n—of whichever of R and S represents the foreign key side of the join.

- Now consider the more general case of a many-to-many join. Let dCR be the number of distinct values of the join attribute C in relation R, and let dCS be defined analogously. If we assume *uniform distribution* of values (so that any given value of C is as likely to occur as any other), then for a given tuple of R there will be n/dCS tuples of S with the same value for C as that tuple; hence the total number of tuples in the join (i.e., the cardinality of the result) will be $(m * n)/dCS$. Or, if we start by considering a given tuple of S instead of R, the total number will be $(n * m)/dCR$; the two estimates will differ if $dCR \neq dCS$, i.e., if there are some values of C that occur in R but not in S or *vice versa*, in which case the lower estimate is the one to use.

In practice, of course, as stated in Section 18.2, it is *page* I/O's that matter, not tuple I/O's. Suppose, therefore, that the tuples of R and S are stored pR to a page and pS to a page, respectively (so that the two relations occupy m/pR pages and n/pS pages, respectively). Then it is easy to see that the procedure of Fig. 18.3 will involve (m/pR) + $(m * n)/pS$ page reads. Alternatively, if we interchange the roles of R and S (making S the outer relation and R the inner), the number of page reads will be (n/pS) + $(n * m)/pR$.

By way of example, suppose $m = 100$, $n = 10,000$, $pR = 1$, $pS = 10$. Then the two formulas evaluate to 100,100 and 1,001,000 page reads, respectively. *Conclusion:* It is desirable in the brute force approach for the smaller relation of the two to be chosen as the outer relation (where "smaller" means smaller number of pages).

We conclude this brief discussion of the brute force technique by observing that brute force should be regarded as a worst-case procedure; it assumes that relation S is neither indexed nor hashed on the join attribute C. Experiments by Bitton *et al.* [18.12] indicate that, if that assumption is in fact valid, matters will usually be improved by constructing such an index or hash dynamically and then proceeding with an index or hash lookup join (see the next two subsections). Reference [18.32] supports this idea, as mentioned at the end of the previous section.

Index Lookup

We now consider the case in which there is an index X on attribute $S.C$ of the inner relation (refer to Fig. 18.4). The advantage of this technique over brute force is that for a given tuple of the outer relation R we can go "directly" (via the index X) to the matching tuples of the inner relation S. The total number of tuple reads to relations R and S is thus simply the cardinality of the joined result (see "Brute force" above); the total num-

```
/* assume index X on S.C */

do i := 1 to m ;                              /* outer loop */
    /* let there be k index entries X[1], ..., X[k] with    */
    /* indexed attribute value = R[i].C                      */
    do j := 1 to k ;                          /* inner loop */
        /* let tuple of S indexed by X[j] be S[j] */
        add joined tuple R[i] * S[j] to result ;
    end ;
end ;
```

FIG. 18.4 Index lookup

ber of page reads to R and S is $(m/pR) + (mn/dCS)$, making the worst-case assumption that every tuple read to S is in fact a separate page read.

If relation S happens to be stored in sequence by values of the join attribute C, however, the page read figure reduces to $(m/pR) + (mn/dCS)/pS$. Taking the same sample values as before ($m = 100$, $n = 10,000$, $pR = 1$, $pS = 10$), and assuming $dCS = 100$, the two formulas evaluate to 10,100 and 200, respectively. The difference between these two figures clearly points up the advantage of keeping stored relations in a "good" physical sequence.

However, we must of course include the overhead for accessing the index X itself. The worst-case assumption is that each tuple of R requires an "out of the blue" index lookup to find the matching tuples of S, which implies reading one page from each level of the index. For an index of l levels, this will add an extra ml page reads to the overall page read figure. In practice, l will typically be 3 or less (moreover, the top level of the index will very likely reside in a main memory buffer throughout processing, thereby reducing the page read figure still further).

Hash Lookup

Hash lookup is similar to index lookup, except that the "fast access path" to the inner relation S on the join attribute $S.C$ is a hash instead of an index (refer to Fig. 18.5). Derivation of cost estimates for this case is left as an exercise for the reader.

```
/* assume hash table H on S.C */

do i := 1 to m ;                          /* outer loop */
   k := hash (R[i].C) ;
   /* let there be h tuples S[1], ..., S[h] stored at H[k] */
   do j := 1 to h ;                       /* inner loop */
      if S[j].C = R[i].C then
      add joined tuple R[i] * S[j] to result ;
   end ;
end ;
```

FIG. 18.5 Hash lookup

Merge

The merge technique assumes that the two relations R and S are both physically stored in sequence by values of the join attribute C. If such is in fact the case, the two relations can be scanned in physical sequence, the two scans can be synchronized, and the entire join can be done in a single pass over the data (refer to Fig. 18.6). Such a technique is unquestionably optimal, because every page is touched just once (at least, this is true if the join is one-to-many; it might not be quite true for the many-to-many case). In other words, the number of page reads is just $(m/pR) + (n/pS))$. It follows that:

```
/* assume R and S are both sorted on attribute C ; */
/* following code assumes join is many-to-many ;   */
/* simpler many-to-one case left as an exercise    */

r := 1 ;
s := 1 ;
do while r ≤ m and s ≤ n ;                    /* outer loop */
   v := R[r].C ;
   do j := s by 1 while S[j].C < v ;
   end ;
   s := j ;
   do j := s by 1 while S[j].C = v ;    /* main inner loop */
      do i := r by 1 while R[i].C = v ;
         add joined tuple R[i] * S[j] to result ;
      end ;
   end ;
   s := j ;
   do i := r by 1 while R[i].C = v ;
   end ;
   r := i ;
end ;
```

FIG. 18.6 Merge (many-to-many case)

- Physical clustering of logically related data is one of the most critical performance factors of all; i.e., it is highly desirable that data be clustered in such a way as to match the joins that are most important to the enterprise [18.6].

- In the absence of such clustering, it is often a good idea to sort either or both relations at run time and then do a merge join anyway (of course, the effect of such sorting is precisely to produce the desired clustering dynamically). This technique is referred to (logically enough) as **sort/merge** [18.7].

See reference [18.30] for further discussion.

Hash

Like the merge technique just discussed, the hash technique requires a single pass over each of the two relations (refer to Fig. 18.7). The first pass builds a hash table for relation S on values of the join attribute $S.C$; the entries in that table contain the join attribute value—possibly values of other S-attributes also—and a pointer to the corresponding tuple. The second pass then scans relation R and applies the same hash function to the join attribute $R.C$. When an R-tuple collides in the hash table with one or more S-tuples, the algorithm checks to see that the values of $R.C$ and $S.C$ are indeed equal, and if so generates the appropriate joined tuple(s). The great advantage of this technique over the merge technique is that relations R and S do not need to be stored in any particular order, and hence that no sorting is necessary.

As with the hash lookup technique, we leave the derivation of cost estimates for this approach as an exercise for the reader.

```
/* build hash table H on S.C */

do j := 1 to n ;
   k := hash (S[j].C) ;
   add S[j] to hash table entry H[k] ;
end ;

/* now do hash lookup on R */
```

FIG. 18.7   Hash

18.8   Summary

We began by stating that optimization represents both a *challenge* and an *opportunity* for relational systems. In fact, optimizability is a **strength** of such systems, for several reasons; a relational system with a good optimizer might very well outperform a non-relational system. Our introductory example gave some idea of the kinds of improvement that might be achievable (a factor of over 10,000:1 in that particular case).

The four broad stages of optimization are:

■ Cast the query into some **internal form** (typically a **query tree** or **abstract syntax tree,** but such representations can be thought of as just an internalized form of the relational algebra)

■ Convert to **canonical form,** using various **laws of transformation**

■ Choose candidate **low-level procedures** for implementing the various operators in the canonical representation of the query

■ Generate **query plans** and choose the cheapest, using **cost formulas** and knowledge of **database statistics**

Next, we discussed the general **distributive, commutative,** and **associative** laws and their applicability to relational operators such as join (also their applicability to **arithmetic, logical,** and **comparison** operators), and we mentioned another general law, called **idempotence.** We also discussed some specific transformations for the **restriction** and **projection** operators. Then we introduced the important idea of **semantic** transformations—i.e., transformations based on the system's knowledge of **integrity constraints.**

By way of illustration, we sketched some of the statistics maintained by the **DB2** and **INGRES** products. Then we described a "divide and conquer" strategy called **query decomposition** that was introduced with the INGRES prototype, and mentioned that such strategies might be very attractive in a parallel processing or distributed environment.

Finally, we examined certain **implementation techniques** for certain of the relational operators, especially **join.** We presented pseudocode algorithms for five join techniques—**brute force, index lookup, hash lookup, merge** (including **sort/merge**), and **hash**—and briefly considered the costs associated with these techniques.

In conclusion, we should mention that many of today's products do unfortunately include certain **optimization inhibitors,** which users should at least be aware of (even though there is little they can do about them, in most cases). An optimization inhibitor is a feature of the system in question that prevents the optimizer from doing as good a job as it might otherwise do (i.e., in the absence of that feature). The inhibitors in question include *duplicate rows* (see reference [4.11]), *three-valued logic* (see Chapter 20), and *SQL's implementation of three-valued logic* (see references [20.9] and [20.11]).

Exercises

18.1 Some of the following pairs of expressions on the suppliers-parts-projects database are equivalent, some are not. Which pairs are indeed equivalent?

(a1) `S JOIN ( ( P JOIN J ) WHERE CITY = 'London' )`

(a2) `( P WHERE CITY = 'London' ) JOIN ( J JOIN S )`

(b1) `( S MINUS ( ( S JOIN SPJ ) WHERE P# = 'P2' )`
`              [ S#, SNAME, STATUS, CITY ] ) [ S#, CITY ]`

(b2) `S [ S#, CITY ] MINUS`
`     ( S [ S#, CITY ] JOIN`
`       ( SPJ WHERE P# = 'P2' ) ) [ S#, CITY ]`

(c1) `( S [ CITY ] MINUS P [ CITY ] ) MINUS J [ CITY ]`

(c2) `( S [ CITY ] MINUS J [ CITY ] )`
`        MINUS ( P [ CITY ] MINUS J [ CITY ] )`

(d1) `( J [ CITY ] INTERSECT P [ CITY ] ) UNION ( S [ CITY ] )`

(d2) `J [ CITY ] INTERSECT ( S [ CITY ] UNION P [ CITY ] )`

(e1) `( ( SPJ WHERE S# = 'S1' ) UNION ( SPJ WHERE P# = 'P1' ) )`
`     INTERSECT`
`     ( ( SPJ WHERE J# = 'J1' ) UNION ( SPJ WHERE S# = 'S1' ) )`

(e2) `( SPJ WHERE S# = 'S1' ) UNION`
`     ( ( SPJ WHERE P# = 'P1' ) INTERSECT ( SPJ WHERE J# = 'J1' ) )`

(f1) `( S WHERE CITY = 'London' ) UNION ( S WHERE STATUS > 10 )`

(f2) `S WHERE CITY = 'London' AND STATUS > 10`

(g1) `( S [ S# ] INTERSECT ( SPJ WHERE J# = 'J1' ) [ S# ] )`
`     UNION ( S WHERE CITY = 'London' ) [ S# ]`

(g2) `S [ S# ] INTERSECT ( ( SPJ WHERE J# = 'J1' ) [ S# ]`
`                    UNION ( S WHERE CITY = 'London' ) [ S# ] )`

(h1) `( SPJ WHERE J# = 'J1' ) [ S# ]`
`     MINUS ( SPJ WHERE P# = 'P1' ) [ S# ]`

(h2) `( ( SPJ WHERE J# = 'J1' )`
`     MINUS ( SPJ WHERE P# = 'P1' ) ) [ S# ]`

18.2 Show that join, union, and intersection are commutative and difference is not.

18.3 Show that join, union, and intersection are associative and difference is not.

18.4 Show that (a) union distributes over intersection; (b) intersection distributes over union.

18.5 Show that for all *A* and *B* (a) *A* UNION (*A* INTERSECT *B*) = *A;* (b) *A* INTERSECT (*A* UNION *B*) = *A*. *Note:* These two rules are called the **absorption** laws. Like the idempotence, commutative, etc., laws, they also can be useful for optimization purposes.

18.6 Show that (a) restriction is unconditionally distributive over union, intersection, and difference, and conditionally distributive over join; (b) projection is unconditionally distributive over union and intersection, is conditionally distributive over join, and is not distributive over difference. State the relevant conditions in the conditional cases.

18.7 Extend the transformation rules of Section 18.4 to take account of EXTEND and SUMMARIZE.

18.8 Can you find any useful transformation rules for the relational division operation?

18.9 Give an appropriate set of transformation rules for conditional expressions involving AND, OR, and NOT. An example of such a rule would be "commutativity of AND"—i.e., *A* AND *B* is the same as *B* AND *A*.

18.10 Extend your answer to the previous exercise to include conditional expressions involving the quantifiers EXISTS and FORALL. An example of such a rule would be the rule given in Chapter 7 (Section 7.2) that allows an expression involving a FORALL to be converted into one involving a negated EXISTS instead.

18.11 Here is a list of integrity constraints for the suppliers-parts-projects database (extracted from the exercises in Chapter 16):

- The only legal cities are London, Paris, Rome, Athens, Oslo, Stockholm, Madrid, and Amsterdam.
- No two projects can be located in the same city.
- At most one supplier can be located in Athens at any one time.
- No shipment can have a quantity more than double the average of all such quantities.
- The highest-status supplier must not be located in the same city as the lowest-status supplier.
- Every project must be located in a city in which there is at least one supplier of that project.
- There must exist at least one red part.
- The average supplier status must be greater than 15.
- Every London supplier must supply part P2.
- At least one red part weighs less than 50 pounds.
- Suppliers in London supply more different kinds of part than suppliers in Paris.
- Suppliers in London supply more parts in total than suppliers in Paris.

And here are some sample queries against that database:

(a) Get suppliers who do not supply part P2.

(b) Get Paris suppliers who supply all projects in Athens with all Helsinki parts.

(c) Get suppliers such that no supplier supplies fewer kinds of parts.

(d) Get London suppliers who supply some project in Athens with all Helsinki parts.

(e) Get Oslo suppliers who supply at least two distinct Paris parts to at least two distinct Stockholm projects.

(f) Get pairs of colocated suppliers who supply pairs of colocated parts.

(g) Get London suppliers who supply some project in Athens with some Helsinki part.

(h) Get pairs of colocated suppliers who supply pairs of colocated projects.

(i) Get parts supplied to at least one project only by suppliers not in the same city as that project.

(j) Get suppliers such that no supplier supplies more kinds of parts.

Use the integrity constraints to transform these queries into simpler forms (still in natural language, however; you are not asked to perform this exercise *formally*).

18.12 Investigate any DBMS that might be available to you. Does that system perform any expression transformations? (not all do). If so, what transformations does it perform?

18.13 Try the following experiment: Take a simple query, say "Get names of suppliers who supply part P2," and state that query in as many different ways as you can think of in whatever query language is available to you (probably SQL). Create and populate a suitable test database, run the different versions of the query, and measure the execution times. If those times vary significantly, you have empirical evidence that the optimizer is not doing a very good job of expression transformation. Repeat the experiment with several different queries. If possible, repeat it with several different DBMSs also.

Note: Of course, the different versions of the query should all give the same result. If they don't, you have probably made a mistake—or it might be an optimizer bug; if so, report it to the DBMS vendor!

18.14 Investigate any DBMS that might be available to you. Does that system maintain any database statistics? (not all do). If so, what are they? How are they updated?—dynamically, or via some utility? If the latter, what is the utility called? How frequently is it run? How selective is it, in terms of the specific statistics that it can update on any specific execution?

18.15 We saw in Section 18.5 that among the database statistics maintained by DB2 are the second highest and second lowest value for each column of each base table. Why the *second* highest and lowest, do you think?

18.16 Devise a set of implementation procedures for the restriction and projection operations (along the lines of the procedures sketched for join in Section 18.7). Derive an appropriate set of cost formulas for those procedures. Assume that page I/O's are the only quantity of interest, i.e., do not attempt to include processor or other costs in your formulas. State and justify any other assumptions you make.

References and Bibliography

The following list represents a relatively small selection from the vast literature on optimization and related issues. It is divided roughly into groups, as follows. References [18.1–18.3] provide introductions to, or overviews of, the general optimization problem. References [18.4–18.14] are concerned with the efficient implementation of individual relational operations, such as join or aggregation. References [18.15–18.28] describe a variety of techniques based on expression transformation as discussed in Section 18.4; in particular, references [18.23–18.28] consider *semantic* transformations. References [18.29–18.39] discuss the techniques used in System R, DB2, and INGRES, and the general problem of optimizing SQL-style nested queries (see Chapter 8). References [18.40–18.49] address a miscellaneous set of techniques, tricks, ideas for future research, and so forth. Reference [18.50] is a recent (and extensive) tutorial. *Note:* Publications that are specifically concerned with optimization in distributed systems are deliberately excluded from the list (see Chapter 21).

18.1 Won Kim, David S. Reiner, and Don S. Batory (eds.). *Query Processing in Database Systems.* New York, N.Y.: Springer-Verlag (1985).

This book is an anthology of papers on the general topic of query processing (not just on optimization specifically). It consists of an introductory survey paper by Jarke, Koch, and Schmidt (similar but not identical to reference [18.3]), followed by groups of papers that discuss query processing in a variety of contexts: distributed database, heterogeneous-DBMS systems, view updating (reference [17.9] is the sole paper in this section), nontraditional applications (e.g., CAD/CAM), cross-statement optimization (see reference [18.43]), database machines, and physical database design.

18.2 IEEE. *Database Engineering 5,* No. 3: Special Issue on Query Optimization (September 1982).

Contains 13 short papers (from both academic and commercial environments) on various aspects of query optimization.

18.3 Matthias Jarke and Jürgen Koch. "Query Optimization in Database Systems." *ACM Comp. Surv. 16,* No. 2 (June 1984).

An excellent tutorial. The paper gives a general framework for query evaluation, much like the one in Section 18.3 of the present chapter (which was heavily influenced by this paper), but based on the relational calculus rather than the algebra. It then discusses a large number of optimization techniques within that framework: syntactic and semantic transformations, low-level operation implementation, and algorithms for generating query plans and choosing among them. An extensive set of syntactic transformation rules for calculus expressions is given. A lengthy bibliography (not annotated) is also included; note, however, that the number of papers on the subject published since 1984 is probably at least an order of magnitude greater than the number prior to that time (see reference [8.50]).

The paper also briefly discusses certain other related issues: the optimization of higher-level query languages (i.e., languages that are more powerful than the algebra or calculus), optimization in a distributed database environment, and the role of database machines with respect to optimization.

18.4 S. Bing Yao. "Optimization of Query Evaluation Algorithms." *ACM TODS 4,* No. 2 (June 1979).

A general model is developed of query evaluation that includes many known algorithms as special cases. The model includes the following set of low-level operations, together with an associated set of cost formulas:

1. Restriction indexing
2. Join indexing
3. Intersection
4. Record access
5. Sequential scan
6. Link scan
7. Restriction filter
8. Join filter
9. Sort
10. Concatenation
11. Projection

A given query processing algorithm expressed in terms of these low-level operations can be evaluated in accordance with the cost formulas. The paper identifies various classes of query processing algorithms and assigns a cost formula to each class. The problem of query optimization then becomes the problem of solving a simple set of cost equations to find a minimum cost, and then selecting the class of algorithm corresponding to that minimum cost.

18.5 Robert M. Pecherer. "Efficient Evaluation of Expressions in a Relational Algebra." Proc. ACM Pacific Conference, San Francisco, Calif. (April 1975).

One of the first papers to discuss techniques for implementing the relational operators. The paper begins by presenting a slightly revised version of the original algebra (the revisions are motivated by efficiency considerations). The implementation of individual operations of that revised algebra is then discussed. It is assumed that relations are stored as sorted files and that tuples can be retrieved only in the sequence in which they are stored. Performance bounds are given for each operation. The paper claims that, under the stated assumptions, the operations requiring the most careful attention are projection and division.

18.6 M. W. Blasgen and K. P. Eswaran. "Storage and Access in Relational Databases." *IBM Sys. J. 16,* No. 4 (1977).

Several techniques for handling queries involving restriction, projection, and join operations are compared on the basis of their cost in disk I/O. The techniques in question are basically those implemented in System R [18.29].

18.7 T. H. Merrett. "Why Sort/Merge Gives the Best Implementation of the Natural Join." *ACM SIGMOD Record 13,* No. 2 (January 1983).

Presents a set of intuitive arguments to support the position statement of the title. The argument is essentially that the join operation itself will be most efficient if the two relations are each sorted on values of the join attribute (because in that case—as we saw in Section 18.7— merge is the obvious technique, and each data page will be retrieved exactly once, which is clearly optimal), and the cost of sorting the relations into that desired sequence, on a large enough machine, is likely to be less than the cost of any scheme for circumventing the fact that they are not so sorted.

However, the author does admit that there could be some exceptions to his extreme position. For instance, one of the relations might be sufficiently small (e.g., it might be the result of a previous restriction operation) that direct access to the other relation via an index or a hash could be more efficient than sorting it. References [18.8–18.11] below give further examples of cases where sort/merge is probably not the best technique in practice.

18.8 Giovanni Maria Sacco. "Fragmentation: A Technique for Efficient Query Processing." *ACM TODS 11,* No. 2 (June 1986).

Presents a "divide and conquer" method of performing joins by recursively splitting the relations to be joined into tuple subsets ("fragments") and performing a series of sequential scans on those subsets. Unlike sort/merge, the technique does not require the relations to be sorted first. The paper shows that the fragmentation technique always performs better than sort/merge in the case where sort/merge requires both relations to be sorted first, and usually performs better in the case where sort/merge requires just one relation (the larger) to be sorted first. The author claims that the technique can also be applied to other operations, such as intersection and difference.

18.9 M. Negri and G. Pelagatti. "Distributive Join: A New Algorithm for Joining Relations." *ACM TODS 16,* No. 4 (December 1991).

Another "divide and conquer" join method. "[The method] is based on the idea that . . . it is not necessary to sort both relations completely . . . It is sufficient to sort one completely and the other only partially, thus avoiding part of the sort effort." The partial sort breaks the affected relation down into a sequence of unsorted tuple subsets $S1, S2, \ldots, Sn$ (somewhat as in Sacco's method [18.8], except that Sacco uses hashing instead of sorting), with the property that $MAX(Si) < MIN(S[i+1])$ for all i $(1, 2, \ldots, n-1)$. The paper claims that this method performs better than sort/merge.

18.10 David J. DeWitt *et al.* "Implementation Techniques for Main Memory Database Systems." Proc. 1984 ACM SIGMOD International Conference on Management of Data, Boston, Mass. (June 1984).

18.11 Leonard D. Shapiro. "Join Processing in Database Systems with Large Main Memories." *ACM TODS 11,* No. 3 (September 1986).

Presents three new hash join algorithms, one of which is "especially efficient when the main memory available is a significant fraction of the size of one of the relations to be joined." The algorithms work by partitioning the relations into tuple subsets that can be processed in main memory. The author contends that hash-based methods are destined to become the technique of choice, given the rate at which memory costs are decreasing.

18.12 Dina Bitton, David J. DeWitt, and Carolyn Turbyfill. "Benchmarking Database Systems: A Systematic Approach." Proc. 9th International Conference on Very Large Data Bases, Florence, Italy (October/November 1983).

The first paper to describe what is now usually called "the Wisconsin benchmark" (since it was developed by the authors at the University of Wisconsin). The benchmark defines a set of relations with precisely specified attribute values, and then measures the performance of certain precisely specified algebraic operations on those relations (for example, various projections, involving different degrees of duplication in the attributes over which the projections are taken). It thus represents a systematic test of the effectiveness of the system optimizer on those fundamental operations.

18.13 Dina Bitton and David J. DeWitt. "Duplicate Record Elimination in Large Data Files." *ACM TODS 8,* No. 2 (June 1983).

The traditional technique for eliminating duplicates is simply to sort the records and then do a sequential scan. This paper proposes an alternative approach that has significantly better performance characteristics if the file is large.

18.14 Dina Bitton, Haran Boral, David J. DeWitt, and W. Kevin Wilkinson. "Parallel Algorithms for the Execution of Relational Database Algorithms." *ACM TODS 8,* No. 3 (September 1983).

Presents algorithms for implementing sort, projection, join, aggregation, and update operations in a multiprocessor environment. The paper gives general cost formulas that take into account I/O, message, and processor costs, and can be adjusted to different multiprocessor architectures.

18.15 Frank P. Palermo. "A Data Base Search Problem." In *Information Systems: COINS IV* (ed., J. T. Tou). New York, N.Y.: Plenum Press (1974).

One of the earliest papers on optimization. Starting from an arbitrary expression of the relational calculus, the paper shows how that expression can be reduced to an equivalent algebraic expression by means of Codd's reduction algorithm (see Chapter 7), and then introduces a number of improvements on that algorithm, among them the following:

■ No tuple is ever retrieved more than once.

■ Unnecessary values are discarded from a tuple as soon as that tuple is retrieved—"unnecessary values" being either values of attributes not referenced in the query or values used solely for restriction purposes. This process is equivalent to projecting the relation over the "necessary" attributes, and thus not only reduces the space required for each tuple but can also reduce the number of tuples that need to be retained.

■ The method used to build up the result relation is based on a least growth principle, so that the result tends to grow slowly. This technique has the effect of reducing both the number of comparisons involved and the amount of intermediate storage required.

■ An efficient technique is employed in the construction of joins, involving the dynamic factoring out of values used in join terms such as S.S# = SP.S# into **semijoins** (which are effectively a kind of dynamically constructed secondary index), and the use of an internal representation of each join called an *indirect join* (which makes use of internal tuple reference numbers to identify the tuples that participate in the join). These techniques are designed to reduce the amount of scanning needed in the construction of the join, by ensuring for each join term that the tuples concerned are logically ordered on the values of the join attributes. They also permit the dynamic determination of a "best" sequence in which to access the required database relations.

Note: The term **semijoin** is frequently encountered in more recent database literature with a meaning somewhat different from that originally ascribed to it by Palermo. See reference [21.26].

18.16 James B. Rothnie, Jr. "An Approach to Implementing a Relational Data Management System." Proc. 1974 ACM SIGMOD Workshop on Data Description, Access, and Control, Ann Arbor, Mich. (May 1974).

18.17 James B. Rothnie, Jr. "Evaluating Inter-Entry Retrieval Expressions in a Relational Data Base Management System." Proc. NCC *44,* Anaheim, Calif. Montvale, N.J.: AFIPS Press (May 1975).

Two more early optimization papers. They describe some techniques used in an experimental system called DAMAS (built at MIT) for implementing a calculus-based language—specifically, techniques for implementing what INGRES would call "two-variable queries" [18.31–18.32] within that system. Reference [18.17] is more tutorial in nature, reference [18.16] gives some experimental results and more internal details. The papers discuss, specifically, the implementation of expressions involving a single existentially quantified tuple variable in terms of simpler expressions known as "primitive Boolean conditions" or PBCs. A PBC is a condition that can be established as *true* or *false* for a given tuple by examining that tuple in isolation—i.e., it is a simple restriction condition. The DAMAS storage modules, which manage the stored database, support the following operations directly:

- Get next tuple where p is *true*
- Test the existence of a tuple such that p is *true*
- Eliminate from consideration all tuples where p is *true*

(where p is a PBC). Using these operations, the system handles a retrieval involving relations—or rather range variables—$R1$ (unquantified) and $R2$ (existentially quantified) as follows. Note that the target of the retrieval must be some projection of $R1$. (Here and throughout the following explanation we use "$R1$" and "$R2$" as shorthand for the relations corresponding to range variables $R1$ and $R2$, respectively.)

Step 1: In the original condition, set all terms involving $R2$ to *true* and simplify. The result is a PBC, $p1$ say. Tuples of $R1$ not satisfying $p1$ can be eliminated from further consideration.

Step 2: Get a (noneliminated) tuple from $R1$. Substitute values from that tuple in the original condition and simplify, yielding $p2$. Does there exist a tuple in $R2$ such that $p2$ is *true?*

Step 3A (Yes): Fetch the identified $R2$ tuple. Extract target values from the $R1$ tuple and append them to the result relation. Build $p3$, selecting all $R1$ tuples containing the same value for the target attributes, and use it to eliminate from consideration all $R1$ tuples that would generate duplicates. (This elimination can be performed whenever a tuple is added to the result.) Also, substitute values from the fetched $R2$ tuple in the original condition and simplify, yielding $p4$. Get all $R1$ tuples satisfying $p4$ and append target values to the result.

Step 3B (No): Build $p5$, selecting all $R1$ tuples that would yield (in Step 2) a PBC for which there cannot exist an $R2$ tuple to make it *true* (because no $R2$ tuple made $p2$ *true*). Eliminate those $R1$ tuples.

Step 4: Repeat Steps 2–3 until no $R1$ tuples remain.

The design of the foregoing algorithm is based on the principle that as much information as possible should be derived from each database access. In practice, however, it might prove more expensive to eliminate tuples from further consideration (for example) than simply to examine and reject them. For this reason, certain steps of the algorithm might or might not be applied in a given situation. In DAMAS the choice of whether or not to apply those steps is left to the user, but the papers give some suggestions for automating that choice.

18.18   James Miles Smith and Philip Yen-Tang Chang. "Optimizing the Performance of a Relational Algebra Database Interface." *CACM 18*, No. 10 (October 1975).

Describes the algorithms used in the "Smart Query Interface for a Relational Algebra" (SQUIRAL). The techniques used include the following.

- Transforming the original algebraic expression into an equivalent but more efficient sequence of operations (along the lines indicated in Section 18.4)
- Assigning distinct operations in the transformed expression to distinct processes and exploiting concurrency and pipelining among them
- Coordinating the sort orders of the temporary relations passed between those processes
- Exploiting indexes and attempting to localize page references

18.19   P. A. V. Hall. "Optimisation of a Single Relational Expression in a Relational Data Base System." *IBM J. R&D. 20*, No. 3 (May 1976).

This paper describes some of the optimizing techniques used in the system PRTV [7.15]. PRTV, like SQUIRAL [18.18], begins by transforming the given algebraic expression into some more efficient form before evaluating it. A feature of PRTV is that the system does not automatically evaluate each expression as soon as it receives it; rather, it combines each new expression with those it has already accepted to build a larger and more complex expression, and defers actual evaluation until the last possible moment (see the discussion of step-at-a-time query formulation in Chapter 6, Section 6.6). Thus the "single relational expression" of the paper's title might actually represent an entire sequence of user operations. The optimizations described resemble those of SQUIRAL but go further in some respects; they include the following (in order of application).

- Restrictions are performed as early as possible
- Sequences of projections are combined into a single projection
- Redundant operations are eliminated
- Expressions involving empty relations and trivial conditions are simplified
- Common subexpressions are factored out

The paper concludes with some experimental results and some suggestions for further investigations.

18.20   Matthias Jarke and Jörgen Koch. "Range Nesting: A Fast Method to Evaluate Quantified Queries." Proc. 1983 ACM SIGMOD International Conference on Management of Data, San Jose, Calif. (May 1983).

Defines a variation of the relational calculus that permits some additional (and useful) syntactic transformation rules to be applied, and presents algorithms for evaluating expressions of that calculus. The particular version of the calculus described allows range variables to be bound to expressions, instead of just to a named relation. The expressions in question involve exactly one free variable and an arbitrary number of existentially or universally quantified bound variables. (Actually, the version of the calculus defined in Chapter 7 is very close to Jarke and Koch's version.) The paper describes the optimization of a particular class of expressions of the revised calculus, called "perfect nested expressions." Methods are given for converting apparently complex queries—in particular, certain queries involving FORALL—into perfect expressions. The authors show that a large subset of the queries that arise in practice correspond to perfect expressions.

18.21   A. Makinouchi, M. Tezuka, H. Kitakami, and S. Adachi. "The Optimization Strategy for Query Evaluation in RDB/V1." Proc. 7th International Conference on Very Large Data Bases, Cannes, France (September 1981).

RDB/V1 was the prototype forerunner of the Fujitsu product AIM/RDB (which is an SQL system). This paper describes the optimization techniques used in that prototype and briefly compares them with the techniques used in the INGRES and System R prototypes. One particular technique seems to be novel: the use of dynamically obtained MAX and MIN values to induce additional restrictions. This technique has the effect of simplifying the process of choosing a join order and improving the performance of the joins themselves. As a simple example of the latter point, suppose relations S and P are to be joined over city values. First relation S is sorted on attribute S.CITY. During the sort, the maximum and minimum values, HIGH and LOW say, of S.CITY are determined. Then the restriction

```
LOW ≤ P.CITY AND P.CITY ≤ HIGH
```

can be used to (try to) reduce the number of tuples of P that need to be inspected in building the join.

18.21a Hamid Pirahesh, Joseph M. Hellerstein, and Waqar Hasan. "Extensible Rule Based Query Rewrite Optimization in Starburst." Proc. 1992 ACM SIGMOD International Conference on Management of Data, San Diego, Calif. (June 1992).

"Query rewrite" is another name for expression transformation. Rather surprisingly, current relational DBMSs—according to the authors—do little in the way of such transformations. The paper describes the expression transformation mechanism of the IBM Starburst prototype [25.17–25.19]. Suitably qualified users can add new transformation rules to the system at any time (hence the "extensible" of the paper's title).

18.22 Inderpal Singh Mumick, Sheldon J. Finkelstein, Hamid Pirahesh, and Raghu Ramakrishnan. "Magic is Relevant." Proc. 1990 ACM SIGMOD International Conference on Management of Data, Atlantic City, N.J. (May 1990).

The infelicitous term "magic" refers to an optimization technique originally developed for use with queries—especially queries involving recursion—expressed in the "logic database" language Datalog (see Appendix C). The present paper extends the approach to conventional relational systems, claiming on the basis of experimental measurements that it is often more effective than traditional optimization techniques (note that the query does not have to be recursive for the method to be applicable). The basic idea is to decompose the given query into a number of smaller queries that define a set of "auxiliary relations" (somewhat as in INGRES's query decomposition approach [18.31–18.32]), in such a way that those auxiliary relations can be used to filter out tuples that are irrelevant to the problem at hand. The following example is based on one given in the paper. The original query is:

```
R   :=  EX.ENAME WHERE EX.JOB = 'Clerk' AND EX.SAL >
                AVG ( EY WHERE EY.DEPT# = EX.DEPT#, SAL ) ;
```

("Get names of clerks whose salary is greater than the average for their department"). If this query is executed "directly"—i.e., more or less as written—the system will scan the employees relation tuple by tuple and hence compute the average salary for any department that employs more than one clerk several times. A traditional optimizer might therefore break the query down into the following two smaller queries:

```
T1  :=  ( EX.DEPT#,
            AVG ( EY WHERE EY.DEPT# = EX.DEPT#, SAL ) AS ASAL ) ;

T2  :=  EMP.ENAME WHERE EMP.JOB = 'Clerk' AND
                EXISTS T1 ( EMP.DEPT# = T1.DEPT# AND
                            EMP.SALARY > T1.ASAL ) ;
```

Now no department's average will be computed more than once, but some *irrelevant* averages will be computed—namely, those for departments that do not employ clerks.

The "magic" approach avoids both the repeated computations of the first approach and the irrelevant computations of the second, at the cost of generating extra "auxiliary" relations:

```
/* first auxiliary relation : name, department, and salary    */
/* for clerks                                                  */
T1  :=  ( EMP.ENAME, EMP.DEPT#, EMP.SAL )
                                    WHERE EMP.JOB = 'Clerk' ;

/* second auxiliary relation : departments employing clerks    */
T2  :=  T1.DEPT# ;

/* third auxiliary relation : departments employing clerks     */
/* and corresponding average salaries                          */
T3  :=  ( T2.DEPT#,
            AVG ( EMP WHERE EMP.DEPT# = T2.DEPT#, SAL )
                                            AS ASAL ) ;

/* result relation */
R   :=  T1.ENAME WHERE EXISTS T3 ( T1.DEPT# = T3.DEPT# AND
                                    T1.SAL > T3.ASAL ) ;
```

The "magic" consists in determining exactly which auxiliary relations are needed.

18.23 Jonathan J. King. "QUIST: A System for Semantic Query Optimization in Relational Databases." Proc. 7th International Conference on Very Large Data Bases, Cannes, France (September 1981).

The paper that introduced the idea of semantic optimization (see Section 18.4 of the present chapter). It describes an experimental system called QUIST ("query improvement through semantic transformation") that is capable of performing such optimizations.

18.24 Sreekumar T. Shenoy and Z. Meral Ozsoyoglu. "A System for Semantic Query Optimization." Proc. 1987 ACM SIGMOD International Conference on Management of Data, San Francisco, Calif. (May/June 1987).

Extends the work of King [18.23] by introducing a scheme that dynamically selects, from a potentially very large set of integrity constraints, just those that are likely to be profitable in transforming a given query. The integrity constraints considered are of two basic kinds, *implication constraints* (e.g., "if the shipment quantity is greater than 300 then the supplier city must be London") and *subset constraints* (e.g., "every supplier in London must supply at least one part"). Such constraints are used to transform queries by eliminating redundant restrictions and joins and introducing additional restrictions on indexed attributes. Cases in which the query can be answered from the constraints alone are also handled efficiently.

18.25 Michael Siegel, Edward Sciore, and Sharon Salveter. "A Method for Automatic Rule Derivation to Support Semantic Query Optimization." *ACM TODS 17*, No. 4 (December 1992)

As explained in Section 18.4, semantic optimization makes use of integrity constraints to transform queries. However, there are several problems associated with this idea:

1. How does the optimizer know which transformations will be effective (i.e., will make the query more efficient)?

2. Some integrity constraints are not very useful for optimization purposes. E.g., the constraint that part weights must be positive, though important for integrity purposes, is essentially useless for optimization. How does the optimizer distinguish between useful and useless constraints?

3. Some conditions might be valid for some states of the database—even for most states—and hence be useful for optimization purposes, and yet not strictly be an integrity constraint as such. An example might be the condition EMP.AGE $\leq$ 50; though not an integrity constraint *per se* (employees can be older than 50), it might well be the case that no current employee is in fact older than 50.

This paper describes the architecture for a system that addresses the foregoing issues.

18.26 Upen S. Chakravarthy, John Grant, and Jack Minker. "Logic-Based Approach to Semantic Query Optimization." *ACM TODS 15*, No. 2 (June 1990).

To quote from the abstract: "In several previous papers [the authors have] described and proved the correctness of a method for semantic query optimization . . . This paper consolidates the major results of those papers emphasizing the techniques and their applicability for optimizing relational queries. Additionally, [it shows] how this method subsumes and generalizes earlier work on semantic query optimization. [It also indicates] how semantic query optimization techniques can be extended to [recursive queries] and integrity constraints that contain disjunction, negation, and recursion."

18.27 A. V. Aho, Y. Sagiv, and J. D. Ullman. "Efficient Optimization of a Class of Relational Expressions." *ACM TODS 4*, No. 4 (December 1979).

The class of relational expressions referred to in the title of this paper is those expressions that involve only (equality-based) restriction (referred to as selection in the paper), projection, and natural join operations—so-called *SPJ-expressions*. SPJ-expressions correspond to relational calculus queries involving only equality comparisons, ANDs, and EXISTS quantifiers. The paper introduces **tableaus** as a means of symbolically representing SPJ-expressions. A tableau is a rectangular array, in which columns correspond to attributes and rows to conditions—specifically, to *membership conditions*, which state that a certain tuple of values must exist in a certain relation. Rows are logically connected by the appearance of common symbols in the rows concerned. For example, the tableau

S#	STATUS	CITY	P#	COLOR	
	a1				
b1	a1	London			— relation S
b1			b2		— relation SP
			b2	Red	— relation P

represents the query "Get status (*a1*) of suppliers (*b1*) in London who supply some red part (*b2*)." The top row of the tableau lists all attributes mentioned in the query, the next row is the "summary" row (corresponding to the target commalist in a calculus query or the final projection in an algebraic query), and the remaining rows (as already stated) represent membership conditions. We have tagged those rows in the example to indicate the relevant relations. Notice that the "*b*"s refer to bound variables and the "*a*"s to free variables; the summary row contains only "*a*"s.

Tableaus represent another candidate for a canonical formalism for queries (see Section 18.3), except of course that they are not general enough to represent all possible relational expressions. (In fact, they can be regarded as a syntactic variation on Query-By-Example, one that is however strictly less powerful than QBE.) The paper gives algorithms for reducing any tableau to another, semantically equivalent tableau in which the number of rows is reduced to a minimum. Since the number of rows (not counting the top two, which are special) is one more than the number of joins in the corresponding SPJ-expression, the converted tableau represents an optimal form of the query—optimal, in the very specific sense that the number of joins is minimized. (In the example above, of course, the number of joins is already the minimum possible for the query, and such optimization has no effect.) The minimal tableau can then be converted back if desired into some other representation for subsequent additional optimization.

The idea of minimizing the number of joins has applicability to queries formulated in terms of join views (in particular, queries formulated in terms of a "universal relation"; see the References and Bibliography section in Chapter 11). For example, suppose the user is presented with a view V that is defined as the join of relations S and SP over S#, and the user issues the query:

```
V [ P# ]
```

A straightforward view processing algorithm would convert this query into the following:

```
( SP JOIN S ) [ P# ]
```

As pointed out in Section 18.4, however, the following query produces the same result, and does not involve a join (i.e., the number of joins has been minimized):

```
SP [ P# ]
```

Note therefore that, since the algorithms for tableau reduction given in the paper take into account any explicitly stated functional dependencies among the attributes (see Chapter 9), those algorithms provide a limited example of a *semantic* optimization technique.

18.28 Y. Sagiv and M. Yannakakis. "Equivalences Among Relational Expressions with the Union and Difference Operators." *JACM 27,* No. 4 (October 1980).

Extends the ideas of reference [18.27] to deal with queries that include the union and difference operations.

18.29 P. Griffiths Selinger *et al.* "Access Path Selection in a Relational Database System." Proc. 1979 ACM SIGMOD International Conference on Management of Data, Boston, Mass. (May/June 1979).

Discusses some of the optimization techniques used in the System R prototype. *Note:* The

System R optimizer was the forerunner of the DB2 optimizer. Reference [18.30] gives some additional information that is specific to DB2.

A query in System R is an SQL statement and thus consists of a set of "SELECT–FROM–WHERE" blocks (*query blocks*), some of which might be nested inside others (see Chapter 8). The System R optimizer first decides on an order in which to execute those query blocks. It then seeks to minimize the total cost of the query by choosing the cheapest implementation for each individual block. Note that this strategy (choosing block order first, then optimizing individual blocks) means that certain possible query plans will never be considered; in effect, it amounts to a technique for "reducing the search space" (see the remarks on this subject near the end of Section 18.3). *Note:* In the case of nested blocks, the optimizer effectively just follows the nested order as specified by the user—i.e., the innermost block will be executed first, loosely speaking. See references [18.35–18.39] for criticism and further discussion of this strategy.

For a given query block, there are basically two cases to consider (the first of which can in fact be regarded as just a special case of the second):

1. For a block that involves just a restriction and/or projection of a single relation, the optimizer uses statistical information from the catalog, together with formulas (given in the paper) for intermediate result size estimates and low-level operation costs, to choose a strategy for performing that restriction and/or projection.

2. For a block that involves two or more relations to be joined together, with (probably) local restrictions and/or projections on individual relations, the optimizer (a) treats each individual relation as in Case 1, and (b) decides on a sequence for performing the joins. The two operations (a) and (b) are not independent of one another; for example, a given strategy for accessing an individual relation A might well be chosen precisely because it produces tuples of A in the order in which they are needed to perform a subsequent join of A with some other relation B.

Joins are implemented by sort/merge, index lookup, or brute force. One point that is stressed in the paper is that, in evaluating (for example) the nested join (A JOIN B) JOIN C, it is not necessary to compute the join of A and B in its entirety before computing the join of the result and C; on the contrary, as soon as any tuple of A JOIN B has been produced, it can immediately be passed to the process that joins such tuples with tuples of C. Thus it might never be necessary to materialize the relation "A JOIN B" in its entirety at all. (This general idea was discussed briefly in Chapter 6, at the end of Section 6.2.)

The paper also includes a few observations on the cost of optimization. For a join of two relations, the cost is said to be approximately equal to the cost of between 5 and 20 database retrievals—a negligible overhead if the optimized query will subsequently be executed a large number of times. (Note that System R is a compiling system, like DB2 [B.8], and hence that an SQL statement might be optimized once and then executed many times, perhaps many thousands of times.) Optimization of complex queries is said to require "only a few thousand bytes of storage and a few tenths of a second" on an IBM System 370 Model 158. "Joins of eight tables have been optimized in a few seconds."

18.30   J. M. Cheng, C. R. Loosley, A. Shibamiya, and P. S. Worthington. "IBM DATABASE 2 Performance: Design, Implementation, and Tuning." *IBM Sys. J. 23,* No. 2 (1984).

Includes a brief description of optimization tactics in DB2 (as of first release): query transformation techniques, the handling of nested query blocks, join methods, access path selection, and index-only processing. The paper also includes much interesting material concerning other performance-oriented aspects of DB2.

18.31   Eugene Wong and Karel Youssefi. "Decomposition—A Strategy for Query Processing." *ACM TODS 1,* No. 3 (September 1976).

18.32   Karel Youssefi and Eugene Wong. "Query Processing in a Relational Database Management System." Proc. 5th International Conference on Very Large Data Bases, Rio de Janeiro, Brazil (September 1979).

18.33 Robert Epstein. "Techniques for Processing of Aggregates in Relational Database Systems." University of California, Berkeley: Electronics Research Laboratory Memorandum No. UCB/ERL M79/8 (21 February 1979).

Describes the algorithms used in the INGRES prototype for dealing with the aggregate functions COUNT, SUM, AVG, etc., including in particular a number of optimizations that can be applied during such processing.

18.34 Lawrence A. Rowe and Michael Stonebraker. "The Commercial INGRES Epilogue." In Michael Stonebraker (ed.): *The INGRES Papers: The Anatomy of a Relational Database Management System*. Reading, Mass.: Addison-Wesley (1985).

"Commercial INGRES" is the product that grew out of the "University INGRES" prototype. Some of the differences between the University and Commercial INGRES optimizers are as follows:

1. The University optimizer used "incremental planning"— i.e., it decided what to do first, did it, decided what to do next on the basis of the size of the result of the previous step, and so on. The Commercial optimizer decides on a complete plan before beginning execution, based on estimates of intermediate result sizes.

2. The University optimizer handled two-variable (i.e., join) queries by tuple substitution, as explained in Section 18.6. The Commercial optimizer supports a variety of preferred techniques for handling such queries, including in particular the sort/merge technique described in Section 18.7.

3. The Commercial optimizer uses a much more sophisticated set of statistics than the University optimizer.

4. The University optimizer did incremental planning, as noted under 1. above. The Commercial optimizer does a more exhaustive search. However, the search process stops if the time spent on optimization exceeds the current best estimate of the time required to execute the query (for otherwise the overhead of doing the optimization might well outweigh the advantages).

5. The Commercial optimizer considers all possible index combinations, all possible join sequences, and "all available join methods—sort/merge, partial sort/merge, hash lookup, ISAM lookup, B-tree lookup, and brute force" (see Section 18.7).

18.35 Won Kim. "On Optimizing an SQL-Like Nested Query." *ACM TODS 7,* No. 3 (September 1982).

See reference [18.39] below.

18.36 Werner Kiessling. "On Semantic Reefs and Efficient Processing of Correlation Queries with Aggregates." Proc. 11th International Conference on Very Large Data Bases, Stockholm, Sweden (August 1985).

See reference [18.39] below.

18.37 Richard A. Ganski and Harry K. T. Wong. "Optimization of Nested SQL Queries Revisited." Proc. 1987 ACM SIGMOD International Conference on Management of Data, San Francisco, Calif. (May 1987).

See reference [18.39] below.

18.38 Günter von Bültzingsloewen. "Translating and Optimizing SQL Queries Having Aggregates." Proc. 13th International Conference on Very Large Data Bases, Brighton, England (September 1987).

See reference [18.39] below.

18.39 M. Muralikrishna. "Improved Unnesting Algorithms for Join Aggregate SQL Queries." Proc. 18th International Conference on Very Large Data Bases, Vancouver, Canada (August 1992).

The SQL language allows "nested subqueries"—i.e., a SELECT–FROM–WHERE block that is nested inside another such block, loosely speaking (see Chapter 8). This construct has caused a certain amount of trouble for implementers. Consider the following SQL query ("names of suppliers who supply part P2"), which we refer to as query Q1:

```
SELECT S.SNAME
FROM   S
WHERE  S.S# IN
     ( SELECT SP.S#
       FROM   SP
       WHERE  SP.P# = 'P2' ) ;
```

In System R [18.29], this query will be implemented by evaluating the inner block first to yield a temporary relation, R say, containing supplier *numbers* for the required suppliers; it will then scan relation S one tuple at a time, and, for each such tuple, will scan relation R to see if it contains the corresponding supplier number. This strategy is likely to be quite inefficient (especially as relation R will not be indexed).

Now consider the following query (Q2):

```
SELECT S.SNAME
FROM   S, SP
WHERE  S.S# = SP.S# ;
```

This query is readily seen to be semantically identical to the previous one, but System R will now consider additional implementation strategies for it. In particular, if relations S and SP happen to be physically stored in supplier number sequence, it will use a merge join, which will be very efficient. And given that the two queries are logically equivalent, but that the second is more immediately susceptible to efficient implementation, the possibility of transforming queries of type Q1 into queries of type Q2 seems worth exploring. That possibility is the subject of references [18.35–18.39].

Kim [18.35] was the first to address the problem. Five types of nested query were identified and corresponding transformation algorithms described. Kim's paper included some experimental measurements that showed that the proposed algorithms improved the performance of nested queries by (typically) one to two orders of magnitude.

Subsequently, Kiessling [18.36] showed that Kim's algorithms did not work correctly if a nested subquery (at any level) included a COUNT aggregate in its target commalist (it did not properly handle the case where the argument of the COUNT evaluated to an empty relation). The "semantic reefs" of the paper's title referred to the difficulties that users have to navigate around in order to get consistent and correct answers to such queries. Furthermore, Kiessling also showed that Kim's algorithm was not easy to fix ("there seems to be no uniform way to do these transformations efficiently and correctly under all circumstances"). By way of an aside, the paper also showed that QUEL was superior to SQL in this general area (see Epstein [18.33]).

The paper by Ganski and Wong [18.37] provides a fix to the problem identified by Kiessling, by using an *outer join* (see Chapter 20) instead of the regular inner join in the transformed version of the query. (The fix is not totally satisfactory, in the present writer's opinion, because it introduces an undesirable ordering dependence among the operators in the transformed query.) The paper also identifies a further bug in Kim's original paper, which is fixed in the same way. However, the transformations in this paper contain additional bugs of their own, some having to do with the problem of duplicate rows (a notorious "semantic reef" [18.36]) and others with the flawed behavior of the SQL EXISTS quantifier [20.9].

The paper by von Bültzingsloewen [18.38] represents an attempt to put the entire topic on a theoretically sound footing (the basic problem being that, as several writers have observed, the behavior—both syntactic and semantic—of nesting and aggregate functions is not well understood). It defines extended versions of both the relational calculus and the relational algebra (the extensions having to do with aggregates and nulls), and proves the equivalence of those two extended formalisms (using, incidentally, a new method of proof that seems more elegant than those previously published). It then defines the semantics of SQL by mapping SQL into the extended calculus just defined. However, it should be pointed out that:

1. The dialect of SQL discussed, though closer to the dialect typically supported in commercial products than that discussed in references [18.35–18.37], is still not completely orthodox: It does not include UNION, it does not directly support ALL-type quantifications, and its treatment of *unknown* truth-values is different from (actually better than) that of conventional SQL.

2. The paper omits consideration of matters having to do with control over duplicate elimination "for technical simplification." But the implications of this omission are not clear, given that (as indicated above) the possibility of duplicates has significant consequences for the validity or otherwise of certain transformations [4.11].

Finally, Muralikrishna [18.39] claims that Kim's original algorithm [18.35], though incorrect, can still be more efficient than "the general strategy" of reference [18.37] in some cases, and therefore proposes an alternative correction to Kim's algorithm. It also provides some additional improvements.

18.40 David H. D. Warren. "Efficient Processing of Interactive Relational Database Queries Expressed in Logic." Proc. 7th International Conference on Very Large Data Bases, Cannes, France (September 1981).

Presents a view of query optimization from a rather different perspective—namely, that of formal logic. The paper reports on techniques used in an experimental database system based on Prolog. The techniques are apparently very similar to those of System R, although they were arrived at quite independently and with somewhat different objectives. The paper suggests that, in contrast to conventional query languages such as QUEL and SQL, logic-based languages such as Prolog permit queries to be expressed in such a manner as to highlight:

- What the essential components of the query are—namely, the logic goals;
- What it is that links those components together—namely, the logic variables;
- What the crucial implementation problem is—namely, the order in which to try to satisfy the goals.

As a consequence, it is suggested that such a language is very convenient as a base for optimization. Indeed, it could be regarded as yet another candidate for the internal representation of queries originally expressed in some other language. See Section 18.3.

18.41 Yannis E. Ioannidis and Eugene Wong. "Query Optimization by Simulated Annealing." Proc. 1987 ACM SIGMOD International Conference on Management of Data, San Francisco, Calif. (May 1987).

The number of possible query plans grows exponentially with the number of relations involved in the query. In conventional commercial applications, the number of relations in a query is usually small and so the number of candidate plans (the "search space") usually stays within reasonable bounds. In future applications, however, having to with, e.g., CAD/CAM applications or deductive DBMSs (see Appendix C), the number of relations in a query might easily become quite large. Furthermore, such applications are also likely to need "global" (i.e., multi-query) optimization [18.43] and recursive query support, both of which also have the effect of increasing the search space significantly, in general. Exhaustive search rapidly becomes out of the question in such an environment; some effective technique of reducing the search space becomes imperative.

The present paper gives references to previous work on the problems of optimization for large numbers of relations and multi-query optimization, but claims that no previous algorithms have been published for recursive query optimization. It then presents an algorithm that it claims is suitable whenever the search space is large, and in particular shows how to apply that algorithm to the recursive query case. The algorithm (called "simulated annealing" because it models the annealing process by which crystals are grown by first heating the containing fluid and then allowing it to cool gradually) is a probabilistic, hill-climbing algorithm that has successfully been applied to optimization problems in other contexts.

See also reference [18.42] immediately following.

18.42 Arun Swami and Anoop Gupta. "Optimization of Large Join Queries." Proc. 1988 ACM SIGMOD International Conference on Management of Data, Chicago, Ill. (June 1988).

The general problem of determining the optimal join order in queries involving large numbers of relations (as arise in connection with, e.g., deductive database systems) is combinatorially hard. This paper presents a comparative analysis of a number of algorithms that address this problem: perturbation walk, quasi-random sampling, iterative improvement, sequence heuristic, and simulated annealing [18.43] (the names add a pleasing element of poetry to a subject that might otherwise be thought a trifle prosaic). According to that analysis, iterative improvement is superior to all the other algorithms; in particular, simulated annealing is not useful "by itself" for large join queries.

18.43 Timos K. Sellis. "Multiple-Query Optimization." *ACM TODS 13,* No. 1 (March 1988).

Classical optimization research has focused on the problem of optimizing individual relational expressions in isolation. In future, however, the ability to optimize several distinct queries as a unit is likely to become important. One reason for this is that what starts out as a single query at some higher level might involve several queries at the relational level. The paper gives the following example. The natural language query "Is Mike well paid?" might conceivably lead to the execution of three separate relational queries:

- "Does Mike earn more than $40,000?"
- "Does Mike earn more than $35,000 and have less than five years of experience?"
- "Does Mike earn more than $30,000 and have less than three years of experience?"

This example illustrates the point that sets of related queries are likely to share some common subexpressions, and hence lend themselves to global optimization.

The paper considers queries involving conjunctions of restrictions and/or equijoins only. Some encouraging experimental results are included, and directions are identified for future research.

18.44 Guy M. Lohman. "Grammar-Like Functional Rules for Representing Query Optimization Alternatives." Proc. 1988 ACM SIGMOD International Conference on Management of Data, Chicago, Ill. (June 1988).

In some respects, a relational optimizer can be regarded as an expert system; however, the rules that drive the optimization process have historically been embedded in procedural code, not separately and declaratively stated. As a consequence, extending the optimizer to incorporate new optimization techniques has not been easy. Future "extendable" database systems (see the References and Bibliography section in Chapter 25) will exacerbate this problem, because there will be a clear need for individual installations to extend the optimizer to incorporate (e.g.) support for specific user-defined data types. Several researchers have therefore proposed structuring the optimizer as a conventional expert system, with explicitly stated declarative rules.

However, this idea suffers from certain performance problems: A large number of rules might be applicable at any given stage during query processing, and determining the appropriate one might involve complex computation. The present paper describes an alternative approach (currently being implemented in the Starburst prototype [25.17–25.19]), in which the rules are stated by means of production rules in a grammar somewhat like the grammars used to describe formal languages. The rules, called STARs (strategy alternative rules), permit the recursive construction of query plans from other plans and "low-level plan operators" (LOLEPOPs), which are basic operations on relations such as join, sort, etc. LOLEPOPs come in various different *flavors;* for example, the join LOLEPOP has a sort/merge flavor, a hash flavor, etc.

The paper claims that the foregoing approach has several advantages: The rules (STARs) are readily understandable by people who need to define new rules, the process of determining which rule to apply in any given situation is simpler and more efficient than the more traditional expert system approach, and the extendability objective is met.

18.45 Ryohei Nakano. "Translation with Optimization from Relational Calculus to Relational Algebra Having Aggregate Functions." *ACM TODS 15,* No. 4 (December 1990).

As explained in Chapter 7 (Section 7.4), queries in a calculus-based language can be implemented by (a) translating the query under consideration into an equivalent algebraic expression, then (b) optimizing that algebraic expression, and finally (c) implementing that optimized expression. In this paper, Nakano proposes a scheme for combining steps (a) and (b) into a single step, thereby translating a given calculus expression directly into an *optimal* algebraic equivalent. This scheme is claimed to be "more effective and more promising . . . because it seems quite difficult to optimize complicated algebraic expressions." The translation process makes use of certain *heuristic* transformations, incorporating human knowledge regarding the equivalence of certain calculus and algebraic expressions.

18.46 Kyu-Young Whang and Ravi Krishnamurthy. "Query Optimization in a Memory-Resident Domain Relational Calculus Database System." *ACM TODS 15,* No. 1 (March 1990).

The most expensive aspect of query processing (in the main memory environment assumed by this paper) is shown to be the evaluation of conditional expressions. Optimization in that environment is thus aimed at minimizing the number of such evaluations.

18.47 Johann Christoph Freytag and Nathan Goodman. "On the Translation of Relational Queries into Iterative Programs." *ACM TODS 14,* No. 1 (March 1989).

Presents methods for compiling relational expressions directly into executable code in a language such as C or Pascal. Note that this approach differs from the approach discussed in the body of the chapter, where the optimizer effectively combines *prewritten* (parameterized) code fragments to build the query plan.

18.48 Kiyoshi Ono and Guy M. Lohman. "Measuring the Complexity of Join Enumeration in Query Optimization." Proc. 16th International Conference on Very Large Data Bases, Brisbane, Australia (August 1990).

Given that join is basically a dyadic operation, the optimizer has to break a join involving N relations ($N > 2$) down into a sequence of dyadic joins. Most optimizers do this in a strictly nested fashion; that is, they choose a pair of relations to join first, then a third to join to the result of joining the first two, and so on. In other words, an expression such as A JOIN B JOIN C JOIN D might be treated as, say, ((D JOIN B) JOIN C) JOIN A, but never as, say, (A JOIN D) JOIN (B JOIN C). Further, traditional optimizers are usually designed to avoid Cartesian products if at all possible. Both of these tactics can be seen as ways of "reducing the search space"—see Section 18.3—though heuristics for choosing the sequence of joins are still needed, of course.

   The present paper describes the relevant aspects of the optimizer in the IBM Starburst prototype [25.17–25.19]. It argues that both of the foregoing tactics can be inappropriate in certain situations, and hence that what is needed is an *adaptable* optimizer that can be instructed to use different tactics for different queries. *Note:* Unlike the typical commercial optimizers of today, Starburst is able to treat an expression of the form $R.A = S.B + c$ as a "join" condition. It also applies "predicate transitive closure" (see Section 18.4).

18.49 Yannis E. Ioannidis, Raymond T. Ng, Kyuseok Shim, and Timos K. Sellis. "Parametric Query Optimization." Proc. 18th International Conference on Very Large Data Bases, Vancouver, Canada (August 1992).

Consider the following query:

```
EMP WHERE SALARY > salary
```

(where *salary* is a run-time parameter). Suppose there is an index on the SALARY attribute. Then:

■ If *salary* is $10,000/month, then the best way to implement the query is to use the index (because presumably most employees will not qualify).

■ If *salary* is $1,000/month, then the best way to implement the query is by a sequential scan (because presumably most employees *will* qualify).

This example illustrates the point that some optimization decisions are best made at run time, even in a compiling system. The present paper explores the possibility of generating *sets* of query plans at compilation time (each plan being "optimal" for some subset of the set of all possible values of the run-time parameters), and then choosing the appropriate plan at execution time when the actual parameter values are known. In particular, it focuses on one particular parameter, namely the amount of buffer space available to the query. Experimental results show that the approach described imposes very little time overhead on the optimization process and sacrifices very little in terms of quality of the generated plans; accordingly, it is claimed that the approach can significantly improve query performance. "The savings in execution cost of using a plan that is specifically tailored to actual parameter values . . . could be enormous."

18.50   Goetz Graefe. "Query Evaluation Techniques for Large Databases." *ACM Comp. Surv. 25,* No. 2 (June 1993).

Answers to Selected Exercises

18.1   (a) Valid. (b) Valid. (c) Valid. (d) Not valid. (e) Valid. (f) Not valid (it would be valid if we replaced the AND by an OR). (g) Not valid. (h) Not valid.

18.2   By way of example, we show that join is commutative. The join A JOIN B of relations $A\{X,Y\}$ and $B\{Y,Z\}$ is a relation with heading $\{X,Y,Z\}$ and body consisting of the set of all tuples $\{X:x,Y:y,Z:z\}$ such that a tuple appears in A with X-value x and Y-value y and a tuple appears in B with Y-value y and Z-value z. This definition is clearly symmetric in A and B. Thus, A JOIN B is the same as B JOIN A.

18.3   By way of example, we show that union is associative. The union A UNION B of two type-compatible relations A and B is a relation with the same heading as each of A and B and with a body consisting of the set of all tuples t belonging to A or B or both. Thus, if C is another type-compatible relation:

   - The union (A UNION B) UNION C is a relation with the same heading and with a body consisting of all tuples t belonging to (A UNION B) or C or both;
   - The union A UNION (B UNION C) is a relation with the same heading and with a body consisting of all tuples t belonging to A or (B UNION C) or both.

   These two relations have the same heading, and the body in each case is the set of all tuples t such that t belongs to at least one of A, B, C. The two relations are thus identical.

18.4   We show that union distributes over intersection.

   - If $t \in A$ UNION (B INTERSECT C), then $t \in A$ or $t \in B$ INTERSECT C.
   - If $t \in A$, then $t \in A$ UNION B and $t \in A$ UNION C and hence $t \in$ (A UNION B) INTERSECT (A UNION C).
   - If $t \in B$ INTERSECT C, then $t \in B$ and $t \in C$, so $t \in A$ UNION B and $t \in A$ UNION C and hence (again) $t \in$ (A UNION B) INTERSECT (A UNION C).
   - Conversely, if $t \in$ (A UNION B) INTERSECT (A UNION C), then $t \in A$ UNION B and $t \in A$ UNION C. Hence $t \in A$ or $t \in$ both of B and C. Hence $t \in A$ UNION (B INTERSECT C).

18.5   We show that A UNION (A INTERSECT B) = A. If $t \in A$ then clearly $t \in A$ UNION (A INTERSECT B). Conversely, if $t \in A$ UNION (A INTERSECT B), then $t \in A$ or $t \in$ both of A and B; either way, $t \in A$.

18.6   By way of example, we consider the distributivity of projection over join. The projection (A JOIN B)[X] is equivalent to the join $A[Y]$ JOIN $B[Z]$ if and only if the set of attributes X is equal to the union of the sets of attributes Y and Z and includes all of the common attributes of A and B.

18.9   A good set of such rules can be found in reference [18.3].

18.10   A good set of such rules can be found in reference [18.3].

18.11   (a)   Get "nonLondon" suppliers who do not supply part P2.

  (b)   Get Paris suppliers.

  (c)   Get "nonLondon" suppliers such that no supplier supplies fewer kinds of parts.

  (d)   Get London suppliers.

  (e)   Get the empty set of suppliers.

  (f)   No simplification possible.

  (g)   Get the empty set of suppliers.

  (h)   Get the empty set of pairs of suppliers.

  (i)   Get the empty set of parts.

  (j)   Get "nonParis" suppliers such that no supplier supplies more kinds of parts.

Note that certain queries—to be specific, queries (e), (g), (h), and (i)—can be answered directly from the integrity constraints themselves.

18.15   For processing reasons, the true highest and/or lowest value is sometimes some kind of *dummy* value—e.g., the highest "employee name" might be a string of all Z's, the lowest might be a string of all blanks. Estimates of (e.g.) the average increment from one column value to the next in sequence would be skewed if they were based on such dummy values.

19 Domains, Relations, and Data Types

19.1 Introduction

In Chapter 4 we said that a domain is essentially a data type—possibly a primitive, builtin, system-defined data type such as INTEGER or FLOAT or BOOLEAN, more generally a **user-defined** data type such as "supplier number" or "part number" or "weight" or "color." Each domain provides a conceptual pool of scalar values—**scalars** for short—from which various attributes in various relations take their actual values; those attributes are said to be **defined on** the domain in question. Each attribute is defined on just one underlying domain.

Before we go any further, we should make it clear that the user who defines a new user-defined data type is unlikely to be an ordinary end user; the job of defining a new type clearly requires certain special IT skills—not least because (as we will see in the next section) an intrinsic part of the task of defining a new data type involves the definition of the **operators** that apply to instances of that type. Thus, the user in question will certainly be an IT professional, probably a member of the DBA staff. *Note:* The term "database customizer" is sometimes used to refer to such a specialist user.

In passing, we should also mention the term "**abstract** data type" (ADT), which is often used with much the same meaning as user-defined data type.

Now, we explained in Chapter 4 how domains constrain comparisons, in the sense that the comparands in any given comparison are generally required to come from the same domain (but see Section 19.2). It follows that, as explained in Chapter 6, domains also constrain certain operations of the relational algebra, *viz.* those operations that involve scalar comparisons, either explicitly (as in restrict) or implicitly (as in divide). In particular, the union, intersection, and difference operations require their operands to be "the same shape" or **type-compatible** (more usually called *union-compatible,* but this term is deprecated, for reasons to be discussed in Section 19.3). And we defined type-compatibility by saying that two relations are type-compatible if they have *identical headings*—i.e., they have the same set of attribute names, and attributes with the same name are defined on the same domain (we will make this definition more precise in Section 19.3).

We also indicated in our earlier discussions, however, that there is considerably more to these concepts than might appear at first glance, and promised to return to them in a later chapter. This is that chapter.

19.2 Domains

We begin by elaborating on domains *per se*. First we take a closer look at the effect of domains on scalar comparison operations such as =, ≠, <, etc.

"Domain-Check Override" *vs.* Strong Typing

We have said that domains constrain comparisons. In the context of the suppliers-and-parts database, for instance, the comparison SP.S# = S.S# is clearly valid, because the comparands come from the same domain, while the comparison SP.P# = S.S# is clearly *not* valid, because the comparands come from different domains. In reference [4.4], however, Codd proposes **"domain-check override"** versions of some (not all) of the relational algebra operations, which allow the operations in question to be performed even if they involve a comparison across different domains. A domain-check override version of join, for example, will cause the join to be done even if the joining attributes are defined on different domains.

The justification for such domain-check override (DCO) operations is that *there will be occasions when the user knows more than the system does*. In a database concerning suppliers and customers, for example, the query "Get suppliers who are also customers" might well involve a comparison between a supplier number and a customer number, and it might equally well be the case that supplier numbers and customer numbers are two different domains. And if this is indeed a reasonable query, then the system must certainly not prevent the user from asking it. So we do need a way of overriding domain checks on occasion. In this writer's opinion, however, "DCO operations" are not the appropriate way of dealing with this requirement, for reasons we now proceed to discuss.

First of all, the legality of even such a simple expression as P.WEIGHT > 15 is sufficient to show that *some* means of performing cross-domain comparisons is required; after all, we are comparing a weight and an integer in this example, and weights and integers are (presumably) different domains. But there is more to it than that. Let us consider a slightly more complex example, the comparison

```
P.WEIGHT > SP.QTY
```

(part weight *vs.* shipment quantity). Assuming that weights and quantities are different domains, we can surely agree that this comparison does not make sense, i.e., is not valid. But suppose we write it slightly differently:

```
P.WEIGHT - SP.QTY > 0
```

According to reference [4.4], this revised comparison is now to be regarded as valid—the system now does *not* perform the same domain checking as before, but merely confirms that all values concerned are of the same "basic data type" (i.e., are all numbers, in the example). In other words, the two expressions, which are clearly identical from a logical point of view, apparently have different semantics. Now, this state of affairs *cannot* be correct, or acceptable. So there seems to be something suspect in the basic notion of domain checking as described in reference [4.4], which implies *a fortiori* that there is something suspect in the "domain-check override" notion too.

Next, consider the comparisons (or conditional expressions)

```
S.S# = 'X3'
P.P# = 'X3'
S.S# = P.P#
```

Of these three expressions:

■ The first is valid, and might even evaluate to *true;*

■ The second is valid, and might even evaluate to *true;*

■ The third is not valid.

In other words, we can apparently have three values, *a, b,* and *c,* say, such that *a = c* is *true* and *b = c* is *true* and yet *a = b* is not *true!*—in fact, the expression *a = b* cannot even legitimately be written. How can this state of affairs be explained?

The answer, of course, is that the (valid) expressions above involve certain **implicit data type conversions** (sometimes called **coercions**). In the first comparison, the character string literal value "X3" is implicitly converted to type S#, and the comparison is between two supplier numbers—which is clearly valid. In the second comparison, the "X3" is implicitly converted to type P#, and the comparison is between two part numbers, which again is clearly valid. But in the third case, *there is no conversion known to the system* that can convert a supplier number to a part number or *vice versa,* and so the comparison fails on a **type error**.

(When we talk of implicit conversions, of course, it is important to understand that the conversion itself might raise an error. In particular, it will do so if the value to be converted has no counterpart in the target domain. For example, consider an attempt to convert the character string "Red" to type S#.)

So we see that the domains S# and P# are (to repeat) really user-defined data types, each of which is represented in terms of the underlying system-defined data type "character string." Part of the process of defining the domains S# and P# will, in all likelihood, consist of defining suitable **conversion functions** (also called S# and P#, respectively, in the example above) for converting a character string to a supplier number or part number, as applicable; these functions will be used implicitly by the system in dealing with expressions such as the two valid comparisons discussed above. In addition, the domain definer might also provide a function, say CHAR, for "going the other way"—i.e., for converting a supplier number or a part number to a character string. And if we really did want to test a supplier number and a part number for equality, then presumably what we really want to know is whether *their character string representations* are the same:

```
CHAR ( S.S# ) = CHAR ( P.P# )
```

This kind of mechanism, making use of either implicit or explicit conversion functions, provides the "domain-check override" capability, but does so in a manner that is clean, systematic (i.e., not *ad hoc*), and fully orthogonal. In particular, there is now no need to clutter up the relational algebra with new operations such as "DCO join" (etc.).

To summarize matters so far: Instead of saying that the comparands in a given comparison must be defined on the same domain, it would be better—more accurate—to say they must be **type-compatible**. That is, given a comparison such as "$A \theta B$" (where A and B denote scalar values and θ denotes a scalar comparison operator), *either* (a) A and B must be of the same type (i.e., come from the same domain), *or* (b) there must be some conversion function known to the system such that A and B can at least be converted to the same type (i.e., same domain).

By now some readers will have realized that what we have been talking about is what is known in programming language circles as **strong typing**. Actually, different writers have slightly different definitions for this concept; as we use the term, however, it means, among other things, that (a) everything *has* a type, and (b) whenever we write an expression, the system checks that *either* the operands of each operator in that expression are of the right type for that operator *or* there exist appropriate conversion functions for converting them to the right type. (And note carefully that "expression" here does not mean comparison expressions only. See the next subsection below.) Strong typing is a good idea, because it provides a basis for catching type errors at compilation time instead of at run time.

One final remark: Some writers would argue for a particularly strong form of strong typing, according to which type conversions would always be explicit, never implicit. Under such a scheme, even such a simple comparison as P.WEIGHT > 15 would be syntactically invalid (assuming the domain of weights is not just integers, of course), and would instead have to be expressed as—for example—P.WEIGHT > WEIGHT(15). For the purposes of this chapter, however, we will continue to assume that conversions can indeed be implicit.

Other Scalar Operations

Recognizing that the concept under discussion is really strong typing allows us to recognize also that it is not just comparisons to which the concept is relevant (despite the emphasis on comparisons in most of the database literature). For example, consider the following expressions:

```
P.WEIGHT + SP.QTY

P.WEIGHT * SP.QTY
```

The first of these presumably makes no sense, and the DBMS should reject it. The second, on the other hand, does make sense: It represents the computation of the total weight for all parts involved in the shipment (the result thus also belongs to the domain of weights, i.e., is of type WEIGHT—see paragraph 4 below).

Complete support for the domain notion would thus include at least all of the following:

1. The ability to specify, for each domain *Di,* the valid monadic operators that apply to values *di* from that domain. This will tell the system, among other things, that a character string can be converted to a supplier number, and (by exclusion) that a supplier number cannot be converted to a part number.

2. The ability to specify, for each pair of domains *Di* and *Dj* (not necessarily distinct), the valid dyadic operators that apply to pairs of values *di* and *dj* from those domains *Di* and *Dj.* This will tell the system, for example, that the expressions SP.S# = S.S# and P.WEIGHT * SP.QTY are valid, and (by exclusion) that the expressions SP.P# = S.S# and P.WEIGHT + SP.QTY are invalid. Note in particular that this is how the system knows which comparison operators (i.e., which "θ"s) apply to which domains; recall from Chapter 6, for example, that the only "θ"s that make sense for the domain SEX (with values "Male" and "Female") are "=" and "≠"— "<" does not make sense.

3. More generally, the ability to specify, for each combination of *n* not-necessarily-distinct domains ($n \geq 0$), the valid *n*-adic operators that apply to collections of *n* values, one from each of those *n* domains.

4. The ability to specify, for each valid operator, the domain of the result of that operator. This will tell the system, for example, that multiplying a part weight by a shipment quantity produces another weight.

The foregoing points have a number of significant implications, which we briefly summarize here:

■ First, and most important, they imply that the system will know (a) exactly which scalar expressions are **legal,** and (b) the **domain of the result** for each such legal expression.

■ They also imply that the total set of domains (for a given database or other operational unit of "data in the large") must be a **closed set**—that is, the domain of the result of every legal scalar expression must be a domain that is known to the system. Observe in particular that that closed set of domains *must* include the domain "Boolean" (i.e., the domain of truth values), if comparisons are to be legal expressions!

■ Finally, the fact that the system knows the domain of the result of every legal expression implies that it also knows which scalar **assignments** are valid. Note that it needs this information in order to handle INSERT and UPDATE operations correctly, since those operations both implicitly involve certain scalar assignments.

Scalars

So far we have said nothing about the nature of the values that can appear inside a domain, except to refer to them as scalars. Our examples have tended to suggest that those values are typically very simple—numbers, strings, etc.—but it is important to understand that *there is absolutely nothing in the relational model that requires them to be limited to such simple forms*. In fact, those "scalar" values can be **as complex as we like**. Thus, we can have domains of engineering drawings, domains of legal contracts, domains of geometric figures, etc., etc. The only requirement is that any internal structure those values might possess must be *invisible to the DBMS*—i.e., as far as the DBMS is concerned, the values are indeed scalar (or "atomic"), as explained in Chapter 4. To use the jargon, the values must be **encapsulated**.

Incidentally, it might be felt in view of the foregoing that the term "scalar" is not very apt. But it is. After all, atoms in the world of physics are likewise "atomic" only when seen from a certain perspective; they actually do have internal structure, but it is useful and convenient to ignore that internal structure when operating at a certain level of abstraction. Thus, we will continue to use the term "scalar" in this book, even though we recognize that *at a lower level of abstraction* those "scalars" can have a structure of arbitrary complexity (they might even be relations!—see the further remarks on this topic later in this section and in Section 19.5).

An example is in order. Suppose we have a database concerning plane figures (circles, polygons, rectangles, etc.). In such a database, we might very well want to have a domain of *points*. One way of defining such a domain might be as follows:

```
CREATE DOMAIN POINT REP ( X FLOAT, Y FLOAT ) ;
```

REP here stands for *representation*—the internal representation of an individual point consists of two FLOAT numbers X and Y, corresponding to the Cartesian *x*- and *y*-coordinates of the point in question.

Alternatively, points might be represented in terms of their *polar* coordinates instead:

```
CREATE DOMAIN POINT REP ( R FLOAT, THETA FLOAT ) ;
```

For simplicity, we will assume the Cartesian representation throughout the following discussion; either way, it makes little difference, because the internal representation will be **hidden from the user** (see the discussion of functions below).

Now we can define relations that make use of the POINT domain. For example:

```
CREATE BASE RELATION TRIANGLES
     ( TRIANGLE_ID ... ,
       A DOMAIN ( POINT ),
       B DOMAIN ( POINT ),
       C DOMAIN ( POINT ) )
     CANDIDATE KEY ( TRIANGLE_ID )
     CANDIDATE KEY ( A, B, C ) ;
```

Note that this relation has four attributes, not seven; the fact that the values in three of those attributes happen to be represented internally as two FLOAT numbers is irrelevant so far as the user (and, in a sense, the DBMS too) is concerned.

As indicated in the previous subsection, it is also necessary to define the *operations* or *functions* (we use the terms interchangeably) that apply to data of type POINT. In particular, we need a function, which we might as well call just POINT, that will create a point out of specified *x*- and *y*-coordinates:

```
CREATE FUNCTION POINT ( A FLOAT, B FLOAT ) RETURNS ( POINT )
    AS BEGIN ;
            DECLARE P POINT ;
            P.X   := A ;
            P.Y   := B ;
            RETURN ( P ) ;
        END ;
```

POINT converts a pair of FLOAT numbers into a point (it is an example of what is sometimes called a **constructor function**). The expressions P.X and P.Y refer to the X and Y components, respectively, of the internal representation of point P. In other words, functions such as POINT are privy to the internal representation of points as two FLOAT numbers, but *users of those functions are not* (this is precisely what it means to say that points are encapsulated—see further discussion below).

Note, incidentally, that invoking a conversion (or "constructor") function such as POINT with literal arguments effectively provides a way of writing a *literal* of the applicable type. For example, the expression POINT(0,0) represents a certain "POINT literal"—in this particular example, the origin point (0,0).

What other functions do we need for data of type POINT? Well, here are two obvious ones:

```
CREATE FUNCTION X ( P POINT ) RETURNS ( FLOAT )
    AS BEGIN ;
            RETURN ( P.X ) ;
        END ;

CREATE FUNCTION Y ( P POINT ) RETURNS ( FLOAT )
    AS BEGIN ;
            RETURN ( P.Y ) ;
        END ;
```

X and Y are functions that return the *x*- and *y*-coordinates of their POINT argument. *Note carefully that we would probably want such functions even if the internal representation of points was in terms of polar, not Cartesian, coordinates.* Indeed, we would probably also want functions R and THETA that returned the polar coordinates of their argument, as well as the functions X and Y just defined, regardless of the internal representation.

Here is an example of the use of the X and Y functions:

```
P   :=   POINT ( X(P), -Y(P) ) ;
```

P here is a variable of type POINT, representing point *p,* say. The effect of the assignment is to update P to represent the point, *p'* say, that is the reflection of *p* in the *x*-axis; i.e., if P previously represented the point (*x,y*), it now represents the point (*x,-y*).

Note very carefully that functions such as POINT, X, Y (etc.) constitute the *only* way that users can operate on data of type POINT; in particular, note that, as already stated, the internal representation of a point as two FLOAT numbers is visible to such functions but is *not* visible to users of those functions, nor indeed to the DBMS. Another way of saying the same thing is that such functions are allowed to **break encapsulation** but users are not.

By the way, the fact that it is necessary to define the functions that apply to a given domain should *not* be taken to imply that those definitions must be "bundled in" with the definition of the domain in question. While it might possibly be argued that such bundling makes sense for functions such as X and Y that apply to a single domain, it obviously does not make sense for functions that apply to *combinations* of domains. For example, we have said that we should be able to multiply a weight by a quantity. So should the definition of the multiplication operation be bundled with the definition of the WEIGHT domain or the QTY domain? The best answer is surely "Neither of the above." We will have more to say on this issue in Chapter 24 (Section 24.3).

To return to the POINT example: Another useful domain for our plane geometry database might be LINESEG (line segments), with definition as follows:

```
CREATE DOMAIN LINESEG REP ( START POINT, END POINT ) ;
```

In other words, the internal representation for a given domain might be specified in terms of previously known *user-defined* domains, not just system-defined domains as in all of our previous examples.

We should not leave this discussion without a couple of forward pointers and a retraction. First, we have shown that domains are data types, possibly user-defined, of (in general) arbitrary internal complexity. Now, if we turn our attention for a moment to **object-oriented** (OO) databases, we find that one of the fundamental OO concepts, the *object class,* is a data type, possibly user-defined, of (in general) arbitrary internal complexity. In other words, domains and object classes are *the same thing.* And so we have here the key to marrying the two technologies (relational and OO) together. We will elaborate on this important issue in Chapter 25.

Second, if domain values can be of arbitrary internal complexity, it follows that it must be possible for a given domain (and hence for attributes defined on that domain) to contain, very specifically, values that are **relations**. In other words, it must be possible to have relations that contain other relations nested inside themselves (the requirements of normalization notwithstanding). This issue we will also revisit later, in Section 19.5.

Third, the retraction. Previous editions of this book distinguished between *simple* and *composite* domains, where a "simple" domain was one that contained primitive values only (e.g., numbers, strings), and a "composite" domain was basically just a combination of simple domains. For example, given the three simple domains YEAR, MONTH, and DAY, we might define a composite domain called DATE in a fairly obvious way. However, it should be clear from everything discussed in this chapter so far that such a capability is not really necessary—it is totally subsumed by the user-defined data type mechanism outlined above. Thus, we no longer agree with the requirement of reference [4.4] that support for "composite" domains in the foregoing sense be explicitly included in the relational model.

CREATE and DESTROY DOMAIN

We conclude this section on domains by summarizing the syntax and semantics of CREATE DOMAIN and DESTROY DOMAIN as discussed so far. First, CREATE DOMAIN:

```
CREATE DOMAIN domain representation [ conditional-expression ] ;
```

Here *domain* is the name of the new domain, the optional *conditional-expression* is a domain integrity constraint (see Chapter 16), and *representation* takes the form

```
REP ( component-rep-commalist )
```

Each *component-rep* in turn consists of an optional component name, followed by the name of the domain corresponding to the component in question. For some examples, see the previous subsection. *Note:* If the commalist contains exactly one *component-rep* and the component name is omitted, the keyword REP and the parentheses can be omitted too, and the CREATE DOMAIN statement reduces to the form shown in all examples prior to this chapter.

As for DESTROY DOMAIN, the syntax is as given in Chapter 4:

```
DESTROY DOMAIN domain ;
```

We said in Chapter 4 that this operation will fail if any base relation currently includes an attribute that is defined on the domain in question. It will also fail if any other domain uses this domain as part of its representation, or if the result of any legal scalar operation is defined to yield values in this domain, or if any other domain is defined as a subtype of this domain (see Section 19.4).

19.3 Relations

Now we turn our attention to relations. As with our discussion of domains in Section 19.2, we begin by taking a closer look at comparison operations—specifically, of course, *relational* comparisons such as "subset of" (see Chapter 6, Section 6.10).

Relational Comparisons

We have seen that domains are scalar data types (with the proviso that the "scalars" in question might actually have an internal structure of arbitrary complexity, but that—at a certain level of abstraction—any such internal structure is hidden from the user and from the DBMS). Now, programming languages additionally recognize certain *composite* data types, which are built up out of other data types (which can be scalar or composite in turn) by means of certain **type constructors**. For example, **arrays** and **lists** are type constructors; thus, we can construct a composite data type that is an array of integers, or a list of arrays of integers, or an array of lists of arrays of character strings, etc., etc.

By the same token, **relations** constitute a type constructor in the relational model.

If we create a new relation—either base or derived—we are, among other things, defining a new composite data type "set of tuples," where the tuples in turn are all of a certain composite type, namely the type specified by the heading of the new relation (see the subsection "Tuples" below). It follows that just as (a) when we compare two scalars, those two scalars must be type-compatible, so (b) when we compare two relations, those two relations must also be type-compatible. And we can now define this latter concept precisely, as follows: Two relations are said to be **type-compatible** if and only if

1. They each have the same set of attribute names (note, therefore, that they must *a fortiori* have the same degree);

and

2. Corresponding attributes—i.e., attributes with the same name in the two relations—are type-compatible in turn, in the sense defined in Section 19.2.

Other Relational Operations

It should be clear that with relations, as with scalars, the notion of type compatibility applies to much more than just comparison operations. To be specific, it applies to relational *assignments* (i.e., if we assign relation B to relation A, then A and B must be type-compatible); also, of course, it applies to the *union, intersection,* and *difference* operations of the relational algebra. All of these possibilities raise the question of the type (or heading) for the result of an arbitrary relational expression—i.e., for a *derived relation*—which we now consider.

Now, we already have a set of rules defining the *attribute names* for an arbitrary derived relation (refer to Chapter 6 if you need to refresh your memory). But a relational heading is not just a set of attribute names, it is a set of attribute-name/domain-name pairs. The distinction was unimportant in Chapter 6, since we were assuming in that chapter that whenever a scalar comparison was involved the comparands had to come from the *same* domain. Now, however, we know that it is sufficient merely that the comparands be type-compatible. Thus, for example, we might wish to join two relations $A\{X,Y\}$ and $B\{Y,Z\}$, where the common attribute Y is defined on domain YA in relation A and some distinct domain YB in relation B. Provided domains YA and YB are type-compatible, such a join is a perfectly feasible proposition, and we obtain a result relation—C, say—with attributes $\{X,Y,Z\}$ (of course). But what is the domain of Y in that result relation C? It must be either YA or YB—but which is it?

Well, the fact that YA and YB are type-compatible implies that either values of type YA can be converted to values of type YB or *vice versa,* or possibly both. Only in the "both" case is there any possible ambiguity. In that case, the answer has to be that the result domain is whichever of YA and YB has **higher precedence**.* For example, if YA

---

* The notion of precedence would be unnecessary if implicit conversions were not supported. As a consequence, the "slightly strange implication" noted in the next paragraph (q.v.) also would not arise.

is the domain of supplier numbers and *YB* is the domain of character strings, we would presumably prefer the result domain to be *YA;* i.e., we would presumably regard supplier numbers as having higher precedence than character strings. Such precedence rules will be builtin for the system-defined data types but will have to be specified by the domain definer(s) in other cases. In fact, we were tacitly assuming the existence of such rules in Section 19.2 when we suggested that the system should be capable of implicitly converting a character string to a supplier number but not the other way about.

The concepts of type compatibility and (in many cases) type precedence apply not only to join but also to most of the other relational operations, including in particular union, intersection, and difference; the details are tedious but straightforward, and we omit them here. (Well, perhaps we should note one slightly strange implication of the precedence rules, which is that the result of, e.g., a union might quite legitimately include a tuple that does not appear in either of the two operands!)

Incidentally, we can now see why "union compatibility" is not a very good term. For one thing, the concept does not apply only to union, as we already know. For another, it does not really apply to union as such anyway, but rather to the special kind of union found in the relational algebra—and to say that *A* and *B* are compatible for (relational) union if and only if they are (relationally) union-compatible seems a trifle tautological. Finally, different DBMSs, different languages, and different writers all have different definitions of the concept; the definition of reference [4.4], for example, is much more *ad hoc* than the one we have given in this chapter. For these reasons among others, we prefer our term *type-compatible*.

Tuples

We have now discussed *domains* (which are scalar types), also *relations* (which are not themselves types but are certainly *of* some [composite] type), but we have skipped over *tuples,* which likewise are of some [composite] type (**tuple** is another type constructor). Basically, a tuple is a set of ordered pairs

```
{ <A1:v1>, <A2:v2>, ..., <An:vn> }
```

in which each *Ai* is an attribute name and each *vi* is a value from the (unique) domain *Di* corresponding to attribute *Ai*. (Note that—at least in the relational algebra as defined in this book—tuples can appear only in a context in which the corresponding relation is always at least implicitly known, and hence the domain corresponding to each attribute is likewise always known.) Each tuple thus has a type, *viz.*, the heading

```
{ <A1:D1>, <A2:D2>, ..., <An:Dn> }
```

So the notions of type and type compatibility apply to tuples also. Without going into details, we observe that these notions apply (of course) to tuple assigments and tuple comparisons. **Tuple assignments** are not directly supported by the relational model in its present form; however, **tuple comparisons** certainly are (albeit implicitly), in the following contexts among others:

- Union, intersection, and difference processing
- Join and divide processing
- Summarize processing
- Testing a tuple for membership in a relation via the set membership operator ϵ (see Chapter 6, Section 6.10)
- Referential integrity checking

19.4   Type Inheritance

The basic idea of type inheritance was introduced and discussed briefly in Chapter 12 (Section 12.3). We now examine that idea, and the related concepts of *subtype* and *supertype,* in more depth.

It is perhaps as well to state right at the outset that there is little true consensus regarding the meanings of these terms (see, e.g., reference [19.1], which lists at least eight different candidate interpretations). Broadly speaking, however, type Y is said to be a **subtype** of type X—equivalently, type X is said to be a **supertype** of type Y—if and only if every instance of Y is necessarily an instance of X. For instance, the type CIRCLE is a subtype of the type ELLIPSE—equivalently, the type ELLIPSE is a supertype of the type CIRCLE—because every individual circle can be regarded as a special case of an ellipse. The converse is not true, of course (i.e., some ellipses are not circles).

Why are such concepts useful? One reason—again broadly speaking—is that if the system knows that every Y is an X, then it immediately knows that properties that apply to instances of type X also apply to instances of type Y. We say that type Y **inherits** the properties that apply to type X. As a consequence, the user can always use a Y wherever an X is permitted (i.e., in expressions of various kinds): the principle of **substitutability**. For example, a function that expects an argument of type ELLIPSE can always be invoked with an argument of type CIRCLE instead. (*Note:* Substitutability does not apply to functions that *break encapsulation,* since the supertype and subtype might have different representations. See point 2 in the subsection "Domains" below.)

The term **reusability** is also frequently encountered in the literature in this context. Reusability refers to the fact that, e.g., the code to perform a certain operation on an X might (perhaps!) be usable without change on a Y. For example, the code to rotate an ellipse through 90 degrees, if applied to a circle, will certainly work, even though (for obvious reasons) it might not be a very efficient way of "rotating" a circle.

The foregoing ideas can be applied at both the domain and the relation level. We consider each case in turn.

Domains

Suppose we define a domain of ellipses:

```
CREATE DOMAIN ELLIPSE REP ( A FLOAT, B FLOAT ) ;
```

We assume for simplicity that the only ellipses we are interested in are those that are centered on the origin; A and B are the lengths of the semiaxes of the ellipse in question (the equation for an ellipse is $x^2/a^2 + y^2/b^2 = 1$).

Let us also define a function that returns the area of a specified ellipse:

```
CREATE FUNCTION AREA ( E ELLIPSE ) RETURNS ( FLOAT )
     AS BEGIN ;
            RETURN ( PI * E.A * E.B ) ;
          END ;
```

PI here is the mathematical constant π (the area of an ellipse is πab). Note that this function breaks the encapsulation of ellipses (because it refers to components of the internal representation).

Now let us define a domain of circles, specifying that circles are a subtype of ellipses:

```
CREATE DOMAIN CIRCLE REP ( R FLOAT ) ISA ( ELLIPSE ) ;
```

Points arising:

1. The keyword ISA ("is a") is conventionally used as shown in this example to specify a subtype-supertype relationship.

2. Note that the fact that "every *Y* is an *X*" does not necessarily imply that the *representation* of *Y's* is the same as that of *X's* (it might in fact be so, and then again it might not). In the example, ellipses are represented by their two semiaxis lengths A and B, whereas circles are represented by just their radius R. However, the fact that every *Y* is an *X* certainly does imply that any instance of type *Y* can be **converted** to type *X*. *Exercise for the reader:* Write the conversion function for converting a value of type CIRCLE to type ELLIPSE.

3. Circles are ellipses, and hence functions such as AREA that apply to ellipses apply to circles as well, necessarily. Because of the difference in representation discussed in the previous paragraph, however, it is necessary to *redefine* that function, as follows:

```
CREATE FUNCTION AREA ( C CIRCLE ) RETURNS ( FLOAT )
     AS BEGIN ;
            RETURN ( PI * ( C.R ** 2 ) ) ;
          END ;
```

Note: Of course, we could always compute the area of a given circle by converting it to type ELLIPSE and then applying the *ellipse* AREA function to the result.

4. Because a circle is a special kind of ellipse, there might well exist functions that apply to circles but not to ellipses in general. For example:

```
CREATE FUNCTION DIAMETER ( C CIRCLE ) RETURNS ( FLOAT )
     AS BEGIN ;
            RETURN ( 2 * C.R ) ;
          END ;
```

In order to avoid a possible confusion here, it is worth pointing out explicitly that (as the example illustrates) the *sub*type has a *super*set of the functionality.

5. Observe now that if we write an expression such as

   ```
   AREA ( figure )
   ```

   (where *figure* is a variable), the system might not be able to determine at compilation time whether the argument is actually a circle or just an ellipse. If it cannot, the question as to which version of the AREA function to invoke will have to be deferred until run time—**"run-time binding."**

6. The types ELLIPSE and CIRCLE constitute a very simple example of a **type hierarchy**. In general, of course, type hierarchies can be arbitrarily complex; see Fig. 19.1 for an extended example. *Note:* In order to avoid a possible confusion, we should point out that Fig. 19.1 assumes that TRIANGLE is a *domain,* whereas in Section 19.2 we defined TRIANGLES (plural) as a *base relation.*

   Type hierarchies are also known variously as *class* hierarchies ("class" is sometimes used as a synonym for "type"), *generalization* hierarchies (on the grounds that, e.g., an ellipse is a generalization of a circle), *specialization* hierarchies (on the grounds that, e.g., a circle is a specialization of an ellipse), *inclusion* hierarchies (on the grounds that, e.g., the set of circles is included in the set of ellipses), or simply *ISA* hierarchies. In this book, we will stay with the term "type hierarchy."

7. The concept of *type compatibility* needs to be refined and extended slightly if the types concerned are part of a type hierarchy. Basically:

   - In the comparison $A \theta B$, A and B need not be of the same type, but if not, then they must share a common supertype (at some level);

   - In the assignment $A := B$, A and B need not be of the same type, but if not, then A must be a supertype of B (at some level).

8. To sum up: Any given entry in a given type hierarchy automatically inherits all functions that apply to the parent of that entry (and, of course, such inheritance is recursive—i.e., the entry actually inherits the functions that apply to *all ancestors*

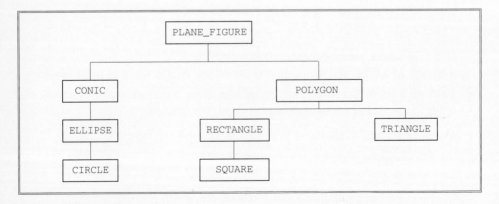

FIG. 19.1 Example of a type hierarchy

of that entry). Such functions can always be redefined at any given level, however. Furthermore, any given entry can have functions of its own that do not apply to ancestors of that entry. *Note:* The ability to apply the "same" function to different types (or, rather, the ability to apply different functions with the same name to different types) is referred to as **polymorphism**. Polymorphism is also known by various different names, including *generic functions, function instances,* and *operator overloading.*

One final point: We stated in the introduction to this section that inheritance applied to "properties" of types. In the case of domains specifically, the "properties" that are inherited are, precisely, *operators* or *functions* as discussed above. In the case of relations, by contrast, the "properties" that are inherited are (principally) the *attributes* of the relation in question, as we will see in the next subsection.

Relations

As indicated earlier, the idea of inheritance can make sense at the relation level as well as at the domain level. Suppose we have a base relation representing employees:

```
CREATE BASE RELATION EMP
     ( EMP#    ... ,
       ENAME   ... ,
       DEPT#   ... ,
       SALARY ... )
     PRIMARY KEY ( EMP# ) ;
```

Now suppose that some employees are programmers (and all programmers are employees). Then we might create a PGMR base relation looking like this:

```
CREATE BASE RELATION PGMR ISA ( EMP )
     ( LANG ... ) ;
```

LANG here represents the particular programming language skill (e.g., C, SQL) possessed by the programmer in question. Points to note:

1. The (composite) type corresponding to relation PGMR can be regarded as a subtype of the (composite) type corresponding to relation EMP. Equivalently, the composite type corresponding to EMP can be regarded as a supertype of the composite type corresponding to PGMR.

2. The CREATE BASE RELATION for relation PGMR can be regarded (in part) as shorthand for the following definition:

```
CREATE BASE RELATION PGMR
     ( EMP#    ... ,
       LANG    ... )
     PRIMARY KEY ( EMP# )
     FOREIGN KEY ( EMP# ) REFERENCES EMP
                          DELETE CASCADES
                          UPDATE CASCADES ;
```

In other words, relation PGMR has exactly two attributes of its own: EMP#, which is both the primary key and also a foreign key referencing the primary key of EMP, and LANG. In addition, the system knows—because of the "ISA (EMP)" specification—that (a) a given EMP tuple has at most one corresponding PGMR tuple, and (b) a given PGMR tuple can be regarded as inheriting the ENAME, DEPT#, and SALARY attribute values from the (unique) corresponding EMP tuple (see Fig. 19.2). Thus, an expression such as (e.g.) PGMR.DEPT#—in a query, say— can be accepted as legal. Note, therefore, that the *sub*type has a *super*set of the attributes, conceptually speaking.

3. Any function that works for employees should work for programmers too. Note, incidentally, that application programs can be regarded as "functions" in this context.

4. In the case of domains, as explained in the previous subsection, we can define a function at the subtype level that effectively overrides a function with the same name at the supertype level. In the case of relations, analogously, we can define an attribute at the subtype level that effectively overrides an attribute with the same name at the supertype level. For example, we might define an attribute HIREDATE for relation EMP (meaning the date the employee was hired into the company), and another attribute HIREDATE for relation PGMR (meaning the date the employee was hired into the programming department). The expression PGMR.HIREDATE would then refer to the latter of these two attributes, not the former. (However, it would be possible to include the former as an attribute of programmers as well by making use of the "attribute RENAME" operator. See Chapter 6.)

5. Again, type hierarchies can be arbitrarily complex. For example, some programmers might be application programmers and others might be system programmers; thus we might say that APPLICATION_PROGRAMMER and SYSTEM_ PROGRAMMER are both subtypes of the PROGRAMMER supertype. And so on, recursively, to any number of levels.

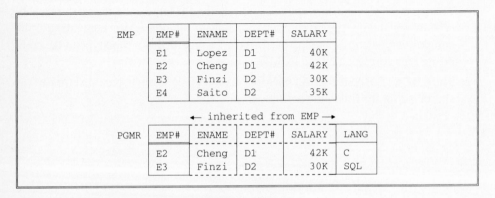

FIG. 19.2 Employees and programmers (sample values)

Multiple Inheritance

Note: We mention this topic merely for completeness; we deliberately do not go into very much detail.

Throughout this discussion so far, we have assumed that every subtype has a single immediate supertype. However, some writers and systems have proposed (and in some cases implemented) the possibility of **multiple inheritance,** on the grounds that "single inheritance" is too simplistic a concept to capture the richness of real-world situations. Multiple inheritance allows a given type to be a subtype of several distinct supertypes simultaneously. For example, the type WHALE might be a subtype of the types MAMMAL and MARINE_ANIMAL simultaneously, meaning that every individual whale inherits all properties of mammals *and* all properties of marine animals (but, of course, some mammals are not marine animals and some marine animals are not mammals, so neither one is a subtype of the other). Refer to Fig. 19.3.

Note, incidentally, that the term "type hierarchy" is no longer totally appropriate if multiple inheritance is involved. For this reason, some writers use the term "type **lattice**" instead.

One problem that arises with multiple inheritance is that of *naming conflicts;* that is, several of the supertypes for a given subtype might have a property with the same name. Furthermore, those several properties might or might not be semantically equivalent; for example, mammals and marine animals might both have a LIFESPAN property (semantically equivalent) or a TAIL property (yes or no for mammals and tail length for marine animals, and hence semantically distinct). Some mechanism for dealing with such situations is needed.

Another, more fundamental problem is that the basic notion of multiple inheritance is itself subject to several different interpretations. For example, consider the situation illustrated in Fig. 19.4, in which some employees are full-time and some are part-time, and further there are both full- and part-time programmers (PGMR) and full- and part-time secretaries (SECY). This example differs from that of Fig. 19.3 in that (for example) an individual programmer inherits *either* the properties of full-time employees *or* the properties of part-time employees, but not both.

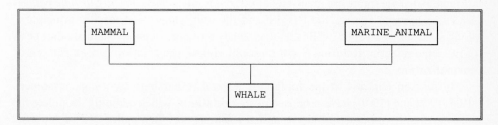

FIG. 19.3 Multiple inheritance

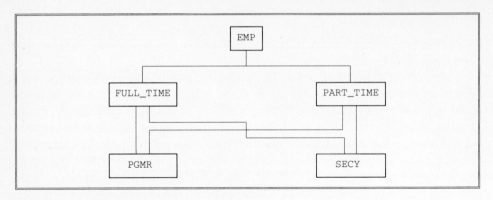

FIG. 19.4 Multiple inheritance (another example)

19.5   Relation-Valued Attributes (A Digression)

In our discussion of scalars in Section 19.2, we explained that such "scalars" can have a structure of arbitrary complexity when viewed at a lower level of abstraction, and we mentioned that they might even be relations. In other words, we can have domains, and therefore attributes, that are relation-valued, and thus have relations that contain other relations inside themselves (and so on, recursively, to any number of levels). In this section we digress briefly to examine this idea in a little more detail. *Note:* The following discussion is heavily based on reference [19.3]. Refer to that paper for further information.

Fig. 19.5 shows an example of a relation with a relation-valued attribute (abbreviated RVA). One point to note immediately about that relation is that the empty set of parts supplied by supplier S5 is represented by an empty set! (more precisely, an empty relation)—not by some ill-advised "null," as it would be if we formed the "outer join" of suppliers and shipments over S# (see Chapter 20). In fact, one immediate advantage of RVAs is that they deal more elegantly with the problem that outer join is intended to solve than outer join does itself. Indeed, the outer join operator as usually understood would be quite unnecessary if the system supported RVAs.

Another point that must be made absolutely clear is the following: The values of attribute PQ in the figure are indeed relations, *but those values (like all attribute values) are encapsulated.* That is, the DBMS, and the user, cannot—at least in principle—"look inside" those values while simultaneously looking "outside" them at other parts of the same relation. **Relation S_SP does not violate the relational requirement of normalization**.

In marked contrast to the foregoing, several researchers (see, e.g., references [19.6–19.7] and [19.9]) have proposed **nested relations,** which certainly do violate the normalization requirement. Indeed, nested relations are often called "NF^2 relations," where NF^2 = NFNF = "non first normal form"—meaning, specifically, that such relations are quite definitely *not* normalized. (Relation S_SP, by contrast, *is* in first normal

S_SP	S#	SNAME	STATUS	CITY	PQ	
	S1	Smith	20	London	P#	QTY
					P1	300
					P2	200
					..	...
					P6	100
	S2	Jones	10	Paris	P#	QTY
					P1	300
					P2	400
	..	.....	..	......	....	
	S5	Adams	30	Athens	P#	QTY

FIG. 19.5 Example of a relation with a relation-valued attribute

form, as already indicated.) Attributes in a nested relation can be relation-valued, as in Fig. 19.5, but those values are not encapsulated. Nested relations therefore typically require significant additions and revisions to the relational algebra, including in particular new **NEST** and **UNNEST** operations for converting between nested and unnested forms of a relation:

- Given a relation and a set of attributes, NEST returns a corresponding nested relation. For example, nesting the usual suppliers relation "along" S#, SNAME, and STATUS yields a nested relation containing three tuples, one for each of the three CITY values (London, Paris, and Athens); each of those tuples contains the appropriate city name and a relation with heading {S#,SNAME,STATUS}, representing the suppliers in that city.

- UNNEST is the opposite of NEST, loosely speaking—though if we unnest *R* "along" some set of attributes and then nest the result "along" those same attributes again, we do not necessarily obtain *R* again! See the annotation to reference [19.9] for an example and further discussion.

The proposals of reference [19.3], by contrast, merely involve some comparatively minor extensions to the EXTEND operator (for both NEST- and UNNEST-like operations).

Detailed discussion of relation-valued attributes would be out of place here. We content ourselves with the following brief list of benefits that proper RVA support could provide:

- RVAs avoid the need for outer join, as already indicated

- RVAs solve certain "zero-case SUMMARIZE" problems (see Section 6.8 and reference [6.3])

- RVAs solve certain "zero-case DIVIDE" problems (see Section 6.6 and reference [6.4])

- RVAs make certain "complex" queries very simple

- RVAs seem to be precisely what is needed to model certain kinds of "complex" data (in rare situations, in other words, we might even want to have RVAs in *base relations*)

19.6   SQL Support

This section is included primarily as a placeholder. The fact is, SQL currently supports almost none of the ideas we have been discussing in this chapter. Refer back to Chapter 8, Section 8.2 (especially the subsection entitled "Domains") to refresh your memory regarding exactly what support SQL does provide in this area.

19.7   Summary

We have discussed the general question of domains, relations, and data types. First, a **domain** is nothing more nor less than a data type—more specifically, a **scalar** data type, possibly system-defined, more generally user-defined, of potentially arbitrary internal complexity. Second, a **relation,** although it is not a type *per se,* certainly *has* a type, namely the **composite** type "set of tuples," where the tuples in turn have a composite type also, namely the type specified by the relation **heading**. And note carefully that these remarks apply to *all* relations, derived relations as well as base relations.

Regarding domains specifically: Any given domain is defined to have a **representation** in terms of previously existing domains, either builtin or user-defined. When a new domain is defined (or possibly at some later time, of course), all **operations** or **functions** that apply to that domain must be defined also (including in particular an operation for specifying "literals" belonging to that domain). Thus, the DBMS will know exactly **which scalar expressions are legal,** and, for those that are, it will also know **the domain of the result**. In particular, it will therefore know the domain for the **derived attributes** that appear in the result of EXTEND and SUMMARIZE operations* (and so we have now tidied up a loose end left over from Chapter 6). We also discussed the syntax and semantics of **CREATE DOMAIN** and **DESTROY DOMAIN**.

Turning now to relations: We did not discuss the question of defining operations

---

* Note that SUMMARIZE involves the use of certain *aggregate* functions (COUNT, SUM, etc.)—i.e., functions that return scalar values but take entire relations as (one of) their arguments. There thus needs to be a mechanism for defining such functions. We omit the details here.

on relations, because of course several such operations—namely the operations of the relational algebra, including certain assignment, update, and comparison operators (see Chapter 6)—are already very familiar and are indeed builtin. Furthermore, those operations are effectively *generic,* in that they apply to all relations. However, there is no reason why those builtin operations should not be augmented with a set of additional, user-defined, relation-specific operations, if the system provides a means for defining them. In some respects, in fact, it could be argued that any given application program is exactly such an "additional, user-defined, relation-specific operation" (except that such operations usually cannot be nested inside general relational expressions, unfortunately).

Next, certain operations—in particular, certain **comparison** operations, and hence certain operations of the relational algebra, such as **union**—require their operands (be they scalars, tuples, or relations) to be **type-compatible**. Type compatibility is also required for the source and target in **assignment** operations. Type compatibility means that either (a) the two types are the same, or (b) there exists some conversion function known to the system such that one type can be converted to the other. We stress the point that the concept applies at both the domain level and the relation level.

We then discussed the question of **subtypes and supertypes** and the related questions of **inheritance** and **type hierarchies** (touching briefly on the possibility of **multiple inheritance** and **type lattices**). All of these concepts also apply at both the domain level and the relation level:

- First, if domain *Y* is defined as a subtype of domain *X,* any function that applies to instances of domain *X* necessarily applies to instances of domain *Y* also (though such functions might possibly need to be redefined for domain *Y*). In addition, there might be certain functions that apply to instances of domain *Y* but not to instances of domain *X*.

- Second, if base relation *Y* is defined to have a type that is a subtype of the type of base relation *X,* any attribute of base relation *X* can be regarded as an implicit attribute of base relation *Y* also. In addition, base relation *Y* might possess attributes of its own that do not apply to base relation *X*.

In both cases the *sub*type has a *super*set of the functionality.

Note: Do not confuse type hierarchies with what might be called *representation* hierarchies. That is, the fact that (e.g.) POINTs and ELLIPSEs are both represented by two FLOAT numbers certainly does not imply that either is a subtype of the other. Equally, the fact that CIRCLEs are a subtype of ELLIPSEs does not imply that either one's representation is a subset of the other's (it might be, or then again it might not).

Next we digressed briefly to introduce the idea of **relation-valued attributes** (RVAs), and claimed that such attributes—if correctly implemented—do not violate the relational requirement for normalization. We contrasted "proper" RVA support (i.e., support that does not violate the relational model's requirement for normalization) with **nested relation** support (which does violate that requirement). We also listed some of the benefits that would accrue from proper RVA support.

Finally, we pointed out that SQL in its present form supports almost none of the ideas discussed in the body of this chapter.

Exercises

19.1 Define the following terms:

type compatibility

coercion

encapsulation

strong typing

type constructor

subtype, supertype

inheritance

substitutability

polymorphism

union compatibility

domain-check override

Why are the last two terms deprecated?

19.2 Give an example of a query requiring "domain-check override" on the supplier-parts-projects database.

19.3 In a system that supported strong typing as discussed in this chapter, which of the following scalar expressions on the suppliers-parts-projects database would be legal? State the domain of the result in the legal cases.

(a) `J.CITY = P.CITY`

(b) `JNAME || PNAME`

(c) `QTY + 100`

(d) `QTY * 100`

(e) `P.COLOR = P.CITY`

(f) `J.CITY < P.CITY`

(g) `J.CITY = P.CITY || 'burg'`

19.4 Spell out in detail the implications for update operations of the implicit foreign key specification in the EMP/PGMR example in Section 19.4.

19.5 Using the syntax sketched in the present chapter, define a *rectangle* data type and a *square* data type, where *square* is a subtype of *rectangle*. For simplicity, assume that all rectangles are "square on" to the axes, so that all sides are either vertical or horizontal. Give (a) an answer involving RECTANGLE and SQUARE domains, (b) an answer involving RECTANGLE and SQUARE base relations.

19.6 Consider the "type lattice" of Fig. 19.4. We could avoid the apparent need for multiple inheritance in that example (and thereby convert the lattice into a true hierarchy) by defining a single supertype (EMP) and four immediate subtypes, representing full-time programmers, part-time programmers, full-time secretaries, and part-time secretaries, respectively. What—if anything—is wrong with this idea?

19.7 What catalog support is needed in order to deal with strong typing?

19.8 What catalog support is needed in order to deal with type inheritance?

References and Bibliography

19.1 J. Craig Cleaveland. *An Introduction to Data Types*. Reading, Mass.: Addison-Wesley (1986).

19.2 E. F. Codd. "Extending the Relational Database Model to Capture More Meaning." *ACM TODS 4*, No. 4 (December 1979).

Codd's paper on the extended version of the relational model known as RM/T includes a discussion of the use of relations—but not domains—to represent subtypes and super-types. Multiple inheritance and implementation issues (specifically, catalog design issues) are also discussed. *Note:* References [5.1] and [12.5] are also references to this paper; see the annotation to those references for further elaboration.

19.3 Hugh Darwen. "Relation-Valued Attributes." In C. J. Date and Hugh Darwen, *Relational Database Writings 1989–1991*. Reading, Mass.: Addison-Wesley (1992).

19.4 C. J. Date. "What Is a Domain?" In C. J. Date, *Relational Database Writings 1985–1989*. Reading, Mass.: Addison-Wesley (1990).

As indicated in the annotation in Chapter 4 (reference [4.8]), this paper is an attempt to provide a systematic and comprehensive tutorial on the relational domain concept. It identifies the following aspects of domain support (i.e., the following is a necessary but not sufficient list of features that a DBMS must provide in order to be able to claim full support for domains):

- An operator for defining new domains (specifying at least a name and a representation for the domain)
- The ability to specify the relevant domain for each attribute of each base relation
- Operators to drop and alter domains
- Domain-level integrity constraints
- Support for appropriate literals
- Appropriate data type conversion or coercion rules, including in particular certain type inheritance rules
- The ability to specify the operators that apply to each domain or combination of domains
- Appropriate catalog support for all of the foregoing

The paper also includes an extensive list of the advantages of proper domain support.

19.5 Linda G. DeMichiel, Donald D. Chamberlin, Bruce G. Lindsay, Rakesh Agrawal, and Manish Arya. "Polyglot: Extensions to Relational Databases for Sharable Types and Functions in a Multi-Language Environment." IBM Research Report RJ8888 (July 1992).

To quote from the abstract: "Polyglot is an extensible relational database type system that supports inheritance, encapsulation, and dynamic method dispatch." (*Dynamic method dispatch* is another term for run-time binding. To continue:) "[Polyglot] allows use from multiple application languages and permits objects to retain their behavior as they cross the boundary between database and application program. This paper describes the design of Polyglot, extensions to the SQL language to support the use of Polyglot types and meth-ods, and the implementation of Polyglot in the Starburst relational database [prototype]." (See references [25.17–25.19] for further discussion of Starburst.)

Polyglot is clearly addressing the kinds of issues that are the subject of the present chapter. A couple of comments are worth making here, however. First, the relational term **domain** is (surprisingly) never mentioned. Second, Polyglot provides the builtin type con-structors (the Polyglot term is *metatypes*) **base-type, tuple-type, rename-type, array-type,** and **language-type,** but (again surprisingly) not **relation-type**. However, the system is designed to allow the introduction of additional type constructors.

19.6 G. Jaeschke and H. Schek. "Remarks on the Algebra of Non First Normal Form Relations." Proc. ACM SIGACT-SIGMOD Symposium on Principles of Database Systems, Los Angeles, Calif. (March 1982).

An early paper on nested relations. It discusses the case in which the nesting is at most one level deep (i.e., relations can have set-valued attributes, but the elements of those sets cannot be decomposed any further). This is the paper that introduced the original versions of the NEST and UNNEST operators.

19.7 A. Makinouchi. "A Consideration on Normal Form of Not-Necessarily-Normalized Relations in the Relational Data Model." Proc. 3rd International Conference on Very Large Data Bases, Tokyo, Japan (October 1977).

Makinouchi seems to have been the first researcher to have addressed the idea of nested relations seriously, although the "quotient relation" ideas of reference [6.10] can be regarded as an early attack on the same problem.

19.8 Sylvia L. Osborn and T. E. Heaven. "The Design of a Relational Database System with Abstract Data Types for Domains." *ACM TODS 11,* No. 3 (September 1986).

Describes an experimental prototype (only partly implemented at the time the paper was written) called RAD that supports the introduction of new abstract (i.e., user-defined) data types, somewhat along the lines sketched in the body of this chapter. The syntax of the CREATE DOMAIN operation (RAD version) gives some idea of the capabilities of the system:

```
CREATE DOMAIN domain AS
        OUTPUT     IS   proc
        INSERT     IS   proc
        UPDATE     IS   proc
        CONSTANTS  ARE  proc
        EQUAL      IS   proc
        LESSTHAN   IS   proc
        PREDICATES ARE  entry-commalist
```

where each *entry* is of the form

```
pred proc ( domain-commalist )
```

The *procs* are procedures (written in "implementation-level code") that define how instances of the data type are to be displayed (OUTPUT) and entered (INSERT) and modified (UPDATE), what the valid format is for literals of the data type (CONSTANTS), and how equality and ranking comparisons are to be performed on instances of the data type (EQUAL and LESSTHAN). The *preds* are predicates (i.e., truth-valued functions) that allow conditional expressions involving user-defined data types to be used in WHERE clauses. For example, we might have a user-defined data type called (plane) FIGURE and a predicate called OVERLAPS that allows us to test whether two given plane figures overlap:

```
CREATE DOMAIN FIGURE AS
        .......
        PREDICATES ARE OVERLAPS olapfun ( FIGURE, FIGURE ) ...
```

Here *olapfun* is the user-provided procedure that performs the actual test for overlapping. Thus, if F1, F2 are plane figures, we might write a query along the following lines:

```
RETRIEVE ... WHERE OVERLAPS ( F1, F2 )
```

When fully implemented, the system will also allow user-defined aggregate functions on attributes containing such user-defined data types, and user-defined "transformations" (i.e., operations that transform one relation into another).

19.9 Mark A. Roth, Henry F. Korth, and Abraham Silberschatz. "Extended Algebra and Calculus for Nested Relational Databases." *ACM TODS 13,* No. 4 (December 1988).

Defines a calculus and an algebra for arbitrarily nested relations and shows their equivalence. *Note:* The paper explicitly prohibits the possibility of relation-valued attributes having an empty relation as their value (see below). As suggested in the body of this chapter, however, such a capability seems to be precisely what is needed to treat certain "outer join" applications correctly.

We add a remark concerning the *reversibility* of the NEST and UNNEST operations. If we nest relation *R* along some set of attributes, there is always an inverse unnesting that will take us back to *R* again. However, if we unnest (nested) relation *R* along some set of attributes, an inverse nesting to take us back to *R* might or might not exist. Here is an example (based on one given in reference [19.3]). Suppose we have the nested relation TWO shown below and we unnest it along RVX to obtain THREE. If we now nest THREE along X (and name the resulting relation-valued attribute RVX once again), we obtain not TWO but ONE:

TWO	A	RVX
	1	X a b
	1	X a c

THREE	A	X
	1	a
	1	b
	1	c

ONE	A	RVX
	1	X a b c

Note that in ONE, RVX is (necessarily) functionally dependent on A, which is thus a candidate key. If we now unnest ONE along RVX, we return to THREE, and we have already seen that THREE can be nested to give ONE; thus, the nest and unnest operations are indeed inverses of one another for this particular pair of relations. In general, it is the FD that is crucial in determining whether or not a given unnesting is reversible. In fact, if relation *R* has a relation-valued attribute *RVX,* then *R* is reversibly unnestable along *RVX* if and only if the following are both true:

- No tuple of *R* has an empty relation as its *RVX* value.

- *RVX* is functionally dependent on the set of all of the other attributes of *R*. Another way of saying the same thing is that there must be some candidate key of *R* that does not include *RVX* as a component.

19.10 Michael Stonebraker. "Inclusion of New Types in Relational Data Base Systems." Proc. 2nd International Conference on Data Base Engineering, Los Angeles, Calif. (February 1986).

Describes the implementation of a set of extensions to the INGRES prototype to support:

- The definition of new data types
- The definition of operators for such data types
- The definition of new storage structures and access methods for such data types
- The optimization of expressions involving such data types and operators

19.11 Michael Stonebraker, Jeff Anton, and Eric Hanson. "Extending a Database System with Procedures." *ACM TODS 12,* No. 3 (September 1987).

Proposes treating "database procedures" (i.e., collections of database operations, or possibly whole programs in a general-purpose programming language) as a data type, so that attributes of a relation could include such procedures. As a trivial example, the suppliers relation S might be extended to include a attribute called PARTS, and the value of the PARTS attribute for supplier S1 might be the QUEL query

```
RETRIEVE ( SP.P#, SP.QTY ) WHERE SP.S# = "S1"
```

A new operator, EXECUTE, is provided to execute such a procedure. In the example, the effect of executing the procedure would be to allow the user to regard the S1 tuple as *unnormalized,* because (conceptually) it would now include the regular supplier information (S#, SNAME, STATUS, and CITY), together with a *repeating group* of corresponding part information (P# and QTY). Note that this is a rather different approach to the "nested relations" idea (see references [19.3], [19.6–19.7], and [19.9]).

The paper claims that user-defined data types, as advocated in, e.g., references [19.4] and [19.8], are useful for supporting "relatively simple objects that do not require shared subobjects," but that database procedures are better for more complex objects. Certainly one advantage is that most database systems do already have some notion of database procedures anyway; for example, views in a relational system can be regarded in such a light, and so too can the "stored procedures" of systems such as INGRES and SYBASE. Thus, regarding such procedures as "full-fledged database objects" (this is the term used in the paper) has the potential of unifying the treatment of various features that might otherwise be treated in an *ad hoc* and unsystematic manner. Other advantages include the possibility of providing some of the facilities of "semantic" and/or object-oriented DBMSs (see Parts III and VI of this book) in a way that does not do too much violence to the precepts of the relational model. For example, aggregation and generalization [12.22–12.23] and component sharing all seem to be amenable to the approach.

The paper reports on an extended version of the INGRES language QUEL called QUEL+ that incorporates the foregoing ideas, and on an extended version of the INGRES prototype called INGRES+ that implements that language. Benchmark results are included, which show that the performance of INGRES+ is quite competitive with that of the original unmodified INGRES code. Some ideas are offered on how performance might be improved.

19.12   Michael Stonebraker, Erika Anderson, Eric Hanson, and Brad Rubinstein. "QUEL as a Data Type." Proc. 1984 ACM SIGMOD International Conference on Management of Data, Boston, Mass. (June 1984).

An earlier version of reference [19.11].

Answers to Selected Exercises

19.1   The term "union compatibility" is deprecated because, first, it is not very apt; second, its meaning is not sufficiently precise (it is defined differently in different languages, in different systems, and by different writers). The term "domain-check override" is deprecated because the *concept* is deprecated.

19.2   An example might be "Get all parts whose part number has the same character string representation as some project number."

19.3   (a) Legal; result type Boolean. (b) Probably illegal—it depends whether "||" (concatenation) has been defined as a valid operator for the NAME domain. (c) Legal; result type QTY. (d) Legal; result type QTY—though both this one and the previous one might produce a result that violates some QTY domain constraint (see Chapter 16). (d) Probably illegal. (f) Legal, provided "<" is valid for the CITY domain; result type Boolean. (g) Probably illegal (the following, by contrast, would be legal: J.CITY = CHAR(P.CITY) || 'burg').

19.4   For EMP, (a) updating EMP# cascades to update EMP# in the corresponding PGMR tuple (if any); (b) deleting an EMP tuple cascades to delete the corresponding PGMR tuple (if any). For PGMR, (a) inserting a PGMR tuple fails if no corresponding EMP tuple currently exists; (b) updating EMP# fails if no EMP tuple with the new EMP# value currently exists. Note that inserting a PGMR tuple does not require the user to supply ENAME,

DEPT#, and SALARY values; note moreover that it would be inconsistent to allow those inherited attributes to be directly updated (it would seem a little strange to be able to update something that cannot be inserted). It would, however, be possible to define EMP JOIN PGMR as a view, V say, and view *V* could then (in principle) support such INSERT and UPDATE operations. See Chapter 17.

19.5 (a)
```
CREATE DOMAIN RECTANGLE REP ( A POINT, B POINT ) ;
   /* A and B are bottom left and top right corners */

   /* following functions break encapsulation of RECTANGLEs */

CREATE FUNCTION RECTANGLE ( A POINT, B POINT )
                           RETURNS ( RECTANGLE ) ;

     AS BEGIN ;
          DECLARE R RECTANGLE ;
          R.A  := A ;
          R.B  := B ;
          RETURN ( R ) ;
        END ;

CREATE FUNCTION BL ( R RECTANGLE ) RETURNS ( POINT )
     AS BEGIN ;
          RETURN ( R.A ) ;
        END ;

CREATE FUNCTION TR ( R RECTANGLE ) RETURNS ( POINT )
     AS BEGIN ;
          RETURN ( R.B ) ;
        END ;

   /* following assignment transposes rectangle R */

R  :=  RECTANGLE ( BL(R),
              POINT ( X(BL(R)) + Y(TR(R)) - Y(BL(R)),
                      Y(BL(R)) + X(TR(R)) - X(TR(R)) ) ) ;

CREATE DOMAIN SQUARE REP ( BL POINT, TR POINT )
                          ISA ( RECTANGLE ) ;
   /* could optionally change the representation */

CREATE FUNCTION IS_SQUARE ( R RECTANGLE ) RETURNS ( BOOLEAN )
   /* operator to test a rectangle for "squareness"; */
   /* this function does NOT break encapsulation     */
     AS BEGIN ;
          IF X(TR) - X(BL) = Y(TR) - Y(BL)
          THEN RETURN ( true ) ;
          ELSE RETURN ( false ) ;
        END ;
```

(b)
```
CREATE BASE RELATION RECTANGLE
     ( BL DOMAIN ( POINT ),
       TR DOMAIN ( POINT ) )
     CANDIDATE KEY ( BL, TR ) ;

CREATE BASE RELATION SQUARE ISA ( RECTANGLE ) ;
   /* could optionally add new attributes */
```

19.6 One consequence would be that properties that applied just to programmers or just to secretaries would now have to be defined in two places instead of one. Similarly for properties that applied just to full-time employees or just to part-time employees.

20 | Missing Information

20.1 Introduction

We stated in Chapter 5 (Section 5.6) that the problem of missing information is one that is encountered very frequently in the real world. To paraphrase the introduction to that section, entries such as "Date of birth unknown," "Speaker to be announced," "Present whereabouts unknown," etc., are only too common in real-world situations, and so it is necessary to have some way of dealing with such situations in our formal database systems.

Section 5.6 went on to say that the approach to this problem most commonly found in the literature (and in commercial products) is based on **nulls** and **three-valued logic**. For instance, we might say, loosely, that the weight of some part is null. What we mean by such a statement is, more precisely, that (a) we know that the part exists, and of course (b) it does have a weight, but (c) we do not know what that weight is. In other words, we do not know a genuine weight value that can sensibly be put in the WEIGHT position in the tuple for the part in question. Instead, therefore, we *mark* that position as "null," and we interpret that mark to mean, precisely, that we do not know what the real value is.

Note: Informally, we might think of the WEIGHT position in the foregoing example as "containing a null," or of the corresponding value as "being null," and indeed we will often speak in such terms in this book, for brevity and convenience. But the previous paragraph should serve to show that such a manner of speaking *is* only informal, and indeed not very accurate. That is why the expression "null value" (which is heard very frequently) is deprecated: The whole point about nulls is precisely that they are not values.

Section 5.6 also mentioned one additional—and crucial—aspect of nulls, namely the fact that any scalar comparison in which either of the comparands is null evaluates to the *unknown* truth value, instead of *true* or *false*. The justification for this state of affairs is the intended interpretation of null as "value unknown": If the value of A is unknown, then clearly it is *unknown* whether, for example, $A > B$, **regardless of the value of** B (even—perhaps especially!—if the value of B is also unknown). Note in particular, therefore, that two nulls are not considered to be equal to one another; that is, the comparison $A = B$ evaluates to *unknown*, not *true*, if A and B are both null. Hence the term "three-valued logic" (abbreviated 3VL): The concept of nulls—at least as that term is usually understood—inevitably leads us into a logic in which there are three truth values, namely *true, false,* and *unknown.*

We also made it clear in Section 5.6 that it is our opinion (and the opinion of many other writers) that nulls and 3VL are a mistake and have no place in a clean formal system like the relational model. In fact, it is our opinion that the missing information problem is still not completely understood and that *no* fully satisfactory solution to the problem is known at this time. Be that as it may, it would be doing the reader a major disservice to exclude discussion of nulls and 3VL entirely from this book; hence this chapter.

The plan of the chapter, then, is as follows. Following this introduction, in Section 20.2 we "suspend disbelief" and describe the basic ideas behind nulls and 3VL, without offering much in the way of criticism of those ideas. (The point is, of course, that it is not possible to criticize the ideas properly or fairly without first explaining what the ideas *are.*) Then in Section 20.3 we discuss some of the more important consequences of those ideas, in an attempt to justify our own position that nulls are a mistake. Section 20.4 digresses to consider an operation commonly encountered in the context of nulls and 3VL, *viz.* the *outer join* operation. Section 20.5 sketches the relevant aspects of SQL. Section 20.6 presents a summary.

One further preliminary remark: There are of course many reasons why some particular piece of information might be missing—"value unknown" is only one possible reason. Others include "value not applicable," "value does not exist," "value undefined," "value not supplied," and so on [20.8]. Indeed, in reference [4.4] Codd proposes that the relational model should include not one but two distinct nulls, one meaning "value unknown" and the other "value not applicable," and hence proposes that systems should deal in terms of not three- but **four-**valued logic. We have argued against such a proposal elsewhere [20.8]; in this chapter we limit our attention to a single kind of null only, namely the "value unknown" null, which we will henceforward often—but not invariably!—refer to, for definiteness, as **UNK** (for unknown).

20.2   An Overview of the 3VL Approach

In this section we attempt* to explain the principal components of the 3VL approach to missing information. We begin by considering the effect of nulls—i.e., UNKs—on scalar operators and expressions.

Scalar Computational Expressions

Consider the numeric expression

```
WEIGHT * 454
```

---

* Emphasis on *attempt* . . . "it all makes sense if you squint a little and don't think too hard" [20.17].

where WEIGHT represents the weight of some part, P*x* say. What if the weight of part P*x* happens to be UNK?—what then is the value of the expression? The answer is that it too must be considered to be UNK. In general, in fact, *any* scalar numeric expression is considered to evaluate to UNK if any of the operands of that expression is itself UNK. Thus, e.g., if WEIGHT happens to be UNK, then all of the following expressions also evaluate to UNK:

```
WEIGHT + 454    454 + WEIGHT    + WEIGHT
WEIGHT - 454    454 - WEIGHT    - WEIGHT
WEIGHT * 454    454 * WEIGHT
WEIGHT / 454    454 / WEIGHT
```

(Perhaps we should point out right away that the foregoing treatment of numeric expressions immediately gives rise to certain anomalies. For example, the expression WEIGHT − WEIGHT, which should clearly yield zero, actually yields UNK, and the expression WEIGHT/0, which should clearly raise a "zero divide" error, also yields UNK— assuming in both cases that WEIGHT is UNK in the first place, of course.)

Analogous considerations apply to all other scalar data types and operators, except for (a) the comparison operators (see the subsection "Conditional expressions" below), and (b) certain special operators to be discussed in the next paragraph. Thus, e.g., the character string expression *A* ‖ *B* returns UNK if *A* is UNK or *B* is UNK or both. (Again there are certain anomalous cases, details of which we omit here.)

In addition to the scalar operators discussed above, it is necessary to introduce a couple of special operators that do *not* evaluate to UNK if they have an UNK operand:

■ The first, IS_UNK, takes a single operand and returns *true* if that operand evaluates to UNK and *false* otherwise; in other words, the operator is effectively a "test for UNK."

■ The second, IF_UNK, takes two operands and returns the value of the first operand unless that operand evaluates to UNK, in which case it returns the value of the second operand instead; in other words, the operator is effectively a "convert UNK to some nonUNK value."

Note, incidentally, that the second of these operators can be defined in terms of the first. To be specific, the expression

```
IF_UNK ( exp1, exp2 )
```

(where expressions *exp1* and *exp2* must be type-compatible) is equivalent to the expression

```
( IF IS_UNK ( exp1 ) THEN exp2 ELSE exp1 )
```

Example: Suppose UNKs are permitted for the CITY attribute in relation P. Then the expression

```
EXTEND P ADD IF_UNK ( CITY, 'City unknown' ) AS PCY
```

will yield a relation in which the PCY value is "City unknown" for any part for which the city is given as UNK in relation P.

Conditional Expressions

We have already explained in Section 20.1 that any scalar comparison in which either of the comparands is UNK evaluates to the *unknown* truth value, instead of *true* or *false,* and hence that we are dealing with three-valued logic (3VL). *Unknown* (which we will henceforward often—but not invariably!—abbreviate to just *unk*) is "the third truth value." Here then are the 3VL truth tables for AND, OR, and NOT (t = *true,* f = *false,* u = *unk*):

```
AND │ t  u  f        OR │ t  u  f        NOT │
────┼────────        ───┼────────        ────┼───
 t  │ t  u  f         t │ t  t  t         t  │ f
 u  │ u  u  f         u │ t  u  u         u  │ u
 f  │ f  f  f         f │ t  u  f         f  │ t
```

Suppose, for example, that A = 3, B = 4, and C is UNK. Then the following expressions have the indicated truth values:

```
A > B AND B > C   :   false
A > B OR  B > C   :   unk
A < B OR  B < C   :   true
NOT ( A = C )     :   unk
```

AND, OR, and NOT are not sufficient in themselves, however [20.12]; another important operator is MAYBE [20.8], with truth table as follows:

```
MAYBE │
──────┼───
  t   │ f
  u   │ t
  f   │ f
```

To see why MAYBE is desirable, consider the query "Get employees who *may be*—but are not definitely known to be—programmers born before January 18th, 1941, with a salary less than $50,000." With the MAYBE operator, the query can be stated quite succinctly as follows:

```
EMP WHERE MAYBE ( JOB = 'Programmer' AND
                  DOB < DATE ('1941-1-18') AND
                  SALARY < 50000.00 )
```

Without the MAYBE operator, the query would look something like this:

```
EMP WHERE ( IS_UNK ( JOB ) AND
            DOB < DATE ('1941-1-18') AND
            SALARY < 50000.00 )
OR        ( JOB = 'Programmer' AND
            IS_UNK ( DOB ) AND
            SALARY < 50000.00 )
OR        ( JOB = 'Programmer' AND
            DOB < DATE ('1941-1-18') AND
            IS_UNK ( SALARY ) )
OR        ( IS_UNK ( JOB ) AND
            IS_UNK ( DOB ) AND
            SALARY < 50000.00 )
```

```
OR          ( IS_UNK ( JOB ) AND
              DOB < DATE ('1941-1-18') AND
              IS_UNK ( SALARY ) )
OR          ( JOB = 'Programmer' AND
              IS_UNK ( DOB ) AND
              IS_UNK ( SALARY ) )
OR          ( IS_UNK ( JOB ) AND
              IS_UNK ( DOB ) AND
              IS_UNK ( SALARY ) )
```

Note: The foregoing should not be construed as suggesting that MAYBE is the *only* additional logical operator needed for 3VL. In practice, for example, a TRUE_OR_MAYBE operator could be very useful [20.8]. See also reference [20.12], which discusses this issue in the specific context of SQL.

EXISTS and FORALL

As explained in Chapter 7, we define the quantifiers EXISTS and FORALL as iterated OR and AND, respectively. In other words, if (a) R is a relation with tuples $T1$, $T2, \ldots Tm$, (b) T is a tuple variable that ranges over that relation, and (c) $f(T)$ is a conditional expression involving T, then the conditional expression

```
EXISTS T ( f ( T ) )
```

is defined to be equivalent to the conditional expression

```
false OR ( f ( T1 ) ) OR ... OR ( f ( Tm ) )
```

Likewise, the conditional expression

```
FORALL T ( f ( T ) )
```

is defined to be equivalent to the conditional expression

```
true AND ( f ( T1 ) ) AND ... AND ( f ( Tm ) )
```

For example, let relation R contain the following tuples:

```
(   1,   2,   3    )
(   1,   2,   UNK  )
( UNK, UNK, UNK  )
```

Assuming for simplicity that we can refer to tuple components by subscripted references of the form $T[i]$ (with the obvious interpretation), the following expressions have the indicated values:

```
EXISTS T ( T[3] > 1 )               :  true
EXISTS T ( T[2] > 2 )               :  unk
EXISTS T ( MAYBE ( T[1] > 3 ) )     :  true
EXISTS T ( IS_UNK ( T[3] ) )        :  true

FORALL T ( T[1] > 1 )               :  false
FORALL T ( T[2] > 1 )               :  unk
FORALL T ( MAYBE ( T[3] > 1 ) )     :  false
```

UNK Is Not *unk*

It is worth pointing out explicitly that UNK (the "value unknown" null) and *unk* (the *unknown* truth value) are **not the same thing**. Indeed, this state of affairs is an immediate consequence of the fact that *unk* is a value (specifically, a truth value), whereas UNK is not a value at all. But let us be a little more specific. Suppose *X* is a variable of data type "truth value." Then *X* must have one of the values *true, false,* or *unk*. Thus, the statement "*X* is *unk*" means, precisely, that the value of *X* is **known to be** *unk*. By contrast, the statement "*X* is UNK" means that the value of *X* is **not known**.

Can a Domain Contain an UNK?

It is also an immediate consequence of the fact that UNK is not a value that UNKs cannot appear in domains. Indeed, if it *were* possible for a domain to contain a null, then a variety of further issues would arise, the following among them:

- For all values *v,* the expression $v \in D$ would always return *unk* or *true* (never *false*) if domain *D* did in fact contain an UNK.

- As a consequence of the previous point, if domain *D* did contain an UNK, then attribute integrity checks for attributes defined on *D* would never fail!

On the other hand, since domains in fact *cannot* contain UNKs, a relation that contains an UNK cannot be a subset of the Cartesian product of its underlying domains, counter to Codd's original definition of relation [4.1]. In other words, such a "relation"—whatever else it might be—is in fact not a relation at all! We will return to this point at the end of the chapter.

Relational Expressions

Now we turn our attention to the effect of UNKs on the operators of the relational algebra. For simplicity we limit ourselves to the five primitive operators restrict, project, product, union, and difference (the effect of UNKs on the other operators can be inferred from their effect on these five).

First of all, **product** is unaffected.

Second, the **restriction** operation is (slightly) redefined to return only those tuples for which the restriction condition evaluates to *true,* i.e., not to *false* and not to *unk*. We were tacitly assuming this redefinition in our MAYBE example earlier.

Next, projection. Projection of course involves the elimination of redundant duplicate tuples. Now, in two-valued logic (2VL), two tuples are duplicates of one another if and only if all corresponding components are equal (the tuples in question must be type-compatible, of course). In 3VL, however, some of those components might be UNK, and UNK (as we have seen) is not equal to *anything,* not even itself. Are we then forced to conclude that a tuple that contains an UNK can never be a duplicate, not even of itself?

According to Codd [20.1], the answer to this question is *no:* Two UNKs, even though they are not equal to one another, are still considered as duplicates of one another for purposes of duplicate elimination. The apparent contradiction is explained away as follows:

> ". . . identification for duplicate removal is . . . at a lower level of detail than equality testing in the evaluation of retrieval conditions. Hence, it is possible to adopt a different rule" [20.1].

We leave it to the reader to judge whether this rationale is a reasonable one; at any rate, let us agree to accept it for now, and hence to accept the following definition:

■ Tuples *t1* and *t2* are **duplicates** of one another if and only if (a) they are type-compatible, and (b) for every pair of corresponding attribute values *a1* and *a2* in the two tuples, either *a1* and *a2* are both "real" (nonUNK) values and *a1* = *a2*, or *a1* and *a2* are both UNK.

We can now define the **projection** of relation *R* on the set of attributes *A* to be the result obtained by eliminating all attributes of *R* not mentioned in *A* and then eliminating redundant duplicate tuples from what remains.

Union likewise involves the elimination of redundant duplicate tuples. We define the **union** of two type-compatible relations *R1* and *R2* to be that type-compatible relation *R* that contains all possible tuples *t* such that *t* is a duplicate of some tuple of *R1* or of some tuple of *R2* (or both).

Finally—even though they do not involve any duplicate elimination as such—**intersection** and **difference** are defined analogously. Thus, a tuple *t* appears in *R1* INTERSECT *R2* if and only if it is a duplicate of some tuple of *R1* and of some tuple of *R2,* and it appears in *R1* MINUS *R2* if and only if it is a duplicate of some tuple of *R1* and not a duplicate of any tuple of *R2*. The significance of this point is that if (e.g.) *R1* and *R2* both include a tuple of the form (*x*,UNK), say, then such a tuple will also appear in *R1* INTERSECT *R2* and will not appear in either *R1* MINUS *R2* or *R2* MINUS *R1*.

Update Operations

There are two general points to make under this heading:

1. If attribute *A* of relation *R* permits UNKs, and if a tuple is inserted into *R* and no value is provided for *A*, the system will automatically place an UNK in the *A* position in that tuple. If attribute *A* of relation *R* does not permit UNKs, an attempt to create a tuple in *R* (via INSERT or UPDATE) in which the *A* position is UNK is an error.

2. An attempt (via INSERT or UPDATE) to create a duplicate tuple in *R* is—as always—an error. The definition of "duplicate tuples" here is as given in the previous subsection.

20.3   Some Consequences of the Foregoing Scheme

The 3VL approach as described in the previous section has a number of logical consequences, not all of them immediately obvious. We discuss some of those consequences,
and their significance, in the present section.

Expression Transformations

First, we observe that several expressions that always evaluate to *true* in two-valued logic
do *not* necessarily always evaluate to *true* in three-valued logic. Here are some examples, with commentary. Please note that the following list is not meant to be exhaustive.

1. $x = x$ is not necessarily *true*

    In 2VL, any variable x is always equal to itself. In 3VL, however, x is not equal to
    itself if it happens to be UNK.

2. p OR NOT (p) is not necessarily *true*

    Here p is a conditional expression. Now, in 2VL, the expression "p OR NOT(p)"
    necessarily evaluates to *true,* regardless of the value of p. In 3VL, however, if p
    happens to evaluate to *unk,* the overall expression evaluates to *unk* OR NOT(*unk*),
    i.e., to *unk* OR *unk,* which reduces to *unk,* not *true.*

    This particular example accounts for a well-known counterintuitive property
    of 3VL, which we illustrate as follows: If we issue the query "Get all suppliers in
    London," followed by the query "Get all suppliers not in London," and take the
    union of the two results, we do *not* necessarily get all suppliers. Instead, we need
    to include "all suppliers who **may be** in London."

    The point about this example is, of course, that while the two states "location
    is London" and "location is not London" are mutually exclusive and exhaust the
    full range of possibilities in the real world, the database does *not* contain the real
    world—instead, it contains **knowledge about** the real world. And there are three
    states, not two, of knowledge about the real world; in the example, the three states
    are "location is known to be London," "location is known not to be London," and
    "location is not known." Furthermore, of course (as reference [20.9] puts it), we
    obviously cannot ask the system questions about the real world, we can only ask it
    questions about its knowledge of the real world as represented by the values in the
    database. The counterintuitive nature of the example thus derives from a confusion
    over *realms:* The user is thinking in terms of the real world realm, but the system
    is operating in terms of the realm that is *its knowledge concerning* that real world.

    Note: It seems to this writer, however, that such a confusion over realms is a
    trap very easily fallen into. Note that *every single query* mentioned in previous
    chapters (examples, exercises, etc.) has been stated in "real world" terms, not "knowl-
    edge about the real world" terms—and this book is certainly not unusual in this regard.

    Incidentally, as the foregoing discussion suggests, an expression that does al-
    ways evaluate to *true* in 3VL—i.e., the 3VL analog of the 2VL expression p OR
    NOT(p)—is p OR NOT(p) OR MAYBE(p).

3. *R* JOIN *R* does not necessarily yield *R*

   In 2VL, forming the natural join of a relation *R* with itself always returns the original relation *R* (i.e., natural join is *idempotent*). In 3VL, however, a tuple with an UNK in any position will not join to itself, because join, unlike union, is based on testing for equality, not on testing for duplicates.

4. INTERSECT is no longer a special case of JOIN

   This fact is likewise a consequence of the fact that join is based on the definition of equality, while intersection, like union, is based on the definition of duplicates.

5. *A* = *B* AND *B* = *C* does not necessarily imply that *A* = *C*

   An extended illustration of this point is given below in the subsection "The departments-and-employees example."

Thus we see that many equivalences that are valid in two-valued logic break down in three-valued logic. One very serious consequence of such breakdowns is as follows. In general, simple equivalences such as *R* JOIN *R* ≡ *R* lie at the heart of the various **laws of transformation** that are used to convert queries into some more efficient form (see Chapter 18). Furthermore, those laws are used not only by the *system* (when doing optimization), but also by *users* (when trying to decide the "best" way to state a given query). And if the equivalences are not valid, then the laws of transformation are not valid. And if the laws are not valid, then the transformations are not valid. And if the transformations are not valid, then we will get *wrong answers* out of the system.

The Departments-and-Employees Example

In order to illustrate the problem of incorrect transformations, we discuss a specific example (taken from reference [20.10]) in some detail. Suppose we are given the simple departments-and-employees database shown in Fig. 20.1. Now consider the conditional expression

```
DEPT.DEPT# = EMP.DEPT# AND EMP.DEPT# = 'D1'
```

(which might be part of a query, of course). For the only tuples in the database, this expression evaluates to *unk* AND *unk*, i.e., to *unk*. However, a "good" optimizer will observe that the expression is of the form *A* = *B* AND *B* = *C*, will therefore infer that *A* = *C*, and hence will append an additional restriction term "*A* = *C*" to the original expression (as discussed in Chapter 18, Section 18.4), yielding the expression

FIG. 20.1 The departments-and-employees database

```
DEPT.DEPT# = EMP.DEPT# AND EMP.DEPT# = 'D1'
                       AND DEPT.DEPT# = 'D1'
```

This modified expression now evaluates to *unk* AND *unk* AND *false,* i.e., to *false* (for the only two tuples in the database). It follows, therefore, that the expression (e.g.)

```
EMP.EMP# WHERE EXISTS DEPT
   ( NOT ( DEPT.DEPT# = EMP.DEPT# AND EMP.DEPT# = 'D1' ) )
```

will return employee E1 if "optimized" in the foregoing sense and will not do so otherwise. In other words, the "optimization" is in fact not valid. Thus we see that certain optimizations that are perfectly valid—and useful—under conventional two-valued logic are no longer valid under three-valued logic.

Note the implications of the foregoing for extending a 2VL system to support 3VL! At best, such an extension is likely to require a certain amount of reengineering of the existing system, since portions of the existing optimizer code are likely to be invalidated; at worst, it will introduce bugs. More generally, note the implications for extending a system that supports *n*-valued logic to one that supports (*n*+1)-valued logic for any *n* greater than 1; analogous difficulties will surely arise for every discrete value of *n*.

The Interpretation Issue

Now let us examine the departments-and-employees example a little more carefully. Since employee E1 does have *some* corresponding department, the UNK does stand for some real value, say *d*. Now, either *d* is D1 or it is not. If it is, the original expression

```
DEPT.DEPT# = EMP.DEPT# AND EMP.DEPT# = 'D1'
```

evaluates (for the given data) to *false,* because the term DEPT.DEPT# = EMP.DEPT# evaluates to *false.* Alternatively, if *d* is not D1, the expression also evaluates (for the given data) to *false,* because the term EMP.DEPT# = 'D1' evaluates to *false.* In other words, the original expression is always *false* in the real world, **regardless of what real value the UNK stands for**. Thus, the result that is correct according to three-valued logic and the result that is correct in the real world are not the same thing! In other words, three-valued logic does not behave in accordance with the way the real world behaves; i.e., 3VL does not seem to have a sensible **interpretation** in terms of how the real world works.

Note: This question of interpretation is very far from being the only problem arising from nulls and 3VL (see references [20.2–20.12] for an extensive discussion of several others), but it is perhaps the most fundamental. In this writer's opinion, in fact, it is a showstopper.

20.4 Outer Join (A Digression)

In this section we digress briefly to discuss a frequently encountered operation known as **outer join** (see references [20.6–20.7] and [20.14–20.15]). Outer join is an extended form of the ordinary or "inner" join operation. It differs from the inner join in that tuples in one relation having no counterpart in the other appear in the result with nulls in the other attribute positions, instead of simply being ignored as they are in the ordinary join. It is not a primitive operation; for example, the following expression could be used to construct the outer natural join of suppliers and shipments on supplier numbers (assuming for the sake of the example that "NULL" is a legal scalar expression):

```
( S JOIN SP )
  UNION
( EXTEND ( ( S [ S# ] MINUS SP [ S# ] ) JOIN S )
                          ADD NULL AS P#, NULL AS QTY )
```

The result includes tuples for suppliers who supply no parts, extended with nulls in the P# and QTY positions.

Let us examine this example a little more closely. Refer to Fig. 20.2. In that figure, the top portion shows some sample data values, the middle portion shows the corresponding inner natural join, and the bottom portion shows the corresponding outer natural join. As the figure indicates, the inner join "loses information"—speaking *very* loosely, please note!—for suppliers who supply no parts (supplier S5, in the example), whereas the outer join "preserves" such information. Indeed, this distinction is the whole point of outer join.

Now, the problem that outer join is intended to solve—*viz.*, the fact that inner join sometimes "loses information"—is certainly an important problem. Some writers would therefore argue that the system should provide direct, explicit support for outer join, instead of requiring the user to indulge in circumlocutions to achieve the desired effect. Codd in particular now considers outer join to be an intrinsic part of the rela-

S	S#	SNAME	STATUS	CITY		SP	S#	P#	QTY
	S2	Jones	10	Paris			S2	P1	300
	S5	Adams	30	Athens			S2	P2	400

Regular (inner) natural join:

S#	SNAME	STATUS	CITY	P#	QTY	
S2	Jones	10	Paris	P1	300	"Loses"
S2	Jones	10	Paris	P2	400	information for supplier S5

Outer natural join:

S#	SNAME	STATUS	CITY	P#	QTY	
S2	Jones	10	Paris	P1	300	"Preserves"
S2	Jones	10	Paris	P2	400	information for
S5	Adams	30	Athens	UNK	UNK	supplier S5

FIG. 20.2 Inner *vs.* outer join (example)

tional model [4.4]. However, we do not propose any explicit outer join support here, for the following reasons among others:

■ First of all, of course, the operation involves nulls, and we are opposed to nulls anyway, for numerous good reasons.

■ Second, we have already mentioned the point (in Chapter 19) that *relation-valued attributes* provide an alternative approach to solving the problem that outer join is intended to solve—an approach that does not involve nulls and does not involve outer join either and is in fact (in this writer's opinion) altogether more elegant [19.3].

■ Third, note that there exist several different varieties of outer join—left, right, and full outer θ-*join,* and left, right, and full outer *natural* join (the "left" joins preserve information from the left-hand relation, the "right" joins preserve information from the right-hand relation, and the "full" joins do both; the example of Fig. 20.2 is a left join—a left outer natural join, to be precise). Note further that there is no very straightforward way of deriving the outer natural joins from the outer θ-joins [20.7]. As a result, it is unclear as to exactly which outer joins need to be explicitly supported.

■ Next, the outer join question is far from being as trivial as the simple example of Fig. 20.2 might suggest. In fact, as reference [20.7] puts it, outer join suffers from a number of Nasty Properties, which together imply that adding outer join support to existing languages—in particular, to SQL—tends to be difficult to do gracefully. Several DBMS products have tried to solve this problem and dismally failed (i.e., they have tripped over those Nasty Properties). See reference [20.7] for an extensive discussion of this issue.

■ Finally, there is an interpretation problem regarding the nulls that appear in the result of an outer join. What do they mean in the example of Fig. 20.2, for instance? They certainly do not mean either "value unknown" or "value does not apply." See reference [20.7] for further discussion of this problem. (Indeed, the reader might have noticed that we have reverted to the generic term "null" in this section, in place of UNK. This is because it is precisely one of the problems of outer join that it is unclear what *kind* of nulls should appear in the result.)

We remark also that outer join will sometimes produce a relation that has nulls in the primary key position and hence cannot be converted into a base relation without violating the entity integrity rule (ignoring for the moment the point that we do not fully subscribe to the entity integrity rule anyway, as explained in Chapter 5). Indeed, this comment applies to the example of Fig. 20.2.

Note: It is also possible to define "outer" versions of certain other operations of the relational algebra—specifically, the union, intersection, and difference operations [20.1]—and again Codd now regards at least one of these, namely outer union, as part of the relational model [4.4]. Such operations permit unions (etc.) to be performed between two relations even if those relations are not type-compatible. They basically work by extending each operand to include those attributes that are peculiar to the other (so that the operands *are* now type-compatible), putting nulls in every tuple for all such added attributes, and then performing a normal union or intersection or difference, as applicable.* We do not discuss these operations in detail, however, for the following reasons:

- Outer intersection is guaranteed to return an empty relation, except in the special case in which the original relations are type-compatible in the first place, in which case it degenerates to the normal intersection.

- Outer difference is guaranteed to return its first operand, except in the special case in which the original relations are type-compatible in the first place, in which case it degenerates to the normal difference.

- Outer union has *major* problems of interpretation (they are much worse than the outer join interpretation problem). See reference [20.2] for further discussion.

20.5   SQL Support

SQL's support for nulls and 3VL follows the broad outlines of the approach described in the foregoing sections. Thus, for example, when SQL applies a WHERE clause to some table *T,* it eliminates all rows of *T* for which the conditional expression in that WHERE clause evaluates to *false* or to *unk* (i.e., not to *true*). Likewise, when it applies a HAVING clause to some grouped table *G,* it eliminates all groups of *G* for which the conditional expression in that HAVING clause evaluates to *false* or to *unk* (i.e., not to *true*). In what follows, therefore, we merely draw the reader's attention to certain features that are specific to SQL *per se,* instead of being an intrinsic part of the 3VL approach as previously discussed.

Note: The full implications and ramifications of SQL's null support are very complex. For additional information, refer to the official standard document [8.1] or the tutorial treatment in reference [8.5].

Data Definition

As explained in Chapter 8, columns in base tables usually have an associated default value, and that default value is often defined, explicitly or implicitly, to be null. Furthermore, columns in base tables always *permit* nulls, unless there is an integrity constraint—probably just NOT NULL—for the column in question that expressly bans them. The representation of nulls is implementation-dependent; however, it must be such that the system can distinguish nulls from all possible nonnull values.

---

* This explanation refers to the operations as originally defined [20.1]. Reference [4.4] changed the definitions somewhat; the interested reader is referred to that book for the specifics.

Table Expressions

Recall from Chapter 8 that the most recent version of the SQL standard (SQL/92) added explicit JOIN support to the language. Furthermore, if the keyword JOIN is prefixed with LEFT, RIGHT, or FULL (with an optional OUTER noiseword in each case), then the join in question is an *outer* join. Here are some examples:

```
S LEFT [ OUTER ] JOIN SP ON S.S# = SP.S#

S LEFT [ OUTER ] JOIN SP USING ( S# )

S LEFT [ OUTER ] NATURAL JOIN SP
```

These three expressions are effectively all equivalent, except that the first produces a table with two supplier number columns and the second and third produce a table with just one such column.

SQL also supports an approximation to outer union, which it calls *union join*. The details are beyond the scope of this chapter.

Conditional Expressions

Conditional expressions—not surprisingly—are the part of SQL most dramatically affected by nulls and 3VL. The following description is necessarily very selective and superficial.

- *Tests for null:* SQL provides two special comparison operators, IS NULL and IS NOT NULL, to test for the presence or absence of nulls. The syntax is:

  row-constructor IS [NOT] NULL

  There is one trap for the unwary: The two expressions *r* IS NOT NULL and NOT (*r* IS NULL) are *not* equivalent! For explanation, see reference [8.5].

- *Tests for true, false, unknown:* If *p* is a conditional expression enclosed in parentheses, then the following are also conditional expressions:

  p IS [NOT] TRUE
  p IS [NOT] FALSE
  p IS [NOT] UNKNOWN

  The meanings of these expressions are as indicated in the following truth table:

p	*true*	*false*	*unk*
p IS TRUE	*true*	*false*	*false*
p IS NOT TRUE	*false*	*true*	*true*
p IS FALSE	*false*	*true*	*false*
p IS NOT FALSE	*true*	*false*	*true*
p IS UNKNOWN	*false*	*false*	*true*
p IS NOT UNKNOWN	*true*	*true*	*false*

Observe, therefore, that the expressions *p* IS NOT TRUE and NOT *p* are not equivalent! *Note:* The expression *p* IS UNKNOWN corresponds to our MAYBE(*p*).

- *MATCH conditions:* The syntax of match-conditions includes a "PARTIAL or FULL" option, not shown and not discussed in Chapter 8, that can affect the result if nulls are present:

```
row-constructor MATCH [ UNIQUE ]
                      [ PARTIAL | FULL ] ( table-expression )
```

There are thus six different cases, depending on (a) whether the UNIQUE option is omitted or not and (b) whether the "PARTIAL or FULL" option is omitted or not (and if not, which it is). The details are complex, however, and beyond the scope of this chapter. See reference [8.5] for further discussion.

- *EXISTS conditions:* See the annotation to reference [20.9].

Scalar Expressions

- *"Literals":* The keyword NULL can be used as a kind of literal representation of null (e.g., in an INSERT statement). Note, however, that this keyword cannot appear in all contexts in which literals can appear; as the standard puts it, "there is no <literal> for a null value, although the key word NULL is used in some places to indicate that a null value is desired" [8.1]. Thus, for example, it is not possible to specify NULL explicitly as an operand of a simple comparison—e.g., "WHERE X = NULL" is illegal.

- *COALESCE:* COALESCE is the SQL analog of our IF_UNK function (see Section 20.2).

- *Aggregate functions:* The SQL aggregate functions SUM, AVG, etc. do *not* behave in accordance with the rules for scalar operators explained in Section 20.2, but instead simply ignore any nulls in their argument (except for COUNT(*), where nulls are treated just like nonnull values). Also, if the argument to such a function happens to evaluate to an empty set, SQL defines the result to be null, except for COUNT, which does correctly return zero. (Contrast the treatment of empty set arguments defined in Chapter 6.)

- *Table expressions in parentheses:* If a scalar expression is in fact a table expression enclosed in parentheses—for example, (SELECT S.CITY FROM S WHERE S.S# = 'S1')—then normally that table expression is required to evaluate to a table containing exactly one column and exactly one row. The value of the scalar expression is then taken to be, precisely, the single scalar value contained within that table. But if the table expression evaluates to a table that contains no rows at all, then SQL defines the value of the scalar expression to be null.

Integrity Constraints

In SQL, an integrity constraint is basically a conditional expression that must not evaluate to *false*. In other words, an SQL constraint is not considered to be violated if it evaluates to *unk*. Technically, of course, we should say in such a case that it is *not known* whether the constraint is violated, but, just as SQL regards *unk* as *false* for the purposes of a WHERE clause, so it regards *unk* as *true* for the purposes of an integrity constraint (speaking a trifle loosely).

The foregoing remarks are directly applicable to SQL domain constraints, general constraints ("assertions"), and check constraints, and effectively dispose of the issue for these three cases. Candidate keys and foreign keys require additional consideration, however.

- *Candidate keys:* Let *C* be a column that is a component of some candidate key *K* of some base table. If *K* is a primary key, SQL will not permit *C* to contain any nulls (in order to enforce the entity integrity rule). If *K* is not a primary key, however, SQL will permit *C* to contain *any number* of nulls (together with any number of nonnull values, of course).

- *Foreign keys:* The rules defining what it means for a given foreign key value to match some value of the corresponding candidate key (in the presence of nulls) are fairly complicated; we omit the details here, except to say that they are basically the same as the details of the MATCH condition (see earlier).

  Nulls also have implications for the referential actions (CASCADE, SET NULL, etc.) specified in the ON DELETE and ON UPDATE clauses. Once again, the details are quite complex, and beyond the scope of the present text; see reference [8.5] for the specifics.

Embedded SQL

- *Indicator variables:* Consider the following example of an embedded SQL "singleton SELECT" (a repeat of Example 8.8.1 from Chapter 8):

```
EXEC SQL SELECT STATUS, CITY
         INTO   :RANK, :CITY
         FROM   S
         WHERE  S# = :GIVENS# ;
```

Suppose there is a possibility that the value of STATUS might be null for some supplier. Then the SELECT statement shown above will fail if the STATUS selected is null (SQLSTATE will be set to the exception value 22002). In general, if it is possible that a value to be retrieved might be null, the user should specify an *indicator value* in addition to the normal target variable for that value, as we now illustrate:

```
EXEC SQL SELECT STATUS, CITY
         INTO   :RANK INDICATOR :RANKIND, :CITY
         FROM   S
         WHERE  S# = :GIVENS# ;
IF RANKIND = -1 THEN /* STATUS was null */ ... ;
```

If the value to be retrieved is null and an indicator variable has been specified, then that indicator variable will be set to the value minus 1 (the effect on the ordinary target variable is implementation-dependent).

- *Ordering:* The ORDER BY clause is used to impose an ordering on the rows resulting from the evaluation of the table expression in a cursor definition. The question arises: What is the relative ordering for two scalar values *A* and *B* if *A* is null or *B* is null (or both)? The SQL answer is as follows:

1. For ordering purposes, all nulls are considered to be equal to one another.

2. For ordering purposes, all nulls are considered *either* to be greater than all nonnull values *or* less than all nonnull values (which of the two possibilities applies is implementation-defined).

20.6   Summary

We have discussed the problem of **missing information** and an approach to the problem based on **nulls** and **three-valued logic** (3VL). We stressed the point that null is not a value, though it is common to speak as if it were (saying, e.g., that some particular attribute position in some particular tuple "is null"). Any comparison in which one comparand is null evaluates to "the third truth value" *unknown* (abbreviated *unk*), which is why the logic is three-valued. We also mentioned that there are many different reasons why information might be missing, and hence many different kinds of null, and introduced **UNK** as a convenient (and explicit) shorthand for the "value unknown" kind of null.

We then explored the implications of UNKs and 3VL for **computational** expressions, **conditional** expressions, the quantifiers **EXISTS** and **FORALL,** and the **relational** operators (in particular the restriction, projection, union, intersection, and difference operators, also INSERT and UPDATE). We introduced the operators **IS_UNK** (which tests for UNK), **IF_UNK** (which converts UNK into a nonUNK value), and **MAYBE** (which converts *unk* into *true*). We discussed the question of **duplicates** in the presence of UNKs, and pointed out also that UNK and *unk* are not the same thing.

Next, we examined some consequences of the foregoing ideas. First, we explained that **certain equivalences break down** in 3VL—equivalences, that is, that are valid in 2VL but not in 3VL. As a result, both users and optimizers are likely to make **mistakes in transforming expressions**. And even if such mistakes are not made, 3VL suffers from the very serious ("showstopper") problem that **it does not match reality**—that is, results that are correct according to 3VL are sometimes incorrect in the real world.

We then digressed to explain **outer join**. However, we do not advocate direct support for that operation (at least as usually understood), because we believe there are better solutions to the problem that outer join is intended to solve. We also briefly mentioned the possibility of other "outer" operations, in particular **outer union**.

Next we examined the **SQL support** for the foregoing ideas. SQL's treatment of missing information is broadly based on 3VL, but it does manage to include a large number of additional complications, most of them beyond the scope of the present book. Indeed, SQL manages to introduce a number of **additional flaws,** over and above the flaws that are inherent to 3VL *per se* [20.9,20.11]. What is more, those additional flaws serve as an additional **inhibitor to optimization** (as mentioned in Chapter 18).

We close with the following observations.

- The reader will appreciate that we have merely scratched the surface of the problems that can arise from nulls and 3VL. However, we have tried to cover enough ground to make it clear that the "benefits" of the 3VL approach are more than a little doubtful.

- We should also make it clear that, even if the reader is not convinced regarding the problems of 3VL *per se*, it would still be advisable to avoid the corresponding features of SQL. This is because of the "additional flaws" referred to above.

- Our recommendation to DBMS users would thus be to ignore the vendor's 3VL support entirely, and to use a disciplined "default values" scheme instead (thereby staying firmly in two-valued logic). Such a scheme is described in detail in reference [20.13].

- Finally, we repeat the following (important) point from earlier in the chapter: If the value at a given attribute position within a given relation "is null," then that position actually contains **nothing at all** . . . which implies that the "relation" (whatever else it might be) is no longer a relation, and the foundation for what we are doing (whatever else it might be) is no longer mathematical relation theory. In other words, it seems to this writer that nulls and 3VL *undermine the entire foundation of the relational model*.

Exercises

20.1 If A = 6, B = 5, C = 4, and D is UNK, state the truth values of the following expressions:

(a) A = B OR (B > C AND A > D)

(b) A > B AND (B < C OR IS_UNK (A - D))

(c) A < C OR B < C OR NOT (A = C)

(d) B > D OR D > B OR D = B

(e) MAYBE (A > B AND B > C)

(f) MAYBE (IS_UNK (D))

(g) MAYBE (IS_UNK (A + B))

(h) IF_UNK (D, A) > B AND IF_UNK (C, D) < B

20.2 If relation *R* contains the following tuples—

```
(   6,    5,    4    )
(  UNK,   5,    4    )
(   6,   UNK,   4    )
(  UNK,  UNK,   4    )
(  UNK,  UNK,  UNK   )
```

—and T is a tuple variable that ranges over R, state the truth values of the following expressions:

(a) EXISTS *T* (*T*[2] > 5)

(b) EXISTS *T* (*T*[2] > 2 AND *T*[3] > 5)

(c) EXISTS *T* (MAYBE (*T*[3] > 3))

(d) EXISTS T (MAYBE (IS_UNK ($T[3]$)))

(e) FORALL T ($T[1] > 1$)

(f) FORALL T ($T[2] > 1$ OR IS_UNK ($T[2]$))

(h) FORALL T (MAYBE ($T[1] > T[2]$))

(We are using subscripted references of the form $T[i]$ to refer to tuple components, as in the body of the chapter.)

20.3 Strictly speaking, the IS_UNK operator is unnecessary. Why?

20.4 Reference [20.1] proposes "maybe" versions of some (not all) of the relational algebra operators. For example, "maybe-restrict" differs from the normal restrict operator in that it returns those tuples for which the restriction condition evaluates to *unk* instead of *true*. However, such operators are strictly unnecessary. Why?

20.5 In two-valued logic, there are exactly two truth values, *true* and *false*. As a consequence, there are exactly four possible *monadic* (single-operand) logical operators—one that maps both *true* and *false* into *true*, one that maps them both into *false*, one that maps *true* into *false* and vice versa (this is NOT, of course), and one that leaves them both unchanged. And there are exactly 16 possible dyadic (two-operand) operators, as indicated by the following table:

A	B																
t	*t*	*t*	*t*	*t*	*t*	*t*	*t*	*t*	*t*	*f*	*f*	*f*	*f*	*f*	*f*	*f*	*f*
t	*f*	*t*	*t*	*t*	*t*	*f*	*f*	*f*	*f*	*t*	*t*	*t*	*t*	*f*	*f*	*f*	*f*
t	*t*	*t*	*t*	*f*	*f*	*t*	*t*	*f*	*f*	*t*	*t*	*f*	*f*	*t*	*t*	*f*	*f*
t	*f*	*t*	*f*	*t*	*f*	*t*	*f*	*t*	*f*	*t*	*f*	*t*	*f*	*t*	*f*	*t*	*f*

Prove that all four monadic operators and all 16 dyadic operators can be formulated in terms of suitable combinations of NOT and either AND or OR (and hence that it is not necessary to support all 20 operators explicitly).

20.6 How many logical operators are there in 3VL? What about 4VL? More generally, what about nVL?

20.7 (Taken from reference [20.8].) Fig. 20.3 represents some sample values for a slight variation on the usual suppliers-and-parts database (the variation is that relation SP includes a new *shipment number* attribute SHIP#, and attribute P# in that relation now has "UNKs allowed"; relation P is irrelevant to the exercise and has been omitted). Now consider the expression

```
S WHERE NOT EXISTS SP ( SP.S# = S.S# AND SP.P# = 'P2' )
```

Which of the following is the correct interpretation of this query?

(a) Get suppliers who do not supply P2.

(b) Get suppliers who are not known to supply P2.

S					SP			
S#	**SNAME**	**STATUS**	**CITY**		**SHIP#**	**S#**	**P#**	**QTY**
S1	Smith	20	London		SHIP1	S1	P1	300
S2	Jones	10	Paris		SHIP2	S2	P2	200
S3	Blake	30	Paris		SHIP3	S3	UNK	400
S4	Clark	20	London					

FIG. 20.3 A variation on suppliers-and-parts

(c) Get suppliers who are known not to supply P2.

(d) Get suppliers who are either known not or not known to supply P2.

20.8 Design a physical representation scheme for SQL base tables in which columns are permitted to contain nulls.

20.9 Suppose for simplicity that the parts relation has just two attributes, P# and COLOR. Suppose too that P# has "nulls not allowed" but COLOR has "nulls allowed." What is the relation predicate for this relation?

References and Bibliography

20.1 E. F. Codd. "Extending the Database Relational Model to Capture More Meaning." *ACM TODS 4,* No. 4 (December 1979).

This was the first of Codd's papers to discuss the missing information problem (although that problem was not the paper's primary focus). It proposes extensions to the algebra to deal with nulls and 3VL—"maybe" versions of θ-join, θ-select (i.e., restrict), and division (see Exercise 20.4), and "outer" versions of union, intersection, difference, θ-join, and natural join.

20.2 Hugh Darwen. "Into the Unknown." In C. J. Date, *Relational Database Writings 1985–1989*. Reading, Mass.: Addison-Wesley (1990).

Raises a number of additional questions concerning nulls and 3VL, of which the following is perhaps the most searching: If (as stated in the answer to Exercise 4.5 in Chapter 4) TABLE_DEE corresponds to *true* and TABLE_DUM corresponds to *false,* and TABLE_DEE and TABLE_DUM are the only possible instances of the nullary relation, then **what corresponds to** *unk?*

20.3 Hugh Darwen. "Outer Join with No Nulls and Fewer Tears." In C. J. Date and Hugh Darwen, *Relational Database Writings 1989–1991*. Reading, Mass.: Addison-Wesley (1992).

Proposes a simple variant of "outer join" that does not involve nulls and does solve many of the problems that outer join is supposed to solve.

20.4 C. J. Date. "Data Models." Chapter 5 of C. J. Date, *An Introduction to Database Systems: Volume II*. Reading, Mass.: Addison-Wesley (1983).

Includes this writer's first questioning of nulls and 3VL.

20.5 C. J. Date. "Null Values in Database Management." In C. J. Date, *Relational Database: Selected Writings*. Reading, Mass.: Addison-Wesley (1986).

A revised and expanded treatment of the material of reference [20.4].

20.6 C. J. Date. "The Outer Join." In C. J. Date, *Relational Database: Selected Writings* (Reading, Mass.: Addison-Wesley, 1986).

Discusses the outer join problem in depth and presents some proposals for supporting the operation in relational languages such as SQL.

20.7 C. J. Date. "Watch Out for Outer Join." In C. J. Date and Hugh Darwen, *Relational Database Writings 1989–1991*. Reading, Mass.: Addison-Wesley (1992).

Section 20.4 of the present chapter mentioned the fact that outer join suffers from a number of "Nasty Properties." This paper summarizes those properties as follows:

1. Outer θ-join is not a restriction of Cartesian product

2. Restriction does not distribute over outer θ-join

3. "A ≤ B" is not the same as "A < B OR A = B" (in 3VL)

4. The θ-comparison operators are not transitive

5. Outer natural join is not a projection of outer equijoin

The paper goes on to consider what is involved in adding outer join support to the SQL SELECT–FROM–WHERE construct. It shows that the foregoing Nasty Properties imply that:

1. Extending the WHERE clause does not work

2. ANDing outer joins and restrictions does not work

3. Expressing the join condition in the WHERE clause does not work

4. Outer joins of more than two relations cannot be formulated without nested expressions

5. Extending the SELECT clause (alone) does not work

The paper also shows how many existing products have fallen foul of such considerations.

20.8   C. J. Date. "NOT Is Not "Not"! (Notes on Three-Valued Logic and Related Matters)." In C. J. Date, *Relational Database Writings 1985–1989.* Reading, Mass: Addison-Wesley (1990).

Suppose *X* is a variable of data type "truth value." Then *X* must have one of the values *true, false,* or *unk.* Thus, the statement "*X* is not *true*" means that the value of *X* is either *unk* or *false.* By contrast, the statement "*X* is NOT *true*" means that the value of *X* is *false* (see the truth table for NOT!). Thus the NOT of 3VL is not the not of ordinary English . . . This fact has already caused several people (including the designers of the SQL/92 standard) to stumble, and will doubtless do so again.

20.9   C. J. Date. "EXISTS Is Not "Exists"! (Some Logical Flaws in SQL)." In C. J. Date, *Relational Database Writings 1985–1989.* Reading, Mass: Addison-Wesley (1990).

Points out that the SQL EXISTS operator is not the same thing as the existential quantifier of 3VL, because it always evaluates to *true* or *false,* never to *unk,* even when *unk* is the logically correct answer.

20.10   C. J. Date. "Three-Valued Logic and the Real World." In C. J. Date and Hugh Darwen, *Relational Database Writings 1989–1991.* Reading, Mass.: Addison-Wesley (1992).

20.11   C. J. Date. "Oh No Not Nulls Again." In C. J. Date and Hugh Darwen, *Relational Database Writings 1989–1991.* Reading, Mass.: Addison-Wesley (1992).

20.12   C. J. Date. "A Note on the Logical Operators of SQL." Part I, *The Relational Journal 5,* No. 1 (February/March 1993); Part II, to appear (1994).

3VL has three truth values *true, false,* and *unk* (here abbreviated to *t, f,* and *u,* respectively); hence there are 3 * 3 * 3 = 27 possible monadic 3VL operators, because each of the three possible inputs *t, f,* and *u* can map to each of the three possible outputs *t, f,* and *u.* And there are three to the ninth power = 19,683 possible dyadic 3VL operators, as the following table suggests:

	t	u	f
t	t/u/f	t/u/f	t/u/f
u	t/u/f	t/u/f	t/u/f
f	t/u/f	t/u/f	t/u/f

More generally, in fact, *n*-valued logic involves *n to the power n* monadic operators and *n to the power n^2* dyadic operators (see the table below).

	monadic operators	dyadic operators
2VL	4	16
3VL	27	19,683
4VL	256	4,294,967,296
...	....	....
nVL	$(n)**(n)$	$(n)**(n^2)$

For any nVL with $n > 2$, the following questions arise:

- What is a suitable set of *primitive* operators? (E.g., either of the sets {NOT,AND} or {NOT,OR} is a suitable primitive set for 2VL.)

- What is a suitable set of *useful* operators? (E.g., the set {NOT,AND,OR} is a suitable useful set for 2VL.)

Part I of the present paper shows that the SQL/92 standard (under a *very* charitable interpretation) does at least support, directly or indirectly, all *monadic* 3VL operators. Part II does the same for the *dyadic* operators. However, the point should be made that in logic the operators operate on *predicates* as well as propositions, whereas in SQL (even under the aforementioned charitable interpretation) the operators operate on propositions only.

20.13 C. J. Date. "The Default Values Approach to Missing Information." In C. J. Date and Hugh Darwen, *Relational Database Writings 1989–1991*. Reading, Mass.: Addison-Wesley (1992).

Describes a systematic approach to the missing information problem that is based on default values and 2VL instead of nulls and 3VL. The paper argues strongly that default values are what we use in the real world—"there is no such thing as a null in the real world"—and hence that it would be desirable for our database systems to behave in this respect in the same way as the real world does.

20.14 I. J. Heath. IBM internal memo (April 1971).

The paper that introduced the term (and the concept) "outer join."

20.15 M. Lacroix and A. Pirotte. "Generalized Joins." *ACM SIGMOD Record 8,* No. 3 (September 1976).

20.16 Ken-Chih Liu and Rajshekhar Sunderraman. "Indefinite and Maybe Information in Relational Databases." *ACM TODS 15,* No. 1 (March 1990).

Contains a set of formal proposals for extending the relational model to deal with *maybe information* (e.g., "part P7 may be black") and *indefinite* or *disjunctive information* (e.g., "part P8 or part P9 is red"). *I-tables* are introduced as a means of representing normal (definite) information, maybe information, and indefinite information. The restrict, project, product, union, intersect, and difference operators are extended to operate on I-tables.

20.17 David Maier. *The Theory of Relational Databases*. Rockville, Md.: Computer Science Press (1983).

20.18 David McGoveran. "Nothing from Nothing" (in four parts). *Database Programming & Design 6,* No. 12 (December 1993); *7,* No. 1 (January 1994); *7,* No. 2 (February 1994); *7,* No. 3 (March 1994).

Part I of this four-part series explains the crucial role of logic in database systems. Part II shows why that logic must be two-valued logic (2VL) specifically, and why attempts to use three-valued logic (3VL) are misguided. Part III examines the problems that three-valued logic (3VL) is supposed to "solve." Finally, Part IV describes a set of pragmatic solutions to those problems that do not involve 3VL.

20.19 Nicholas Rescher. *Many-Valued Logic*. New York, N.Y.: McGraw-Hill (1969).

The standard text.

Answers to Selected Exercises

20.1 (a) *unk.* (b) *true.* (c) *true.* (d) *unk* (note the counterintuitive nature of this one). (e) *false.* (f) *false* (note that IS_UNK never returns *unk*). (g) *false.* (h) *true.*

20.2 (a) *unk.* (b) *unk.* (c) *true.* (d) *false.* (e) *unk.* (f) *true.* (g) *false.*

20.3 Because "IS_UNK(x)" returns *true* if and only if "$x \theta y$" returns *unk* (for arbitrary θ and arbitrary y), and it returns *false* if and only if "$x = y$ OR $x \neq y$" returns *true* (for arbitrary nonUNK y).

20.4 Because (e.g.) "MAYBE_RESTRICT R WHERE p" is the same as "R WHERE MAYBE(p)."

20.5 The four monadic operators can be defined as follows (A is the single operand):

```
A
NOT(A)
A OR NOT(A)
A AND NOT(A)
```

The 16 dyadic operators can be defined as follows (A and B are the two operands):

```
A OR NOT(A) OR B OR NOT(B)
A AND NOT(A) AND B AND NOT(B)
A
NOT(A)
B
NOT(B)
A OR B
A AND B
A OR NOT(B)
A AND NOT(B)
NOT(A) OR B
NOT(A) AND B
NOT(A) OR NOT(B)
NOT(A) AND NOT(B)
(NOT(A) OR B) AND (NOT(B) OR A)
(NOT(A) AND B) OR (NOT(B) AND A)
```

Incidentally, to see that we do not need both AND and OR, observe that, e.g.,

```
A OR B  ≡  NOT(NOT(A) AND NOT(B))
```

20.6 See the annotation to reference [20.12].

20.7 (c). For further discussion, see reference [20.8].

20.8 We briefly describe the representation used in IBM's DB2 product. In DB2, a column that can accept nulls is physically represented in the stored database by two columns, the data column itself and a hidden indicator column, one byte wide, that is stored as a prefix to the actual data column. An indicator column value of binary ones indicates that the corresponding data column value is to be ignored (i.e., taken as null); an indicator column value of binary zeros indicates that the corresponding data column value is to be taken as genuine. But the indicator column is always (of course) hidden from the user.

20.9 It seems to this writer that this relation does not have a well-formed predicate at all. The best we can say is something like the following: *The part with the specified part number EITHER has the specified color OR has no color*. But this statement is essentially meaningless! To say that each x either has a y or it doesn't is to say **nothing at all**. It certainly does not serve as a very meaningful "criterion for update acceptability." To this writer, therefore, it looks strongly as if (once again) the notion of nulls undermines the very foundations of the relational model.

21 Distributed Database and Client/Server Systems

21.1 Introduction

We touched on the subject of **distributed databases** at the end of Chapter 2, where we said that " . . . full support for distributed database implies that a single application should be able to operate transparently on data that is spread across a variety of different databases, managed by a variety of different DBMSs, running on a variety of different machines, supported by a variety of different operating systems, and connected together by a variety of different communication networks—where the term *transparently* means that the application operates from a logical point of view as if the data were all managed by a single DBMS running on a single machine." We are now in a position to examine these ideas in some detail. To be specific, in this chapter we will explain exactly what a distributed database is, why distributed databases are important, and what some of the unsolved technical problems are in the distributed database field.

Chapter 2 also briefly discussed **client/server** systems, which can be regarded as a particularly simple special case of distributed systems in general. We will consider client/server systems specifically in Section 21.6.

The overall plan of the chapter is explained at the end of the next section.

21.2 Some Preliminaries

We begin with a working definition (necessarily a little imprecise at this stage):

■ A distributed database system consists of a collection of **sites,** connected together via some kind of communications network, in which

  1. Each site is a database system site in its own right, but

  2. The sites have agreed to work together so that a user at any site can access data anywhere in the network exactly as if the data were all stored at the user's own site.

It follows that the so-called "distributed database" is really a kind of *virtual* object, whose component parts are physically stored in a number of distinct "real" databases at a number of distinct sites (in effect, it is the logical union of those real databases). Fig. 21.1 provides an example.

Note that, to repeat, **each site is a database system site in its own right**. In other words, each site has its own local "real" databases, its own local users, its own local DBMS and transaction management software (including its own local locking, logging, recovery, etc., software), and its own local data communications manager (DC manager). In particular, a given user can perform operations on data at that user's own local site exactly as if that site did not participate in the distributed system at all (at least, this is an objective). The distributed database system can thus be regarded as a kind of **partnership** among the individual local DBMSs at the individual local sites; a new software component at each site—logically an extension of the local DBMS—provides the necessary partnership functions, and it is the combination of this new component

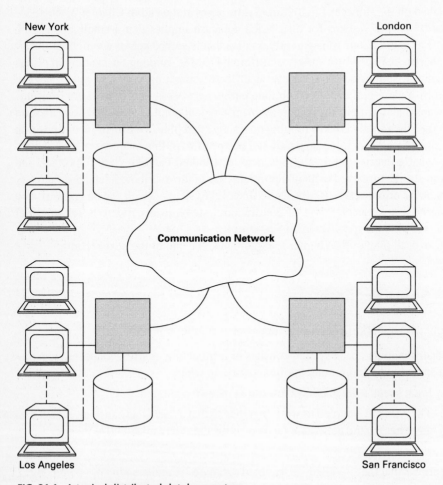

FIG. 21.1 A typical distributed database system

together with the existing DBMS that constitutes what is usually called the **distributed database management system** (sometimes abbreviated DDBMS).

Incidentally, it is common to assume that the component sites are physically dispersed—possibly in fact geographically dispersed also, as suggested by Fig. 21.1—although actually it is sufficient that they be dispersed *logically*. Two "sites" might even coexist on the same physical machine (especially during the period of initial system installation and testing). Indeed, the emphasis in distributed systems has shifted over the past few years: Whereas most of the original research tended to assume geographic distribution, most of the early commercial installations have involved *local* distribution instead, with (e.g.) several "sites" all in the same building and connected together by means of a local area network (LAN). From the database point of view, however, it makes little difference—essentially the same technical problems still have to be solved—and so we can reasonably regard Fig. 21.1 as representing a typical system for the purposes of this chapter.

Note: In order to simplify the exposition, we will assume until further notice that the system is *homogeneous,* in the sense that each site is running a copy of the same DBMS. We will refer to this as the **strict homogeneity** assumption. We will explore the possibility of relaxing this assumption in Section 21.5.

Advantages

Why are distributed databases desirable? The basic answer to this question is that enterprises normally *are* distributed already, at least logically (into divisions, departments, workgroups, etc.), and very likely physically too (into plants, factories, laboratories, etc.)—from which it follows that data normally is distributed already as well, because each organizational unit within the enterprise will necessarily maintain data that is relevant to its own operation. Thus, a distributed system enables the structure of the database to mirror the structure of the enterprise: Local data can be kept locally, where it most logically belongs, while at the same time remote data can be accessed when necessary.

An example will clarify the foregoing. Consider Fig. 21.1 once again. For simplicity, suppose there are only two sites, Los Angeles and San Francisco, and suppose the system is a banking system, with account data for Los Angeles accounts stored in Los Angeles and account data for San Francisco accounts stored in San Francisco. Then the advantages are surely obvious: The distributed arrangement combines **efficiency of processing** (the data is stored close to the point where it is most frequently used) with **increased accessibility** (it is possible to access a Los Angeles account from San Francisco and *vice versa,* via the communications network).

Allowing the structure of the database to mirror the structure of the enterprise is (as just explained) probably the number one advantage of distributed systems. Numerous additional benefits do also accrue, of course, but we will defer discussion of such additional benefits to appropriate points later in the chapter. However, we should mention that there are some disadvantages too, of which the biggest is the fact that distributed systems are *complex,* at least from a technical point of view. Ideally, of course, that complexity should be the implementer's problem, not the user's, but it is likely—to be pragmatic—that some aspects of that complexity will show through to users, unless very careful precautions are taken.

Sample Systems

For purposes of subsequent reference, we briefly mention some of the better known distributed system implementations. First, prototypes. Out of numerous research systems, three of the best known are (a) *SDD-1,* which was built in the research division of Computer Corporation of America in the late 1970s and early 1980s [21.26]; (b) *R** (pronounced "R star"), a distributed version of the System R prototype, built at IBM Research in the early 1980s [21.30]; and (c) *Distributed INGRES,* a distributed version of the INGRES prototype, also built in the early 1980s at the University of California at Berkeley [21.28].

As for commercial implementations, most of today's relational products offer some kind of distributed database support (with varying degrees of functionality, of course). Some of the best known include (a) *INGRES/STAR,* from The ASK Group Inc.'s Ingres Division; (b) the *distributed database option* of ORACLE7, from Oracle Corporation; and (c) the *distributed data facility* of DB2, from IBM. *Note:* These two lists are obviously not meant to be exhaustive; rather, they are meant to identify certain systems that either have been or are being particularly influential for one reason or another, or else have some special intrinsic interest.

It is worth pointing out that all of the systems listed above, both prototypes and products, are relational. Indeed, there are several reasons why, for a distributed system to be successful, that system *must* be relational; relational technology is a prerequisite to (effective) distributed technology [21.14]. We will see some of the reasons for this state of affairs as we proceed through the chapter.

A Fundamental Principle

Now it is possible to state what might be regarded as **the fundamental principle of distributed database** [21.13]:

■   *To the user, a distributed system should look exactly like a NONdistributed system.*

In other words, users in a distributed system should behave exactly as if the system were *not* distributed. All of the problems of distributed systems are—or should be—internal or implementation-level problems, not external or user-level problems.

Note: The term "users" in the foregoing paragraph refers specifically to users (end users or application programmers) who are performing *data manipulation* operations. All data manipulation operations should remain logically unchanged. Data *definition* operations, by contrast, will require some extension in a distributed system—for example, so that a user at site *X* can specify that a given stored relation be divided into "fragments" that are to be stored at sites *Y* and *Z* (see the discussion of fragmentation in the next section).

The fundamental principle identified above leads to a number of subsidiary rules or objectives*—actually twelve of them—which will be discussed in Section 21.3. For reference, we list those twelve objectives here:

1. Local autonomy
2. No reliance on a central site
3. Continuous operation
4. Location independence
5. Fragmentation independence
6. Replication independence
7. Distributed query processing
8. Distributed transaction management
9. Hardware independence
10. Operating system independence
11. Network independence
12. DBMS independence

These twelve objectives are *not* all independent of one another, nor are they necessarily exhaustive, nor are they all equally significant (different users will attach different degrees of importance to different objectives in different environments). However, they *are* useful as a basis for understanding distributed technology and as a framework for characterizing the functionality of specific distributed systems. We will therefore use them as an organizing principle for the rest of the chapter. Section 21.3 presents a brief discussion of each objective; Sections 21.4 and 21.5 then home in on certain specific issues in more detail. Section 21.6 (as previously mentioned) discusses client/server systems. Finally, Section 21.7 addresses the question of SQL support, and Section 21.8 offers a summary and a few concluding remarks.

One final introductory point: It is important to distinguish true, generalized, distributed database systems from systems that merely provide some kind of remote data access (which is all that client/server systems really do, incidentally). In a "remote data access" system, the user might be able to operate on data at a remote site, or even on data at several remote sites simultaneously, but *the seams show;* the user is definitely aware—to a greater or lesser extent—that the data is remote, and has to behave accordingly. In a true distributed database system, by contrast, the seams are *hidden*. (Much of the rest of this chapter is concerned with what it means in this context to say that the seams are hidden.) In what follows, we will use the term "distributed system" to refer specifically to a true, generalized, distributed database system, as opposed to a simple remote data access system (barring explicit statements to the contrary).

---

* "Rules" was the term used in the paper in which they were first introduced [21.13] (and the "fundamental principle" was referred to as *Rule Zero*). However, "objectives" is really a better term—"rules" sounds much too dogmatic. We will stay with the milder term "objectives" in the present chapter.

21.3   The Twelve Objectives

1. Local Autonomy

The sites in a distributed system should be **autonomous**. Local autonomy means that all operations at a given site are controlled by that site; no site X should depend on some other site Y for its successful operation (for otherwise the fact that site Y is down might mean that site X is unable to run, even if there is nothing wrong with site X itself—obviously an undesirable state of affairs). Local autonomy also implies that local data is locally owned and managed, with local accountability: All data "really" belongs to some local database, even if it is accessible from other, remote sites. Such matters as security, integrity, and storage representation of local data thus remain under the control and jurisdiction of the local site.

Actually, the local autonomy objective is not wholly achievable; there are a number of situations in which a given site X *must* relinquish a certain degree of control to some other site Y. The autonomy objective would thus more accurately be stated: Sites should be autonomous **to the maximum extent possible**. See the annotation to reference [21.13] for more specific information.

2. No Reliance on a Central Site

Local autonomy implies that **all sites must be treated as equals;** thus, there must not be any reliance on a central "master" site for some central service—for example, centralized query processing, centralized transaction management, or centralized naming services—such that the entire system is dependent on that central site. This second objective is therefore in fact a corollary of the first (if the first is achieved, the second follows *a fortiori*). But "no reliance on a central site" is desirable in its own right, even if full local autonomy is not achieved. It is therefore worth spelling it out as a separate objective.

Reliance on a central site would be undesirable for at least the following two reasons: First, that central site might be a bottleneck; second, and more important, the system would be *vulnerable*—if the central site were to go down, the whole system would be down.

3. Continuous Operation

An advantage of distributed systems in general is that they should provide greater *reliability* and greater *availability:*

- **Reliability** (which can be defined as the probability that the system is up and running at any given moment) is improved because distributed systems are not an all-or-nothing proposition—they can continue to function (at a reduced level) in the face of failure of some individual component, such as an individual site.

- **Availability** (which can be defined as the probability that the system is up and running continuously throughout a specified period) is improved also, partly for the same reason and partly because of the possibility of data replication (see further discussion under No. 6 below).

The foregoing discussions apply to the case where an **unplanned shutdown** (i.e., a failure of some kind) has occurred at some point within the system. Unplanned shutdowns are obviously undesirable, but difficult to avoid entirely. **Planned** shutdowns, by contrast, should *never* be required; that is, the system should ideally never require itself to be shut down in order to perform some function, such as adding a new site, or upgrading the DBMS at an existing site to a new release level.

4. Location Independence

The basic idea of **location independence** (also known as location **transparency**) is simple: Users should not have to know where data is physically stored, but rather should be able to behave—at least from a logical standpoint—as if the data were all stored at their own local site. Location independence is desirable because it simplifies user programs and terminal activities. In particular, it allows data to migrate from site to site without invalidating any of those programs or activities. Such migratability is desirable because it allows data to be moved around the network in response to changing performance requirements.

Note: The reader will doubtless realize that location independence is just an extension of the familiar concept of (physical) *data* independence, as that concept applies to the distributed case. In fact—to jump ahead of ourselves for a moment—every objective in our list that has "independence" in its name can be regarded as an extension of data independence, as we will see.

We will have a little more to say regarding location independence in Section 21.4 (in our discussion of object naming, under the heading "Catalog management").

5. Fragmentation Independence

A system supports **data fragmentation** if a given stored relation can be divided up into pieces or "fragments" for physical storage purposes. Fragmentation is desirable for performance reasons: Data can be stored at the location where it is most frequently used, so that most operations are purely local and network traffic is reduced. For example, consider the employees relation EMP shown at the top of Fig. 21.2. In a system that supports fragmentation, we might define two fragments as follows:

```
FRAGMENT EMP INTO
   N_EMP AT SITE 'New York' WHERE DEPT# = 'D1' OR DEPT# = 'D3',
   L_EMP AT SITE 'London'   WHERE DEPT# = 'D2' ;
```

(refer to the lower portion of Fig. 21.2). *Note:* We are assuming that (a) employee tuples map to physical storage in some fairly direct manner); (b) D1 and D3 are New York departments and D2 is a London department. In other words, tuples for New York employees will be stored at the New York site and tuples for London employees will be stored at the London site. Note the system's internal fragment names N_EMP and L_EMP.

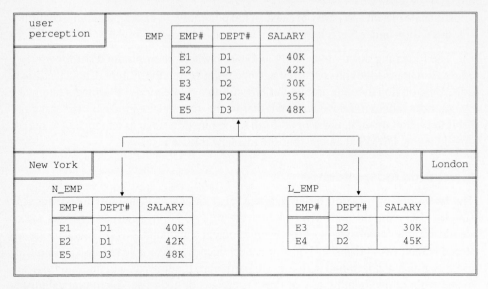

FIG. 21.2   An example of fragmentation

There are basically two kinds of fragmentation, horizontal and vertical, corresponding to the relational operations of restriction and projeetion, respectively (Fig. 21.2 illustrates a horizontal fragmentation). More generally, a fragment can be *any arbitrary subrelation* that is derivable from the original relation via restriction and projection operations—arbitrary, that is, except that:

- We assume without loss of generality that all fragments of a given relation are *disjoint,* in the sense that none of the fragments can be derived from the other fragments, or has a restriction or a projection that can be derived from the other fragments. (If we really do want to store the same piece of information in several different places, we can do so by means of the system's *replication* mechanism. See the next subsection.)

- In the case of projection, the projections must be nonloss (see Chapters 10–11).

Reconstructing the original relation from the fragments is done via suitable join and union operations (join for vertical fragments, union for horizontal ones). In the case of union, incidentally, observe that no duplicate elimination will be required (why not?).

Note: We should elaborate slightly on the question of vertical fragmentation. It is true that, as stated above, such a fragmentation must be nonloss, and hence that, e.g., fragmenting the EMP relation into its projections on (EMP#,DEPT#) and (SALARY) would not be valid. In some systems, however, stored relations are regarded as having a hidden "tuple ID" or TID attribute, where the TID for a given stored tuple is a physical or logical address for that tuple. That TID attribute is clearly a candidate key for the relation in question; thus, for example, if the EMP relation included such an attribute, the relation *could* validly be fragmented into its projections on (TID,EMP#,DEPT#) and (TID,SALARY), since this fragmentation is clearly nonloss.

Note, incidentally, that ease of fragmentation and ease of reconstruction are two of the many reasons why distributed systems are relational; the relational model provides exactly the operations that are needed for these tasks [21.14].

Now we come to the main point: A system that supports data fragmentation should also support **fragmentation independence** (also known as fragmentation **transparency**)—i.e., users should be able to behave, at least from a logical standpoint, as if the data were in fact not fragmented at all. Fragmentation independence (like location independence) is desirable because it simplifies user programs and terminal activities. In particular, it allows the data to be refragmented at any time (and fragments to be redistributed at any time) in response to changing performance requirements, without invalidating any of those user programs or activities.

Fragmentation independence implies that users will be presented with a view of the data in which the fragments are logically combined together by means of suitable joins and unions. It is the responsibility of the *system optimizer* to determine which fragments need to be physically accessed in order to satisfy any given user request. Given the fragmentation shown in Fig. 21.2, for example, if the user issues the request

```
EMP WHERE SALARY > 40K AND DEPT# = 'D1'
```

the optimizer will know from the fragment definitions (which will be stored in the catalog, of course) that the entire result can be obtained from the New York site—there is no need to access the London site at all.

Let us examine this example a little more closely. The EMP relation as perceived by the user can be regarded as a **view** of the underlying fragments N_EMP and L_EMP:

```
EMP = N_EMP UNION L_EMP
```

The optimizer thus transforms the user's original request into the following:

```
( N_EMP UNION L_EMP ) WHERE SALARY > 40K AND DEPT# = 'D1'
```

This expression can then be transformed further:

```
( N_EMP WHERE SALARY > 40K AND DEPT# = 'D1' )
  UNION
( L_EMP WHERE SALARY > 40K AND DEPT# = 'D1' )
```

From the definition of fragment L_EMP in the catalog, the optimizer knows that the second of these two expressions evaluates to an empty relation (the restriction condition DEPT# = 'D1' AND DEPT# = 'D2' can never evaluate to *true*). The overall expression can thus be simplified to just

```
N_EMP WHERE SALARY > 40K AND DEPT# = 'D1'
```

Now the optimizer knows that it need access only the New York site. *Exercise for the reader:* Consider what is involved on the part of the optimizer in dealing with the request

```
EMP WHERE SALARY > 40K
```

As the foregoing indicates, the problem of supporting operations on fragmented relations has certain points in common with the problem of supporting operations on join and union views (in fact, the two problems are one and the same—they just manifest themselves at different points in the overall system architecture). In particular, the problem of *updating* fragmented relations is the same as the problem of updating join and union views (see Chapter 17). It follows too that updating a given tuple might cause that tuple to migrate from one fragment to another, if the updated tuple no longer satisfies the relation predicate for the fragment it previously belonged to.

6. Replication Independence

A system supports **data replication** if a given stored relation—or, more generally, a given *fragment*—can be represented by many distinct copies or *replicas,* stored at many distinct sites. For example:

```
REPLICATE N_EMP
    LN_EMP AT SITE 'London' ;

REPLICATE L_EMP
    NL_EMP AT SITE 'New York' ;
```

(see Fig. 21.3). Note the system's internal replica names NL_EMP and LN_EMP.

Replication is desirable for at least two reasons: First, it can mean better performance (applications can operate on local copies instead of having to communicate with remote sites); second, it can also mean better availability (a given replicated object remains available for processing so long as at least one copy remains available, at least for retrieval purposes). The major *dis*advantage of replication, of course, is that when a

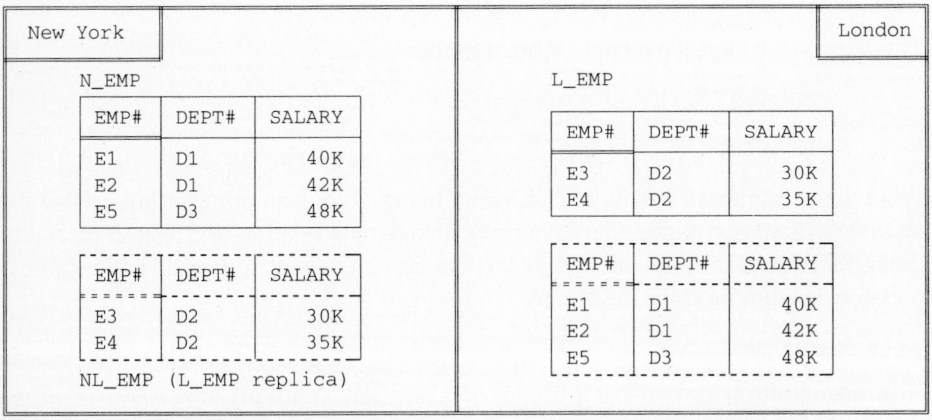

New York				London

N_EMP

EMP#	DEPT#	SALARY
E1	D1	40K
E2	D1	42K
E5	D3	48K

EMP#	DEPT#	SALARY
E3	D2	30K
E4	D2	35K

NL_EMP (L_EMP replica)

L_EMP

EMP#	DEPT#	SALARY
E3	D2	30K
E4	D2	35K

EMP#	DEPT#	SALARY
E1	D1	40K
E2	D1	42K
E5	D3	48K

FIG. 21.3 An example of replication

given replicated object is updated, *all copies* of that object must be updated—the **update propagation** problem. We will have more to say on this problem in Section 21.4.

We remark in passing that replication in a distributed system represents a specific application of the idea of *controlled redundancy* as discussed in Chapter 1.

Now, replication, like fragmentation, ideally should be "transparent to the user." In other words, a system that supports data replication should also support **replication independence** (also known as replication **transparency**)—i.e., users should be able to behave, at least from a logical standpoint, as if the data were in fact not replicated at all. Replication independence (like location independence and fragmentation independence) is desirable because it simplifies user programs and terminal activities; in particular, it allows replicas to be created and destroyed at any time in response to changing requirements, without invalidating any of those user programs or activities.

Replication independence implies that it is the responsibility of the system optimizer to determine which replicas physically need to be accessed in order to satisfy any given user request. We omit the specifics of this issue here.

We close this subsection by pointing out that many commercial products currently provide a form of replication support that does *not* include full replication independence (i.e., is *not* entirely "transparent to the user"). See the further remarks on this topic in Section 21.4, in the subsection on update propagation.

7. Distributed Query Processing

There are two broad points to be made under this heading.

- First, consider the query "Get London suppliers of red parts." Suppose the user is at the New York site and the data is stored at the London site. Suppose too that there are *n* suppliers that satisfy the request. If the system is relational, the query will basically involve two messages—one to send the request from New York to London, and one to return the result set of *n* tuples from London to New York. If, on the other hand, the system is not relational but record-at-a-time, the query will basically involve 2*n* messages—*n* from New York to London requesting "the next" supplier, and *n* from London to New York to return that "next" supplier. The example thus illustrates the point that a relational system is likely to outperform a nonrelational one (at least for set-level requests) by possibly orders of magnitude.

- Second, **optimization** is even more important in a distributed system than it is in a centralized one. The basic point is that, in a query such as the one above involving several sites, there will be many possible ways of moving data around the network in order to satisfy the request, and it is crucially important that an efficient strategy be found. For instance, a request for (say) the union of a relation *Rx* stored at site *X* and a relation *Ry* stored at site *Y* could be carried out by moving *Rx* to *Y* or by moving *Ry* to *X* or by moving both to a third site *Z* (etc.). A compelling illustration of this point, involving the query mentioned above ("Get London suppliers of red parts"), is presented in the next section. To summarize the findings from that example briefly, six different strategies for processing the query are analyzed under a certain set of plausible assumptions, and the response time is shown to vary from a minimum of one tenth of a second to a maximum of nearly six *hours* . . . ! Optimization is thus clearly crucial, and this fact in turn can be seen as yet another reason why distributed systems are always relational—the point being that set-level requests are optimizable, while record-level requests are not.

8. Distributed Transaction Management

There are two major aspects to transaction management, recovery control and concurrency control, each of which requires extended treatment in the distributed environment. In order to explain that extended treatment, it is first necessary to introduce a new term, "agent." In a distributed system, a single transaction can involve the execution of code at many sites; in particular, it can involve updates at many sites. Each transaction is therefore said to consist of several **agents,** where an agent is the process performed on behalf of a given transaction at a given site. And the system needs to know when two agents are both part of the same transaction—for example, two agents that are part of the same transaction must obviously not be allowed to deadlock with each other.

Turning now to recovery control specifically: In order to ensure that a given transaction is atomic (all-or-nothing) in the distributed environment, therefore, the system must ensure that the set of agents for that transaction either all commit in unison or all roll back in unison. This effect can be achieved by means of the **two-phase commit** protocol, already discussed (although not in the distributed context) in Chapter 13. We will have more to say regarding two-phase commit for a distributed system in Section 21.4.

As for concurrency control: Concurrency control in most distributed systems is typically based on **locking,** just as it is in nondistributed systems. (Several more recent systems have begun to implement *multiversion controls* [14.1]; however, conventional locking still seems to be the technique of choice for most systems.) Again, we will discuss this topic in a little more detail in Section 21.4.

9. Hardware Independence

There is actually not a great deal to be said on this topic—the heading says it all. Real-world computer installations typically involve a multiplicity of different machines— IBM machines, DEC machines, HP machines, PCs and workstations of various kinds, etc., etc.—and there is a real need to be able to integrate the data on all of those systems and present the user with a "single-system image." Thus, it is desirable to be able to run the same DBMS on different hardware platforms, and furthermore to have those different machines all participate as equal partners in a distributed system.

10. Operating System Independence

This objective is partly a corollary of the previous one, and also does not really require very much discussion here. It is obviously desirable, not only to be able to run the same DBMS on different hardware platforms, but also to be able to run it on different operating system platforms as well—including different operating systems on the same hardware—and have (e.g.) an MVS version and a UNIX version and a PC/DOS version all participate in the same distributed system.

11. Network Independence

Once again there is not very much to say; if the system is to be able to support many disparate sites, with disparate hardware and disparate operating systems, it is obviously desirable to be able to support a variety of disparate communication networks also.

12. DBMS Independence

Under this heading, we consider what is involved in relaxing the strict homogeneity assumption. That assumption is arguably a little too strong: All that is really needed is that the DBMS instances at different sites **all support the same interface**—they do not necessarily all have to be copies of the same DBMS software. For example, if INGRES and ORACLE both supported the official SQL standard, then it *might* conceivably be possible to get an INGRES site and an ORACLE site to talk to each other in the context of a distributed system. In other words, it might be possible for the distributed system to be *hetero*geneous, at least to some degree.

Support for heterogeneity is definitely desirable. The fact is (to repeat), real-world computer installations typically run not only many different machines and many different operating systems, they very often run different DBMSs as well; and it would be nice if those different DBMSs could all participate somehow in a distributed system. In other words, the ideal distributed system should provide **DBMS independence**.

This is such a large topic, however (and such an important one in practice), that we devote a separate section to it. See Section 21.5.

21.4   Problems of Distributed Systems

In this section, we elaborate a little on some of the problems that were mentioned only briefly in Section 21.3. The overriding problem is that communication networks—at least, "long-haul" or wide area networks (WANs)—are *slow*. A typical WAN might have an effective data rate of around 5 to 10 thousand bytes per second; the typical disk drive, by contrast, has a data rate of around 5 to 10 *million* bytes per second [13.11]. (Local area networks, on the other hand, are beginning to support data rates of the same order of magnitude as disk drives.) As a consequence, an overriding objective in distributed systems is, typically, **to minimize network utilization**—i.e., to minimize the number and volume of messages. This objective in turn gives rise to problems in a number of subsidiary areas, the following among them (this list is not meant to be exhaustive):

- Query processing
- Catalog management
- Update propagation

- Recovery control
- Concurrency control

Query Processing

The objective of minimizing network utilization implies that the query optimization process itself needs to be distributed, as well as the query execution process. In other words, the overall optimization process will typically consist of a **global optimization** step, followed by **local optimization** steps at each affected site. For example, suppose a query Q is submitted at site X, and suppose Q involves a union of a relation Ry of a hundred tuples at site Y with a relation Rz of a million tuples at site Z. The optimizer at site X will choose the global strategy for executing Q; and it is clearly important that it decide to move Ry to Z and not Rz to Y (and certainly not Ry and Rz both to X). Then, once it has decided to move Ry to Z, the strategy for performing the actual union at site Z will be decided by the local optimizer at Z.

The following more detailed illustration of the foregoing point is based on an example given in reference [21.12], which adopted it in turn from a paper by Rothnie and Goodman [21.25].

Database (suppliers and parts, simplified):

```
S  { S#, CITY }          10,000 stored tuples at site A
P  { P#, COLOR }        100,000 stored tuples at site B
SP { S#, P# }         1,000,000 stored tuples at site A
```

Assume that every stored tuple is 25 bytes (200 bits) long.

Query (supplier numbers for London suppliers of red parts):

```
S.S# WHERE EXISTS SP EXISTS P ( S.CITY = 'London' AND
                                S.S# = SP.S# AND
                                SP.P# = P.P# AND
                                P.COLOR = 'Red' )
```

Estimated cardinalities of certain intermediate results:

Number of red parts   =   10

Number of shipments by London suppliers = 100,000

Communication assumptions:

Data rate   = 50,000 bits per second

Access delay = 0.1 second

We now briefly examine six possible strategies for processing this query, and for each strategy i calculate the total communication time $T[i]$ from the formula

```
T[i] = total access delay + ( total data volume / data rate )
     = ( number of messages / 10 ) + ( number of bits / 50000 )
```

1. Move relation P to site A and process the query at A.

```
T[1] = 0.1 + ( 100000 * 200 ) / 50000
     = 400 seconds approx. (6.67 minutes)
```

2. Move relations S and SP to site B and process the query at B.

```
T[2] = 0.2 + ( ( 10000 + 1000000 ) * 200 ) / 50000
     = 4040 seconds approx. (1.12 hours)
```

3. Join relations S and SP at site A, restrict the result to tuples for London suppliers, and then, for each of those tuples in turn, check site B to see whether the corresponding part is red. Each of these checks will involve two messages, a query and a response. The transmission time for these messages will be small compared with the access delay.

```
T[3] = 20000 seconds approx. (5.56 hours)
```

4. Restrict relation P at site B to tuples for red parts, and then, for each of those tuples in turn, check site A to see whether there exists a shipment relating the part to a London supplier. Each of these checks will involve two messages; again, the transmission time for these messages will be small compared with the access delay.

```
T[4] = 2 seconds approx.
```

5. Join relations S and SP at site A, restrict the result to tuples for London suppliers, project the result over S# and P#, and move the result to site B. Complete the processing at site B.

```
T[5] = 0.1 + ( 100000 * 200 ) / 50000
     = 400 seconds approx. (6.67 minutes)
```

6. Restrict relation P at site B to tuples for red parts and move the result to site A. Complete the processing at site A.

```
T[6] = 0.1 + ( 10 * 200 ) / 50000
     = 0.1 second approx.
```

Fig. 21.4 summarizes the foregoing results. Points arising:

- Each of the six strategies represents a plausible approach to the problem, yet the variation in communication time is enormous (the slowest technique is *two million times* slower than the quickest).

- Data rate and access delay are both important factors in choosing a strategy.

Strategy	Technique	Communication time
1.	Move P to A	6.67 mins
2.	Move S and SP to B	1.12 hrs
3.	For each London shipment, check if part is red	5.56 hrs
4.	For each red part, check if a London supplier exists	2.00 secs
5.	Move London shipments to B	6.67 mins
6.	**Move red parts to A**	**0.10 secs (best)**

FIG. 21.4 Distributed query processing strategies (summary)

■ Computation and I/O times are likely to be negligible compared with communication time for the poor strategies. (For the better strategies, on the other hand, this might or might not be the case [21.27].)

In addition, some strategies permit parallel processing at the two sites; thus, the response time to the user might actually be less than in a centralized system. Note, however, that we have ignored the question of which site is to receive the final result.

Catalog Management

In a distributed system, the system catalog will include not only the usual catalog data regarding base relations, views, indexes, users, etc., but also all the necessary control information to enable the system to provide the desired location, fragmentation, and replication independence. The question arises: Where and how should the catalog itself be stored? Here are some possibilities:

1. *Centralized:* The total catalog is stored exactly once, at a single central site.
2. *Fully replicated:* The total catalog is stored in its entirety at every site.
3. *Partitioned:* Each site maintains its own catalog for objects stored at that site. The total catalog is the union of all of those disjoint local catalogs.
4. *Combination of 1 and 3:* Each site maintains its own local catalog, as in paragraph 3; in addition, a single central site maintains a unified copy of all of those local catalogs, as in paragraph 1.

Each of these approaches has its problems. Approach 1 obviously violates the "no reliance on a central site" objective. Approach 2 suffers from a severe loss of autonomy, in that every catalog update has to be propagated to every site. Approach 3 makes nonlocal operations very expensive (finding a remote object will require access to half the sites, on average). Approach 4 is more efficient than Approach 3 (finding a remote object requires only one remote catalog access), but violates the "no reliance on a central site" objective again. In practice, therefore, systems typically do not use *any* of these four approaches! By way of example, we describe the approach used in R* [21.30].

In order to explain how the catalog is structured in R*, it is first necessary to say something about R* **object naming**. Now, object naming is a significant issue for distributed systems in general; the possibility that two distinct sites A and B might both have an object, say a stored relation, called R implies that some mechanism—typically qualification by site name—will be required in order to guarantee system-wide name uniqueness. If qualified names (such as A.R and B.R) are exposed to the user, however, the location independence objective will clearly be violated. What is needed, therefore, is a means of mapping the names known to users to their corresponding system-known name.

Here then is the R* approach to this problem. First, R* distinguishes between an object's **printname**, which is the name by which the object is normally referenced by users (e.g., in an SQL SELECT statement), and its **system-wide name,** which is a globally unique internal identifier for the object. System-wide names have four components:

- *Creator ID* (the ID of the user who created the object)
- *Creator site ID* (the ID of the site at which the CREATE operation is entered)
- *Local name* (the unqualified name of the object)
- *Birth site ID* (the ID of the site at which the object is initially stored)

For example, the system-wide name

```
MARILYN @ NEWYORK . STATS @ LONDON
```

identifies an object (e.g., a stored relation) with local name STATS, created by the user called Marilyn at the New York site and initially stored at the London site. This name is **guaranteed never to change**—not even if the object migrates to another site (see below).

As already indicated, users normally refer to objects by their *printname*. A printname consists of a simple unqualified name—either the "local name" component of the system-wide name (STATS in the example above), or a **synonym** for that system-wide name, defined by means of the special R* SQL statement CREATE SYNONYM. Here is an example:

```
CREATE SYNONYM MSTATS FOR MARILYN @ NEWYORK . STATS @ LONDON ;
```

Now the user can say either (e.g.)

```
SELECT ... FROM STATS ... ;
```

or

```
SELECT ... FROM MSTATS ... ;
```

In the first case (using the local name), the system infers the system-wide name by assuming all the obvious defaults—namely, that the object was created by this user, it was created at this site, and it was initially stored at this site. Incidentally, one consequence of these default assumptions is that old System R applications will run unchanged on R* (once the data has been redefined to R*, that is).

In the second case (using the synonym), the system determines the system-wide name by interrogating the relevant **synonym table**. Synonym tables can be thought of as the first component of the catalog; each site maintains a set of such tables for each user known at that site, mapping the synonyms known to that user to their corresponding system-wide names.

In addition to the synonym tables, each site maintains:

1. A catalog entry for every object **born** at that site
2. A catalog entry for every object **currently stored** at that site

Suppose now that the user issues a request referring to the synonym MSTATS. First, the system looks up the corresponding system-wide name in the appropriate synonym table (a purely local lookup). Now it knows the birthsite, namely London in the example, and it can interrogate the London catalog (which we assume for generality to be a remote lookup—first remote access). The London catalog will contain an entry for the object, by virtue of point 1 above. If the object is still at London, it has now been found. However, if the object has migrated to (say) Los Angeles, then the catalog entry in London will say as much, and so the system can now interrogate the Los Angeles catalog (second remote access). And the Los Angeles catalog will contain an entry for the object, by virtue of point 2 above. So the object has been found in at most two remote accesses.

Furthermore, if the object migrates again, say to San Francisco, then the system will:

■ Insert a San Francisco catalog entry

■ Delete the Los Angeles catalog entry

■ Change the London catalog entry to point to San Francisco instead of Los Angeles

The net effect is that the object can still be found in at most two remote accesses. And this is a completely distributed scheme—there is no central catalog site, and no single point of global failure within the system.

We remark that the object naming scheme used in the DB2 distributed data facility is similar but not identical to the one described above.

Update Propagation

The basic problem with data replication, as pointed out in Section 21.3, is that an update to any given logical object must be propagated to all stored copies of that object. A difficulty that arises immediately is that some site holding a copy of the object might be unavailable (because of a site or network failure) at the time of the update. The obvious strategy of propagating updates immediately to all copies might thus be unacceptable, because it implies that the update—and therefore the transaction—will fail if any one of those copies is currently unavailable. In a sense, in fact, data is *less* available under this strategy than it would be in the nonreplicated case, thereby undermining one of the advantages claimed for replication in the previous section.

A common scheme for dealing with this problem (not the only one possible) is the so-called **primary copy** scheme, which works as follows:

■ One copy of each replicated object is designated as the *primary* copy. The remainder are all secondary copies.

■ Primary copies of different objects are at different sites (so this is a distributed scheme once again).

■ Update operations are deemed to be logically complete as soon as the primary copy has been updated. The site holding that copy is then responsible for propagating the update to the secondary copies at some subsequent time. (That "subsequent time" must be prior to COMMIT, however, if the ACID properties of the transaction are to be preserved. See the further remarks on this subject below.)

Of course, this scheme leads to several additional problems of its own, most of them beyond the scope of this book. Note too that it does represent a violation of the local autonomy objective, because a transaction might now fail because a remote (primary) copy of some object is unavailable—even if a local copy is available.

Note: As mentioned above, the requirements of transaction atomicity (etc.) imply that all update propagation must be completed before the relevant transaction can complete. At the time of writing, however, several commercial products support a less ambitious form of replication, in which update propagation is guaranteed to be done at some future time (possibly at some user-specified time) but *not* necessarily within the scope of the relevant transaction. Indeed, the term "replication" has unfortunately been more or less usurped by those products, with the result that—in the commercial marketplace, at least—it is almost always taken to imply that update propagation is delayed past the commit point of the relevant transaction. The problem with this "delayed propagation" approach, of course, is that the database can no longer be guaranteed to be consistent at all times; indeed, the user might not even know whether it is consistent or not.

We close this subsection with a couple of additional observations on the delayed propagation approach:

1. The concept of replication in a system with delayed update propagation can be thought of as a limited application of the idea of *snapshots* as discussed in earlier chapters of this book.

2. One reason (perhaps the major reason) why products are implementing replication with delayed propagation is that the alternative— i.e., updating all replicas prior to COMMIT—requires two-phase commit support (see below), which in turn requires all relevant sites to be up and running at commit time and can be costly in performance. This state of affairs explains the articles sometimes encountered in the trade press with mystifying titles like "Replication *vs.* Two-Phase Commit"— mystifying, because on the surface they appear to be comparing the merits of two totally different things.

Recovery Control

As explained in Section 21.3, recovery control in distributed systems is typically based on the **two-phase commit** protocol (or some variant thereof). Two-phase commit is required in *any* environment in which a single transaction can interact with several autonomous resource managers; however, it is particularly important in a distributed system, because the resource managers in question—i.e., the local DBMSs—are operating at distinct sites and are hence *very* autonomous.

Points arising:

1. The "no reliance on a central site" objective dictates that the Coordinator function must not be assigned to one distinguished site in the network, but instead must be performed by different sites for different transactions. Typically it is handled by the site at which the transaction in question is initiated; thus, each site must be

capable of acting as the Coordinator site for some transactions and as a participant site for others (in general).

2. The two-phase commit process requires the Coordinator to communicate with every participant site—which means more messages and more overhead.

3. If site Y acts as a participant in a two-phase commit process coordinated by site X, then site Y *must* do what it is told by site X (commit or rollback, whichever applies)—a (minor?) loss of local autonomy.

4. Ideally, of course, we would like the two-phase commit process to work even if site or network failures occur at any point; ideally, in fact, we would like the process to be resilient to *any conceivable* kind of failure. Unfortunately, it is easy to see that this problem is fundamentally unsolvable—that is, there does not exist any finite protocol that will *guarantee* that all agents will commit a successful transaction in unison, or roll back an unsuccessful one in unison, in the face of arbitrary failures. For suppose, conversely, that such a protocol does exist. Let N be the minimum number of messages required by such a protocol. Suppose now that the last of these N messages is lost because of some failure. Then either that message was unnecessary, which is contrary to the assumption that N was minimal, or the protocol now does not work. Either way there is a contradiction, from which we deduce that no such protocol exists.

5. The two-phase commit protocol described in this book (Chapter 13) might be regarded as a *basic* protocol. However, there are numerous improvements on that basic protocol that can and probably should be adopted in practice. For example, reference [21.22] describes a variant called *presumed commit* that reduces the number of messages in the case where the transaction completes successfully, at the cost of incurring additional messages in the case where the transaction fails. Reference [21.14] includes a brief tutorial on such matters.

Concurrency Control

As explained in Section 21.3, concurrency control in most distributed systems is based on locking, just as it is in most nondistributed systems. In a distributed system, however, requests to test, set, and release locks become *messages* (assuming that the object under consideration is at a remote site), and messages mean overhead. For example, consider a transaction T that needs to update an object for which there exist replicas at n remote sites. If each site is responsible for locks on objects stored at that site (as it will be under the local autonomy assumption), then a straightforward implementation will require at least $5n$ messages:

  n lock requests

  n lock grants

  n update messages

  n acknowledgments

  n unlock requests

Of course, we can easily improve on the foregoing by "piggybacking" messages—for example, the lock request and update messages can be combined, and so can the lock grant and acknowledgment messages—but even so, the total time for the update could still be several orders of magnitude greater than it would be in a centralized system.

The usual approach to this problem is to adopt the **primary copy** strategy outlined under "Update propagation" above. For a given object R, the site holding the primary copy of R will handle all locking operations involving R (remember that the primary copies of different objects will be at different sites, in general). Under this strategy the set of all copies of an object can be considered as a single object for locking purposes, and the total number of messages will be reduced from $5n$ to $2n + 3$ (one lock request, one lock grant, n updates, n acknowledgments, and one unlock request). But notice once again that this solution entails a (severe) loss of autonomy—a transaction can now fail if a primary copy is unavailable, even if the transaction is read-only and a local copy is available. (Note that not only update operations, but also retrieval operations, need to lock the primary copy [21.14]. Thus, an unpleasant side-effect of the primary copy strategy is to reduce performance and availability for retrievals as well as for updates.)

Another problem with locking in a distributed system is that it can lead to **global deadlock**. A global deadlock is a deadlock involving two or more sites. For example (refer to Fig. 21.5):

1. The agent of transaction *T2* at site *X* is waiting for the agent of transaction *T1* at site *X* to release a lock;

2. The agent of transaction *T1* at site *X* is waiting for the agent of transaction *T1* at site *Y* to complete;

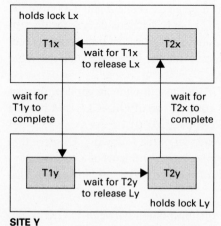

SITE X

SITE Y

FIG. 21.5 An example of global deadlock

3. The agent of transaction *T1* at site *Y* is waiting for the agent of transaction *T2* at site *Y* to release a lock;

4. The agent of transaction *T2* at site *Y* is waiting for the agent of transaction *T2* at site *X* to complete. Deadlock!

The problem with a deadlock such as this one is that *neither site can detect it using only information that is internal to that site*. In other words, there are no cycles in the local Wait-For Graphs, but a cycle will appear if those two local graphs are combined to form a global Wait-For Graph. It follows that global deadlock detection incurs further communication overhead, because it requires individual local graphs to be brought together somehow.

An elegant (and distributed) scheme for global deadlock detection is described in the R* papers. See, e.g., reference [21.30].

21.5   Gateways

The last of the twelve objectives in Section 21.3 was *DBMS independence*. As explained in the brief discussion in that section, it might be argued that the strict homogeneity assumption is really too strong; all that is really needed is that the DBMSs at different sites support the same interface. As Section 21.3 put it: If, e.g., INGRES and ORACLE both supported the official SQL standard, then it might conceivably be possible to get them to behave as equal partners in a heterogeneous distributed system (indeed, such a possibility is one of the arguments usually advanced in favor of the SQL standard). Let us consider this possibility in detail. *Note*: We base our discussion on the specific case of INGRES and ORACLE merely to make matters a little more concrete. The concepts are generally applicable, of course.

Suppose, therefore, that there are two sites *X* and *Y* running INGRES and ORACLE respectively, and suppose some user *U* at site *X* wishes to see a single distributed database that includes data from the INGRES database at site *X* and data from the ORACLE database at site *Y*. By definition, user *U* is an INGRES user, and the distributed database must therefore be an INGRES database so far as that user is concerned. The onus is thus on INGRES, not ORACLE, to provide the necessary support. What must that support consist of?

In principle, it is quite straightforward: INGRES must provide an application program—usually referred to as a **gateway**—that runs on top of ORACLE and has the effect of "making ORACLE look like INGRES" (see Fig. 21.6).

The functions of the gateway must thus include all of the following. Observe that several of these functions present technical implementation problems of a very nontrivial nature. *Note:* The RDA and DRDA standards to be discussed briefly in Section 21.6 (*q.v.*) do address some of these issues.

■   Implementing protocols for the exchange of information between INGRES and ORACLE—which involves (among other things) understanding the message format in which SQL source statements are sent from INGRES, and mapping

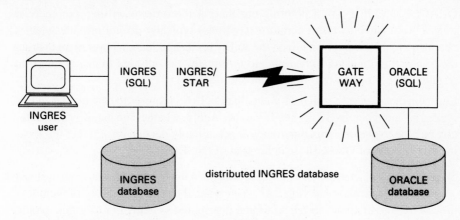

FIG. 21.6   A hypothetical INGRES-provided gateway to ORACLE

ORACLE results (data values, return codes, etc.) into the message format that INGRES expects.

- Providing a "relational server" function for ORACLE (analogous to the function provided by the interactive SQL processor found in most SQL products already). In other words, the gateway must be able to execute arbitrary unplanned SQL statements on the ORACLE database. In order to be able to provide this function, the gateway will have to make use of the **dynamic SQL** support (see Chapter 8)—or a call interface—at the ORACLE site.

- Mapping between the ORACLE and INGRES data types. This problem includes a variety of subproblems having to do with such matters as processor differences (e.g., different machine word lengths), character code differences (string comparisons and ORDER BY requests can give unexpected results), floating point format differences (a notorious problem area), differences in date and time support (no two DBMSs known to this writer currently provide identical support in this area), etc., etc. See reference [21.14] for further discussion of these issues.

- Mapping the INGRES dialect of SQL to the ORACLE dialect. Note that INGRES and ORACLE both support certain SQL features that the other does not, and that there are also some features that have identical syntax in the two products but different semantics.

- Mapping ORACLE feedback information (return codes, etc.) to INGRES format.

- Mapping the ORACLE catalog to INGRES format, so that the INGRES site, and users at the INGRES site, can find out what the ORACLE database contains.

- Serving as a participant in (the INGRES variant of) the two-phase commit protocol (assuming that INGRES transactions are to be allowed to perform updates on the ORACLE database). Whether the gateway will actually be able to perform this function will depend on the facilities provided by the transaction manager at the

ORACLE site. It is worth pointing out that, at the time of writing, commercial transaction managers (with certain exceptions) typically do *not* provide what is necessary in this respect—namely, the ability for an application program to instruct the transaction manager to "prepare to terminate" (as opposed to instructing it to terminate, i.e., commit or rollback, unconditionally).

■ Ensuring that data at the ORACLE site that INGRES requires to be locked is in fact locked as and when INGRES needs it to be. Again, whether the gateway will actually be able to perform this function will presumably depend on whether the locking architecture of ORACLE matches that of INGRES or not.

So far we have discussed DBMS independence in the context of relational systems only. What about nonrelational systems?—i.e., what about the possibility of including a nonrelational site in an otherwise relational distributed system? For example, would it be possible to provide access to an IMS site from an INGRES or ORACLE site? Again, such a feature would be very desirable in practice, given the enormous quantity of data that currently resides in IMS and other prerelational systems. But can it be done?

If the question means "Can it be done at the 100 percent level?"—meaning "Can all nonrelational data be made accessible from a relational interface, and can all relational operations be performed on that data?"—then the answer is definitely *no,* for reasons explained in detail in reference [21.15]. But if the question means "Can some useful level of functionality be provided?", then the answer is obviously *yes*. This is not the place to go into details; the interested reader is referred to references [21.13-21.15] for further discussion.

To summarize, there are clearly significant problems in providing satisfactory gateways, especially if the target system is not relational. However, the potential payoff is dramatic, even if the solutions are less than perfect; for this reason, many gateway products have already appeared in the marketplace, and more are likely to appear over the next few years. But the reader is warned that the solutions will necessarily be less than perfect—vendor claims to the contrary notwithstanding. *Caveat emptor*.

21.6 Client/Server Systems

As mentioned in Section 21.1, **client/server** systems can be regarded as a simple special case of distributed systems in general. More precisely, a client/server system is a distributed system in which (a) some sites are *client* sites and others are *server* sites, (b) all data resides at the server sites, (c) all applications execute at the client sites, and (d) "the seams show" (full location independence is not provided). Refer to Fig. 21.7 (a repeat of Fig. 2.5 from Chapter 2).

At the time of writing, there is a great deal of commercial interest in client/server systems, and comparatively little in true general-purpose distributed systems. We continue to believe that true distributed systems represent an important long-term trend, which is why we have concentrated on such systems in the present chapter; however, it

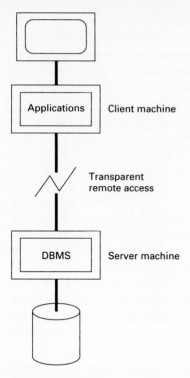

FIG. 21.7 A client/server system

is clearly appropriate to say something here regarding client/server systems specifically.

Recall from Chapter 2 that the term "client/server" refers primarily to an *architecture,* or logical division of responsibilities; the **client** is the application (also known as the *frontend*), and the **server** is the DBMS (also known as the *backend*). Precisely because the overall system can be so neatly divided into two parts, however, the possibility arises of running the two on different machines. And this latter possibility is so attractive (for so many reasons—see Chapter 2) that the term "client/server" has come to apply almost exclusively to the case where the client and the server are indeed on different machines. To repeat from Chapter 2, this usage is sloppy but very, very common, and we adopt it ourselves in what follows.

We remind the reader also that several variations on the basic theme are possible:

1. First, several clients might be able to share the same server (indeed, this is the normal case).

2. Second, a single client might be able to access several servers. This latter case in turn subdivides into two further cases:

   ▪ The client is limited to accessing just one server at a time—i.e., each individual database request must be directed to just one server; it is not possible, within a single request, to combine data from two or more different servers. Furthermore, the user has to know which particular server stores which pieces of data.

- The client can access many servers simultaneously—i.e., a single database request can combine data from several servers, which means that the servers look to the client as if they were really just one server, and the user does not have to know which servers store which pieces of data.

But the last case here is effectively a true distributed database system ("the seams are hidden"); it is not what is usually meant by the term "client/server." We therefore ignore it in what follows.

Client/Server Standards

There are several standards that are applicable to the world of client/server processing. First, certain client/server features have been incorporated into the the the most recent version of the **SQL** standard (*viz.*, SQL/92), including in particular **CONNECT** and **DISCONNECT** operations for establishing and breaking client/server connections. In fact, an SQL application *must* execute a CONNECT operation to connect to the server before it can issue any database requests at all (though that CONNECT might be implicit). Once the connection has been established, the application—i.e., the client—can issue SQL requests in the usual way, and the necessary database processing will be carried out by the server.

The standard also allows an SQL client that is already connected to one server to connect to another. Establishing that second connection causes the first to become **dormant;** subsequent SQL requests are processed by the second server, until such time as the client either (a) switches back to the previous server (via another new operation, **SET CONNECTION**) or (b) connects to yet another server, which causes the second connection to become dormant as well (and so on). At any given time, in other words, a given SQL client can have one **active** connection and any number of **dormant** connections, and all database requests from that client are directed to, and processed by, the server on the active connection.

Note: The standard also permits (but does not require) the implementation to support *multi-server transactions*. That is, the SQL client might be able to switch from one server to another in the middle of a transaction, so that part of the transaction is executed on one server and part on another. Note in particular that if *update* transactions are permitted to span servers in this way, the implementation *must* presumably support (some variant of) two-phase commit in order to provide the transaction atomicity that the standard requires.

Finally, every connection established by a given client (whether currently active or currently dormant) must eventually be broken via an appropriate DISCONNECT operation (though that DISCONNECT, like the corresponding CONNECT, might be implicit in simple cases).

So much for SQL *per se.* The next standard that must be mentioned is the ISO **Remote Data Access** standard, RDA [21.1–21.2]. RDA exists only in draft form at the time of writing, but it is important nonetheless—most especially because something very close to it has already been implemented by members of the **SQL Access Group** (SAG), which is a consortium of database software vendors committed to open systems and interoperability. *Note:* For our purposes it is not worth bothering to distinguish between the ISO and SAG versions of RDA; we will simply use the name "RDA" to refer to them both generically.

The intent of RDA is to define **formats and protocols** for client/server communication. It assumes that (a) the client expresses database requests in a standard form of SQL (basically a subset of the SQL/92 standard), also that (b) the server supports a standard catalog (also basically as defined in the SQL/92 standard). It then defines specific representation formats for passing messages (SQL requests, data and results, and diagnostic information) between the client and the server. *Note:* At the time of writing RDA supports only the Open Systems Interconnection (OSI) network environment, but work is in hand to extend it to TCP/IP and other environments.

The third and last standard we discuss here is IBM's **Distributed Relational Database Architecture** (DRDA) standard [21.3] (which is a *de facto* standard, not a *de jure* standard). DRDA and RDA have similar objectives; however, DRDA differs from RDA in several important respects—in particular, it does tend to reflect its IBM origins. For example, DRDA does not assume that the client is using a standard version of SQL, but instead allows for any dialect of SQL whatsoever. One consequence is (possibly) better performance, since the client might be able to exploit certain server-specific features; on the other hand, portability suffers, precisely because those server-specific features are exposed to the client (i.e., the client has to know what kind of server it is talking to). In a similar vein, DRDA does not assume any particular catalog structure at the server. The DRDA formats and protocols are quite different from those of RDA (essentially, DRDA is based on IBM's own architectures and standards, while RDA is based on international, non-vendor-specific standards).

Further details of RDA and DRDA are beyond the scope of this book; see references [21.19] and [21.23] for some analysis and comparisons.

Client/Server Application Programming

We have said that a client/server system is a simple special case of distributed systems in general. As suggested in the introduction to this section, a client/server system can be thought of as a distributed system in which all requests originate at one site and all processing is performed at another (assuming for simplicity that there is just one client site and just one server site). Note, however, that under this simple definition the client site is not really "a database system site in its own right" (and thus contravenes our definition of a general distributed database system in Section 21.2); in practice the client site might well have its own local databases, but those databases will not play a direct part in the client/server arrangement as such.

Now, the client/server approach does have certain implications for application programming (as indeed do distributed systems in general). One of the most important points has already been touched on in our discussion of Objective No. 7 (distributed query processing) in Section 21.3—namely, the fact that relational systems are, by definition and design, **set-level** systems. In a client/server system (and indeed in distributed systems in general), it is more important than ever that the application programmer *not* just "use the server like an access method" and write record-level code. Instead, as much functionality as possible should be bundled up into set-level requests; for otherwise performance will suffer, because of the number of messages involved.

Note: In SQL terms, the foregoing implies *avoiding cursors*—i.e., avoiding FETCH loops and the CURRENT forms of UPDATE and DELETE (see Chapter 8).

The number of messages between client and server can be reduced still further if the system provides some kind of **stored procedure** mechanism. A stored procedure is basically a precompiled program that is *stored at the server site* (and is known to the server). It is invoked from the client by a **remote procedure call** (RPC). In particular, therefore, the performance penalty associated with record-level processing can be partly offset by creating a suitable stored procedure to do that processing directly at the server site.

Note: Although it is somewhat tangential to the topic of client/server processing as such, we should point out that improved performance is not the only advantage of stored procedures. Others include:

- Such procedures can be used to conceal a variety of system-specific and/or database-specific details from the user, thereby providing a greater degree of data independence than might otherwise be the case.

- One stored procedure can be shared by many clients.

- Optimization can be done at the time the stored procedure is created instead of at run time. (This advantage applies only to interpretive systems, of course.)

- Stored procedures can provide better security. For example, a given user might be authorized to invoke a given procedure but not to operate directly on the data accessed by that procedure.

One disadvantage is that there are currently no standards in this area, and different products provide very different facilities.

21.7 SQL Support

SQL currently provides no support at all for true distributed database systems. Of course, no support is *required* in the area of data manipulation—the whole point of distributed database (so far as the user is concerned) is that data manipulation capabilities should remain unchanged. However, data definition operations such as FRAGMENT, REPLICATE, etc., *are* required [21.14], but are not currently supported.

On the other hand, SQL does include certain client/server capabilities; specifically, it provides facilities for connecting to and disconnecting from servers, as we have seen. For additional details (over and above the material already presented in Section 21.6 above), refer to the SQL standard document [8.1] or the tutorial treatment in reference [8.5].

21.8 Summary

In this chapter, we have presented a brief discussion of distributed database systems. We used the **"twelve objectives"** of distributed database [21.13] as a basis for structuring the discussion, though we stress the point once again that not all of those objectives will be relevant in all situations. We also briefly examined certain technical problems arising in the areas of **query processing, catalog management, update propagation, recovery control,** and **concurrency control**. In particular, we discussed what is involved in trying to satisfy the **DBMS independence** objective (the discussion of **gateways** in Section 21.4). We then focused in on **client/server** processing, which can be regarded as a special case of distributed processing in general, one that is currently very important in the marketplace. In particular, we summarized those aspects of SQL that are relevant to client/server processing, and we stressed the point that users should **avoid record-level code** (cursor operations, in SQL terms). We also briefly described the concept of **stored procedures** and **remote procedure calls**.

One problem we did not discuss at all thus far is the (physical) **database design** problem for distributed systems. In fact, even if we ignore the possibility of fragmentation and/or replication, the problem of deciding which relations should be stored at which sites—the so-called **allocation problem**—is a notoriously difficult one [21.25]. Fragmentation and replication support only serve to complicate matters further.

Another point that is worthy of mention is that certain so-called *massively parallel* computer systems are beginning to make their presence felt in the marketplace. Such systems typically consist of a large number of separate processors connected together by means of a high-speed bus; each processor has its own main memory and its own disk drives and runs its own copy of the DBMS software, and the complete database is spread across the complete set of disk drives. In other words, such a system essentially consists of a distributed database system "in a box"!—and all of the issues we have been discussing in the present chapter regarding (e.g.) query processing strategies, two-phase commit, global deadlock, etc., are relevant.

By way of conclusion, we remark that the "twelve objectives" of distributed database (or possibly some subset of them that includes at least Nos. 4, 5, 6, and 8), taken together, seem to be equivalent to Codd's "distribution independence" rule for relational DBMSs [21.10]. For reference, we state that rule here:

■ *Distribution independence* (Codd): "A relational DBMS has distribution independence . . . [meaning that the] DBMS has a data sublanguage that enables application programs and terminal activities to remain logically unimpaired:

  1. When data distribution is first introduced (if the originally installed DBMS manages nondistributed data only);

  2. When data is redistributed (if the DBMS manages distributed data)."

Note finally that (as mentioned earlier in the chapter) objectives 4–6 and 9–12— that is, all of the objectives that include the word "independence" in their name—can be regarded as extensions of the familiar notion of data independence, as that concept applies to the distributed environment. As such, they all translate into **protection for the application investment**.

Exercises

21.1   Define location independence, fragmentation independence, and replication independence.

21.2   Why are distributed database systems almost invariably relational?

21.3   What are the advantages of distributed systems? What are the disadvantages?

21.4   Explain the following terms:

primary copy update strategy

primary copy locking strategy

global deadlock

two-phase commit

global optimization

21.5   Describe the R* object naming scheme.

21.6   We pointed out in Section 21.5 that successful implementation of a gateway depends on reconciling the interface differences between the two DBMSs under consideration (among many other things). Take any two DBMSs with which you might be familiar (preferably both relational—better yet, both SQL-based), and identify as many differences as you can between the two user interfaces. Consider both syntactic and semantic differences.

21.7   Investigate any client/server system that might be available to you. Does that system support explicit CONNECT and DISCONNECT operations? Does it support SET CONNECTION or any other "connection-type" operations? Does it support multi-server transactions? Does it support two-phase commit? What formats and protocols does it use for client/server communication? What network environments does it support? What client and server hardware platforms does it support? What software platforms (operating systems, DBMSs) does it support?

21.8   Investigate any relational DBMS that might be available to you. Does that DBMS support stored procedures? If so, how are they created? How are they invoked? What language are they written in? Do they support the whole of SQL? Do they support conditional branching (IF–THEN–ELSE)? Do they support loops? How do they return results to the client? Can one stored procedure invoke another? At a different site? Does the stored procedure execute as part of the invoking transaction?

References and Bibliography

21.1   International Organization for Standardization (ISO). *Information Processing Systems, Open Systems Interconnection, Remote Data Access Part 1: Generic Model, Service, and Protocol (Draft International Standard)*. Document ISO DIS 9579-1 (March 1990).

21.2   International Organization for Standardization (ISO). *Information Processing Systems, Open Systems Interconnection, Remote Data Access Part 2: SQL Specialization (Draft International Standard)*. Document ISO DIS 9579-2 (February 1990).

21.3   IBM Corporation. *Distributed Relational Database Architecture Reference*. IBM Form No. SC26-4651.

IBM's DRDA defines four levels of distributed database functionality, as follows:

1. Remote request

2. Remote unit of work

3. Distributed unit of work

4. Distributed request

Since these terms show signs of becoming *de facto* standards in the industry, we briefly explain them here. *Note:* "Request" and "unit of work" are IBM's terms for *SQL statement* and *transaction,* respectively.

1. **Remote request** means that an application at one site X can send an individual SQL statement to some remote site Y for execution. That request is executed *and committed* (or rolled back) entirely at site Y. The original application at site X can subsequently send another request to site Y (or possibly to another site Z), regardless of whether the first request was successful or unsuccessful.

2. **Remote unit of work** (abbreviated RUW) means that an application at one site X can send all of the database requests in a given "unit of work" (i.e., transaction) to some remote site Y for execution. The database processing for the transaction is thus executed in its entirety at the remote site Y; however, the local site X decides whether the transaction is to be committed or rolled back. *Note:* RUW is effectively client/server processing with a single server.

3. **Distributed unit of work** (abbreviated DUW) means that an application at one site X can send some or all of the database requests in a given unit of work (transaction) to one or more remote sites $Y, Z, \ldots$ for execution. The database processing for the transaction is thus spread across multiple sites, in general; each individual request is still executed in its entirety at a single site, but different requests can be executed at different sites. However, site X is still the cooordinating site, i.e., the site that decides whether the transaction is to be committed or rolled back.

4. **Distributed request** is the only one of the four levels that approaches what is commonly accepted as true distributed database support. Distributed request means everything that distributed unit of work means, *plus* it permits individual database requests (SQL statements) to span multiple sites—for example, a request originating from site X might ask for a join or union to be performed between a table at site Y and a table at site Z. Note that it is only at this level that the system can be said to be providing genuine location independence; in all three previous cases, users do have to have some knowledge regarding the physical location of data.

21.4 David Bell and Jane Grimson. *Distributed Database Systems.* Reading, Mass.: Addison-Wesley (1992).

This is the most recent of several textbooks devoted to the topic of the present chapter (two others are mentioned below [21.9,21.24]). A notable feature of this particular book is the inclusion of an extended case study involving a health care network. It is also a little more pragmatic in tone than the other two.

21.5 Philip A. Bernstein, James B. Rothnie, Jr., and David W. Shipman (eds.). *Tutorial: Distributed Data Base Management.* IEEE Computer Society, 5855 Naples Plaza, Suite 301, Long Beach, Calif. 90803 (1978).

A collection of papers from various sources, grouped under the following headings:

1. Overview of relational database management

2. Distributed database management overview

3. Approaches to distributed query processing

4. Approaches to distributed concurrency control

5. Approaches to distributed database reliability

21.6 Philip A. Bernstein *et al..* "Query Processing in a System for Distributed Databases (SDD-1)." *ACM TODS 6,* No. 4 (December 1981).

See the annotation to reference [21.26].

21.7 Philip A. Bernstein, David W. Shipman, and James B. Rothnie, Jr. "Concurrency Control in a System for Distributed Databases (SDD-1)." *ACM TODS 5,* No. 1 (March 1980).

See the annotation to reference [21.26].

21.8 Yuri Breitbart, Hector Garcia-Molina, and Avi Silberschatz. "Overview of Multidatabase Transaction Management." *The VLDB Journal 1,* No. 2 (October 1992).

The term **multidatabase system** is sometimes used to mean a distributed system—usually *heterogeneous*—with full local autonomy. (The term "federated system" is also sometimes used with much the same meaning.) In such a system, purely local transactions are managed entirely by the local DBMSs, but global transactions are a different matter. This paper provides a survey of recent results and current research in this latter ("increasingly important") field.

21.9 Stefano Ceri and Giuseppe Pelagatti. *Distributed Databases: Principles and Systems*. New York, N.Y.: McGraw-Hill (1984).

21.10 E. F. Codd. "Is Your DBMS Really Relational?" *Computerworld* (October 14th, 1985); "Does Your DBMS Run by the Rules?" *Computerworld* (October 21st, 1985).

21.11 D. Daniels *et al.* "An Introduction to Distributed Query Compilation in R*." In *Distributed Data Bases* (ed., H.-J. Schneider): Proc. 2nd International Symposium on Distributed Data Bases (September 1982). New York, N.Y.: North-Holland (1982).

See the annotation to reference [21.30].

21.12 C. J. Date. "Distributed Databases." Chapter 7 of C. J. Date, *An Introduction to Database Systems: Volume II*. Reading, Mass.: Addison-Wesley (1983).

Portions of the present chapter are based on this earlier publication.

21.13 C. J. Date. "What Is a Distributed Database System?" In C. J. Date, *Relational Database Writings 1985–1989*. Reading, Mass.: Addison-Wesley (1990).

The paper that introduced the "twelve objectives" for distributed systems (Section 21.3 is modeled fairly directly on this paper). As mentioned in the body of the chapter, the objective of *local autonomy* is not 100 percent achievable; there are certain situations that necessarily involve compromising on that objective somewhat. We summarize those situations below for purposes of reference.

- Individual fragments of a fragmented relation cannot normally be accessed directly, not even from the site at which they are stored.

- Individual copies of a replicated relation (or fragment) cannot normally be accessed directly, not even from the site at which they are stored.

- Let P be the primary copy of some replicated relation (or fragment) R, and let P be stored at site X. Then every site that accesses R is dependent on site X, even if another copy of R is in fact stored at the site in question.

- A relation that participates in a multi-site integrity constraint cannot be accessed for update purposes within the local context of the site at which it is stored, but only within the context of the distributed database in which the constraint is defined.

- A site that is acting as a participant in a two-phase commit process must abide by the decision (i.e., commit or rollback) of the corresponding coordinator site.

21.14 C. J. Date. "Distributed Database: A Closer Look." In C. J. Date and Hugh Darwen, *Relational Database Writings 1989–1991*. Reading, Mass.: Addison-Wesley (1992).

A sequel to reference [21.13], discussing most of the twelve objectives in considerably more depth (albeit still in tutorial style).

21.15 C. J. Date. "Why Is It So Difficult to Provide a Relational Interface to IMS?" In C. J. Date, *Relational Database: Selected Writings*. Reading, Mass.: Addison-Wesley (1986).

21.16 R. Epstein, M. Stonebraker, and E. Wong. "Distributed Query Processing in a Relational Data Base System." Proc. 1978 ACM SIGMOD International Conference on Management of Data, Austin, Texas (May/June 1978).

See the annotation to reference [21.28].

21.17 John Grant, Witold Litwin, Nick Roussopoulos, and Timos Sellis. "Query Languages for Relational Multidatabases." *The VLDB Journal 2,* No. 2 (April 1993).

Proposes extensions to the relational algebra and relational calculus for dealing with multidatabase systems [21.8]. Issues of optimization are discussed, and it is shown that every multirelational algebraic expression has a multirelational calculus equivalent ("the converse of this theorem is an interesting research problem").

21.18 J. N. Gray. "A Discussion of Distributed Systems." Proc. Congresso AICA 79, Bari, Italy (October 1979). Also available as IBM Research Report RJ2699 (September 1979).

A sketchy but good overview and tutorial.

21.19 Richard D. Hackathorn. "Interoperability: DRDA or RDA?" *InfoDB 6,* No. 2 (Fall 1991).

21.20 Michael Hammer and David Shipman. "Reliability Mechanisms for SDD-1: A System for Distributed Databases." *ACM TODS 5,* No. 4 (December 1980).

See the annotation to reference [21.26].

21.21 B. G. Lindsay *et al.* "Notes on Distributed Databases." IBM Research Report RJ2571 (July 1979).

This paper (by some of the original members of the R* team) is divided into five chapters:

1. .Replicated data

2. Authorization and views

3. Introduction to distributed transaction management

4. Recovery facilities

5. Transaction initiation, migration, and termination

Chapter 1 discusses the update propagation problem. Chapter 2 is almost totally concerned with authorization in a *non*distributed system (in the style of System R), except for a few remarks at the end. Chapter 3 considers transaction initiation and termination, concurrency control, and recovery control, all rather briefly. Chapter 4 is devoted to the topic of recovery in the *non*distributed case (again). Finally, Chapter 5 discusses distributed transaction management in some detail; in particular, it gives a very careful presentation of two-phase commit.

21.22 C. Mohan and B. G. Lindsay. "Efficient Commit Protocols for the Tree of Processes Model of Distributed Transactions." Proc. 2nd ACM SIGACT-SIGOPS Symposium on Principles of Distributed Computing (1983).

See the annotation to reference [21.30].

21.23 Scott Newman and Jim Gray. "Which Way to Remote SQL?" *Database Programming & Design 4,* No. 12 (December 1991).

21.24 M. Tamer Öszu and Patrick Valduriez. *Principles of Distributed Database Systems.* Englewood Cliffs, N. J.: Prentice-Hall (1991).

21.25 James B. Rothnie, Jr., and Nathan Goodman. "A Survey of Research and Development in Distributed Database Management." Proc. 3rd International Conference on Very Large Data Bases, Tokyo, Japan (October 1977). Also published in reference [21.5].

A very useful early survey. The field is discussed under the following headings:

1. Synchronizing update transactions

2. Distributed query processing

3. Handling component failures

4. Directory management

5. Database design

The last of these refers to the *physical* design problem—what we called the *allocation* problem in Section 21.8.

21.26 J. B. Rothnie, Jr., *et al.* "Introduction to a System for Distributed Databases (SDD-1)." *ACM TODS 5,* No. 1 (March 1980).

References [21.6–21.7], [21.20], [21.26], and [21.31] are all concerned with the early distributed prototype SDD-1, which ran on a collection of DEC PDP-10s interconnected via the ARPANET. It provided full location, fragmentation, and replication independence. We offer a few comments here on selected aspects of the system.

Query processing: The SDD-1 query optimizer (see references [21.6] and [21.31]) made extensive use of an operator called **semijoin,** which we explain as follows. (*Note:* The term "semijoin" first appeared with a somewhat different meaning in a paper by Palermo [18.15].) Given two relations *A* and *B,* the expression "*A* semijoin *B*" is defined to be equal to the join of *A* and *B,* projected back on to the attributes of *A.* In other words, the semijoin operation yields that subset of the tuples of *A* that match at least one tuple in *B* under the joining condition. For example, the semijoin of the supplier relation S and the shipment relation SP (over supplier numbers) is the set of S tuples for suppliers who supply at least one part—namely, the set of S tuples for suppliers S1, S2, S3, and S4, given our usual sample data values. Note that the expressions "*A* semijoin *B*" and "*B* semijoin *A*" are not equivalent, in general.

The advantage of using semijoins in distributed query processing is that they can have the effect of reducing the volume of data shipped across the network. For example, suppose that the supplier relation S is stored at site A and the shipment relation SP is stored at site B, and the query is "Compute the join of S and SP over S#." Instead of shipping the entire relation S to B (say), we can do the following:

- Compute the projection (TEMP1) of SP over S# at B.
- Ship TEMP1 to A.
- Compute the semijoin (TEMP2) of TEMP1 and S over S# at A.
- Ship TEMP2 to B.
- Compute the semijoin of TEMP2 and SP over S# at B. The result is the answer to the original query.

This procedure will obviously reduce the total amount of data movement across the network if and only if

size (TEMP1) + *size* (TEMP2) < *size* (S)

where the *size* of a relation is the cardinality of that relation multiplied by the width of an individual tuple (in bits, say). The optimizer thus clearly needs to be able to estimate the size of intermediate results such as TEMP1 and TEMP2.

Update propagation: The SDD-1 update propagation algorithm is "propagate immediately" (there is no notion of a primary copy).

Concurrency control: Concurrency control is based on a technique called **timestamping,** instead of on locking; the objective is to avoid the message overhead associated with locking, but the price seems to be that there is not in fact very much concurrency! The details are beyond the scope of this book (though the annotation to reference [14.2] does describe the basic idea very briefly); see reference [21.7] or reference [21.12] for more information.

Recovery control: Recovery is based on a *four*-phase commit protocol; the intent is to make the process more resilient than the conventional two-phase commit protocol to a failure at the Coordinator site, but unfortunately it also makes the process considerably more complex. The details are (again) beyond the scope of this book.

Catalog: The catalog is managed by treating it as if it were ordinary user data—it can be arbitrarily fragmented, and the fragments can be arbitrarily replicated and distributed, just like any other data. The advantages of this approach are obvious. The disadvantage is, of course, that since the system has no *a priori* knowledge of the location of any given piece of the catalog, it is necessary to maintain a higher-level catalog—the **directory locator**—to provide exactly that information! The directory locator is fully replicated (i.e., a copy is stored at every site).

21.27   P. G. Selinger and M. E. Adiba. "Access Path Selection in Distributed Data Base Management Systems." In S. M. Deen and P. Hammersley (eds.), Proc. International Conference on Data Bases, Aberdeen, Scotland (July 1980). London, England: Heyden and Sons Ltd. (1980).

See the annotation to reference [21.30].

21.28 M. R. Stonebraker and E. J. Neuhold. "A Distributed Data Base Version of INGRES." Proc. 2nd Berkeley Conference on Distributed Data Management and Computer Networks, Lawrence Berkeley Laboratory (May 1977).

References [21.16] and [21.28–21.29] are all concerned with the distributed INGRES prototype. Distributed INGRES consists of several copies of University INGRES, running on several interconnected DEC PDP-11s. It supports location independence (like SDD-1 and R*); it also supports data fragmentation (via restriction but not projection), with fragmentation independence, and data replication for such fragments, with replication independence. Unlike SDD-1 and R*, Distributed INGRES does not necessarily assume that the communication network is slow; on the contrary, it is designed to handle both "slow" (long-haul) networks and local (i.e., comparatively fast) networks. The query optimizer understands the difference between the two cases. The query optimization algorithm is basically an extension of the INGRES decomposition strategy described in Chapter 18 of this book; it is described in detail in reference [21.16].

Distributed INGRES provides two update propagation algorithms: a "performance" algorithm, which works by updating a primary copy and then returning control to the transaction (leaving the propagated updates to be performed in parallel by a set of slave processes); and a "reliable" algorithm, which updates all copies immediately (see reference [21.29]). Concurrency control is based on locking in both cases. Recovery is based on two-phase commit (with certain improvements that are beyond the scope of this book, as in the case of R*; again, see reference [21.29] or reference [21.14]).

As for the catalog, Distributed INGRES uses a combination of full replication for certain portions of the catalog—basically the portions containing a logical description of the relations visible to the user and a description of how those relations are fragmented—together with purely local catalog entries for other portions, such as the portions describing local physical storage structures, local database statistics (used by the optimizer), and security and integrity constraints.

21.29 M. R. Stonebraker. "Concurrency Control and Consistency of Multiple Copies in Distributed INGRES." *IEEE Transactions on Software Engineering SE-5,* No. 3 (May 1979).

See the annotation to reference [21.28].

21.30 R. Williams *et al.* "R*: An Overview of the Architecture." In P. Scheuermann (ed.), *Improving Database Usability and Responsiveness.* New York, N.Y.: Academic Press (1982). Also available as IBM Research Report RJ3325 (December 1981).

References [21.11], [21.22], [21.27], and [21.30] are all concerned with R*, the distributed version of the original System R prototype. R* provides location independence, but no fragmentation and no replication, and therefore no fragmentation or replication independence either. The question of update propagation does not arise, for the same reason. Concurrency control is based on locking (note that there is only one copy of any object to be locked; the question of a primary copy also does not arise). Recovery is based on two-phase commit, but with certain improvements that have the effect of reducing the number of messages required (see reference [21.22] or reference [21.14]).

21.31 Eugene Wong. "Retrieving Dispersed Data from SDD-1: A System for Distributed Databases." In reference [21.5].

See the annotation to reference [21.26].

21.32 C. T. Yu and C. C. Chang. "Distributed Query Processing." *ACM Comp. Surv. 16,* No. 4 (December 1984).

A tutorial survey of techniques for query optimization in distributed systems. Includes an extensive bibliography.

OBJECT-ORIENTED SYSTEMS

Object-oriented technology is an important new area within the overall field of database management. Unfortunately, it is also an area in which there is a certain amount of confusion, as the reader will soon see. Part of the problem is that there is no universally accepted, abstract, formally defined "object data model" (contrast the situation with relational technology). Rather, the term **OO**—which we use generically as an abbreviation for "object-oriented" or "object orientation," as the context demands— is best thought of as a convenient label for a collection of interconnected ideas. Of those ideas, moreover, some are tightly interwoven and some are not; some are essential and some are not; some are good and some are not; some are new and some are not (very few are truly new, as a matter of fact); some really do apply to databases and some do not; and so on.

Regarding this latter point, incidentally, another source of confusion is the fact that the OO label is applied to a variety of quite distinct disciplines. For example, it is used to describe a certain *graphic interface* style, a certain *programming* style, a certain set of programming *languages* (not the same thing as programming style!), a certain set of *analysis and design* methodologies, and so on, as well as a certain approach to database management *per se*. And just because OO might be good for some of these problems, it does not follow that it is necessarily good for others.

In the chapters that follow, we attempt to clarify these matters. Specifically, we present a tutorial on OO as it applies to database systems, an analysis (not uncritical) of OO database concepts, and a proposal for a rapprochement between OO and relational database technology. *Note:* We assume throughout that the reader has a reasonable prior understanding of conventional (relational) database technology.

22 Basic OO Concepts

22.1 Introduction

"Everyone knows" that today's relational products are inadequate in a variety of ways. And some people—not this writer!—would argue that the relational model is inadequate too. Be that as it may, some of the new features that seem to be needed in DBMSs have existed for many years in **object-oriented programming languages;** it is thus natural to investigate the idea of incorporating those features into database systems, and hence to consider the possibility of **object-oriented database systems**. And, of course, many researchers, and some vendors, have been doing exactly this over the past few years.

To repeat, OO database systems have their origins in OO programming languages. And the basic idea in both disciplines is the same—to wit: Users should not have to wrestle with computer-oriented constructs such as bits and bytes (or even records and fields), but rather should be able to deal with **objects,** and **operations** on those objects, that more closely resemble their counterparts in the real world. For example, instead of having to think in terms of a "DEPT tuple" plus a collection of corresponding "EMP tuples" that include "foreign key values" that "reference" the "primary key value" in that "DEPT tuple," the user should be able to think directly of a *department object* that actually contains a corresponding set of *employee objects*. And instead of, e.g., having to "insert" a "tuple" into the "EMP relation" with an appropriate "foreign key value" that "references" the "primary key value" of some "tuple" in the "DEPT relation," the user should be able to *hire* an *employee* object directly into the relevant *department* object. In other words, the fundamental idea is to **raise the level of abstraction**.

Now, raising the level of abstraction is unquestionably a desirable goal, and the OO paradigm has been very successful in meeting that goal in the programming languages arena [22.3]. It is natural to ask, therefore, whether the same paradigm can be applied in the database arena also. Indeed, the idea of dealing with a database that is made up of **encapsulated objects** (e.g., department objects that "know what it means" to hire an employee or change their manager or cut their budget), instead of having to understand relations, tuple updates, foreign keys, etc., is naturally much more attractive from the user's point of view—at least at first sight.

A word of caution is appropriate, however. The point is, although the programming language and database management disciplines certainly do have a lot in common, they also differ in certain important respects. In particular, an application program (by definition) is intended to solve some specific problem, whereas a database (by definition) is intended to solve a variety of different problems, some of which might not even be known at the time the database is established. In the application programming environment, therefore, embedding a lot of "intelligence" into encapsulated objects is clearly a good idea: It reduces the amount of manipulative code that has to be written to use those objects, it improves programmer productivity, it increases application maintainability, and so on. In the database environment, by contrast, embedding a lot of intelligence into the database might or might not be a good idea: It might simplify some problems, but it might at the same time make others more difficult or even impossible.

(Incidentally, the foregoing point is exactly one of the arguments against prerelational database systems such as IMS. A department object that contains a set of employee objects is conceptually very similar to an IMS *hierarchy* in which department "segments"—this is the IMS term—are superior to employee "segments." Such a hierarchy is well suited to problems like "Find employees that work in the accounting department." It is not well suited to problems like "Find departments that employ MBAs." Thus, many of the arguments that were made against the hierarchic approach in the 1970s are surfacing again in the OO context.)

The foregoing caveat notwithstanding, many people believe that OO systems are the next big step forward in database technology. In particular, many believe that OO techniques are the approach of choice for new application areas such as

- **computer-aided design and manufacturing** (CAD/CAM)
- **computer-integrated manufacturing** (CIM)
- **computer-aided software engineering** (CASE)
- **geographic information systems** (GIS)
- **science and medicine**
- **document storage and retrieval**

and so forth (note that all of the above represent areas in which today's relational products do tend to run into trouble). There have certainly been numerous technical papers on such matters in the literature over the past few years, and more recently several commercial products have begun to appear. In this part of the book, therefore, we will take a look at what OO technology is all about.

The aim of this first chapter is simply to introduce the most important concepts of the OO approach, and in particular to describe those concepts **from a database perspective** (much of the literature, by contrast, presents the ideas very much from a *programming* perspective instead). The structure of the chapter is as follows. Following this introductory section, Section 22.2 presents a motivating example—an example, that is, that today's relational products do *not* handle satisfactorily, and hence one that OO technology stands a good chance of doing better on. Next, Section 22.3 presents an overview of *objects, object classes, messages,* and *methods;* Sections 22.4–22.6 then focus in on certain specific aspects of these concepts and discuss them in more depth. Section 22.7 briefly considers *class hierarchies;* Section 22.8 discusses a few miscellaneous topics, and Section 22.9 presents a summary.

One last preliminary remark: Despite the fact that OO systems were originally meant specifically for "complex" applications such as CAD/CAM, CIM, CASE, etc., we deliberately use only very simple examples in our discussions, for reasons of space and familiarity. Of course, adopting this simplifying approach in no way invalidates the presentation. In any case, OO technology is intended to be suitable for "simple" applications too.

22.2   A Motivating Example

We begin with a simple example, due to Stonebraker [19.10] and elaborated by the present author in reference [22.5], that illustrates some of the problems with today's relational products. The database (which might be thought of as a grossly simplified approximation to a CAD/CAM database) concerns *rectangles,* all of which are assumed for simplicity to be "square on" to the X and Y axes—i.e., all sides are either vertical or horizontal. Each rectangle can thus be uniquely represented by the coordinates (*x1,y1*) and (*x2,y2*), respectively, of its bottom left and top right corners (see Fig. 22.1). In SQL:

```
CREATE TABLE RECTANGLES
    ( RECTID ... , X1 ... , X2 ... , Y1 ... , Y2 ... , ... ,
      UNIQUE ( RECTID ) ,
      UNIQUE ( X1, X2, Y1, Y2 ) ) ;
```

Now consider the query "Find all rectangles that overlap the unit square (0,1,0,1)" (see Fig. 22.2). The "obvious" representation of this query in SQL is:

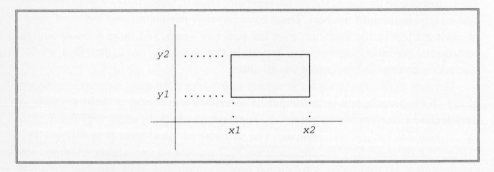

FIG. 22.1 The rectangle (*x1, x2, y1, y2*)

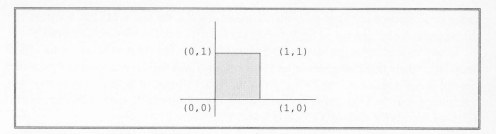

FIG. 22.2   The unit square (0,1,0,1)

```
SELECT ...
FROM     RECTANGLES
WHERE    ( X1 >= 0 AND X1 <= 1 AND Y1 >= 0 AND Y1 <= 1 )
                         — bottom left corner inside unit square
OR       ( X2 >= 0 AND X2 <= 1 AND Y2 >= 0 AND Y2 <= 1 )
                         — top right corner inside unit square
OR       ( X1 >= 0 AND X1 <= 1 AND Y2 >= 0 AND Y2 <= 1 )
                         — top left corner inside unit square
OR       ( X2 >= 0 AND X2 <= 1 AND Y1 >= 0 AND Y1 <= 1 )
                         — bottom right corner inside unit square
OR       ( X1 <= 0 AND X2 >= 1 AND Y1 <= 0 AND Y2 >= 1 )
                         — rectangle totally includes unit square
OR       ( X1 <= 0 AND X2 >= 1 AND Y1 >= 0 AND Y1 <= 1 )
                         — bottom edge crosses unit square
OR       ( X1 >= 0 AND X1 <= 1 AND Y1 <= 0 AND Y2 >= 1 )
                         — left edge crosses unit square
OR       ( X2 >= 0 AND X2 <= 1 AND Y1 <= 0 AND Y2 >= 1 )
                         — right edge crosses unit square
OR       ( X1 <= 0 AND X2 >= 1 AND Y2 >= 0 AND Y2 <= 1 )
                         — top edge crosses unit square
;
```

Readers should take the time to convince themselves that this formulation is indeed correct before continuing. Diagrams will probably prove helpful in this regard.

With a little further thought, however, it can be seen that the query can be expressed somewhat more simply as:

```
SELECT ...
FROM     RECTANGLES
WHERE    ( X1 <= 1 AND Y1 <= 1
                     — bottom left corner is "downwind" of (1,1)
AND        X2 >= 0 AND Y2 >= 0 )
                     — top right corner is "upwind" of (0,0)
;
```

Again, diagrams will probably prove helpful in understanding this formulation.

The question now is: Could the system optimizer transform the original long form of the query into the corresponding short form? In other words, suppose the user expresses the query in the "obvious" (and obviously inefficient) long form; would the system be capable of reducing that query to the more efficient short form before executing it? Reference [22.5] gives evidence to suggest that the answer to this question is almost certainly *no,* at least so far as today's commercial optimizers are concerned.

In any case, despite the fact that we just referred to the short form as "more efficient," it is likely that performance on the short form will still be unacceptably poor in most of today's relational products, given the usual storage structures—typically B-trees—supported by those products (on average, the system will examine 50 percent of the index entries for each of X1, X2, Y1, and Y2).

Thus we see that today's relational products are indeed inadequate in certain respects. To be specific, problems like the rectangles problem show clearly that certain "simple" user requests

1. are unreasonably difficult to express, and

2. execute with unacceptably poor performance,

in those products. Such considerations provide much of the motivation behind the current interest in OO systems.

Note: We will give a "good" solution to the rectangles problem in Chapter 25 (Section 25.3).

22.3   Objects, Methods, and Messages

In this section, we introduce some of the principal terms and concepts of the OO approach, namely *object* itself (of course), *object class, method,* and *message.* We will also relate these notions to more familiar terms and concepts wherever possible or appropriate. In fact, it is probably helpful to show a rough mapping of the OO terms to traditional programming terms right at the outset (refer to Fig. 22.3).

Caveat: Before we start getting into details, it is as well to warn readers not to expect the kind of precision they are accustomed to in the relational world. Indeed, many OO concepts—or the published definitions of those concepts, at any rate—are quite imprecise, and there is very little true consensus and much disagreement, even at the most basic level (see references [22.2], [22.10–22.11], [22.14], and [22.16]). In particular, there is no abstract, formally defined "object data model," nor is there even consensus on an *in*formal model. (For such reasons we will always place phrases such

OO term	Programming term
object	variable (if "mutable") or value (if "immutable")
object class	data type
method	function
message	call

FIG. 22.3 OO terminology

as "the OO model" in quotes in this book.) In fact, there seems, rather surprisingly, to be much confusion over *levels of abstraction*—specifically, over the distinction between the model *per se* and its implementation.

The reader should also be warned that, as a consequence of the foregoing state of affairs, the definitions and explanations offered in this part of the book are *not* universally agreed upon and do *not* necessarily correspond to the way that any given OO system actually works. Indeed, just about every one of those definitions and explanations could well be challenged by some other worker in this field, and probably will be.

An Overview of OO Technology

Question: What is an object?
Answer: Everything!

It is a basic tenet of the OO approach that **"everything is an object"** (sometimes "everything is a **first-class** object"). Some objects are builtin, primitive, and **immutable;** examples might be integers (e.g., 3, 42) and character strings (e.g., "Mozart", "Hayduke Lives!"). In traditional terminology, such objects correspond to simple *values.* Other objects—typically user-created and typically **mutable**—are more complex; examples might be EMPs, DEPTs, VEHICLEs, etc. These more complex objects correspond to *variables,** of arbitrary internal complexity (where the phrase "arbitrary internal complexity" is meant to imply that such objects can make use internally of any or all of the usual programming language data types and type constructors—numbers, strings, lists, arrays, stacks, etc.). *Note:* In some systems the term *object* is used to mean the mutable case only (the term *value* then being used for the immutable case). Even in those systems where the term "object" does strictly refer to both cases, the reader should be aware that it is common in informal contexts to take the term to mean a mutable object specifically, barring explicit statements to the contrary.

Every object has a *type* (the OO term is **class**). Individual objects are sometimes referred to as object **instances** specifically, in order to distinguish them clearly from the corresponding object type or class. Please note also that the term *type* here is used with its usual programming language meaning; that is, an intrinsic aspect of any given type consists of the set of *operators* or *functions* (the OO term is **methods**) that can be applied to objects of that type (see the discussion of *encapsulation* below). We will normally assume that the type of an object is fixed at object creation time, although as we will see in Section 22.7—when we discuss class hierarchies—an object might be of several types simultaneously, and might acquire and lose types dynamically.

As an aside, we remark that some OO systems support both types and classes and therefore make a distinction between the two concepts. We will discuss this possibility further in Section 22.6.

All objects are **encapsulated**. What this means is that the representation—i.e., the

---

* Note, however, that the (unqualified) term *variable* in OO systems refers specifically to a *program* variable that is used to hold an *object ID* (see later).

internal structure—of a given object, say a given DEPT, is not visible to users of that object; instead, users know only that the object is capable of performing certain functions ("methods"). For example, the methods that apply to DEPT objects might be HIRE_EMP, FIRE_EMP, CUT_BUDGET, etc. *Note carefully that such methods constitute the ONLY operations that can be applied to the objects in question.* The code that implements those methods *is* permitted to see the internal representation of the objects, of course; to use the jargon, those methods—and only those methods—are allowed to "break encapsulation."

The advantage of encapsulation is that it allows the internal representation of objects to be changed without requiring any of the applications that use those objects to be rewritten—provided, of course, that any such change in internal representation is accompanied by a corresponding change to the code that implements the applicable methods. In other words, encapsulation implies **data independence**.

In accordance with the idea of encapsulation, objects are sometimes described, a little loosely, as having a **private memory** and a **public interface:**

■ The private memory consists of **instance variables** (also known as *members* or *attributes*), whose values represent the internal state of the object. In a "pure" OO system, instance variables are completely private and hidden from users, but—as indicated above—they are of course visible to the code that implements the methods. However, we should add that many OO systems are *not* "pure" in this sense but do expose certain of their instance variables to users, a point we will return to later.

■ The public interface consists of interface definitions—i.e., definitions of the inputs and outputs—for the methods that apply to this object. The code that implements those methods, like the instance variables, is hidden from the user. *Note:* It would be more accurate to say that the public interface is part of the **class-defining object** for the object in question (i.e., the object that defines the class of which the object in question is an instance), rather than part of the object itself. The code that implements those methods is kept with the class-defining object, not with the object itself.

Incidentally, note that if it is really true that predefined methods are the only way to manipulate objects, then *ad hoc* query is impossible!—unless objects are designed in accordance with a certain very specific discipline, another topic we will come back to later (in Chapter 24).

Methods are invoked by means of **messages**. A message is essentially just a function call, possibly asynchronous, in which one argument (the *receiver* or *target*) is distinguished and given special syntactic treatment. For instance, the following might be a message to department D, asking it to hire employee E:

```
D HIRE_EMP ( E )
```

(hypothetical syntax; see Section 22.6 for an explanation of the arguments D and E). The *receiver* or *target* in this example is the object denoted by D. A conventional programming language analog of this message might look like this:

```
HIRE_EMP ( D, E )
```

For convenience, an OO system will typically come equipped with certain builtin classes and methods. In particular, the system will almost certainly provide such classes as NUMERIC (with methods "=", "<", "+", "-", etc.), CHAR (with methods "=", "<", "||" (string concatenation), SUBSTRING, etc.), and so forth.

Instance Variables

We now take a slightly closer look at the concept of instance variables. The fact is, there is a certain amount of confusion in this area. As stated previously, instance variables would be completely hidden from the user in a pure OO system, but many systems are not pure. As a consequence, it is necessary to distinguish between *public* and *private* instance variables.

For example, suppose we have an object class of LINESEGs (line segments). Then the user might be able to think of each individual LINESEG as having a START point and an END point, and be able, e.g., to ask what the START point is for a given LINESEG. Internally, however, LINESEGs might be represented by MIDPOINT, LENGTH, and SLOPE, and these would be the variables seen by the code that implements the LINESEG methods (whatever those might be). In this example, then, START and END would be **public** instance variables and MIDPOINT, LENGTH, and SLOPE would be **private** instance variables.

It should be pointed out that—the foregoing notwithstanding—the concept of public instance variables is logically unnecessary. That is, even if the user is allowed to write an expression such as (say) *ls*.START to refer to the START point of LINESEG *ls,* that expression can still be regarded as shorthand for a function call that invokes a *method* called START that returns the START point for the LINESEG *ls.* In accordance with common practice, however, we will normally assume (until further notice) that objects typically do have one or more public instance variables.

It is worth pointing out too that just because certain "instance variable" arguments happen to be required in order to create objects of a particular class, it does not follow that those instance variables are available for arbitrary purposes. Suppose, for example, that creating a LINESEG requires START and END values. It does not follow that we can ask for, e.g., all LINESEGs with a given START value; whether this is possible will depend on whether a suitable method has been defined.

Finally, note that some systems support a variation on private instance variables called **protected** instance variables. If objects of class *C* have a protected instance variable *P,* then *P* is visible to the methods defined for class *C* (of course) *and* to the methods defined for any *subclass* (at any level) of class *C.* See Section 22.7 for a discussion of subclasses.

Object Identity

Every object has a unique **identity** called its "object ID" or OID. Primitive ("immutable") objects like the integer 3 are *self-identifying,* i.e., they are their own OIDs; other ("mutable") objects have (conceptual) *addresses* as their OIDs, and these addresses can be used elsewhere in the database as (conceptual) *pointers* to refer to the objects in

question. One implication—and one point of difference *vis-à-vis* the relational model—
is that objects do not necessarily have to have any user-defined candidate keys. Note,
however, that OIDs are not directly visible to the user. See Section 22.5 and Chapters
23–25 for further discussion.

We remark that it is sometimes claimed that it is an advantage of OO systems that
two distinct objects can be identical in all user-visible respects—i.e., be duplicates of
one another—and yet be distinguished via their OIDs. To this writer, however, this
claim seems specious. For how can the *user* distinguish between two such objects, externally? (See references [4.5] and [4.11] for further discussion of this issue in a specifically relational context.)

22.4   Objects and Object Classes Revisited

Let us now consider a detailed example. Suppose we wish to create two object classes,
DEPT (departments) and EMP (employees). Suppose also that the user-defined classes
MONEY and JOB have already been created and the class CHAR is builtin. Then the
necessary class creation operations for DEPT and EMP might look something like the
following (hypothetical syntax):

```
CREATE OBJECT CLASS DEPT
       PUBLIC  ( DEPT#      CHAR,
                 DNAME      CHAR,
                 BUDGET     MONEY,
                 MGR        REF ( EMP ),
                 EMPS       REF ( SET ( REF ( EMP ) ) ) ) ...
       METHODS ( HIRE_EMP ( REF ( EMP ) ) ... code ... ,
                 FIRE_EMP ( REF ( EMP ) ) ... code ... , ... ) ... ;

CREATE OBJECT CLASS EMP
       PUBLIC  ( EMP#       CHAR,
                 ENAME      CHAR,
                 SALARY     MONEY,
                 POSITION   REF ( JOB ) ) ...
       METHODS ( ... ) ... ;
```

Points arising:

1. We have chosen to model departments and employees by means of a **containment
   hierarchy,** in which EMP objects are conceptually contained within DEPT objects. Thus, objects of class DEPT include a public instance variable called MGR,
   representing the given department's manager, and another one called EMPS representing the given department's employees. More precisely, objects of class DEPT
   include a public instance variable called MGR whose value is a reference ("REF")
   to an employee, and another one called EMPS whose value is a reference to a set
   of references to employees. ("Reference to" here really means *OID of*—see further
   discussion below.) We will elaborate on the containment hierarchy notion in a few
   moments.

2. For the sake of the example, we have chosen *not* to include a "foreign key" instance variable within objects of class EMP that refers to objects of class DEPT. This decision is consistent with our decision to model departments-and-employees by means of a containment hierarchy. However, it does mean that there is no direct way to get from a given EMP object to the corresponding DEPT object. See Chapter 24 (Section 24.3, subsection entitled "Relationships") for further discussion.

3. Note that each CREATE OBJECT CLASS operation includes definitions (coding details omitted) of the **methods** that apply to objects of that class.

Fig. 22.4 shows some sample object instances corresponding to the DEPT and EMP classes as just defined. Let us consider the EMP object at the top of that figure (with OID *eee*), which contains:

■ The primitive value object "E001" (a character string) in the public instance variable EMP#

■ The primitive value object "Smith" (another character string) in the public instance variable ENAME

■ The user-defined object $50,000 (an object of class MONEY) in the public instance variable SALARY

■ **The OID of** a user-defined object of class JOB in the public instance variable POSITION

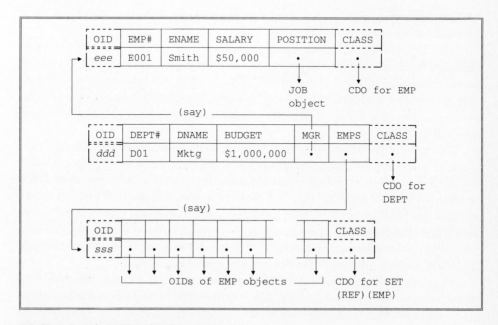

FIG. 22.4 Sample DEPT and EMP instances

It also contains at least two private instance variables, one that contains the OID *eee* of the EMP object itself, and one that contains the OID of the **class-defining object** (CDO) for EMPs (so that the implementation can find the code for the methods that apply to this object). *Note:* These two OIDs might or might not be physically stored with the object. For instance, the value *eee* need not necessarily be stored as part of the relevant EMP object; it is necessary only that the implementation have some way of locating that EMP object given that value *eee* (i.e., some way of mapping that value *eee* to that EMP object's physical address). But conceptually the user can always think of the OID as being part of the object, as shown.

Now let us turn to the DEPT object in the center of the figure (with OID *ddd*). That object contains:

- The primitive value object "D01" in the public instance variable DEPT#
- The primitive value object "Mktg" in the public instance variable DNAME
- The user-defined object $1,000,000 (an object of class MONEY) in the public instance variable BUDGET
- The OID *eee* of a user-defined object of class EMP in the public instance variable MGR (this is the OID of the object that represents the department manager)
- The OID *sss* of a user-defined object of class SET(REF(EMP)) in the public instance variable EMPS (see below)
- Two private instance variables containing in turn the OID *ddd* of the DEPT object itself and the OID of the corresponding class-defining object

And the object with OID *sss* consists of a set of OIDs of individual EMP objects (plus the usual private instance variables).

Now, Fig. 22.4 represents the sample instances "as they really are"; i.e., the figure illustrates the *data structure* component of "the OO model," and such figures must be clearly understood by users of that model. OO texts and presentations, however, typically do *not* show diagrams like that in Fig. 22.4; instead, they typically represent the situation as shown in Fig. 22.5 (which might be regarded as being at a higher level of abstraction).

The representation shown in Fig. 22.5 is certainly more consistent with the "containment hierarchy" interpretation. However, it obscures the important fact, already discussed above, that objects often contain, not other objects as such, but rather **OIDs** of other objects. For example, Fig. 22.5 clearly suggests that the DEPT object shown includes the EMP object for employee E001 *twice* (implying, among many other things, that employee E001 might be shown—inconsistently—as having two different salaries in its two different appearances). This sleight-of-hand is the source of much confusion, which is why we prefer pictures like that of Fig. 22.4.

As an aside, we note that real OO data definitions tend to increase the confusion, because they typically do *not* define instance variables as "REFs" (as in our hypothetical syntax above) but instead directly reflect the containment hierarchy interpretation. Thus, for example, instance variable EMPS in object class DEPT would typically be

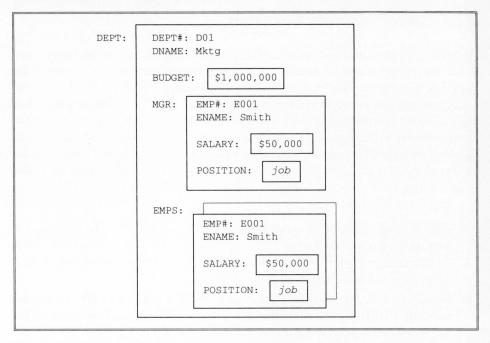

FIG. 22.5 Sample DEPT and EMP instances as a containment hierarchy

defined not as REF(SET(REF(EMP))) but just as SET(EMP). Although clumsy, we prefer our style of data definition, for clarity.

It is worth pointing out too that all of the old criticisms of hierarchies in general (as implemented in, e.g., IMS) apply to containment hierarchies in particular. Space does not permit detailed consideration of those criticisms here; suffice it to say that the overriding issue is **lack of symmetry**. In particular, hierarchies do not lend themselves well to the representation of many-to-many relationships. Consider suppliers and parts, for instance. Do the suppliers contain the parts, or *vice versa?* Or both? What about suppliers, parts, and projects?

Thus, it is our feeling, despite the common talk of "containment hierarchies," that objects are not really hierarchies at all. Instead, as Fig. 22.4 suggests, they are **tuples**—where the tuple components can be any of the following:

1. self-identifying values (e.g., integers)

2. simple nonshared "subobjects" (e.g., MONEY objects)

3. OIDs of other, possibly shared, "subobjects" (see Section 22.6)

4. sets, lists, arrays, . . . of 1., 2., 3., or 4.

(plus certain hidden OID, CDO OID, etc., components). Note carefully, however, that (in a pure system) such tuples are **encapsulated**.

22.5   Object Identity Revisited

Today's relational DBMSs typically rely on user-defined, user-controlled keys ("user keys" for short) for entity identification and referencing purposes. It is well known, however, that user keys suffer from a number of problems; reference [12.12] discusses such problems in some detail and argues that relational DBMSs should support *system-*defined keys ("surrogates") instead. And the argument in favor of OIDs in OO systems is very similar to the argument in favor of surrogates in relational systems. (Do not, however, make the mistake of equating the two: Surrogates are *values* and are visible to the user; OIDs are *addresses* or *pointers*—at least conceptually—and are hidden from the user.)

Points and questions arising:

1. First, it is very important to understand that OIDs do not avoid the need for user keys, as we will see in Chapter 23. To be more precise, user keys are still needed for interaction with the outside world, although inside the database all object cross-referencing can now be performed via OIDs.

2. What is the OID for a *derived* object?—e.g., the join of a given EMP and the corresponding DEPT, or the projection of a given DEPT over BUDGET and MGR? This is another important question that we will have to defer for now. See Chapter 25 (Section 25.4).

3. OIDs are the source of the oft-heard criticisms to the effect that OO systems look like "CODASYL warmed over"—where "CODASYL" refers generically to certain network (i.e., prerelational) database systems such as IDMS. Certainly OIDs tend to lead to a rather low-level, pointer-chasing style of programming (see Section 22.6 and Chapter 23) that is very reminiscent of the old CODASYL style. Also, the fact that OIDs are pointers and not values accounts for the claims, also sometimes heard, to the effect that CODASYL systems are closer to OO systems than relational systems are.

22.6   Classes, Instances, and Collections

OO systems make clear distinctions among the concepts of *class, instance,* and *collection.* First of all, an object **class** is (as previously explained) basically a data type, possibly builtin, possibly user-defined, of arbitrary internal complexity. (As an aside, however, we remark that—as mentioned in Section 22.3—some OO systems use both "type" and "class," in which case "type" means *data type* and "class" means *collection.* We will not adopt this usage in this book.)

Every class understands a **NEW** message, which causes a new **instance** of the class to be created (the method invoked by the NEW message is sometimes referred to as a *constructor function*). For example (hypothetical syntax):

```
E   :=   EMP NEW ( 'E001', 'Smith', $50000, POS ) ;
```

Here POS is a program variable that contains the OID of some JOB object. The NEW method is invoked on the object class EMP; it creates a new instance of that class, initializes it to the specified values, and returns that new instance's OID. That OID is then assigned to the program variable E.

Next, because objects can contain pointers (OIDs) to other objects instead of objects *per se,* the very same object can be *shared* by many objects. In particular, the very same object can belong to multiple **collection** objects simultaneously. To continue with our example:

```
CREATE OBJECT CLASS EMP_COLL_CLASS
       PUBLIC ( EMP_COLL REF ( SET ( REF ( EMP ) ) ) ) ... ;

ALLEMPS  :=  EMP_COLL_CLASS NEW ( ) ;

ALLEMPS ADD ( E ) ;
```

Explanation:

- An object of class EMP_COLL_CLASS contains a single public instance variable, called EMP_COLL, whose value is a pointer (OID) to an object whose value is a set of pointers (OIDs) to individual EMP objects.

- ALLEMPS is a variable whose value is the OID of an object of class EMP_COLL_CLASS. After the assignment operation, it contains the OID of such an object whose value in turn is the OID of an *empty* set of OIDs of EMP objects.

- ADD is a method that is understood by objects of class EMP_COLL_CLASS. In the example, that method is applied to the object of that class whose OID is given in the variable ALLEMPS; its effect is to append the OID of the EMP object whose OID is given in the variable E to the (previously empty) set of OIDs whose OID is given in the EMP_COLL_CLASS object whose OID is given in the variable ALLEMPS.

After the foregoing sequence of operations, we can say, loosely, that the variable ALLEMPS denotes a collection of EMPs that currently contains just one EMP, namely employee E001. By the way, note the need to mention a user key value in this latter sentence!

Of course, we can have any number of distinct, and possibly overlapping, "sets of employees" at any given time:

```
PROGRAMMERS  :=  EMP_COLL_CLASS NEW ( ) ;
PROGRAMMERS ADD ( E ) ;

   .....

HIGHLY_PAID  :=  EMP_COLL_CLASS NEW ( ) ;
HIGHLY_PAID ADD ( E ) ;
```

and so on. Contrast the state of affairs in relational systems. For example, the SQL statement

```
CREATE TABLE EMP
    ( EMP# ... ,
      ENAME ... ,
      SALARY ... ,
      POSITION ... ) ... ;
```

creates a type *and* a collection simultaneously; the (composite) type corresponds to the table heading, and the (initially empty) collection corresponds to the table body. Likewise, the SQL statement

```
INSERT INTO EMP ( ... ) VALUES ( ... ) ;
```

creates an individual EMP row *and* appends it to the EMP collection simultaneously. In SQL, therefore:

1. There is no way for an individual EMP "object" to exist without being part of some "collection"—in fact, exactly one "collection" (but see below).
2. There is no direct way to create two distinct "collections" of the same "class" of EMP "objects" (but see below).
3. There is no direct way to share the same "object" across multiple "collections" of EMP "objects" (but see below).

At least, the foregoing are claims that are sometimes heard. In fact, however, they do not stand up to close scrutiny. To be specific, the relational foreign key mechanism can be used to achieve an equivalent effect in each case; for example, we could define two more base tables called PROGRAMMERS and HIGHLY_PAID, each of them consisting of just the employee numbers for the relevant employees. Alternatively, the relational view mechanism can be used to achieve a similar effect. For example, we could define PROGRAMMERS and HIGHLY_PAID as views of the EMP base table:

```
CREATE VIEW PROGRAMMERS
    AS SELECT EMP#, ENAME, SALARY, POSITION
       FROM    EMP
       WHERE   POSITION = 'Programmer' ;

CREATE VIEW HIGHLY_PAID
    AS SELECT EMP#, ENAME, SALARY, POSITION
       FROM    EMP
       WHERE   SALARY > some threshold, say $75000 ;
```

And now, of course, it is perfectly possible for the very same employee "object" to belong to two or more "collections" simultaneously. What is more, membership in those collections that happen to be views is handled automatically by the system, not manually by the programmer.

We close this discussion by mentioning an illuminating parallel between the *objects* of OO systems and the **explicit dynamic variables** of certain programming language systems (PL/I's BASED variables are a case in point). Like an OO object, an explicit dynamic variable can have any number of distinct instances, the storage for which is allocated by explicit programmer action. Furthermore, those instances, again like individual object instances, *have no name,* and thus can be referenced only through pointers. In PL/I, for example, we might write:

```
DCL XYZ ... BASED ;              /* XYZ is a BASED variable */
DCL P POINTER ;                  /* P is a pointer variable */

ALLOCATE XYZ SET ( P ) ;      /* create a new XYZ instance */
                              /* and set P to point to it  */

P -> XYZ = 3 ;             /* assign the value 3 to the XYZ */
                           /* instance pointed to by P      */
```

(and so on). This PL/I code bears a striking resemblance to the OO code discussed earlier; in particular, the declaration of the BASED variable is akin to the creation of an object class, and the ALLOCATE operation is akin to the creation of a NEW instance of that class. We can thus see that the reason OIDs are necessary in "the OO model" is precisely because, in general, the objects they identify do not possess any other unique name—just like BASED variable instances in PL/I.

22.7   Class Hierarchies

No treatment of basic OO concepts would be complete without some discussion of **class hierarchies** (not to be confused with containment hierarchies). However, the OO "class hierarchy" concept is essentially the same as the type hierarchy concept discussed in Chapter 19 (Section 19.4); we therefore content ourselves here with a few brief definitions (paraphrased from Chapter 19, for the most part) and a couple of relevant observations.

First, object class Y is said to be a **subclass** of object class X—equivalently, object class X is said to be a **superclass** of object class Y—if and only if every object of class Y is necessarily an object of class X ("Y **ISA** X"). Objects of class Y then **inherit** the instance variables and methods that apply to class X. As a consequence, the user can always use a Y object wherever an X object is permitted (i.e., as an argument to various methods)—this is the principle of **substitutability**—and thereby take advantage of **code reusability**. *Note:* Inheriting instance variables is referred to as **structural** inheritance; inheriting methods is referred to as **behavioral** inheritance. The ability to apply the same method to different classes—or, rather, the ability to apply different methods with the same name to different classes (a class X method might need to be **redefined** for use with class Y)—is referred to as **polymorphism**.

Here is an example. Suppose RECTANGLE is a subclass of POLYGON, which in turn is a subclass of PLANE_FIGURE. The object class declarations might look as follows:

```
CREATE OBJECT CLASS PLANE_FIGURE
       PUBLIC ( AREA ... ) ...
       METHODS ( OVERLAP ... ) ... ;
```

```
CREATE OBJECT CLASS POLYGON
       ISA ( PLANE_FIGURE )
       PUBLIC ( VERTICES ... ) ...
       METHOD ( COUNT_VERTICES ... ) ... ;

CREATE OBJECT CLASS RECTANGLE
       ISA ( POLYGON )
       PUBLIC ( DIAGONAL_LENGTH ... )
       METHODS ( TRANSPOSE ... ) ... ;
```

A sample RECTANGLE instance is shown in Fig. 22.6. Note in particular that it includes the instance variables of PLANE_FIGURE and POLYGON as well as the instance variables of RECTANGLE *per se*. Note too the implications for creating a "NEW" instance of RECTANGLE, and contrast the situation with Fig. 22.7, which shows a relational representation of the same data.

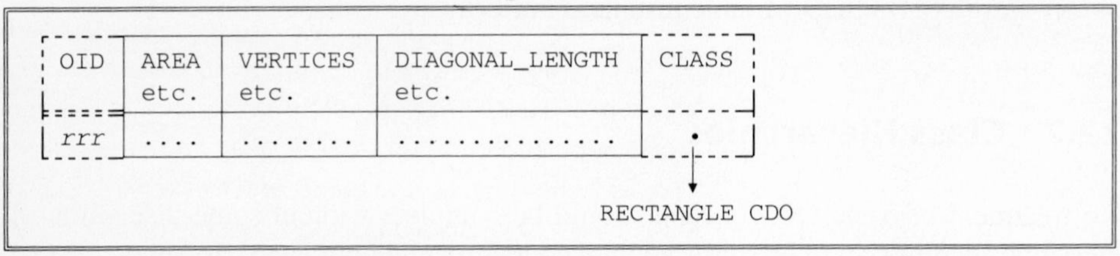

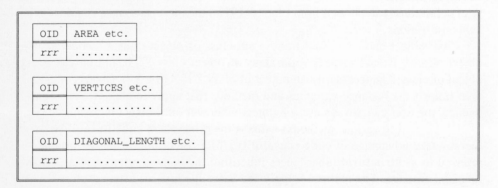

FIG. 22.6 Sample RECTANGLE instance

OID	AREA etc.
rrr	....

OID	VERTICES etc.
rrr	....

OID	DIAGONAL_LENGTH etc.
rrr	....

FIG. 22.7 Relational version of Fig. 22.6

The system will come equipped with some builtin class hierarchies. In OPAL, for example (see Chapter 23), every class is considered to be a subclass (at some level) of the builtin class OBJECT. Builtin subclasses of OBJECT include BOOLEAN, CHAR, INTEGER, COLLECTION (etc.); COLLECTION in turn has a subclass called BAG (a *bag* is the same as a set, except that it permits duplicates), and BAG has another called SET (etc., etc.).

Finally, we repeat another point from Chapter 19, *viz.*: Some systems support the notion of **multiple inheritance,** in which a given class can be a subclass of several superclasses simultaneously. In such a system, class "hierarchies" really become class **lattices,** in the sense that a given "child" class might have several distinct "parent" classes (but the "hierarchy" terminology is usually retained nonetheless).

22.8   Miscellaneous Remarks

In this section we make a few miscellaneous observations regarding objects in general.

1. A given object might acquire new types and lose existing types dynamically. For example, a given employee might become or cease to be a stockholder. The system must therefore support the ability for a given object to change its position within the class hierarchy—e.g., to "move up and down" a given branch, or (more complex) to be attached to or detached from an arbitrary node, at any time.

2. It is often suggested that OO technology simplifies database design and development (as well as database use) by providing high-level modeling constructs and supporting those constructs directly in the system. (By contrast, relational systems involve an extra level of indirection in mapping real-world objects into relations, attributes, foreign keys, etc.) But this claim raises the question: How exactly do we do OO database design? For instance, how do we decide whether to represent a given collection as a set or a bag or a list or an array? How do we decide whether to represent data explicitly (via instance variables) or procedurally (via methods)? And so on.

3. Finally, we remark that in an OO system, objects—that is, individual objects *per se,* not object classes—are:
   - the natural unit of security and authorization
   - the natural unit of recovery
   - the natural unit of concurrency

   (except where prohibited by the requirements of integrity constraints that span objects).

22.9   Summary

This brings us to the end of the first of our series of chapters on the OO approach. Following our discussion of the motivating RECTANGLES example, we explained:

- **Objects** (i.e., object **instances**), which correspond in traditional terms to *variables* (if "mutable") or *values* (if "immutable")
- **Object classes,** which correspond to *data types*
- **Methods** and **messages,** which correspond to *functions* and *calls* (possibly asynchronous calls), respectively

In addition, we pointed out that "mutable" objects correspond specifically to **explicit dynamic** variables, in programming parlance, which is why they have to be accessed through pointers (i.e., OIDs—see below).

Objects are **encapsulated** (i.e., their internal representation is not visible to users of the object; instead, users know only that the object can be manipulated via certain methods). Objects are sometimes described as having a **private memory** and a **public interface:** The private memory is the **instance variables,** the public interface is the definitions of the interfaces to the **methods.** In a "pure" OO system, only the methods— or, rather, the method *externals*—are visible to the user, but many systems are not pure. The methods are kept with the the **class-defining object** (CDO) for the object in question.

Every object has a unique **object ID** (OID). A given object's OID is used to refer to the object from other objects. Program variables also refer to objects by means of their OID. We stressed the point that an OID is a *pointer,* not a *value,* and left some rather important questions regarding OIDs unanswered. See Chapter 25 for further discussion.

We also described **containment hierarchies**—despite our feeling that the concept is misleading; in fact, it would be more accurate to regard objects not as hierarchies, but as (encapsulated) **tuples,** where the tuple components can be (a) self-identifying values, (b) simple nonshared "subobjects," (c) OIDs of other (possibly shared) subobjects, or (d) various combinations of the foregoing.

We then elaborated on the concepts of **class, instance,** and **collection.** OO systems make clear distinctions among these concepts; we gave some simple coding examples to illustrate the point, and compared and contrasted the situation with relational systems.

We then briefly touched on the OO **class hierarchy** concept, without however going into very much detail (because the concept has already been described, in slightly different terms, in Chapter 19). Finally, we offered a few further miscellaneous comments regarding objects in general.

Exercises

22.1 What is an object?

22.2 What does the term *encapsulated* mean?

22.3 Instance variables can be *public, private,* or *protected.* Explain.

22.4 What is the difference between *class* and *type?*

22.5 Define the concept *object ID.* What are the advantages of OIDs? What are the disadvantages?

22.6 How might OIDs be implemented?

22.7 What is a class-defining object?

22.8 What do you understand by the term "constructor function"? What analogs (if any) of such functions exist in traditional programming languages?

22.9 Explain and justify the *containment hierarchy* concept.

22.10 Explain the idea and conceptual implementation of "shared subobjects."

22.11 Give an example of multiple inheritance.

22.12 In Section 22.2 we gave two SQL formulations—a long form and a short form—of the query "Find all rectangles that overlap the unit square." Prove that those two formulations are equivalent.

References and Bibliography

References [22.1–22.3], [22.6], and [22.11] are textbooks on OO topics and related matters. References [22.9] and [22.16] are collections of research papers. References [22.7–22.8], [22.10], and [22.12] are tutorials.

22.1 Grady Booch. *Object Oriented Design, with Applications.* Redwood City, Calif.: Benjamin/ Cummings (1991).

22.2 R. G. G. Cattell. *Object Data Management.* Reading, Mass.: Addison-Wesley (1991).

The first book-length tutorial on the application of OO technology to databases specifically. The following edited extract suggests that the field is still a long way from any kind of consensus: "Programming languages may need new syntax . . . swizzling [see Chapter 24, Section 24.2], replication, and new access methods also need further study . . . new end-user and application development tools [are] required . . . more powerful query-language features [must be] developed . . . new research in concurrency control is needed . . . timestamps and object-based concurrency semantics need more exploration . . . performance models are needed . . . new work in knowledge management needs to be integrated with object and data management capabilities . . . this [will lead to] a complex optimization problem [and] few researchers have [the necessary] expertise . . . federated [OO] databases require more study."

22.3 Brad J. Cox. *Object Oriented Programming: An Evolutionary Approach.* Reading, Mass.: Addison-Wesley (1986).

A tutorial text on object-oriented ideas in the programming world, with the emphasis on the use of OO techniques for software engineering.

22.4 O. J. Dahl, B. Myhrhaug, and K. Nygaard. *The SIMULA 67 Common Base Language.* Pub. S-22, Norwegian Computing Center, Oslo, Norway (1970).

SIMULA 67 was a language designed expressly for writing simulation applications. OO programming languages grew out of such languages; in fact, SIMULA 67 was really the first OO language.

22.5 C. J. Date. "An Optimization Problem." In C. J. Date and Hugh Darwen, *Relational Database Writings 1989–1991.* Reading, Mass.: Addison-Wesley (1992).

22.6 Adele Goldberg and David Robson. *Smalltalk-80: The Language and its Implementation.* Reading, Mass.: Addison-Wesley (1983).

The definitive account of the pioneering efforts at the Xerox Palo Alto Research Center to design and build the Smalltalk-80 system. The first part of the book (out of four parts) is a detailed description of the Smalltalk-80 programming language, on which the OPAL language of GemStone is based (see Chapter 23).

22.7 Nathan Goodman. "Object Oriented Database Systems." *InfoDB 4,* No. 3 (Fall 1989).

See the annotation to this paper in Chapter 25 (reference [25.5]).

22.8 Nathan Goodman. "The Object Database Debate," "The Object Data Model," and "The Object Data Model in Action." *InfoDB 5*, No. 4 (Winter 1990–91); *6*, No. 1 (Spring/Summer 1991); and *6*, No. 2 (Fall 1991).

22.9 Won Kim and Frederick H. Lochovsky (eds.). *Object-Oriented Concepts, Databases, and Applications*. Reading, Mass.: Addison-Wesley (1989).

22.10 Roger King. "My Cat Is Object-Oriented." In reference [22.9].

22.11 Kamran Parsaye, Mark Chignell, Setrag Koshafian, and Harry Wong. *Intelligent Databases*. New York, N.Y.: John Wiley & Sons (1989).

22.12 Jacob Stein and David Maier. "Concepts in Object-Oriented Data Management." *Database Programming & Design 1*, No. 4 (April 1988).

A good tutorial on OO concepts by two of the GemStone designers.

22.13 Michael Stonebraker. *Introduction to* "New Data Models"; and *Introduction to* "Extendibility." Both in M. Stonebraker (ed.): *Readings in Database Systems*. San Mateo, Calif.: Morgan Kaufmann (1988).

These two introductions include Stonebraker's translation of OO concepts to traditional terms and his own brief analysis of what OO technology is trying to do and where it is likely to lead in the future.

22.14 D. C. Tsichritzis and O. M. Nierstrasz. "Directions in OO Research." In reference [22.9].

This paper lends further weight to the contention of the present writer that OO database technology is a long way from consensus: "There are disagreements on basic definitions; e.g., what is an object? . . . There is no reason to worry: Loose definitions are inevitable and sometimes welcome during a dynamic period of scientific discovery. They should and will become more rigorous during a period of consolidation that will inevitably follow." But OO concepts have been around for well over 25 years! (see reference [22.4]).

22.15 Gottfried Vossen. *Data Models, Database Languages, and Database Management Systems*. Reading, Mass.: Addison-Wesley (1991).

22.16 Stanley B. Zdonik and David Maier (eds.). *Readings in Object-Oriented Database Systems*. San Mateo, Calif.: Morgan Kaufmann (1990).

Answers to Selected Exercises

22.1 Part of the problem in discussing OO technology is that some of the most fundamental OO concepts lack a clear, universally accepted definition. Here, for example, are some "definitions" from the OO literature of the term **object:**

■ "Objects are reusable modules of code that store data, information about relationships between data and applications, and processes that control data and relationships" (from a commercial product announcement).

■ "An object is a chunk of private memory with a public interface" [22.12].

■ "An object is an abstract machine that defines a protocol through which users of the object may interact" (introduction to reference [22.16]).

■ "An object is a software structure that contains data and programs" [22.7].

■ " . . . everything is an object . . . an object has a private memory and a public interface" [22.15].

■ ". . the object-oriented model is based on a collection of objects. An object contains values stored in *instance variables* within the object . . . these values are themselves objects . . . An object also contains bodies of code that operate on the object . . . called methods" [3.7].

Our own understanding of what an object is is explained in Section 22.3.

22.5   Some of the advantages of OIDs are as follows:

- They are not "intelligent." See reference [12.8] for an explanation of why this state of affairs is desirable.

- All objects in the database are identified in the same uniform way (contrast the situation with relational databases).

- They never change so long as the object they identify remains in existence.

- There is no need to repeat user keys in referencing objects. There is thus no need for an "ON UPDATE" foreign key rule.

- They are noncomposite. See references [5.5–5.7] for an explanation of why this state of affairs is desirable.

Some of the *dis*advantages—the fact that they do not avoid the need for user keys, the fact that they lead to a low-level "pointer-chasing" style of programming, and the fact that they apply to "base" objects only—were discussed briefly in Section 22.5.

22.6   Possible implementation techniques include:

- Physical disk addresses (fast but poor data independence).

- Logical disk addresses (i.e., page and offset addresses; fairly fast, better data independence).

- Artificial IDs (e.g., timestamps, sequence numbers; need mapping to actual addresses).

22.12   See reference [22.5].

23 | A Cradle-to-Grave Example

23.1 Introduction

In the previous chapter we introduced the basic concepts of the OO approach. Now we show how those concepts fit together by presenting a "cradle-to-grave" example—i.e., we show how an OO database is defined, how it is populated, and how retrieval and update operations can be performed against that database. Our example is based on one of the best known OO systems, namely **GemStone** (available from Servio Corporation [23.2]) and its data language **OPAL**. *Note:* OPAL in turn was heavily influenced by Smalltalk-80 (see references [22.6] and [23.1]).

We introduce the example below. Section 23.2 then discusses data definition operations and Sections 23.3–23.5 discuss data manipulation operations. Section 23.6 presents a summary and a few additional comments.

The Example

The example is based on a simplified version of the education database from Exercise 5.3 in Chapter 5. To recap:

- An education database contains information about an inhouse company education training scheme. For each training course, the database contains details of all offerings of that course; for each offering it contains details of all student enrollments and all teachers for that offering. The database also contains information about employees.

A relational version of this database looks something like this:

```
EMPLOYEE ( EMP#, ENAME, JOB )
        PRIMARY KEY ( EMP# )

COURSE ( COURSE#, TITLE )
        PRIMARY KEY ( COURSE# )

OFFERING ( COURSE#, OFF#, ODATE, LOCATION )
        PRIMARY KEY ( COURSE#, OFF# )
        FOREIGN KEY ( COURSE# ) REFERENCES COURSE
```

```
ENROLLMENT ( COURSE#, OFF#, EMP#, GRADE )
          PRIMARY KEY ( COURSE#, OFF#, EMP# )
          FOREIGN KEY ( COURSE#, OFF# ) REFERENCES OFFERING
          FOREIGN KEY ( EMP# ) REFERENCES EMP

TEACHER ( COURSE#, OFF#, EMP# )
        PRIMARY KEY ( COURSE#, OFF#, EMP# )
        FOREIGN KEY ( COURSE#, OFF# ) REFERENCES OFFERING
        FOREIGN KEY ( EMP# ) REFERENCES EMP
```

Fig. 23.1 gives a referential diagram for this database. Refer to the Exercises and Answers in Chapter 5 if you require further explanation.

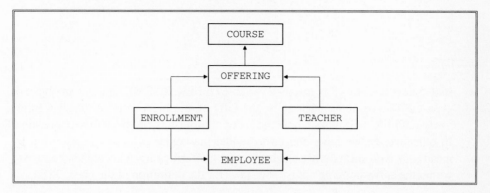

FIG. 23.1 Referential diagram for the education database

23.2 Data Definition

We now proceed to show an OPAL definition for the education database. Here first is the definition for an object class called EMPLOYEE (the lines are numbered for purposes of subsequent reference):

```
1 OBJECT SUBCLASS : 'EMPLOYEE'
2    INSTVARNAMES : # [ 'EMP#', 'ENAME', 'JOB' ]
3    CONSTRAINTS  : # [ # [ # EMP#, STRING ] ,
4                       [ # ENAME, STRING ] ,
5                       [ # JOB, STRING ] ] .
```

Explanation:

■ Line 1 defines an object class called EMPLOYEE, a subclass of the builtin class called OBJECT. (In OPAL terms, line 1 is sending a message to the object called OBJECT, asking it to execute the method called SUBCLASS; INSTVARNAMES and CONSTRAINTS specify parameters to that method. Defining a new class—like everything else—is thus done by sending a message to an object.)

- Line 2 states that objects of class EMPLOYEE have three public instance variables called EMP#, ENAME, and JOB, respectively.

- Line 3 constrains the instance variable EMP# to contain objects of class STRING. Lines 4 and 5 are analogous.

Note: Throughout this chapter we omit discussion of purely syntactic details (such as the ubiquitous "#" signs in the foregoing example) that are essentially irrelevant for our purposes.

Next the COURSE class:

```
1 OBJECT SUBCLASS : 'COURSE'
2    INSTVARNAMES : # [ 'COURSE#', 'TITLE', 'OFFERINGS' ]
3    CONSTRAINTS  : # [ # [ # COURSE#, STRING ] ,
4                         [ # TITLE, STRING ] ,
5                         [ # OFFERINGS, OSET ] ] .
```

Explanation:

- Line 5 here specifies that instance variable OFFERINGS will contain an object of class OSET—or, more accurately, the OID of an object of class OSET.* Informally, OFFERINGS will denote the set of all offerings for the course in question. In other words, we have chosen to model the course-offerings relationship by means of a **containment hierarchy,** in which offerings are conceptually contained within the corresponding course. See later for the definition of the class OSET.

Now the OFFERING class:

```
1 OBJECT SUBCLASS : 'OFFERING'
2    INSTVARNAMES : # [ 'OFF#', 'ODATE', 'LOCATION',
3                        'ENROLLMENTS', 'TEACHERS' ]
4    CONSTRAINTS  : # [ # [ # OFF#, STRING ] ,
5                         [ # ODATE, DATETIME ] ,
6                         [ # LOCATION, STRING ] ,
7                         [ # ENROLLMENTS, NSET ] ,
8                         [ # TEACHERS, TSET ] ] .
```

Explanation:

- Line 7 specifies that instance variable ENROLLMENTS will contain (the OID of) an object of class NSET; informally, NSET will denote the set of all enrollments for the offering in question. Likewise, TSET will denote the set of all teachers for the offering in question. Again, therefore, we are adopting a "containment hierarchy" representation. See later for the NSET and TSET definitions.

- Note that we have chosen not to include a "foreign key" instance variable within objects of class OFFERING referring back to objects of class COURSE. This decision is consistent with our decision to use a containment hierarchy. However, it

---

* The hypothetical syntax introduced in Chapter 22 would have made this point more explicit, defining the instance variable OFFERINGS to be of type REF(SET(REF(OFFERING))).

does mean that there is no direct way to get from a given OFFERING instance to the corresponding COURSE instance. We will return to this issue in the next chapter.

Now the ENROLLMENT class:

```
1 OBJECT SUBCLASS : 'ENROLLMENT'
2    INSTVARNAMES : # [ 'EMP', 'GRADE' ]
3    CONSTRAINTS   : # [ # [ # EMP, EMPLOYEE ] ,
4                          [ # GRADE, STRING ] ] .
```

Explanation:

- Again, objects of class ENROLLMENT do not include a "foreign key" instance variable referencing objects of class OFFERING. Note, however, that objects of class ENROLLMENT do include a *kind* of foreign key: Instance variable EMP (line 3) contains the OID of an object of class EMPLOYEE, representing the individual employee to whom this enrollment pertains. *Note:* The "containment hierarchy" interpretation would regard that EMPLOYEE object as actually being contained within the ENROLLMENT object, of course. But note the asymmetry: Enrollments are a many-to-many relationship, but the two participants in that relationship (employees and offerings) are treated quite differently.

Now we turn to teachers. For the sake of the example, we depart slightly from the original relational version of the database and treat teachers as a **subclass** of employees:

```
1 EMPLOYEE SUBCLASS : 'TEACHER'
2    INSTVARNAMES  : # [ 'COURSES' ]
3    CONSTRAINTS   : # [ # [ # COURSES, CSET ] ] .
```

Explanation:

- Line 1 defines an object class called TEACHER, a subclass of the previously defined class EMPLOYEE (in other words, TEACHER "ISA" EMPLOYEE). Thus, each individual TEACHER object has instance variables EMP#, ENAME, and JOB (all inherited from EMPLOYEE), plus COURSES, which will contain the OID of an object of class CSET. This CSET object will denote the set of all courses this teacher can teach.

Now, we saw in Chapter 22 that OO systems make a clear distinction between *classes* and **collections**. Indeed, the foregoing class definitions assumed the existence of several object collections—collections of offerings, collections of enrollments, collections of teachers, and so on—but no such collections have yet been defined. Let us therefore define a "collection" object class for each of the five classes defined above; we will name them ESET, CSET, OSET, NSET, and TSET, respectively. An object of class CSET, for example, will consist of a set of OIDs for individual objects of class COURSE. Here then are the definitions:

```
1 SET SUBCLASS    : 'ESET'
2    CONSTRAINTS : EMPLOYEE .
```

Explanation:

■ Line 1 defines an object class called ESET, a subclass of the builtin class called SET.

■ Line 2 constrains objects of class ESET to be sets of (OIDs of) objects of class EMPLOYEE. In general, there could be any number of objects of class ESET, but we will create just one (see Section 23.3), which will contain the set of OIDs of *all* EMPLOYEE objects (referred to loosely in what follows as "the set of all employees"). Informally, that ESET object will be the OO analog of the EMPLOYEE base relation in the relational version of the database.

■ Observe that objects of class ESET have no public instance variables.

The CSET, OSET, NSET, and TSET definitions are analogous (see below). In each of these cases, however, we will definitely have to create several objects of the relevant class, not just one. For example, there will be as many OSET objects as there are individual COURSE objects. See Section 23.3 for the details of actually creating these several "set" objects.

```
SET SUBCLASS    : 'CSET'
    CONSTRAINTS : COURSE .

SET SUBCLASS    : 'OSET'
    CONSTRAINTS : OFFERING .

SET SUBCLASS    : 'NSET'
    CONSTRAINTS : ENROLLMENT .

SET SUBCLASS    : 'TSET'
    CONSTRAINTS : TEACHER .
```

To conclude this section, Fig. 23.2 (opposite) gathers together all of the foregoing definitions (and reorders them) for ease of subsequent reference. That figure will serve as a basis for the manipulative examples to be presented in the rest of this chapter.

23.3 Populating the Database

Now we consider what is involved in populating this database. We consider each of the five basic object types (employees, courses, offerings, enrollments, teachers) in turn.

Employees

Recall that we intend to collect together the OIDs of all EMPLOYEE objects in an ESET object, so first we need to create that ESET object:

```
OID_OF_SET_OF_ALL_EMPS  :=  ESET NEW .
```

Explanation:

■ The expression on the right-hand side of this assignment returns the OID of a new, empty instance of class ESET (i.e., an empty set of EMPLOYEE OIDs); the OID

```
SET SUBCLASS    : 'ESET'
    CONSTRAINTS : EMPLOYEE .

SET SUBCLASS    : 'CSET'
    CONSTRAINTS : COURSE .

SET SUBCLASS    : 'OSET'
    CONSTRAINTS : OFFERING .

SET SUBCLASS    : 'NSET'
    CONSTRAINTS : ENROLLMENT .

SET SUBCLASS    : 'TSET'
    CONSTRAINTS : TEACHER .

OBJECT SUBCLASS : 'EMPLOYEE'
   INSTVARNAMES : # [ 'EMP#', 'ENAME', 'JOB' ]
   CONSTRAINTS  : # [ # [ # EMP#, STRING ] ,
                        [ # ENAME, STRING ] ,
                        [ # JOB, STRING ] ] .

OBJECT SUBCLASS : 'COURSE'
   INSTVARNAMES : # [ 'COURSE#', 'TITLE', 'OFFERINGS' ]
   CONSTRAINTS  : # [ # [ # COURSE#, STRING ] ,
                        [ # TITLE, STRING ] ,
                        [ # OFFERINGS, OSET ] ] .

OBJECT SUBCLASS : 'OFFERING'
   INSTVARNAMES : # [ 'OFF#', 'ODATE', 'LOCATION',
                               'ENROLLMENTS', 'TEACHERS' ]
   CONSTRAINTS  : # [ # [ # OFF#, STRING ] ,
                        [ # ODATE, DATETIME ] ,
                        [ # LOCATION, STRING ] ,
                        [ # ENROLLMENTS, NSET ] ,
                        [ # TEACHERS, TSET ] ] .

OBJECT SUBCLASS : 'ENROLLMENT'
   INSTVARNAMES : # [ 'EMP', 'GRADE' ]
   CONSTRAINTS  : # [ # [ # EMP, EMPLOYEE ] ,
                        [ # GRADE, STRING ] ] .

EMPLOYEE SUBCLASS : 'TEACHER'
   INSTVARNAMES   : # [ 'COURSES' ]
   CONSTRAINTS    : # [ # [ # COURSES, CSET ] ] .
```

FIG. 23.2   Data definition for the education database (OO version)

of that new instance is then assigned to the program variable OID_OF_SET_ OF_ALL_EMPS. Informally, OID_OF_SET_OF_ALL_EMPS will be used to identify "the set of all employees."

Now, every time we create a new EMPLOYEE object we want the OID of that object to be inserted into the ESET object identified by the OID saved in the variable OID_OF_SET_OF_ALL_EMPS. We therefore define a **method** for creating such an EMPLOYEE object and inserting its OID into that ESET object:

```
 1 METHOD : ESET                              /* anonymous!    */
 2   ADD_EMP#  : EMP#_PARM                     /* parameters    */
 3   ADD_ENAME : ENAME_PARM
 4   ADD_JOB   : JOB_PARM
 5 | EMP_OID |                                 /* local variable */
 6   EMP_OID := EMPLOYEE NEW .                  /* new employee   */
 7   EMP_OID SET_EMP# : EMP#_PARM ,            /* initialize     */
 8           SET_ENAME : ENAME_PARM ,
 9           SET_JOB : JOB_PARM .
10   SELF ADD: EMP_OID .                        /* insert         */
11 %
```

Explanation:

- Line 1 defines the code that follows (up to the terminating percent sign in line 11) to be a method that applies to objects of class ESET. (In fact, of course, *exactly one* object of that class will exist in the system at run time.)

- Lines 2–4 define three parameters, with external names ADD_EMP#, ADD_ ENAME, and ADD_JOB. These names will be used in messages that invoke the method. The corresponding internal names EMP#_PARM, ENAME_PARM, and JOB_PARM will be used in the code that implements the method.

- Line 5 defines EMP_OID to be a local variable, and line 6 then assigns to that variable the OID of a new, uninitialized EMPLOYEE instance.

- Lines 7–9 send a message to that new EMPLOYEE instance; the message specifies three methods (SET_EMP#, SET_ENAME, and SET_JOB) and passes one parameter to each of them (EMP#_PARM to SET_EMP#, ENAME_PARM to SET_ ENAME, and JOB_PARM to SET_JOB). *Note:* We are assuming here that SET_ EMP# is a method that applies to an EMPLOYEE object and has the effect of setting the EMP# instance variable within that object to the specified value, and similarly for SET_ENAME and SET_JOB. We will have a little more to say regarding these three methods in just a moment.

- Line 10 sends a message to SELF, which is a special variable that represents the object to which the method being defined is currently being applied (i.e., the current *receiver* or *target* object). The message causes the builtin method ADD to be applied to that object (ADD is a method that is understood by every "collection"- type class); the effect in the case at hand is to insert the OID of the object identified by EMP_OID into the object identified by SELF. *Note:* The reason the special variable SELF is required is that the parameter corresponding to the receiver object is otherwise unnamed.

■ Note that—as pointed out by the comment in line 1—the method being defined is likewise unnamed. In general, in fact, methods do not have names in OPAL, but instead are identified by their **signature** (i.e., the combination of the name of the class to which they apply and the external names of their parameters). This convention leads to awkward circumlocutions, as can be seen. Note too another slightly unfortunate implication—namely, that if two methods both apply to the same class and take the same parameters, those parameters must be given arbitrarily different external names in the two methods.

Now we have a method for inserting new EMPLOYEEs into the database, but we still have not actually inserted any. So let us do so:

```
OID_OF_SET_OF_ALL_EMPS ADD_EMP#   : 'E009',
                       ADD_ENAME : 'Watt',
                       ADD_JOB   : 'Janitor' .
```

This statement (a) creates an EMPLOYEE object for employee E009 and (b) adds (the OID of) that EMPLOYEE object to the set of (OIDs of) all EMPLOYEE objects.

Note, incidentally, that the builtin NEW method must now never be used on class EMPLOYEE other than as part of the method we have just defined—for otherwise we might create some dangling EMPLOYEE objects, i.e., employees who are not represented in "the set of all employees." *Note:* We apologize for the burdensome repetition of cumbersome circumlocutions like "the set of all employees" and "the method we have just defined," but it is not easy to talk about things that have no name.

To conclude our discussion of the employees case, we must say something regarding the methods SET_EMP#, SET_ENAME, and SET_JOB. As explained in Chapter 22, a pure OO system will not expose instance variables to the user; instead, it will permit objects to be manipulated solely by means of methods (**encapsulation**). In accordance with this principle, we will adopt the convention throughout this chapter that instance variables are indeed hidden; if a class definition in fact defines a "public" instance variable v, we will treat that definition as shorthand for the definition of a pair of methods GET_v and SET_v, where GET_v returns the value of v to the caller and SET_v sets v to the value specified by the caller.

Courses

Employees really represent the simplest possible case, since they correspond to "regular entities" (to use the terminology of the E/R model), and moreover do not contain any other objects embedded within themselves. We now move on to consider the more complex case of *courses,* which—although still "regular entities"—do conceptually include certain other objects embedded within them. In outline, the steps we must go through are as follows:

1. Apply the NEW method to class CSET to create an initially empty "set of all courses" (actually COURSE OIDs).

2. Define a method for creating a new COURSE object and inserting its OID into "the set of all courses." That method will take a specified COURSE# and TITLE as parameters and will create a new COURSE object with the specified values. It will also apply the NEW method to class OSET to create an initially empty set of offerings (actually OFFERING OIDs), and will then place the OID of that empty set of offerings into the OFFERINGS position within the new COURSE object.

3. Invoke the method just defined for each individual course in turn.

Offerings

The "offerings" steps are as follows:

1. Define a method for creating a new OFFERING object. That method will take a specified OFF#, ODATE, and LOCATION as parameters and will create a new OFFERING object with those specified values. It will also:

   ▪ Apply the NEW method to class NSET to create an initially empty set of enrollments (actually ENROLLMENT OIDs), and then place the OID of that empty set of enrollments into the ENROLLMENTS position within the new OFFERING object.

   ▪ Apply the NEW method to class TSET to create an initially empty set of teachers (actually TEACHER OIDs), and then place the OID of that empty set of teachers into the TEACHERS position within the new OFFERING object.

2. The method will also take a COURSE# parameter, and will use that COURSE# value to:

   ▪ Find the corresponding COURSE object for the new OFFERING object. See Section 23.4 for an explanation of how this might be done. *Note:* Of course, the method must reject the attempt to create a new offering if the corresponding course cannot be found. We omit further consideration of such exception cases from the rest of our discussions.

   ▪ Hence, locate "the set of all offerings" for that COURSE object.

   ▪ Hence, add the OID of the new OFFERING object to the appropriate "set of all offerings."

   Note carefully, therefore, that (as mentioned in Chapter 22) OIDs do *not* avoid the need for user keys such as COURSE#. Indeed, such keys are needed, not just to refer to objects in the outside world, but also to serve as the basis for lookups inside the database.

3. Finally, invoke the method just defined for each individual offering in turn.

Note, incidentally, that (in keeping with our containment hierarchy representation) we have chosen not to create a "set of *all* offerings." One implication of this omission is that any query that requires that set as its scope—e.g., "Find all offerings in New York"—will involve a certain amount of procedural workaround code.

Enrollments

The difference in kind between the enrollments and offerings cases is that ENROLLMENT objects include a instance variable of class EMPLOYEE—namely, the variable EMP, whose value is the OID of the relevant EMPLOYEE object. Hence the necessary sequence of steps is as follows:

1. Define a method for creating a new ENROLLMENT object. That method will take a specified COURSE#, OFF#, EMP# and GRADE as its parameters and will create a new ENROLLMENT object with the specified GRADE value. It will then:

   - Use the COURSE# and OFF# values to find the corresponding OFFERING object for the new ENROLLMENT object.

   - Hence, find "the set of all enrollments" for that OFFERING object.

   - Hence, add the OID of the new ENROLLMENT object to the appropriate "set of all enrollments."

   It will also:

   - Use the EMP# value to find the relevant EMPLOYEE object.

   - Hence, place the OID of that EMPLOYEE object in the EMP position within the new ENROLLMENT object.

2. Invoke the method just defined for each individual enrollment in turn.

Teachers

The difference in kind between the teachers and offerings cases is that TEACHER is a subclass of EMPLOYEE. Hence:

1. Define a method for creating a new TEACHER object. That method will take a specified COURSE#, OFF#, and EMP# as its parameters. It will then:

   - Use the EMP# value to find the relevant EMPLOYEE object.

   - Convert that EMPLOYEE object into a TEACHER object (since that employee is now additionally a teacher; refer back to Section 22.7 if you need to refresh your memory regarding the representation of superclass/subclass objects in an OO system).

   It will also:

   - Use the COURSE# and OFF# values to find the corresponding OFFERING object for the new TEACHER object.

   - Hence, find "the set of all teachers" for that OFFERING object.

   - Hence, add the OID of the new TEACHER object to the appropriate "set of all teachers."

2. In addition, the set of courses this teacher can teach must be specified somehow and the COURSES instance variable set appropriately in the new TEACHER object. We omit the details of this step here.

3. Invoke the method just defined for each individual teacher in turn.

Relational Analogs

For comparison purposes, we close this section with a reminder of what is involved in populating the *relational* version of the education database. Here, for example, is the SQL code to insert employee E009 into the database:

```
INSERT INTO EMPLOYEE ( EMP#, ENAME, JOB )
       VALUES ('E009', 'Watt', 'Janitor') ;
```

Some further examples:

```
INSERT INTO COURSE ( COURSE#, TITLE )
       VALUES ('C001', 'Database Technology') ;

INSERT INTO OFFERING ( COURSE#, OFF#, ODATE, LOCATION )
       VALUES ('C001', '004', DATE '94/01/18', 'CDG') ;

INSERT INTO ENROLLMENT ( COURSE#, OFF#, EMP#, GRADE )
       VALUES ('C001', '004', 'E009', '') ;
```

And so on. Note in particular that the information the (end) user must provide in order to insert, say, a new enrollment is *exactly the same* in both the relational and the OO case.

23.4 Retrieval Operations

Before getting into details of retrieval operations as such, we make the point (though it should already be obvious) that OPAL—like OO languages in general—is essentially record-at-a-time, not set-at-a-time. Hence, most problems will require some programmer to write a block of procedural code.

We consider a single example—the query "Find all New York offerings of course C001." We suppose for the sake of the example that we have a variable called OOSOAC whose value is the OID of "the set of all courses." Here then is the code:

```
1 | COURSE_C001 , C001_OFFS , C001_NY_OFFS |
2   COURSE_C001
3      := OOSOAC DETECT : [ :CX | 'C001' = CX GET_COURSE# ] .
4   C001_OFFS
5      := COURSE_C001 GET_OFFERINGS .
6   C001_NY_OFFS
7      := C001_OFFS SELECT : [ :OX | 'New York' = OX GET_LOCATION ] .
8 ^ C001_NY_OFFS .
```

Explanation:

■ Line 1 declares three local variables—COURSE_C001, which will be used to hold the OID of course C001; C001_OFFS, which will be used to hold the OID of "the set of all offerings" for course C001; and C001_NY_OFFS, which will be used to hold the OID of the set of OIDs of the required offerings.

■ Lines 2–3 send a message to the object denoted by the OOSOAC variable. The message calls for the builtin **DETECT** method to be applied to that object. The DETECT argument is a block of code of the form

```
[ :x | p(x) ]
```

Here $p(x)$ is a conditional expression involving the variable x, and x is effectively a range variable that ranges over the members of the set to which the DETECT is applied (i.e., the set of COURSE objects, in the example). The result of the DETECT is the OID of the first object encountered in that set that makes $p(x)$ evaluate to *true*—i.e., it is the COURSE object for course C001, in the example. The OID of that COURSE object is then assigned to the variable COURSE_C001.

Note: It is also possible to specify an "escape" argument to DETECT to deal with the case in which $p(x)$ never evaluates to *true*. We omit the details here.

■ Lines 4–5 assign the OID of "the set of all offerings" for course C001 to the variable C001_OFFS.

■ Lines 6–7 are rather similar to lines 2–3: The operation of the builtin **SELECT** method is the same as that of DETECT, except that it returns the OID of the set of OIDs of *all* objects (instead of just the first) that make $p(x)$ evaluate to *true*. In the example, therefore, the effect is to assign the OID of the set of OIDs of New York offerings of course C001 to the variable C001_NY_OFFS.

■ Finally, line 8 returns that OID to the caller (the symbol ^ is used to mean "Display" or "Return result").

Points arising from this example:

1. First, note that the block of code in SELECT and DETECT can involve (at its most complex) a set of simple scalar comparisons all ANDed together—i.e., it is a limited form of restriction condition.

2. The square brackets surrounding the block of code in SELECT and DETECT can be replaced by curly brackets (braces). If curly brackets are used, OPAL will attempt to use an index (if an appropriate index exists) in applying the method. If square brackets are used, it will not.

3. When we say that DETECT returns the OID of the "first" object encountered that makes $p(x)$ evaluate to *true*, we mean, of course, the first according to whatever sequence OPAL uses to search the set (sets have no intrinsic ordering of their own). In our example it makes no difference, because the "first" object that makes the condition *true* is in fact the *only* such.

4. The observant reader will have noticed that we have been using expressions such as "the DETECT method," whereas we pointed out previously that methods have no names in OPAL. Indeed, DETECT and SELECT are not method names (and phraseology such as "the DETECT method" is strictly incorrect). Rather, they are external parameter names for certain builtin (and unnamed) methods. For brevity and simplicity, however, we will continue to talk as if DETECT and SELECT (and other similar items) were indeed method names.

5. The observant reader might also have noticed that we have been using (many

times!) the expression "the NEW method." This usage is in fact *not* incorrect: Methods that take no arguments other than a receiver are an exception to the general OPAL rule that methods are unnamed.

Now, the foregoing simple example does not illustrate the point, but (because of the record-at-a-time level of the OPAL language) many retrieval problems will naturally require the execution of one or more *loops*. OPAL supports loops by means of a special **DO** method. A message that invokes DO is similar in form to one that invokes SELECT or DETECT:

```
object DO : [ :x | block-of-code ]
```

Here *x* ranges over the members of the set denoted by *object,* and *block-of-code* is executed for each such member in turn. Using GET_*v* and SET_*v* methods, that code can retrieve instance variables within the individual objects of the set (or update them, of course, but retrieval is the topic currently under discussion).

IFTRUE and **IFFALSE** methods are also available to support conditional code execution. We omit the details here.

23.5 Update Operations

The OO analog of INSERT has already been discussed in Section 23.3. The OO analogs of UPDATE and DELETE are discussed below.

Update

Updating operations are performed in essentially the same manner as retrieval operations, except that SET_*v* methods are used instead of GET_*v* methods.

Delete

The builtin method REMOVE is used to delete objects. More precisely, it is used to remove the OID of a specified object from a specified collection. When an object reaches a point when there are no remaining references to it—i.e., it cannot be accessed at all—then OPAL deletes it automatically by means of some kind of "garbage collection" process. Here is an example:

```
OID_OF_SET_OF_ALL_EMPS
    REMOVE : DETECT : [ :EX | 'E001' = EX GET_EMP# ] .
```

("remove employee E001 from the set of all employees").

But what if we want to enforce (say) a "DELETE CASCADES" rule?—for example, a rule to the effect that deleting an employee is to cascade and delete (e.g.) all enrollments for that employee as well? The answer, of course, is that we have to implement an appropriate method once again; in other words, we have to write some more procedural code.

Incidentally, it might be thought that the garbage collection approach to deletion does at least implement a kind of "DELETE RESTRICTED" rule, inasmuch as an object is not actually deleted so long as any references to that object exist. However, such is not necessarily the case. For example, OFFERING objects do not include the OID of the corresponding COURSE object, and hence offerings do not "restrict" DELETEs on courses.

(In fact, containment hierarchies tacitly imply a kind of "DELETE CASCADES" rule, *unless* the user chooses either

- to include the parent OID in the child, or
- to include the child OID in some other object elsewhere in the database,

in which case the "containment hierarchy" interpretation no longer makes sense anyway. See the discussion of *inverse variables* in Chapter 24.)

Note finally that REMOVE can be used to emulate a relational DESTROY or SQL DROP operation—e.g., to destroy the ENROLLMENT class object. The details are left as an exercise (highly nontrivial) for the reader.

23.6 Summary

This brings us to the end of our "cradle-to-grave" example. Our example was based on **OPAL,** a dialect of **Smalltalk-80** supported by the **GemStone product**. We began by discussing **data definition** operations, showing how object classes are created in OPAL and pointing out that we typically need both (a) a "base" object class, such as EMPLOYEE, that allows us to create individual object instances, and (b) a "collection" object class, such as ESET, that allows us to gather together sets of such object instances into one or more collections. The reason both are needed, of course, is that the base object class is just a type declaration; thus, some collection object class is required to hold (pointers to) actual object instances.

We then considered in some detail what is involved in **populating** the database, showing how appropriate methods might be written. Those methods were fairly nontrivial, involving as they did a great deal of procedural adjustment of existing objects in order to maintain (OO analogs of) certain referential constraints. (*Note:* We will have more to say regarding referential constraints in the next chapter.) We stressed the point that *all* "insert" operations must be performed via those defined methods, not directly via the builtin NEW method. We also pointed out that user keys are still necessary; in particular, the information the end user has to provide on "insert" is exactly the same in the OO case as it would be in the relational case.

Next, we considered **retrieval** operations. Since OO systems are essentially record-at-a-time, retrieval operations (like everything else) tend to be fairly procedural in nature. However, we did give examples of the OPAL **DETECT** and **SELECT** methods, which are slightly less procedural than some.

Last, we considered **update** operations. "Update" *per se* is very similar to retrieval, except for the use of **SET_*v*** methods instead of **GET_*v*** methods. "Deletion" is done via the **REMOVE** method and a garbage collection process (in OPAL, that is; some

OO systems do support deletion in a more explicit manner). We briefly discussed the implications of this latter fact for foreign key rules such as RESTRICTED and CASCADES.

Miscellaneous Issues

We close this section (and this chapter) with a few miscellaneous remarks regarding OO database operations in general.

- First, consider the following two methods:
  1. Find the courses attended by employee E
  2. Find the employees attending course C

These two methods are clearly inverses of each other, but they must be separately defined—i.e., two separate pieces of procedural code must be written. What is more, of course, matters get combinatorially worse as the number of unknowns increases. For instance, suppose we have courses, employees, and grades. Then each of the following queries will require a different method to be explicitly defined:

  1. Find the grade obtained by employee E on course C.
  2. Find the employees who obtained an "A" on course C.
  3. Find the courses on which employee E obtained an "A".
  4. Find the grades obtained by employee E on all courses.

(etc., etc., etc.). Furthermore, it is not at all clear which object(s) these method(s) should be applied to; to find the grade obtained by employee E on course C, for example, do we send a message to E or to C? (See Chapter 24 for further discussion of this latter point.)

The relational approach, of course, solves all of the foregoing problems very nicely. First, we have the ENROLLMENT relation, which represents all relevant information in a completely symmetric manner:

```
ENROLLMENT ( COURSE#, OFF#, EMP#, GRADE )
```

Each of the queries mentioned above can then be represented by a single relational request against this relation; there is no need to define lots of different methods, with different (in some cases, arbitrarily different) arguments. The details are left as an exercise to the reader. Relational systems thus provide **symmetric exploitation** [4.1]: The user can access any given relation with any combination of attribute values as "knowns" and retrieve the other attribute values as the corresponding "unknowns." OO systems, by contrast, do not provide symmetric exploitation.

- Note that we have said nothing so far in this chapter regarding relational operators such as **join**. What would it mean to join two objects? What class of object would the result be? What would its OID be?

In fact, OO systems typically support **path expressions** instead of join. For example, we might write

```
ENROLL . OFFERING . COURSE . COURSE#
```

to obtain the course number of the course of the offering of the enrollment whose

OID is given in the variable ENROLL. Such an expression is the OO equivalent of a certain relational expression (involving two joins and a projection). But note that such "joins" are therefore limited (a) to predefined paths only, and (b) to many-to-one joins only. Note too that such "joins" do *not* yield new objects, i.e., they simply navigate through the database to locate existing objects.

■ We must not conclude our discussion of OO database operations without considering the question of how much of what we have seen is intrinsic to OO systems in general and how much is due merely to quirks of OPAL specifically. It seems to this writer that—in principle, at least—certain of the complexities we have been examining could have been avoided; for example, the fact that receiver parameters are unnamed and the fact that methods are unnamed both seem to lead to unnecessary complications. But other aspects of "the OO model," such as the heavy emphasis on pointers and the record-at-a-time nature of programming and the fact that objects themselves are unnamed, seem to be more inherent, and some of the complexity we have seen is due to such matters also.

Exercises

23.1 Design an OO version of the suppliers-and-parts database. *Note:* This design will be used as a basis for Exercises 23.2–23.4 below.

23.2 Write a suitable set of OPAL data definition statements for your OO version of the suppliers-and-parts database.

23.3 Sketch the details of the necessary "database populating" methods for your OO version of the suppliers-and-parts database.

23.4 Write OPAL code for the following queries on your OO version of the suppliers-and-parts database:

(a) Get all London suppliers.

(b) Get all red parts.

23.5 Consider the education database once again. Show what is involved in (a) deleting an enrollment, (b) deleting an employee, (c) deleting a course (assuming in every case that the OPAL-style garbage collection process applies). State any assumptions you make regarding such matters as "DELETE CASCADES," "DELETE RESTRICTED," etc.

23.6 Suppose the suppliers-parts-projects database is to be represented by means of a single OO containment hierarchy. How many possible such hierarchies are there? Which one is best?

23.7 Consider a variation on the suppliers-parts-projects database in which, instead of recording that certain suppliers supply certain parts to certain projects, we wish to record only that (a) certain suppliers supply certain parts, (b) certain parts are supplied to certain projects, and (c) certain projects are supplied by certain suppliers. How many possible OO designs are there now (with or without containment hierarchies)?

References and Bibliography

23.1 George Copeland and David Maier. "Making Smalltalk a Database System." Proc. 1984 ACM SIGMOD International Conference on Management of Data, Boston, Mass. (June 1984). Republished in M. Stonebraker (ed.), *Readings in Database Systems*. San Mateo, Calif.: Morgan Kaufmann (1988).

Describes some of the enhancements and changes that were made to Smalltalk-80 [22.6] in order to create GemStone and OPAL.

23.2 Servio Corporation. *GemStone Reference Manual*. Beaverton, Ore. (1990).

Answers to Selected Exercises

23.5 We do not give a detailed answer to this question, but we do make one remark concerning its difficulty. First, let us agree to use the term "delete" as a shorthand to mean "make a candidate for physical deletion" (i.e., by erasing all references to the object in question). Then in order to delete an object X, we must first find all objects Y that include a reference to X; for each such object Y, we must then either delete that object Y, or at least erase the reference in that object Y to the object X (by setting that reference to the special value *nil*). And part of the problem is that it is not possible to tell from the data definition alone exactly which objects include a reference to X, nor even how many of them there are. Consider employees, for example, and the object class ESET. In principle, there could be any number of ESET instances, and any subset of those ESET instances could include a reference to some specific employee.

23.6 There are obviously six possible hierarchies:

```
S contains ( P contains ( J ) )
S contains ( J contains ( P ) )
P contains ( J contains ( S ) )
P contains ( S contains ( J ) )
J contains ( S contains ( P ) )
J contains ( P contains ( S ) )
```

"Which is best?" is unanswerable without additional information, but almost certainly *all* of them are bad.

23.7 There are at least twelve "obvious" containment hierarchy designs. Here are four of them:

```
S contains ( P contains ( J ) )
S contains ( J contains ( P ) )
S contains ( first P then J )
S contains ( first J then P )
```

There are many other candidate designs—for example, an "SP" object that shows directly which suppliers supply which parts and also includes two embedded sets of projects, one for the supplier and one for the part.

There is also a very simple design involving no hierarchies at all, consisting of an "SP" object, a "PJ" object, and a "JS" object.

24 | Additional OO Concepts

24.1 Introduction

In this chapter we take a brief look at a somewhat mixed bag of issues. The issues in question are all part of what is usually thought of as the general subject of OO systems, though in fact—despite the overall title of this chapter—every one of those issues is actually quite independent of whether the system is object-oriented or not; there is no reason, for example, why a database programming language should not be used with a relational system (see, e.g., reference [24.2]). The issues are:

- Database programming languages
- Versioning
- Transaction management
- Schema evolution
- Performance considerations

We also consider some more traditional aspects of database management and see how they look in an OO context. Specifically, we examine:

- "Relationships" (i.e., referential integrity)
- General integrity constraints
- "Methods that span classes" (i.e., multi-argument functions)
- *Ad hoc* query

plus a few miscellaneous items. Our discussions will lead to a number of important questions regarding OO systems.

24.2 The Issues

Database Programming Languages

The OPAL examples in the previous chapter illustrate the point that OO systems typically do not employ the *embedded database language* approach found in most (SQL) relational products today. Instead, the same **integrated language** is used for both database operations and nondatabase operations. To use the terminology of Chapter 2, the host language and the database language are *tightly coupled* in OO systems (in fact, of course, the two languages are one and the same).

Now, it is undeniable that there are many advantages to such an approach [24.2]. One important one is the improved type checking that becomes possible, as discussed in Chapter 19. And reference [22.12] argues that the following is another:

> "With a single unified language, there is no *impedance mismatch* between a proce-dural programming language and an embedded DML with declarative semantics."

The term **impedance mismatch** refers to the difference in level between today's typi-cal programming languages, which are *record-at-a-time,* and relational languages such as SQL which are *set*-at-a-time. And it is true that this difference in level does give rise to certain practical problems in relational products. However, the solution to those problems is *not* to bring the database language down to the record-at-a-time level (which is what OO systems do)!—it is to introduce set-at-a-time facilities into pro-gramming languages instead. The fact that OO languages are record-at-a-time is a throwback to the days of prerelational systems such as IMS and IDMS.

To pursue this latter point a moment longer: It is indeed the case that most existing OO languages are quite procedural or "3GL" in nature. As a consequence, all of the relational set-level advantages are lost; in particular, the system's ability to optimize user requests is severely undermined, which means that—as in prerelational systems—performance issues are largely left to some human user (the application programmer or the DBA). What is more, (a) most installations currently use several distinct host lan-guages anyway, not a "single language" (unified or otherwise); (b) in an OO system, that "single unified language" is likely to be OPAL, C++, or some other OO language that is unfamiliar to most installations.

As an aside, we remark that although many OO languages have been defined, the two most commonly seen in the marketplace are indeed OPAL (or some other dialect of Smalltalk) and C++. C++ in particular [24.6,24.10] is supported by most commercial products and looks like becoming a *de facto* standard (despite the fact that it is not very "OO-pure"). Efforts are also under way to define an official standard version of C++.

Note: Our discussions in this subsection have been concerned specifically with *programming* languages, not with query languages. Indeed, as mentioned in Chapter 22, the idea of *ad hoc* query is somewhat at odds with the "pure" OO idea of object encapsulation; however, most OO systems do provide some kind of query language (usually a derivative of SQL, with a name like **"Object SQL"** or **"OSQL,"** though the reader is cautioned that such languages often do not look much like conventional SQL). Another point of difference *vis-à-vis* relational systems, therefore, is that OO systems typically use two different languages, one for application programming and one for interactive query; thus, they typically do not support the *dual-mode principle* (see Chapter 8, Section 8.8).

We will consider the question of *ad hoc* query further in Section 24.3.

Versioning

Many applications need the concept of multiple **versions** of a given object; examples include software development, hardware design, document creation, and so forth (see, e.g., references [24.4,24.8-24.9]). And some OO systems support this concept directly. Such support typically includes:

■   The ability to create a new version of a given object, typically by **checking out** a copy of the object and moving it from the database to the user's private workstation, where it can be kept and modified over a possibly extended period of time (e.g., hours or days)

■   The ability to establish a given object version as the current database version, typically by **checking it in** and moving it from the user's workstation back to the database (which might in turn require some kind of mechanism for **merging** distinct versions)

■   The ability to **delete** (and perhaps **archive**) obsolete versions

■   The ability to interrogate the **version history** of a given object

Note that—as Fig. 24.1 suggests—version histories are not necessarily linear (version V.2 in that figure *branches* into two distinct versions V.3a and V.3b, which are subsequently *merged* to produce version V.4).

Next, because objects are typically interrelated in various ways, the concept of versioning leads to the concept of *configurations*. A **configuration** is a collection of mutually consistent versions of interrelated objects. Configuration support typically includes:

■   The ability to **copy** an object version from one configuration to another (e.g., from an "old" configuration to a "new" one)

■   The ability to **move** an object version from one configuration to another (i.e., to add it to the "new" configuration and remove it from the "old" one)

Internally, such operations basically involve a lot of pointer juggling—but there are major implications (beyond the scope of this book) for language syntax and semantics in general and *ad hoc* query in particular.

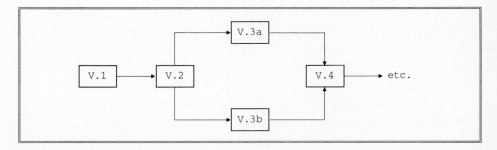

FIG. 24.1 Typical version history

Transaction Management

OO applications often involve complex processing requirements for which the classical transaction management controls described in Chapters 13 and 14 are not well suited. The basic problem is that (as suggested under "Versioning" above) complex transactions might last for hours or days, instead of for a few milliseconds at most as in traditional systems. As a consequence:

1. Rolling back a transaction all the way to the beginning might cause the loss of an unacceptably large amount of work

2. The use of conventional locking might cause unacceptably long delays (waiting for locks to be released)

Point 1 here implies the need to be able to perform *partial* rollbacks; point 2 implies the need for some *nonlocking* concurrency control mechanism. *Long transactions* and *nested transactions* both address these requirements somewhat. We do not discuss these concepts in detail here, but content ourselves with the following observations:

- **Long transactions:** Here the concept of **savepoints** [13.10] and the concept of **sagas** [13.8] are both relevant, since both effectively provide some kind of partial rollback capability. Furthermore, **multiversion** concurrency control [14.1] also looks attractive (especially if the system supports versioning anyway as discussed above), because it implies among other things that:

  - Reads are never delayed (in particular, they are not delayed by any concurrent long transaction)

  - Reads never delay updates (in particular, they do not delay any concurrent long transaction)

  - It is never necessary to roll back a read-only transaction

  - Deadlock is possible only between update transactions

- **Nested transactions:** The nested transaction idea can be thought of as a generalization of savepoints [13.10]. Savepoints allow a transaction to be organized as a sequence of actions that can be rolled back individually; nesting, by contrast, allows a transaction to be organized (recursively) as a *hierarchy* of such actions (see Fig. 24.2). In other words:

  - BEGIN TRANSACTION is extended to support subtransactions (i.e., if BEGIN is issued when a transaction is already running, it starts a *child* transaction)

  - COMMIT TRANSACTION "commits" but only within the *parent scope* (if this transaction is a child)

  - ROLLBACK TRANSACTION undoes work back to the start of this particular subtransaction (including child, grandchild, etc., transactions)

See the answer to Exercise 13.2 in Chapter 13 for further discussion.

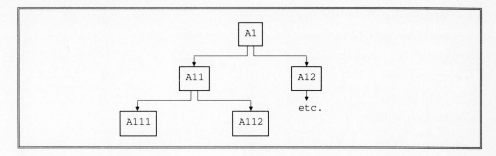

FIG. 24.2 Typical nested transaction

Schema Evolution

Traditional database products typically support only rather simple changes to an existing schema (e.g., the addition of a new attribute to an existing base relation). However, some applications require more sophisticated schema change support, and some OO prototypes have investigated this problem in depth. Note, incidentally, that the problem is actually more complex in an OO environment, because the schema is more complex.

The following taxonomy of possible schema changes is based on one given in a paper on the OO prototype ORION [24.3]:

- Changes to an object class
  1. Instance variable changes
     - add instance variable
     - delete instance variable
     - rename instance variable
     - change instance variable default value
     - change instance variable data type
     - change instance variable inheritance source
  2. Method changes
     - add method
     - delete method
     - rename method
     - change method internal code
     - change method inheritance source
- Changes to the class hierarchy (assuming multiple inheritance)
  - add class *A* to superclass list for class *B*
  - delete class *A* from superclass list for class *B*

- Changes to the overall schema
  - add class (anywhere)
  - delete class (anywhere)
  - rename class
  - partition class
  - coalesce classes

It is not clear how much transparency can be achieved with respect to the foregoing changes, however, especially since view support is typically not included in "the OO model" (see Section 24.3). In fact, the possibility of schema evolution implies a significant problem for OO systems, owing to their record-at-a-time nature. As reference [25.10] puts it: "If the number of indexes changes or the data is reorganized to be differently clustered [see the next subsection below], there is no way for [methods] to automatically take advantage of such changes."

Performance Considerations

Raw performance is one of the biggest objectives of all for OO systems. To quote Cattell [22.2]: "An order-of-magnitude performance difference can effectively constitute a *functional* difference, because it is not possible to use the system at all if performance is too far below requirements" (slightly paraphrased).

Many factors are relevant to the performance issue. Here are a few of them:

- **Clustering:** As we saw in Chapter 18, physical clustering of logically related data on the disk is one of the most important performance factors of all. OO systems typically use the logical information from the schema (regarding type hierarchies, containment hierarchies, or other explicitly declared interobject relationships) as a hint as to how the data should be physically clustered. Alternatively (and preferably), the DBA might be given some more explicit and direct control.

- **Caching:** As suggested under "Versioning" above, OO systems are typically used in a client/server environment, in which users "check out" data from the database and bring it down to their workstation and keep it there for an extended period of time. Caching logically related data at the client site obviously makes sense in such an environment.

- **Swizzling:** The term "swizzling" refers to the process of replacing OID-style pointers by main memory addresses when objects are read into memory (and *vice versa* when the objects are written back to the database). The advantages for applications that process "complex objects" and thus require extensive pointer chasing are obvious.

Reference [22.2] discusses a benchmark called OO1 for measuring system performance on a bill-of-materials database (see also reference [24.5]). The benchmark involves:

1. Random retrieval of 1000 parts, applying a user-defined function to each
2. Random insertion of 1000 parts

3. Random part explosion (up to 7 levels), applying a user-defined function to every part encountered

According to reference [22.2], comparison of an (unspecified) OO product with an (unspecified) state-of-the-art relational product showed up to two orders of magnitude difference in favor of OO—especially on "warm" accesses (after the cache had been populated). However, reference [22.2] is also careful to say that "The differences . . . should *not* be attributed to a difference between the relational and OO models. . . . There is reason to believe that most of the differences can be attributed to [implementation matters]." This disclaimer is supported by the fact that the differences were much smaller when the database was "large" (i.e., when it was no longer possible to accommodate the entire database in the cache).

24.3   Some Questions

As promised in the introduction, we now turn our attention to some aspects of database management that are usually regarded as traditional, see how they look in an OO context, and use them as a basis for raising a number of questions regarding OO technology. The aspects in question are as follows:

- Relationships
- Integrity
- Methods that span classes
- *Ad hoc* query
- Miscellaneous

Relationships

OO products and the OO literature typically use the term "relationships" to refer specifically to those relationships that would be represented by foreign keys in a relational database. But they distinguish:

1. Subclass-to-superclass ("ISA") relationships
2. One-to-many relationships
3. Many-to-many relationships

We discuss each case in turn.

1. Subclass-to-superclass relationships are represented by the **class hierarchy**—e.g.,

   ```
   ... RECTANGLE ISA ( POLYGON ) ...
   ```

   (to use the hypothetical syntax of Chapter 22).

2. One-to-many relationships are represented *either* by a **containment hierarchy**—e.g.,

   ```
   ... DEPT ... ( ... EMPS REF ( SET ( REF ( EMP ) ) ) ) ...
   ```

   or by a mechanism called "inverse variables" (see below).

3. Many-to-many relationships are represented *either* by **object sharing**—e.g., supplier and part objects might both "contain" (and thus share) shipment objects—*or* by "inverse variables" again.

Inverse variables: Consider departments and employees once again. Instead of adopting a containment hierarchy representation, we might decide to define two separate object classes (rather as in a relational database), *and* to include both (a) an EMPS instance variable in each DEPT, corresponding to the set of employees in the department, and (b) an EDEPT instance variable (say) in each EMP, corresponding to the department for this employee:

```
... DEPT ... ( ... EMPS REF ( SET ( REF ( EMP ) ) )
                                      INVERSE EMP.EDEPT ) ...
... EMP  ... ( ... EDEPT REF ( DEPT ) INVERSE DEPT.EMPS ) ...
```

The *reference* instance variable EDEPT and the *references set* instance variable EMPS are said to be **inverses** of each other. Inverse variables obviously need to be kept mutually consistent; this is one aspect of *referential integrity* (as that concept applies to OO systems), and we will return to it in just a moment.

The foregoing example illustrates the one-to-many case. Here is an example of the many-to-many case:

```
... S ... ( ... PARTS REF ( SET ( REF ( P ) ) )
                                   INVERSE P.SUPPS ) ...
... P ... ( ... SUPPS REF ( SET ( REF ( S ) ) )
                                   INVERSE S.PARTS ) ...
```

Here the inverse variables are both *reference set* variables.

One obvious question that arises is the following: How does OO deal with relationships that involve more than two object classes—e.g., suppliers, parts, and projects? The best (i.e., most symmetric) answer to this question, of course, is that an "SPJ" object class is created, in which each SPJ object has an "inverse variables" relationship with the appropriate supplier, the appropriate part, and the appropriate project. Given that creating a new object class is apparently the best approach for "relationships" of degree greater than two, the question arises as to why "relationships" of degree two are not treated in the same way.

Also—regarding inverse variables specifically—why is it necessary to introduce the asymmetry, the directionality, and two different names for what is essentially one thing? For example, the OO analogs of the two relational expressions

```
SP.P# WHERE SP.S# = 'S1'
SP.S# WHERE SP.P# = 'P1'
```

look something like this:

```
S.PARTS.P# WHERE S.S# = 'S1'
P.SUPPS.S# WHERE P.P# = 'P1'
```

(hypothetical syntax, deliberately chosen to avoid irrelevant distinctions).

Referential integrity: As promised, we now take a slightly closer look at OO support for referential integrity (frequently claimed as a strength of OO systems, incidentally).

Various levels of support are possible. The following classification scheme is taken from Cattell [22.2]:

- **No system support:** Referential integrity is the responsibility of the user or user-written methods (just as it was in the original SQL standard, incidentally).

- **Reference validation:** The system checks that all references are to objects of the correct type; however, object deletion might not be allowed (instead, objects might be "garbage collected" when there are no remaining references to them, as in OPAL). As explained in Chapter 23, this level of support is roughly equivalent (but only roughly) to a "DELETE CASCADES" rule for nonshared subobjects within a containment hierarchy and to a "DELETE RESTRICTED" rule for other objects.

- **System maintenance:** Here the system keeps all references up to date automatically (e.g., by setting references to deleted objects to *nil*). This rule is somewhat akin to a "DELETE NULLIFIES" rule in a relational system.

- **"Custom semantics":** "DELETE CASCADES" (outside of the containment hierarchy) might be an example of "custom semantics." Such cases are typically not supported by OO systems at the time of writing, and must therefore be handled by appropriate methods—in other words, by user-written procedural code.

Integrity

We now turn to **general integrity constraints**. Here is an example (taken from Section 16.7): "Suppliers with status less than 20 must not supply any part in a quantity greater than 500." Using the integrity language developed in Chapter 16, this constraint might be expressed as follows in a relational system:

```
CREATE INTEGRITY RULE C95
      IF S.STATUS < 20 AND S.S# = SP.S#
      THEN SP.QTY ≤ 500 ;
```

In an OO system, by contrast, this constraint will almost certainly have to be enforced by *procedural code* (though reference [24.7] does describe a prototype implementation of declarative integrity constraints in an OO system). Such procedural code will have to be included in at least all of the following:

- Method for creating a shipment
- Method for changing a shipment quantity
- Method for changing a supplier status
- Method for assigning a shipment to a different supplier

Points and questions arising:

1. We have obviously lost the possibility of the system determining for itself when to do the integrity checking.

2. How do we ensure that all necessary methods include all necessary enforcement code?

3. How do we prevent the user from (e.g.) bypassing the "create shipment" method

and using the builtin method NEW directly on the shipment object class (thereby bypassing the integrity check)?

4. How do we ensure uniformity of error messages:

   ▪ across all methods involved in enforcing "the same" constraint?

   ▪ across all constraints (e.g., all referential constraints) that bear a strong family resemblance?

5. If the constraint changes, how do we find all methods that need to be rewritten?

6. How do we ensure that the enforcement code is correct?

7. How do we do deferred (commit-time) integrity checking?

8. How do we query the system to find all constraints that apply to a given object or combination of objects?

9. Will the constraints be enforced during load and other utility processing?

10. What about semantic optimization (i.e., using integrity constraints to simplify queries, as discussed in Chapter 18)?

And what are the implications of all of the above for productivity, both during application creation and subsequent application maintenance?

(As a practical matter, incidentally, the SQL/92 standard [8.1] does include declarative support for integrity constraints, and DBMS products, OO or otherwise, are going to have to support that standard. The implications for OO systems are not clear.)

A note on functional dependencies: Functional dependencies (FDs) are a special kind of integrity constraint, and we have seen elsewhere in this book that the system needs to know about FDs in order to behave in a variety of "intelligent" ways. But OO systems provide no way of declaring FDs. In fact, some writers seem to regard such a lack almost as a *virtue.* As we know, FDs are important for database design; however, reference [22.12] says:

> "Complex [data] can be represented directly [in an OO system], without the need to normalize . . ."

Now, it might be true that OO eliminates the "need to normalize," in the sense that it directly supports unnormalized objects (i.e., hierarchies). However, it does not follow that OO automatically eliminates the problems that unnormalized objects cause! The point cannot be overemphasized that "the need to normalize" is not something that is peculiar to relational systems, i.e., something that can be ignored if the system is not relational. On the contrary, the problems that normalization solves are *inherent* problems, and do not go away just because the data structure happens to be something other than relational.

Methods That Span Classes

Consider the education database from Chapter 23 and the query "Find the grade obtained by employee *E* on course *C*" (where *E* and *C* are parameters). Let us suppose a method *M* has been written to implement this query. Is *M* part of the EMPLOYEE object class or the COURSE object class? Whichever it is, why? How does the user know? What are the implications?

To state matters differently: The idea of a function or method being bundled in with an object class works fine *so long as* the function in question takes just one argument. But as soon as two or more arguments are involved, a degree of arbitrariness inevitably creeps in. In fact, some methods—NEW is an example—are bundled, not with the object class of one of their parameters, but rather with that of their *result,* which seems to introduce yet another element of arbitrariness.

So let us step back for a moment. Why are methods bundled in with an object class anyway? The answer is that they need *privileged access*—access, that is, to the internal representation (i.e., private instance variables) of objects of the class in question. (Access to other objects, by contrast, is by means of the usual GET and SET methods.)

But we already have a mechanism for dealing with privileged access, namely the **security** mechanism.* Would it not be better to unbundle methods from object classes, and instead use the security mechanism to control which methods are allowed to access the internals of which objects? Such an approach would have the advantages that:

- Methods could be permitted to access the internals of any number of objects instead of being limited to just one.

- The asymmetry, arbitrariness, and awkwardness inherent in the bundling scheme would be eliminated.

- In particular, the *ad hoc* distinction between private and protected instance variables would be unnecessary.

In other words, it is the opinion of this writer that the bundling of methods with object classes should not be regarded as a fundamental component of "the OO model." Please note that this is not a criticism of methods as such, only of the bundling aspect of such methods.

Ad Hoc Query

We have suggested a couple of times already that OO systems might have some difficulty over *ad hoc* query. As we put it in Chapter 22, ". . . if it is really true that predefined methods are the only way to manipulate objects, then *ad hoc* query is impossible!—unless objects are designed in accordance with a certain very specific discipline." For example, if the only methods defined for DEPT objects are HIRE_EMP, FIRE_EMP, and CUT_BUDGET, then even a query as simple as "Who is the manager of the programming department?" cannot be handled.

Careful consideration of examples such as the foregoing leads to the following conclusion. If we are indeed to be able to permit *ad hoc* queries against objects of some given class, then we must do the following two things:

---

* Note that we are talking about OO *database* systems specifically here. OO programming systems typically did not have a security mechanism, and this historical lack probably accounts for the current situation.

1. Define and maintain a "collection" that is the set of all currently existing objects of that class. This collection will serve as a defining scope for queries, much as base relations do in a relational system.

2. Define the public interface for that class in such a way as to expose *one candidate representation* of the objects to the user.

For example, consider the classes POINT and LINESEG (line segment). If we define GET methods for the start and end points of line segments, and GET methods for the *x*- and *y*-coordinates of points—and if we permit references to such methods to be nested within scalar expressions in arbitrary ways—and if we do indeed define and maintain a collection that is the set of all line segments, and another collection that is the set of all points—then we can indeed define an *ad hoc* query language that will permit the user to ask arbitrary unplanned queries against objects of those classes. For example:

■ Find all line segments starting at the origin (0,0)

■ Find all line segments of length one unit

■ Find the midpoint of a specified line segment

(and so on). *Note very carefully that the fact that line segments might internally be represented by MIDPOINT, LENGTH, and SLOPE, and points by polar coordinates R and THETA, is neither here nor there.*
Points arising:

1. GET methods are sufficient for query *per se,* of course. SET methods are needed to permit arbitrary updates.

2. There is nothing wrong with the idea of exposing more than one candidate representation for a given class. In the case of class POINT, for example, we could define methods GET_x and GET_y *and* methods GET_r and GET_θ, thereby making queries that are expressed in terms of polar coordinates just as easy to formulate as ones expressed in terms of Cartesian coordinates. In effect, we would be telling the user that each point has an x property and a y property and an r property and a θ property. However, we could not pretend that these properties were all independent of one another; we would have to explain that, e.g., changing the value of x or y will have the side-effect of changing both r and θ, in general. (Furthermore, we would have to explain the exact nature of the relationship between (x,y) and (r,θ), so that the details of those side-effects would be explicable and predictable.)

Note: We do not mean to suggest by the foregoing that the various GET and SET methods should be the *only* methods defined for a given class. At the very least, there needs to be an appropriate constructor function (NEW or some analog thereof) to create new instances of the class, also a corresponding "destructor" function to destroy such instances again. In addition, there almost certainly need to be methods for comparing class instances, assigning class instances, etc.

Miscellaneous

We close this section with some comments and questions regarding a few miscellaneous topics: views, the catalog, missing information, and closure.

- **Views:** What is the analog of views in an OO system?

  Some OO systems do support **derived** (public) **instance variables**—e.g., the instance variable AGE might be derived by subtracting the value of the instance variable BIRTHDATE from the current date—but such a capability falls far short of a full view mechanism. *Note:* This question is related to the question of derived objects in general (see Chapter 25). See also reference [24.1], which describes some research ideas for view support in an OO system.

- **The catalog:** Where is the catalog in an OO system? What does it look like? Are there any standards?

  Incidentally, this is as good a place as any to point out that there is really a **difference in kind** between an OO DBMS and a relational DBMS. A relational DBMS comes *ready for use:* As soon as the system is installed, users can start building databases, writing applications, running queries, and so on. An OO DBMS, by contrast, is best thought of as a kind of *DBMS construction kit:* It provides a set of building blocks—object library maintenance tools, method compilers, etc.—that can be used by technical staff (i.e., database professionals) to *construct* a DBMS in the more familiar sense of the term. In particular, those database professionals will have to construct an appropriate *catalog* for the objects and methods they create. What is more, that constructed DBMS will be *application-specific:* It might, for example, be tailored for a certain set of CAD/CAM applications, but be essentially useless for, e.g., medical applications.

- **Missing information:** Missing information is far from being a fully solved problem in relational systems (see Chapter 20). But OO systems mostly seem to ignore the problem altogether; at best, the evidence suggests that the OO community lags some way behind the relational community in this regard. For example: "Is *nil* a member of every [class]?" [22.12].

- **Closure:** What is the OO analog of the relational closure property? *Note:* This question is actually an extremely important one. We will revisit it in Chapter 25.

24.4 Summary

In this chapter we have concerned ourselves with the following major topics.

- *Database programming languages:* We explained the **impedance mismatch** problem, and claimed that the solution to that problem was not to bring the database language down to the record-at-a-time level, but rather to raise the programming language to the set-at-a-time level. Indeed, the fact that OO languages are so procedural is a severe disadvantage of those languages; in particular, it seriously undermines optimizability.

■ *Versioning:* We briefly described the ideas of **version** and **configuration** support and the basic notions of **checking out** database objects and subsequently **checking in** those objects again.

■ *Transaction management:* OO transactions might last for hours or days, instead of just a few milliseconds. As a result, support for **long** and **nested transactions** becomes desirable. We briefly considered the use of **multiversion concurrency control** in this connection and summarized some of its advantages.

■ *Schema evolution:* We presented a taxonomy of possible schema changes, and pointed out in passing that the schema evolution problem is actually more complex for an OO system, because (a) the schema itself is more complex, (b) "the OO model" typically does not include any view support, and (c) OO code is typically record-at-a-time.

■ *Performance considerations:* We stressed the point that performance is one of the biggest objectives of all for OO systems, and briefly considered certain performance-related issues, *viz.* **clustering, caching,** and **pointer swizzling**. We also mentioned the **OO1 benchmark**.

■ *Relationships:* The term "relationships" is typically used in OO contexts to refer specifically to the OO analog of foreign key relationships in the relational world. However, **subclass-to-superclass** relationships, **one-to-many** relationships, and **many-to-many** relationships are typically all treated differently. In particular, we discussed the use of **inverse variables** and various possible **levels** of referential integrity support—none at all, "reference validation," system maintenance, and "custom semantics." Where possible, we related these cases to their relational analogs.

■ *Integrity:* We were very critical of the fact that OO systems typically handle integrity constraints procedurally (via methods), not declaratively.

■ *Methods that span classes:* We were also critical of the fact that OO systems bundle methods in with object classes, especially as the choice of which particular class the method is to be bundled with is often arbitrary. We suggested that methods in fact *not* be so bundled, and that suitable extensions to the system's **security** mechanism would be a preferable means of controlling which methods have access to the internals of which objects.

■ *Ad hoc query:* We proposed a particular discipline that would allow OO systems to provide full *ad hoc* query support. The key component of that discipline consisted in exposing *one candidate representation* of objects to the user (through appropriate GET methods).

■ *Miscellaneous:* Finally, we offered a few comments regarding **views,** the **catalog, missing information,** and **closure**. In particular, we pointed out that there is really a *difference in kind* between an OO DBMS and a relational DBMS, inasmuch as a relational DBMS comes ready for use, whereas an OO DBMS, by contrast, is more of a *construction kit* for building application-specific DBMSs.

To pursue this last point a little further: We could speculate that the difference in kind referred to reflects a difference in origins between the two disciplines. It appears to this writer that OO database technology most likely grew out of a desire on the part of OO application programmers—for a variety of application-specific reasons—to keep their application-specific objects in persistent memory. That "persistent memory" could then certainly be regarded as a database, but (a) it was indeed application-specific, and as a consequence (b) there was little perceived need to be able to perform *ad hoc* queries against it. Thus, the notions that

1. Such a database might be shared among several applications, and hence that
2. The data should be subject to certain application-independent integrity constraints, and also that
3. The data should likewise be subject to certain security constraints,

all surfaced later, after the basic idea of storing objects in a database was first conceived, and thus all constitute "add-ons" to the original "OO model."

Now, the foregoing speculations might be a little wide of the mark, but they do seem to this writer to explain some of the differences in emphasis that can be observed in OO database systems *vis-à-vis* traditional database systems.

Exercises

24.1 What do you understand by the terms *version* and *configuration?*

24.2 Why are *long* transaction support and *nested* transaction support desirable?

24.3 Sketch an implementation mechanism for multiversion concurrency control.

24.4 Consider the performance factors discussed briefly in Section 24.2. Are any of them truly OO-specific? Justify your answer.

24.5 OO systems typically support integrity constraints in a *procedural* fashion, via methods; the main exception is that *referential* constraints are typically supported (at least in part) *declaratively*. What are the advantages of procedural support? Why do you think referential constraints are handled differently?

24.6 Explain the concept of *inverse variables*.

24.7 Consider the *schema evolution* taxonomy presented in Section 24.2. Which items in that taxonomy have counterparts in a relational system? What are those counterparts?

24.8 What are the implications of schema evolution for existing data?

24.9 Investigate any OO system that might be available to you. What programming language does that system support? Does it support a query language? If so, what is it? In your opinion, is it more or less powerful than conventional SQL? Does the system support versioning and configurations? If so, what is involved on the part of the user in managing versions and in interrogating version histories? Does the system support long or nested transactions? Does the system have any schema evolution capabilities? What does the catalog look like? How does the user interrogate the catalog? Is there any view support? If so, how extensive is it? (e.g., what about view updating?) How is missing information handled?

References and Bibliography

See also the references in Chapters 22 and 23.

24.1 Serge Abiteboul and Anthony Bonner. "Objects and Views." Proc. ACM International Conference on Management of Data, Denver, Colo. (May 1991).

Proposes a view mechanism for OO systems. The proposal appears to be the first to take *behavior* (methods) into account.

24.2 Malcolm P. Atkinson and O. Peter Buneman. "Types and Persistence in Database Programming Languages." *ACM Comp. Surv. 19,* No. 2 (June 1987).

This paper is recommended as the best starting point for reading in the area of database programming languages in general.

24.3 J. Banerjee *et al.* "Data Model Issues for Object-Oriented Applications." *ACM TOOIS (Transactions on Office Information Systems) 5,* No. 1 (March 1987). Republished in M. Stonebraker (ed.), *Readings in Database Systems.* San Mateo, Calif.: Morgan Kaufmann (1988). Also republished in reference [22.16].

24.4 Anders Björnerstedt and Christer Hultén. "Version Control in an Object-Oriented Architecture." In reference [22.9].

24.5 R. G. G. Cattell and J. Skeen. "Object Operations Benchmark." *ACM TODS 17,* No. 1 (March 1992).

24.6 Margaret A. Ellis and Bjarne Stroustrup. *The Annotated C++ Reference Manual.* Reading, Mass.: Addison-Wesley (1990).

24.7 H. V. Jagadish and Xiaolei Qian. "Integrity Maintenance in an Object-Oriented Database." Proc. 18th International Conference on Very Large Data Bases, Vancouver, Canada (August 1992).

Proposes a declarative integrity mechanism for OO systems, showing how an integrity constraints compiler can incorporate the necessary integrity checking code into methods for the appropriate object classes.

24.8 R. H. Katz and E. Chang. "Managing Change in a Computer-Aided Design Database." Proc. 13th International Conference on Very Large Data Bases, Brighton, UK (September 1987).

24.9 John F. Roddick. "Schema Evolution in Database Systems—An Annotated Bibliography." *ACM SIGMOD Record 21,* No. 4 (December 1992).

24.10 Bjarne Stroustrup. *The C++ Programming Language.* Reading, Mass.: Addison-Wesley (1986).

Answers to Selected Exercises

24.3 The following brief description is taken from reference [21.14]. First of all, the system must keep:

1. For each data object, a stack of committed versions (each stack entry giving a value for the object and the ID of the transaction that established that value; i.e., each stack entry essentially consists of a pointer to the relevant entry in the log). The stack is in reverse chronological sequence, with the most recent entry being on the top.

2. A list of transaction IDs for all committed transactions (the *commit list*).

When a transaction starts executing, the system gives it a private copy of the commit list.

Read operations on an object are directed to the most recent version of the object produced by a transaction on that private list. Update operations, by contrast, are directed to the actual current data object (update/update conflict testing is thus still necessary). When the transaction commits, the system updates the commit list and the data object version stacks appropriately.

24.4 The performance factors discussed were *clustering, caching,* and *pointer swizzling.* All of these techniques are applicable to any system that provides a reasonable level of data independence; they are thus not truly "OO-specific." In fact, the idea of using the logical database definition to decide what physical clustering to use, as some OO systems do, could be seen as potentially *undermining* data independence. *Note:* It should be pointed out too that another very important performance factor, namely **optimization,** typically does *not* apply to OO systems.

24.5 It is the opinion of this writer that declarative support, if feasible, is *always* better than procedural support (for everything, not just for integrity constraints). In a nutshell, declarative support means that the system does the work instead of the user. This is why relational systems support declarative queries, declarative view definitions, declarative cursor definitions (see Chapter 8), declarative integrity constraints, and so on.

25 | Toward an OO/Relational Rapprochement

25.1 Introduction

We have now examined all of the major aspects of OO systems. We began by claiming (in Chapter 22) that today's relational products are inadequate in a variety of ways, and we gave an example ("Find all rectangles that overlap the unit square") in support of that claim. And we went on to say that some of the new features that seem to be needed in DBMSs have existed for many years in OO programming languages, and hence the idea of **OO database systems** is a natural one to investigate. *BUT*—and it is a very big "but"—it does not follow that OO database systems can or will replace relational systems. On the contrary, we should be looking for a *rapprochement* between the two technologies—that is, a way of marrying the two technologies together, so as to get the best of both worlds. The purpose of this final chapter is to investigate the possibility of such a rapprochement.

Now, it is this writer's strong opinion that any such rapprochement should be firmly founded on the relational model (which is after all the foundation of modern database technology in general, as explained in Part II of this book). That is, what we want is for relational systems to evolve to incorporate the features—or, at least, the good features—of OO. We do *not* want to discard relational systems entirely, nor do we want two totally disparate systems, relational and OO, existing side by side as equals but (perhaps) competitors. And this opinion is shared by many other writers, including in particular the authors of the "Third Generation Database System Manifesto" [25.10], who state categorically that **third-generation DBMSs must subsume second-generation DBMSs**—where "second-generation DBMSs" basically means relational systems, and "third generation DBMSs" means whatever comes next. The opinion is apparently *not* shared, however, by some of the early OO products, nor by certain OO researchers. Here, for example, is a typical quote:

"Computer science has seen many generations of data management, starting with indexed files, and later, network and hierarchical DBMSs ... [and] more recently relational DBMSs ... Now, we are on the verge of another generation of database systems . . . [that] provide *object management*, [supporting] much more complex kinds of data" [25.4].

Here the writer is clearly suggesting that just as relational systems displaced the older hierarchic and network systems, so OO systems will displace relational systems in exactly the same kind of way.

The reason we disagree with this position is that (to quote reference [3.2]) *relational really is different*. It is different because it is not *ad hoc*. The older, prerelational systems were *ad hoc;* they might have provided solutions to certain important problems of their day, but they did not rest on any solid theoretical foundation.* Unfortunately, relational advocates—this writer included—did themselves a major disservice in the early days when they argued the relative merits of relational and prerelational systems; such arguments were necessary at the time, of course, but they had the unlooked-for effect of reinforcing the idea that relational and prerelational DBMSs were essentially the same kind of thing. And this mistaken idea in turn supports the position of the quotation above from reference [25.4]—to wit, that OO is to relations as relations were to hierarchies and networks.

In what follows, therefore, we take it as an axiom that what we want to do is enhance relational systems to incorporate the good features (but not the bad features!) of OO. To repeat, we do *not* want to discard relational systems entirely. It would be a great pity to walk away from 25 years of solid relational research and development.

The plan of the chapter is as follows. Section 25.2 reviews the features of OO, in an attempt to separate the good from the bad. Sections 25.3 and 25.4 then discuss ways in which the good features might be added to relational systems; Section 25.3 concentrates on domains and Section 25.4 on relations *per se*. Section 25.5 describes the benefits of a true rapprochement. Section 25.6 offers a summary.

25.2 A Review of "the OO Model"

Below is a summary of the principal features of "the OO model," with a subjective assessment as to which features are essential, which are "nice to have" but not essential, which are bad, etc.

■ **Objects:** Objects themselves, both *mutable* (variables) and *immutable* (values), are clearly essential.

---

* What about OO? Is OO *ad hoc?* The following quote from "The Object-Oriented Database System Manifesto" [25.1] is interesting in this regard: "With respect to the specification of the system, we are taking a Darwinian approach: We hope that, out of the set of experimental prototypes being built, a fit [object-oriented] model will emerge. We also hope that viable implementation technology for that model will evolve simultaneously."

- **Object IDs:** Unnecessary, and in fact undesirable (see the "Conclusion" subsection at the end of Section 25.3).

- **Object classes** (meaning **types**): Essential. The associated notion of a *constructor function*—which among other things effectively provides a way of writing a *literal value* of the relevant type—is essential too.

- **Encapsulation:** See the subsection "A note on encapsulation" below.

- **Instance variables:** First of all, *private* and *protected* instance variables are by definition merely implementation matters and are thus not relevant to the definition of an abstract, user-oriented model, which is what we are concerned with here. Second, *public* instance variables do not exist in a pure OO system and are thus also not relevant. Third, *derived* instance variables are a special case of public instance variables and are thus *a fortiori* irrelevant also. We conclude that instance variables can be ignored; objects should be manipulable solely by methods.

- **Containment hierarchy:** We have already explained in Chapter 22 that in our opinion the containment hierarchy concept is misleading and in fact an illusion. Objects are really *tuples,* not hierarchies.

- **Methods:** This concept is essential, of course (although we would prefer the more conventional terms "function" or "operator" in place of the term "method"). Bundling method definitions with object classes is *not* essential, however, and leads to several problems. We would prefer to use the *security* mechanism to control which functions have access to the internals of which objects.

- **Messages:** Again, the concept is essential, though we would prefer to replace the term by the more conventional term "call" or "invocation"—always recognizing that such calls or invocations are not necessarily synchronous.

- **Class hierarchy:** Essential. So too is the related notion of *inheritance,* although—since we have no notion of (public) instance variables—there is no need to distinguish between *structural* and *behavioral* inheritance (all inheritance is by definition behavioral). **Polymorphism** is thus essential too, with its likely implication of *run-time binding* (discussed in Chapter 19)— though this latter notion is an implementation matter and should not be regarded as part of "the OO model" as such.

- **Multiple inheritance:** Secondary. (Actually this concept is likely to prove quite important, but it seems to this writer that there are some significant conceptual and definitional issues to be resolved before we can include such a feature in a well-defined abstract "OO model" with any significant degree of confidence. More study is required.)

- **Class *vs.* instance *vs.* collection:** The distinctions are essential, of course, but not really exclusive to OO (the *concepts* are distinct, and that is really all that needs to be said).

- **Database programming language:** Nice to have, but not exclusive to OO.

- **3GL nature:** A giant step backward.

- **Versions:** Nice to have, but not exclusive to OO. The same goes for the related concept of **configurations.**

- **Long and nested transactions:** Nice to have, but not exclusive to OO.

- **Schema evolution:** Nice to have, but not exclusive to OO.

And here is a list of features that "the OO model" typically does *not* support:

- *Ad hoc* **query:** As explained in Chapter 24, early versions of "the OO model" typically did not include *ad hoc* query capabilities, because (a) the need for such capabilities was not so pressing in the environment in which OO systems originated, and (b) such capabilities seem to imply *either* that objects must be designed according to some discipline such as that outlined in Section 24.3 *or* that queries will have to break encapsulation.

- **Closure:** Generic operators such as (object-level) union, join, projection, etc., are not supported. Derived objects in general are not supported.

- **Symmetric exploitation:** Not supported. Each and every access request involves a distinct, precoded, procedural method.

- **Foreign keys:** The "OO model" has several different mechanisms for dealing with referential integrity, none of which is the same as the relational model's more uniform foreign key mechanism. Such matters as "DELETE RESTRICTED" and "DELETE CASCADES" are typically left to procedural code (probably methods, possibly application code).

- **Declarative integrity constraints:** Currently not supported (for reasons not unrelated to the reasons *ad hoc* query is typically not supported).

- **Views:** Currently not supported (for reasons not unrelated to the reasons *ad hoc* query is typically not supported).

- **Catalog:** Must be built by the professional staff whose job it is to tailor the OO DBMS for whatever application it has been installed for. There is no universal "common catalog" (nor was there for relational systems, of course, prior to SQL/92).

To summarize, the good (and essential) features of the "OO model"—i.e., the ones we would like relational systems to support—are as follows:

- **Objects** and **object classes,** plus corresponding constructor functions (returning *objects,* however, not OIDs—see Section 25.3) and other access and maintenance **functions,** together with a (necessarily) clear distinction among classes, instances, and collections

- **Class hierarchies,** with (behavioral) **inheritance,** and therefore *polymorphism* and run-time binding (though this latter is not part of the model as such)

A Note on Encapsulation

We have said that the system should support encapsulated objects, i.e., objects that are accessible *only* via appropriate access functions (there should be no "public instance variables" in those objects at all). The advantage of such encapsulation is basically that it provides **data independence,** as explained in Chapter 22. (In fact, OO systems are sometimes said to provide a *particularly strong form* of data independence [22.7]. It is important to understand, however, that—at least in principle—OO systems cannot provide any more data independence than relational systems can. For example, there is absolutely no reason—at least in principle—why a base relation called POINT, with Cartesian coordinate attributes X and Y, should not map to a stored relation that represents points by their polar coordinates R and θ instead. As we remarked in Chapter 3, however, today's relational products unfortunately do not provide nearly as much data independence as we would really like, or as much as relational systems are theoretically capable of.)

Note, however, that it is possible to take the encapsulation idea too far. There will always be a need to access the data in ways that were not foreseen when the database was originally created, and the notion of having to write new procedural code every time a new data access requirement arises is simply not acceptable. Indeed, such was exactly the state of affairs with prerelational systems, and it was a major contributor to their downfall.

Thus we see that the system should additionally support "objects" that are *not* encapsulated but expose their "instance variables" for all the world to see. And—to jump ahead of ourselves for a moment—those nonencapsulated "objects" are, precisely, **tuples** in **relations** (see Section 25.3). Note that, at least in principle, nonencapsulated relations can provide just as much data independence as can encapsulated objects (as explained above); note too that, again in principle, the ideas of type hierarchies, inheritance, etc., apply at least as well to nonencapsulated relations as they do to encapsulated objects (as explained in Chapter 19). And, of course, relations can be accessed by the well-known, builtin, generic operators of the relational algebra instead of just by methods that are specific to the particular relation in question, thus satisfying the "unforeseen requirements" objective.

25.3 Domains *vs.* Objects

In this section we argue that the key to the desired rapprochement is the relational notion of **domains** (indeed, we stated this as our position on the subject in Chapter 19). For consider:

■ The fundamental construct in OO systems is the **object class,** which is basically a user-defined, encapsulated data type of arbitrary internal complexity.

■ The fundamental construct in relational systems—mostly not implemented, unfortunately, in today's relational products—is the **domain,** which is (again) basically a user-defined, encapsulated data type of arbitrary internal complexity.

In other words, a domain and an object class are *the same thing!* Thus, a relational system that implemented domains properly would be able to do all the things that (it is claimed) OO systems can do and relational systems cannot.

Let us review the principal properties of domains as discussed in Chapter 19. We showed in that chapter:

■ How domains really are data types of arbitrary complexity

■ How the "scalar" values in such a domain can therefore have arbitrarily complex internal structure

■ How those values are encapsulated, however, and can be operated on only by pre-defined functions

We also discussed:

■ The fact that the function definitions are typically *not* bundled with the domain definitions

■ The relevance of the "strong typing" concept from programming languages

■ The ideas of inheritance and polymorphism as they apply to domains

Indeed, domains and object classes really are one and the same. Thus, domains (and therefore relational attributes) can contain absolutely anything—arrays, lists, stacks, documents, photographs, maps, blueprints, etc., etc. Another way of saying this is: **Domains encapsulate, relations don't**.

The Rectangles Problem Revisited

So now we can give a "good" solution to the rectangles problem. First of all, we define a domain of rectangles ("we" here probably meaning the DBA):

```
CREATE DOMAIN RECTANGLE REP ( ... ) ;
```

We assume here that the representation ("REP") is in terms of one of the newer storage structures (quadtrees, grid files, R-trees, etc.) that are specifically intended to support spatial data such as geometric figures efficiently—see Appendix A, references [A.48–A.59].

Next we define a "constructor" function for creating new rectangles (i.e., for converting a set of four floating-point numbers into a rectangle):

```
CREATE FUNCTION RECTANGLE
     ( A FLOAT, B FLOAT, C FLOAT, D FLOAT )
       RETURNS ( RECTANGLE )
    AS BEGIN ;
         DECLARE R RECTANGLE ;
         R.X1  :=  A ;  R.X2  :=  B ;
```

```
R.Y1  :=  C ;  R.Y2  :=  D ;
RETURN ( R ) ;
END ;
```

Here we assume that R.X1 refers to the *x*-coordinate of the bottom left-hand corner of rectangle R, etc., and that a rectangle can be defined by specifying these four coordinates. Note, incidentally, that we do *not* bundle the RECTANGLE function with the RECTANGLE "object class" (domain).

We also define a function to test two rectangles to see whether they overlap:

```
CREATE FUNCTION OVERLAP
   ( R1 RECTANGLE, R2 RECTANGLE. )
     RETURNS ( BOOLEAN )
  AS BEGIN ;
     ... code ... ;
     END ;
```

The *code* here is low-level implementation code, probably written in a language like C, to implement the *efficient* (short) form of the "overlaps" test against the *efficient* (R-tree or whatever) storage structure.

Now an SQL user can create a base table with a column defined on the rectangles domain:

```
CREATE TABLE RECTANGLES
      ( RECTID ... , R RECTANGLE ... , ... ,
      UNIQUE ( RECTID ) ,
      UNIQUE ( R ) ) ;
```

And the query "Find all rectangles that overlap the unit square" now becomes simply:

```
SELECT ...
FROM    RECTANGLES
WHERE   OVERLAP ( R, RECTANGLE ( 0, 1, 0, 1 ) ) ;
```

Note that the expression RECTANGLE(0,1,0,1) in this query effectively constitutes a kind of "rectangle literal."

Conclusion

The system should support *relations,* with the "extension" (actually not an extension at all) that *domains* are properly supported and can be user-defined data types of arbitrary complexity. Now, we can call the elements of such domains *objects* if we like (they are totally encapsulated); note, however, that at the relational level **there is no need for OIDs**—the relational model requires relations to contain *actual objects* (at least conceptually), not pointers to objects. Thus, for example, the RECTANGLE function (which is the relational analog of "NEW" for rectangles) does not return a rectangle OID, it returns (at least conceptually) *an actual rectangle.*

As for the "class *vs.* instance *vs.* collection" distinctions:

■   The *class* is the domain.

■   An *instance* is an element of the domain. So far as the database is concerned, such instances exist only within attribute positions within tuples within relations; however, we can create new "literal" instances at any time for use as arguments to whatever operations or functions are defined for the domain in question.

- A *collection* is the collection of values of any attribute defined on the domain. As for sharing the very same instance among several collections, the *effect* of such sharing can be achieved by means of foreign keys; actually placing two copies of the same instance in two distinct base relations is *not* sharing in the same sense (and in fact is typically contraindicated by the principles of further normalization). *Note:* The very same instance can of course be shared among exactly one base relation and any number of other (named) relations if those other relations are all *views.*

To sum up: Relational vendors should do all in their power to extend their systems to include proper domain support. Indeed, an argument can be made that the whole reason that OO systems look attractive is precisely because the relational vendors to date have failed to support the relational model adequately. But this fact should not be seen as an argument for abandoning relational systems entirely (or at all!).

25.4 Relations *vs.* Objects

In the previous section we equated object classes and domains. Many products and prototypes, however, are equating object classes and *relations* instead.* In this section we argue that this latter equation is a serious mistake.

We begin by considering a simple example. Here is a slightly simplified version of one of the very first CREATE OBJECT CLASS examples from Chapter 22:

```
CREATE OBJECT CLASS EMP
PUBLIC ( EMP#  CHAR,
         ENAME CHAR,
         SAL   NUMERIC ) ... ;
```

And here is a relational (SQL) analog:

```
CREATE TABLE EMP
        ( EMP#   CHAR,
          ENAME  CHAR,
          SAL    NUMERIC ) ... ;
```

---

* Regarding the general question of whether any two concepts *A* and *B,* such as relations and object classes, are "the same" and can thus be equated, there is a simple general principle—previously articulated by this writer in reference [4.12], and well worth repeating here—that can usefully be applied: Simply ask yourself "Is every instance of *A* an instance of *B?*" and, conversely, "Is every instance of *B* an instance of *A?*" Only if the answer is *yes* to both of these questions is it true that *A* and *B* are identical.

It is very tempting to equate the two! And many systems have done exactly that, including Iris [25.3,25.7], POSTGRES [25.13-25.16], UniSQL [25.11], and others. UniSQL, for example, supports an extended form of SQL called SQL/X, which we illustrate by means of the following example (based on one in the SQL/X user's manual [25.11]). We start with a conventional, self-explanatory SQL CREATE TABLE statement:

```
CREATE TABLE EMP
       ( EMP#       CHAR(5),
         ENAME      CHAR(20),
         SAL        NUMERIC,
         HOBBY      CHAR(20),
         WORKS_FOR  CHAR(20) ) ;
```

Two points arise immediately:

1. SQL/X does not currently support the SQL PRIMARY and FOREIGN KEY clauses. Furthermore, since the intent is to equate CREATE TABLE and "CREATE OBJECT CLASS"—as a matter of fact, SQL/X allows the keyword TABLE in CREATE TABLE to be replaced by the keyword CLASS—the implications of adding such support are not clear, since primary and foreign keys are not part of the object class concept.

2. SQL/X also does not support domains. Indeed, those who espouse the "relation = object class" equation typically never even mention domains. This omission is probably due to the widespread failure on the part of the relational vendors to implement domains, which in turn is due to the failure of the original SQL language to include any domain support in the first place.

Anyway, to get back to the example: The first SQL/X extension is to add **composite column** support. Thus, e.g., we can replace the original CREATE TABLE by the following (refer to Fig. 25.1):

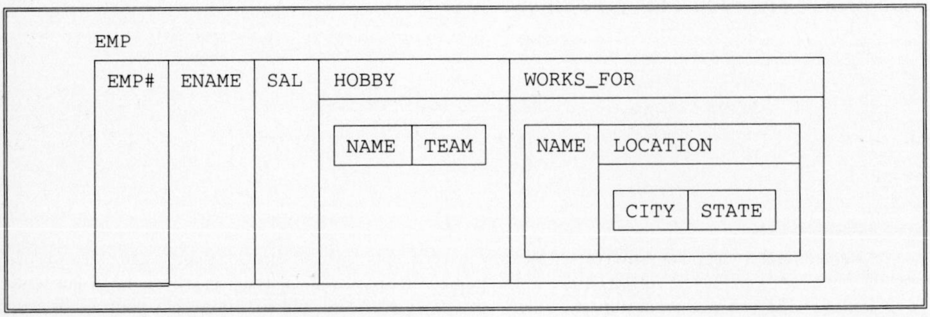

FIG. 25.1 SQL/X table with composite columns

```
CREATE TABLE EMP
     ( EMP#        CHAR(5),
       ENAME       CHAR(20),
       SAL         NUMERIC,
       HOBBY       ACTIVITY,
       WORKS_FOR   COMPANY ) ;

CREATE TABLE ACTIVITY
     ( NAME   CHAR(20),
       TEAM   INTEGER ) ;

CREATE TABLE COMPANY
     ( NAME        CHAR(20),
       LOCATION    CITYSTATE ) ;

CREATE TABLE CITYSTATE
     ( CITY        CHAR(20),
       STATE       CHAR(2) ) ;
```

Explanation:

- The column HOBBY in table EMP is declared to be of type ACTIVITY. ACTIVITY in turn is a table of two columns, NAME and TEAM, where TEAM represents the number of players in the corresponding team—e.g., a possible "activity" might be (Soccer,11). Each HOBBY value is thus actually an ordered pair of values, a NAME value and a TEAM value. (More precisely, it is an ordered pair of values that currently appears in the ACTIVITY table.) Incidentally, those HOBBY values are *not* encapsulated (Fig. 25.1 notwithstanding); thus, e.g., a "path expression" of the form EMP.HOBBY.NAME is legal (see below).

- Similarly, column WORKS_FOR in table EMP is declared to be of type COMPANY, and COMPANY is also a table of two columns, one of which is defined to be of type CITYSTATE, which is another two-column table, and so on.

In other words, tables ACTIVITY, COMPANY, and CITYSTATE are all considered to be *types* as well as tables (the same is true for table EMP also, of course). Thus, the first SQL/X extension is roughly analogous to allowing objects to contain other objects (it is SQL/X's version of support for the containment hierarchy).

The next extension is to add **table-valued columns**. Suppose, for example, that employees can have an arbitrary number of hobbies, instead of just one (see Fig. 25.2):

```
CREATE TABLE EMP
     ( EMP#        CHAR(5),
       ENAME       CHAR(20),
       SAL         NUMERIC,
       HOBBIES     SET OF ( ACTIVITY ),
       WORKS_FOR   COMPANY ) ;
```

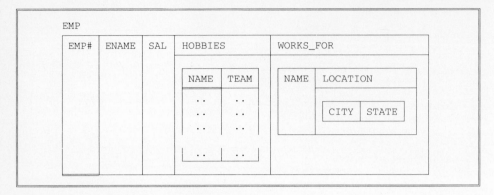

FIG. 25.2 SQL/X table with a table-valued column

Explanation:

■ The HOBBIES value within any given row of table EMP is now (conceptually) a *set* of zero or more (NAME,TEAM) pairs from the ACTIVITY table. This second extension is thus roughly analogous to allowing objects to contain "aggregate" objects—a more complex version of the containment hierarchy. *Note:* The aggregate object types supported by SQL/X are *sets, sequences,* and *multisets* (bags).

The third extension is to permit tables to have associated **methods**. For example:

```
CREATE TABLE EMP
     ( EMP#        CHAR(5),
       ENAME       CHAR(20),
       SAL         NUMERIC,
       HOBBIES     SET OF ( ACTIVITY ),
       WORKS_FOR   COMPANY )
METHOD RETIREMENT_BENEFITS ( ) : NUMERIC ;
```

Explanation:

■ RETIREMENT_BENEFITS is a function (method) that takes a given EMP instance as its argument and produces a result of type NUMERIC. *Note:* The parentheses are required; they surround a commalist (empty in the example) of data type specifications for additional arguments to the function.

■ The code that implements the method is written in C plus embedded SQL/X and resides in an operating system file (whose name can be specified explicitly as part of the CREATE TABLE statement; if it is not, a default name derived from the method name is assumed).

■ The method is invoked by a CALL statement of the form

```
CALL method ( argument-commalist ) ON variable INTO variable ;
```

For example:

```
CALL RETIREMENT_BENEFITS ( ) ON E INTO F ;
```

Here E and F are program variables; E contains the OID of some particular EMP instance, and the OID of the result of executing the method is assigned to F.

■ Note, incidentally, that RETIREMENT_BENEFITS is *not* a "derived column." SQL/X does not currently support derived columns (though such support is promised for a future release).

The final extension is to permit the definition of **subclasses**. For example (refer to Fig. 25.3):

```
CREATE TABLE PERSON
     ( SS#          CHAR(9),
       BIRTHDATE    DATE,
       ADDRESS      CHAR(50) ) ;

CREATE TABLE EMP
     AS SUBCLASS OF PERSON
     ( EMP#         CHAR(5),
       ENAME        CHAR(20),
       SAL          NUMERIC,
       HOBBIES      SET OF ( ACTIVITY ),
       WORKS_FOR    COMPANY )
METHOD RETIREMENT_BENEFITS ( ) : NUMERIC ;
```

Explanation:

■ EMP now has three additional columns (SS#, BIRTHDATE, ADDRESS) inherited from PERSON. If PERSON had any methods, it would inherit those too.

Along with the data definition extensions sketched above, numerous data manipulation extensions are required also. They include:

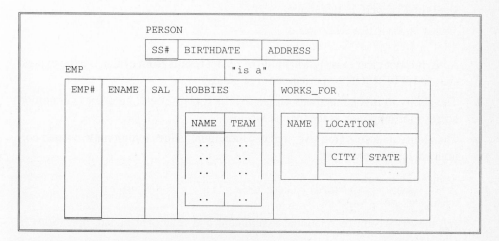

FIG. 25.3 SQL/X superclasses and subclasses (example)

■ Path expressions (e.g., EMP.WORKS_FOR.LOCATION.STATE)—a new kind of scalar expression. For example:

```
SELECT  ENAME, WORKS_FOR.NAME
FROM    EMP
WHERE   WORKS_FOR.LOCATION.STATE = 'CA' ;
```

We remark that these path expressions go *down* the containment hierarchy, whereas the path expressions discussed briefly at the end of Chapter 23 go *up*.

■ An extended kind of path expression that is multi-valued instead of single-valued (e.g., EMP.HOBBIES.NAME). Example:

```
SELECT  ENAME, WORKS_FOR.NAME
FROM    EMP
WHERE   { 'Soccer', 'Bridge' } SUBSETEQ HOBBIES.NAME ;
```

The operator SUBSETEQ means "proper subset of or equal to" (see below).

■ The ability to write literal instances of complex objects. One simple example appears in the WHERE clause just shown. Here is a more complex example (a literal EMP):

```
( 'E001', 'Smith', $50000,
        { ( 'Soccer', 11 ), ( 'Bridge', 4 ) },
                     ( 'IBM', ( 'San Jose', 'CA' ) ) )
```

■ Table comparison operators such as SUBSET, SUBSETEQ, SETEQ, etc. (see example above).

■ Operations for traversing the class hierarchy. For example:

```
SELECT  SS#, ENAME
FROM    EMP ;
```

The FROM clause "FROM *T*" allows the user to refer to all columns of *T,* including those inherited from superclasses (at any level) of *T*. By contrast, the FROM clause "FROM ALL *T*" allows the user to refer to columns of subclasses (at any level) of *T* as well. For example:

```
SELECT  SS#, BIRTHDATE, ENAME
FROM    ALL PERSON ;
```

Note: It is not clear exactly what kind of object results from evaluating the expression "ALL PERSON"—perhaps a set of tables?

■ The ability to invoke methods within WHERE clauses etc., in order to condition access (not supported at the time of writing).

■ The ability to access (retrieve, update) individual values within multi-valued column values. For example:

```
UPDATE EMP
SET    HOBBIES = HOBBIES - { 'Soccer,' 11 }
WHERE  ENAME = 'Smith' ;
```

(*cf.* the discussion of relational assignment and relational update operations in Chapter 6).

We now proceed to examine some consequences of the foregoing. **Please understand clearly that the following remarks are NOT intended as an attack on SQL/X
*per se;*** rather, they are applicable to any system or language that attempts to equate
relations and object classes. We use SQL/X merely by way of illustration.

1. The first point is that this system is a long way from being a true OO system. (As
   an aside, we remark that it is not really a "nested relation" or "RVA" system either—see Chapter 19—because of the points discussed in paragraphs 4 and 5
   below.) It might best be characterized as **an SQL system with extensions**—which
   means, first and foremost, that it *is* an SQL system. *Note:* This comment is not
   meant as a criticism; it is just that an appreciation of this point will help the reader
   to understand the points that follow.

2. SQL/X "objects" are *rows in tables* (and are thus totally unencapsulated); the corresponding "instance variables" are *columns. Note:* Again, these comments are not
   necessarily criticisms—they are just observations.

3. Note, therefore, that whereas a pure OO class has methods and no (public) instance
   variables, an SQL/X "class" has public instance variables and does not necessarily
   have any methods. Thus, the "relation = class" equation looks a little suspect already.

4. We remark that there is a difference in kind between the column definitions (e.g)

   ```
   ENAME CHAR(20)
   ```

   and

   ```
   WORKS_FOR COMPANY
   ```

   "CHAR(20)" is a true data type (equivalently, a true— albeit primitive—domain);
   it places a time-independent constraint on the values that can appear in column
   ENAME. "COMPANY" by contrast is *not* a true data type; the constraint it places
   on the values that can appear in column WORKS_FOR is *time-dependent* (it depends, obviously, on the set of values currently appearing in table COMPANY). In
   fact, the "class *vs.* instance *vs.* collection" distinctions are muddied here, and the
   concept of true domains has been lost. The full implications of this state of affairs
   are unclear.

5. SQL/X objects are regarded (in general) as containing other objects—i.e., they are
   containment hierarchies. In fact, however, subobject sharing is done via pointers
   (OIDs), and users must understand this point clearly. For instance, referring back
   to the example of EMP objects "containing" COMPANY objects: Suppose the user
   updates one particular EMP object, changing (say) the name of the "contained"
   COMPANY object. Then that change will immediately be propagated to all other
   EMP objects for employees of the same company.

   Here are some further implications and questions arising from this same point:

   ▪ Can we insert a new EMP instance and specify a value for the contained
     COMPANY instance that does not currently exist in the COMPANY table? If

the answer is yes, the definition of column WORKS_FOR as being of type COMPANY does not mean very much, since it does not significantly constrain the INSERT operation. If the answer is no, the INSERT operation becomes unnecessarily complex—the user has to specify, not just a legal COMPANY.NAME "foreign key" value (as would be required in the analogous relational situation), but an entire legal COMPANY object. Moreover, specifying an entire COMPANY object means—at best—having to tell the system something it already knows; at worst, it means that if the user makes a mistake, the INSERT will fail when it could perfectly well have succeeded.

- Suppose we want a "DELETE RESTRICTED" rule for COMPANY (i.e., an attempt to delete a company must fail if the company has any employees). Presumably this rule must be enforced by a suitable method, M say. Furthermore, native SQL DELETE operations must not be performed on COMPANY objects other than within that method M. How is this latter requirement enforced?

- Analogous remarks apply to "DELETE CASCADES," though possibly not to "DELETE NULLIFIES."

- DELETE on an EMP presumably does *not* delete the corresponding COMPANY, despite the pretense that the corresponding COMPANY is contained within the EMP.

- It follows from all of the above that we are not really talking about the relational model any more. The fundamental data object is not a relation containing values, it is a table containing values *and pointers*. As a consequence, operators such as projection and join require careful and subtle reinterpretation. This is a big issue, and we therefore make it our next major point.

6. Let us simplify the EMP table slightly, as follows (the notation is intended to be self-explanatory):

```
EMP ( EMP#, SAL, WORKS_FOR ( NAME, LOCATION ( CITY, STATE ) ) )
```

Now suppose we project this EMP table over SAL and the corresponding company CITY. Does the result look like this?—

```
( SAL, ( ( CITY ) ) )
```

or like this?—

```
( SAL, CITY )
```

Refer to Fig. 25.4.

- If it is the former (which is more logically correct)—see the left-hand side of the figure—then what is the name of the column that contains the relation that contains the CITY value? And what is the name of the column that contains the relation that contains the relation that contains the CITY value? *Note:* Lest the reader be tempted to reply "LOCATION.CITY" and "WORKS_FOR.LOCATION.CITY," respectively, we point out that these con-

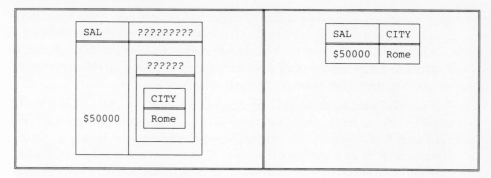

FIG. 25.4   Which projection is correct?

structs are not proper column names. They cannot be used in CREATE TABLE, after all.

- If it is the latter—see the right-hand side of the figure—then do we conclude that hierarchic objects make sense only at the "base object" level and that, as soon as we create any derived objects, we are back in the relational world? If so, why did we leave it in the first place?

- Assuming that the left-hand result, with heading (SAL,((CITY))), is indeed the correct one, can we now join that result to the CITYSTATE table over cities? That is, is the following comparison legal?

```
CITY = ( ( CITY ) )
```

Note that the CITY values on the right-hand side will at least have to be doubly unnested before the actual comparison can be done (for otherwise the comparison will certainly either give *false* or else raise a type error).

   The foregoing discussion illustrates the two points that (a) if join is going to apply to hierarchic objects, it is going to require very careful definition, and (b) even if that definition can be properly worked out, the resultant operation is likely to be quite complex. In particular, the rules regarding the kind of object that is produced by the join are likely to be *very* complicated. The details are left to the reader to meditate on.

7. Referring again to the projection example from the previous discussion: Whichever is the correct result, **what class is it? What methods apply?**

   In our example, EMPs had only one method, namely RETIREMENT_BENE-FITS, and that method clearly does not apply to the result of the projection; in fact, it hardly seems reasonable that *any* methods that applied to EMP objects would apply. And there certainly are no others. So it looks as if we are forced to conclude that *no methods at all* apply to the result of a projection—i.e., the result, whatever it is, is not really an object class at all. (We might *say* it is an object class, but that does not make it one!—it will have instance variables and no methods, whereas we have already observed that a true object class has methods and no instance variables.)

In fact, it is quite clear that when people equate relations and object classes, it is specifically *base* relations they are referring to.* The relational **closure** property applies to relational tables but not to object classes.

8. Following on from the previous point: Suppose we are given a base relation R and we project it over *all* of its columns. In the version of the relational algebra defined in Chapter 6 of this book, the syntax for such a projection is simply R. So the expression "R" is now ambiguous! If we think of it as referring to base relation R, then it is an object class, with methods. If we think of it as referring to the projection of base relation R over all of its columns, then it is not an object class and it has no methods. How do we tell the difference?

9. Finally, it has to be said that SQL/X represents a *major* increase in complexity *vis-à-vis* plain SQL. Such additional complexity is an inevitable consequence of making the wrong equation (i.e., "relation = object class" instead of "domain = object class").

25.5   Benefits of True Rapprochement

In this section we briefly summarize the benefits of a true OO/relational rapprochement (i.e., a rapprochement that exploits the relational concept of domains properly, not one that makes the mistaken equation of relations and object classes).

First of all, the system is still a relational system, so all the usual relational benefits apply [3.2]. In particular, the advantage of *familiarity* applies—the OO capabilities represent a very natural "extension" (actually not an extension at all) to the relational model.

Second, the system is also an OO system, which implies the following additional benefits:

■ *Open architecture (extendability):* Users are no longer limited to the predefined, builtin data types. The system can be tailored and extended in arbitrary ways to meet the needs of specific application areas.

■ *User-defined data types and functions, with inheritance:* These in a nutshell are **the** advantages of OO systems in general.

■ *Strong typing:* Proper domain support provides a sound basis for catching type violations (preferably at compilation time), as discussed in Chapter 19.

■ *Improved performance:* Performance is improved because methods are executed

---

* Or at least *named* relations. SQL/X does support *views,* which are regarded as "virtual classes"—see the annotation to reference [25.11]. Virtual classes do not inherit methods from the classes from which they are derived, however.

by the server, not the client.* As a trivial example, consider the query "Find all books with more than 20 chapters." In a traditional relational system, books might be represented as "BLOBs" (a **BLOB** or *basic large object* is essentially just an arbitrarily long byte string), and the client will have to retrieve each book in turn and scan it to see if it has more than 20 chapters. But with proper OO support, the "number of chapters" method will be executed by the server, and only those books actually desired will be transmitted to the client.

    Note: The foregoing is not really an argument for OO, it is an argument for *stored procedures* (see Chapter 21). A traditional relational system with stored procedures will give the same performance benefits here as an OO system with methods.

- *Improved productivity:* Once the appropriate object classes (domains) have been defined, users of those classes can obviously be much more productive, both in application development and—probably more important—in application mainte-nance also.

- *Object-level recovery, concurrency, and security:* As pointed out in Chapter 22, objects—that is, individual objects, not object classes—are the natural unit for re-covery, concurrency, and security purposes in an OO system (integrity constraints permitting).

- *Accessibility:* Complex objects now become available via the relational query lan-guage (probably SQL) to end users.

Furthermore, all of the criticisms we leveled at OO systems in previous chapters no longer apply. To be specific, the system can now support all of the following without any undue difficulty:

- *Ad hoc* query
- Dual-mode access (i.e., using the same language for programmed and interactive database access)
- Relationships of degree greater than two
- Methods that span classes
- Symmetric exploitation
- Declarative integrity constraints
- Integrity constraints that span classes
- "Foreign key rules" (DELETE CASCADES, etc.)
- Semantic optimization

In addition:

- OIDs and pointer chasing are now totally "under the covers" and hidden from the user
- "Difficult" OO questions (e.g., what does it mean to join two objects?) go away

---

* Not true at the time of writing for SQL/X. A future release will offer an option by which the DBA can specify where a given method is to be executed.

- The benefits of encapsulation still apply (to values within relations, not to relations themselves)
- Relational systems can now handle "complex" application areas such as CAD/CAM, as previously discussed

And the approach is conceptually clean.

25.6 Summary

The message of this chapter (and indeed its three predecessors) can be summed up as follows. First of all, OO unquestionably has some good ideas, namely:

- **User-defined data types** (including user-defined functions)
- **Inheritance** (behavioral, not structural)

However, it also has some ideas that would be better rejected, or at least kept under the covers:

- **OIDs** and pointer chasing
- Strong **procedural** (3GL) orientation
- Function **bundling**
- Complex and asymmetric treatment of **relationships**
- Lack of declarative **integrity** support

What we need to do is enhance relational systems to incorporate the good ideas of OO (but not the bad ones!), and we have argued that **domains** are the key to achieving this goal. Specifically, we have argued that the equation "domain = object class" is correct, and the equation "relation = object class" is incorrect.

References and Bibliography

See also the references in Chapter 19 and Chapters 22–24.

25.1 Malcolm Atkinson *et al.* "The Object-Oriented Database System Manifesto." Proc. First International Conference on Deductive and Object-Oriented Databases, Kyoto, Japan (1989). New York, N.Y.: Elsevier Science (1990).

One of the first attempts to build a consensus on what "the OO model" should include. See reference [25.10] for another attempt.

25.2 François Bancilhon. "A Logic-Programming/Object-Oriented Cocktail." *ACM SIGMOD Record 15,* No. 3 (September 1986).

To quote the introduction: "The object-oriented approach . . . seems to be particularly well fitted to [handling] new types of applications such as CAD, software [engineering], and AI. However, the natural extension to relational database technology is . . . the logic pro-gramming paradigm, [not] the object-oriented one. [This paper addresses the question of] whether the two paradigms are compatible."

25.3 David Beech. "A Foundation for Evolution from Relational to Object Databases." In Schmidt, Ceri, and Missikoff (eds.): *Extending Database Technology*. New York, N.Y.: Springer-Verlag (1988).

This is one of several papers that discuss the possibility of extending SQL to become some kind of "Object SQL" or "OSQL" (see also reference [25.7], which gives more detail on this particular proposal). In common with most such papers it has little or nothing to say regarding domains, closure, or relational operators such as join; i.e., it falls into the "relation = class" trap. It also makes a number of somewhat contentious claims regarding (among other things) the "smooth adaptation" of SQL. Here, for example, is an OSQL CREATE FUNCTION statement (taken from reference [25.7]):

```
CREATE FUNCTION RaiseAllSalaries (Integer incr) AS
     UPDATE Salary(e) = newsal
     FOR EACH Employee e, Integer newsal
     WHERE newsal = Salary(e) + incr ;
```

The following might seem to many people to be more in keeping with the style of conventional SQL:

```
CREATE FUNCTION RaiseAllSalaries (Integer incr) AS
     UPDATE Employee
     SET Salary = Salary + incr ;
```

As in SQL/X, "types" (tables) are not encapsulated. *Note:* One interesting aspect of OSQL is that (in contrast to some other OO languages) methods—i.e., functions—are themselves regarded as objects.

25.4 R. G. G. Cattell. "What Are Next-Generation DB Systems?" *CACM 34,* No. 10 (October 1991).

25.5 Nathan Goodman. "Object Oriented Database Systems." *InfoDB 4,* No. 3 (Fall 1989).

The previous edition of this book included the following quote from this paper:

"At this stage it is futile to compare [the] relational and object-oriented [approaches]. We have to compare like to like: apples to apples, dreams to dreams, theory to theory, and mature products to mature products."

And it (the previous edition) went on to say:

"Dreams aside, the relational approach has been in existence for some time: It rests on a very solid theoretical foundation, and it is the basis for a large number of mature products. The OO approach, by contrast, is new (at least in the database arena); it does not possess a theoretical foundation that can meaningfully be compared with the relational model, and the few products that exist can scarcely be described as mature. Thus, a great deal remains to be done before we can seriously begin to consider the question of whether OO technology will ever represent a viable alternative to the relational approach."

While many of the foregoing remarks are still applicable, matters have crystallized somewhat since the previous edition was published. In many ways, in fact, relational *vs.* OO can now be seen to be somewhat of an apples-and-oranges comparison; as explained in Chapter 24, a relational DBMS comes *ready for use,* whereas an OO DBMS by contrast is best thought of as a kind of *construction kit* for building application-specific DBMSs.

25.6 Michael Kifer, Won Kim, and Yehoshua Sagiv. "Querying Object-Oriented Databases." Proc. ACM International Conference on Management of Data, San Diego, Calif. (June 1992).

Proposes another "Object SQL" called XSQL.

25.7   Peter Lyngbaek *et al.* "OSQL: A Language for Object Databases." Technical Report
HPL-DTD-91-4, Hewlett-Packard Company (January 15th, 1991).

See the annotation to reference [25.3].

25.8   Gail M. Shaw and Stanley B. Zdonik. "A Query Algebra for Object-Oriented
Databases." Proc. 6th International Conference on Data Engineering (February 1990).
Also Technical Report TR CS-89-19, Dept. of Computer Science, Brown University,
Providence, RI (March 1989).

This paper serves to support the present writer's contention that any "OO algebra" will
be inherently complex (because objects are complex). In particular, *equality* of arbitrarily nested hierarchic objects requires very careful treatment. The basic idea behind the
specific proposals of this paper is that each query algebra operator produces a *relation*,
in which each tuple contains OIDs for certain database objects. In the case of join, for
example, each tuple contains OIDs of objects that match one another under the joining
condition. Those tuples do not inherit any methods from the component objects.

25.9   David W. Shipman. "The Functional Data Model and the Data Language DAPLEX."
ACM TODS 6, No. 1 (March 1981). Republished in M. Stonebraker (ed.): *Readings in
Database Systems.* San Mateo, Calif.: Morgan Kaufmann (1988).

There have been several attempts to construct systems based on *functions* instead of
relations, and DAPLEX is one of the best known. The functional approaches share certain ideas with the OO approach, including in particular a somewhat navigational (i.e.,
path-following) style of addressing objects that are functionally related to other objects
(that are functionally related to other objects, etc.). Note, however, that a function in one
of the so-called "functional" models is typically not a mathematical function at all; it
might, for example, be multi-valued. In fact, considerable violence has to be done to the
function concept in order to make it capable of all the things required of it in the "functional data model" context. Be that as it may, it seems to this writer that the functional
approach and the OO approach are in large part the same thing under different names.

25.10 Michael Stonebraker *et al.* "Third Generation Database System Manifesto." *ACM
SIGMOD Record 19,* No. 3 (September 1990).

In part, this paper is a response to—i.e., counterproposal to—the proposals of reference
[25.1]. A quote: "Second generation systems made a major contribution in two areas,
nonprocedural data access and data independence, and these advances must not be compromised by third generation systems." The following features are stated to be essential
requirements of a "third generation DBMS" (the list is somewhat paraphrased):

  1. Provide traditional DB services plus richer object structures and rules

  ▪ Rich type system

  ▪ Inheritance

  ▪ Functions and encapsulation

  ▪ Optional system-assigned tuple IDs [there seems to be some confusion here between
    object IDs and tuple IDs]

  ▪ Rules (e.g., integrity rules), *not* tied to specific objects

  2. Subsume second generation DBMSs

  ▪ Navigation only as a last resort

  ▪ Intensional and extensional set definitions [meaning collections that are maintained
    automatically by the system and collections that are maintained manually by the user]

- Updatable views
- Clustering, indexes, etc., hidden from the user

3. Support open systems
   - Multiple languages
   - Persistence
   - SQL [characterized as "intergalactic dataspeak" (!)]
   - Queries and results must be the lowest level of client/server communication

Regarding SQL support for "complex objects," incidentally, it seems to this writer that such support can be made part of a clean, abstract OO model only if the object design discipline from Section 24.3 is made an essential part of that model too. Assuming that such query capabilities *are* incorporated into the model, we could then extend the requirement to permit those capabilities to be invoked from within application code, thereby:

1. Moving away from the present 3GL orientation of OO systems, and

2. Providing support for the dual-mode principle, as in relational systems.

We would also have a basis for stating integrity constraints declaratively and providing declarative view support.

25.11 UniSQL Inc. *UniSQL/X Database Management System User's Manual: Release 1.2* (1991).

See Section 25.4 for an extended discussion of this product. It is worth noting that, precisely because (as stated in that section) it is really an extended SQL system, not a true OO DBMS, some of the criticisms leveled at OO systems in general in Chapter 24 and elsewhere do not apply to UniSQL in particular. To be more specific:

■ UniSQL does support views ("virtual classes"). They have their own methods, however—i.e., they do not inherit methods from the tables (classes) from which they are derived. Incidentally, the manual talks in terms of "classes and virtual classes," which suggests that virtual classes are not classes. This situation is reminiscent of the SQL standard's talk of "tables and views" (see Chapter 3), which suggests that views are not tables.

■ In fact, UniSQL does support derived objects in general— i.e., the relational operators join, union, etc., are all supported. However, those derived objects are not regarded as classes, and it is not clear exactly what *kind* of objects (e.g., how nested they are) those operations produce.

■ UniSQL does have a single language (SQL/X) for both programmed and interactive access to the database. Moreover, that language is set-level, and SQL/X requests are thus optimizable. It also supports symmetric exploitation.

■ UniSQL does have support for missing information—it provides both SQL-style nulls and (limited) support for user-defined default values.

■ It also presumably supports a predefined system catalog.

■ Finally, it provides a separate CREATE CLUSTER statement, which means that (unlike some OO systems) it does not make the mistake of undermining data independence by letting the logical database definition dictate what physical clustering to use.

25.12 Carlo Zaniolo. "The Database Language GEM." Proc. 1983 ACM SIGMOD International Conference on Management of Data, San Jose, Calif. (May 1983). Republished in

M. Stonebraker (ed.): *Readings in Database Systems*. San Mateo, Calif.: Morgan Kaufmann (1988).

GEM is an acronym, standing for "General Entity Manipulator." It is effectively an extension to QUEL that supports non1NF relations (i.e., relations with set-valued attributes) and relations with alternative attributes (e.g., exempt EMPs have a SALARY attribute, nonexempt EMPs have HOURLY_WAGE and OVERTIME attributes). It also makes use of the OO idea that objects conceptually contain other objects (instead of foreign keys that reference those other objects), and extends the familiar dot notation to provide a simple way of referring to attributes of such contained objects (in effect, by implicitly traversing certain preferred join paths). For example, the qualified name EMP.DEPT.BUDGET could be used to refer to the budget of the department of some given employee. Many other systems, including POSTGRES [25.13-25.16] and UniSQL [25.11], have adopted and/or adapted this idea.

Extendable Systems

A variety of research projects have been under way for some years to build systems that are essentially relational and yet (like OO systems) are *extendable*—that is, they allow knowledgeable users (sometimes called "database customizers") to tailor the system in various ways, e.g., by defining their own data types, their own functions, their own storage structures, and so on. Two of the best known projects are **POSTGRES** from the University of California at Berkeley and **Starburst** from IBM Research. The following is a brief selection from the numerous publications on these two projects. Note, however, that neither of these systems adheres to the "domain = object class" equivalence advocated in the body of this chapter.

25.13 Michael Stonebraker and Lawrence A. Rowe. "The Design of POSTGRES." Proc. ACM SIGMOD International Conference on Management of Data, Washington, D.C. (June 1986).

The stated objectives of POSTGRES are:

1. To provide better support for complex objects

2. To provide user extendability for data types, operators, and access methods

3. To provide active database facilities (alerters and triggers) and inferencing support

4. To simplify the DBMS code for crash recovery

5. To produce a design that can take advantage of optical disks, multiple-processor workstations, and custom-designed VLSI chips

6. To make as few changes as possible (preferably none) to the relational model

25.14 Michael Stonebraker. "The Design of the POSTGRES Storage System." Proc. 13th International Conference on Very Large Data Bases, Brighton, England (September 1987).

25.15 Lawrence A. Rowe and Michael R. Stonebraker. "The POSTGRES Data Model." Proc. 13th International Conference on Very Large Data Bases, Brighton, England (September 1987).

25.16 Michael Stonebraker and Greg Kemnitz. "The POSTGRES Next Generation Database Management System." *CACM 34,* No. 10 (October 1991).

25.17 Bruce Lindsay, John McPherson, and Hamid Pirahesh. "A Data Management Extension Architecture." Proc. ACM SIGMOD International Conference on Management of Data, San Francisco, Calif. (May 1987).

Describes the overall architecture of the Starburst prototype. Starburst "facilitates the implementation of data management extensions for relational database systems." Two kinds of extensions are described in this paper, user-defined storage structures and access methods, and user-defined integrity constraints and triggered procedures. However (to quote the paper), "there are, of course, other directions in which it is important to be able to extend [DBMSs, including] user-defined abstract data types [and] query evaluation techniques." See reference [25.18] below.

25.18   Laura M. Haas, J. C. Freytag, G. M. Lohman, and Hamid Pirahesh. "Extensible Query Processing in Starburst." Proc. ACM SIGMOD International Conference on Management of Data, Portland, Ore. (June 1989).

The aims of the Starburst project expanded somewhat after reference [25.17] was first written: "Starburst provides support for adding new storage methods for tables, new types of access methods and integrity constraints, new data types, functions, and new operations on tables." The system is divided into two major components, Core and Corona, corresponding respectively to the RSS and RDS in the original System R prototype [8.12–8.16]. Core supports the extendability functions described in reference [25.17]. Corona supports the Starburst query language Hydrogen, which is a dialect of SQL that (a) eliminates most of the implementation restrictions of System R SQL, (b) is much more orthogonal than System R SQL, (c) supports recursive queries, and (d) is user-extendable. The paper includes an interesting discussion of "query rewrite," i.e., Hydrogen transformation rules that are used by the optimizer to convert queries to a semantically equivalent but more efficient form (see Chapter 18). See also reference [18.44].

25.19   Guy M. Lohman *et al.* "Extensions to Starburst: Objects, Types, Functions, and Rules." *CACM 34,* No. 10 (October 1991).

APPENDIXES

The following appendixes cover a somewhat mixed bag of topics. Appendix A provides a tutorial survey of common storage structures and access techniques. Appendix B gives a brief overview of a commercial relational implementation—namely, IBM's DB2 product—in order to give some idea of how a real relational DBMS actually works. Appendix C is an introduction to the ideas underlying logic-based systems (i.e., systems that attempt to marry ideas from the logic programming world with database ideas). Finally, Appendix D presents a list of the more important abbreviations and acronyms introduced in the text, together with their meanings.

A | Storage Structures and Access Methods

A.1 Introduction

In this appendix we present a tutorial survey of techniques for physically representing and accessing the database on the disk. (*Note:* We use the term "disk" throughout to stand generically for all direct-access media, including, e.g., RAID arrays, mass storage, and more recently optical disks, as well as conventional moving-head magnetic disks *per se*). The reader is assumed to have a basic familiarity with disk architecture and to understand what is meant by such terms as **seek time, rotational delay, cylinder, track, read/write head,** and so on. Good tutorials on such material can be found in many places; see, for example, reference [A.4].

The basic point motivating all storage structure and access method technology is that disk access times are *much* slower than main memory access times. Typical seek times and rotational delays are both on the order of 10 milliseconds or so, and typical data transfer rates are somewhere in the range 5 to 10 million bytes per second; main memory access is likely to be at least four or five orders of magnitude faster than disk access on any given system. An overriding performance objective is thus *to minimize the number of disk accesses* (disk I/O's). This appendix is concerned with techniques for achieving that objective—i.e., techniques for arranging stored data on the disk so that a required piece of data, say a required stored record, can be located in as few I/O's as possible.

As already suggested, any given arrangement of data on the disk is referred to as a **storage structure**. Many different storage structures can be and have been devised, and of course different structures have different performance characteristics; some are good for some applications, others are good for others. There is no single structure that is optimal for all applications. It follows that a good system should support a variety of different structures, so that different portions of the database can be stored in different ways, and the storage structure for a given portion can be changed as performance requirements change or become better understood.

The structure of the presentation is as follows. Following this introductory section, Section A.2 explains in outline what is involved in the overall process of locating and accessing some particular stored record,* and identifies the major software components involved in that process. Section A.3 then goes into a little more detail on two of those components, the *file manager* and the *disk manager*. Those two sections (A.2 and A.3) need only be skimmed on a first reading, if the reader desires; a lot of the detail they contain is not really required for an understanding of the subsequent material. The next four sections (Sections A.4–A.7) should not be just skimmed, however, since they represent the most important part of the entire discussion; they describe some of the most commonly occurring storage structures found in present-day systems, under the headings *indexing, hashing, pointer chains,* and *compression techniques,* respectively. Finally, Section A.8 presents a summary and a brief conclusion.

Note: The emphasis throughout is on *concepts,* not detail. The objective is to explain the general idea behind such notions as indexing, hashing, etc., without getting too bogged down in the details of any one specific system or technique. The reader who needs such detail is directed to the books and papers listed in the References and Bibliography section at the end of the appendix.

A.2   Database Access: An Overview

Before we get into our discussion of storage structures *per se,* we first briefly consider what is involved in the overall process of database access in general. Locating a specific piece of data in the database and presenting it to the user involves several layers of data access software. Of course, the details of those layers vary considerably from system to system, and so too does the terminology, but the principles are fairly standard and can be explained in outline as follows (refer to Fig. A.1).

1. First, the DBMS decides what stored record is required, and asks the **file manager** to retrieve that record. (We assume for the purposes of this simple explanation that the DBMS is able to pinpoint the exact record desired ahead of time. In practice it might need to retrieve a set of several records and search through those records in main memory to find the specific one desired. In principle, however, this only means that the sequence of steps 1–3 must be repeated for each stored record in that set.)

2. The file manager in turn decides what page contains the desired record, and asks the **disk manager** to retrieve that page.

3. Finally, the disk manager determines the physical location of the desired page on the disk, and issues the necessary disk I/O request. *Note:* Sometimes, of course, the required page will already be in a buffer in main memory as the result of a previous retrieval, in which case it obviously should not be necessary to retrieve it again.

Loosely speaking, therefore, the DBMS has a view of the database as a collection of stored records, and that view is supported by the file manager; the file manager, in

---

* Throughout this appendix, since our discussions are all at the storage level, we use storage-level terminology (files, records, fields, etc.) in place of their relational analogs.

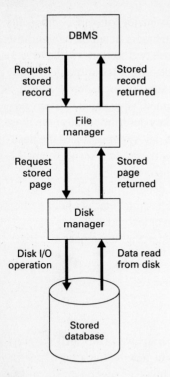

FIG. A.1 The DBMS, file manager, and disk manager

turn, has a view of the database as a collection of pages, and that view is supported by the disk manager; and the disk manager has a view of the disk "as it really is." The three subsections below amplify these ideas somewhat. Section A.3 then goes into more detail on the same topics.

Disk Manager

The disk manager is a component of the underlying operating system. It is the component responsible for all physical I/O operations (in some systems it is referred to as the "basic I/O services" component). As such, it clearly needs to be aware of **physical disk addresses**. For example, when the file manager asks to retrieve some specific page *p*, the disk manager needs to know exactly where page *p* is on the physical disk. However, the user of the disk manager—namely, the file manager—does *not* need to know that information. Instead, the file manager regards the disk simply as a logical collection of **page sets,** each one consisting of a collection of fixed-size pages. Each page set is identified by a unique **page set ID**. Each page, in turn, is identified by a **page number** that is unique within the disk; distinct page sets are disjoint (i.e., do not have any pages in common). The mapping between page numbers and physical disk addresses is understood and maintained by the disk manager. The major advantage of this arrangement (not the only one) is that all device-specific code can be isolated within a single system component, namely the disk manager, and all higher-level components—in particular, the file manager—can thus be *device-independent.*

As just explained, the complete set of pages on the disk is divided into a collection of disjoint subsets called page sets. One of those page sets, the **free space** page set, serves as a pool of available (i.e., currently unused) pages; the others are all considered to contain significant data. The allocation and deallocation of pages to and from page sets is performed by the disk manager on demand from the file manager. The operations supported by the disk manager on page sets—i.e., the operations the file manager is able to issue—include the following:

- Retrieve page *p* from page set *s*
- Replace page *p* within page set *s*
- Add a new page to page set *s* (i.e., acquire an empty page from the free space page set and return the new page number *p*)
- Remove page *p* from page set *s* (i.e., return page *p* to the free space page set)

The first two of these operations are of course the basic page-level I/O operations the file manager needs. The other two allow page sets to grow and shrink as necessary.

File Manager

The file manager uses the disk manager facilities just described in such a way as to permit its user—*viz.,* the DBMS—to regard the disk as a collection of **stored files** (remember from Chapter 1 that a stored file is the collection of all occurrences of one type of stored record). Each page set will contain one or more stored files. *Note:* The DBMS does need to be aware of the existence of page sets, even though it is not responsible for managing them in detail, for reasons indicated in the next subsection. In particular, the DBMS needs to know when two stored files share the same page set or when two stored records share the same page.

Each stored file is identified by a **file name** or **file ID,** unique at least within its containing page set, and each stored record, in turn, is identified by a **record number** or **record ID** (RID), unique at least within its containing stored file. (In practice, record IDs are usually unique, not just within their containing file, but actually within the entire disk, since they typically consist of the combination of a page number and some value that is unique within that page. See Section A.3, later.)

The operations supported by the file manager on stored files—i.e., the operations the DBMS is able to issue—include the following:

- Retrieve stored record *r* from stored file *f*
- Replace stored record *r* within stored file *f*
- Add a new stored record to stored file *f* and return the new record ID *r*
- Remove stored record *r* from stored file *f*
- Create a new stored file *f*
- Destroy stored file *f*

Using these primitive file management operations, the DBMS is able to build and manipulate the storage structures that are the principal concern of this appendix (see Sections A.4–A.7).

Note: In some systems the file manager is a component of the underlying operating system, in others it is packaged with the DBMS. For our purposes the distinction is not important. However, we remark in passing that, although operating systems do invariably provide such a component, it is often the case that the general-purpose file manager provided by the operating system is not ideally suited to the requirements of the special-purpose "application" that is the DBMS. For more discussion of this topic, see reference [A.44].

Clustering

We should not leave this overview discussion without a brief mention of the subject of *data clustering.* The basic idea behind clustering is to try and store records that are logically related (and therefore frequently used together) physically close together on the disk. Physical data clustering is an extremely important factor in performance, as can easily be seen from the following. Suppose the stored record most recently accessed is record *r1,* and suppose the next stored record required is record *r2.* Suppose also that *r1* is stored on page *p1* and *r2* is stored on page *p2.* Then:

1. If *p1* and *p2* are one and the same, then the access to *r2* will not require any physical I/O at all, because the desired page *p2* will already be in a buffer in main memory.

2. If *p1* and *p2* are distinct but physically close together—in particular, if they are physically adjacent—then the access to *r2* will require a physical I/O (unless, of course, *p2* also happens to be in a main memory buffer), but the seek time involved in that I/O will be small, because the read/write heads will already be close to the desired position. In particular, the seek time will be *zero* if *p1* and *p2* are in the same cylinder.

As an example of clustering, we consider the usual suppliers-and-parts database:*

■ If sequential access to all suppliers in supplier number order is a frequent application requirement, then the supplier records should be clustered such that the supplier S1 record is physically close to the supplier S2 record, the supplier S2 record is physically close to the supplier S3 record, and so on. This is an example of **intra-file** clustering: The clustering is applied within a single stored file.

■ If, on the other hand, access to some specific supplier together with all shipments for that supplier is a frequent application requirement, then supplier and shipment records should be stored interleaved, with the shipment records for supplier S1 physically close to the supplier S1 record, the shipment records for supplier S2

---

* We assume for simplicity throughout this appendix that each individual supplier, part, or shipment tuple maps to a single stored record on the disk (barring explicit statements to the contrary).

physically close to the supplier S2 record, and so on. This is an example of **inter-file** clustering: The clustering is applied across more than one stored file.

Of course, a given file or set of files can be physically clustered in one and only one way at any given time.

The DBMS can support clustering, both intra- and inter-file, by storing logically related records on the same page where possible and on adjacent pages where not (this is why the DBMS must know about pages as well as stored files). When the DBMS creates a new stored record, the file manager must allow it to specify that the new record be stored "near"—i.e., on the same page as, or at least on a page logically near to—some existing record. The disk manager, in turn, will do its best to ensure that two pages that are logically adjacent are physically adjacent on the disk. See Section A.3.

Of course, the DBMS can only know what clustering is required if the database administrator is able to tell it. A good DBMS should allow the DBA to specify different kinds of clustering for different files. It should also allow the clustering for a given file or set of files to be changed if the performance requirements change. Furthermore, of course, any such change in physical clustering should not require any concomitant changes in application programs, if data independence is to be achieved.

A.3 Page Sets and Files

As explained in the previous section, a major function of the disk manager is to allow the file manager to ignore all details of physical disk I/O and to think in terms of (logical) "page I/O" instead. This function of the disk manager is referred to as **page management**. We present a very simple example to show how page management is typically handled.

Consider the suppliers-and-parts database once again. Suppose that the desired logical ordering of records within each table is (loosely) *primary key sequence*—that is, suppliers are required to be in supplier number order, parts in part number order, and shipments in part number order within supplier number order.* To keep matters simple, suppose too that each stored file is stored in a page set of its own, and that each stored record requires an entire page of its own. Suppose also that the disk contains a total of $64K = 65,536$ pages (not at all unreasonable, by the way). Now consider the following sequence of events.

1. Initially the database contains no data at all. There is only one page set, the free space page set, which contains all the pages on the disk—except for page zero, which is special (see later). The remaining pages are numbered sequentially from one.

2. The file manager requests the creation of a page set for supplier records, and inserts

---

* We say "loosely" because the term *primary key sequence* is not well-defined if the primary key is composite. In the case of shipments, for example, it might mean either part number order within supplier number order or the other way about.

the five supplier records for suppliers S1–S5. The disk manager removes pages 1–5 from the free space page set and labels them "the suppliers page set."

3. Similarly for parts and shipments. Now there are four page sets: the suppliers page set (pages 1–5), the parts page set (pages 6–11), the shipments page set (pages 12–23), and the free space page set (pages 24, 25, 26, . . .). The situation at this point is as shown in Fig. A.2.

To continue with the example:

4. Next, the file manager inserts a new supplier stored record (for a new supplier, supplier S6). The disk manager locates the first free page in the free space page set—namely, page 24—and adds it to the suppliers page set.

5. The file manager deletes the stored record for supplier S2. The disk manager returns the page for supplier S2 (page 2) to the free space page set.

6. The file manager inserts a new part stored record (for part P7). The disk manager locates the first free page in the free space page set—namely, page 2—and adds it to the parts page set.

7. The file manager deletes the stored record for supplier S4. The disk manager returns the page for supplier S4 (page 4) to the free space page set.

And so on. The situation at this juncture is as illustrated in Fig. A.3. The point about that figure is the following: After the system has been running for a while, it can no longer be guaranteed that pages that are logically adjacent are still physically adjacent, even if they started out that way. For this reason, the logical sequence of pages in a given page set must be represented, not by physical adjacency, but by *pointers*. Each page will contain a **page header,** i.e., a set of control information that includes (among

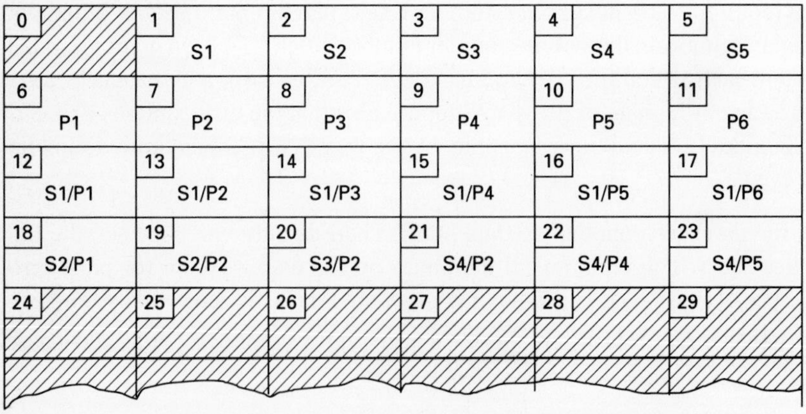

0	1	2	3	4	5
	S1	S2	S3	S4	S5
6	7	8	9	10	11
P1	P2	P3	P4	P5	P6
12	13	14	15	16	17
S1/P1	S1/P2	S1/P3	S1/P4	S1/P5	S1/P6
18	19	20	21	22	23
S2/P1	S2/P2	S3/P2	S4/P2	S4/P4	S4/P5
24	25	26	27	28	29

FIG. A.2 Disk layout after creation and initial loading of the suppliers-and-parts database

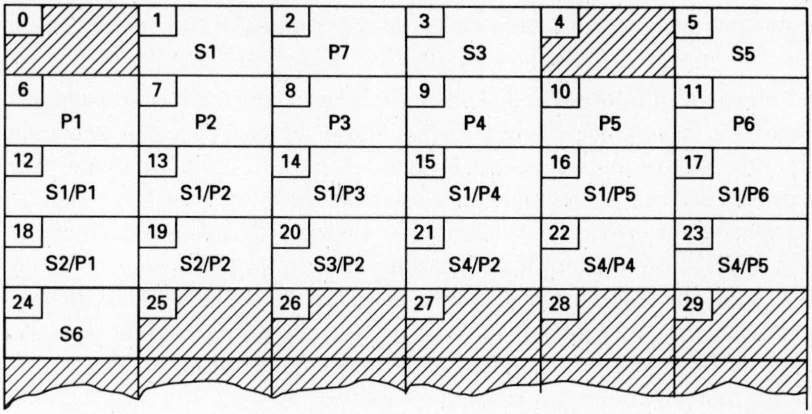

0 (free)	1 S1	2 P7	3 S3	4 (free)	5 S5
6 P1	7 P2	8 P3	9 P4	10 P5	11 P6
12 S1/P1	13 S1/P2	14 S1/P3	15 S1/P4	16 S1/P5	17 S1/P6
18 S2/P1	19 S2/P2	20 S3/P2	21 S4/P2	22 S4/P4	23 S4/P5
24 S6	25 (free)	26 (free)	27 (free)	28 (free)	29 (free)

FIG. A.3 Disk layout after inserting supplier S6, deleting supplier S2, inserting part P7, and deleting supplier S4

other things) the physical disk address of the page that immediately follows that page in logical sequence. See Fig. A.4.

Points arising from the foregoing example:

- The page headers—in particular, the "next page" pointers—are managed by the disk manager; they should be completely invisible to the file manager.

- As explained in the subsection on clustering at the end of Section A.2, it is desirable to store logically adjacent pages in physically adjacent locations on the disk (as far as possible). For this reason, the disk manager normally allocates and deallocates pages to and from page sets, not one at a time as suggested in the ex-

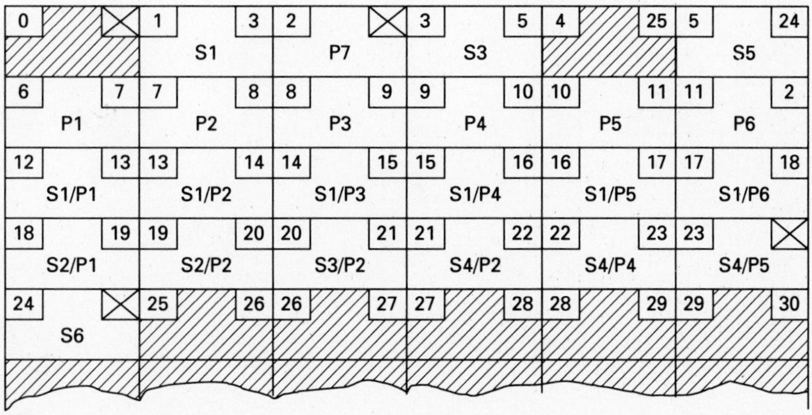

Each cell below shows: page number (top left), "next page" pointer (top right), and contents.

0 → [X] (free)	1 → 3 S1	2 → [X] 3 P7	3 → 5 S3	4 → 25 (free)	5 → 24 S5
6 → 7 P1	7 → 8 P2	8 → 9 P3	9 → 10 P4	10 → 11 P5	11 → 2 P6
12 → 13 S1/P1	13 → 14 S1/P2	14 → 15 S1/P3	15 → 16 S1/P4	16 → 17 S1/P5	17 → 18 S1/P6
18 → 19 S2/P1	19 → 20 S2/P2	20 → 21 S3/P2	21 → 22 S4/P2	22 → 23 S4/P4	23 → [X] S4/P5
24 → [X] S6	25 → 26 (free)	26 → 27 (free)	27 → 28 (free)	28 → 29 (free)	29 → 30 (free)

FIG. A.4 Fig. A.3 revised to show "next page" pointers (top right corner of each page)

ample, but rather in physically contiguous groups or **extents** of (say) 64 pages at a time.

■ The question arises: How does the disk manager know where the various page sets are located?—or, more precisely, how does it know, for each page set, where the (logically) first page of that page set is located? (It is sufficient to locate the first page, of course, because the second and subsequent pages can then be located by following the pointers in the page headers.) The answer is that some fixed location on the disk—typically cylinder zero, track zero—is used to store a page that gives precisely that information. That page (variously referred to as the *disk table of contents,* the *disk directory,* the *page set directory,* or simply *page zero*) thus typically contains a list of the page sets currently in existence on the disk, together with a pointer to the first page of each such page set. See Fig. A.5.

Now we turn to the file manager. Just as the disk manager allows the file manager to ignore details of physical disk I/O and to think for the most part in terms of logical pages, so the file manager allows the DBMS to ignore details of page I/O and to think for the most part in terms of stored files and stored records. This function of the file manager is referred to as **stored record management**. We discuss that function very briefly here, once again taking the suppliers-and-parts database as the basis for our examples.

Suppose, then (rather more realistically now), that a single page can accommodate several stored records, instead of just one as in the page management example. Suppose too that the desired logical order for supplier records is supplier number order, as before. Consider the following sequence of events.

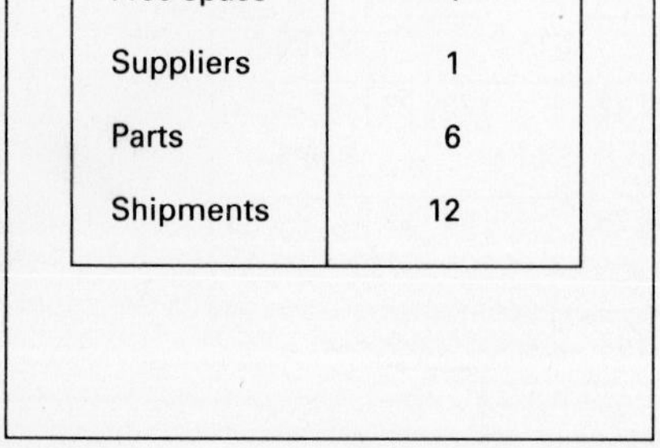

Page set	Address of first page
Free space	4
Suppliers	1
Parts	6
Shipments	12

FIG. A.5 The disk directory ("page zero")

1. First, the five stored records for suppliers S1–S5 are inserted and are stored together on some page *p*, as shown in Fig. A.6. Note that page *p* still contains a considerable amount of free space.

2. Now suppose the DBMS inserts a new supplier stored record (for a new supplier, say supplier S9). The file manager stores this record on page *p* (because there is still space), immediately following the stored record for supplier S5.

3. Next, the DBMS deletes the stored record for supplier S2. The file manager erases the S2 record from page *p*, and shifts the records for suppliers S3, S4, S5, and S9 up to fill the gap.

4. Next, the DBMS inserts a new supplier stored record for another new supplier, supplier S7. Again the file manager stores this record on page *p* (because there is still space); it places the new record immediately following that for supplier S5, shifting the record for supplier S9 down to make room. The situation at this juncture is illustrated in Fig. A.7.

And so on. The point of the example is that the logical sequence of stored records within any given page can be represented by *physical* sequence within that page. The file manager will shift individual records up and down to achieve this effect, keeping all data records together at the top of the page and all free space together at the bottom. (The logical sequence of stored records *across* pages is of course represented by the sequence of those pages within their containing page set, as described in the page management example earlier.)

As explained in Section A.2, stored records are identified internally by *record ID* or RID. Fig. A.8 shows how RIDs are typically implemented. The RID for a stored

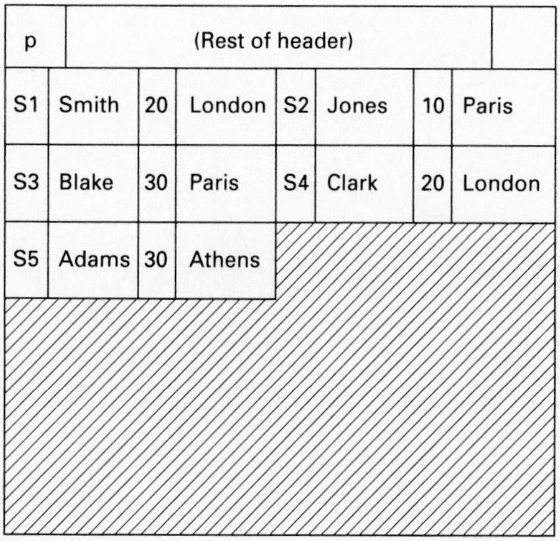

p	(Rest of header)						
S1	Smith	20	London	S2	Jones	10	Paris
S3	Blake	30	Paris	S4	Clark	20	London
S5	Adams	30	Athens				

FIG. A.6 Layout of page *p* after initial loading of the five supplier records for S1–S5

p	(Rest of header)						
S1	Smith	20	London	S3	Blake	20	Paris
S4	Clark	20	London	S5	Adams	10	Athens
S7	...	..	....	S9	...	..	....

FIG. A.7 Layout of page *p* after inserting supplier S9,
deleting supplier S2, and inserting supplier S7

record *r* consists of two parts—the page number of the page *p* containing *r*, and a byte offset from the foot of *p* identifying a slot that contains, in turn, the byte offset of *r* from the top of *p*. This scheme represents a good compromise between the speed of direct addressing and the flexibility of indirect addressing: Records can be shifted up and down within their containing page, as illustrated in Figs. A.7 and A.8, without having to change RIDs (only the local offsets at the foot of the page have to change); yet access to a given record given its RID is fast, involving only a single page access. (It is desir-

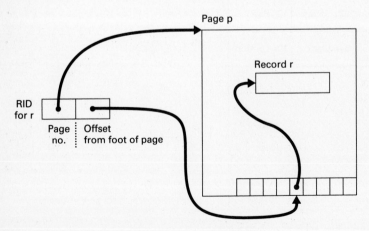

FIG. A.8 Implementation of stored record IDs (RIDs)

able that RIDs not change, because they are used elsewhere in the database as pointers to the records in question—for example, in indexes. If the RID of some record did in fact change, then all such pointer references elsewhere would have to be changed too.)

Note: Access to a specific stored record under the foregoing scheme might in rare cases involve two page accesses (but never more than two). Two accesses will be required if a varying length record is updated in such a way that it is now longer than it was before, and there is not enough free space on the page to accommodate the increase. In such a situation, the updated record will be placed on another page (an **overflow** page), and the original record will then be replaced by a pointer (another RID) to the new location. If the same thing happens again, so that the updated record has to be moved to still a third page, then the pointer in the original page will be changed to point to this newest location.

We are now almost ready to move on to our discussion of storage structures. From this point forward, we will assume for the most part (just as the DBMS normally assumes) that a given stored file is simply a collection of stored records, each uniquely identified by a record ID that never changes so long as that record remains in existence. A few final points to conclude this section:

■ Note that one consequence of the preceding discussion is that, for any given stored file, it is *always* possible to access all of the stored records in that stored file sequentially—where by "sequentially" we mean "stored record sequence within page sequence within page set" (typically, ascending RID sequence). This sequence is often referred to loosely as **physical** sequence, though it should be clear that it does not necessarily correspond to any obvious physical sequence on the disk. For convenience, however, we will adopt the same term.

■ Notice that access to a stored file in physical sequence is possible even if several files share the same page set (i.e., if stored files are interleaved). Records that do not belong to the stored file in question can simply be skipped over during the sequential scan (see the note below regarding record prefixes).

■ It should be stressed that physical sequence is often at least adequate as an access path to a given stored file. Sometimes it might even be optimal (especially if the stored file is small, say not more than ten or so pages). However, it is frequently the case that something better is needed. And, as indicated in Section A.1, an enormous variety of techniques exist for achieving such a "something better."

■ For the remainder of this appendix, we will usually assume for simplicity that the (unique) "physical" sequence for any given stored file is *primary key sequence* (as defined in Section A.3), barring any explicit statement to the contrary. Please note, however, that this assumption is made purely for the purpose of simplifying subsequent discussion; we recognize that there might be good reasons in practice for physically sequencing a given stored file in some other manner, e.g., by the value(s) of some other field(s), or simply by time of arrival (**chronological** sequence).

■ For various reasons, a stored record will probably contain certain control information in addition to its user data fields. That information is typically collected together at the front of the record in the form of a **record prefix**. Examples of the kind of information found in such prefixes are the ID of the containing stored file (necessary if one page can contain records from several stored files), the record length (necessary for varying length records), a delete flag (necessary if records are not physically deleted at the time of a logical delete operation), pointers (necessary if records are chained together in any way), and so on. But of course all such control information will normally be concealed from the user (i.e., end user or application programmer).

■ Finally, note that the user data fields in a given stored record will be of interest to the DBMS *but not to the file manager* (and not to the disk manager). The DBMS needs to be aware of those fields because it will use them as the basis for building indexes and the like. The file manager, however, has no need to be aware of them at all. Thus, another distinction between the DBMS and the file manager is that a given stored record has a known internal structure to the DBMS but is basically just a byte string to the file manager.

In the remainder of this appendix we describe some of the more important techniques for achieving the "something better" referred to above (i.e., an access path that is better than physical sequence). The techniques are discussed under the general headings of *indexing, hashing, pointer chains,* and *compression techniques.* One final general remark: The various techniques should not be seen as mutually exclusive. For example, it is perfectly feasible to have a stored file with (say) both hashed and indexed access to that file based on the same stored field, or with hashed access based on one field and pointer chain access based on another.

A.4 Indexing

Consider the suppliers table once again. Suppose the query "Find all suppliers in city *C* " (where *C* is a parameter) is an important one—i.e., one that is frequently executed and is therefore required to perform well. Given such a requirement, the DBA might choose the stored representation shown in Fig. A.9. In that representation, there are two stored files, a supplier file and a city file (probably in different page sets); the city file, which we assume to be stored in city sequence (because CITY is the primary key), includes pointers (RIDs) into the supplier file. To find all suppliers in London (say), the DBMS now has two possible strategies:

1. Search the entire supplier file, looking for all records with city value equal to London

2. Search the city file for the London entries, and for each such entry follow the pointer to the corresponding record in the supplier file

If the ratio of London suppliers to others is small, the second of these strategies is likely to be more efficient than the first, because (a) the DBMS is aware of the physical sequencing of the city file (it can stop its search of that file as soon as it finds a city that

City file (index)   Supplier file (data)

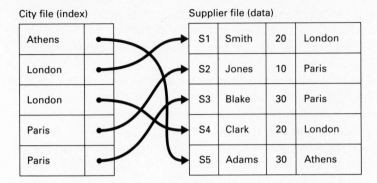

FIG. A.9 Indexing the supplier file on CITY

comes later than London in alphabetic order), and (b) even if it did have to search the entire city file, that search would still probably require fewer I/O's overall, because the city file is physically smaller than the supplier file (because the records are smaller).

In this example, the city file is said to be an **index** ("the CITY index") to the supplier file; equivalently, the supplier file is said to be *indexed by* the city file. An index is thus a special kind of stored file. To be specific, it is a file in which each entry (i.e., each record) consists of precisely two values, a data value and a pointer (RID); the data value is a value for some field of the indexed file, and the pointer identifies a record of that file that has that value for that field. The relevant field of the indexed file is called the *indexed field,* or sometimes the *index key* (we will not use this latter term, however).

Note: Indexes are so called by analogy with conventional book indexes, which also consist of entries containing "pointers" (page numbers) to facilitate the retrieval of information from an "indexed file" (i.e., the body of the book). Note, however, that unlike our CITY index, book indexes are *hierarchically compressed*—i.e., entries typically contain several page numbers, not just one. See Section A.7.

More terminology: An index on a primary key—e.g., an index on field S# of the supplier file—is sometimes called a *primary* index. An index on any other field—e.g., the CITY index in the example—is sometimes called a *secondary* index. Also, an index on a primary key, or more generally on any candidate key, is sometimes called a *unique* index.

How Indexes Are Used

The fundamental advantage of an index is that it speeds up retrieval. But there is a disadvantage too: It slows down updates. For instance, every time a new stored record is added to the indexed file, a new entry will also have to be added to the index. As a more specific example, consider what the DBMS must do to the CITY index of Fig. A.9 if supplier S2 moves from Paris to London. In general, therefore, the question that must be answered when some field is being considered as a candidate for indexing is:

Which is more important, efficient retrieval based on values of the field in question, or the update overhead involved in providing that efficient retrieval?

For the remainder of this section we concentrate on retrieval operations specifically.

Indexes can be used in essentially two different ways. First, they can be used for **sequential** access to the indexed file—where *sequential* means "in the sequence defined by values of the indexed field." For instance, the CITY index in the example above will allow records in the supplier file to be accessed in city sequence. Second, indexes can also be used for **direct** access to individual records in the indexed file on the basis of a given value for the indexed field. The query "Find suppliers in London" discussed at the start of the section illustrates this second case.

In fact, the two basic ideas just outlined can each be generalized slightly:

- *Sequential access:* The index can also help with *range* queries—for instance, "Find suppliers whose city is in some specified alphabetic range" (e.g., begins with a letter in the range L–R). Two important special cases are (a) "Find all suppliers whose city alphabetically precedes (or follows) some specified value," and (b) "Find all suppliers whose city is alphabetically first (or last)."

- *Direct access:* The index can also help with *list* queries—for instance, "Find suppliers whose city is in some specified list" (e.g., London, Paris, and New York).

In addition, there are certain queries—e.g., *existence tests*—that can be answered from the index alone, without any access to the indexed file at all. For example, consider the query "Are there any suppliers in Athens?" The response to this query is clearly "Yes" if and only if an entry for Athens exists in the CITY index.

A given stored file can have any number of indexes. For example, the supplier stored file might have both a CITY index and a STATUS index (see Fig. A.10). Those indexes could then be used to provide efficient access to supplier records on the basis of given values for either *or both* of CITY and STATUS. As an illustration of the "both" case, consider the query "Find suppliers in Paris with status 30." The CITY

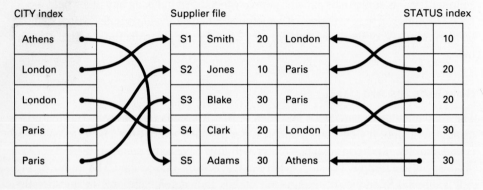

FIG. A.10 Indexing the supplier file on both CITY and STATUS

index gives the RIDs—*r2* and *r3,* say—for the suppliers in Paris; likewise, the STATUS index gives the RIDs—*r3* and *r5,* say—for suppliers with status 30. From these two sets of RIDs it is clear that the only supplier satisfying the original query is the supplier with RID equal to *r3* (namely, supplier S3). Only then does the DBMS have to access the supplier file itself, in order to retrieve the desired record.

More terminology: Indexes are sometimes referred to as **inverted lists,** for the following reason. First, a "normal" file—the supplier file of Figs. A.10 and A.11 can be taken as a typical "normal file"—lists, for each record, the values of the fields in that record. By contrast, an index lists, for each value of the indexed field, the records that contain that value. (The inverted-list database systems mentioned briefly at the end of Chapter 1 draw their name from this terminology.) And one more term: A file with an index on every field is sometimes said to be *fully inverted.*

Indexing on Field Combinations

It is also possible to construct an index on the basis of values of two or more fields in combination. For example, Fig. A.11 shows an index to the supplier file on the combination of fields CITY and STATUS, in that order. With such an index, the DBMS could respond to the query discussed above—"Find suppliers in Paris with status 30"—in a single scan *of a single index.* If the combined index were replaced by two separate indexes, then (as described earlier) that query would involve two separate index scans. Furthermore, it might be difficult in that case to decide which of those two scans should be done first; since the two possible sequences might have very different performance characteristics, the choice could be significant.

Note that the combined CITY/STATUS index can also serve as an index on the CITY field alone, since all the entries for a given city are at least still consecutive within the combined index. (Another, separate index will have to be provided if indexing on STATUS is also required, however.) In general, an index on the combination of fields

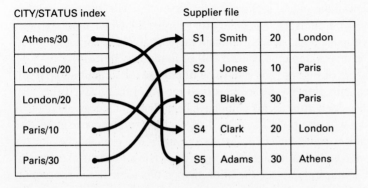

FIG. A.11 Indexing the supplier file on the combination of CITY and STATUS

F1, F2, F3, . . . Fn (in that order) will also serve as an index on *F1* alone, as an index on the combination *F1F2* (or *F2F1*), as an index on the combination *F1F2F3* (in any order), and so on. Thus the total number of indexes required to provide complete indexing in this way is not as large as might appear at first glance (see Exercise A.9 at the end of this appendix).

Dense *vs.* Nondense Indexing

As stated several times already, the fundamental purpose of an index is to speed up retrieval—more specifically, to reduce the number of disk I/O's needed to retrieve some given stored record. Basically, this purpose is achieved by means of *pointers;* and up to this point we have assumed that all such pointers are *record* pointers (i.e., RIDs). In fact, however, it would be sufficient for the stated purpose if those pointers were simply *page* pointers (i.e., page numbers). It is true that to find the desired record within a given page, the system would then have to do some additional work to search through the page in main memory, but the number of I/O's would remain unchanged. *Note:* As a matter of fact, the book index analogy mentioned earlier provides an example of an index in which the pointers are page pointers rather than "record" pointers.

We can take this idea further. Recall that any given stored file has a single "physical" sequence, represented by the combination of (a) the sequence of stored records within each page and (b) the sequence of pages within the containing page set. Suppose the supplier file is stored such that its physical sequence corresponds to the logical sequence as defined by the values of some field, say the supplier number field; in other words, the supplier file is *clustered* on that field (see the discussion of intra-file clustering at the end of Section A.2). Suppose also that an index is required on that field. Then there is no need for that index to include an entry for every stored record in the indexed file (i.e., the supplier file, in the example); all that is needed is an entry for each *page,* giving the highest supplier number on the page and the corresponding page number. See Fig. A.12 (where we assume for simplicity that a given page can hold a maximum of two supplier records).

As an example, consider what is involved in retrieving supplier S3 using this index. First the system must scan the index, looking for the first entry with supplier number greater than or equal to S3. It finds the index entry for supplier S4, which points to page *p* (say). It then retrieves page *p* and scans it in main memory, looking for the required stored record (which in this example, of course, will be found very quickly).

An index such as that of Fig. A.12 is said to be **nondense** (or sometimes **sparse**), because it does not contain an entry for every stored record in the indexed file. (By contrast, all indexes discussed prior to this point have been **dense**.) One advantage of a nondense index is that it will occupy less storage than a corresponding dense index, for the obvious reason that it contains fewer entries. As a result, it will probably be quicker to scan also. A disadvantage is that it might no longer be possible to perform existence tests on the basis of the index alone (see the brief note on this topic in the subsection "How indexes are used" earlier in this section).

Note that in general a given stored file can have at most one nondense index,

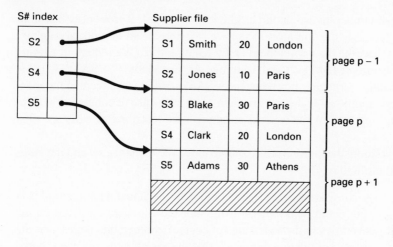

FIG. A.12 Example of a nondense index

because such an index relies on the (unique) physical sequence of the file in question. All other indexes must necessarily be dense.

B-trees

A particularly common and important kind of index is the **B-tree**. Although it is true that there is no single storage structure that is optimal for all applications, there is little doubt that if a single structure must be chosen, then B-trees of one kind or another are probably the one to choose. B-trees do generally seem to be the best all-around performer. For this reason, in fact, most relational systems support B-trees as their principal form of storage structure, and several support no other.

Before we can explain what a B-tree is, we must first introduce one more preliminary notion, namely the notion of a **multi-level** or **tree-structured** index.

The reason for providing an index in the first place is to remove the need for physical sequential scanning of the indexed file. However, physical sequential scanning is still needed in the *index*. If the indexed file is very large, then the index can itself get to be quite sizable, and sequentially scanning the index can itself get to be quite time-consuming. The solution to this problem is the same as before: We treat the index simply as a regular stored file, and build an index to it (an index to the index). This idea can be carried to as many levels as desired (three are common in practice; a file would have to be very large indeed to require more than three levels of indexing). Each level of the index acts as a nondense index to the level below (it *must* be nondense, of course, for otherwise nothing would be achieved—level n would contain the same number of entries as level $(n+1)$, and so would take just as long to scan).

Now we can discuss B-trees. A B-tree is a particular type of tree-structured index. B-trees as such were first described in a paper by Bayer and McCreight in 1972 [A.16]. Since that time, numerous variations on the basic idea have been proposed, by Bayer himself and by many other investigators; as already suggested, B-trees of one kind or another are now probably the commonest storage structure of all in modern database systems. Here we describe the variation given by Knuth [A.1]. (We remark in passing that the index structure of IBM's "Virtual Storage Access Method" VSAM [A.18] is very similar to Knuth's structure; however, the VSAM version was invented independently and includes additional features of its own, such as the use of compression techniques. In fact, a precursor of the VSAM structure was described as early as 1969 [A.19].)

In Knuth's variation, the index consists of two parts, the *sequence set* and the *index set* (to use VSAM terminology).

■ The **sequence set** consists of a single-level index to the actual data; that index is normally dense, but could be nondense if the indexed file were clustered on the indexed field. The entries in the index are (of course) grouped into pages, and the pages are (of course) chained together, such that the logical ordering represented by the index is obtained by taking the entries in physical order in the first page on the chain, followed by the entries in physical order in the second page on the chain, and so on. Thus the sequence set provides fast *sequential* access to the indexed data.

■ The **index set,** in turn, provides fast *direct* access to the sequence set (and hence to the data too). The index set is actually a tree-structured index to the sequence set; in fact, it is the index set that is the real B-tree, strictly speaking. The combination of index set and sequence set is sometimes called a "B-plus"-tree (B^+-tree). The top level of the index set consists of a single node (i.e., a single page, but of course containing many index entries, like all the other nodes). That top node is called the **root**.

A simple example is shown in Fig. A.13, which we explain as follows. First, the values 6, 8, 12, . . . 97, 99 are values of the indexed field, F say. Consider the top node, which consists of two F values (50 and 82) and three pointers (actually page numbers). Data records with F less than or equal to 50 can be found (eventually) by following the left pointer from this node; similarly, records with F greater than 50 and less than or equal to 82 can be found by following the middle pointer; and records with F greater than 82 can be found by following the right pointer. The other nodes of the index set are interpreted analogously; note that (for example) following the right pointer from the first node at the second level takes us to all records with F greater than 32 *and also less than or equal to 50* (by virtue of the fact that we have already followed the left pointer from the next higher node).

The B-tree (i.e., index set) of Fig. A.13 is somewhat unrealistic, however, for the following two reasons:

■ First, the nodes of a B-tree do not normally all contain the same number of data values;

■ Second, they normally do contain a certain amount of free space.

In general, a "B-tree of order n" has at least n but not more than $2n$ data values at any given node (and if it has k data values, then it also has $k+1$ pointers). No data value

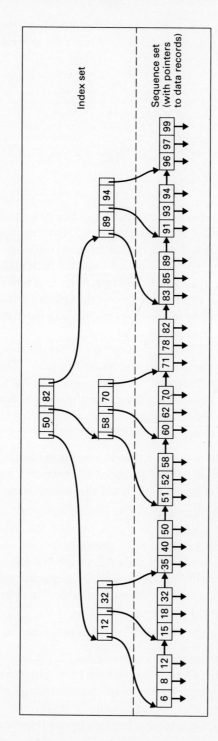

FIG. A.13 Part of a simple B-tree (Knuth's variation)

appears in the tree more than once. We give the algorithm for searching for a particular value V in the structure of Fig. A.13; the algorithm for the general B-tree of order n is a simple generalization.

```
set N to the root node ;
do until N is a sequence-set node ;
    let X, Y (X < Y) be the data values in node N ;
    if V ≤ X     then set N to the left   lower node of N ;
    if X < V ≤ Y then set N to the middle lower node of N ;
    if V > Y     then set N to the right  lower node of N ;
end ;
if V occurs in node N then exit /* found */ ;
if V does not occur in node N then exit /* not found */ ;
```

A problem with tree structures in general is that insertions and deletions can cause the tree to become *unbalanced*. A tree is unbalanced if the leaf nodes are not all at the same level—i.e., if different leaf nodes are at different distances from the root node. Since searching the tree involves a disk access for every node visited, search times can become very unpredictable in an unbalanced tree. *Note:* In practice, the top level of the index—possibly portions of other levels too—will typically be kept in main memory most of the time, which will have the effect of reducing the average number of disk accesses. The overall point remains valid, however.

The notable advantage of B-trees, by contrast, is that the B-tree insertion/deletion algorithm guarantees that the tree will always be balanced. (The "B" in "B-tree" is sometimes said to stand for "balanced" for this reason.) We briefly consider insertion of a new value, V say, into a B-tree of order n. The algorithm as described caters for the index set only, since (as explained earlier) it is the index set that is the B-tree proper; a trivial extension is needed to deal with the sequence set also.

- First, the search algorithm is executed to locate, not the sequence set node, but that node (N say) at the lowest level of the index set in which V logically belongs. If N contains free space, V is inserted into N and the process terminates.

- Otherwise, node N (which must therefore contain $2n$ values) is *split* into two nodes $N1$ and $N2$. Let S be the original $2n$ values plus the new value V, in their logical sequence. The lowest n values in S are placed in the left node $N1$, the highest n values in S are placed in the right node $N2$, and the middle value, W say, is promoted to the parent node of N, P say, to serve as a separator value for nodes $N1$ and $N2$. Future searches for a value U, on reaching node P, will be directed to node $N1$ if $U \le W$ and to node $N2$ if $U > W$.

- An attempt is now made to insert W into P, and the process is repeated.

In the worst case, splitting will occur all the way to the top of the tree; a new root node (parent to the old root, which will now have been split into two) will be created, and the tree will increase in height by one level (but even so will still remain balanced).

The deletion algorithm is of course essentially the inverse of the insertion algorithm just described. Changing a value is handled by deleting the old value and inserting the new one.

A.5   Hashing

Hashing (also called **hash-addressing,** and sometimes—confusingly—**hash indexing**) is a technique for providing fast *direct* access to a specific stored record on the basis of a given value for some field. The field in question is usually but not necessarily the primary key. In outline, the technique works as follows.

- Each stored record is placed in the database at a location whose address (RID, or perhaps just page number) is computed as some function (the **hash function**) of some field of that record (the *hash field,* or sometimes *hash key;* we will not use this latter term, however). The computed address is called the **hash address**.

- To store the record initially, the DBMS computes the hash address for the new record and instructs the file manager to place the record at that position.

- To retrieve the record subsequently given the hash field value, the DBMS performs the same computation as before and instructs the file manager to fetch the record at the computed position.

As a simple illustration, suppose (a) that supplier number values are S100, S200, S300, S400, S500 (instead of S1, S2, S3, S4, S5), and (b) that each stored supplier record requires an entire page to itself, and consider the following hash function:

```
hash address (i.e., page number) =
    remainder after dividing numeric part of S# value by 13
```

This is a trivial example of a very common class of hash function called **division/ remainder**. (For reasons that are beyond the scope of this appendix, the divisor in a division/remainder hash is usually chosen to be prime, as in our example.) The page numbers for the five suppliers are then 9, 5, 1, 10, 6, respectively, giving us the representation shown in Fig. A.14.

It should be clear from the foregoing description that hashing differs from indexing inasmuch as, while a given stored file can have any number of indexes, it can have *at most one* hash structure. To state this differently: A file can have any number of indexed fields, but only one hash field. (These remarks assume the hash is *direct*. By contrast, a file can have any number of *indirect* hashes. See reference [A.24].)

In addition to showing how hashing works, the example also shows why the hash function is necessary. It would theoretically be possible to use an "identity" hash function—e.g., to take the primary key value directly as the hash address (assuming, of course, that the primary key is numeric). Such a technique would generally be inadequate in practice, however, because the range of possible primary key values will usually be much wider than the range of available addresses. For instance, suppose that supplier numbers are in fact in the range S000–S999, as in the example above. Then there would be 1000 possible distinct supplier numbers, whereas there might in fact be only ten or so actual suppliers. Thus, in order to avoid a considerable waste of storage space, we would ideally like to find a hash function that would reduce any value in the range 000–999 to one in the range 0–9 (say). To allow a little room for future growth,

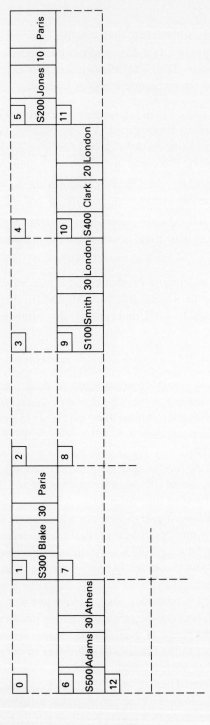

FIG. A.14 Example of a hashed structure

it is usual to extend the target range by 20 percent or so; that was why we chose a function that generated values in the range 0–12 rather than 0–9 in our example above.

The example also illustrates one of the disadvantages of hashing: The "physical sequence" of records within the stored file will almost certainly not be the primary key sequence, nor indeed any other sequence that has any sensible logical interpretation. (In addition, there may be gaps of arbitrary size between consecutive records.) In fact, the physical sequence of a stored file with a hashed structure is usually—not invariably— considered to represent no particular logical sequence.

(Of course, it is always possible to *impose* any desired logical sequence on a hashed file by means of an index; indeed, it is possible to impose several such sequences, by means of several indexes, one for each sequence. See also references [A.35] and [A.37], which discuss the possibility of hashing schemes that do preserve logical sequence in the file as stored.)

Another disadvantage of hashing in general is that there is always the possibility of **collisions**—that is, two or more distinct records ("synonyms") that hash to the same address. For example, suppose the supplier file (with suppliers S100, S200, etc.) also includes a supplier with supplier number S1400. Given the "divide by 13" hash function discussed above, that supplier would collide (at hash address 9) with supplier S100. The hash function as it stands is thus clearly inadequate—it needs to be extended somehow to deal with the collision problem.

In terms of our original example, one possible extension is to treat the remainder after division by 13, not as the hash address *per se,* but rather as the start point for a sequential scan. Thus, to insert supplier S1400 (assuming that suppliers S100–S500 already exist), we go to page 9 and search forward from that position for the first free page. The new supplier will be stored on page 11. To retrieve that supplier subsequently, we go through a similar procedure. This **linear search** method might well be adequate if (as is likely in practice) several records are stored on each page. Suppose each page can hold n stored records. Then the first n collisions at some hash address p will all be stored on page $p,$ and a linear search through those collisions will be totally contained within that page. However, the next—i.e., $(n+1)$st—collision will of course have to be stored on some distinct **overflow** page, and another I/O will be needed.

Another approach to the collision problem, perhaps more frequently encountered in real systems, is to treat the result from the hash function, a say, as the storage address, not for a data record, but rather for an **anchor point**. The anchor point at storage address a is then taken as the head of a chain of pointers (a **collision chain**) linking together all records—or all pages of records—that collide at a. Within any given collision chain, the collisions will typically be kept in hash field sequence, to simplify subsequent searching.

Extendable Hashing

Yet another disadvantage of hashing as described above is that as the size of the hashed file increases, so the number of collisions also tends to increase, and hence the average access time increases correspondingly (because more and more time is spent searching through sets of collisions). Eventually a point might be reached where it becomes desirable to reorganize the file—i.e., to unload the existing file and to reload it, using a new hashing function.

Extendable hashing [A.28] is a nice variation on the basic hashing idea that alleviates the foregoing problems. In fact, extendable hashing guarantees that the number of disk accesses needed to locate a specific record (i.e., the record having a specific primary key value) is never more than two, and will usually be only one, no matter what the file size might be. (It therefore also guarantees that file reorganization will never be required.) *Note:* Values of the hash field must be unique in the extendable hashing scheme, which of course they will be if that field is in fact the primary key as suggested at the start of this section.

In outline, the scheme works as follows.

1. Let the basic hash function be h, and let the primary key value of some specific record r be k. Hashing k—i.e., evaluating $h(k)$—yields a value s called the *pseudokey* of r. Pseudokeys are not interpreted directly as addresses but instead lead to storage locations in an indirect fashion as described below.

2. The stored file has a *directory* associated with it, also stored on the disk. The directory consists of a header, containing a value d called the *depth* of the directory, together with 2^d pointers. The pointers are pointers to data pages, which contain the actual stored records (many records per page). A directory of depth d can thus handle a maximum file size of 2^d distinct data pages.

3. If we consider the leading d bits of a pseudokey as an unsigned binary integer b, then the ith pointer in the directory ($1 \le i \le 2^d$) points to a page that contains all records for which b takes the value $i-1$. In other words, the first pointer points to the page containing all records for which b is all zeros, the second pointer points to the page for which b is $0 \ldots 01$, and so on. (These 2^d pointers are typically not all distinct; that is, there will typically be fewer than 2^d distinct data pages. See Fig. A.15.) Thus, to find the record having primary key value k, we hash k to find the pseudokey s and take the first d bits of that pseudokey; if those bits have the numeric value $i-1$, we go to the ith pointer in the directory (first disk access) and follow it to the page containing the required record (second disk access).

   Note: In practice the directory will usually be sufficiently small that it can be kept in main memory most of the time. Thus the "two" disk accesses will usually reduce to one in practice.

4. Each data page also has a header giving the *local depth* p of that page ($p \le d$). Suppose, for example, that d is three, and that the first pointer in the directory (the 000 pointer) points to a page for which the local depth p is two. Local depth two here means that, not only does this page contain all records with pseudokeys starting 000, it contains *all* records with pseudokeys starting 00 (i.e., those starting 000 and also those starting 001). In other words, the 001 directory pointer also points to this page. Again, see Fig. A.15.

5. Continuing the example from paragraph 3 above, suppose now that the 000 data page is full and we wish to insert a new record having a pseudokey that starts 000

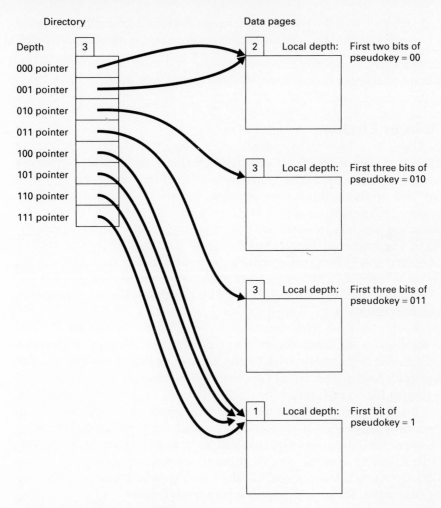

FIG. A.15   Example of extendable hashing

(or 001). At this point the page is split in two; that is, a new, empty page is acquired, and all 001 records are moved out of the old page and into the new one. The 001 pointer in the directory is changed to point to the new page (the 000 pointer still points to the old one). The local depth p for each of the two pages will now be three, not two.

6. Again continuing the example, suppose that the data page for 000 becomes full again and has to split again. The existing directory cannot handle such a split, because the local depth of the page to be split is already equal to the directory depth. Therefore we *double the directory;* that is, we increase d by one and replace each pointer by a pair of adjacent, identical pointers. The data page can now be split; 0000 records are left in the old page and 0001 records go in the new page; the first pointer in the directory is left unchanged (i.e., it still points to the old page), the

second pointer is changed to point to the new page. Note that doubling the directory is a fairly inexpensive operation, since it does not involve access to any of the data pages.

So much for our discussion of extendable hashing. Numerous further variations on the basic hashing idea have been devised; see, for example, references [A.29–A.36].

A.6 Pointer Chains

Suppose again, as at the beginning of Section A.4, that the query "Find all suppliers in city *C*" is an important one. Another stored representation that can handle that query reasonably well—possibly better than an index, though not necessarily so—uses *pointer chains*. Such a representation is illustrated in Fig. A.16. As can be seen, it involves two stored files, a supplier file and a city file, much as in the index representation of Fig. A.9 (this time both files are probably in the same page set, for reasons to be explained in Section A.7). In the pointer chain representation of Fig. A.16, however, the city file is not an index but what is sometimes referred to as a *parent* file. The supplier file is accordingly referred to as the *child* file, and the overall structure is an example of **parent/child organization**.

In the example, the parent/child structure is based on supplier city values. The parent (city) file contains one stored record for each distinct supplier city, giving the city value and acting as the head of a *chain* or *ring* of pointers linking together all child (supplier) records for suppliers in that city. Note that the city field has been removed from the supplier file; to find all suppliers in London (say), the DBMS can search the city file for the London entry and then follow the corresponding pointer chain.

The principal advantage of the parent/child structure is that the insert/delete algorithms are somewhat simpler, and might conceivably be more efficient, than the corresponding algorithms for an index; also, the structure will probably occupy less storage than the corresponding index structure, because each city value appears exactly once instead of many times. The principal disadvantages are as follows:

- For a given city, the only way to access the *n*th supplier is to follow the chain and access the 1st, 2nd, ... $(n - 1)$st supplier too. Unless the supplier records are appropriately clustered, each access will involve a separate seek operation, and the time taken to access the *n*th supplier could be considerable.

- Although the structure might be suitable for the query "Find suppliers in a given city," it is of no help—in fact, it is a positive hindrance—for the converse query "Find the city for a given supplier" (where the given supplier is identified by a given supplier number). For this latter query, either a hash or an index on the supplier file is probably desirable; note that a parent/child structure based on supplier numbers would not make much sense (why not?). And even when the given supplier record has been located, it is still necessary to follow the chain to the parent record to discover the desired city (the need for this extra step is our justification for claiming that the parent/child structure is actually a hindrance for this class of query).

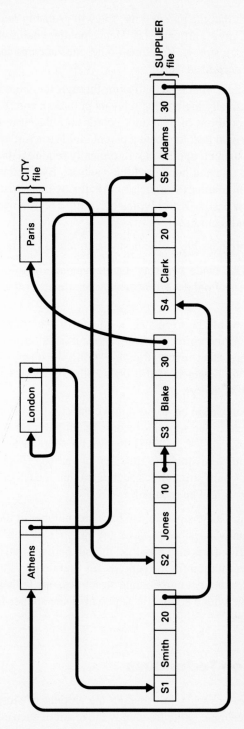

FIG. A.16 Example of a parent/child structure

Note, moreover, that the parent (city) file will probably require index or hash access too if it is of any significant size. Hence pointer chains alone are not really an adequate basis for a storage structure—other mechanisms such as indexes will almost certainly be needed as well.

- Because (a) the pointer chains actually run through the stored records (i.e., the record prefixes physically include the relevant pointers), and (b) values of the relevant field are factored out of the child records and placed in the parent records instead, it is a nontrivial task to create a parent/child structure over an existing set of records. In fact, such an operation will typically require a database reorganization, at least for the relevant portion of the database. By contrast, it is a comparatively straightforward matter to create a new index over an existing set of records. *Note:* Creating a new hash will also typically require a reorganization, incidentally, unless the hash is indirect [A.24].

Several variations are possible on the basic parent/child structure. For example:

- The pointers could be made two-way. One advantage of this variation is that it simplifies the process of pointer adjustment necessitated by the operation of deleting a child record.

- Another extension would be to include a pointer (a "parent pointer") from each child record direct to the corresponding parent; this extension would reduce the amount of chain-traversing involved in answering the query "Find the city for a given supplier" (note, however, that it does not eliminate the need for a hash or index to help with that query).

- Yet another variation would be *not* to remove the city field from the supplier file but to repeat the field in the supplier records (a simple form of controlled redundancy). Certain retrievals—e.g., "Find the city for supplier S4"—would then become more efficient. Note, however, that that increased efficiency has nothing to do with the pointer chain structure as such, also that a hash or index on supplier numbers will probably still be required.

Finally, of course, just as it is possible to have any number of indexes over a given stored file, so it is equally possible to have any number of pointer chains running through a given stored file. (It is also possible, though perhaps unusual, to have both.) Fig. A.17 shows a representation for the supplier file that involves two distinct pointer chains, and therefore two distinct parent/child structures, one with a city file as parent (as in Fig. A.16) and one with a status file as parent. The supplier file is the child file for both of these structures.

A.7 Compression Techniques

Compression techniques are ways of reducing the amount of storage required for a given collection of stored data. Quite frequently the result of such compression will be not only to save on storage space, but also (and probably more significantly) to save on

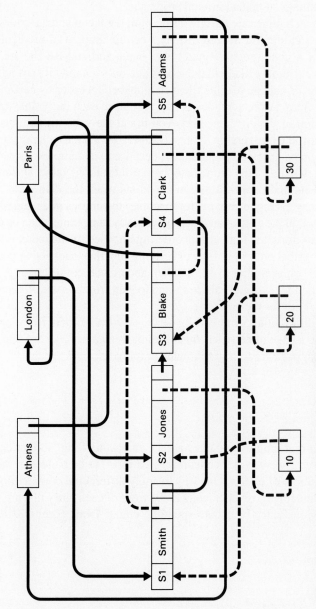

FIG. A.17 Example of a multiple parent/child organization

disk I/O; for if the data occupies less space, then fewer I/O operations will be needed to access it. On the other hand, extra processing will be needed to decompress the data after it has been retrieved. On balance, however, the I/O savings will probably outweigh the disadvantage of that additional processing.

Compression techniques are designed to exploit the fact that data values are almost never completely random but instead display a certain amount of predictability. As a trivial example, if a given person's name in a name-and-address file starts with the letter R, then it is extremely likely that the next person's name will start with the letter R also—assuming, of course, that the file is in alphabetical order by name.

A common compression technique is thus to replace each individual data value by some representation of the difference between it and the value that immediately precedes it—**differential compression**. Note, however, that such a technique requires that the data in question be accessed sequentially, because to decompress any given stored value requires knowledge of the immediately preceding stored value. Differential compression thus has its main applicability in situations when the data must be accessed sequentially anyway, as in the case of (for example) the entries in a single-level index. Note moreover that, in the case of an index specifically, the pointers can be compressed as well as the data—for if the logical data ordering imposed by the index is the same as, or close to, the physical ordering of the underlying file, then successive pointer values in the index will be quite similar to one another, and pointer compression is likely to be beneficial. In fact, indexes almost always stand to gain from the use of compression, at least for the data if not for the pointers.

To illustrate differential compression, we depart for a moment from suppliers-and-parts and consider a page of entries from an "employee name" index. Suppose the first four entries on that page are for the following employees:

```
Roberton
Robertson
Robertstone
Robinson
```

Suppose also that employee names are 12 characters long, so that each of these names should be considered (in its uncompressed form) to be padded at the right with an appropriate number of blanks. One way to apply differential compression to this set of values is by replacing those characters at the front of each entry that are the same as those in the previous entry by a corresponding count: **front compression**. This approach yields:

```
0 - Roberton++++
6 - son+++
7 - tone+
3 - inson++++
```

(trailing blanks now shown explicitly as "+").

Another possible compression technique for this set of data is simply to eliminate all trailing blanks (again, replacing them by an appropriate count): an example of **rear compression**. Further rear compression can be achieved by dropping all characters to the right of the one required to distinguish the entry in question from its two immediate neighbors, as follows:

```
0 - 7 - Roberto
6 - 2 - so
7 - 1 - t
3 - 1 - i
```

The first of the two counts in each entry here is as in the previous example, the second is a count of the number of characters recorded. We have assumed that the next entry does not have "Robi" as its first four characters when decompressed. Note, however, that we have actually lost some information from this index. That is, when decompressed, it looks like this:

```
Roberto?????
Robertso????
Robertst????
Robi????????
```

(where "?" represents an unknown character). Such a loss of information is obviously permissible only if the data is recorded in full *somewhere*—in the example, in the underlying employee file.

Hierarchic Compression

Suppose a given stored file is physically sequenced (i.e., clustered) by values of some stored field *F,* and suppose also that each distinct value of *F* occurs in several (consecutive) records of that file. For example, the supplier stored file might be clustered by values of the city field, in which case all London suppliers would be stored together, all Paris suppliers would be stored together, and so on. In such a situation, the set of all supplier records for a given city might profitably be compressed into a single **hierarchic** stored record, in which the city value in question appears exactly once, followed by supplier number, name, and status information for each supplier that happens to be located in that city. See Fig. A.18.

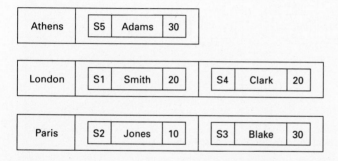

FIG. A.18 Example of hierarchic compression (intra-file)

The stored record *type* illustrated in Fig. A.18 consists of two parts: a fixed part, namely the city field, and a varying part, namely the set of supplier entries. (The latter part is varying in the sense that the number of entries it contains—i.e., the number of suppliers in the city in question—varies from one occurrence of the record to another.) As explained in Chapter 3, such a varying set of entries within a record is usually referred to as a **repeating group**. Thus we would say that the hierarchic record type of Fig. A.18 consists of a single city field and a repeating group of supplier information, and the repeating group in turn consists of a supplier number field, a supplier name field, and a supplier status field (one instance of the group for each supplier in the relevant city).

Hierarchic compression of the type just described is often particularly appropriate in an index, where it is commonly the case that several successive entries all have the same data value (but of course different pointer values).

It follows from the foregoing that hierarchic compression of the kind illustrated is feasible only if intra-file clustering is in effect. As the reader might already have realized, however, a similar kind of compression can be applied with *inter*-file clustering also. Suppose that suppliers and shipments are clustered as suggested at the end of Section A.2—that is, shipments for supplier S1 immediately follow the supplier record for S1, shipments for supplier S2 immediately follow the supplier record for S2, and so on. More specifically, suppose that supplier S1 and the shipments for supplier S1 are stored on page *p1,* supplier S2 and the shipments for supplier S2 are stored on page *p2,* etc. Then an inter-file compression technique can be applied as shown in Fig. A.19.

Note: Although we describe this example as "inter-file," it really amounts to combining the supplier and shipment files into a single file and then applying *intra*-file compression to that single file. Thus this case is not really different in kind from the case already illustrated in Fig. A.18.

We conclude this subsection by remarking that the pointer chain structure of Fig.

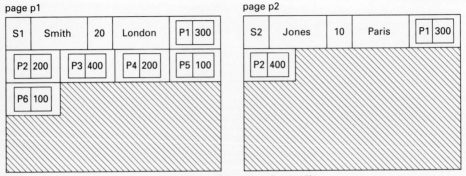

(and similarly for pages p3, p4, p5)

FIG. A.19 Example of hierarchic compression (inter-file)

A.16 can be regarded as a kind of inter-file compression that does not require a corresponding inter-file clustering (or, rather, the pointers provide the logical effect of such a clustering—so that compression is possible—but do not necessarily provide the corresponding physical performance advantage at the same time—so that compression, though possible, might not be a good idea).

Huffman Coding

"Huffman coding" [A.39] is a character encoding technique, little used in current systems, but one that can nevertheless result in significant data compression if different characters occur in the data with different frequencies (which is the normal situation, of course). The basic idea is as follows: Bit string encodings are assigned to represent characters in such a way that different characters are represented by bit strings of different lengths, and the most commonly occurring characters are represented by the shortest strings. Also, no character has an encoding (of n bits, say) such that those n bits are identical to the first n bits of some other character encoding.

As a simple example, suppose the data to be represented involves only the characters A, B, C, D, E, and suppose also that the relative frequency of occurrence of those five characters is as indicated in the following table:

```
Character   Frequency   Code

E               35%      1
A               30%      01
D               20%      001
C               10%      0001
B                5%      0000
```

Character E has the highest frequency and is therefore assigned the shortest code, a single bit, say a 1-bit. All other codes must then start with a 0-bit and must be at least two bits long (a lone 0-bit would not be valid, since it would be indistinguishable from the leading portion of other codes). Character A is assigned the next shortest code, say 01; all other codes must therefore begin 00. Similarly, characters D, C, and B are assigned codes 001, 0001, and 0000 respectively. *Exercise for the reader:* What English words do the following strings represent?

1. 00110001010011

2. 010001000110011

Given the encodings shown, the expected average length of a coded character, in bits, is

```
0.35 * 1 + 0.30 * 2 + 0.20 * 3 + 0.10 * 4 + 0.05 * 4 = 2.15  bits,
```

whereas if every character were assigned the same number of bits, as in a conventional character coding scheme, we would need three bits per character (to allow for the five possibilities).

A.8 Summary

In this appendix we have taken a lengthy—by no means exhaustive!—look at some of the most important storage structures used in current practice. We have also described in outline how the data access software typically functions, and have sketched the ways in which responsibility is divided up among the **DBMS,** the **file manager,** and the **disk manager.** Our purpose throughout has been to explain overall concepts, not to describe in fine detail how the various system components and storage structures actually work; indeed, we have tried hard not to get bogged down in too much detail, though of course a certain amount of detail is unavoidable.

By way of summary, here is a brief review some of the major topics we have touched on. First, we described **clustering,** the basic idea of which is that records that are used together should be stored physically close together. We also explained how stored records are identified internally by **record IDs** or **RIDs.** Then we considered some of the most important storage structures encountered in practice:

- **Indexes** (several variations thereof, including in particular **B-trees**) and their use for both **sequential** and **direct** access

- **Hashing** (including in particular **extendable** hashing) and its use for **direct** access

- **Pointer chains** (also known as **parent/child structures**) and numerous variations thereof

We also examined a variety of **compression** techniques.

We conclude by stressing the point that most users are (or should be) unconcerned with most of this material most of the time. The only "user" who needs to understand these ideas in detail is the DBA, who is responsible for the physical design of the database and for performance monitoring and tuning. For other users, such considerations should preferably all be under the covers, though it is probably true to say that those users will perform their job better if they have some idea of the way the system functions internally. For DBMS implementers, on the other hand, a working knowledge of this material (indeed, an understanding that goes much deeper than this introductory survey does) is clearly desirable, if not mandatory.

Exercises

Exercises A.1–A.8 might prove suitable as a basis for group discussion; they are intended to lead to a deeper understanding of various physical database design considerations. Exercises A.9 and A.10 have rather a mathematical flavor.

A.1 Investigate any database systems (the larger the better) that might be available to you. For each such system, identify the components that perform the functions ascribed in the body of this appendix to, respectively, the disk manager, the file manager, and the DBMS proper. What kind of disks or other media does the system support? What is the page size? What are the disk capacities, both theoretical (in bytes) and actual (in pages)? What are the data rates? The access times? How do those access times compare with the speed of main memory? Are there any limits on file size or database size? If so, what are they? Which of the storage structures described in this appendix does the system support? Does it support any others? If so, what are they?

A.2 A company's personnel database is to contain information about the divisions, departments, and employees of that company. Each employee works in one department; each department is part of one division. Invent some sample data and sketch some possible corresponding storage structures. Where possible, state the relative advantages of each of those structures—i.e., consider how typical retrieval and update operations would be handled in each case. *Hint:* The constraints "each employee works in one department" and "each department is part of one division" are structurally similar to the constraint "each supplier is located in one city" (they are all examples of **many-to-one relationships**). A difference is that we would probably like to record more information in the database for departments and divisions than we did for cities.

A.3 Repeat Exercise A.2 for a database that is to contain information about customers and items. Each customer can order any number of items; each item can be ordered by any number of customers. *Hint:* There is a **many-to-many** relationship here between customers and items. One way to represent such a relationship is by means of a *double index*. A double index is an index that is used to index two data files simultaneously; a given entry in such an index corresponds to a pair of related data records, one from each of the two files, and contains two data values and two pointers. Can you think of any other ways of representing many-to-many(-to-many-...) relationships?

A.4 Repeat Exercise A.2 for a database that is to contain information about parts and components, where a component is itself a part and can have lower-level components. *Hint:* How does this problem differ from that of Exercise A.3?

A.5 A stored file of data records with no additional access structure (i.e., no index, no hash, etc.) is sometimes called a **heap**. New records are inserted into a heap wherever there happens to be room. For small files—certainly for any file not requiring more than (say) nine or ten pages of storage—a heap is probably the most efficient structure of all. Most files are bigger than that, however, and in practice all but the smallest files should have some additional access structure, say (at least) an index on the primary key. State the relative advantages and disadvantages of an indexed structure when compared with a heap structure.

A.6 We referred several times in the body of this appendix to physical clustering. For example, it might be advantageous to store the supplier records such that their physical sequence is the same as or close to their logical sequence as defined by values of the supplier number field (the *clustering field*). How can the DBMS provide such physical clustering?

A.7 In Section A.5 we suggested that one method of handling hash collisions would be to treat the output from the hash function as the start point for a sequential scan (the *linear search* technique). Can you see any difficulties with that scheme?

A.8 What are the relative advantages and disadvantages of the multiple parent/child organization? (See the end of Section A.6. It might help to review the advantages and disadvantages of the multiple index organization. What are the similarities? What are the differences?)

A.9 Let us define "complete indexing" to mean that an index exists for every distinct field combination in the indexed file. For example, complete indexing for a file with two fields A and B would require two indexes, one on the combination AB (in that order) and one on the combination BA (in that order). How many indexes are needed to provide complete indexing for a file defined on (a) 3 fields; (b) 4 fields; (c) N fields?

A.10 Consider a simplified B-tree (index set plus sequence set) in which the sequence set contains a pointer to each of N stored data records, and each level above the sequence set (i.e., each level of the index set) contains a pointer to every page in the level below. At the top (root) level, of course, there is a single page. Suppose also that each page of the index set contains n index entries. Derive expressions for the number of *levels* and the number of *pages* in the entire B-tree.

A.11 The first ten values of the indexed field in a particular indexed file are as follows:

```
Abrahams,GK
Ackermann,LZ
Ackroyd,S
Adams,T
Adams,TR
Adamson,CR
Allen,S
Ayres,ST
Bailey,TE
Baileyman,D
```

Each is padded with blanks at the right to a total length of 15 characters. Show the values actually recorded in the *index* if the front and rear compression techniques described in Section A.7 are applied. What is the percentage saving in space? Show the steps involved in retrieving (or attempting to retrieve) the stored records for "Ackroyd,S" and "Adams,V". Show also the steps involved in inserting a new stored record for "Allingham,M".

References and Bibliography

The following references are organized into groups, as follows. References [A.1–A.10] are textbooks that either are devoted entirely to the topic of this appendix or at least include a detailed treatment of it. References [A.11–A.15] describe some formal approaches to the subject. References [A.16–A.23] are concerned specifically with indexing, especially B-trees; references [A.24–A.38] represent a selection from the very extensive literature on hashing; references [A.39–A.40] discuss compression techniques; and, finally, references [A.41–A.59] address some miscellaneous storage structures and related issues (in particular, references [A.48-A.59] discuss certain new storage media and new kinds of applications, and new storage structures for those media and applications).

A.1 Donald E. Knuth. *The Art of Computer Programming. Volume III: Sorting and Searching.* Reading, Mass.: Addison-Wesley (1973).

Volume III of Knuth's classic series of volumes contains a comprehensive analysis of search algorithms. For *database* searching, where the data resides in secondary storage, the most directly applicable sections are 6.2.4 (Multiway Trees), 6.4 (Hashing), and 6.5 (Retrieval on Secondary Keys).

A.2 James Martin. *Computer Data-Base Organization* (2nd edition). Englewood Cliffs, N.J.: Prentice-Hall (1977).

This book is divided into two major parts, "Logical Organization" and "Physical Organization." The latter part consists of an extensive description (well over 300 pages) of storage structures and corresponding access techniques.

A.3 Toby J. Teorey and James P. Fry. *Design of Database Structures.* Englewood Cliffs, N.J.: Prentice-Hall (1982).

(Same as reference [12.27].) A tutorial and handbook on database design, both physical and logical. Over 200 pages are devoted to physical design.

A.4 Gio Wiederhold. *Database Design* (2nd edition). New York, N.Y.: McGraw-Hill (1983).

This book (15 chapters) includes a good survey of secondary storage devices and their performance parameters (one chapter, nearly 50 pages), and an extensive analysis of secondary storage structures (four chapters, over 250 pages).

A.5 T. H. Merrett. *Relational Information Systems.* Reston, VA.: Reston Publishing Company, Inc. (1984).

Includes a lengthy introduction to, and analysis of, a variety of storage structures (about 100 pages), covering not only the structures described in the present appendix but also several others.

A.6   Jeffrey D. Ullman. *Principles of Database and Knowledge-Base Systems: Volume I*. Rockville, MD.: Computer Science Press (1988).

Includes a treatment of storage structures that is rather more theoretical than that of the present appendix.

A.7   Henry F. Korth and Abraham Silberschatz. *Database System Concepts* (2nd edition). New York, N.Y.: McGraw-Hill (1991).

A.8   Peter D. Smith and G. Michael Barnes. *Files and Databases: An Introduction*. Reading, Mass.: Addison-Wesley (1987).

A.9   Ramez Elmasri and Shamkant B. Navathe. *Fundamentals of Database Systems* (2nd edition). Redwood City, Calif.: Benjamin/Cummings (1994).

References [A.7], [A.8], and [A.9] are all textbooks on database systems. Each includes material on storage structures that goes beyond the treatment in the present appendix in certain respects (extensively so, in the case of [A.8]).

A.10 Sakti P. Ghosh. *Data Base Organization for Data Management* (2nd edition). Orlando, Fla.: Academic Press (1986).

The primary emphasis of this book is on storage structures and associated access methods—of the book's ten chapters, at least six are devoted to these topics. The treatment is fairly abstract.

A.11 David K. Hsiao and Frank Harary. "A Formal System for Information Retrieval from Files." *CACM 13,* No. 2 (February 1970).

This paper represents what was probably the earliest attempt to unify the ideas of different storage structures—principally indexes and pointer chains—into a general model, thereby providing a basis for a formal theory of such structures. A generalized retrieval algorithm is presented for retrieving records from the general structure that satisfy an arbitrary Boolean combination of "*field = value*" conditions.

A.12 Dennis G. Severance. "Identifier Search Mechanisms: A Survey and Generalized Model." *ACM Comp. Surv. 6,* No. 3 (September 1974).

This paper falls into two parts. The first part provides a tutorial on certain storage structures—basically hashing and indexing. The second part has points in common with reference [A.11]; like that paper, it defines a unified structure, here called a *trie-tree* structure, that combines and generalizes ideas from the structures discussed in the first part. (The term *trie*, pronounced *try*, derives from a paper by Fredkin [A.42].) The resulting structure provides a general model that can represent a wide variety of different structures in terms of a small number of parameters; it can therefore be used (and has in fact been used) to help in choosing a particular structure during the process of physical database design.

A difference between this paper and reference [A.11] is that the trie-tree structure handles hashes but not pointer chains, whereas the proposal of reference [A.11] handles pointer chains but not hashes.

A.13 M. E. Senko, E. B. Altman, M. M. Astrahan, and P. L. Fehder. "Data Structures and Accessing in Data-Base Systems." *IBM Sys. J. 12,* No. 1 (1973).

This paper is in three parts:

1. Evolution of Information Systems

2. Information Organization

3. Data Representations and the Data Independent Accessing Model

The first part consists of a short historical survey of the development of database systems prior to 1973. The second part describes "the entity set model," which provides a basis for describing a given enterprise in terms of entities and entity sets (it corresponds to the conceptual level of the ANSI/SPARC architecture). The third part is the most original and significant part of the paper: It forms an introduction to the *Data Independent Accessing Model* (DIAM), which is an attempt to describe a database in terms of four successive levels of abstraction, namely the entity set (highest), string, encoding, and physical device levels. These four levels can be thought of as a more detailed, but still abstract, definition of the conceptual and internal portions of the ANSI/SPARC architecture. They can be briefly described as follows:

- *Entity set level:* Analogous to the ANSI/SPARC conceptual level.

- *String level:* Access paths to data are defined as ordered sets or "strings" of data objects. Three types of string are described—atomic strings (example: a string connecting stored field occurrences to form a part stored record occurrence), entity strings (example: a string connecting part stored record occurrences for red parts), and link strings (example: a string connecting a supplier stored record occurrence to part stored record occurrences for parts supplied by that supplier).

- *Encoding level:* Data objects and strings are mapped into linear address spaces, using a simple representation primitive known as a *basic encoding unit.*

- *Physical device level:* Linear address spaces are allocated to formatted physical subdivisions of real recording media.

The aim of DIAM, like that of references [A.11–A.12], is (in part) to provide a basis for a systematic theory of storage structures and access methods. One criticism (which applies to the formalisms of references [A.11] and [A.12] also, incidentally) is that sometimes the best method of dealing with some given access request is simply to sort the data, and sorting is of course dynamic, whereas the structures described by DIAM (and the models of [A.11] and [A.12]) are by definition always static.

A.14 S. B. Yao. "An Attribute Based Model for Database Access Cost Analysis." *ACM TODS 2,* No. 1 (March 1977).

The purpose of this paper is similar to that of references [A.11] and [A.12]; in some respects, in fact, it can be regarded as a sequel to those earlier papers, in that it presents a generalized model of database storage structures that can be seen as a combination and extension of the proposals of those papers. It also presents a set of generalized access algorithms and cost equations for that generalized model. References are given to a number of other papers that report on experiments with an implemented physical file design analyzer based on the ideas of this paper.

A.15 D. S. Batory. "Modeling the Storage Architectures of Commercial Database Systems." *ACM TODS 10,* No. 4 (December 1985).

Presents a set of primitive operations, called *elementary transformations,* by which the mapping from the conceptual schema to the corresponding internal schema (i.e., the conceptual/internal mapping—see Chapter 2) can be made explicit, and hence properly studied. The elementary transformations include *augmentation* (extending a stored record by the inclusion of prefix data as well as user data), *encoding* (converting data to an internal form by, e.g., compression), *segmentation* (splitting a record into several pieces for storage purposes), and several others. The paper claims that any conceptual/internal mapping can be represented by an appropriate sequence of such elementary transformations, and hence that the transformations could form the basis of an approach to automating the development of data management software. By way of illustration, the paper applies the ideas to the analysis of three real-world systems: INQUIRE, ADABAS, and System 2000.

A.16 R. Bayer and C. McCreight. "Organization and Maintenance of Large Ordered Indexes." *Acta Informatica 1,* No. 3 (1972).

A.17 Douglas Comer. "The Ubiquitous B-tree." *ACM Comp. Surv. 11,* No. 2 (June 1979).

A good tutorial on B-trees.

A.18 R. E. Wagner. "Indexing Design Considerations." *IBM Sys. J. 12,* No. 4 (1973).

Describes basic indexing concepts, with details of the techniques—including compression techniques—used in IBM's Virtual Storage Access Method, VSAM.

A.19 H. K. Chang. "Compressed Indexing Method." *IBM Technical Disclosure Bulletin II*, No. 11 (April 1969).

A.20 Gopal K. Gupta. "A Self-Assessment Procedure Dealing with Binary Search Trees and B-trees." *CACM 27*, No. 5 (May 1984).

A.21 Vincent Y. Lum. "Multi-Attribute Retrieval with Combined Indexes." *CACM 13*, No. 11 (November 1970).

The paper that introduced the technique of indexing on field combinations.

A.22 James K. Mullin. "Retrieval-Update Speed Tradeoffs Using Combined Indices." *CACM 14*, No. 12 (December 1971).

A sequel to reference [A.21] that gives performance statistics for the combined index scheme for various retrieval/update ratios.

A.23 Ben Shneiderman. "Reduced Combined Indexes for Efficient Multiple Attribute Retrieval." *Information Systems 2*, No. 4 (1976).

Proposes a refinement of Lum's combined indexing technique [A.21] that considerably reduces the storage space and search time overheads. For example, the index combination *ABCD, BCDA, CDAB, DABC, ACBD, BDAC*—see the answer to Exercise A.9(b)—could be replaced by the combination *ABCD, BCD, CDA, DAB, AC, BD*. If each of *A, B, C, D* can assume 10 distinct values, then in the worst case the original combination would involve 60,000 index entries, the reduced combination only 13,200 entries.

A.24 R. Morris. "Scatter Storage Techniques." *CACM 11*, No. 1 (January 1968).

This paper is concerned primarily with hashing as it applies to the symbol table of an assembler or compiler. Its main purpose is to describe an **indirect** hashing scheme based on *scatter tables*. A scatter table is a table of record addresses, somewhat akin to the directory used in extendable hashing [A.28]. As with extendable hashing, the hash function hashes into the scatter table, not directly to the records themselves; the records themselves can be stored anywhere that seems convenient. The scatter table can thus be thought of as a single-level *index* to the underlying data, but an index that can be accessed directly via a hash instead of having to be sequentially searched. Note that a given stored data file could conceivably have several distinct scatter tables, thus in effect providing hash access to the data on several distinct hash fields (at the cost of an extra I/O for any given hash access).

Despite its programming language orientation, the paper provides a good introduction to hashing techniques in general, and most of the material is applicable to database hashing also.

A.25 W. D. Maurer and T. G. Lewis. "Hash Table Methods." *ACM Comp. Surv. 7*, No. 1 (March 1975).

A good tutorial, though now somewhat dated (it does not discuss any of the newer approaches, such as extendable hashing). The topics covered include basic hashing techniques (not just division/remainder, but also random, midsquare, radix, algebraic coding, folding, and digit analysis techniques); collision and bucket overflow handling; some theoretical analysis of the various techniques; and alternatives to hashing (techniques to be used when hashing either cannot or should not be used). *Note:* A **bucket** in hashing terminology is the unit of storage—typically a page—whose address is computed by the hash function. A bucket normally contains several records.

A.26 V. Y. Lum, P. S. T. Yuen, and M. Dodd. "Key-to-Address Transform Techniques: A Fundamental Performance Study on Large Existing Formatted Files." *CACM 14*, No. 4 (April 1971).

An investigation into the performance of several different "basic" (i.e., nonextendable) hashing algorithms. The conclusion is that the division/remainder method seems to be the best all-around performer.

A.27 M. V. Ramakrishna. "Hashing in Practice: Analysis of Hashing and Universal Hashing." Proc. 1988 ACM SIGMOD International Conference on Management of Data, Chicago, Ill. (June 1988).

As this paper points out (following Knuth [A.1]), any system that implements hashing has to solve two problems that are almost independent of one another: It has to choose among the wide variety of possible hash functions to provide one that is effective, and it also has to provide an effective technique for dealing with collisions. The author claims that, while much research has been devoted to the second of these problems, very little has been done on the first, and few attempts have been made to compare the performance of hashing in practice with the performance that is theoretically achievable (reference [A.26] is an exception). How then does a system implementer choose an appropriate hash function? This paper claims that it is possible to choose a hash function that in practice does yield performance close to that predicted by theory, and presents a set of theoretical results in support of this claim.

A.28 Ronald Fagin, Jurg Nievergelt, Nicholas Pippenger, and H. Raymond Strong. "Extendible Hashing—A Fast Access Method for Dynamic Files." *ACM TODS 4*, No. 3 (September 1979).

A.29 G. D. Knott. "Expandable Open Addressing Hash Table Storage and Retrieval." Proc. 1971 ACM SIGFIDET Workshop on Data Description, Access, and Control, San Diego, Calif. (November 1971).

A.30 P.-Å. Larson. "Dynamic Hashing." *BIT 18* (1978).

A.31 Witold Litwin. "Virtual Hashing: A Dynamically Changing Hashing." Proc. 4th International Conference on Very Large Data Bases, Berlin, FDR (September 1978).

A.32 Witold Litwin. "Linear Hashing: A New Tool for File and Table Addressing." Proc. 6th International Conference on Very Large Data Bases, Montreal, Canada (October 1980).

A.33 Per-Åke Larson. "Linear Hashing with Overflow-Handling by Linear Probing." *ACM TODS 10*, No. 1 (March 1985).

A.34 Per-Åke Larson. "Linear Hashing with Separators—A Dynamic Hashing Scheme Achieving One-Access Retrieval." *ACM TODS 13*, No. 3 (September 1988).

References [A.28–A.34] all present extendable hashing schemes of one kind or another. The proposals of [A.29] for "expandable" hashing predate (and are therefore of course quite independent of) all of the others. Nevertheless, expandable hashing is fairly similar to extendable hashing as defined in reference [A.28], and so too is "dynamic" hashing [A.30], except that both schemes use a tree-structured directory instead of the simple contiguous directory proposed in reference [A.28]. "Virtual" hashing [A.31] is somewhat different; see the paper for details. "Linear" hashing, introduced in [A.32] and refined in [A.33] and [A.34], is an improvement on virtual hashing.

A.35 Witold Litwin. "Trie Hashing." Proc. 1981 ACM SIGMOD International Conference on Management of Data, Ann Arbor, Mich. (April 1981).

Presents an extendable hashing scheme with a number of desirable properties:

- It is *order-preserving* (that is, the "physical" sequence of stored records corresponds to the logical sequence of those records as defined by values of the hash field).

- It avoids the problems of complexity, etc., usually encountered with order-preserving hashes.

- An arbitrary record can be accessed (or shown not to exist) in a single disk access, even if the file contains many millions of records.

- The file can be arbitrarily volatile (by contrast, many hash schemes, at least of the nonextendable variety, tend to work rather poorly in the face of high insert volumes).

The hash function itself (which changes with time, as in all extendable hashing algorithms) is represented by a trie structure [A.42], which is kept in main memory whenever the file is in use and grows gracefully as the data file grows. The data file itself is, as already mentioned, kept in "physical" sequence on values of the hash field; and the logical sequence of leaf entries in the trie structure corresponds, precisely, to that "physical" sequence of the data records. Overflow in the data file is handled via a page-splitting technique, basically like the page-splitting technique used in a B-tree.

Trie hashing looks very interesting. Like other hash schemes, it provides better performance than indexing for direct access (one I/O *vs.* typically two or three for a B-tree); and it is preferable to most other hash schemes in that it is order-preserving, which means that sequential access will also be fast. No B-tree or other additional structure is required to provide that fast sequential access. However, note the assumption that the trie will fit into main memory (probably realistic enough). If that assumption is invalid (i.e., if the data file is too large), or if the order-preserving property is not required, then linear hashing [A.32] or some other technique might provide a preferable alternative.

A.36 David B. Lomet. "Bounded Index Exponential Hashing." *ACM TODS 8,* No. 1 (March 1983).

Another extendable hashing scheme. The author claims that the techniques proposed in this paper:

- Provide direct access to any record in close to one I/O on average (and never more than two);
- Yield performance that is independent of the stored file size (by contrast, most extendable hashing schemes suffer from temporary performance degradation at the time a directory page split occurs, because typically all such pages need to be split at approximately the same time);
- Make efficient use of the available disk space (i.e., space utilization can be very good);
- Are straightforward to implement.

A.37 Anil K. Garg and C. C. Gotlieb. "Order-Preserving Key Transformations." *ACM TODS 11,* No. 2 (June 1986).

As explained in the annotation to [A.35] above, a hash (or "key transformation") function is *order-preserving* if the physical sequence of stored records corresponds to the logical sequence of those records as defined by values of the hash field. Order-preserving hashes are desirable for obvious reasons. One simple function that is clearly order-preserving is the following:

hash address = quotient after dividing hash field value
by some constant (say 10,000)

However, an obvious problem with a function such as this one is that it performs very poorly if hash field values are nonuniformly distributed (which is the usual case, of course). Hence some researchers have proposed the idea of *distribution-dependent* (but order-preserving) hash functions, i.e., functions that transform nonuniformly distributed hash field values into uniformly distributed hash addresses, while maintaining the order-preserving property. (*Note:* Trie hashing [A.35] is an example of such an approach.) The present paper gives a method for constructing such hash functions for real-world data files and demonstrates the practical feasibility of those functions.

A.38 M. V. Ramakrishna and Per-Åke Larson. "File Organization Using Composite Perfect Hashing." *ACM TODS 14,* No. 2 (June 1989).

A hash function is called *perfect* if it produces no overflows. (*Note:* "No overflows" does not mean "no collisions." For example, if we assume that the hash function generates page addresses, not record addresses—see the remark on "buckets" in the annotation to [A.25] above—and if each page can hold *n* stored records, then the hash function will be perfect if it never maps more than *n* records to the same page.) A perfect hash function has the property that any record can be retrieved in a single disk I/O. This paper presents a practical method for finding and using such perfect functions.

A.39 D. A. Huffman. "A Method for the Construction of Minimum Redundancy Codes." Proc. IRE 40 (September 1952).

A.40 B. A. Marron and P. A. D. de Maine. "Automatic Data Compression." *CACM 10,* No. 11 (November 1967).

Gives two compression/decompression algorithms: NUPAK, which operates on numeric data, and ANPAK, which operates on alphanumeric or "any" data (i.e., any string of bits).

A.41 Dennis G. Severance and Guy M. Lohman. "Differential Files: Their Application to the Maintenance of Large Databases." *ACM TODS 1,* No. 3 (September 1976).

Discusses "differential files" and their advantages. The basic idea is that updates are not made directly to the database itself, but instead are recorded in a physically distinct file—the differential file—and are merged with the actual database at some suitable subsequent time. The following advantages are claimed for such an approach:

- Database dumping costs are reduced.
- Incremental dumping is facilitated.
- Dumping and reorganization can both be performed concurrently with updating operations.
- Recovery after a program error is fast.
- Recovery after a hardware failure is fast.
- The risk of a serious data loss is reduced.
- "Memo files" are supported efficiently. (A memo file is a kind of scratchpad copy of some portion of the database, used to provide quick access to data that is probably up to date and correct but is not guaranteed to be so. See the discussion of *snapshots* in Chapter 17.)
- Software development is simplified.
- The main file software is simplified.
- Future storage costs might be reduced.

One problem not discussed is that of supporting efficient sequential access to the data—e.g., via an index—when some of the records are in the real database and some are in the differential file.

A.42 E. Fredkin. "TRIE Memory." *CACM 3,* No. 9 (September 1960).

A **trie** is a tree-structured data file (rather than a tree-structured access path to such a file; that is, the data is represented *by* the tree, it is not pointed to *from* the tree—unless the "data file" is really an index to some other file, as it effectively is in trie hashing [A.35]). Each node in a trie logically consists of n entries, where n is the number of distinct symbols available for representing data values. For example, if each data item is a decimal integer, then each node will have exactly ten entries, corresponding to the ten symbols 0, 1, 2, . . . 9. Consider the data item "4285." The (unique) node at the top of the tree will include a pointer in the "4" entry. That pointer will point to a node corresponding to all existing data items having "4" as their first digit. That node in turn (the "4 node") will include a pointer in its "2" entry to a node corresponding to all data items having "42" as their first two digits (the "42 node"). The "42" node will have a pointer in its "8" entry to the "428" node, and so on. And if (for example) there are no data items beginning "429," then the "9" entry in the "42" node will be empty (there will be no pointer); in other words, the tree is pruned to contain only nodes that are nonempty. (A trie is thus generally not a balanced tree.)

Note: The term *trie* derives from "retrieval," but is nevertheless usually pronounced *try.* Tries are also known as *radix search trees* or *digital search trees.*

A.43 Eugene Wong and T. C. Chiang. "Canonical Structure in Attribute Based File Organization." *CACM 14,* No. 9 (September 1971).

Proposes a novel storage structure based on Boolean algebra. It is assumed that all access requests are expressed as a Boolean combination of elementary "*field* = *value*" conditions, and that those elementary conditions are all known. Then the file can be partitioned into disjoint subsets for storage purposes. The subsets are the "atoms" of the Boolean algebra consisting of the set of all sets of records retrievable via the original Boolean access requests. The advantages of such an arrangement include the following:

- Set intersection of atoms is never necessary.

- An arbitrary Boolean request can easily be converted into a request for the union of one or more atoms.

- Such a union never requires the elimination of duplicates.

A.44 Michael Stonebraker. "Operating System Support for Database Management." *CACM 24,* No. 7 (July 1981).

Discusses reasons why various operating system facilities—in particular, the operating system file manager—frequently do not provide the kind of services required by the DBMS, and suggests some improvements to those facilities.

A.45 M. Schkolnick. "A Survey of Physical Database Design Methodology and Techniques." Proc. 4th International Conference on Very Large Data Bases, Berlin, FDR (September 1978).

A.46 S. Finkelstein, M. Schkolnick, and P. Tiberio. "Physical Database Design for Relational Databases." *ACM TODS 13,* No. 1 (March 1988).

In some respects, the problem of physical database design is more difficult in a relational system than it is in other kinds of system. This is because it is the system, not the user, that decides how to "navigate" through the storage structure; thus, the system will only have a chance of performing well if the storage structures chosen by the database designer are a good fit with what the system actually needs—which implies that the designer has to understand in some detail how the system works internally. And designers typically will not have such knowledge (nor is it desirable that they should). Hence some kind of automated physical design tool is highly desirable. This paper reports on such a tool, called DBDSGN, which was developed to work with System R [8.12–8.13]. DBDSGN takes as input a workload definition (i.e., a set of user requests and their corresponding execution frequencies), and produces as output a suggested physical design (i.e., a set of indexes for each stored table, typically including a "clustering index"—see the answer to Exercise A.6—for each such table). It interacts with the system optimizer (see Chapters 3 and 18) to obtain information such as the optimizer's understanding of the database (i.e., table sizes, etc.) and the cost formulas that the optimizer uses.

   DBDSGN was used as the basis for an IBM product called RDT, which is a design tool for SQL/DS (see Appendix B).

A.47 Kenneth C. Sevcik. "Data Base System Performance Prediction Using an Analytical Model." Proc. 7th International Conference on Very Large Data Bases, Cannes, France (September 1981).

As its title implies, the scope of this paper is broader than that of the present appendix—it is concerned with overall system performance issues, not just with storage structures as such. The author proposes a layered framework in which various design decisions, and the interactions among those decisions, can be systematically studied. The layers of the framework represent the system at increasingly detailed levels of description; thus, each layer is more specific (i.e., at a lower level of abstraction) than the previous one. The names of the layers give some idea of the corresponding levels of detail: abstract world, logical database, physical database, data unit access, physical I/O access, and device loadings. The author claims that an analytical model based on this framework could be used to predict numerous performance characteristics, including device utilization, transaction throughput, and response times.

   The paper includes an extensive bibliography on system performance (with commentary). In particular, it includes a brief survey of work on the performance of different storage structures.

A.48 Hanan Samet. "The Quadtree and Related Hierarchical Data Structures." *ACM Comp. Surv. 16,* No. 2 (June 1984).

The storage structures described in the present appendix work well for traditional commercial databases. However, as the field of database technology expands to include new kinds of data—e.g., spatial data, such as might be found in image-processing or cartographic applications—so new methods of data representation at the storage level are needed also. This paper is a tutorial introduction to some of those new methods. See Samet's book [A.49] for further discussion, also references [A.50–A.59].

A.49 Hanan Samet. *The Design and Analysis of Spatial Data Structures*. Reading, Mass.: Addison-Wesley (1990).

See the annotation to the previous reference.

A.50 Stavros Christodoulakis and Daniel Alexander Ford. "Retrieval Performance Versus Disc Space Utilization on WORM Optical Discs." Proc. 1989 ACM SIGMOD International Conference on Management of Data, Portland, Ore. (May/June 1989).

See the annotation to reference [A.51].

A.51 David Lomet and Betty Salzberg. "Access Methods for Multiversion Data." Proc. 1989 ACM SIGMOD International Conference on Management of Data, Portland, Ore. (May/June 1989).

A "WORM disk" is an optical disk with the property that once a record has been written to the disk, it can never be rewritten—i.e., it cannot be updated in place. (WORM is an acronym, standing for "Write Once, Read Many times.") WORM technology has reached the point where the use of WORM disks in database applications has become a practical proposition. Such disks have obvious advantages for certain applications, particularly those involving some kind of archival requirement. Traditional storage structures such as B-trees are not adequate for such disks, however, precisely because of the fact that rewriting is impossible. Hence (as explained in the annotation to reference [A.48], though for different reasons), new storage structures are needed. References [A.50] and [A.51] propose and analyze some such structures; reference [A.51], in particular, concerns itself with structures that are appropriate for applications in which a complete historical record is to be kept (i.e., applications in which data is only added to the database, never deleted).

A.52 J. Encarnação and F. L. Krause (eds.). *File Structures and Data Bases for CAD*. New York, N.Y.: North-Holland (1982).

Computer-aided design (CAD) applications are a major driving force behind the research into new storage structures. This book consists of the proceedings of a workshop on the subject, with major sections as follows:

1. Data modeling for CAD

2. Data models for geometric modeling

3. Databases for geometric modeling

4. Hardware structures

5. CAD database research issues

6. Implementation problems in CAD database systems

7. Industrial applications

A.53 R. A. Finkel and J. L. Bentley. "Quad-Trees—A Data Structure for Retrieval on Composite Keys." *Acta Informatica 4* (1974).

A.54 J. Nievergelt, H. Hinterberger, and K. C. Sevcik. "The Grid File: An Adaptable, Symmetric, Multikey File Structure." *ACM TODS 9*, No. 1 (March 1984).

A.55 Antonin Guttman. "R-Trees: A Dynamic Index Structure for Spatial Searching." Proc. ACM SIGMOD International Conference on Management of Data, Boston, Mass. (June 1984).

A.56 Nick Roussopoulos and Daniel Leifker. "Direct Spatial Search on Pictorial Databases Using Packed R-Trees." Proc. ACM SIGMOD International Conference on Management of Data, Austin, Texas (May 1985).

A.57 D. A. Beckley, M. W. Evens, and V. K. Raman. "Multikey Retrieval from K-D Trees and Quad-Trees." Proc. ACM SIGMOD International Conference on Management of Data, Austin, Texas (May 1985).

A.58 Michael Freeston. "The BANG File: A New Kind of Grid File." Proc. ACM SIGMOD International Conference on Management of Data, San Francisco, Calif. (May 1987).

A.59 Michael F. Barnsley and Alan D. Sloan. "A Better Way to Compress Images." *BYTE 13,* No. 1 (January 1988).

Describes a novel compression technique for images called *fractal compression*. The technique works by not storing the image itself at all, but rather storing code values that can be used to recreate the desired image as and when needed by means of appropriate fractal equations. In this way "compression ratios of 10,000 to 1—or even higher" can be achieved.

Answers to Selected Exercises

A.5 The advantages of indexes are as follows:

- They speed up direct access based on a given value for the indexed field or field combination. Without the index, a sequential scan would be required.

- They speed up sequential access based on the indexed field or field combination. Without the index, a sort would be required.

The disadvantages are as follows:

- They take up space on the disk. The space taken up by indexes can easily exceed that taken up by the data itself in a heavily indexed database.

- While an index will probably speed up retrieval operations, it will at the same time slow down update operations. Any INSERT or DELETE on the indexed file or UPDATE on the indexed field or field combination will require an accompanying update to the index.

A.6 In order to maintain the desired clustering, the DBMS needs to be able to determine the appropriate physical insert point for a new supplier record. This requirement is basically the same as the requirement to be able to locate a particular record given a value for the clustering field. In other words, the DBMS needs an appropriate access structure—for example, an index—based on values of the clustering field. *Note:* An index that is used in this way to help maintain physical clustering is sometimes called a **clustering index**. In general, a given stored file can have at most one clustering index, by definition.

A.7 Let the hash function be h, and suppose we wish to retrieve the record with hash field value k.

- One obvious problem is that it is not immediately clear whether the record stored at hash address $h(k)$ is the desired record or is instead a collision record that has overflowed from some earlier hash address. Of course, this question can easily be resolved by inspecting the value of the hash field in the stored record.

- Another problem is that, for any given value of $h(k)$, we need to be able to determine when to stop the process of sequentially searching for any given record. This problem can be solved by keeping an appropriate flag in the stored record prefix.

- Third, as pointed out in the introduction to the subsection on extendable hashing, when the stored file gets close to full, it is likely that most records will not be stored at their hash address location but will instead have overflowed to some other position. If record $r1$ overflows and is therefore stored at hash address $h2$, a record $r2$ that subsequently hashes to $h2$ might be forced to overflow to $h3$—even though there might as yet be no records that actually hash to $h2$ as such. In other words, the collision-handling technique itself can lead to further collisions. As a result, the average access time will go up, perhaps considerably.

A.9 (a) 3. (b) 6. For example, if the four fields are $A, B, C, D,$ and if we use the appropriate ordered combination of field names to denote the corresponding index, the following indexes will suffice: *ABCD, BCDA, CDAB, DABC, ACBD, BDAC.* (c) In general, the number of indexes required is equal to the number of ways of selecting n elements from a set of N elements, where n is the smallest integer greater than or equal to $N/2$—i.e., the number is $N! / (n! * (N\text{-}n)!)$. For proof see Lum [A.21].

A.10 The number of *levels* in the B-tree is the unique positive integer k such that $n^{k-1} < N \le n^k$. Taking logs to base n, we have $k - 1 < \log_n N \le k$; hence

$$k = \text{ceil}(\log_n N),$$

where ceil(x) denotes the smallest integer greater than or equal to x.

Now let the number of pages in the ith level of the index be P_i (where $i = 1$ corresponds to the lowest level). We show that

$$P_i = \text{ceil}\left(\frac{N}{n^i}\right)$$

and hence that the total number of pages is

$$\sum_{i=1}^{i=k} \text{ceil}\left(\frac{N}{n^i}\right)$$

Consider the expression

$$\text{ceil}\left(\frac{\text{ceil}\left(\dfrac{N}{n^i}\right)}{n}\right) = x, \text{ say.}$$

Suppose $N = qn^i + r$ ($0 \le r \le n^i - 1$). Then

(a) If $r = 0$,
$$x = \text{ceil}\left(\frac{q}{n}\right)$$

$$= \text{ceil}\left(\frac{qn^i}{n^{i+1}}\right)$$

$$= \text{ceil}\left(\frac{N}{n^{i+1}}\right)$$

(b) If $r > 0$,
$$x = \text{ceil}\left(\frac{q+1}{n}\right)$$

Suppose $q = q'n + r'$ ($0 \le r' \le n - 1$). Then $N = (q'n + r')n^i + r = q'n^{i+1} + (r'n^i + r)$; since $0 < r \le n^i - 1$ and $0 \le r' \le n - 1$,

$$0 < (r'n^i + r) \le n^{i+1} - (n^i - n^{i+1}) < n^{i+1};$$

hence $\text{ceil}\left(\dfrac{N}{n^{i+1}}\right) = q' + 1$.

But

$$x = \text{ceil}\left(\frac{q'n + r' + 1}{n}\right)$$

$$= q' + 1$$

since $1 \le r' + 1 \le n$. Thus in both cases (a) and (b) we have that

$$\text{ceil}\left(\frac{\text{ceil}\left(\dfrac{N}{n^i}\right)}{n}\right) = \text{ceil}\left(\frac{N}{n^{i+1}}\right).$$

Now, it is immediate that $P_1 = $ ceil (N/n). It is also immediate that $P_i + 1 = $ ceil(P_i/n), $1 \leq i < k$. Thus, if $P_i = $ ceil (N/n^i), then

$$P_{i+1} = \text{ceil}\left(\frac{\text{ceil}\left(\dfrac{N}{n^i} \right)}{n} \right) = \text{ceil}\left(\frac{N}{n^{i+1}} \right)$$

The rest follows by induction.

A.11   *Values recorded in index*   *Expanded form*

```
0 - 2 - Ab                  Ab
1 - 3 - cke                 Acke
3 - 1 - r                   Ackr
1 - 7 - dams,T+             Adams,T+
7 - 1 - R                   Adams,TR
5 - 1 - o                   Adamso
1 - 1 - l                   Al
1 - 1 - y                   Ay
0 - 7 - Bailey,             Bailey,
6 - 1 - m                   Baileym
```

Points arising:

1. The two figures preceding each recorded value represent, respectively, the number of leading characters that are the same as those in the preceding value and the number of characters actually stored.

2. The expanded form of each value shows what can be deduced from the index alone (via a sequential scan) without looking at the indexed records.

3. The "+" characters in the fourth line represent blanks.

4. We assume that the next value of the indexed field does not have "Baileym" as its first seven characters.

The percentage saving in storage space is $100 * (150 - 35) / 150$ percent $= 76.67\%$.

The index search algorithm is as follows. Let V be the specified value (padded with blanks if necessary to make it 15 characters long). Then:

```
found := false ;
do for each index entry in turn ;
    expand current index entry and let expanded length = N  ;
    if expanded entry = leftmost N characters of V
    then do ;
            retrieve corresponding stored record ;
            if value in that record = V
            then found := true ;
            leave loop ;
        end ;
    if expanded entry > leftmost N characters of V
    then leave loop ;
end ;
if found = false
then /* no stored record for V exists */ ;
else /* stored record for V has been found */ ;
```

For "Ackroyd,S" we get a match on the third iteration; we retrieve the corresponding record and find that it is indeed the one we want.

For "Adams,V" we get "index entry high" on the sixth iteration, so no corresponding record exists.

For "Allingham,M" we get a match on the seventh iteration; however, the record retrieved is for "Allen,S", so it is permissible to insert a new one for "Allingham,M". (We are assuming here that the indexed field values are required to be unique.) Inserting "Allingham,M" involves the following steps.

1. Finding space and storing the new record

2. Adjusting the index entry for "Allen,S" to read

    ```
    1 - 3 - lle
    ```

3. Inserting an index entry between those for "Allen,S" and "Ayres,ST" to read

    ```
    3 - 1 - i
    ```

Note that the preceding index entry has to be changed. In general, inserting a new entry into the index may affect the preceding entry or the following entry, or possibly neither—but never both.

B | DB2: A Relational Implementation

B.1 Introduction

In order to give the reader some idea of how a real relational DBMS actually works—i.e., how it implements the features of the relational model*—we devote this appendix to a brief overview of one particular relational system, namely DB2 ("IBM DATABASE 2") from IBM Corporation [B.1–B.7]. *Note:* DB2 runs in the MVS environment. IBM also provides some other relational products for its other operating environments, as follows:

- DB2/6000 for the AIX environment
- DB2/2 (originally called the OS/2 Database Manager) for the OS/2 environment
- SQL/DS for the VM and VSE environments (IBM has recently begun to refer to this product as "DB2 for VM and VSE")
- DB2/400 (originally called SQL/400) for the OS/400 environment

These products are meant to bear a strong family resemblance, of course; in this appendix, however, we will concentrate on the MVS product specifically—i.e., the name "DB2" should be understood throughout to refer to the original DB2 product specifically (where it makes any difference). Our discussions are essentially accurate as of the release level current at the time of writing, namely DB2 Version 3 Release 1. However, we do not hesitate to omit material that is irrelevant to the purpose at hand, nor to make significant simplifications in the interests of brevity.

DB2, like most other commercial relational products, supports a dialect of SQL. In particular, it permits SQL statements to be **embedded** in programs written in a variety of languages (C, COBOL, PL/I, etc.). What this means is that a program written in (say) COBOL can include SQL statements that are intermixed with the COBOL statements, as explained in Chapter 3 (and discussed in more detail in Chapter 8). In this appendix we will concentrate on this embedded use of the language, for reasons that will quickly become apparent.

---

* Or some of them, at any rate. As explained in Chapter 3, many aspects of the model are in fact not implemented in today's commercial products.

Note: Since DB2 is an SQL system and uses the SQL terms *table, row,* and *column* in place of the relational terms *relation, tuple,* and *attribute,* we will do likewise in this appendix (as indeed we have been doing throughout this book whenever we have been dealing with SQL specifically).

B.2 Storage Structure

We begin by briefly examining the way DB2 physically represents data in storage. Fig. B.1 is a schematic representation of DB2's principal storage objects and their interrelationships. The figure is meant to be interpreted as follows:

- The total collection of stored data is divided up into a number of disjoint **databases**—several user databases and several system databases, in general. (As explained in Chapter 1, there are often good practical reasons for dividing the data among several distinct databases, and DB2, like most other systems, supports this idea.) Note that the DB2 catalog is stored in one of the system databases.

    Databases (meaning *user* databases specifically) are *the unit of start and stop,* in the sense that the system operator can make a given database available or unavailable for processing via an appropriate START or STOP command.

- Each database is divided up into a number of disjoint *spaces*—several **table spaces** and several **index spaces,** in general. A "space" corresponds to what we called a

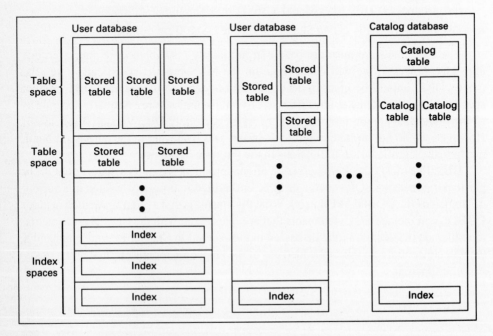

FIG. B.1 The major storage objects of DB2

page set in Appendix A; in other words, it is a dynamically extendable collection of **pages**. The pages in a given "space" are all the same size—4K bytes for index spaces, and either 4K bytes or 32K bytes for table spaces (K = 1024). At the physical level, DB2 uses the MVS access method VSAM ("Virtual Storage Access Method") to store its "spaces" on the disk.

- Each table space contains one or more **stored tables**. A stored table is the physical representation of a base table; it consists of a collection of **stored records,** one for each row of the corresponding base table.* A stored table thus corresponds to what we called a *stored file* in Appendix A (except that, for operational reasons, very large stored tables might be "partitioned" across several stored files—but this fact does not materially affect the discussions of the present appendix). A given stored table must be wholly contained within a single table space.

- Each index space contains exactly one **index** (a B-tree). A given index must be wholly contained within a single index space. A given stored table and all of its associated indexes must be wholly contained within a single database.

  Note: If a given stored table has any indexes at all, then exactly one is the **clustering index** for that stored table. A clustering index is one for which the sequence defined by the index is the same as, or close to, the physical sequence (see Exercise A.6 in Appendix A); note, therefore, that "clustering" in DB2 refers specifically to intrafile clustering, not interfile clustering. Clustering indexes are extremely important for optimization purposes—the DB2 optimizer will always try to use a clustering index, if there is one, and if the sequence represented by that index is appropriate for the user request under consideration.

- Each stored record must be wholly contained within a single page; however, one stored table can be spread over several pages, and one page can contain stored records from several stored tables. As explained above, each stored record corresponds to one row from one base table; however, a given stored record is *not* identical to the corresponding base table row. Instead, it consists of a byte string, made up of a **stored record prefix** (containing such information as the internal system identifier for the stored table of which this stored record is a part) and a set of **stored fields**. Each stored field, in turn, has (usually) a **stored field prefix** (containing such things as the data length, if the field is varying length) and an encoded form of the actual data value. *Note:* Stored data is encoded in such a manner that the IBM System/360 (/370, /390, . . .) "compare logical" instruction CLC will always yield the appropriate response when applied to two values of the same SQL data type. For example, binary integers are stored with their sign bit reversed.

  Internally, stored records are addressed by **record ID** or RID, as discussed in Appendix A.

---

* In other words, base tables in DB2 "physically exist," in the sense that they have a direct storage representation—despite the fact that, strictly speaking, physical existence is *not* the distinguishing characteristic of base tables in the relational model, as explained in Chapters 3 and 4.

B.3 System Components

The internal structure of DB2 is quite complex, as is only to be expected of a state-of-the-art system that provides all of the functions typically found in a modern DBMS. The product thus contains a very large number of internal components. From a high-level point of view, however, it can be regarded as having just four *major* components, each of which divides up into numerous subcomponents. The four major components are as follows:

1. The **system services** component, which supports system operation, operator communication, logging, and similar functions

2. The **locking services** component, which provides the necessary controls for managing concurrent access to data

3. The **database services** component, which supports the definition, retrieval, and update of user and system data

4. The **distributed data facility** component, which provides DB2's distributed database support

Of these four components, the one that is most directly relevant to the user is, of course, the database services component. We therefore concentrate here on that component specifically. That component in turn divides into five principal subcomponents, which we refer to as the *Precompiler, Bind,* the *Run Time Supervisor,* the *Stored Data Manager,* and the *Buffer Manager* (these terms are not always the ones used by IBM). Together, these components support (a) the preparation of application programs for execution and (b) the subsequent execution of those programs. The functions of the individual components, in outline, are as follows (refer to Fig. B.2):

- The **Precompiler** is a preprocessor for application programs that contain embedded SQL statements. It collects those statements into a **Database Request Module** (DBRM), replacing them in the original program by host language CALLs to the Run Time Supervisor.

- The **Bind** component compiles one or more related DBRMs to produce an **application plan** (i.e., executable code to implement the SQL statements in those DBRMs, including in particular calls to the Stored Data Manager). *Note:* The functions of the Bind component have been significantly extended since the DB2 product was first released. We content ourselves here with a description of the basic (original) functions only.

- The **Run Time Supervisor** oversees SQL programs during their execution. When such a program requests some database operation, control goes first to the Run Time Supervisor, thanks to the CALL inserted by the Precompiler. The Run Time Supervisor then routes control to the application plan, and the application plan in turn invokes the Stored Data Manager to perform the required function.

- The **Stored Data Manager** manages the stored database, retrieving and updating records as requested by application plans. In other words, the Stored Data Manager

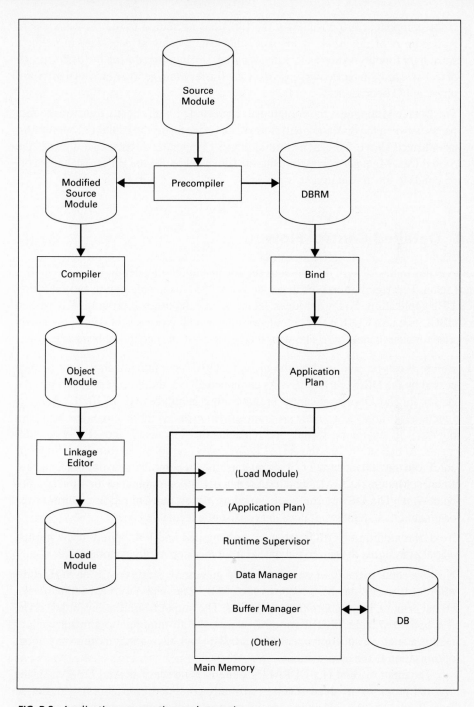

FIG. B.2 Application preparation and execution

is the component responsible for the functions attributed to the *file manager* in Appendix A of this book. It invokes other components as necessary to perform subsidiary functions such as locking, logging, sorting, etc., during the performance of its basic task; in particular, it invokes the Buffer Manager (see below) to perform physical I/O operations.

■ The **Buffer Manager** is the component responsible for physically transferring data pages between the disk and main storage; i.e., it performs the actual I/O operations, as indicated above. To use the terminology of Appendix A once again, just as the Stored Data Manager corresponds to the file manager, so the Buffer Manager corresponds to the *disk manager*.

B.4 Detailed Control Flow

Let us examine the ideas of the previous section in a little more depth. Refer to Fig. B.2 once again. That figure shows the major steps involved in the preparation and execution of a DB2 application. To fix our ideas, let us assume the original program *P* is written in COBOL (we take COBOL for definiteness; the overall process is of course essentially the same for other languages). The steps that program *P* must go through are as follows:

1. Before *P* can be compiled by the regular COBOL compiler, it must first be processed by the DB2 *Precompiler*. As explained above, the Precompiler is a preprocessor for the DB2 application programming languages (C, COBOL, etc.). Its function is to analyze a source program written in one of those languages, stripping out the SQL statements it finds and replacing them by host language CALL statements. At execution time those CALLs will pass control to the Run Time Supervisor. From the SQL statements it encounters, the Precompiler constructs a Database Request Module (DBRM), which subsequently becomes input to the Bind component. *Note:* The DBRM can be regarded as just an internal representation of the original SQL statements. It does *not* consist of executable code.

2. Next, the modified COBOL program is compiled and link-edited in the normal way. Let us agree to refer to the output from this step as "load module *P*."

3. Now we come to the *Bind* step. As already suggested, Bind is really an **SQL compiler:** It converts database requests (i.e., SQL statements) into executable code. (What is more, it is an *optimizing* compiler: The output from Bind is not just code, it is *optimized* code. In DB2, in other words, the all-important optimizer component is actually a subcomponent of Bind. We shall have a litle more to say about optimization in the next section.)

   The input to Bind is a DBRM (or more likely a set of several DBRMs, if the original program involved several separately compiled procedures). The output from Bind—i.e., the compiled code, which as already mentioned is called an *application plan*—is stored away in the DB2 catalog, where it can be found when needed by the Run Time Supervisor.

4. Finally we come to execution time. Since the original program has effectively been broken into two pieces (load module and application plan), those two pieces must somehow be brought back together again at execution time. This is how it works (refer to Fig. B.2). First, the load module *P* is loaded into main memory; it starts to execute in the usual way. Sooner or later it reaches the first of the CALLs inserted by the Precompiler. Control goes to the *Run Time Supervisor.* The Run Time Supervisor then retrieves the application plan from the catalog, loads it into main memory, and passes control to it. The application plan in turn invokes the *Stored Data Manager,* which performs the necessary operations on the actual stored data (invoking the *Buffer Manager* as necessary) and passes results back to the executing application as appropriate.

B.5 Compilation and Recompilation

Our discussions so far have glossed over one extremely important point, which we now explain. First, as already indicated, DB2 is a compiling system: Database requests are *compiled* (by Bind) into internal form. By contrast, many other systems—certainly all prerelational systems, to this writer's knowledge—are *interpretive* in nature. Now, compilation is certainly advantageous from the point of view of performance; it will nearly always yield better run-time performance than will interpretation [B.10]. However, it does suffer from one significant drawback: *It is possible that decisions made by the "compiler"* (actually Bind) *at compilation time are no longer valid at execution time.* The following simple example will serve to illustrate the problem:

1. Suppose program *P* is compiled on Monday, and the optimizer decides to use an index—say index *X*—in its access strategy for *P*. Then the application plan for *P* will include explicit references to *X* by name; in other words, the generated code will be *tightly bound to* (i.e., highly dependent on) the optimizer's choice of strategy.

2. On Tuesday, some suitably authorized user issues the statement

```
DROP INDEX X ;
```

3. On Wednesday, some suitably authorized user tries to execute program *P*. What happens?

What does happen is the following. When an index is dropped, DB2 examines the catalog to see which plans are dependent on that index. Any such plans it finds it marks "invalid." When the Run Time Supervisor retrieves such a plan for execution, it sees the "invalid" marker, *and therefore invokes Bind to produce a new plan*—i.e., to choose some different access strategy and then to recompile the original DBRM (which has been kept in the catalog) in accordance with that new strategy. Assuming the recompilation is successful, the new plan then replaces the old one, and the Run Time Supervisor continues with that new plan. Thus the entire recompilation process is "transparent to the user"; the only effect that might be observed is a slight delay in the execution of certain SQL statements (possibly some change in overall program performance also, of course; the point is, however, that there should be no effect on program *logic*).

Note carefully that the automatic recompilation we are talking about here is an *SQL* recompilation, not a *COBOL* recompilation. It is not the COBOL program that is invalidated by the dropping of the index, only the application plan associated with that program.

We can now see how it is possible for programs to be independent of physical access structures—more specifically, how it is possible to create and drop (destroy) such structures without at the same time having to rewrite programs. As explained in Chapter 3, SQL statements such as SELECT and UPDATE never include any explicit mention of such structures. Instead, they simply indicate what data the user is interested in; and it is DB2's responsibility—actually Bind's responsibility—to choose a way of getting to that data, and to change to another way if the old way no longer works. We say that systems like DB2 provide a high degree of data independence (more specifically, **physical** data independence, so called to distinguish it from *logical* data independence, discussed in Chapter 17): Users and user programs are not dependent on the physical structure of the stored data—even though this is a compiling system.

Note: Data independence is easier to provide in an interpretive system, because the process of "compilation" and optimization is effectively repeated every time the program is executed. But that repetition represents a significant overhead, of course, which is precisely why DB2 chose to go the compiling route.

One further point concerning the foregoing: Our example was in terms of a dropped *index,* and perhaps that is the commonest case in practice. However, a similar sequence of events occurs when other objects (not just indexes) are dropped. Thus, for example, dropping a base table will cause all plans that refer to that table to be flagged as invalid. Of course, the automatic recompilation will work in this case only if another table has been created with the same name as the old one by the time the recompilation is done (and maybe not even then, if there are significant differences between the old table and the new one).

Let us return to the index case for a moment. Given the fact that DB2 does automatic recompilations if an existing index is dropped, the reader might be wondering whether it will also do such automatic recompilations if a new index is created. The answer is no, it will not. And the reason is that there can be no guarantee in such a case that recompiling will actually be profitable; recompilation might simply mean a lot of unnecessary work (existing compiled code might already be using an optimum strategy). The situation is different with DROP—a program will simply not work if it relies on a nonexistent object (index or otherwise), so recompiling is mandatory in this case. Thus, if some user—typically the DBA—creates a new index, and suspects that some plan could now profitably be replaced, then he or she must explicitly request that replacement by means of an explicit "REBIND" command.* Even then, of course, there is no guarantee that the new plan will in fact use the new index.

---

* It is not impossible that DB2 might be extended in some future release to perform automatic rebinds on index creation as well.

We conclude this section by noting that SQL is *always* compiled in DB2, never interpreted, even when the statements in question are submitted interactively. In other words, if the user enters (say) a SELECT statement at the terminal, then that statement will be compiled and an application plan generated for it; that plan will then be executed; and finally, after execution has completed, that plan will be discarded. Experiments have indicated that, even in the interactive case, compilation almost always results in better overall performance than interpretation [B.10]. The advantage of compilation is that the actual process of physically accessing the required data is more efficient, since it is done by tailored, compiled code. The disadvantage, of course, is that there is a cost in doing the compilation, i.e., in producing that compiled code in the first place. But the advantage almost always outweighs the disadvantage, sometimes dramatically so.

B.6   Utilities and Related Matters

In this section we take a brief look at what is involved in controlling and managing the day-to-day operation of a system like DB2. There are numerous administration and operational tasks that need to be performed, and the system provides a variety of utility programs and similar tools to assist in those tasks. We briefly describe some of the DB2 utilities in a little more detail in order to give a slightly clearer picture of the kinds of functions that need to be performed by such utilities in general. We also offer a brief description of a few miscellaneous topics of a general "utilities" nature. Please note, however, that our descriptions are very much simplified; more details can be found in reference [B.7], from which the following outline descriptions have been extracted.

- **CHECK:** The CHECK utility is used to perform certain checks on the stored data—e.g., to check that a given index is consistent with the table it indexes, or to check that a given table does not contain any "dangling" foreign key references (i.e., foreign key values for which no corresponding row exists in the target table; note that such dangling references might occur as a result of running the LOAD utility—see below—with referential integrity checking disabled).

- **COPY:** The COPY utility creates a full or incremental backup copy (an *image copy*) of a database or some portion thereof (see the discussion of MERGECOPY and RECOVER below). An incremental copy is a copy of just the pages that have been updated since the previous full or incremental copy was taken.

- **LOAD:** The LOAD utility loads data from a sequential file into one or more stored tables within a specified database. The tables in question need not be initially empty. Note that LOAD can be run with either logging or referential integrity checking disabled (or both, of course).

- **MERGECOPY:** The MERGECOPY utility merges a full copy and one or more incremental copies to produce an up-to-date full copy, or a set of incremental copies to produce an up-to-date composite incremental copy.

- **QUIESCE:** The QUIESCE utility is used to quiesce operations (temporarily) on a specified collection of base tables. The quiesced state corresponds to a single point in the log, so that the collection of tables can subsequently be recovered as a unit. In particular, QUIESCE can be useful in establishing a *point of consistency* for a collection of tables that are related via referential constraints, thus ensuring that subsequent recovery to that point will restore the data to a consistent state (see the discussion of RECOVER below).

- **RECOVER:** The RECOVER utility uses the most recent full copy, any subsequent incremental copies, and any subsequent log data to recover data after (e.g.) a media failure has occurred. RECOVER can also be used to perform *point-in-time recovery* by recovering from a specific image copy or recovering to a specific point in the log.

- **REORG:** The REORG utility reorganizes a stored database or some portion thereof to reclaim wasted space and to reestablish clustering sequence (if applicable).

- **RUNSTATS:** The RUNSTATS utility computes certain specified statistics on specified stored data (e.g., cardinality for a specified stored table), and writes those statistics to the system catalog. Bind uses such statistics in its process of optimization (see Chapter 18). They can also be useful for determining when reorganization is necessary. RUNSTATS should be executed whenever a table has been loaded, an index has been created, data has been reorganized, or generally whenever there has been a significant amount of update activity on some table. It should then be followed by an appropriate set of application plan REBINDs.

Explain

EXPLAIN is a special SQL statement that can be used to obtain information regarding the optimizer's choice of access strategy for a specified SQL query. (*Note:* EXPLAIN is not included in the SQL standard [8.1], but many SQL products support it in one form or another.) The information provided includes indexes used, details of any sorts that will be needed, and—if the specified query involves any joins—the order in which tables will be joined and the methods by which the individual joins will be performed (see Chapter 18). Such information can be useful for tuning existing applications, also for determining how projected applications will perform. Here is an example:

```
EXPLAIN PLAN FOR
        SELECT S.S#, P.P#
        FROM    S, P
        WHERE   S.CITY = P.CITY ;
```

The output from EXPLAIN is placed in a special table in the database called PLAN_TABLE. The user can then interrogate that table by means of ordinary SQL SELECT statements in order to discover, for example, whether a particular index is being used or whether creating a new index might obviate the need for a sort.

Instrumentation Facility

The DB2 **Instrumentation Facility** gathers system diagnostic information, system-wide statistics, performance information, and accounting and audit data. The information can subsequently be analyzed by the DB2 **Performance Monitor** to produce a variety of reports, including the following:

- Graphical summaries of accounting and system statistics data
- Processing time information for SQL statement, Bind, utility, and command execution
- I/O summaries
- Information on locking efficiency (number of deadlocks, number of waits, etc.)
- A detailed trace of SQL statement execution

Resource Limit Facility

The DB2 **Resource Limit Facility** is a "DB2 governor." Its principal use is to allow the DBA to limit (on an individual user basis) the amount of processor time that can be consumed during the execution of SQL data manipulation operations that are entered interactively. If the specified limit is exceeded, the offending operation is canceled.

B.7   Summary

We have presented a brief overview of DB2 in order to give the reader some idea as to what is involved in a real relational implementation. First we described the principal DB2 storage objects—**databases, table** and **index spaces** (analogous to the *page sets* of Appendix A), **stored tables** (analogous to the *stored files* of Appendix A) and **indexes** (B-trees in DB2). A stored table is the stored version of a base table; DB2—like most other relational products on the market today—thus maps base tables to physical storage in a fairly direct manner, and so does not provide as much data independence as it really should (as discussed in Chapters 3 and 4).

We then took a look at application program preparation and execution. First, the **Precompiler** removes the SQL statements from the program (replacing them by CALLs) and uses those SQL statements to build a **Database Request Module** (DBRM). The program can then be compiled and link-edited in the usual way. The DBRM(s) for a given program are processed by **Bind** to produce an **application plan**—in effect, a compiled version of the original SQL statements (Bind can be thought of as an **optimizing SQL compiler**). At run time, the CALLs inserted by the Precompiler cause control to go to the **Run Time Supervisor,** which invokes the **Stored Data Manager** (DB2's analog of the *file manager* of Appendix A) to perform the desired operations on the stored data. The Stored Data Manager in turn invokes the **Buffer Manager** (DB2's analog of the *disk manager* of Appendix A) to carry out the physical page I/O's.

We also discussed the fact that SQL requests are compiled, not interpreted, in DB2, and explained how DB2 performs **automatic recompilation** if necessitated by a change in the physical storage structure— in particular, if an existing index is dropped.

Finally, we gave a very brief overview of some of the most important DB2 **utilities** (CHECK, LOAD, COPY, etc.), together with certain related facilities such as **EXPLAIN**.

Exercises

B.1 Name the four major components of DB2.

B.2 Draw a diagram showing the overall process of program preparation and program execution in DB2.

B.3 Explain how DB2 provides physical data independence.

B.4 List the principal storage objects of DB2.

B.5 What is the maximum length in bytes of a DB2 stored record? Note that the maximum width of a base table is less than this figure; why is this?

B.6 What is a clustering index? Why can a given stored table have a maximum of one such index? What are the advantages of such an index?

B.7 The DB2 Bind component includes the optimizer as an important subcomponent. The optimizer is responsible for deciding on a strategy for implementing database requests (i.e., SQL statements); in particular, it decides when and when not to make use of indexes. How does the optimizer know what indexes exist? How does it know whether a given index is a clustering index?

B.8 Explain EXPLAIN.

References and Bibliography

References [B.1–B.5] are the principal DB2 manuals from IBM. References [B.8–B.10] are concerned with various aspects of System R, the prototype predecessor to DB2 and to IBM's other SQL products (in this regard, see also references [8.12–8.16] and [18.29–18.30]). *Note:* The reader should be aware that after several commercial releases of the product, the details of DB2's internals—particularly its compilation and optimization mechanisms—have evolved considerably and no longer display much trace of their System R origins. From a DB2 perspective, therefore, the System R references are now primarily of historical interest.

B.1 IBM Corporation. *IBM DATABASE 2 Version 3 General Information.* IBM Form No. GC26-4373.

B.2 IBM Corporation. *IBM DATABASE 2 Version 3 Administration Guide* (three volumes). IBM Form No. SC26-4374.

B.3 IBM Corporation. *IBM DATABASE 2 Version 3 SQL Reference.* IBM Form No. SC26-4380.

B.4 IBM Corporation. *IBM DATABASE 2 Version 3 Application Programming and SQL Guide.* IBM Form No. SC26-4377.

B.5   IBM Corporation. *IBM DATABASE 2 Version 3 Command and Utility Reference*. IBM Form No. SC26-4378.

B.6   Various authors. *IBM Sys. J. 23,* No. 2 (DB2 Special Issue, 1984).

A series of technical articles on DB2 as it was at first release. Topics discussed include:

- DB2 under IMS
- DB2 under TSO
- Data recovery
- DB2 design, performance, and tuning [18.30]
- DB2 buffer management
- The Query Management Facility QMF

B.7   C. J. Date and Colin J. White. *A Guide to DB2* (4th edition). Reading, Mass.: Addison-Wesley (1993).

Provides an extensive and thorough overview of DB2 and some of its companion products. Much of the present appendix is based on material from this book.

B.8   Raymond A. Lorie and Bradford W. Wade. "The Compilation of a High-Level Data Language." IBM Research Report RJ2598 (August 1979).

The DB2 compilation/recompilation scheme was pioneered by System R. This paper describes the System R mechanism in some detail, without however getting into questions of optimization (see reference [18.29] for information on this latter topic).

B.9   Raymond A. Lorie and J. F. Nilsson. "An Access Specification Language for a Relational Data Base System." *IBM J. R&D. 23,* No. 3 (May 1979).

Gives more details on one particular aspect of compilation in System R. For any given SQL statement, the System R optimizer generates a program in an internal language called ASL (Access Specification Language). That language serves as the interface between the optimizer and the *code generator*. (The code generator, as its name implies, converts an ASL program into machine code.) ASL consists of operators such as "scan" and "insert" on objects such as indexes and stored files. The purpose of ASL was to make the overall translation process more manageable, by breaking it down into a set of well-defined subprocesses.

B.10   Donald D. Chamberlin *et al.* "Support for Repetitive Transactions and Ad-Hoc Queries in System R." *ACM TODS 6,* No. 1 (March 1981).

Gives some measurements of System R performance in both the *ad hoc* query and "canned transaction" environments. (A "canned transaction" is a simple application that accesses only a small part of the database and is compiled prior to execution time. It corresponds to what we called a *planned request* in Chapter 2.) The measurements were taken on an IBM System 370 Model 158, running System R under the VM operating system. They are described as "preliminary"; with this caveat, however, the paper shows, among other things, that (a) compilation is almost always superior to interpretation, even for *ad hoc* (interactive) queries, and (b) a system like System R is capable of processing several canned transactions a second, provided appropriate indexes exist in the database.

Since this paper was first published, several relational products, including in particular DB2, have achieved performance figures that are comparable to the best figures obtained with *any* database system, relational or otherwise. In particular, transaction rates in the hundreds and even thousands of canned transactions per second have been demonstrated.

Answers to Selected Exercises

B.1 The four major components of DB2 are the system services, locking services, database services, and distributed data facility components. The database services component, in turn, divides into the Precompiler, Bind, Run Time Supervisor, Data Manager, and Buffer Manager components.

B.4 The principal DB2 storage objects are databases, table spaces, index spaces, stored tables, and indexes.

B.5 Since each stored record must be wholly contained within a single page, the maximum length of a DB2 stored record is constrained by the page size (either 4K or 32K bytes). The maximum width of a base table is less than this figure because the stored record includes certain control information—e.g., in the stored record prefix—that is concealed from the user.

B.6 A clustering index is an index for which the physical sequence of the indexed data is the same as, or very close to, the logical sequence of that same data as represented by the index entries (see Appendix A). A given stored table cannot have more than one such index because—by definition—that stored table can have only one physical sequence. The advantage of a clustering index is that sequential access via the index will access each data page once only and will thus be as fast as possible.

B.7 All such information is kept in the catalog.

C | Logic-Based Systems

C.1 Introduction

A significant new trend has emerged within the database research community over the past few years. That trend is toward **database systems that are based on logic**. Expressions such as *logic database, inferential DBMS, expert DBMS, deductive DBMS, knowledge base, knowledge base management system (KBMS), logic as a data model, recursive query processing,* etc., etc., are now frequently encountered in the research literature. But it is not always easy to relate such terms and the ideas they represent to familiar database terms and concepts, nor to understand the motivation underlying the research from a traditional database perspective. There is a clear need for an explanation of all of this activity in terms of conventional database ideas and principles. This appendix is an attempt to meet that need.

Our aim is thus to explain what logic-based database systems are all about from the viewpoint of someone who is familiar with database technology but not necessarily with logic *per se*. As each new idea from logic is introduced, therefore, we will explain it in conventional database terms, where possible or appropriate. Of course, we have discussed certain ideas from logic in this book already, particularly in the chapter on relational calculus (Chapter 7), which is directly based on logic. However, there is more to logic-based systems than just the relational calculus, as we will see.

The structure of this appendix is as follows. Following this preliminary background section, Section C.2 provides a brief overview of the subject, with a little history. Sections C.3 and C.4 then provide an elementary (and very much simplified) treatment of *propositional calculus* and *predicate calculus,* respectively. Next, Section C.5 introduces the so-called *proof-theoretic* view of a database, and Section C.6 builds on the ideas of that section to explain what is meant by the term *deductive DBMS*. Section C.7 then discusses some approaches to the problem of *recursive query processing,* and finally Section C.8 offers a summary and a few concluding remarks.

C.2 Overview

Research on the relationship between database theory and logic goes back to at least the late 1970s, if not earlier—see, for example, references [C.5], [C.7], and [C.13]. However, the principal stimulus for the recent considerable expansion of interest in the subject seems to have been the publication in 1984 of a landmark paper by Reiter [C.15]. In that paper, Reiter characterized the traditional perception of database systems as **model-theoretic**—by which he meant, very loosely speaking, that (a) the database is seen as a set of explicit (i.e., base) relations, each containing a set of explicit tuples, and (b) executing a query can be regarded as evaluating some specified formula (i.e., truth-valued expression) over those explicit relations and tuples. (We will explain the meaning of the term "model-theoretic" a little more precisely in Section C.5.)

Reiter then went on to argue that an alternative **proof-theoretic** view was possible, and indeed preferable in certain respects. In that alternative view—again very loosely speaking—the database is seen as a set of **axioms** ("ground" axioms, corresponding to domain values and tuples in base relations, plus certain "deductive" axioms, to be discussed), and executing a query is regarded as proving that some specified formula is a logical consequence of those axioms—in other words, proving that it is a **theorem**. (Again, we will explain the term "proof-theoretic" a little more precisely in Section C.5.)

An example is in order. Consider the following query (expressed in relational calculus) against the usual suppliers-and-parts database:

```
SPX WHERE SPX.QTY > 250
```

In the traditional—i.e., model-theoretic—interpretation, we examine the shipment tuples one by one, evaluating the formula "QTY > 250" for each one in turn; the query result then consists of just those shipment tuples for which the formula evaluates to *true*. In the proof-theoretic interpretation, by contrast, we consider the shipment tuples (plus certain other items) as *axioms* of a certain **"logical theory"**; we then apply theorem-proving techniques to determine for which possible values of the variable SPX the formula "SPX.QTY > 250" is a logical consequence of those axioms within that theory. The query result then consists of just those particular values of SPX.

Of course, this example is extremely simple—so simple, in fact, that the reader might be having difficulty in seeing what the difference between the two interpretations really is. The point is, however, that the reasoning mechanism employed in the attempted proof (in the proof-theoretic interpretation) can of course be much more sophisticated than our simple example is able to convey; indeed, it can handle certain problems that are beyond the capabilities of classical relational systems, as we will see. Furthermore, the proof-theoretic interpretation carries with it an attractive set of additional features [C.15]:

- **Representational uniformity:** It becomes possible to define a database language in which domain values, tuples in base relations, "deductive axioms," queries, and integrity constraints are all represented in essentially the same way.

- **Operational uniformity:** Proof theory provides a basis for a unified attack on a variety of apparently distinct problems, including query optimization (especially semantic optimization), integrity constraint enforcement, database design (dependency theory), program correctness proofs, and other problems.

- **Semantic modeling:** Proof theory also provides a good basis on which to define various semantic modeling extensions, such as events, type hierarchies, and certain types of entity aggregation.

- **Extended application:** Finally, proof theory also provides a basis for dealing with certain issues that classical approaches have traditionally had difficulty with—for example, *disjunctive information* (e.g., "Supplier S5 supplies either part P1 or part P2, but it is not known which").

Deductive Axioms

We offer a brief and preliminary explanation of the concept, referred to a couple of times above, of a **deductive axiom** (also known as a **rule of inference**). Basically, a deductive axiom is a rule by which, given certain facts, we are able to deduce additional facts. For example, given the facts "Anne is the mother of Betty" and "Betty is the mother of Celia," there is an obvious deductive axiom that allows us to deduce that Anne is the grandmother of Celia. To jump ahead of ourselves for a moment, therefore, we might imagine a *deductive DBMS* in which the two given facts are represented as tuples in a relation, as follows:

MOTHEROF

MOTHER	DAUGHTER
Anne	Betty
Betty	Celia

These two facts would represent **ground axioms** for the system. Let us suppose also that the deductive axiom has been formally stated to the system somehow, e.g., as follows:

```
IF    MOTHEROF       ( x, y )
AND   MOTHEROF       ( y, z )
THEN GRANDMOTHEROF ( x, z ) ;
```

(hypothetical and simplified syntax). Now the system can apply the rule expressed in the deductive axiom to the data represented by the ground axioms (in a manner to be explained in Section C.4) to deduce the result GRANDMOTHEROF (Anne,Celia). Thus, users can ask queries such as "Who is the grandmother of Celia?" or "Who are the granddaughters of Anne?" (More precisely, they can ask "Who is Anne the grandmother of?"—see Section C.4.)

Let us now attempt to relate the foregoing ideas to traditional database concepts. In traditional terms, the deductive axiom can be thought of as a *view definition*—for example:

```
CREATE VIEW GRANDMOTHEROF AS
     ( MX.MOTHER AS GRANDMOTHER, MY.DAUGHTER AS GRANDDAUGHTER  )
       WHERE MX.DAUGHTER = MY.MOTHER ;
```

(here MX and MY are tuple variables ranging over MOTHEROF). Queries such as the ones mentioned above can now be framed in terms of this view:

```
GX.GRANDMOTHER WHERE GX.GRANDDAUGHTER = 'Celia'

GX.GRANDDAUGHTER WHERE GX.GRANDMOTHER = 'Anne'
```

(GX is a tuple variable ranging over GRANDMOTHEROF).

So far, therefore, all we have really done is presented a different syntax and different interpretation for material that is already basically familiar. However, we will see in later sections that there are in fact some significant differences, not illustrated by the simple examples of the present section, between logic-based systems and more traditional DBMSs.

C.3 Propositional Calculus

In this section and the next, we present a very brief introduction to some of the basic ideas of logic. The present section considers propositional calculus and Section C.4 considers predicate calculus [C.1–C.3]. We remark immediately, however, that so far as we are concerned, propositional calculus is not all that important as an end in itself; the major aim of the present section is really to pave the way for an understanding of the next one. The aim of the two sections taken together is to provide a basis on which to build in the rest of the appendix.

The reader is assumed to be familiar with the basic concepts of Boolean algebra. For purposes of reference, we state certain laws of Boolean algebra that we will be needing later on:

■ *Distributive laws:*

```
f AND ( g OR  h )  ≡  ( f AND g  ) OR  ( f AND h )
f OR  ( g AND h )  ≡  ( f OR  g  ) AND ( f OR  h )
```

■ *De Morgan's laws:*

```
NOT ( f AND g )  ≡  NOT f OR  NOT g
NOT ( f OR  g )  ≡  NOT f AND NOT g
```

Here *f, g,* and *h* are arbitrary truth-valued expressions.

Now we turn to logic *per se*. Logic can be defined as **a formal method of reasoning**. Because it is formal, it can be used to perform formal tasks, such as testing the validity of an argument by examining just the structure of that argument as a sequence of steps (i.e., without paying any attention to the meaning of those steps). In particular, of course, because it is formal, it can be mechanized—i.e., it can be programmed, and thus applied by the machine.

Propositional calculus and predicate calculus are two special cases of logic in general (in fact, the former is a subset of the latter). The term "calculus," in turn, is just a general term that refers to any system of symbolic computation; in the particular cases at hand, the kind of computation involved is the computation of the truth value (*true* or *false*) of certain formulas or expressions. *Note:* Naturally we assume throughout that we are dealing with two-valued logic only.

Terms

We begin by assuming that we have some collection of objects, called **constants,** about which we can make statements of various kinds. In database parlance, these constants are the elements of the underlying domains. We define a **term** as a statement involving such constants that:

- Does not involve any quantifiers (see Section C.4), and
- Either does not involve any logical connectives (see below) or is contained in parentheses, and
- Evaluates unequivocally to either *true* or *false*.

For example, "Supplier S1 is located in London" and "Supplier S2 is located in London" and "Supplier S1 supplies part P1" are all terms (they evaluate to *true*, *false*, and *true* respectively, given our usual sample data values). By contrast, "Supplier S1 supplies some part *p*" is not a term, because it contains a quantifier ("some part *p*"). Another counterexample: "Supplier S5 will supply part P1 at some time in the future" is also not a term, because it does not evaluate unequivocally to either *true* or *false*.

Formulas

Next, we define the concept of a **formula**. Formulas of the propositional calculus—more generally, of the *predicate* calculus (see the next section)—are used in database systems to represent the conditional expression that defines the result of a query (among many other things).

```
formula
    ::=    term
        | NOT term
        | term AND formula
        | term OR formula
        | term ⇒ formula

term
    ::=    atomic-formula
        | ( formula )
```

Formulas are evaluated in accordance with the truth values of their constituent terms and the usual truth tables for the connectives. Points arising:

1. An *atomic formula* is a term that involves no connectives and is not contained in parentheses.
2. The symbol "⇒" represents the *logical implication* connective. The expression $f \Rightarrow g$ is defined to be logically equivalent to the expression NOT *f* OR *g*. *Note:* We used "IF . . . THEN . . . " for this connective in Chapter 7 and elsewhere in the body of the text.
3. We adopt the usual precedence rules for the connectives (NOT, then AND, then OR, then ⇒) in order to allow us to reduce the number of parentheses that the grammar would otherwise require.

Rules of Inference

Now we come to the **rules of inference** for the propositional calculus. Many such rules exist. Each such rule is a statement of the form

$\vDash f \Rightarrow g$

(where the symbol $\vDash$ can be read as **"It is always the case that"**; note that we need some such symbol in order to be able to make *metastatements*, i.e., statements about statements). Here are some examples of inference rules:

1. $\vDash$ (f AND g) $\Rightarrow f$
2. $\vDash$ f $\Rightarrow$ (f OR g)
3. $\vDash$ ((f $\Rightarrow$ g) AND ($g \Rightarrow h$)) $\Rightarrow$ ($f \Rightarrow h$)
4. $\vDash$ (f AND (f $\Rightarrow$ g)) $\Rightarrow g$

Note: This one is particularly important. It is called the **modus ponens** rule. Informally, it says that if *f* is *true* and *f* implies *g*, then *g* must be *true* as well. For example, given the fact that each of the following (a) and (b) is *true*—

(a) I have no money;

(b) If I have no money then I will have to wash dishes;

—then we can infer that (c) is *true* as well:

(c) I will have to wash dishes.

To continue with our inference rules:

5. $\vDash$ (f $\Rightarrow$ (g $\Rightarrow$ h)) $\Rightarrow$ ((f AND g) $\Rightarrow$ h)
6. $\vDash$ ((f OR g) AND (NOT g OR h)) $\Rightarrow$ (f OR h)

Note: This is another particularly important one. It is known as the **resolution** rule. We will have more to say about it under "Proofs" below and again in Section C.4.

Proofs

We now have the necessary apparatus for dealing with formal proofs (in the context of the propositional calculus). The problem of proof is the problem of determining whether some given formula *g* (the **conclusion**) is a logical consequence of some given set of formulas *f1, f2, . . . fn* (the **premises**)*—in symbols:

f1, f2, ..., fn $\vdash$ g

(read as "*g* **is deducible from** *f1, f2, . . . fn*"; observe the use of another metastatement symbol, $\vdash$). The basic method of proceeding is known as **forward chaining**. Forward chaining consists of applying the rules of inference repeatedly to the premises, and to formulas deduced from those premises, and to formulas deduced from those formulas, etc., etc., until the conclusion is deduced; in other words, the process "chains forward"

---

* Also spelled **premisses** (singular *premiss*).

from the premises to the conclusion. However, there are several variations on this basic theme:

1. **Adopting a premise:** If g is of the form $p \Rightarrow q$, adopt p as an additional premise and show that q is deducible from the given premises plus p.

2. **Backward chaining:** Instead of trying to prove $p \Rightarrow q$, prove the **contrapositive** NOT $q \Rightarrow$ NOT p.

3. **Reductio ad absurdum:** Instead of trying to prove $p \Rightarrow q$ directly, assume that p and NOT q are both *true* and derive a contradiction.

4. **Resolution:** This method uses the resolution inference rule (No. 6 in the list shown earlier).

We discuss the resolution technique in some detail, since it is of wide applicability (in particular, it generalizes to the case of predicate calculus also, as we will see in Section C.4).

Note first that the resolution rule is effectively a rule that allows us to **cancel sub-formulas;** that is, given the two formulas

```
f OR g    and    NOT g OR h
```

we can derive the simplified formula

```
f OR h
```

In particular, given f OR g and NOT g (i.e., taking h as *true*), we can derive f.

Observe, therefore, that the rule applies in general to a *conjunction* (AND) of two formulas, each of which is a *disjunction* (OR) of two formulas. In order to apply the resolution rule, therefore, we proceed as follows. (To make our discussion a little more concrete, we explain the process in terms of a specific example.) Suppose we wish to determine whether the following putative proof is in fact valid:

```
A ⇒ ( B ⇒ C ), NOT D OR A, B ⊢ D ⇒ C
```

(where A, B, C, and D are formulas). We start by adopting the negation of the conclusion as an additional premise, and then writing each premise on a separate line, as follows:

```
A ⇒ ( B ⇒ C )
NOT D OR A
B
NOT ( D ⇒ C )
```

Note that these four lines are implicitly all "ANDed" together. We now convert each individual line to **conjunctive normal form,** i.e., a form consisting of one or more formulas all ANDed together, each individual formula containing (possibly) NOTs and ORs but no ANDs (see Chapter 18). Of course, the second and third lines are already in this form. In order to convert the other two lines, we first eliminate all appearances of "⇒" (using the definition of that connective in terms of NOT and OR); we then apply the distributive laws and De Morgan's laws as necessary (see the beginning of this section). We also drop redundant parentheses and pairs of adjacent NOTs (which cancel out). The four lines become

```
NOT A OR NOT B OR C
NOT D OR A
B
D AND NOT C
```

Next, any line that includes any explicit ANDs we replace by a set of separate lines, one for each of the individual formulas ANDed together (dropping the ANDs in the process). In the example, this step applies to the fourth line only. The premises now look like this:

```
NOT A OR NOT B OR C
NOT D OR A
B
D
NOT C
```

Now we can start to apply the resolution rule. We choose a pair of lines that can be "resolved," i.e., a pair that contain (respectively) some particular formula and the negation of that formula. Let us choose the first two lines, which contain NOT *A* and *A* respectively, and resolve them, giving

```
NOT D OR NOT B OR C
B
D
NOT C
```

(*Note:* We also need to keep the two original lines, in general, but in this particular example they will not be needed any more.) Now we apply the rule again, again choosing the first two lines (resolving NOT *B* and *B*), giving

```
NOT D OR C
D
NOT C
```

We choose the first two lines again (NOT *D* and *D*):

```
C
NOT C
```

And once again (*C* and NOT *C*); the final result is the empty proposition (usually represented thus: []), which represents a contradiction. By reductio ad absurdum, therefore, the desired result is proved.

C.4 Predicate Calculus

We now turn our attention to the predicate calculus. The big difference between propositional calculus and predicate calculus is that the latter allows formulas to contain quantifiers, which makes it very much more powerful and of very much wider applicability. For example, the statement "Supplier S1 supplies some part *p*" is not a legal formula in propositional calculus, but it is a legal formula in predicate calculus. Hence predicate calculus provides us with a basis for expressing queries such as "What parts are supplied by supplier S1?" or "Find suppliers who supply some part" or even "Find suppliers who do not supply any parts at all."

Predicates

A **predicate** is a *truth-valued function*, i.e., a function that, given appropriate arguments, returns either *true* or *false*. For example, ">" is a predicate; the expression ">(x,y)"—more conventionally written "$x > y$"—returns *true* if the value of x is greater than the value of y and *false* otherwise. A predicate that takes n arguments is called an n-place predicate. A proposition—or for that matter a formula—in the sense of Section C.3 can be regarded as a zero-place predicate: It has no arguments and evaluates to either *true* or *false,* unconditionally.

It is convenient to assume that the predicates "=", ">", "≥", etc., are builtin (i.e., they are part of the formal system we are defining) and that expressions using them can be written in the conventional manner, but of course users should be able to define their own additional predicates as well. Indeed, that is the whole point, as we will quickly see: The fact is, in database terms, a user-defined predicate is nothing more nor less than a user-defined *relation.* The suppliers relation S, for example, can be regarded as a predicate with four arguments (S#, SNAME, STATUS, and CITY). Furthermore, the expressions S(S1,Smith,20,London) and S(S6,White,45,Rome) represent "instances" or "invocations" of that predicate that evaluate to *true* and *false* respectively (within the particular database that is represented by our usual sample set of values). Informally, we can regard such predicates—together with any applicable integrity constraints, which are also predicates—as defining what the corresponding relation "means," as explained in Part II of this book.

Well-Formed Formulas

The next step is to extend the definition of "formula." In order to avoid confusion with the formulas of the previous section (which are actually a special case), we will now switch to the term **well-formed formula** (WFF, pronounced "weff") that we first introduced in Chapter 7. Here is a simplified syntax for WFFs:

```
wff    ::=    term
            | NOT ( wff )
            | ( wff ) AND ( wff )
            | ( wff ) OR ( wff )
            | ( wff )  ⇒  ( wff )
            | EXISTS variable ( wff )
            | FORALL variable ( wff )

term   ::=    [ NOT ] predicate [ ( argument-commalist ) ]
```

Points arising:

1. A *term* is simply a possibly negated predicate instance. Each *argument* must be a constant, a variable, or a function reference, where each argument to a function

reference in turn is a constant or variable or function reference. The *argument commalist* (and enclosing parentheses) are omitted for a zero-place predicate. *Note:* Functions are permitted in order to allow WFFs to include computational expressions such as "$+(x,y)$"—more conventionally written "$x + y$"—and so forth.

2. As in Section C.3, we adopt the usual precedence rules for the connectives (NOT, then AND, then OR, then $\Rightarrow$) in order to reduce the number of parentheses that the grammar would otherwise require.

3. The reader is assumed to be familiar with the quantifiers EXISTS and FORALL.*

4. De Morgan's laws can be generalized to apply to quantified WFFs, as follows:

```
NOT ( FORALL x ( f ) )  ≡  EXISTS x ( NOT ( f ) )
NOT ( EXISTS x ( f ) )  ≡  FORALL x ( NOT ( f ) )
```

This point was also discussed in Chapter 7.

5. To repeat yet another point from Chapter 7: Within a given WFF, each occurrence of a variable is either **free** or **bound**. An occurrence of a variable is bound if (a) it is the variable immediately following a quantifier (the "quantified variable") or (b) it is within the scope of a quantifier and has the same name as the applicable quantified variable. A variable occurrence is free if it is not bound.

6. A **closed WFF** is one that contains no free variable occurrences. An **open WFF** is a WFF that is not closed.

Interpretations and Models

What do WFFs *mean?* In order to provide a formal answer to this question, we introduce the notion of an **interpretation**. An interpretation of a WFF—or more generally of a set of WFFs—is defined as follows:

■ First, we specify a **universe of discourse** over which the WFFs are to be interpreted. In other words, we specify a *mapping* between the permitted constants of the formal system (the domain values, in database terms) and objects in "the real world." Each individual constant corresponds to precisely one element in the universe of discourse.

■ Second, we specify a meaning for each predicate in terms of objects in the universe of discourse.

■ Third, we also specify a meaning for each function in terms of objects in the universe of discourse.

Then the interpretation consists of the combination of the universe of discourse, plus the mapping of individual constants to objects in that universe, plus the defined meanings for the predicates and functions with respect to that universe.

By way of example, let the universe of discourse be the set of integers

---

* We are concerned here only with the *first order* predicate calculus, which basically means that there are no predicate variables (i.e., variables whose value is a predicate), and hence that predicates cannot themselves be subjected to quantification. See Exercise 7.9 in Chapter 7.

{0,1,2,3,4,5}, let constants such as "2" correspond to elements of that universe in the obvious way, and let the predicate ">" be defined to have the usual meaning. (We could also define functions such as "+", "-", etc., if desired.) Now we can assign a truth value to WFFs such as the following, as indicated:

```
2 > 1                  — true
2 > 3                  — false
EXISTS x ( x > 2 )     — true
FORALL x ( x > 2 )     — false
```

Note, however, that other interpretations are possible. For example, we might specify the universe of discourse to be a set of security classification levels, as follows:

```
destroy before reading (level 5)
destroy after reading  (level 4)
top secret             (level 3)
secret                 (level 2)
confidential           (level 1)
unclassified           (level 0)
```

The predicate ">" could now mean "more secure (i.e., higher classification) than."

Now, the reader will probably realize that the two possible interpretations just given are *isomorphic*—that is, it is possible to set up a one-to-one correspondence between them, and hence at a deep level the two interpretations are really one and the same. But it must be clearly understood that interpretations can exist that are genuinely different in kind. For example, we might once again take the universe of discourse to be the integers 0–5, but define the predicate ">" to mean *equality*. (Of course, we would probably cause a lot of confusion that way, but at least we would be within our rights to do so.) Now the first WFF above would evaluate to *false* instead of *true*.

Another point that must be clearly understood is that two interpretations might be genuinely different in the foregoing sense and yet give the same truth values for the given set of WFFs. This would be the case with the two different definitions of ">" in our example if the WFF "2 > 1" were omitted.

Note, incidentally, that all of the WFFs we have been discussing in this subsection so far have been *closed* WFFs. The reason is that, given an interpretation, it is always possible to assign a truth value unambiguously to a closed WFF, but the truth value of an open WFF will depend on the values assigned to the free variables. For example, the open WFF

```
x > 3
```

is (obviously) *true* if the value of x is greater than 3 and *false* otherwise (whatever "greater than" and "3" mean in the interpretation).

Now we define a **model** of a WFF, or more generally of a set of (closed) WFFs, to be an interpretation for which all WFFs in the set are *true*. The two interpretations given above for the four WFFs

```
2 > 1
2 > 3
EXISTS x ( x > 2 )
FORALL x ( x > 2 )
```

in terms of the integers 0-5 were not models for those WFFs, because some of the WFFs evaluated to *false* under that interpretation. By contrast, the first interpretation (in which ">" was defined "properly") *would* have been a model for the set of WFFs

```
2 > 1
3 > 2
EXISTS x ( x > 2 )
FORALL x ( x > 2 OR NOT ( x > 2 ) )
```

Note finally that, since a given set of WFFs can admit of several interpretations in which all of the WFFs evaluate to *true,* it can therefore have several *models* (in general). Thus, a database can have several models (in general), since—in the model-theoretic view—a database *is* basically a set of WFFs. See Section C.5.

Clausal Form

Just as any propositional calculus formula can be converted to conjunctive normal form, so any predicate calculus WFF can be converted to **clausal form,** which can be regarded as an extended version of conjunctive normal form. One motivation for making such a conversion is that (again) it allows us to apply the resolution rule in constructing or verifying proofs, as we will see.

The conversion process proceeds as follows (in outline; for more details, see reference [C.10]). We illustrate the steps by applying them to a sample WFF, namely

```
FORALL x ( p ( x ) AND EXISTS y ( FORALL z ( q ( y, z ) ) ) )
```

Here p and q are predicates and $x, y,$ and z are variables.

1. Eliminate "⇒" symbols as in Section C.3. In our example, this first transformation has no effect.
2. Use De Morgan's laws, plus the fact that two adjacent NOTs cancel out, to move NOTs so that they apply only to terms, not to general WFFs. (Again this particular transformation has no effect in our particular example.)
3. Convert the WFF to **prenex normal form** by moving all quantifiers to the front (systematically renaming variables if necessary):

```
FORALL x ( EXISTS y ( FORALL z ( p ( x ) AND q ( y, z ) ) ) )
```

4. Note that an existentially quantified WFF such as

```
EXISTS v ( r ( v ) )
```

is equivalent to the WFF

```
r ( a )
```

for some (unknown) constant *a;* that is, the original WFF asserts that some such *a* does exist, we just don't know its value. Likewise, a WFF such as

```
FORALL u ( EXISTS v ( s ( u, v ) ) )
```

is equivalent to the WFF

```
FORALL u ( s ( u, f ( u ) ) )
```

for some (unknown) function f of the universally quantified variable u. The constant a and the function f in these examples are known, respectively, as a **Skolem constant** and a **Skolem function*** (where a Skolem constant is really just a Skolem function with no arguments). So the next step is to eliminate existential quantifiers by replacing the corresponding quantified variables by (arbitrary) Skolem functions of all universally quantified variables that precede the quantifier in question in the WFF:

```
FORALL x ( FORALL z ( p (. x ) AND q ( f ( x ), z ) ) )
```

5. All variables are now universally quantified. We can therefore adopt a convention by which all variables are *implicitly* universally quantified and so drop the explicit quantifiers:

```
p ( x ) AND q ( f ( x ), z )
```

6. Convert the WFF to conjunctive normal form, i.e., to a set of clauses all ANDed together, each clause involving possibly NOTs and ORs but no ANDs. In our example, the WFF is already in this form.

7. Write each clause on a separate line and drop the ANDs:

```
p ( x )
q ( f ( x ), z )
```

This is the clausal form equivalent of the original WFF.

Note: It follows from the foregoing procedure that the general form of a WFF in clausal form is a set of clauses, each on a line of its own, and each of the form

```
NOT A1 OR NOT A2 OR ... OR NOT Am OR B1 OR B2 OR ... OR Bn
```

where the A's and B's are all nonnegated terms. We can rewrite such a clause, if we like, as

```
A1 AND A2 AND ... AND Am  ⇒  B1 OR B2 OR ... OR Bn
```

If there is at most one B ($n = 0$ or 1), the clause is called a **Horn clause**.[†]

Using the Resolution Rule

Now we are in a position to see how a logic-based database system can deal with queries. We use the example from the end of Section C.2. First, we have a predicate MOTHEROF, which takes two arguments, representing mother and daughter respectively, and we are given the following two terms (predicate instances):

1. MOTHEROF (Anne, Betty)

2. MOTHEROF (Betty, Celia)

We are also given the following WFF (the "deductive axiom"):

3. MOTHEROF (x, y) AND MOTHEROF (y, z) ⇒ GRANDMOTHEROF (x, z)

---

* After the logician T. A. Skolem.
[†] After the logician Alfred Horn.

(note that this is a Horn clause). In order to simplify the application of the resolution rule, let us rewrite the clause to eliminate the "⇒" symbol:

4. NOT MOTHEROF (x, y) OR NOT MOTHEROF (y, z) OR GRANDMOTHEROF (x, z)

We now show how to prove that Anne is the grandmother of Celia—i.e., how to answer the query "Is Anne Celia's grandmother?" We begin by negating the conclusion that is to be proved and adopting it as an additional premise:

5. NOT GRANDMOTHEROF (Anne, Celia)

Now, to apply the resolution rule, we must systematically substitute values for variables in such a way that we can find two clauses that contain, respectively, a WFF and its negation. Such substitution is legitimate because the variables are all implicitly universally quantified, and hence individual (nonnegated) WFFs must be *true* for each and every legal combinations of values of their variables. *Note:* The process of finding a set of substitutions that make two clauses resolvable in this manner is known as **unification**.

To see how the foregoing works in the case at hand, note first that lines 4 and 5 contain the terms GRANDMOTHEROF(x,z) and NOT GRANDMOTHEROF(Anne, Celia), respectively. So we substitute Anne for x and Celia for z in line 4 and resolve, to obtain

6. NOT MOTHEROF (Anne, y) OR NOT MOTHEROF (y, Celia)

Line 2 contains MOTHEROF(Betty,Celia). So we substitute Betty for y in line 6 and resolve, to obtain

7. NOT MOTHEROF (Anne, Betty)

Resolving line 7 and line 1, we obtain the empty clause []: Contradiction. Hence the answer to the original query is "Yes, Anne is Celia's grandmother."

What about the query "Who are the granddaughters of Anne?" Observe first of all that the system does not know about granddaughters, it only knows about grandmothers. We could add another deductive axiom to the effect that z is the granddaughter of x if and only if x is the grandmother of z (no males are allowed in this database). Alternatively, of course, we could rephrase the question as "Who is Anne the grandmother of?" Let us consider this latter formulation. The premises are (to repeat)

1. MOTHEROF (Anne, Betty)
2. MOTHEROF (Betty, Celia)
3. NOT MOTHEROF (x, y) OR NOT MOTHEROF (y, z) OR GRANDMOTHEROF (x, z)

We introduce a fourth premise, as follows:

4. NOT GRANDMOTHEROF (Anne, r) OR RESULT (r)

Intuitively, this says that either Anne is not the grandmother of anyone, or alternatively she is the grandmother of some person r. We wish to discover the identity of all such persons r, assuming they exist. We proceed as follows.

First, substitute Anne for x and r for z and resolve lines 4 and 3, to obtain

5. `NOT MOTHEROF ( Anne, y ) OR NOT MOTHEROF ( y, z ) OR RESULT ( z )`

Next, substitute Betty for y and resolve lines 5 and 1, to obtain

6. `NOT MOTHEROF ( Betty, z ) OR RESULT ( z )`

Now substitute Celia for z and resolve lines 6 and 2, to obtain

7. `RESULT ( Celia )`

Hence Anne is the grandmother of Celia.

Note: If we had been given an additional term, as follows—

`MOTHEROF   ( Betty, Delia )`

—then we could have substituted Delia for z in the final step (instead of Celia) and obtained

`RESULT ( Delia )`

The user expects to see both names in the result, of course. Thus, the system needs to apply the unification and resolution process exhaustively to generate *all possible* result values. Details of this refinement are beyond the scope of the present discussion.

C.5   A Proof-Theoretic View of Databases

As explained in Section C.4, a *clause* is an expression of the form

`A1 AND A2 AND ... AND Am ⇒ B1 OR B2 OR ... OR Bn`

where the A's and B's are all terms of the form

`r ( x1, x2, ... xt )`

(here r is a predicate and $x1, x2, \ldots xt$ are the arguments to that predicate). Following reference [C.12], we now consider a couple of important special cases of this general construct.

1. *Case 1:* $m = 0$, $n = 1$

In this case the clause can be simplified to just

`⇒ B1`

or in other words (dropping the implication symbol) to just

`r ( x1, x2, ..., xt )`

for some predicate r and some set of arguments $x1, x2, \ldots, xt$. If the x's are all constants, the clause represents a **ground axiom**—i.e., it is a statement that is unequivocally *true*. In database terms, such a statement corresponds to a tuple of some relation $R*$. The predicate r corresponds to the "meaning" of relation R, as explained elsewhere in this book. For example, in the suppliers-and-parts database, there is a relation called SP, the meaning of which is that the indicated supplier (S#) is supplying the indicated part (P#) in the indicated quantity (QTY). Note that this meaning corresponds to an **open WFF,** since it contains some free variables (S#, P#, and QTY). By contrast, the tuple (S1,P1,300)—in which the arguments are all constants—is a ground axiom or **closed WFF** that asserts unequivocally that supplier S1 is supplying part P1 in a quantity of 300.

2. *Case 2:* $m > 0$, $n = 1$

In this case the clause takes the form

    A1 AND A2 AND . . . AND Am ⇒ B

which can be regarded as a **deductive axiom;** it gives a (partial) definition of the predicate on the right-hand side of the implication symbol in terms of those on the left (see the definition of the GRANDMOTHEROF predicate earlier for an example).

Alternatively, such a clause might be regarded as defining an **integrity constraint**. Suppose for the sake of the example that the suppliers relation S contains only two attributes, S# and CITY. Then the clause

    S (s, c1) AND S (s, c2) ⇒ c1 = c2

expresses the constraint that CITY is functionally dependent on S#. Note the use of the builtin predicate "=" in this example.

As the foregoing discussions demonstrate, tuples in relations ("ground axioms"), derived relations ("deductive axioms"), and integrity constraints can all be regarded as special cases of the general *clause* construct. Let us now try to see how these ideas can lead to the "proof-theoretic" view of a database mentioned in Section C.2.

First, the traditional view of a database can be regarded as **model**-theoretic. By "traditional view" here, we simply mean a view in which the database is perceived as a collection of explicitly named (base) relations, each containing a set of explicit tuples, together with an explicit set of integrity constraints that those tuples are not allowed to violate. It is this perception that can be characterized as "model-theoretic," as we now explain.

■   The underlying domains contain values or constants that are supposed to stand for certain objects in the "real world" (more precisely, in some **interpretation,** in the sense of Section C.4). They thus correspond to the universe of discourse.

■   The base relations (more precisely, the base relation *headings*) represent a set of predicates or open WFFs that are to be interpreted over that universe. For example, the heading of relation SP represents the predicate "Supplier S# supplies part P# in quantity QTY."

---

* Or to an element of a domain.

- Each tuple in a given relation represents an instance of the corresponding predicate; i.e., it represents a proposition (a closed WFF—it contains no variables) that is unequivocally *true* in the universe of discourse.

- The integrity constraints are also closed WFFs, and they are interpreted over the same universe. Since the data does not (i.e., *must* not!) violate the constraints, these constraints necessarily evaluate to *true* as well.

- The tuples and the integrity constraints can together be regarded as the set of axioms defining a certain **logical theory** (loosely speaking, a "theory" in logic *is* a set of axioms). Since those axioms are all *true* in the interpretation, then by definition that interpretation is a **model** of that logical theory, in the sense of Section C.4. Note that, as pointed out in that section, the model might not be unique—that is, a given database might have several possible interpretations, all of which are equally valid from a logical standpoint.

In the model-theoretic view, therefore, the "meaning" of the database *is* the model, in the foregoing sense of the term "model." And since there are many possible models, there are many possible meanings, at least in principle.* Furthermore, query processing in the model-theoretic view is essentially a process of evaluating a certain open WFF to discover which values of the free variables in that WFF cause the WFF to evaluate to *true* within the model.

So much for the model-theoretic view. However, in order to be able to apply the rules of inference described in Sections C.3 and C.4, it becomes necessary to adopt a different perspective, one in which the database is explicitly regarded as a certain logical theory, i.e., as a set of axioms. The "meaning" of the database then becomes, precisely, the collection of all *true* statements that can be deduced from the axioms using those axioms in all possible combinations—i.e., it is the set of **theorems** that can be proved from those axioms. This is the **proof-theoretic** view. In this view, query evaluation becomes a theorem-proving process (conceptually speaking, at any rate; in the interests of efficiency, however, the system is likely to use more conventional query processing techniques, as we will see in Section C.7).

Note: It follows from the foregoing paragraph that one difference between the model-theoretic and proof-theoretic views (intuitively speaking) is that, whereas a database can have many "meanings" in the model-theoretic view, it typically has precisely one "meaning" in the proof-theoretic view—except that (a) as pointed out earlier, that one meaning is really *the* canonical meaning in the model-theoretic case, and in any case (b) the remark to the effect that there is only one meaning in the proof-theoretic case ceases to be true, in general, if the database includes any negative axioms [C.9-C.10].

---

* However, if we assume that the database does not explicitly contain any negative information (e.g., a proposition of the form "NOT S#(S9)," meaning that S9 is not a supplier number), there will also be a "minimal" or *canonical* meaning, which is the intersection of all possible models [C.10]. In this case, moreover, that canonical meaning will be the same as the meaning ascribed to the database under the proof-theoretic view, to be explained.

The axioms for a given database (proof-theoretic view) can be informally summarized as follows [C.15]:

1. Ground axioms, corresponding to the elements of the domains and the tuples of the base relations. These axioms constitute what is sometimes called the **extensional database** (EDB).

2. A "completion axiom" for each relation, which states that no tuples of that relation exist other than those explicitly appearing in that relation. These axioms correspond to what is usually called the **Closed World Assumption** (CWA), which states that omission of a given tuple from a given relation implies that the proposition corresponding to that tuple is *false*. For example, the fact that the suppliers relation S does not include the tuple (S6,White,45,Rome) means that the proposition "There exists a supplier S6 named White with status 45 located in Rome" is *false*.

3. The "unique name" axiom, which states that every constant is distinguishable from all the rest (i.e., has a unique name).

4. The "domain closure" axiom, which states that no constants exist other than those in the database domains.

5. A set of axioms (essentially standard) to define the builtin predicate "=". These axioms are needed because the axioms in Nos. 2, 3, and 4 above each make use of the equality predicate.

We conclude this section with a brief summary of the principal differences between the two perceptions (model-theoretic and proof-theoretic). First of all, it has to be said that from a purely pragmatic standpoint there might not be very much difference at all!—at least in terms of present-day systems. However:

■ Nos. 2–5 in the list of axioms for the proof-theoretic view make explicit certain assumptions that are implicit in the notion of interpretation in the model-theoretic view [C.15]. Stating assumptions explicitly is generally a good idea; furthermore, it is necessary to specify those additional axioms explicitly in order to be able to apply general proof techniques, such as the resolution method described in Sections C.3 and C.4.

■ Note that the list of axioms makes no mention of integrity constraints. The reason for that omission is that (in the proof-theoretic view) adding such constraints converts the system into a **deductive** DBMS. See Section C.6.

■ The proof-theoretic view does enjoy a certain elegance that the model-theoretic view does not, inasmuch as it provides a uniform perception of several constructs that are usually thought of as more or less distinct: base data, queries, integrity constraints (the previous point notwithstanding), virtual data (etc.). As a consequence, the possibility arises of more uniform interfaces and more uniform implementations.

■ The proof-theoretic view also provides a natural basis for treating certain problems that relational systems have traditionally always had difficulty with—**disjunctive information** (e.g., "Supplier S6 is located in either Paris or Rome"), the derivation of **negative information** (e.g., "Who is not a supplier?"), and **recursive queries** (see the next section)—though in this last case, at least, there is no reason in principle why a classical relational system could not be extended appropriately to deal with such queries (a proposal for doing so can be found in reference [C.14]). We will have more to say regarding such matters in Sections C.6 and C.7.

- Finally, to quote Reiter [C.15], the proof-theoretic view "provides a correct treatment of [extensions to] the relational model to incorporate more real world semantics" (including—to repeat from Section C.2—events, type hierarchies, and certain kinds of entity aggregation).

C.6 Deductive Database Systems

A **deductive DBMS** is a DBMS that supports the proof-theoretic view of a database, and in particular is capable of deducing additional facts from the extensional database by applying specified **deductive axioms** or **rules of inference** to those facts. The deductive axioms, together with the integrity constraints (discussed below), form what is sometimes called the **intensional database** (IDB), and the extensional database and the intensional database together constitute what is usually called the *deductive database* (not a very good term, since it is the DBMS, not the database, that carries out the deductions).

As just indicated, the deductive axioms form one part of the intensional database. The other part consists of additional axioms that represent integrity constraints (i.e., rules whose primary purpose is to constrain updates, though actually such rules can also be used in the deduction process to generate new facts).

Let us see what the suppliers-and-parts database would look like in "deductive DBMS" form. First, there will be a set of ground axioms defining the legal domain values. *Note:* In what follows, we omit the (necessary) quotes surrounding string constants purely for reasons of readability.

```
S# ( S1 )    NAME ( Smith )    STATUS (  5 )    CITY ( London )
S# ( S2 )    NAME ( Jones )    STATUS ( 10 )    CITY ( Paris  )
S# ( S3 )    NAME ( Blake )    STATUS ( 15 )    CITY ( Rome   )
S# ( S4 )    NAME ( Clark )    etc.             CITY ( Athens )
S# ( S5 )    NAME ( Adams )                     etc.
S# ( S6 )    NAME ( White )
S# ( S7 )    NAME ( Nut   )
etc.         NAME ( Bolt  )
             NAME ( Screw )
             etc.

etc., etc., etc.
```

Next, there will be ground axioms for the tuples in the base relations:

```
S ( S1, Smith, 20, London )
S ( S2, Jones, 10, Paris )
etc.
```

```
P ( P1, Nut, Red, 12, London )
etc.

SP ( S1, P1, 300 )
etc.
```

Note: We are not seriously suggesting that the extensional database will be created by explicitly listing all of the ground axioms as indicated above; rather, of course, traditional data defnition and data entry methods will be used. In other words, deductive DBMSs will typically apply their deductions to conventional databases that already exist and have been constructed in the conventional manner. Note, however, that it now becomes more important than ever that the extensional database not violate any of the declared integrity constraints!—because a database that does violate any such constraints represents (in logical terms) an inconsistent set of axioms, and it is well known that *absolutely any proposition whatsoever* can be proved to be "true" from such a starting point (in other words, contradictions can be derived). For exactly the same reason, it is also important that the stated set of integrity constraints be consistent.

Now for the intensional database. Here are the domain constraints:

```
S ( s, sn, st, sc ) ⇒ S# ( s ) AND
                       NAME ( sn ) AND
                       STATUS ( st ) AND
                       CITY ( sc )

P ( p, pn, pl, pw, pc ) ⇒ P# ( p ) AND
                          NAME ( pn ) AND
                          COLOR ( pl ) AND
                          WEIGHT ( pw ) AND
                          CITY ( pc )
etc.
```

Candidate key constraints:

```
S ( s, sn1, st1, sc1 ) AND S ( s, sn2, st2, sc2 )
                   ⇒     sn1 = sn2 AND
                         st1 = st2 AND
                         sc1 = sc2
etc.
```

Foreign key constraints:

```
SP ( s, p, q ) ⇒ S ( s, sn, st, sc ) AND
                 P ( p, pn, pl, pw, pc ) AND
                 QTY ( q )
```

And so on. *Note:* We assume for the sake of the exposition that variables appearing on the right-hand side of the implication symbol and not on the left (*sn, st,* etc., in the example) are existentially quantified. (All others are universally quantified, as explained in Section C.4.) Technically, we need some Skolem functions; *sn,* for example, should really be replaced by (say) SN(*s*), where SN is a Skolem function.

Note, incidentally, that most of the constraints shown above are not pure clauses in the sense of Section C.5, because the right-hand side is not just a disjunction of simple terms.

Now let us add some more deductive axioms:

```
S ( s, sn, st, sc ) AND st > 15
                      ⇒  GOOD_SUPPLIERS ( s, st, sc )
```

(compare the sample view definition in Chapter 17, Section 17.1).

```
S ( sx, sxn, sxt, sc ) AND S ( sy, syn, syt, sc )
                      ⇒   SS_COLOCATED ( sx, sy )

S ( s, sn, st, c ) AND P ( p, pn, pl, pw, c )
                      ⇒   SP_COLOCATED ( s, p )
```

And so on.

In order to make the example a little more interesting, let us now extend the suppliers-and-parts database to incorporate a part structure relation, showing which parts *px* contain which parts *py* as immediate (i.e. first-level) components. First a constraint to show that *px* and *py* must both identify existing parts:

```
PART_STRUCTURE ( px, py ) ⇒ P ( px, xn, xl, xw, xc ) AND
                            P ( py, yn, yl, yw, yc )
```

Some data values:

```
PART_STRUCTURE ( P1, P2 )
PART_STRUCTURE ( P1, P3 )
PART_STRUCTURE ( P2, P3 )
PART_STRUCTURE ( P2, P4 )
etc.
```

(In practice PART_STRUCTURE would probably also have a "quantity" argument, showing how many *py*'s it takes to make a *px,* but we omit this refinement for simplicity.)

Now we can add a pair of deductive axioms to explain what it means for part *px* to contain part *py* as a component *at any level:*

```
PART_STRUCTURE ( px, py )  ⇒  COMPONENTOF ( px, py )

PART_STRUCTURE ( px, pz ) AND COMPONENTOF ( pz, py )
                      ⇒  COMPONENTOF ( px, py )
```

In other words, part *py* is a component of part *px* (at some level) if it is either an immediate component of part *px* or an immediate component of some part *pz* that is in turn a component (at some level) of part *px*. Note that the second axiom here is recursive—it defines the COMPONENTOF predicate in terms of itself. Classical relational systems, by contrast, do not permit view definitions (or queries or integrity constraints or . . .) to be recursive in such a manner. This ability to support recursion is one of the most immediately obvious distinctions between deductive DBMSs and their classical counterparts—although, as mentioned in Section C.5 and also at earlier points in this book, there is no fundamental reason why the classical relational algebra should not be extended to support an appropriate set of recursive operators.

We will have more to say regarding this recursive capability in the next section.

Datalog

From the foregoing discussion, it should be clear that one of the most directly visible portions of a deductive DBMS will be a language in which the deductive axioms (usually called **rules**) can be formulated. The best known example of such a language is called (by analogy with Prolog) **Datalog** [C.9]. We present a brief discussion of Datalog in this subsection. *Note:* The emphasis in Datalog is on its descriptive power, not its computational power (as was also the case with the original relational model, incidentally). The objective is to define a language that ultimately will have greater expressive power than conventional relational languages [C.9]. As a consequence, the stress in Datalog—indeed, the stress throughout logic-based database systems in general—is very heavily on query, not update, though it is possible, and desirable, to extend the language to support update also (see later).

In its simplest form, Datalog supports the formulation of rules as simple Horn clauses without functions. In Section C.4, we defined a Horn clause to be a WFF of either of the following two forms:

    A1 AND A2 AND ... AND An

    A1 AND A2 AND ... AND An ⇒ B

(where the *A*'s and *B* are nonnegated predicate instances involving only constants and variables). Following the style of Prolog, however, Datalog actually writes the second of these the other way around:

    B ⇐ A1 AND A2 AND ... AND An

To be consistent with other publications in this area, therefore, we will do the same in what follows. In such a clause, *B* is the **rule head** (or conclusion) and the *A*'s are the **rule body** (or premises or **goal**; each individual *A* is a **subgoal**). For brevity, the ANDs are often replaced by commas. A **Datalog program** is a set of such clauses separated in some conventional manner—e.g., by semicolons (in this book, however, we will not use semicolons but instead will simply start each new clause on a new line). No meaning attaches to the order of the clauses within such a program.

Note that *the entire "deductive database"* can be regarded as a Datalog program in the foregoing sense. For example, we could take all of the axioms stated above for suppliers-and-parts (the ground axioms, the integrity constraints, and the deductive axioms), write them all in Datalog style, separate them by semicolons or by writing them on separate lines, and the result would be a Datalog program. As noted earlier, however, the extensional part of the database will typically *not* be created in such a fashion, but rather in some more conventional manner. Thus, the primary function of Datalog is to support the formulation of deductive axioms specifically. As already pointed out, that function can be regarded as an extension of the view definition mechanism found in conventional relational DBMSs today.

Datalog can also be used as a query language (again, much like Prolog). For example, suppose we have been given the following Datalog definition of GOOD_SUPPLIERS:

```
GOOD_SUPPLIERS ( s, st, sc ) ⇐ S ( s, sn, st, sc ) AND st > 15
```

Here are some typical queries against GOOD_SUPPLIERS.

1. Find all good suppliers:

   ```
   ? ⇐ GOOD_SUPPLIERS ( s, st, sc )
   ```

2. Find good suppliers in Paris:

   ```
   ? ⇐ GOOD_SUPPLIERS ( s, st, Paris )
   ```

3. Is supplier S1 a good supplier?

   ```
   ? ⇐ GOOD_SUPPLIERS ( S1, st, sc )
   ```

And so on. In other words, a query in Datalog consists of a special rule with a head of "?" and a body consisting of a single term that denotes the query result; the head "?" means (by convention) "Display."

It should be pointed out that, despite the fact that Datalog does support recursion, there are quite a few features of conventional relational languages that Datalog in its original form does not support—scalar operations ("+", "−", etc.), aggregate operations (COUNT, SUM, etc.), set difference (because clauses cannot be negated), grouping, etc. It also does not support attribute naming (the significance of a predicate argument depends on its relative position), nor does it provide full domain support (i.e., user-defined data type support in the sense of Chapter 19). As noted earlier, it also does not provide any update operations, nor (as a special case of the latter) does it support the declarative specification of foreign key delete and update rules in the sense of Chapter 5 (DELETE CASCADES, etc.).

In order to address some of the foregoing shortcomings, a variety of extensions to basic Datalog have been proposed. Those extensions are intended to provide the following features, among others:

- *Negative premises*—for example:

  ```
  SS_COLOCATED ( sx, sy )  ⇐   S ( sx, sxn, sxt, sc ) AND
                               S ( sy, syn, syt, sc ) AND
                               NOT ( sx = sy )
  ```

- *Scalar functions* (builtin and user-defined)—for example:

  ```
  P_WT_IN_GRAMS ( p, pn, pl, pg, pc ) ⇐
                       P ( p, pn, pl, pw, pc ) AND pg = pw * 454
  ```

  In this example we have assumed that the builtin function "*" (multiplication) can be written in conventional infix notation. A more orthodox logic representation of the term following the AND would be "=(pg,*(pw,454))".

- *Aggregate functions and grouping* (somewhat along the lines of our relational SUMMARIZE operator—see Chapter 6). Such operators are necessary in order to address (for example) what is sometimes called the *gross requirements* problem, which is the problem of finding, not only which parts *py* are components of some part *px* at any level, but also *how many py*'s (at all levels) it takes to make a *px* (naturally we are assuming here that PART_STRUCTURE includes a QTY attribute).

- *Update operations:* One approach to meeting this obvious requirement [C.10]— not the only one—is based on the observation that in basic Datalog, any predicate in a rule head must be nonnegated, and that every tuple generated by the rule can be regarded as being "inserted" into the result relation. A possible extension would thus be to allow negated predicates in a rule head and to treat the negation as requesting the *deletion* (of pertinent tuples).

- *NonHorn clauses in the rule body*—in other words, allow completely general WFFs in the definition of rules.

A survey of the foregoing extensions, with examples, can be found in the book by Gardarin and Valduriez [C.10], which also discusses a variety of Datalog implementation techniques.

C.7 Recursive Query Processing

As indicated in the previous section, one of the most notable features of deductive database systems is their support for recursion (recursive rule definitions, and hence recursive queries also). As a consequence of this fact, the past few years have seen a great deal of research into techniques for implementing such recursion—indeed, just about every database conference since 1986 or so has included one or more papers on the subject (see the References and Bibliography section at the end of this appendix). Since recursive query support represents a problem that typically has not existed in classical DBMSs, we discuss it briefly in the present section.

By way of example, we repeat from Section C.6 the recursive definition of the "part structure" relation (for brevity, however, we now abbreviate PART_STRUC-TURE to PS and COMPONENTOF to COMP; we also convert the definition to Datalog form).

```
COMP ( px, py ) ⇐ PS ( px, py )

COMP ( px, py ) ⇐ PS ( px, pz ) AND COMP ( pz, py )
```

Here is a typical recursive query against this database ("Explode part P1"):

```
? ⇐ COMP ( P1, py )
```

To return to the definition *per se:* The second rule in that definition—i.e., the recursive rule—is said to be **linearly** recursive because the predicate in the rule head appears just once in the rule body. As a matter of fact, it would be possible to restate the definition in such a way that the recursion would not be linear:

```
COMP ( px, py ) ⇐ PS ( px, py )

COMP ( px, py ) ⇐ COMP ( px, pz ) AND COMP ( pz, py )
```

However, there is a general feeling that linear recursion represents "the interesting case," in the sense that most recursions that arise in practice are naturally linear, and furthermore there are known efficient techniques for dealing with the linear case [C.16]. We therefore restrict our attention to linear recursion for the remainder of this section.

Note: For completeness, we should point out that it is necessary to generalize the definition of "recursive rule" (and of linear recursion) to deal with more complex cases such as the following:

```
P ( x, y ) ⇐ Q ( x, z ) AND R ( z, y )
Q ( x, y ) ⇐ P ( x, z ) AND S ( z, y )
```

For brevity, we ignore such refinements here. The interested reader is referred to reference [C.16] for more details.

As in classical (nonrecursive) query processing, the overall problem of implementing a given recursive query can be divided into two subproblems, namely (a) transforming the original query into some equivalent but more efficient form and (b) actually executing the result of that transformation. The literature contains descriptions of a variety of attacks on both of these problems. Reference [C.16] provides an excellent survey, analysis, and comparison of published techniques as of about 1988. In the present section, we briefly discuss some of the simpler techniques. We will illustrate them by showing their application to the query "Explode part P1," using the following set of sample values for the PS relation (based on Fig. 4.4 from Chapter 4, but ignoring QTY for simplicity):

PS	PX	PY
	P1	P2
	P1	P3
	P2	P3
	P2	P4
	P3	P5
	P4	P5
	P5	P6

Unification and Resolution

One possible approach, of course, is to use the standard Prolog techniques of **unification and resolution,** as described in Section C.4. In the example, this approach works as follows. The first premises are the deductive axioms, which look like this in conjunctive normal form:

1. NOT PS (px, py) OR COMP (px, py)
2. NOT PS (px, pz) OR NOT COMP (pz, py) OR COMP (px, py)

We construct another premise from the desired conclusion:

3. `NOT COMP ( P1, ` *py* ` ) OR RESULT ( ` *py* ` )`

The ground axioms form the remaining premises. Consider, for example, the ground axiom

4. `PS ( P1, P2 )`

Substituting P1 for *px* and P2 for *py* in line 1, we can resolve lines 1 and 4 to yield

5. `COMP ( P1, P2 )`

Now substituting P2 for *py* in line 3 and resolving lines 3 and 5, we obtain

6. `RESULT ( P2 )`

So P2 is a component of P1. An exactly analogous argument will show that P3 is also a component of P1. Now, of course, we have the additional axioms COMP(P1,P2) and COMP(P1,P3); we can now apply the foregoing process recursively to determine the complete part explosion. The details are left as an exercise for the reader.

In practice, however, unification and resolution can be quite costly in performance. It will thus often be desirable to find some more efficient strategy. The remaining subsections below discuss some possible approaches to this problem.

Naive Evaluation

Naive evaluation [C.25] is probably the simplest approach of all. As the name suggests, the algorithm is very simple-minded; it can most easily be explained (for our sample query) in terms of the following pseudocode.

```
COMP := PS ;
do until COMP reaches a "fixpoint" ;
   COMP := COMP UNION ( COMP ⨝ PS ) ;
end ;
DISPLAY := COMP WHERE PX = 'P1' ;
```

Relations COMP and DISPLAY (like relation PS) each have two attributes, PX and PY. Loosely speaking, the algorithm works by repeatedly forming an intermediate result consisting of the union of the join of relation PS and the previous intermediate result, until that intermediate result reaches a **"fixpoint"**—i.e., until it ceases to grow. *Note:* The expression "COMP ⨝ PS" is shorthand for "join COMP and PS over COMP.PY and PS.PX and project the result over COMP.PX and PS.PY." For brevity, we ignore the attribute renaming operations that our dialect of the algebra would require to make this work (see Chapter 6).

Let us step through the algorithm with our sample set of data values. After the first iteration of the loop, the value of the expression COMP ⨝ PS is as shown below on the left and the resulting value of COMP is as shown below on the right (with tuples added on this iteration flagged with an asterisk):

COMP ⋈ PS	PX	PY
	P1	P3
	P1	P4
	P1	P5
	P2	P5
	P3	P6
	P4	P6

COMP	PX	PY	
	P1	P2	
	P1	P3	
	P2	P3	
	P2	P4	
	P3	P5	
	P4	P5	
	P5	P6	
	P1	P4	⋆
	P1	P5	⋆
	P2	P5	⋆
	P3	P6	⋆
	P4	P6	⋆

After the second iteration, they look like this:

COMP ⋈ PS	PX	PY
	P1	P3
	P1	P4
	P1	P5
	P2	P5
	P3	P6
	P4	P6
	P1	P6
	P2	P6

COMP	PX	PY	
	P1	P2	
	P1	P3	
	P2	P3	
	P2	P4	
	P3	P5	
	P4	P5	
	P5	P6	
	P1	P4	
	P1	P5	
	P2	P5	
	P3	P6	
	P4	P6	
	P1	P6	⋆
	P2	P6	⋆

Note carefully that the computation of COMP ⋈ PS in this second step repeats the entire computation of COMP ⋈ PS from the first step but additionally computes some extra tuples (actually just two extra tuples—(P1,P6) and (P2,P6)—in the case at hand). This is one reason why the naive evaluation algorithm is not very intelligent.

After the third iteration, the value of COMP ⋈ PS (after more repeated computation) turns out to be the same as on the previous iteration; COMP has thus reached a fixpoint, and we exit from the loop. The final result is then computed as a restriction of COMP:

COMP	PX	PY
	P1	P2
	P1	P3
	P1	P4
	P1	P5
	P1	P6

Another glaring inefficiency is now apparent: The algorithm has effectively computed the explosion for *every* part—in fact, it has computed the **transitive closure** of relation PS (see below)—and has then thrown everything away again except for the tuples actually wanted. In other words, again, a great deal of unnecessary work has been performed.

A note regarding transitive closure: The **transitive closure** of a binary relation $R\{X,Y\}$ is a superset of R, defined as follows: The tuple (x,y) appears in the transitive closure of R if and only if it appears in R or there exists a sequence of values $z1$, $z2, \ldots zn$ such that the tuples $(x,z1)$, $(z1,z2)$, $\ldots (zn,y)$ all appear in R.

Note in conclusion that the naive evaluation technique can be regarded as an application of forward chaining: Starting from the extensional database (i.e., the actual data values), it applies the premises of the definition (i.e., the rule body) repeatedly until the desired result is obtained. In fact, the algorithm actually computes the *minimal model* for the Datalog program (see Sections C.5 and C.6).

Seminaive Evaluation

The first obvious improvement to the naive evaluation algorithm is to avoid repeating the computations of each step in the next step: **semi**naive evaluation [C.28]. In other words, in each step we compute just the new tuples that need to be appended on this particular iteration. Again we explain the idea in terms of the "Explode part P1" example. Pseudocode:

```
NEW  := PS ;
COMP := NEW ;
do until NEW is empty ;
    NEW  := ( NEW ⋈ PS ) MINUS COMP ;
    COMP := COMP UNION NEW ;
end ;
DISPLAY := COMP WHERE PX = 'P1' ;
```

Let us again step through the algorithm. On initial entry into the loop, NEW and COMP are both identical to PS:

NEW	PX	PY		COMP	PX	PY
	P1	P2			P1	P2
	P1	P3			P1	P3
	P2	P3			P2	P3
	P2	P4			P2	P4
	P3	P5			P3	P5
	P4	P5			P4	P5
	P5	P6			P5	P6

At the end of the first iteration, they look like this:

NEW	PX	PY		COMP	PX	PY	
	P1	P4			P1	P2	
	P1	P5			P1	P3	
	P2	P5			P2	P3	
	P3	P6			P2	P4	
	P4	P6			P3	P5	
					P4	P5	
					P5	P6	
					P1	P4	*
					P1	P5	*
					P2	P5	*
					P3	P6	*
					P4	P6	*

COMP is the same as it was at this stage under naive evaluation, and NEW is just the new tuples that were added to COMP on this iteration; note in particular that NEW does *not* include the tuple (P1,P3) (compare the naive evaluation counterpart).

At the end of the next iteration we have:

NEW	PX	PY		COMP	PX	PY	
	P1	P6			P1	P2	
	P2	P6			P1	P3	
					P2	P3	
					P2	P4	
					P3	P5	
					P4	P5	
					P5	P6	
					P1	P4	
					P1	P5	
					P2	P5	
					P3	P6	
					P4	P6	
					P1	P6	*
					P2	P6	*

The next iteration makes NEW empty, and so we leave the loop.

Static Filtering

Static filtering is a refinement on the basic idea from classical optimization theory of performing restrictions as early as possible. It can be regarded as an application of backward chaining, in that it effectively uses information from the query (the conclusion) to modify the rules (the premises). It is also referred to as *reducing the set of relevant facts,* in that it (again) uses information from the query to eliminate useless tuples in the extensional database right at the outset. The effect in terms of our example can be explained in terms of the following pseudocode:

```
NEW   := PS WHERE PX = 'P1' ;
COMP :=  NEW ;
do until NEW is empty ;
   NEW   := ( NEW ⋈ PS ) MINUS COMP ;
   COMP := COMP UNION NEW ;
end ;
DISPLAY := COMP ;
```

Once again we step through the algorithm. On initial entry into the loop, NEW and COMP both look like this:

At the end of the first iteration, they look like this:

At the end of the next iteration we have:

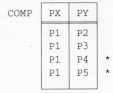

The next iteration makes NEW empty, and so we leave the loop.

This concludes our brief introduction to recursive query processing strategies. Of course, many other approaches have been proposed in the literature, most of them considerably more sophisticated than the rather simple ones discussed above; however, there is insufficient space in a book of this nature to cover all of the background material that is needed for a proper understanding of those approaches. See references [C.16–C.43] for further discussion.

C.8 Summary

This brings us to the end of our short introduction to the topic of database systems that are based on logic. The idea is still comparatively new, but it looks very interesting. Several potential advantages were identified at various points in the preceding sections.

One further advantage, not mentioned explicitly in the body of the appendix, is that logic could form the basis of a genuinely seamless integration between general-purpose programming languages and the database. In other words, instead of the "embedded data sublanguage" approach supported by most DBMS products today—an approach that is not particularly elegant, to say the least—the system could provide a single logic-based language in which "data is data," regardless of whether it is kept in a shared database or local to the application. (Of course, there are a number of obstacles to be overcome before such a goal can be achieved, not the least of which is to demonstrate to the satisfaction of the IT community at large that logic is suitable as a basis for a general-purpose programming language in the first place.)

Quite apart from the foregoing possibility, it is certain that some applications, at least, will need Datalog-style access (or similar) to data stored in a shared database. The question thus arises: How exactly can such access be provided? There are two broad answers to this question, referred to generically as *loose coupling* and *tight coupling* [C.11].

■ The loose coupling approach consists essentially of taking an existing DBMS and an existing logic programming language system and providing a call interface between the two. In such an approach, the user is definitely aware of the fact that there are two distinct systems involved—database operations (e.g., SQL statements) must be executed to retrieve data before logic operations (e.g., Prolog rules) can be applied to that data. This approach thus certainly does *not* provide the "seamless integration" referred to above.

■ The tight coupling approach, by contrast, involves a proper integration of the DBMS and the logic programming system; in other words, the DBMS query language includes direct support for the logical inferencing operations (etc.). Thus, the user deals with one language, not two.

The pros and cons of the two approaches are obvious: Loose coupling is more straightforward to implement but is not so attractive from the user's point of view; conversely, tight coupling is harder to implement but is more attractive to the user. In addition, tight coupling is likely to perform better (the scope for logic query optimization is necessarily very limited in a loose coupling system). For obvious reasons, however, the first commercial products (a few do exist) are based on loose coupling.

Let us quickly review the major points of the material we have covered. We began with a brief tutorial on **propositional calculus** and **predicate calculus,** introducing the following concepts among others:

■ An **interpretation** of a set of WFFs is the combination of (a) a universe of discourse, (b) a mapping from individual constants appearing in those WFFs to objects in that universe, and (c) a set of defined meanings for the predicates and functions appearing in those WFFs.

■ A **model** for a set of WFFs is an interpretation for which all WFFs in the set evaluate to *true*. A given set of WFFs can have any number of models (in general).

■ A **proof** is the process of showing that some given WFF g (the **conclusion**) is a logical consequence of some given set of WFFs *f1, f2, . . . fn* (the **premises**). We discussed one proof method, known as **resolution and unification,** in some detail.

We then examined the **proof-theoretic** view of databases. In such a view, the database is regarded as consisting of the combination of an **extensional** database and an **intensional** database. The extensional database contains **ground axioms,** i.e., the base data (loosely speaking); the intensional database contains integrity constraints and **deductive axioms,** i.e., views (again, loosely speaking). The "meaning" of the database then consists of the set of **theorems** that can be deduced from the axioms; executing a query becomes (at least conceptually) a **theorem-proving** process. A **deductive DBMS** is a DBMS that supports this proof-theoretic view. We briefly described **Datalog,** a user language for such a DBMS.

One immediately obvious distinction between Datalog and traditional relational languages is that Datalog supports **recursive** axioms, and hence recursive queries—though there is no reason why the traditional relational algebra and calculus should not be extended to do likewise.* We discussed some simple techniques for evaluating such queries.

In conclusion: We opened this appendix by mentioning a number of terms—"logic database," "inferential DBMS," "deductive DBMS," etc., etc.—that are often met with nowadays in the research literature (and indeed in vendor advertising). Let us therefore close it by providing some definitions for those terms. We warn the reader, however, that there is not always a consensus on these matters, and different definitions can probably be found in other publications. Following are the definitions preferred by the present writer.

■ *Recursive query processing:* This is an easy one. Recursive query processing refers to the evaluation (and in particular optimization) of queries whose definition is intrinsically recursive. See Section C.7.

■ *Knowledge base:* This term is sometimes used to mean what we called the intensional database in Section C.6—i.e., it consists of the *rules* (the integrity constraints and deductive axioms), as opposed to the base data, which constitutes the extensional database. But then other writers use "knowledge base" to mean the combination of both the intensional and extensional databases (see "deductive database" below)—except that, as reference [C.10] puts it, "a knowledge base often includes complex objects [as well as] classical relations." (See Part VI of this book for a discussion of "complex objects.") Then again, the term has another, more specific meaning altogether in natural language systems. It is probably best to avoid the term entirely.

■ *Knowledge:* Another easy one! Knowledge is what is in the knowledge

---

* In this connection it is interesting to observe that relational DBMSs need to be able to perform recursive processing under the covers anyway, because the catalog will contain certain recursively structured information (e.g., domain definitions expressed in terms of other domain definitions, view definitions expressed in terms of other view definitions, etc.).

base . . . This definition thus reduces the problem of defining "knowledge" to a previously unsolved problem.

- *Knowledge base management system (KBMS):* The software that manages the knowledge base. The term is typically used as a synonym for deductive DBMS, *q.v.*

- *Deductive DBMS:* A DBMS that supports the proof-theoretic view of databases, and in particular is capable of deducing additional information from the extensional database by applying inferential (i.e., deductive) rules that are stored in the intensional database. A deductive DBMS will almost certainly support recursive rules and so perform recursive query processing.

- *Deductive database:* (Deprecated term.) A database that is managed by a deductive DBMS.

- *Expert DBMS:* Synonym for deductive DBMS.

- *Expert database:* (Deprecated term.) A database that is managed by an expert DBMS.

- *Inferential DBMS:* Synonym for deductive DBMS.

- *Logic-based system:* Synonym for deductive DBMS.

- *Logic database:* (Deprecated term.) Synonym for deductive database.

- *Logic as a data model:* A data model consists of objects, integrity rules, and operators. In a deductive DBMS, the objects, integrity rules, and operators are all represented in the same uniform way, namely as axioms in a logic language such as Datalog; indeed, as explained in Section C.6, a database in such a system can be regarded, precisely, as a logic program containing axioms of all three kinds. In such a system, therefore, we might legitimately say that the abstract data model for the system *is* logic itself.

Exercises

C.1 Use the resolution method to see whether the following statements are valid in the propositional calculus:

(a) $A \Rightarrow B$, $C \Rightarrow B$, $D \Rightarrow (A \text{ OR } C)$, $D \vdash B$

(b) $(A \Rightarrow B)$ AND $(C \Rightarrow D)$, $(B \Rightarrow E$ AND $D \Rightarrow F)$,
     NOT $(E$ AND $F)$, $A \Rightarrow C \vdash$ NOT A

(c) $(A \text{ OR } B) \Rightarrow D$, $D \Rightarrow$ NOT $(E \text{ OR } F)$,
     NOT $(B$ AND C AND $E) \vdash$
                    NOT $(G \Rightarrow$ NOT $(C$ AND $H))$

C.2 Convert the following WFFs to clausal form:

(a) FORALL x (FORALL y ($p (x, y) \Rightarrow$ EXISTS z ($q (x, z)$)))

(b) EXISTS x (EXISTS y ($p (x, y) \Rightarrow$ FORALL z ($q (x, z)$)))

(c) EXISTS x (EXISTS y ($p (x, y) \Rightarrow$ EXISTS z ($q (x, z)$)))

C.3 The following is a fairly standard example of a logic database:

```
MAN     ( Adam )
WOMAN   ( Eve )
MAN     ( Cain )
MAN     ( Abel )
MAN     ( Enoch )

PARENT ( Adam, Cain )
PARENT ( Adam, Abel )
PARENT ( Eve, Cain )
PARENT ( Eve, Abel )
PARENT ( Cain, Enoch )
```

FATHER (x, y) $\Leftarrow$ PARENT (x, y) AND MAN (x)
MOTHER (x, y) $\Leftarrow$ PARENT (x, y) AND WOMAN (x)

SIBLING (x, y) $\Leftarrow$ PARENT (z, x) AND PARENT (z, y)

BROTHER (x, y) $\Leftarrow$ SIBLING (x, y) AND MAN (x)

SISTER (x, y) $\Leftarrow$ SIBLING (x, y) AND WOMAN (x)

ANCESTOR (x, y) $\Leftarrow$ PARENT (x, y)
ANCESTOR (x, y) $\Leftarrow$ PARENT (x, z) AND ANCESTOR (z, y)

Use the resolution method to answer the following queries:

(a) Who is the mother of Cain?

(b) Who are Cain's siblings?

(c) Who are Cain's brothers?

(d) Who are Cain's sisters?

(e) Who are Enoch's ancestors?

C.4 Define the terms *interpretation* and *model*.

C.5 Write a set of Datalog axioms for the definitional portion (only) of the suppliers-parts-projects database.

C.6 Give Datalog solutions, where possible, to Exercises 6.13–6.48.

C.7 Give Datalog solutions, where possible, to Exercises 16.1–16.16.

C.8 Complete (to your own satisfaction) the explanation given in Section C.7 of the unification and resolution implementation of the "Explode part P1" query.

References and Bibliography

The field of logic-based systems has mushroomed within the last few years. The following list represents a tiny fraction of the literature currently available. It is partially arranged into groups, as follows. First, references [C.1–C.9] are books that either are devoted to the subject of logic in general (particularly in a computing and/or database context) or are collections of papers on logic-based database systems specifically. References [C.10–C.12] are tutorials, as are the books by Ceri *et al.* [C.46] and Das [C.47]. References [C.14], [C.17–C.20], [C.30], and [C.49–C.50] are concerned with the transitive closure operation and its implementation. References

[C.21–C.24] describe an important recursive query processing technique called "magic sets" (and variations thereon). The remaining references are included principally to show just how much investigation is going on in this field; they address a variety of aspects of the subject, and are presented for the most part without further comment.

C.1 Robert R. Stoll. *Sets, Logic, and Axiomatic Theories*. San Francisco, Calif.: W. H. Freeman and Company (1961).

A good introduction to logic in general.

C.2 Zohar Manna and Richard Waldinger. *The Logical Basis for Computer Programming. Volume I: Deductive Reasoning* (1985); *Volume II: Deductive Techniques* (1990). Reading, Mass.: Addison-Wesley (1985, 1990).

C.3 Peter M. D. Gray. *Logic, Algebra and Databases*. Chichester, England: Ellis Horwood Ltd. (1984).

Contains a good gentle introduction to propositional calculus and predicate calculus (among a number of other relevant topics) from a database point of view.

C.4 Adrian Walker, Michael McCord, John F. Sowa, and Walter G. Wilson. *Knowledge Systems and Prolog* (2nd edition). Reading, Mass.: Addison-Wesley (1990).

This book is about logic programming in general, not logic-based database systems specifically, but it contains a great deal that is relevant to the latter topic.

C.5 Hervé Gallaire and Jack Minker. *Logic and Data Bases*. New York, N.Y.: Plenum Publishing Corp. (1978).

One of the first, if not *the* first, collections of papers in the field.

C.6 Larry Kershberg (ed.). *Expert Database Systems* (Proc. 1st International Workshop on Expert Database Systems, Kiawah Island, S.C.). Menlo Park, Calif.: Benjamin/Cummings (1986).

An excellent and thought-provoking collection of papers. Not all of them are directly related to the main subject of the present appendix, however. Indeed, the titles of the sections betray a certain degree of confusion as to what the subject of "expert database systems" really is! Those titles are as follows:

1. Theory of knowledge bases

2. Logic programming and databases

3. Expert database system architectures, tools, and techniques

4. Reasoning in expert database systems

5. Intelligent database access and interaction

In addition, there is a keynote paper by John Smith on expert database systems, and reports from working groups on (1) knowledge base management systems, (2) logic programming and databases, and (3) object-oriented database systems and knowledge systems. As Kershberg remarks in his preface, the expert database system concept "connotes diverse definitions and decidedly different architectures."

C.7 Jack Minker (ed.). *Foundations of Deductive Databases and Logic Programming*. San Mateo, Calif.: Morgan Kaufmann (1988).

C.8 John Mylopoulos and Michael L. Brodie (eds.). *Readings in Artificial Intelligence and Databases*. San Mateo, Calif.: Morgan Kaufmann (1988).

C.9 Jeffrey D. Ullman. *Database and Knowledge-Base Systems* (two volumes). Rockville, Md.: Computer Science Press (1988, 1989).

Volume I of this two-volume work includes one (long) chapter (out of a total of 10 chapters) that is entirely devoted to the logic-based approach. That chapter (which is the origin of Datalog, incidentally) includes a discussion of the relationship between logic and relational algebra, and another on relational calculus—both domain and tuple versions—as a special case of the logic approach. Volume II includes five chapters (out of seven) on various aspects of logic-based systems.

C.10 Georges Gardarin and Patrick Valduriez. *Relational Databases and Knowledge Bases.* Reading, Mass.: Addison-Wesley (1989).

Contains a chapter on deductive systems that (although tutorial in nature) goes into the underlying theory, optimization algorithms, etc., in much more detail than the present appendix does.

C.11 Michael Stonebraker. *Introduction to* "Integration of Knowledge and Data Management." In M. Stonebraker (ed.): *Readings in Database Systems.* San Mateo, Calif.: Morgan Kaufmann (1988).

C.12 Hervé Gallaire, Jack Minker, and Jean-Marie Nicolas. "Logic and Databases: A Deductive Approach." *ACM Comp. Surv. 16,* No. 2 (June 1984).

C.13 Veronica Dahl. "On Database Systems Development through Logic." *ACM TODS 7,* No. 1 (March 1982).

A good and clear description of the basic ideas underlying logic-based database systems, with examples taken from a Prolog-based prototype implemented by Dahl in 1977.

C.14 Rakesh Agrawal: "Alpha: An Extension of Relational Algebra to Express a Class of Recursive Queries." *IEEE Transactions on Software Engineering 14,* No. 7 (July 1988).

Proposes a new operator called *alpha* that supports the formulation of "a large class of recursive queries" (actually a superset of linear recursive queries) while staying within the framework of conventional relational algebra (more or less; the operator actually produces a non1NF result, i.e., a relation one of whose attributes is relation-valued, but then places bounds on how that result can be used in order to avoid having to define a complete algebra for such unnormalized relations). The contention is that the *alpha* operator is sufficiently powerful to deal with most practical problems involving recursion, while at the same time being easier to implement efficiently than any completely general recursion mechanism would be. The paper gives several examples of the use of the proposed operator; in particular, it shows how the transitive closure and "gross requirements" problems (see reference [C.17] and Section C.6 respectively) can both easily be handled.

Reference [C.19] describes some related work on implementation. Reference [C.18] is also relevant.

C.15 Raymond Reiter. "Towards a Logical Reconstruction of Relational Database Theory." In *On Conceptual Modelling: Perspectives from Artificial Intelligence, Databases, and Programming Languages* (eds., Michael L. Brodie, John Mylopoulos, and Joachim W. Schmidt). New York, N.Y.: Springer-Verlag (1984).

As mentioned in Section C.2, Reiter's work was by no means the first in this area—many researchers had investigated the relationship between logic and databases before (see, e.g., references [C.5], [C.7], and [C.13]). However, it seems to have been Reiter's "logical reconstruction of relational theory" that spurred much of the current activity and high degree of interest in the field.

C.16 François Bancilhon and Raghu Ramakrishnan. "An Amateur's Introduction to Recursive Query Processing Strategies." Proc. 1986 ACM SIGMOD International Conference on Management of Data, Washington, D.C. (May 1986). Republished in revised form in M. Stonebraker (ed.), *Readings in Database Systems.* San Mateo, Calif.: Morgan Kaufmann (1988). Also republished in reference [C.8].

An excellent overview. The paper starts by observing that there is both a positive and a negative side to all of the research on the recursive query implementation problem. The positive side is that numerous techniques have been identified that do at least solve the problem; the negative side is that it is not at all clear how to choose the technique that is most appropriate in a given situation (in particular, most of the techniques are presented in the literature with little or no discussion of performance characteristics). Then, after a section describing the basic ideas of logic databases, the paper goes on to describe a number of proposed algorithms—naive evaluation, seminaive evaluation, iterative query/subquery, recursive query/subquery, APEX, Prolog, Henschen/Naqvi, Aho-Ullman, Kifer-Lozinskii, counting, magic sets, and generalized magic sets. The paper compares these different approaches on the basis of application domain (i.e., the class of problems to which the algorithm can be applied), performance, and ease of implementation. The paper also includes performance figures (with comparative analysis) from testing the various algorithms on a simple benchmark.

C.17 Yannis E. Ioannidis. "On the Computation of the Transitive Closure of Relational Operators." Proc. 12th International Conference on Very Large Data Bases, Kyoto, Japan (August 1986).

Transitive closure is an operation of fundamental importance in recursive query processing [C.18]. This paper proposes a new algorithm (based on a "divide and conquer" approach) for implementing that operation. See also references [C.14], [C.18–C.20], and [C.49–C.50].

C.18 H. V. Jagadish, Rakesh Agrawal, and Linda Ness. "A Study of Transitive Closure as a Recursion Mechanism." Proc. 1987 ACM SIGMOD International Conference on Management of Data, San Francisco, Calif. (May 1987).

To quote from the abstract: "[This paper shows] that every linearly recursive query can be expressed as a transitive closure possibly preceded and followed by operations already available in relational algebra." The suggestion is that providing an efficient implementation of transitive closure is therefore sufficient as a basis for providing an efficient implementation of linear recursion in general, and hence for making deductive DBMSs efficient on a large class of recursive problems.

C.19 Rakesh Agrawal and H. Jagadish. "Direct Algorithms for Computing the Transitive Closure of Database Relations." Proc. 13th International Conference on Very Large Data Bases, Brighton, England (September 1987).

Proposes a set of transitive closure algorithms that "do not view the problem as one of evaluating a recursion, but rather obtain the closure from first principles" (hence the term *direct*). The paper includes a useful summary of earlier work on other direct algorithms.

C.20 Hongjun Lu. "New Strategies for Computing the Transitive Closure of a Database Relation." Proc. 13th International Conference on Very Large Data Bases, Brighton, England (September 1987).

More algorithms for transitive closure. Like reference [C.19], the paper also includes a useful survey of earlier approaches to the problem.

C.21 François Bancilhon, David Maier, Yehoshua Sagiv, and Jeffrey D. Ullman. "Magic Sets and Other Strange Ways to Implement Logic Programs." Proc. 5th ACM SIGMOD-SIGACT Symposium on Principles of Database Systems (1986).

The basic idea of "magic sets" is to introduce new sets of rules ("magic rules") dynamically that are guaranteed to produce the same result as the original query but are more efficient, in the sense that they reduce the set of "relevant facts" (see Section C.7). The details are a little complex, and beyond the scope of these notes; the reader is referred to the paper or to Bancilhon and Ramakrishnan's survey [C.16] or the books by Ullman [C.9] or Gardarin and Valduriez [C.10] for more explanation. We remark, however, that numerous variations on the basic idea have been devised—see, e.g., references [C.22–C.24] below.

See also reference [18.22] in Chapter 18.

C.22 Catriel Beeri and Raghu Ramakrishnan. "On the Power of Magic." Proc. 6th ACM SIGMOD-SIGACT Symposium on Principles of Database Systems (1987).

C.23 Domenico Saccà and Carlo Zaniolo. "Magic Counting Methods." Proc. 1987 ACM SIGMOD International Conference on Management of Data, San Francisco, Calif. (May 1987).

C.24 Georges Gardarin. "Magic Functions: A Technique to Optimize Extended Datalog Recursive Programs." Proc. 13th International Conference on Very Large Data Bases, Brighton, England (September 1987).

C.25 A. Aho and J.D. Ullman. "Universality of Data Retrieval Languages." Proc. 6th ACM Symposium on Principles of Programming Languages, San Antonio, Texas (January 1979).

Given a sequence of relations $R, f(R), f(f(R)), \ldots$ (where f is some fixed function), the **least fixpoint** of the sequence is defined to be a relation R^* derived in accordance with the following naive evaluation algorithm (see Section C.7):

```
R* := R ;
do until R* stops growing ;
   R* := R* UNION f(R*) ;
end ;
```

This paper proposes the addition of a least fixpoint operator to the relational algebra.

C.26 Jeffrey D. Ullman. "Implementation of Logical Query Languages for Databases." *ACM TODS 10*, No. 3 (September 1985).

Describes an important class of implementation techniques for possibly recursive queries. The techniques are defined in terms of "capture rules" on "rule/goal trees," which are graphs that represent a query strategy in terms of clauses and predicates. The paper defines several such rules—one that corresponds to the application of relational algebra operators, two more that correspond to forward and backward chaining respectively, and a "sideways" rule that allows results to be passed from one subgoal to another. Sideways information passing later became the basis for the so-called *magic set* techniques [C.21–C.24].

C.27 Shalom Tsur and Carlo Zaniolo. "LDL: A Logic-Based Data-Language." Proc. 12th International Conference on Very Large Data Bases, Kyoto, Japan (August 1986).

LDL includes (1) sets as a primitive data object, (2) negation (based on set difference), (3) data definition operations, and (4) update operations (for data definitions, base relations, and derived relations—the last of these not implemented at the time of publication of the paper). It is a pure logic language (no ordering dependencies among statements) and is compiled, not interpreted.

See also the book by Naqvi and Tsur [C.45] on the same subject.

C.28 François Bancilhon. "Naive Evaluation of Recursively Defined Relations." In M. Brodie and J. Mylopoulos (eds.): *On Knowledge Base Management Systems: Integrating Database and AI Systems*. New York, N.Y.: Springer-Verlag (1986).

C.29 Eliezer L. Lozinskii. "A Problem-Oriented Inferential Database System." *ACM TODS 11*, No. 3 (September 1986).

The source of the concept of "relevant facts." The paper describes a prototype system that makes use of the extensional database to curb the otherwise very fast expansion of the search space that inferential techniques typically give rise to.

C.30 Arnon Rosenthal *et al..* "Traversal Recursion: A Practical Approach to Supporting Recursive Applications." Proc. 1986 ACM SIGMOD International Conference on Management of Data, Washington, D.C. (June 1986).

C.31 Georges Gardarin and Christophe de Maindreville. "Evaluation of Database Recursive Logic Programs as Recurrent Function Series." Proc. 1986 ACM SIGMOD International Conference on Management of Data, Washington, D.C. (June 1986).

C.32 Louiqa Raschid and Stanley Y. W. Su. "A Parallel Processing Strategy for Evaluating Recursive Queries." Proc. 12th International Conference on Very Large Data Bases, Kyoto, Japan (August 1986).

C.33 Nicolas Spyratos. "The Partition Model: A Deductive Database Model." *ACM TODS 12,* No. 1 (March 1987).

C.34 Jiawei Han and Lawrence J. Henschen. "Handling Redundancy in the Processing of Recursive Queries." Proc. 1987 ACM SIGMOD International Conference on Management of Data, San Francisco, Calif. (May 1987).

C.35 Weining Zhang and C. T. Yu. "A Necessary Condition for a Doubly Recursive Rule to be Equivalent to a Linear Recursive Rule." Proc. 1987 ACM SIGMOD International Conference on Management of Data, San Francisco, Calif. (May 1987).

C.36 Wolfgang Nejdl. "Recursive Strategies for Answering Recursive Queries—The RQA/FQI Strategy." Proc. 13th International Conference on Very Large Data Bases, Brighton, England (September 1987).

C.37 Kyu-Young Whang and Shamkant B. Navathe. "An Extended Disjunctive Normal Form Approach for Optimizing Recursive Logic Queries in Loosely Coupled Environments." Proc. 13th International Conference on Very Large Data Bases, Brighton, England (September 1987).

C.38 Jeffrey F. Naughton. "Compiling Separable Recursions." Proc. 1988 ACM SIGMOD International Conference on Management of Data, Chicago, Ill. (June 1988).

C.39 Cheong Youn, Lawrence J. Henschen, and Jiawei Han. "Classification of Recursive Formulas in Deductive Databases." Proc. 1988 ACM SIGMOD International Conference on Management of Data, Chicago, Ill. (June 1988).

C.40 S. Ceri, G. Gottlob, and L. Lavazza. "Translation and Optimization of Logic Queries: The Algebraic Approach." Proc. 12th International Conference on Very Large Data Bases, Kyoto, Japan (August 1986).

C.41 S. Ceri and L. Tanca. "Optimization of Systems of Algebraic Equations for Evaluating Datalog Queries." Proc. 13th International Conference on Very Large Data Bases, Brighton, England (September 1987).

C.42 Allen Van Gelder. "A Message Passing Framework for Logical Query Evaluation." Proc. 1986 ACM SIGMOD International Conference on Management of Data, Washington, D.C. (June 1986).

C.43 Ouri Wolfson and Avi Silberschatz. "Distributed Processing of Logic Programs." Proc. 1988 ACM SIGMOD International Conference on Management of Data, Chicago, Ill. (June 1988).

C.44 Jeffrey F. Naughton *et al.* "Efficient Evaluation of Right-, Left-, and Multi-Linear Rules." Proc. 1989 ACM SIGMOD International Conference on Management of Data, Portland, Ore. (June 1989).

C.45 Shamim Naqvi and Shalom Tsur. *A Logical Language for Data and Knowledge Bases.* New York, N.Y.: Computer Science Press (1989).

An indepth, book-length presentation of the language LDL [C.27].

C.46 S. Ceri, G. Gottlob, and L. Tanca. *Logic Programming and Databases.* New York, N.Y.: Springer-Verlag (1990).

C.47 Subrata Kumar Das. *Deductive Databases and Logic Programming.* Reading, Mass.: Addison-Wesley (1992).

C.48 Michael Kifer and Eliezer Lozinskii. "On Compile-Time Query Optimization in Deductive Databases by Means of Static Filtering." *ACM TODS 15,* No. 3 (September 1990).

C.49 Rakesh Agrawal, Shaul Dar, and H. V. Jagadish. "Direct Transitive Closure Algorithms: Design and Performance Evaluation." *ACM TODS 15,* No. 3 (September 1990).

C.50 H. V. Jagadish. "A Compression Method to Materialize Transitive Closure." *ACM TODS 15,* No. 4 (December 1990).

Proposes an indexing technique that allows the transitive closure of a given relation to be stored in compressed form, such that testing to see whether a given tuple appears in the closure can be done via a single table lookup followed by an index comparison.

C.51 Serge Abiteboul and Stéphane Grumbach. "A Rule-Based Language with Functions and Sets." *ACM TODS 16,* No. 1 (March 1991).

Describes a language called COL ("complex object language")—an extension of Datalog—that integrates the ideas of deductive and object-oriented databases.

Answers to Selected Exercises

C.1 (a) and (b) are valid, (c) is not.

C.2 In the following, *a, b,* and *c* are Skolem constants and *f* is a Skolem function with two arguments.

(a) $p (x, y) \Rightarrow q (x, f (x, y))$

(b) $p (a, b) \Rightarrow q (a, z)$

(c) $p (a, b) \Rightarrow q (a, c)$

C.6 In accordance with our usual practice, we have numbered the following solutions as C.6.*n*, where 6.*n* is the number of the original exercise in Chapter 6.

C.6.13 ? ⇐ J (j, jn, jc)

C.6.14 ? ⇐ J (j, jn, London)

C.6.15 RES (s) ⇐ SPJ (s, p, J1)
? ⇐ RES (s)

C.6.16 ? ⇐ SPJ (s, p, j, q) AND 300 ≤ q AND q ≤ 750

C.6.17 RES (pl, pc) ⇐ P (p, pn, pl, w, pc)
? ⇐ RES (pl, pc)

C.6.18 RES (s, p, j) ⇐ S (s, sn, st, c) AND
P (p, pn, pl, w, c) AND
J (j, jn, c)
? ⇐ RES (s, p, j)

C.6.19–C.6.20 Cannot be done without negation.

C.6.21 RES (p) ⇐ SPJ (s, p, j, q) AND
                            S (s, sn, st, London)
        ? ⇐ RES (p)

C.6.22 RES (p) ⇐ SPJ (s, p, j, q) AND
                            S (s, sn, st, London) AND
                            J (j, jn, London)
        ? ⇐ RES (p)

C.6.23 RES ($c1$, $c2$) ⇐ SPJ (s, p, j, q) AND
                                S (s, sn, st, $c1$) AND
                                J (j, jn, $c2$)
        ? ⇐ RES ($c1$, $c2$)

C.6.24 RES (p) ⇐ SPJ (s, p, j, q) AND
                            S (s, sn, st, c) AND
                            J (j, jn, c)
        ? ⇐ RES (p)

C.6.25 Cannot be done without negation.

C.6.26 RES ($p1$, $p2$) ⇐ SPJ (s, $p1$, $j1$, $q1$) AND
                                SPJ (s, $p2$, $j2$, $q2$)
        ? ⇐ RES ($p1$, $p2$)

C.6.27–C.6.30 Cannot be done without grouping and aggregate functions.

C.6.31 RES (jn) ⇐ J (j, jn, jc) AND
                            SPJ (S1, p, j, q)
        ? ⇐ RES (jn)

C.6.32 RES (pl) ⇐ P (p, pn, pl, w, pc) AND
                            SPJ (S1, p, j, q)
        ? ⇐ RES (pl)

C.6.33 RES (p) ⇐ P (p, pn, pl, w, pc) AND
                            SPJ (s, p, j, q) AND
                            J (j, jn, London)
        ? ⇐ RES (p)

C.6.34 RES (j) ⇐ SPJ (s, p, j, q) AND
                            SPJ (S1, p, $j2$, $q2$)
        ? ⇐ RES (j)

C.6.35 RES (s) ⇐ SPJ (s, p, j, q) AND
                            SPJ ($s2$, p, $j2$, $q2$) AND
                            SPJ ($s2$, $p2$, $j3$, $q3$) AND
                            P ($p2$, pn, Red, w, c)
        ? ⇐ RES (s)

C.6.36 RES (s) ⇐ S (s, sn, st, c) AND
                            S (S1, $sn1$, $st1$, $c1$) AND $st < st1$
        ? ⇐ RES (s)

C.6.37–C.6.39 Cannot be done without grouping and aggregate functions.

C.6.40–C.6.44 Cannot be done without negation.

C.6.45 RES (c) ⇐ S (s, sn, st, c) AND
        RES (c) ⇐ P (p, pn, pl, w, c)

```
     RES ( c ) ⇐ J ( j, jn, c )
     ? ⇐ RES ( c )
```

C.6.46
```
     RES ( p ) ⇐ SPJ ( s, p, j, q ) AND
                 S ( s, sn, st, London )
     RES ( p ) ⇐ SPJ ( s, p, j, q ) AND
                 J ( j, jn, London )
     ? RES ( p )
```

C.4.47–C.4.48 Cannot be done without negation.

C.7 We show the constraints as conventional implications instead of in the "backward" Datalog style. We have numbered them C.7.n, where 16.n is the number of the original exercise in Chapter 16.

C.7.1
```
     CITY ( London )
     CITY ( Paris )
     CITY ( Rome )
     CITY ( Athens )
     CITY ( Oslo )
     CITY ( Stockholm )
     CITY ( Madrid )
     CITY ( Amsterdam )

     S ( s, sn, st, c )       ⇒ CITY ( c )
     P ( p, pn, pc, pw, c )   ⇒ CITY ( c )
     J ( j, jn, c )           ⇒ CITY ( c )
```

C.7.2 `P ( p, pn, Red, pw, pc ) ⇒ pw < 50`

C.7.3 Cannot be done without negation.

C.7.4
```
     S ( s1, sn1, st1, Athens ) AND
     S ( s2, sn2, st2, Athens ) ⇒ s1 = s2
```

C.7.5–C.7.6 Cannot be done without grouping and aggregate functions.

C.7.7 `J ( j, jn, c ) ⇒ S ( s, sn, st, c )`

C.7.8
```
     J ( j, jn, c ) ⇒ SPJ ( s, p, j, q ) AND
                      S ( s, sn, st, c )
```

C.7.9
```
     P ( p1, pn1, pl1, pw1, pc1 ) ⇒
     P ( p2, pn2, Red, pw2, pc2 )
```

C.7.10 Cannot be done without grouping and aggregate functions.

C.7.11 Cannot be done without negation.

C.7.12
```
     P ( p1, pn1, pl1, pw1, pc1 ) ⇒
     P ( p2, pn2, Red, pw2, pc2 ) AND pw2 < 50
```

C.7.13 Cannot be done (this is a transition constraint).

C.7.14–C.7.15 Cannot be done without grouping and aggregate functions.

C.7.16 Cannot be done (this is a transition constraint).

Abbreviations
and Acronyms

ACID	atomicity/consistency/isolation/durability
ACM	Association for Computing Machinery
ADT	abstract data type
AK	alternate key
ANSI	American National Standards Institute
ANSI/SPARC	literally, ANSI/Systems Planning and Requirements Committee; used to refer to the three-level database system architecture described in Chapter 2
BCNF	Boyce/Codd normal form
BCS	British Computer Society
BLOB	basic (*or* binary) large object
BNF	Backus/Naur form *or* Backus normal form
CACM	Communications of the ACM (ACM publication)
CAD/CAM	computer-aided design/computer-aided manufacturing
CASE	computer-aided software engineering
CDO	class-defining object
CIM	computer-integrated manufacturing
CK	candidate key
CODASYL	literally, Conference on Data Systems Languages; used to refer to certain prerelational (network) systems such as IDMS
CPU	central processing unit
CS	cursor stability (DB2)
DA	data administrator
DB/DC	database/data communications
DBA	database administrator
DBMS	database management system
DBRM	database request module (DB2)
DBTG	literally, Data Base Task Group; used interchangeably with CODASYL

DB2	IBM DATABASE 2
DC	data communications
DDB	distributed database
DDBMS	distributed DBMS
DDL	data definition language
DES	Data Encryption Standard
DK/NF	domain-key normal form
DL/I	Data Language/I (IMS)
DML	data manipulation language
DRDA	Distributed Relational Database Architecture (IBM)
DSL	data sublanguage
DUW	distributed unit of work
E/R	entity/relationship
EDB	extensional database
EKNF	elementary key normal form
EMVD	embedded MVD
FD	functional dependence
FK	foreign key
I/O	input/output
IDB	intensional database
IDMS	Integrated Database Management System
IMS	Information Management System
IND	inclusion dependence
INGRES	Interactive Graphics and Retrieval System
INGRES/STAR	distributed version of INGRES
IRDS	Information Resource Dictionary Systems
IS	intent shared (lock), *also* information systems
ISO	International Organization for Standardization
IT	information technology
IX	intent exclusive (lock)
JD	join dependence
LAN	local area network
MLS	multilevel secure
MVD	multivalued dependence
NF^2	"NF squared" = non1NF
OID	object ID
OO	object-oriented *or* object-orientation
OODB	object-oriented database
OOPL	object-oriented programming language

OSI	Open Systems Interconnection
OSQL	Object SQL
PJ/NF	projection-join normal form
PK	primary key
PRTV	Peterlee Relational Test Vehicle
QBE	Query-By-Example
QMF	Query Management Facility
QUEL	Query Language (INGRES)
R*	"R star" (distributed version of System R)
RAID	redundant array of inexpensive disks
RDA	Remote Data Access
RDB	relational database
RDBMS	relational DBMS
RID	(stored) record ID
RM/T	relational model/Tasmania
RM/V1	relational model/Version 1
RM/V2	relational model/Version 2
RPC	remote procedure call
RR	repeatable read (DB2)
RUW	remote unit of work
RVA	relation-valued attribute
S	shared (lock)
SAG	SQL Access Group
SDD-1	System for Distributed Databases - 1
SIGMOD	Special Interest Group on Management of Data (ACM special interest group)
SIX	shared intent exclusive (lock)
SPARC	*see* ANSI/SPARC
SQL	(originally) Structured Query Language
SQL/DS	SQL/Data System
SQL/92	the current ISO/ANSI SQL standard
TCB	Trusted Computing Base
TCP/IP	Transmission Control Protocol/Internet Protocol
TID	(stored) tuple ID
TODS	Transactions on Database Systems (ACM publication)
U	update (lock)
unk	*unknown* (truth value)
UNK	unknown (null)
UOW	unit of work

VLDB	Very Large Data Bases (annual conference)
VSAM	Virtual Storage Access Method (IBM)
WAL	write-ahead log
WAN	wide area network
WFF	well-formed formula
WORM	write-once/read-many-times
WYSIWYG	what you see is what you get
X	exclusive (lock)
X3H2	ANSI database committee
1NF	first normal form
2NF	second normal form
2PC	two-phase commit
2PL	two-phase locking
2VL	two-valued logic
3GL	third generation language
3VL	three-valued logic
3NF	third normal form
4GL	fourth generation language
4NF	fourth normal form
4VL	four-valued logic
5NF	fifth normal form (same as PJ/NF)

Index